MW01483031

Fertility, class and gender in Britain, 1860–1940 offers an original interpretation of the history of falling fertilities. It integrates the approaches of the social sciences and of demographic, gender and labour history with intellectual, social and political history. Dr Szreter excavates the history and exposes the statistical inadequacy of the long-standing orthodoxy of a national, unitary class-differential fertility decline. A new analysis of the famous 1911 fertility census presents evidence for over 200 occupational categories, showing many diverse fertility régimes, differentiated by distinctively gendered labour markets and changing family roles. Surprising and important findings emerge: births were spaced from early in marriage; sexual abstinence by married couples was far more significant than previously imagined. A new general approach to the study of fertility change is proposed; also a new conception of the relationship between class, community and fertility change; and a new evaluation of the positive role of feminism. *Fertility, class and gender* continually raises central issues concerning the relationship between history and social science.

Fertility, class and gender in Britain, 1860–1940

Cambridge Studies in Population, Economy and Society in Past Time 27

Series Editors

Recent work in social, economic and demographic history has revealed much that was previously obscure about societal stability and change in the past. It has also suggested that crossing the conventional boundaries between these branches of history can be very rewarding.

This series exemplifies the value of interdisciplinary work of this kind, and includes books on topics such as family, kinship and neighbourhood; welfare provision and social control; work and leisure; migration; urban growth; and legal structures and procedures, as well as more familiar matters. It demonstrates that, for example, anthropology and economics have become as close intellectual neighbours to history as have political philosophy or biography.

For a full list of titles in the series, please see end of book

Fertility, class and gender in Britain, 1860–1940

SIMON SZRETER
University of Cambridge

Published by the Press Syndicate of the University of Cambridge
The Pitt Building, Trumpington Street, Cambridge CB2 1RP
40 West 20th Street, New York, NY 10011-4211, USA
10 Stamford Road, Oakleigh, Melbourne 3166, Australia

First published 1996

Printed in Great Britain at the University Press, Cambridge

A catalogue record for this book is available from the British Library

Library of Congress cataloguing in publication data

Szreter, Simon.
Fertility, class and gender in Britain, 1860–1940 / Simon Szreter.
p. cm. – (Cambridge studies in population, economy, and society in past time; 27)
Includes bibliographical references.
ISBN 0 521 34343 7
1. Population – Great Britain – History – 19th century.
2. Population – Great Britain – History – 20th century. 3. Fertility, Human – Great Britain – History – 19th century. 4. Fertility, Human – Great Britain – History – 20th century. 5. Social classes – Great Britain – History – 19th century. 6. Social classes – Great Britain – History – 20th century. 7. Sex role – Great Britain – History – 19th century. 8. Sex role – Great Britain – History – 20th century.
I. Title. II. Series.
HB3583.S97 1995
304.6'0941 – dc20 94-42262 CIP

ISBN 0 521 34343 7

VN

In memory of
Ryszard Szreter (1927–89)
Ian Cooper (1964–85)

Contents

Figures

Tables

Acknowledgements

How innumerable and unenumerable are all the influences which have contributed to the making of this book. There can be no enterprise more dependent on the work and the support of others and upon the wider collectivity than the strangely solitary activity of intellectual inquiry. In the ensuing footnotes and bibliography lie the record of many of the most important direct influences. All the stimulus provided by colleagues and students, at seminars, conferences and in the course of teaching, inevitably remains unattributable, but not forgotten. It falls to me here to try to acknowledge some, at least, of the other pleasurable debts.

Family and friends, of course, come first and last. It is they who are always there at the beginning and the end: of my life, of my day and of each year. For all this, I can only record the offering of thanks.

In becoming interested in the kinds of historical problems pursued in this book, there have been a number of guides along the way, beginning with my father, Ryszard Szreter. As an undergraduate in history at Pembroke College, Clive Trebilock was a model, supportive teacher. It was a particularly histrionic lecture from Peter Laslett at his inimitable best which first drew me towards the subject of his passion: the sociological and demographic history of the family. I then discovered and entered the community of scholars working on these problems in Cambridge, with the particular encouragement of Roger Schofield, Richard Smith and Tony Wrigley. I wish to record my thanks also to all the other members, past and present, of the Cambridge Group for the History of Population and Social Structure, who have between them sustained such a positive place for learning. The Fellowships and other members of Gonville and Caius College and St John the Evangelist, where I am currently so happily ensconced, are also to be thanked for the same reason. This book was gestating during Barry Supple's tenure of the Cambridge Chair in Economic History and I remain grateful for his patient support throughout.

Several individuals have read all or part of the drafts of the book at various stages and I wish to record my gratitude for their many helpful comments: Eilidh

Garrett, Boyd Hilton, Alice Reid, Alastair Reid, Emma Rothschild, Simon Schaffer, Roger Schofield, Libby Schweber, Richard Smith, Pat Thane and Tony Wrigley. Others have helped with specific issues and I hope I have acknowledged them in the appropriate places. Remaining errors are of my own making. I would additionally like to thank all those involved at Cambridge University Press for their work in producing this book. I am grateful to Basil Blackwell Ltd for permission to reproduce, in part of chapter 3, material which was originally published in L. Bonfield *et al.*, *The World We Have Gained*, ch. 12.

Finally, there must be a very special mention of gratitude to my mother, Dulcie Szreter, and to Sam and Ben's mother, Hilary Cooper, my partner in all, my most rigorous critic and fairest friend.

Abbreviations

ARRG	Annual Report of the Registrar-General
BA	British Academy for the Advancement of Science
FMR	*Fertility of Marriage Report*
GRO	General Register Office
JRRS	*Journal of the Royal Statistical Society*
LGB	Local Government Board
MOH	Medical Officer of Health
NBRC	National Birth Rate Commission
PDC	Physical Deterioration Committee
PP	Parliamentary Papers
PRO	Public Record Office
RC	Royal Commission
RG	Registrar-General

Introduction

The period 1860–1940 witnessed a dramatic fall in fertility in British society. There was a marked decline in the number of live births experienced by each married woman in the population from an average of nearly six to an average of just over two.[1] *Fertility, class and gender in Britain, 1860–1940* is intended as a contribution to the collective effort of trying to explain and to understand how and why this happened.

By the early twentieth century there was widespread international recognition by officials and social scientists that this phenomenon had occurred in many of the economically advanced countries of the world. In fact it is now clear that both within Austro-Hungary and France there had been a substantial reduction in the birth rate in certain rural quarters from the late eighteenth century, while some aristocratic and urban bourgeois groups display reduced marital fertility in the previous century.[2] Despite the somewhat rudimentary facilities for demographic observation possessed by most nineteenth-century states, awareness of these developments had prompted a certain amount of speculative discussion. This was particularly so in France after the disaster of the Franco-Prussian War, where the menace of her demographically more vigorous neighbour, the newly unified German Empire of *Blut und Eisen*, gave particular impetus to such concerns.[3] Towards the end of the nineteenth century the pioneering anthropological and sociological work of the peculiar obsessive, Arsène Dumont, represented the most thorough attempt, in the continuing absence of appropriately constructed official statistics, to study and explain fertility restraint in French society.[4]

[1] *Report of the Royal Commission on Population*, ch. 23, para. 617.

[2] For a helpful, accessible summary of this range of evidence, see Livi-Bacci, 'Social group forerunners of fertility control in Europe'.

[3] Zeldin, *France 1848–1945. Vol. II*, ch.19; Spengler, 'French population theory since 1800', Parts I and II; Spengler, *France faces depopulation*.

[4] His most influential publication was *Dépopulation et civilisation*; additionally he published *Natalité et démocratie* and *La Morale basée sur la démographie*. Having failed to acquire a permanent academic position, Dumont committed a bizarre suicide in 1902, fulfilling a plan he had formed in 1892 to

However, examination and discussion of falling fertility was placed on an entirely new footing of observational rigour in the next century, with the initiative taken by the British state in 1911 to use the decennial census of that year to conduct and (eventually) to publish a comprehensive survey of the fertility patterns for an entire, large nation.[5] The 1911 fertility census was taken throughout the British Isles but the results were separately analysed using somewhat different approaches by the General Register Offices of Scotland, of Ireland and of England and Wales.[6] It was the comprehensive investigation published by the GRO for England and Wales which has been by far the most intellectually and historiographically influential of these reports and for this reason it is the main focus of attention in the following study.

It is to be noted, therefore, that although the term 'Britain' is used in this book's title and frequently in the ensuing pages this almost always refers only to England and Wales and not to Scotland. This is certainly not because this author believes that the experience of fertility change in Scotland (or in Ireland, for that matter) was essentially similar to, or can be subsumed within, an account based on England and Wales.[7] As will become obvious in the course of Parts III and IV, it is one of the principal contentions of this study that there was no single national story of fertility decline in England or in Wales, let alone in 'Britain'. It will be argued below that the evidence from the 1911 census in fact shows that there were many distinct fertility and nuptiality régimes changing alongside each other within England and Wales. Michael Anderson and Donald Morse have recently published an important analysis of Scottish evidence which has also emphasised the existence there of a number of distinct regional demographic régimes.[8]

devote himself, unsalaried, to research for ten years by dividing his then-current capital into ten parts, one for each year. For further information, see Sutter, 'Un démographe engagé: Arsène Dumont (1849-1902)'.

[5] Although the US census of 1910 also asked for detailed fertility information, apparently there were no funds available for analysis or publication. It was only following the stimulus provided by prior publication of the British results that such work began to be undertaken in the late 1920s on the US census of 1910 (see below, pp. 14–15). It is to be noted that there was also a precedent on a much smaller scale in an official inquiry in Australia. In the new Australian Commonwealth (which came into existence on 1 January 1901 as a federation of the existing colonies), there had been a Royal Commission *On the Decline in the Birth-Rate and on the Mortality of Infants in New South Wales*, which published 2 volumes in 1904 (Government Printer: Sydney), using demographic statistics analysed and first published by T. A. Coghlan: *The decline of the birth rate of New South Wales*. Timothy A. Coghlan, 1857–1926, KCMG 1918, was an eminent civil servant, brought up in Sydney, who had supervised both the 1891 and 1901 censuses of New South Wales while holding the post of Government Statistician for New South Wales, 1886-1905. Source: *Who was who 1916–28*. For further information on Coghlan and the Royal Commission, see Hicks, *This sin and scandal*.

[6] The report of the fertility census in Scotland is to be found in *Census of Scotland, 1911*, Vol. III, Section F (PP 1914 XLIV); the report on Ireland's marital fertility is in *Census of Ireland, 1911*, General Report, Section XIV, (PP 1912–13 CXVIII).

[7] The standard recent secondary source on modern demographic history in Scotland is: Flinn (ed.), *Scottish population history*. There is no similar integrated volume for Ireland's modern demographic history but see: Connell, *The population of Ireland*; Arensberg and Kimball, *Family and community in Ireland*; O'Gráda, *Ireland before and after the famine*; O'Gráda, 'New evidence on the fertility transition in Ireland'.

[8] Anderson and Morse, 'High fertility, high emigration, low nuptiality'.

The *Fertility of Marriage Report* was published by the General Register Office of England and Wales in two parts, in 1917 and in 1923.[9] It made available in full the results of the massive census investigation of 1911, with numerous useful tabulations and an exhaustive accompanying explanatory report. That this happened despite the intervention of the First World War and the Office's fulfilment of numerous additional duties, was largely a tribute to the dedication of its Superintendent of Statistics, Dr T. H. C. Stevenson, who had in fact been the original moving force behind the nation's fertility census, as will be shown in Part II, below.

The appearance in the 1920s of this authoritative confirmation and comprehensive description of changing fertility behaviour on a national scale fuelled international scientific curiosity and interest. A continuous flow of theories, studies and explanations to account for this remarkable cross-cultural phenomenon has subsequently proliferated. Indeed, the post-Second World War era has seen a further redoubling of efforts devoted to the study of human fertility change, so that the scale of institutional resources involved in such research has become quite unrecognisable by early twentieth-century standards. This has been especially the case since the 1960s, the decade in which the emotive ecological term 'Population Bomb' was first applied to the high-fertility populations of poor countries, as part of a campaign which successfully induced the US Congress to dispense massive funds for the design and implementation of family planning programmes for the populations of poor countries.[10]

Fertility, class and gender in Britain, 1860–1940 necessarily follows in the wake of this complex historiographical inheritance: a long line of several generations of international social scientific and historical studies addressed to the problem of understanding how and why a widespread change in human fertility could occur. It is of the greatest importance that any new study should seek to comprehend the characteristics of this intellectual inheritance and its preoccupations. A particular burden in discharging this task follows from the early recognition of the international and cross-cultural nature of the phenomenon. Affecting virtually all societies of European extraction by the 1920s, it has always seemed an eminently reasonable methodological assumption that there must be some form of 'general' causation at work in the secular fertility falls that have occurred. As a result it is not only those studies which have been explicitly based upon British historical source materials which have been considered to throw light on falling fertility in Britain; nor are inquiries into the causes of historical fertility change in Britain considered entirely irrelevant to the explication of such change in other historical or even in contemporary, non-European societies. Consequently, to undertake a critical historiographical review is in principle an almost boundless enterprise and

[9] Census of 1911, Vol. XIII, *FMR*, Pt 1, Cd 8678, PP 1917–18 XXXV; Pt 2, Cd 8491, was published separately (not as a Parliamentary Paper) by HMSO in 1923.

[10] Paul Ehrlich's *The population bomb* was the most widely read of a number of such admonitory publications in the 1960s. The continuity throughout the period ever since is symbolised in the publication of *The population explosion*, on the same theme by the same author (with Anne Ehrlich) in 1990.

therefore in practice an inevitably selective one. In a sense this task takes up fully half of this study: Parts I and II.

Part I provides a critical historiographical review of the field since the 1920s. While much has been learned in detail from the many and varied approaches, it is noted that they have all shared, explicitly or by default, the same general conception of the nature – the social and historical *form* – of the phenomenon which they address. Falling fertility in England and Wales has been treated by all as essentially a unitary, national process or event. It is usually acknowledged that it was a process differentiated in its social incidence according to the graded class structure of society at this time, but the object of study is decidedly '*the* fertility decline'.

Part II of this study is entirely taken up with investigation of exactly how and why falling fertility in Britain came to be so unanimously conceptualised as taking this particular social form. Ever since the phenomenon of a secular fall in fertility was first noticed in Britain around the turn of the century, contemporary social scientists and commentators appear to have assessed and measured its incidence and significance in terms of social class. The official *Fertility of Marriage Report* compiled by T. H. C. Stevenson from the 1911 census inquiry is no exception to this. In fact it was this document which was the *fons* – if not the ultimate *origo* – of this particular empirical representation of the phenomenon. There is nothing necessarily untoward in this consensus, supposing, of course, that it is empirically well founded. It is somewhat disconcerting, therefore, to realise that no independent assessment of the validity of this representation of the 1911 census evidence has ever been undertaken throughout the many decades which have since elapsed.

Part II shows how it was the occasion of the national fertility inquiry of 1911 which itself gave birth to the particular unitary, hierarchical model of the nation's class structure which I have termed 'the professional model'. The professional model of fertility decline formed the original, authoritative official interpretation of the empirical evidence collected in 1911 and it is this which has remained the largely unquestioned point of departure for all subsequent students of the subject. The professional model was, therefore, simultaneously a depiction of the social incidence of falling fertility in England and Wales and an implicit general model of the nation's social structure, in which role it has been officially retained to the present day.

Part II shows that the professional model of class-differential fertility decline was a classification scheme imposed in advance upon the empirical data collected at the 1911 census. It was a classification generated by a long-running and intense, but now defunct, contemporary policy debate between hereditarian eugenicists and environmentalists of the public health movement. This professional model of social classes has never, therefore, had any formal correspondence with any currently recognised social or political theory of class or of stratification – Marxist, Weberian or other.

More importantly for the central concerns of this study, nor has the professional model of fertility decline ever been the subject of any independent exercise to verify or assess its adequacy as a summary of the evidence collected in 1911. Its ancient claims to adequacy rest purely on incumbency. Part III therefore commences with a statistical examination of this official, class-differential model of fertility decline. It is found wanting in many respects.

Once thus emancipated from the intellectual strait-jacket of the professional model, the rich source of social and demographic evidence contained in the published tables of the 1911 census is then re-examined in the remaining chapters of Part III for the new light which it may be capable of throwing upon how and why fertility and marriage patterns changed in England and Wales during the critical period before the Great War. The ensuing empirical analysis exploits the detailed fertility and nuptiality information for over 200 male and female occupational subdivisions of the population of England and Wales. This shows that during this period there were many distinct histories of fertility change among the different social groups and industrial communities of Britain. The occupational fertility evidence is also used to mount a thorough examination of the current 'spacing' versus 'stopping' debate regarding family limitation. Part III concludes with an evaluation of the possible methods used to restrict fertility, combining what has been learned from the 1911 census data with a reappraisal of other contemporary sources of testimony.

In addition to the central theme of fertility, the book's title focuses attention on the concepts of class and gender. In fact, the relationship between class and fertility change is subjected to substantial revision and deconstruction in Part II of this study. As will become apparent in Parts III and IV, occupation, communication communities, social identity and sexuality are considered to be every bit as important as class and gender in coming to an understanding and explanation of fertility change in nineteenth- and twentieth-century Britain.

In conclusion in Part IV it is suggested that a general approach can be formulated for the study of changing fertility in British history. This provides the basis for the new historical interpretation that is offered of falling fertilities in modern Britain and it is suggested that it may also have a wider application and viability as an heuristic framework for use in a variety of historical and even contemporary contexts.

PART I

Historiographical introduction: a genealogy of approaches

The way that most men deal with traditions, even traditions of their own country, is to receive them all alike as they are delivered, without applying any critical test whatever.

. . . My conclusions have cost me some labour from the want of coincidence between accounts of the same occurrences by different eye-witnesses, arising sometimes from imperfect memory, sometimes from undue partiality for one side or the other. The absence of romance in my history will, I fear, detract somewhat from its interest; but if it be judged useful by those enquirers who desire an exact knowledge of the past as an aid to the interpretation of the future, which in the course of human things must resemble if it does not reflect it, I shall be content. In fine, I have written my work, not as an essay which is to win the applause of the moment, but as a possession for all time.

Thucydides, *History of the Peloponnesian War*, transl. R. Crawley
(Everyman Library edn), pp. 13, 15

1

The construction and the study of the fertility decline in Britain: social science and history

Fertility decline as a national, unitary phenomenon: the interwar intellectual inheritance

Since the end of the Second World War virtually all social scientific and historical research into large-scale change in fertility behaviour has been strongly influenced by the 'theory', or idea, of demographic transition. The seminal statement is considered to have been published in 1945, the product of the collective efforts of the group of social scientists who had spent much of the war producing strategic population projections for the US State Department, working under the leadership of F. W. Notestein at the Princeton Office of Population Research.[1]

The original theory of demographic transition posited a general historical model, purporting to explain the course of any nation's changing demographic history during industrialisation. Reduced to its essentials, the model envisaged a three-stage process. In an initial pre-industrial era, high rates of gross fertility were more or less cancelled out by equally high rates of mortality. This was a 'high pressure' equilibrium exhibiting little secular trend of population growth or decline. A subsequent period of industrialisation and sustained economic growth then effected a period of transition – the second stage – to a new post-industrial 'low pressure' equilibrium. Rapid population growth typically occurred during the transition, or second stage, which normally lasted for several decades, as mortality rates fell more rapidly than fertility rates. In the third and final stage relatively low mortality rates would be offset by low fertility rates, once again resulting in population stasis.

[1] Notestein, 'Population – the long view'; Davis, 'The world demographic transition'. The theory had an important pre-history of prototype formulations by demographers in a number of countries throughout the first half of the century, especially during the interwar years. D. Hodgson finds key elements of the theory adumbrated among various US demographers such as E. A. Ross as early as 1909: 'Demography as social science'. W. S. Thompson's 1929 statement was in virtually all important respects a full dress rehearsal for the 1945 version: 'Population'. Although there can certainly be no disputing that 'demographic transition' has been very much the product and instrument of the US community of demographers, at least four other distinct European antecedents include: Landry, 'Les Trois Théories' and *La Révolution démographique*; Carr-Saunders, *The population problem*; Stevenson, 'The laws governing population'; and Rabinowicz, *Le Problème de la population*.

The theory explained that this pattern occurred because the economic forces, which supplied this peculiar general historical model's *primum mobile*, acted first and most directly to depress mortality. This was envisaged as an almost automatic concomitant of the rising material living standards and advances in natural and medical science and technology which seemed self-evidently to comprise an integral part of the economic growth process. Decrease in fertility occurred only somewhat later, after the cultural consequences of rising material affluence had had sufficient time to break down beliefs and customs characterised as religious, 'traditional' or 'non-rational', which had for centuries put a high value on human fecundity. Until this had happened, rapid population growth would occur.

This general theory of historical change was widely endorsed by demographers, sociologists, economists of growth and policy-makers from the mid-1940s. It was treated as if it was securely established on a wide-ranging, authoritative empirical basis. In fact it was not. Its universal geographical pretensions perhaps obscured the fact that it rested upon the support of precariously little independent empirical research of a genuinely comparative sort. Indeed, in the 1940s there was only one country whose modern economic, social and demographic history had been researched in anything like the degree of empirical detail necessary to justify some confidence among social scientists in the credibility of their theory. That single country was Britain, and most specifically England.[2] Reliance on the properly documented economic and demographic history of only a single industrialised country was not, perhaps, initially perceived to be the potential liability which it clearly was. Partly this was because the more fragmentary knowledge available of other countries' histories could appear plausibly to fit such a general model. But it was also because this was a community of social and policy scientists who believed – witness transition theory itself – in *general* laws of economic and concomitant demographic development: one empirical example was enough.

By the end of the decade following the First World War a generation of new historical studies had arrived at an authoritative and apparently well-researched interpretation of the course of economic and demographic change over the previous two centuries in Britain. This interpretation found its definitive statement in the influential synthesis of J. H. Clapham, *An economic history of modern Britain*, published in three volumes between 1926 and 1938.[3] It was the general viewpoint offered by Clapham, and the various detailed studies associated with his

[2] Sweden was the only other country whose historical demographic record was considered at this time to rest upon a sound empirical basis; but the wider economic and social history of Sweden was less fully developed as a subject of scholarly research. The principal demographic source for Sweden was the continuous record provided by the *Tabellverket* established in 1749. The original data had been subject to careful scholarly evaluation, correction and retabulation by Gutav Sünbärg in work published in the first decade of the century: Heckscher, 'Swedish population trends'; Hofsten and Lundström, *Swedish population history*, Appendix 1.

[3] John H. Clapham (1873–1946), FBA, was the first Professor of Economic History in Cambridge, 1928–38, and Vice-Provost at King's College, 1933–43. On the historiography of economic history in Britain and Clapham's place within the field, see Koot, *English historical economics*.

synthesis, which provided the generation of demographers who developed transition theory with their apparently most trustworthy long-term historical evidence. Clapham was the champion of a self-consciously revisionist and 'optimistic' interpretation of the social consequences of early economic growth in English society. He stressed the importance of the gradually accumulating material benefits of economic growth, as against an earlier view that the industrial revolution had represented a cataclysmic and immiserating episode in the lives of the common people. The hard core of Clapham's case in this respect was based on the time-series wage-data for the nineteenth century assembled by A. L. Bowley and G. H. Wood in combination with a new prices index compiled by Norman J. Silberling.[4] Clapham had argued that this evidence showed a clear trend of uninterrupted rising real (disposable) income among the vast majority of English workers, urban and rural, from 1790 onwards.[5]

Support for this 'optimistic' interpretation came also from the leading Manchester University historian, A. Redford. His major research publication of 1926 argued that careful scrutiny of migration patterns during the first half of the nineteenth century showed that those who became the earliest generation of urban factory workers were not cruelly 'pushed' off the land by their avaricious enclosing landlords, as previously claimed by the Hammonds.[6] Rather, they voluntarily moved to the expanding towns, responding to the incentive 'pull' of the higher wages to be found there. Additionally, there were the supportive findings of two independent social and medical histories of Britain, which both appeared to confirm that the spectacular population growth which occurred during the period of the industrial revolution, *c.*1760–1850, was mainly due to decreases in mortality rather than to any changes in fertility or nuptiality.[7] A fall in mortality, supposedly accounting for the population surge accompanying industrialisation, had apparently long preceded any fall in fertility.

Thus, in reconstructing England's modern economic history, detailed, quantitative information on historical wages and prices and an index of industrial output, as well as demographic data, had already been the subject of intensive scholarly analysis, whereas much of this kind of data had not even been located in the cases

4 Clapham, *An economic history of modern Britain I.* The new prices index was presented in graphic form by Clapham on p. 128, with an accompanying explanatory Appendix (pp. 601–2). It was derived from: Silberling, 'British prices'. The historical work by Bowley and Wood was originally published in a long series of articles appearing between 1895 and 1906 in the *Journal of the Royal Statistical Society.*

5 Clapham, *An economic history of modern Britain I*, pp. 128, 561.

6 Redford, *Labour migration*; Hammond and Hammond, *The village labourer*; Hammond and Hammond, *The town labourer.*

7 Griffith, *Population problems*; Buer, *Health, wealth and population* (although it is worth noting that Griffith was a student of Clapham's). Modern historical demographic research has, of course, established quite the opposite: that the evidence in fact points to fertility change, as affected by nuptiality behaviour, as the major source of changes in the rate of population growth. See Wrigley and Schofield, *The population history.* It should be noted that there always were significant sceptics of the emerging 'optimistic' view of the 1920s: see in particular Marshall, 'The population problem'.

of many other national economies.[8] Hence, because of the relative abundance of the available historical evidence, the most important new quantitative project mounted by American economic historians during the 1930s was the Columbia University study of fluctuations in *Britain's* economic growth, a subject also addressed by the eminent German economic historian, Walther Hoffmann.[9] Thus, despite the predominantly US intellectual genesis and exposition of demographic transition theory, the empirically researched historical basis upon which it rested was primarily that of a particular interpretation, presented in a cluster of interwar historical monographs, of Britain's modern social and economic history and the nature of the attendant demographic changes there.[10]

In the British case, there was also a uniquely comprehensive body of processed and tabulated demographic data covering the entire nation's falling fertility in the recent past. The findings of the 1911 census, reported in the official *Fertility of Marriage Report*, analysed the fertility patterns of the entire population during the period 1851–1911. Furthermore, the results of the sample survey conducted for the Royal Commission on Population of 1944–9 were fast becoming available, covering the period 1901–46. Between them, these two official inquiries apparently provided transition demographers with a complete record of the process of falling fertility as it had occurred in modern British society.[11] In particular it was the picture of fertility decline presented in the first of these official documents which had predominantly influenced transition demographers when formulating their theory in the 1930s and 1940s.

The 1911 census was interpreted by British officials through an adopted scheme of social classification of all male occupations in the economy into a linear hierarchy of five grades of social position. This has been termed 'the professional model' and the complex history of its genesis will occupy much of Part II, below. Class I, the professional upper and middle class, appeared to have taken to the new practice of controlling their fertility earlier and more rigorously than their social inferiors. They were followed most closely by class II, those occupying an intermediate status between class I and the skilled manual workers of class III,

[8] Indeed, there remain to this day substantial discrepancies in the available historical data sources for different nations: on, for instance, real wages, see the essays in Scholliers, *Real wages*.

[9] The Columbia project began in 1936 and the main publication was in 1953: Gayer, Rostow and Schwartz, *Growth and fluctuations of the British economy, 1790–1850*. The aim had been to analyse in the light of the most recent economic theory of business cycles a vast range of historical data on prices, trade, investment, pay and sectoral output for the early industrialising economy in Britain. This British empirical orientation was despite the fact that the authors were consciously developing an indigenous US analytical approach, pioneered by W. C. Mitchell and A. F. Burns of the National Bureau of Economic Research (Mitchell's *Business cycles* had been published in 1913; Burns and Mitchell, *Measuring business cycles*, was published in 1946 by the National Bureau). Walther G. Hoffmann's *British industry 1700–1950* was first published in German in 1940.

[10] To the above could also be added Ivy Pinchbeck's rather optimistic view of the gains from industrialisation ultimately accruing to women: *Women workers*.

[11] F. W. Notestein, the leading transition demographer, published two reviews of the Royal Commission's work in 1949, signifying the importance he attached to the British historical record: 'Notes on the report'; and 'The report'.

who followed class II; they were followed in turn by another intermediate group, class IV, with the unskilled labourers of class V bringing up the rear. This aspect of the results was first made public in 1920, in an unofficial publication, by Dr T. H. C. Stevenson, the Superintendent of Statistics at the GRO and the chief designer and analyst of the inquiry.[12] It was officially confirmed in the second part of the *Fertility of Marriage Report* published in 1923.[13]

In a synthesis and summary, presented in 1924 and published in 1925, Stevenson particularly dwelled on the significance of both the class-differential aspect of the phenomenon and also the broad international simultaneity of fertility decline.[14] Falling fertility appeared to be a process which had commenced during the last quarter of the nineteenth century in virtually all populations of the 'European cultural sphere'. This seemed to Stevenson to comprise strong independent confirmation of the self-same theory most obviously suggested by the class-differential pattern of incidence recorded for England and Wales in the 1911 census: that the cause of fertility decline was the social and international diffusion of new ideas and techniques regarding birth control.

In his own independent contribution also published in 1925, this thesis was championed by W. H. Beveridge, the influential Director of the LSE, who claimed that fertility decline should primarily be understood as another case of technology spreading.[15] He graphically likened the diffusion of contraceptive practices to that of the increasing use of anaesthetics in medical operations or of motor vehicles for travel and transport. Wherever geographical and chronological variation was observed Beveridge claimed that this should be attributed either to low density of population or to Roman Catholicism, both of which tended to delay the dissemination of the new birth controlling practices.

In 1927, at the important conference founding the International Union for the Scientific Study of Population, a third leading British authority on contemporary population problems, Alexander Carr-Saunders, publicly added his weight to this viewpoint, enthusiastically supporting the professional model of fertility decline.[16] Carr-Saunders recommended the new British official model of social classes to the assembled international delegates as a methodological vehicle well suited to all forms of demographic and social science research. The unanimity of this new orthodoxy among the country's most eminent demographic social scientists was thereby sealed.

The professional model of fertility decline was soon publicised and adopted by a diversity of leading social scientists interested in population problems in North

[12] Stevenson, 'Fertility of various social classes', esp. pp. 412–23. For further information on Stevenson, see p. 74 and ch. 5.

[13] *FMR*, Pt 2. Pt 1 of the *Report* (aggregate tables without any commentary or analysis) had been published in Parliamentary Papers in 1917. See Introduction, n. 9.

[14] Stevenson, 'The laws governing population'.

[15] Beveridge, 'The fall of fertility'. Beveridge presented comparative data to support the contention that the birth rate had fallen almost simultaneously in all industrialised countries.

[16] Carr-Saunders, 'Differential fertility'.

America, such as R. M. MacIver, Raymond Pearl, William Ogburn, Warren Thompson, F. W. Notestein and Norman Himes.[17] Warren Thompson, the first American incumbent of a university post specifically in demography, had attended the conference in 1927 in Geneva and proceeded to include Stevenson's classification scheme and its findings in his textbook, *Population problems*, published in 1930.[18] This was to provide the first generation of American students of demography with their standard text throughout the 1930s and 1940s. Thompson still noted in his third edition of 1942 that 'In the author's judgement the most satisfactory study of fertility that has ever been made is that of England and Wales, based on information collected at the census of 1911.'[19]

The hierarchical social assumptions underlying the official classification scheme developed by the GRO were unflinchingly spelled out and apparently endorsed in an influential, encyclopaedic study of the medical history of contraception published in 1936 by the American social and medical scientist, N. E. Himes:

> Such a differential is what one would expect. The upper classes are, on the whole, more intelligent. They have more foresight and probably more personal ambition. As with mechanical improvements newly placed on the market, the lower classes ape the upper classes. In the masses, strongholds of the mores, there are more impediments to the prompt adoption of improved contraceptive methods.[20]

The significance of this quotation is that Himes was in fact commenting here, in 1936, on the class-differential fertility patterns of his *own* country, the USA.

Once the British findings from the 1911 census had been internationally publicised, US demographers (and those of several other nations, too) seem to have become intent upon testing for this possible pattern in their own societies. The wide appeal of this project was no doubt partly because of the acknowledged comprehensive nature and scientific rigour of the British inquiry. This therefore represented a kind of disciplinary standard for the members of a youthful discipline, population studies, one of whose principal attractions was the promise of a seriously scientific study of certain aspects of society. Hence, the young F. W. Notestein, the leading postwar exponent of demographic transition theory, was one of the principal individuals involved in an intriguing process of transatlantic transfusion of the British professional model of social classes, whereby it also became adopted in 1933 as the official census model of social classes in the USA.[21]

[17] Szreter, 'The official representation of social classes', pp. 291–305.

[18] In 1922 W. S. Thompson had been the recipient of an award from the Scripps Foundation, which endowed him with his own department for research in population problems at Miami University in Oxford, Ohio.

[19] Thompson, *Population problems*, p. 176.

[20] Himes, *Medical history*, p. 390.

[21] In order to produce a comparative historical study of US class differences in fertility, Notestein had exploited an opportunity in the late 1920s which had enabled him to work in close collaboration with the officials of the US Census Bureau on the project of retrospectively classifying the official demographic data collected at the US census of 1910. It seems to have been this close contact with the

Hence, it was as a result of Notestein's efforts that Himes was able to follow his observation that 'until recently we have lacked a study half-way comparable to that published in 1911 as part of the census Report for England and Wales' by proudly reviewing in his 1936 publication the parallel results now published by Notestein on historic US class-differentials in fertility decline.[22]

According to Himes it had been the publicity surrounding the famous trial in England from 1876 to 1879 of the Freethinkers, Charles Bradlaugh and Annie Besant (they had provoked a test-case over the publication and sale of birth control propaganda), which had finally been the catalytic cause of rapid diffusion of the knowledge and practices of birth control in Anglophone countries.[23] By invoking this contingent event in social and legal history as a galvanising force, Himes had been able to explain an otherwise anomalous discontinuity in the diffusion process. His careful account of the historical trajectory of expansion in Anglophone birth control literature on both sides of the Atlantic had found a modest but steady flow of propaganda appearing, since an original flurry of pamphleteering in the 1820s and 1830s. Yet this had apparently failed to induce any general behavioural change in Britain for several decades.[24]

Himes was not, however, a simple Beveridge-style diffusionist. He in fact envisaged a more encompassing process, which equally fitted both the class-differential pattern in Britain and the observation of transnational simultaneity in fertility decline. This was Himes's notion of the 'democratisation' of society as a fundamental enabling force, producing the individual motivation necessary to control births. Himes produced a long list of all the associated factors which had paved the way for the sweeping 'Vital Revolution' of mass birth control. The panoptic scope of this inventory can be readily appreciated by citing merely the first few items listed by Himes: 'the growth of hedonism, utilitarianism, materialism; the declining hold of orthodox religion and the rise of rationalism and the scientific spirit; growing emancipation or independence of women and feminism'.[25] Hence,

relevant US Census Bureau staff which catalysed the Bureau's adoption of the British professional model of social classes for its own classification of the US population at the subsequent 1940 census. For a full account of these developments, see Szreter, 'The official representation of social classes', pp. 291–305.

22 Himes, *Medical history*, p. 379. The fact that none of the parts of the 1911 census of fertility was actually published in 1911 suggests that Himes, scrupulous about most of his sources, had uncharacteristically not bothered to consult any of these official British documents first hand. This indirectly attests to the high status which the *Fertility of Marriage Report* and its findings enjoyed, as 'common knowledge' at this time among the international community of scholars interested in population problems.

23 Himes, *Medical history*, ch. 10. For a full, recent historical account, see Chandrasekhar, '*A dirty, filthy book*'.

24 Himes, *Medical history*, ch. 9. On this earlier history of birth controllers in Britain, see also Langer, 'Origins of the birth control movement'; and on the subsequent history, see Ledbetter, *A history of the Malthusian League*; D'Arcy, 'The Malthusian League'.

25 Cited in Banks, *Prosperity and parenthood*, p. 7.

Himes had introduced an explicitly ideological dimension into the explanation of diffusion, whereas this had remained at most an unarticulated assumption in the more rudimentary thesis of diffusion of techniques. In fact, the application of this concept, democratisation, to the explanation of national fertility decline had already received its most thorough and extreme exposition over four decades before Himes's publication, in the remarkable work of the French pronatalist demographer and anthropologist, Arsène Dumont.

The Dumont thesis of *capillarité sociale* or *attraction capillaire* was formulated as a law of nature, in the Newtonian sense.[26] Dumont had claimed that it was an essential property of liberal democratic polities that the individual citizens comprising them were subject to an intense competitive struggle for social status, due to the dynamic tension created by an inevitable inconsistency between the *de jure* myth of a collectivity of sovereign and equal citizens and the *de facto* situation of an unequal social and economic order. The sacrifice of fertility – and even of conventional family life itself in extreme cases (such as his own) – were considered by Dumont to be the inevitable corollary of the more ambitious individuals' preoccupation with their personal advance and gain and the self-gratifications to be had from individual success in this sense. Dumont believed that this problem was especially true of France where the highly centralised state preached to all its individual citizens through a uniform, universal education system the same – unattainable – myth of their equality and equal opportunities.

Not surprisingly, since the basic tenets and assumptions behind Dumont's political model chimed well with the cherished libertarian and individualist myths regarding the nature of their own society, Dumont's work was rapidly absorbed into a long stream of commentary from economists and social scientists in the USA on the observed relationship between rising living standards, rising aspirations and reduced fertility.[27] This phenomenon had long been seen by American social theorists as offering hope for an optimistic, supposedly 'anti-Malthusian' view of the human potential for rational self-improvement and social progress.[28] In fact, as J. A. Banks showed, similar views had once been current in British society, too, among the apologists of liberal political economy in the early and mid-nineteenth century, the era of Smilesian self-help and the myth of the self-made man.[29] But in Britain the highly visible and entrenched class system which had since developed rendered such a Dumontian analysis seemingly unrealistic. As D. E. C. Eversley has acutely remarked of Dumont's theory of *capillarité sociale*, at the end of the

[26] Dumont, *Dépopulation et civilisation*, ch. 6. On Dumont, see Introduction, n. 4.

[27] See Hodgson, 'Demography as social science', pp. 5–6; and also n. 2 in the same article, regarding the early publicisation of Dumont's thesis in the USA in 1903 by Frederick Bushee in *Popular Science Monthly*.

[28] On the early conflict with Malthusianism in US social thought, especially from the Boston Unitarians, see Cocks, 'The Malthusian theory'.

[29] Banks, *Prosperity and parenthood*, pp. 26–31, citing the views of Nassau William Senior in debate with Malthus in the 1820s.

nineteenth century 'No such observation could have been made in England!'[30]

It is not therefore surprising to find a complete absence of analysis along the lines proposed by Dumont among British social scientists, until the work of the socialist Enid Charles in the changed circumstances of the mid-1930s (though it was not until the *Report of the Royal Commission on Population*, published in 1949, that Dumont's thesis was explicitly referred to in print in Britain).[31] By this time it had of course become clear that all social classes in Britain, rich and poor, were restricting their fertility very considerably. Enid Charles's book was a major contribution to an intense public debate in interwar Britain over the nation's apparent reluctance to reproduce itself, essentially a bout of the same pronatalist anxieties which had been preoccupying French public opinion for over half a century by this time. In *The twilight of parenthood* Charles echoed Dumont's diagnosis of the causes of 'dépopulation', when arguing that the blind economic forces of unplanned competitive capitalist societies with inegalitarian income distributions were driving all classes towards voluntary sterility.[32] Charles claimed that the middle classes limited their fertility in an effort to husband resources and preserve their privileged status; the working classes, on the other hand, had done so because the economic value of their children had been progressively curtailed through restrictive factory and education acts.[33] Though not in principle opposed to the protective and pedagogic aims of such central state intervention, Charles was concerned to point out that such legislative acts had undesirable and unintended consequences for the nation's biological survival because they were isolated pieces of *ad hoc* interventionism, and not an integrated part of a 'scientific' overall plan for society, as would be possible in the socialist state which she advocated.[34]

Following in the train of this more sociologically sophisticated analysis of the 1930s, as represented by Himes and by Charles, F. W. Notestein seems to have strongly rejected any simplistic diffusionism in coming to his classic formulation of transition theory in 1944. Notestein was convinced of the culturally embedded nature of fertility behaviour and the need to approach its modification through changing the context in which individuals' intentions and motivations were formed, rather than through the mere provision of contraceptive information and

30 Eversley, *Social theories of fertility*, p. 152.

31 *Report of the Royal Commission on Population*, ch. 5, para. 100.

32 Charles, *The twilight of parenthood*, ch. VI. The second, more widely read, edition was entitled *The menace of under-population* and was published in 1936. Enid Charles was wife and collaborator with the prominent socialist, Professor Lancelot Hogben. Both were based at the LSE as a result of its Director – W. H. Beveridge – inviting Hogben to head the new Rockefeller-funded Social Biology Unit established in 1934.

33 Charles, *The twilight of parenthood*, pp. 140–2, 185, 205–6.

34 Charles, *The twilight of parenthood*, ch. VI. Of course, in the aftermath of the mayhem of the Great Crash this was how socialists in the 1930s tended to conceive of their ideal alternative to free-market capitalism, with an eye on the Soviet Union as an apparently successful working model. On socialist scientists in the 1930s, see Werskey, *The visible college*.

devices.[35] This was based on a powerful logical inference from his reading of the most authoritative historical and comparative research into human fertility variation then available to him, particularly that of Carr-Saunders summarising anthropological and ethnographic findings and Himes's work on the historical evidence.[36] Such research seemed to show that the availability of at least some form of contraception was virtually a cultural universal: the variety of methods found was stupefying. It therefore followed that the general absence of any systematic recourse to contraceptive behaviour by a population was not the result of sheer ignorance but rather due to lack of sufficient motivation. This important inference was empirically confirmed by his own work with Regine Stix on the fertility behaviour of those attending at a contemporary US clinic in the 1930s.[37]

Hence, in his original version of demographic transition theory Notestein invoked 'the whole process of modernisation' in all its economic and cultural aspects as the necessary precondition for the emergence of the appropriate motivational context for systematic, mass fertility control to appear in any society.[38] Notestein was certainly not alone in following in this way the potentially wide-ranging implications of Himes's thesis of 'democratisation'. Where most earlier hypotheses to explain fertility decline – whether biological, economic, or cultural (diffusionist) – had posited a nomic mono-causality, multi-causality was now the watchword in the 1940s.[39] The Royal Commission on Population likewise produced a catalogic list: 'a complex of causes' which 'acted and reacted on each other' as 'a complex web, rather than a chain, of cause and effect' and among which it did not wish to adjudicate as to relative importance; and therefore it also accepted the cultural diffusionist interpretation as an important part of the overall explanation of fertility decline.[40]

Thus, by the beginning of the postwar era a range of intellectual positions on the causation involved in fertility decline had already found their respective representatives among scholars and officials. First, Stevenson and Beveridge had championed simple diffusion of techniques and information. This is the stance which has consistently found most favour among family planning activists, since the early days of Francis Place, Charles Knowlton, Richard Carlile through to the late nineteenth-century neo-Malthusian League of Annie Besant, Charles Bradlaugh, as well as the celebrated interwar birth controllers, Marie Stopes and Margaret Sanger. It would seem that versions of such diffusionism have continued in currency in the post-Second World War era, despite the notion's patent intellectual

35 Hodgson, Demeny and the Caldwells are all agreed that this aspect of Notestein's approach was fundamental: Hodgson, 'Orthodoxy and revisionism', pp. 542–3; Demeny, 'Social science', pp. 458–9; Caldwell and Caldwell, *Limiting population growth*, pp. 6–7.

36 Carr-Saunders, *The population problem*; Himes, *Medical history*.

37 Stix and Notestein, *Controlled fertility*.

38 Notestein, 'Population – the long view', p. 39.

39 On earlier, mono-causal theories, see below, chapters 4 and 5.

40 Cited in Banks, *Prosperity and parenthood*, pp. 5–6; *Report of the Royal Commission on Population*, ch. 5.

superficiality.[41] This may be because the discipline of demography has been so powerfully influenced by its client-relationship with the enormous funds and resources available as spin-off from the international family planning programmes which have been set up since the 1960s by 'the family planning industry' (as one critical observer has termed it).[42] Simple diffusionism has always been the most appealing and easily grasped explanatory concept, advocated by those seeking a simple and compelling rationale for a pro-active birth control policy.[43]

Secondly, Himes had both incorporated and superseded simple diffusion in a more generalised socio-cultural and politico-ideological theory, the 'democratisation' of birth control. Himes's comprehensive list of preconditions was intended as a potential heuristic framework, and as such anticipates much of the essence of the structural functionalist 'modernisation' approach with which the dominant Princeton school's research programme on the demographic transition has been intimately associated throughout much of the postwar era. Additionally, there have appeared during this more recent period complementary historical accounts of the rise of the birth control movement and its incorporation into institutions of the state, which can be read as providing the detailed political and cultural narratives implied by Himes's original 'democratisation' thesis.[44]

Thirdly, Enid Charles's widely read and influential intervention, published even before Himes's *magnum opus*, also took issue with Beveridge's narrowly cultural notion of simple diffusion. But Charles's counter-thesis emphasised instead the importance of the changing household economy as the analytical focus of attention. In championing 'household economics' as the proper approach to the study of changing fertility behaviour, Charles also raised several of the key issues which have since dominated debate between economists and sociologists over the use of this approach. Although Charles offered a recognisably Dumontian status-and-aspiration-driven analysis for the middle classes, she perceived the significance of a rather different set of influences where the working classes were concerned. Here she envisaged the imposition of certain central state legislative restrictions on child labour and education as a critical factor. Charles, therefore, clearly acknowledged that an important methodological adjunct to the economic approach was a recognition that the economic logic of different groups or social classes in the population might be quite distinct, governed as they were by their differing social and cultural circumstances. She also raised, in principle, issues relating to the

41 For a frequently cited diffusionist statement, made as a balanced judgement in full knowledge of the range of historical evidence, see Knodel and van de Walle, 'Lessons from the past'. This was also republished in 1986 as ch. 9 in Coale and Watkins (eds.), *The decline of fertility*.

42 Demeny, 'Social science'.

43 Marie Stopes perfectly exemplifies the direct connection between simple diffusionism as an historical interpretation and as an activist policy for promoting fertility decline. Her *Early days of birth control* was an example of the former; and her *Contraception: its theory, history and practice* an example of the latter. On Stopes and birth control, see Soloway, *Birth control*; and Rose, *Marie Stopes*.

44 For instance in regard to British history: Fryer, *The birth controllers*; Leathard, *The fight for family planning*. Also, on USA, Gordon, *Woman's body, woman's right*; Reed, *From private vice to public virtue*.

actions of the central state, and therefore formal political developments, as a potentially determinative influence upon fertility behaviour.

Finally, there was Notestein's early attention to the question of the extent to which birth controlling behaviour really was a novel departure in human history and the nature of the evidence for and against such a view. The apparent force and explanatory sufficiency of Beveridge's elegant diffusionist thesis would be undermined if it could be shown that contraceptive techniques of some efficacy were *not* something entirely new, after all. That would tend to suggest that factors related to the motivational and encompassing socio-economic contexts might after all be crucial in accounting for the differential adoption of such techniques in different times and places. Notestein was impressed with the significance of comparative historical and cultural evidence on the existence and practice of contraception before the modern era. The implications of the extent and kind of contraceptive behaviour practised in non-industrialised cultures have again become an extremely active focus of debate during the last decade or so.[45]

Thus, the central issues of most post-Second World War debates over the relative importance of economic and social or cultural and political forces in determining changes in fertility behaviour were in fact already on the agenda before demographic transition theory had become the predominant heuristic framework. Once the basic empirical form of the phenomenon in question – national, unitary fertility decline – had become an established fact for all parties concerned, this alone was enough to fuel most of these debates. The official and comprehensive inquiry into falling fertility in Britain had apparently demonstrated that it was, indeed, a national unitary process, exhibiting a socially graded pattern of incidence in conformity with British society's well-known social class or status hierarchy. Even Enid Charles, offering the most politically critical and methodologically independent input to the interwar debates, nevertheless accepted this representation of the phenomenon. In rejecting the diffusionist theory of Beveridge and proposing her own alternative, Charles nevertheless accepted Stevenson's socially graded empirical model of the fertility decline as a sufficient description of the phenomenon itself.[46] The official, class-differential, 'professional model' of fertility decline was not merely unchallenged, but was thereby positively reinforced as the correct depiction of the phenomenon in question, since all the burgeoning debate was premised upon it.

Since 1945 demographic transition has come and gone and, according to some at least, even come once again as scientific theory.[47] Meanwhile social scientists of

[45] McLaren, *Reproductive rituals*; McLaren, *A history of contraception*; Noonan, *Contraception*; Riddle, 'Oral contraceptives'; Riddle, *Contraception and abortion*.

[46] Charles, *The twilight of parenthood*, pp. 114–18.

[47] Jean-Claude Chesnais has emerged as a champion of Notestein's original demographic transition theory, in a substantial work: Chesnais, *La Transition démographique*. (This has now been translated by Kreager and Kreager, as *The demographic transition*.)

various methodological persuasions continue to disagree over the primacy of economic versus cultural factors in causing fertility decline.[48] But throughout all this, the underlying notion of fertility decline as national unitary phenomenon has never been subjected to rigorous or radical critique. The conviction has simply continued that this was first and most conclusively demonstrated in the case of Britain's socially regimented fertility decline. Perhaps, then, it is the uncritical acceptance of this representation which partly explains the relative absence of conceptual development or heuristic change within the field of fertility study throughout the many decades that have elapsed since the range of positions set out above was first articulated in the interwar period. As long as this empirical model of a unitary, socially graded national process remains unrefuted as the predominant conception, it will govern, as a premise, the form in which all attempts at explanation are framed.

The postwar study of fertility behaviour within the social sciences

This section reviews the main approaches which have characterised social scientists' study of fertility change since the Second World War.[49] The ideas of demographic transition and modernisation will first be discussed, as they influenced sociologists and demographers. There will then be sections looking at the approach of anthropologists and of micro-economists, the other two main social science disciplines involved in the study of fertility.

During the course of the 1950s US transition demographers had begun to appreciate the limitations of their theory when confronted with a widening spectrum of historical and contemporary evidence. In fact it is quite clear that the two leading exponents of the concept of a demographic transition, F. W. Notestein and K. Davis, had already by the beginning of the 1950s each abandoned the empirically testable, theoretical content of their classic formulations of 1944–5.[50] Primary causation was no longer envisaged as being necessarily provided by economic development and it was recognised that a fall in mortality might be preceded by a fall in fertility, as had clearly been the case in late eighteenth-century France. All that really remained of transition theory was a broad, inductive generalisation: that mortality and fertility rates tended to be higher in a country before it had experienced the process of industrialisation than was the case after. It was the encompassing conceptual framework of structural

48 For a well-informed survey of this long-standing impasse, see Cleland and Wilson, 'Demand theories'.

49 Although it was published a quarter of a century ago in a field which has seen an enormous volume of publications, Geoffrey Hawthorn's *The sociology of fertility* still provides a stimulating, wide-ranging but concise introduction to the various approaches of social scientists; and it is accompanied by a very helpful annotated bibliography, integrated with the text, of much of the important early postwar literature whose formative influence upon current preoccupations is not to be discounted.

50 Hodgson, 'Demography as social science'; Hodgson, 'Orthodoxy and revisionism'; Szreter, 'The idea of demographic transition'.

functionalist modernisation which kept the basic idea of demographic transition alive throughout the 1950s and 1960s at a time when the accumulating historical and contemporary demographic evidence was suggesting a more murky and complicated picture.[51] Hence, in 1959 the demographer N. B. Ryder had explicitly spelled out that 'demographic transition', if it was to continue to be seen as a theory at all, entailed a larger set of general laws, which he identified as substantially those of the 'modernisation' school of thought.[52]

There were certain specific intellectual influences which lay beneath and behind the particular appeal that 'transition theory' had for liberal social scientists in the post-Second World War era. This was a school of thought emanating from the structural functionalist theory of Talcott Parsons which was at this time a new orthodoxy enjoying its heyday, a temporary all-engrossing pre-eminence.[53] Originating from within the discipline of sociology, the theory posited the validity of general principles of social and political organisation, in a tightly constrained relationship with the forces of economic and technological change.

The core of Parsons's functionalist theory consisted in the innovative attempt to analyse 'society' rigorously and comprehensively as a self-equilibriating *system*. The cybernetic concepts of systems theory, initially developed in the control engineering and the biological sciences, were deployed: in particular the powerful homeostatic concept of feedback control. This approach produced a theory which purported to explain how most social, economic and cultural features of societies necessarily interacted and how this occurred according to a hierarchy of implicit goals which functioned to maintain the society in a state of dynamic healthy stability. In the 1950s sociologists were increasingly appreciative of this intellectual framework, as it enabled them to admonish those economists and policy-makers who were insufficiently respectful of the systemic effects of cultural and social forces in their designs for stimulating economic development, an intellectual and political enterprise of fast-growing status and vigour at this time.

The theory of a tightly interactive, cybernetic system constrained Parsons to assert that such a stable society would be characterised by a single, unitary value system. Other conflicting sanctions for morality would represent a form of

51 Kingsley Davis and Judith Blake began giving much greater attention to the social and cultural variables which mediated the process of demographic transition. Davis went on to formulate a more flexible model of 'multi-phasic' demographic response to economic change, in which migration, nuptiality and other demographic processes were all seen as mutually related functional substitutes alongside fertility and mortality: any combination of short- and longer-term responses was possible under conditions of economic change. Davis and Blake, 'Social structure and fertility'; Davis 'The theory of change and response'.

52 Ryder, 'Fertility'.

53 Parsons's first major work expounding structural functionalism was *The structure of social action* (1937). However, it was *The social system* (1951) which initiated what has been described as the only brief period of normal science, in the Kuhnian sense, in the history of American empirical sociology (R. W. Friedrichs, cited in Kent, *A history*, p. 192).

'deviance', which the system's controls would flush out.[54] In the case of modern liberal US society, Parsons believed that this single dominant value system could be characterised according to his celebrated 'pattern variables', a set of related fundamental dispositions in the personality of individuals, which strongly conditioned all actions. This framework was eagerly adopted by the 'modernisation' theorists, a highly influential policy-oriented school of what might be termed 'development sociology' or sociological history.[55] This was conceived by its chief progenitors, B. F. Hoselitz, Marion Levy, E. E. Hagen, J. J. Spengler and Wilbert Moore (one of Notestein's wartime colleagues at the Princeton Office), as a corrective to any narrowly economic blueprints for fostering growth and development in low-income societies.[56] The modernisation school operationalised Parsons's pattern variables, or action-orientations, as empirical criteria for diagnosing the characteristics of all possible societies along a dichotomous continuum from the 'traditional' to the 'modern'.[57]

According to structural functionalist theory, since the family was the central institution of socialisation, it was the primary agency of cultural determination of individuals' personality traits, inculcating the dominant value system and its pattern variables. Economic growth and the emergence of an industrialised and urbanised society, in succession to an agrarian 'traditional' society, entailed certain necessary changes in the family and its functions, both *vis-à-vis* the society and the economy, and also between the family's constituent members. This inevitable transition was characterised as a shift, in terms of the pattern variables, to a 'modern' universalist, individualist and rationalist value system, replacing a 'traditional' particularist, collectivist and localist one. The small, socially insulated, nuclear family household of income-earning parents and dependent, consuming children was envisaged as the historical product of the process of industrialisation and urbanisation, replacing the extended family of traditional communities. It became the new normal socialising environment, incubating the modern versions of the pattern variables. There was, thus, an exact homology between the theory of demographic transition and Parsonian sociology, in terms of their model of historical change in the form and functions of the family. This was no coincidence:

54 Although it is to be noted that the phenomenon of deviance also seems to have constituted the theory's main possibility for envisaging a process of historical change from one dominant value system to another, something which occurred in the event of the controls failing to contain such deviance. This potential was embodied in E. E. Hagen's thesis regarding the nonconformist socialisation of entrepreneurs as the agency of social change causing the industrial revolution itself: Hagen, *On the theory of social change*.

55 For a critique of modernisation as a social evolutionary theory of historical change, see Burke, *History and social theory*, pp. 131–41.

56 The 'Modernisation School' founded its journal, *Economic Development and Cultural Change*, in 1952, *pari passu* with the fast-emerging discipline of development economics.

57 The pattern variables were a set of binary opposites: affectivity versus affective neutrality; self-orienation versus collective orientation; universalism versus particularism; ascription versus achievement; specificity versus diffuseness. Parsons, *The social system*, pp. 58–67; Parsons and Shils, *Toward a general theory of action*, pp. 56–60.

all of the Princeton demographers, and especially W. E. Moore, Marion Levy and K. Davis, were well versed in Parsonian sociology.

From the late 1950s until the 1970s the related disciplines of the economics and sociology of development formed probably the most well-resourced intellectual project in the US social sciences. This was because of the keen interest which US foreign policy had in competing with the USSR to offer third world client states a liberal alternative to centrally planned models for economic development. From the perspectives of both liberal development economics and the closely associated Parsonian 'modernisation school' of evolutionary sociology and sociological history, the continued portrayal by transition demographers of a dichotomy between 'traditional' and 'modern' demographic régimes still seemed a helpful descriptive generalisation, even though the idea of demographic transition itself had already suffered conclusive empirical refutation, *qua* general *theory*. Thus, during this period Notestein encouraged A. J. Coale's successful collaboration with the economist, E. M. Hoover, to consolidate and formalise a link between transition demography and development economics. They did this by producing an extremely influential model of the dynamic relationships between economic and demographic factors for a low income country during its early phases of economic growth.[58]

It was A. J. Coale who became Notestein's successor as the head of the Princeton Office, when the latter was appointed Chairman of the Population Council in 1959. From this pre-eminent disciplinary position within the field of population studies, Coale launched in 1963 the Princeton European Fertility Project. This was an ambitious research programme aiming to use the relatively detailed quantitative data available for administrative subdivisions of the nation-states of Europe to map the historical decline in fertility which had taken place there over the previous century or so.[59] It was intended to correlate these patterns, recording a demographic transition from high to low fertility, with a range of other quantifiable socio-economic and cultural data, where available for the appropriate administrative units. The programme's ultimate aim and justification was to offer an empirical test of some of the key propositions derived from the modernisation-economic development conglomerate of ideas, regarding the differences between traditional and modern societies and the mechanisms of demographic change between the two states.

Throughout the 1960s and 1970s modernisation theory, therefore, provided the conceptual backdrop for the most comprehensive programme yet of empirical research into recent European demographic history. The causal primacy assigned to autonomous economic and technological change and the chronological priority

[58] Coale and Hoover, *Population growth*. Their exposition was adumbrated in the work of H. Leibenstein: *A theory of economic-demographic development*. Another important contemporary contribution from outside the Princeton Office was: Nelson, 'A theory of the low-level equilibrium trap'.

[59] These territorial subdivisions were referred to in the project as 'provinces' and were usually the approximate equivalent of British counties.

of mortality decline, as in classic transition theory, were both abandoned, in favour of a more exploratory approach which avoided pre-judgement of the direction of causal relationships between various factors. Nevertheless, those subscribing to the new approach tended to believe that certain generalisable causal processes would be indicated. These could then be used to inform contemporary population policies in developing countries.

This search for underlying general causes was sustained by the belief that an important clue to follow, in trying to explain the fertility decline as a genus of historical event, was its supposed simultaneity of occurrence throughout the nations of European extraction.[60] The inference was implicitly drawn that fertility decline must therefore be the consequence of discoverable common features of the generic process of industrialisation and associated urbanisation.[61] With hindsight, it could apparently be seen that the fertility decline was concomitant with a wide variety of other changes in the institutions, work patterns and values of society, which in each case could be characterised as moving from a traditional to a modern status. What was required, then, was a 'shopping list' of all these variables of potential interest and, for empirical research, the construction of various surrogate quantifiable indices from the available historical sources to measure the influence of the different items on the list. Given certain conceptual advances in the application of statistical techniques, such as multivariate regression analysis and the availability of relatively cheap computing facilities, changes in dependent fertility indices could then be statistically correlated with changes in other independent variables to discover the most consistent or marked inter-relationships.[62]

It has been predominantly through the momentum of this long-running project that the neo-evolutionary dichotomies of 'modernisation' have retained, right through to the late 1980s, a dominance over the mainstream demographic approach to the study of historical fertility declines. The Princeton Project has thus succeeded in granting to the idea of demographic transition a scientific life after death. What had been a refutable theory, refuted, now lived on as an extremely non-specific general model.

[60] Coale, 'Factors associated'.

[61] Coale, 'Factors associated'; Coale, 'The voluntary control'.

[62] The most important philosophical justification for the validity of the statistical methods of correlation and regression in empirical research has been the concept of stochastic processes (i.e. probabilistic relationships). According to this argument statistics can legitimately be used to establish the existence of post-hoc descriptive regularities between variables without this entailing any necessary claim that a deterministic predictive form of causation has been revealed. See Lazarsfeld, 'Notes on the history of quantification', pp. 303–4. Strictly speaking, therefore, the question of causation would then require further research and a different methodology for its resolution. This latter stage in the methodological strategy has been exemplified by at least one contributor to the series of Princeton Project volumes, in the separate, carefully contextualised work on German village populations undertaken by J. Knodel. The difference between the two methodologies is illustrated by a comparison of the methodology and findings of Knodel's *The decline of fertility in Germany* published in 1974, with his subsequent *Demographic behaviour in the past*, published in 1988.

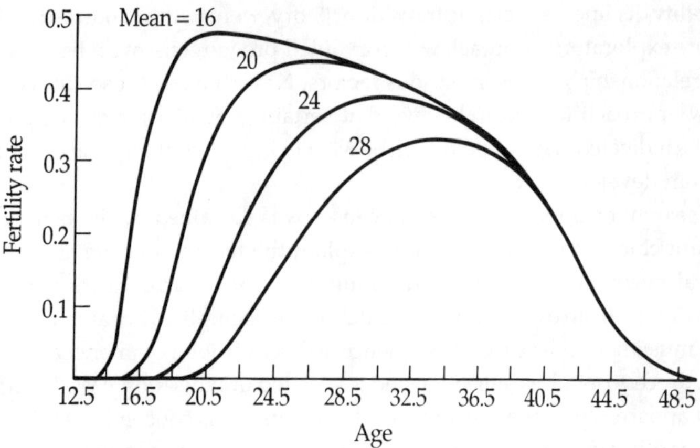

Figure 1.1 Age-specific fertility rates when marital fertility is 'natural' for four mean ages at marriage

Adapted from Trussel, Menken and Coale, 'A general model', p. 9

The task of breathing life back into the model was achieved by demographers through deployment of what purported to be an extremely powerful measuring instrument based on the dichotomous concepts of 'natural fertility' and 'controlled fertility'. This apparently provided demographers with empirically measurable analogues to the sociologists' concepts of the 'traditional' and the 'modern', respectively. Traditional societies were characterised by a natural fertility schedule of age-specific birth rates. The schedule always exhibited a particular functional form with respect to age regardless of the absolute level of fertility prevailing (see Figure 1.1). The transition to a modern régime could therefore be reliably diagnosed from the demographic evidence by the distortions evident in the functional form of this schedule: the detection of age-specific interference with the natural fertility pattern, producing a characteristically concave back slope, instead of the 'natural', convex form.

Natural fertility was significantly *not* defined as the absence of *any* kind of birth control, but only as the absence of that kind of birth control which could be detected as a deviation from the 'natural' age-specific functional form. The original inventor of the technique, Louis Henry, had classically defined controlled fertility only as parity-specific birth control: where a woman's fertility is deliberately curtailed after reaching a target number of live births. This artificially restrictive definition of birth controlling behaviour had been proposed by Henry for the purely pragmatic reason that testing for its presence or absence could be achieved in a relatively wide range of historical and contemporary information sources, as it only required data on age-specific fertility.[63]

[63] Wilson, Oeppen, and Pardoe, 'What is natural fertility?', p. 5; and see below, pp. 368–70.

A. J. Coale and his colleagues adopted, extended and perfected Henry's concepts and his measuring instrument for the Princeton cross-national historical research project. They added complementary methods for measuring variations in nuptiality and illegitimate fertility and they calibrated these measures according to an absolute level of maximum 'natural fertility', the so-called Hutterite scale based on the age-specific fertility characteristics of the most prolific population for which reliable records were deemed to exist: this resulted in the familiar system of arithmetically related Princeton fertility indices.[64] The provision of an absolute maximum value for total fertility was methodologically essential for the Princeton Project. This enabled the empirical results for the component fertility indices (I_g, I_h, I_m), whose values were derived from the empirical evidence for the territorial subdivisions in each country, to be referred to a common interval scale of measurement. This legitimated both their cross-cultural, direct comparison; and it also meant that they could be deployed as standard dependent variables in multivariate statistical analyses. This was the methodological mainstay of the Princeton Project, which aimed to use the cross-national databases to adjudicate between the causal significance of different variables on the shopping list, by measuring the relative strength of ecological relationships of correlation and regression between dependent fertility variables and a range of socio-economic and cultural variables representing the hypotheses of the modernisation school.[65] A series of national studies using this methodology has since appeared for many of the countries of Europe. This is based on analyses of the data collected by the regular censuses and the vital registration systems which most European states established during the second half of the nineteenth century, such that the continuous demographic record is usually available from a point before the dramatic falls in fertilities occurred. The volume on Britain was published in 1984 and a summary volume for the Project appeared in 1986.[66]

The British study offered three broad findings which, while suggestive, were barely more than hypotheses for further testing given the somewhat cumbersome

[64] Coale, 'Factors associated with the development of low fertility'; Coale, 'Age patterns of marriage', p. 207. The Hutterites' remarkable fertility had first been rigorously documented in Eaton and Mayer, 'The social biology of very high fertility'. The arithmetic relationship of the Princeton fertility indices is expressed by the equation, $I_f = I_g.I_m + I_h.(1 - I_m)$. Where I_f = total fertility of the population in question (expressed as a decimal fraction of the total fertility which a Hutterite population with the same female age structure would have had). I_g = marital fertility (also expressed as a fraction, measuring the degree to which the number of births experienced by the married women in the study population approaches the number that Hutterites with the same age structure would have had). I_m = a fraction expressing the extent to which all fecund women in the population are married and therefore at risk to pregnancy, adjusted to reflect the fact that on average female fertility declines with age (and therefore, for instance, a high proportion of unmarried women in their early twenties will reduce the value of this fraction much more than a high proportion unmarried in their thirties). I_h = illegitimate fertility: the fertility of unmarried women measured in exactly the same way, with reference to the Hutterite age-specific rates of childbearing, as I_g.

[65] Subject to the methodological considerations specified in n. 62.

[66] Teitelbaum, *The British fertility decline*; Coale and Watkins (eds.), *The decline of fertility*.

nature of the basic taxonomic units of analysis (registration counties), the statistical limitations of the general approach (ecological correlation of co-varying indices), and the somewhat inconsistent statistical results in the measures of correlation that were reported. First, there was little variation between registration counties in the date at which they passed below a given level of aggregate marital fertility. Secondly, what statistical variance there was, was 'explained' (in the statistical sense) largely by variables related to the male occupation of mining; to male illiteracy; and to the percentage of females employed in non-traditional occupations (this latter not being true for Scotland). Thirdly, a strong cultural divide between England-and-Wales and Scotland, and also, of course, Ireland, was in evidence in the timing of fertility change.

Indeed, many of the Princeton Project studies seemed to indicate the importance of broadly 'cultural' factors, such as linguistic and religious variables and those related to female work patterns, as being of great significance as determinants of the timing of marked regional and local differentials in fertility decline within national populations.[67] Some of the contributors to the summary volume of 1986 seemed also to be impressed with the extent to which national populations appeared to be significantly fissured into various types of family household depending on highly localised employment opportunities, determined by the character of the community's industry.[68] Furthermore, it was observed that cultural and political factors – often related to both the region's social history and its degree of urbanisation – may have been extremely important.[69]

However, the most recently published attempt to give a unified interpretation to the results of the Princeton Project seeks to incorporate and interpret these findings and those of early modern demographic historians once again within a modified version of the linear, neo-evolutionary, modernisation framework of thinking. In *From provinces into nations* Susan Watkins argues that each nation's Princeton data exhibits a marked historical trend of a movement from pre-industrial local and regional intra-national variance and diversity in family-building behaviour towards a post-industrial situation of national convergence and relative homogeneity.[70] Watkins is offering a transposition on the Princeton Project's

[67] For instance: Livi-Bacci, *A century of Portuguese fertility*, pp. 125–31, on Portugal; Knodel, *The decline of fertility*, especially pp. 130–47, on Germany; Lesthaeghe, *The decline of Belgian fertility*, pp. 40–4, 227–31, on Belgium. Note that this is a reiteration of one of Beveridge's main findings in his 1925 article: that the unitary 'national' experience of fertility decline has been moderated by those ethnic divisions which are related to historical religious and linguistic differences within a national population. Beveridge, 'The fall of fertility'. In the Princeton studies the influence of such ethnic diversity has tended to be conceptualised only in a relatively simple manner, as functioning rather like social classes in the British case, in either delaying or facilitating the pace of the unitary phenomenon of fertility decline, rather than as rendering it into distinct phenomena, as will be argued here, below.

[68] Lesthaeghe and Wilson, 'Modes of production'; and Knodel, 'Demographic transitions in German villages'.

[69] Sharlin, 'Urban–rural differences in fertility'; Watkins, 'Regional patterns of nuptiality'.

[70] Watkins, *From provinces into nations*.

animating theme of 'modernisation'. The 'traditional' is now allowed the mosaic of variety which three decades of detailed research by early modern demographic historians has conclusively demonstrated to have been the case (see below, pp. 31–3 and n. 164). However, all still converges towards the single state of 'the modern', now defined as national homogeneity.

Yet even a cursory glance at modern British society indicates that the assumption of homogeneity is untenable for this country, alone. There is the direct evidence of the urban anthropologists of London's East End and various other communities in the 1950s, which demonstrates the massive intra-county (indeed, intra-urban) variety in family forms to be found in British society still in 1960.[71] Added to this, the bald summary statistics of rising rates of cohabitation, marital separation and single-parent families, apart from other forms of extended and multiple family households related to first and even second remarriages and to the customs of immigrant ethnic communities, all strongly indicate that the degree of heterogeneity in family formation and residence patterns in Britain has only increased all the more in the period since Watkins's cut-off date of 1960.[72]

Furthermore, a fundamental flaw in the argument from the statistical evidence for increased homogeneity should be exposed. It may well be that if each national population is divided into the geographical units used by the Princeton Project – equivalent to Britain's administrative counties – there will appear to be less variance in the averaged fertility and nuptiality behaviour between such counties in 1960 than existed in 1870. But this is almost certainly for the obvious reason that at the earlier date most counties were in the midst of a massive shift in the proportions of the population living and working in the countryside as against the town. They therefore exhibited enormous heterogeneity in these terms, whereas by 1960 virtually all counties had a uniformly relatively low proportion of truly rural families. It seems probable that much of the change in statistical variance which Watkins observes is simply a statistical artefact attributable to this effect, whose importance in interpreting differentials in demographic behaviour was demonstrated long ago by David Goldberg.[73]

Thirdly, the crucial issue of the agency of the state, as something which

[71] Young and Willmott, *Family and kinship*; Bott, *Family and social network*.

[72] See Joshi (ed.), *The changing population*, especially, chs. 1, 3–5, 7–8, 10–11; also Coleman and Salt, *The British population*, chs. 5–6, 12.

[73] In a salutary and deservedly influential article on the putative relationship between social class and fertility in the USA, David Goldberg has shown the importance of the simple compositional effect of the proportions having rural as against urban origins. Through a rigorous local study Goldberg was able to show that the much-vaunted pattern of class-differential fertility behaviour in the USA, graded according to the professional model of occupational classification, was primarily a function of the different classes' compositions in terms of rural immigrants versus first- and second-generation urbanites. Since these compositional effects have varied so enormously in all countries across the period surveyed by Watkins, it is essential that they be correctly acknowledged before drawing any wider inferences regarding the kinds of diachronic trends which Watkins has emphasised. Goldberg, 'The fertility of two-generation urbanites'.

should be brought more centrally into an account of changing fertility behaviour, is also raised by Watkins as an important part of the story; and this is undoubtedly important. But there is a failure to consider the state as anything more complex than the monolithic homogeniser of market conditions and regional cultures, which thereby supposedly accounts for the national uniformities in family formation patterns obtaining *c.* 1960. But the state's workings are complex and may be as divisive as they are productive of uniformities. For instance, one of the primary functions of the central state which Watkins refers to is its direction of the nation's evolving education system. In the case of English society, however (but not Scottish), the national education system was intentionally designed by the British state (the nineteenth-century Education Department and the twentieth-century Board of Education) to act as a fundamentally élitist, hierarchical and socially divisive institution throughout the period under review by Watkins.[74] This is quite to the contrary of Watkins's assumption, regarding the necessarily homogenising influence of the institutions of the state. Certainly, any degree of convergence in family-building practices in Britain which may have occurred during this period was in despite of – perhaps even in reaction against – the positively class-divisive educational policies pursued by the British state. The rise of the nation-state and its many functions has not, therefore, had any single general linear influence towards convergence in forms of reproduction.

Ultimately, then, as a contribution to the central issue of the causation involved in fertility declines, Watkins does not offer an approach which can escape from the conceptual shackles of the dichotomous neo-evolutionism of modernisation, which has throughout animated the Princeton Project's notion of a demographic transition from natural to controlled fertility. Nor does the explicit reference to the state result in a formulation of its role which carries immediate conviction in the British historical context. The relationship between 'the state' and changing fertility behaviour clearly requires a more nuanced and flexible conceptualisation.

Thus, almost despite itself and its clinging to the modernisation conceptual framework along with the 'natural fertility' measurement technology, the work done within the Princeton Project's tradition is beginning to point towards the need for appreciation and study of the non-generalisable elements within societies: their particular political authority structures in different regions and towns; the relation of these to different communities' economic bases; relationships within the family, especially between the sexes. The study of fertility change

[74] On the character of the Victorian state's education policy, see below, pp. 148–65. The famous Butler Education Act of 1944, coming towards the end of Watkins's period of analysis, was remarkable for its masterly preservation of the principles of social class division in the nation's educational institutions as laid down in the Victorian era. The perniciously inegalitarian nature of the system perpetuated by the Act was brilliantly analysed and exposed in: Banks, *Parity and prestige*.

through aggregated statistics is confirming, through its own limitations, the value of more carefully contextualised studies of communities and social groupings, such as those pioneered, for the mid- and later nineteenth-century period of British history, in the publications of Joe Banks, Michael Anderson and Michael Haines.[75]

Demographic social scientists working within the methodological terms of reference of the Princeton Project were far from being alone in their continuing endorsement of the modernisation perspective. From the early 1950s onwards there appeared a stream of influential treatments of change in the family from sociologists and historians, each, in effect, charting a different variation on the master-theme of a Parsonian shift from the traditional to the modern: Riesman, Smelser, Ariès, Shorter, de Mause and Stone.[76] Nevertheless, throughout the same period there were also historians and anthropologists involved in more careful and independent-minded investigative research on family forms and fertility behaviour, both in the past and present of post-industrial and less developed societies.[77] They were producing a range of empirical findings profoundly at variance with the linear, evolutionary perspective of modernisation theory.[78]

Many historians interested in the family, kinship and the functioning of local communities in the past adopted methodologies having much in common with ethnological and anthropological approaches, paying careful attention to local contexts and institutions. The historical work on medieval and early modern English society by the anthropologist Alan Macfarlane or the 'ethnographic' work on French society by the historian Emmanuel Le Roy Ladurie most clearly demonstrate this virtual identity of interests and methods across the disciplines.[79] Demographic and social historians of early modern Europe such as Louis Henry, Pierre Goubert, E. A. Wrigley, K. Wrightson and D. Levine, using the powerful family reconstitution technique, have demonstrated the potential value of this

[75] Banks, *Prosperity and parenthood*; Banks and Banks, *Feminism and family planning*; Banks, *Victorian values*; Anderson, *Family structure*; Haines, *Fertility and occupation*; see also Johansson (unpublished PhD dissertation).

[76] Riesman, *The lonely crowd*; Smelser, *Social change*; Ariès, *L'Enfant et la vie familiale* (translated as *Centuries of childhood*); de Mause (ed.), *The history of childhood*; Shorter, *The making of the modern family*; Stone, *The family, sex and marriage*.

[77] For example, in the same the year that Stone published his triumphalist chronicle of the rise of the egalitarian nuclear family in early modern Protestant society (seemingly unaware of the implications of demographic historians' research over the previous two decades, which showed the nuclear family generally in existence long before it had 'risen' – according to Stone's chronology), an altogether much more sophisticated and penetrating account of such relationships also became available: Greven, *The Protestant temperament* (1977). Trumbach's *The rise of the egalitarian family* was also a more nuanced approach. Greven's study effectively built upon and amplified Morgan's *The Puritan family*, published in 1944, which should have given Stone and others more pause for thought.

[78] The most effective and scathing attack on the modernisation school's Whig history of family relations has been Pollock's *Forgotten Children*.

[79] Macfarlane, *The origins of English individualism*; Le Roy Ladurie, *Montaillou*.

approach as the basis for an understanding of the complexity of demographic processes in the pre-industrial past.[80]

This historical demographic work on pre-industrial English society has, for instance, conclusively shown that 'modern' nuclear family households were not so much concomitant with as antecedent to industrialisation, constituting the typical form of residential group throughout the early modern period. The early modern socio-demographic régime was characterised by nuclear family household and late prudential marriage which typically followed a period of waged work and saving on the part of young adults while they lived away from their household and parish of birth.[81] There was in effect a taboo in this culture against marriage if the prospective married couple did not have their own physically separate household and the reasonable expectation of the stream of income necessary to maintain their economic independence from kin and neighbours (which is not to say that, having been seen to have correctly observed these ground rules for family formation, kin, neighbours and community would not thereafter provide assistance at times of special need). The taboo was apparently sufficiently rigorously observed that in addition to a late age at marriage, as much as 10–20% of each cohort were regularly prepared to remain celibate to age forty-five rather than flout these prudential rules. Whatever illicit sexual activity there was, seems to have issued in remarkably few illegitimate births.[82]

The régime's effective nuptiality controls functioned, therefore, as an extremely sensitive regulator of the society's fertility potential, tying rates of reproduction closely to the prevailing conditions of relative economic opportunity for saving and setting up households, the prerequisite for marriage and commencement of reproduction. Clearly these were cultural and economic institutions of supreme importance, which no theory of population change nor any historical sociological account can afford to ignore. The relationship between population growth, economic development, fertility and mortality levels was seen to be an infinitely

[80] From the first years of the 1950s Pierre Goubert and Louis Henry had independently begun to investigate the possibility of family reconstitution from French parish registers. A methodological handbook first appeared in 1956 and the first such systematic reconstitution was published in 1958: Fleury and Henry, *Des registres paroissiaux*; Gautier and Henry, *La Population de Crulai*. Goubert's much more substantial work, placing the demographic evidence revealed by reconstitution within the context of a broad social and economic historical interpretation, appeared in 1960: Goubert, *Beauvais et les Beauvaisis*. The pioneering Anglophone reconstitution was, of course, E. A. Wrigley's work on Colyton first published in 1966: 'Family limitation', followed by Wrightson and Levine, *Poverty and piety*. On the pre-history of family reconstitution during the first half of the twentieth century, see Dupâquier, *Pour la démographie historique*.

[81] This régime was first identified in John Hajnal's celebrated article, 'European marriage patterns in perspective', first published in 1965. Peter Laslett's best-selling *The world we have lost*, published in the same year, also drew attention to these features. Kussmaul, *Servants in husbandry*, was an important further contribution. See also previous footnote for references to the pioneering methodological work.

[82] Laslett and Oostereven, 'Long-term trends in bastardy'. See also Laslett, Oostereven and Smith (eds.), *Bastardy*; Laslett, *Family life and illicit love*.

more complex and variable one than the linear evolution envisaged under the rubric of transition theory and modernisation.[83]

Similar embarrassments for Parsonian grand theory emerged from contemporary research by urban anthropologists on the post-industrial family in Britain and the USA in the 1950s and 1960s. This work has shown that, rather than 'disappearing', extended and complex family households and localist value systems were very much in existence, if not positively proliferating in many industrialised urban communities. The continuing existence in many social groups of strongly localised extended kinship networks and considerable gender segregation of social life was, from the point of view of Parsonian theory, a surprise 'discovery'.[84] These communities were additionally subjected to a thorough functionalist anthropological treatment, through the analysis of the relationship between networks of kin, neighbours, friends and the quality of the conjugal role relationships enjoyed by the spouses. The latter were categorised on a spectrum from 'joint' (i.e. relatively full sharing of decisions and responsibilities) to 'segregated'.[85] Joint conjugal relationships were, in general, found to be associated with loose-knit social networks outside the family, especially those of kinship; whereas in the case of segregated conjugal relationships, the individual spouses had closer-knit social networks outside the nuclear family.

The general implications of all this work were clear: that conjugal relationships, differences in roles between the sexes, networks of kinship, patterns of socialisation with friends and neighbours all still varied widely in the post-industrial world, depending on such influences as community, class, occupation, income level and education. Meanwhile, in the USA, the phenomenon of chronic poverty, as a continuing affliction of certain families even within an extremely affluent society, was provoking studies of these 'deviant' minorities in an attempt to account for their plight. One of the principal observable characteristics of the members of these underprivileged sections of society was found to be their strong association with large family size, either as siblings or as parents or both. This came to be identified as the demographic element in a syndrome of characteristics termed 'the culture of poverty'. The theoretically important point of this term, coined by Oscar Lewis in *Scientific American* in 1966, was that it successfully conveyed the strongly anti-Parsonian thesis, which American sociologists were now coming to entertain, that two or more separate value systems might co-exist as permanent features: carrying the implication that 'modern' society was not necessarily the unitary, integrated monolith envisaged in Parsonian theory after all.

The anthropological study of human fertility behaviour has a long pedigree, as

[83] For a synthesis of this more nuanced view of the relationship between economic and demographic growth, see Wrigley, *Continuity, chance and change*.

[84] Young and Willmott, *Family and kinship*, p. 11. It was a surprise in the context of Parsonian theory, which predicted that the modern urban family was nuclear and privatised.

[85] Bott, *Family and social network*.

one would expect in a discipline which has always placed the comparative study of family forms and kinship functions at its centre.[86] However, the specifically demographic perspective of rigorously quantified vital rates and their inter-relations has not, until very recently, attracted anthropologists' attentions. While demographers have periodically shown systematic interest in anthropologists' findings – two prominent English-language examples being A. M. Carr-Saunders's comprehensive survey published in 1922 and F. Lorimer's UN report of 1954 – only a small number of trained anthropologists have shown sufficient interest in the demographers' agenda to devote their powerful, intensive investigative methodology specifically to the study of changing fertility (this may also be because of the dominance of the functionalist approach for so long within modern anthropology, which militates against a focus on change in the societies studied).

The principal early exception to this in the postwar era was the work of J. M. Stycos and associates.[87] Stycos and his colleagues were able to show, for instance, the importance of local mores and norms governing gender relations as strong determinants of the quality of conjugal relationships between husbands and wives, in turn influencing their capacity to formulate family planning goals and to put such aims into effective practice.[88] More recently it has been predominantly those working within a self-consciously anthropological approach who have come to place more and more emphasis on all aspects of local, national and even international power relations – as well as gendered inequalities – as playing an important part in explanations of historical change in fertility patterns.[89]

By contrast, the functionalist, liberal sociology of Parsons and evolutionary modernisation theory were both notoriously evasive on such issues of power relations and socio-political conflict.[90] This criticism was first made within the demographic field as a call in the late 1970s for more 'institutional' analysis of fertility change, combining anthropological respect for context with a rigorous micro-demography. The Population Council's Centre for Policy Studies emerged as something of a base for this approach, exemplified in the work of Mead Cain,

[86] On the institutional and cognitive history of the discipline of anthropology as practised in Britain, see Stocking, *Victorian anthropology*; and Kuklick, *The savage within*.

[87] Stycos, *Family and fertility in Puerto Rico*; Hill *et al.*, *The family and population control*; Stycos, 'Culture and differential fertility'; Stycos and Weller, 'Female working roles'; Stycos, *Human fertility in Latin America*.

[88] Stycos, *Family and fertility in Puerto Rico*: the first chapter dealt with the 'Differential status ideologies of the sexes', an overwhelming force in such a *machismo* culture. Stycos *et al.*, 'Problems of communication', showed that family planning was very ineffective in Puerto Rico because the '*respeto*' ethic of wifely deference reduced communication between spouses on this issue to a minimum.

[89] For examples of such work, see McCormack (ed.), *Ethnography of fertility*; Bledsoe and Isiugo-Abanihe, 'Strategies of child fosterage'; Bledsoe, 'The politics of children', in Handwerker (ed.), *Births and power*. Greenhalgh, 'Toward', is a stimulating guide to this body of work.

[90] Wright Mills's *The sociological imagination* contains the classic and eloquent indictment, on these grounds, of the intellectual adequacy of both Parsonian sociology and Lazarsfeld's philosophy of statistical empiricism.

G. McNicoll, W. Arthur and others.[91] The fieldwork of J. C. and P. Caldwell, discussed below, should certainly also be included among the 1970s revivalists of an anthropological micro-demographic approach. Their work has contributed a plethora of intriguing insights into the operation and rationale of the demographic régimes of urban and rural Nigeria, such as the notable finding that pioneers of marital birth control among the urban élite of their study town, Ibadan, did not perceive themselves as doing anything innovative but merely as extending a practice which had now become 'normal' – but in the context of illicit sexual relations. This finding was related to the important additional discovery that confiding 'companionate' relations between the sexes were expected and sought more frequently in the context of freely chosen, extra-marital affairs. It was simply accepted that there would often be no freedom of choice over marriage partners and therefore there was little expectation there by either spouse of a companionate conjugal relationship.[92]

The relative successes of the intensive, contextual approach characteristic of anthropological fieldwork seem now to be attracting more and more demographers to such local micro-studies, even where the ultimate aim remains the elucidation of large-scale demographic change, such as nation-wide fertility decline.[93] An increasingly penetrating, empirically grounded debate has ensued over the relative importance, inter-relationship and mode of operation of the various dimensions of household and community power (patterns of land-holding, parental authority, and labour, status and security considerations) in accounting for and giving an institutional and individual rationality to different kinds of fertility strategies in agrarian, low-income contexts and under changing economic conditions.[94] There has also been increasingly fruitful exchange and debate between anthropologically inclined demographers of contemporary, less developed societies and demographic historians of early modern Europe. These early modern historians have been able to combine detailed demographic data with various other forms of local, historical evidence to sustain theoretical debates that match in complexity and sophistication the debates of present-day researchers with the ability to design and collect their own material. There has, for instance, been much exchange between the two sets of scholars over the relationship

91 Arthur and McNicoll, 'An analytical survey'. At the same time Geoffrey Hawthorn's reportage of field studies in India identified absence of appreciation of these factors as a problem for the successful implementation of family planning programmes there: Hawthorn (ed.), *Population and development*, pp. 15–17; also in the same volume, the article by McNicoll, 'Population and development', especially pp. 84ff. Mead Cain's earliest contributions included: 'The economic activities of children'; 'The household life cycle'.

92 Caldwell and Caldwell, 'The role of marital sexual abstinence'.

93 Caldwell, Hill and Hull (eds.), *Micro-approaches to demographic research*; McNicoll and Cain (eds.), *Rural development and population*, contains contributions from a number of researchers in this vein.

94 For examples of two recent substantial contributions to this wide-ranging debate, both entering into critical dialogue with Mead Cain's work, see Thomas, 'Land fertility'; Vlassof, 'The value of sons'.

between different forms of family household, institutionalised community provision for the elderly, and fertility patterns.[95]

There has also been a significant attempt from within this anthropological perspective to formulate a general theory of fertility decline as an explicit alternative to demographic transition theory. This has been J. C. Caldwell's theory that fertility behaviour is determined by 'inter-generational wealth-flows'.[96] If parents were the net gainers of the wealth generated by children's labours, benefiting and buttressing their position of authority, this would favour high and relatively unrestrained fertility. If this net flow was significantly disrupted or reversed, then lower levels of fertility would be favoured instead. Although ostensibly an economic theory of fertility decline, the Caldwells unequivocally identified a specific socio-cultural institution as the key historical cause of shifts in the pattern of wealth-flows. The Caldwells claimed that mass education in modern Nigeria and in both historical Australia and Britain had been the key development. Both its short- and its longer-term effects were the primary cause of a reversal in the direction of intergenerational wealth-flows.

According to the Caldwells the specifically 'western' education system equipped many of the younger generation with the skills for an enhanced personal earning power. It also influenced their expectations through exposure to its liberal individualist value system, legitimising personal merit and achievement as against familial responsibilities. It thereby contained an immanent counter-gerontocratic message. The elder generation were nevertheless keen to sponsor their children through education because of the widely appreciated prospect of the higher familial earnings which this produced. But an unintended consequence was that the bargaining position of the educated young, *vis-à-vis* their land/cattle-holding and wealth-allocating parents, was transformed by virtue of the children's possession of an independent and superior earning potential in the urban service economy, as a result of the portable, personal skills they had acquired from formal education. The Caldwells argued that with parental control over children gradually but inexorably thereby eroded, the established wealth-flows rationale for high fertility as a source of parental income and old-age security was also diminished: children were no longer prepared to view their earnings as a family, rather than an individual resource. The setting up of private and state insurance and pension schemes was both response to and reinforcement of the *de facto* emergence of this trend of a decreasing hold of the elderly over the young.

The Caldwells' thesis is that in Nigeria it was specifically the 'westernisation' of key values in the education system, replacing extended family loyalties with more individualist aims, which was the cause of shifting wealth-flows and fertility

[95] Smith, 'Transfer incomes'; Smith, 'Welfare and the management of demographic uncertainty'; Schofield, 'Family structure'.

[96] Caldwell, 'Towards a restatement'. A stream of articles over the ensuing years was collected together in: Caldwell, *Theory of fertility decline*.

strategies. This was propounded by the Caldwells as an explicit alternative to and 'restatement' of demographic transition theory. 'Westernisation', primarily through a national education system – and not the all-embracing forces of 'modernisation' more generally associated with industrialisation – was now proposed as the true cause of fertility decline.[97]

However, as will be seen below, 'westernisation' does not in fact represent a genuine conceptual alternative to 'modernisation', being once again an attempt to reduce the explanation of fertility variation to a single specific cause. It is, moreover, inconsistent with the thrust of much of the most valuable, detailed anthropological fieldwork in this area, including some of the Caldwells' own researches.

Since Malthus, the relationship between household size and its economic resources has, of course, been seen as an important perspective from which to approach the question of variations in human fertility. The economics of household formation, widely defined, has been one of the most important and stimulating areas of genuine conceptual growth in the research into fertility that has been conducted during the last three decades. It is now becoming fully appreciated that the scope for questions concerning the variable economics of children constitutes a formidably broad empirical research agenda.[98] In fact it is something which involves addressing quintessentially cultural issues: in particular the changing definitions of childhood, parenting and motherhood, upon which the more economic evaluations are premised. This is not, after all, merely a sub-branch of neoclassical micro-economics, although historiographically micro-economics was a source of reinvigoration for this approach in the postwar era.

It was always a direct implication of the modernisation-transition school and the supposed applicability of the Parsonian pattern variables, that the individuals of a 'modern' society could be expected to exhibit a more or less economically rational relationship between their fertility, their production and their consumption behaviour: deploying their scarce resources of time and money in such a way as to maximise overall benefit to themselves, or 'utility'. Not surprisingly, therefore, in 1960 the neoclassical economist Gary Becker was to be found offering a formal extension of the range of marginal utility models for the analysis of household decision-making – part of the growing analytical theory of consumer demand – so as to include decisions relating to family size. From the point of view of neoclassical micro-economists, it was evidently desirable that such models attempt to take into account consumers' propensities to invest their time and money in child-related goods and services as against other forms of consumption, as part of their efforts to develop models offering more accurate predictions of market behaviour. Over the ensuing decade there has followed much skirmishing

[97] Caldwell, 'Towards a restatement' (reprinted as ch. 4 of Caldwell, *Theory of fertility decline*).

[98] McCormack (ed.), *Ethnography of fertility*; Gillis *et al.* (eds.), *The European experience of declining fertility*, especially the essays in Parts II and IV. Folbre, *Who pays for the kids?*

between the proponents of this neoclassical, micro-economic utility modelling approach and their opponents, mainly social and economic psychologists. The pattern of much of this debate has continued in broadly the same vein as that established at the outset: Becker's first presentation of his model in 1960 immediately provoked the pithy retort from J. S. Duesenberry, which cannot be bettered as a summary of the limitations of the utility modelling approach, that 'Economics is all about how people make choices. Sociology is all about why they don't have any choices to make.'[99]

There are a number of differences between the utility modellers and their critics and, over the years, further models have appeared, attempting to respond to some of the criticisms of the latter.[100] However, there remains a generic problem in all of the economic, modelling approaches, which constitutes a debilitating and invalidating one in the eyes of many of its critics, and one which is particularly salient when it comes to the problems of understanding historical change in fertility behaviour. This is the question of what kind or degree of rationality applies: an issue which is automatically omitted from the inquiry by the utility modelling approach, where the form of rationality obtaining is a given, and fixed.

This underlying notion of a fixed form of economically rational behaviour, both as a general proposition and as a supposedly helpful assumption for the modelling of economic behaviour in real societies, as embodied in micro-economic consumer theory, has received pulverising and radical criticism in the theoretical work of H. A. Simon, a leading figure among those within the economics

99 Becker, 'An economic analysis of fertility', immediately followed by Duesenberry's 'Comment'.

100 As a result at least two distinct types of utility model have been propounded in the study of fertility change, the fixed-preference and the variable-preference models. Until very recently, Gary Becker's 'new home economics' or 'Chicago–Columbia school' has stuck relentlessly to his original approach, as propounded in the second edition of Becker's *A treatise*. This was a conventional neoclassical utility modelling approach, in which 'preferences' (i. e. what sociologists call values or aspirations, in relation to childrearing) were assumed to be fixed and the sources of their variation were outside (exogenous) the remit of the model. The resulting model was constrained to explain observed differences in fertility between different social or historical groups only in terms of shifts in the relative prices of child-related commodities (including the time resources required of parents), as against other forms of consumption commodities. Changes in norms, attitudes, values were excluded from consideration. This was justified on the division of academic labour argument: that study of these was not the economist's job. Pollak and Watkins, 'Cultural and economic approaches to fertility', p. 490. The criticisms of the obvious limitations of this approach flowed forth: Blake, 'Income and reproductive motivation' and 'Are babies consumer durables?'; Namboodiri, 'Some observations'; Busfield and Paddon, *Thinking about children*, ch. 3; Miller and Goodwin, *Psyche and demos*, chs. 3 and 5. In response to these critiques, the alternative, 'relative income model' of the 'Pennsylvania school' has attempted to incorporate the possibility of changing preferences within the specification of the utility model and has also attempted to render the reasons for their change internal to the model (i. e. preferences are variable and endogenous): Easterlin, 'The economics and sociology of fertility'; Lindert, *Fertility and scarcity*. While this results in more complex and cumbersome models, it is not obvious that they gain much in predictive power (which remains the only justifiable reason for the modelling exercise), over the more simple and abstract, fixed preference variants.

discipline who do not subscribe to the tenets of neoclassical micro-economics.[101] Simon has drawn attention to the important distinction between the procedural and the substantive rationality attributable to any observable behaviour.[102] Neoclassical economic theory is predicated on a 'substantive' rationality, in which rational economic agents exhibit perfect utility maximising behaviour in accordance with their professed goals (which such economists call 'preferences' and which comprise a supposedly complete and rank-ordered set of reflexive and transitive options). 'Procedural' rationality, by contrast, involves a varying range of 'satisficing' behaviours, which satisfy intermediate or modified goals, consistent with the imperfect economic information available to most individuals for most of the time. Indeed, Simon has shown that the amount and character of relevant information available to individuals crucially governs the degree to which their procedural rationality can appear to be consonant with the standards of substantive rationality, as understood by economic theorists and modellers.[103]

A fundamental implication of H. A. Simon's work is that the huge variety of forms and flows of relevant information available to individuals necessarily relativises the rationality of agents' behaviour, even in a population substantially sharing the same economic and cultural values. Observable behaviour derived from the same principles of economic rationality will inevitably vary widely in its manifestations, purely as a result of the contingent properties and variability of the information environment which different individuals enjoy. This is a highly generalisable proposition and one with penetrating and proliferating relevance for the study of historical variation in human fertility behaviour.

Differences in the cultural values and the social and political institutions of different times or different places (or indeed of different social groups in the same time and place) will significantly affect the forms and flows of information perceived by individuals as relevant to their economic priorities. Hence, the effects of these cultural, social and political differences are catastrophic, in the sense that they are both formative and, therefore, determinative of people's economic preferences. Differences of this kind, which produce the informational context for

101 It is far from obvious to disciplinary outsiders, including many demographers and demographic historians, that neoclassical micro-economics is not co-extensive with the modern discipline of economics. Indeed, it is arguably a minority taste only. It is an interesting question in its own right why it is that this section of the economics discipline has been so heavily and continuously involved in dialogue with demographers over fertility behaviour during the last three to four decades, whereas other schools of thought, such as Keynesians and other macro-economists, seem to have been less involved. However, for an important recent initiative from a different kind of economist, see the discussion on pp. 590–3 below, of the work of Partha Dasgupta.

102 Simon, 'From substantive to procedural rationality'.

103 Harvey Leibenstein, one of the founding exponents of the neoclassical approach to fertility behaviour, has subsequently fully accepted this important qualification on the utility of such micro-economic theory: Leibenstein, 'Relaxing the maximisation assumption'. Others have continued to retail the original approach: Becker, *A treatise on the family*.

individual decision-makers, therefore have enormous implications for observable patterns of fertility behaviour – even holding constant the prior assumption: that fertility behaviour is, indeed, something primarily determined by considerations based on (some form of) an economic rationality. It follows that a priority for research should therefore be in elucidating the character and the causes of change in these information contexts, rather than in modelling exercises which do not address these issues.

Simon's analysis has, in effect, been independently verified and its wide-ranging implications exemplified in the findings of a number of historical researchers, notably in the work of Paul David in the USA on the supply side and Paul Johnson in Britain on the demand side of the economy. Paul Johnson has shown how the requirements of Victorian and Edwardian working-class 'respectability' produced consumption behaviour which, while completely different from that of the contemporary middle classes and even castigated by them as imprudent and wasteful, can in fact be demonstrated to have been perfectly economically rational.[104] A classic example of this was the institutionalised practice of frequently pawning a 'Sunday best' suit for the other six days of the week, thereby incurring punitive interest charges on short-term loans which could amount to as much as 100% over the fifty-two weeks of a year. However, the utility of 'Sunday best' was social and of high value. In a relatively low-income community it acted as the visible public guarantee of a family's continuing respectability.[105] It demonstrated the family's financial sufficiency and therefore maintained its local status and credit-worthiness (the fact that a man had nothing to wear on his day off other than his work-clothes, being the sure sign of the family's financial distress). Johnson points out that the problem was that 'Sunday best', like many other key status-conferring items – such as a piano for the parlour – was a 'lumpy' good requiring to be of a certain minimal quality and cost or else it was not worth having at all (because it would have failed to confer the status-enhancement which was its primary ostentation function). These considerations mean that it was actually rational and logical for a working-class family with low and irregular income to buy and use a suit which they could not actually afford to own all the time, periodically borrowing at high interest rates (via pawning) to maintain use of the asset.

Indeed, more generally Johnson points out that, given their pressing liquidity needs, 'for working class households portable durable goods were the near-money equivalent of demand deposits today'.[106] Before the introduction in 1905 of a 'withdrawal on demand' facility by the Post Office Savings Bank (rapidly followed by banks and building societies), 'no major thrift institution gave the same degree of liquidity as the pawnshop'; and hence only after 1914 did pledging permanently

[104] Johnson, *Saving and spending*; Johnson (unpublished paper).

[105] On working-class respectability see also below, pp. 56–7, 460–1.

[106] Johnson, *Saving and spending*, p. 179.

decline from the 200 million items per annum of the Edwardian period.[107] Even more remarkable, in terms of their procedural economic rationality, the same families were often simultaneously saving while incurring these punitively high interest pawning charges. They were typically saving small amounts on a relatively short-term basis for two other status-related activities: a decent burial and Christmas expenditures. What did not, however, make sense in their circumstances – a small and unpredictable margin above current subsistence and 'respectability' levels – was any significant, long-term saving – including for old age. Hence, before state pensions began on 1 January 1909 the Poor Law was the principal source of maintenance for those aged proletarians whose families could not support them.

Paul Johnson concludes that it is quite conceivable, therefore, that for the best of rational reasons, workers with low incomes might choose to borrow, to buy on credit, to save only for short-run ends, and to abstain from long-term accumulation. By contrast he graphically demonstrates how, once above a certain level of income and – in particular – once guaranteed of that income's *regularity* (the crucial change in the nature of the informational environment), the entirely distinct practices typical of the Victorian bourgeoisie became economically rational, as well as financially feasible. All consumer goods could now be paid for fully in cash out of savings. To be in debt and paying punitive interest was now unnecessary as well as abhorrent; longer-term financial planning was possible; there was much more interest-earning saving – indeed investment – for old age and for lumpy status-related items, notably children's private education. This, of course, merely contrasts the two opposite poles of a spectrum of varying forms of household economic rationality found in Britain at that time.

Paul Johnson's analysis is fruitful in indicating and illustrating the ways in which the great variety in the information environments of different social groups manifested themselves in radically varying forms of economic behaviour – divergent procedural rationalities. Without the need for invoking any substantial differences between the families in terms of the degree to which they acted according to the general principles of an economic rationality, fundamental differences in their procedural rationality can be understood. This indicates, also, the great extent to which politically mediated changes in many key aspects of the institutional, informational environment, such as in the functioning of sources of credit or mutual assistance, the possibility of pensions, or alterations in a range of labour market features such as pay, conditions, age of entry or gender restrictions, could account for significant historical change, by critically altering the economic rationale behind households' consumption and reproductive behaviours.

Yet, as Robert Pollak and Susan Watkins have pointed out, despite the fundamental nature of H. A. Simon's critique, the popularity of the 'rational actor' model of human behaviour has, if anything, been increasing in the social

[107] Johnson, *Saving and spending*, pp. 179, 168.

sciences.[108] Apparently the profound implications of Simon's work have simply been politely ignored by many practitioners. Indeed, there is a tendency to refer to Simon's work only as having resulted in a concept of 'bounded' – but still substantive – rationality, rather than acknowledging the radically alternative concept of 'procedural' rationality: 'The folk wisdom among economists is that bounded rationality may retard the timing or muffle the magnitude of behavioural responses, but is unlikely to reverse their direction. Thus, the qualitative predictions of the rational actor model are likely to remain valid in the presence of bounded rationality.'[109] But Johnson's detailed, historical case study shows, to the contrary of this complacent assumption, exactly how likely 'reversals of direction' are: the direction in which economic rationality manifests itself is highly sensitive to the informational field in which it is exercised and this has varied and does vary enormously between different social groups in any community in the past or the present. It would seem to be an urgent matter for neoclassical micro-economists to set about investigating empirically the dimensions of the phenomenon which has been identified by H. A. Simon's theoretical insights, rather than assuming its unimportance and continuing to apply unreconstructed rational actor models to problems as complex as changing fertility.

Paul David has also argued for the extremely limited applicability of neoclassical economic models for historical research even in an area in which it should be at its most appropriate. In his careful empirical study of technological change and the diffusion of innovations, such as the McCormick reaping machine, David found that, in real historical markets, decisions by firms or entrepreneurs over choice of techniques were typically made myopically, 'having their objective in the minimisation of current (as distinct from future) private costs of production.'[110] It was always the specific details of the current method of production (and not some future optimal configuration or some cost-benefit calculation based on perfect market information available only with hindsight) which determined how problems, such as bottle-necks and the costs of technical change, were defined, learned about and then dealt with by entrepreneurs and managers. David showed that the historical course of technical change is far from the paradigm of a 'substantively' economically rational sequence of modifications to correctly interpreted market signals. The existing forms of production always exerted a determinative and, from the viewpoint of neoclassical pure market theory, essentially baleful and distorting influence over the actual historical course of events. These events unfolded as the unintended consequences of a series of reactions and responses.

108 Pollak and Watkins, 'Cultural and economic approaches to fertility', p. 467. This article, incidentally, provides the inestimable service of a clear and balanced, critical introduction to the utility modelling approach.

109 Pollak and Watkins, 'Cultural and economic approaches to fertility', p. 476.

110 David, *Technical choice*, p. 4.

This suggests that in order to know how and why economic history happened as it did, rather than as it should have according to a theory of timelessly optimal allocation of resources, it is always necessary to inquire into the imperfect informational context and the associated decisions, which populated the past. The motivations behind these decisions are only comprehensible within those contexts and they did not conform to a pattern of rationality which was substantively rational with hindsight. It is therefore fundamentally anti-historical to rely on an abstract theory to sort and order that past according to an artificial set of consistent rules and relationships. Not only did this never exist as the conscious aim and 'rationality' of the actors involved but it is also actually demonstrably antithetical to the economic conditions which were the essence of the historical reality: namely imperfect information.

According to both the theory of H. A. Simon and the empirical research of P. A. David, then, one of the few certainties concerning economic history is that the model economic behaviour of neoclassical theory has been conspicuous in its absence. Indeed, David's conclusions are dismissive both of the motives and of the cognitive limitations of those employing such an approach for explanation in the social and historical sciences: 'Like the mechanical conception of the physical universe, this construction of man bespeaks a longing for permanence in human affairs, for the certainty of laws governing a natural order based on uniform matter.'[111] David further points out that this 'aspiration of the neoclassical school to imitate the great success which Newtonian mechanics achieved' has all the intellectual status of defunct ancestor worship, given the cadaverous nature of the object of their veneration. He cites Georgescu-Roegen:

> But by the time Jevons and Walras began laying the cornerstones of modern [neoclassical] economics, a spectacular revolution in physics had already brought the downfall of the mechanistic dogma both in the natural sciences and in philosophy. And the curious fact is that none of the architects of 'the mechanics of utility and self-interest' and even none of the latter-day model builders seem to have been aware at any time of this downfall. Otherwise, one could not understand why they have clung to the mechanistic framework with the fervour with which they have.[112]

As will be argued in Part IV, below, in the field of the historical analysis of changing fertility behaviour there is, nevertheless, some value in an approach which focuses on changes in different kinds of households' economic predicaments. But the potential value of this approach is *only* valid if full attention is given to the relevant historical political, cultural and ideological forces which determine the changing contexts in which individuals form their economic priorities. This means that the full force of Simon's and David's critique of the abstract modelling approach is valid and that in fact, as an exclusive method, such modelling remains

[111] David, *Technical choice*, p. 12.
[112] Georgescu-Roegen, *The entropy law*, pp. 2–3.

an unhelpful approach for understanding the varying economics of historical fertility change.

Nancy Folbre's work, combining a 'household economics' approach with an ethnographic sensitivity to social and political context, comprises an altogether much more promising departure. Folbre has argued that the neoclassical modelling approach suffers a crippling loss in explanatory power where the analysis of changing fertility behaviour is concerned because of the methodology's refusal to analyse the interior workings of the 'black box' of the family household. In the neoclassical model the shifting costs and benefits of children are determined by the market relations of the family as a whole, considered as a unit of production or consumption. Folbre argues that these costs and benefits are also endogenously determined by the internal household relations of changing bargaining powers between the generations and the sexes. She observes of the utility modelling approach that 'the possibility that changes in bargaining power [between family members] might affect fertility decisions has never been conceded . . . Such a concession . . . invites consideration of the role of non-market forces – such as political struggle – in economic change.'[113]

Folbre has additionally produced much impressively detailed and relevant evidence from her fieldwork, a household survey conducted in 1975 in the Laguna province of the Philippines. She has quantified the extent of wives' self-exploitation, relative to husbands, in terms of hours worked, absence of leisure and nutrition not consumed.[114] This was found to be especially marked where household wealth was low and male wages low or where infants or several children were present in the household, unless in the latter case an elder sibling was available to share some of the hard work. Folbre's conclusion was that the principal cause of females' chronically weak bargaining position within the home in this society was a prevailing set of closely related 'patriarchal' customs and formal laws. Of central importance among the latter was the fact that married women's rights over conjugal property were legally subordinate to their husbands' rights. Another specific law, itself the product of a recent 'liberalising' revision of the Penal Code previously in force, ensured that under certain, broad-ranging circumstances a husband had the right to prevent a wife from any income-earning activity.[115] Not surprisingly, marked differentials in the wage-rates for female and male labour were conventional in this economy.

Thus, Folbre was able to document in detail her important theoretical point that the ground rules of the market – the premises for its schedules of economically rational behaviour – are set by the environment of laws endorsed by the state. A relatively low female earning power in the formal economy resulted from these laws. This in turn created the situation in which there was little opportunity cost in

113 Folbre, 'Of patriarchy born', p. 267.
114 Folbre, 'Household production', pp. 316–25.
115 Folbre, 'Household production', p. 323.

the exhaustive use of female time on domestic chores and in childrearing activities. In the Philippines at this time the state's relevant laws primarily reflected an accommodation of interests between male employers and male trades unionists. Their principal concern was to perpetuate the patriarchal principles of traditional kinship loyalties, which ensured greatest power and influence in this society for senior males. 'Patriarchy' not only connotes gender but also generational subordination.

Folbre's theoretical arguments and empirical analysis have much in common with the Caldwells' emphasis on contextualised micro-demography, as the appropriate method for examining intergenerational wealth-flows, as well as with the 'institutional' approach to demographic change advocated by McNicoll, Cain and others. Thus, from within the social sciences there has emerged over the last decade or so a clear set of parallel intellectual developments, from a range of disciplinary perspectives including demography, historical sociology, anthropology and economics. These developments challenge the whole basis of the modernisation-transition framework for studying falling fertilities, through their emphasis on the importance of understanding local contexts and socio-political institutions. It is the conviction of this study that the way forward in the analysis of changing human fertility behaviour does indeed lie in following an approach which focuses upon the economic relationships involved, but only once these have been properly culturally contextualised in all their local variety, and provided they are seen as primarily determined by the influence of highly negotiated, socio-political and ideological forces of change.

Historical studies of falling fertility in modern Britain

In addition to this range of social scientific approaches in the postwar period there has been a distinct line of historical studies of falling fertility in Britain. Of course, there is no hard and fast boundary dividing social scientific from historical studies of changing fertility. The extent to which some historians of the family were influenced by the modernisation perspective has already been remarked upon.[116] While the most important, independent products of historical scholarship have remained relatively detached from any specific social scientific 'school' of thought, historians studying changing fertility have inevitably been influenced by the ideas and methods of the social sciences; similarly the most able social scientists have always wished to learn from the findings of historians. Both have contributed equally to the overall historiographical inheritance which this chapter is attempting to elucidate and, equally, both were heirs to the intellectual inheritance of the interwar period analysed in the opening section of this chapter.

The starting point for all serious historical study of falling fertility in Britain

[116] See above, n. 76.

remains the pioneering historical sociology of J. A. Banks, partly co-authored with Olive Banks.[117] Joe Banks's original contribution published in 1954, *Prosperity and parenthood*, remains a classic which continues to provide stimulus for all students of the problem.[118] It presented a detailed empirical description of the changing conventional definitions of a comfortable standard of living among the Victorian upper and middle classes, as their prosperity and aspirations increased. Furthermore, he demonstrated in detail how such ideals infiltrated into the sphere of family building. This was both through changes in the materialist implications of the long-established prudential concept of 'the right age to marry'; and through the perceived need to equip dynastic heirs with an increasingly expensive education so as to ensure their status retention in an increasingly competitive, professionalised job market.[119]

Banks has never, however, analysed the changing fertility behaviour of the reciprocal, plebeian or working-class section of the nation in a comparable degree of detail to his work on the Victorian bourgeoisie. This partly reflects the inevitable social bias in the main body of primary source material which he analysed: birth control pamphlets, household manuals and the relevant literature of the period. Through these sources, Banks has provided a carefully researched historical interpretation of how the smaller part of the population, the bourgeoisie, came to incur ever-increasing direct and opportunity costs in having and rearing children, and the way in which this ultimately led to their adoption of birth controlling

117 The principal contributions have been the trilogy: Banks, *Prosperity and parenthood*; Banks and Banks, *Feminism and family planning*; Banks, *Victorian values*.

118 Banks's study constituted the first explicitly historical interpretation of the phenomenon, i.e. a study which was not seeking in any way to comment upon fertility trends for a policy-related reason, but treating the phenomenon purely as a matter for historical research. In a necessarily selective historiographical survey such as the present exercise, many studies will inevitably be omitted from consideration. For the sake of clarity and brevity of exposition, between p. 21 and this section I have 'jumped' twenty years, in terms of indigenous British studies of falling fertility, from the work of Enid Charles, published in 1934, to that of J. A. Banks, published in 1954. In the intervening period there were a large number of important, policy-related, official, institutional and individual studies of Britain's declining birth rate. There is certainly an enormous amount of historical interest in these various works, as contributions to the political history of the period and as part of the intellectual history of the social sciences. Also considerable advances were made in the techniques for measuring changing fertility in different sections of the population. But as a contribution to explaining the nation's historical fall in fertility, they did not, in sum, provide any significant conceptual extension to the range of alternative positions as outlined on pp. 12–21. Many of the specific findings of the most important of these studies, the Royal Commission on Population of 1944–9, will be considered in Part III, below; and many of the other significant publications, such as those of D. V. Glass, John Hajnal, John Innes and Mass-Observation, will be also mentioned at various points in the text below. Other important studies from the period include: Hogben (ed.), *Political arithmetic*; Leybourne and White, *Education and the birth-rate*; Titmuss and Titmuss, *Parents revolt*; and PEP, *Population policy in Great Britain*. The most comprehensive historical account of the range of demographic studies in this period is Soloway, *Demography and degeneration*; see also Grebenik, 'Demographic research'; Thane, 'The debate on the declining birthrate'; Pfeffer, *The stork and the syringe*.

119 Banks, *Prosperity and parenthood*, chs. 10 and 11; Banks, *Victorian values*, amplifies this theme in chs. 6 and 8.

practices. Banks initially believed this to have occurred during the decades of the so-called Great Depression, 1873–96, but he has subsequently emphasised the golden age of mid-Victorian prosperity.[120] These mid-century decades were host to a virulent status war within the upper and middle classes as rising incomes chased spiralling consumption aspirations.

However, this interpretation could not, with consistency, be simultaneously offered as an explanation of how the new form of behaviour – family planning and the household accountancy that accompanied it – could have become so rapidly adopted by vast numbers of working-class people who did not experience the rising expectations of affluence, which Banks charted for the upper and middle classes. His silence on this in 1954 could only be interpreted as a *de facto* acceptance of the then-current, broadly diffusionist viewpoint. But, by 1964, in a second major contribution to the field, J. A. and Olive Banks had begun explicitly to acknowledge the sociological deficiencies in such a view.[121]

In his most recent contribution Banks has replaced simple diffusion with an analogous but sociologically more elaborate theory: that of the conscripted 'socialisation' of the non-planning elements of the population into a 'bourgeois future-time perspective'. According to Banks this occurred through the childhood experience of competitive examination with their peers and social equals in the new compulsory schooling system put in place in British society over the last three decades of the nineteenth century. For the children of the working classes:

> Success in school tests, and more especially in external examinations, thus became for them the measure of achievement in conformity with the performance of people in broadly the same social circumstances as themselves; . . .[122]
>
> . . . the majority moved through the school together. Thus, that standard of expectation, which was . . . consolidated at this time to establish the special sort of future-time perspective, relevant for family planning, was not confined to the children of the upper and upper middle classes but extended by the popularity of examining to all those sections of the community whose children could be persuaded or compelled to attend school.[123]

Banks's socialisation thesis, therefore, represented an attempt to delineate the course of change in those cultural and normative features of late nineteenth-century British society which most significantly influenced the degree to which rational planning, in the economists' sense, became internalised in social groups beyond the bourgeoisie. An increasing majority of young proletarians adopted a planning perspective on their own lives as a general approach because this was the underlying symbolic message imbibed in the nation's new elementary schools.

[120] Banks, *Victorian values*, ch. 4.

[121] Banks and Banks, *Feminism and family planning*, ch. 9, published in 1964, contains the skeleton of the subsequent 'socialisation' thesis of 1981. However, 'diffusion' was still emphasised in the 1964 'Conclusion' (p. 132).

[122] Banks, *Victorian values*, p. 133. [123] Banks, *Victorian values*, p. 134.

Once acquired, the habit of planning was in due course applied to sexual and reproductive behaviour.

There are interesting implications, but also serious limitations in this latest interpretation from Banks. The revised emphasis on the importance of political and ideological developments related to the expansion of schooling carries a strong implicit thesis of the causal significance of political processes. The formulation, and effective realisation, of a national policy of compulsory elementary education becomes a key determining causal factor in Banks's most recent interpretation. He identifies such educationalists in society as a small but significant minority acting as a political pressure group. They successfully promoted their view 'that *all* children, including their own, should be given an education which was of value both to them personally and to the society in which they would live when adult' (emphasis added),[124] as against the prevailing 'very false philosophy' that education was simply a means to 'material advantage'.[125] This latter belief produced in many a conservative view that the appropriate amount of education was simply that which parents themselves had enjoyed, on the assumption that children would take up the same kind of occupations and life-styles as their parents. Alternatively, among the ambitious or the deferential education was viewed as a means to buy status and social advance for one's own children, but not necessarily to be available to others in society. There is the important implication in Banks's most recent thesis, therefore, that explicit political and ideological developments, not just impersonal, 'structural' economic forces, are to be considered as causes of fertility change.

However, it has to be acknowledged that the 'socialisation' thesis as it stands is closely related to the flawed 'social control' school of thought on class relations in late Victorian Britain. This views schooling as a process whose significance and function was principally that of 'disciplining' the raw and unruly proletariat to the more ordered forms of behaviour and thought already internalised by the governing class.[126] As such, it is subject to the full force of the powerful criticisms which have been levelled against social control theory.[127] These criticisms include the fact that, first, a general national uniformity of the disciplining or socialising process is assumed, which simply cannot be corroborated in the history of highly varied working-class take up and response to educational provision in different parts of the country. Secondly, formal education has never been more than one of a range of children's educative processes, which include the family, the wider kinship group, the neighbourhood and work-training environments,

[124] Banks, *Victorian values*, p. 119.

[125] These last two phrases are drawn from Horace Mann's censuring of the attitudes of the labouring masses in the 'Education Report' published in 1854, which was derived from the results of the 1851 census. Cited in Banks, *Victorian values*, p. 118.

[126] Banks's principal source for the idea of 'socialisation' is cited as the essays in McCann (ed.), *Popular education*. For the social control thesis, see Donajgrodzki (ed.), *Social control*, especially 'Introduction'.

[127] In particular: Thompson, 'Social control'; Stedman Jones, 'Class expression versus social control?'.

all of which varied enormously in different parts of Britain at this time.[128]

Thirdly, socialisation, like social control suffers from an extremely one-sided conception of the nature of the cultural and ideological exchanges occurring in the relationship between plebeian communities and the educational resources made available to them. The working classes actively selected from the educational system what was of most use and value to them, rather than merely passively receiving and being moulded by it. Hence, the government's infamous economy-motivated Revised Code of 'payment by results' of 1862, which was castigated as unrelieved philistinism by middle-class educationists – famously so in Matthew Arnold's *Culture and anarchy* – was actually very popular among those working-class parents who paid for their children's attendance. This was because many simply wanted their children to obtain the basic skills, 'the three Rs' (reading, 'riting and 'rithmetic), as quickly as possible and with as little religious and moral indoctrination from their social betters as possible; payment by results encouraged teachers to deliver education in precisely this way.[129] Furthermore, the notion that the 'middle-class' school system was able to impose its values and message upon the labouring poor has been radically undermined by David Vincent's important research, showing that the extent to which proletarian culture remained rooted in its oral dialect sharply delimited the penetrative power of the literacy-based culture of the schools.[130]

There are further fundamental problems with the 'socialisation' thesis. As the work of H. A. Simon and Paul Johnson demonstrates, the reasons why many working-class communities did not manifest a 'future-time' planning perspective in the conventional bourgeois sense was because it was entirely rational *not* to do so, given that their lives were subject to chronic insecurity and irregularity of income. Indeed, this rationale in working-class behaviour was precisely recognised by the Edwardian social worker, Helen Bosanquet. In spite of her disapproval of the popularity of taking credit at exorbitant rates of interest, she nevertheless recognised that 'the uncertainty of the future becomes a powerful argument against anticipatory provision and in favour of credit. There is no doubt that saving is regarded, and perhaps justifiably regarded, as the sacrifice of present and certain advantages for the meeting of evils which may, possibly, never occur.'[131]

It is the notion that schooling could act autonomously, or even as the single most important influence, to transform the peculiar, fatalistic rationality of the working poor which is an unrealistic one. The rationale informing their behaviour and values was firmly embedded in and well adapted to the harsh economic realities of their neighbourhoods and labour markets. The social control and socialisation

[128] Sutherland, 'Education', p. 119, citing E. Durkheim, *Education and sociology* (Glencoe 1956), p. 71.

[129] Thompson, *The rise of respectable society*, pp. 148–9.

[130] Vincent, *Literacy and popular culture*. See below, pp. 549–50.

[131] H. Bosanquet, *The standard of life* (1906), p. 68, cited in the superb article by McKibbin: 'Class and poverty in Edwardian England', p. 173.

perspectives slip too easily into assuming that elementary schools could mobilise the conditioning powers of Goffman-like 'total institutions', an analysis which has been applied with some greater validity to nineteenth-century asylums, prisons and workhouses.[132] But, unlike these institutions, the elementary school competed as an educative influence with the family home, the street-culture of the neighbourhood and the work-culture of the town. It could not significantly modify the rising generation's attitudes toward the adoption of more bourgeois evaluations of time, planning and order, if all the signals imbibed from these other socialising environments indicated that this remained an inappropriate approach to the economic facts of life.

Apart from Banks's 'socialisation' thesis, there have appeared several other important general interpretations of the British fertility decline by historians, which also deal specifically with the major problem remaining after Banks's classic account of fertility control among the upper and middle classes: how this new form of behaviour came to be adopted among the working classes all around the country. This work has additionally pioneered the exploration of a further range of issues: the political significance of birth control and of different methods, notably abortion; and the importance of gender and spouse relations in fertility behaviour.

Angus McLaren's work was the first of these alternative interpretations to appear and he has recently reiterated his views.[133] McLaren made two firm demands: first, that the entirely different circumstances of life and work among the manual, labouring population call for a separate historical treatment for them from that accorded by Banks to the upper classes.[134] Secondly, that the role of women and female techniques of birth control would be much more important in these different circumstances.[135] In particular, McLaren stressed that 'the traditional female form of fertility control – abortion – would be one of the options considered.'[136] According to McLaren abortion represented appropriate technology for the poor. It was essentially a form of crisis-management, a last-ditch expedient to avoid the burden of yet another mouth to feed, and not part of a deliberate prudential strategy of family planning, such as Banks had traced evolving in the upper and middle classes. McLaren argued that 'In allowing the working class couple to postpone the decision of controlling pregnancy to a later date in the reproductive cycle abortion gave the family living at a subsistence level time to assess whether they could support an additional child.'[137] Thus, according to McLaren, to achieve the traditional 'working woman's goal . . . of maintaining and

[132] Goffman, *Asylums*. The principal historical exponent has been Scull, *Museums of madness*; an approach reaffirmed in his address, 'Museums of madness revisited'.

[133] McLaren, 'A woman's work'; and McLaren *Birth control*; McLaren, 'The sexual politics of reproduction', p. 98.

[134] McLaren, 'A woman's work', pp. 71, 77–80.

[135] McLaren, 'A woman's work', pp. 74–6.

[136] McLaren, 'A woman's work', p. 71.

[137] McLaren, *Birth control*, p. 245.

protecting her family'[138] she was quite prepared to 'violate bourgeois morality'.[139]

McLaren has, therefore, offered a diametrically opposed political interpretation of the ideological significance of the practice of birth control among the working population before the Great War to that suggested by 'diffusion' or by 'socialisation'. For McLaren, the fact that proletarian regulation of births included the widespread practice of abortion shows that it was quite different from the middle-class individualistic strategy of prudential birth control. Since abortion was a criminal and clandestine act, the practice of birth control by the working classes in fact represents a rejection of the cultural values and conventional morality of the bourgeoisie, rather than constituting a proof of the expansion and spread of this ideological code throughout society.[140] McLaren's work was especially significant, therefore, in introducing into the historiography an explicit awareness of the political and ideological dimensions of the relationship between the fertility behaviour of different parts of the population during the period of falling fertility and their distinctive class, status and gender relations.

McLaren's specific hypothesis cannot be assessed absolutely conclusively because of the absence of reliable evidence on the characteristics of abortion during the nineteenth century.[141] But McLaren certainly provided sufficient evidence from contemporary commentators and professional medical journals to establish that attempted abortion through ingesting lead (usually by swallowing the lead contained in cheap diachylon plasters) did occur in some places on a scale sufficiently widespread to have brought the problem of 'plumbism' (i.e. lead poisoning) to the attention of the local medical authorities.[142]

However, an entirely different interpretation of the incidence of abortion to that proffered by McLaren can be maintained. The crucial point of contention is whether the practice of abortion can only signify, as McLaren argued, sporadic desperation; or whether its practice might not be compatible with a more measured strategy of fertility regulation. Banks's own overall conclusion that coitus interruptus, or withdrawal, was probably the most commonly employed technique by those couples who limited births in the nineteenth century, itself implies that abortion, and the willingness to countenance abortion, would, therefore, almost certainly have been a crucial concomitant of this most unreliable of techniques.[143] The most effective contraceptive means then available, the early, rather thick and uncomfortable rubber condoms retailing at between 2 shillings and 10 shillings per dozen in the 1890s, was probably beyond the pocket of all but the highest paid manual workers as a regular form of contraception and also, crucially, tainted by association with prostitution, venereal

[138] McLaren, 'A woman's work', p. 77. See also Roberts, 'Working class standards of living', for oral evidence of female self-sacrifice in their families' interests.

[139] McLaren, 'A woman's work', p. 80.

[140] McLaren, 'A woman's work', pp. 78, 79; McLaren, *Birth control*, p. 255.

[141] For a full evaluation of the available evidence on the incidence of abortion, see below, pp. 424–31.

[142] McLaren, *Birth control*, ch. 13. [143] Banks, *Victorian values*, p. 110.

disease and irreligion.[144] The counter-argument open to Banks is that if coitus interruptus were, indeed, the principal contraceptive technique practised by this population (as McLaren himself has acknowledged), then, considering its unreliability, the willingness to resort to abortion would be essential if this low-budget strategy were to be effective.[145] Abortion did, indeed, violate bourgeois morality, as McLaren has observed; however, so did the use of artificial forms of contraception and also the resort to prostitutes. Nevertheless, it is quite certain that the latter activity, at least, was privately practised by substantial numbers of the bourgeoisie themselves at this time.[146] Hence, although abortion may have transgressed moral precepts, it cannot, therefore, automatically be seen as signifying the rejection of the prudential morality and individualistic strategy of the bourgeoisie towards birth control.

However, Diana Gittins has further elaborated and extended McLaren's argument. She has produced oral history evidence which helps to assess the relationship between such complex issues as contemporaries' perceptions of the importance of experiences at work and their personal relationships with other family and community members as sources of information and knowledge of contraceptive techniques and as possible influences over the formulation of ideals of family size.[147] Gittins has further developed McLaren's thesis on the importance of proletarian abortion by postulating a rigid dichotomy between coitus interruptus and abortion, as both class- and sex-specific practices.[148] The former Gittins sees as a private activity, which was typical of the middle class and was a reflection of the male's dominance in the conjugal relationship. Abortion, on the other hand, was the characteristic working-class method of birth control. It was a hidden but collective and social action, carried out by a collusive community of womenfolk. For Gittins, working-class women's use of abortion was an expression of their relatively greater power and control in these matters than their socially superior sisters in the middle classes. This greater independence flowed from their greater access to employment and thereby evasion of complete economic dependence on their menfolk.

Gittins's principal findings seem to be quite compatible with McLaren's thesis. Gittins argues that the arrival of real family planning, as opposed to mere *ad hoc*

144 On prices of condoms, see Peel, 'The manufacture and retailing of contraceptives'; on their unrespectable associations, see Davenport-Hines, *Sex, death and punishment*, chs. 5–6.

145 Although McLaren has devoted much effort to showing that abortion was more important than had been previously recognised by students of falling fertility in Britain – an important revisionist achievement – it is to be noted that he never claimed that abortion was the most quantitatively important practice. He agreed with Banks that for the working classes 'withdrawal was their main form of contraception until well into the 20th century': McLaren, 'A woman's work', p. 71.

146 On the incidence of prostitution, see ch. 8, n. 54.

147 Gittins (unpublished MA thesis); Gittins, *Fair sex*. The latter also utilises two other historical sources: the vital statistics provided by the GRO and the surviving interwar case records of the Manchester and Salford birth control clinic.

148 Gittins, *Fair sex*, pp. 160–4.

occasional and desperate efforts to avert a particular birth, did not really arrive until the interwar period for the urban working class.[149] She argues that it was changes in work and occupational practices in the 1920s and 1930s, and their inter-relationship with family life, which were particularly important in bringing this about, such that 'More women were experiencing greater independence prior to marriage and, paradoxically, less after marriage.'[150] This was due to an increase in the ratio of single to married women who went out to work in the interwar period, which Gittins traces to the expanding influence and acceptability of the bourgeois model of female domesticity. She sees this as being disseminated largely through the effects of state policies such as the sex-differentiated education curriculum and the infant and maternity welfare movement.[151] According to Gittins, 'Thus, one of the crucial developments during this period among the working classes was an increase in joint marital role-relationships, but a decrease in equal relationships.'[152] This was because 'Central to this ideology was the concept of a happy, clean home environment; the responsibility for creating and maintaining this environment was invariably seen as the married woman's principal role.'[153]

According to Gittins her work experience before marriage in office or factory was very likely to equip the future working-class wife with knowledge of effective contraceptive techniques through discussion with workmates. The continuing decrease in working hours for many working-class husbands allowed the increased leisure which facilitated closer communication and co-operation between spouses. This aided successful pursuit both of their family planning and of their joint consumption aspirations. Gittins has produced evidence and arguments to show that during the interwar period there was an expansion beyond the middle classes of certain social and cultural characteristics which significantly affected both contraceptive motivation and its effective usage: knowledge and accessibility of techniques; quality of decision-sharing and communication between spouses; high evaluation of material control over the domestic environment.

There would, therefore, seem to be no major incompatibility between Banks's most recent thesis of 'socialisation' and the findings of McLaren and Gittins. Socialisation into a future-time rational perspective of an increasing proportion of each generation increasingly compulsorily educated from the 1870s onwards would seem to help to explain the dramatic change in attitudes and behaviour between the late nineteenth century and the interwar period, which is apparently

149 Always excepting, of course, the workers in textiles factories in Lancashire and West Yorkshire.

150 Gittins, *Fair sex*, p. 182.

151 Gittins, *Fair sex*, p. 177. On the curriculum and educational experience, see C. Dyhouse, *Girls growing up*, and Hunt (ed.), *Lessons for life*. On the infant welfare movement, see Davin, 'Imperialism and motherhood'; Lewis, *The politics of motherhood*; Dwork, *War is good for babies*. See also Rowbotham, *Good girls make good wives*.

152 Gittins, *Fair sex*, p. 182.

153 Gittins, *Fair sex*, p. 183.

documented by McLaren's and Gittins's studies.[154] This would account for the transformation from McLaren's conjugally segregated, harassed and subordinated Victorian working wife, sporadically resorting to abortion in desperation, to Gittins's interwar domesticated, privatised, non-working member of a joint conjugal relationship, pursuing together their co-ordinated aims of a small family, to enable them to live in a 'happy, clean home'.

There is undoubtedly much of analytical value in each of these three interpretations. Gittins's work is certainly of lasting importance in having focused attention so firmly on the question of power relations between the sexes in marriage and its relationship with the gendered labour market. However, as an account which fits the detailed evidence of the early stages of falling fertility during the half-century or so before the Great War, these three interpretations are distinctly less convincing, either separately or when combined together in the above fashion. The conceptual limitations of socialisation have already been discussed. But neither does the socialisation thesis match up well with the empirical evidence. In particular, it was in the textiles districts, where school attendance rates were the lowest in the country until the end of the century, that fertility regulation was most firmly established as a general practice well before the turn of the century.[155] In putting such emphasis on the importance of the arrival of the ideal of domesticity in the working-class home during the interwar years, Gittins's interpretation would also seem to have difficulty in accounting for textiles workers' fertility control up to two generations earlier, as well as among several other elements of the working classes.

Furthermore, it is far from obvious that a wife's relative power in the conjugal relationship should manifest itself in having to subject herself to the dangers and ignominies of repeated abortions as a contraceptive technique, rather than in having a husband who submitted to the less than satisfactory practice of coitus interruptus or any of the other male techniques (principally the use of the highly unsatisfactory condoms or some form of abstinence). Gittins's suggestion that these two methods were practised quite separately as alternatives (either the male method of coitus interruptus *or* the female method of abortion) seems quite artificial. As argued above, they might be more realistically seen as complementary components of a 'low tech.' (i.e. without appliances) contraceptive strategy, adopted by many of those couples who were attempting to regulate their fertility before 1911, regardless of their social position. Finally, although abortion must certainly be brought into the reckoning as playing some part in the story, the emphasis by Gittins on abortion as the principal method systematically used by the working class seems to go well beyond the evidence presented (mainly by McLaren) on the extent of its practice.

154 Implementation of compulsory elementary school attendance did not become truly effective until the 1890s. See Hurt, *Elementary schooling*, ch. 8.

155 See Marsden, *Unequal educational provision*, especially, pp. 65–7.

The thesis of the primacy of proletarian abortion is vulnerable, therefore, to the criticism that a more plausible – because less dramatic – alternative interpretation is entirely consistent with the resort to abortion: that it represented a reluctantly deployed entailment of the not infrequent failure of other methods. It may well have been certain *other* methods which were primarily and preferentially deployed: coitus interruptus, prolonged breast-feeding, post-coital douching and various forms of supposedly spermicidal or obstructive pessaries and blocks, and attempted abstinence. The resort to abortion played a secondary but necessary role in all of these cases. In conclusion, there are undoubtedly insights and findings of value in each of these contributions by Banks, McLaren and Gittins. But as general interpretations and explanations of the fertility patterns actually found among the working classes, they suffer from conceptual shortcomings and inconsistencies with the demographic evidence.

There are not dissimilar problems with the two most recent historical interpretations of changing fertility in modern Britain. These are the separate attempts at unified, wide-ranging general interpretations of population changes in Britain over the entire modern and early modern periods published by David Levine and by Wally Seccombe.[156] They both approach the problem through a wide-angle, post-Marxian lens, which attempts to incorporate the process of falling fertility in the modern period within an interpretative framework of very long-term social and economic change. Although 'we are all Marxists now', social historians are debating with Marx (alongside all the other classics), in all manner of ways; and it is not at all clear that a very long-term perspective focusing primarily on economic relations and their implications is necessarily the most helpful for understanding this particular episode in the histories which they each recount.

Both Levine and Seccombe see fertility change as primarily explained through alterations in the family household production unit due to its relationship with transformations in the material mode of production. But these are in no sense crude materialist interpretations: the importance of the 'superstructure' is addressed. The wider questions of labour relations and working-class culture are central to each of their interpretations of fertility change, in the form of a 'respectability' thesis. Insofar as the period of falling fertility is concerned, Levine has endorsed Caldwell's theory of intergenerational wealth flows as a stimulating departure point, acknowledging the importance of the fact that children's net economic contribution to the family budget was, indeed, radically diminished during the last third of the nineteenth century broadly in the manner described by Caldwell.[157] But Levine argues that the provision of an education system and its putative cultural effects 'upon' the *mentalité* of the working classes are properly seen only as secondary causes in the process of fertility decline. The primary causation for Levine lies in a dialectical combination of both objective economic developments

156 Levine, *Reproducing families*; Seccombe, *A millennium of family change*; Seccombe, *Weathering the storm*.

157 See above, pp. 36–7, for description of Caldwell's thesis.

and also politicised, cultural adaptations to those developments by a working class conceived as a relatively autonomous historical force in itself.

While working people were to some extent at the mercy of the market (as, indeed, were most capitalist employers – a crucial point often insufficiently stressed by social historians), Levine argues that their autonomous capacity for a significant degree of collective, political organisation in pursuit of certain moral and economic goals remains to be properly taken into account. This requires that the labouring masses should not be conceptualised simply as malleable receivers, passively reflecting the impress 'upon' them of the moulding powers either of market forces or of the state policies devised for them by their social superiors, the governing class. Both of these were mediated by the working class's own cultural forms and political powers. This argument provides the driving force of the socio-political side of Levine's dialectical model of causation.

The economic side was generated by the logic of the national and international market. During the last quarter of the nineteenth century Britain's capitalists and her governing class were having to respond to the changing human capital demands generated by competition for economic growth in a maturing economic structure. This resulted in, first, pressures for an increasingly capitalised mode of material production in most branches of industry involving the operation of ever more expensive forms of mechanisation. Industrial bosses became increasingly disinclined to employ non-responsible minors to supervise their equipment. Secondly, this period saw the expansion of a widening range of literacy-based jobs relating to the distributional, managerial, clerical and service sectors of the diversifying economy. Economic development also enforced upon the nation's legislators a perception of the necessity of implementing a universal compulsory education system for the sake of national economic survival, increasingly aware of their competitors' initiatives in this respect.[158]

Levine's socio-political interpretation is critically based upon the work of certain labour historians, regarding the development of a specifically working-class cultural concept of respectability. Levine follows in particular the research and interpretation of Geoffrey Crossick and R. Q. Gray, on the autonomous nature and meaning of 'respectability' for the English working class.[159] These authors have importantly and helpfully pointed out that working-class 'respectability' was no simple mimesis of middle-class proprieties. Mere use of the same term by propertied and working classes, alike, hides quite distinct schedules of priorities. Middle-class preoccupations were with privacy, piety, cleanliness and hygiene, personal 'worth' and achievement and possession of the public 'paraphernalia of gentility', so well documented by J. A. Banks in 1954. Tied to the different circumstances, problems and privations of the working-class economy and

[158] Levine, *Reproducing families*, pp. 161, 173–5, 192.

[159] Levine, *Reproducing families*, pp. 174–6, following the work of Gray, *The labour aristocracy*; Crossick, *An artisan elite*.

community, proletarian 'respectability' drew on the radical tradition of working men's 'independence'. This was to be achieved through collective strength and solidarity and membership of the principal institutions of mutual support, such as Friendly Societies, burial societies, building societies, workingmen's clubs, the Co-operative movement or trade unions. Working-class 'respectability' emphasised instead: thrift and living within one's means; stoical forbearance in the face of material and cultural deprivations; and a neighbourliness which could yet provide the mutual aid vital in periods of extreme crisis when the spectre of the Poor Law beckoned.[160] These were threats to the proletarian family's very survival which still remained all too real, given the fundamental insecurity of those relying on both the market's demand for their labour and their physical fitness for the ability to offer that labour. Of particular significance where the explanation of fertility change is concerned, the respectable paradigm entailed the ideal of a male breadwinner, wife at home and children at school which, according to the Caldwell wealth-flows thesis which Levine endorses, created powerful forces conducive to fertility regulation.

The period of fertility decline broadly coincides with the several decades after 1870 during which social historians have argued that relatively more stable working-class communities began to reconstitute themselves in their novel urban and industrial environments, after the previous century or so of extraordinary, hectic mobility and chaotic urban growth.[161] Historians have consequently identified this period of increasing relative residential stability among a growing proportion of the urban working class as one in which new sets of social and moral rules and customs, functional to more established community relations, were rekindled and elaborated in the new urban settings. Levine and Seccombe have each cogently argued that a return to a greater degree of community regulation of the sexual and reproductive behaviour of the young would have been an integral and normal part of the cultural rebuilding of such self-surveillant neighbourhoods, hence the well-attested fall in illegitimacy and rise in church weddings among proletarian communities during this period.[162]

Levine also has an intriguing passage in which he argues that where the respectable 'male breadwinner' ideology of Victorian artisans and craftsmen was successfully established as industrial practice, it had the effect of turning the family's source of livelihood into a *reprise* for the classic 'peasant' land tenancy: a fixed fund of wealth supporting the family, with primary control in the hands of the patriarchal head of household.[163] Levine contrasts this with the intervening régime of the earlier proletarian family of the eighteenth-century cottage industries

160 In addition to the work of Gray and Crossick and Paul Johnson (pp. 40–1, above), on the complexities of working-class respectability, see Bailey, '"Will the real Bill Banks please stand up?"'; Ross, '"Not the sort that would sit on the doorstep"'.

161 See Stedman Jones, 'Working class culture'; and Hobsbawm, 'The making'.

162 Seccombe, 'Starting to stop', p. 169.

163 Levine, *Reproducing families*, p. 172.

and the early nineteenth-century factories, where the family's earning power depended more on the number of young hands it could call upon. In terms both of the conventional economic logic of the household budget and of Caldwell's intergenerational wealth-flows, this proto-industrial situation of the earlier period had favoured high fertility and relatively early marriage, as the demographic record confirms, whereas now the attainment of working-class respectability reversed this.

Within its own terms, Levine's thesis is a coherent, persuasive and elegant general interpretation of the course of proletarian family history over two centuries. However, specifically as an explanation of the course of falling fertilities among the working class in Britain, Levine's analysis is directly refuted by some of the most well-known evidence of the striking social variations in fertility behaviour evident within the working class during the period in which fertilities fell. Levine is fully cognisant of the relative complexity and variety of forms of demographic and social behaviour that can be found in pre- and proto-industrial times, having himself been one of the principal historians whose primary researches, along with Keith Wrightson, have uncovered and raked through this rich subsoil.[164] Although appreciative of the importance of local cultural contexts and economic circumstances for interpretation of demographic behaviour in the era before industrialisation, Levine has, however, insufficiently considered the significance of these fine-grade, local factors in mediating the changing fertility behaviour of the late nineteenth and early twentieth centuries. This was, after all, a society containing several times the number of persons and communities than had been the case two centuries earlier. The Smithian division of labour and the increasing range of specialised goods and services meant that this was a society which was much more variegated and fissured. It incorporated a much greater range of socio-economic contexts than ever before, in terms of the variety of forms of employment and kinds of community extant: new suburbs of office workers might be only a few miles from rural enclaves, which were living and working substantially as they had two centuries earlier. The analysis offered by Levine, while plausible for some elements of the population some of the time, breaks down critically for others.

Foremost among these failures is the fact that the principal 'respectability' characteristic – male breadwinner, single earner family – applies paradigmatically to coal-mining communities and yet these were, of course, the highest fertility section of the working classes throughout the period and the last to rein in their marital fertility. Equally damning for Levine's respectability-driven thesis of fertility decline is the fact that family and work patterns in the textiles industry corresponded to the paradigm of 'non-respectability', in terms of the ideal-typical model set out by Levine: relatively low male wages and ineffective political

164 Wrightson and Levine, *Poverty and piety*; Levine and Wrightson, *The making*.

organisation; girls and married women working outside the home more frequently than in most other parts of the economy; juveniles endemically at work, both part time and after school, throughout the period. And yet, of course, this was the pioneer area of working-class fertility decline on a large scale. Levine talks of the miners as a 'special case', but a general interpretation of working-class fertility decline in Britain cannot retain credibility when such important groups as miners and textile workers remain not merely exceptions, but flat contradictions to the main thrust of the thesis on offer.

In fact the fundamental, internally contradictory problem with Levine's interpretation is that it ends up proposing a proletarian variant of 'trickle down'. This is despite Levine's correctly targeted hostility at the outset of his chapter on the decline of working-class fertility to 'the so-called modernisation of mentalities', neo-evolutionary school of 'trickle-down demography'; and despite his accurate criticism of Caldwell for in effect 'saving' modernisation theory through his argument that the institution of schooling performed the essential 'modernising' function (which Caldwell termed 'westernisation'), via its impact on the wealth-flows of the family economy.[165]

Levine argues that the working classes increasingly sent their children to the state's schools instead of out to work and simultaneously decided to have fewer children, as and when they became respectable. Levine, following Crossick and Gray, has conceptualised this as a relatively autonomous process within working-class culture and has thereby correctly rejected the most condescending and naïvely ethnocentric assumptions of modernisation theory. However, in putting forward yet another cultural '-isation' – a single sweeping process accounting generally for falling proletarian fertility throughout the land – Levine is ultimately offering a rather rigid and sterile conception of political, cultural and ideological forces. For all the dialectical mode of mediation which he insists on, these forces are in the end economically determined towards a single outcome. Levine's 'respectabilisation' is a one-way street, which families or communities progress along at different speeds according to their willingness to ride upon the trams going down that street – the engines of economic change which are all progressing toward the same destination of 'respectability' (instead of 'modernity').

Thus, the underlying methodological assumptions of the transition-modernisation viewpoint remain intact – or are unwittingly reproduced in parallel – in Levine's approach, insidiously determining his explanatory agenda and strategy. There is still a linear evolutionism in his conception of the phenomenon to be explained: 'the' working-class fertility decline. There is still the search for a general causal narrative account that can apply to the whole of the social extent under review, in this case the English working class. In confronting the contradiction of the miners,

165 Levine, *Reproducing families*, pp. 160–2.

Levine does not consider the possibility that the project of constructing a single *general* causal account of *the* proletarian fertility decline may be not just occasionally inaccurate with respect to certain special cases, but a fundamentally heuristically misleading project.

This same kind of criticism can be applied to the similarly stimulating work on Britain's fertility decline contributed by Levine's colleague at Toronto, Wally Seccombe.[166] In focusing on the notion of working-class 'respectability', Levine had re-emphasised the power of culturally negotiated social and moral norms for influencing family roles and fertility strategies. Seccombe has followed up this lead and attempted to provide evidence bearing on these issues. Of course, oral historians of the family in modern Britain, such as Diana Gittins and Elizabeth Roberts, had also generated a considerable amount of evidence on these matters and Gittins had produced the interpretation discussed above. Wally Seccombe, drawing on a distinct set of contemporary documents on spouse relations, sexual and contraceptive behaviour, has come to a somewhat different emphasis from Gittins, more in line with the findings of Elizabeth Roberts.[167]

The principal source which Seccombe has analysed is the published sample of letters written to Marie Stopes during the 1920s in response to the publication in 1918 of *Married love*, her controversial, best-selling guide to sex in marriage.[168] Seccombe has concluded that there is substantial evidence from this source which suggests that it was the active co-operation of husbands with their wives which facilitated successful fertility control among many interwar couples. Whereas Gittins tended to emphasise (though not exclusively) female initiative where working-class birth control was concerned, Seccombe argues that it was full male involvement which was vital, while nevertheless acknowledging that this arrived somewhat late in the day.[169]

Beyond this, Seccombe concurs with Levine and others that state-imposed compulsory schooling importantly altered the long-run economic costs and benefits of large families and he also interestingly draws attention to a range of other aspects of state interventions which had the potential to affect relations between spouses.[170] The reforms of divorce laws and matrimonial separation procedures gave middle- and working-class women, respectively, slightly improved recourse in law against the worst excesses of unreasonable husbands. Following on the increased state control over childrearing through the developing education

166 Seccombe, 'Starting to stop'; and Seccombe, *Weathering the storm*, especially chs. 4 and 5.

167 Roberts, *A woman's place*, especially ch. 3.

168 Stopes (ed.), *Mother England*. Stopes published 200 letters written to her in 1926. Seccombe also refers to some of the working-class women's letters published in 1915 in Margaret Llewellyn Davies's celebrated collection, *Maternity*, and he additionally cites – somewhat uncritically – some of the relevant results of the Lewis-Faning survey for the Royal Commission on Population 1944–9. For further discussion of these sources, see below, pp. 398–424.

169 Seccombe, 'Starting to stop', pp. 176–7. For a more extensive analysis of the Stopes letters which is consistent with Seccombe's interpretation, see Hall, *Hidden anxieties*.

170 Seccombe, *Weathering the storm*, chs. 4 and 5.

system of the late nineteenth century, the processs of childbearing was itself increasingly brought within official purview during the first decades of the twentieth century.[171] Midwives were licensed, the system of health visitors organised, child and maternity health centres grew apace into a national system of provision, and the attendance of male doctors at births became more frequent.[172]

Despite the stimulating points and insights, Seccombe is nevertheless ultimately drawn back, as have been virtually all other students of the problem, towards the quest for a single, unitary view of 'the' fertility decline. In the case of both Seccombe and Levine, to some extent this is almost inevitable because of the extremely long-term perspective they have both taken, wishing to integrate the history of falling fertility within an ambitious general interpretation of change in the family over many centuries. Seccombe assents to a view of the phenomenon as a whole in which the professional middle class and bourgeoisie led the process and the respectable skilled working class followed next, with the proletariat bringing up the rear, agreeing with Levine that 'respectabilisation' of the working class is central to the explanation of fertility decline.[173]

There are, then, intrinsic problems in adopting the perspective of *la longue durée*, when it comes to understanding the highly differentiated empirical patterns of fertility change in late nineteenth-century Britain. But, additionally, a major problem with the interpretations offered by Levine and Seccombe is that they are, in fact, consistent only with an historiographically obsolescent representation of the structure and character of the British working class in the late nineteenth and early twentieth centuries, as a graded status hierarchy in which gender differences played little part. The work of Levine and Seccombe reflects the orthodoxy among labour historians as it was until the early 1980s. This was derivative from Eric Hobsbawm's influential essays of 1949 and 1954, regarding the trends of political activism among the working classes during the seventy-odd years between the collapse of Chartism and the outbreak of the Great War.[174] In turn this rested on a view of the working class as graded into horizontal strata. The concept of a 'labour aristocracy', a popularly used contemporary term to denote a better-paid, regularly employed, more capable subsection of the manual labouring population,

171 For documentation of this in London, see Ross, *Love and toil*, especially ch. 7.

172 Note that this last development was almost certainly to the detriment of mothers' health in both the short and the medium term: Loudon, 'On maternal and infant mortality'. Irvine Loudon's statistical demonstration of the incompetence and dangers of the medical profession's interference with childbirth at this time is graphically confirmed in many of the letters printed in Llewellyn Davies, *Maternity*. The insult added to the injury was the ill-afforded payment which had to be found for the doctor's attendance.

173 Seccombe, 'Starting to stop', p. 186.

174 Hobsbawm's 'Trends in the British labour movement since 1850' was originally published in the journal, *Science and Society*, in 1949; 'The labour aristocracy in nineteenth-century Britain' was published in 1954 in John Saville's edited collection, *Democracy and the labour movement*. Both articles were reprinted in 1964 (the former in a revised form) in Hobsbawm, *Labouring men*.

was invoked as the key load-bearing empirical concept to sustain this interpretation.[175]

It was claimed by Hobsbawm that the relative political quiescence of the working classes after 1848 and until the 1880s was the result of the formation of this privileged, reformist (as opposed to revolutionary) 'stratum', in place of a unified oppressed working class. The 'labour aristocracy' constituted a relatively ubiquitous horizontal stratum of skilled and unionised workers enjoying higher pay and seeing themselves as 'respectable' by contrast with their less fortunate brethren. By the 1880s this manual aristocracy began to find itself displaced in the status hierarchy by a growing white-collar stratum, and so a period of intense labour unrest ensued as the 'aristocracy' defensively switched tactics and sought to ally itself organisationally with the lower strata of the labour force, through the new 'all-grades' unions.[176]

A corollary of this model of social structure has been a tendency to envisage other, similarly coherent, nationwide horizontal layers of social strata, ranged above and below the 'labour aristocracy', also possessing distinctive attributes and interests. These have been the subjects of empirical studies, such as Crossick's work on 'the lower middle class' and the 'petite bourgeoisie'.[177] A unified governing and ruling class of employers, administrators and professionals, with supposedly identical shared interests and outlook, was also posited to exist, mobilised in the work of the 'social control' theorists.[178] There has, however, always been considerable opposition to Hobsbawm's 'materialist' interpretation from within the ranks of labour historians, long represented by H. M. Pelling in his work on the political activities of the trade unions and on geographical variations in voting patterns.[179] However in the 1970s, greater emphasis on the significance of the political sphere, as in Pelling's work, also began to emerge in British labour history from within the Marxist tradition itself, as the influence of the remarkable writings of Antonio Gramsci was more fully absorbed.[180] After initially broadly

175 See Reid, 'Intelligent artisans', for the historical origins of the term's contemporary currency.

176 Labour history has, of course, moved some distance from this formulation of the nature of working-class and popular politics in the period 1848–1914. The most recent contributions have stressed the importance of the accommodations to be found between working-class aspirations and political Liberalism, through the continuity across the entire period of their shared participation in the ideological and rhetorical resources of the long-standing radical tradition: Biagini and Reid (eds.), *Currents of radicalism*; Biagini, *Liberty, retrenchment and reform*. This was an approach originally opened up by Peter Clarke: *Lancashire and the New Liberalism*.

177 Crossick, *The lower middle class in Britain*; Crossick and Haupt (eds.), *Shopkeepers and master-artisans*.

178 For all the attempts to imbue considerable subtlety to this theory, its weaknesses remain as described above: see pp. 48–9.

179 Pelling, 'The concept of the labour aristocracy'; Pelling, *Social geography of British elections*.

180 The first English translation of Gramsci's work was published in 1971: *Selections from the prison notebooks*. The incarcerated Gramsci had spent the interwar years in Fascist Italy reflecting on the importance for political stability of the 'primordial' institutions of civil society in western liberal democracies: those 'taken for granted' components of the moral landscape such as the concept of private property itself or 'the rule of law'. Acceptance of these institutions constituted 'the problem of commonsense', insidiously channelling people's common perceptions of everyday reality along paths most conducive to maintaining the interests of the governing and exploiting groups. The

following the Hobsbawm approach in *Outcast London,* Gareth Stedman Jones became increasingly critical both of the historical accuracy of the economic-determinist behavioural model of class consciousness and, more importantly for present purposes, of the associated social structural one of layered, monolithic 'classes' within the working class and within society more generally.[181]

Stedman Jones argued that the currency of this model was due to a proliferating confused conflation of Marxist and post-Weberian terminology in the usage of the term 'class', and associated concepts such as status and power.[182] Furthermore, in emphasising the peculiarity of the metropolitan working classes, Stedman Jones provided an early example of research documenting the great social, cultural and political variation between different urban, industrial communities in Britain during this period.[183] E. H. Hunt was responsible for an important material backdrop for such a new interpretation, by establishing empirically the intense regional variation in wage levels, even within the same industry, found throughout the economy in this period.[184]

This dissatisfaction with Hobsbawm's concept of the labour aristocracy has continued to grow among the latest generation of labour historians, mounting their attack from a variety of ideological directions and resting their respective cases primarily on grounds of empirical authenticity.[185] For instance, studies by W. Lazonick, A. Reid, J. Zeitlin, M. Savage and R. Whipp have each demonstrated the divergences to be found in workplace and community politics and culture in different industries and the different ways in which employers and workers came to negotiated accommodations with each other.[186] Meanwhile W. D. Rubinstein's research on the propertied status groups similarly demolished the credibility of the reciprocal category – a ubiquitous coherent and distinct nationwide stratum corresponding to 'the bourgeoisie', 'the middle class' or 'the governing class'.[187]

'hegemony' of the ruling class was thereby attained with the apparent consent of the exploited, which in fact occurred because of their inability to formulate coherent, viable alternatives to the cultural values and political institutions and structures of the hegemonic class. In other words, cultural consensus was by default and there was a failure by the working class to define properly and in a unified manner its conflicting values and ideals, a fundamental prerequisite for effective political action. I am grateful to Alastair Reid for discussion of Gramsci's thought. On Gramsci, see Femia, *Gramsci's political thought.*

181 Stedman Jones, 'Class struggle and the industrial revolution'.

182 Stedman Jones, 'From historical sociology to theoretical history'.

183 Stedman Jones: *Outcast London* and 'Working class culture'. 184 Hunt, *Regional wage variations.*

185 For early statements, see: Field, 'British historians'; Reid, 'Politics and economics'; Reid, 'The labour aristocracy'; and Joyce, *Work, society and politics.*

186 On the textiles industry, see Lazonick, 'Industrial relations'. See the collection of essays in Harrison and Zeitlin (eds.), *Divisions of labour*: especially McClelland and Reid, 'Wood, iron and steel' on the shipbuilding industry; and Zeitlin, 'Engineers and compositors: a comparison'. Savage, *The dynamics of working class politics*; Whipp, *Patterns of labour.* In the form of the 'institutional rigidities' perspective on British economic performance, these findings have also been extended by Elbaum and Lazonick into a broader thesis, explaining the declining efficiency of twentieth-century British industry in comparative international terms: Elbaum and Lazonick, *The decline.*

187 Rubinstein, 'Wealth, elites, and the class structure'.

Local studies of class relations have produced, instead, the picture of a much more highly fragmented and organic, locally diverse and chaotically changing society, economy and set of associated political cultures throughout the nineteenth century.[188]

In this light it can now be seen that even those formally subscribing to Hobsbawm's interpretation, such as R. Q. Gray and G. C. Crossick, whose admirably detailed local researches into class structure in Victorian Edinburgh and South London provided the main basis for Levine's views, had in fact illustrated the strength and importance of unique internal community relations and localised status hierarchies in those places.[189] The process of revision has now gone sufficiently far that some of the most important introductory and reference works on the period now reproduce the view that Britain in the late nineteenth century cannot be seen simply as a hierarchically stratified national society and that Victorian society was essentially fractured along industrial and community lines.[190] Britain was, then, a congeries of extremely localised communities, each possessing a relatively unique cultural and even economic existence.

In principle, all of these matters of local politics and economics are of relevance for a satisfactory account of the drastic falls in fertility which occurred in each of these various communities at some point during the period 1860–1940. Given the current state of historiography in the study of fertility behaviour itself, it is the aspects of this research on working-class life which relate to the detailed mechanisms involved in the stratification of the manual labour market (as between the interests of men and women, adults and children) which most obviously have implications. As has been noted above, social scientific debate over the causes of 'fertility decline' has increasingly focused upon the significance of shifts in the short-, medium- and longer-term relative financial contributions of the different members of the family household, according to age and gender. A seemingly irresolvable battle continues between those who ascribe such shifts primarily to socio-cultural developments and those subscribing to the view that economic forces, and adjustments to them, were the prime mover. However, the work of some of the local labour historians, such as Mike Savage and Richard Whipp, exemplifies important ways in which this rather tired debate could be reconceptualised and revived as a more fruitful heuristic framework for research into the sources of falling fertilities.[191]

The fundamental message of the detailed historical work by Savage on the

[188] For instance, Koditschek, *Class formation*; Morris, *Class, sect and party*. The most recent contributions have proceeded to explore the extent of local and regional variety in political consciousness and symbols which prevailed throughout the period. For instance: Stedman Jones, 'The "cockney" and the nation'; Joyce, *Visions of the people*.

[189] Gray, *The labour aristocracy*; Crossick, *An artisan elite in Victorian society*.

[190] For instance, Thompson, *The rise of respectable society*; Benson, *The working class in Britain*. Notably also, Volume I of the recent *Cambridge social history of modern Britain*, edited by F. M. L. Thompson, was devoted to *Regions and communities*.

[191] Savage, *Dynamics of working class politics*; Whipp, *Patterns of labour*. For a detailed account of the work of Whipp and Savage, see below, pp. 498, 509–12, 554.

Lancashire textiles industry and Whipp on the North Staffordshire potteries is that of massive variation (both synchronic and diachronic) in labour market practices. However, the great variation which they report does not simply sum to intellectual anarchy or radical indeterminacy. Rather, from the basis of their detailed comparative knowledge, Whipp and Savage are each able to point to certain strategically significant 'variables', which primarily account for the historical development of the important differences between towns and communities in each of their regional industries. In particular both have independently come to the conclusion that a key issue correlated with major differences between towns and between different industrial sectors, in terms of relative wage-rates and employment opportunities for females and youths, was the way in which control over recruitment and acquisition of skills occurred. It may also be possible, therefore, in the study of changing fertility behaviour to identify certain general strategic factors or variables which were of particular importance in determining the manner in which fertility fell in different places or among different social groups in Britain, just as mode of recruitment has been identified by these local studies as having been so important in determining the evolving character of local labour markets.

Prognosis

Thus, in accounting for fertility change among the mass of the population, no less than in accounting for political, economic and cultural change, a general model of social structure as more or less invariant both over time and between localities – differing only in the proportions of the population assigned to each of its few hierarchic grades – has contributed to a fundamental distortion of the investigative process and a gross limitation upon the forms of explanation which can be attained. This kind of model has sent those seeking explanations down a cul-de-sac where only highly general, nationally applicable, sweeping causal mechanisms are attended to. The unitary, professional model of fertility decline is essentially the tool and premise appropriate for those seeking a quick and approximate explanation for a phenomenon as complex as Britain's fall in fertility, just as the 'labour aristocracy' model has served so well those wishing to advance grand, sweeping explanations for the supposedly quiescent (relative to a revolutionary model of political behaviour) character of British working-class politics. However, for those prepared to invest more time and effort in the search for a more rigorous, discerning and complex, but ultimately more comprehensive and satisfactory account, the profound limitations involved in accepting this kind of representation must be explicitly acknowledged and challenged head on by demographic historians, as they have been by social and labour historians.

What is now under critical investigation in Part II, therefore, is how this graded, class-differential 'professional model' of fertility decline came into existence in the first place. This forms part of an examination of whether it is a justifiable or helpful representation of the process of falling fertility. This will in turn lead on, in Part III, to an exploration of the alternative possible lessons that can be learned from the social and demographic evidence collected at the 1911 census, once the professional model of fertility decline has been put on one side. Finally, in Part IV, there is a return to the issues of interpretation raised, but not answered, in this critical historiographical review. An effort is made to put forward a new framework for analysing changing fertility which can accommodate the goal of general explanation while incorporating and acknowledging the importance of local and cultural variation, and the political and ideological aspects of historical change, including demographic change.

PART II

The professional model of social classes: an intellectual history

Of all vulgar methods of escaping from the consideration of the effect of social and moral influences on the human mind, the most vulgar is that of attributing the diversities of conduct and character to inherent and natural differences.

John Stuart Mill, *Principles of political economy I*, p. 390, cited by Arthur Newsholme, *Vital Statistics* (1923 edn), p. 556

Prologue: the fertility census of 1911 and the professional model of social classes

With the approach of the census year of 1911, the senior staff of the GRO were to be found making preparations for a massive retrospective survey of the entire nation's marital fertility patterns as an integral part of the forthcoming census.[1] For the first time ever the statutory census duty of every household head in the country was to include a response to questions eliciting detailed information on the number of children everborn and surviving to all extant marriages.[2] Parliament could occasionally be prevailed upon to authorise such exceptional inquiries through the machinery of the nation's decennial census if there was sufficient public anxiety over a topical issue that could be sensibly investigated in this way.[3] Hence, in 1851 there had been an attempt to use the census to assess the

[1] The GRO was established in 1837 under the aegis of the Home Office (subsequently transferring to the Local Government Board on its formation in 1871) by the Registration Act and the Marriage Act, both passed in 1836. Its duties were the supervision of a new civil registration system for recording all births, deaths and marriages, in replacement of the defunct parish registration scheme originally established by Thomas Cromwell in 1538 in Henry VIII's reign. From the 1841 census onwards, the Office was also regularly invested by Parliament with responsibility for undertaking the series of decennial censuses begun in 1801. On this early history of the national census and the GRO for England and Wales, see Glass, *Numbering the people*; Cullen, 'The making of the Civil Registration Act'; Cullen, *The statistical movement*, ch. 2; Eyler, *Victorian social medicine*, ch. 3. There has been no attempt to write a definitive institutional history of the GRO. On the GRO in the Victorian and Edwardian periods, see the special issue of *Social History of Medicine* 4, 3 (1991): 'The GRO of England and Wales and the public health movement 1837–1914, a comparative perspective'.

[2] Not until 1951 was the national census again used to provide a fertility survey (although there had also been an official 'Family Census' taken in 1946 – a 10% sample survey for the Royal Commission on Population of 1944–9).

[3] Before the Census Act of 1920 established the taking of the decennial census on a routine and permanent basis through the mechanism of an Order in Council, each decennial census had previously been authorised by the passing of a separate Act of Parliament. The consequent lack of permanent facilities and staff for processing the census was a perennial (or rather 'perdecennial') grouse on the part of the hard-pressed staff of the GRO. The demand for a permanently established office to manage the national census was often linked with arguments in favour of a more frequent, quinquennial census. The GRO was supported in this dual call by such bodies as the Royal Statistical Society Census Committee and its representatives in Parliament (e.g. Sir Charles Dilke in 1910: see Hansard (1910), Vol. XIV col. 1875; Vol. XVII cols. 1233–8).

proportions of religious adherents of different denominations within the nation; and in 1931 there would be an attempt to assess the incidence of unemployment in different industries, occupations and regions.

In 1911, there was an analogous burning issue, at least among an influential section of the political nation. This was the desire to know the facts concerning recent, apparently alarming changes in the nation's birth rate, and associated variations in fertility between different sections of society. Not, of course, that this was the only object of concern and speculation at this time: there were other issues competing for inclusion on the census form. For instance, proposals for a religious census or for a census of the unemployed each found their champions in debates in the House of Commons.[4] Nevertheless, it was to be the fertility inquiry that triumphed, despite opposition from some MPs on grounds of privacy and propriety.[5]

It is important not to take this event – a national census of fertility in 1911 – at face value, as simply nothing more than a statistical exercise and an impartial source of quantitative evidence. We must ask why and how it was that, during the interval since the previous census of 1901, the issue had come to be perceived as important enough, at least in the debating chamber of the House of Commons, to justify the state's expenditure on such a costly and prying intelligence exercise. In the answers to those questions we shall begin to gain some clues as to the reasons for the particular treatment afforded to the data when it came to be tabulated and presented by the GRO in its official *Report on the Fertility of Marriage*.[6] It has been the conceptual framework that informed that original, official analysis and presentation of the evidence collected in 1911 that we today, and all students of the phenomenon for the past seventy years, have had to take as our point of departure.[7] It seems eminently reasonable, therefore, to attempt to understand how and why the evidence that was presented in that seminal document was classified and ordered in the particular ways that it was. To fail to ask such questions merely perpetuates the received orthodoxy by default and for no explicit reason other than its longevity.

The Office of the Registrar-General was a senior civil service post, directly responsible to the President of the Local Government Board. This was a junior

4 Hansard (1910), Vol. XIV cols. 1071, 1241–56, respectively, and Vol. XVIII cols. 246–57; 257–76, respectively. Proposals for *additional* questions to be asked of the populace – beyond the standard inquiries as to age, sex, relation to household head, occupation, etc. – were to some extent seen as mutually exclusive alternatives, since it was generally considered that the populace could not be overburdened with demands for additional information by the census exercise without risking serious 'response fatigue' and consequent inaccuracy in the information collected.

5 Hansard (1910), Vol. XVIII cols. 289–91; 300–3.

6 Pt 1, the General Report, was published in 1917 and Pt 2 in 1923. The latter is much the more important for demographic historians, containing as it does a wealth of detailed analyses and tabulations of the data. See above, Introduction, n. 9.

7 The 'raw data' – the manuscript census schedules – do not, of course, become available to the public for 100 years under present law (a 1966 Order of the Lord Chancellor under the Public Records Act 1958).

Cabinet position held by John Burns during 1910, when the Census Bill was before Parliament.[8] It was the President's responsibility to argue the case in the Commons for any innovations in census procedure. If we examine the arguments which he and his supporters were putting to MPs in 1910, we find the following:

For the first time in the English census we are making a provision for information being obtained from married couples as to the duration of marriage and the number of children born of the marriage. We believe that this will furnish data of the highest value for the study of certain social problems, such as comparative fertility in classes of different social positions, and in occupations, bearing on age and upon certain questions relating to infant and child mortality, to which increasingly the community is giving closer attention.[9]

This was Burns's opening statement in debate after the second reading. There was no suggestion of opposition to these proposals until the bill entered committee stage, on 21 June 1910. Burns was then forced to elaborate somewhat on his justifications for the investigation. He replied to suspicions of the inquiry's 'inquisitional' nature that 'The reason for this question is that nearly all the countries of the world are confronted with a very remarkable diminution of the birth-rate.'[10] He continued: 'I would repeat that the sole object of the question which we ask the House to sanction is to get at the fertility of married couples in various social positions and occupations, and at various ages, and to ascertain the cause of the heavy child mortality.'[11] He expanded on this latter interest: 'We hope to obtain information as to the strain to which the mother and father may be subjected in consequence of their occupation instead of what I believe to be the ideal rule being followed, in which a father does the work and not the mother, by which the money to keep the family is earned.'[12] Meanwhile he found an ally in Dr Christopher Addison, new to Parliament but very experienced in public health matters, who ably defended the value of the census inquiry against one MP's objection that the census would add nothing new to the information already available from vital registration.[13] Addison emphasised the rapidity with which

[8] John Burns (1858–1943) had been elected as an independent Labour MP for Battersea in 1892 after playing a leading role with Tom Mann in the famous London dock strike of 1889. In 1906 he joined the Liberal administration as the only working-class member of Campbell-Bannerman's (and later Asquith's) Cabinet, holding the post of President of the LGB until 1914. Brown, *John Burns*; Gilbert, *The evolution of national insurance*, p. 33 n. 28. Also see below, ch. 4, n. 49; ch. 5, n. 20.

[9] Hansard (1910), Vol. XVII cols. 1229–30. [10] Hansard (1910), Vol. XVIII col. 291.

[11] Hansard (1910), Vol. XVIII col. 296. [12] Hansard (1910), Vol. XVIII col. 248.

[13] Christopher (later Viscount) Addison (1869–1951), son of a Lincolnshire tenant farmer, had been appointed Sheffield University's first Professor of Anatomy in 1897 and subsequently held posts at Charing Cross and St Batholomew's Hospitals before entering Parliament in 1910 as Liberal MP for Hoxton in London's East End. Having made an effective maiden speech on 24 February 1910 on social issues, he was immediately involved at this time in the formulation of Lloyd George's National Health Insurance scheme. Addison was the future first Minister of Health under Lloyd George, 1919–21, but broke with him over the cuts to the postwar housing scheme and subsequently joined Labour as MP for Swindon and Minister for Agriculture, 1930–1. At the end of his life he was Labour's leader of the House of Lords throughout Attlee's administration, 1945–51: Morgan and Morgan, *Portrait of a progressive*.

the census would supply comprehensive and relevant information on the urgent issues at stake.[14]

Thus, the RG was empowered to undertake the fertility of marriage investigation on Parliament's understanding that it would provide the quickest route to reliable information on a cluster of three explicitly inter-related issues. First, 'comparative fertility in classes of different social positions'; secondly, the relationship of fertility variation with the age of couples; finally, 'the cause of the heavy child mortality' was to be examined through an occupational analysis of the population, paying special attention to the supposed evil effects of a mother's occupation. The suspected class differentials in fertility were always presented by Burns as the prime justification for the fertility questions. It was clearly considered that this was the aspect most likely to secure Parliamentary sanction for a survey of the nation's fertility behaviour. Yet in 1910, at the time Burns was speaking, the GRO was not even in possession of a means with which to measure phenomena and analyse data with reference to 'social position'.

Why, then, since the last census of 1901, had the relationship between fertility and 'social position' suddenly become such a concrete focus of attention in national politics? To anticipate in brief the more complex story to be recounted in the course of the following chapters of Part II, this development was a by-product of the intense social policy debates that racked British politics during the first decade of the new century. A palpable sense of crisis seems to have been generated in the public consciousness by the reverberating shock to national pride – for a generation used to a sense of global superiority – represented by the ignominious performance of the Imperial army in the Boer War.[15] Along with the formal end to the Victorian era with the Queen Empress's death in the first year of the new century, these traumas provoked a period of national self-examination and political reappraisal. The wide-ranging policy debates drew on several lines of thought critical of conventional liberal political and economic assumptions, reflecting a current of ideas that was relatively new to the national political stage, though it had been articulated by various intellectuals since the 1880s, and even earlier in some cases.[16] The emergence of a national political organisation of the working classes, with the formation of the Labour Representation Committee in February 1900, was itself both a symptom of the established political parties' failure to

[14] Hansard (1910), Vol. XVIII cols. 301–3 replying to Sir F. Banbury's argument made at 291. Ironically, the intervention of the Great War was to ensure that the full report on the 1911 fertility census was to be one of the most delayed publications in the GRO's history, Part 2 not appearing until 1923.

[15] See Searle, *The quest for national efficiency*, especially ch. 2 on the galvanising effects of the reverses of the second Boer War. Also Semmel, *Imperialism and social reform*.

[16] On the 1880s developments in social thought and their relationship with the earlier intellectual watershed of the 1860s, see Stedman Jones *Outcast London* (1984 edition, including new 'Preface'); and on some of the associated forms of intellectual critique: Richter, *The politics of conscience*; MacKenzie and MacKenzie, *The first Fabians*; Freeden, *The New Liberalism*; Collini, *Liberalism and sociology*; Kadish, *The Oxford economists*.

confront Britain's apparently mounting social and economic ills and also a further political spur to them to do so before it was too late.

In the 1890s a few isolated doom-mongers, notably the eugenicist Karl Pearson, had already been trying to draw public attention to differentials between the fertility and survival rates of the nation's social classes. Pearson's (in)famous claim was that approximately one quarter of the current generation were producing about one half of the next, as a result of social class differences in propensity to marry and to produce surviving children in marriage. He cited class-fertility statistics from Copenhagen, as showing that it was the lowly artisan class whose stock was thereby predominating over the elevated professional classes, an undesirable evolutionary trend which he suspected to be similar in Britain.[17] In the 1890s all this was to little avail. However, in the transformed atmosphere that prevailed after the Boer War, these supposedly scientific admonitions began to be taken sufficiently seriously for the government to find itself compelled to appoint a commission of inquiry at the very least, in order to forestall the prospect of a full-scale Royal Commission.[18] Thus, the famous Inter-departmental Inquiry into Physical Deterioration of 1903–4 was set up to examine the alarming claims of these Darwinian 'sociologists'. Broadly speaking, it was out of this inquiry's recommendations for more information on the subject, along with the continuing heated speculations of the ensuing five years which were stoked up by further eugenic revelations, that the need for an authoritative, scientific fertility survey gained sufficient public recognition to appear on the agenda for possible inclusion in the next national census.

However, this is merely to summarise the barest bones of a much more complex story. To understand fully why, in 1911, the GRO was undertaking these novel ventures – a fertility census and an associated social classification of the nation – and especially to comprehend the particular form which its solution to these duties took, we must venture in the next two chapters some way into the maelstrom of the history of ideas in this period. It is completely misleading to treat the statistical products of the GRO as if they were created in an intellectual vacuum. Their creation was intimately related to certain policy aims and to the contemporary methods of investigative empirical social science. These can only be properly understood within the appropriate context of that period's social thought, social scientific practices and relevant political contests. In undertaking such an exercise we have to bear in mind Michael Freeden's counsel that 'social and political thought were indistinguishable as separate specialisms before the First World War'.[19] To this we might add that the claims of 'science' – in particular an evolutionary biology – also bulked particularly large where issues of the

17 Pearson, 'Reproductive selection'; Pearson, 'Contributions to the mathematical theory of evolution'. Pearson's data came from Rubin and Westergaard, *Ægteskabsstatistik paa Grundlag (Statistics of marriages)*.

18 On the reluctance of the Balfour government to become embroiled, see Gilbert, 'Health and politics'.

19 Freeden, *The New Liberalism*, p. 7.

public's physical and moral health and the significance of changes in its reproductive behaviour were the centre of attention.

For reasons that will become abundantly clear in due course, the official model of the nation's class structure, which is the centre of attention in the ensuing account, is most aptly described as a *professional* model or representation of the nation's social class structure. It will perhaps be most helpful to start with a simple description of the basic form of this professional model of society. It comprises a linear scale of five ranked grades of 'social position' or status, which were arranged as follows:

I Professional
II Intermediate
III Skilled Manual
IV Intermediate
V Unskilled Manual

This was the form in which the official model was first rendered by its progenitor, Dr T. H. C. Stevenson, after several years of experimentation.[20] It is also the basic form that was used to interpret the 1911 census fertility data.[21] All individual male heads of household and their families (female heads, if no male present) were assigned to one of these five grades according to their recorded gainful occupation. These social classes are, therefore, primarily aggregations of (male) occupational unit groups, according to some notion of the relative social status of such occupations. Such relative prestige was judged to fall into three clearly demarcated zones standing in an ordinal relationship to each other, while the two intermediate categories were created for marginal, mixed or imprecisely defined occupations. As well as producing five grades of social position, the model also provided for a bipartite distinction between a non-manual 'upper and middle class' supposedly represented most unequivocally by the professions of class I, as against the various grades of the manual working class, in classes III–V.

There would appear to have been three fundamental methodological premises

20 Thomas Henry Craig Stevenson (1870–1932), MB, MD (University College, London). Born Strabane, Co. Tyrone. Stevenson was William Farr's third successor as Superintendent of Statistics at the GRO, holding the post from 1909 until his retirement through illness in 1931. Before his appointment to the GRO he was Assistant Medical Officer to Sir Arthur Newsholme (Brighton's Medical Officer of Health, 1888–1908); and during 1905–6 Stevenson was a medical officer for the Education Committee of the LCC. The intellectual direction of the 1911 census and the development of the associated social class model were primarily Stevenson's responsibility. (See below, ch. 5.) For further information on Stevenson, see ch. 5, n. 48; *Who was who* 1929–40; obituary in *JRSS* 96 (1933), 151–5.

21 Originally, there were three anomalous 'industrial' classes which stood apart from the five graded classes. These were for textiles workers, coal miners, and agricultural labourers. Not until 1927 did Stevenson feel that he had satisfactorily integrated these three groups into the five-class system. These developments are dealt with in detail in chapter 5, below.

which defined the original, essential characteristics of this professional model of social classes:

(i) that occupation of the individual male household head provided the most reliable and accessible single piece of information upon which to base an empirical social classification system of the nation's families
(ii) that there was a primary division between, on the one hand, the higher-status *non-manual* occupations which could be assessed according to the extent to which they were *professional* and, on the other hand, the lower-status *manual* occupations, which were assessed according to their *skill* level
(iii) that overall there could be a single, exhaustive *uni-dimensional hierarchical* social grading of *all* members of the nation according to such occupational criteria.

The model in fact spent about eighteen years being developed, 'in the workshop' so to speak, at the GRO. The first mention of T. H. C. Stevenson's intention to build such a classification scheme is recorded in an internal memorandum of February 1910. He finally pronounced himself satisfied with his work in a paper delivered to the Royal Statistical Society on 21 February 1928. If durability is a test of strength or value, it seems to have been an extremely well-crafted instrument that resulted. It is still in commission today, subject only to minor modifications over the intervening decades.[22] Like any structure that has endured, the official representation of the nation's class structure also has deep foundations: a pre-history which stretches back in time long before Stevenson's interest in the project was first announced at the end of the first decade of the twentieth century. As well as a protracted birth, the model's gestation was long and tortuous, the product of a warring parentage, as the following chapters will reveal.

22 Initially in the 1910s and 1920s, the graded scheme comprised five categories, with an attempt to keep separate the higher-status 'non-manual' workers in classes I and II, as against lower-status 'manual' workers in classes III, IV and V. However, already by the end of the 1920s routine clerical work had suffered such an obvious relative decline in both remuneration and social status that white-collar clerical workers were 'demoted' to class III, where they were classed alongside skilled manual occupations in the publications derived from the 1931 census. Since the 1971 census, however, the categorical distinction between manual and non-manual has been revived by splitting class III into class IIIN and class IIIM for non-manual and manual occupations respectively. There are, therefore, six social classes but because IIIN and IIIM notionally have equivalent social status, there are still only five grades of social position, something that has remained consistent from the outset. Furthermore, the two 'intermediate' classes have since acquired positive identities. At the 1951 census the intermediate manual class (IV) began to be referred to as 'partly skilled' and from the 1991 census the intermediate non-manual class (II) began to be described as 'Managerial and technical'. See 1991 Census, *Definitions Great Britain* (HMSO 1992), para. 7.51, 'Social class based on occupation', p. 40.

2

Social classification of occupations and the GRO in the nineteenth century

The GRO's nineteenth-century social classification of occupations

In searching for the origins of the professional model of social classes, it would seem most likely at first sight that Stevenson's model might have been in some way influenced by, or even have been a direct replacement for, the previous official classification of occupations.[1] This had been nominally in use at the Office until

[1] The questions of the deeper historical origins and philosophical implications of the application of the concept of 'class' to humans and to society and of the prior history of 'classification' are extremely interesting. Only a brief reference can be made here to what remains a vast and under-researched subject, suitable for a separate study. As the first footnote of Asa Briggs's subsequent study attests, Raymond Williams first drew attention to this problematic 'key word' in his *Culture and society*. The term 'class', as a socio-economic category, was introduced into the English language principally through the popularisation of the terminology of political economy. In political economy 'class' originally referred to each of Adam Smith's three analytical categories of economic agents: landlords, capitalists and labourers. In his pioneering article, Asa Briggs argued that in the early decades of the nineteenth century the subsequent popularisation of the term was an essentially political process: Briggs, 'The language of "class"'. Briggs argued that the term 'class' was deployed by political economists, by radicals and by the commercial classes more generally (both masters and artisans) so as to challenge the traditional, neo-aristocratic, paternalistic conception of society as a finely graded hierarchy of 'ranks', a continuous 'chain of connection' linking protective superiors and deferential inferiors. In the hands of radicals the class terminology of political economy could be deployed to marginalise landowning aristocrats as 'unproductive' rentiers. Indeed, William Farr at the GRO categorised those without an 'occupation' in this way (see pp. 122–3). However, since Adam Smith believed that his three economic agents interacted to their common good (the 'invisible hand') a more harmonious view could also be derived from political economy. Geoffrey Crossick has noted this, referring to the unpublished original research of S. Wallech on Ricardo's more hierarchical and politically concessionary reading of the relationship between the three economic agents as higher, middle and lower classes: Crossick, 'From gentlemen to the residuum', pp. 151–4. Of course, subsequently in the 1840s and 1850s Karl Marx and Friedrich Engels developed the terminology and concepts in the opposite direction, emphasising the exclusive historical and political significance of a conflict of interests between two of Smith's three classes, the property-accumulating capitalists and the property-less, wage-labouring proletarians. The key passages, including those from *The manifesto of the Communist party* (1848) and *The eighteenth Brumaire of Louis Bonaparte* (1852), are conveniently collected together in Giddens and Held (eds.), *Classes, power and conflict*, pp. 12–38. Note that Keith Wrightson's work has shown, since Briggs published, a similarly politically-contested field of terms for social representation throughout the early modern period: Wrightson, 'Estates, degrees, and

1900 and had originally been devised by Dr William Farr for the 1861 census.[2] It consisted of six classes constituted out of eighteen industrial orders of occupations.[3] Edward Higgs has helpfully clarified the predominantly medical rationale behind this scheme and shown that the highest level of aggregation of occupations and orders into six great classes was merely a fanciful rhetorical flourish (complete with classical Greek names), giving a superficial 'economic' gloss to a scheme that was in fact constructed primarily for medical purposes.[4] The main aim was always to elucidate the nature of occupation-specific causes of death, explicitly following Bernardino Ramazzini's (1633–1714) views that the materials and activities involved in each distinct occupation entailed specific health risks.[5] Farr's attempt

sorts'. On the earlier history of the development of measurement and classification from the sixteenth century, as embodying a 'scientific' epistemological disposition, in the sense of an intellectual 'technology' of representation for ordering empirical information and facilitating inductive generalisation, see Foucault, *The order of things*; Kula, *Measures and men*. For an historical exposition of the way in which this technology of representation has become deeply embedded within statistics, in both its disciplinary and its social sense, as the modern state's mathematically based knowledge of society and economy, see Desrosières, *La Politique des grands nombres*. Additionally, see Corrigan and Sayer, *The great arch*, ch. 6, for a post-Foucauldian interpretation of English state formation, which explains the particular importance to the state of developing and expanding its statistical and classificatory powers during the first half of the nineteenth century in terms of the social surveillance requirements of a new liberal, rationalist theory of the sources of authority, 'representative democracy'. Since property ownership above an arbitrary point, rather than birth and reputation, was now the formal criteria for admission to 'Society', there was a critical, political and 'policing' need for intelligence regarding the character and extent of the masses on and below this boundary, the rest of 'society' clamouring for admission within the pale of the constitution.

2 William Farr (1807–83) was the first specialist statistician to be employed at the GRO (appointed 'compiler of abstracts' in July 1839, he retired from the prestigious post he had created of Superintendent of Statistics in 1880). Apparently with the full support of his almost equally long-serving superior, George Graham, (Registrar-General 1842–79), Farr established the GRO as the nation's leading institution of epidemiological expertise and as a vociferous champion of the public health movement. The definitive intellectual biography of William Farr is John Eyler's *Victorian social medicine*.

3 Its original specification is to be found in: PP 1863 LIII, Pt I: 1861 Census General Report Vol. III, Appendix, pp. 225–48. The six classes were: Professional (*Andrici*); Domestic (*Oikici*); Commercial (*Agorici*); Agricultural (*Georgici*); Industrial (*Technici*); and a residual for 'Indefinite, or Unoccupied'. While these six classes were introduced in 1861, the principle of grouping occupations into 'orders' had already been deployed at the previous census of 1851, a scheme which William Farr had designed in association with Horace Mann and George Graham. However, somewhat confusingly the 'Orders' of 1861 had initially been called 'classes' when they were first introduced in 1851 (and there had been seventeen such 'classes' in 1851, whereas there were eighteen 'Orders' in 1861). For further details, see Banks, 'The social structure of England', pp. 190–1.

4 E. Higgs, 'Disease, febrile poisons'; on the enduring tensions between economic and medical interests in the national census, see also Higgs, 'The struggle for the occupational census'.

5 This was an integral part of the complex, broader etiological position, which Farr held during the mid-century decades before microscope technology had finally confirmed the validity of the germ theory of disease. Farr, in common with many others, had subscribed to a broadly 'pythogenic' or chemical etiology. This permitted a kind of intellectual compromise between the two theoretical extremes of pure contagionism and miasmatism, which defined the limits of the field of scientific discourse (with many degrees of nuance lying between these two poles). According to Farr each distinct epidemic, endemic or contagious disease was caused by its own specific chemical agent or matter. But it was not the case that such matter could only spread between victims by their mutual contact (strict contagionism). The pythogenic theory supposed that disease was caused by the

to imbue this ambivalent overall scheme with a supposedly unifying scientific rationale rightly failed to impress his contemporaries.[6] Farr himself was clearly never entirely happy with this effort at an occupational classification and never attempted to analyse demographic data using the six major classes.[7]

The formal abandonment of these six classes is recorded in a memorandum from 'R.M.' (Reginald Macleod, briefly the Registrar-General 1900–2) to John Tatham (T. H. C. Stevenson's predecessor), dated October 1900. Abandonment was justified on the grounds that the scheme was of no use to any government department and potentially misleading as a social classification.[8] Macleod complained that 'the dangers of fallacious deductions being made from the figures is a very real one', since 'A scrutiny of the details suggests that such a title as "Professional Class" is misleading when the class includes postmen.'[9] Farr's 1861 scheme is, thus, a false lead in trying to trace the intellectual origins of the professional model. Not only had it been dropped several years before Stevenson entered service at the Office in 1909, but also it had never even been considered of any analytical importance while in use.

In fact, it can be shown that by the mid-1880s senior statistical staff at the GRO had already been publicly expressing their interest, for a variety of reasons, in the possibility of constructing a new empirical representation of the nation's social class structure in order to illustrate various socio-demographic and epidemiological aspects of the population's life-experience. By implication at least, if not by explicit acknowledgement, the extant 1861 scheme bequeathed by Farr was considered

fermentation of the poisonous matter in the victim's body. However, such 'zymotic' matter (the general term Farr gave to all such fermenting poisons) could also proliferate outside the body under appropriate environmental conditions (for instance where piles of filth were subject to heat and moisture). Exposure to such conditions might therefore act as a separate, environmental (i.e. not communicated between persons) source of primary infection. Human beings chronically exposed to such insalubrious environments both ran a higher risk of infection and also would be more likely to succumb once attacked. All aspects of individuals' 'environments', notably including the workplace, were therefore potentially associated with the chances of contracting different types of lethal 'zymotic' or 'pythogenic' disease. Overall, the pythogenic theory directed practical attention to the amelioration of unhygienic and insanitary aspects of the environment as the appropriate means to promote the public's health. Occupations were therefore grouped into orders mainly according to the supposed pythogenic potentialities and implications of the different types of occupational environment involved, including the material or product worked upon. See Pelling, *Cholera, fever*, especially ch. 8; Eyler, *Victorian social medicine*, pp. 102–18; Eyler, 'William Farr on the cholera'.

6 Farr's attempted justifications are to be found in PP 1863 LIII, Pt I: 1861 Census General Report Vol. III, pp. 27–39; and Appendix, 'The new classification of the people according to their employments', pp. 225–32. See the scathing critique by T. A. Welton (whose apprenticeship in such matters had been served as Headlam Greenhow's assistant in the 1850s): 'On the classification of the people by occupations'.

7 It is obvious from the section entitled 'Proposed enquiry into the occupations of the people', immediately following his section on 'The new classification', that Farr ideally envisaged much more work in this area, though his extraordinarily ambitious projected inquiry failed to materialise: PP 1863 LIII, Pt I: 1861 Census General Report Vol. III, Appendix, pp. 233–48.

8 PRO RG 19/10, Item 15.

9 PRO RG 19/10, Item 15.

totally inadequate to these purposes. Public arguments in favour of such a new classification scheme by staff of the GRO were first expounded by Noel Humphreys, a relatively unknown but in fact extremely important presence in the Office, Farr's loyal and long-standing factotum.[10] In a paper read to the Royal Statistical Society in 1887, Humphreys had proposed the innovation of class-specific mortality statistics: envisaging that ideally a life table should be compiled for each social class to enable valid comparisons to be made.[11] He referred to several types of previous work that had already been done in this direction: the Experience Tables drawn up by commercial life insurance companies for calculating insurance and assurance premia for their relatively well-off clients;[12] William Farr's Healthy District Life Tables;[13] and the occupational mortality tables for males engaged in different occupations begun by Farr in the supplement to the 25th ARRG, published in 1865.[14]

Humphreys did not, however, mention at all the various other early labours in this direction by the likes of Headlam Greenhow, W. L. Sargant and H. W. Rumsey.[15] The last-named in particular, in criticising the GRO's 'national system' for analysis and publication of the data in its care, had put forward strong arguments for measurements of class effects on mortality. In 1871 Dr H. W. Rumsey had discussed the occupational mortality tables, then recently published

[10] Noel Algernon Humphreys (1837–1923) was from a family of independent means and was privately educated. He entered the GRO in 1856 as a Junior Clerk and spent exactly fifty years there, rising to the highest administrative rank beneath the Registrar-General, which he held from 1890 until his retirement in 1905. Although the archival records of the nineteenth-century GRO are relatively sparse and staff did not leave memoirs, it is certain that Humphreys had considerable status and influence within the Office, especially, of course, during his last fifteen years when his authority was probably on a par with both Ogle and Tatham, Farr's successors. This was only partly due to his length of service and experience. It was also because of his intimate association with much of Farr's founding work. He edited for the Sanitary Institute of Great Britain the important posthumous anthology of Farr's work, *Vital statistics: a memorial volume*. Humphreys successfully established an independent reputation as a social statistician, in recognition of which from 1874 he was a Fellow of the Statistical Society of London (the Royal Statistical Society from 1887); and he was appointed one of its honorary secretaries from the mid-1880s and was awarded the Society's Guy medal in silver in 1907. (Sources: *Who was who 1916–28*; *JRSS* Obituary, March 1923.)

[11] Humphreys, 'Class mortality statistics', p. 256.

[12] These included the well-known data of Ansell, Jr, *On the rate of mortality*; the Healthy Male and Healthy Female Tables compiled by the Institute of Actuaries; and various Experience Tables of thirty or so US life assurance societies. Humphreys, 'Class mortality statistics', pp. 258–60.

[13] First presented by Farr to the Royal Society in 1859: 'On the construction of life-tables'.

[14] This was subsequently improved as age-corrected rates by his immediate successor (Humphreys's current colleague), Dr William Ogle, in the decennial supplement to the 45th ARRG (although the age-correction procedure was very simple: the 100 occupations in this exercise were simply corrected for the proportion above and below age 45, among those aged 25–65 in each occupation). 45th ARRG Supplement, pp. xxi–xxv.

[15] Greenhow, 'Illustrations of the necessity'; Greenhow, *Papers relating to the sanitary state*; Sargant, 'On certain results and defects', p. 170; Rumsey, 'On certain fallacies'. Possibly the reason for this was Humphreys's sense of loyalty to his former superior and recently deceased mentor. Humphreys was at this time engaged in collating the memorial volume of Farr's demographic writings for the Sanitary Institute. (Note that although Farr's relations with both Greenhow and Sargant were probably not entirely cordial, Rumsey was in fact a lifelong personal friend of his.)

for the first time in the decennial supplement to the 25th ARRG and concluded that: '"occupations" as returned in the decennial Census . . . do not correctly express the conditions of CLASS, which may have as much to do with mortality and disease as OCCUPATION itself' (sic).[16] Rumsey defined 'class' after Edwin Chadwick's earlier usage in his famous *Report on the sanitary conditions of the labouring population*, published in 1842, where he divided the self-supporting population into three great classes: Gentry and Professional Families; Farmers, Tradesmen; Labourers, Artisans (and there was a fourth category for paupers).[17] These were 'distinguished chiefly by apparent differences in their means of subsistence, in their style or mode of living'.[18] There is, then, a clear notion here that the classification should rest on criteria of social status and on the closely associated question of mode of gaining a living.

Sixteen years after this suggestion by Rumsey, Humphreys, also referring to the results of (a subsequent edition of) the RG's decennial tables of occupational mortality, was to be found writing:

> Valuable as are the RG's statistics of occupational mortality for throwing light upon the excessive death-rates of adult males engaged in different occupations, they do not afford much help in the direction of class mortality statistics. As the most important differences between the mortality statistics of the upper classes and of the general population occur in infancy and childhood, it is absolutely necessary to obtain information of the mortality in childhood among the working classes.[19]

In this paper Humphreys defined class influences in explicit socio-economic terms related to questions of income: 'class hardships' were those 'arising from poverty and its attendant penalties of bad housing, bad feeding, and bad clothing'.[20]

Humphreys's 1887 suggestions were not merely prospective, for he was also able to cite an experimental social classification of occupations already in operation by the Irish Registrar-General, Dr T. W. Grimshaw, for the city of Dublin.[21] This scheme was the result of the efforts of the Dublin Sanitary

16 Rumsey, 'On certain fallacies', p. 22.

17 Edwin Chadwick (1800–90), Jeremy Bentham's amanuensis at the end of the latter's life, was the 'civil servant genius' of the reforming Whig administrations of the 1830s and 1840s: principal architect, *inter alia*, of the Factory Inspectorate, the New Poor Law of 1834, the County Constabulary created in 1839 and the nation's first Public Health Act of 1848, as well as the Acts which created the General Register Office itself (see Prologue, n. 1). On Chadwick: Finer, *The life and times*; Lewis, *Edwin Chadwick*; Brundage, *England's Prussian Minister*. There is an excellent 'Introduction' by M. W. Flinn to the 1965 reprinted edition of Chadwick's *Report*.

18 Rumsey, 'On certain fallacies', p. 22.

19 Humphreys, 'Class mortality statistics', pp. 264–5.

20 Humphreys, 'Class mortality statistics', p. 264.

21 In fact Humphreys displayed a detailed acquaintance with, and enthusiasm for, the Irish social classification and its potential application to demographic statistics as early as May 1886, when he informally presented a calculation of class-differential rates for child mortality, total fertility and old-age dependency derived from the Irish data. This can be found – somewhat obscurely – in Humphreys's contribution to the discussion following Charles Booth's paper to the Statistical Society of London: Booth, 'Occupations of the people', pp. 440–1.

Association in successfully impressing upon the Irish administration a request for class-differentiated mortality information, following the serious smallpox epidemic of 1878, which had resulted in a Royal Commission to inquire into the sewerage and drainage of the city of Dublin.[22] Consequently, the 1881 Irish census report and, since January 1883, the *Weekly Returns of Births and Deaths* contained an attempted social classification for the heads of families in Dublin.[23]

Why were senior staff at the GRO only now, in 1887, prepared to back a form of mortality analysis that had been publicly argued for nearly twenty years earlier by a colleague and friend of Farr's (Rumsey) and had been in use since the beginning of the decade in one part of the United Kingdom? As recently as 1884 Humphreys had given a paper covering similar ground in which the possibility of class-differential statistics had simply been ignored.[24] What had changed? One direct stimulus seems to have been the appearance, during the three years elapsing between Humphreys's two articles, of the RG's decennial supplement for 1871–80, authored by Farr's successor, William Ogle. The most significant mortality trend which it reported for the 1870s was a decline in the nation's death rates, but concentrated mostly among young and middle-aged adults and conspicuously not shared by children and infants. Hence Humphreys's new concern to construct an empirical measure of the harmful effects of the living conditions most relevant to this particular sector of the population, something which could not be inferred from the GRO's established practice of publishing occupational mortality patterns, as these reflected only the differential hazards endured by adults in the workplace.

In the mid-1880s the GRO did in fact undertake an apparently long-forgotten research initiative aimed at the broad area identified as important by Humphreys: the living conditions of the working classes. Of course, studies of the employment, wages and budget patterns of the working classes were shortly to become a principal activity of an entire department of government, the new Labour Statistical Bureau of the Board of Trade created in 1886 and upgraded to a Labour Department in 1893. However, in the period of growing concern over industrial unrest and unemployment which preceded the formation of the Bureau itself, the GRO, under its new leadership 'team' of Brydges P. Henniker (Registrar-General)

22 This account is given in the *Dublin Journal of Medical Science* 70 (1880), pp. 325–30.

23 There were five classes: Professional and Independent; Middle Class; Artisan Class and Petty Shopkeepers; General Service Class; and Inmates of Workhouses. The same scheme was used for detailed class mortality statistics by age and by cause (though these were not cross-classified), issued as Table VIII of the *Weekly Returns of Births and Deaths in Dublin*. The Irish social classification of the population of Dublin was used continuously in the *Weekly Returns* until 1922 (when it was abandoned by the officials of the newly consitituted Free State). Yet despite Humphreys's discussion of the Irish scheme in 1887, it is not mentioned at all by T. H. C. Stevenson, the author of the subsequent English scheme. During his protracted deliberations over a method for classifying the population into social grades, the only previous work of social classification which Stevenson referred to directly was that of Charles Booth's famous survey, conducted in the late 1880s and early 1890s, of London's *Life and labour*: Stevenson, 'Suggested lines of advance', pp. 696–7.

24 Humphreys, 'How far may the average death-rate'.

and Dr William Ogle (Statistical Superintendent), had apparently launched its own inquiry. Ogle's investigation took the form of a self-administered voluntary questionnaire survey in four selected working-class districts in London. It was carried out by the GRO in 1884. The results from the 29,451 responses (it was not stated what response rate this represented) seem only ever to have been reported as a paper that Ogle delivered to the third meeting of the International Statistical Institute in Vienna in 1891, which he attended as the official British delegate.[25] Presumably the reason for the relative neglect of this exercise by the GRO, and the evident low priority accorded to its publication, was the speed with which its limited and unverifiable findings (because self-attributed by the voluntary respondents) were superseded by the more systematic and massive material generated by Charles Booth's project and by the Board of Trade's Labour office.

Ogle's report of 1891 focused mainly on questions of the typical household and family size in his sample and on the distribution of its members as between earners and dependants. (The most significant result, which Ogle did not, however, dwell upon, was the 27% unemployment rate apparently reported by the adult males who responded!) Ogle chose to emphasise the economic consequences of the finding that relatively early marriage habits prevailed among his sample. He pointed out that this burdened them with an unusually large number of resident dependants, which also required an extremely high proportion of their average wages to be absorbed by rents (20% or more, a figure which Ogle contrasted with the estimate of the Director of the Prussian Bureau of Statistics, Ernst Engel (1821–96) – the progenitor of Engel's Law – who claimed that the average for European urban workers was around 12%). These views in fact bear strong affinities with those expressed by Ogle in another of his contemporaneous investigations: a study of bachelors' occupational marriage ages, which appeared in 1886. The most marked pattern that Ogle claimed to detect in these occupational samples was a class distinction between the early marrying 'working men' and the 'more prudent classes', who married much later in life.[26]

However, instead of launching a social class analysis, as seemed to be adumbrated in Humphreys's address of 1887 and in Ogle's investigations, the GRO chose to pursue the central issue of infant and child mortality by the

[25] Ogle, 'On certain conditions of life'.

[26] 48th ARRG, p. ix. This was the last of several studies of marriage behaviour in the ARRGs. The first inquiry of this sort seems to have been produced by Farr in the 17th ARRG (published 1856), pp. ii–iv. Indeed, Farr had himself offered a 'class analysis' of nuptiality behaviour, something that was virtually forced upon him by the structure of the data collected. He distinguished between the 'higher and middle classes' who could afford the 50 shilling licence, as against 'artisans and labourers' who opted for the cheap alternative of having banns read only, at a cost of 1 shilling. The GRO's statistics showed the latter to be 5.35 times more numerous than the former. Farr noted that there was much greater amplitude of fluctuation in the latter's numbers from year to year, inversely correlated with movements in the price of wheat; whereas at mid-century the domestic plans of the wealthy apparently remained relatively insulated from such direct economic influences.

extension of its traditional methodology of comparative epidemiology: more exact temporal and spatial analysis of the relevant vital registration data. Hence, from the 51st ARRG onwards (relating to registered deaths during 1888), infant cause of death data was published for England and Wales, distinguishing the first and second three-month periods and the last six months as three separate durations for observation.[27] Separate studies then followed up some of the leads suggested by this more detailed tabulation.[28] The following year three rural counties (Hertfordshire, Wiltshire and Dorset) were compared with five mining and manufacturing counties (Staffordshire, Leicestershire, Lancashire, the West Riding and County Durham) and also with three selected towns (Preston, Leicester and Blackburn).[29] Henniker and Ogle then presented the first ever highly detailed life table comparison between the three grouped towns and the three combined rural counties, showing the wide differentials that existed in infants' cause-specific mortality rates over each day of the first week, each week of the first month and each month of the first year of life.[30]

In general, infant mortality in the three towns was shown to be twice as high as in the rural counties. The contrast between the towns and the rural counties was most extreme with regard to the classic hygiene and sanitation diseases, diarrhoea and enteritis, which were seven times more lethal in the towns.[31] Of particular significance, this detailed analysis strongly supported a generally environmentalist interpretation of the urban–rural differential: 'the periods when the town rates are most in excess of the rural rates are not the earliest weeks or months of infancy but the later months . . . showing a progressive or accumulative increase in the deleterious effects of town conditions as compared with rural conditions upon

[27] 51st ARRG (published 1889), p. ix. Analysis by such precise age divisions within the first year of life, as a standard feature of the annual reports, was only possible if there was sufficient confidence in the death registration machinery to suppose that these details were being recorded accurately. Initially, in the first few years of publication, the Registrar-General's annual reports had carried an analysis of infant mortality for registration districts distinguishing such precise age divisions. But this was soon dropped from the presentation and the reason would seem to be contained in William Farr's subsequent discussion, at some length, of the importance of the ambiguities and local variations found in the simple practice of recording ages, showing how especially significant this was in introducing biases over the first years of life: Farr, 'On infant mortality'. The Births and Deaths Registration Act of 1874 was the basis for the improved uniformity of practices in this as in other respects, since it was also made compulsory for death registration to be accompanied by a certificate signed by a medical practitioner, specifying cause of death.

[28] For instance, two years later a special analysis showed that the excessive mortality from accidental suffocation experienced by urban infants was principally due to overlaying on Saturday nights. To B. P. Henniker, the Registrar-General, this suggested that 'the real cause of this accident is the drunkenness of parents'. 54th ARRG, p. xvi (referring to the results reported in the previous year's, 53rd ARRG).

[29] The latter were specifically chosen because they seemed consistently to exhibit the highest infant mortality in the land. 54th ARRG, p. xi.

[30] 54th ARRG, pp. xii–xvi.

[31] 54th ARRG, p. xvi.

infantile life.'[32] In the next decennial supplement, published three years later, John Tatham, who had succeeded Ogle in 1893, presented his own further analysis of the problem for the years 1881–90, giving a life table comparison of infant mortality during these years in the 263 'New Healthy Districts' and in Manchester Township, the latter taken to represent an unhealthy inner city. He pronounced himself content to repeat most of his predecessor's substantive conclusions, since they were identical to his own.[33]

These developments amounted to an impressive refinement in the armoury of techniques deployed by the comparative geographical approach, the tried and tested methods which had served the GRO so well for many decades. But the much-trailed social class analysis simply never materialised.

It would be reasonable to conclude, then, that the GRO, in common with a wide range of other social investigators and political commentators during the 1880s, had certainly been manifesting signs of considerable and increasing interest in the social class-differential aspect of economic and demographic behaviour and its relationship with the divergent material conditions of the nation's social classes.[34] But all this only makes it all the harder to account for the much delayed emergence, almost a quarter of a century later, of an official social classification scheme for British society. Humphreys had demanded in 1887 that 'it is absolutely necessary to obtain information of the mortality in childhood among the working classes'.[35] As well as Ogle's evident interest in social class as an explanatory category, John Tatham, who was to succeed Ogle in 1893 as Statistical Superintendent, can be shown to have long been in favour, in principle at least, of following the Irish example.[36] Yet, far from introducing a new system of social classification of

32 54th ARRG, p. xiii.

33 55th ARRG decennial supplement, Part 2, pp. cvi–cx. Tatham's presentation was a comparison of the national life table with that for the 263 'Healthy Districts'; and for different parts of Manchester and Salford, where he had been the Medical Officer of Health, until his appointment to the GRO.

34 Considering his important subsequent influence upon T. H. C. Stevenson, it is worth noting that in his contemporary textbook of 1889, *The elements of vital statistics* (pp. 149–52), the young Arthur Newsholme was also one of those interested in the issue of social classification of occupations. In a lively discussion, he examined the GRO's current scheme (i.e. the old sixfold classification of 1861), the additional suggestions of H. W. Rumsey and those of a Dr Russell of Glasgow, as well as presenting his own classification, which he used in his Annual Report of 1886 as MOH in Clapham. Newsholme divided all reported deaths into four classes according to occupation: nobility and gentry; professional classes; middle and trading classes; industrial and labouring classes. However, in his 3rd edition of 1899 the relevant passage (pp. 169–71) was replaced by a section directing his fellow professionals to the GRO scheme only, and repeating the somewhat deflationary adverse comments by Ogle, in the 1891 census Report, on the general validity and precision of the occupational information collected at the census.

35 Humphreys, 'Class mortality statistics', p. 265.

36 See his comments of approval and recommendation after hearing the Irish Registrar-General, T. W. Grimshaw, describe the scheme at the annual meeting of the Public Medicine Section of the British Medical Association (*British Medical Journal* 13 August 1887, p. 343). Against this, it might be claimed that the Irish experiment was not considered a wholehearted success. It was drastically altered in the 1901 Irish census Report, because of the difficulties caused by the absence of information regarding the employment status of respondents (i.e. whether employer, self-employed or employee): Census

occupations following up on Humphreys's proposals, the only development which eventually occurred, as was mentioned at the beginning of this section, was that in 1900 Reginald Macleod, the Registrar-General, authorised the abandonment of Farr's old scheme, dating from 1861 – but without replacing it with anything more satisfactory!

The public health programme of the GRO

It would seem that during the late 1880s the GRO mysteriously and quietly backed off from the possibility of a major investment of its time and energies in the construction of an empirical social classification for the nation, along the lines pioneered in Ireland. A paper on a relevant theme given by Humphreys to the Royal Statistical Society in 1891 was curiously silent on the subject.[37] The GRO's evanescent interest in the middle of the 1880s in the demographic and epidemiological properties of social classes was, of course, part of a much wider concern with such issues in a period of mounting economic hardship. Hence, it appears that the GRO strangely lost interest in a social class analysis at precisely the point in time when various *other* social scientists were increasingly coming to see the socio-economic phenomenon of class-differentiation as a vital clue in explaining the great affliction of modern, urban society – the persistence of poverty and unemployment.

The change that occurred in the GRO's disposition can only be explained properly through an understanding of the thoroughly political role which the Office assumed for itself, a conception which informed all its analytical work. Furthermore, its performance of this role needs to be seen within the appropriate contemporary intellectual and administrative context. The GRO necessarily promoted its own preferred policies within a competitive and changing environment comprising various other informal 'schools of thought', all vying for sway and influence over the politically negotiated processes of social change. The GRO's detailed decisions regarding the development and deployment of its principal tools of influence – the flow of reports and statistics that it published – depended ultimately on a calculation of how these would best promote its own institutionalised practices and its vision of ordered progress and social improvement, as against giving possible assistance to any seriously antagonistic, alternative programmes. As will be shown below, although the GRO had formed its own epidemiological reasons for constructing an official social classification scheme, it soon became

of Ireland 1901, General Report, 'Social position of inhabitants of Dublin', pp. 26–7, and Tables 92–4 on pp. 402–35. PP 1902 CXXIX, Cd1190. And yet at the 1891 census of England and Wales and Scotland (paradoxically not Ireland) questions were included, for the first time, using special columns on the face of the household schedule, to elicit exactly this information on the employment status of individuals. On the historical provenance of this innovation and the GRO's distrust of the employment status information, see below pp. 115–18.

[37] Humphreys, 'Results of the recent census'.

apparent that certain of its rivals would actually benefit most from its involvement in such an undertaking; and that this would be in a way that was directly inimical to the interests of the GRO. The Office would simply be devoting its precious energies to creating a heavy stick, which others would promptly wrench from its grasp and proceed to beat it with.

It is, then, first necessary to form a clear understanding of the nature of the GRO's long-standing, institutional disposition towards a particular programme of social change. As has been argued at greater length elsewhere, this broadly corresponded to the environmental ameliorationism of the public health movement.[38] All three of Farr's direct successors in the key technical post of Superintendent of Statistics at the GRO were, like him, medically trained men and all came from a background of professional experience in public health and preventive medicine.[39] Most cognitive aspects of the published output of the GRO throughout the entire period from its foundation to the Great War cannot be deciphered and correctly understood without reference to this medical, epidemiological perspective and the associated professional interests and aims of the public health movement. The Office's publications espoused this in their relentless battle to expose 'preventable' causes of death especially in the growing towns and cities. Since its establishment in 1837 the GRO had developed a strong tradition of deployment of its expertise in comparative epidemiology for the primary purpose of graphical exposure of the extent of *preventable* mortality afflicting the towns and cities of Britain. The work and publications of the GRO in the nineteenth century therefore comprise an important, formative contribution to what has become the well-defined subdiscipline of medical epidemiology.[40]

The central notion of preventability was scientifically premised on a predominantly environmentalist etiology and was therefore intimately associated with the promotion of public health measures such as sanitary engineering works and regulatory administrative structures. Politically the programme was premised on a liberal philosophy of rational, 'democratic' reform through local self-government. This was allied to a rationalist belief in the power of empirical science to reveal the important positive laws of the social organism, the prerequisite for effective remedial action.[41] This institutional position was something that had been built up

[38] The following paragraphs represent a brief summary of the material presented in: Szreter, 'The G.R.O. and the public health movement'.

[39] William Ogle (1827–1912) was Farr's first successor at the GRO, holding the post from 1880 to 1893. He was recommended for the position by George Buchanan (Sir John Simon's successor as the Chief Medical Officer to the LGB), who had unsuccessfully fought to prevent the East Hertfordshire combination sanitary authority from dismissing Ogle in 1879 for his too assiduous services, as their local Medical Officer of Health. On this incident, see Young (unpublished BLitt thesis), p. 183. Ogle's successor was J. F. W. Tatham (1844–1924), who then held the post at the GRO from 1893 until 1909. From 1873 until 1892 Tatham had been a Medical Officer of Health, first for Salford and then, from 1888, for Manchester. T. H. C. Stevenson became the third of Farr's successors in 1909. For more on Tatham and Ogle, see nn. 47, 98. On Stevenson, see Prologue, n. 20.

[40] Lilienfeld, *Foundations of Epidemiology*.

[41] As John Eyler pointed out, and as Lawrence Goldman has recently re-emphasised, Adolphe

during the long-enduring partnership of George Graham and William Farr, Registrar-General and Statistical Superintendent, respectively, from the beginning of the 1840s until 1880. Farr had no doubt partly derived his strongly environmentalist predisposition and his reverence for the careful but creative use of taxonomic and quantitative methods of inquiry from his first-hand experience of the French medical school of *hygiène publique* during his period of study in Paris 1829–30, the heyday of such figures as Pierre Louis, Parent-Duchâtelet and Villermé.[42]

M. J. Cullen has shown how the GRO's approach was part of a wider consensus emerging during the 1830s and 1840s.[43] This was reflected in the labours of a widely dispersed 'statistical movement' of metropolitan and provincial statistical societies, containing both many industrialists and many doctors. They diligently observed and investigated, producing the empirical evidence to confirm their earnest beliefs: that urbanism and public ignorance, not industrialism, were to blame for proletarian poverty. The solution they proposed was that of locally devised measures to promote sanitation, hygiene and public education. This suited equally the interests of the growing numbers of doctors and of employers and other local worthies, whose instincts were to emulate the tutelary paternalism of past generations of landowning gentry. At the centre of government a complementary corresponding development was taking place, illuminated in a contribution by A. F. La Berge, which examines the evolving views of the key figure, Edwin Chadwick.[44] La Berge shows that Chadwick, fluent in French, had become deeply versed in the reports of the French school of *hygiène publique* since the late 1820s, even before his personal introduction to Bentham. Over the next ten years or so Chadwick digested and transformed the works of the leading French exponents, Villermé and Parent-Duchâtelet. Where their researches had led them to the inescapable conclusion that poverty caused disease, Chadwick claimed their authority for his reinterpretation: that disease caused poverty – and therefore

Quetelet (1796–1874) was in many ways the inspiration and direct stimulus for the efflorescence in England in the 1830s of this new, liberal putative science of ameliorationism: Eyler, *Victorian social medicine*, p. 13; Goldman, 'Statistics and the science of society'.

42 Hilts, 'William Farr and the human unit', p. 144. Eyler, *Victorian social medicine*, pp. 1–2, 6–8. For direct evidence of Villermé's influence on Farr, see, for instance, 5th ARRG, p. 440. The most important study of L. R. Villermé (1782–1863), the French pioneer of the comparative epidemiology of wealth and poverty, is: Coleman, *Death is a social disease*. On the numerous French hygienists of this period, see: Ackernecht, 'Hygiene in France, 1815–48'; Lécuyer, 'Médecins et obervateurs sociaux'; La Berge, 'The early nineteenth-century French public health movement'. Flinn saw this French influence as also having had a major impact upon Farr's contemporary, Edwin Chadwick, in determining Chadwick's post-1834 public 'conversion' to an environmentalist view of the cause of poverty and disease: Flinn, 'Introduction', p. 52. La Berge has since shown that Chadwick had been even more strongly influenced by the French hygienists than Flinn suspected – from the late 1820s, well before his work on the Poor Law (see immediately below).

43 As Cullen has put it: 'The real function of the G.R.O. was to be another government-sponsored pulpit for reforming ideas.' Cullen, *The statistical movement*, p. 38.

44 La Berge, 'Edwin Chadwick and the French connection'. The following account is based on La Berge's article.

cost British property-holders their rising Poor Law rates. In Chadwick's *Report* of 1842 – the English public health movement's seminal document – he replaced the French socio-economic theory of disease with his own 'filth theory' and its entailed sanitary message.[45]

Chadwick's 'Sanitary Idea' departed from the premise that his 1834 reform of the Poor Laws had eliminated unjustifiable sources of poverty and that the British working class were now on average better paid than ever before. By the sleight of hand of narrowing the discussion to 'fevers' rather than diseases in general, Chadwick and his colleagues, Drs Arnott and Southwood Smith, concluded that the epidemiological evidence showed that disease could only be caused either by individuals' misuse of their generally adequate wages or by the environmental filth that was due to an absence of proper sanitation. Solution of the former problem was in the hands of the educators; but their efforts would be in vain if attention were not also given to the insanitary conditions of the teeming new towns. The first goal of a public health programme therefore should be the provision of satisfactory urban sewering facilities, entailing also the regular supply of clean water. However, impressed also with the French model of a centralised public health agency – an infatuation for which he was later to pay dearly – Chadwick wished to proceed far beyond the statistical movement's cautious endorsement of local remedies. As a Benthamite, Chadwick envisaged central state intervention as quite legitimate where the pursuit of private self-interest was demonstrably failing to produce the most efficient net outcome – the utilitarian goal of the greatest happiness of the greatest number. Chadwick's essential argument was that collective investment in sanitary and hygienic facilities was not merely a humane but also in the end a more efficient option for property-holders than that of paying to support the incapacitated through the higher Poor Law rates that resulted from families losing their breadwinners to disease.

The centralising side of Chadwick's Sanitary Idea was rapidly killed off as a political non-starter but the environmentalist medical and pedagogic 'science' of urban and personal self-improvement was retained. This became the orthodox liberal bourgeois and professional response to the plight of the deserving, non-pauper poor. Where Chadwick's programme importantly chimed in harmony with the diagnosis and interests of industrialists and propertied dignitaries was in its firm refusal to follow the French lead in questioning the social relations and economic principles of industrial capitalism. Chadwick's 'sanitised' public health version of the French *hygiène publique* permitted the anxious middle and upper classes a politically safe, medical discourse with which to attempt to wrestle with

[45] Of course, the Edinburgh school under W. P. Alison (Professor of Medicine, 1820–56), also provided an important independent source of 'environmentalist' socio-medical reformers; and Alison himself did not accept Chadwick's reversal of the causation discerned by the French: Flinn, 'Introduction', pp. 18–26, 63–6.

the disturbing spectacle of urban suffering and squalor amid their own guilty prosperity. The sources of poverty were attributed either to disease or to ignorance, but not to inadequate wages; attempts to tackle the problem were directed accordingly.

The fundamental nature of the GRO's commitment to this ameliorationist policy of *practical* alleviation of the poverty–disease complex is demonstrated by its response to a particular threat to the public health programme, emanating from a somewhat surprising corner in the mid-1870s. The episode (below) demonstrates that this commitment constituted the ethical centre of motivation and rationale for their work in the eyes of these medically oriented officials, scientists and improvers of society, providing them with a preoccupation in common with both evangelical religionists and secular moralists.[46] While maintaining in principle an open and inquiring mind on the difficult scientific questions of causation – heredity versus environment and miasmas versus microbes – the GRO nevertheless became practically committed as an institution to the ameliorationist and preventive policies of the public health movement. This was broadly consistent both with the precepts of a serious Christian belief in the dignity and ultimate equality of all human beings, and with those simultaneously implied by the terms of the medical profession's Hippocratic Oath.[47]

In order to promote the public health movement on the ground all around the country Farr had always aimed to publicise simple, graphic, but authoritative information on the relative state of health in all towns and cities of the nation. Politicians, ratepayers and local government officials had to be kept to their resolve during the long periods between cholera attacks, (undoubtedly a most effective stimulus to organised public health measures). The index of comparison chosen by Farr was the general or total mortality rate: the crude death rate per thousand inhabitants. Its variations supposedly showed the relative success or failure of each community's leaders and health authorities to do the best possible for their locality. The GRO was able from 1840 onwards to issue weekly bulletins on total mortality rates in the metropolis and from 1842 was able to establish quarterly publication for the 114 most populous districts in the country.[48]

Farr and his superior, George Graham, had a very clear conception of the basic intelligence and propagandist role which their most regular and rapidly produced publications performed. The more time-consuming, rigorous analysis of the same

[46] As Sir Arthur Newsholme remarked, 'William Farr, like Chadwick, was a friend of [Benjamin Ward] Richardson for twenty or thirty years, and all of them were possessed, one might say obsessed, with the spirit of missionary fervour.' Newsholme, *Fifty years in public health*, p. 103.

[47] Explicit religious convictions were evidently important in the lives of Farr's two immediate successors, William Ogle and John Tatham. Ogle had been a Deacon in his twenties, before leaving the church to take up medicine; Tatham, after retiring from his distinguished career in public medicine, took Holy Orders at the age of 73 in 1917 and served as a curate (in Tandridge, Surrey).

[48] This system was pioneered for the metropolis by Sir John Simon in collaboration with Farr. See Lambert *Sir John Simon*, p. 114.

data appeared somewhat later in the annual reports and the decennial supplements, inevitably exerting less political impact because of their necessarily delayed publication. The GRO's position on the utility of publicising the more easily produced crude mortality rate figures was entirely pragmatic and political. Given the quantity and quality of staff available at the central office, it was the only kind of mortality figure that could be quickly produced from the raw data of hundreds of thousands of death certificates regularly sent in through the new postal system by the enormous network of 2,000 or so provincial registrars and subregistrars. Having decided that it was of the utmost importance to do all in its relatively limited powers to engender a climate of opinion all around the country that was conducive to the promotion of public and preventive health measures, it was considered that frequent publication of the crude mortality rate was broadly adequate for these propagandist purposes, as a generally robust index of gross differences in mortality between different places.

The senior staff of the GRO finally felt moved in the 1870s publicly to defend this strategy vigorously because they perceived that both wider public confidence in these regularly published mortality figures and also professional accord between themselves and the ranks of the Medical Officers of Health seemed to be seriously threatened.[49] The acute danger signals came in the form of the address delivered in 1874 by Dr Henry Letheby, that year's President of the Society of Medical Officers of Health.[50] Letheby began by observing that the total death rate in the Metropolitan area had remained virtually stationary at 25 per thousand for three decades despite all the efforts that had been made during this period in the direction of sanitary improvements.[51] He proceeded to argue that this proved, as had been argued for some time, that the total death rate (crude mortality rate) was not an authentic indicator of sanitary conditions in a locality, nor was it an aid to public health officers in their tasks of devising appropriate strategies to improve local health and hygiene.

On 15 December 1874, Farr and Letheby were both present at a paper read to the Statistical Society of London by N. A. Humphreys. The speaker strongly supported the GRO's 'national system' against Letheby's criticisms. Humphreys's main defence of total mortality rates was not their scientific value or accuracy – the limitations of which had long been recognised by Farr, witness his definitive work

[49] For a fuller analysis of the significance of the episode recounted in the following paragraphs, see Szreter, 'The G.R.O. and the public health movement', pp. 449–54.

[50] In 1855 Henry Letheby had succeeded John Simon as Medical Officer of Health of the City of London, when the latter left to take up his new duties as Medical Officer to the Privy Council. Letheby had been a defeated candidate for the post in 1848, when Simon had been originally appointed by the City's Commission of Sewers as the first incumbent of the post, under the Sewers Act of 1848. In the interim Letheby held the position of City gas analyst. Letheby resigned as Medical Officer in 1873. See Lambert, *Sir John Simon*, pp. 77, 88, 209, 213.

[51] Letheby's address is reported in the *Sanitary Record* 1 (1874), pp 305–8, and reiterated in his contribution to the recorded 'Discussion' following N. A. Humphreys's paper to the Statistical Society of London in 1874: Humphreys 'The value of death rates', pp. 472–3.

on life tables – but rather their suitability for 'statist' purposes and 'popularisation'.[52] Humphreys complained that Letheby was misguidedly leading a new generation of public health officers into barren technical arguments: 'The want of confidence that would be engendered among health officers were the adverse criticisms on the death-rates and other figures of the Registrar-General to remain unanswered, would materially impede sanitary progress.'[53] Humphreys therefore proceeded to demonstrate conclusively, with the aid of various hypothetical test data designed to illustrate the scale of the likely distortionary statistical effects involved, 'that not one of these disturbing influences,' (such as differing age and sex distributions, the practice of intercensal interpolation, and migration effects) 'or the combined result of them all, would so affect a death-rate, calculated upon the "national system" as to warrant its being disregarded as a test of sanitary conditions'.[54] Indeed, as one would expect in such a virtuoso of the life table technique, William Farr himself had always been well aware that general mortality rates for any given population were disproportionately influenced by infant and child mortality components: the combined effect of the mortality rates prevailing among children under five years old and the proportion of the population which they constituted. For instance, long before Rumsey's piece of 1871 cited above, Farr, in his supplement to the 25th ARRG (published 1865), had demonstrated that four-fifths of the difference in overall mortality levels between the nation's 'Healthy Districts' and a sample of thirty densely populated, industrial towns was due to the wide divergence between the two in the frequency of deaths to those under age five.[55]

However, Farr had never drawn from this the conclusion that an illustration of the social class-specific incidence of heavy infant and child mortality could be a useful undertaking in the public health battle. The positive reasons for Farr's lack of interest in such a class analysis lie in his pragmatic understanding and realistic appraisal of the political mechanisms of effective social change in mid-Victorian society. These were considered to reside less in the agencies of the central state and more in the hands of elected local authorities. The GRO's propaganda campaign was primarily aimed not at central government but at neglectful local authorities, hence the relentless emphasis on identifying specific places, and not social classes, as exhibiting deficient health and mortality patterns.

Before involving itself in any such computationally onerous undertaking as a social class analysis of national mortality rates, the GRO would want to be satisfied as to the practical political benefits that would ensue from such an *exposé*. The decisions of Farr, his superior Graham and their successors, regarding how best to analyse and present the information at their disposal, were not determined simply

52 Humphreys, 'The value of death rates', p.438.

53 Humphreys, 'The value of death rates', p.465.

54 Humphreys, 'The value of death rates', p.464.

55 25th ARRG Supplement, pp. xxvii–xxviii. Farr had also taken care further to publicise his work on infant and child mortality: Farr, 'On infant mortality and on alleged inaccuracies'; Farr, 'Mortality of children'.

by purely etiological and scientific considerations, important though these were. It was equally their aim to promote as effectively as possible the public health message. This involved evangelising and energising a predominantly lay public of ratepayers and local councillors. Although these two aims, etiological precision and political impact, might not necessarily conflict, they often did in the circumstances prevailing in Victorian Britain. The science of disease incidence was a relatively esoteric subject but hotly debated among the experts. It was therefore not comprehended in any detail or with any confidence by most of those ratepayers and elected local dignitaries whose opinions would ultimately determine whether or not significant local public health measures were promoted by each and every locality around the country.

As has been explained, the optimal propaganda strategy adopted by the GRO was to disseminate very straightforward, apparently unambiguous, hard-hitting indices of death and preventable disease, aimed as directly as possible at the local executive authorities concerned. In this role as campaigner for remedial public health measures, the GRO had developed the extremely effective political and propagandist strategy of using its publications to identify and publicise local 'blackspots' and recalcitrant local authorities, so as literally to shame them into acting for their community's good, by following their Medical Officer's advice, or at least by appointing one as a first step. From this point of view, therefore, a class-differentiated analysis of infant mortality statistics would have seemed an unjustifiably expensive exercise. It was a purely academic embellishment when the main aim was to generate political momentum at the local authority level to clean up towns and cities and provide them with strategic, comprehensive sanitary facilities. Farr had not needed an elaborate and expensive class analysis to make the telling point stick as effective rhetoric: that excessive infant mortality in the nation's wealth-creating cities such as Liverpool constituted a 'death-tax which the great city populations of England now pay'.[56]

In a still as yet undemocratic political age, before the notion of government or central state responsibility for the health of its citizenry had acquired any general currency in British society, there was no politically energising capital to be derived from a demonstration of the class inequity of infant mortality. The GRO was intent upon the extremely practical concern of getting something done about the nation's *preventable* health problems, by identifying the responsible 'culprits', who supposedly had it in their power to ameliorate the situation. Such responsible agencies were considered to come in two sizes: elected local authorities and individual citizens. National class-differentials in infant mortality did not point the finger of blame at any set of responsible elected representatives; politically it was altogether too nebulous.[57] Such an analysis might have value on abstract, scientific grounds, as

[56] 35th ARRG Supplement, pp. xxi–xxii.

[57] Farr and Graham may even have suspected that a class analysis would have been politically counter-productive, if it would have had the effect of defusing a sense of urgency on the part of the

illuminating a significant aspect of the problem of infant mortality, but it carried no political charge to assist the public health movement in its battle against preventable disease.

The GRO in adversity, 1880–1900

While the foregoing has provided a necessary outline of the particular mix of political and analytical aims which was established by Graham and Farr as the characteristic GRO approach, this is not, alone, an entirely sufficient explanation for the GRO's long continuing failure to innovate a social class analysis at either the 1891 or 1901 censuses. However, with an appreciation of the GRO's intellectual and policy disposition established, the remainder of the explanation can now be sought. At a time when social class was increasingly being invoked as a quasi-analytical concept by those concerned with poverty and destitution, why did it not now become available to the epidemiologists of the GRO as a rhetorical device of use to their public health campaign?

To anticipate the story which unfolds below, the broad answer is that a social class analysis was at this time fast becoming intimately associated with certain new approaches to economic, social and health problems not at all in harmony with the practical environmentalist ameliorationism of the GRO. Moreover, during the last quarter of the nineteenth century, the GRO was also suffering a relative decline in its scientific and administrative status, for reasons entirely outside its control. This combined to put the GRO firmly on the defensive. The Office became unwilling to embroil itself in the innovation of a new social classification scheme because such an undertaking increasingly came to be seen as something of a Trojan horse, providing a means for its intellectual and administrative rivals to divert the uses of the nation's census away from the GRO's own epidemiological, preventive health aims.

There were three cognitive aspects to the difficulties which the GRO came to experience in the late Victorian period. First, public health environmentalists were to find their efforts and achievements challenged by the nagging scepticism of those arguing, from Darwinian selectionist principles, that society should not strive too officiously to keep alive those whose greater mortality could be presumed to be a sign of their unfitness. As subsequent chapters will show, debate over this issue was to provide the central context of intellectual conflict from which the official, professional model of social classes was finally to emerge in the Edwardian period. In this section, a much earlier example of the deployment of this argument from within the public health movement will be presented. The episode illuminates the pervasive nature of these scientific anxieties and their

better-off leaders of local communities by suggesting that their own health and that of their own infants was considerably less in danger than that of the rest of their district's population.

direct impact on the GRO's own activities long before the eugenics movement took up the cudgels in the next century.

Secondly, in the intervening period of the last two decades of the century the GRO also found itself faced with a closely related but distinct intellectual Siren. This was the less rigorous and shorter-lived 'fall-out' from Darwin's conceptual bomb: the so-called theory of 'urban degeneration'. Thirdly, with the rise of the new scientific orthodoxy of germ theory the GRO's expertise in comparative epidemiology suffered a relative decline in scientific status as a mode of etiological inquiry. Finally, to these three cognitive considerations should be added the fact that, as a department of the Local Government Board (LGB), the GRO suffered during this period from the same Treasury-imposed policy of morale-sapping retrenchment and deliberate down-grading that Roy MacLeod has documented, both for the LGB as a whole and for its medical activists in particular.[58] For the GRO this problem of administrative weakness most relevantly manifested itself in a challenge to their control over the census, sponsored by a powerful coterie predominantly drawn from the first generation of professional academic economists. This group compared the GRO's capabilities unfavourably against those of the new Labour Statistical Bureau of the Board of Trade and the Factory Inspectorate of the Home Office.[59]

An early warning of the serious threat that the selectionist, social Darwinian argument could pose for the unity of the public health movement had appeared in another part of Letheby's public attack of 1874 on the GRO's publications. Letheby had followed up the assertions discussed in the last section by arguing that since the level of the overall mortality rate was largely determined by deaths of the young a high mortality rate in fact simply reflected a high birth rate, which he claimed was generally agreed to be the invariable concomitant of prosperity, so arriving at the conclusion that high mortality rates merely reflected the prosperity of a town.[60] Although not an inaccurate observation of a short-term statistical association met with under certain economic and demographic conditions, the implication that nothing needed to be done about high urban death rates was unhelpful to the public health movement to say the least; and, if regarded as a long-term prescription, it was downright misleading as an inference and counter to the entire preventive health project. However, Letheby then proceeded to elaborate an evolutionary justification for such sanitary do-nothingism. He expressed the fear that preventive health measures only tended to preserve the ailing and weakly, who then reproduced themselves in ever larger numbers, placing the public health official in an unwinnable position in his battle to bring down the local death rate, while increasingly burdening society with these biological inadequates.

For Letheby this pessimistic social Darwinist insight had seemed to provide a

[58] MacLeod, *Treasury Control*; MacLeod, 'The frustration of state medicine'.

[59] This important episode will be dealt with in some detail, below, pp. 114–20.

[60] The source for Letheby's views is the same as that cited in n. 51, above.

most convenient explanation for a vexing problem, one which several other MOHs (Medical Officers of Health) had also had to confront at various times. This was the frustration he felt at the monotonous failure of the City of London's high death rates to respond to the sanitary measures undertaken under his direction. The problem seems to have privately plagued and obsessed him for years, something which he must have taken to represent a personal, professional failing. Letheby has actually been shown to have engaged in falsifying his own figures of annual death rates to present a more optimistic picture of the effects of sanitary reform in his yearly reports across the period 1856–73 until, in effect, 'coming clean' in this speech of 1874.[61] In fact in the case of Letheby and the City of London, part of the reason for these persistently high death rates may well have been an insufficient commitment to the goals of public health in the face of particularly powerful and seductive commercial vested interests. For instance, it was Letheby himself whom Bill Luckin has identified as one of those specialist consultants assisting the London water companies in resisting Edward Frankland's attempts to impose upon them stricter standards of water purity.[62]

During the course of the discussion which followed Humphreys's delivery of his paper defending the GRO's practices against Letheby's assertions, it is recorded that Farr himself contributed the apparent *coup de grâce* by turning Letheby's logic on its head. Farr argued that a stationary death rate in the metropolis, despite the massive expansion and intensification of urban conditions over the last thirty years, usefully measured the fact that sanitary improvements had kept pace with this and prevented a deterioration in life-chances that would otherwise have occurred – so proving how valuable were the efforts and skills of medical and sanitation officers.[63] The mutiny appears to have been at least temporarily squashed.

Letheby's views, although not entirely coherent and to some extent self-contradictory, were nevertheless significant in at least one respect. They show how, already in this period, there was a keen sensitivity among those medical men most involved in public health matters to the potential importance of the theoretical issues raised by Darwinian evolutionism. This episode was an accurate presage of much to come: the kind of argument deployed by Letheby was to return again in a more virulent form, with the rise of the eugenics movement. Here we have one of the earliest statements from within the heart of the public health movement – from no less a figure than a President of the Society of MOHs – of a position fundamentally questioning the wisdom of preventive medicine and public health measures in general.

61 Lambert, *Sir John Simon*, p. 213.

62 Frankland was sponsored in this by Farr and Graham at the GRO, who gave him a publicity platform in the publications of the GRO. Luckin, 'Evaluating the sanitary revolution', p. 117. Hamlin, *A science of impurity*, chs. 6–7.

63 Humphreys,'The value of death rates', pp. 476–7.

Of course, the general issues which Letheby raised were certainly not new. For instance, it had long been a commonplace observation that the advances of civilisation seemed to produce the medical paradox of freeing the privileged classes from many epidemic scourges, while simultaneously bringing an increased incidence of chronic afflictions, the 'diathetic' diseases of 'luxury', such as gout, hysteria, even tuberculosis.[64] Rousseau had perhaps most influentially stirred these waters with his championing of the virtues of *Emile*'s 'state of nature'.[65] During the 1820s the debate in France finally came to the boil within the medical world, with the leaders of the great post-Napoleonic French school of *hygiène publique*, Louis René Villermé in Paris and Frédéric Bérard in Montpelier, apparently resolving the matter in favour of the benefits of civilisation: the diseases of civilisation were a necessary price paid for the indubitable net advantages of economic and cultural progress.[66] An evolutionary typology of diseases came to be envisaged, with the uncivilised races and the labouring poor dying in droves from their epidemics, while the advanced social classes endured their diathetic conditions as the worthwhile price paid for their enhanced state of civilisation.[67] Subsequently in England in the 1830s and 1840s medical observers and government investigators had registered their disquiet at the physical size and condition of the new class of factory workers.[68] The precocious evolutionist and atheistic individualist, the young Herbert Spencer, was one of the first to complain of the apparent increased survival of the physically unfit.[69] But on the whole this generation of early Victorians was persuaded of the urban and environmental causes of the problem and therefore of the engineering solution which was at hand – the 'Sanitary Idea'.[70]

Now, a generation later, a pessimistic version of social Darwinism was raising all the old fears and doubts once again, posing a direct challenge and threat to those who believed in the value of the disease prevention rationale of a public health infrastructure. Ironically it was precisely those most committed to the rationalist programme of scientific improvement of society (including many

64 See Bynum, 'Darwin and the doctors', pp. 46–7.
65 Ackernecht, 'Hygiene in France', p. 140.
66 Ackernecht, *Medicine at the Paris Hospital*, p. 156.
67 Bynum, 'Darwin and the doctors', p. 47.
68 For observations on physical deterioration, see Chadwick, *Report on the sanitary condition*, pp. 247–67. According to the recent historical research on anthropometric evidence from the past, these social observers were, indeed, accurate in their perception that the generations born from the 1820s until the 1850s were suffering a shortfall in their achieved growth, relative to earlier birth cohorts: Floud *et al.*, *Height, health and history*, esp. pp. 304–6.
69 Spencer, *Social statics*, pp. 414–15.
70 As propounded most famously by Edwin Chadwick in his *Report* of 1842, this envisaged the primary solution in terms of ensuring private hygiene and public cleanliness, ideally through the construction of the necessary urban utilities to achieve a regular supply of clean water and, reciprocally, an effective system of waterborne drainage and sewering through an arterial network of ingenious self-scouring sewers (because of the pipes' inverted egg-shape in cross-section). See above, pp. 87–8.

Medical Officers of Health themselves) who were among the most vulnerable potential victims of the illusion that the most powerful, recent product of rational science – evolutionary theory – impugned the wisdom of many of the preventive health measures central to the ameliorationist public health programme.[71] In the mid-1870s the fate of the public health movement hung in the balance, as the terms of the important consolidating Public Health Act of 1875 were being decided upon by Parliament. At such a time of crisis the public health movement could not easily withstand the loss of confidence in the environmentalist strategy that would ensue if it were seen to be divided within itself, as Humphreys, Farr and Graham well knew. They were determined that a pernicious, hereditarian social Darwinism should not be allowed to gain a hold on the public or on fellow professionals' imagination for lack of effective public refutation.

However, during the ensuing 1880s and early 1890s the blunt and ruthless selectionist argument, though by no means absent, was much less in evidence than its conceptual cousin, the more nebulous and populist notion of 'urban degeneration'. This became the principal vehicle for the political expression of a supposedly scientific, 'Darwinist' perspective on public health and poverty issues. The 1880s was, of course, a decade of severe and mounting industrial unrest, whose epicentre, unlike the many previous bouts of economic dislocation, was located in the metropolis. As Gareth Stedman Jones has shown, in 1886 this had even mounted – albeit momentarily – to a crescendo of guilt-ridden hysteria among the geographically segregated, propertied classes of the West End, fearing the possible effects that the material deprivation being experienced in the East End might be having on the political allegiances of that vast, anonymous mass.[72] The hopeful, optimistic mid-Victorian 'faith in Progress' of the 1860s and 1870s was turning sour. It now seemed to many that years of costly sanitary ameliorationism and devoted evangelical toil in the slums had eradicated neither poverty and squalor nor the accompanying vicious behaviour of the ungrateful recipients. As serious economic distress returned in the mid-1880s, the dreaded degraded behaviour of the lower orders was once again believed to be rearing its head. In this atmosphere of disillusionment with their working-class probationers, the

[71] Fifteen years after the skirmish between Letheby and the GRO, in his statistical manual for fellow MOHs, Arthur Newsholme considered the selectionist (which he chose to call 'the Malthusian doctrine') and the demographic arguments raised by Letheby once again. Evidently he considered these anti-public health ideas still sufficiently threatening to merit a formal treatment, in order to demonstrate their deficiencies to his colleagues: Newsholme, *The elements of vital statistics*, pp. 66–70 and ch. 5. Letheby appeared again as an 'Aunt Sally' in the 3rd edition of 1899 (pp. 96–7). But by this time Newsholme did not think it necessary to repeat the critical discussion of 'the Malthusian hypothesis' (p. 83). It is interesting that Newsholme no longer judged such evolutionary selectionist arguments a threat in the late 1890s, just as they were about to be revived in their most virulent form – by the Edwardian eugenicists. As shown below in chapters 4 and 5, Newsholme would have to devote significant energies to countering these views in the next century, when appointed to the senior post in the public health movement, as Chief Medical Officer to the LGB.

[72] Stedman Jones, *Outcast London*, ch. 16.

notion gained in popularity among some of the middle classes that there existed in the slums a persistent rotten core of irremediable atavistic types, the so-called 'residuum' whose existence undermined the health and morals, and prevented the recuperation, of those around them.

Daniel Pick has shown that degeneration was a pronounced literary theme of the period, although, as José Harris has pointed out, there was never a strong belief among practical social workers and officials that deterioration was actually occurring.[73] An important part of the reason for this was in the stout scientific resistance and scepticism to the idea provided by the official epidemiological authorities. But whilst a liberal faith in developmental progress remained the dominant sentiment, this entailed a capacity to fear the *possibility* of evolutionary regression or deterioration, the pessimistic obverse side of the belief in Progress. Degeneration was a nightmare in abeyance, ready to come to the fore in times of perceived public crisis, and even educated public opinion was prey to this anxiety throughout the closing decades of the Victorian era. The idea gained ground in Britain and especially in London, both among scientists and writers and in the genre of didactic popularising addresses, pamphlets and periodicals, which peddled their heady new mixture of science and morality to an expanding mass market for such wares.[74] For a section of the British middle classes a 'degeneration' or deterioration from the fondly imagined higher standards of yesteryear provided a tempting explanatory mechanism for a propertied élite who found themselves beset with a domestic economy labouring through a 'Great Depression' while other nations, notably the USA and Germany, were apparently experiencing the kind of dynamic economic growth which they had once believed to be a purely British prerogative.[75]

In this more defensive and anxious climate of opinion the degeneration notion and fantasy flourished. In terms of broad swings in national political mood, it would seem legitimate to characterise the twenty years after 1885 as a period of defensive conservatism and corresponding Conservative political ascendancy, in contrast with both the preceding and subsequent periods. Perhaps the most valid brief illustration of this is provided by the voting patterns at general elections. These attest to such a shift in the centre of gravity across the transitional period 1880–6. In the wider context of secular trends towards both an increasing electorate and an increasing turn out, the Liberal vote had been consistently a clear

[73] Harris, *Private lives*, pp. 241–5; Pick, *Faces of degeneration*. The scientistic notion of 'degeneration' seems to have become a recurrent *Leitmotif* in several European cultures during the last quarter of the century, providing a self-consciously rational urban bourgeoisie with a pseudo-explanatory metaphor to describe their many anxieties over the internal and external, political and biological threats which they felt themselves to be facing. See also Chamberlin and Gilman (eds.), *Degeneration*.

[74] Young, *Darwin's metaphor*, ch. 5.

[75] The historiography on the theme of Britain's relative or absolute decline from global economic pre-eminence has grown in volume over the decades since contemporaries began to express disquiet, to such an extent that it is almost in danger of becoming co-extensive with the field of British economic history post 1870. For an introduction, see Pollard, *Britain's prime and Britain's decline*.

majority of all votes cast in each of the seven elections from 1852 to 1880 inclusive; only once did the Conservative total even reach above four-fifths of the Liberal total (and only marginally so at that – in 1874). Yet at each of the four elections between 1886 and 1900 the Conservatives polled absolutely more votes than the Liberals, after which the pattern reversed again, taking in the subsequent three elections held before the outbreak of the Great War.[76]

If the notion of cumulative racial decline gained some currency in the more pessimistic political mood among Britain's urban liberal middle class in the 1880s and 1890s, it was partly because, initially at least, the idea was not lacking in respected scientific supporters. E. Ray Lankester's address to the British Association in 1879 was an important occasion on which the notion of degeneration was discussed as a putatively scientific phenomenon.[77] Lankester deliberately juxtaposed evidence of anatomical, *physical* degeneration in nature with discussion of the possibility of *cultural* degeneration in man (leaving the audience to draw its own analogies).[78] The British Association had long been the respectable cockpit for radical evolutionary speculation, since the famous encounter in 1860 between Bishop Wilberforce and 'Darwin's bulldog', T. H. Huxley. It was an Anthropometric Committee of the British Association, originally convened in 1875, whose reports during the early 1880s probably gave the most substantial apparent scientific support to the idea of urban degeneration (this work will be examined in great detail in the next chapter as it is of central importance in the genesis of the professional model). It was accepted in this Committee's Final Report that, on average, citizens born and bred in the countryside were better developed than their urban counterparts, something which seemed to confirm fears of urban degeneration.[79] This summary report played down the fact that the Committee's evidence suggested that there were also good grounds for supposing that the average urban physique was now improving and might therefore in the long run be expected to catch up its rural counterpart.[80]

The degeneration threat conveniently seemed to justify for some influential, mainstream liberals the necessity of countenancing some very illiberal solutions to urban poverty. Forcible segregation of the unfit was a policy advanced on

76 The only other election in this period, that of 1885, was exactly transitional according to these criteria: the Liberals for the first time failed to poll a majority of all votes cast (achieving 47%), but the Conservatives also failed to poll more votes than their opponents (obtaining 44%). Craig, *British electoral facts*, Tables 4.01, 7.01, 7.02, 7.05.

77 Lankester, *Degeneration*. Edwin Ray Lankester (1847–1929) was son of Charles Darwin's close friend, Edwin Lankester (1814–74), who was an eminent meteorologist and editor of the natural history section of the *Penny encyclopaedia*. E. Ray Lankester, himself, was generally considered to be Britain's leading zoologist at the time of his address to the British Association. Elected to the Royal Society in 1875, he was Professor of Zoology at University College, London (1874–91).

78 Bowler, 'Holding your head up high', pp. 335–6.

79 Final Report of Anthropometric Committee of the British Association, paragraphs 16–34, in *British Association Report* (1883), pp. 253–306. See next chapter, pp. 132–48, for a full account of the Committee's work.

80 Final Report of Anthropometric Committee of the British Association, paragraph 65.

several fronts at this time:[81] by economists led by Alfred Marshall;[82] in the work edited by the great social investigator Charles Booth;[83] by Christian social workers led by General William Booth (no relation) under the Salvation Army banner;[84] and, towards the end of the century, by the vanguard of the eugenics movement.[85] Stedman Jones has documented the growing acceptance in conservative social thought in the 1880s of the 'scientific' urban degeneration theory of poverty, as the successor to the earlier, 'demoralisation', neo-religious theory that poverty was due to pauperism – the corruption of the individual's character and morals.[86] He has concluded that 'It can now be seen that the theory of urban degeneration bore little relation to the real situation of the London casual poor in the late Victorian period. What it provided, was . . . a mental landscape within which the middle class could recognise and articulate their own anxieties about urban existence.'[87]

Nevertheless the anxieties were sufficiently strong and widely felt for the theory to grow in popularity among the privileged classes over a number of years, so that many other social problems with a strongly economic basis came for a time to be seen partly in these terms. This is conspicuously the case with the issues of rural depopulation and alien immigration in the 1890s.[88] During the 1890s even the new Labour Department of the Board of Trade under its first Commissioner, H. Llewellyn Smith, appointed the rural labour market specialist, A. Wilson Fox, to investigate *inter alia* agricultural labour colonies as a possible solution to 'urban degeneration'.[89] Popular fears of such a process of urban degeneration finally reached their climax at the turn of the new century, with the public scandal over physical unfitness of urban recruits for the Boer War. This was to be the point at which the eugenicist biometricians, led by Karl Pearson and Francis Galton, made their bid to capitalise on the temporarily widespread public anxieties, in order to gain acceptance for the reinstatement of their rigorously selectionist understanding of health and welfare issues. They were to offer a rerun of the Letheby type of

81 In general, see Harris, *Unemployment and politics*, pp. 102–44.

82 For instance, Marshall, 'The housing of the London poor'; Marshall, 'Some aspects of competition'.

83 Booth, *Life and labour* ser. 1, Vol. I, ch. VI, 'Class relations', especially pp. 165–71.

84 Booth, *In darkest England*.

85 Pearson, *The chances of death*.

86 Stedman Jones, *Outcast London*, chs. 6 and 16.

87 Stedman Jones, *Outcast London*, p. 151.

88 For instance, the success of the German army was sometimes explained in terms of its supposedly superior supply of healthy rural stock, being a less urbanised society. Also the problem of rural depopulation (in fact caused by the collapse of food prices and agricultural rents due to cheap, predominantly North and South American imports) was seen by some primarily through this perspective: White, *The destitute alien*; Longstaff, 'Rural depopulation'; Drage, 'Alien immigration'. Other such studies incorporating an urban degenerationist interpretation included: White, *The problems of a great city*; Freeman-Williams, *The effect of town life*; Booth, *In darkest England*. In Gareth Stedman Jones's opinion, the most thorough empirical exposition was provided by H. Llewellyn Smith's two contributions to Charles Booth's *Life and labour*: 'Influx of population' (Vol. I) and 'Migration' (Vol. II): Stedman Jones, *Outcast London*, ch. 6.

89 Davidson and Lowe, 'Bureaucracy and innovation', p. 272.

argument; but with a considerable weight of new, purportedly scientific evidence behind it.

By contrast, 'urban degenerationism' of the late 1880s and 1890s never was a definitively formulated, precise theory. It was popular at a time when the status and moral authority of science, scientists and medical doctors in British society was higher than ever before, and yet confusion reigned supreme in the relevant scientific fields – those of etiology and evolutionary theory – partly because most scientists themselves had not yet fully recognised the provisional nature of the knowledge they offered society.[90] In these circumstances, the ambivalence of 'urban degeneration' was in fact its chief strength. It offered a scientific-sounding – and therefore authoritative – explanation to the anxious lay majority, while remaining sufficiently plausible and imprecise as an hypothesis that it avoided outright rejection by any influential group of scientists.

Far from being a purely hereditarian notion, urban degeneration, if it meant anything specific at all at this time, envisaged a neo-Lamarckian, environmentally induced process in operation.[91] Individuals' constitutions were supposedly damaged by physical or psychological insults and stresses thrown up by the deleterious 'unnatural' conditions of urban existence. At the beginning of the twentieth century the term 'degeneration' was to acquire a more definite association with a purely hereditary understanding of the supposed mechanism involved, thanks to the eugenicist proselytising of Francis Galton and his disciple Karl Pearson. In fact it was as a result of their insistence on this point that the Lamarckian notion of 'urban degeneration' finally ceased to be invoked at all by the would-be scientists of racial decay.[92] But until this much later, forcing move on the part of the Edwardian eugenicists, there was no rigid distinction generally made between the operation of hereditary and of environmental factors in accounting for the putative phenomenon of degeneration.[93] It is therefore

[90] Again, see Bynum, 'Darwin and the doctors', on the chronic state of speculation in medicine during the period 1865–95, as doctors were attempting to adjust to the novelties of both evolutionary theory and germ theory (on the latter see below, pp. 105–7). Confusion was particularly intense during the 1880s, when germ theory had been accepted in principle but a comprehensive grasp remained elusive; while great debate continued over the implications of evolutionary theory, especially between Herbert Spencer and August Weismann (see n. 93 and pp. 220–1).

[91] On Lamarckian use-inheritance, see ch. 3, n. 19.

[92] See Soloway, *Demography and degeneration*, pp. 42–3. Digby, 'The extinction of the Londoner', published in 1904, is the latest serious study I have found still apparently accepting the tenets of undiluted urban degenerationism.

[93] As Ruth Schwartz Cowan has carefully shown, it was only the obsessive Francis Galton who, since the 1860s, had always insisted on a distinction between hereditary 'inheritance' and socially or culturally 'acquired characters', believing unconditionally that physiologically 'everything was hereditary': Cowan, 'Nature and nurture'. Darwin himself remained unconvinced by his younger cousin, Galton, and – like many other social evolutionists in Britain, even until the 1890s – continued to subscribe instead to Herbert Spencer's authoritative endorsement of a form of Lamarckian inheritance of acquired characteristics, thereby combining environmental and hereditary forces. Herbert Spencer, the doyen of secular, libertarian social philosophy, exalted by his English-speaking contemporaries on both sides of the Atlantic, was the most influential exponent of this viewpoint,

anachronistic to read the 1880s popular and medical discourse as a 'nature versus nurture' issue. Once this point has been taken, it is not surprising to find several public health medical figures playing a leading role in discussing and disseminating degenerationist views (although it was never the predominant viewpoint of public health professionals as a group). For instance, B. W. Richardson, G. B. Longstaff and Sir T. Lauder Brunton could all be found among the many subscribing to notions of urban degeneration at various points.[94]

Indeed, it was a leading figure within the public health medical establishment who gave the theory its most well-publicised 'airing'. Dr J. L. Cantlie was Honorary Secretary of the College of State Medicine when in January 1885 he delivered the Parkes Memorial Lecture on Public Hygiene in which he sensationally claimed to have established from personal investigation that it was impossible to find a born and bred third-generation Londoner, owing to the life-inhibiting influences of the metropolitan environment, particularly its stagnant air, which he found to be lacking in ozone.[95] Quite unlike Letheby, however, Cantlie saw all this as an environmentalist argument for the further heroic extension of the public health infrastructure of the capital: seriously suggesting that the solution was for pure air to be piped into the centre of the largest cities, just as was already done with water. Not surprisingly these engineering proposals were greeted with scorn and derision in the press. Far from promoting the status of public health environmentalism, his address only succeeded in further reinforcing the vague popular notion that some kind of almost subhuman 'residuum' of degraded urbanites existed, requiring urgent attention.[96]

Degenerationism was a poisoned chalice to the public health movement. To attempt to invoke the spectre of degeneration to back the call for an expansion in environmentalist preventive health measures, as Cantlie did in 1885, was to misunderstand the political and ideological function of the metaphor. For all the apparent logic in Cantlie's assertions, which followed from the supposedly environmental mechanism of urban degeneration as he understood it, the popular attraction and plausibility of 'degenerationism' did not derive from its status as a potentially fruitful scientific analysis. It derived instead from its provision of a suitably scientific-sounding sanction for a negative attitude towards the entitlements of the poor.

continuing to resist even August Weismann's microscopic evidence in favour of a germ plasm/soma distinction between heredity and environment until the early 1890s. See Bowler, *Evolution*, pp. 251–3. Of course, 'nature versus nurture' already had a long previous history in the context of post-Enlightenment educational debate; see, for instance, Bloch, 'Rousseau and Helvétius'.

94 Richardson, *Diseases of modern life* (for more on Richardson, see ch. 4, n. 73); G. B. Longstaff was the author of *Studies in statistics* and 'Rural depopulation'; for more on Lauder Brunton, see ch. 4, n. 89.

95 Cantlie, *Degeneration amongst Londoners*. Note that although Cantlie's argument looks initially like a strongly hereditarian one because of his talk of generations, in fact the mechanism of deterioration envisaged is primarily environmental.

96 This was Cantlie's own retrospective opinion, twenty years later, on the effect of his 1885 address and the response to it: see Cantlie, *Physical efficiency* (1906).

The 'theory of urban degeneration' was an emotionally charged negative metaphor and not a positive scientific hypothesis, although some of those using it no doubt believed they were acting scientifically. As such it was a defensive reaction to perceived hard times on the part of a supremely status-conscious urban society of *les nouveaux riches*. Those with a precarious hold on a little property and prestige were consumed with fear at what they might lose in the long drawn-out recession. 'Degeneration' justified a witch-hunt against their feared *alter egos*, the supposed failures and scroungers in society.

It was this attitude which resulted in a gradual cutting to the minimum of all obligatory personal outlay on support for the indigent poor through the poor rates. During the Great Depression a period of almost unprecedented general meanness of public spirit became entrenched in the operation of both official and voluntary provision for the poor (though at the same time calling forth a conscience-stricken response from among the more sensitive and idealist of the privileged minority, exemplified by the Oxbridge colleges' settlement movement – see ch. 3, n. 4). An official 'crusade' against out-relief was launched by the Poor Law, following upon the infamous Goschen circular of 1869, which urged guardians to apply the 'workhouse test' more rigorously so that only those prepared to enter under its portals should be granted relief, as the genuinely destitute. The 1834 principles of 'less eligibility' were revitalised, supposedly discriminating between the respectable and the unrespectable applicants for relief. This was also a goal and strategy to which, as a voluntary association, the COS, or the Society for Organising Charitable Relief and Repressing Mendicity to give it its proper title, dedicated itself. Its self-appointed mission went from strength to strength in this new climate of opinion.[97]

Once again, as in the mid-1870s, the GRO was to be found seeking to investigate and challenge the claims made for 'urban degeneration', recognising the importance of so doing because of the potential of such ideas to inflict damaging divisions within the public health movement. Thus, when the popularity of this viewpoint was at its height during the mid-1880s William Ogle published a carefully argued demographic demonstration of the implausibility of the claims.[98] It was being

[97] The COS is long overdue for an historical reassessment: the extant history is Mowat, *The Charity Organisation Society*. For some interesting comments of reappraisal, see Harris, 'The Webbs, the C.O.S. and the Ratan Tata Foundation'; and Harris, *Private lives*, pp. 229–31, 242. On the Poor Law's policy, see Williams, *From pauperism to poverty*, ch. 3. According to David Thomson, by 1890 the proportion of the elderly receiving some form of public assistance was only half that of 1870; and the value of the pensions paid to this dwindling group had also halved since the 1860s: Thomson, 'Welfare and the historians', p. 374.

[98] William Ogle, son of a Regius Professor of Medicine at Oxford, was one of Arnold's last pupils at Rugby. He studied natural science at Oxford, where he became a Fellow of Corpus Christi at 21 years of age before taking Deacon's orders – only to leave the church within a few years to take up medical science. Aristotle was his lifelong true passion, and it is perhaps no surprise to find that the translator of an authoritative edition of *De Partibus Animalium* (published in 1882) was a friend of several of the leading scientific naturalists of his day including E. Ray Lankester (see n. 77), Charles Darwin and J. D. Hooker. Biographical information on Ogle from: Munk's *Roll*; his obituary in *JRSS*

asserted that the supposed phenomenon of 'urban degeneration' proved that expensive public health improvements were misguided because they only led to the artificial preservation of 'unfit', stunted children, who then died in droves at slightly more advanced ages. Using the GRO's historical record of the nation's vital statistics, Ogle compared the life table experience of those born into the mortality conditions prevailing in 1871–80 with those of 1835–54. He was able to show that, by 1885 at least, there had been no rise in mortality at higher ages consequent on increased survivorship in infancy:

> The changes in the death-rates therefore have given to the community an annual addition of 1,800,047 years of life shared among its members; and allowing that the changes in death-rates are the direct consequences of sanitary interference, we must regard this addition of nearly two million years of life as an annual income derived from the money invested in sanitation.[99]

Ogle himself did not, incidentally, take a dogmatic position on this issue. There is even evidence that at the end of the 1880s he was prepared to speculate in a non-official capacity on the possibility that physical degeneration of the British nation might after all be occurring, contrary to his conclusion of 1885. This was apparently largely because, in a subsequent examination of the nation's historical mortality record, Ogle had found that although an increased proportion of the population were now surviving childhood than earlier in the century, average life expectancy after reaching the age of thirty seemed to have deteriorated.[100] Noel Humphreys had himself closely questioned Ogle on this point in the discussion that followed Ogle's presentation of these results in a paper of 1889. Ogle had concluded by leaving the matter open: 'After the next census some other person would doubtless take up the question and deal with it in the light of the new figures.'[101] Ogle retired before the results of that next census and its associated decennial supplement were processed. But when the relevant calculations from the new information had finally been completed in 1896 the long-serving Humphreys, keenly aware of the potential significance of this issue, made certain to publicise, in a short report to the Royal Statistical Society, that Ogle's fears were now officially laid to rest. The new age-specific mortality rates, covering the most recent decade of the 1880s and published by Ogle's successor, John Tatham, showed a virtually universal fall in mortality at all ages for both sexes, including those above age thirty.[102]

The central point remains, however, that during the last quarter of the century

75 (1912), 659–61; and Robb-Smith, 'A history of the College's nomenclature', pp. 11–13. Also, see above n. 39, n. 47.

99 45th ARRG Supplement, p. xi.

100 Ogle, 'On the alleged depopulation', pp. 239–40.

101 Ogle, 'On the alleged depopulation', pp. 236–7, 240.

102 Humphreys, 'The Registrar-General's decennial supplement', p. 544.

the GRO found itself increasingly on the defensive, scientifically and politically. In an earlier era Farr and Graham had been firmly on the offensive, authoritatively demonstrating with a multitude of graphs and tables the extent to which the nation's death rates were preventable through implementation of public health measures. While continuing to deploy epidemiological statistics to demonstrate the range of preventable health problems in society, the GRO now found its preferred programme and overall strategy of environmentalist ameliorationism assailed by the wailing would-be Cassandras of 'social Darwinism'.

At the same time the GRO was struggling to maintain its high status within the public health movement following the impact of germ theory. The GRO's social scientific authority had been successfully established during the founding era of Graham and Farr on the basis of its position as the leading practitioner of the important science of comparative epidemiology ('vital statistics' as it was then called). Until the last few years of William Farr's reign as Superintendent of Statistics at the GRO, 1840–80, scientific understanding of disease etiology had remained in a sufficient state of conjecture for the methods of comparative epidemiology to be considered among the leading investigative techniques available for furthering scientific medical knowledge. Several of the most celebrated studies of disease outbreaks in this period were conducted through an epidemiological approach, some with Farr's collaboration.[103] With the GRO's unparalleled information resources in the form of its vital registration and census data, its chief analyst therefore enjoyed a considerable contemporary reputation as a medical scientist.

However, the basis for this was undermined in the last quarter of the century with the rise to prominence of the germ theory of disease and its associated microscopial and laboratory techniques of investigation.[104] During the course of the late 1870s and throughout the 1880s, therefore, the leading edge of medical science was increasingly seen to be leaving behind the statistical methods of comparative epidemiology.[105]

103 Farr participated with John Snow in his famous studies of London cholera outbreaks of 1849 and 1854: Eyler, *Victorian social medicine*, pp. 114–18.

104 The efforts of two generations of germ theorists, led by Jacob Henle (1809–85) of Berlin, to give visible proof for their theories were finally fulfilled when Henle's student, Robert Koch, published definitive results between 1876 and 1884, exploiting the new aniline dye techniques for staining and identifying bacteria devised by Carl Weigert and Paul Ehrlich between 1871 and 1875. Shryock, *The development of modern medicine*, ch. XIV.

105 It is important to note, however, that this was a gradual process. Although many doctors in Britain, including such public health leaders as Sir John Simon and William Farr, himself, had come to accept the outlines of germ theory by the mid-1870s, intense medical debate continued throughout the 1880s over the scope and implications of the new ideas. The central issue at stake was that of disease specificity: whether each different disease had a differentiated microbial agent as direct cellular cause, or whether some diseases might be due to the chemical by-products of parasite–host relationships. Such was the state of conjecture that, as W. F. Bynum has pointed out, although the longer-term consequence of the promulgation of the germ theory resulted, as we all know, in the

Nevertheless, for the wider public health movement the triumph of germ theory, once its implications had been fully digested by the end of the 1880s, actually had an empowering and reinvigorating effect without causing any sudden changes in practice. During this period most public health officials dropped their flirtation with the problematic theory of 'urban degeneration', for the compelling reason that its Lamarckian environmentalist etiology was inconsistent with the more powerful etiological principles of the new germ theory. Their investigative centre of attention had already been shifting somewhat away from the overall physical and climatic conditions of the urban environment as a whole, towards a new focus upon the most likely vectors and pathways for communication of the specific micro-organisms responsible for identifiable diseases.[106] The control of animal products and foodstuffs from the 1870s was an early example of such attentions, with the MOHs' powers extended towards overseeing sources of supply (though only within their local authority area of jurisdiction – a continuing problem with urban milk supply from the countryside, for instance).[107] By the 1890s bacteriological studies had shown the usually limited survival of germs away from the human body or in the immediate domestic environment. This legitimated efforts to 'interfere' even more in the working-class home in the interests of promoting greater domestic hygiene, but it was also used to justify the call for the provision of better standards of housing.[108] For the MOHs, germ theory only seemed to add more and more compelling arguments for the extension of further powers of surveillance, regulation and inspection to the growing administrative apparatus under their command.

Of course contagionism also stressed the need to identify and isolate the primary victims of disease to forestall secondary infections and outbreaks. Hence, MOHs were the leading figures to put into effect local and national surveillance structures and isolation facilities to enable this counter-contagionist medical technology to work properly.[109] But most trained and practising MOHs would not have seen this development as anything but a sensible extension of the traditional environmentalist aims and principles of the public health movement: to maintain and promote as effectively as possible a pathogen-free environment in the locality

adoption of the correct concept of disease specificity and the closely associated etiological principle of contagionism, paradoxically in the shorter term the immediate effect in British medicine, in the late 1870s and early 1880s, was actually to reinforce the opposite and incorrect viewpoint. See Bynum, 'Darwin and the doctors', pp. 49–51.

106 See Hardy, *The epidemic streets*, pp. 6–7 and 116–28, on the emergence of the contagionist 'stamping out' policy as the main preventive health strategy in the public health movement during the last two decades of the nineteenth century; and see below, pp. 199–200.

107 Raymond, 'Science in the service of medicine'; Atkin 'White poison?'.

108 Raymond, 'Science in the service of medicine'.

109 Bolton was the first local authority to institute such a system on a permanent basis (notification schemes were often set up on a temporary basis during epidemic scares), taking a private bill through Parliament in 1877: Newsholme, *Fifty years*, p. 280. An Act to re-establish notification for infectious diseases in the capital (see next footnote) was finally secured in 1889 and eventually the whole country was covered under an Act of 1899: Hardy, 'Public health and the expert'.

under their supervision. Indeed, MOHs had collectively campaigned for an efficient notification system since the mid-century, long before the germ theory of disease had become orthodoxy.[110]

In other words, segregationist policies were easily adopted by MOHs because they could be seen not so much as a new master-principle of therapeutic practice, but as merely a part – albeit an important part – of a comprehensive community health strategy, still conceived within the spirit of public health environmentalist prevention. As more scientific techniques for the identification and control of dangerous micro-organisms became available, so the MOH's responsibility to keep the locality pathogen-free inevitably became an ever-more complex and resource-using task. The period from the early 1880s to the outbreak of the Great War was an era of unprecedented expansion in the duties and powers of local health officers and their administrations. MOHs came to oversee the foods and drugs inspectors appointed alongside their sanitary officers, the setting up of the notification and isolation facilities to deal with outbreaks of infectious diseases, and even in some cases the diagnostic laboratories built to serve many towns and areas.

Nevertheless, the central point insofar as the fortunes of the GRO are concerned is that the advent of the germ theory and its microscopial methodology signalled a relative decline in the status of the GRO within the public health movement. This was both because of its lost claim to 'scientific' leadership and also because of the increasing powers and *élan* of the Medical Officers of Health themselves. Their new professional journal, *Public Health*, now superseded the annual and decennial publications of the GRO as the most significant and respected institutional voice of the public health movement.

Liberal economic and social science, 1870–1900: the evolutionary perspective

If the relatively esoteric field of vital statistics was experiencing something of a temporary loss of *cachet* during the last quarter of the nineteenth century, the 1870s and 1880s was also a period of crisis for the liberal master-science of political economy. Its intellectual authority was buckling in the face of a protracted depression in the domestic economy, which it apparently could neither explain nor solve. As Eugenio Biagini has shown, employers in the 1870s found that after over half a century of faithful service the science of political economy was no longer to be trusted as a source of intellectual support in their continual

110 There was a long history of struggle by public health medical professionals to have a national scheme for notification of diseases established. But it was not until the triumph of the germ theory of disease that the utility of notification was finally officially endorsed. A short-lived scheme had been instigated by Sir John Simon for the metropolis in the 1850s, collapsing for lack of Treasury support in 1858: Lambert, *Sir John Simon*, pp. 246–7.

confrontation with labour. Classical political economy had particularly served the bargaining interests of employers because of its abhorrence of combinations of working men as a supposed impediment to the free workings of the labour market and because of its (in)famous wages fund theory and its derivative 'iron law of wages'. This sanctioned the claim by employers that any increase of wages paid to one section of workers must mean a smaller amount left for the others from the employer's supposedly fixed fund of circulating capital.[111]

For over a decade before the onset in 1873 of the 'Great Depression' a dislocating theoretical revisionism had been emerging from within the citadel of political economy itself, as the moral Achilles heel of liberal economic theory – the question of the politics of information – became the centre of attention. The new focus on the imperfections of markets led in the early 1860s to a recognised place for workers' collective bargaining as the appropriate market determinant of the price of labour.[112] By 1869 this had led on further to Mill's celebrated 'recantation' of the wages fund doctrine of classical political economy and by 1872 to the 'heretical' derivative proposition, articulated in a best-seller from the authoritative pen of one of the most successful employers of the period, Thomas Brassey, that higher wages and shorter hours could be perfectly compatible with increased productivity.[113]

The British discipline of political economy itself fractured into two main camps, led on the one hand by those in Toynbee's Oxford, who drew the relativist conclusion that the laws of economic behaviour were historically contingent and not universals. On the other hand, in Cambridge Alfred Marshall was striving to maintain a Newtonian paradigm, a 'neo-classical' replacement for Ricardian political economy through his careful redefinition of the subject as an academic discipline analysing the behaviour of markets, firms and prices through the infinitesimal calculus of marginal utility.[114] Marshall, himself, continued to see his

111 For an accessible brief summary of the wages fund theory, see the excellent article by Eugenio Biagini, 'British trade unions and popular political economy', p. 820.

112 The 1862 edition of J. S. Mill's classic textbook, *Principles of political economy*, had taken up with alacrity the arguments independently presented by J. T. Dunning of the London Consolidated Society of Bookbinders and Henry Fawcett, the political economist, in influential articles they each published in 1860. Their argument was that bargaining between employer and employee was the essential process for a free market to allocate wage-levels efficiently and to reflect correctly the comparative value of the labour offered (the equivalent of competitive pricing of commodities by producers/suppliers, who thereby 'bargained' for their share of the consumers' demand). Since an isolated labourer could no more bargain effectively than could a producer without information on the price and quality of the goods of his competitors, this led, as J. S. Mill acknowledged, to a powerful theoretical justification for trade unions and collective bargaining in order to make free markets work properly. See Biagini, 'British trade unions and popular political economy', pp. 812–15.

113 Biagini, 'British trade unions and popular political economy', pp. 820–2, 838–9. Thomas Brassey (1805–70) made his fortune primarily in domestic and international rail construction.

114 The marginalist revolution in economic theory, pioneered in Britain during the late 1860s and early 1870s by W. S. Jevons, was the basis for Marshall's comprehensive theoretical overhaul of the discipline, resulting in the new orthodoxy of neoclassical economics. This was formally announced in 1890 with his publication of the masterly and conciliatory (towards the classical theorists) synthesis, *Principles of political economy*. Thereafter Marshall was the leading force in the

economic analysis as integral to a larger moral and political programme for the improvement of society. But the direct effect upon the subsequent, first generation of university-trained professional economists was to lead them away from the grandiose pretensions of classical economics to a general moral authority and guidance over the principles of government policy. The primary disciplinary focus now moved to the elucidation of the technical calculus of market supply and demand.[115] This relative withdrawal of economics (though not Marshall) from overt political and moral engagement was additionally part of the wider process of nascent professionalisation which affected many putative academic specialisms during the last third of the nineteenth century. As Stefan Collini and James Moore have each shown, such disciplines sought to differentiate their activities as scientific and non-partisan in order to argue their case for national financial support and institutional resources in the reformed and multiplying universities.[116]

Thus, with the passing of the mid-Victorian decades of unparalleled prosperity, confusions and disagreements within 'the bourgeois science' of political economy were now added to extant religious doubts, creating a general problem of ideological self-justification for members of the educated and propertied class. They were now deprived of their comforting certainty in the 'iron laws' as the moral legitimation of their pursuit of self-interest in the market place of society. For many of the propertied class, political economy had come to be understood as an integral part of their personal, Christian viewpoint on the world: the discovery and preaching of the harmonising natural laws of society.[117] Hence, chronic doubts about the validity of classical economic science added to the theological dilemma.

As a result, from the 1870s until the 1930s mainstream conservative ideology drew its intellectual support instead from a bastard conglomerate of idealist formulations and materialist 'evidence', which together sanctioned a social evolutionary belief in the possibility of Progress.[118] This provided a supposedly rational and scientific understanding of the positive direction in which society and individuals were destined to be heading. It thereby offered the all-important

professional consolidation of economics as a demarcated academic discipline, founding the new Economics Tripos in Cambridge in 1903. The definitive formulation of marginalism by W. S. Jevons had been his *Theory of political economy* of 1871. Apart from Jevons's own earlier work, it is clear that the 'marginalist revolution' in economic theory was in fact a highly protracted process of applying ideas that had been in circulation among various European economists since at least the 1830s. Hence, the Austrians, Menger and Walras, are generally considered to have simultaneously formulated marginal utility theory independently of Jevons. See Blaug, *Economic theory in retrospect*, ch. 8. More generally on the ensuing division within economics, see Kadish, *The Oxford economists*; Koot, *English historical economics*.

115 However, for Marshall's own intellectually imperialist and morally charged inclinations, see Collini, Winch and Burrow, *That noble science*, ch. X, 'A separate science: polity and society in Marshall's economics'. J. M. Keynes, who in the 1930s was to reinfuse economics with overtly political claims, was not, of course, a university-trained economist.

116 Collini, *Public moralists*, ch. 6; Moore, 'Deconstructing Darwinism', pp. 388–9, 404–8.

117 Hilton, *The age of atonement*, *passim*.

118 For a fuller discussion of the formation of the classical liberal ideology, see below, ch. 3.

legitimating moral code – now secularised – by which the governing and propertied class could justify their social position and behaviour. They were representatives of the most evolved and progressive life-forms, towards which their lesser brethren were to be encouraged to approach. These were moral and socio-political derivates from 'Darwinian' evolutionary biology, improvised on the strength of the idealist convictions which underpinned the ideology of the liberal intellectual class. It was the product of a symbiosis between the self-justifying ideals of Liberal rationalism and the increasingly confident pronouncements of the biological, anthropological and medical empirical sciences on the enviable place of the liberal, educated Anglo-Saxon male in the grand evolutionary scheme.

With Marshall's new marginalist orthodoxy, mainstream 'neoclassical' economics itself abandoned the more pessimistic classical disposition regarding the stasis of Ricardo's diminishing marginal returns and Malthus's glum population principle as popularly understood. In his social and political beliefs Marshall embraced instead the apparently biologically sanctioned dynamic principles of evolutionary change, the winnable battle between the forces of progress and degeneration. Indeed, with economic conditions worsening, conservative and reformist intellectuals recognised during the 1880s that there was an urgent need for a convincing response to the many novel branches of radical and socialist thought and their associated 'movements': Henry George's 'land tax' campaign; Hyndman's 'Marxist' Social Democratic Federation; William Morris's splinter Socialist League; the Fabian Society. These critiques threw into the public domain a variety of intellectual and political challenges. Liberal economists were spurred on by the goads of these critics, facing some of them directly and in person at the Industrial Remuneration Conference held in London in January 1885.[119] The criticisms put forward by these groups demanded some kind of reply from conservative and reformist intellectuals, trying to justify, explain, defuse or correct the deplorable situation that was acknowledged to prevail in the economy of the London labour market, where all economic laws seemed to have ground to a halt.

The growing appreciation of the significance of imperfections in the market economy was gradually leading orthodox liberal economists to focus on the issues of income distribution, low wages, underemployment and unemployment as the most important symptoms of the metropolitan economy's tendencies to imperfections. An early harbinger of this had been J. E. Cairnes's important sociological insight into the potential fracturing of the labour market into a set of non-competing groups, although the term 'unemployment' was apparently only first publicly utilised as an economist's term by Marshall in 1888 and not formally defined as such until 1895 by the underconsumptionist, J. A. Hobson.[120] As early as 1884 and again in 1885, Marshall publicly advocated schemes to remove – forcibly if

[119] For an account of the public criticism of their discipline that Marshall and others faced at this conference, see: Kadish, *The Oxford economists*, pp. 127–30.

[120] Cairnes, *Some leading principles*, pp. 70–3; Harris, *Unemployment and politics*, p. 4.

necessary – the poorest, least regularly employed section of the capital's workforce – the 'residuum' – from the slums and hovels which they occupied.[121] These unorganised, inadequate workers and their demoralised families were the root cause of the capital's market imperfections, choking the economy's progressive workings. The solution was to resettle them in the more salubrious environment of rural labour colonies, providing them with an ordered régime of regular, albeit low-paid, employment.[122] According to Marshall the resultant freeing up of the metropolitan labour market would also benefit those who were not removed, a slightly superior stratum of families headed by more disciplined and able – albeit unskilled – workers. A glutted labour market at this level had resulted in chronic competition between this slightly superior segment and the residuum for the lowest-paid jobs and lowest-rent housing, to the mutual detriment of both groups.[123]

Thus, Marshall had been among the earliest of mainstream liberals to countenance authoritarian, interventionist and segregationist means to achieve liberal ends, on the basis of his reasoned analysis of the causes of persistent mass unemployment in the capital's peculiarly imperfect labour market. The capital's economic problems were seen as a remediable awkward case within the 'optimistic', new, liberal Marshallian economics. This was generally characterised by a faith in the operation of the free market to evolve towards a 'moralised capitalism' of self-improved individuals. But progress was not claimed to be an inevitable process, especially given the imperfections of markets. Progress was crucially dependent on careful direction by intelligent human agency. In the exceptional conjunction in London of an overstocked, anarchic and non-unionised labour market at the lower levels, it was diagnosed that a vicious circle of underemployment and associated physical and moral degeneration of those involved had developed. However, this could be 'righted' by a simple act of state intervention, once the problematic individuals had been correctly identified so that they could be appropriately treated. Furthermore, according to Brassey and Marshall alike, more favourably remunerated, higher quality workers were likely to be a prime source of greater productivity. For Marshall the unionised, prudential elements of the working classes were the living proof and vanguard of this evolutionary process towards responsible self-improvement on the part of the working classes.[124]

There was, then, a crucial interventionist, regulatory role to be performed by a properly informed state agency, to preserve the proper, progressive working of the market economy. The new generation of liberal economists gave their blessing, therefore, to the creation, in response to much pressure from trade unions also, of a separate new sub-department of government in 1886 to study and even if necessary to intervene in a conciliating role in the grievances of labour with their

[121] See above, n. 82.

[122] Stedman Jones, *Outcast London*, p. 304.

[123] Brown, 'Charles Booth and labour colonies'; Hennock, 'Poverty and social theory', p. 84.

[124] Stedman Jones, *Outcast London*, pp. 7–10.

employers.[125] The new Labour Statistical Bureau was established within the Board of Trade with Robert Giffen as its statistical head.[126] Initially, the Bureau appeared to be a sickly child, suffering alongside many other government departments from the Treasury's relentless economising policy, dubbed 'Lingenism' after the Permanent Secretary who had established the policy.[127] Nevertheless, the Bureau survived to become a full Department of Labour within the Board of Trade from January 1893. Thereafter it quickly became a centre of recruitment for those who had served a social science apprenticeship as assistants on Charles Booth's great social survey of London, reflecting his contributory influence (as President of the Royal Statistical Society 1892–4) in campaigning for the Department's permanent establishment.[128] Meanwhile many of the leading economists in the encompassing Board of Trade were former Cambridge students of Marshall's.[129]

There was much common ground between Marshall and Booth, respectively the most influential economic and social inquirers of this late Victorian generation. Charles Booth's monolithic survey of the capital's working people acted in a sense as the empirical demonstration of the accuracy of Marshall's view of the nation's workforce and his diagnosis of the particular problems of the London labour market. Booth had decided to dedicate himself and his substantial private funds to his great work of social survey in 1886, after several years of increasing interest in 'social diagnosis'.[130] After being contacted by Marshall in this first year of his project, Booth had lost no time in consulting him for criticism of his plans, so as to ensure that his proposed methods would satisfy Marshall's criteria 'to describe analytically the industrial and social status of the population of London, that is to state the proportions in which different classes exist'.[131] Booth's principal aim was

[125] On the belated conversion of trade unionists in the 1870s, and thereafter their stubborn pressure in favour of officially recognised collective bargaining and arbitration procedures, see Biagini, 'British trade unions and popular political economy', pp. 832–40. Apparently it had been the uncomfortable encounter for liberal economists at the Industrial Remuneration conference of 1885 which had finally provided the stimulus for the formation of the Labour Statistical Bureau of the Board of Trade in 1886: Davidson, *Whitehall*, p. 82.

[126] Robert Giffen (1837–1910) had been chief of the Board of Trade's statistical department since 1876. He had been a participant in the Industrial Remuneration conference and was the author of several ameliorationist studies such as his inaugural Presidential address to the Statistical Society of London, demonstrating 'The progress of the working classes' through a comparison of real wage-levels in 1831 and 1881.

[127] Davidson, *Whitehall*, pp. 86–92. Baron R. R. W. Lingen (1819–1905), Permanent Secretary of the Treasury, 1869–85.

[128] O'Day and Englander, *Mr Charles Booth's inquiry*, pp. 13–14; 16–17. In the Labour Department its chief, Hubert Llewellyn Smith, and also Clara Collet and David Schloss, were all ex-Booth.

[129] The Department's most influential independent statistical adviser, A. L. Bowley, had come under Marshall's influence at Cambridge, as also had several of the Board of Trade's first division economists. See, Davidson, *Whitehall*, p. 239, n. 68.

[130] O'Day and Englander, *Mr Charles Booth's inquiry*, pp. 28–9. This contains an important reassessment of the sociological value of the project which Booth directed and advertises the historical value of the massive, largely unexploited archive of working materials generated by Booth and his assistants.

[131] Letter from Booth to Marshall, 18 October 1886, cited in Simey and Simey, *Charles Booth*, p. 86; and see O'Day and Englander, *Mr Charles Booth's inquiry*, p. 42.

to demonstrate the Marshallian case: the need for the removal of his class 'B', those in casual and irregular labour who were 'unfit' in the Darwinian sense, from the London labour market.[132]

Booth's work shows the extent to which the evolutionary forms of both economic and biological analysis of poverty and underemployment were able to concur on the essential nature of the social problem and the remedies needed. The inefficient individuals were to be identified and then segregated from the healthy majority, both to ameliorate their own lot and to contain their contaminating influence upon others. The notion of a 'residuum' – a section of the urban population which was both superfluous to the local labour requirements and biologically or morally incapable of productive labour – expressed the common diagnostic and political ground between the two approaches, due to their evolutionary social assumptions. The residuum was simultaneously a descriptive and analytic term.

Herbert Spencer's systematic philosophy was the overarching intellectual framework for this consensus among reforming, mainstream liberal social scientists in the 1880s. The important characteristics of Spencer's work, in this context, were: his adherence to a 'faith in the universality of natural causation';[133] his evolutionism (specifically a form of Lamarckism);[134] and his commitment to 'the liberal, individualistic, rational bourgeois society par excellence' as the endpoint of the super-organic evolution, which he claimed was the highest human potentiality.[135] Marshall's new liberal economics seems to have almost entirely absorbed this conditionally optimistic, Spencerian assessment of the evolutionary potentialities available to a well-adjusted liberal society.[136] If Booth was Marshall's

132 Hennock, 'Poverty and social theory', pp. 76, 84. Peter Hennock has successfully unravelled a tortuous, complex historiographical misinterpretation of Booth's motives and aims in constructing the specific classification system which he used in this survey. Hennock shows that the classification system has been anachronistically misinterpreted to try to show that Booth was an early anti-individualist who was making an argument that poverty and unemployment were not caused by individual character failings but by impersonal 'conditions of employment'. However, Booth 'had no way of distinguishing between individual failings and impersonal economic causes' of poverty (p. 82). Hennock has shown that Booth was an eclectic of socially conservative and reformist ideas, 'a systematiser using the categories familiar from the immediate past' (p. 69), and therefore his work could be interpreted as potentially supporting either side in the prevailing conservative versus liberal reformist debate of 'urban degeneration' versus Marshallian 'progress': contemporaries of both hues could draw from Booth's survey 'scientific' support for their views: the massive and authoritative documentation provided by mountains of 'facts'.

133 This phrase was used by J. W. Burrow, *Evolution and society*, p. 75. Burrow was referring there to the young J. S. Mill, whilst observing that this faith was: 'something which was to exercise a profound influence on the development of sociological theory' (Burrow, *Evolution and society*, p. 75). There seems to be little doubt that it was the systematic philosophy of Herbert Spencer (1820–95), enunciated in a series of works commencing in 1850 with *Social statics*, which was the specific agency through which early British sociology was thoroughly imbued with this faith. See Burrow, *Evolution and society*, ch. 6, esp. pp. 188–9, 205; Abrams, *The origins of British sociology*, pp. 66–75; and, more generally, Peel, *Herbert Spencer*.

134 Jones, *Social Darwinism*, pp. 78–80. See below, ch. 3, n. 19 for Lamarckian use-inheritance.

135 Burrow, *Evolution and society*, pp. 190–213, 222.

136 See Marshall, *The economics of industry*, p. 9, for use of Spencerian physiological terminology.

right arm, his empirical demonstrator, Marshall could in a sense be cast as Spencer's master-builder, providing him with the blueprint of the socio-economic mechanism whereby his evolutionary goal might be attained.

The battle for control of the census

Marshall and Booth came into head-on conflict with the GRO in early 1890 over the specific issue of the Office's occupational classification scheme. A Committee had been 'appointed by the Treasury to enquire into certain questions connected with the taking of the census'.[137] This Committee was an official response to issues raised by a high-powered delegation, organised primarily by the Royal Statistical Society, which had obtained a joint interview with the Chancellor of the Exchequer and the President of the Local Government Board on 11 December 1888. It was a measure of Booth's status and the effectiveness of his connections, which were especially concentrated in the community of social investigators gathered in the neighbouring premises on the Strand of Somerset House (housing the GRO) and the Royal Statistical Society, that he uniquely acted as both a Committee member and witness to the inquiry.[138] Sir Brydges P. Henniker, the Registrar-General, was one of the seven other Committee members, while Marshall and Ogle both appeared as witnesses (as did the Registrar-Generals of Scotland and of Ireland, who were simultaneously the chief statistical experts for their respective Offices).[139] Judging by the active presence on this small, time-consuming Committee of Sir Reginald Welby, himself, the Permanent Secretary at the Treasury and a zealous exponent of his predecessor's eponymous cost-cutting régime of 'Lingenism', this was no mere routine inquiry. Evidently Welby was taking the opportunity thrown up by the delegation to have a close look at how the GRO operated and how it managed the census, no doubt with a keen eye to any economies that could be imposed upon either the GRO or the census procedure.[140]

The Committee examined a wide range of issues and incidentally provided a

137 PP, 1890 LVIII, Cmd 6071, *Report of the Committee Appointed by the Treasury*, Minutes of Evidence and Appendices.

138 Charles Booth (1840–1916), the son of a wealthy Liverpool corn merchant, was as well connected a member of the charmed circle of 'the intellectual aristocracy' as was possible (as was his wife and collaborator, Mary Catherine Macaulay, niece of T. B. Macaulay): O'Day and Englander, *Mr Charles Booth's inquiry*, pp. 12–16, 30, 144; Annan, 'The intellectual aristocracy'.

139 Leonard H. Courtney, MP and Deputy Speaker (an ex-Professor of Political Economy of University College, London, 1872–5), was Committee Chairman; Mr T. H. Elliott, Principal Secretary to the President of the LGB, was Committee Secretary; the other four members being the two most senior civil servants involved: Sir Reginald Welby, Permanent Secretary of the Treasury (1885–94); and Sir Hugh Owen, Permanent Secretary of the LGB (1882–99); and two MPs, Mr C. A. Whitmore and Mr Munro Ferguson.

140 The Labour Statistical Bureau of the Board of Trade provides an exactly contemporary example of Welby's capacity to impose economies even to the detriment of operational efficiency: see Davidson, *Whitehall*, p. 87.

forum for a productive exchange of opinions between the GRO and the principal medical users of the information that it collected at the census: four of the twenty witnesses called were senior Medical Officers of Health.[141] In general the inquiry went well for the GRO. Welby seems to have been satisfied that there was no serious extravagance to be found at the GRO and that its management of the census should continue. All but one of the ten summary recommendations of the Report conformed with preferences expressed by Henniker and Ogle during the Committee's proceedings. The single exception was that new columns should be added to the face of the census schedule to attempt to elicit the supplementary information from the population as to whether a worker, after returning his or her occupation, was an employer, employee or self-employed; and that this information should then be published if the response was adequate.[142] This represented a very partial victory for Marshall and Booth.

In arguing for this change Booth and Marshall presented an essentially similar case in their respective depositions, the former's being a subset and amplification of a part of the much more comprehensive and cogently argued case laid out by Marshall. In his evidence Marshall began by pointing out that there was a clear distinction between vital statistics and statistics useful for studying questions of industrial and economic change. He began by diplomatically praising 'the Registrar-General's Department' for 'the excellent work they have done in vital statistics, to which they give their chief attention' and then proceeded to argue that what was required was an 'Industrial Statistics Department . . . at least as large as the whole work of the Registrar-General's Department; and that a strong body of men ought to be always working at it . . . trained people, with full knowledge of detail.'[143]

The essential point of conflict with the interests of the GRO was over the use of the occupational questions in the national census. This was a massive intelligence resource for the social sciences which Marshall wanted to see deployed to assist in answering the social and economic questions which he regarded as most important to the country's future. He gave a detailed account of the German industrial census as a model of useful occupational information from the social and economic point of view. The German census enabled crucial distinctions to be made within each occupational category that were unavailable in the British census: between dealers and makers; between the skilled or supervisory workers and others; between employers, subcontractors and the self-employed. And all this information, along with the distribution of large and small firms in each branch of industry, was published for each of the major towns in the German Empire.[144]

[141] Shirley Murphy, MOH to the LCC; B. A. Whitelegge, MOH, West Riding; H. E. Armstrong and J. F. J. Sykes, respectively President and Secretary of the Society of MOHs.

[142] *Report of the Committee Appointed by the Treasury*, p. xii.

[143] *Report of the Committee Appointed by the Treasury*, Minutes of Evidence, para. 1462.

[144] *Report of the Committee Appointed by the Treasury*, Minutes of Evidence, paras. 1531–40.

The GRO's expressed objections to all this were primarily practical: Marshall and Booth's scheme was a chimerical fantasy that had not worked well even in Germany. It aspired to a degree of detail which could not be trusted for its authenticity or consistency. Furthermore, by overburdening with a whole battery of extra questions the fragile human machinery of data collection in the field – the census schedule, the householder and the enumerator – it was most likely to produce worse and more confused occupational information than was attained under the present system.[145] Ogle and Henniker received broad support for these objections from both Irish and Scottish Registrars-General.[146] Robert Giffen, Assistant Secretary and head of the Statistical and Commercial Departments of the Board of Trade, also assisted the GRO's refusal of Marshall's case, by pointing out that his own Department's special wage inquiries, conducted by its new Labour Statistical Bureau, would be furnishing information of just this kind, on the distribution of grades of skill in different industries.[147] Under cross-questioning, Marshall acknowledged that a separately undertaken 'industrial census' was probably the best way forward, to produce the information that he and Booth desired. Following the suggestion of the Irish Registrar-General, he envisaged this inquiry as a follow-up after the main census had established the identity and location of the nation's employers.[148] But this further emphasised the need for the census at least to attempt to distinguish between employers, employees and the self-employed; Ogle's objections that this would overburden the census schedule notwithstanding. Hence, the partial victory for Booth and Marshall in the single recommendation that went against the GRO's wishes.

Ogle was certainly far from enthusiastic about the experimental recording of employment status recommended by the Committee and foisted on the 1891 census schedule more or less in the form requested by Booth.[149] After the census had been taken he succeeded in evading tabulation of the results on grounds of inaccuracy and internal inconsistency of the information collected. Nevertheless, the experiment became a permanent part of the census, thanks mainly to the insistent requests of the vigorous Labour Department of the Board of Trade. But the reasons for the GRO's resistance to the most sweeping aspects of the Booth–Marshall proposals for reforms of the occupational classification scheme

[145] *Report of the Committee Appointed by the Treasury*, Minutes of Evidence, paras. 1–356A *passim* (Ogle's evidence). The Registrar-General's views are recorded in Appendix 6, pp. 120–1: his original response to the petition of 1888 which prompted the setting up of the inquiry.

[146] *Report of the Committee Appointed by the Treasury*, Minutes of Evidence, paras. 517–32, 2023–32.

[147] *Report of the Committee Appointed by the Treasury*, Minutes of Evidence, para. 1627. Giffen had his own reasons for trumpeting the capacities of the Labour Bureau and underlining its 'product differentiation' from the GRO, as a producer of statistics. Since its formation in 1886, Giffen had been fighting Welby's underfunding of the Labour Bureau, even threatening resignation at one point: Davidson, *Whitehall*, p. 87.

[148] *Report of the Committee Appointed by the Treasury*, Minutes of Evidence, paras. 1541–60. Irish Registrar-General at para. 517.

[149] *Report of the Committee Appointed by the Treasury*, Minutes of Evidence, para. 1357.

were not simply those of technical impracticality, though they were certainly wise to mount their defence in 1890 on these grounds, as it was by far the most difficult argument for those without actual experience of conducting a national census exercise to refute. Neither were their objections merely the product of obscurantist, bureaucratic do-nothingism as has been tentatively suggested in at least one historian's account of the relationship between the Labour Department and the GRO.[150]

There were really two, intimately related reasons for the GRO's resistance to any far-reaching and rapid changes in the manner in which the census occupational data was to be collected or tabulated: one technical and the other politico-professional. The particular function that such occupational information had come to perform in the GRO's established battery of epidemiological statistics has to be understood. Edward Higgs's illuminating account of the GRO's use of its occupational data to develop disease-specific occupational mortality statistics has already been mentioned.[151] This was something to which Ogle had given his particular attention, developing significantly the early work done by Farr. This represented a relatively unexplored area of research and one in which the epidemiological approach of the GRO could still contribute novel scientific and practical insights since, regardless of the germ theory, the as yet unspecified proximate causes of marked occupational differences in disease incidence were most likely to lie in the conditions of the occupational environment and its working materials. It was certainly the most intellectually stimulating and challenging investigative work open to Ogle in his official capacity, an opportunity which he firmly grasped – to improve significantly upon Farr's pioneering forays into the field.

In order to compile valid occupational mortality indices, the GRO combined the vital registration data, recording deaths at every age for every occupation, with the census record of the number of persons at risk to die in each age group in each corresponding occupation. The crucial technical problem was that of matching up the census's occupational information with that derived separately from the nation's death registration system. Discrepancies between the two data sources in the way they defined and recorded occupations could seriously invalidate the results. The trouble was that the nation's registration system was inevitably much less exacting in this respect than the census: at least the employed individuals entered their own occupation on the census form; by definition they did not do so on their death certificates. On the whole, the latter provided less accurate and less detailed occupational information for cross-referencing with the census's categories. Ogle had therefore devoted great efforts to ensuring that at least 100 meaningful, corresponding occupational groups could be constructed from this combined source, in order to study their comparative disease patterns both synchronically and diachronically. The far-reaching proposals of Marshall and Booth, to change

150 Davidson, *Whitehall*, pp. 193–6. 151 See above, p. 77.

the occupational census in a number of ways simultaneously, automatically jeopardised the future of this difficult exercise of cross-classification between census and vital registration.

Of course, what we have here is only the specific circumstance or proximate reason for the GRO's rejection of the overtures of Booth and Marshall, compelling as it no doubt seemed to Ogle, who had by 1890 devoted a decade of his professional energies to the rather intractable problems of perfecting measures of occupational mortality. The wider politico-professional and institutional context for this clash of interests lies in the varying scientific agenda and associated policy aims of the two distinct disciplinary perspectives of public health medicine and liberal economics. This was essentially a dispute over access to and use of a unique national information resource – the census – which each side considered to be of great importance to its own discipline's scientific efficacy. It is perhaps somewhat surprising that the economists' claim to the fruits of the national census was only now being strongly pressed. Almost a century had passed since the first decennial census was taken and those now arguing that the census should serve the interests of economists faced an incumbent public health interest well 'dug-in' with half a century of experience in administering and processing the census for its own requirements.[152]

With both vital statistics and economics experiencing something of a nadir in their respective claims to scientific status, public authority and importance, there was no evidence of Booth's or of Marshall's appreciation or detailed knowledge of the GRO's established epidemiological uses for the census occupational data, the latter's polite opening remarks notwithstanding. And in return there was no explicit acknowledgement by Ogle of the validity of Marshall's aims. In the longer run there would be a rapprochement between the two sets of demands at the 1921 census (see pp. 323–4), when it came to be mutually acknowledged that *both* the economic/industrial and the socio-demographic were important dimensions of occupational information which could in fact be collected together and classified separately from the same single census exercise. But in 1890 the two sides seemed

[152] Much earlier in the century government recognition of its growing need for systematic and co-ordinated national 'economic' data had led to the formation in 1833 of a Statistical Department within the Board of Trade, headed by G. R. Porter. As Lucy Brown has shown, this Department (and the Board as a whole) in fact devoted its early energies to a successful propaganda campaign supporting the Free Trade movement, while failing to develop as the intended central statistical office. This failure was formally acknowledged in the 1854 Northcote–Trevelyan Report on the Board of Trade and there was no further attempt to create a central intelligence agency for economic data: Brown, *The Board of Trade*, ch. 5. If there ever had been a possibility of the national census passing into the administrative control of a department with a primarily economic perspective, that opportunity had apparently passed without the Free Trade partisans at the Board of Trade even noticing. During the year of 1840 their attentions were thoroughly absorbed by the Select Committee on Import Duties: Brown, *The Board of Trade*, chs. 4, 8–12. It was exactly at that time, in 1840, that the crucial recommendations of a Committee of the London Statistical Society determined that the census should be administered by the recently established GRO: Glass, *Numbering the people*, ch. 3.

to be at loggerheads, believing that their designs for the occupational census were simply incompatible. As Ogle had stated as early as 1886, in response to Booth's first salvo in his campaign to modify the official classification: 'a classification of occupations which was good for a political economist would be very different to that which would approve itself to a sanitary administrator.'[153]

However, the GRO sensibly took the episode in 1890 to heart, as a warning shot. The Treasury's Committee of Inquiry represented the most serious administrative threat that the Office had ever faced to its previously undisputed authority to manage all detailed aspects of the census. As a result of the GRO's rejection of most suggestions on grounds of impracticality, Ogle had found himself having to describe – and implicitly justify – in meticulous detail all the technical arrangements for taking and processing the census in response to the probing questions of the Committee, led by Booth, who had himself prepared a detailed alternative method for tabulating occupational information.[154] Moreover, the initiative which had originally led to the setting-up of the Committee had also represented the most serious attempt so far by an alternative disciplinary perspective to that of public health medicine to exert control over the analytical output of the GRO. Of the forty-six signatories to the original memorandum handed to the Chancellor and the President of the LGB in December 1888, only three were medical practitioners, while no less than eighteen are identifiable as eminent economists, including eleven Professors of Political Economy.[155] Indeed, at the end of his evidence Marshall even mooted the idea of a permanent central statistical office to oversee all government statistics, something that might easily take control of the census out of the hands of the GRO altogether.[156]

Ogle and his successor, Tatham, subsequently made a whole series of voluntary, gradual changes in the occupational classification at each of the next two censuses, starting at the 1891 census with an attempt to separate dealers from makers more effectively. It was now understood that the requirements of the professional economists and statisticians of the increasingly powerful Labour Department of the Board of Trade could no longer be simply ignored. In view of this, the main aim of the GRO was therefore to satisfy their reasonable requests as well as possible, in order to fend off any larger demands for more direct control over any aspect of the census. So long as it could retain exclusive control over the census machinery, the GRO could at least itself determine the pace at which its occupational classification

153 Booth, 'Occupations of the people', p. 437 (W. Ogle's contribution to the 'Discussion').

154 The Committee also made similar comparative detailed inquiries of the Irish and Scottish Registrar-Generals. As a result, the minutes of evidence taken by this Committee provide the most informative description of the detailed mechanics of the administration and taking of the nineteenth-century censuses in the United Kingdom that I have come across.

155 *Report of the Committee Appointed by the Treasury*, Appendix 5. Most of the balance was composed of ten MPs and six social workers/investigators (e.g. Booth himself, C. S. Loch of the COS, H. Llewellyn Smith of Toynbee Hall – also one of Booth's main collaborators).

156 *Report of the Committee Appointed by the Treasury*, Minutes of Evidence, para. 1566.

scheme changed – so as to be able to marry the registration information to such changes wherever possible and so maintain their epidemiological usefulness. Thus, the Registrar-General saw to it that the next census of 1901 was preceded by a set of planned, interdepartmental consultations with the Labour Department under H. Llewellyn Smith and the Factory Inspectorate of the Home Office, under Dr B. A. Whitelegge.[157] (The Inspectorate's expertise had been reserved for special praise by Marshall in 1890.[158]) The GRO invited and received detailed advice on the information that these departments would like to see collected, how to frame the census schedule accordingly, and also on the principles of classification they would like to see adopted. Among the most important results of this consultation was an inquiry for the first time of those working at home in each industry, in response to a request from the Factory Inspectorate;[159] several of the many examples of occupational imprecision specified by Alfred Marshall in his evidence in 1890 were also improved in due course, usually along the lines he had suggested.[160]

Conclusion: the professional model, occupation and skill

This chapter has examined the preceding, nineteenth-century history of empirical occupational and social classification in the work of the GRO, in order to ascertain whether the professional model adopted at the 1911 census should be seen as a development of the Office's earlier schemes. It has been shown that, in strict terms of continuity, there is an absolute break in 1900 in the official practice of socially classifying occupations. The scheme of 1861 was abandoned and the official report of the 1901 census is almost unique in this respect, in that it is the only one since the very earliest censuses lacking a representation of the nation in terms of a systematic model of a few large socio-economic categories.

However, in other ways, the importance of which will become more apparent as the rest of this study unfolds, the historical origins of fundamental methodological precedents and of formative influences upon the professional model of social classes have been uncovered in the preceding sections of this chapter, even though official work on the professional model itself was not to commence until the beginning of the second decade of the next century.

It has been shown that during the nineteenth century the GRO was not simply unaware of social class as an important phenomenon influencing the demographic patterns which it analysed. Quite to the contrary, the officials of the GRO were only too well aware of the potential significance of such a form of analysis. But they

157 The correspondence is to be found in PRO RG 19/9 and RG 19/10.

158 *Report of the Committee Appointed by the Treasury*, Minutes of Evidence, para. 1566.

159 PRO RG 19/10, Item 13.

160 *Report of the Committee Appointed by the Treasury*, Minutes of Evidence, paras. 1462–4, 1489. For instance, coal workers above and below ground were separated, as were several categories of skilled tradesmen from their respective labourers, such as masons and bricklayers from masons' labourers and bricklayers' labourers.

weighed and evaluated its importance primarily in terms of its potential for contributing to the practical, ameliorationist and environmentalist public health movement, whose political promotion was the Office's heart and soul throughout this period. The battles which have been recounted above, which the Office fought in the 1870s, 1880s and 1890s, demonstrate the paramount importance of these environmentalist, preventive health considerations in the Office's intellectual disposition. In order to understand fully the provenance of the professional model in the next century, it is of crucial importance to appreciate the thoroughness and consistency of the GRO's institutional commitment to this programme, as it will be shown that there is a strong continuity manifest in T. H. C. Stevenson's work, when he came to construct the professional model. Without proper appreciation of the environmentalist, public health tradition of the Office, to which Stevenson was the heir, it is only too easy to misinterpret the rather lapidary evidence available regarding the motivations and intentions behind the professional model.

The single most important of the nineteenth-century methodological precedents which was so strongly to influence the form of the professional model was the establishment of the principle that the adult male head of household's gainful occupation was to be treated as the fundamental generic social category, or unit of identity, for the Office's empirical social and demographic analysis. As outlined in the Prologue this was the first of the three essential premises in the ensuing professional model. It may seem today relatively unremarkable that male occupation would be used as the primary criterion for evaluating social status or prestige. But it must be recalled that until the early nineteenth century title, rank, office, calling, tenancy and trade – or lack of any of these – were the principal modes of assigning social identity and status in the oligarchic hierarchy that was British society (as well as age and sex, of course).[161] These were not simply older, historical terms for essentially the same concept of 'occupation'. After all, to enjoy an elevated social position, rank or office, above the ruck and insecurity of mere farming, commerce and trade, was synonymous with *not* having a gainful occupation among the gentleman aristocrats of the eighteenth century. Furthermore, the classic form which an occupation took by the latter half of the nineteenth century – the waged employee of a single 'master' (the term for employers before the end of the nineteenth century) – was widely considered before the mid-nineteenth century to be a demeaning state of affairs for a grown man and head of household.[162]

The gainful male occupation, in the sense of a singular, definable form of employment as something which was the primary source of social identity and differentiation, was an historical development of the nineteenth century. In its long campaign for professional autonomy, broadly demarcated by the activities leading

[161] On the many and varied terminologies used in early modern representations of social hierarchy, see Wrightson, 'Estates, degrees, and sorts'; Corfield, 'Class by name and number'.

[162] Hill, 'Pottage for freeborn Englishmen'; and see below, pp. 484–8, on how and why this was transformed, primarily through the Chartist movement.

to the attainment of the Licensed Apothecaries Act of 1815 and culminating in the Medical Act of 1858 which set up the General Medical Council, the medical profession was both the paradigm and the leading case exemplifying the emergence of gainful personal occupation as the fundamental category of male social identity.[163] William Farr, formulator of the 1851 official taxonomy and the 1861 census classification of occupations, was himself a 'textbook example' of the upwardly mobile, professionalising medical man. A provincial medical 'Licensiate' (apothecary) of humble birth trained in the 1820s, he was a leading advocate of the reforms necessary to organise the practice of medicine into a carefully regulated occupational profession with membership to be based on examinable scientific knowledge.

Individuals had been asked to record their personal 'occupations' for the first time at the 1841 census, the first supervised by Farr and the GRO.[164] It was intended thereby to render the census data compatible with the civil registration scheme, which the GRO had been set up to administer from 1837, and which had recorded occupations of the deceased from the start. This feature of vital registration had almost certainly been due to the careful design of Edwin Chadwick, that archetypal reformer of aristocratic, patronage-based governmental institutions (information on personal occupation was a deliberately political, anti-aristocratic innovation).[165] Introduction of the occupational variable by the likes of Chadwick and Farr, as the fundamental unit of socially identifying information into the state's most powerful intelligence apparatus, should be recognised as the important political and cultural innovation that it was. This both reflected and reinforced the *de facto* arrival in government of a new ideology which evaluated personal occupation and abilities, and not title or rank and connections, as the primary criterion of social identity and status.[166] The profoundly political

[163] On the history of the medical profession at this time, see Reader, *Professional men*, chs. 2 and 4; Porter (ed.), *Patients and practitioners*, chs. 6–10; Peterson, *The medical profession*; Waddington, *The medical profession*; Loudon, *Medical care*.

[164] In 1811 and 1821 paid enumerators had simply been asked to state for their allocated district the number of families either in agriculture or in trade, manufacture and handicraft, or in 'other'. A transitional step towards the notion of personal, individual occupation as a universal attribute, as used in the 1841 census, is reflected in the procedure at the 1831 census. In addition to the information requested as in 1811 and 1821, enumerators were asked to state the number of adult males aged 20 and above found in nine types of employment: agricultural employers; self-employed agriculturalists; agricultural labourers; employees in manufacturing; employees in retail or handicrafts; capitalists, bankers, professional and other educated men; non-agricultural labourers; servants; and others.

[165] Glass, *Numbering the people*, pp. 139–41. On Chadwick's anti-patronage reforms of local government through the Poor Law Amendment Act, see Finer, *The life and times*, pp. 39–114.

[166] Of course, this development only very imperfectly reflected the conditions of employment and income earning actually experienced by most working men and their families at mid-century. Although many more households than ever before were now reliant on the wages of their male head in performance of a single activity for a specific employer, multiple forms of by-employment both for the head and for other members of the household were still common – indeed, they never disappeared and are again increasingly important in the later twentieth-century economy: Pahl, *Divisions of Labour*, ch. 2.

nature of this development is reflected in the fact that William Farr and his colleagues ostentatiously classified those living off private means and returning no personal occupation alongside paupers in a residual category, designated as the unproductive class.[167] For a hard-working medical professional, civil servant and social scientist like Farr, the landed rentier who could not own to any definable personal occupation was here proclaimed to be in some senses the equivalent of a pauper – in terms of his active contribution to society!

Under Farr's direction the concept of gainful male occupation was progressively established in the census as the most favoured official unit of social information on the nation's households. Initially the large number of unpaid occupations of females – acting as their husbands' partners in craft, retailing, inn-keeping, etc., as well as those of female relatives working in the home and on farms – were all formally recognised as occupations in the censuses from 1851 to 1871. From 1881, however, following various earlier ditherings and dissatisfactions with this arrangement, the GRO summarily removed all these categories to a residual 'unoccupied' class.[168] The timing is suggestive of the influence upon official thinking of the relatively successful campaigns of the 1870s by working men's associations. Privileged recognition of the status of organised male breadwinners was achieved through the highly favourable trade union legislation of 1871–6, while the position of female workers was further marginalised through restrictions upon their hours and conditions in the Factory and Workshops Acts of that decade.[169] This development, at least, was something about which Marshall had no qualms whatever. It was his diagnosis – in common with the most powerful male trade unionists' – that the proliferation of casual, part-time and low-paid work constituted the core of the labour market problem of chronic underemployment; and female 'amateurs' were therefore contributory to this problem. In the disagreements between Booth, Marshall and the GRO this was not, therefore, a bone of contention. The terms of reference of their debate simply presumed that male occupational identity was the most significant item of information with which to group and class divisions of the national population for the purposes of social and economic analysis: the only question was what kind of male occupational classification there should be.

Although Marshall's arguments for a new system of occupational classification certainly did not prevail upon the GRO in 1890, in the longer run the Marshallian agenda did, indeed, come to exert a very considerable influence upon the GRO's empirical social classification scheme. And here we come to the way in which the subject matter of this chapter has uncovered the deeper historical origins of important aspects of the second and third of the three methodological premises underlying the professional model, as outlined in the Prologue. This specifically

167 See PP 1863 LIII, Pt I: 1861 Census General Report Vol. III, pp. 27–39; and Appendix, 'The new classification of the people according to their employments', especially p. 225.

168 Higgs, 'Women, occupations and work'.

169 McKibbin, 'Why was there no Marxism?', p. 320; Rose, *Limited livelihoods*, pp. 53–74, 90–9.

relates to the grading of all manual occupations according to level of skill, and the neo-evolutionary notion that these grades form part of a single, unidimensional social hierarchy.

The chief legacy of Marshall in this respect was reflected in the bottom half of the professional model of social classes: the tripartite linear grading of all male manual occupations according to degree of skill, and regardless of industrial sector. The intellectual vehicle which transmitted this influence to T. H. C. Stevenson in the next century was Charles Booth's great survey of life and labour in London, which acted as a conduit for the relevant aspects of Marshall's powerful, neo-evolutionary political and economic sociology.[170]

It may seem paradoxical, in view of some of his arguments at the 1890 Treasury inquiry, to attribute to Marshall the primary role in forming the professional model's emphasis on the *skill* level of male occupations, as opposed to the economic and industrial aspects of their jobs, as the principal status-signifying dimension of information on the manual population. But it has to be appreciated that Marshall's motives for reform of the occupational census were due to much more than merely his interest *qua* economist in trends in the size of firms, in the specialisation of labour and in the growth and decline of different branches of industry. He had beyond this a quite explicit ulterior interest in the social, political and moral significance of the census's occupational information.

At the beginning of his testimony in 1890 Marshall had echoed exactly the politically defensive sentiments expressed three years earlier by Booth when explaining to the Royal Statistical Society the purposes of his social survey in London.[171] Marshall declared to the Committee:

If one reads the newspapers, particularly those that circulate among the masses of the people; if one reads statements as to the condition of the working classes in England, in foreign

170 It is frequently reiterated that Britain produced no great indigenous classical sociological theorist at this time to compare with Durkheim or Weber (though, of course, Marx worked in London and his work was read in England – for instance *Das Kapital* was reviewed by, among others, W. E. Gladstone in the *Church Quarterly Review* in 1879). Various hypotheses have been advanced to account for this: see, for instance, Abrams, *The origins*; Yeo (unpublished PhD dissertation); Goldman, 'A peculiarity of the English?'. However, one might argue that Marshall's *corpus*, for all its formal focus on the elucidation of economics, was the disguised British sociological 'classic' of its time. Certainly, Talcott Parsons seems to have treated Marshall's work in this way, as more directly relevant and stimulating to his own sociological project than that of any other British thinker of the previous generation, including Herbert Spencer, L. T. Hobhouse and, even, Karl Marx: in *The structure of social action*, Parsons focused on the work of Durkheim, Weber, Pareto and Marshall.

171 In 1887 Booth had justified his attempt to sectionalise the working masses in his pilot survey into distinct classes according to their material means because 'The question of those who actually suffer from poverty should be considered separately from that of the true working classes, whose desire for a larger share of wealth is of a different character. It is the plan of agitators . . . to talk of "starving millions" . . . Against this method I strongly protest'; 'In attempting the work I had one leading idea: that every social problem, as ordinarily put, must be broken up to be solved or even to be adequately stated.' Booth, 'Inhabitants of Tower Hamlets', p. 375. Marshall had also been present on this occasion and had taken the opportunity, in discussion after Booth's paper, to outline his views on the overstocked metropolitan labour market.

treatises based, to some extent, upon newspaper reports, one finds that disproportionate importance is often attached to facts relating to classes of the community which one knows really to be very small; but how small they are we cannot tell, the census does not give us the requisite information.[172]

Therefore:

It seems to me that the first aim of the classification of an industrial census should be to group together, as far as possible, those homogeneous industrial groups of people who have skill of about the same kind and degree, who are of the same social status, who are able to act together in industrial and social questions, and who are fitted for being the subject of generalisations of importance in economic and social studies. There is no attempt in the existing census to bring out the existence of any such classes of people.[173]

Here we have a clear statement of the notion of homogeneous skill levels existing throughout the economy and of an equation between skill level and social status, as being of primary importance for an empirical classification scheme of relevance for economic and social studies. The highly political nature, both of Marshall's motivation to create ('bring out the existence of') these classes and in how he saw their essential character and historical function, was very candidly expressed. In fact Marshall's neoclassical economic analysis and his socio-political views were closely tied together. The classical economists' vicious circle, tied to the wages fund theory, had envisaged that increasing wages to labour could only in the end produce a corresponding and ultimately self-defeating decrease in profits, investment and economic activity. With the wages fund theory demolished, Marshall believed that both his own most recent revisions of economic theory and the actual economic history of the nineteenth century demonstrated that this was mistaken: workers' rising real wages had provided the material basis for an improvement in their moral character and mental strength. The capacity shown by skilled craftsmen for responsible self-organisation in trade unions was, for Marshall, the clearest proof of this higher evolution occurring in their self-discipline and character. This process of improvement in the quality of 'human capital' therefore generated consequent efficiency gains in the productivity of labour. This issued in a virtuous circle of mutually reinforcing rises in wages *and* profits.[174] For Marshall, therefore, the existence of a respectable, unionised section of the working class was critical, being the key to the nation's future positive evolution. Its legitimate aspirations to gradual self-improvement, in mimesis of its social superiors, comprised for him the engine of true cultural, ethical and economic progress in British society, whereby the fruits of material affluence would be ever more equitably *and* productively distributed.

In 1890 Marshall was therefore complaining of an official failure to acknowledge even the very existence of this important class of skilled, respectable workers, the

[172] *Report of the Committee Appointed by the Treasury*, Minutes of Evidence, para. 1462.
[173] *Report of the Committee Appointed by the Treasury*, Minutes of Evidence, para. 1462.
[174] Kadish, *The Oxford economists*, p. 135.

agents of progress as he saw it. Marshall seems to have perceived that this very lack of official recognition might seriously jeopardise the capacity of that social group to perform the vital political and historical function which he wished and envisaged for it. If this, the class of the essential agents of progress, went unacknowledged and submerged in the 'starving millions', the progress of society generally was threatened. Entailed within this viewpoint was a clear understanding of the precariously political and cultural nature of the process whereby a potential social grouping with a putative cultural identity might or might not become a collective, institutional and political 'reality', capable of determining events according to its own interests (a close analogy with Marx's celebrated distinction between class 'in itself' and 'for itself').

Marshall evidently believed in the importance of achieving 'official' recognition, as part of this process. Luc Boltanski has analysed this phenomenon in detail in the case of the dramatic emergence of 'les cadres' as a social and political group in twentieth-century France.[175] Boltanski has suggested that 'representation' is the key concept in the process, in both its linguistic/cultural and its political senses: the latter follows from the successful establishment of the former. But the fight for this linguistic and juridical, official recognition is also itself a highly political activity. Marshall saw that formal recognition of his favoured social class in an official representation of the nation's occupational structure could give valuable (though, of course, by no means determinative) assistance in the overall political battle to achieve their cultural 'representation' and consequently to fulfil their historical, political mission, which he saw as a highly desirable outcome.

Booth's work on London had also focused obsessively on the demarcation of putative social gradings within the working classes. As he had stated in 1887, his driving conviction, which he shared with Marshall, was that social scientific inquiry would show that the labouring population of Britain was not a uniform, impoverished mass. In Edwardian London Booth continued to enjoy unparalleled eminence as a social investigator, especially in the official circles with which he was so well-connected through his ex-assistants. This and the apparent continuing topicality of Booth's social survey project (the last volumes of the series were not published until the first years of the twentieth century, when the mammoth third edition of seventeen volumes appeared) ensured that when T. H. C. Stevenson eventually came to contemplate the construction of an official classification scheme for the GRO in the first decade of the new century, it was the experience and methods of the great man's London survey that seemed to provide the obvious point of departure, especially for grappling with the practical problems involved in such large-scale work. Indeed, Booth's methodology was the only work in empirical social classification explicitly discussed in detail by Stevenson during his protracted deliberations: it was still considered to be the state of the art.

[175] Boltanski, *The making of a class.*

Booth devised and published a number of different grading schemes but they all reinforced the same generic model of social structure. Although he subsequently became distinctly less convinced than Marshall of the socially progressive and constructive character of trade unions, Booth's social classifications nevertheless reflected the formative framework of the social evolutionary set of assumptions and aims which he shared with Marshall.[176] This held that the forces of material and cultural Progress within the working class should be recognised, requiring discrimination of a hierarchy of grades within the working classes, according to occupational skills: 'homogeneous industrial groups of people who have skill of about the same kind and degree, who are of the same social status'. It was the essential, linear hierarchical core of this view which was adopted into the official classification of occupations, and from which was eventually derived a simple, tripartite classification of all the nation's manual occupations according to the degree of skill involved.

But if the broad form of the manual half of the professional model can be traced ultimately to the influence of Alfred Marshall's optimistic evolutionist economics, it seems certain that if Marshall had been able to exert similar influence over the construction of the reciprocal half of an official social classification scheme for Britain, to apply to the non-manual occupations, there would have been an important place – possibly even a pre-eminent place – reserved for the class of businessmen and employers. As Collini, Winch and Burrow have emphasised, the captains of Britain's industry occupied a special place in Marshall's pantheon.[177] At the very least it would have been inconceivable to Marshall to ignore their existence as a social category altogether, as monstrous a crime against his grand evolutionary design as the omission of the skilled manual vanguard. And yet this is precisely what the official, professional model of the nation's social structure subsequently proceeded to do throughout all stages of its protracted construction. This testifies to the hybrid nature of the professional model of social structure. While Marshall's ideas influenced the form of the lower, manual half of the grading scheme, the particular character of the upper half of the professional model derives its animating force from a somewhat different intellectual locus. In

[176] O'Day and Englander, *Mr Charles Booth's inquiry*, pp. 151–4. In examining Booth's views on trade unions and related economic issues, O'Day and Englander (pp. 147–55) emphasise the influence of the writings of the eminent American economist and marginal theorist, F. A. Walker, much of whose work closely paralleled Marshall's (although O'Day and Englander also clearly acknowledge the early and close personal contact between Booth and Marshall). The account here has considered only the relationship between Booth's and Marshall's thought because of their joint contribution to the Treasury Committee. It is intriguing and indicative of the close affinities between Walker's and Marshall's intellectual projects that Walker had exploited his position as Superintendent of the previous US censuses of 1870 and 1880 to analyse the changing occupational composition of the US workforce in order to assess the nation's socio-economic and moral progress in almost exactly the same way that Marshall envisaged it. Walker believed this to be demonstrated in his own country by a shrinking proportion of unskilled labourers recorded in successive US censuses: Conk, *The United States census*, pp. 11, 72–5.

[177] Collini, Winch, and Burrow, *That noble science*, chapter X.

order to discern the intellectual origins and genealogy of the other main organising concept adopted in the official classification of occupations – the privileged and exclusive position accorded to 'the professions' at the apex of the hierarchy – we need now to leave Booth and Marshall and turn to a different kind of evolutionary social science, also dating from the last quarter of the nineteenth century: the anthropometric school of physical anthropology, whose leading light was Francis Galton.

3

Social classification and nineteenth-century naturalistic social science

Introduction

Charles Booth's social survey methodology was to form the principal practical reference point for T. H. C. Stevenson when he came to consider the construction of a new official model of social classes for the 1911 census. As a result, Marshall's specific influence, conducted via Booth, was reflected in the linear skill gradings for the working classes which were to be adopted. But it was another social science product of the 1880s which was to provide the most fundamental conceptual influence – albeit through a dialectical process of political antagonism and intellectual critique.

This was the eugenic, or Galtonian, or meritocratic model of the nation's class structure. The model was first formalised within the empirical social sciences in the work of the Anthropometric Committee of the British Association for the Advancement of Science, completed in 1883.[1] It is therefore to this 'school' of naturalistic social science that we now turn to discover the original investment of British empirical social science with the core political and moral ideals ensconced in the official, professional model of social structure.

The Anthropometric Committee's work was part of an attempt to interpret the observable phenomena of physiological and mental variation between individuals, social and ethnic groups in terms of the disputed insights of the Darwinist theory of evolution. It was also significantly motivated by the aspiration of contributing to the long-standing, ultimately theologically derived controversy over the origins of man's racial varieties: whether monogenist or polygenist.[2] The work of the BA

[1] Appointed at the Bristol meeting of the British Association in 1875, the Anthropometric Committee submitted several substantial interim papers published in the *British Assocation Annual Reports* and submitted its Final Report at the Southport meeting in 1883, published in *British Association Annual Reports* (1883).

[2] Polygenism was the theory of fundamentally different racial types of mankind, akin to distinct species. Monogenism was the alternative theory of a single humanity manifested in a variety of merely superficially different forms. The latter was more consistent with Enlightenment rationalist,

Anthropometric Committee, 1875–83, represents the point at which differences between social groups or classes in British society were first formally studied and analysed as explicitly 'scientific' matters, and with reference to the same body of evolutionary scientific theory and the same empirical measurement methods as those used to explain putative 'racial', ethnic or international differences between populations.[3] Among at least one influential section of the Victorian professional and scientific establishment, racial and class differences had now come to be viewed as essentially similar kinds of phenomena, having a probable relationship with the master-principles of evolutionary biological theory.[4]

humanitarian and egalitarian ideals and closely allied to an environmentalist and Lamarckian understanding (see below, n. 19) of human and animal variation and evolution. For the best general account of the debate and its context, see J. W. Burrow, *Evolution and society*. See also N. Stepan, *The idea of race*, ch. 4. The monogenist orthodoxy was originally established on the firm bedrock of the great ethnographic and comparative philological scholarship of James Cowles Prichard during the first half of the century. James Cowles Prichard (1786–1848) was a Quaker resident of Bristol and founder-member in 1843 of the Ethnological Society, as well as being highly active in the short-lived Bristol Statistical Society. His four decades of major publications dominated the field of philology in Britain: *Researches into the physical history of man* (1808); *Analysis of Egyptian mythology* (1819); *The natural history of man* (2 vols. 1843). See Stocking, 'Introductory essay'. The death of Prichard in 1848 and the publication two years later of Robert Knox's *The races of man* are considered to demarcate, respectively, the end in Britain of an era of undisputed Prichardian environmentalist monogenism and the first significant indigenous, anti-environmentalist polygenist work. Knox's racist ideas were championed after his death in 1862 by James Hunt's colourful 'Cannibal Clique' and especially through the Anthropological Society, which Hunt founded in 1863 and which was initially and briefly more popular and successful than its more respectable rival, the polygenist Ethnological Society, from which Hunt had resigned in 1862. Stocking, 'What's in a name?'; Curtin, *The image of Africa*, Vol. II, pp. 363–87; Stepan, *The idea of race*, ch. 2; Richards, 'The "moral anatomy" of Robert Knox', especially pp. 421–6, 429–31. The debates of the 1850s and 1860s between these two opposing camps had climaxed in the public blood-letting among mid-Victorian intellectuals over the Governor Eyre controversy, 1866–9. Eyre had indiscriminately fired upon black freedmen in Jamaica. Such figures as J. S. Mill, T. H. Huxley, Darwin and Spencer formed the 'Jamaica Committee', which brought the prosecution, while Eyre was defended by those such as Carlyle, Ruskin, Tyndall and Charles Dickens, who formed the Eyre Defence and Aid Committee. Lorimer, *Colour, class and the Victorians*, ch. 9, and pp. 155–6, 197–204. The early death in 1869 of James Hunt, the chief proponent of racist polygenism and the anthropologist most closely associated with Eyre, ensured an ensuing decade of silence from the polygenists. Nevertheless, the proponents of polygenist scientific racism subsequently reappeared in the later 1870s and 1880s stronger then ever, primarily in the form of Francis Galton's eugenic and anthropometric projects. Lorimer's argument is that this later reappearance should correctly be seen as an almost entirely distinct intellectual enterprise from the polygenism of the 1850s and 1860s: Lorimer, 'Theoretical racism'.

3 Independently of the BA Anthropometric Committee, Beddoe's *The races of Britain* was also important at this time in apparently establishing the hereditary bases of ethnic differences, which supposedly determined differential physical attributes and mental abilities of the races. See Stepan, *The idea of race*, pp. 89–90, 100–1; and n. 20, below.

4 Douglas Lorimer has helpfully delineated the course of prior developments in mid-Victorian anthropological conceptions of race and class relations which had led to this. An equation of class distinctions as being essentially similar to racial ones first became conventional in British educated society during the 1850s and 1860s, with the rise of a neo-evolutionary Anglo-Saxonism, which envisaged the white – preferably English – 'Gentleman' as the ultimate product of civilisation and 'progress'. Lorimer, *Colour, class and the Victorians*, especially pp. 101–2, 157–60, 204; and see also Horsman, *Race and manifest destiny*. The members of other classes and races were, alike, seen as inferior charges awaiting improvement through the tutelage of their superiors. This altruistic mission

The most significant figure in this new development was the scientist, Francis Galton. As early as 1853 Galton had first published his views on the innate racial inferiority of the Africans he had encountered during his travels in south-west Africa, 1850–2.[5] But from the mid-1870s Galton provided an important new intellectual leadership for the view that factors of heredity, and not environment, were the source of all observable class and race differences. This he did through his revolutionising of the ancillary science of anthropometrics in a series of path-breaking innovations in methods of statistical analysis.

Anthropometrics, the science of the measurement and analysis of variation in the physical dimensions of the human body, offered Victorian social scientists the prospect of a forum in which the quantitative methods and rigour of the empirical natural sciences could apparently be legitimately applied to the study of man. In addition to analysing sources of physical variation by age and sex, humans could of course be classified according to any criterion in order to examine whether there were differences in the average physical proportions of such different groupings of individuals. Hair colour, eye colour, complexion and head shape were among the classifying principles attempted in the late nineteenth century which have justifiably caused some retrospective amusement.[6] But other classifications made at this time according to 'race' and social class were far more ominous matters, appearing as they did to give valuable scientific support to those wishing to believe that the visible differences between the peoples of different lands and those of different social classes within the British Isles reflected unbridgeable barriers in nature, thereby justifying inegalitarian political relationships.

Galton himself was almost exclusively interested in social class differentials in British society and it was through his work with the Anthropometric Committee of the British Association that he finally acquired the *imprimatur* of scientific respectability for his project. It was his anthropometric work which was instrumental in lending empirical, scientific credence to the core notion underlying the hereditarian version of the professional model of society: that different categories of employment recruited different levels of naturally inherited ability and physique, reflecting a linear hierarchy – or normal distribution – of ability in society.

to civilise gave to those who no longer possessed an unquestioning religious faith, a worthy life-work to live for. The working classes were therefore inferior but improvable – in response to the evangelising initiatives of their social superiors. Thus, in the early 1870s the East End came to be colonised by the Oxford students of Samuel Barnett, inspired by their settlement martyr, Edward Denison, who had died in 1868 after his pioneering stay there in the slums. Meanwhile social consciences in Cambridge were playing a broadly parallel role in pioneering the university extension movement. Meacham, *Toynbee Hall*; Simon, *Education and the labour movement*. The rapid upsurge in such optimistic missionary work at this time drew additional strength from its apparent consistency with the reinvigorated monogenist orthodoxy following the collapse of Hunt's polygenism (see n. 2), which provided scientific sanction for belief in the efficacy of the tutelary, missionary relationship between the privileged and their subordinates.

[5] Fancher, 'Francis Galton's African ethnology'.

[6] Gould, *The mismeasure of man*.

The British Association Anthropometric Committee, 1875–83

The Anthropometric Committee was formed in 1875 by several interested members of the British Association.[7] However, it was only subsequently, during the course of its eight years of deliberations that the two principal figures in the ensuing account, first Francis Galton and then Charles Roberts, came to the fore in playing their leading roles.[8] Both men began their interest in anthropometrics with a similar scientific goal: that of establishing the 'typical' physical proportions of the British population.

Francis Galton had first proposed in the early 1870s that a national anthropometric survey be conducted in order to establish whether 'the general physique of the nation' was deteriorating or improving, both absolutely and comparatively with that of other nations.[9] His initial goal was to establish a *national* standard age-specific growth profile to compare the performance of the English with their competitors. Galton's underlying motivation for this project, the hereditarian perfectibility of man – or rather of Englishmen – had already been publicly announced in his eugenic manifesto of 1869, *Hereditary genius*. This aim represented an exact inversion of the Enlightenment's broadly environmentalist ambitions. Galton claimed that since 'Civilisation is a new condition imposed upon man'[10] so 'The needs of centralisation, communication, and culture, call for more brains and mental stamina than the average of our race possess.'[11] In the competitive struggle with other nations and races, imperial mastery would only be won by the nation breeding these desirable characteristics most efficiently.[12] Galton was especially concerned that far from a desirable raising of the nation's average abilities, blind social conditions seemed to be conspiring to exert the opposite effect.

A paper which Galton had delivered to the Statistical Society of London (later the Royal Statistical Society) in January 1873 had lamented that 'the more energetic of our race, and therefore those whose breed is the most valuable to our nation, are

[7] For a full list of the original thirteen committee members and the twenty other individuals associated with its work during its eight years, see Szreter, 'The first scientific social structure', n. 1.

[8] The original Chairman and Secretary were William Farr and Francis Galton, respectively. On Farr's retirement through ill-health in 1880, Galton became the Chairman and a new member, Edward Brabrook (assistant Registrar of Friendly Societies at that time), became the Secretary. However, as will be discussed below, the Committee's important Final Report was written by Charles Roberts (on whom see below) and Rawson W. Rawson (a civil servant who had been Governor of the Bahamas and the Windward Islands before his retirement in 1875; he was President of the International Statistical Institute, 1885–98). For more information on the context and the interests of many of the figures involved on the Committee, see Kuklick, *The savage within*, *passim*.

[9] Galton, 'Proposal to apply'.

[10] Galton, *Hereditary genius*, p. 344. [11] Galton, *Hereditary genius*, p. 345.

[12] Galton's increasing involvement in the late 1860s with these issues of imperial supremacy was part of a general sense of unease which the Victorians experienced at this time, following the less than impressive military performance in the Crimea, the Indian mutiny and the new unifications of Germany and the USA. With the defeat of the Austrians at Sadowa in 1866, and then the French in 1871, the sense of growing Prussian strength and menace heightened sensitivities further. See Searle, *The quest for national efficiency*, ch. 4.

attracted from the country to our towns'.[13] Galton had then presented a series of demographic calculations based on the difference between the GRO's urban (Manchester) and 'Healthy Districts' life tables, purporting to show that the pernicious effects of the urban, high mortality environment meant that 'the adult grandchildren of artisan townsfolk are little more than half as numerous as those of labouring people who live in healthy country districts'.[14] Thus, Galton feared that dysgenic rather than eugenic social selection was in fact occurring and that the average ability of each generation was actually declining. (The notion that the observable and measurable dimensions of a race's or a class's average physical size were in some important way correlated with the less measurable property of their average mental 'ability' was, of course, the fundamental but untested assumption which underwrote the significance which Galton attached to his anthropometric work.)

At the same time that Galton was coming to the conclusion that an anthropometric survey was required, as a result of his social Darwinist speculations, Mr Charles Roberts was already engaging in such an inquiry in an official capacity. This was for the quite separate purposes of practical administration of the state's protective factory legislation.[15] Roberts was one of five doctors appointed to take anthropometric surveys of factory children for the Parliamentary Commission of 1872, which reported in 1876 on the working of the Factory and Workshop Act.[16] As a result of

[13] Galton, 'The relative supplies', p. 19.

[14] Galton, 'The relative supplies', p. 23. This, of course, was exactly the form of argument which was to be repeated to greater public effect by Karl Pearson in the 1890s and 1900s in the context of falling fertility (see pp. 73, 238–46).

[15] The administrative problem in question was that of devising a procedure for Factory Surgeons to enable them to certify whether or not a child or young person was physically capable of work, within the age limits set by Parliament. It was recognised that birth certificates, even if produced, were insufficient evidence of an individual's physical fitness for factory work, since there was such wide variation in individuals' physical development at given ages. Hence the project of determining empirically the typical proportions of children of the labouring class, so as to fix uniform minimum standards of age-specific physique to facilitate enforcement of the laws. The collection of anthropometric data by the Commission was in keeping with the precedent set by Edwin Chadwick's 1833 Factory Commission and also a subsequent inquiry by Leonard Horner in 1837. See Tanner, *A history of the study of human growth*, pp. 147–61.

[16] I have been unable to discover Charles Roberts's date and exact place of birth in Yorkshire; or his education before attending St George's Medical School in London (he died on the last day of 1901). Apparently he was an individual of ample private means. Whilst at St George's he assisted Henry Gray in the preparation of the first edition of the famous *Anatomy*. He qualified from St George's in 1859, the same year as Rugby-educated John Henry Bridges (1832–1906). (Bridges had left the Fellowship of Oriel College, Oxford, in 1855 to undertake medical training at St George's and in Paris.) Roberts then practised in York, becoming the surgeon to the North Riding prison, and FRCS in 1871. With Bridges's appointment in 1870 as one of Sir John Simon's medical inspectors at the LGB, Roberts was one of the five doctors appointed by his former colleague from medical school to work on the Parliamentary Commission. Roberts simultaneously acted as surgeon to the outpatients department at the Victoria hospital for children. Bridges is an extremely interesting figure: as well as a leading public health practitioner he was at this time becoming one of the country's principal Comtist philosophers, as translator of several of Comte's major works and lecturer to the London Positivist Society 1870–1900. On Comtism in England, see below, nn. 87, 115. Sources: for Charles

this official work, Roberts had become fascinated with anthropometrics and conceived the (never-completed) project of mounting a general scientific study of the dimensions and physical development of the British peoples.[17] As a first contribution in this direction Roberts published in 1878 *A manual of anthropometry*. This was not a major empirical study, presenting an analysis of only a few data sets which he had culled from various sources including his own official labours. It was predominantly a methodological discussion and survey of this new, international field of research. Roberts justified his proposed scientific project on a host of pragmatic grounds, concerning the advantages such knowledge would bring to the individual and to the state for maintenance of personal health and longevity, efficiency of occupational and military recruitment and so on.[18] What Roberts conspicuously did not deem it necessary to discuss at all throughout the *Manual* was the relationship of his work on the proportions of the British race to the theory of evolution.

This does not, however, mean that contemporary developments in socialised Darwinism were unimportant to Roberts's work. The reason for Roberts's lack of any detailed discussion of these issues in 1878 was probably the conventionality of his views as he saw them at this time: comprising a very gradualist, broadly Lamarckian and environmentalist understanding of evolution allied to a monogenist stance on racial differences.[19] Roberts believed that each of the 'races' of mankind was a relatively fundamental and unchanging unit produced by a process of very long-term adaptation to a characteristic set of environmental conditions prevailing over many generations during the prehistoric past. By contrast the current observable variations between individuals of the same race, for instance those found between the representatives of the middle and working classes of 'the British race', were conceptualised as due to relatively superficial current environmental influences which could not alter the long-established characteristics of the race, but merely lead to their under or overexpression in individual

Roberts, Plarr's *Lives*, and his Obituary, *British Medical Journal* 1, 181 (1902); for J. H. Bridges, *Munk's Roll* IV. For more on Bridges, see Liveing, *A nineteenth-century teacher*, with preface by L. T. Hobhouse and introduction by Patrick Geddes; and Collini, *Liberalism and sociology*, pp. 152, 216.

17 Roberts was particularly inspired towards this by reading the latest publication of the veteran Belgian statistician, Adolphe Quetelet: Quetelet, *Anthropométrie.*

18 Roberts, *Manual*, pp. 1–4.

19 This is explicitly confirmed by C. Roberts in his statement of 1891 that, 'When I first began my observations, I held with Lamarck and Herbert Spencer that acquired characters are transmitted by heredity . . . but I have more recently come to believe with Weismann and others, that acquired characters are not transmitted.' Roberts, 'On the uses', p. 13. The Lamarckian notion of use-inheritance, which Roberts implicitly endorsed in the *Manual*, emphasised the importance of the social environment in selecting, over the long term, only those variations which were 'useful' or 'fitted' to society from among the many mutations which nature spontaneously generated. With Darwin's adoption of this mode of argument in *The descent of man*, published in 1871, the early 1870s seems to have been a brief period of relative unanimity among evolutionary social theorists, during which this view held sway. See Jones, *Social Darwinism*, pp. 78–82. It was principally Francis Galton who continued to work against this consensus (see below, pp. 141–2). On Lamarckianism, see also pp. 170–3, 220–1.

specimens.[20] Thus Roberts's statement that 'The permanent and constant elements which modify the development of the human body are age, sex and race, and some of the secondary and temporary ones are disease, occupation, social habits, nurture, food, exercise, rest, etc.'[21]

Hence Roberts's initial goal at this stage in his thinking was formulated as 'fixing the typical forms of man for each age as they exist at present'.[22] He warned that

> It is necessary to bear in mind that the typical form . . . is not necessarily the most perfect form of man, but represents the equilibrium, as it were, of many contending forces which may be disturbed by the future predominance of any one of them; hence the typical form is not the same for the working and non-working man, for the man living in towns and the man living in the rural districts.[23]

During the account that follows it is important to remember this distinction which Roberts himself had so carefully made at the outset, between the neutral *descriptive* notion of the typical or average form and the *prescriptive* notion of the most perfect form.

Roberts was soon able to carry out the analysis of further anthropometric data-sets under the aegis of the Anthropometric Committee. Galton had recognised that until the government could be persuaded to fund an assay of the nation's physical attainments, anthropometry could only hope to obtain the relevant data in a relatively unsystematic way, principally wherever it might prevail upon a school teacher to take a record of the requisite measurements. This Galton did where he could, mainly through members and correspondents of the British Association. Hence, Roberts was now able to compare the large dataset of measurements generated by the Parliamentary Commission, relating predominantly to children in factory towns, with a growing miscellany relating to public and secondary school children.

In order to study the problem of *national* deterioration from such a miscellany of *ad hoc* sources, Galton had originally proposed an ingenious methodology, akin to the notion of taking a stratified sample. Galton reasoned that since 'different grades of school represent different grades of the community' the anthropometric datasets which he proposed to collect from various schools could be socially and occupationally categorised into four grades according to the type of school from which they came.[24] The four broad groupings of occupations to which each

[20] Of course, race was itself a very imprecise notion at this time, in both its putatively scientific ('analytical') and its popular ('folk') meanings. Roberts seems to have envisaged three historical racial groupings – Celtic, Scandinavian and Teutonic – as constituting 'the British race'. On the complexities of the scientific idea of race at this time, see: Banton, *The idea of race*; Lorimer, *Colour, class*; Stepan, *The idea of race*. Burrow, *Evolution and society* is excellent for a more general coverage. On the range of more popular, conventional understandings of the notion of 'race', see the helpful comments in Harris, *Private lives*, pp. 234–7. On the distinction between scientific and popular meanings, see Banton, 'Analytical and folk concepts'.

[21] Roberts, *Manual*, p. 95. [22] Roberts, 'The physical development', p. 16.

[23] Roberts, 'The physical development', pp. 16–17 (repeated verbatim in Roberts, *Manual*, p. 24).

[24] Galton, 'Proposal to apply', p. 309.

category of school supposedly applied could then be identified in the occupational returns of the 1871 census. This would show what proportion of the national population each of the four groupings of occupations constituted, and therefore what proportion of the nation each equivalent grade of school served and represented. These proportions would then provide appropriate weightings for the calculation of the overall national average figures of age-specific growth from the data collected in each of the four grades of school.

However, the classification scheme which Roberts had, independently, originally devised for his analysis of the official data was not premised on the meritocratic or status-graded image of the nation's class structure that Galton had proposed. It testifies more to his strongly environmentalist interpretation of the causes of the physical variation exhibited, which predisposed him to examine the effects on growth of urban and industrial conditions rather than social class affiliation.[25] The primary distinction drawn by Roberts was between Urban and Rural populations. The Rural category was then subdivided into Factory Districts (rural industry) and Agricultural Districts. The Urban category was also subdivided into Factory (additionally distinguishing Cotton from Woollen mills) and Non-Factory (further distinguishing those residing in Factory towns from those in Country towns). Use of this classification confirmed the strong influence of urban conditions in affecting children's growth rates.

Roberts did, however, in effect introduce a form of classification according to paternal occupation, distinguishing between the non-labouring and labouring, artisan and operative classes. His early work seemed to show that the children of the 'non-labouring' class completed their growth at younger ages and finished taller and heavier than those of the 'labouring class'.[26] This was important because it confirmed for Roberts the significance of the concept of development, or ontogeny, over that of mere 'growth' as being essential to the correct interpretation of the anthropometric data. The evidence indicated that there was a specific trajectory of physical development, in which each sequential stage had to be as fully and effectively completed to enable the proper consummation of all subsequent stages. An inadequate environment both delayed the completion of earlier stages and prejudiced the full expression of the later stages of development. As will be shown below, Roberts's ontogenic interpretation (specifically in a recapitulationist form) of the anthropometric data which he collected and analysed was to be of great significance in subsequently accounting for his opposed analysis to that offered by Galton.

Publication of *A manual of anthropometry* in 1878 established Roberts as the foremost practitioner of the new science in Britain and he was then co-opted on to the British Association's Committee, where he became its most active member. Before summarising his work to date, Roberts explained in his first contribution to the Committee that

[25] Roberts, 'The physical requirements', p. 683. [26] Roberts, 'The physical development', Table 1.

to obtain the typical proportions of the British race it would be necessary to measure a proportionate number of individuals of each class . . . If we take the census of 1871 we shall find that such a model community would consist of 14.82% of the non-labouring class, 47.46% of the labouring class, and 37.72% of the artisan and operative classes.[27]

This method was of course the same as that which had originally been suggested by Galton.[28] Roberts contrasted this with his own methods so far: 'As the statistics which I have collected in England represent various classes rather than the general population, I have arranged them in a double series – a most favoured class and a least favoured class – and I have adopted the average of the two extremes as typical of the English nation.'[29] Whichever method he referred to, it is quite clear, therefore, that at this stage the goal of Roberts's empirical work, and of the associated classification of occupations which he had now developed, was still the elucidation of the descriptive average or typical form of 'the English nation' and not the prescriptive 'most perfect form', which he had carefully distinguished at the outset of his work as a separate concept.

However, within a year of being co-opted on to the British Association Committee this had all changed. The beginning of the next Annual Report of the BA Committee described 'the scheme of classification' prepared by Mr Roberts as follows:

It is based on the principle of collecting into a standard class as large a number of cases as possible which imply the most favourable conditions of existence in respect to fresh air, exercise, and wholesome and sufficient food – in one word, nurture – and specialising into classes which may be compared with this standard, those which depart more or less from the most favourable condition.[30]

Yet as recently as 1878 Roberts had written in the *Manual*, that the difference in growth rates between 'the non-labouring and the artisan class . . . shows the marked effect of social surroundings on the development of the body; the one class being retarded and depressed by laborious occupations and insanitary influences, the other *expanded and probably exaggerated*, by the prevalence of circumstances favourable to growth' (emphasis added).[31] In other words, in his publication of 1878 Roberts considered that those individuals exhibiting characteristics which were more developed than the national average were to be considered as much a deviation from the true national type as those showing relative underdevelopment. That those subject to the 'most favourable conditions' could now in 1880 be used as a standard from which all else was to be considered a deviation or departure was clearly a radical change from Roberts's earlier emphasis on the average or modal type of the nation as a whole as the fundamental reference point for measuring variation or deviation.

[27] Report of the Anthropometric Committee, *British Association Reports* (1879), pp. 202–3. These figures were based on a calculation which Roberts had made in his *Manual*, pp. 42–3.

[28] Galton, 'Proposal to apply', pp. 308–9.

[29] Report of the Anthropometric Committee, *British Association Reports* (1879), p. 203.

[30] Report of the Anthropometric Committee, *British Association Reports* (1880), p. 121.

[31] Roberts, *Manual*, p. 99.

Roberts's new classification scheme first appeared as Table III of the 1880 Report of the Anthropometric Committee and was confirmed virtually unchanged in the Final Report of the Committee three years later.[32] As can be seen in Figure 3.1, the miscellaneous collected data on children's growth records were to be divided, *a priori*, into a series of bifurcating classifications so as to arrive at a rank order of social groups commencing with the most 'favoured' and ending with the least 'favoured'. The social units corresponded to groupings of the male parents' occupations, as distinguished for every household at the decennial census. The primary division between these social groups was that between the 'Non-labouring Classes' and the 'Labouring Classes' of the nation. This was a distinction based on the 'social condition' of each occupational milieu, by which was meant 'influences of leisure, mental and manual labour'. This division, then, was clearly felt to be the most fundamental and determinative criterion for a scale measuring achieved physical development of individuals. A modern student might be excused for supposing that this was done because that part of the nation engaged in physical labour would be much more physically developed; the reasoning was the reverse, of course! The assumption locked within this procedure was that 'social condition', in the sense of achieved social status as reflected by the prestige of the (male) parental occupation, was most strongly and reliably correlated with some kind of natural differential in physique between the individuals who were their children.[33] Social position, then, as measured by paternal occupation, was the sign by which the Elect and the Reprobate of Nature could be most unequivocally identified.

Next, these two primary conditions of existence were subdivided according to the secondary influence of 'Nurture', which was defined as 'the influences of food, clothing, nursing, domestic surroundings etc.'. The children of the 'Non-labouring Classes' were judged to have received 'Very Good' nurture if the head of household's occupation was 'Professional'. This subdivision formed the standard class, class I (including under this heading only bankers and wholesale merchants from the commercial community). The remainder of the 'Non-labouring Classes' were judged to experience only 'Good' nurturing – this applied to the Commercial Class of occupations, who were assigned to class II. For the 'Labouring Classes', their children's nurturing was judged to be either 'Imperfect' or plain 'Bad'. The former applied to class III, all artisan and skilled trades; but also to class IV, all types of labourer whose working conditions were considered to be 'Out-door' or 'Country'. Presumably, miners were included under the latter head not because of the father's occupational environment (which was clearly not 'Out-door') but because of the likely environment of his growing children. 'Bad' was then reserved for the sedentary trades and factory operatives of class V (although it is not clear why the conditions entailed by the working practices of these adults should

[32] Table XII of the Final Report of the Anthropometric Committee. *British Association Reports* (1883).

[33] Whether or not this differential was seen as ultimately due to environmental factors, as in Roberts's interpretation, or solely to heredity, as Galton believed, was still an open question (see below, pp. 144–6).

Table III.—Classification of the British Population according to *Media*, or the conditions of life.

*Social Condition.**—Non-labouring Classes			Labouring Classes.			
Nurture.†—Very Good		Good	Imperfect		Bad	Selected Classes
Professional Classes ‡ (Upper and Upper Middle Classes) 4·46 per cent.		Commercial Class (Lower Mid. Classes) 10·30 per cent.	Labourers 47·46 per cent.	Artisans 26·82 per cent.	Industrial Classes (Sedentary Trades) 10·90 per cent.	
Out-door Country §	In-door Towns	In-door Towns	Out-door Country	In-door Towns	In-door Towns	
Class I. Country-gentlemen. Gentlemen-farmers. Officers of Army and Navy. Auxiliary Forces. Clergymen. Lawyers. Doctors. Civil Engineers. Architects. Dentists.	Civil Servants. Authors. Artists. Teachers. Musicians. Actors. Bankers. Merchants (Wholesale).	Class II. Teachers in Elementary Schools. Clerks. Shopkeepers. Shopmen. Dealers in " Drugs. " Books. " Wool. " Silk. " Cotton. " Foods. " Drinks. " Furniture. " Metals. " Glass. " Earthenware. " Fuel, &c.	Class III. Labourers and Workers on Agriculture. " Gardens. " Roads. " Railways. " Quarries. Navvies. Porters. Guards. Woodmen. Brickmakers. Labourers, &c., on Water. " Sailors. " Fishermen. " Watermen. Labourers, &c., in Mines. " Coal. " Minerals.	Class IV. Workers in " Wood. " Metal. " Stone. " Leather. " Paper. &c. Engravers. Photographers. Printers. &c.	Class V. Factory Operatives. Tailors. Shoemakers. &c.	Class VI. Policemen. Fire Brigade. Soldiers. Recruits. Messengers? Industrial-Schools. Criminals. Idiots Lunatics.

* Social Condition; (influences of leisure, mental and manual labour).
† Nurture; (influences of food, clothing, nursing, domestic surroundings, &c.)
‡ Occupation; (influences of external physical conditions, exercise, &c.) Percentage of male population, including male children (Census of 1871).
§ Climatic and sanitary surroundings.

Figure 3.1 Reproduction of Table III from British Association Anthropometric Committee Report of 1880

directly influence their children's nurturing when those of the miners presumably were not supposed to do so). Thus, this process of a two-stage, *a priori* division of the data, first by 'social condition' and then by 'Nurture', had produced an ordinal scale of four hypothesized subdivisions of the population (one of which contained two classes, III and IV), each synonymous with certain groupings of male occupations.

Finally a distinction was made within the third of these four 'Nurture' categories to account for differences in 'Climate and sanitary surroundings', by which was meant a rural–urban dichotomy of the environment. This enabled class III, 'Labourers', to be divided off from class IV, 'Artisans', on the grounds that the former were 'Out-door', rural and the latter 'In-door', urban occupations. Additionally, within class I (the 'Professional Classes' of the 'Very Good' 'Nurture' category) there was an attempt to grade the occupations into an ordinal scale of three zones: entirely rural, entirely urban and intermediate.[34] Notice that the vector which Roberts had used as the primary discriminant in his first classification of 1876, the rural–urban dimension, was now relegated to the status of a third order scale of effect, whilst pride of place was assigned instead to 'social condition', that is social position according to occupational status.

The following extract from the Final Report illustrates a number of pertinent points. In particular, the classes (groupings of paternal occupations) that Roberts had developed had now come to be viewed as concrete social units, or phenomena in their own right. They were therefore generating their own derivative procedures for scientific study. We find that the classes are being invoked as basic analytical units and the anthropometric data was now being fashioned to expose most effectively the differences between these classes:

> The classification has been constructed on the physiological and hygienic laws which are familiar to the students of sanitary science, and on a careful comparison of the measurements of different classes of the people, and especially of school children of the age from eleven to twelve years. This age has been selected as particularly suited to the study of the *media* or conditions of life which influence the development of the human body, as it is subject to all the wide and more powerful agencies which surround and divide class from class, but is yet free from the disturbing elements of puberty and the numerous minor modifying influences, such as occupation, personal habits, etc., which in a measure shape the physique of older boys and adults. The data on which the classification has been based are given below. The most obvious facts which the figures disclose are the check which growth receives as we descend lower and lower in the social scale, and that a difference of five inches exists between the average statures of the best and worst nurtured classes of children of corresponding ages, and of 3 and a half inches in adults.[35]

[34] In addition to these five graded classes, there was a residual one for anomalous 'Selected Classes', by which was meant datasets which the Committee had acquired, which were evidently biased in their composition through selection of individuals on physical or mental criteria: such as policemen, military recruits, lunatics.

[35] Final Report of Anthropometric Committee, para. 53.

It had now, therefore, become a primary aim of the whole anthropometric exercise simply to measure the average physical properties of these artificially created categories, rather than those of the nation as a whole, as an empirical aid to expounding the causes of the differences between them.

Moreover, the 'national standard' had now come to be defined *prescriptively* as that of the 'best' identifiable 'class' of individuals – those who could be isolated by controlling for various influences which were considered in some sense prejudicial to the human organism obtaining its most complete, that is its physically largest, development.[36]

This was an important moment in the development of the 'scientific' study of social structure in modern Britain. It was the point at which an explicitly moral and social evaluation was introduced into a purportedly natural scientific exercise. The class of professional occupations was held up as the desirable standard in society, a natural Clerisy. The properties of this particular section of society henceforth became the main objective of analysis, rather than the more neutral descriptive concept of the national average or mode, with which the project had begun. The episode is a near-perfect historical example of the insidious manner in which the initial *ad hoc* introduction of a model – reflecting a hierarchic image of society in this case – for a specific methodological purpose (namely, to calculate a weighted average from a set of disparate data sources) can subsequently subvert the entire investigative procedure by becoming the principal subject of investigation in and for itself.

Why, then, did this change occur: from the Committee's original aim of establishing, through measurement, the nation's *average* physique, to the aim of identifying a national *ideal*? It seems most probable from the published writings available that the new hierarchical method of classification was not adopted autonomously by Roberts in 1880 but was a change which was initially foisted upon him by other(s) on the Committee, Galton's influence being strongly implicated.[37]

By the later 1870s Galton had succeeded to his own satisfaction in discrediting the weak Lamarckism which had become generally accepted since Darwin's endorsement of it in 1871.[38] Galton now gained confidence in his own strongly hereditarian predilections for a theory of natural selection and inheritance. As he put it in his memoirs: 'I had long tried to gain some insight into the relative power of Nature and Nurture, in order that due allowance might be made for Environment, neither too much nor too little.'[39] In his autobiography he claimed of a study of human twins (in fact little more than a highly selective and small-scale

[36] Final Report of Anthropometric Committee, para. 52.

[37] Galton's considerable involvement with the work of the Committee at this time is signified by his assumption of the Chairmanship during 1880 and his major contribution to the Report of the following year.

[38] See above, pp. 134–5. [39] Galton, *Memories of my life*, p. 294.

accumulation of anecdotal material) which he published in 1875 that 'The evidence was overwhelming that the power of Nature was far stronger than that of Nurture'.[40] Galton now conceived of naturally inherited characteristics as a finite number of discrete and fixed elements each determining correspondent observable mental and physical properties. This led him to an exclusive interest in that section of the nation which supposedly 'possessed' the most valuable sets of these elemental units of inheritance. Such well-endowed individuals would be instantly recognisable by their highly developed mental and physical abilities. Only they could pass on these desirable qualities to future generations. A further corollary, then, was his increased emphasis on breeding alone as the correct eugenic strategy, since the overall average abilities of the nation could only be improved or raised – always Galton's ultimate motivating aim – by this élite segment of the nation increasing itself as a proportion of subsequent generations, through out-breeding the more feeble sections.

Thus, for Galton, by the later 1870s the most important aspect of any exploratory survey of the current range of human faculties in Britain would be the clear delineation of the nature and extent of the élite section of the population, so as to establish the 'standard', which it could be hoped that the British nation would approximate in the future, given the implementation of the appropriate eugenic breeding policies. Simultaneously this would provide the yardstick to judge the scale of deterioration among the remainder of the nation. It is possible, therefore, that Galton, after being introduced to Roberts's proposed scheme in 1879, somehow prevailed upon its author to alter the focus to conform more closely with his own designs.

However, it can also be shown that by 1883, at the latest, Roberts had subsequently developed his own reasons, independent of Galton's, for presenting the classification in this hierarchical way (but it can also be shown that he does not appear to have subscribed to these more extreme views in 1880, when the new scheme was first presented). By 1883 Roberts had moved in quite the opposite direction from Galton, to an extreme form of environmental determinism. The principal evidence to support this contention is a bizarre paragraph and accompanying footnote in the Final Report of the Anthropometric Committee, submitted in 1883.[41] First, a table of statistics of height and weight of liveborn infants at birth was presented as follows: 'The table is one of great interest to the student examining the physical development and the physical improvement of a

[40] Galton, *Memories of my life*, p. 295. It seems likely that Galton may have been retrospectively encouraged to exaggerate the value of his rather flimsy positive evidence in favour of his hereditarian theory because of the more robust work of demolition, of Darwin's pro-Lamarckian 'provisional hypothesis of pangenesis', which Galton carried out in a separate study completed at the same time in 1875. For an account of the latter, see the excellent MacKenzie, *Statistics in Britain*, p. 60. MacKenzie does not mention the twins-study, despite its evident importance to Galton himself.

[41] This report was co-authored by Charles Roberts and Sir Rawson W. Rawson. But it is clear from internal evidence that the relevant part of the Report referred to here was the work of Roberts alone.

race, as it presents the materials with which he has to deal in its earliest and simplest form.'[42] It was noted that this table confirmed the slightly larger average size of viable male babies and also suggested a tendency to their greater variation around the mean than female babies. Next, the established fact of a higher rate of stillbirths among male babies in Britain was invoked. Finally the astounding inference was offered that

> the largest surviving infants are those of males. It would appear, therefore, that the physical (and most probably the mental) proportion of a race, and their uniformity within certain limits, are largely dependent on the size of the female pelvis, which acts as a gauge, as it were, of the race, and eliminates the largest infants especially those with large heads (and presumably more brains), by preventing their survival at birth [*sic*].[43]

This may seem a little overimaginative but there was more to follow, in the appended footnote. All pretensions to scientific rigour were abandoned as a handful of skeletons from the Museum of the Royal College of Surgeons were pressed into service by Roberts 'To ascertain if there is any difference between the circumference of the skull as compared with that of the pelvis in adults of different races of man.'[44] The 'hypothesis' being tested here was that European races were more intelligent than primitive ones because of their larger brains inside their larger heads. The 'proof' – and proximate cause – of this difference was supposedly found in the larger pelvic size of European females which permitted the survival of larger-headed infants.

As D. J. Cunningham, Professor of Anatomy at Edinburgh University, was to point out many years later, Roberts's comparison of European and Andaman Islanders' skeletons was not only based on a statistically meaningless sample (only a single European female skeleton was used) but furthermore the female pelvic ring was compared with adult skull circumferences, not infant ones![45] The conclusion drawn by Roberts from this exercise was that 'it is not improbable that the relatively small pelvis of the female Andamanese has been instrumental, in some measure, in differentiating that diminutive race'.[46] But the real *pièce de résistance* was the next sentence, concluding this section of the Report:

> It is probably in this direction we must look for an explanation of the degenerating influences of town life and sedentary occupations, as they, together with the new movement for the higher education of women, favour the productions of large heads and imperfectly developed bodies of women in this and other civilised countries, and a corresponding disproportion between the size of the head and the circumference of the pelvis.[47]

[42] Final Report of the Anthropometric Committee, para. 55.

[43] Final Report of the Anthropometric Committee, para. 55.

[44] Final Report of the Anthropometric Committee, footnote on p. 285.

[45] *Interdepartmental Committee on Physical Deterioration* (Evidence), para. 2241. See below, pp. 225–8.

[46] Final Report of the Anthropometric Committee, footnote on p. 287. The intrinsic inferiority of the diminutive Andamanese was, of course, assumed to be self-evidently true!

[47] Final Report of the Anthropometric Committee, footnote on p. 287.

It seems certain that Roberts did not hold this specific set of views in 1880, since it was quite deliberately pointed out in his original specification of the Committee's classification scheme that 'at birth children are of the same average size in all classes',[48] a statement that would be inconsistent with the implications of the above passages, and which was omitted from the 1883 Report, where the remainder of the paragraph from which it was drawn was reproduced *verbatim*.

In his early work Roberts had – due to his gradualist Lamarckism – attributed to environmental forces the status only of secondary effects after 'age, sex and race'. By 1883, however, the more extreme form of environmentalism which he was now espousing meant that he was prepared to argue that short-term influences acting over the lifetime of a single individual had the power to modify the dimensions of the female pelvis and thereby to exert a determining influence over the average physical size – and supposedly correlated mental abilities – of future generations. Furthermore, the environment was not only supposed to be able to exert a profound and rapid influence, but also it was now assumed that in the British, increasingly urban and industrial, context this influence was an entirely negative and degrading one. It followed that the most common human form found in Britain would simply reflect the prevalence of these degenerating urban conditions rather than the true national type. Therefore only among 'the most favoured' class of the population, the children of the upper middle professional classes, educated and brought up in their predominantly rural public schools, could the true national type be discovered.

The reasons why Roberts should have so significantly shifted his position during the period between 1880 and 1883 are obscure. It seems possible that it may partly have been a polarising reaction precipitated by closer exposure to the strongly hereditarian ideas of Galton. Apart from the more deterministic environmentalism, the attitudes and the assumptions behind the reasoning in the extracts cited, also have much in common with the pronouncements of certain craniologists such as Carl Vogt, Paul Broca and Gustave Le Bon, who worked within the ontogenic, recapitulationist evolutionary paradigm.[49] However, since Roberts was already familiar with their work by 1878 (witness the bibliography in his *Manual*), there still remains the question of why he should have become so much more attached to this school of thought between 1880 and 1883.

There is the obvious point that the relatively new theory of recapitulation was continually gaining ground during the relevant years.[50] But a more specific answer may be that recapitulation appeared to offer an explanation for an apparent anthropometric conundrum which had been increasingly vexing Roberts, something

[48] Report of the Anthropometric Committee, *British Association Reports* (1880), p. 121.

[49] See Gould, *The mismeasure of man*, pp. 100–7. For a more comprehensive treatment of recapitulation theory and its influence, see the same author's *Ontogeny and phylogeny*.

[50] Ernst Haeckel's *Generelle Morphologie*, published in Berlin in 1866, was the first coherent formulation of the recapitulationist ideas evident in the earlier work of craniologists such as Paul Broca.

to which his great mentor Quetelet had not given much attention. This was the sex-differential growth pattern, whereby girls achieved their mature adult form earlier and quicker than boys.[51] Recapitulation theory entails that the ontogeny of the individual recapitulates a putative phylogenesis of its species, conceived as a linear process of development through all supposedly lower life forms. This purported to 'explain' earlier cessation of growth in humans by the smaller female sex as being consistent with the assumption that the female was the simpler form of the more developed, larger bodied, and larger brained male sex. It seems significant that Roberts retrospectively attached great importance to this aspect of his work.[52]

Thus, Roberts can be seen in this period passing from under the spell of Quetelet and the empiricist project of simply discovering and recording the proportions of the human races, and moving on to an attempt to explain his findings in terms of evolutionary theory, and so coming under the influence of the recapitulationists.[53] The net result was an abandonment by Roberts of the search for the typical member of the British race, defined descriptively as simply the most frequently observed combination of dimensions, the modal type. The extreme form of environmentalism adopted by him, because it was asymmetrically determinist (envisaging current environmental influences only as a negative, degrading force), drove him to focus upon the children of the professional, upper middle class as the only repository of the nation's true 'genius', providing an accurate record of its developmental profile. As a result the derivative representation of social structure paradoxically came to approximate – but for entirely opposed reasons – that which was expounded by the extreme hereditarian determinist, Francis Galton.[54] This was a hierarchy of grades, defined as groupings of certain occupations which departed increasingly from the prescriptive standard of the professional upper and middle classes at the apex.

[51] Roberts's preoccupation with this matter can be found in the *Manual*, p. 25, and chs. 5, 6; and also in his contributions to the Anthropometric Committee's work: *British Association Reports* (1879), pp. 206–8, and (1880), pp. 141–7.

[52] See Charles Roberts's letter to the editor, published in *Nature* 21 August 1890; also his 'Memorandum on the medical inspection'.

[53] Quetelet's work seems to have remained entirely independent of this later school of thought: there is no reference to Haeckel in *Anthropométrie*. For further details regarding Quetelet's project, see Lazarsfeld, 'Notes on the history of quantification', pp. 299–311.

[54] Roberts remained staunchly committed to this environmentalist understanding of observable variation between individuals. Even when, subsequently, it came to be accepted that Weismann's researches had conclusively ruled out the intergenerational transmission of acquired characters, Roberts was quite prepared in 1891 to refute, head on, the support for hereditarianism, which Galton drew from this. Roberts deployed further detailed anthropometric evidence to argue that Weismann's non-transmission of physical variation simply meant that the influence upon their physical development of the conditions under which children lived was even more powerful than previously suspected, since all the observable difference between classes must be due to the differential childhood conditions currently experienced by each individual generation. Roberts, 'On the uses', especially pp. 17–18 and Diagrams II–IV; this took issue with the views expressed in the immediately preceding 'Communication from Mr. Francis Galton on international anthropometry' (pp. 10–12).

Thus, at just the point in the mid-1880s when the GRO was becoming potentially interested in the possibility of a social classification of the nation for its own epidemiological purposes, as shown in the last chapter, the practice of empirical social classification was becoming strongly associated with an evolutionist and naturalistic approach to the study of the dimensions and attributes of inequality in society. This was something potentially hostile to the interests of the moderate environmentalist ameliorationism of the public health movement, as propounded by the GRO. The principal officials of the GRO were only too well aware of all this: both Farr and his successor, William Ogle, were themselves members of the Anthropometric Committee, able to keep a close eye on its work and findings. In case it might be thought that after the mid-1880s, the anthropometric agenda might have faded into the background for the GRO, it should be noted that when, for instance, William Ogle attended the meeting of the International Statistical Institute in Vienna in 1891, virtually the first business conducted was the communication to the assembled audience of a letter from Sir Francis Galton on the subject of anthropometrics. This was followed by a formal paper by Charles Roberts, disagreeing with Galton's reading of the relationship between evolutionary theory and anthropometrics and displaying his tables of the approximate correlation between the social status grading of the nation's occupational structure and the growth patterns of children.[55]

It was Roberts's scheme that had originally demonstrated that it was feasible to identify empirically social classes or grades as groupings of male occupations, and that these classes apparently corresponded to differentials in natural endowment within the nation. However, the anthropometric data with which he was concerned did not exhibit a unidimensional pattern following conventional status gradings. As can be seen from Figure 3.2, the reproduction of Table IV of the Anthropometric Committee's 1880 Report, although all three categories of manual workers fell comfortably below the two non-manual categories, it was the lowest-status labourers who recorded the 'best' anthropometric measurements amongst the manual classes, followed by the artisans – of highest manual status – with the medium-status factory operatives coming last. In other words the graded social classes were shown to exhibit differential life-chances, as measured by average achieved physical development, but it appeared that this primary association could be modified to a significant degree by other factors associated with the extent to which the occupations within a class entailed an urban existence. This seemed to confirm the notion of 'urban degeneration': from agricultural labourers to factory operatives.

While these findings corresponded to the idea with which Francis Galton had started in the early 1870s, after 1875 the clarification and hardening of his understanding of differences as due only to heredity made such a finding at best a

[55] Roberts, 'On the uses'; see n. 54.

Table IV.—Table showing the Relative Statures of Boys of the age of 11 to 12 years, under different social and physical conditions of life. The zig-zag line running through the means shows the degradation of stature as the boys are further and further removed from the most favourable conditions of growth. (C. Roberts.)

Height in inches	Total No. of Obs.	Public Schools		Middle-class Schools		Elementary Schools				Military Asylums	Pauper Schools	Industrial Schools	Total per-centages
		Country	Towns	Upper — Towns	Lower — Towns	Agricultrl. Labourers — Country	Artisans — Towns	Factories and Work-shops: Country	Factories and Work-shops: Towns		?		
60 to 61	6	2 1			3 1		1						2
59–	16	2 1		3 1	5 1	2 1	2 1			1			5
58–	35	9 6		9 3	8 2	5 1	0 1	2 1		2			15
57–	66	11 8		17 6	13 4	4 2	4 2	5 1	5 1	7 1		1 1	25
56–	118	21 14		23 8	27 7	14 4	4 2	10 3	3 1	15 2			42
55–	230	28 19		35 12	57 14	32 10	15 8	13 6	17 5	33 4			78
54–	329	33 22		53 18	68 17	47 16	24 13	36 12	20 6	46 6		2 3	113
53–	361	15 10		55 19	58 15	47 16	26 15	34 13	38 11	84 10		4 6	115
52–	441	14 9		37 12	61 15	58 19	36 20	52 17	59 17	118 14		6 9	132
51–	370	6 5		25 9	40 10	36 12	28 15	45 16	57 17	123 14		10 15	113
50–	367	7 4		23 7	27 7	32 10	17 10	46 15	61 18	143 17		11 18	106
49–	252	2 1		8 3	20 5	14 5	12 6	31 10	40 12	114 14		11 18	74
48–	132			3 1	1 1	7 2	4 3	11 4	20 6	76 9		10 15	41
47–	102			3 1	4 1	5 1	7 3	5 1	13 3	59 7		6 9	28
46–	22					1 1	1 1	3 1	7 2	7 1		3 4	10
45–	12								1 1	10 1		1 1	3
44–	1									0		1 1	1
43–	1									1			
42 to 43	1									1			
Total	2862	150 100		294 100	392 100	304 100	181 100	293 100	341 100	840 100		66 100	90
Average height	52·60	54·98		53·85	53·70	53·01	52·60	52·17	51·56	51·20		50·02	
Mean height	52·5	55·0	54·5	54·0	53·5	53·0	52·5	52·0	51·5	51·0	50·5	50·0	

Figure 3.2 Reproduction of Table IV from British Association Anthropometric Committee Report of 1880

diversion, if not a positive embarrassment to his new view that breeding was everything. The British Association's summary findings, principally Roberts's interpretation as published in the Final Report, had indicated that somatic environmental conditions – the principal source of differences between town and countryside – were, after all, of great import. Hence Francis Galton rarely if ever mentioned the British Association work and its results in any of his subsequent writings on anthropometrics.

Instead, in the (in)famous Huxley lecture of 1901 Francis Galton finally formally united the two social science 'schools', whose previously independent interests in empirical social classification had so inhibited the GRO's own earlier curiosity. Galton fused his own anthropometric and the Marshallian evolutionary conceptions of the nation's social structure when he invoked Charles Booth's (not Charles Roberts's) social classification of occupations as representing a hierarchy of 'civic worth'.[56] The immense political conservatism and social élitism embodied in this 'ill-grounded fantasy'[57] cannot be better illustrated than by quoting the fundamental Galtonian belief which was being rationalised in this way: 'It follows that men who achieve eminence and those who are naturally capable are to a large extent identical.'[58] This model of society was precisely the one being actively utilised by the biometric school in the first years of the twentieth century for its empirical researches into both physical deterioration and class-differential mortality, as well as the alarming, and only recently perceived, related danger that the supposedly least fit part of the nation – the manual working class – was reproducing most of the subsequent generation. Ultimately, it was only in reaction to the aggressive claims regarding social policy, derived from this naturalistic hereditarian exposition of social structure, that the environmentalists of the public health and public service professions mobilised their own alternative, collectivist and interventionist, 'sociological' analysis of social stratification, as we shall see in the next chapter.

Ideological origins of Galton's professional model: the aristocratic liberal meritocracy

In the above account, the grading of children and society into socially classed categories of schools, supposedly unambiguously associated with occupationally

[56] Henrika Kuklick has suggested that another aspect of Booth's social survey methodology may well have been borrowed just a couple of years previously by Galton's anthropological colleague, W. H. R. Rivers, when he adopted Booth's 'genealogical method' for the rapid compilation of family histories from his informants in the Torres Straits expedition: Kuklick, *The savage within*, p. 140 (and see p. 225). The close relationship and possibilities for intellectual exchange between those studying the poor in Britain and the 'primitive' abroad flowed, of course, from the encompassing social evolutionary perspective within which these phenomena were addressed. But it should be borne in mind that the genealogical method of focusing on family households had a longer pedigree in social investigation, dating back at least to Frédéric Le Play's classic mid-century monographs (published in Paris in 1855 as *Les Ouvriers Européens*) on the patriarchal stem family, which were also pioneering studies in urban anthropology and industrial ethnography.

[57] This is Bernard Norton's term: 'Psychologists and class', p. 291.

[58] Galton, *Hereditary genius* (1892 edition), p. 33: cited in Norton, 'Psychologists and class', p. 295.

defined grades of social position, was an all-important methodological threshold, over which both Galton and Roberts rapidly and apparently quite unworriedly strode in pursuit of their anthropometric endeavours. But where did this fateful categorisation come from? The short answer is that it represented the common-sense consensus of the liberal intellectual class, the social status group (in the Weberian sense of identity group) to which Roberts and Galton belonged. The amplification of this short answer – what exactly this all-important common sense constituted – requires the remainder of this section to describe.

In his proposals in the 1870s Francis Galton set out his original taxonomy of four grades of school, and the assertion that they each closely represented a particular socio-occupational class. In this Galton was merely following the apparently authoritative official views expressed in the Report of the Taunton Commission of 1864–8, the last of the three major Royal Commissions on the nation's schools which had successively sat over the course of the previous decade.[59] The Commissioners had concluded that both as a matter of fact and as a matter of preferred policy there existed – and should exist – three grades of secondary school each serving a distinct grading of the populace, occupationally defined and quite clearly hierarchically differentiated. In its Report the Commission inconsistently claimed that this tripartite classification was merely a *de facto* distinction corresponding to already established patterns of parental wishes and behaviour (see quotation immediately below in the text), while also citing the views of Viscount Sandon, who had presented this tripartite classification as one that he would like to see implemented, clearly thereby implying that it was not as yet the extant state of affairs.[60]

Commencing with the boarding public schools and a few of the most promising urban grammar schools, this first grade was seen as a corps of 'classical schools' appropriate for the children of the most cultured, the upper middle class of future Gentlemen: public leaders, senior professionals and administrators. Second grade grammar schools were to be for the middle middle class, those with a managerial life in commerce and industry or as junior professionals ahead of them. The third grade was for the lower middle class: 'commerce of the shop and town', including higher craft trades.[61] The Commission recognised, overall, four grades of educational establishment and vocational training. The fourth grade was defined by attendance at the elementary school only, appropriate for the majority of the children of the propertyless, manual working classes, who were destined to remain in the same

[59] The Newcastle Commission on the state of popular education 1858–61; the Clarendon Commission on the revenues and management of certain colleges and schools (the nine ancient public schools), 1861–4; and the Taunton Commission, (known as the Schools Inquiry Commission and investigating other forms of endowed and secondary schooling), 1864–8.

[60] Viscount Sandon (Dudley F. S. Ryder, 1831–1900), later known as 3rd Earl of Harrowby and responsible for the 1876 Elementary Education Act when he was Vice-President of the Committee of Council on Education, had been Baron Taunton's Private Secretary when, as the commoner Henry Labouchere, Taunton had been at the Colonial Office, 1856–8). Simon, *Studies in the history*, p. 323.

[61] The class terms, 'upper middle', 'middle middle' and 'lower middle', were those of Viscount Sandon, reproduced by the Commissioners in their Report: Simon, *Studies in the history*, p. 323.

social position as their parents. As the Report acknowledged of its three grades of secondary school, 'It is obvious that these distinctions correspond roughly, but by no means exactly, to the gradations of society. Those who can afford to pay more for their children's education will also, as a general rule, continue that education for a longer time.'[62]

The Commission took it that apart from discussing curricula, its main business was the relatively technical matter of prescribing clearly demarcated leaving-age limits and fee levels for each of the three grades of secondary school, to make sure that they each catered properly for their distinct, occupationally and socially graded constituency within the nation, without any economically wasteful or socially confusing overlap. Where the third grade of secondary school should charge no more than £4 per annum, the first grade should charge no less than £60 (and no more than £120). Education in the first grade was to be primarily geared to entrance through examination into the reformed universities and so was to continue until eighteen or nineteen years of age; completion of education at sixteen years of age was deemed sufficient for those attending second grade schools; while those destined for the lower middle class had finished their education at fourteen.[63] In summary of its approach and vision, the Committee stated:

> It will be seen that we also propose to accept the distinction that we already find, and to classify schools side by side, so that a parent, according to the destination for which he intends his son, may place him from the first in a school of the third grade, or of the second, or of the first. The three grades do not lead one into the other, but stand side by side, starting it may be said from the same point, but leading to different ends.[64]

There could hardly be a clearer statement of endorsement for a simultaneously hierarchical and conservative model of social structure.

The Commissioners quite explicitly envisaged a linear status hierarchy of distinct grades defined by male occupational, vocational position. This is amply illustrated in the terminology of their opening discussions of the relationships between these grades and the appropriate curricula for them.[65] Motives of those paying for the first grade schools were 'to keep their sons on a high social level. And they would not wish . . . to let their children sink in the social scale.'[66] The immediately following discussion of the second grade of schooling commenced with 'When we *come down* to the second grade of education', and thence to 'The third grade of education [which] belongs to a class distinctly *lower* in the scale' (emphases added).[67]

The content of the curriculum was similarly to be linearly graded according to degree of classical content. Again the discussion in the Report takes the form of a

[62] *Report of the Schools Inquiry Commission* PP 1867–8 XXVIII (hereafter Taunton Report), p. 16.
[63] Taunton Report, pp. 78–88.
[64] Taunton Report, pp. 94–5; cited in Sutherland, *Ability, merit and measurement*, p. 105.
[65] Taunton Report, ch. 1 (pp. 15–21).
[66] Taunton Report, p. 18. [67] Taunton Report, pp. 18, 20.

conflation between the prescriptive views of the Commissioners themselves and the supposedly inescapable facts of the blind forces of demand – the parents' socially graded wishes. On the assumption that the necessarily protracted process of a thorough acquaintance with the classics was the only true source of the liberal culture requisite for an imperial governing class, this was to be the core curriculum for the first grade, including a direct knowledge of ancient Greek. A modest leavening of mathematics and other more purely vocational 'modern' subjects, such as modern languages, natural science and modern history was, however, admissible in these schools. In second grade schools, these were expected to play a more central role, with classics relatively diminished such that it was expected that while there would be 'a high place to Latin', 'they would hardly give Greek any place at all'.[68] In the third grade there was no talk of classics at all. The Commissioners reported that

> The need of this class is described briefly . . . to be 'very good reading, very good writing, very good arithmetic' . . . they merely 'wish to learn whatever their betters learn' . . . their wish . . . is . . . a clerk's education; namely, a thorough knowledge of arithmetic, and ability to write a good letter. It cannot be said that this is aiming at much, and it is to be wished that parents even of this rank should learn the value of a somewhat higher cultivation. But the more their demand is considered the more thoroughly sensible it seems.[69]

The Commission's Report was a masterpiece of disguised ideology *à la mode anglaise*: a highly specific piece of social engineering for the design of the nation's future educational institutions presented as little more than a down-to-earth summary of current practices as expressed in the simple patterns of consumer demand. The Commissioners took it that their prime task was to ensure that the design of society's educational institutions continued to perform the essential function of the reproduction of this class structure from parent to son.

This patriarchal, dynastic model of social structure and educational policy was, of course, profoundly socially conservative. As the first two quotations from the Report illustrate, it was hardly a positive programme for educationally developing the nation's individuals. Its technical justification depended on the crude reiteration of the by now rather worn and rusting iron laws of classical political economy: the inevitable market outcomes of individual preferences (parental intentions) constrained by costs (of different lengths of education). There was a bland acceptance that parental – specifically paternal – market position necessarily must continue strongly to determine both educational aspirations and attainments, as a general rule.

But where, in turn, did this socially conservative, neo-aristocratic, hierarchical conception of British society in the mid-Victorian decades come from? Unlike most of the previous and subsequent government interest and official inquiries into education in Victorian Britain, there was strong unanimity of opinion among

[68] Taunton Report, p. 18. [69] Taunton Report, p. 20.

the great and the good called upon to participate in the Taunton Commission. Unusually for an education inquiry there was a cosy consensus and this was also true of the closely related predecessor, the Clarendon Commission of 1861–4, which examined the nine great public schools. Partly this was simply because of the lower profile, in the elective and voluntary matter of secondary education, of the fraught issue of denominational religious instruction, which had bedevilled and sunk all the many parliamentary efforts to provide some kind of universal elementary education for over a generation (until Forster's compromise of 1870 subsequently broke the deadlock).

But it was also a reflection of the extremely high degree of consensus among the principal figures and officials most intimately involved with the construction of these two seminal Reports. This was no accident of circumstance. The unanimity of viewpoint resulted from an incestuous overlap in the key institutions and personnel participating. Two of the most active participants, Stafford Northcote and Frederick Temple, were paradigms of this on both counts. Northcote was educated at Eton and Balliol College, Oxford, before becoming Gladstone's Private Secretary in 1842; he co-authored the famous Northcote–Trevelyan Report on the Home Civil Service of 1853; influenced the important Report on the Indian Civil Service of the following year; and served on both the Clarendon and the Taunton Commissions.[70] Frederick Temple was also an undergraduate (and then Fellow) of Balliol from 1839 to 1848 and was a principal leading light within Benjamin Jowett's Balliol coterie.[71] Jowett and Temple were two of the seven contributors to the famous *Essays and reviews* of 1860, which laid down the liberal, Broad Church gauntlet challenging the incumbent Tory Anglican hierarchy, and they therefore shared the same baptism of fire in the subsequent vilification from their fellow clergymen. As Headmaster of Arnold's revered Rugby from 1857 to 1868, Frederick Temple's views carried great weight with the Clarendon Commissioners.[72] He was also both member, witness and author of large parts of the Taunton Report itself![73]

As if this were not enough, from its formation in 1849 until 1900, through its four successive Permanent Secretaries, Balliol and Jowett enjoyed uninterrupted direct

[70] Sir Stafford Henry Northcote (1818–87), 1st Earl Iddesleigh. His political career began as Gladstone's Private Secretary in 1842 and culminated as Disraeli's Chancellor of the Exchequer, 1874–80.

[71] Benjamin Jowett (1817–93), Regius Professor of Greek at Oxford 1855–93 (Vice-Chancellor of the university 1882–6); was College Tutor, 1842–70, and became Master, 1870–93. See below, pp. 157–8. Frederick Temple (1821–1902), was a mere Major's son born in the Ionian Islands and educated at Blundell's School, Tiverton. Following his career in education, he subsequently became Bishop of Exeter, 1869–85, Bishop of London, 1885–97, and eventually Archbishop of Canterbury, 1897–1902. His son William Temple (1881–1944), also Balliol (after Rugby, of course), also rose to be Archbishop of Canterbury (1942–4)! To complete the circle, William Temple also played a considerable role in seeing through the major educational legislation of his age: the 1944 Education Act.

[72] The popular, retrospective apotheosis of Dr Thomas Arnold's headmastership of Rugby school (1828–41) appeared in the year Temple took over the Headmastership, with the publication of Thomas Hughes's *Tom Brown's schooldays*.

[73] Sutherland, *Ability, merit and measurement*, p. 105.

influence over the Privy Council's Education Department – the administrative office of government responsible for advising on educational policy and for managing all inquiries.[74] Where the detailed design of the nation's education policy was concerned, therefore, the main actors and their formative institutions principally comprised a small and powerful caucus. It was Benjamin Jowett's Balliol College which was the true epicentre of this nexus of influence over the official education reports.

Indeed, the reverberating ideological and political influence of the Balliol and Jowett connection over the design of that part of the nation's social policy most relevant to the genesis of the Registrar-General's professional model was a continuous one through to the 1920s. The crucial Interdepartmental Physical Deterioration Committee of 1903–4, whose inquiry will be dealt with in great detail in the next chapter, was chaired, and in fact largely organised behind the scenes, by the powerful Clerk of the Privy Council, Sir Almeric Fitzroy, another product of Jowett's Balliol.[75] And T. H. C. Stevenson's superior during the period he was developing the professional model, Bernard Mallet, the Registrar-General 1909–20, was, again, from the same stable, eight years Fitzroy's junior.[76]

What this group predominantly shared, which is important in accounting for the particular representation of society informing their reports, was a specific ideological solution to the common social and moral predicament which all in the educated, governing class of their generation faced. This was the fundamental dilemma for liberal rationalists of their age: what to believe in, in an age which had convincingly questioned the authenticity of the biblical scriptures, and how to construct an associated collective moral code to order social and political relationships in a fast-changing and commercial culture. Jeremy Bentham and his felicific calculus of utilitarianism had produced a rational solution to this problem, which had certainly had some influence in the 1830s and 1840s; but its rigorous materialism, hedonistic sensation psychology and the hollow pleasure-maximiser at its centre were guaranteed to offend the more Romantic and idealist sensibilities of precisely those who were most exercised by this problem of moral uncertainty and reasoned legitimacy.[77]

[74] The four Balliol Permanent Secretaries were: R. R. W. Lingen (1849–69); F. R. Sandford (1870–84); P. Cumin (1884–90); G. W. Kekewich (1890–1900). For more on the extensive Balliol connections, with their virtual fiefdom in the Education Department (and also, to some extent, the influence of Trinity College, Cambridge), see: Roach, *Public Examinations*, ch. 1; R. Johnson, 'Administrators in Education before 1870'.

[75] Fitzroy was a Modern History graduate in 1874. He spent the intervening decades before his appointment to the Clerkship in 1898 climbing the civil service hierarchy – inevitably within the Privy Council's Education Department! For more on Sir Almeric William Fitzroy (1851–1935), see below, ch. 4, n. 11.

[76] For more on Bernard Mallet, see below, pp. 249 (n. 49), 267.

[77] The range of debate which was provoked by pondering these metaphysical and (ultimately) ontological questions was both complex and vast. Theology, philosophy, literature, political economy, natural science, sociology and all the nascent sciences of man all participated in this vital debate, making Britain's intellectual history in the first two-thirds of the nineteenth century a subject

Since the post-Newtonian flowering of natural theology – the peculiarly Anglican variant of the Enlightenment – the Church of England had long ago allowed prescriptive religious truth to become embroiled with the dangerously provisional 'truths' revealed by descriptive empirical science. During the nineteenth century liberal, rationalist scholarship had successfully claimed a right to have its say in the matter of the interpretation of the truths of the scriptures themselves.[78] The disputes which then arose from the products of critical biblical exegesis, over such fundamentals as the exact course and significance of the life, actions and teachings of Jesus, had devastating consequences for the authority of Christian religion in general and for the theological unity of the established, Anglican church in particular.

Essays and reviews, published in 1860, was not simply a late contribution to theological debate. It was also an incendiary device, constructed by those, led by Jowett, who wished to see the colleges of Oxford University transformed from a set of stolid Anglican seminaries into a central institution in the nation's political and cultural life, training its secular leaders. Jowett's vision informed what was ultimately a relatively successful campaign, whereby the colleges of Oxbridge did sufficiently reform themselves so that they effectively acquired and 'nationalised' the education of the governing élite, drawing their sons (and later daughters) away from both the new provincial universities and the older Scottish universities (which had been so influential in the early nineteenth century).[79] But the earlier stages of the process were anything but foregone conclusions and created seismic ructions within the church and the universities.

There was a considerable degree of common ground between the reformers and the long-standing, wider politics of reforming radicalism and liberalism, with its attack on Old Corruption, of which the Established Church and its vested interests offered many prime examples. The university reformers were attempting, against a bitterly fought rearguard action, to lever the Established Church out of its central, controlling position within the nation's most prestigious institutions of learning. This they did by exposing the intellectual weaknesses of the prescriptive claims of clerical dogma to scriptural and scientific authority and by drawing attention to the intellectually illiberal nature of its extensive institutional powers of

of almost inexhaustible proliferation in its scope. All that can be offered in the text here is an attempt briefly to abstract one or two strands relating to the aspects most relevant for uncovering the deeper ideological origins of the official professional model of social classes of 1911. Apart from the studies referred to in the following footnotes, other relevant contributions on important aspects of the intellectual history of the period have included: Soloway, *Prelates and people*; Young, *Mind, brain and adaptation*; Stocking, *Victorian anthropology*; Desmond, *The politics of evolution*.

[78] The pioneering work of this kind was *The life of Jesus, critically examined*, published in German in 1835–6 by David Friedrich Strauss (1808–74) and translated into English by George Eliot as her first published work, in 1846. Strauss argued that much that was reported in the gospels regarding Jesus had a mythic rather than factual status.

[79] Harvie, *The lights of Liberalism*, pp. 14, 21. Harvie points out that this was an almost contemporary analysis: Campbell, *The nationalisation of the old English universities* (1901).

patronage and influence.[80] Christopher Harvie has seen this as an early part of a larger process, more or less successfully promulgated, of cultural formation of an anti-clerical Liberal Academy committed to the principles of free inquiry, symbolically completed in 1903 with the foundation of the British Academy.[81]

The principal idea which provided these mid-Victorian liberal rationalists with a substitute for the moral certainty which had been supplied by the ancient revealed truths of scripture was the dynamic concept of evolution. This was not, of course, specifically Darwinian evolution, but the more general idea which long antedated his theories and can be found in the conjectural histories of the eighteenth century: social, human evolution, taken in its broadest, metaphorical sense to include the related but separable notions of development and progress.[82] In other words, history with a direction to it.

It was this concept, envisaging a positive evaluation of change in social relations and possibly even in the mental constitution of human beings themselves, which was for these Victorians fundamental to the solution of the beckoning moral hiatus. The concept of evolution offered the promise that absolute, transcendental moral order could, in fact, be discerned by the sufficiently discriminating mind. From the radically dynamic phenomena of material, historical change in an industrialising landscape, from the great cultural variation evident to the travellers and administrators of a far-flung empire, and even from the relativist confusion of differing faiths and theologies, the idea of evolution meant that it was possible in principle to chart a direction. This was both descriptive and prescriptive: an

[80] These mid-Victorian reforms also represented the long-term flowering of the Reform generation of Dissenter and Evangelical educationists, most active from the second decade of the nineteenth century onwards. From their first efforts can be traced a very slow transforming movement through the structure and content of the nation's education system from the bottom up. This started with elementary schooling for the poor and then the foundation or reconstruction of non-Anglican secondary schools for the commercial and well-to-do middle classes, offering an efficient course in the 'modern' vocational subjects for which there was massive demand among the increasingly affluent urban, commercial and artisan class: economics, accounting, sciences, languages. Simon, *Studies in the history*; Gardner, *The lost elementary schools*. A small core of reform-minded headmasters of Anglican public schools, such as Arnold of Rugby, G. H. Moberly of Winchester and Christopher Wordsworth at Harrow, began to respond to this challenge, supplementing their exclusively classics orientation with modern studies. They also began the process of converting England's almost defunct public schools into model institutions for infusing their privileged and sometimes aristocratic wards with their own leadership version of the new, dutiful Puritan ethos of 'godliness and good learning': Newsome, *Godliness and good learning*. The influence of this vanguard of the movement was rapidly magnified through the subsequent careers in education, as masters and headmasters in other public and secondary schools and as administrators and university academics, of many of the most able and favoured students of this first generation of reformed patrician institutions, the hand-picked prefects of the sixth form. For instance, at least eighteen of Arnold's own pupils and four of his assistant teachers at Rugby themselves became renowned headmasters, including James Prince Lee at King Edward's School, Birmingham (1839–47), J. D. Collis at Bromsgrove School (1843–67), Rev. Herbert Hill at Warwick School (1843–76) and Dawson W. Turner at Liverpool Royal Institution (1846–74). Honey, *Tom Brown's universe*, ch. 1.

[81] Harvie, *The lights of Liberalism*, pp. 19–21.

[82] Burrow, *Evolution and society*.

evolutionary viewpoint both ranked and ordered the evidence and – critically – provided a moral guide through it.

If it was possible to discern the direction of movement, the direction of history, then it was possible to know what was right and what was wrong; and how to act in order best to pursue the path of history. As Boyd Hilton's *Age of atonement* has shown, the 1850s and 1860s were the decades during which such an optimistic, dynamic belief in social and human evolution became conventional in educated society. The mid-Victorians talked of Progress, and the improvement in this life of 'character': the divine presence was incarnational and inspirational. This vanquished the soteriological preoccupations with atonement of a previous generation, which had still been committed to a static conception of man and society: the Adam and Eve of the Fall condemned forever to toil and anguish in a Malthusian world of limits. The sheer undeniable facts of an ever-increasing material prosperity sustained throughout these two decades, allied to the accumulating weights of geological and biological evidence against Genesis and of scriptural criticism questioning the gospels, had discredited the cosmology of centuries; and in its place an incarnational optimism had arisen, a new faith – in Progress.

But progress and improvement towards what? Exactly how to know and to define the nature of Progress remained the necessarily tautological proposition at the heart of the new teleology. As Stefan Collini has argued, the Victorian ethical ideal of manly 'character' was the essence of the solution to this conundrum.[83] The mid-Victorians believed that the historical and the desirable direction of social evolution was towards the production of a society of high-minded, spiritually and aesthetically superior, ethically impeccable, physically resilient individuals (in fact, adult males: patriarchs).[84]

The Victorian ideal of manly 'character' – *Das Gentlemanideal* – was the key concept which performed the intellectual sleight-of-hand of simultaneously providing the goal, the purpose, the means and the explanation for the occurrence of social evolution. Those who had it, or were near approximations, could help others towards it, simply by being it to the best of their ability. Moreover for those who were the incarnation of this state of grace there was a compelling public duty upon them to be as active as possible in proselytising and improving those less fortunate than themselves: the uncivilised 'races' abroad and at home.

[83] Collini, *Public moralists*, chs. 2–3, 5; and Hilton, 'Manliness'.

[84] As José Harris has pointed out ethical idealists in fact experienced little problem in adopting a social evolutionist perspective: 'Political thought', p. 124. Because the term 'evolution' has been so closely associated with Darwin's theories and because of the relentless materialism of the blind mechanism of natural selection, the ease with which a social evolutionist and an idealist perspective can be combined has not always been obvious. Correspondingly, it has only been established by modern scholarship, with the publication and interpretation of his early notebooks, how 'social' and implictly moral Darwin's own views of evolution were from the very beginning of his project: Greene, 'Darwin as a social evolutionist'; Schweber, 'The origin'. Darwin's work was an integral part of the wider, anthropological rationalist project of 'naturalising morality' described by Gay Weber: the search to replace the theological with a natural scientific sanction for the moral order. Weber, 'Science and society', p. 280.

The Cambridge historian, J. R. Seeley, published – anonymously – in 1865 the most eloquent and persuasive text of the new incarnational creed: *Ecce homo*, a new life of Jesus for the age of scientific progress.[85] Many other colleagues and students, apart from Jowett's circle, were also involved in this generational phenomenon of recasting an ideology of leadership and active intervention in the world in terms that appeared to reconcile the dictates of both religious ethics and rationalist science.[86] An important feature of this wave of reinvigorating intellectual reassessment was its championing of self-sacrificing active leadership on the part of the ruling classes as their new road to Damascus. As such it was influential in leading to a culturally improved and spiritually uplifted nation. The 1867 Reform Act granting votes to a part of the working class for the first time, the environmentalist Sanitary revival of 1866–75, the momentous educational reforms and much of the other legislation enacted by Gladstone's great reforming administration of 1868–74 were to a considerable extent inspired by this reinvigorated, optimistic political and social philosophy, which had flowered in the 1860s.

This, then, was how this generation of liberal rationalists solved their dilemma of moral legitimation and the construction of social values for an individualist, commercial age. The active cultivation by moral individuals of an altruistic 'character' of public leadership provided the concept which enabled a smooth articulation to take place between the fierce, rhetorical individualism of mid-Victorian society, the idea of universal social evolution, and the resurgent ethical idealism, which was quite definitely at the heart of Benjamin Jowett's belief system and teaching.[87]

It was specifically through the direct medium of Jowett's circle that the design

[85] Rothblatt, *The revolution of the dons*, ch. 5.

[86] For further information on such other important figures as A. L. Smith in Oxford, Henry Sidgwick, John Graham or F. D. Maurice in Cambridge, see the classic accounts of Richter, *The politics of conscience*, and Rothblatt, *Revolution of the dons*; and also Harvie, *The lights of Liberalism*. For various other important dimensions of this movement see, for instance: Stedman Jones, *Outcast London*; Turner, *The Greek heritage in Victorian Britain*; Meacham, *Toynbee Hall*; Kadish, *The Oxford economists*.

[87] Through his early championing and popularising of Plato, rather than the more fashionable Aristotle, Jowett was able to maintain an idealist philosophical critique of commercial and industrial society across the mid-century decades, when materialist, Comtian Positivism, as refined by J. S. Mill, seemed to be sweeping all before it as a social science or philosophy. See Turner, *The Greek heritage*, pp. 414–56. Jowett's major publication was the four-volume *The Dialogues of Plato, translated into English with analyses and introductions* (Oxford 1871; and five-volume 2nd edition in 1875). On the rising popularity of Comtian thought in England (unlike elsewhere in Europe) in the 1860s and 1870s, see Harvie, *The lights of Liberalism*, pp. 21–4; Cashdollar, *The transformation of theology*; and, more generally, Annan, *The curious strength of Positivism*. Alongside Matthew Arnold, Jowett was the primary intellectual link between the Romantic, paternalist idealism of Coleridge and Carlyle and the ethical idealism of his charismatic younger colleague at Balliol, T. H. Green, whose influence was to proliferate so widely in English thought throughout the closing decades of the century, ultimately transforming the nature of political Liberalism. Collini, 'Hobhouse, Bosanquet and the state'; Collini, *Arnold*, ch. 5. T. H. Green (1836–82) was not only a Jowett product but also, before entering Balliol, a product of Temple's Rugby. He symbolised the nature of Temple and Jowett's educational and university reforms even in the terms of his own appointment as a Fellow of Balliol College in 1860: Green was its first ever non-clerical Fellow. On Green, see Richter, *The politics of conscience*.

of the nation's education system and the intimately associated representation of society which it both served and created came so closely to reflect this idealist and paternalist vision of social evolution led by a Gentlemanly élite. As Frank Turner has noted: 'Jowett was not a democrat. He remained all his life a thoroughgoing elitist and paternalist. Jowett desired enlightened change and progress, but he did not want reform at the cost of order',[88] and 'the elitism of both Plato and Jowett meshed quite neatly with the growing conservatism of the British intellectual nation during the latter part of the century'.[89] Furthermore, it was integral to the idealist position of both Jowett and Matthew Arnold, in opposition to the natural right philosophy, that they were intensely hostile to what they saw as the character-corroding philistinism of commercialism, utilitarianism and the mere pursuit of material self-interests, which characterised the activities of those involved in a market society. Hence the clarity and confidence of their ranking of society and the grading of the educational system according to how distant each social group was from the sordid exchanges of the market place; and hence the blindness in the scheme to the place of the business class, born of a deep disdain.

The two inquiries on secondary schools in the 1860s and their resulting definitions of the social and economic roles of different kinds of school were an administrative follow-up and response to the implications of the previous decade's reforms of Oxford and Cambridge, the Indian civil service, and the statutory formation of the General Medical Council as a model for self-regulation of the nation's professions. In all these cases the 1850s was the decade of the arrival of the examination; and in the Northcote–Trevelyan Report of 1853 examination was proposed even for the Home Civil Service – though this did not arrive formally until 1870.[90] A new apparatus spawned by the ideology of meritocracy, the written examination, had now emerged to challenge (though never quite to replace) the nobility's traditional method of personal recommendation and patronage as the central cultural mechanism for acquiring position and status in civil society.[91] The reports of the reform commissions of the 1850s, like those of the 1860s, were principally conceived, staffed and written by the scions of this ascendant, meritocratic liberal intelligentsia.[92]

Given the flavour and consistency of the recommendations of the official educational inquiries, it becomes somewhat more understandable that Galton's contemporaneous eugenic manifesto and his subsequent proposals for an empirical

[88] Turner, *The Greek heritage*, p. 429. [89] Turner, *The Greek heritage*, p. 415.

[90] Roach, *Public examinations in England*. [91] Bourne, *Patronage and society*.

[92] A paradoxical result of the 1832 Great Reform Act's abolition of much aristocratic patronage in politics had been to render Parliamentary politics and ministerial careers less accessible than before for many young men of talent but only modest means. Those with political aspirations and the requisite ability therefore subsequently tended instead to carve out administrative careers for themselves in the departments of the central government and its famous inspectorates. Hence the peculiar importance, especially during the central third of the nineteenth century, of these 'statesmen in disguise' in shaping British government and society, as famously emphasised by MacDonagh, 'The nineteenth-century revolution in government'; and Clark, 'Statesmen in disguise'.

anthropometric analysis should have been alike suffused with an apparently unquestioned belief in an actual, empirically visible social hierarchy of occupational and vocational achievements similar in all essentials to that envisioned in the Taunton Report. Galton was himself in 1822 born into that set of intermarrying families who have been identified as an élite within the liberal, middle-class reform movement including, as well as his own Galton, Wedgwood, Darwin 'extended family', the Macaulays, Trevelyans, Venns, Stephens, Arnolds, Huxleys, Keyneses, Haldanes, Maurices, Potters and Butlers (into whom Galton married – remaining childless).[93] This 'intellectual aristocracy' was predominantly drawn from the three religious constituencies at the heart of the radical and liberal, Evangelical reform movement of the first part of the nineteenth century: Anglican Evangelicals such as notably the Claphamites; Quakers; and Unitarians.[94]

The intellectual, institutional and administrative products of these families and their peers created the moral code of the culturally dominant status-group of mid- and late-Victorian society. This was the new class of professional 'gentlemen' bearing a new code of honour: diligence and personal culture harnessed to active public service according to the highest standards of a serious personal, ostensibly Christian morality. They were a fusion of landowners, politicians, clergy, writers, administrators, professionals, officers, financiers and the more cultured and philanthropically inclined big businessmen. They were all alike created through their shared personal formation as individuals experiencing their *rites de passage* in the Evangelically reformed and reforming first grade schools and thence under the eyes of their earnest young tutors at the reviving colleges of Oxford and Cambridge.

There is one final issue to be considered: an apparent contradiction in the case that has been made so far for seeing the social and intellectual origins of Galton's professional model lying within the political ideology of the status group into which he was born, the liberal 'intellectual aristocracy'. Galton has been accurately identified as one of the principal ideologues and champions of a professional meritocracy as providing the constitutional ideal for British society.[95] Indeed, as we shall see, his hereditarian, professional model was the paradigm English meritocratic representation of social structure. How can this be consonant with his adoption of substantially the same model of society entertained by the 1860s Royal

[93] Annan, 'The intellectual aristocracy'.

[94] I follow here the convention recommended by D. W. Bebbington, in using the capitalised form, 'Evangelical', to refer to all aspects of the popular Protestant movement which originated as Methodism in Britain and as the Great Awakening in New England in the 1730s, and was increasingly attractive to a section of the Anglican church itself after the 1780s. According to Bebbington, it reached its historical climax of general influence during the 1850s and 1860s, a judgement with which Boyd Hilton would concur, though distinguishing between the soteriological preoccupations (the theological essence of Evangelicalism) which were in decline from the later 1850s, and the outward Evangelicalism of earnest attitudes and sober manners, which continued strong into the early 1860s. Bebbington, *Evangelicalism in modern Britain*, esp. p. 105; Hilton, *The age of atonement*.

[95] MacKenzie, *Statistics in Britain*, pp. 51–6.

Commissions, something which has been characterised, above, as that of a socially conservative, neo-aristocratic dynasticism? The solution to this paradox goes to the heart of the questions surrounding the central meaning, the cultural and semiotic significance of the professional model as a representation of society.

For, the socio-occupational linear graded status hierarchy, which the Taunton Commissioners presumed to discuss and which Francis Galton was to clothe in the metric of naturalistic social science, was simultaneously both an aristocratic and a meritocratic construct. The peculiarly English political ideology of merit in fact involved a socially exclusionary institutionalisation of the dynamic process of merit election at its heart. This ideology and its practical expression had been fashioned through a protracted process of conflict and negotiation over many decades. The contest had been both with the established practices and values of the incumbent patrician class of landed and mercantile wealth-holders and also with, and in response to, the radical claims of the industrial capitalist and proletarian 'parties' (that is, ideologically motivated political movements in Weber's sense of 'party', such as, respectively, the Anti-Corn Law League; and Owenite socialism and radical Chartism).

Merit was the particular ideological weapon of the Whig-liberal, Evangelical reforming status group, wielded by its own 'aristocracy' of intellectuals in their ultimately successful campaign for cultural and ideological dominance in British society. But that success was only achieved through the construction of an elaborate cultural and institutional compromise with the country's landed élite, its code of noble honour and its interests in continued access to political power. This resulted in the construction of the peculiarly aristocratic form of English meritocracy. It is a great pity that the excellent manuscript by Dr Keith Hope summarising his primary historical research on this subject and offering an exceptionally stimulating interpretation of the origins of this political conception of merit remains unpublished.[96] All that can be offered here is a brief summary of this crucially important text in support of the argument made above: it is to be emphasised that the remainder of this section is deeply indebted to Hope's unpublished work.

Hope has confirmed the central significance of T. B. Macaulay (1800–59) as the chief ideologist of the English political conception of merit.[97] Macaulay had an impeccable Evangelical and prototypical 'intellectual aristocrat' upbringing. Born into the bosom of the Claphamite Saints, his father Zachary was Wilberforce's right hand in the abolitionist crusade. In Hope's interpretation Macaulay's particular achievement was to fuse the (originally Scottish) twinned ideas of intelligence and merit as attributes of individuals (equivalent to talent, allied to

[96] Hope (unpublished typescript). See also, Hope, *As others see us*.

[97] Of course, many of Macaulay's most eminent contemporaries can be found also proffering views on the virtues of meritocracy: for instance, J. S. Mill's pronouncement in 1829 that 'The intelligent classes lead the government, and the government leads the stupid classes' (cited in Corfield, 'Class by name and number', p. 52). Following this quotation, Corfield observes 'But brainpower proved notoriously difficult to fit into a social hierarchy.' This was precisely Macaulay's project and achievement.

probity and strength of character) with the neo-aristocratic code of honour of his Whig political masters and patrons. Through the device of his unashamedly populist and highly popular mythic historical works, Macaulay made a fortune propagating the view that the guardianship of the essential central values of society was divinely vested in a virtuous, industrious, independent 'middle class', the stalwart yeomen cavalry of ancient and modern times alike – the *equites* of the battle of Lake Regillus, the Roundheads of the English Civil Wars. Their equivalent in nineteenth-century Britain was to be found in the liberal intelligentsia, whose particular sense of honour combined with their unrivalled aptitude meant that they should be seen as the true custodians of the Imperial British state and entrusted with its administration.

Macaulay's flow of propaganda began with a stream of rumbustious, highly readable essays on diverse meritorious individuals such as Milton (1825), Sir Francis Bacon (1837), Clive of India (1840).[98] These were followed by his immediately successful ballads, *Lays of Ancient Rome* published in 1842, which became a school-room classic. And, of course, there was also the more scholarly, unfinished *History of England – the* 'Whig' interpretation of history, which was the principal object of Herbert Butterfield's celebrated denunciatory essay against all forms of teleological evolutionism in historiography.[99] Hope argues that although Macaulay himself was an early secularist, in reaction to his father's obsessive, dutiful piety, he nevertheless looked to religious morality (a proto-Durkheimian in this, as were several of his more thoughtful, non-believing contemporaries) as a source of vital social cement for a liberal, secular society of hard-working individuals striving in Smithian competition with each other. Macaulay's moral code taught that the mere holding and inheriting of land, the traditional source of formal economic independence and its consequent noble virtues of political independence and personal cultivation, was, alone, an insufficient sanction of 'gentility'. The active exhibition of merit was what was now required for honour: diligent, inspiring dutiful public leadership by chaste, erudite and Christian public servants. Macaulay's 'merit' therefore strongly bore the moral charge of his Evangelical pedigree and remained essentially a transcendent concept. Hence its relative acceptability to the aristocracy as a replacement – as they saw it an adaptation – of their own code of personal honour.

This was in marked contrast to the meaninglessness – to the landowning nobility – of the philosophic radicals' deliberately impersonal utilitarian calculus for achieving 'the greatest happiness of the greatest number'. During the 1820s and 1830s the Benthamites of the *Westminster Review* (founded 1824) proposed that this 'objective' rationalist tool should be adopted as the polity's principal guide for defining moral action. It was therefore the centre-piece of a competing reform

[98] These were collected together as *Critical and historical essays*.

[99] Macaulay, *The history of England from the accession of James II* (5 vols., 1858–61). Butterfield, *The Whig interpretation*.

ideology to that preferred by the Whig-liberals, championed in their *Edinburgh Review* (refounded in 1802 by Lord Henry Brougham, Lord Francis Jeffrey and the cleric Sydney Smith, all disciples of Dugald Stewart).[100] Hope argues that the Whig ideology's greater political influence in the 1830s and greater cultural staying power thereafter (greater than the philosophic radicals') were considerably due to the aristocratic support it enjoyed as a result of the appeal contained in Macaulay's moral idea of merit (and this is a thesis which would draw broad support from Peter Mandler's more recent interpretation of the period, envisaging a decline of Whig influence only after the 1840s).[101]

But philosophic radicalism was not the only competing ideology. The Whig-liberals also had to compete on their right flank with the political attractions of the alternative neo-aristocratic and profoundly socially conservative programme of the sacerdotal Tory blue-print: that society should approximate a National Church led by a Clerisy, a cultural élite performing a role analogous to that of the clergy. Coleridge's *Church and state*, published at the end of his life in 1830, was the seminal statement, but politically the most significant adherent was the young Gladstone (expounded in his *The state in its relations with the church*, published in 1838). This ideological platform, and its associated, fundamentally conservative belief in the desirability of a politico-cultural hierarchy more or less congruent with the current distribution of wealth, was highly influential when it came to the political process of actually devising a system of merit election for British society.

It was during this process of practically constructing a system of merit election, in which Macaulay himself was intimately involved, that the crucial compromises between the Whig-liberal ideology and this alternative neo-aristocratic interest were forged. This was particularly manifest through the civil service and educational reforms of the 1850s and 1860s. These reforms were cautiously implemented with Gladstone's direct participation so that they would not disturb the extant status hierarchy, but rather act in the aggregate so as to maintain the exclusive access to these coveted positions of the propertied and privileged families of the nation. This was at variance with the original Scottish meaning and pedagogic practice of merit election, which explicitly attempted to remain socially unbiased in its continual search through the nation for persons of talent and probity.

Indeed, Hope has shown that in the key forum where Macaulay's ideas on merit were given an official vehicle for their expression, the 1854 Parliamentary Report

[100] For more on Brougham, Jeffrey and Smith, see Stewart, *Henry Brougham*. Dugald Stewart (1753–1828) was Professor of Mathematics, 1775–85, before becoming Professor of Moral Philosophy at the University of Edinburgh, 1785–1810. Lord Lansdowne and Palmerston were also among his students. Stewart's importance was not least as an authoritative disseminator to his highly influential students of both Adam Smith's economics and the 'common-sense' philosophy of Smith's successor as Professor of Moral Philosophy in Glasgow, Thomas Reid (1710–96). Collini, Winch, and Burrow, *That noble science of politics*, ch. 1: 'The system of the North: Dugald Stewart and his pupils'. On Reid, see below, n. 118.

[101] Mandler, *Aristocratic government in the age of reform*.

on the Indian civil service and its implementation in the following year, Macaulay's own championship of what was potentially a socially egalitarian form of radically open merit election, as the means of entry into the service, was crucially transformed into a socially exclusionist one. Only the gentlemanly products of public schools and university colleges were to be considered appropriate to enter the competition in the first place. This occurred through priority being given to the ideas contained in the concluding six paragraphs of the Report, which were the work of Macaulay's formidable brother-in-law, Charles Trevelyan, in consultation with 'a small group of men': his political master as Chancellor of the Exchequer, W. E. Gladstone; Gladstone's Private Secretary, Stafford Northcote, with whom Trevelyan had recently completed the 1854 Report on Examination and Recruitment into the Home Civil Service; and, of course, Benjamin Jowett, the great *éminence grise* of the all-pervasive Balliol connection.[102]

Macaulay had originally envisaged that entrance examinations should explicitly take account of the different kinds of curricula taught in the country's various educational institutions so as to make sure that selection occurred on grounds of ability and aptitude only and regardless of the content of what had been taught: he did not want to see these various curricula modified. However, Gladstone, Trevelyan and Northcote were all agreed that on grounds of promoting efficiency the first priority for reform of the civil service was to make an effective primary division within the service between an 'intellectual' administrative grade and an 'inferior' executive one, with differential recruitment to each. Furthermore, politicians such as Gladstone and, after him, Disraeli were, of course, as much concerned with issues of loyalty, honour and trustworthiness in their civil servants as with intellectual capacities: precisely the considerations which had sustained the patronage system for so long (and which had, paradoxically, seen it recently revitalised in the USA, as the spoils system of President Jackson). It was concurred that the honourable character of the recruits to the administrative grade must be as unquestionable as their intellectual talents. They must be gentlemen, preferably with glowing recommendations of their gentility from reliable gentlemanly sources: Oxbridge tutors, for instance.

Here Gladstone found his wishes dovetailed perfectly with Jowett's cherished ambitions regarding his conception of the proper pedagogic function of reformed Oxbridge colleges, free of the Anglican stranglehold.[103] They were to act as the

[102] Sir C. E. Trevelyan (1807–86) was administrative head (Assistant Secretary) of the Treasury, 1840–59. Trevelyan had married Macaulay's sister while both men were in India in 1834, when Trevelyan was a Deputy Secretary in the East India Company, after attending its Haileybury College. Macaulay had been serving as a Whig nominee on the Supreme Council of India, 1834–8, to considerable effect: Stokes, *The English utilitarians and India*.

[103] Note that there was no simple unanimity on this in Oxbridge even among the committed reformers. For instance the views of Jowett's powerful contemporary, Mark Pattison (1813–84, tutor of Lincoln College since 1843 and its Rector after 1861), were in marked contrast. Pattison believed that the principal *raison d'être* of the university should be the professionalised pursuit of academic and scientific excellence, eschewing worldly aims.

cultural incubators of the imperial nation's governing élite. Society was to evolve under the guidance of an impartial, Olympian class of imperial administrators, having only the good of the state as their aim and not the promotion of vested interest. This was a view which, despite its entailed élitism, had considerable appeal to the radical critique which empowered reforming Gladstonian liberalism. At a time when only the ancient status professions, principally the clergy and the bar, seemed to offer a guaranteed gentlemanly career, Jowett was concerned that his almost Jesuit ideal of a carefully nurtured Clerisy of college graduates suffered from an insufficiency of vocational openings for its graduates to fulfil their destiny as political and cultural leaders of their increasingly complex society. It was most appropriate to Jowett's aims that an upper, administrative grade of the civil service should become a career destination for the best of his graduates. Personally fascinated with India, Jowett jumped at the opportunity to set up a scholarship scheme at Balliol to prepare candidates in the right gentlemanly environment for the proposed Indian civil service exams – he and Gladstone consequently persuading Trevelyan to close down his own *alma mater*, the now-redundant East India Company college at Haileybury.

The technical key to the overwhelming bias in favour of a public school and university education for successful candidates to the new exam for the Indian service was in the marking system. The subject of 'English language, literature and history' was worth 1,500 of a possible total of 6,875 marks. Assessment through mastery of language, literature and history was also responsible for a further 3,750 of the remaining potential marks in papers on Ancient Greece and Rome (750 each), France, Germany, Italy, Sanskrit and Arabic (375 each). Moral sciences accounted for another 500 marks, leaving 500 for natural sciences and 1,000 for mathematics. Only the most distinguished candidates ever proved able to attain more than a third of the possible total. The scheme's historian, John Roach, has reserved himself to the bald comment that 'The large total given for the English subjects is surprising, since they did not form at that time a separate part of a higher academic education.'[104]

Thus was the examination devised so as to test primarily the candidate's degree of informal assimilation of the most subtle and sophisticated aspects of the cultural code of the liberal intelligentsia: the expressive and discursive use of its language. Furthermore, knowledge of and ability in manipulation of its explicit value system would, of course, be essential in scoring highly in all the other subjects examined, with the relative exception only of mathematics and natural sciences. Hence, Hope's conclusion that 'the competition gave success to young men from a narrow range of institutions'.[105] Once the Indian experiment was seen to perform this function safely and effectively, political anxieties over 'open competition' melted away and the system was extended to the Home Civil Service from 1870.[106]

[104] Roach, *Public examinations*, p. 196. [105] Hope (unpublished typescript), p. 157.
[106] Although its adoption was gradual and uneven, taking longest to penetrate the Foreign Office,

The official, model English practice of merit election was, therefore, a highly conditional one relative to the Scottish original, permitting the open competition of examination only between the members of that select social stratum whose prior attendance at a first grade school and university confirmed their membership of the élite status group of cultivated, honourable gentlemen. This exclusionary, hierarchical edifice did offer, however, one critical concession to the original meaning of merit election, the institution which became known as the 'scholarship ladder'. It was freely acknowledged by the 1860s inquiries that individuals of 'real ability' and determined 'character' were sometimes born among the masses and that there should be provision on a modest but adequate basis all around the country for the identification of these exceptional individuals and for their funding through the higher grades of schools and on to university if appropriate. No doubt ideologically important in convincing contemporaries of their own meritocratic credentials, this remained, however, an almost spectral tokenism throughout the Victorian era: as late as 1900 fewer than one in a thousand elementary school children were gaining such assistance for their secondary schooling.[107]

Thus, the institutionalised model of a practical working system of merit election for British society, established through the civil service and educational reforms of the 1850s and 1860s, was essentially that of a highly aristocratic, hierarchically graded kind of 'meritocracy'. This comprehends the conceptualisation of the essential nature of his society which Francis Galton unquestioningly brought with him to his study of anthropometrics and his eugenic project. But, more importantly, it needs to be grasped that this was also an encompassing, default representation of their society which virtually all members of the liberal intelligentsia, regardless of political sympathy, religious denomination or lack thereof, had come to share in common by the end of the Victorian era. Their elders were the makers of this social selection system which they had been willing into existence since the 1820s, while the younger members of this status group of the governing class were themselves the products of it.

Galton's 'Great Chain'

Galton belonged to the next generation of the intellectual aristocracy after Macaulay's. He therefore spent his formative adolescent and young adult years, from the late 1830s to the early 1850s, maturing within the brave new aristocratic-

where the international contacts of noble families were arguably of some functional value. Even here patronage and connection were being supplemented if not entirely replaced by a professional corps by the first decade of the next century: Steiner, *The Foreign Office*.

107 The 1907 Free Place Regulations were the first serious attempt to make the scholarship ladder a reality, resulting in an almost tenfold increase in scholarships from 1900 to 1912. But this still, of course, represented less than 1% of the elementary school population in 1912: Sutherland, *Ability, merit and measurement*, p. 111.

meritocratic world which the likes of Thomas Arnold and Thomas Macaulay were actively battling to create. Galton above all others should perhaps be seen as Macaulay's truest intellectual heir in that subsequent generation. He shared with Macaulay a positive absence of religious faith, allied to an obsessive preoccupation with the shared conservative and liberal problem of how to find a moral basis for the social order and for its stability. Macaulay's answer was in the mythic power revealed through the lessons of human history; Galton's was in the compelling implications of the laws of natural history. This reflected the different modes of 'scientific' discourse rhetorically dominant in the two halves of the nineteenth century. Although born only twenty-two years apart, Macaulay's precocity meant that his literary campaign commenced forty years before Galton's first scientific foray on behalf of meritocracy, which was only published several years after Macaulay's somewhat premature death.[108] But both were offering similar linear, evolutionary accounts of forms of 'Progress': teleological tales to justify the deriving of a socio-political 'ought' from an historical or natural 'is'.

The essential affinities are also confirmed in Keith Hope's intriguing demonstration that in the course of his elaboration of the concept of merit, Macaulay was additionally responsible for outlining all the essential elements of the specific notion of 'general intelligence', which was to be the key concept underwriting the subsequently unfolding eugenic enterprise of Galton, Spearman, Burt and others. For Macaulay this was a supposedly general capacity for abstract intellectual work, distinct from any specialised talents, whose strength of manifestation among the individuals of the nation could be shown, by any genuinely comparative examination, to vary according to Quetelet's binomial law of distribution (the 'normal distribution' in today's parlance).[109] The subsequent labours of Galton, Spearman, Burt *et al.*, on the notion of an intelligence quotient, were an attempt to operationalise this concept as an empirically measurable attribute of individuals, through development of the technology of psychometric testing. Their work can in a sense be seen as a scientistic footnote to the ideologue, Macaulay's, supreme abilities to conjure with metaphysical notions, weaving and spinning moral judgements into the illusion of tangible characteristics and measurable properties.[110]

[108] It was Macaulay's essay on Milton in the *Edinburgh Review* of 1825 which launched his career under Whig sponsorship. Galton did publish accounts from his explorations and travels in the 1850s (see above n. 5), but his first fully formulated meritocratic salvo was: 'Hereditary talent and character', published in 1865. For this Galton chose the same forum, *Macmillan's Magazine*, in which the high priest of Clerisy, Matthew Arnold, had publicised his own views the previous year under the title, 'A French Eton'. As a senior Board of Education HMI, Arnold had been commissioned to undertake various comparative international studies for the 1860s Royal Commissions (Arnold's *Culture and anarchy* was published in 1869).

[109] Hope (unpublished typescript), pp. 78, 154–65. Hope traces Macaulay's first formulation of the notion of 'general intelligence' to an article of his on 'The Athenian orators' in *Knight's Quarterly* in 1824. Hope found that the specific idea of Quetelet's binomial distribution, as describing the way in which general intelligence was supposedly distributed through the population, was finally adopted by Macaulay in his 1853 Parliamentary speech on the India Bill.

[110] For an important, critical collection of articles on the historical construction of the IQ concept and scale, see Smith and Hamilton (eds.), *The meritocratic intellect*.

The social and political views implicit in Galton's intellectual project can be fairly summarised as those of an authoritarian élitist, though he did not consciously hold such views for politically conservative or socially pro-aristocratic reasons. As an outgrowth of his radically materialist and naturalistic belief in the hereditarian perfectibility of human society, Galton believed that the direction of society should be entrusted to a natural oligarchy of intelligence, openly recruited and identifiable through their personal achievements in matters of science and learning. Ideally, over a sufficient period of time the proportion of these intelligent beings in the national population should be increased through their differentially higher reproduction to a maximum consonant with securing the efficient working of the more mundane aspects of the supporting economy (positive eugenics). This therefore entailed a proportionate decrease in the less intelligent classes (negative eugenics), which for Galton included not only uneducated plebeians but also the indolent rich living off the fruits of a more capable ancestor, whose meritorious traits they had evidently failed to inherit. Indeed, he reserved his sharpest invective for this latter group and their lackeys, the clergy of the Established Church, dealing in what Galton – as committed a naturalistic rationalist as can be found in the nineteenth century – regarded as muddled superstition.[111]

However, lest this apparently even-handed treatment of the idle rich and the labouring poor be thought to indicate that Galton's radical rationalism and hereditarian viewpoint were relatively untainted by political and social bias, an important inconsistency should be pointed out. Galton was well aware that in certain rather obvious – and to him particularly irksome – circumstances, social and cultural factors intervened quite massively to effect a divorce, or non-correlation, between individuals' apparent attainments – their position in life – and the all-important innate, hereditary capacities in their biological make-up. These were the idle rich of high society, living off their secure, rentier incomes. However, Galton was quite incapable of working up anything like the same degree of animus to denounce the reciprocal of the same set of factors, whereby economic and cultural forces conspired to handicap those individuals among the lower classes with great inborn intelligence, who were unable to attain the position of great eminence to which their germ plasm entitled them, according to Galton's views.

Galton's understanding of the probable mechanisms of biological inheritance was not simplistic: he accommodated an explanation for social mobility in terms of natural selection through his particular statistical interpretation of the genetic phenomenon of regression to the mean.[112] This envisaged plenty of scope for normal variance between parents and offspring in their respective endowments, leading to a degree of upward and downward social mobility between generations. So in theory this particular discrepancy among the lowborn should have been an

[111] Galton's disdain for works spiritual drove him to the publication in the *Fortnightly Review* in 1872 of his heavily ironic 'Statistical inquiries into the efficacy of prayer'.

[112] See Norton, 'Psychologists and class', pp. 296–9.

even greater scandal for Galton than the case of the idle rich, since it affected much larger numbers of 'misplaced' persons, owing to the much greater numerical size of the working classes.

Yet, although there might be a generous sprinkling of duds among the highborn, while the gifted sometimes had to find their way up the social ladder from relatively humble origins, Galton seems to have been confident that the vast generality of beings were broadly speaking correctly located within the hierarchical status structure of society. This was precisely because of his *a priori* belief that pure heredity played much the largest role in determining individuals' manifest abilities (conceived as a relatively one-dimensional characteristic, 'intelligence' or 'civic' worth). This necessarily meant that he could not seriously entertain the possibility that mere economic or cultural forces might significantly or systematically distort or impede the accurate and faithful expression in society of individuals' innate, inherited capacities. Hence his axiomatic belief in the prepotent significance of heredity also precluded such cultural and economic factors from being of any great importance in allocating individuals to their occupational grades in the biological hierarchy that was, for him, society.

From the perspective of this naturalistic form of sociology, the social structure inevitably corresponded to a hierarchy in nature, the consequence of selective breeding. This led directly to an anti-public health and anti-welfare political disposition. Galton believed that the vast majority of the manual working poor performed relatively simple and unremunerative tasks in society because that is all that their hereditary material suited them for, rather than this being an indication of the degree of economic and cultural disadvantages they had suffered and the attenuated life-chances open to them. Given the flimsiness of Galton's claims, as articulated in his autobiography, to have established scientifically the preponderant importance of heredity over environment (see above, n. 40), this non-negotiable belief is perhaps best characterised as a moral and political conviction, the non-rational basis of which Galton apparently had little personal insight into.

It is significant that despite his professed meritocratic ideals Galton did not or could not countenance the radically 'democratic', or egalitarian, possibility that all individuals in every generation might be born everywhere with a substantially equal chance of having received, through their natural inheritance, the physiological basis for the development of any of those abilities which their society particularly valued and rewarded. This betrays the nature of his directly political and ideological rather than scientific motivation for studying these phenomena. To allow that all individuals might have a relatively equal chance of social and cultural success, regardless of their biological provenance, would have vastly downgraded the *social* and *political* significance of Galton's efforts to study the laws governing the *hereditary* germ material from which individuals grew. But note that the existence of such a biologically democratic possibility would not have affected at all the *scientific* importance of study leading to the elucidation of the laws of inheritance. The clear implication is that Galton's motivation sprang primarily from his unexamined political and neo-religious naturalistic convictions: his desire to show that the social and natural world was in conformity with his prior moral beliefs, rather than from a scientific curiosity – a desire to understand as precisely as possible how the phenomena of human variation occurred.[113] Galton's was essentially a deductivist socio-biological approach, for all that it masqueraded as inductivist, empirical natural science.

Furthermore, Galton did not particularly care about the fate of the lowborn because for him they were a mass of lesser beings, from among whom even the most exceptional products, thrown up by the processes of reproductive variance, would hardly ever match up even to the average of the august class of their social superiors, those who constituted the nation's knowledge élite: its scientists, artists, writers and professionals. The fundamentally conservative nexus of political premises which underpinned Galton's life-work is here exposed for inspection. As well as presuming that social position was a relatively faithful reflection of individuals' differential genetic endowment, Galton simply assumed that the linear, hierarchical social structure of status gradings, to which he constantly referred, was *itself* 'correct'. 'Correct' both in the sense of synthetically true as an accurate description of British society as it existed, and also in the analytical or prescriptive sense: that it was a just and desirable social arrangement. Despite the radicalism of his rational materialist naturalism and scientific empiricism, Galton held to an implicit model of society, which he apparently never questioned. This model was profoundly reactionary, backward-looking, neo-aristocratic and in fact, for all his detestation of the clergy, thoroughly theological and clerical in its origins.

Galton pictured society as a linear and hierarchical set of grades, degrees or ranks – almost exactly as the theological theory of the Great Chain of Being had. Pre-Enlightenment theologians, in rationalising and eulogising a static monarchical and aristocratic feudal polity, had construed the teleological explanation of the Great Chain. The cosmos was as an unbroken line of dyadic links between superiors and inferiors, from its divine head down through the sovereign crown, the lords spiritual and temporal, greater and lesser men, women and children and finally higher and lower animals and other life-forms. Linnaean taxonomy addressed itself to this conceptual framework such that eighteenth-century problems in biological taxonomy and early evolutionary theory were seen in terms

[113] R. S. Cowan has pointed to the outstanding example of Galton's explicit commitment to his neo-religious political programme of eugenics in preference to his commitment to scientific inquiry. When justifying the support he gave to his eugenic disciples Pearson and Weldon, in their attack on the Mendelian saltationism of William Bateson, Galton, who in fact had always been a saltationist, had written in January 1904 to the aggrieved Bateson that 'the achievement of a eugenic society was a more important goal than the achievement of scientific truth'. Cowan, 'Nature and nurture', pp. 147, 194–7.

of gaps and inconsistencies in the Chain. Although the fundamental Enlightenment idea of Progress introduced a dynamic aspect, the teleological form of the thought system remained intact: a 'temporalised' Great Chain resulted. Nineteenth-century evolutionary thought and science unwittingly inherited the linear and hierarchical epistemological premises of the Great Chain, as constitutive of the intellectual field of problems it sought to address.[114]

Thus, Galton was to be found in the second half of the nineteenth century supposedly providing a biological and evolutionary scientific explanation of the nation's social structure, which simply assumed that the *explicandum* – society – could be validly conceived as a linear hierarchy of grades, without ever questioning where that assumption came from. Simultaneously he was deploying as his explanatory intellectual framework – the *explicans* – a biological evolutionary approach, which was itself also broadly premised on the same theologically derived, Great Chain, linear and hierarchical conceptualisation.

Thus, it was that in Galton's anthropometric project, the main empirical expression of his social science of eugenics, he successfully (in the sense of not falling victim to a fatal contemporary critique for so doing) fused and conflated his own status group's meritocratic moral evaluations and social prejudices with the authority of scientific rationalism. This he achieved through application of the statistical methodology of physical observation and metrication. The latter had originally been brought from the natural sciences to the study of human physical dimensions by the Belgian astronomer Quetelet from the late 1820s onwards. Quetelet's earlier work had already inspired the 'Statistical movement' in Britain in the 1830s. However, it was his mature writings from the latter 1840s, on regularities in human behaviour and the applications of probability theory, which generated a second wind of enthusiasm in Britain.[115] Among others, J. Clark Maxwell and W. S.

[114] Darwin's blind and passive mechanism, natural selection, may have been intended by him to be a radical materialist, non-teleological and anti-hierarchical break with the fundamental assumptions of any linear view of evolution, as influenced by the Great Chain. But it was not at all understood in this way by his contemporaries because of the failure – until the rediscovery of Mendelism – to produce any convincing, detailed empirical description or theoretical specification of the blind and passive process of genetic inheritance that was supposed to be involved. As a result, nineteenth-century 'Darwinism', including eventually even Darwin's own published version (the 'provisional hypothesis of pangenesis' in *The descent of man*), has been termed 'neo-Lamarckian' by P. J. Bowler because it permitted the continued teleological conceptualisation of evolution as 'Progress'. This neo-Lamarckian interpretation was most influentially insisted upon in Anglophone culture by Herbert Spencer: Bowler, *Evolution*, chs. 1, 3, 8–10. (See above, pp. 134–5; and below, pp. 220–1)

[115] This was transmitted through the widely read popularisation of these ideas by H. T. Buckle in his *History of civilisation in England* (first volume published 1857, second volume 1861). Buckle's popularisation was certainly preceded and accompanied by various other English-language disseminators of Quetelet (see next footnote). The notable popularity in England from the 1860s of both Quetelet's positivist empiricism and Comte's epistemologically compatible positivist social philosophy was no doubt mutually reinforcing (on the latter, see above, nn. 16, 87). On Quetelet, see Stigler, *The history of statistics*, pp. 226–8; Porter, *The rise of statistical thinking*, pp. 60–5. On positivism, see Annan, *The curious strength of positivism*.

Jevons in the 1860s both derived from Quetelet fundamentally important elements for their own theoretical reformulations in mechanics and economics, respectively.[116] As Reba Soffer has pointed out, whereas both Maxwell and Jevons were acutely aware of the epistemological status of probabilistic statistics as a form of deductive thought, Galton seems to have mistakenly believed he was dealing with an ontology.[117]

It seems extremely likely that this was due to Galton's immersion in and exclusive acceptance of the inductivism and positivism of the 'common-sense', empiricist epistemology, originally bequeathed in a rigorous form to the Evangelical tradition of thought by Thomas Reid.[118] Galton's mentor and cousin, Charles Darwin, was, of course, strongly motivated in his work precisely by the aim of invalidating the religious teleology which had issued from this strain of thought, culminating in the Paleyan natural theology of the *Bridgewater treatises* of the 1830s. However, Darwin's chosen rhetorical method for achieving this was the presentation of an apparently all-encompassing and overwhelmingly comprehensive inductive edifice, where the compelling general explanatory principles seemed to emerge from the particulars of specific observations drawn from a vast range of phenomena. Furthermore, as Peter Bowler has pointed out, the reception and cultural digestion of Darwinian evolutionary theory itself was initially largely subsumed within the overwhelmingly teleological, optimistic faith in Progress, which dominated liberal thought during the 1850s and 1860s. The original intentions of the atheist, Darwin, may have been to enunciate the blind, morally neutral, relentlessly materialist, scientific principles whose operation might unravel the mystery of the origin of species – natural selection and survival of the fittest (although recent research casts doubt on this even for Darwin).[119] But even if this was Darwin's original aim, his work was almost unanimously reinterpreted by contemporaries through the conceptual framework of an inherently moral and

116 Maxwell's statistical mechanics was influenced by the astronomer Sir John Herschel's 1850 review of Quetelet's work: Gigerenzer *et al., The empire of chance*, p. 62; Jevons was much impressed with George Boole's interpretation of Quetelet, as part of Boole's founding work on mathematical logic (*An investigation of the laws of thought* published in 1854): Soffer, 'The revolution in English social thought', p. 1955.

117 Soffer, 'The revolution in English social thought,' pp. 1948, 1955.

118 Thomas Reid (1710–96) was Adam Smith's successor as Professor of Moral Philosophy at Glasgow University, 1764–80. His pro-Baconian and Newtonian, inductivist, 'common-sense' philosophy of the mind's direct apprehension of reality (*Inquiry into the human mind, on the principles of common sense*, published 1764), in rejection of Lockean sensation psychology, was extremely important as the foundation of the Evangelically inspired intellectual project of Natural Theology: the law-governed universe as material proof of divine existence, beneficence and the correct forms of moral conduct. This was brought to its fullest Evangelical fruition in the teleological work of Thomas Chalmers (1780–1847), Professor of Moral Philosophy at St Andrews in 1823, Professor of Theology at Edinburgh after 1828, and author in 1833 of the first of the *Bridgewater treatises*: 'The adaptation of external nature to the moral and intellectual constitution of man'. Bebbington, *Evangelicalism in modern Britain*, ch. 2; Hilton, *The age of atonement*. Also, see above, nn. 94, 100.

119 See above, n. 84.

teleological discourse on the means to ensure 'Progress'.[120] Galton was no exception in this: he rejected an explicitly theological teleology only to replace it with a materialist one, all within an inductivist empiricism.

Thus it was that Galton equated the structure of his chosen theoretical tool – Quetelet's normal law of error – with a supposedly independent, inductively revealed structure of the physical world being studied. It seems eminently possible that it was this positivist misapprehension, the belief that he was actually discovering and not merely creating an order in the nature of man, which may have imbued Galton with the necessary crusading energy and zeal to produce the startling and ingenious series of successful innovations of statistical concepts designed to measure relationships between the various social and biological phenomena which he chose to study. It was this achievement which justifiably drew great contemporary interest and admiration, particularly from his peers in the natural and biological sciences, regardless of whether they concurred exactly with his particular views on the mechanisms of evolution, which, it was accepted, remained a field of intense and complex conjecture.

The notion that characteristics of the *social* world also necessarily reflected the form of the statistical tool, now known as the law of normal distribution – Galton's canny re-christening of Quetelet's normal error law – had no more philosophical sense or logical force than the original mistaken assumption that the natural world was so constituted.[121] But those more discerning and fastidious thinkers who knew this only too well seem to have remained too aloof from the messy business of empirical social science and related policy discussions to have provided the kind of serious, direct challenge to this positivist, naturalistic programme, which would have been necessary to deflate its pretensions, in view of Galton's apparently impeccable scientific credentials.

Those in the immediate intellectual environment of fellow empirical scientists – natural, biological and social – were not inclined to question the validity or perceive the relativity of the common-sense moral values and social categorisations which premised their shared view of the world. These were smuggled into the anthropometric project via the titles, definitions and relationships posited to exist between the basic social categories which comprised the objects to be measured:

[120] Bowler, *Evolution*, chs. 8–10. Indeed, as noted above, n. 114, this has led Peter Bowler to argue that the term 'social Darwinism', used to describe these many late nineteenth-century variants of a moralised, teleological selection mechanism, should really be seen as the resurgence of various forms of an essentially pre-Darwinian or Lamarckian notion of evolution, an era of 'neo-Lamarckism'. However, since even Darwin himself seems to have substantially endorsed this kind of interpretation of his principles with respect to human affairs, 'social Darwinism' would seem to remain a fair description for this protracted period of conceptual conflation prevailing throughout the last third of the nineteenth century. See Moore, 'Socialising Darwinism'; and for an important narrative account of the interplay of political, professional and scientific factors in the early 'evolution' of Darwinian theory, see Moore, 'Deconstructing Darwinism'; and see n. 84.

[121] MacKenzie, *Statistics in Britain*, pp. 56–9.

the occupations; the social classes; the linear hierarchy which they composed; the pre-eminence in all this of their own class, the professional and administrative intelligentsia who provided society and empire with the inestimable public service of moral, cultural and political leadership. Provided that the evolutionary premises were recognisable, the mathematics sound, the statistics innovative, the inferences logical, Galton was practising high science so far as his audience and immediate peers were concerned. The arbitrary infiltration into the project of an entire ideological code and its derivative social and moral precepts simply went through unexamined.

In effect Galton's procedures for classifying and judging humans amounted to a scientistic analogue to then contemporary medical practice, once germ theory had been established. Galton was measuring a physical attribute of an individual and treating this observable and quantifiable datum in the same way as bacteriological scientists and medical practitioners were treating the physical symptoms and ascertainable infections of patients: as legitimate means of identification with which to classify them, so as to segregate (or demarcate) them as candidates for differential treatment for health-promotion purposes (from both their own and the wider community's point of view). However, for all the similarities in methodology, the supporting identification theory lying behind Galton's classificatory taxonomy and the justifying body of scientific theory and evidence, were both extraordinarily speculative and frail by comparison with that deployed by the bacteriological and medical practitioners. Galton's methods were formally identical with those of empirical medical and bacteriological science but they were surreptitiously admixed with a consensual moral scale, which, via a simple process of circular reasoning provided most of the 'theory' and the associated diagnostic signs. It defined the vast majority of individuals in the nation as being in the equivalent of varying grades of illness or unfitness, to the extent that they departed in their occupational employments from the highest category on the moral, prestige scale: the professional upper and middle class.

Naturalistic social science, liberalism and social policy at the turn of the century

The first decade of the twentieth century witnessed a virtual revolution in the social and economic policies of the Liberal party in power: the New, or Progressive, or collectivist Liberalism. Although collectivist state welfare policies were not adopted by the Liberal party at Westminster until the first decade of the new century, it is well known that an increasing preoccupation with these themes can be seen in advanced Liberal political and social thought throughout the last quarter of the nineteenth century. The rising generation of New Liberals was inspired by the neo-Hegelian, idealist teachings associated with their charismatic mentor, T. H. Green of Balliol, before his premature death at forty-two years old in

1882.[122] How do these important developments within liberal political philosophy and social theory relate to the account offered here: of the influence of the main concurrent forms of empirical and policy-related social science upon the technology of social classification in the late Victorian decades?

In fact, progressive liberal thinkers seen to have exerted relatively little direct impact upon empirical social science throughout the period before the landslide Liberal general election victory of 1906. Stefan Collini and Michael Freeden, from their varying perspectives, have each done much to delineate the nature of the reorientation in liberal social and political theory that occurred during the last two decades of the nineteenth century. This produced the main philosophical alternative to the politically conservative evolutionisms of both the Spencerian 'socio-biological' and the Marshallian economic theories, as guides to political action.[123] This Oxford idealist, ethical school of moral philosophy was the principal intellectual force behind the new, collectivist liberalism, which eventually crystallised in the political arena during the Asquith premiership. It was a school of thought powerful in philosophical and moral disputation and abstract reasoning, as the works of Hobson and Robertson on economics, and Ritchie, Hobhouse and Bosanquet on social theory attest, following the ultra academic approach of their great mentors, J. S. Mill and T. H. Green. But it is notable that as an intellectual project with moral and political pretensions, the elaboration of the new ideas into practical policies and as new departures in empirical social science was surprisingly muted.[124]

Certainly in the cases of both Hobhouse and Hobson this was because of acute awareness on their part of the fragility of the distinction between personal values and 'facts' in any process of empirical investigation.[125] It was also for Hobhouse due to his positive conviction that sociology was an academic specialism whose domain of study was 'the discovery of the connecting links between other specialisms', in pursuit of his ultimate aim of 'a general synthesis of moral philosophy and social analysis'.[126] Indeed, it was this extreme lack of direct engagement with matters of practical social policy and research for their own sake which resulted in the historic split between social philosophy and social work in

[122] The definitive study is Melvin Richter's *The politics of conscience.*

[123] Collini, *Liberalism and sociology;* Freeden, *The New Liberalism.*

[124] Perhaps the most important extension of the new idealist and collectivist principles into empirical investigation was actually embodied in the historical research undertaken by the Oxford historical economists, such as Thorold Rogers, Arnold Toynbee, William Ashley. However, their empirical research remained explicitly historical and only implicitly and indirectly concerned with lessons for the arrangement of society in the present and future. Ultimately, in the formidable shape of R. H. Tawney, and, in a somewhat less scholarly manifestation in the work of the Hammonds, this historical approach was to produce a genuine, full dialogue between historical insight and contemporary social investigation. But, again, this was not to be until the period after 1905. See Kadish, *The Oxford economists;* Koot, *English historical economics.*

[125] For Hobhouse's views, see Abrams, *The origins*, pp. 94–6; and more generally Collini, *Liberalism and sociology;* for Hobson, see Freeden, *The New Liberalism*, p. 8.

[126] Abrams, *The origins*, pp. 135, 30.

the newly endowed discipline of sociology in the first years of its university existence in Britain. Hobhouse, the first Professor of Sociology in the country (at the London School of Economics), surrendered the editorship of the *Sociological Review* in 1911 in response to the protests for a more practical orientation by Patrick Geddes, the great exponent of town planning and 'civics'. The following year a separate chair in Social Science and Administration was established at the LSE for E. J. Urwick, where he began to put into practice his belief that, in R. J. Halliday's terms, 'sociology was a science for social work'.[127] The work of this new department at the LSE was a direct extension and development of the long-established practices of the COS, being created by a merger with its training school for social workers.[128]

It was in fact certain progressive elements within the COS which represented the main empirical, social science arm of the idealist school of social thought. The COS had, of course, been immersed in practical social work for several decades, and as a result has been considered responsible for the important innovation of individual case work in social work.[129] But its activities had also for decades represented the embodiment of the conventional, individualism of nineteenth-century, socially conservative evangelism, premised on the moralistic idea that failure of personal character was a sufficient explanation for the existence of poverty. However, there was a new line of idealist thought developing within the COS during the late nineteenth century, which ultimately issued in institutionalised form in Urwick's new department at the LSE in 1912. The question here is whether this new approach within the COS sufficiently embraced a collectivist position before the inauguration of the Progressive Liberal administration, that it can be regarded as an important independent influence upon empirical social science in Britain. Was it a new development which was offering something different from the evangelical, philanthropic, individualist nostrums of the past; and something distinct from the anti-welfare stance of the eugenic biometricians?

José Harris has recently attempted to argue precisely this revisionist interpretation of the significance of the COS: that new developments, represented primarily in the writings of the idealist philosopher Bernard Bosanquet, indicate that by the beginning of the twentieth century the leading lights in the COS were advocating a much more socially collectivist and less individualist and evangelically philanthropist approach. However, José Harris acknowledges that for this to be a convincing thesis, there needs to be an explanation of exactly how Bernard Bosanquet's 'grandiose vision of comprehensive state power' can 'be reconciled with Bosanquet's opposition to such apparently modest forms of public welfare provision as free

[127] Halliday, 'The sociological movement', p. 390.

[128] Harris, 'The Webbs, the C.O.S. and the Ratan Tata Foundation'. Also see above, p. 103 and n. 97.

[129] See Mowat, 'Charity and case work'; and Woodruffe, 'The Charity Organisation Society'. However, George Behlmer has argued that the NSPCC was, in fact, more important as the real champion of this development: Behlmer, *Child abuse*, pp. 167–8.

school dinners and state old-age pensions'.[130] But in attempting to derive this explanation from Bosanquet's tortuous position, it seems to me that José Harris identifies precisely the internal contradiction which marks him out, in the final analysis and regardless of the implications of his abstract, collectivist Hegelian theorising, as a paternalist, philanthropist individualist, when it comes to the concrete and practical implementation of social policy. José Harris's explanation of Bosanquet's social collectivist position on matters of practical social policy is exactly as follows: 'A benefit was allowable (even a state benefit) if it took place within an ethical context (that is, a reciprocal personal relationship between giver and receiver) and if its end was rational (that is, the promotion of independent citizenship in the recipient)' (*sic*).[131] The internal contradiction in this is that the independence of the recipient is precisely compromised by the unequal, tutelary relationship of charity between giver and receiver which Bosanquet, the paternalist, believes to be so essential.

José Harris is undoubtedly right to emphasise the much more flexible attitude of the COS by the end of the nineteenth century and its greater willingness to consider working with the agencies of the state. But it does not seem justifiable on the strength of this to represent the COS as a leading force in the development of such new ways of conceptualising social problems. While the most progressive elements in the COS certainly recognised that the effects of transindividual, environmental factors had to be taken into account, they still viewed the crux of the poverty issue as that of the individual's independence and strength of character:

> the individual member of society is above all things a character and a will . . . Among the influences which operate upon the will, . . . some . . . are due to material or economic conditions . . . but in watching the social process, . . . the skilled observer becomes aware that circumstance is modifiable by character, and so far as circumstance is a name for human action, by character alone.[132]

Social work was still for the COS a missionary calling, only more secular now that it worked to modify the environment, too; not simply wrestling with the naked souls of degraded individuals. However, the fundamentally individualist approach to social problems continued, and therefore placed most of its practitioners within the broadly conservative consensus that viewed the Poor Law as either desirable

[130] Harris, 'Political thought and the welfare state', p. 132.

[131] Harris, 'Political thought and the welfare state', p. 132.

[132] Bosanquet (ed.), *Aspects of the social problem*, Preface, pp. v–vi. This was a series of studies based on 'prolonged and systematic experience in practical efforts to improve the condition of the poor' (*ibid.*, p. v.). As well as his own six chapters, it comprised contributions from C. S. Loch, M. McCallum and Helen Dendy (she was married to Bernard Bosanquet that year and thereafter took his name). On the Bosanquets, see also McBriar, *An Edwardian mixed doubles*. It might also be pointed out that the idea that individual charitable *givers* should not necessarily themselves give in person to the needy had been central to the founding rationale of the COS in 1869, which was to act as the organising and administering agency to deliver charitable resources; so that an absence of a pure and thoroughgoing 'individualism' in charitable activity was, in any case, not new to the COS, but integral to its operation.

or necessary, and collectivist state intervention as fundamentally problematic and potentially counter-productive, unless delivered in a paternalistic way. In looking for the practical roots of the collectivist approach to social policy which emerged in the Edwardian era, the account offered here in the ensuing chapters will emphasise, instead, the public service professions working in local government, particularly the environmentalists of the public health branch of medicine, as key innovators, rather than the COS.

With the exception, therefore, of the idealist thinkers within the COS, the novel collectivist strain of liberal thought did not produce a collectivist school of empirical sociology. It contributed to the inspiration for the settlement movement of the last third of the Victorian century and it is certainly true that many of the most important social scientists and policy-makers of the Progressive Liberal era, such as Asquith himself and the young W. H. Beveridge, for instance, served their political apprenticeship in these East End missionary institutions. But the ethics of community, which these settlements attempted to foster in London's slums, remained a morally charged *praxis*, and was not developed into a secular *doxa*: community signified a prescriptive moral sentiment, not a sociological descriptive category.

This distinction between moral values and social facts was something with which idealist philosophers of the liberal academy were becoming increasingly preoccupied in this period; and it provides an important additional reason why the new idealist liberal thought exerted only a very limited impact upon practical social science and policy before 1905. This ultimately issued in the publication in 1903 of G. E. Moore's *Principia ethica*, the classic formulation of the so-called naturalistic fallacy. Paradoxically, it was partly because of this philosophical preoccupation that Galton's naïvely positivist and empiricist 'scientific' programme was, in a sense, 'protected' from too close a critical scrutiny by social and political philosophers with more respect for defining and exploring premises and propositions. Furthermore, a consequence of these academicians' increasing sensitivity to this distinction was their relatively general withdrawal from the dangers of synthetically derived pronouncements on contemporary society. There was a disinclination towards involvement with the treacherous shifting sands of empirical social research and a growing distaste for the former favourite pastime of social philosophers: the confident discussion of and arbitration upon matters moral and politic (which before the 1870s had simultaneously meant matters economic).

Growing institutional, intellectual, indeed quintessentially professional and disciplinary pressures – towards specialisation and the separation of the diverse philosophical and methodological approaches that can be brought to the study of human and social affairs – were also partially responsible for this 'protective' division between synthetic and analytical approaches to the study of social problems. The foundation of innumerable scholarly journals during the last two decades of the nineteenth century marks the proliferation and differentiation of claims to specific forms of demarcated disciplinary and even subdisciplinary expertise within the Anglophone academic world at this time.[133] In the first decade of the new century this phenomenon of intellectual fragmentation was further compounded in those areas of economics, sociology and medicine where issues of public social and economic policy were unavoidably concerned, since there was also a vast concurrent explosion of explicit political concern and related research into such practical but complex matters as pensions, insurance, personal hygiene, infant mortality, child growth and welfare, as well as continuing further exploration of the long-established areas of interest such as unemployment, preventive health measures, housing and education.

The tendency to abdicate active critique and engagement with practical politics and policies among those with idealist intellectual pretensions therefore left the field of substantive and detailed, reasoned policy debate on these kinds of issues to the combined efforts of various kinds of self-styled rational empiricists. These included, first, academic natural scientists like Galton and Pearson who believed in positivistically studying man and society as one would study the natural world. Either unaware of (Galton) or undeterred by (Pearson) the idealists' philosophical niceties, they enjoyed considerable influence and authority by virtue of being 'scientists'.[134] Secondly, there were those officials, public health doctors and other public service professionals, as well as philanthropic voluntary social workers, who could legitimately claim specialist knowledge and expertise by virtue of their practical experience in specific areas of social policy and social work. Thirdly, there were those political figures and social investigators espousing non-revolutionary, reformist programmes who were prepared to invest their energies in empirical inquiry in order to devise effective policy. Chiefly these last were to be found among the ranks of the 'intellectual aristocracy': encompassing a range of political dispositions from 'conservatives' (Booth and Marshall, for instance) to Fabian socialists. Through their common educational formation all of these empirical social scientists shared the values of the liberal, rationalist meritocratic status group to which they predominantly belonged, as a matter of personal biography.

Furthermore, it was also true that to the extent that liberal philosophers of this generation did contemplate practical social affairs, they did so from within the same encompassing set of hierarchical, evolutionary social assumptions which framed the empiricists' views, as exemplified at length, above, with respect to Galton's project. The self-glorification of the position, both within English society and in relation to the civilisations of the whole world, of the white Anglo-Saxon

[133] Young, *Darwin's metaphor*, ch. 5; Collini, *Public moralists*, ch. 6.

[134] Karl Pearson's *The grammar of science* was an epistemologically sophisticated defence of positivist empirical science, much influenced by Ernst Mach and substantially anticipating the position of the logical positivists in the next century.

classical, liberal arts educated male was just too seductive for all concerned. Liberal social philosophers across the spectrum from Bosanquet, through Hobhouse, to Hobson believed in the global, moral superiority of the humane, liberal, rational values of their class, as a virtuous product of history. They could not, on the whole, sufficiently distinguish between the merit of the abstract values which their class advocated and the merit of the class itself, and all its interests.[135] As a result they could not see through, underneath or behind the smuggled moral premises and social evolutionary supports for the 'evidence' presented to them by empirical scientists sharing the same assumptions: anthropologists, biologists, sociologists – many of them trained in medicine, the ultimate materialist science of 'man'. Materialist and idealist approaches to the study of humankind simply concurred with each other because of their shared evolutionary perspective, a sort of cosmological 'Whig' (in fact, liberal) interpretation – of all history.

However, despite the shared framework of moral and social assumptions there were, of course, significant differences in methodology of investigation. It was these differences which determined that the GRO and the public health environmentalist medical professionals, as practical empirical social scientists, would find that their principal political and intellectual antagonists and competitors would be the empirical biometricians, and not idealist social and economic theorists. Whereas the liberal, ethical philosophers and economists were proudly deductivist and distrusted the status of empirical information, the hereditarian biometricians believed themselves to be thoroughly and rigorously inductive, armed with the means to subjugate all living objects to an ordered place within the evolutionary framework, through employment of the appropriate tools of analysis: mathematical statistics. They did not recognise the crucial distinction between the animal world and the human, social world that lay at the core of the Oxford ethical approach to the study of society. For the latter group, the difference was that humans, in distinction to animals, were determined by their own motives, and that this fact constituted the real object of study, in the manner appropriate: philosophical reflection and dialectical discourse. The biometric eugenicists, on the other hand, tended to assume that social reality, or quantifiable aspects of it, could simply be measured in the same way as data from the natural world concerning other, less autonomous organisms.

The GRO, given its medical, public health interests and environmentalist, epidemiological approach, subscribed broadly to the same epistemology and methodology of scientific empiricism when analysing social, economic and health problems as was ostensibly exhibited by social Darwinists. Both shared a commitment to a materialistic scientific empiricism that sought general and

[135] Although J. A. Hobson, in his theories of underconsumption and imperialism, was highly critical of defects in the liberal capitalist culture which permitted gross inequalities of incomes to arise, this was a reformist and not revolutionary critique, designed to bring the liberal society into line with its own ethical premises. On Hobson, see Freeden, *J. A. Hobson*; Clarke, *Liberals and social democrats*.

uniform laws. The implicitly agreed rules of combat were those of a positivist epistemology: logical inference from the statistically expressed 'facts' to demonstrate Humean, constant conjunction, cause–effect relationships, according to the rules of induction classically laid down by J. S. Mill in his celebrated treatise of 1843.[136] As will be seen in the next chapter each side deployed its recognised expertise in statistical techniques and inferential reasoning as the primary rhetorical, intellectual weapon in a crucial scientific battle during the opening decades of the new century over the wisdom of welfare policies.

Summary: the professional model of social evolution

Galton's professional model was really no more than an extremely simple linear hierarchy, an essentially naïve representation directly reproducing the common-sense social prejudices, social evolutionary beliefs and moral code of his own status group: the liberal, classically educated upper middle class. Indeed, as has been shown, both Galton's and Roberts's model initially came into existence as little more than the consequence of a methodological expedient based on an *ad hoc* summary categorisation – supplied by the spokesmen of this status group who had served on the Royal Commissions of the 1860s – of the four different social grades of school which they chose to recognise as currently in existence in the 1870s. It was, ultimately, little more than the transposition on to the current structure of society, of that social evolutionary view of history which several generations of Britain's liberal intelligentsia had since mid-Victorian times found so congenial. The professional model is the static social analogue for the dynamic concept of a teleological evolution.

Such a social evolutionary perspective was shared alike by materialist and by idealist poles within the broad liberal consensus, from Spencer, Darwin and Galton to Jowett, Green and Hobhouse. And it seemed all the more convincing because both empirical, socio-biological science and abstract reason, seeking respite from doubt, concurred upon it, as independently both 'is' and 'ought', apparently both ontological and ethical truth.

This chapter has elucidated how it was, through the further elaboration of the scientific project of anthropometrics, that this banal initial combination of unexamined, conventional social presumptions, allied to methodological expedience, became insidiously reified into a naturalistic theory or model of British society's essential structure. The prototype professional model thereby acquired the full 'scientific' status of an empirically tested intellectual construct because it had apparently been demonstrated to have been in accord with the observable facts of correlated social and biological variation in British society (although, as has been noted, the empirical verification of a linear social grading in the anthropometric

[136] Mill, *A system of logic*, in particular Books III and VI.

data was in fact highly attenuated in Roberts's scheme, though even Roberts himself eventually seems to have 'forgotten' this). The model then began to take on a life of its own, independent of its origins, as an established and authoritative fact about British society and its class structure – something which therefore began to provoke and generate its own derivative agenda of 'scientific' questions, issues and debates.

4

The emergence of a social explanation of class inequalities among environmentalists, 1901–1904

Introduction: the National Efficiency crisis

In the previous chapters it has been shown how it was that the GRO pulled back from launching a new official social classification scheme for the 1891 census after an initial expression of interest in the mid-1880s. It had become clear during the intervening few years that such an innovation was both likely to undermine the Office's long-standing autonomy in utilising its vital statistics for medical, epidemiological purposes and was also certain to provide intellectual ammunition for other, competing 'schools' of empirical social science that had emerged during the course of the troubled 1880s. They offered diagnoses of the causes of and remedies for urban poverty and disease that rivalled those of the environmentalist public health movement, to which the GRO continued to owe its primary allegiance.

In this respect relatively little had changed by the late 1890s, when preparations for the succeeding census of 1901 were beginning to be made. Financial restraint was still the order of the day in central government and especially at the closely-watched LGB; the main departmental rival for the GRO's control of the census – the Labour Bureau of the Board of Trade – was stronger than ever, having become a fully fledged Department in 1893. The segregationist proposals of Marshall and Booth regarding rural labour colonies had now become an experimental reality, enjoying something of a vogue among several important social work institutions, such as the Salvation Army, the Church Army and the Home Colonisation Society.[1] The same defensive and conservative climate of public political opinion still prevailed.[2] 'Urban degeneration' remained a still-credible public anxiety. In the late 1880s, the Director-General of the Army Medical Department had overhastily proclaimed a physical deterioration in the masses on

[1] Harris, *Unemployment and Politics*, ch. 3.

[2] See pp. 98–9 for political voting patterns in illustration of this point.

the strength of his statistics of medical rejections among recruits.[3] He was to do so once again, with even more publicity, at the beginning of the new century: an important episode which will be analysed in some detail in this chapter. Preparing for the 1901 census in this inhospitable climate of opinion, the GRO was content simply to drop the obsolete 1861 classification scheme as quietly as possible and without reopening the question of a new one to replace it.[4]

It was not until the years immediately after the turn of the new century that relevant new factors began to come into play. These were to lead the GRO into a renewed interest in the possibility of a social classification scheme, without, however, abandoning its continuing commitment to the public health movement. Indeed, as will become apparent, it was the rapid emergence within the social science and policy arena of Edwardian Britain of a confident, revitalised and more comprehensive environmentalist analysis of the causes of poverty and social inequality that was to provide the essential precondition and intellectual impetus behind the GRO's new resolve to construct an official model of the nation's social classes. This mobilisation of intellectual resources by the environmentalist, rehabilitationist approach occurred as a spontaneous defensive response to a sudden upsurge of hostile pronouncements issuing from the hereditarian and segregationist schools of thought.

By the beginning of the twentieth century Fabian socialists had been advocating collectivist social legislation for well over a decade, on grounds of functional efficiency, national defence and, increasingly, congruence with the lessons of evolutionary science. In this respect their analysis and aims coincided to a considerable extent with those of the eugenicist Karl Pearson. Both shared a nationalist interpretation of evolutionary theory: 'social Darwinism' as it has come to be termed. The specific form of social Darwinism espoused by the Fabians and by the biometricians would be more accurately termed 'nationalist Darwinism', since there were so many other social Darwinisms.[5]

Sidney Webb and Karl Pearson had both come to the conclusion quite separately that, amongst humans, national populations were the fundamental unit of evolution, to whom the unavoidable laws of survival of the fittest applied in all their rigour. The collective protection – or even positive enhancement – of the

[3] On this occasion the Director-General's dramatic claims were duly debunked by Dr T. Graham Balfour (an Associate of the BA Anthropometric Committee of 1875–83), in his inaugural address in 1888 as President of the Royal Statistical Society.

[4] See above pp. 78, 85.

[5] Even liberals such as Ritchie, Kidd and Hobson were deeply involved in the 'socialising' of Darwinian theory. Herbert Spencer was initially responsible for tying together biology and sociology within a social evolutionary perspective: Spencer, *The study of sociology*; and Spencer, *The principles of sociology*. Only Huxley and Hobhouse among the Progressive Liberals staunchly argued against the direct applicability of a theory of selection by 'natural' characteristics of individuals to a theory of man and society. Hobhouse developed his concept of 'orthogenic development' as an idealist alternative to the Spencerian notion of superorganic evolution (see below, pp. 220–1). See Collini, *Liberalism and sociology*, ch. 6; Freeden, *The New Liberalism*, pp. 80 and 186–9; Abrams, *The origins*, pp. 90–2.

health of the domestic, national population was therefore deemed to be an appropriate task for the state to take upon itself. Evolutionary logic dictated that the goal of national physical efficiency was the prerequisite for national survival against the competition represented by other nations. Such responsibilities required the state to undertake a prudential policy of rational and scientific regulation of the economic system's motor force of capitalism in order to prevent its individualistic, internally competitive forces from outrunning their overall national, social utility.[6] Karl Pearson and the Webbs shared a belief in the rational perfectibility of human society, a reverence for the efficacy of scientific empiricism, an acceptance that the state could and should direct its citizens in the means to improve themselves, and a meritocracy as the ultimate goal.[7]

Until the opportunity created by the public outcry over the army's poor performance in the Boer War, however, these two precocious apologists for the scientific state had been largely preaching in the wilderness. Their unremitting collectivising and regulating prescriptions were unable to find an appreciative national audience in a society that still cherished its liberal and libertarian myths. Albion's self-image was still that of the home of the radical, independent free-born Englishman, who may not have the vote but knew – or thought that he knew – that he lived free of the continental blight of 'despotism': the anonymous and capricious interference of the inherently corrupt and costly hand of central government. This mythic libertarian national identity, first fully and powerfully reinforced upon an entire generation by the propaganda machine which helped to mobilise the nation into arms to defeat the Napoleonic dictator, had of course – even for a myth – become extraordinarily divorced from reality by the end of the nineteenth century.[8] It was true that central government had grown only relatively slowly since its explosive expansion in the second quarter of the century. But, compensatingly, local government functions and expenditure had mushroomed in the second half of the Victorian era, while administration of the Empire had, of course, become a global 'despotism' for many of those on its receiving end.

At the commencement of the new century, therefore, the individualist libertarian myth was over-ripe for its fall. Public opinion was more than ready for a rapid conversion to more collectivist norms, reflecting ideas long-propounded by a variety of political theorists and policies already long-practised in an *ad hoc* manner as good municipal government. With the much-heralded public scandal

[6] For early expression of this thesis by two Fabians in 1896, see Fabian Tracts 69 and 72, respectively: Webb, *The difficulties of individualism*; and Ball, *The moral aspects of socialism*. The best general study of the Fabians remains McBriar, *Fabian socialism*. For Pearson's social Darwinism, see MacKenzie, *Statistics in Britain*, p. 83.

[7] They were still essentially in agreement on all this as late as 1930, six years before Pearson's death: Soloway, *Demography and degeneration*, pp. 189–90. As a result of its capacity to appeal to materialist rationalists in this way, there was a complex relationship throughout the first four decades of the century between eugenics and political positions of the right and the left. See Paul, 'Eugenics and the left'.

[8] On the significance of anti-Napoleonic propaganda in propagating the popular myth of libertarian Britain, see Linda Colley, *Britons*, especially ch. 7.

over the deplorable physical condition of so many of the urban recruits offering themselves for service in the South African Wars, the full force of the National Efficiency analysis and the apparent logic of their radical collectivist policies came flooding into the public mind, within and without Parliament. The maverick journalist of popular jingoism and *ressentiment*, Arnold White, seems to have played a prominent role in linking 'degenerationist' notions with the recruitment fears. He first drew attention to the recruitment rejection rates in October 1899 and from May to December 1900 White followed up with a series of thirty-three articles in the *Weekly Sun*.[9] Other influential figures thereafter took up the hue and cry, amongst whom General Sir (John) Frederick Maurice seems to have been responsible for two of the most influential articles.[10] Ultimately, public anxiety was stirred up sufficiently to make it inevitable that the government be seen to do something, leading to Balfour's reluctant appointment of the famous inquiry of the Interdepartmental Committee on Physical Deterioration.[11]

There was, however, a wide and fundamental divergence of scientific interpretation as to the causes of the problem across the spectrum of opinion that was mobilised into demanding state intervention to remedy the dangers exposed by the Boer War. Sidney Webb's Fabian socialism and Karl Pearson's eugenic socialism were in fact representative of the two most opposed political extremes, for all that they had shared a pioneering preoccupation with promoting 'national efficiency'. Once serious discussion of remedial policies began, this difference was bound to become manifest. As MacKenzie has pointed out, Fabians were in favour of extending the franchise; Pearson was not.[12] The Fabian advocates of scientific

[9] These were collected together and published with some other material as *Efficiency and empire* (1901). The original article of October 1899 was entitled 'The cult of infirmity', published in the *National Review*. For further information on Arnold White (1848–1925), see G. R. Searle's 'Introduction' to the 1973 reprinted edition of *Efficiency and empire*.

[10] 'Where to get men' (published under the pseudonym 'Miles'), and 'National health: a soldier's study' published in the *Contemporary Review* in January 1902 and January 1903, respectively. See PDC, Evidence, paras. 283–8. Major-General Sir J. F. Maurice (1841–1912), son of (J.) F. D. Maurice (the leading Christian Socialist), was a prominent army reformer.

[11] See Gilbert, 'Health and politics', pp. 144–7, on the reluctance of the Balfour government to become embroiled in the issue. The Clerk to the Privy Council, Sir Almaric Fitzroy, was, however, very keen to have an inquiry appointed; and was able to ensure this through his great ally, the Duke of Devonshire (Spencer Compton Cavendish, 1833–1908), Balfour's President of the Privy Council. Fitzroy had worked continuously with Devonshire, first as his Private Secretary and then as Clerk to the Council, since Devonshire's appointment in 1895 as Salisbury's President of the Council in the previous Conservative and Unionist administration. Fitzroy was to repeat this initiating role when he successfully encouraged another friend and subsequent Lord President of the Council, the great Liberal John Morley, to back the setting up of the Royal Commission on Venereal Disease in 1913. Apparently Fitzroy's diaries reveal that his determination to investigate the threats of physical deterioration and venereal disease was prompted by more than just a sense of the public interest: they record a long-standing quasi-romantic infatuation with the bodily perfection which he perceived to be manifest in young peers and peeresses of the realm. He was forced to resign his high office in 1923 after being charged with importuning girls in Hyde Park. See Davenport-Hines, *Sex, death and punishment*, pp. 213–14. On Fitzroy's earlier career, see above, ch. 3, n. 75.

[12] MacKenzie, *Statistics in Britain*, p. 78.

administration and avoidance of 'human waste' believed that the agencies of local government, public health, hygiene and all the official powers of regulatory enforcement should be expanded, infused with scientific principles and so made more effective as the means to improve the 'quality' of the nation's human material. The selectionist hereditarian eugenists, while sharing the same ultimate aims, believed that such efforts to improve the poor were mistaken, since the poor corresponded more or less to the inherently unfit. The population's quality could only be scientifically raised through policies to encourage reproduction of the fit, or to discourage it in the unfit.

The peculiarly penetrating influence of Galton's eugenics and the associated professional model as a scientific representation of society in the debates of the early years of the century is intriguing, given its relatively low profile throughout the preceding decade. Galton had continued with anthropometric work at his Kensington Laboratory from 1884 until 1894, but overall the period after his work with the BA Committee appears as something of a lull in his eugenic activism, until the post-Boer War opportunity to proselytise presented itself. This is despite the boost received during these years from the apparent vindication of his extreme hereditarianism from the refinement of August Weismann's theory of the fixity of the germ plasm during the period 1883–93.[13] In fact Galton's ideas were being gradually absorbed at this time, among others by a small number of influential COS figures working in the field of early mental health policy and administration, notably Mary Dendy, Ellen Pinsent and G. E. Shuttleworth. It was to be their efforts in the new century which resulted in the only pre-Great War formal victory for the eugenics movement in terms of social policy legislation (the Mental Deficiency Act of 1913).[14]

There was a sharply increased interest among social and policy scientists after 1900 in the eugenic, meritocratic social class model and its doom-laden depictions of current demographic trends. Undoubtedly this was sparked into life by the post-Boer War incendiaries of imperial inefficiency; but the interest was also premised on a general perception that these were genuinely scientific products and prognostications. How did the model acquire this scientific status?

[13] Weismann, *The germ plasm*, was the definitive statement of 1893 following a decade of active debate with his critics and opponents, particularly with the Lamarckian, Herbert Spencer, who had marshalled a number of telling counter-arguments, which Weismann successfully strove to overcome. See below, pp. 220–1.

[14] Sutherland, *Ability, merit and measurement*; see esp. p. 34, for comparison between the first (1895) and second (1900) editions of G. E. Shuttleworth's important textbook, *Mentally deficient children*, illustrating the progressive acceptance of Galton's notions of heritability among this group. For further details, see below, pp. 205–6; and ch. 5, n. 111 for later attempts at further mental deficiency legislation. As David Feldman has shown, the Aliens Act of 1905 substantially owed its place on the statute book to the Conservative party's calculations of the electoral advantage which would accrue in the marginal seats of London's East End by pandering to popular racism. Although the race science of eugenics is not unrelated to popular forms of racism, the Aliens Act cannot be attributed in any direct sense to the eugenics movement, which was not formally launched until 1907. Feldman, *Englishmen and Jews*, ch. 11.

Of course, it helped that Galton himself as well as his two principal, biometric disciples, W. F. R. Weldon and Karl Pearson, were all established, respected natural scientists.[15] Hence, Galton's early popularity with the Sociological Society in the first years after its founding in 1903 reflects the urgent need felt for endorsement by 'real scientists' on the part of an as yet uninstitutionalised discipline extremely unsure of itself. But this alone could not have guaranteed the eugenists' professional model its 'scientific' status. In accounting for both the scientific plausibility of Galton's social class model as well as the political acceptability of its segregationist implications in the hands of the eugenicists, it seems relevant to point out that the contemporaneous rise and rise of contagionist germ theory, which had occurred during the intervening period since Galton's work in the mid-1880s, probably gave great assistance, albeit in a somewhat indirect way.

In the context of British empirical social, medical and policy-related science, germ theory appeared to impart an enormously increased general legitimacy to the intimately related twin-practices of classification and segregation of groups of individual humans. Because of the preventive health practices sanctioned by the contagionism of germ theory, the classification of individuals and their families into groups on grounds of visually observable bio-medical signs was rapidly becoming a generally accepted, scientifically sanctioned social procedure, accompanied by the justification that such treatment of individuals facilitated the greater good and welfare of the society or community as a whole. Germ theory strongly reinforced a general approach which focused administrative and investigative powers and attention on the problems of classifying – and thereby identifying and locating – and segregating those individuals and their families who could be authentically, scientifically diagnosed as infected and infectious. By contrast the sanitary and environmentalist approach previously dominant in preventive medicine and very wary of the strength of libertarian sentiments, had also sought to measure, classify and improve: but with a focus on places not persons. As illustrated in the comparative geographical methodology of the GRO, this ecological approach assumed that the relative incidence of a disease condition among the individuals of a community was indicative of the strength and character of certain transindividual malevolent forces active in their shared environment. This led to a strategy of egalitarian rehabilitation: the same environmental improvements were assumed to benefit all equally.

Contagionist germ theory indicated instead that the most effective preventive health strategy was an 'inegalitarian' programme of differential treatments, extending even to enforced physical segregation of identified victims and their

[15] W. F. R. Weldon (1860–1906), Professor of Zoology at University College, London, 1890–9, Linacre Professsor of Comparative Anatomy, Oxford University, 1899–1906; Karl Pearson (1857–1936), Goldsmid Professor of Applied Mathematics and Mechanics, 1884–1911, and Galton Professor of Eugenics, University College, London, 1911–33.

families. As a result preventive public health measures increasingly came to revolve around the classification and control of afflicted persons, instead of environments. Removal to controlled conditions under the watchful eye of those experts who supposedly understood best the nature of the afflicted's condition came to be seen as the most thorough policy, simultaneously promoting the recovery of the victim, while protecting the community of origin from further contamination. Germ theory meant that for reasons of executive efficiency in both treating the victims and preventing their contact with others at risk, classification and temporary segregation of affected individuals was a scientifically reasonable and administratively legitimate preventive policy with respect to those persons properly identified to be suffering from notifiable infectious diseases. However, the unquestionable validity of such procedures and of such an approach in these circumstances seems to have lent a cloak of spurious legitimacy to a host of other concurrent attempts to classify and allocate individuals 'scientifically', according to supposedly biologistic criteria relating to their visible, physical characteristics.

The treatment provided for the mystifying affliction of respiratory tuberculosis was an example of this which is of central importance, because it provided a bridge between the genuinely medical and the decidedly non-medical, and also between the temporary and the permanent detention of individuals. There are, of course, several grounds on which historians have found cause for complaint over the British medical establishment's lack-lustre record in dealing with the white plague.[16] Whatever its longer-term inadequacies, however, the initial late Victorian and Edwardian extension of the segregationist approach to TB treatment – in the form of rural sanatoria – was not entirely unreasonable. It was at least known that a specific micro-organism, the tubercle bacillus identified by Koch in 1882, was responsible – although the precise etiology remained an enigma.

However, if such a classification and segregation policy was admissible for a disease as little understood as tuberculosis, there was no obvious dividing line between this condition and others such as venereal diseases, alcoholism, sexual promiscuity, imbecilism, dementia, or perhaps just plain old age or inability to keep a job. These 'conditions' were all considered by contemporaries to be major social problems as well as personal afflictions, in which a much-debated mix of cultural and/or biological mechanisms of contagion or heritability were generally believed to be implicated. Where etiology was more soundly based and diagnostics were most well developed, quarantine and detention was temporary: individuals' segregated status ended with the lifting of their classification as potentially infectious. But TB, with its uncertain course and uncertain symptoms, could and did provide the pretext for months and even years of protected segregation. Of course it had been the Poor Law practice for decades to classify and segregate individuals, often detaining them on a long-term basis on grounds of the

16 Bryder, *Under the magic mountain*; Smith, *The retreat of tuberculosis*; and a review article including these two publications: Szreter, 'Healthy government?'.

moralised economics of 'less eligibility' (and Poor Law practice was itself changing in the 1890s, introducing more finely graded distinctions).[17] But it was the medical, biological and 'scientific' involvement and justification for such segregation that was new.

From this perspective anthropometrics, the empirical centre-piece of early eugenics, can be seen as another 'scientific' field in which this late Victorian bio-medical methodology of classification and differentiation was being extended way beyond the legitimate confines of pathological preventive medicine. The anthropometricians wished to discover and demonstrate the dimensions of the supposedly permanent systematic physical differences existing between social and 'racial' groups of normal, non-pathogenic individuals: differences of physiognomy, cranial shape and size, complexion, and, especially, height attainment.[18] These were to provide illustrations for their evolutionary and biologically determinist theory of both intercultural distinctions between nations and intracultural differences between social classes within nations (both were loosely referred to as forms of 'racial' difference by the proponents of anthropometry).

It is probable therefore that after nearly two decades of acquaintance with classification and segregation as an increasingly routine and demonstrably effective scientific and administrative procedure for dealing with issues of health, where individuals defined as unfit were to be temporarily – or not so temporarily in the case of TB – segregated, the notion of a global social classification of the nation according to supposedly biological criteria may have seemed not only less novel and contentious than previously but even positively normal: as the kind of scientific procedure that was appropriate for dealing with human beings, especially in matters relating to the health of the community. Nearly two decades of bacteriological contagionism and the appropriate preventive health measures had also thoroughly accustomed the public to the idea that certain persons – not places or smells – were unhealthy.[19]

Categories of persons whom the relevant experts had scientifically tested and judged unfit were a hazard and a threat to all. Eugenic scientists were now arguing, by extension, that the relative overall unhealthiness, unfitness, inefficiency and burdensomeness of certain people in general – not just during episodes of illness – could be judged or classed (to judge is to classify and vice versa), relative to that of the most healthy, efficient and productive individuals. This was supposedly demonstrated by the professional model of social structure and the results it showed for the differential growth patterns, heights, fertility and mortality of the graded social classes.

17 Williams (Thane) (unpublished PhD thesis).

18 Gould, *The mismeasure*, chs. 2–4; Stepan, *The idea of race*, ch. 4. On 'race', see ch. 3, n. 20.

19 On the increasing acceptability during the last two decades of the century, even among the working classes, of previously much-resisted preventive measures, including the removal and isolation of persons, see Hardy, *The epidemic streets*, ch. 9.

The silent revolution in nineteenth-century government: the public service professions and local government

Apart from the somewhat speculative and grandiose analyses of Fabian and eugenist intellectuals, there were other significant constituencies of informed opinion that had developed powerful convictions regarding the nature, causes and remedies of the urban poverty which the recruiting statistics had so dramatically implicated in the early years of the new century. Prominent among these other voices were those who had dedicated their professional careers to the task of improving the conditions of life in towns and communities all over the land – the largely local authority-employed public service professionals. These included sanitary engineers, surveyors, food and drugs analysts, sanitary inspectors and – above all – the Medical Officers of Health and the Town Clerks, who were the executive élite among these trained cadres of officials. Others whose professional activities entailed a direct interest in urban poverty and the domestic conditions of the working classes included such local and central government officials as school attendance officers, building inspectors, HM Inspectors of Factories, and of Schools, school managers, and the newly regulated profession of midwife. Finally, of course, there were the swelling ranks of teachers in the nation's recently consolidated universal elementary school system, a large occupational group perhaps more directly and fully in contact with the lives of the poor than any other. In the course of the last three decades of the nineteenth century this proliferating mass of salaried posts for suitably trained officials had emerged and promptly professionalised itself with examining bodies, subscription to national associations, annual conferences and journals.[20]

To this must be added a second major category of practical worker in the poverty industry, the self-appointed ranks of volunteer philanthropists and social workers throughout the country, such as the Settlement House residents, Salvation

[20] The country's earliest MOH appointments dated from the 1840s and an Association of Metropolitan MOHs had been founded as early as 1856, immediately after the 1855 Metropolis Local Management Act had established forty-eight such posts for London's newly defined vestries and districts. But it was not until the Public Health Act of 1872 that there was a statutory obligation laid on all local health authorities to appoint MOHs. By the end of the nineteenth century there were 1,770 MOHs in post. Brand, *Doctors and the state*, p. 109. It was not until 1888 that the growing subprofession launched its influential national journal, *Public Health*, which accompanied the formation of its national organisation, the Incorporated Society of MOHs formed by the amalgamation of various regional societies. One of the earliest other such national associations of local preventive health officials had been the Society of Public Analysts, founded in 1874 and comprising 224 members by 1882: Wohl, *Endangered lives*, pp. 54, 195. The sanitary inspectors' Royal Sanitary Institute of Britain held its founding conference at Leamington in 1877, with Burdon Richardson in the chair (Edwin Chadwick himself, the pioneer exponent of 'the Sanitary Idea' a generation earlier, chaired the second year's conference held at Stafford). Its transactions ran as a journal from the next year. The Institution of Public Health Engineers, the Association of Municipal and Sanitary Engineers and Surveyors, the Sanitary Inspectors' Association and the National Union of Sanitary Inspectors were among the other public service professional organisations all founded at this time, their journals commencing in the 1890s.

Army and Temperance League workers, the National Society for the Prevention of Cruelty to Children (NSPCC), Dr Barnardo's and the Lady Health Visitors, many of long pedigree and increasingly professional in their self-organisation and training under the auspices of such institutions as the COS.[21] At one remove from these official and voluntary social workers in the front line, but still close enough to have personal experience of these communities of the poor, were those investigative philanthropists who were anxious to define for themselves the true nature and extent of urban poverty. Charles Booth and Seebohm Rowntree were, of course, the outstanding examples of such social investigators at this time, hoping both to promote deeper understanding of the perplexing problems, and simultaneously thereby to contribute to more effective legislation and social action.[22] Most of those giving evidence to the Interdepartmental Committee on Physical Deterioration were practical students of the problem of poverty, drawn from one of these various constituencies.[23]

In the numerous studies that have appeared of social policy in the Edwardian period, the third of these three categories, local government employees and related officials and educationists, have rarely been given the attention they deserve as an empowering and progressive agency. In these studies they have usually ceded pride of place to New Liberal intellectuals and other thinkers, and to politicians and Fabian civil servants;[24] or else to the various categories of philanthropists.[25] Nevertheless, it was precisely these local officials, teachers and school managers – often working in co-operation with local voluntary bodies – whose collectivist

21 Meacham, *Toynbee Hall*; Dowling (unpublished MA thesis); Behlmer, *Child abuse*; Prochaska, *Women and philanthropy*.

22 As B. S. Rowntree saw it: 'two great departments of human effort . . . may be brought to bear upon the problem of poverty. All history speaks of the enormous and far-reaching influence of *law* upon the character of a people'; 'Wise legislation must, however, be based upon facts, and it was as a contribution to the knowledge of facts in relation to poverty that my inquiry was undertaken.' Rowntree, *The poverty line*, pp. 29–30. O'Day and Englander have speculated that an identical disposition in Booth's case may be traceable to his formative immersion in the Comtian Positivist 'religion', which swept the liberal intellectuals of his generation, and particularly his family in the 1860s and 1870s (his cousins included the Crompton brothers, E. S. Beesly and W. S. Jevons): O'Day and Englander, *Mr Charles Booth's inquiry*, pp. 20, 144–6.

23 Of the sixty-seven witnesses before the PDC, there were five MOHs and sixteen public servants whose professional activities would fall into the first category outlined above. There were eleven philanthropists – the second category. Of the remaining thirty-five witnesses to be accounted for, nearly two-thirds were other medical experts, leaving four investigative philanthropists of the third category, four military witnesses and five miscellaneous, including the MPs John Gorst and Thomas Macnamara. It should be remembered that those giving evidence often represented many more. For example, Dr Alfred Eicholz claimed to represent 'the members and officers of the Education Committees of Manchester, Salford, Leeds and many officers of the London School Board' (PDC, Evidence, para. 432).

24 For instance: Semmel, *Imperialism*; Searle, *The quest for national efficiency*; Freeden, *The New Liberalism*; Collini, *Liberalism and sociology*; McBriar, *An Edwardian mixed doubles*.

25 Prochaska, *Women and philanthropy*; Harris, 'The Webbs, the COS and the Ratan Tata Foundation'. However, for an earlier study which did acknowledge the local government contribution to new initiatives in social thought in this period, see Harris, *Unemployment and politics*, chs. IV–V.

initiatives and schemes were so to impress Sir Frederick Maurice when he first began to campaign for greater attention to the nation's health in the aftermath of the Boer War.[26] Maurice was to confess himself quite overwhelmed by the response from these quarters which he received when he raised the issue of the nation's health in 1903: 'it was the accidental circumstance of my happening to touch, without knowing it, upon a subject about which all who had really been studying it were red hot, that has made me appear to have more to do with it than I have had . . .'.[27] It was the temporary resonance between the beliefs and practices of these increasingly powerful and prestigious personnel, proliferating in local and central government positions of social responsibility, the programmatic diagnosis of Britain's ills offered by the various nationalist Darwinists, and the loud alarum sounded by national figures such as Maurice, which ultimately swept into the forum of national politics a novel collectivist, interventionist language for addressing the nation's social problems, an ideology and practice of social reform.[28]

Local welfare administrators and executive agents, and their various provincial political allies on local councils, had been steadily growing in numbers and powers for many decades. The stereotype image of local councillors and ratepayers as a uniformly myopic 'shopocracy' preoccupied only with economising on the rates needs to be informed by a more realistic acknowledgement of the diversity of opinion in such a body; and also by a recognition of the historical importance of the growing participation of women in local politics, as well as working men (deemed to have the local vote by virtue of their votes being 'compounded' within the rents they paid to their absentee landlords), after they were both admitted to the municipal franchise in 1869. These were two new constituencies both of whom could be more favourably disposed towards health and welfare measures and services, and increasingly were after 1869. A system of localised self-government and social responsibility had been asserted in the Local Government Act of 1858, consolidated by the major Public Health Act of 1875 and finally made universal with the Local Government Acts of 1888 (defining County Councils) and 1894 (defining district and parish authorities). As well as acting as full Council members, locally elected political representatives could serve on Poor Law Boards of Guardians, where women were also eligible and were increasingly elected after 1875. Additionally both women and working-class men could serve on local School Boards, established with a householder franchise in 1870.[29]

26 See his eulogy of the schemes for feeding school children in Glasgow, and of Lady Health Visitors in Manchester, which he had encountered on being asked to speak in each of these cities over the previous year. PDC, Evidence, paras. 279–81, 283.

27 Sir F. Maurice, in PDC, Evidence, para. 325.

28 Note that the emphasis here on the narrative importance of practical policy implementers is complementary rather than antagonistic to Freeden's emphasis on the ideological context for the efflorescence of the new policies, as he himself acknowledges: Freeden, *The New Liberalism*, p. 195.

29 On the political impact of these newly admitted sections of the populace – middle-class women and the male working class – see, for instance, Simon, *Education and the labour movement*; and Hollis, *Ladies elect*. In general, see Read, *The age*; Waller, *Town, city*.

The increasing activism and dynamism of local authorities during the last decades of the Victorian era provides something of a contrast with the activities of the main corresponding central government department. Roy MacLeod long ago exposed the many and varied stratagems by which the Treasury deliberately sought to stymie initiative and expansion in the LGB, especially its medical activities, during the last two decades of the nineteenth century.[30] This was the era of 'Lingenism', when the pre-eminence of the generalist over the technical specialist was being established throughout the civil service.[31] A Gladstonian policy of retrenchment and control over central expenditure was prosecuted in pursuit of the *laissez-faire* virtues of minimal taxation and minimal central state interference, appealing to a widespread and ingrained radical ethos in favour of local self-government.[32] But it has been insufficiently appreciated by historians that precisely because this Treasury-implemented strategy of devolution in social policy – casting off executive and financial responsibilities onto the provinces – was so successful, the last quarter of the century witnessed an unprecedented expansion of administrative and organisational initiatives at the local authority level. Not surprisingly there was a corresponding growth in the numbers and strength of the public service professional groups involved in this activity.

In other words, the inevitable and actual corollary of the success of central government retrenchment and the refusal to be drawn into executive responsibility for all the collectively funded facilities and services required to avoid the urban public squalor against which late Victorians recoiled was a compensating growth in government and policy initiatives at the local authority level. Central government provided concessionary grants-in-aid and technical advice if requested, but it was primarily local government that initiated, staffed, sometimes devised and mostly funded the enormous expansion in urban infrastructure and social services that occurred throughout the period, 1858–1914.[33] As H. J. Hanham has observed: 'In retrospect the extent of local self-government during the nineteenth century appears stupefying. As a matter of principle Whitehall thrust every type of administration on to elected local bodies.'[34] This is unequivocally borne out by the basic quantitative evidence: the expenditure of local government as a share of all government expenditure (itself a continually increasing figure) rose dramatically from 1870, when it stood at just under 30%, to 1905 when it peaked at over 50%.[35] It

[30] MacLeod, 'The frustration of state medicine'; MacLeod, *Treasury control*; MacLeod, 'Introduction', pp. 16–18.

[31] Although Maurice Wright's argument must be respected: tight control of the Treasury over the rest of the civil service as a whole (as opposed to the LGB in particular) can be exaggerated for this period and probably applies most rigorously to the interwar period: Wright, 'Treasury control 1854–1914'. For more on 'Lingenism', see ch. 2, nn. 58, 127, and pp. 114–15.

[32] On the importance of local self-government throughout the nineteenth century, see Bellamy, *Administering local–central relations*; Prest, *Liberty and locality*.

[33] This was true even in the early part of the period: Lambert, 'Central and local relations'.

[34] Hanham, *The nineteenth century constitution*, p. 373.

[35] Figures for 1870 calculated from Mitchell and Deane, *Abstract*, pp. 416 and 426. Figures for 1905 from A. T. Peacock and Wiseman, *The growth of public expenditure*, Table A-20.

was only at this juncture that the political desirability of a shift in the fiscal burdens and formal responsibilities for social policies, back towards the central state and direct taxation, became sufficiently pressing and widely acknowledged that such a policy programme was adopted by a national party – the New Liberals.[36]

Not surprisingly all this produced considerable fiscal strains for local authorities. They attempted to manage this in various ways, notably through the innovations of 'municipal trading' and deficit financing – borrowing on the money-markets.[37] As ever, under the illogical yet compelling pressures from ratepayers both to deliver the services and improvements to their environment that they wanted while not adding a penny to the local rates bills, town councils had increasingly found it expedient to supplement the funds for local services collected in from the rate base with income generated by running municipal services such as tramways and gas supply. This phenomenon, and the innovations in local revenue generation devised to fund it, was broadly referred to by its contemporary, anti-collectivist detractors as 'gas and water socialism' and 'municipal trading'.[38]

The peculiar invisibility of the massive local government-based preventive health achievement during the period 1870–1914, and of the degree of its informal integration with an associated penumbra of both proletarian and genteel institutions of voluntary support and philanthropic assistance seems to be due to a set of compounding historiographical factors.[39] First, as Sidney Webb's celebrated and oft-repeated fictional anecdote suggested, the invisibility started with contemporaries' perceptions. The preventive and regulatory public health apparatus grew with the collusive protection of a kind of Victorian ideological blind spot: 'The individualist town councillor will walk along the municipal pavement, lit by municipal gas and cleansed by municipal brooms with municipal water...[while declaring, many 'municipals' later] . . . "Self-help, Sir, individual self-help, that's what made our city what it is".'[40] This creed was also manifested on the stage of national politics by the strict adherence throughout the century to the ritual formula of local self-government.[41] In such expensive matters as preventive public health measures, central government merely enabled and advised, leaving local ratepaying property-holders to decide. But decide they did, slowly and reluctantly

36 See pp. 252–3.

37 For important new research on the expansion of local government expenditure and sources of finance during this period, see Wilson *et al.* (unpublished paper); Millward and Sheard (unpublished paper).

38 See Offer, *Property and politics*, for the most penetrating analysis of the resulting conflict between interest groups, in particular chs. 15–16.

39 Against this historiographical invisibility, the study which has most fully documented and advocated the interpretation favoured here is: Behlmer, *Child abuse*. In his summary ch. 7 (p. 218), Behlmer notes that at least one contemporary analyst of government growth, the economist Kirkman Gray, was fully aware of the devolutionary nature of British government and the consequent mix of voluntary and local government activism in influencing its policies and providing its execution: Gray, *Philanthropy and the state*.

40 Sidney Webb, *Times*, 23 August 1902.

41 Bellamy, *Administering local–central relations.*

responding over the course of several decades to conscience-pricking scenes of poverty and offensive public squalor.

Secondly, and probably of most importance in the historiographical vanishing act of local government has been the long-lasting effect of the two most influential studies of the history of local government that were both produced in this period, by A. V. Dicey and by the Webbs. These were written by opposed partisans in the heated contemporary debate over the ideological and economic rights and wrongs of elected local authorities, collectivising and running commercial services in their localities. Both were highly critical of the recent practices of local government throughout the land, but for diametrically opposed reasons: one because they had done too little, the other because they had done too much.[42]

Sidney Webb, as a leading force behind the Progressives' 'gas and water socialism' programme of the new London County Council (LCC), believed that most local authorities had done nothing like enough to use and co-ordinate the administrative and financial resources at their disposal to transform the lives of their citizens. As Anne Hardy has pointed out, it has been particularly unfortunate for the historical reputation of Victorian public health that it was under the London vestries that a geographically comprehensive set of metropolitan MOH jurisdictions was first established, by the 1855 Metropolis Local Management Act.[43] Their reputation has consequently suffered from guilt by association with the vestries, the principal target of Sidney Webb and the Progressives, in their successful campaign to vilify the vestries in order to change the structure of government in London.[44] More generally, the monumental nine-volume Fabian history of local government by Beatrice and Sidney Webb exposed severe limitations, inefficiencies and absurdities in an administrative apparatus of great antiquity. It had grown in an entirely *ad hoc* and non-systematic way through a long series of accretions and half-hearted reforms into a set of overlapping, partial jurisdictions, none of which were quite the same in any two parts of the country.[45]

On the other hand, the more concise interpretation of the nineteenth-century history of local government that was published in 1905 by the old-style liberal, A. V. Dicey, deplored, on libertarian political and economic grounds, the novel trend towards collectivism. It was both an abrogation of the sacred free market,

[42] Webb and Webb, *English local government*. Dicey, *Law and public opinion*.

[43] Wilkinson (now Hardy) (unpublished DPhil thesis), p. 320.

[44] After languishing for almost a century, the London vestries have recently been treated to a revisionist account, which at least salvages something of their reputation for the last two decades of the century: Davis, *Reforming London*.

[45] Webb and Webb, *English local government*. The obvious point must be made that the attention which they lavished on this subject reflected the high hopes they held for the gradualist transforming potential of local government in British society, also, of course, practically manifested in Sidney Webb's prominent role in the Progressive party of the new LCC of the 1890s. This reflected the political strategy of Fabian 'permeation' for the introduction of socialism, named after Rome's defender against Hannibal, Quintus Fabius Maximus, 'Cunctator' ('the delayer').

'crowding-out' private firms, and a supposedly dangerous accretion of unaccountable sources of income and therefore power on the part of local governments and their unelected officials.[46] The local authorities seem, then, to have been caught in this ideological crossfire, with their historical reputation being the chief victim.[47]

Thirdly, there is the closely intertwining relationship that local government health and social services always had with the parochial operation of the dreaded Victorian Poor Law, despite their statutory separation in 1834.[48] The two parallel systems for provision of local 'welfare' services were administered under the same department of central government from 1871 onwards, the Local Government Board. This department always remained under the predominant influence of the parsimonious Poor Law tradition, something which the first definitive history of the period, published in 1936, pointed to as especially fateful.[49] Through this association with the Poor Law, therefore, Victorian local government and the Local Government Board itself have both been tarred with perhaps the largest of the several dirty brushes that reside in the nineteenth-century historian's capacious pot of tar.

But all this conceals a positive history of numerous local initiatives in research and expansion in service provision and funding during the last decades of the Victorian era, led in many respects by the MOHs. As the following section will exemplify, a major consequence of the Treasury's successful stifling of the LGB at the centre was that new ideas, experiments and their revisions were carried out in scores of local contexts instead. Thus, when plans for ambitious social services to combat urban poverty, infant mortality and unemployment came to be required in the Edwardian period by a Liberal central government at last interested in nationally funded social policy, an embarrassment of choice came flooding forth from locally employed professional and administrative experts and their associations. By then they had a long history behind them of developing and improving their schemes on the ground, out in the provinces and in London. They worked with their local government employers where they could, and cajoled them with

46 Dicey, *Law and public opinion*.

47 It is symptomatic of this historiographical distortion that Gray's more balanced and perceptive account (see n. 39), though published at the same time as the Webbs' and Dicey's work, has exerted relatively little historiographical influence and had to be 'rediscovered' by Behlmer in 1982.

48 For instance, a particular, direct problem for the public health movement was the difficulty experienced in gaining working-class co-operation for the vaccination programme against smallpox, due to its administration by the Poor Law. Wilkinson (unpublished DPhil thesis), pp. 168, 182. On the Poor Law generally, see Crowther, *The workhouse system*; Rose (ed.), *The poor and the city*.

49 R. C. K. Ensor's influential contribution to the Oxford History of England, *England 1870–1914*, pp. 126, 516–17. As a Fabian in close contact with Beatrice Webb at the time of her work as an appointed commissioner to the Royal Commission on the Poor Laws, Ensor had been made keenly aware of the enormous disappointment experienced by those with progressive ideas, when confronted with the attitudes of the ex-Poor Law secretariat of the LGB and its completely assimilated political 'master', the President John Burns. On Ensor and Beatrice Webb, and on Beatrice Webb's view of Burns, see McBriar, *An Edwardian mixed doubles*, pp. 215–16, 108, 309.

scientific investigations and reports when they could not.[50] The rough and tumble of relationships with local authorities over three decades had done much to cement the professional *esprit de corps* which had developed within the national associations of the public service professions by the turn of the century.[51]

The influence of local government experience in the public health field

As Anne Hardy has pointed out, whereas central government 'did not provide a career for any significant number of doctors during the period', it 'was in local government that there proved to be real opportunities for both professional and administrative expansion'.[52] Many then went on to pursue later careers in central government bringing their experience and ideas with them. The obvious and outstanding examples of this at this time are George Newman and Arthur Newsholme, both of whom launched their successful careers in Whitehall from a background as MOHs in local government. The Factory Inspectorate provides another case in point: Peter Bartrip has found a rather sluggish late Victorian Factory Inspectorate in Whitehall, labouring under the same blight of 'Lingenism' as everybody else. It was finally transformed with the arrival from the provinces of B. A. Whitelegge, appointed as Chief Inspector in 1896. He was a medical professional qualified in public health with twelve years' experience and practice in the field, as MOH for Nottingham and then for the county of Yorkshire's West Riding.[53]

It was assiduous MOHs who actively inquired into the reasons for the stubbornly high levels of mortality from certain specific diseases in the area under their jurisdiction, and who pioneered locally the research and the preventive systems which were subsequently to influence national solutions and legislation. For instance the first notification systems for tuberculosis were initiated in the late 1880s by Robert Philip in Edinburgh and by James Niven in Manchester (who became Tatham's successor as MOH there, 1894–1922). This was noticed and then advocated by Newsholme when he became MOH in Brighton and finally became embodied as part of a national scheme in 1913, after Newsholme had become the LGB's Chief Medical Officer.

John Tatham, Stevenson's predecessor as Superintendent of Statistics at the GRO, perfectly illustrates this process of recruitment of initiative and ideas into

[50] There is a wealth of detail on the difficulties which MOHs faced – and frequently surmounted – in their dealings with their local authority employers in Young (unpublished BLitt thesis).

[51] For instance, from her detailed work on MOHs in several London vestries, Anne Wilkinson has concluded that the relatively poor pay of Victorian MOHs was on the whole a paradoxical source of strength and independence in their dealings with their local authority employers. As they usually had an additional source of income from a teaching post or from medical practice, they were not so much in fear of dismissal and could afford to ride their luck when proposing unpopular measures. Wilkinson (unpublished DPhil thesis), pp. 321–2.

[52] Hardy, 'Public health and the expert', p. 129.

[53] Bartrip, 'Expertise and the dangerous trades'.

the central government service from the experienced local government sphere. As an MOH for twenty years (first for Salford and then for Manchester) he had a number of significant public health administrative innovations to his credit when he joined the GRO as its Statistical Superintendent in 1893. Chief among these, he had instigated a comprehensive scheme for the notification of infectious diseases and he had asked for and obtained the resources for a domiciliary house-to-house health visiting team of thirteen female health visitors in Manchester.[54] Thus, Tatham was drawing on highly relevant personal administrative experience when he gave evidence in 1897 to the House of Lords Committee for their Bill for the Better Protection of Infant Life and, again, to the important Interdepartmental Inquiry into Physical Deterioration of 1904. His views on the problems of urban poverty and disease and on the realistic means to remedy them derived from this apprenticeship and career of practical prevention in local government; and this was therefore reflected in the kinds of analysis he elected to perform on the statistics collected by the GRO, which he presented in evidence to these central government inquiries.

Another important example of the way in which local authority initiatives did not simply occur in a vacuum, hermetically sealed off from Whitehall and Westminster, is provided by the innovation of school medical inspection. It is well known that in 1907 a national system of inspection was established by the New Liberal government. What is much less well known is that the origins of this policy lay in local government. In June 1893 W. P. Byles and James Hanson, respectively the only female and the only working-class member of Bradford's School Board (this was before the arrival in Bradford of Margaret McMillan), prevailed upon their colleagues to appoint Dr Kerr to the country's first full-time post of school medical officer.[55] In 1902 the LCC itself followed suit, poaching the impressive Kerr in the process. Finally, twelve years after Bradford's pioneering scheme and following its endorsement by the Interdepartmental Inquiry on Physical Deterioration, central government duly took up the policy, enacting a nationwide school medical inspection service in 1907.

By the opening years of the new century, therefore, the numbers, powers and self-organisation of local officials, inspectors and civic servants had grown and matured enormously. Above all, the leaders of this diffused movement were medical professionals, especially the widening stream of graduates who had been emerging from the nation's postgraduate public health courses each year since the

[54] The Manchester and Salford Sanitary Association had pioneered in 1860 a system for weekly notification of sickness and infections, launched by the public health campaigner, Arthur Ransome. Tatham significantly expanded upon this in 1888 by co-ordinating a mutual exchange of the weekly information then being collected in various places by thirty-three different local authorities, which had each independently set up such schemes. See Newsholme, 'A national system'. On the health visitors, see Dowling (unpublished MA thesis), p. 227.

[55] Hollis, *Ladies elect*, pp. 182–3, 117. On Margaret McMillan's subsequent role in Bradford education, see Steedman, *Childhood, culture and class*, ch. 2.

mid-1870s.[56] Clause 21 of the 1888 Local Government Act had made possession of a sanitary diploma compulsory for appointment as MOH to any large local authority (above 50,000 population). Such accredited MOHs numbered 263 in 1886, and nearly 700 by 1900.[57] Hence, two-thirds of the witnesses, who were to appear before the 1903–4 Interdepartmental Inquiry of the Physical Deterioration Committee were medically trained, mostly in public health.[58] The strong sense of professional continuity and solidarity within the public health branch of the medical profession by the beginning of the twentieth century is nicely illustrated by the desire of the founding editorial board of the new *Journal of Hygiene* (Arthur Newsholme, G. H. F. Nuttall and J. S. Haldane) to obtain a contribution to their first issue in 1900 from the eighty-six-year-old Sir John Simon, active over half a century earlier as the City of London's and then the nation's first Chief Medical Officer (to the Privy Council).[59]

The first generation of sanitarians had been preoccupied with cleaning up the unpaved, dung-laden streets and stagnant cesspools which substituted for sewers, so as to avoid the poisonous miasmas which they believed these nose-sores emitted.[60] By the early 1890s, MOHs had begun to direct the growing investigative resources at their disposal towards the related knot of problems surrounding working-class diet, housing, domestic hygiene practices and social behaviour. Increasingly MOHs and their staffs were concerned, first, with the disease-promoting mores of urban working-class communities; and, secondly, with the gross inadequacies of hygienic facilities inside the overcrowded, unplumbed, working-class back-to-backs, huddled together around tiny courtyards where they often shared a single, irregular water supply and a single, indescribable privy.[61] Germ theory suggested that together these created perfect conditions for the spread of infectious micro-organisms both directly between people and from the infected, unclean foods they prepared for themselves in their inadequately equipped homes.

However, this new focus of attention was by no means due only to the contagionist implications of the germ theory of disease (fully accepted in Britain

56 The first diploma in state medicine was offered by Trinity College, Dublin, in 1871. This initiative was then followed by the universities of Cambridge (1875), London (1876) and Durham (1879). The examination for Diploma in Public Health was standardised by resolution of the General Medical Council, 1 June 1889, which recognised fourteen licensing bodies. Watkins (now Porter) (unpublished PhD thesis), pp. 114, 121.

57 MacLeod, *Treasury control*, p. 224.

58 Of the sixty-seven witnesses, twenty-two were acknowledged medical experts from the Royal Colleges of Physicians and of Surgeons; and a further twenty-one were local and central government administrators and inspectors with medical qualifications and duties, such as Medical Officers of Health, Factory and School Inspectors.

59 They were duly gratified by the short dedication which he wrote to them and which they printed at the commencement of the first volume.

60 Wohl, *Endangered Lives*, and Hardy, *The epidemic streets*, are the best general accounts of the work of local Medical Officers of Health during the second half of the nineteenth century.

61 For instance, the normal response to serious sickness among the poor unfortunately entailed increased rather than diminished social contacts. Wilkinson (unpublished DPhil thesis), pp. 301–6.

only from the late 1880s).[62] The only systematic research showing the practical activities of Britain's local public health professionals across the period as a whole is Anne Hardy's important study of London MOHs. She shows that the much greater attention paid to the homes and habits of the population in the last decade was primarily an extension of earlier practices and policies. It was a spin-off from the success that the MOHs finally achieved in their decades-long efforts to establish a fully integrated preventive system to 'stamp out' communicable diseases. This system involved the co-ordinated mechanisms of: outbreak notification, isolation of victims and disinfection of all contacts and premises. It had been culturally rooted libertarian objections to forcible detention or isolation of persons which delayed the adoption of such an integrated plan to deal with human afflictions. The public health movement was not granted the essential machinery of compulsory notification for diseases recognised to be infectious until the 1890s. As Anne Hardy has pointed out, in consequence it was only in the field of veterinary policy, specifically in response to the rinderpest epidemic of 1865, that such 'stamping out' policies were first fully implemented. It was the spectacular practical successes of this approach over the ensuing decades which particularly impressed the hard-nosed empiricist Anglo-Saxon mind, rather than the perfection of germ theory. It was this efficacy which gradually convinced medical professionals and wider public opinion, alike, that the cost to human liberty of such a comprehensive preventive apparatus was worth paying.[63]

Thus, an increasingly powerful, professionalised body of medically trained public servants had, for a quarter of a century, been arguing for and expanding, piecemeal, a variety of local forms of regulation of industrial capitalism and of collectivist responsibility for poverty. Following the war in South Africa, they found themselves in possession of a great opportunity to advance their cause, as the nation's saviour in the face of crisis. They were not unprepared for the moment of opportunity. When Sir Frederick Maurice cast about him for wider evidence and views on the all-important issue of national physique, he found himself surrounded on all sides by a veritable crowd of well-informed professionals, fully organised into national associations actively exchanging ideas and information through their journals, offering evidence, roundly formed opinions and experimental policies with which to combat many aspects of the problem he had identified. What was occurring in the early years of the new century was a spontaneous political offensive into the national arena by the phalanxes of locally employed professional public servants. The vast majority were, by virtue of their chosen vocation, practitioners of an interventionist, implicitly 'environmentalist' approach to the problems associated with the urban population's standards of health. Organised into their professional associations, they were the agents of a *de facto*

62 Since publication of Margaret Pelling's *Fever, disease and medicine*, it has been clear that a mix of miasmatist and contagionist ideas had always co-existed within the British public health movement.

63 Wilkinson (unpublished DPhil thesis). Hardy, *The epidemic streets*, ch. 1; and see above, pp. 106–7.

acknowledged collectivist responsibility on the part of most local authorities for the conditions of their poor. This responsibility had been gradually and haphazardly but nevertheless widely assumed by the beginning of the new century, through a protracted sequence of policy decisions, albeit often grudgingly taken, stretching over many decades (see below, pp. 516–20).

These professionals were men and women who had had a voice only in local affairs and at specialist conferences of fellow professionals. For instance, both the *Journal of State Medicine* (*Journal of Preventive Medicine* from 1905), organ of the Royal Institute of Public Health founded in 1892, and *Public Health*, the journal of the Incorporated Society of MOHs, had each provided for over a decade a forum for detailed discussion and for organised political lobbying on preventive health issues. The former concentrated more exclusively on matters relating to administrative control of environmental factors in infectious diseases and relevant developments in bacteriology, while the latter also included coverage of diet, domestic hygiene and education.[64] But certainly they had always entertained strong aspirations for greater influence: from 1889 the Society of MOHs was served by a Committee devoted to vetting all relevant parliamentary legislation, often resulting in important proposals for amendments.[65]

Of course, there always remained wide differences of opinion among the hundreds of doctors involved and interested in public health work, including even those such as C. K. Millard (MOH, Leicester) and Sir James Barr (Professor of Clinical Medicine, Liverpool University) who had strong eugenic leanings.[66] But, as G. R. Searle has argued, apart from specialists in certain pathological and hereditary conditions, the vast majority of medical practitioners were hostile to the hereditarianism of eugenics, especially those who were Medical Officers of Health, who by the Edwardian period inclined, he claims, towards Fabian socialism, if anything.[67] This general point would certainly be borne out by the diminutive membership of doctors in the Eugenics Education Society as a proportion of the profession (though doctors were a major occupational group within the relatively small membership of the Eugenics Education Society).[68]

[64] Porter and Porter, 'What was social medicine?', pp. 97–100.

[65] Watkins (unpublished PhD thesis), pp. 187–8.

[66] Greta Jones has interestingly pointed out that membership of the eugenics movement was geographically highly clustered, with its main centres of activism apparently confined to London, Birmingham, Leicester, Manchester, Liverpool, Brighton, Cambridge, Edinburgh, Glasgow and Belfast. Jones, *Social hygiene*, pp. 26–7, 55. There has been little systematic research into this local aspect of the eugenics movement and its implications. For some further details on Manchester and, especially, Birmingham, see Lowe: 'Eugenicists, doctors' and 'Eugenics and education'. Note, however, that Gillian Sutherland offers a different interpretation of the wider significance of this local evidence: *Ability, merit and measurement*, pp. 25–6.

[67] Searle, 'Eugenics and class', pp. 224–6.

[68] They probably formed about 20–5% of the membership, about equal with 'academics' in 1914, when total national membership was 1,047: MacKenzie, *Statistics in Britain*, pp. 22–3. This, then, represented approximately 1% of the 23,469 men and women returning themselves as 'Physicians, surgeons and registered practitioners' at the 1911 census (Census, 1911, Volume X, Table 3).

Furthermore, it needs to be pointed out that for many persons who became members of this Eugenics Society, both before and after the Great War, their membership reflected a more general disposition in favour of 'science'. For many it was their commitment to the search for and promotion of scientifically rational methods for dealing with social problems in an ordered fashion that put them in sympathy with the broad aims of the eugenics movement, rather than any strong belief in an exclusively hereditarian evolutionism. An increasingly scientific medical profession was therefore particularly likely to yield a certain degree of openminded interest in the possibilities that might be offered by knowledge of hereditary aspects of incapacity. Such members included, for instance, the MOHs Dr James Niven of Manchester and Dr John Robertson of Birmingham (of whom more later), neither of whom can be accurately characterised as hereditarian eugenicists.[69]

Only the most politically and ideologically astute minds within the profession – Arthur Newsholme and Alfred Eicholz among them – could clearly discern at this time the political importance of the illiberal and exclusionary implications that lay at the hereditarian core of the eugenicist position. A 'leading caucus' of such percipients has been identified within the Edwardian Society of MOHs.[70] This included E. W. Hope, G. F. McCleary, George Newman and Arthur Newsholme. As a group these men also shared the ambitious long-term aim of bringing about a centrally funded and organised preventive health service for the nation, free from the whims and capricious parsimonies of local politics. This was conceived as a grander, more rational and efficient vision of the social role of medicine than the mere reactive, curative conception of clinical medicine. There were compelling ideological and professional reasons for the attractions of this strategy to a relatively new and young, and therefore inevitably low-status, section of that most gerontocratic of professions, medicine. Public health doctors were attempting to throw off the Poor Law Medical Officer connotations of public work in medicine and experiencing some difficulty in establishing satisfactory tenure arrangements with a melange of corporate employers.[71]

However, there was an equally important and independent set of wider scientific and political developments during the first years of the century which were also impelling the organised public health movement towards the novelty of an explicit, positive endorsement for a programme of collectivist health and welfare systems for the nation as a whole. It is these intellectual factors which were

[69] Their membership is mentioned by Greta Jones: *Social hygiene*, p. 20.

[70] Porter and Porter, 'What was social medicine?', especially p. 101.

[71] Porter and Porter, 'What was social medicine?'; and see also Watkins (unpublished PhD thesis). While MOHs were certainly well aware of their distinct aims as a group and were politically well organised through the Society of MOHs, it is possible to exaggerate the degree of separation that existed in practice between public health doctors and others at this time, since many MOHs combined their public health duties with a variety of other medical work. In general on professional rivalries within medicine, see Honigsbaum, *The division in British medicine*.

of particular significance in bringing forth the new official representation of social classes from the GRO and which are, therefore, central to the account offered here.

The environmentalist response to hereditarian eugenics

Previously, public health professionals had broadly acquiesced in the conventional individualist, liberal *Weltanschauung* of Victorian educated society, which is to say no more than that these Victorian medical practitioners were normal educated men of their class and times. *Laissez-faire*, free trade and self-help were, of course, popular, rhetorical slogans, not accurate descriptions of Victorian society. They most accurately expressed not so much a shared conviction in the social ideal of a free market anarchy of perfect competition (itself an oxymoron as a normative idea) as a pervasive belief in the desirability of economic independence as an ideal and moral way of life for the individual – particularly for the adult male, voting head of household, as sanctioned in Lockean constitutional theory.[72] As a result of their acceptance of these conventional Victorian tenets, public health environmentalists were constrained within a consensus that accepted the economic relations of the market – in particular the labour market – as simply not amenable to any form of systematic policy manipulation. Any attempt to tamper with the invisible hand was immoral and doomed to failure. Wages, wage levels and the demand for labour were, generally speaking, among the givens of nature. It was simply not considered a worthwhile subject for discussion where the main issues which preoccupied the public health movement were concerned: the poverty, disease and unfitness of the urban poor and how practically to alleviate their plight.

Despite this prevailing normative consensus, radical ideas for a more comprehensive system of state intervention to promote the nation's health had been mooted by some medical men, although the institutionalised heads of the public health movement such as Chadwick, Farr, Simon and his successors as Chief Medical Officers at the LGB had not found it politic – some to their cost – to champion too zealously such schemes.[73] In the first decade of the twentieth century, however, leading figures in the public health movement such as those identified by the Porters, were now showing their heads above the parapet, displaying a willingness to argue for certain national measures to be taken, notably the provision of school meals for needy children, which amounted to state-sponsored income support for the poor.

It is certainly not the intention here to give the impression that such limited

[72] For discussion of the complex issues of 'character', 'manliness' and the franchise, see pp. 156–7 and below, pp. 460–2 and 484–8.

[73] Of course, Chadwick himself was the first and foremost such casualty, 'let go' by his Whig masters in 1854. His biographer, Benjamin Ward Richardson (1828–98), evidently took the lesson to heart, presenting his own most radical ideas in 1876 as a utopian excursion: *Hygiea*. Richardson also published in 1879 *A ministry of health*; H. W. Rumsey's *Essays on state medicine* is often cited as an early exposition of an ambitious system of state medicine.

proposals by public health professionals represented *the* leading edge of new ideas and policies concerning the relationships between the state, fiscal redistribution and citizenship. Since the 1880s unemployment and old-age dependency had been the principal fields in which such innovations in municipal and official policy had been pioneered. Local authorities and the local government-groomed President of the LGB, Joseph Chamberlain, can be seen from the mid-1880s groping towards an implicit acknowledgement of collective responsibility for the vagaries of the labour market and a recognition of the social value of schemes designed to deflect its harshest aspects. Chamberlain's famous circular of March 1886 authorised non-pauperising municipal public works for the unemployed.[74] Furthermore, there had been much radical new thinking, especially during the 1890s, on the problems of dependency in old age (although the nettle of full state provision of old-age pensions was not finally grasped until 1908).[75] Edwardian public health specialists were, then, joining social theorists, political figures and progressive civil servants who were already involved in radically redefining the legitimacy of a much expanded role for the collectivist state.[76]

However, these new views among public health professionals were not merely derivative from the initiatives pioneered in other fields of social policy. They were also an independently generated product of a galvanising clash over the correct 'scientific' analysis of the causes of urban poverty, physical unfitness and child development, issues which were specific to their own field of expertise. In this confrontation with the views of hereditarian eugenicists, environmentalist public health officials found themselves substantially making common cause with those involved in implementing the nation's evolving universal education policy over the cluster of issues surrounding child development and appropriate measures for the abnormal child.

It had not been until the final two decades of the nineteenth century that children of the poorest of the poor were finally being forcibly drafted into the nation's elementary schools. Indeed it was only in the closing decade of the century that schooling was being made effectively compulsory – through the diligence of the school attendance officers – and also genuinely free, through the assiduous implementation under A. H. D. Acland's Vice-Presidency of the Committee of Council on Education, 1892–5, of the Assisted Education Act of

74 Harris, *Unemployment and politics*; Davidson, *Whitehall*.

75 Williams (Thane) (unpublished PhD thesis); Hennock, *British social reform*, Part II. Charles Booth's call in 1891 for universal, non-contributory pensions of 5 shillings per week for all above age 70 had originally created a minor sensation, coming as it did from a socially conservative quarter (*ibid.*, p. 122).

76 The principal administrative innovations concerned were those of the Progressive, or New Liberal Asquith government after 1908, creating overtly redistributive fiscal arrangements for centrally funded mechanisms of social security and insurance against sickness, old age and unemployment. This entailed an altogether new degree of regulatory intervention into the workings of the economy, particularly the conditions of the labour market. The best general introductions are: Hay, *The origins*; Thane, *The foundations*; Fraser, *The evolution*. There has also been a definitive narrative account of the politics of the birth of the insurance scheme: Gilbert, *The evolution of national insurance*.

1891.[77] The appearance in elementary schools of the very poor stimulated a wave of renewed concern among the local health and education professionals involved. This was not merely disquiet at the contagionist health risk that such children represented for their fellow class-mates. Confronted with the appalling condition of many of these new child wards emerging from the slums, teachers, attendance officers and school managers now joined MOHs and their staffs and the NSPCC as first-hand, professional observers of the effects of chronic material deprivation. They experienced for themselves the impaired powers of concentration and learning capacities of the hungry poor. Even in London, for instance, this eventually led to a formal survey of hunger among school children conducted in 1889 and the immediate setting up of the London School Dinners Association in response to the results.[78]

The sheer numbers involved and the financial implications of different potential solutions were forcing those in positions of responsibility to address more rigorously than ever before the difficult administrative decisions of how best to accommodate and teach those with learning difficulties and special needs, where scarce resources of teachers and buildings were already overstretched. These were policy questions whose answers crucially depended upon matters of correct definition and classification of different kinds and degrees of impairment, an area of scientific speculation where issues closely paralleled those at the heart of the nature–nurture conflict.[79] Which kinds of defect – blind, deaf, dumb, lame, as well as mental – rendered children truly ineducable in a normal school? Which problems were food- or health-related only? And was the pedagogically adequate remedy (free school meals) also politically acceptable in such cases? What were the visible or behavioural signs for diagnosis of these varying conditions? These were the practical problems, demanding scientific and administrative solutions, which the local health and education professionals were facing in the last decade of the century.

Central government commissions took evidence while Local Government School Boards took initiatives. By the beginning of the new century, there were therefore a growing number of medically trained or pedagogic practical professional experts: managers of asylums and of special schools; local or central inspectors of schools; some MOHs, some teachers; and the country's first School Board Medical Officers (Dr W. R. Smith and his assistant Dr F. D. Harris in London, James Kerr in Bradford). The NSPCC and the COS were also considered important sources of expertise and experience. The COS in particular had a long-standing interest in devising the most efficient and appropriate care for the feeble-minded as these

[77] Sutherland, *Policy-making*, chs. 10–11. [78] Rubinstein, *School attendance*, pp. 81–2.

[79] Sutherland, *Ability, merit and measurement*, ch. 1. In addition to Gillian Sutherland's important study, these formative debates in the discipline of educational psychology have received an extremely stimulating treatment in: Rose, *The psychological complex*. For further explorations of related fields, see the collection edited by Roger Cooter: *In the name of the child*; and Wooldridge (unpublished DPhil thesis).

were disproportionately represented among its destitute clientage. Its own specialists in these affairs at the turn of the century were: Dr Francis Warner (Physician to the London Hospital); Dr G. E. Shuttleworth (Superintendent of the Royal Albert Asylum); Miss Mary Dendy and Mrs Ellen Pinsent (both School Board members, from Manchester and Birmingham, respectively). These individuals were the leading campaigners in the National Association for Promoting the Welfare of the Feeble-Minded, founded in 1896. Their principal policy priorities were to deal with the danger and 'waste' (i.e. cost) to society that the uncontrolled proliferation of defectives represented, on the assumption that deficiencies in their age-specific physical and mental development and in apparent learning capacities were primarily something naturally inherited, or at least an ingrained familial character which was best not reproduced. Segregation and control were the main measures they envisaged, as practised from 1902 on Mary Dendy's 'Farm' at Sandlebridge, Cheshire. There were strong affinities with Francis Galton's anti-environmentalist eugenics, an association formally signalled in Francis Warner's anthropometric survey of 100,000 school children, 1888–93, inspired by Galton's earlier work and supported by the COS.[80]

Opposed to these segregationist policies were to be found those educationists who preferred instead to emphasise the importance of the vast number and range of subnormal, disabled or underachieving children who could be assisted to develop positively and without the need for institutionalised segregation. Among these were such figures as Dr W. Leslie MacKenzie, Dr James Kerr, Dr Nathan Eicholz, Dr George Newman, Rachel and Margaret McMillan, W. H. Libby and the MPs, Thomas Macnamara and Sir John Gorst, several of whom will appear in the account which unfolds below in this chapter and the next.[81] There was much overlap and experience held in common with public health environmentalists, as the doctors' names, above, suggest. Rachel McMillan originally trained and worked as a sanitary inspector; her sister, as an Independent Labour Party (ILP) representative on Bradford School Board, had participated in James Kerr's first recorded official school medical inspection in 1899.[82] They were impressed with the importance of environmental deprivations in causing many of the children's problems and with the devising of effective measures to alleviate these hindrances. They stressed the great possibilities for rehabilitation of deficient individuals, rather than their segregation, as the most promising means to attain greater social and economic national efficiency (although conceding that a small group of the grossly defective would still have to be detained). These were the voices alongside whom public health environmentalists found themselves testifying for similar measures at the 1903 and 1904 official inquiries and thereafter.

The remainder of this chapter charts the manner in which the 'physical

80 Sutherland, *Ability, merit and measurement*, ch. 2; and see above p.186.

81 For further information on Gorst and Macnamara, see ch. 5, nn. 17, 18.

82 Aldrich and Gordon, *Dictionary of British educationists.*

deterioration' public inquiries of 1903–4 provided the forum in which practically experienced, public health and pedagogic professionals were directly confronted with the views of the hereditarian eugenicists. In meeting and beating off this challenge, the rudiments of a sophisticated, alternative, 'environmentalist' explanation for the dynamic phenomenon of social class differentiation was developed, envisaging self-reinforcing cycles of cultural and economic deprivation from one generation to the next. This, along with the increasing scientific discomfiture of the biometric hereditarians over the ensuing years, as Mendelism gained in strength, finally cleared the ground and encouraged the GRO to embark upon the project of constructing a new social classification scheme for the nation's demographic statistics. For only then could it be seen by the GRO that such a representation could be given a cogent environmentalist rationale, and that it had central and direct relevance for public health debates over the significance of recent trends in the nation's demographic behaviour and over the issue of collective provision for the nation's health.

The environmentalist understanding of social classes

The consonance of interests between practising environmentalists among local government officials and administrators, educationists, Fabian collectivist 'permeators' and eugenic academic biologists, briefly welded together by nationalist and imperialist politicians, was, then, sufficient to secure government recognition of the gravity of the public's anxieties over the nation's physical condition. Finally, an Interdepartmental Committee on Physical Deterioration was appointed, despite the fact that a Royal Commission on Physical Training in schools (in Scotland) was currently examining strongly related issues.[83] The terms of reference of the PDC were:

> (1) To determine with the aid of such counsel as the medical profession are able to give, the steps that should be taken to furnish the Government and the Nation at large with periodical data for an accurate comparative estimate of the health and physique of the people; (2) to indicate generally the causes of such physical deterioration as does exist in certain classes; and (3) to point out the means by which it can be most effectually diminished.[84]

These terms of reference in fact represented an amplification of the original remit, which had been merely to inquire into 'allegations concerning the deterioration of certain classes of the population'.[85] The final formulation was the product of an extremely significant exchange of views which had preceded the setting up of the Committee. Evidently the Committee itself recognised the importance of this preliminary debate because the relevant correspondence and memoranda were reproduced as Appendix 1 of their report, from which the following account is reconstructed. It fully reveals the nature of the fundamental scientific division of

[83] See Gilbert, 'Health and politics'. [84] PDC, Report, p. v. [85] PDC, Report, p. v.

opinion between the hereditarians and the environmentalists and shows that this was keenly appreciated on both sides. It can, broadly speaking, be labelled a nature–nurture division, but it was simultaneously a reflection of the political and ethical differences between vocational ideologies.

The public health branch of the medical profession was the most coherently organised and prestigious unit within the constellation of interventionist public servants who were involved in a daily battle with the social and environmental causes of poverty and disease. They were very much on their mettle, and on the offensive to wrest the direction of practical social policy from what they correctly perceived to be the meddling and dangerously quixotic opinions of certain biological scientists, economists and moralising politicians, who were comfortably removed from the harsh realities of the urban slums. As far as they were concerned winning the battle against the entrenched individualist and *laissez-faire* attitudes to secure a greater level of state intervention to combat destitution would be a hollow victory if such intervention were to take the segregationist form of labour colonies and prohibitions on marriage of the poor. Public health environmentalists wanted an enlarged attack on inadequate living conditions and ignorance, a strategy which they believed had already proved itself to be effective. A battle to establish the correct scientific interpretation of poverty and disease, in order to control the strategy of remedial social policy, therefore began in earnest in 1903.

This conflict is particularly important to our study of the twinned genesis of an official social classification system and a fertility inquiry. For, these two creations of the social sciences were themselves largely born out of the disputes over substantive scientific issues involved in this political–professional conflict. In the preliminary exchange recounted below, it will be noted that the notion of hereditary causation was immediately singled out for attack by the public health leaders of the medical profession. Whereas the Fabians wanted national efficiency whatever the means, and biometricians believed in the importance of heredity, whatever the consequences, public health doctors and other public officials would not relinquish their vocational conviction in a thoroughgoing environmentalist analysis of the sources of disease and debility. As we shall see, under the pressure of having to respond to the claims being advanced by hereditarians, leading practical exponents of this environmentalism were to be found broadening and deepening their analysis to encompass, ultimately, a theory of the socially structured and economically induced causes of poverty and social inequality. Such, then, were the conflicting aims of the important interest groups within the National Efficiency movement.

The preliminary terms of reference of the Interdepartmental Inquiry, referring to 'allegations concerning the deterioration of certain classes of the population', had certainly implied that some form of physiological, hereditary degeneration was under discussion. This reflected the suspicions of the original memorandum sent to the Secretary of State for the Home Department on 2 April 1903 by Sir William Taylor, Director-General of the Army Medical Service. It was this suggestion which was taken as read and which was therefore addressed by both the Royal Colleges, of Physicians and of Surgeons, when Taylor's memo was forwarded to them by the Secretary of State to sound their opinions on the need for, and terms of reference of, a possible official investigation. Both Colleges immediately pointed out that the statistical evidence, presented by Taylor, concerning rejection ratios at recruiting stations and reasons for those rejections over the period 1893–1902, was inadequate to support the contention that a physical deterioration had occurred in the classes referred to.[86] On being reconsulted, Sir William Taylor clarified his position, agreeing that the figures he himself had produced did not support an interpretation of progressive physical deterioration but rather attested to a disturbing current state of affairs, which nevertheless merited investigation.[87]

The impression that he had been making a case for hereditary degeneration was overwhelming in the original memo, as the responses of the two Colleges indicate. That impression had been due initially to Taylor's extensive quotation in that document of the views of General Sir Frederick Maurice[88] and Sir Lauder Brunton,[89] both of whom strongly suggested that the low standard of physique was more prevalent among the urban dwelling population.[90] Taylor had then juxtaposed the recent work of Rowntree on York, and it was noted that his finding of a total of 28% of the town's population in poverty was similar to the figure of 30% found for London some years previously by Booth.[91] Thus, a putative rise in poverty in the growing towns was strongly, but only implicitly and not formally, linked to a deterioration of national physique. In fact the PDC Report itself only referred to one official source in which it was specifically stated that there was a gradual deterioration of the physique of the working classes. This was the 1902 Annual Report of the Inspector-General for Recruiting (Major-General H.C. Barrett, one of the witnesses called before the inquiry).[92] The Physicians and

[86] Their replies to this first inquiry by the Home Office are reproduced as Appendices Ib and Ic in the PDC Report.

[87] PDC, Report, Appendix Id.

[88] From both of his articles in the *Contemporary Review*: 'Where to get men' and 'National health'.

[89] Uncited. But from Brunton's later evidence, we learn that Sir William Taylor was quoting from Brunton's letter to the *Lancet*, 14 February 1903, calling for the appointment of a commission. The National League for Physical Education and Improvement was the organisation which Brunton was promoting at this time, following upon the recommendations of the Royal Commission on Physical Training of 1903.

[90] PDC, Report, Appendix Ia, paras. 2 and 3 respectively. Sir Frederick Maurice was again quoted in the conclusion: Appendix Ia, para. 12.

[91] PDC, Report, Appendix Ia.

[92] PDC, Report, para. 8. When examined as a witness Major-General Barrett acknowleged that the basis on which he had made this statement (in para. 150 of his Report for 1902) was statistically unsound: PDC, Evidence, paras. 163–73.

Surgeons had imputed that this was Taylor's meaning – an inheritable and cumulative deterioration – because of the stridency at this time of the claims being made by the hereditarian eugenists.

The interchange of correspondence which preceded the setting up of the Physical Deterioration Committee's inquiry additionally reveals the first signs of the process whereby the significance of social classification for interpreting 'data' was coming to be perceived by anti-hereditarian environmentalists in the medical profession as a central methodological issue. The Royal College of Physicians had appointed a subcommittee of five to deal with the issues preliminary to setting up the inquiry.[93] The subcommittee focused their attention on Sir William Taylor's usage of the established system of the Army Medical Department for classifying candidates presenting themselves for medical inspection prior to recruitment into six different categories according to their former occupation.[94] They took him to task for his assertion that examination of a series of figures classified into these six categories showed that 'the proportion of the different classes remains remarkably constant from year to year, and the figures indicate that the bulk of our soldiers are drawn from the unskilled labour class, and consequently from the stratum of the population living in actual poverty or close to the poverty line'.[95] The subcommittee pointed out that this classification scheme could not adequately capture significant changes in the proportions recruiting into the army from different parts of the labour market, and so did not support the main point which Taylor was trying, rather obliquely, to make: that an alleged change in the average physique was not simply due to changes in the proportions recruiting from different strata. Of the six classes used by the Army Medical Department, Category 1, which accounted for over 60% of all recruits examined, compounded together all kinds of labourers: rural and urban, regularly employed factory 'hands' and the casual 'residuum of the labour market'. It was observed that there was strong reason to believe that a well-documented recent trend rise in the relative real wages of agricultural labourers could have caused a serious fall-off in the recruitment into the army of this, the most physically fit section of the overlarge Category 1.[96] The classification system's inadequacies were, thus, rigorously exposed.

In fact, by the time the PDC report was written this critique was already being acted upon:

[93] This included: Dr G. B. Longstaff (see ch. 2, n. 94); Dr J. F. W. Tatham, the immediate predecessor to T. H. C. Stevenson, as medical statistician at the G R O; and Arthur Newsholme (for more on Newsholme, see below, pp. 232–4, 240–6, 254–6). (The other two were a Dr Poore and a Dr Pringle.)

[94] The six were: 'Labourers, servants, husbandmen, etc.'; 'Manufacturing artisans (cloth workers, weavers, lace makers, etc.)'; 'Mechanics employed in occupations favourable to physical development'; 'Shopmen and clerks'; 'Professional occupations, students, etc.'; and 'Boys under 17 years of age'. Clearly these categories were designed with some idea in mind of classifying by physique as well as by average income or status of occupation. PDC, Report, Appendix Ia, para. 5.

[95] PDC, Report, Appendix Ia, para. 6.

[96] PDC, Report, Appendix Ib.

> In supplement of the request for a more detailed subdivision of the classes denominated 'Labourers' in the Recruiting Returns . . . it was subsequently suggested to both the Admiralty and the War Office that the subheads might with advantage follow the classification shown in the Census Summary Volume for 1901 and the Committee have reason to believe that the Admiralty have already adopted the suggestion.[97]

Although this incident shows a keen awareness amongst the Physicians that classification of the population into large categories for purposes of hypothesis testing and presentation of evidence was a practice requiring great care and scrutiny, it does not establish conclusively that any strong notion of social class or socio-economic stratification had been at issue in their eyes. However, when it comes to the proceedings of evidence taken by the Physical Deterioration Committee, we do indeed encounter ideas and research which explicitly utilise the notion of a socio-economic stratification in society and which refer to the existence of social classes as institutions which are in some way strong causal determinants of the substantive issue at stake: the extent, causes and remedies for the current state of physical health in the nation. What is important, though, about those witnesses to the inquiry who did mobilise and argue and give evidence using social classes in this way is that they did so with the aim of discrediting the entire hereditarian interpretation of poverty and social structure. Thus, conflict over the implicit meaning of social classes – whether they were 'natural' as the hereditarians maintained, or socially formed as the environmentalists would argue – became a critical issue in the battle over interpretation of empirical evidence, which ensued between these two camps.

To anticipate the following account, it was the environmentalists who ultimately prevailed in 1904 with their environmentalist interpretation of the sources of social class inequalities. In the PDC's summary Report, it was concluded that, with the exception of syphilis and possibly alcoholism: 'So far as the Committee is in a position to judge, the influence of heredity in the form of the transmission of any direct taint is not a considerable factor in the production of degenerates.'[98] In coming to this conclusion the Committee expressed itself strongly influenced by the evidence of D. J. Cunningham, Professor of Anatomy at Edinburgh University; Dr Alfred Eicholz, Her Majesty's Inspector (HMI); and Dr W. Leslie MacKenzie, MOH for Leith and Medical Inspector for the Local Government Board of Scotland.[99] The last-named had also been an important witness before the 1903 Royal Commission on Physical Training (Scotland), as had Mr J. G. Legge, HMI of Reformatory and Industrial Schools, who was now cast in the role of investigator, as member of the PDC.

It is known from the evidence Legge presented in 1903 to the Scottish Royal Commission that he was quite convinced of the powerful effect that environmental factors could have, at least on physical development, from his own analysis of

[97] PDC, Report, para. 10. [98] PDC, Report, para. 246. [99] PDC, Report, para. 250.

anthropometric data in Scottish and English reform schools.[100] Leslie MacKenzie had also stated to that inquiry: 'What I wish to emphasise is that the scope for improvement by improved nurture is almost unlimited.'[101] He had distinguished there between 'transmissible degeneration' and 'generational degeneration . . . confined to the particular generation concerned, and . . . capable of removal by the improvement of the environment – improvement that is in housing and nurture'.[102] MacKenzie had specified that this included precisely those diseases whose symptoms might easily, to the untrained eye, be imagined as evidence of the nation's alleged hereditary physical deterioration: 'rickets, anaemia, tubercular bone disease, and the multitude of diseases that result in deformities, in impairment of physique'. He was even prepared to conclude this list with 'malnutrition of the nervous system, with consequent mental deterioration' as a condition definitely open to environmental improvement.[103]

In the proceedings of the Physical Deterioration Committee, it was to be Dr Eicholz's evidence which provided by far the most intellectually penetrating and extensive case that had yet been made for the environmentalist interpretation of the social statistics of physical deterioration.[104] Although others went politically further in their evidence – notably both Rowntree and H. J. Wilson (HM Inspector of Factories) in suggesting that the wages of the very poor should be improved – Eicholz's analysis was the most conceptually advanced in relation to social classification. His presentation to the inquiry constitutes, in effect, the extension of the environmentalist view of debility into a comprehensive social (as opposed to naturalistic) understanding of the dynamic cultural and economic forces producing the measurable phenomena of inequalities between the social classes in developmental growth and the incidence of fatal disease. This was an important antecedent for the eventual emergence of an official social classification system, constructed by the GRO.

Eicholz commenced his presentation by invoking a simple notion of social stratification, with the urban nation divided into three broad classes distinguished

[100] J. G. Legge's cross-national comparative data showed no trend physical degeneration over the previous twenty years among the most underprivileged elements of the town population: Royal Commission on Physical Training (Scotland) (hereafter RC on P T), Appendix 1. This reform school data showed Scottish boys with a marginally better physique at age 14 than the English boys; but by age 17, after at least two years at reform school in each case, the English boys were ahead. Legge attributed this change to the fact that physical training was more developed in English reform schools than in the Scottish equivalent. RC on PT, Evidence, paras. 740–3.

[101] RC on PT, para. 6893. [102] RC on PT, para. 6893. [103] RC on PT, para. 6893.

[104] Alfred Eicholz (1869–1933) had been the first Jew to be elected to a Cambridge Fellowship (Emmanuel College, 1893). After medical training at St Bartholomew's, he became an HMI, 1898–1907, and then an Inspector for the new Medical Department of the Board of Education, created on the recommendation of the Report of the PDC. He succeeded George Newman as Chief Medical Officer at the Board of Education (a post he held until 1930), when Newman left in 1919 to become the new Ministry of Health's first Chief Medical Officer. Sources: *Who was who 1929–40*; Aldrich and Gordon, *Dictionary of British educationists*.

by their employment and income prospects and associated consumption and social habits:

> elementary education has contributed to the stratification of the large urban population into a distinct series of social levels. There is an upper class well to do and well cared for, to whom our methods of education afford every chance of mental and physical improvement . . . At the other end of the scale we find the aggregations of slum population ill-nourished, poor, ignorant, badly housed, to a small extent only benefited by our methods of training. They are the degenerates for whom this inquiry is presumably instituted. Between these two is the third and largest stratum consisting of the average industrial artisan population in which bread-winners are in regular employment.[105]

He then distinguished, as had Leslie MacKenzie to the Scottish inquiry, between 'physical degeneracy' and 'inherited retrogressive deterioration'. Eicholz's investigations of schools in London, Manchester, Salford and Leeds consisted, first, in measuring the heights of random samples of twenty students at each age and, secondly, in interviewing the head teacher, the manager, local medical officers and lay workers 'as regards the circumstances and signs of degeneracy and their causes, and as to the evidence of hereditary deterioration'.[106] His measurements showed clear signs that poverty was causing temporary debilitation, but no justification for assuming a cumulative inherited effect. More significantly, Eicholz was able to demonstrate from his secondary investigations that 'In every case of alleged progressive hereditary deterioration among the children frequenting an elementary school, it is found that the neighbourhood has suffered by the migration of the better artisan class or by the influx of worse population from elsewhere'.[107] In fact, of thirty-five head teachers interviewed, nineteen thought that if anything there had been an improvement in children's health and fitness and only four spoke for the view that deterioration had occurred.[108]

> The main strength of opinion in favour of progressive deterioration came from Salford. I therefore made a special point of visiting their black spot Greengate, as I have observed and discovered that the schools which are now free as regards fees used to charge a 6d. fee, and drew from a good artisan population which has now gone outwards.[109]

In the case of London, Eicholz generalised this point to note that over the years there had been a 31% increase in the number of children scheduled on the London School Board census, and attendance had been raised from 74% to 85%, therefore increasingly including the children of the poor and the very poor: 'in other words the schools are touching a much larger percentage of children than formerly'.[110] In his evidence Eicholz had summarised this view, on the various effects of the increase in school attendance through the operation of the compulsory system:

> the more rigorous scheduling of children of school age and the abolition of school fees in elementary schools, have swept into the schools an annually increasing proportion of

105 PDC, Evidence, para. 429. 106 PDC, Evidence, paras. 439, 433.
107 PDC, Report, para. 69; and Evidence, para. 435.
108 PDC, Evidence, para. 552. 109 PDC, Evidence, para. 556. 110 PDC, Evidence, para. 556.

children during the last 30 years. These circumstances are largely responsible for focusing public notice on the severer cases of physical impairment, just as at a previous stage in educational development, they established the need for special training of the more defined types of physical deficiency.[111]

This was, of course, the same kind of argument as that used by the Royal College of Physicians to question the validity of hereditarian inferences from the recruiting ratio figures: that the degeneration scare was a statistical artefact of unrecognised changes in the underlying social composition of the observed population.

But, whereas the Colleges had talked only in terms of sectors within the labour market to make this point, Eicholz proceeded to articulate a wider socio-economic theory of stratification in the labour market, which quite clearly attributed to such stratification the *causality* for the kind of physical defects and debilities which he had found among the school children. Eicholz saw the structured labour market as an integral part of an encompassing, repetitive social process which systematically inflicted differential environments and life experiences on various parts of the population. This created the consistent, wide divergences in living conditions and economic opportunities which sustained the marked differences in behaviour and culture which characterised the division of society into social classes.

Eicholz elucidated as the causes of the social class differentiation of the poor from the rich, a process amounting to a transgenerational cycle of poverty or deprivation, entirely due to environmental economic and social factors. His analysis was certainly not the first in the new century to invoke the central importance of impersonal, systematic socio-economic forces in both causing and perpetuating working-class poverty. It had been Rowntree's study of York, published in 1901, that had demonstrated the inevitability of a demographically induced pattern of life-cycle poverty for virtually all proletarian family households. During the period when the number of small growing children was greatest, the family's income was usually at its lowest, dependent solely upon the father's wages because of the wife's full-time engagement in domestic work and the lack as yet of adolescent children (who would be able to earn for the household). Taking in a lodger was almost the only source of additional income available for families at this stage of their development, at the cost of even greater overcrowding in the home. J. M. Winter has also pointed to W. L. MacKenzie's evidence, presented to the Scottish Royal Commission of 1903, as the first classic description of the self-reinforcing vicious circle of childhood malnutrition, overcrowding, chronic disease and high infant and child mortality.[112] But Eicholz's presentation was the first time in a highly influential official document that the environmentalist approach to poverty and illness had been fully developed, in the context of a compelling, concrete empirical analysis, to its logical conclusion as a dissection and critique of the fundamental social and economic causes of inequality.

Eicholz dismissed the hereditarian arguments, often advanced to support a

[111] PDC, Evidence, para. 435 (9). [112] Winter, *The Great War*, p. 17.

eugenic policy, that the greater mortality and morbidity of the poor was due to their inherent unfitness. The biometricians believed that congenital physiological weaknesses and deficiencies in intellectual or learning capacities resulted in the hierarchical stratification of society. Eicholz advanced strong environmentalist interpretations to account for both these conditions:

To discuss more closely the question of heredity may I in the first instance recall a medical factor of the greatest importance . . . In no single case has it ever been asserted that ill-nourished or unhealthy babies are more frequent at the time of birth among the poor than among the rich or that hereditary diseases affect the new born of the rich and the poor unequally . . . The interpretation would seem to follow that Nature gives every generation a fresh start.[113]

In his summary of the conclusions, Eicholz spelt out the policy implications thus:

Other than the well-known specifically hereditary diseases which affect poor and well-to-do alike, there appears to be very little real evidence on the pre-natal side to account for the widespread physical degeneracy among the poor population. There is, accordingly, every reason to anticipate RAPID amelioration of physique so soon as improvement occurs in external conditions particularly as regards food, clothing, overcrowding, cleanliness, drunkenness and the spread of common practical knowledge of home management [*sic*].[114]

As to broad differences between the children of the well-fed upper classes and those of the labouring poor in their apparent learning abilities and 'intelligence' – differences which were being talked of as inherited conditions by Francis Galton and his supporters – Eicholz did not deny that such differences existed. But he offered a radically alternative, environmental analysis of why they existed and where the learning problems of the children of the poor originated:

There is very little memory power, and with children, who in a normal condition depend entirely upon their memory for getting hold of things and who only reason later this is a fatal handicap for any mental progress. The want of food, the absence of any home training and self-control will account for any absent power of endurance.[115]

Hence his conviction that: 'I hold a very firm opinion . . . that food is at the base of all the evils of child degeneracy.'[116]

It has already been noted that Leslie MacKenzie was prepared to attribute poor mental performance to feeding deficiencies. The Committee heard evidence in similar vein from other experienced educationists: W. H. Libby, an elementary school teacher and secretary of the East Lambeth Teachers' School Dinner Association; the MPs Sir John Gorst and Dr Macnamara; and Dr O. Airy, HMI. In the Report, they singled out the latter's evidence of the long-established system of school dinners for the needy, something which had been initiated twenty years

[113] PDC, Evidence, para. 556.
[114] PDC, Evidence, para. 435 (7).
[115] PDC, Evidence, para. 438.
[116] PDC, Evidence, para. 475.

earlier in Birmingham by George Dixon, MP, as a model of thrifty organisation.[117] Significantly, the Report noted that 'The testimony of the teachers is unanimous that the system pursued enables the children to do the ordinary school work, and they report that the difference is perfectly extraordinary.'[118]

Proceeding from the establishment of this fundamentally environmentalist premise that bad feeding was the ultimate root cause of most of the evils which they were charged to investigate, the Committee sought the reasons for this, weighing the evidence before them in regard to the issue of parental responsibility. They expressed concurrence with their witnesses amongst whom 'With scarcely an exception, there was a general consensus of opinion that the time has come when the State should realise the necessity of ensuring adequate nourishment to children in attendance at school.'[119] But this did not apparently necessarily imply a positive policy endorsement. Indeed, the rider on this recommendation showed quite clearly the residual retention in the Report of the 'less eligibility' Poor Law anxiety that indiscriminate welfare could pauperise. The Committee declared itself against the somewhat dangerous doctrine that free meals are the necessary concomitant of free education;[120] and declared that society 'should aim in the first instance, at the restoration of self respect and the enforcement of parental duty'.[121]

However, where the Committee most definitely did depart from nineteenth-century moralising individualism, the significance of which seems to have been missed by many commentators, was in its acceptance of the findings of an alternative method of *analysis* of the causes of poverty. Individual integrity was maintained only as the ultimate *aim* of social work and social policy, but there was no longer a relentless methodological individualism employed as the direct

[117] PDC, Report, para. 345. It was reported that in Birmingham sixteen centres fed 2,500 children daily – 2.5% of the relevant school population – at a cost of 1/2d. *p.cap. p.diem*. George Dixon (1820–98) had been co-founder (with Joseph Chamberlain, R. W. Dale and George Dawson) of the National Education League in 1869, an early campaigner for universal compulsory education involving payment of fees for the poor. Dixon had been Mayor of Birmingham in 1866, and was Liberal MP 1867–76, and Liberal Unionist MP 1885–98. Dixon succeeded Chamberlain as Chairman of Birmingham's School Board, 1876–97. George Dixon and the National Education League represent the strength of provincially organised pedagogic opinion, something which was distinct from that of the better known Oxford Balliol nexus. The latter was given such prominence in the account in the previous chapter because of their relative dominance over national educational thinking and policy through control of the pro-active central government Education Department. Incidentally, the latter was the only major example of strong programmatic central government leadership in 'social policy' issues during the second half of the nineteenth century and the only major exception to the general thesis being argued in this chapter: that provincial and local government was more active and was the true originator of most social policy inititiatives, belatedly adopted by central government. In the capital, where the influence of the COS was at its strongest, the London School Board never formally broached the problem of 'underfeeding' of schoolchildren until 1884, concentrating instead on the problems of extracting fees and arrears from impoverished parents: Lewis, 'Parents, school fees', p. 308; and see below, ch. 9, n. 204.

[118] PDC, Report, para. 347.

[119] PDC, Report, para. 348.

[120] PDC, Report, para. 365.

[121] PDC, Report, para. 365.

approach to and diagnosis of the problems under discussion.[122] Rather, the Committee came to an appreciation and public acknowledgement of the operation of certain *transindividual*, social and economic forces which would have to be reckoned with in order to prevent the evils of poor infant and child feeding. They were particularly impressed here with the study presented to them by Miss A. M. Anderson, HM principal Lady Inspector of Factories.[123] The Report referred to her convincingly argued evidence for clear connections between infant mortality, bad feeding, overcrowding of one- and two-roomed tenements and the factory employment of mothers. These were elements of a syndrome.[124]

Anderson enumerated the causes of mothers having to work as including: death or desertion of the husband; or his lack of employment; or inadequacy of his wage.[125] It was true that the mother's factory employment led to such apparently culpable practices as feeding babies with stale cow's milk and other even more unsuitable foods instead of from the breast; leaving them in the care of siblings too young to cope; and not maintaining household cleanliness or adequate cooking arrangements to feed the family properly. Nevertheless, it was conclusively shown by Anderson that the original need for the mother to work all day often in exhausting conditions, from which the supposed neglect of her parental duties all followed, was usually a compelling requirement, if destitution was to be avoided. The Committee concluded that it had no doubt that the employment of mothers in factories had evil consequences but that it could not suggest remedies such as prohibition because of the genuine needs for the income required by many of the mothers who did work.[126]

The direct implication contained in this conclusion was the nearest approach the Committee's Report made to an overt acknowledgement of the extremely politically charged issues of the adequacy of wage-levels and of availability of work for certain sections of the working-class poor.[127] Rowntree and H. J. Wilson in their evidence to the PDC, had each explicitly raised lack of adequately paid employment as a primary cause of the problem of poverty, the former offering a careful analysis of the vicious circle of malnutrition and overcrowding that resulted from it.[128] But the summary Report of 1904 cautiously shaded around such contentious matters, retaining certain 'individualist' caveats, as exemplified above over the issue of free school meals.

For the professionals of the public health movement, however, it was the evidence that the Committee heard, and not the hesitancies in the final Report that mattered most. The inquiry had provided an official and public forum in which the

122 On the many different possible manifestations of 'individualism' in the social sciences, see Lukes, *Individualism*.

123 PDC, Report, para. 241.

124 PDC, Report, Appendix V.

125 PDC, Report, para. 255.

126 PDC, Report, para. 260.

127 The 'Right to work' campaign of Keir Hardie's ILP was at this time running alongside the Fabians' slogan of the 'National Minimum' as two major political demands on behalf of organised labour.

128 This was noted by Winter, *The Great War*, pp. 17–18.

default 'individualist', pessimistic, 'social Darwinist', moral and scientific predisposition of a quarter of a century's standing had been thoroughly reviewed, tested and found wanting. The potential power of a more thoroughly environmentalist and collectivist strategy to deal with a set of old and vexing problems had now been very publicly rehearsed in a forum which brought together a host of previously disparate professionals, each approaching from their own particular sphere of responsibility. Certainly Galton, Pearson and the eugenicists were stung by the outcome of the PDC report: the formation of the Eugenics Education Society was a propaganda response by them to this apparent failure of the eugenic message at its first major public test.[129]

The PDC sat and reported on the eve of a subsequent rapid change in the prevailing ideological and political consensus, which it did much to precipitate itself. This was towards a much greater acceptance in national politics of collectivist principles of social responsibility for citizens' health and welfare legislatively embodied in the famous social policy reforms of the New Liberal administration after 1906. Indeed, part of the reason for the historical importance that has always been accorded to this mere interdepartmental inquiry was, of course, that several of its most significant detailed recommendations – of a decidedly collectivist and environmentalist character – were in fact implemented relatively quickly.[130] While certain of the Report's more guarded aspects can easily, with hindsight, be portrayed as backward-looking, there can be little doubt that the effects of the legislative measures it positively promoted acted as a fly-wheel upon the ensuing, rapid momentum in social policy of the next five years. This was towards a much greater acceptance of collectivist provision of health and welfare services at central as well as at local level; and an enhanced confidence in this approach among public service professionals themselves.

The environmentalist scientific alternative to the hereditarians

Eicholz can be seen in 1904 confidently expounding a relatively coherent social, cultural and economic, as opposed to individualist, naturalistic formulation of the causes of social stratification and inequality. It will have been observed that an essential analytical step in Eicholz's dismissal of the hereditarians' claims – that many individuals of poor physique were inherently and congenitally weak – was the conceptual distinction which he operated between two different potential sources of weakness: inherited and environmentally caused. He claimed, in direct contradiction of the biometricians' views on this matter, that the 'physical deterioration' visible in the progeny of the poor was almost entirely attributable to

[129] Soloway, *Demography and degeneration*, pp. 29–33, 46.

[130] This was, for instance, in marked contrast to the fate of the proposals emanating from the great, lumbering Royal Commission on the Poor Laws, which sat 1905–9.

the current environment of the individuals in question, and was in no significant sense transmissible from one generation to the next.

Such a distinction was, of course, not new; it was fundamental in the long-standing scientific controversy over the relative importance of nature as opposed to nurture in accounting for the observable phenomena of human variation, both within and between cultures. The fortunes of each side in this debate had swung back and forth during the nineteenth century, as succeeding schools of thought and forms of evidence had been presented: philological, geological, archaeological, anatomical, and anthropological. Through marshalling their various forms of evidence, the scientists saw themselves as contributing to two larger issues: the theologically derived debate over monogeny versus polygeny;[131] and the post-Enlightenment pursuit of the rational means to the perfectibility of man.[132] In the course of the Victorian century the interpretative framework within which this evidence was sifted and assessed had shifted from the theological and Creationist to the natural scientific and evolutionary, principally a result of the impact of geological science in demonstrating the immensely greater age of the earth than that stated in Genesis.[133]

By the latter part of the century biological evolutionary theory had, of course, become the exclusive framework within which the rational discussion of the relative importance of nature and nurture took place. It is essential to a full understanding of the character of the official classification scheme to place its emergence within the context of this increasingly dominant debate within the social and biological sciences over the potential implications of evolutionary theory for social policies. It is certainly true that at this time there were several eminent evolutionists who argued with great cogency that there was no justification whatsoever for the presumption that the provisional and impermanent findings to emerge from the conjectural science of the origin of species should have any direct implications for human social and ethical questions at all.[134] Nevertheless, the inexorably growing reverence for 'science' and its products, whether technological or intellectual, meant that their counsel of caution was only one small voice among many, listened to only by those with the most acute hearing.

The last two decades of the nineteenth century witnessed the gradual rise to scientific prominence of Francis Galton's long-held conviction in the overwhelming importance of hereditarian over environmental factors as the sources of most

[131] See ch. 3, n. 2.

[132] Passmore, *The perfectibility of man*; Frankel, *The faith of reason*.

[133] Porter, *The making of geology*; Secord, *Controversy in Victorian geology*.

[134] Some, like Benjamin Kidd and Karl Pearson himself, argued pragmatically that such inferences were premature, due to the insufficiency of scientific knowledge of such extremely complex matters: Soloway, *Demography and degeneration*, pp. 70–2. Others, notably T. H. Huxley and L. T. Hobhouse, argued more absolutely that ethical and moral issues were simply distinct from matters relating to knowledge of the natural world, a view philosophically formalised with G. E. Moore's famous formulation of 'the naturalistic fallacy', in his *Principia ethica* of 1903.

human variation. Galton's own role in bringing this about was, however, only secondary. During this period he devoted himself primarily to his statistical anthropometry (and not unproductively so, either: correlation; the bivariate normal distribution; and the celebrated work on finger-prints were all developed at this time). But it was the German, August Weismann's, microscopial cytological work during the 1880s which appeared to establish most firmly the empirical basis for a rational belief in the primacy of heredity. Weismann's work revealed that there was a clear distinction to be made between the microscopic 'germ' plasm (what he later began to call the chromosome material) and the macroscopic soma.[135] The latter represented the bodily form and structure attained by any individual of the species and was therefore in principle subject to all the environmental conditions, both positive and negative, which could affect growth during the individual's development. The germ plasm, by contrast, was invariant with respect to the environment. It was the intergenerationally transmissible material carried from birth by each fertile individual of the species in their reproductive cells.

The primary, immediate significance of Weismann's research, as it was interpreted by his British contemporaries in the late 1880s and early 1890s, was that, if correct, it appeared to remove the possibility that mere environmental influences affecting the outward shape and appearance of the body – for good or for bad – could have any important effects upon the permanent, transmissible characteristics of individuals. This struck at the heart of the neo-Lamarckian use-inheritance views which had become something of a consensus by this time.[136] According to the neo-Lamarckians, permanent inheritable changes in organisms could be seen as the result of the individuals' attempts to adapt themselves to the changing environment. It was this which sanctioned Herbert Spencer's invocation, from the unlikely basis of a rigorously mechanistic and materialist philosophical position, of a form of 'super-organic' evolution as the highest creation of the

135 Jones, *Social Darwinism*, pp. 84–6. Weismann's breakthrough came as a result of applying the successful German microscope technology developing at this time, in the field of cytology, to the observation of the elemental growth germs posited by recapitulation theory, a school of thought which was also particularly strongly developed in German biology (see ch. 3, nn. 49–50).

136 Neo-Lamarckism provided one answer to the crucial evolutionary question, relevant to the nature–nurture issue, which concerned the origin of species: whether they were formed by apparently spontaneous and radical transmutations of organisms, with respect to the morphology of their parents (saltationism); or whether they were the product of much more gradual change, due to the demands of the external, competitive environment in selecting certain characteristics as conferring a competitive advantage and, therefore, a greater chance of survival, and so transmission to future generations. Although each of these positions was capable of being expressed in a range of more nuanced versions, this was the essence of their opposed claims. Throughout most of the nineteenth century, those arguing for the direct application of the biological theory of evolution to the analysis of human society favoured the more moderate notion, the Lamarckian theory of use-inheritance, as the explanatory mechanism of social evolution. In a sense, this was an eclectic compromise, which ruled out neither heredity, nor environment, nor conscious and rational manipulation (especially in the case of humans, of course) as important factors; its chief comfort to social theorists being the inclusion of the lattermost element. For more on Lamarckianism, see pp. 134–5.

human mind: to be able to direct its own evolutionary social development was the special prerogative of humankind.[137]

In the resulting controversy with Weismann, Spencer's autonomous super-organic evolution was the most significant intellectual casualty, eventually succumbing after a dogged rearguard action fought out by Spencer into the early 1890s.[138] 'Urban degeneration' was a casualty to Weismannism for similar reasons, since the environmental, neo-Lamarckian mechanism it presupposed was no longer deemed valid. Whether attempting to account for an unwanted trend deterioration in the physique of the nation or to devise policies to improve the average physical health of the nation's individuals, Weismannism seemed to support an hereditarian, selective breeding approach: the superior germ plasm must be given all encouragement to reproduce itself, while the inferior must be prevented from so doing. Those who continued through the 1890s to believe that the race was deteriorating before their eyes were increasingly forced to conceive of this occurring through a more hereditarian, selective breeding mechanism, as Galton had always argued.

It was, therefore, particularly Galton's strongly hereditarian views which initially benefited from the impact of August Weismann's apparent disproof of use-inheritance.[139] Indeed, Galton had already adumbrated Weismann's dichotomy, as a result of his own experiments.[140] During the 1880s Galton had perfected his statistical theory of reversion ('regression') towards the population mean, as the explanatory basis for his proof that individuals' stature was an inherited correlate of that of their parents.[141] It was from the basis of these empirical findings, regarding physical attributes, that Galton believed it to be legitimate – within the self-imposed intellectual confines of his nakedly materialist empiricism and his inductivist epistemology allied to a radical sensation psychology – to argue, by analogy, for the natural inheritance of mental abilities, moral character and, ultimately, even 'civic worth'.[142]

Although there were very significant differences between Galton and Pearson in their understanding of the exact mechanisms of natural inheritance, what importantly united them and defined them both as eugenicists was, first, their

137 Burrow, *Evolution and society*, pp. 190–213, 222.

138 Jones, *Social Darwinism*, p. 86; Halliday, 'The sociological movement', p. 384.

139 Galton had never subscribed to a gradualist, adaptationist theory, accurately observing that nature afforded too many examples of radical discontinuities between species. MacKenzie, *Statistics in Britain*, p. 130; Jones, *Social Darwinism*, p. 78, notes that Darwin was also impressed by this evidence originally in his *Origin of species*. It was only later in the *The descent of man* that he increasingly abandoned 'transmutation' (saltationism) in favour of Lamarckianism.

140 MacKenzie, *Statistics in Britain*, p. 60.

141 MacKenzie, *Statistics in Britain*, pp. 60–8.

142 Norton, 'Psychologists and class', p. 293. According to sensation psychology, the powers of the mind were ultimately a function of the physiological capacities of the senses, through which all information was received. Jones, *Social Darwinism*, pp. 104–5, notes that Galton's methodological notion of 'observability' was identical with that of the phrenological paradigm.

perfectionist goals. The essential difference between the positive programme of eugenicists and the merely negative admonitions of urban degenerationism was that the latter seemed to imply that only the 'pure' selective conditions of a mythical state of nature could guarantee the health of the race through survival of the fittest. Eugenicists accepted that natural selection was in abeyance in any urban and civilised society: they did not advocate a return to primitive or bucolic, rural conditions but proposed instead a perfectionist future to be achieved through artificially selective breeding policies guided by a scientific knowledge of the biological mechanisms involved. Eugenicists were genuine 'reactionary modernists': their techniques and scientific knowledge were contemporary, if not positively futuristic, and they wished to change society. But their goals – describing the society which they desired to create – were profoundly reactionary and neo-aristocratic.[143]

Secondly, as hereditarians, Galton and Pearson shared the conviction that the only means which could successfully improve the nation in this sense were those which worked through direct manipulation of the survival chances of the inherited matter, the germ plasm which individuals transmitted to their progeny.[144] This belief, of course, directly led to the conclusion that no significant evolutionary effects of a perfecting kind could be hoped for from the environmentalist measures proposed by the public health and welfare lobby. Such measures merely affected the superficial, short-term conditions in the somatic environment of individuals. The hereditarians instead threw the weight of their emphasis on the germ plasm itself and therefore on breeding patterns; not on the somatic relationship with the environment. This supported an emphasis on policies to affect breeding – negative or positive eugenics – at the neglect of welfare policies.

This, then, was the critical point of conflict in the new century between hereditarian eugenicists and the environmentalists of the public health movement: their diametrically opposed views on the principles that should inform the overall strategy of a social policy designed positively to raise the standard of the nation's health. The principal focus of attention throughout most of the Victorian era had been on the prevention of disease and the battle against the threat of rising mortality, with the ameliorationist public health movement finding itself dogged by those pessimists such as Letheby who, at bottom, feared that all interference with the processes of nature were doomed to failure. With proof of definite, if modest, gains in the nation's longevity finally becoming evident by the close of the century, the political and cultural discussion shifted towards a debate over the state of physical and mental health of this less mortal population; and to the correct means to effect positive improvements in the nation's health; and, hence, to

[143] On racialist eugenics as a species of reactionary modernism, see, for instance, Herf, *Reactionary modernism*, which, however, uses the term only of Nazi Germany.

[144] See MacKenzie, *Statistics in Britain*, pp. 86–91, for Pearson's views; Norton, 'Psychologists and class', pp. 296–9, for Galton's.

questions of 'quality'. The public health environmentalists were themselves slowly raising their sights and groping towards a more comprehensive strategy of attack on the problems of disease and poverty, designed to enhance the nation's health and not merely protect it. But they now found themselves confronted with a new variant of the evolutionary school of thought, with its own radically alternative, positive programme: the eugenics movement.

The 1890s had represented a period of growing confidence among hereditarian biologists in the correctness of their views, in particular buoyed up by the apparent vindication of the importance of heredity implied in Weismann's work. This was the decade in which a distinct, if at first small, 'school' of 'biometric' evolutionary science began to form around the old master, Francis Galton, as first Karl Pearson, then W. F. R. Weldon and others gravitated towards him as their figurehead.[145] Their intellectual and scientific position was in fact never as strong or coherent as they themselves believed it to be, as the events of the early Edwardian era were to show. In fact Pearson and Galton held opposite views on the central scientific issue of saltationism versus gradualism in the origin of species. It was Pearson who made the running when it came to strong public statements on the importance of heredity and it was quite clearly Pearson who encouraged the ageing Galton to lend his public support to promotion of the eugenics viewpoint after the Boer War débâcle.[146]

However, this was simultaneously the moment of over-reaching for Pearsonian biometric science just at the point when his confident public pronouncements were attracting sufficient attention to help bring about the instigation of a major government inquiry, the Interdepartmental Committee on Physical Deterioration. For this was also the point at which the biometric eugenicists, with their gradualist view of species variation, were beginning to lose ground scientifically to the saltationist alternative, championed in Britain by William Bateson and gaining strength from rediscovered Mendelism.[147] Within the field of evolutionary biology the first fifteen years of the new century were witness to a remarkable period of scientific activity from within the Mendelian framework. The principal landmarks along the way were: Hugo de Vries's rediscovery of Mendel's work in 1900; W. L. Johanssen's specification in 1909 of the phenotype/genotype distinction; and T. H. Morgan's classical exposition of Mendelism in 1915, *Mechanism of Mendelian inheritance*, based on his team's empirical study of sexual reproduction in *Drosophila*.[148]

The Mendelian theory implied significantly different conclusions from those of the biometricians, though sharing a recognition of the importance of the germ/soma distinction. In particular, the validity of the principal biometric methodological

[145] MacKenzie, *Statistics in Britain*, pp. 85–91. [146] Searle, 'Introduction'.

[147] For discussion of whether Mendel or his rediscoverers were truly responsible for the crucial distinction between phenotypic and genotypic analysis, which is basic to modern Mendelian genetic theory, see Olby, 'Mendel no Mendelian'.

[148] MacKenzie, *Statistics in Britain*, ch. 6; Bowler, *Evolution*, chs. 9, 11; Allen, *Thomas Hunt Morgan*.

assumption was called into question: the utility of measuring observable physical characteristics to make inferences regarding the underlying causes and laws of individual variation within a species. Mendelism held that each species, including *homo sapiens*, had a fixed 'centre of regression', for each of its outwardly measurable characteristics. For Mendelians these outwardly visible, morphological properties of the species were the net result of interaction and combination among an immense complex of non-observable underlying, formational genetic elements. The former, phenotype characteristics were invalid as guides for direct inference regarding the nature of, and relationships between, the latter, the underlying genotypes.

Individual organisms in a population exhibited wide variation about the species mean in their physical appearances – individual phenotypes – due to the virtually infinite permutations possible in the exact configuration of the large number of fundamental determinate genotype elements, which all the individuals possessed in equal numbers in common as a species. Environment was important in determining whether or not any given individual actually expressed in phenotypic, observable form, the genetic potential inherent in its particular permutation of genotypic endowment. Therefore, especially given the importance of development through growth, the effects of the individual's biographical history of exposure to varying environmental conditions and influences – more or less favourable to full expression of the different aspects of the genotypic endowment – were hopelessly admixed with underlying hereditary factors in any observable or 'achieved', phenotypic characteristics. However, environmental influences did not significantly affect the content of that genotypic endowment which the individual was most likely, in turn, to pass on to its offspring and therefore each generation had a fresh start. In 1904, the controversy between these two schools over whether measurable characteristics of individuals could be used as an indicator of the underlying principles of genetic inheritance was at the height of its ferocity in Britain; there was a vivid confrontation in that year at the meeting of the British Association when Bateson, the leading Mendelian in Britain, debated face to face with Pearson and Weldon of the biometric school.[149]

The immediate effect after 1900 of the rapidly expanding alternative Mendelian paradigm was to deprive the biometric school of the apparent scientific authority which it had only recently believed itself to have acquired, post-Weismann. Of particular importance to the story being recounted here, this returned the whole field to a state of expectant conjecture. This placed a large question mark over the validity of any attempts to propound rigorously hereditarian views as a 'scientific' basis for the formulation of social policy. Thus, throughout the ten years leading up to the Great War the hereditarian and eugenic science of society was increasingly on the defensive in scientific terms.[150] This certainly provided a

149 See MacKenzie, *Statistics in Britain*, pp. 121–2, and ch. 6 in general for a detailed account of the conflict.
150 In the longer run, by the 1930s, there was to be a reconciliation between the 'populationist',

context which assisted public health environmentalists both to formulate with more conviction and to assert – apparently politically successfully – their radically opposed, environmentalist interpretation of poverty and physical unfitness, a view which in fact seemed to be carrying all before it by the end of the Great War itself.

In the evidence actually submitted to the PDC, the Mendelian resurgence, despite – or perhaps because of – its extreme contemporaneity, did not directly provide the principal positive scientific ammunition against the hereditarian diagnosis of the causes of physical deterioration, and its appropriate remedies. It was, instead, recently reported evidence from novel fieldwork in physical anthropology and experimental psychology derived from A. C. Haddon's expedition to the Torres Straits – alongside palaeontological evidence from Egyptologists – which was presented as appearing to prove conclusively that human racial stocks or 'types' were long-established and essentially immutable 'givens' of the natural world.[151] It followed from this essential fixity of racial type that the perfectionist aims of eugenicists were chimerical: no amount of selective breeding within a racial group could significantly alter the basic configuration of hereditary material which was the blueprint for each of the major racial types. The observable phenomenon of individual variation about the mean value for each such type was due merely to the plasticity of superficial characteristics adaptive to the environment; it did not indicate any potential for fundamental modification to the race's genetic identity, as the eugenic biometricians wished to argue.[152]

The principal expert witness on evolutionary theory before the PDC was D. J.

macroscopic and empiricist approach, still being advocated by Pearson – and independently advanced by many zoologists studying the peculiarities of actual geographical distribution and differentiation of species – with that of the microscopic, laboratory study of genetic structures in chromosomes and their laws of reproductive recombination. The result of this synthesis was to be the emergence of the modern field of population genetics, with the work of R. A. Fisher, J. B. S. Haldane, Sewall Wright and the Russian, Theodosius Dobzhansky, among many others, playing central roles. Bowler, *Evolution*, ch. 11. W. B. Provine has produced the most detailed historical studies: *The origins of theoretical population genetics* and *Sewall Wright*.

151 See Kuklick, *The savage within*, pp. 133–54; Stepan, *The idea of race*, pp. 89–91 and ch. 4. The results of Haddon's famous Cambridge University Torres Straits expedition confirmed the views of W. M. F. Petrie (1853–1940) and Grafton Elliot Smith (1871–1937), who had shown from their analysis of the palaeontological evidence of Egyptian mummies that typical racial characteristics were apparently extremely stable across thousands of years. The expedition's careful and innovative research in experimental psychology and anthropometrics, particularly the work on hearing and vision and especially colour perception and sensitivity, was undertaken on the Melanesians by C. S. Myers, William McDougall, C. G. Seligman, S. Ray and A. Wilkin, under the direction of W. H. R. Rivers (1864–1922). Its significance was that it showed remarkably little differences in natural endowments and sensory perceptions between the islanders and the Europeans who had been studied since 1884 in Galton's anthropometric laboratory in Kensington and also in Dublin, where D. J. Cunningham and A. C. Haddon had worked together in a similar anthropometric laboratory.

152 Although, as has been mentioned, Galton had been one of the principal individuals responsible for a relaunching of the physical anthropology of racial difference in the 1870s and 1880s by reinvigorating its study with his quantitative anthropometric technology, by the beginning of the new century Galton and Pearson were finding it increasingly difficult to enthuse the Anthropological Institute with their eugenic ideas. Soloway, *Demography and degeneration*, pp. 29–30.

Cunningham (1850–1909), Professor of Anatomy at Edinburgh University.[153] He was at that time promoting the establishment of a national anthropometric bureau, through a Committee of the British Association.[154] This project was based on the understanding that no reliable inferences could be made about the nation's physique and changes in it until the basic parameters had been rigorously identified: what variation there was in 'normal' physique within a population; what constituted 'normal' development and growth in an individual. Only then could individuals and groups be confidently identified as abnormal or different and only then would theoretical discussion of causes of abnormality, deterioration or improvement become meaningful and empirically focused. The PDC's formal recommendation that a system of school medical inspection be instituted represented their acceptance of Cunningham's views on the matter.[155]

Professor Cunningham opened his evidence to the Commission with a statement of his own 'anthropological' understanding of evolution in man. Cunningham employed the conceptual distinction between an underlying fixed inheritance for any species, its 'stock', and the possibility of environmentally induced variations between individuals in their superficial, adaptable characteristics, including in the latter category even the eugenicists' favourite item of heritability: intelligence. Cunningham was quite prepared to believe that 'in civilised peoples the volume of the brain, and with it the size of the cranium, are undergoing a slight increase'; but he also believed that this was because 'the range of growth and the period of growth of the brain and cranium *after birth* have both been extended' (emphasis added).[156]

Cunningham took great pains thoroughly to discredit the earlier conclusions of the British Association's Anthropometric Committee, both regarding the notion of a correlation between foetal skull size and mental capacities and the related notion that the female pelvis therefore acted as a constricting gauge on the race's potential to evolve into a higher, more intelligent, form.[157] First, he noted that the sex differential development in the pelvis was almost entirely 'hereditarian' in its structural determination (i.e. part of the fixed 'stock' of inheritance, which defined

153 See n. 151, above, on Cunningham's close association with the anthropometric work of Haddon and Galton. The study of comparative anatomy had been intimately associated with evolutionary theory, since Cuvier's pioneering anatomical and embryological work, arguing for the necessary fixity of species through study of the functional integrity and balance of organisms' developmental growth. The definitive study of Cuvier in the English language is Coleman, *Georges Cuvier*; see also Bowler, *Evolution*, chs. 3, 5; Gould, *Ontogeny and phylogeny*. Anatomy was also used in the attempt to establish a science of racial differences: Stepan, *The idea of race*, p. xiii.

154 See Royal Anthropological Institute Occasional Papers No. 2 (1905).

155 For Cunningham's case put to the Committee, see PDC, Evidence, paras. 2244–61; and for the extensive discussion of such a scheme in the Committee's own Report, see PDC, Report, paras. 46–66. The expeditious embodiment of this idea in legislation, through the Education (Administrative Provisions) Act of 1907, represented a particularly significant triumph for Robert Morant's manipulative arts. Sutherland, *Ability, merit and measurement*, pp. 49–50.

156 PDC, Evidence, para. 2225.

157 See above, p. 143, for an account of this aspect of the British Association Committee's Report.

a species) and therefore not much subject to environmental influences.[158] He proceeded to expose the severe flaws in the method used by the BA Committee to support its case: only a single European female pelvis was used in its comparative calculations; and the pelvic ring was compared with *adult* skull circumferences, not foetal skulls.[159] He further adduced as *prima facie* evidence against the 1883 theory, the fact that the proportion of stillbirths had not risen dramatically in the recent past, according to the available figures.[160] But here he noted that stillbirth registration in Britain was far behind the standards of most other European countries. He then took the opportunity to propagandise the Committee on the need for improved birth registration, not only to help to settle the scientific issue conclusively but also as a valuable complement to his proposals for a permanent physical census of the population, especially of growing school children.[161]

In their Report, the Interdepartmental Committee quoted Cunningham's announcement of the recent theory of 'anthropologists' that differences in physique between classes in Great Britain were entirely due to environmental effects on the individual organism, since there was a mean physical standard which was the inheritance of the people as a whole: 'the tendency of the race as a whole will always be to maintain that inherited mean'.[162] They also quoted extensively from Karl Pearson's ultra-pessimistic Huxley Lecture of 1903 where, in contrast, he had claimed that:

> The mentally better stock in the nation is not reproducing itself at the same rate as it did of old; the less able and the less energetic are more fertile than the better stocks. The only remedy, if one be possible at all, is to alter the relative fertility of the good and the bad stocks in the community. Let us have a census of the effective size of families among the intellectual classes now and a comparison with the effective size of families in the like classes of the first half of the century . . . Compare in another such census the fertility of the more intelligent working man with that of the uneducated hand labourer. You will, I again feel certain, find that grave changes have taken place in relative fertility during the last 40 years. We stand, I venture to think, at the commencement of an epoch which will be marked by a great dearth of ability . . . intelligence can be trained, but no training or education can *create* it. You must breed it.[163]

However, this passage in the Report was followed by the comment that 'The Committee have not been able to obtain decided confirmation of this view' and they then quoted Professor Cunningham's response to Pearson's views: 'I think that the statement is a pure assumption. I do not know how we can possibly measure this supposed loss of inherited intelligence.' And: 'It should be borne in

158 PDC, Evidence, para. 2240. 159 PDC, Evidence, para. 2241.

160 PDC, Evidence, para. 2241. The point was that this was incompatible with the thesis that the size of the female pelvis was being diminished, due either to sedentary activities or to overconcentration on intellectual activity.

161 PDC, Evidence, paras. 2241, 2244–62.

162 PDC, Report, para. 43. For Cunningham's original statement, see Evidence, para. 2210.

163 Cited in PDC, Report, para. 212.

mind that it is stocks and not classes which breed men of intellect . . . No class can claim intellect as its special perquisite.'[164] Finally, the Committee cautiously concluded that: 'in view of the statement made by Professor Pearson it might be as well if here as in America, steps were taken to obtain by means of a proper census, accurate information on the point'.[165]

However, this recommendation for a fertility inquiry cannot be claimed as a 'victory' for the hereditarian eugenists. Cunningham himself had been enthusiastic for it when asked. He was quite certain that the recent decline in fertility amongst the upper classes was due entirely to their employment of 'artificial restraints' and not to any decline in physiological fecundity, and that only a proper census could demonstrate this conclusively.[166] Furthermore, the fertility of the different classes was itself part of the environmentalists' explanation of the possible changes occurring in measures of the nation's average physique. If the wealthiest and healthiest section of the population was steadily contributing proportionately less to each generation because of a tendency – for whatever reason – towards smaller families, then this shift in the compositional make-up of the population as a whole would inevitably produce the appearance of a fall or deterioration in the average value of any measure of the nation's health and physique, as a purely statistical artefact. The form of the argument was exactly the same as has been detailed in the correspondence preliminary to the setting up of the PDC: the identification of a compositional fallacy, in that apparent shifts over time in the average value of some measurable population parameter, such as height, may simply be due to shifts in the proportions of the social groups composing the overall population. Professor Cunningham's colleague, Mr John Gray, Secretary to the recently re-convened Anthropometric Committee of the British Association, encapsulated this point in his evidence. He claimed that the probable reduction of the birth rate amongst 'the superior classes' tended to produce 'a progressive deterioration of the average national physique', meaning that the average measure registered a fall because the well-fed were a shrinking proportion of the population.[167]

The prospect of a fertility census, like the establishment of an anthropometric survey, was, then, equally important to both hereditarian and environmentalist interpretations of social evolution. Both could agree on the apparent gravity of a situation in which the able-bodied, and possibly most able-minded, too, might be a shrinking proportion of the nation. There has, incidentally, been much unnecessary confusion over the aims and motives of various factions within the broad National Efficiency consensus of the early years of the century precisely because of their agreement over this matter, the basic facts of the problem. Their crucial disagreement was over the causes – and therefore the appropriate remedies – for this universally

[164] Quoted in PDC, Report, para. 213, from Cunningham's statements in Evidence, paras. 2270 and 2271, respectively. [165] PDC, Report, para. 215. [166] PDC, Evidence, para. 2268.

[167] PDC, Evidence, para. 3267. Gray was also cited in the same part of the Report as the statements from Pearson and Cunningham (para. 214).

deplored situation. For instance, G. R. Searle claims that it was a fallacious assumption 'that the working classes were made up of people of weak physique and low intelligence'.[168] However, as a descriptive statement and observation, this was accepted by all concerned at the time as a true fact about the nation's dilemma. What was at issue was the question of why the working poor were generally in such a condition and what could be done about it.

Thus, contemporary scientific controversy in biology and physical anthropology was brought squarely into the debate over social policy during the deliberations of the Physical Deterioration Committee. Now that the scientific coherence of the biometricians' hereditarian position was challenged, a more rigorously environmentalist interpretation of the structure of society was able to gain currency, as more than simply the expression of a minority opinion.

Conclusion: the scientific and social emancipation of medical environmentalism

It is not, of course, the case that there was a clean divide in 1903–4. The emergence of a coherent anti-hereditarian interpretation in the deliberations of the official inquiries of 1903 and 1904 was only the start of a protracted scientific and political battle, which was to continue through to the next decade and beyond. It was this which formed the immediate context from which the GRO's official classification was to emerge: a highly visible intellectual struggle on the part of the environmentalists within the medical, educational and public service professions for emancipation from the domineering claims being advanced by a putatively authoritative and scientific hereditarian interpretation of social stratification.

This conflict provided a powerful stimulus for ideological and political reassessment among those trained in preventive medical science, including the relevant staff of the GRO. The default acceptance of a previously conventional assumption, that responsibility for individuals' poverty lay *primarily* with themselves, was overturned as much greater emphasis was now laid on the impersonal economic and cultural forces trapping individuals into their impoverishment. Careful empirical social research pointed toward the mode of operation of these self-reinforcing causes of social inequalities. The urgent need for a response to the diametrically opposed assertions of the hereditarian eugenicists forced the environmentalists to develop fully and to amplify the national policy implications of their analysis. This political dynamic effectively and rapidly drove them towards a strongly collectivist position, since the corollary was that it was the responsibility of the community as a whole to deploy its formidable resources to break these bonds of perpetual impoverishment.

In Britain, the first empirical social survey which really did break with the conservative, individualist consensus had been relatively independent of the

168 Searle, *The quest for national efficiency*, p. 61.

influence of developments in the supposed applicability of evolutionary theory to social analysis. This was Seebohm Rowntree's *Poverty*, published in 1901. This provoked a vitriolic response from the leading representatives of the COS, which forced Rowntree to defend his work by outlining these underlying divergences in approach and policy:

> I imagine that the difference between Mrs Bosanquet and myself goes deeper than anything represented by the criticisms I have been considering. Mrs Bosanquet, as is well known, belongs to the extreme wing of the Individualistic school. This school unduly magnifies what may be done for the amelioration of social conditions through the personal effort and self-reliance of the individual, and correspondingly minimises the sphere of State intervention.[169]

Until recently the methodological novelty and importance of Rowntree's work has remained somewhat obscured by his own deliberate emphasis on the similarities between his survey and that of Charles Booth. In his introduction he lauded Booth on every page and in the text he printed a letter from the great man congratulating him on the closeness of agreement between each of their estimates of poverty.[170] E. P. Hennock has convincingly argued that consequently there has been a failure to appreciate the truly independent significance of Rowntree's work in its contribution both to the framing of the subsequent 'national efficiency' debate, and simultaneously in providing the pioneering outlines of an effective environmentalist brief in this debate.[171]

By explicitly linking his findings to Booth's and emphasising the supposed similarity that about 30% of the population in each city were in poverty, Rowntree claimed that this indicated there was an enormous *national* and general problem, where Booth, Marshall and the Labour Bureau had preferred in the 1890s to envisage only a metropolitan dilemma, due to the supposedly unique problems of the capital. Rowntree further underlined the connections between his findings in York and national problems of health and efficiency by citing the topical rejection rates for recruits which the journalist Arnold White was so publicising at this time. Thirdly, and this is where his work is most clearly original, Rowntree offered a putative 'scientific', hard measurement of poverty, which addressed the essential social and political issue of the relation between economic means and physiological requirements. This was the famous poverty line calculation, where the nutritional science of human dietary needs was used to show that the incomes of many families in York throughout much of their life-cycle were below the costs of an

169 Rowntree, *The poverty line*, p. 28. 170 Rowntree, *Poverty*, p. 355.

171 Although it is to be noted that despite the popular elision of their findings and methods, the President of the COS, C. S. Loch, cogently destroyed the illusion of corroboration between the two surveys in a careful, critical review of their two works for the Physical Deterioration Committee. PDC, Report, Appendix III. However, this analysis by Loch seems to have been virtually ignored by contemporary sociologists and by historians ever since. He anticipated many of the important points concerning Booth's classification system, which were only more recently exposed by E. P. Hennock: 'Poverty and social theory'. See especially PDC, Report, Appendix III, paras. 20–5, for comparison with Hennock's analysis.

indisputably frugal subsistence budget and diet.[172] Mortality indices and anthropometric measures of children's growth rates only reported health outcomes, leaving much room for debate between hereditarians and environmentalists over the causes. Rowntree's approach more directly analysed the relationship between physiological adequacy and economic means.[173] As has been noted, the PDC was particularly impressed with the evidence and argument from educationists relating to the inadequate feeding of many working-class children and the undesirable effect of this, not merely on their physical development but also on their learning capacities.

The more radical novelty of Rowntree's approach can perhaps be explained to some extent by his cultural isolation and independence from the metropolitan tradition of conservative and biologised empirical social science. Here his background is relevant: a provincial upbringing and education outside Oxbridge and London, at Owen's College, Manchester; the strong influence of his father's humanitarianism; and his Quaker faith.[174] This imbued him with a more genuinely egalitarian attitude towards his fellow men than that held at this time by the devout paternalists of the Established Church, whether High Church or Evangelical, self-helpers or the COS. His Quakerism prevented him from seeking explanations for the plight of individuals in terms of their inherent failings and moral inferiority. Furthermore, he explicitly rejected any *a priori* claims for the relevance of biological science to social analysis, following the careful counsel of T. H. Huxley.[175]

Rowntree was definitely rather unusual at this time, in *both* having a conviction in the value of practical, 'scientific', empirical study of the conditions of the poor and yet remaining relatively unimpressed with the findings of the natural sciences as having any direct relevance for questions of social organisation. Other students of social problems, such as the idealist L. T. Hobhouse or the socialist liberal Graham Wallas, were similarly unconvinced that the natural sciences had any direct lessons for human social organisation. But, by virtue of this, they tended

172 However, see the further discussion that has developed over the rigour of Rowntree's methods: Veit-Wilson has shown that Rowntree did not, in fact, use as fully as he could have done the comprehensive income data for York's working class that was undoubtedly at his disposal. Hennock has argued that this was because he preferred to repeat Booth's methodology of counting observers' impressions of 'apparent poverty' in order to carry out his original aim of ensuring comparability between his findings and those of Booth's. Veit-Wilson, 'Paradigms of poverty'; Hennock, 'Concepts of poverty', pp. 194–200.

173 The principal follower of Rowntree's lead in this direction was the mathematical statistician, A. L. Bowley, in his work over the next two decades, both for the Labour Department and also funded by the Ratan Tata foundation. As Hennock shows, Bowley was particularly attracted to the development of statistical probabilistic solutions for the two major measurement issues raised by Rowntree's work: first, the national representativeness of necessarily local, detailed inquiries into household budgets; secondly the problem of the weightings for components of any comparisons of 'cost-of-living' estimates, either over time or between different parts of the country. Hennock, 'The measurement of urban poverty'.

174 Briggs, *Social thought and social action*, pp. 4–14.

175 Briggs, *Social thought and social action*, pp. 23–4.

also to subscribe to a more profound philosophical distrust of the status of inductively derived, practical and positivist knowledge *per se*.

Medical science and medical professionals, on the other hand, hailed from an almost diametrically opposite approach to the study of humankind, in the sense that they had a vocational commitment to practical observation and to positive, empirically based ameliorative action, rather than abstract reflection. There was an understandable general association for medical professionals between the commitment to practical, positive action and a respect for the ordered principles and methods of scientific empiricism. This was the model for a rational and efficacious approach, of which the natural sciences, including evolutionary biology, appeared to offer the most successful and promising examples to medical scientists.

It is interesting, then, to compare Rowntree's intellectual development in this respect with that of the medically trained Arthur Newsholme. There were important similarities. Newsholme was also a Yorkshireman, brought up in Haworth, who recalled in his memoirs the importance of Evangelicalism (Wesleyan in the case of Haworth) 'as a potent factor in determining the social and hygienic as well as the moral uplifting of the nineteenth century' because 'Evangelicalism meant an enormously increased solicitude for one's fellow men and not merely or chiefly that "other-worldliness" attributed to it by Matthew Arnold.'[176] Yet, as a trained medical professional, a particularly able epidemiologist and a bacteriological scientist, Newsholme was inevitably much more cognisant than Rowntree of the claims and apparent validity of the scientific and evolutionary perspective on poverty and disease. With Weismann's ostensible confirmation of Galton's long-standing claim that heredity was all-important, science appeared in the 1890s to be ratifying in biological form the long-standing 'individualist' conviction that poverty and unfitness reflected the reproduction of innate flaws in the individual and not the malfeasance of social forces. Discussing, in retrospect, the views which he held in the 1890s, Newsholme admitted that 'in some measure I then endorsed the "deterrent principle" of the Poor Law Act, 1834. I view with dismay the strict C.O.S views which I then expressed: but I confess them as illustrating the views then generally held and the rapid emergence from them.'[177]

His autobiographical account of his own 'rapid emergence' from such a position towards a thoroughly collectivist view of the need for public health reforms, dated his conversion to some time before 21 October 1904. Appropriately in Rowntree's York, this was the date of a speech in which Newsholme had first expressed the anti-individualist view that 'most poverty is a symptom of disease and not a disease in itself'. He went on proudly to recall that the following year, in an article co-authored with T. H. C. Stevenson, he had made a stand against the 'ultra

176 Newsholme, *Fifty years*, p. 26. This discussion of his articles of faith was one of the few personal details which he permitted himself, in his exceptionally catalogic memoirs.

177 Newsholme, *The last thirty years*, p. 68.

Calvinistic attitude of Galton and his disciples'.[178] He had claimed, echoing Cunningham's dismissal before the PDC of Pearson's 'pure assumption', that: 'Very few would venture to assert that the line of intellectual ability or of physical endurance is horizontal and not oblique, or possibly almost perpendicular in relation to social position.'[179]

For a medical scientist like Newsholme, therefore, a nonconformist prior commitment to certain Christian principles of human fellowship was insufficient, alone, to engender in him a radical alternative to an individualistically and naturalistically premised analysis of the causes of urban poverty. He was subject to the conventional, supposedly scientifically backed wisdom current in the metropolis in the final decades of the nineteenth century where he learnt his trade. For this leading figure in the medical profession, however strong his egalitarian religious beliefs, the apparently compelling claims of advanced biological science were not to be shrugged off lightly. In his retrospective explanation of his own 'conversion' in 1904, Newsholme explicitly linked together the COS moral individualism and Galtonian hereditarian social Darwinism as mutually supporting forces largely responsible for his earlier views. Hence the importance of the dissolution, at the beginning of the first decade of the new century, of the apparent scientific authority of the post-Weismann biometric, hereditarian position on evolution. This facilitated an intellectual emancipation among the leaders of the preventive health tradition in the medical profession, enabling them to reassess the rational grounds for their current social assumptions, and to develop and promote more confidently their own rigorously social and environmentalist analysis of poverty. In formulating a more thorough environmentalist position in rejection of the biological 'Calvinism' of the predestinarian hereditarians, a previously unexamined attachment to the political orthodoxy of liberal individualism also came under scrutiny.

The interpretation offered here differs somewhat from that which has been presented by other accounts of Newsholme's ideas, notably by J. M. Eyler.[180] I have followed through the implications of Newsholme's own recollections in seeing a definite 'conversion', or radical transformation, in his thinking occurring in 1903–4. This was a fundamental change from a previously conventional, predominantly individualist, to a more thoroughgoing collectivist approach. I believe that this was an extremely significant shift and that within the public and preventive health community Newsholme was the leading individual in this respect and one whose influence was important in bringing about a similar (though usually less thorough) shift in priorities among others within the profession. It follows from this that it is vital when addressing any of Newsholme's writings to distinguish whether they were composed before or after the watershed

178 Newsholme, *Fifty years*, p. 298. 179 Newsholme, *Fifty years*, p. 296.

180 Eyler, 'The sick poor and the state'; Eyler, 'Poverty, disease, responsibility'; and see also Porter, '"Enemies of the race"'.

of 1903–4, since it is invalid to cite material from before 1903 as illustrative of his views when Chief Medical Officer and, of course, vice versa.[181]

Thus, by the opening years of the new century the country's leading public health officials and salaried educationists were gradually piecing together a perception of the detailed operation of certain impersonal social and economic forces acting within and upon the country's poorer communities: self-reinforcing circles of impoverishment and disadvantage upon the poor. Employing the methods of the sceptical scientific empiricism in which they had been trained, MOHs and others sifted through the evidence before their eyes to probe for preventable 'causes' in the recurrent patterns which they encountered.[182] Despite a continuing common-sense attachment to an individualistic ontology (the confidential relationship between caring doctor and individual patient was then, as now, the primary ethical rule of medical training), a new understanding of the intractable, imbricate nature of poverty was dawning upon practically involved medical professionals. These were conclusions they were increasingly forced to draw and to articulate to each other *as a professional group* from their close and daily observation of the problems, the families and the individuals involved. The rise of the public service professions, led by the MOHs, was so significant in this period because they brought and sustained the analytical approach of their professional training to the wider issues of poverty and the conditions of life of the poor. This complex subject was now addressed and discussed as the routine business of a potentially powerful social grouping – a set of middle-class professions. Urban distress was no longer only known as the exotic or the moral, 'exposed' by maverick investigators or evangelised by the holy.

However, what seems to have really catalysed this newly emerging social perspective on poverty into a truly self-conscious and assertive programme was the concurrent hardening of the traditional, 'individualist' viewpoint into an

[181] John Eyler is quite right to stress Newsholme's Huxleyan view that humans' capacity for reason, co-operation and morality meant that they were not subject to the brute forces of biological evolution; and his Hobhouseian belief that recent history, such as the abolition of slavery and campaigns against cruelty to children, showed that progressive moral evolution in the individual character was occurring, towards altruism and civilisation and away from the selfishness and vice which were encouraged by a deprived and deficient environment. However, in assessing Newsholme's views on the relative importance of individual responsibility and collective provision, it is important to distinguish his attitude towards the deprived and towards the privileged. After 1904 Newsholme consistently emphasised the priority of collectively organised and collectively resourced environmental improvements as the key to raising the prospects of the poor: a necessary condition to enable and facilitate the desirable moral evolution of individuals' characters to take place. Whereas in discussing the behavioural shortcomings of his own social peers – those individuals already fortunate enough to enjoy a beneficial environment – Newsholme could be severe and censorious, invoking weakness of character in individuals because he believed that they had no (environmental) excuse for their failings and 'selfishness'. See, for instance, Newsholme's *The declining birth rate*, pp. 41–2, 56–63, for this differential approach towards the poor and the comfortable. For Eyler's discussion, see Eyler, 'The sick poor and the state', pp. 202–5.

[182] Wilkinson (unpublished DPhil thesis), pp. 284, 321, 330–4.

uncompromising and extreme variant, the form purveyed by the hereditarian eugenicists. Theirs was an absolutely opposed, alternative analysis of the dynamic causes of poverty and unfitness in society, aggressively claiming full and exclusive scientific authority for their approach. Previously, there had been no absolute and inevitable philosophical or practical conflict between the 'soft' individualism of conventional, high Victorian, Evangelical and revivalist philanthropy and the emerging view among late Victorian educationists and health workers: that impoverished individuals were subject to vicious circles of economic and cultural disadvantage beyond their immediate control. This analysis could be read as simply adding another level of strategic missionary activity – attending to the pernicious circular forces – while not ruling out the continuing value of face-to-face missionary work, encouraging personal independence and so on. That formidable COS figure, Octavia Hill, had, after all, long been the figurehead of sustained philanthropic attention to housing conditions, urban parks and open spaces, an implicit acknowledgement that uplifted individual souls flourished best in an uplifting shared environment, ultimately finding manifestation in the highly statist and collectivist notion of the National Trust.[183] The 'Broad Church' environmentalism that had characterised the hard-pressed and understaffed Victorian public health movement would in fact happily continue to co-operate and live with the much-needed small armies of philanthropic voluntaries right through the interwar period, especially in view of the increasing professionalism of the latter, encouraged by the intellectually formidable COS, which had become particularly active in training and education for social workers during the last decade of the century.[184]

But in its 'first generation' militant and evangelical manifestation (Galton himself viewed the Edwardian eugenics movement as a primarily religious rather than scientific organisation), the eugenicist, hereditarian version of 'individual responsibility' for manifest physical or mental inadequacy was a ruthless and uncompromising one. Its truths excluded all other interpretations. Therefore its rapid rise to public prominence after the turn of the new century clarified the thoughts of practical professional environmentalists. It called forth a necessarily clear and convincing riposte. As a result the relatively tentative findings of systematic vicious cycles of immiseration that were emerging in the course of their professional work, on the part of an extremely practical and empiricist collection of Medical Officers of Health and a small but influential number of school medical officers, were transformed through the forcing school of sharp public contest and debate with the hereditarian eugenicists.

It was the extremism of the hereditarians which pushed the public health movement to rediscover the challenging political and ideological implications – for an English liberal individualist consensus – of a rigorous environmentalism.

183 Darley, *Octavia Hill*.

184 Harris, 'The Webbs, the C.O.S. and the Ratan Tata Foundation', pp. 34–5.

This was the moment at which the radical, socio-economic theory of disease was finally rediscovered and expounded by the most advanced among English mainstream exponents of public health. Originally formulated by the leaders of the French school of *hygiène publique* in the first third of the nineteenth century and championed at the same time by W. P. Alison in Edinburgh, 'the social theory of disease' had been politically castrated by the dominant English influence, Edwin Chadwick, when he adapted its findings to support his merely sanitary idea, 'the filth theory of disease'.[185] In fighting to oppose the exclusive claims being made for nature, the Edwardian public health movement rediscovered and for the first time publicly championed the radical political potential of the argument from nurture.

It was only the close combat with the hereditarians, 1903–4, which crystallised the new ideas for those such as MacKenzie, Newsholme, Newman and Eicholz, identified by the Porters as the leading collectivist and environmentalist caucus; hence, it is difficult to find any mainstream medical figures expressing such views before 1903. The leading environmentalists were being pushed into discerning more clearly the methodological individualism common to both the traditional, moralistic COS position and the new, aggressive hereditarianism; and the limitations which acceptance of such premises entailed for the health and welfare aims which they cherished.[186] It was the polarising ferocity of the hereditarian arguments of the eugenics movement which finally clarified and confirmed for the most politically aware and intellectually cogent leaders of the environmentalist public health movement that their future, their true beliefs and their interests lay with the idea of collective provision for health promotion of the nation as a whole.

Pearson, Galton and those hereditarians writing of degeneration and deterioration in the opening years of the century had succeeded in forcing an hereditarian, national interpretation of evolution on to the national stage as a political issue. As a result, those public service professionals wishing to see the nation's health and welfare services continuing to expand as the major weapon against poverty and disease were forced to mobilise their own national-scale arguments in order not to lose the political debate. Through the forum offered by the wide-ranging government inquiries, particularly the Physical Deterioration Committee, this prompted and facilitated a pooling of their intellectual resources. Representatives of the practical observers and helpers of the nation's poor – educationists, voluntary workers, public health officials and social scientists – found the conclusions emerging from their several specialist perspectives pointing in common towards the kind of comprehensive social analysis most fully expressed by Eicholz. Furthermore, it was increasingly being appreciated that the countervailing scientific evidence of certain anthropologists, comparative anatomists and the new Mendelian geneticists provided an effective challenge to the 'degenerationist' and hereditarian viewpoints. With the Mendelian challenge growing ever stronger

[185] La Berge, 'Edwin Chadwick'. See above, pp. 87–8.

[186] On methodological individualism, see the elucidatory Lukes, *Individualism*.

during the decade or so before the First World War, medically trained proponents of environmentalist policies felt increasingly able to take on their scientific detractors.

However, the hereditarians' social and scientific analysis was far from a broken reed; it was merely under challenge. Thus, over the decade or so following the 1904 inquiry, there ensued a vigorous *scientific* battle over the correct interpretation of demographic statistics of mortality, morbidity and, of course, fertility. The debate was given its particular force and significance because of its *political* importance to the proponents concerned. It was a debate in scientific terms and issues, but with direct political implications, goals and significance, as well as investigative scientific ones; and out of it emerged the 1911 fertility census and the official, professional model of social classes.

5

The emergence of the professional model as the official system of social classification, 1905–1928

Infant mortality: the focus of scientific debate

The official Reports of 1903 and 1904 only represented the initial exchange of hostilities between hereditarians and environmentalists. The post-Boer War inquests proved to be the start of a continuous battle by appeal to the evidence as each side sought to show greater congruence between its own theory and the facts of poverty: the associated class-differential patterns of mortality and fertility. Inspired by Galton's attribution of a eugenic scale of evaluation to Booth's social class scheme, there soon appeared eugenic studies, purporting to measure the reproduction of the various social groups within the nation.

In a research report published in 1906 David Heron, one of Pearson's assistants at the UCL (University College, London) Biometric Laboratory endowed by Galton, attempted the first 'thorough' eugenic treatment of the subject: 'On the relation of fertility in man to social status changes in the last fifty years'. In Heron's study, the main empirical undertaking consisted of producing correlation coefficients between various indices constructed from official sources, relating to the observable socio-demographic traits of the populations of administrative districts. Of course, the assumption involved in such a procedure, for any causal inference to be validly derived, was that the attributes were formally independent. Yet such indices as the numbers of legitimate births per hundred wives, the proportion in each district living more than two to a room, the number of children aged 10–14 employed per hundred children between those ages, and the infant mortality rate were all correlated with the districts' birth rates. Heron considered that this exercise then entitled him to conclude that 'the morally and socially lowest class in the community are those which are reproducing themselves with the greatest rapidity'.[1]

The eugenicists were not really using the statistical method of correlation to seek proof for – or an empirical test of – hypotheses regarding causation. Of the mode of

[1] Heron, 'On the relation', p. 15.

causation they were already sublimely certain. These statistics, showing correlations between far from independent variables, were primarily deployed for rhetorical and illustrative purposes. The biometricians were principally intent upon measurement of whether or not those elements in the population deemed to be most worthwhile, on the *a priori* grounds supplied by Galtonian hereditarianism, were on the increase or decrease. The kinds of factors measured were among many which were assumed to be outward signs both of relative status and simultaneously of biological fitness. This equation was implied by the Galtonian naturalistic model of social structure, the hierarchy of occupations. The empirical findings merely provided information on the extent and location of the predefined problem.

In the following year, the Fabian socialists joined battle, with the publication of Sidney Webb's *The decline in the birth rate* (Fabian Tract 131, 1907), later followed by H. D. Harben's *The endowment of motherhood* (Fabian Tract 149, 1910). The radical disagreement between the Fabians and the hereditarian biometricians over specific remedial policies shows that their sharing of a nationalist interpretation of social Darwinism by no means guaranteed agreement over the causation involved; nor, therefore, over the appropriate political means to achieve national efficiency. This is best illustrated in their entirely opposed view of the crucial issue of wages in relation to the differential birth rate, which resulted from the radical difference in each side's assessment of the relative importance of nature and nurture. Hereditarian eugenists saw material living standards as the outward sign of the individuals' inherited ability and 'civic worth'. Natural endowment was the over-riding determinant of material achievements in society: those individuals best endowed should be most encouraged to reproduce their precious stock. Thus, it was stated, in a co-authored document, by the workers in the Francis Galton Memorial Laboratory (the renamed Biometric Laboratory) in 1913:

Let us conclude with what seems to us almost obvious axioms of the requisite conditions for national progress:

(i) Wages ought to be directly proportional to social value as measured by physique and mentality.
(ii) The size of family ought to be proportional on the average to wages.[2]

The Fabians, by contrast, held that poverty was not the manifestation of inherited and biological deficiencies. The miserable conditions of life surrounding the poor working man caused, rather than reflected, his moral and material degradation. This state of affairs was imposed upon him and his family by the puny remuneration and amenities which the profit-maximising, *laissez-faire*, capitalist economy granted him for his labour. H. D. Harben's Fabian Tract of 1910 proposed

[2] Elderton, Barrington, Jones, Lamotte, Laski, Pearson, 'On the correlation', p. 45. The presence in this list of Harold Laski, the subsequent social democratic political theorist is, of course, of some interest. On Laski's eugenics, see MacKenzie, *Statistics in Britain*, pp. 107, 141; and Martin's, *Harold Laski*, pp. 14–16, for further details. On the provenance of social democratic thought in Britain at this time, see Clarke, *Liberals and social democrats*.

a universal standard 'pension' to be provided by the state of 10 shillings per week for two months at the birth of a child. This sum was to be granted to all families specifically on the grounds that it would most benefit the manual and clerical grades within society; while it was admitted that such a sum would still 'hardly touch the middle classes' as an attraction to increased childbearing.

However, the most effective *scientific* opponent of the biometric statistical work, which, of course, drew its strength and authority from its claim to be based on the rational and scientific analysis of empirical, social demographic data, was not one of the established political figures of the Fabian faction of Britain's 'intellectual aristocracy', but a public health official. Arthur Newsholme, who had been President of the Society of Medical Officers of Health in the first year of the century, was an adroit medical statistician and proved himself to be an extremely able apologist for the cause of public health and welfare. He used to the full the resources available to him in his position as Chief Medical Officer to the Local Government Board from 1908 onwards, to undermine the hereditarian position and to launch a relatively successful counter-attack on behalf of the environmentalist viewpoint.[3]

For this leader of the preventive health movement, with its centre of gravity in the public health branch of the medical profession, the appetite for battle against the biometric pronouncements was all the keener for the knowledge that he had on his hands a fight for the hearts and minds of his own troops. Newsholme well recognised that the appeal of the eugenics prescription was insidious, reinforcing with apparent scientific authority a certain tendency towards censorious and moralising attitudes and policies towards the poor, which he himself had until very recently entertained to some extent. Certainly, the eugenic attitude found influential sympathisers in a number of important voluntary organisations in the Edwardian era, with which Medical Officers of Health inevitably had considerable contact as the other main providers of social services in urban communities.[4]

The significance of Newsholme's efforts can only be fully appreciated when it is understood that this was a crucial contest of persuasion. In addition to voluntary workers and other professionals there were many doctors, even some Medical Officers of Health, who were inclined broadly to accept the hereditarian interpretation

3 Arthur Newsholme (1857–1943) was Chief Medical Officer to the LGB until its disbandment in 1919 and was undoubtedly the most able and influential professional public health figure of this period. A major biographical study by J. M. Eyler is currently in press. Newsholme's appointment to this pre-eminent position in the government medical service was apparently supported through the lobbying of John Burns on his behalf by the Fabian coterie of the two Webbs and Sir Robert Morant. George Newman, who had himself benefited from similar support when gaining preferment as the Education Board's first Chief Medical Officer, was also much in favour of Newsholme's appointment. See Searle, *The quest for national efficiency*, pp. 243–4. Brown, *John Burns*, p. 133, states that Burns was in any case personally impressed with Newsholme.

4 Pauline Mazumdar gives as examples of such organisations: the Moral Education League, from which the Eugenics Education Society itself formed as an offshoot in 1907; the COS; the National Temperance League; and the National Association for the Care and Protection of the Feeble-minded. Mazumdar, 'The eugenists and the residuum'.

and its entailed policies of segregation for the unfit and their regulated suppression.[5] For several years this was a real threat, as the eugenicists, shaken by what they saw as the extremely unfavourable outcome of the PDC's inquiry, redoubled their propaganda efforts, realising that confining their publications to *Biometrika*, the obscure and highly statistical house journal of the Galton Laboratory, was no way to win over wider opinion. Coincident with changing its name from the *Journal of State Medicine* to the *Journal of Preventive Medicine* in 1905, one of the two main established journals of health administration was subject to a flood of eugenic articles, with Galton himself contributing in 1906 on his old haunt, 'Anthropometry in schools'. In the following year the Eugenics Education Society itself was founded. With the founding of its own organ, the *Eugenics Review* commencing in 1909, the eugenic siege of the *Journal of Preventive Medicine* appears to have been lifted, although their activism elsewhere continued unabated: the first international eugenic congress was held in London in 1912.

It was only because of the political significance of the issues at stake that the scientific debate became so polarised, as if it were starkly one of 'Nature versus Nurture'.[6] As Newsholme later acknowledged in his memoirs, 'Both extremes of thought present a distortion of the truth . . . Biological Calvinism and environmental determinism form a double enslavement.'[7] In his second volume of memoirs, Newsholme recalled that what had motivated his scientific efforts to expose the inadequacies of the hereditarians' presumptions was the fear of damage to the public health movement's morale caused by

> biometrical investigations which appear . . . to throw doubt on the value of many public health activities. The usefulness of not a few medical officers of health has been dulled by these doubts; and this diminution of enthusiasm for their life-work has been increased by their inability to check the statistical measures employed by biometricians, and by their too ready belief that pontifical statements based on (to them) incomprehensible statistics must be accepted implicitly.[8]

[5] At the PDC inquiry itself, at least one senior MOH, Sir Charles Cameron of Dublin, was prepared to propound broadly hereditarian views: PDC, Evidence, paras. 10917, 11001–18. A few examples of others can also be found in the journal, *Public Health*. For instance, an article by A. W. Martin (MOH for Gorton) on 'The elimination of the unfit' in the 1907 volume of *Public Health* prompted the editor (Newsholme) prominently to remind his readers that he was not responsible for the opinions expressed in any signed article!

[6] In a somewhat different 'political' context, in the discipline of anthropology in the USA about ten years later, Derek Freeman has noted a similar effect, whereby the suffocating claims of a hereditarian determinism provoked an equally extreme cultural determinism in the defensive intellectual responses of R. H. Lowie and A. Kroeber, fearing for their discipline's professional and institutional survival: Freeman, *Margaret Mead*, pp. 45–6.

[7] Newsholme, *Fifty years*, p. 408. It was the influential post-Second World War study by N. Pastore, *The nature–nurture controversy*, which was historiographically responsible for reinforcing the somewhat simplistic notion that these scientific positions automatically entailed diametrically opposed political positions. Of course, this appeared to be a not unreasonable inference at that time, in view of the recent history of associations between, on the one hand, fascism with racist hereditarian determinism, and, on the other hand, Stalinist communism with the environmental determinism of Lysenko.

[8] Newsholme, *The last thirty years*, p. 208.

Dr Alfred Eicholz was similarly motivated. Shortly after the publication of the Report of the PDC, he was to be found addressing the annual conference of the National Union of Women Workers of Great Britain and Ireland, reassuring them that their activities as social workers to the poor were far from futile, and that the PDC's official inquiry had found that there was nothing of value in the degenerationists' claims that they were merely preserving the evolutionary unfit:

> It is not twelve months ago that the country was shaken with doubt and insecurity as to our national well-being, arising from the dissemination of certain facts, now well-known, tending to indicate that we as a people were physically on the down grade.
>
> With every opportunity for hearing all that could be said on both sides, the Committee has concluded that the evidence before them did not support the belief that there was progressive physical deterioration. We are in fact no worse off than the generation that preceded us, and there is much to show that we are in many respects better. The encouragement in all this is that we may once more take our places in the fighting-line with a firmer hope of meeting successfully the forces which man sets up for his own destruction.

He continued:

> The position which seems to me worth supporting is that Nature endows the vast majority of mankind with a birthright of normal physical efficiency; that it is the duty of those who aspire to be known as social workers each to do his share in confirming his fellow-beings in this possession.[9]

The continuing scientific battle, principally between Arthur Newsholme and Karl Pearson, was fought out over the next few years over the correct interpretation of infant and child mortality rates. In his first report on 'Infant and child mortality' for the Local Government Board (LGB), Newsholme used his statistical expertise to show there was 'no necessary relationship between large families and a high infant mortality';[10] but rather that 'large families are common among the poorest classes, and these classes are especially exposed to the degrading influences producing excessive infant mortality'.[11] Newsholme thereby, in effect, exposed a source of co-variation in the eugenists' statistical indices, adduced as independent forms of evidence by them. He then quite explicitly invoked Bateson's new saltationist theories to argue against any form of control over reproduction such as was called for by policies of positive eugenics.[12] Furthermore, he made the point that the hereditarians' judgement *against* the 'anthropological view' of the late Professor Cunningham – who had held that all recorded and observable physical differences between social classes would disappear *if* their environments were equalised – was arbitrary and quite unscientific, *until* the condition which Cunningham had specified had been fulfilled, and hence tested.[13] This clearly implied the need for a massive expansion in the nation's health and welfare services.

[9] Eicholz, 'The alleged deterioration', p. 409.

[10] Statement made in Newsholme, *The declining birth rate*, p. 44. The original report is in PP, 1910 XXXIX, Cd 5263.

[11] Newsholme, *The declining birth rate*, p. 45.

[12] Newsholme, *The declining birth rate*, p. 54.

[13] Newsholme, *The declining birth rate*, pp. 48–50.

Pearson nevertheless continued to maintain a rigorously Spartan view: that infant mortality weeded out the sickly and weak and so performed a useful evolutionary function which was interfered with at society's cost. This belief was in a certain sense analogous to the old anthropometric notion which held that the pelvic ring acted as a regulating gauge on the nation's progress. It employed precisely the same form of naturalistic mechanistic logic: that a physically measurable statistical 'fact' – the infant mortality rate here, physical size of the female pelvis in 1883 – proved a relationship of inherent superiority or inferiority between 'social classes', or racial groups in the latter case. Non-intervention against poverty was the political message of such élitist, hereditarian biological theories. But Pearson's pessimistic admonitions were insufficient to stem a swelling tide of infant and child welfare work and legislation, accompanied by several successive government investigations into the plight of children.[14]

In 1908 there was the famous Children's Act consolidating several decades of piecemeal protective legislation for children; and a National Association for the Prevention of Infant Mortality and for the Welfare of Infancy was formed, as well as a National League for Physical Education and Improvement.[15] Apart from Newsholme at the LGB and a host of MOHs around the country,[16] other public leaders of this movement included John Gorst,[17] Dr Thomas Macnamara,[18] and John Burns, the first President of the National Conference on Infant Mortality, which began its biannual meetings in 1906; and also the medical civil servant, George Newman.[19] From his position as President of the Local Government Board,

[14] For instance, apart from the already mentioned Royal Commission on Physical Training (Scotland) of 1903 and the Physical Deterioration Inquiry of 1904 there was: the Interdepartmental Committee on the Employment of Children (1902) and the subsequent series of Reports of the Interdepartmental Committee on Wage-Earning Children; the 1909 Interdepartmental Committee on Partial Exemption (from elementary school attendance); also the continual monitoring by the Central Midwives Board of the working of the 1902 Midwives Act, which was itself reviewed by a Departmental Committee under Sir Almeric Fitzroy in 1909. See Behlmer, *Child abuse*, Appendix A, which helpfully lists seventy-nine Acts of Parliament passed between 1870 and 1908 (twenty-one from 1900 onwards) to promote child welfare.

[15] The best of several recent accounts of the twentieth-century infant and child welfare movement is: Dwork, *War is good for babies*. On the late nineteenth-century infant and child protection movement and the legislation preceding the 1908 Act, see the excellent Behlmer, *Child abuse*.

[16] For instance: G. F. McCleary (Battersea), E. W. Hope (Liverpool), Drew Harris (St Helens), Samson Moore (Huddersfield), J. F. J. Sykes (St Marylebone).

[17] Sir John Eldon Gorst (1835–1916) was a Conservative politician who had succeeded the Liberal, A. H. D. Acland, as the last Vice-President of the Education Department of the Privy Council, 1895–1902. He broke with the Conservatives over tariff reform.

[18] T. J. Macnamara (1861–1931) had been elected to the executive of the National Union of Teachers in 1890, was President of the Union in 1896 and editor of its journal, *The Teacher*, 1892–1907. He was a radical Liberal MP for North Camberwell, 1900–24, and Minister of Labour 1920–2.

[19] George Newman (1870–1948), a prominent Quaker, had been MOH for both Finsbury and Bedfordshire, and was the author of *Infant mortality*, a timely, semi-popular publication which appeared in 1906. He was the first Chief Medical Officer of the Board of Education from 1907 until his promotion in 1919 to the nation's premier public health post of Chief Medical Officer of the new Ministry of Health, which he held until his retirement in 1935.

Burns certainly held the greatest potential power to effect policy, though he characteristically moved somewhat slowly.[20] In 1907 he had sanctioned a set of local studies to be undertaken in industrial areas by local Medical Officers of Health to assess more closely the true causal vectors of high infant mortality. These produced findings which lent yet further support to the environmentalist interpretation of the inter-relationship between poverty and infant mortality; and they were summarised and presented to great effect by Newsholme in the supplements on infant and maternal mortality to his official annual reports as Chief Medical Officer to the LGB.

One of the most methodologically thorough of these studies was that supervised by John Robertson, the MOH in Birmingham.[21] Robertson selected two of Birmingham's worst wards, St George's and St Stephen's, where housing was all 60–100 years old and mostly back-to-back. The population density was over three times the city's average, and nearly half of those visited over the two years of the inquiry had incomes of less than one pound (20 shillings) per week. All babies born in the district during 1908 were visited.[22] It was judged that in this generally uniformly depressed area, 'The home conditions of those industrially employed wives do not differ to any large extent from those not so employed and therefore the two groups can be compared without selection.'[23] However, of all the women who bore children in 1908, the 46% who could afford to stay at home enjoyed an average income of 23 shillings per week, whereas those who went out to work (54% of the total) had an average household weekly income of only 20 shillings per week despite their own additional earnings. The approximate uniformity of home conditions between the two groups was, therefore, achieved only by virtue of the working mother, without whom the latter category's income would have been very low. Robertson's data showed that in fact the really significant social variables affecting an infant's *health* over its first year of life, as measured by its weight, were: first, the absolute income level of the household; and, secondly, whether the mother was employed after confinement. The former was positively associated with healthy weight-gain, while the latter was negatively correlated because of the early cessation of breast-feeding.[24]

However, there was also an extremely significant counter-effect visible: a wife's industrial employment after confinement was associated with an actual decrease in infant *mortality*, because of the extra income brought in.[25] Robertson's initial

[20] The initiative for the first British national conference on infant mortality in 1906 came not from Burns but from some of the leading local authorities in the field: Dwork, *War is good for babies*, p. 114. In a progressive era and in a progressive administration, John Burns conspicuously failed to distinguish himself as a leading force in the dramatic social reforms that were being sponsored by some of his Cabinet colleagues, notably Lloyd George and the young Churchill. For more on Burns, see p. 71, and ch. 4, n. 49.

[21] 'Report on industrial employment of married women and infantile mortality', in City of Birmingham Health Department's *Annual Report of Medical Officer* (1909).

[22] 'Report on industrial employment', pp. 1–4.

[23] 'Report on industrial employment', p. 5.

[24] 'Report on industrial employment', pp. 18–19.

[25] 'Report on industrial employment', p. 6.

summary of his findings was forceful, in its emphasis on the household income factor: 'These figures very clearly show the powerful effect of poverty on the infant. It does not very much matter whether the mother is industrially employed or not, or whether the infant is breast-fed or not, if great poverty exists the infant suffers from want of nutrition.'[26] These findings were confirmed the following year by Dr Jessie G. Duncan, the female doctor who, with two assistants, had actually carried out all the visits and weighings on which Robertson's Report had been based:

> The general conclusions to be drawn from another year's study of this question are much the same as those arrived at in 1908. It seems pretty certain that industrial employment of women had a bad effect on the infant mortality principally because it interferes with breast-feeding . . . but the influence of industrial employment is quite small when compared with the influence of acute poverty . . . in so far as the mother's employment reduces the acuteness of poverty it may even tend to improve the infant mortality . . . it is doubtful whether any further interference with the employment of married women would be at all beneficial as long as the acute poverty remains.[27]

Another such study was that by Dr George Reid, MOH for Staffordshire. He compared and contrasted his own findings of 1908 with Robertson's, as cited above, when giving evidence in 1914 to the NBRC. (This was a body sponsored by the influential National Council of Public Morals, as a substitute for the lack of a government-sponsored Royal Commission on the birth rate).[28] Reid had found that in the North Staffordshire pottery towns lack of breast-feeding was the strongest determining factor in infant mortality.[29] However, this was not necessarily inconsistent with the Birmingham findings, where sheer poverty, rather than breast-feeding, was judged to have been the most significant factor. Reid pointed out to the NBRC that the Potteries were a community of artisans, a more prosperous social class than that observed in the particularly poor Birmingham wards selected by Robertson.[30] He argued that as a result there was no comparable pool of extremely poorly paid workers in his North Staffordshire sample and that therefore the women and mothers who went to work in his study did not do so out of absolute necessity in order to supplement the family's otherwise inadequate earnings, but because they 'elect to do so'.[31] The factory 'is a sort of club for them'.[32] Furthermore, it was his opinion that the inadequate artificial feeding, which the female pottery workers administered to their children, was not through a lack of income but simple ignorance of dietetic and hygienic considerations.[33] Here, he saw the growth of the practice of County and District Councils' employment of

26 'Report on industrial employment', p. 19.

27 Dr J. G. Duncan, in appended Report to City of Birmingham Health Department's *Annual Report of Medical Officer* (1910).

28 NBRC, *The declining birth rate*, Evidence, 13 November 1914, pp. 198–312.

29 NBRC, *The declining birth rate*, Evidence, 13 November 1914, pp. 300, 307.

30 NBRC, *The declining birth rate*, Evidence, 13 November 1914, p. 302.

31 NBRC, *The declining birth rate*, Evidence, 13 November 1914, p. 303.

32 NBRC, *The declining birth rate*, Evidence, 13 November 1914, p. 308.

33 NBRC, *The declining birth rate*, Evidence, 13 November 1914, p. 312.

lady health visitors, something which had received support in the Physical Deterioration Report of 1904, as an extremely valuable agency to fight such ignorance as a source of child mortality.[34]

Thus, these two studies, and the comparative conclusions which were drawn from them, illustrate how much it was becoming appreciated by exponents of preventive public health that social class composition was a highly significant factor to be taken into account in any investigation and in interpretation of the results of statistical inquiries into social and health-related problems. Such detailed empirical work continued to confirm and fill out the kind of analysis originally presented to the PDC by Rowntree, Leslie MacKenzie, Eicholz and Anderson: that infant and child mortality varied as a function of the economic conditions experienced and the accompanying habits adopted by different social strata. These strata and their characteristic differences existed as a result of the varying opportunities which their place in the labour market and related patterns of upbringing conferred upon essentially biologically similar individuals.

The role of the GRO in the battle for social welfare legislation

The role of the GRO throughout this Edwardian battle over the expansion of preventive health and welfare services was quite clearly that of an important ally of the environmentalists in the public health movement. Newsholme, in his first Report to the LGB as its Chief Medical Officer, had launched a major offensive against the hereditarian interpretation of the causes of infantile mortality. He was able to produce compelling statistical evidence regarding the co-variation of infant (under one year old) and child (from one to five years old) mortality rates.[35] Since it was accepted even by hereditarians that the latter was caused principally by environmental influences, independent of the infant's congenital viability, Newsholme was able to argue that the co-variation of both rates together proved that infant mortality was likewise mainly influenced by the same environmental conditions and not simply a function of natural selection (where high infant mortality among the poor was interpreted by eugenicists as an index of their innate unfitness).

It was only as a result of the co-operation of T. H. C. Stevenson, the newly appointed Superintendent of Statistics at the GRO, in supplying Newsholme with the relevant unpublished data of death rates since 1855 that he was able to produce this evidence. Furthermore, in making this particular argument Newsholme was borrowing more than just the data from the GRO. For Stevenson's immediate predecessor as Superintendent of Statistics, John Tatham, had, in effect, utilised

[34] PDC, Report, para. 300; and see below, chapter 9 n. 230.

[35] 39th Annual Report of the Local Government Board (1909–10), Supplement to the Report of the Medical Officer, on 'Infant and Child Mortality'. PP, 1910 XXXIX, Cd 5263, pp. 9–18. This was the first of several such reports by Newsholme. See Lewis, *The politics of motherhood*, pp. 28–33, for an account of Pearson's response and the course of the subsequent debate between the two men.

very similar inferences to those that Newsholme was now employing, when six years previously Tatham had presented statistics of infant and child mortality to the PDC, of which he was an appointed member.[36]

This had been the first new initiative by the GRO in this area since the special investigations in the late 1880s and early 1890s.[37] Tatham used the GRO's vital registration data to distinguish mortality in each of the first four weeks of life and thereafter in each of the next eleven months. He also, incidentally, innovated the comparison for legitimacy and for sex of the child while retaining the previous study's overall framework of an urban–rural comparative inquiry, a long-established practice of all analysis at the GRO. Tatham had deployed this analysis to point out to the PDC inquiry a finding of particular relevance to the scientific interpretation of infant mortality rates. A comparison of mortality among legitimate births showed that the London baby actually stood a higher chance of surviving its first week of life than did the rural newborn, presumably on account of the former's access to the hospital facilities and emergency medical treatments that were available in the capital.[38] But once past the first week, the disadvantages of the metropolitan environment began to show themselves fully. From the second week onwards, infants in the capital experienced continually worsening higher differential mortality throughout the remainder of the first year of life.[39] Both of these features strongly supported an environmentalist interpretation. On the one hand, the effectiveness of medical intervention was indicated even at the earliest post-natal stage, provided that it was sufficiently accessible to the populace, as in the capital. On the other hand, the relative maleficence of urban conditions in causing the higher mortality over the first year of life as a whole was confirmed, and the need for the curtailment of these conditions by preventive public health measures was underlined.

From this point onwards, the annual reports produced by the GRO display a strong continuity of interest in the perfection of the accurate measurement of trends in infant mortality and morbidity. This generated certain related modifications in fertility calculations, since measures of infant death were usually calculated as rates per thousand births, so that improvements in fertility measures were also required. The corrections for sex and legitimacy differentials (both of which could be expected to influence mortality rates) in the PDC study were the first steps in this process of improvement. The following year the implications of recent research, including work by Stevenson and Newsholme in collaboration, were taken on board by Tatham, in the form of a modified measure of fertility to correct for secular changes in the proportion of women of childbearing age in the national population.[40] In the next Report, that for 1904 (published in 1906), a new table was

36 PDC, Report, Appendix Va, pp. 130–7. See also 65th ARRG, Supplement Pt1, pp. cv–cxvi, especially p. cix.

37 See pp. 83–4. 38 65th ARRG, p. cix. 39 65th ARRG, p. cix.

40 66th ARRG, pp. xvii–xix; Stevenson and Newsholme, 'An improved method'.

introduced distinguishing each of the first five years of mortality separately.[41] In the following year an entirely novel and potent concept, survivorship rates, made its first appearance.[42] For the moment it was used by W. C. Dunbar, the Registrar-General, to compare in detail the demographic régimes of various localities in Britain: three textiles counties (Leicestershire, Lancashire and the West Riding); three mining counties (Glamorganshire, Staffordshire, County Durham); three agricultural counties (Herefordshire, Cambridgeshire, Wiltshire); the metropolis; and several large townships. This year also saw a comparison between the fifteen towns with the highest and the fifteen with the lowest proportions of married women occupied in gainful employment outside the home. The year after this, in the Report for 1906, great advances in measurement were still being made. Tatham now produced tables for mortality on each day of the first week of life.[43]

Meanwhile, the efforts of the Registrar-General, W. C. Dunbar, on behalf of the movement for preventive health legislation, had not stopped short at publication of information in the most persuasive possible form. In 1907 there had been enacted the Notification of Births Act. This was a measure which Dunbar himself, in his official capacity, had been actively promoting in 1906 to help fight infant mortality.[44] It was something which had, in his own words, 'escaped even the "eagle eye" of that Committee' – referring to the PDC inquiry.[45] In 1908 Dunbar was to be found championing a suggestion made by Dr George Reid and supported by Miss A. M. Anderson, that there should be legislation to restrict mothers from returning to work within three months of giving birth.[46] This was to prolong the period of breast-feeding, so ensuring immunity from most infectious diseases over the highly vulnerable early months of life.[47]

Thus, when the new team of Bernard Mallet, as Registrar-General, and T. H. C. Stevenson, as Superintendent of Statistics, took up their posts in 1909, following

41 67th ARRG, Table J, p. xciv.

42 68th ARRG, p. xxvii and Table C, p. xxviii. This was the concept which was to dominate the politically eye-catching but intellectually somewhat stultifying interwar project of demography: that of constructing comparative replacement rates (i.e. the net fertility of an average woman in the population, after allowing for the depletion effects of mortality, sterility and celibacy) for social classes and for nations – permitting, in the latter case, projections in the 1930s of future population stasis or even decline. Enid Charles's work, described in some detail above in chapter 1 (see pp. 17–20), was in part a contribution to this debate, which involved virtually all demographers in the 1930s. For a full account, see Soloway *Demography and degeneration*, especially chs. 10–11.

43 69th ARRG, Tables Q, R, S, and p. cxxxi.

44 The principle of the compulsory notification of medically relevant events was, of course, a long-standing primary element of the preventive health strategy, comprising the essential intelligence mechanism for its operation. In this instance, it was the means by which the growing network of Lady Health Visitors could be alerted to a new arrival in their district and enabled to deploy their expertise and resources in influencing the immediately post-natal environment of mother and child, which mortality statistics proved to be the most vulnerable stage of life, especially in the big cities.

45 67th ARRG, p. xlix.

46 See previous chapter, p. 217, for Anderson's important evidence to the PDC.

47 69th ARRG, p. lxvi.

the retirements of Dunbar and Tatham in that year, they were the heirs to a strongly pronounced, almost political role, which the GRO's recent publications had been expounding. Stevenson, trained in public health medicine with subsequent experience both as a School Board Medical Officer and as Newsholme's assistant during the latter's post as Brighton's MOH, was a natural heir to this recent tradition of strong involvement – amounting virtually to an open alliance with the Local Government Board's Medical Department under Newsholme's guidance – in promoting the cause of environmentalist public health and welfare.[48] The new Registrar-General, Bernard Mallet, being a non-specialist career civil servant, now took a backseat, leaving Stevenson to undertake full direction of the Office's reports.[49]

In his first full-length report, that for 1909, which was published in 1911, Stevenson was immediately to be found engaged in an analysis of the recent disputed fall in infant mortality. By separating out that portion due to diarrhoeal deaths, which fluctuated markedly as a function of summer temperature, he was able to conclude that the analysis 'supports the conclusion arrived at by Dr. Newsholme in his recent report on Infant and Child Mortality that "the improvement experienced has not been entirely due to more favourable climatic conditions".'[50] Stevenson further followed this up with a strong publicity point, aimed at underlining the effectiveness of the numerous local initiatives which had been made by county and municipal councils and their Medical Officers, after the PDC's Report and the formation of the National Association for the Prevention of Infant Mortality. Stevenson, commenting on his own analysis of the recent infant mortality trends, noted that 'when diarrhoeal deaths are eliminated, the improvement up to 1904 is found to have been comparatively slight though very considerable

[48] A measure of the extent to which Stevenson's post at the GRO, as Superintendent of Statistics, was considered of crucial importance to the success of the Public Health programme can be gauged from Newsholme's statement in his memoirs that in 1907 it had been: '. . . the only appointment under the government which I desired'. Newsholme *The last thirty years*, p. 28. Furthermore, Newsholme had been a short-listed candidate for the post at Tatham's appointment in 1892 (*ibid.*, p. 29). Stevenson's professional relationship with Newsholme was extremely close. Newsholme had been Stevenson's boss in his first post at Brighton and his collaborator on two of Stevenson's first four publications: Stevenson and Newsholme, 'An improved method' and 'The decline'. The relationship between the two men is referred to in Stevenson's obituary, in *JRSS* 96 (1933), pp. 151–5. This was written by Professor Major Greenwood ('M.G.').

[49] This was formally recognised in the 72nd ARRG, in announcing a changed format for the annual reports, whereby the RG's contribution was reduced to a very brief prefatory summary. Bernard Mallet (1859–1932) was Registrar-General from 1909 until his retirement in 1920. A Balliol product (see p. 153), he had served in the Foreign Office and the Treasury before appointment as Commissioner of Inland Revenue, 1897–1909. Although he did later become interested in eugenics, at the time of his appointment as RG, his intellectual interests were still firmly focused on the subject of his previous official position, the analysis of British fiscal policy and structure. This is shown by the fact that his first publication on this subject appeared in 1913, deploring the recent developments in Liberal budgets: *British budgets 1887–1913*. Having established an expert reputation in this field of official fiscal policy, it seems to have remained the primary non-professional call on his time throughout the remainder of his life: his last major publication on the subject appeared the year after his death: Mallet and George, *British budgets*, 3rd Series (1921–2 to 1932–3).

[50] 72nd ARRG, p. xliii.

since that year. It is impossible to avoid associating this decline with the simultaneous increase of effort to reduce infant mortality'.[51]

Two years later, Stevenson was able to give an analysis of novel, occupationally specific details of infant mortality, from combined census and vital registration data, which was entirely aimed at mobilising the information to argue as strongly as possible for the environmentalist interpretation of the causes of infant mortality. The essential preliminary to this was the ordering of the data into a form which represented social classes or grades.[52] This then provided the ammunition for a thoroughly environmentalist message:

> Much may be learnt . . . as to the extent to which infant mortality can be regarded as preventable. For instance, the middle-class mortality [rate] was only 61 per cent. of the total legitimate infant mortality of the country. This at once suggests that at least 40 per cent. of the present infant mortality of this country could be avoided . . . Figures like these show how little of our present infant mortality is essentially inevitable. No doubt it must be long before the average infant can receive the intelligent care bestowed upon that of the officer, solicitor, or doctor, and no doubt also a proportion of the advantage enjoyed by the latter is dependent upon ante-natal causes, so that more than care of the infant is required to equalise matters. It may probably be assumed however that if health conditions were equally good for all classes of society (and till this is so the inferior conditions must always involve preventable mortality) most of any congenital disadvantage which the labourer's infant suffers would disappear. If this is the case there seems no reason to consider the limit of improvement reached till infant mortality in general is reduced to the level where that of the professional classes now stands, or, say, to one-third of its present amount.[53]

These collectivist, interventionist conclusions were given concrete evidential support by showing that between the social grades of the nation, as measured, the difference in terms of causes of death: 'is greatest from the most preventable causes, infectious diseases, diarrhoea, and tubercle'.[54] Infant mortality over the first twelve months from infectious diseases in social class I was only 40% of the figure for class V occupations;[55] and for tubercle and diarrhoea it was only 50%.[56] A further illustration showed infant mortality at different periods for two groups of occupations, the first with the lowest and the second with the highest overall infant mortality levels, regardless of the occupations' social class assignment. This showed that the mortality difference between these two extreme groupings was least over the first month of life but increased steadily as environmental factors came more and more into play, reaching a difference of sevenfold in magnitude at the latest period, i.e. mortality between six and twelve months of age.[57] The substantive scientific conclusions – demonstrating the importance of non-hereditary factors in causing infant mortality – were then simultaneously invoked as directives for future social policy: 'The *causes* leading to the largest proportion of unnecessary deaths, and, by inference, the administrative measures necessary

[51] 72nd ARRG, p. xliv. [52] See below, pp. 255–9, for details of the procedure.
[53] 74th ARRG, p. xli. [54] 74th ARRG, p. xlv. [55] 74th ARRG, p. xliii.
[56] 74th ARRG, p. xliii. [57] 74th ARRG, p. xliv, Table XXIX.

to combat them, can be discerned with equal clearness' (original emphasis).[58]

Thus, it can clearly be seen that in this ten-year period between the post-Boer War inquiry and the outbreak of the First World War, there was a well-coordinated and self-conscious public health and welfare movement, operating in political and scientific opposition to the tenets and legislative aims of politically reactionary hereditarian eugenists. Historians have for some time recognised, though they have given insufficient recognition to, Arthur Newsholme at the LGB, as a leading figure in the championing of this environmentalist policy for national efficiency. However, the very important role played by the GRO has somehow eluded attention. J. M. Eyler's definitive biography of Farr has at least revised an earlier historiographical bias against the nineteenth-century GRO, created, unwittingly perhaps, by Royston Lambert's overenthusiastic treatment of Sir John Simon's role, at the expense of all other participants, in the mid-Victorian public health movement.[59] But it seems to have been assumed that, with Farr's retirement in 1880, the GRO became a much more anaemic and anonymous state department, relatively devoid of independent political influence. There was certainly something of a lull in its activism during the last two decades of the century. But, as has been argued in chapter 2, this should be evaluated within the proper context of the considerable difficulties faced by the GRO during the last quarter of the century both in scientific terms and because of a generalised attempt by the Treasury to circumscribe the activities and expenditure of the LGB.

The evidence presented here shows a powerful twentieth-century resurgence of the 'statist' role – that of leading public and professional medical opinion through the didactic analysis of the nation's vital statistics – which the GRO had originally carved out for itself over its first decades of existence.[60] The GRO's declining profile during the 1880s had been partly due to developments beyond its control, as the leading technology of biomedical scientific investigation temporarily shifted away from statistical epidemiology towards microscopial bacteriology. The marked revival in the scientific and political role of the GRO in the Edwardian period was once again due to shifts within socio-biological science. Paradoxically the GRO had its intellectual opponents – the hereditarian biometricians – to thank for returning issues surrounding the interpretation of epidemiological and demographic statistics to near the top of the scientific and political agenda. The statistical methodology developed by Galton, Pearson and others for the study of evolutionary questions was applied by them to various social and demographic data – especially fertility and infant mortality rates – apparently giving 'scientific' backing to the hereditarian eugenics movement. In these circumstances, the GRO's traditional expertise in statistical inference and its authority as official

[58] 74th ARRG, p. xlii.

[59] Eyler, *Victorian social medicine*; Lambert, *Sir John Simon*; for a fuller exposition of this historiographical point, see Szreter, 'The G.R.O. and the historians'.

[60] See Szreter, 'The G.R.O. and the public health movement'.

custodian of the nation's demographic record had once more placed the Office in the political limelight, as it provided the public health movement with its most effective intellectual resources for a refutation of the eugenicists' views – in their own 'scientific' and statistical terms. Whereas throughout Farr's reign the principal object of the GRO's propagandist attentions had been the lay ratepaying public, in the Edwardian period the major effort was devoted to the hearts and minds of the public health professionals and policy-makers themselves.[61]

There was additionally another important historically new dimension to the political and propagandist role adopted by the GRO in the Edwardian period. This was reflected in the shift away from the exclusive attention previously given to purely local variations in mortality patterns and towards the emphasis, instead, on national, social class variations in health. The emergence of a new thoroughgoing environmentalism among public service health and pedagogic professionals was shown in the previous chapter. At the same time – both cause and effect of this – the terms of *national* politics were rapidly transposing, to the extent that the enormously expensive and ambitious remedial policies on a national scale, which this environmentalist analysis ultimately implied, were now entering the realm of the politically possible. Throughout the latter nineteenth century there had been no policy relevance in attempting a social class analysis of mortality for the nation as a whole, since no executive authority was politically recognised to be responsible for the health of the nation as a whole. However, with the election in 1906 of a Progressive Liberal administration, under pressure to deliver genuine social reforms in response to the rise of a politically organised Labour movement on their exposed left flank, the problems of working-class poverty, health and social insecurity were for the first time publicly acknowledged in politicians' discussions to be structural problems of the society and economy as a whole. Rather than as something always to be solved by local, relatively small-scale measures, it was beginning to be admitted that the burden of dealing with such problems through rate-financed local government was too great, and that national, state-sponsored, collectivist solutions must be devised, entailing a new level of taxation on the nation's major wealth-holders.[62] Hence, the environmentalist

[61] Important 'conversions' could take place, as illustrated by the case of Major Greenwood, a medically trained Pearsonian acolyte of the 1900s, who defected to the environmentalist camp in 1913 (having done epidemiological work for the Lister Institute of Preventive Medicine since 1910). Greenwood was a lively and attractive personality, who subsequently became London University's Professor of Epidemiology and Vital Statistics and was a trusted adviser to the Ministry of Health. MacKenzie, *Statistics in Britain*, pp. 110–11, 176–7. He appears below, in chapter 8 (pp. 409–11), as one of the authors of an important study on the middle-class birth rate.

[62] See Cronin, *The politics of state expansion*, esp. pp. 4–43, on the important nineteenth-century history of the underlying fiscal aspect of these issues. The historic endorsement of free trade in 1846 tied the British state to a polity of direct taxation. This historical ideological commitment was sufficiently strong over fifty years later to prevent the adoption of Chamberlain's option advocated in 1903: that protectionist tariffs be introduced by the Imperial state to raise the necessary public finance to bail out local government and provide the necessary social services. With this option politically closed, the only alternative fiscal source was increased direct taxation. Hence, ultimately, Lloyd George's

public health lobby was able at this juncture to go on to the political as well as the scientific offensive, in the debate over the causes of poverty.

At this point, in this crucially altered climate of political opinion, an analysis of the nation's infant mortality drawing attention to the nationwide social class disadvantage that existed, at last made sense in terms of the practical life-saving aims which provided the consistent rationale behind all the analytical work done by the GRO throughout the period, 1837–1914. The poor families of the unskilled and casually employed manual working class were a social group spread right across the country suffering inadequate living conditions under many different local authorities. But the analysis of 'preventability' no longer had to be aimed exclusively at specific local and municipal authorities in the attempt to shame them into action. There was at last a central government administration prepared to take the deeper causes of the nation's social ills seriously and to contemplate central, state-funded and nationally organised action to alleviate the plight of entire sections of the population, regardless of geographical location. In policy terms the precedent for such a centrally organised approach had already been set by the end of the first decade of the century in the treatment of such problems as sectoral unemployment and the need for old-age pensions, after these had been effectively shown, through social research, to be genuinely national social problems, not truly remediable at the local level.[63]

Stevenson's social class model was therefore used to argue for the renewed expansion, now on a national scale and with the resources of the central state, of the collective public health facilities and services formerly mainly provided only on a local basis. It showed to greatest effect the contrasting living conditions and health of the wealthy and comfortable classes as against the working poor, regardless of geographical location, so as to demonstrate that these aspects of national welfare should also now come under state purview.

Thus, it has been shown that the official professional model was first applied in published form to serve as powerful illustration to support the political and legislative interests and desires of the environmentalist programme for national efficiency. It came almost as the inevitable culmination of a decade of efforts by the directing staff of the GRO to construct ever more telling and effective measurements to promote scientific understanding of, and political action against, an environmentally induced poverty syndrome. It was presented by individuals acting as part of an identifiable movement promoting collectivist public health legislation, who believed that socially preventable privations were the direct cause of much of the excessive infant mortality and physical debility prevalent among the working population.

People's Budget of 1909 and the ensuing constitutional confrontation the following year with the House of Lords, representing the interests of wealth. See also pp. 193–4.

63 Harris, *Unemployment and politics*, chs. IV–VI. Hennock, *British social reform*; Booth, 'Enumeration and classification of paupers'; Booth, *Pauperism*; Booth, *Old age pensions*.

Differential fertility and the social classification of occupations

The first published application of the GRO's official system of social classification, therefore, was to the interpretation of mortality amongst the young, just as Rumsey had called for over forty years before, and Humphreys fifteen years later. Nevertheless, as will become clear from the evidence to be presented in this section, the original and initiating motivation to devise a social classification of occupations in fact derived from the issue of differential fertility, in the dramatic terms in which the eugenicists had posed the question. This is a fact of some importance in explaining the exact nature of the final form of the official classification: the five graded classes of the professional model which have been considered for so long to be an accurate empirical description of the fertility decline in Britain.

Newsholme, in a public address delivered to the Royal Sanitary Institute's Congress at Brighton in 1910, identified two crucial areas of doubt in the biometricians' claims, both of which were in principle empirically verifiable and both of which he would require to be convinced of before accepting their case:

1. Is it certain that the population is being recruited in an increased proportion from the inferior grades of society?
2. Is it certain that a lower infant mortality will produce a survival of an increased proportion of physically inferior children?[64]

The attempt to provide conclusive answers to this pair of critical questions constitutes the core of what was, in effect, an informal research programme pursued by Newsholme and by Stevenson in their respective official capacities over the following years. As we have seen, Newsholme made the running with regard to the second question. Stevenson, through his organisation of the fertility census and its reportage, dealt with the first.

It should not, incidentally, be supposed that both men shared identical views, nor that they necessarily both held the same strong *a priori* positions regarding the scientific answers they expected to find from their inquiries, as many of the hereditarian 'empiricists' seem to have done. It is quite clear that Newsholme was the more convinced of the biometricians' inadequacies and that his determination to prove these was strongly motivated by his keen political awareness of the possible effects of hereditarian propaganda on the morale of his fellow Medical Officers of Health.[65] For Newsholme, therefore, the primary aim in this work was to expose and publicise the inconsistencies and lack of empirical substantiation in the arguments of those who would dismantle the nascent public health and welfare administration in Britain. He held a prior moral and ethical position,

[64] Newsholme, 'The national importance', p. 332. [65] See above, pp. 240–1

which fortified him with a certain scepticism as to the claims of science to act as the basis for the direction of social policy.[66]

Stevenson, although sharing Newsholme's environmentalist interpretation of the causes of infant mortality as we have seen, was more exclusively committed to a positivist, rationalist 'faith in the universality of natural causation' than the Wesleyan Newsholme.[67] Thus, his preoccupation with demographic issues was premised, like the biometricians', upon the belief that 'The Laws Governing Population' existed to be discovered and elucidated through rational investigation.[68] But, *unlike* the biometricians, Stevenson did not premise the process of empirical inquiry with either a biologistic or an hereditarian framework of explanation. Stevenson's intellectual preoccupations with the discovery of 'laws', in the Newtonian sense, hailed from a distinct demographic-economic branch of the rationalist tradition, which did not entail any specific proposition, as did the belief in heredity, regarding the ultimate causes or ultimate significance of individuals' observable physiological variation.[69]

Communication at this time between Newsholme and his ex-assistant, Stevenson, was so close that the former was able to include, in a special insertion in his second supplementary Report for the LGB on Infant and Child Mortality published in 1913, an advanced copy of the class differential statistics of infant mortality which were at the time being compiled by Stevenson for presentation in the 74th ARRG.[70] This was positively the first appearance of the official system of social classification in published form. It is extremely interesting because it illustrates the difference in overall appearance of the classification scheme that might have resulted if an interest in mortality and poverty had been the principal objective of its construction, instead of the issues raised over the nation's declining fertility, as was in fact the case. This evidence demonstrates how an ambivalence in the format of the classification at its introduction reflected the tensions inherent in these two somewhat opposed usages (mortality and fertility analysis), to which it was initially put.

At its formal inception in the Registrar-General's 74th Annual Report for 1911 (published in 1913) the new classification presented was basically a tripartite structure. Three of the social classes were positively identified and placed in order as:

66 Witness the statement in his memoirs, that 'I have been comforted by an ineradicable belief that what is socially desirable or in accord with Christian principles cannot be injurious to the welfare of oncoming generations.' Newsholme, *Fifty years*, p. 400.

67 Burrow's phrase: Burrow, *Evolution and society*, p. 75.

68 The title he chose for an important article published in *JRSS* in 1925. See below, 268–9, for further discussion of this work.

69 Stevenson was drawn to that vein of scientific speculation which had been most thoroughly developed in the previous work of Malthus and Farr: on the possibility of discovering systematic aggregate relationships between population, demographic and reproductive behaviour, and its accompanying technological and resource base.

70 42nd Annual Report of LGB, 1912–13. Report of Medical Officer, Supplement, ch. XIII, p. 73.

Class I 'the upper- and middle-class';
Class III 'those occupations of which it can be assumed that the majority of men classified to them at the census are skilled workmen'; and
Class V 'occupations including mainly unskilled men'.

Two intermediate classes, without any identifying description, were interleaved between each of these three, making five graded classes in total.[71] In addition to the five graded classes there were three separate, so-called 'industrial classes', making an overall total of eight classes.[72]

There was, however, an ambiguity in this original presentation, in that class I was introduced first, on its own; and then classes III to VIII altogether, on the reasoning that they 'as a whole are meant to represent the working class'.[73] Class II was therefore merely a buffer zone of indeterminacy between these two identifiable social groups, 'the upper- and middle-class' and 'the working class'.

The existence of a bipartite view of class is confirmed by the evidence of the early, prototype tabulation of infant mortality by social class, presented in Newsholme's Report for the LGB published in the same year. For there, the primary comparison is that between 'class 1 Upper and Middle Class' and 'class 2 Wage-earning Class'; with an intermediate zone between these two monolithic divisions envisaged for those occupations which are of indeterminable composition. Class 2 is further subdivided into: '2a Skilled Labour'; '2b Unskilled Labour'; and '2c Special Industries', which are 'Agriculture', 'Textiles', and 'Mining'. There is no mention of three or five social grades here. There are simply two opposed primary classes, the 'Upper and Middle Class' and the 'Wage-earning Class', whose infant mortality differed by almost 100% when so measured.

Despite the fact that the first public application of the official classification was to illustrate infant mortality differentials, it can nevertheless be conclusively shown that Stevenson's social classification was originally conceived to deal with the issues of differential fertility, as raised by the eugenicists. This is demonstrated in the valuable unpublished minutes of the GRO 'Committee on the census 1911'. 'The question of the division of the population into social strata' was first discussed there at a meeting of 24 February 1910. It is recorded that 'Dr Stevenson was rather anxious if possible to get fertility coefficients for three grades of society. The upper and middle classes, he said, were constantly being accused of not reproducing themselves and he thought it desirable that statistics should verify or deny this accusation.'[74] It is most fortunate that a record of this preparatory discussion by the officials of the GRO has survived, as few such internal documents and working papers from the GRO have. It records the early official

[71] These definitions are given in the 74th ARRG, p. xli.

[72] See below, pp. 259–61, for discussion and explanation of the three additional classes.

[73] 74th ARRG, p. xli.

[74] PRO RG 19/48B, pp. 61–2. Others present at the meeting were Bernard Mallet (Registrar-General), A. C. Waters (Chief Clerk) and A. Bellingham (Secretary).

deliberations on the subject of a social classification, nearly four years before the publication of the mortality analysis by social class. It shows that Stevenson's original attraction to the project of creating a social classification of occupations was in order to test hereditarian theories and fears regarding the nation's fertility patterns as outlined in the first of Newsholme's two questions in his address at Brighton in 1910. The application to infant mortality was, therefore, a subsequent opportunist decision, even though it was the occasion for the first published appearance of the scheme.

This interpretation is confirmed by a careful reading of Stevenson's introduction to the analysis of infant mortality by social class when it first appeared in the 74th ARRG. First he announced that in the forthcoming decennial supplement, 'it has been decided to show, not only the rate at which persons following each occupation die, but also at which they reproduce themselves'.[75] But in the meantime, while tabulation of the numbers in each occupation from the (new) census data was being completed so that these occupational fertility indices could be computed, Stevenson explained that, as a by-product of this exercise, 'The tabulation by parents' occupation of the births registered in 1911 required for this purpose has been carried out, and has provided an opportunity for calculating the occupational infant mortality rates'.[76] The figures for social class mortality differences were, of course, directly derived by aggregation from this occupational data (in other words the social classes were compared by grouping together numbers of male occupations).

Stevenson's primary interest in fertility was an important determining influence: both over the choice of occupation as the variable for measuring and constructing social grades; and over the form of the classification which resulted. For, those respected social scientists who had previously worked primarily on the problem of urban poverty, with which the issue of infant and child mortality was intimately connected, had found occupational categories to be less useful than a measure of overcrowding or, conversely, of the number of servants employed, as an index of a household's social position.[77] On the other hand, those who were most vociferous in their apocalyptic utterances as to the race suicide which would result from the present differential fertility conceived of the nation in the anthropometric tradition, as composed of a natural hierarchy or distribution of supposedly correlated mental and physical abilities, which had their direct corollary in the level of rational thought or manual dexterity – 'skill' – required by the individual

[75] 74th ARRG, p. xl. The decennial supplement utilised *both* registration and the new 1911 census data.

[76] 74th ARRG, p. xl. The occupational rates of infant mortality were calculated as a rate (of deaths) per thousand births, and were, therefore, arithmetically derivative from the prior compilation of the occupational fertility rates. Hence, Stevenson wrote of the latter computations providing an 'opportunity' for the calculation of occupational and class infant mortality rates.

[77] Booth, *Life and labour. Final volume*, pp. 6–9. Rowntree had, of course, used figures of families' weekly income (partially estimated) per head for classification; but information on income was not available at all to Stevenson. Rowntree, *Poverty*, pp. 53–7.

worker to perform his occupation satisfactorily. It was therefore because his primary aim was to attempt to test empirically the eugenicists' claims regarding fertility differentials, that Stevenson's initial inclination was to use occupation as the basis of his classification.[78]

In fact, according to an interim report by Stevenson on his social classification efforts, the occupational approach was nearly abandoned at an early stage, because of practical difficulties:

> The determination of the stratum to which each couple is to be referred is a matter of considerable difficulty, but it is felt that the task should be undertaken for the purpose of definitely determining the very important question of the relative degrees of fertility of the various grades of society. The use of occupation for this purpose has been considered, but it was found that this would be a very imperfect test. We shall, therefore, probably use Mr. Booth's criteria – numbers of rooms, or of domestic servants, in relation to the number of persons in the family. There are various fallacies in the use of these tests also, but we can devise no better . . . failing improvement we shall be content to work upon a scheme which can claim the high authority of Mr Booth.[79]

Apparently it was not until 1920 that Stevenson had completely convinced himself that the available alternatives were even less satisfactory for his principal objective of fertility analysis (because both size of tenement and number of servants retained were themselves strongly a function of current family size).[80]

However, if mortality and morbidity of the young, the prime index of poverty, had been the main aim of Stevenson's work of social classification, then these *other* variables (and additional ones, such as whether the mother was employed or not) would have been of greatest use and relevance as a basis for stratifying the population. As shown by the above testimony regarding the methodological difficulties he was encountering, it is quite possible that in that case Stevenson would not have persevered against the formidable problems involved in devising the occupational classification, the professional model.

The use of an occupationally based system in order to inquire into the fertility issues raised by the hereditarians, in turn necessarily imposed certain constraints and limitations on the form of the social classification which could be adopted. The principal methodological problem was a consequence of the fact that it was not individuals (or rather individual family households) that were assessed directly in the classification process. They were first gathered together into a (male) occupational grouping and then the whole occupation was assigned to one of the

78 Soloway, *Birth control*, pp. 37–8, states that the Whethams were by far the most effective and widely read propagandists of eugenic ideas (as opposed to the biometricians, discussed above, who were proponents of ostensibly scientific studies). In particular, Soloway refers to the popularisation: Whetham and Whetham, *The family and the nation*. Direct evidence that Stevenson had, indeed, read this work and that his proposals were at least partly prompted by its impact, is available: see Stevenson, 'Suggested lines of advance', p. 697, where reference is made to specific information produced in *The family and the nation* (pp. 140–1).

79 Stevenson, 'Suggested lines of advance', pp. 696–7.

80 Stevenson, 'The fertility of various social classes', pp. 408–10.

classes. Unfortunately, it was well known that some of the occupations were rather imprecisely defined, grouping together rather disparate individuals (and their attached families). The most obvious problem was the fact that many manufacturing occupations contained a mixture of waged employees and their employers. Hence, the need to create the two buffer classes between the three main categories, to cater for the most indeterminate occupations.

Apart from the somewhat laconic statement that the five main classes were 'designed to represent as far as possible social grades',[81] there was no further published amplification of the rationale behind the system from Stevenson himself until the late 1920s, when he was introducing his streamlined five class scheme, which finally did away with the three subsidiary industrial classes which had accompanied the original version of the scheme at the 1911 census. Stevenson latterly claimed, in 1928, that he had simply adopted a common-sense approach, which was to take the crudest possible social division of the nation into a top, a middle and a bottom, with two marginal areas for indeterminable occupations sandwiched in between. The three special industrial classes were created to cater for those forms of employment which would not even fit into this broad scheme.[82] In 1928 Stevenson explained that class VIII, agricultural labourers, had been originally removed from the rest of the national population for the purpose of mortality comparisons because of the peculiar advantages of the rural environment, which would have confounded the attempt to measure the association between 'social position' and infant mortality in the nation as a whole.[83] He also explained that class VI for Textile Workers and class VII for Miners (iron and coal) were each removed from the main analysis for the separate reason that it was felt to be quite impossible to judge, within these numerically very large occupational categories, the average levels of skill they contained.[84]

However, on closer inspection this would seem to have been something of a *post hoc* rationalisation. There is an inconsistency between this latter explanation for classes VI and VII and the original statement, published in 1913, that these important groups of working-class occupations had, from the start, been *deliberately* treated as neither skilled nor unskilled (and this is confirmed by their separation from the rest of the working classes even in the preliminary format, which was published by Newsholme). In fact, originally it had been stated by Stevenson that the three special industrial classes were for 'important groups of the working-class population which it seemed desirable to distinguish separately, and they are therefore not treated either as skilled or unskilled'.[85]

In order to begin to explain this inconsistency in Stevenson's testimony at the two points in time, fifteen years apart, we should now recall the findings of the

81 74th ARRG, pp. xl–xli.

82 Stevenson, 'The vital statistics', p. 211. 83 Stevenson, 'The vital statistics', p. 229.

84 Stevenson first expressed this reason in the RG's decennial supplement for 1921, Part II, p. viii. (HMSO 1927). 85 74th ARRG, p. xli.

preceding, special studies of infant and child mortality by the GRO. W. C. Dunbar's study of 1907 had confirmed, as had the studies of the 1890s, the significance of degree of urbanism and of mothers' occupation, especially in textiles areas, as two major correlates of mortality of the young.[86] Additionally, Dunbar had established the anomalous characteristics of mining communities, which seemed to combine very high fertility with very high infant mortality despite a relatively low level of maternal employment. Thus, when Stevenson, a few years later in the 74th ARRG, talked of 'important groups of the working class which it seemed desirable to distinguish separately', he was simply following his predecessors in isolating occupations related to textiles, agriculture and mining because of the now well-established findings regarding the unusual demographic regimes of these occupational groups. Since his principal aim was to assess the strength of a possible relationship between fertility and mortality on the one hand, and social class or graded social position on the other, it was only wise, in hoping to demonstrate and assess the strength of this latter effect, to attempt to separate out and exclude from the analysis those large-scale, independent effects already known to be related to the special physical environments and social and occupational characteristics of agricultural, mining and textiles communities.

This is confirmed once again by the valuable unpublished evidence of the GRO 'Committee on the census 1911', where it is recorded that Stevenson recognised that a significant problem for valid comparison of 'fertility coefficients for three grades of society' – his original motivating aim – would be that of the known heterogeneity of occupational fertility behaviour. He specifically acknowledged that it would be a difficulty for his aim that the projected 'class III would include the Miners of great fertility and the Cotton operatives of low fertility'.[87] In other words, it appears that, already at this initiating stage in February 1910, Stevenson was envisaging a tripartite scheme of social grading for occupational categories. But he was also aware that it would probably be necessary to exclude certain numerically large categories of the working-class population, because he appreciated, from the outset, that they did not conform in their demographic characteristics to that pattern of social grading which he was attempting to test for in the remainder of the population.

The change of stance on Stevenson's part between 1910–13 and 1927–8, over the rationale behind the creation of the special subsidiary classes, is an indicator of a more significant change in his attitude towards the classification system which he had created. The reasoning given in the late 1920s implies the proposition that skill level alone was the vital criterion for assigning manual occupations to a classification by 'social position'. Furthermore, as we shall see, Stevenson proceeded to assert that 'social position', in turn, was the most highly significant explanatory variable correlated with demographic behaviour. Yet, before the

[86] 68th ARRG, pp. xx–xxxii. See above, previous section.

[87] PRO RG 19/48B, p. 63.

Great War, Stevenson had clearly felt that skill level or social position was no more than one amongst several equally important factors causing differences in demographic behaviour, including mothers' occupation and industrial or community affiliation, at least for the occupations in the special classes VI, VII and VIII (which each represented a large fraction of the national population). Thus, in 1910 Stevenson was to be found before the Royal Statistical Society discussing his plans for a social class analysis of the forthcoming fertility census in the following terms: 'Differences in fertility will very likely be found between persons of the same social class who are connected with different occupations'[88] and: 'It may be, moreover, that the study of occupational fertilities will reveal some other line of cleavage between the fertile and the infertile than that commonly suggested of position in the social scale.'[89]

But by the late 1920s this kind of open, inquiring approach, recognising the potential importance of measuring the variation in demographic behaviour *within* or *across* the artificially created social classes, had given way to a rather partisan overestimate of the adequacy and utility of the five graded classes of the professional model for the analysis of demographic data.[90] As a result, by the late 1920s the unique characteristics of the three special industrial classes had been submerged by spreading their component occupations around the three graded working-class categories, classes III, IV and V, according to putative level of skill.[91]

It was probably true that the uncertainties as to accuracy of occupational definition had originally forced the five class scheme of grouped occupations upon Stevenson, as a pragmatic solution to that problem. Yet, loudly proclaimed and genuine improvements in occupational definition at the 1921 census were not used as the foundation for a more refined, disaggregated and discriminating social classification.[92] Rather, were they seen as perfecting and further justifying the accuracy of the original, self-confessedly crude and simplistic conception of a

88 Stevenson, 'Suggested lines of advance', p. 697.

89 Stevenson, 'Suggested lines of advance', p. 697.

90 Stevenson, 'The vital statistics', p. 212.

91 RG's decennial supplement for 1921, Part 2B, Table A. Class VIII, agricultural workers, were all assigned to class IV. The miners, class VII, went into class III, with the exception of a small number of auxiliary workers, who joined class IV (the separate occupational category of coal mineowners were meanwhile demoted from class I to class II). The textiles workers of class VI were mostly placed in class III, except for dyers, card-room workers, doublers, strippers and grinders, who all went into class IV; foremen and overlookers joined the employers of the textiles industry in class II. The other major alteration was the removal of all clerks, a large body of workers, from class I in the 1911 scheme to class II for the analysis of the 1921 census, appearing to give the latter a more definable sense of representing the lower middle class, rather than simply being an intermediate zone between manual and non-manual.

92 Decennial supplement for 1921, (HMSO 1927), p. viii. The principal innovation resulted from the recognition that it was feasible to construct two parallel classifications, one for socio-medical purposes and the other for economic-industrial analysis from a single set of employment questions, collecting the information at the census. Questions were devised for the 1921 census schedule in order to be able to classify and tabulate occupational data on individuals in these two different ways. See below, n. 140, ch. 6, n. 10, and p. 323.

hierarchy of five grades. The apologies which accompanied the public introduction of the classification scheme in 1913[93] should be contrasted with the eulogy indulged in by Stevenson in 1928, after noting that there was a regular grading from low to high from class I down to class V in returns of the classes' aggregated mortality and fertility experience: 'I would go so far as to suggest that the results now discussed . . . prove that the social classification employed is substantially correct . . . in the social grading of occupation.'[94] In the analysis of the 1921 and 1931 censuses, therefore, occupations continued to be assigned either to class I 'Upper and Middle Class' or to class III 'Skilled Workers' or to class V 'Unskilled Workers' or else to either of the zones of indeterminacy, class II and class IV. Thus, the model of five grades of occupation, originally a methodological expedient to deal with data inadequacies and imprecision of occupational definitions, became established as the officially approved representation of the nation's social classes.

Paradoxically, then, improvement in the quality of occupational returns in 1921 did not result in expansion of the number of social classes used, nor in greater clarity of their definition. Rowntree had distinguished six grades of working-class people, alone, in his study of York.[95] Booth had distinguished eight categories for the whole population of London in his earlier classification and sixteen in his later work; and A. L. Bowley thought that there were at least five types of urban working men distinguishable *a priori*.[96] Yet in its classification of the whole nation the General Register Office moved from eight to five classes, proudly proclaiming that this 'has the great merit of simplicity'.[97]

The theory of diffusion and the professional model of social classes

In fact, by the mid-1920s Stevenson had developed certain quite specific, ulterior motives for championing the official classification scheme in this form. These related to the conclusions he had meanwhile drawn from his analysis of the nation's declining fertility, the problem which had originally stimulated his efforts to devise a social classification in the first place. The real reason for Stevenson's growing enthusiasm in the 1920s for the system of five ordinal grades was that it constituted the star witness in support of his novel general explanation for the recent decline in human fertility, something which was coming to be recognised as a fascinatingly widespread phenomenon, affecting most post-industrial societies.

It was established above, from his interpretation of infant mortality data, that

93 74th ARRG, p. xli: 'This assignment is by no means precise, for in many cases, especially in commerce and industry, the census occupational description gives no certain indication of social position . . . As a result, many men, especially business men belonging to the middle classes, have necessarily been included with the working-class.'

94 Stevenson, 'The vital statistics', p. 213.

95 Rowntree, *Poverty*, pp. 53–7. His classes A, B, C, D, E and G.

96 Bowley, *The nature and purpose*, pp. 91–2.

97 Stevenson, 'The vital statistics', p. 212.

Stevenson was far from being a convert of the hereditarian school of explanation of demographic problems. He adopted the biometricians' notion of social structure as a hierarchy of occupations in order to test, not simply to illustrate, their theories. In effect, he was pursuing one half of the research programme of empirical validation, which Newsholme had outlined in 1910 (see above, n. 64). In pursuit of the answer to Newsholme's first question, regarding the eugenicists' claims, Stevenson hoped that the census of the nation's fertility patterns would establish conclusively, as a matter of *fact*, whether recent trend changes in effective fertility (that is net of mortality, age at marriage differences and other sources of purely demographic variation in the statistics) did, indeed, show that the nation was now being reproduced disproportionately from its lower orders more so than previously in its history. The empirical answer to this question furnished by the census results was broadly in the affirmative.[98]

However, even once this was established as a matter of fact, the issues of causation and significance remained wide open. In the decade before the Great War, when Stevenson was designing his census inquiry and commencing his analysis, he was aware of three alternative scientific interpretations of the causes of the nation's fertility decline.[99] Two of these were entirely hereditarian, positing a secular deterioration in human fecundity. One such theory, of fluctuation in 'germinal vitality', claimed to detect such a decline in the procreative powers of the nation as a whole.[100] The other hereditarian theory – of 'individuation' – maintained that this was something which only afflicted the more able and intellectual members.[101] Hence, the first part of Stevenson's long official report on the results of the 1911 fertility census was devoted to a scrupulous examination (and rejection) of these two possibilities.[102] The third explanatory thesis, popularly expounded by Sidney Webb, and, from the opposite end of the political spectrum by the Whethams, was the correct one: that the proximate cause of the

98 *FMR* Pt 2, pp. xci and xciv.

99 Apparently the Frenchman, A. Dumont's, celebrated thesis of *capillarité sociale* was not known to Stevenson (see pp. 16–17, 269).

100 The theory of cyclical germinal vitality was most vigorously propounded by J. Brownlee: 'The history of birth and death rates'.

101 The theory of individuation derived from Herbert Spencer's work and was favoured by Galton until near the end of his life. Note that Herbert Spencer's theory of 'individuation' exhibited certain similarities to Arsène Dumont's thesis of a necessary association between individual striving and curtailment of reproductive powers (on Dumont see Introduction, n. 4). Although both theories were forms of a mechanistic determinism, the important difference was that Dumont's mechanism was explicitly socio-cultural, Spencer's was biological and materialist, derived from his bizarre notion of the psycho-physical 'spermatic economy', whereby reproductive and intellectual activities were conceived as placing mutually competitive demands upon males' limited funds of vital energy. See Soloway, *Birth control*, pp. 15–19.

102 *FMR* Pt 2, pp. xix–xlvii. In fact, as R. A. Soloway has pointed out, speculative theories of biological variation in human fecundity to account for the recent fertility trends were still being touted by some parties in the late 1920s and beyond – notably by R. A. Fisher – when they were given short shrift by both Stevenson and the Registrar-General, Sir Sylvanus Vivian (RG 1921–45). Soloway, *Demography and degeneration*, pp. 261–3, 323.

phenomenon was in the voluntary restriction of fertility by married couples.[103]

Nevertheless, judgement in favour of the behavioural and against the hereditary, physiological theories still left unanswered two further, vital issues. First, how to explain the observed social differentials in the pattern of fertility decline, which were now, of course, perceived to be differentials in the voluntary practice of birth control. Secondly, the issue of the wider significance of this novel departure in behaviour, for the nation's health, vitality and future: 'In the deficient fertility of the classes, which having achieved most success in life, are presumably best endowed with the qualifications for its achievement, we see that we have to face a new and formidable fact – how formidable is a question which must be left for the consideration of authorities on eugenics.'[104] If cited out of its full context this statement might appear to be a ringing endorsement by Stevenson of the eugenic perspective. But it was not. It was an ironic, rhetorical flourish to precede the presentation of Stevenson's own alternative answer to the two further vital issues.[105] Stevenson proceeded to argue that an optimistic answer to the second issue could in fact be reliably inferred from the answer he provided to the first, without ever having to enter the fraught arena of speculative debate over heritability. In replacement of the discredited theory of individuation to account for the demographic evidence of social class differentials in the fertility decline, Stevenson now proceeded to offer an alternative, sociological explanation: diffusion. 'This sequence appears on the other hand very natural if we regard the decline as due to increasing practice of contraceptive measures. It is natural that the more educated classes should first be affected by a movement such as the neo-Malthusian, which has always depended largely on the printing press for the

[103] Webb, *The decline of the birth rate*; Whetham and Whetham, *The family and the nation*. In fact Stevenson and Newsholme, 'The decline of human fertility', had provided in 1906 the first scientific evidence that this was the case.

[104] Stevenson, 'The fertility of various social classes', p. 417.

[105] There was a very similar passage reproduced in the *FMR* Pt 2, p. xciv. This seems to have misled R.A. Soloway, in his otherwise highly informative account of the many variegated components of the eugenics movement at this time, into considering Stevenson to be 'eugenically minded'. Soloway believes that this statement shows of Stevenson that 'Whatever other interpretation might be put upon the *Fertility of Marriage Census* [*sic*], there was no doubt in his [Stevenson's] mind that it had "much significance from the eugenic point of view."' Soloway, *Demography and degeneration*, pp. 169, 17. However, the full context for this quotation from the *FMR* Pt 2, as used by Soloway, shows a much more circumspect formulation by Stevenson. It reads as follows: 'This result *appears to have* much significance from the eugenic point of view. *If* the more successful classes *may be assumed* to be in bulk better equipped than others with the qualities adapted to command success, the failure of this stock to maintain itself in proportion to the rest of the nation is evidently undesirable from the national point of view' (emphasis added). This single passage is in fact the only one within a large Report of over 150,000 words in which the eugenic point of view is explicitly mentioned. Given the active participation of Stevenson's recently retired superior, Bernard Mallet, in the eugenics movement at this time, the silence on eugenics throughout the rest of the Report seems all the more remarkable and is a more telling indication of Stevenson's true sympathies, than this single, carefully hedged statement (on Mallet's eugenics and his limited input into the fertility inquiry, see below, pp. 266–8).

dissemination of its ideas.'[106] This entailed an optimistic answer to the second issue because, with the continuing diffusion of these new neo-Malthusian ideas in an increasingly educated society, the corollary of this causal hypothesis was the prediction that all classes would soon approximate the same fertility levels, as Newsholme had forecast as early as 1911.[107] The temporary episode of disproportionate recruitment of subsequent generations from the physically less fit and mentally less able part of the nation, which so worried 'the authorities on eugenics', would, therefore, soon be curtailed, provided the poor received an adequate education and opportunities to make such new ideas accessible to them.

Of course, this prescription rested on the egalitarian and environmentalist premise that, given a fair chance, even the poorest in society would respond positively to the new ideas and take effective control over precisely those 'lower' and 'animal' aspects of behaviour – sexual gratification – where hard-line hereditarian eugenicists and 'degeneration' doom-mongers most doubted their capacities for self-control. It was because of this extremely ungenerous estimate of the capacities of the poor to grasp the possible advantages to themselves of family planning that, throughout this period, the Eugenics Education Society under Leonard Darwin's presidency, 1911–28, formally held aloof from the contraceptive propagandist efforts of the Malthusian League (the neo-Malthusians whom Stevenson referred to) and the maverick eugenicist Marie Stopes. They believed such propaganda would only further reduce the fertility of the valuable, prudent class while the poor would remain ignorant, unmoved and prolific. Stevenson's diffusionist position during the early and mid-1920s could, then, be characterised as 'neo-Malthusian' but certainly not as eugenic.[108]

How Stevenson alighted during this period, 1920–4, upon the thesis of diffusion is not stated in his publications. There is a strong sense in which it was entailed in his anti-hereditarian, environmentalist position; but it would seem extremely likely that the proximate reason for his seizing upon the notion at this time was its spectacular, if transient, *cachet* at precisely this point – the five years following the First World War – in the discipline of anthropology.[109] Diffusion, like ameliorationist

106 Stevenson, 'The fertility of various social classes', pp. 417–18.

107 Newsholme, *The declining birth rate*, pp. 55–6.

108 See also comments, above, in n. 105. Note that the fact that some eugenicists *subsequently*, in the late 1920s and during the 1930s, came to accept broadcast birth control propaganda as a eugenic policy does *not*, of course, make Stevenson some kind of retrospective eugenicist. Rather, to the extent that eugenicists later came to accept the premises of diffusionism, they were conceding something to the opposed, egalitarian and environmentalist position (see also next footnote).

109 Kuklick, *The savage within*, ch. 4. In the hands of its most fervent proponents and popularisers Grafton Elliot Smith and W. J. Perry, respectively Professor of Anatomy and Reader in Cultural Anthropology at University College, London (having each held similar positions at the University of Manchester before the First World War), diffusionism purported to provide an integrated biological and cultural analysis of all human history: *ibid.*, pp. 123–4. See also ch. 10, n. 56). While diffusionism did not survive into the 1930s as an influence within anthropology because of the rise to prominence of Durkheimian functionalism under the leadership of Radcliffe-Brown and Malinowski, Kuklick shows that W. H. R. Rivers's diffusionist inheritance continued to exert

environmentalism, was a position logically entailed in the monogenist viewpoint: the belief that humans were everywhere essentially the same in their mental and physical endowment.[110] This entailed the notion that there was no intrinsic barrier to the passing of ideas and cultural practices between different peoples or social groups, just as there was no barrier to the improvability of the poor, or their capacity to grasp the value of a new practice, like contraception.

To advance diffusion, as a general explanatory concept to account for the social class fertility differentials apparently revealed at the 1911 census, was, therefore, thoroughly inimical to the eugenic interpretation, as contemporary eugenicists well knew.[111] An apt and chronologically correct illustration of this is provided by Stevenson's ex-superior, Sir Bernard Mallet, who became a leading figure in the

considerable intellectual influence in the developing ameliorationist fields of social, industrial and organisational psychology, building on what was perceived to be relatively successful ameliorationist work with shell-shock victims.

110 The intellectual origins of diffusionism within anthropology lay in the polygenist–monogenist debate, which has appeared at key points in this account before, notably in the discussions at the PDC inquiry, where Professor Cunningham dismissed Pearson's hereditarian assertions on the grounds that they did not square with the latest anthropological evidence. As explained above, in 1904 Cunningham was referring to the recent monogenist findings of the important psychological experiments supervised by W. H. R. Rivers on the Torres Straits expedition. See above, p. 225.

111 Some historians have recently tended to emphasise the importance of the rise of a moderate or 'reform eugenics' from the mid-1920s, arguing that it became prominent in the Eugenics Society at some point after the appointment of C. P. Blacker as its first full-time Secretary in 1931 (this staffing innovation was made possible by the Henry Twitchin bequest of 1930): Kevles, *In the name of eugenics, passim*; Soloway, *Demography and degeneration*, ch. 8. However, the parallel, mounting strength of those eugenicists intent on expounding a far from moderate set of views and policies right through until the mid-1930s should certainly not be underestimated. In addition to the emergence of 'reform eugenics', the period 1925–35 simultaneously encompassed the high point of a resurgent, apparently scientifically backed, hard-line hereditarianism. Both the Interdepartmental Committee on Mental Deficiency, 1924–9 (the Wood Report) and the Departmental Committee on Sterilisation, 1932–4 (the Brock Report) devoted much of their attentions to 'the Social Problem Group'. This was essentially a new name for the 'residuum'. ('The Social Problem Group' was a term invented by a Poor Law relieving officer, E. J. Lidbetter, who had for twenty years collected details of 'pauper pedigrees': thousands of poor families in London's East End and in Edinburgh, whose documented 'hereditary' inadequacy and associated reproductive incontinence A. F. Tredgold claimed to be representative of 10% of the nation.) Cyril Burt, R. A. Fisher, A. F. Tredgold and E. O. Lewis all provided these official inquiries with various 'scientific' analyses of the hereditary dimensions of this national problem, in pursuit of the Eugenics Society's main formal political objective at this time (including the 'moderate' Blacker): legislation to permit voluntary sterilisation. Greta Jones and R. A. Soloway have shown that the most effective positive intellectual and scientific opposition to the hereditarians in the 1930s emanated from Lancelot Hogben's Social Biology Unit at the LSE, from J. B. S. Haldane and from Lionel Penrose. As a result of their opposition the civil servant generalists, such as Laurence Brock, who wrote the official reports after sifting the evidence, ultimately remained rightly sceptical of the eugenists' claims that policy could be based on the predominant role of heredity: Soloway *Demography and degeneration*, p. 203. However, it was the political implacability of the Labour party and all its assocations at local and national level (except, incidentally, the Women's Co-operative Guild because of its sympathy for birth control on maternalist and feminist grounds) which ensured that sterilisation remained off the statute book: a private Voluntary Sterilisation Bill of 1931 was only positively defeated in Parliament by the votes of the Labour party. See Jones, *Social hygiene*, chs. 4–5.

interwar eugenics movement after his retirement as Registrar-General in 1920.[112] As a eugenicist, Mallet had proclaimed in 1922, at precisely the time when Stevenson was formulating his diffusionist position, that 'it may be noted that the most competent authorities have little confidence in the mere diffusion of wider knowledge of the methods of birth control as likely ever to neutralise their hitherto racially detrimental effects, much less to operate as a positively eugenic influence'.[113]

The fact that Mallet became such a strong advocate of eugenic views after his retirement in 1920 has misled at least one historian into assuming that he must therefore have been the original instigator of the official survey of fertility differentials, on the basis of the compounded misapprehension that the fertility census could only have served eugenic purposes.[114] Certainly, there can be no doubt that, as Registrar-General, Mallet's commitment to the project would have been essential in securing the support of the sponsoring Minister to ensure Parliamentary permission for the innovative inquiry. However, all the evidence available shows that both the fertility inquiry itself and the class-differential interpretation were quite unequivocally Stevenson's initiative and intellectual products, and not in any sense instigated by his superior, Bernard Mallet. In fact, in the first years after his appointment as Registrar-General in 1909 Mallet displayed distinctly less enthusiasm for matters demographic than had his predecessor, apparently remaining to some extent preoccupied with the fiscal issues which had been the central responsibility of his previous official positions, in the Treasury and Inland Revenue.[115] Apart from the burden of all the detailed evidence that has been adduced above, Mallet himself, not a man averse to taking credit for actions where these were genuinely his own,[116] acknowledged and positively confirmed this:

I should like to draw attention to a section of the Census of 1911 the results of which . . . provided material, on a national scale, for analysing the fall in fertility since 1876 . . . by social class, occupation, birthplace, and locality of residence. I am proud to have been associated, as the official in charge of that Census, with this novel departure, but the credit for both the

112 Mallet succeeded Leonard Darwin as President of the Eugenics Society, 1928–32. He was the preferred choice of Darwin, R. A. Fisher and those who did not want a 'negative eugenics' alliance with the birth controllers but preferred instead to pursue the 'positive eugenics' policy options of some form of family allowance or tax concession to encourage the prudent to have more children: Soloway, *Demography and degeneration*, p. 185.

113 Mallet, 'Is England in danger of racial decline?', p. 853.

114 J. Austoker, *British Medical Journal* (10 August 1985), 'Letters'.

115 See above, n. 49. I have examined the small archive of Sir Bernard Mallet's private papers and have found nothing to contradict this conclusion. I am most grateful to the Mallet family for facilitating this.

116 See, for instance, his account of his ambitious attempt during the Great War to establish a permanent national central General Register for all kinds of information on individuals: Mallet, 'Reform of vital statistics'.

initiation and the organisation of the work was due to my colleague, Dr T. H. C. Stevenson, CBE, Superintendent of Statistics at that time.[117]

Thus, both Stevenson and Mallet, despite their diametrically opposed dispositions along the nature–nurture axis, worked together perfectly effectively to initiate and carry through the 1911 fertility census, both conceiving of it as primarily an investigation into class differentials in fertility. This illustrates the point that adoption of the hierarchical, professional model of the nation's social structure did not presuppose a particular theory as to the reasons for the graded social inequality which it demonstrated. Indeed, the construction of an empirical representation of the nation conforming to this hierarchical model of society was itself a vehicle which facilitated the intellectual debate between hereditarian and environmentalist; and enabled it to take on a 'scientific' mode, according to the positivist conception of empirical scientific inquiry which medically trained, public health environmentalists shared with eugenic socio-biologists.

By 1924, Stevenson had consolidated his diffusionist approach into a comprehensive explanation of the recent general transformation of European demographic behaviour. Proceeding from the observation that the decline in fertility seemed to have occurred almost simultaneously in the last quarter of the nineteenth century in all countries of western Europe and north America, the impact of the acquisition of 'knowledge of the methods of contraception' was postulated as the direct cause to account for this 'sudden downward plunge' (in all the birth rates).[118] This mode of causation was doubly attractive as an explanation, since it seemed to fit the other main piece of empirical evidence: the class-differential in the take up of these novel methods, which was apparent in the data from the fertility census in England and Wales. In the *Fertility of Marriage Report* Pt 2 of 1923, Stevenson had written that: 'on the assumption that the decline is due to restriction of natural fertility, the movement must have percolated downwards throughout society from the upper to the lower strata during at least its earlier history'.[119]

In the consolidated presentation of 1924, the potential explanatory scope of Stevenson's theory was extremely ambitious, suggesting (with considerable justice) that he had identified an historical revolution in the driving mechanism of modern nations' demographic systems. Conventional wisdom among actuaries and vital statisticians at this time held that the death rate most importantly determined changes in the overall form of the nation's life table, not surprisingly in view of the dramatic impact of disease and mortality in nineteenth-century urban society. With the new appreciation that fertility could vary just as greatly as mortality, it was now possible to posit trend changes in fertility as being an equally

117 Mallet, 'Registration in relation to eugenics', p. 24. See also Mallet's very similar statement when chairing Stevenson's first public presentation of the fertility census results: Stevenson, 'The fertility of various social classes', p. 432.
118 Stevenson, 'The laws governing population', p. 75.
119 *FMR* Pt 2, p. xcix.

important cause of demographic movements.[120] Hence, Stevenson speculated on the possibility that with the decline in fertility he had discovered that 'a new chapter was opened in the history of the European birth-rate . . . the independence of the birth-rate variable . . . fully equal to that of the death-rate?'.[121]

However, with the demise of the hereditarian theory of individuation, there had emerged several new competing theses in the early 1920s to explain falling fertility. Apart from Brownlee's continuing stubborn adherence to the notion of 'germinal vitality',[122] there were two other explanations – both economic – with which Stevenson's new theory of diffusion was in competition. First, D. S. Thomas demonstrated that the marriage rate fluctuated with the trade cycle, and therefore implied that the latter – through the medium of nuptiality – could cause significant fertility change, though it was not clear how this could cause a secular trend decline in marital fertility over such a long period.[123] Secondly, G. U. Yule had found a correlation between movements in wholesale prices during the latter half of the nineteenth century and fertility fluctuations (after failing to find such a relationship for either 'living standards' or real wages), though admitting that the correlation seemed less strong after 1881, the most important period.[124]

As a result of his long-running interest in the problems of chronic unemployment and his recent involvement in a debate with J. M. Keynes over whether this reflected incipient overpopulation in Britain, the formidable Director of the LSE, W. H. Beveridge, had also developed at this time a strong interest in population matters from a predominantly economic perspective.[125] He was therefore present at the reading of Stevenson's paper to the Royal Statistical Society in December 1924. In the discussion that followed it is recorded that Beveridge enthusiastically

[120] Stevenson's empirical observations were in fact leading him to draw attention to the same important implication emerging from the exactly contemporaneous analytical work being done by Lotka and Dublin in specifying the mathematical properties of demographic systems, through defining the concept of a stable population (finally formalised in Dublin and Lotka, 'On the true rate of natural increase'). Their analytical work also showed that in principle the birth rate was as significant as the death rate in determining the long-term trends in a population's age structure and its dynamic demographic attributes. Ryder, 'Notes on the concept', and Hajnal, 'The study of fertility', are helpful on selected aspects of the historical development of analytical demography.

[121] Stevenson, 'The laws governing population', p. 73.

[122] See his remarks after Stevenson's paper was read: Stevenson, 'The laws governing population', pp. 82–3.

[123] Thomas, *Social aspects*, ch. 2.

[124] Yule, 'Changes in marriages and birth rates'; and Yule, *The fall of the birth-rate*.

[125] In the early 1920s Beveridge had taken issue with certain passages in J. M. Keynes's *The economic consequences of the peace*. Beveridge reported that Keynes had argued that after half a century of rising industrial productivity 'a diminishing yield of Nature to man's efforts was beginning to reassert itself', manifest in rising food prices relative to the prices of manufactures. Birth control was therefore to be welcomed, according to Keynes. Beveridge used the occasion of his Presidential Address to the British Association's Section F to disagree very publicly with Keynes's diagnosis, regarding relative price trends. Beveridge argued that 'The authority of economic science cannot be invoked for the intensification of these practices' (i.e. birth control): Beveridge, 'Population and unemployment', pp. 449, 474 (with ensuing reply from J. M. Keynes). See also, Beveridge, 'Mr Keynes' evidence for overpopulation' (and further reply from J. M. Keynes).

endorsed Stevenson's diffusionist views: 'the one possible explanation could not be mistaken, and that, as Dr Stevenson had said, was the growth of a knowledge of the methods of contraception'.[126] This thesis maintained that the communication of ideas regarding the acceptability and availability of advanced contraceptive techniques was the main determinant of the timing of the spread of the phenomenon throughout society and naturally the wealthy and most well-informed classes benefited first.

Beveridge's forceful intervention in this field was probably crucial in accounting for the relative success of the notion of diffusion over its rivals.[127] His dismissal of both Yule's and Brownlee's interpretations in his own subsequent article of 1925 proved conclusive in both cases. He ridiculed Brownlee's notion of racial fluctuations in 'germinal vitality', pointing out that Frenchmen in Canada were recording markedly different and higher fertility than Frenchmen in France. As regards Yule's suggestions, he observed that although the wholesale price index had, indeed, turned down at the right date, 1877, it had also turned up again in 1897, yet fertility had continued on its downward path. Furthermore, he used the example of Holland to show divergent trends in fertility among ethnically different provinces, despite their shared experience of falling wholesale prices.[128]

Beveridge's simultaneous adoption and well-publicised espousal of the same explanatory thesis as Stevenson seems to have had one further important consequence, apart from accounting for the quick demise of the competing economic theories of the early 1920s and assisting with the international acceptance of the associated professional model of social structure.[129] This has been the apparent eradication of all appreciation and knowledge of Stevenson's equal – indeed prior – role in the formulation of the theory of diffusion. This process of occlusion began with the very first widely read account to question and challenge diffusionism. In her critique of diffusionism, it was Enid Charles's *The twilight of parenthood*, published in 1934, which gave prominence to Beveridge as the progenitor of the theory.[130] Not surprisingly Lancelot Hogben, her husband, followed suit in the introduction which he wrote to the important collection of work emanating from his Social Biology Unit at the LSE, which was published four years later.[131] Stevenson's obscurity ever since, unknown as the true originator of the diffusionist explanation, has crucially contributed to the illusion that the

126 W. H. Beveridge, recorded comments in discussion of the paper given by T. H. C. Stevenson to the Royal Statistical Society, 16 December 1924: Stevenson, 'The laws governing population', p. 84.

127 Beveridge, 'The fall of fertility'.

128 Beveridge, 'The fall of fertility', pp. 17–18.

129 As mentioned in the opening section of chapter 1, in addition to the relative success of the explanatory thesis of diffusion, Stevenson's professional model of social structure was thereafter rapidly endorsed as a suitable framework for analysing fertility change by the leading students of population problems on both sides of the Atlantic, such as A. M. Carr-Saunders and W. S. Thompson. See pp. 13–14.

130 Charles, *The twilight of parenthood*, ch. V, especially pp. 172–85.

131 Hogben, *Political arithmetic*, p. 34. On Hogben, Charles and Beveridge, see ch. 1, n. 32.

theory of diffusion was an independent, *post hoc* explanation of the class-graded demographic evidence from the British census of 1911, upon which it was based.

It has been shown here, however, that, if anything, the relationship was exactly the inverse of this; *explicans* and *explicandum* were intimately related as joint intellectual constructs. It was because of his formulation of the explanatory mechanism of diffusion that Stevenson became exclusively committed to the virtues of the five class graded pattern, which it so neatly explained. The class-differential pattern in the fertility data from the 1911 census was not, therefore, simply an independent, purely empirical finding. Furthermore, the original analysis of this enormous empirical database had actually suggested that various *other* important patterns could be discerned, in particular the anomalous behaviour of the special industrial classes. Yet these indications were subsequently ignored, and the possibility of their detection suppressed by the inclusion of all sections of the nation in a single, ordinally graded, status hierarchy, generating that straightforward patterning of the evidence which most unequivocally appeared to support Stevenson's favoured, monocausal theory of explanation: diffusionism.

The place of the GRO's professional model within British social science and social thought

It had been the naturalistic and evolutionist 'school' of social science which had originally spawned the professional model of society as a unitary, graded hierarchy of occupations, as shown in chapter 3. The fact that the overall form of the GRO's 'professional model' exhibits the stamp of the Galtonian, social Darwinist and eugenic representation of the nation's social structure does not, however, mean that in some insidious way the public health project – or at least T. H. C. Stevenson – was, after all, specifically 'eugenic'. The theory of diffusion had been conceived by Stevenson as a directly alternative socio-cultural explanation, mutually exclusive to any of the socio-biological mechanisms suggested by the hereditarian social Darwinists. But Stevenson's willingness to adopt the same kind of model of society as the eugenicists for empirical research undoubtedly reflects the fact that he held certain significant social and scientific, methodological assumptions in common with the eugenic social scientists.

There were probably three particularly important such assumptions which Stevenson shared with the eugenicists. First, a broad commitment to the emulation in the social and medical sciences of the epistemology and methods of that kind of inductive rational scientific empiricism that was believed to have characterised the apparently successful scientific study of nature over the previous couple of centuries or more. Although this was (and is) only one among several radically different philosophical conceptions of the scientific study of society and of social problems, it should be no surprise that Stevenson, as a medically trained official intimately involved with the study of policy-related social and demographic problems, subscribed to this particular conception of scientific methodology.

Secondly, it needs to be borne in mind that certain elementary conceptual features of an evolutionary perspective were integral to virtually all forms of British social thought at this time. As Lyndsay Farrall has succinctly put it, 'Eugenics, by virtue of taking human evolution as its central concern, was taken very seriously by those social scientists who were convinced that an evolutionary model needed to be used in the social sciences.'[132] The scope for the influence of eugenics claimed in this remark is colossal when it is realised that the use of some form of evolutionary perspective had increasingly characterised virtually all progressive, radical, socialist and ultimately even liberal thinkers as the nineteenth century progressed. This was because, as Reba Soffer has pointed out, the intellectual driving force throughout the second half of the century was the search to replace the deductivist and static certainties of natural theology and classical political economy and even utilitarianism, all modelled on the Newtonian axiomatic system. Something more dynamic and providential, contingential and probabilistic was required to at least correspond more convincingly with – and hopefully explain – the bewildering world of fundamental material and cultural *change* and novelty, with its accompanying freight of personal choice and moral dilemma, which all persons during the second half of the century undeniably knew themselves to be experiencing.[133] Evolution seemed to provide the essential dynamic principle for those desiring a respectably scientific sociology ('development' or 'progress' were its synonyms for those less attached to an empiricist science, to provide their teleological needs).

Thirdly, there was an acceptance by Stevenson that British society could legitimately be characterised as a graded status hierarchy in which 'the professions' comprised an identifiable class of occupations plausibly and justly representing those of highest status, while the vast mass of the population, the manual working class, could usefully be graded according to the imputed skill levels of their various occupations. As has been shown in previous chapters, Roberts and Galton, Marshall and Booth were between them most conspicuously and identifiably responsible for combining the essential elements of this evolutionist representation of society into a plausibly coherent, rational and 'scientific' model. But its cultural power derived ultimately from the underlying premises which resonated with the most fondly cherished beliefs and sources of self-identity shared in common by virtually all members of an imperial liberal intelligentsia, of which Stevenson was inevitably a member.

As has been shown, this was the national status group moulded and produced since the mid-century through the neo-aristocratic, merit-election system of Britain's reformed 'first grade', 'classical' schools, the Oxbridge colleges, the civil service and the liberal professions – paradigmatically the medical profession.

[132] Farrall, 'The history of eugenics', p. 116.

[133] Soffer, 'The revolution in English social thought 1880–1914'. Also, see above, pp. 148–65.

Belief in progress through the scientific reform of society through their own leadership as a rational, liberal élite was their defining ideology; and the members and factions of this powerful group increasingly dominated all forms of ameliorationist social science during the last quarter of the nineteenth century.[134] Their substantial intellectual, scientific and political disagreements – instanced here in the conflicts between environmentalists and hereditarians, eugenicists and Fabians – always remained constrained within the terms of reference of an overall consensus of liberal, meritocratic social assumptions, which comprised the institutional hallmark of the cultural crucible in which they had all been formed. These were, in the end, intellectual sibling rivalries between members of the same ideological family: a highly cohesive liberal intelligentsia who governed British society at the turn of the century, who administered a global Empire and, fortified by an Olympian, evolutionary superiority complex, believed that they dominated the world of science and learning.

The combination of these three shared assumptions would be all but sufficient to account for Stevenson's enthusiastic endorsement of the eugenicists' empirical model of society (while of course simultaneously rejecting their theory of the causes of its existence). Any alternative explanation of the process of fertility decline which he might construe would have to be consistent with the place of privilege and cultural leadership assumed to belong to the liberal professions. But his scientific disposition would additionally predispose Stevenson to search for an all-encompassing, law-like, general and social evolutionary explanation for the phenomena before him. For those – probably the great majority of interested parties in politics and government – broadly sharing Stevenson's methodological conception of the form that policy-relevant empirical social science should take, any explanation that could not at least match – and preferably surpass – the simplicity and elegance of the hereditarian explanation of class-differentials in demographic patterns, would inevitably be perceived as less 'scientific' and, therefore, as less persuasive. Hence, the intellectual appeal of the professional model and the associated theory of diffusion: its 'great merit of simplicity'.

Throughout this account great emphasis has been laid upon the institutionalised epidemiological and 'public health' commitments of the General Register Office as

[134] On the paradigmatic mid-Victorian institution which encapsulated this, the NAPSS (National Association for the Promotion of Social Science), see Goldman, 'The Social Science Association'. The demise of this association in 1886 supports the thesis of Christoper Harvie that the liberal intelligentsia's principled support for Home Rule represented an act of political secession, isolating them from mainstream politics: Harvie, *The lights of Liberalism*, p. 18. However, the extent to which the Royal Statistical Society (which received its charter in 1887) in fact became something of a functional substitute for the NAPSS during the remainder of the period down to the Great War should not be overlooked. Although it did not tend to draw ministerial politicians to its proceedings, as the annual conferences of the NAPSS had, its quarterly meetings in central London attracted regular contributions and attendance from a wide range of the most active civil servants of the period as well as the major social investigators and academics.

determinative of the timing and character of the emergence of the official, professional model of social classes. Its preventive health focus and statistical expertise ensured that the Office became locked into an intellectual contest with the hereditarian eugenicists in the first decade of the new century because of the latter's loudly trumpeted, hostile interpretation of the nation's recent demographic trends. The only other significant influence upon the occupational and social classification practices of the GRO that can be detected during the late nineteenth and early twentieth centuries emanated, not unexpectedly, from the economics-oriented students of the labour force and of industrial relations. Indeed, the unpredictable aspect of this influence was its relative feebleness, in that the economists were unable to impose their agenda upon the GRO. Despite the formation of an embryonic government department, the Labour Bureau, as early as 1886, the GRO was able to deflect for decades the demands being made upon it from the late 1880s by Alfred Marshall and other economists.

In understanding the genesis of the professional model as the official representation of British society, it is the preponderance of only these two influences, the Galtonian and the Marshallian, in dialectical combination with the GRO's own medical preventive health agenda which emerges as the first conclusion of the above account. This selectivity of influence is significant. There were several other perfectly plausible schemes for occupational classification extant, which could have – but apparently did not – directly influenced Stevenson's approach. Many foreign classifications must certainly have been known to Stevenson and the GRO. The International Statistical Institute's 'nomenclature des professions' had been developed between 1871 and 1893 mainly by the French statistician, Jacques Bertillon, in correspondence with many of Europe's official statistical bureaux.[135] The evidence presented by Alfred Marshall to the Treasury Committee on the Census in 1890 shows that the occupational classifications of the USA and Germany were also held in high regard by some.[136] It had been the Danish social classification and Danish data which were employed by Karl Pearson for his earliest, admonitory calculations of fertility differentials in the 1890s.[137] A long and highly informative article appearing in the *Journal of the Royal Statistical Society* in 1894 had detailed many of the different occupational classifications used throughout the dominions, for instance in the censuses of the various parts of Australasia, of India, of Canada and so on.[138] Apart from these, there was the Irish Registrar-

[135] Work had begun on the scheme at the Vienna meeting of the International Statistical Institute in 1871 and the final version was approved at the Chicago meeting of 1893. There were several levels of aggregation: 499 elementary occupational units (*groupes*) were combined into 206 *chapitres*; these were further collected into 61 *classes*, which could in turn be grouped into 12 *Grandes Divisions*. Finally there were 4 ultimate agglomerations: (A) Production de la matière première; (B) Transformation et emploi de la matière première; (C) Administration publique et professions libérales; (D) Divers. This description is drawn from Bertillon, *Cours élémentaire*, pp. 194–6.

[136] See pp. 115, 127. [137] See Prologue, n. 17.

[138] Hooker, 'Modes of census-taking in the British dominions'.

General's social classification for Dublin, which has already been discussed above but which was never mentioned by Stevenson.

There were, furthermore, several other contemporary domestic exponents of occupational classification, whose work could have been explicitly considered by Stevenson as he grappled with his own scheme. The work of A. L. Bowley was certainly the most important of these methodologically. There is strong circumstantial evidence which suggests that Stevenson had, indeed, by 1910 read Bowley's first contribution on the subject of 1908.[139] But Bowley's most significant advances on the issues of occupational and social classification did not appear until his major publication of 1915.[140] This probably therefore came just too late to influence Stevenson's commitment to the professional model during the critical period from 1910 to 1914 (the period from Stevenson's first proposal to survey social differentials in fertility until the first public appearance of the classification scheme itself). There is no evidence that any of the other indigenous occupational classifiers, such as T. A. Welton, had any substantial independent influence upon the form of Stevenson's social classification scheme.[141] The absence of explicit reference to any of these many other classificatory efforts, either foreign or domestic, in Stevenson's official or unofficial writings seems, then, to confirm the relatively exclusive importance, as influences upon Stevenson, of the three forms of 'social science' which have occupied the above account: Galtonian biometrics; Marshallian economics and the social inquiry of Charles Booth; and the tradition of public health environmentalism from which Stevenson himself hailed.

Among the many novel social, economic and political theories and analyses that were thrown up in the turbulent decades between 1880 and 1914, it was, then, primarily only these three 'schools' which exerted a direct, methodological influence over the form that the official, professional model was to take. This was not at all because they necessarily represented the most significant currents of

139 The passage on this subject in Stevenson, 'Suggested lines of advance', p. 701, would appear to be a close paraphrase of the statement in Bowley, 'The improvement of official statistics', p. 476.

140 Bowley, 'The improvement of official statistics'; Bowley, *The nature and purpose*. The latter is a classic of clarity and good sense. Arthur Lyon Bowley (1869–1957), Professor of Mathematics and Economics at University College, Reading, 1907–13, and later the University of London's Professor of Statistics, 1919–36, was the most innovative, policy-oriented social and economic statistician of his generation. Further information can be found in Davidson, *Whitehall*; MacKenzie, *Statistics in Britain*, ch. 5 n. 21; Hennock, 'The measurement of urban poverty'. It was substantially Bowley's considerable authority and influence that resulted both in the important innovation of a parallel classification of the employment information, by personal occupations and by industrial function, which was adopted at the 1921 census; and also in the attempted family dependency analysis at that census. See also Waites, *A class society*, ch. 2, on contemporary images of social class.

141 T. A. Welton had a venerable record of independent analysis and criticism of the GRO's occupational statistics dating back to the 1850s and 1860s (see ch. 2, n. 6). His relevant publications in the Edwardian period were: 'Occupations in England and Wales' and *England's recent progress*. Other contemporary stabs at occupational and social classification included: D'Aeth, 'Present tendencies of class differentiation'; Chapman and Marquis, 'The recruiting of the employing classes'; Chapman and Abbott, 'The tendency of children to enter their fathers' trades'; and Jones, 'Some notes on the census of occupations'.

thought in the wider political drama of the period. It was rather because each of these shared substantially the same social science methodology and policy agenda, despite their varying intellectual and institutional origins. They were speaking the same social scientific language and were looking – from different vantage points – at the same problem. They had in common a positivist, empiricist epistemology associated with a rationalist philosophy of political action and its legitimacy. They were each committed to applying this methodology to the old, vexing problem of poverty; and they each conceived this problem in the same, novel fashion as a *social variable*.

According to this shared approach, poverty was observable and quantifiable (on an ordinal, categorical scale of measurement) for comparative purposes. Of course, the data therefore had to be coded and classified into types and categories (occupations and classes in the case of the professional model; and in Booth's case this included counting 'impressions') in order to construct the ordinal scale of analysis. It was acknowledged by all concerned that to classify raw, observed 'data' according to social class was of primary importance in order to analyse the problems in which they were interested. These three approaches therefore shared an epistemology and methodology which ensured that each reciprocally perceived their various 'scientific' findings as directly mutually competitive. They in effect comprised an informal forum of intellectual peers, involved in the same, contested enterprise of empirical social inquiry. It was the outcome of the resulting intellectual conflict and negotiation between these three 'schools' of empirical social science which most strongly determined the ensuing characteristics of the official model of social classes.

Stevenson's five class model of society, and its subsequent eager utilisation by interwar demographers, as well as by educational psychologists, has considerable significance in the context of developments in social scientific theory and practice. It represents the accommodation into the empiricist branch of the social and human sciences in Britain of a holistic conception of the socially structured, systematic variation of individuals' life-chances within a society. This followed upon and, indeed, was made possible by the thorough absorption into social thought of the powerful and transposing, evolutionary, Darwinist perspective. With its focus both on the destiny of the species or 'race' as a whole, and also upon the pregnant relationship between individuals and their environment, Darwinism acted as a vehicle for the acceptance and integration of the fundamental notions of the social and the collective into an orthodox tradition of profoundly individualist and libertarian English thought and empirical inquiry (which had its distant origins in Lockean contract theory). The early nineteenth-century utilitarian science of government had initiated an attempt to accommodate some notion of collective aims, goods and rights within an individualist ontology and formulation ('the greatest good of the greatest number' – of individuals). But, ironically, it was the empiricist, anthropological, natural 'science of man', once equipped with its fully developed evolutionary perspective, which finally made a social and collective ontology appear to be a necessarily true and important aspect of a world still composed of interacting, rational individuals.[142] Hence, only from the 1850s and 1860s, can we begin to talk without anachronism of a mainstream, continuous tradition of indigenous English political and *social* thought.

Stevenson's public health work in social and medical statistics was, then, centrally located within a firmly established tradition in Britain of a positivist and scientific empiricist methodology which had long embraced the encompassing disciplines of medical epidemiology, demography, practical policy-oriented social science and evolutionary biology. Of course, within the academic social and political sciences in Britain, there was no shortage throughout this period of exponents of much less empiricist approaches: the idealist social philosopher, Hobhouse, and his successors as Professor of Sociology at the LSE, Morris Ginsberg and T. H. Marshall; the English Pluralist political thinkers, A. D. Lindsay and Ernest Barker (who from 1928 held a Professorship in Political Science in Cambridge that had been endowed by the Rockefeller Foundation to promote empirical inquiry, but Cambridge had other ideas); the deductivists of the economics profession; and, by the interwar period, even one or two Marxist theorists, such as Harold Laski.

But there can be no surprise that a hard-pressed civil servant (Stevenson almost certainly suffered from chronic overwork, retiring early due to ill health and dying shortly thereafter) trained in medical science with his attention fixed firmly upon public health policy issues should have remained relatively immune to such alternative intellectual influences in his work of social classification, instead continuing to subscribe exclusively to an epistemology of rational scientific empiricism. After all, other eminent and leading figures within the interwar empirical social sciences, with whom Stevenson was most directly in touch and from whom he would rightly have taken his lead in such methodological matters, were strongly antagonistic towards the value and relevance of any alternative and more elaborate forms of sociological theorising. The dismissive tone that such figures were capable of mobilising can be gauged from the statement in a standard reference work of the period, published in 1927 by A. M. Carr-Saunders and David Caradog Jones, that 'The belief in the existence of social classes . . . is the result of studying social theory of doubtful value and of neglecting social facts.'[143]

[142] On early nineteenth-century comparative physical anthropology (out of which the anthropometric project of Galton in the later nineteenth century emerged) as the primary intellectual vehicle for the early development of an empiricist natural science of 'man', see Weber, 'Science and society'.

[143] Carr-Saunders and Jones, *A survey of the social structure*, p. 72. There is more than an echo in this empiricist, positivistic swipe, of James Fitzjames Stephen's famous, scornful opinion that notions of group identity and social action were no more than a 'bag of words' – a statement made in 1873 (Harris, *Private lives*, p. 224)! Of course, Noel Annan followed his historical biography of Stephen's equally forthright, muscular Christian brother, *Leslie Stephen* (published in 1951), with a study of

Carr-Saunders was shortly to succeed W. H. Beveridge as the Director of the LSE, the single most important institutional centre for the pursuit of policy-related social sciences in the country.[144] Both of these men shared with the Webbs, the LSE's founders and intellectual progenitors, an antipathy towards 'fact-free' deductive theorising in the social and policy sciences and a strong preference for 'value-free' (as they saw it) scientific empiricism. The conviction that sociology was only valid while it was striving to be 'scientific' and empirical – and that in any other form it was a subject that was politically troublesome, overly speculative and insufficiently rigorous – was apparently a view which was, if anything, actually gaining in strength within the British academic establishment during the early interwar years.[145]

Thus, as a potentially comprehensive transformation of causal theories and epistemological assumptions among empirical investigators in the social sciences, the Edwardian episode of the development among public health medical officials of a thoroughgoing, environmentalist analysis of poverty and social inequality proved to be stillborn. The potential for drawing the more radical and critical methodological and philosophical implications of the holistic *social* conception of the forces of inequality, which it entailed, was not further developed or explored by empirical social scientists in the interwar period. It was a revelation that failed to take root as the practically manufactured, critical sociological perspective that it might have become in Britain.[146] In the interwar period the search was resumed

The curious strength of Positivism in English political thought. R. M. Young has interestingly remarked that during the period 1880–1910 the dominant concepts of social evolution changed from those of social Darwinism to those of functionalism, as the market economy itself and the associated ideology and practice of market relations shifted from one of outright competition to one of ordered, managerialism and collective bargaining. Both forms of social evolution were equally positivist. Young, 'Darwinism is social', p. 622.

144 This comes out very clearly from Martin Bulmer's useful sketch survey, predominantly on the twentieth century: 'The development of sociology and of empirical social research'. On social work at the LSE, see also Harris, 'The Webbs, the Charity Organisation Society and the Ratan Tata Foundation'.

145 Thus, as the eminent American sociologist, Edward Shils, a visiting observer of the British social science scene in the 1940s, recalled, succinctly summarising the nature of the prejudice: 'How could sociologists come into existence in Britain when in Oxford and Cambridge sociologists were looked upon as pariahs, as no better than Americans or Germans?' Shils, 'On the eve: a prospect in retrospect', p. 168. José Harris, who has emphasised the increasing significance of idealism in British social thought and social policy during the decades before the Great War, has also noted something of a faltering of this influence after the war. She notices, as symptomatic of this, that A. C. Pigou's innovative interest in 'welfare economics' did not find an enthusiastic audience either in the economics discipline or among social scientists interested in policy, such as Beveridge or Carr-Saunders. Harris, 'Political thought and the welfare state', p. 141.

146 The reasons for this are somewhat obscure and deserving of further investigation. José Harris's pioneering work on the history of empirical social work, social thought and social inquiry throughout this period, 1880–1940, is very helpful in this respect, although it raises many further issues of interpretation (see pp. 175–7). Her argument that the ethos and practice of voluntary social work was not in gradual decline from the 1880s but was relaunched, backed by a reinvigorated idealism derived from Plato, Hegel and T. H. Green is extremely important: Harris, 'Political thought and the welfare state', pp. 121–32. Throughout this period neither local nor central

within the British social science 'Establishment' for elegant, singular, general causal explanations of demographic phenomena, in conformity with the orthodox, logical empiricist notion of what it was to offer a proper and compelling scientific explanation.[147] This continued to constitute the main intellectual objective in using and subsequently 'refining' the official classification scheme. Hence, Stevenson's 'perfection' of the official social classification system in the 1920s took the form which has been recounted above. As the immediate positive endorsements of the resulting professional model by both Beveridge and Carr-Saunders show, according to the opinion of his most professionally eminent social scientific peers, Stevenson's representation of the nation's social structure was perceived to be an exemplary instrument for the kind of empirically oriented social and policy sciences which they recognised as intellectually valid.

The professional model is an extremely simplified, rigid and unilinear representation of an apparently invariant social structure. As such it is ideal for the initial, exploratory function of testing to what degree there may be a broad pattern of social grading visible in any measurable process of national change; or attributable to any one of a wide range of characteristics, from disease incidence to car-ownership. But beyond this, the professional model remains an extraordinarily blunt instrument for any form of investigative empirical inquiry attempting a more discriminating approach to questions of causation. Empirical data which have been classified according to this instrument are therefore ordered and structured in such a way as to be highly resistant to – indeed positively inoperable with – any hypotheses *not* formulated to be testable as a unidimensional national 'effect'. This would seem arbitrarily to preclude an enormous variety of those more precise and less general questions which researchers most need to ask in the

government expansion in social services resulted in a radical diminution in the contribution and influence of voluntary associations, which continued to work in partnership with official agencies. Further research may show that a crucial development was the disciplinary institutionalisation of this late Victorian movement in university departments of social work, thereby establishing that the core of the academic discipline of 'social science' continued to retain a practical, individualist focus throughout the interwar period. Certainly, the moralising attitude towards poverty and disease did not evaporate and disappear during the Edwardian decade. For instance, Linda Bryder's research has shown the prevalence of unreconstructed COS attitudes and policies in the interwar activities of the important National Association for the Prevention of Tuberculosis: Bryder, *Below the magic mountain, passim*; and, more generally, see Jones, *Social hygiene*.

147 It is undoubtedly highly significant in explaining this that, within the natural sciences at this time, the autonomy of the traditional Hume–Mill positivist concept of a unitary scientific methodology was preserved, in the form of the hypothetico-deductive method, despite the revolutionary implications to the contrary of Einstein's development of relativity theory. The philosophical dominance of this logical positivism, or logical empiricism as the Vienna Circle preferred to call it (principally Moritz Schlick, Rudolf Carnap, Otto Neurath, Hans Reichenbach, Herbert Feigl and C. G. Hempel), as the orthodox description of liberal, rational empirical science offered by its philosophers, remained more or less unchallenged until T. S. Kuhn's *The structure of scientific revolutions*, published in 1962. This deployed an historical account which showed that scientific rationality was historically constructed and relative: a series of paradigms or 'styles' of reasoning were evident in the historical record. See Hacking, *Representing and intervening*, pp. 42–4, 142–4; Crombie, *Styles of scientific thinking*, and below, pp. 599–602.

social and historical sciences. The cognitive opportunity cost of the professional model is not just in terms of alternative representations of social structures, but also in terms of its exclusion and marginalisation of an enormous range of other investigative approaches and forms of explanation.

Current research into the history of falling fertility in Britain has long abandoned the simple diffusionist theory, and its radical egalitarian assumption – a rationalistic fallacy – that all individuals would respond to novel information in a similar way. But, in an analogous fashion to that which occurred when 'diffusion' replaced 'individuation', as recounted here, the original professional model of social structure and its derivative empirical account of the fertility decline as a class-differentiated event threatens, once more, to continue its remarkable record of survival, as the unquestioned empirical representation of the phenomena to be explained, and therefore as the unexamined premise for further research. Hence, as long as the professional model of national unitary fertility decline is retained, our attempts to understand how and why fertility changed in late nineteenth-century and early twentieth-century Britain will, in consequence, remain characterised by the retention of a quest for a nationally generalisable, single variable to explain the apparent unidimensional pattern of a social grading in the data: a mere replacement for diffusion, rather than an alternative *form* of causal account.

Methodological conclusions: the professional model and falling fertility

The foregoing revisionist account of the intellectual provenance of the GRO's social classification scheme and its relationship to the 1911 fertility census carries a number of implications regarding the status of the interpretation offered by the seminal document, the *Fertility of Marriage Report*, in the modern study of falling fertility in Britain. It has been shown that the project of devising an official social classification of occupations was clearly prompted and initially sustained not so much by an interest in *mortality* as previously suggested by most commentators, but by a determination to evaluate critically the provocative assertions of eugenicists regarding the social pattern, the supposedly hereditarian causes and the racial significance of the nation's declining *fertility*. Indeed, the design of the empirical exercise of taking a national fertility census and the class-differential interpretation of its results were not at all conceptually independent of each other, as previously thought.

This is of some significance in the assessment of the intellectual sufficiency and rigour of the received professional model of fertility decline. It has always been somewhat uncritically assumed that the class-differential pattern of fertility decline was the most dependable positive empirical finding to have emerged from the 1911 census survey. However, it has not been clearly appreciated that the class-graded model was actually a prior interpretation, imposed from the start and built into the design of the empirical survey conducted through the census. Furthermore, the classification scheme on which it rested was subsequently modified to bring into line the recalcitrant evidence of the three anomalous industrial classes, once the theory of diffusion had been promulgated, a theory which itself presupposed a class-graded model of fertility decline. This has gone unnoticed partly because the first published application of the classification scheme was to the analysis of mortality and partly because Stevenson's involvement with the theory of diffusion has been hidden in the shadow of W. H. Beveridge's robust championing of the same thesis.

The 1911 census survey was primarily designed to yield data that could be socially classified by the professional model. The only question was what kind of social class differentials in fertility would emerge (the main possibilities with a simple set of only five ordinal categories being either a monotonic trend, a U-shaped distribution, or no trend at all). In fact the original exercise conspicuously did not even show the reassuringly straightforward social grading in the onset of fertility decline which has always been portrayed as the principal finding, once the excluded classes of textile workers and miners are brought back into the picture. Yet, there have not been any rigorous, systematic tests of the model's value as an accurate empirical description of the process of falling fertility in England and Wales; and there has been very little in the way of competition from conceptual alternatives.[148]

It has been shown that this inherited empirical view of Britain's fertility decline has little to do with either its tested authenticity or its proven capacity for illumination of the problem. It is rather the derivative residue of a particularly

148 Two important subsequent studies of social variation in fertility classified by fathers' occupations did, indeed, deploy different classification schemes: Hopkin and Hajnal, 'Analysis of the births in England and Wales, 1939'; and Glass and Grebenik, *The trend and pattern of fertility*. However, the results of these studies have never been considered to have challenged the class-differential model of the 1911 census. This is principally because they refer to a somewhat later period when social differentials in fertility had attenuated to a great extent (though, of course, by no means disappearing altogether). But also it is because the more modest social differentials which these later studies depicted were not particularly incompatible with the professional model of fertility decline for the pre-1911 period. For instance, it was found that by the 1940s clerical workers were restricting their fertility to the greatest extent – slightly ahead of professionals even; but, understandably, this was not considered to cast doubt on the validity of the professional model of fertility decline for the earlier period, before the Great War. Glass and Grebenik, *The trend and pattern*, Part I, pp. 106–11. An independent, secondary analysis of the published tables from the 1911 census, along with additional analysis of data from vital registration and for London districts, was performed in the 1930s and early 1940s by J. W. Innes: *Class fertility trends*; and 'Class birth rates'. Although introducing one or two classificatory variants of his own, Innes predominantly accepted the professional model of social class differentials as an approach to the phenomenon. He was principally interested in analysing the differential rates and paces of change over time in the fertility declines of the different social classes. However, such an exercise in dynamic analysis, involving measures of change over time in the reported fertility levels to compare the changing fertility of various social classes and groups, is methodologically flawed. There are unmeasurable mortality and memory selection biases vitiating a diachronic exercise of this sort, which are discused below in chapter 6 (see pp. 289, 293–8).

pervasive, élitist and hierarchical view of the nature of British society prevalent during the decades before and after the taking of the 1911 census among that section of the professional intelligentsia most closely involved in the 'scientific' issues associated with interpretation of the nation's demographic trends. The 1911 census fertility inquiry provided the occasion on which the formal codification of this particular representation of the nation's class structure passed into official practice, thereby achieving a privileged form of institutionalised currency in the nation's consciousness.

There are two direct methodological conclusions to be drawn from the account offered so far. First, we can no longer continue to refer to this classification system as one of social classes or even of status groups. Both of these terms would be better employed if reserved for reference to the specific constructs of Marxian and Weberian social theory. Neither of these bodies of theory, the foregoing account has shown, appears to have any direct reference to the official system of occupational classification, whose intellectual origins are located firmly within the context of a British tradition and form of empirical social science *ante* the influence of the modern classics of sociology. Secondly, the class-differential pattern of fertility decline, as represented by the professional model, needs to be validated to ascertain whether it does, in fact, constitute an accurate summary of the historical processes involved in falling fertility, as has for so long been assumed to be the case. This task is now undertaken at the beginning of Part III, through an examination of the fertility record of the component occupations from which the ordinally graded social classes were aggregated.

PART III

A new analysis of the 1911 census occupational fertility data

But society is possible, precisely because man is not necessarily a brute. Civilization in every one of its aspects is a struggle against the animal instincts. Over some even of the strongest of them, it has shown itself capable of acquiring abundant control. It has artificialized large portions of mankind to such an extent, that of many of their most natural inclinations they have scarcely a vestige or a remembrance left. . . .

. . . That it is possible to delay marriage, and to live in abstinence while unmarried, most people are willing to allow: but when persons are once married, the idea, in this country, never seems to enter any one's mind that having or not having a family, or the number of which it shall consist, is at all amenable to their own control.

J. S. Mill, *Principles of political economy* (Routledge edn, 1900; 1st edn, 1848), pp. 258–9

6

A test of the coherence of the professional model of class-differential fertility decline

Introduction

In the historiographical review at the outset it was observed that it seems always to have been accepted – either explicitly or simply by default – that falling fertility in Britain was a unitary phenomenon primarily characterised by a pattern of graded social class-differentials. This model has acted as a premise for all attempts to explain the causation involved. In the intervening chapters of Part II the ideological roots and the intellectual provenance of this particular model, 'the professional model', have been unearthed. It has been shown how this representation of social structure became so firmly grafted into the tradition of study of Britain's falling fertility. The unitary, hierarchical professional model was adopted as the official classification scheme specifically in order to interpret the data derived from the comprehensive inquiry into the nation's fertility taken as part of the 1911 census. In this way the professional model became intimately associated from the start with the rigorous study of declining fertility in Britain, occupying pride of place in the seminal document which provides the most authoritative historical source of demographic evidence: the *Fertility of Marriage Report* of the 1911 census.

As long as the empirical evidence continues to be looked at through the unitary hierarchical lens of the professional model students of the problem will continue to give greatest respect and consideration only to those kinds of general explanations and hypotheses which might be able to explain an apparently unified general process, socially graded in its incidence. But what if a more careful, high-resolution examination of the phenomenon – the historical process of falling fertility – showed it to have a somewhat different empirical shape? What if the unitary graded social class model proved to be only a poor representation, a very rough first approximation – tolerably accurate only when viewed from a distance – of a much more detailed picture of the social morphology of changing fertility behaviour throughout the British nation at this time? Or, even worse, what if this macroscopic image, the professional model of fertility decline, were shown to be a significantly misleading distortion of the historical picture when examined with a greater degree of social precision than that offered by the official model itself?

Until recently a little-known critical review of the official system of social classification written by D. V. Glass in 1947 remained the only penetrating methodological discussion of any length (five pages) to have reached print.[1] Glass decried the continuing use of the incumbent professional model, noting that its claims to provide a correct grading of occupations' social status had never been independently assessed and that a scrutiny of the actual occupations contained within the classes did not increase confidence in its theoretical or empirical value:

> In sum, the Registrar-General's classification, though purporting to be in terms of 'social position', shows various anomalies. The individual groups [the social classes] contain occupations which do not really belong to them and the groups entitled 'skilled workmen', 'intermediate' and 'unskilled workmen', even if they were homogeneous and consistent, would not necessarily provide a correct gradation of social status.[2]

A later generation of empirical social classifiers, Goldthorpe and Hope of the Oxford Social Research and Social Policy Unit, have written of the same official model of social classes: 'Certainly, no results from attempts to validate them have ever been reported. Thus one can place no more reliance on them than one would intuitively place on the common-sense knowledge and armchair decision-making ability of the officials responsible for their construction.'[3]

The professional model's claims to empirical validity in fact rest purely on prescription. This does not ever seem to have been properly appreciated by students of Britain's fertility decline. As an accurate and sufficient summary of the empirical evidence of social variation in fertility behaviour collected in 1911 the professional model has never been subjected to any critical test to verify its statistical adequacy or reliability. There has never been an assessment of the extent to which the graded class model faithfully and helpfully summarises the more detailed patterns of occupational fertility from which it was constructed. And yet the materials for such an examination have always been available.

The aim of this chapter, then, is to report the results of such a validation exercise. Such a test can be mounted because Part 2 of the extensive official *Fertility of Marriage Report*, based on the results of the 1911 census, contained detailed published tables showing the fertility data recorded for over 200 of the individual occupational divisions of the national population distinguished by the Registrar-General. It was these occupational units which were then directly aggregated into

[1] This was hidden away as Appendix 5, pp. 296–300, to a special study undertaken with the Registrar-General's co-operation by W. A. B. Hopkin and J. Hajnal: 'Analysis of the births in England and Wales, 1939'. Their work involved the sophisticated analysis made possible by the new, high-quality birth registration data available for 1939, following the Population (Statistics) Act, 1938. This introduced the demographically important information on age of mother and number of previous births on to the nation's birth registration forms.

[2] D. V. Glass, in Hopkin and Hajnal, 'Analysis of the births in England and Wales, 1939', p. 299.

[3] Goldthorpe and Hope, *The social classification of occupations*, p. 4.

the graded social classes of the professional model, which have remained such an integral part of the historiography of the fertility decline ever since. Thus, it is possible to examine the internal composition and coherence of the professional model and its social classes according to the fertility behaviour of the component parts.

The occupational fertility tables from the 1911 census

There are two large tables which were published in Part 2 of the 1911 census *Fertility of Marriage Report*. It is these tables which provide the principal source of detailed information on male occupational fertility in the ensuing chapters:

Table 30 'England and Wales – Marriages where the wife had not attained the age of 45 years at census – families and mortality therein, classified by occupation of the husband, duration of marriage, and age of wife at marriage'.

Table 35 'England and Wales – Marriages where the age of the wife exceeded 45 years at census – families and mortality therein, classified by occupation of the husband, duration of marriage, and age of wife at marriage'.

Between them, these two tables give all the collated and verified marital fertility information that was collected in 1911 for 206 different occupational groupings of married males and their wives. In the course of the analysis undertaken in later chapters the information on *incomplete* fertility provided by Table 30 will be utilised. Use will also subsequently be made of a third important table, Table 37, giving similarly detailed information on *incomplete* marital fertility for sixty-six *female* occupational groupings. However, in the present chapter, attention will be focused exclusively on Table 35, in order to use its data on the *completed* marital fertility of male occupations to devise and present a rigorous critical test of the professional model of class-differential fertility decline. This is simply because evidence of incomplete fertility, while extremely revealing for certain well-defined purposes, cannot form the basis for conclusive comparative measures of occupational fertility differentials.

The reader needs to bear in mind at all times the exact format and nature of the published tables, since this largely determines the nature of the technical demographic problems involved in their use as a source. On inspecting Table 35 (see Appendix B), it can be seen that each occupational grouping of the national population has been primarily divided according to the age of wife at marriage into four quinquennial sections between ages 15 and 34, a decennial section for ages 35 to 44, and a residual for all ages above 44. These primary divisions are further subdivided according to the duration of the marriage as of 1911. These duration categories are decennial above 30 years and quinquennial for periods of five to thirty years' duration. The duration categories have been converted (by simple subtraction from 1911) into date of marriage categories in the names of the variables used in the ensuing analysis. As Figure 6.1 shows, for each occupational

Date of marriage	Age of wife at marriage		
	15–19	20–4	25–9
1851–60			
1861–70			
1871–80	AM1/ 71–80		
1881–5		AM2/ 81–5	
1886–90			AM3/ 86–90
1891–5			

Figure 6.1 Representation of the information presented in Table 35 of the *Fertility of Marriage Report*, Part 2

grouping of wives we have, in effect, a matrix of cells, covering the everborn completed fertility history of couples surviving to 1911.

The cells are cross-classified by female age at marriage (hereafter AM1 = age 15–19 at marriage; AM2 = age 20–4 at marriage; and AM3 = age 25–9 at marriage) and date of marriage (where 71–80 = those married 1871–80; 81–5 = those married 1881–5; 86–90 = those married 1886–90). Note that horizontal cells contain those women marrying between the same dates, whilst vertical cells are those marrying between the same age limits. Therefore, cells in a diagonal line, from top left to bottom right, give approximate 'cohort' information for women originally born between the same dates but marrying at different ages, and therefore at different dates (this property of the table is slightly compromised by the change from quinquennial to decennial duration categories for marriage durations above thirty years).

The figures in Table 35 for 'children dead' are unusable as simple child mortality estimates for marriages of completed fertility. Many of the children of these marriages would have attained their majority long before 1911, and so can hardly be considered to have been subject only to the mortality conditions of childhood in their parents' household.[4] The ensuing analysis of occupational differences will therefore deal only with the everborn figures, rather than with any attempts to measure comparative 'effective' fertility (i.e. net of mortality).

The specimen manuscript schedule (see Appendix A) shows that the new fertility questions on the 1911 census schedule can be found under the section 'Particulars as to Marriage'. The instructions asked each married woman in the

[4] This point is fully appreciated in the Report but not stated in an obvious place. See *FMR* Pt 2, p. civ, final paragraph.

household to state the total number of children born alive to the present marriage (requiring additional information on the number who had died, cross-checked by a further statement on the number still living). The date of birth of each liveborn child was not asked (and probably would not have been reliably answered in any case). Wife's age at marriage was deduced in each case by the GRO's clerical staff, by subtracting the figure of completed years of marriage duration from the statement of the woman's present age.[5] Cross-examination of the answers on each schedule for internal consistency was possible and as a result we are told that 122,286 defective schedules from the total of 6,630,284, relating to the married population in 1911, were omitted from the analysis because of internally inconsistent information.[6]

However, in some of the remaining schedules memory loss may have caused distortions in responses that were internally consistent and so escaped detection.[7] Memory loss is an undeniable physiological fact of the ageing process. If manifesting itself in an under-reporting of births, then it would act to underestimate the known trend of decline from high to lower fertility since, on this hypothesis, the older couples enumerated in 1911 representing those marrying earliest (with highest fertility levels) would be most prone to under-reporting. This consideration may become a serious problem for an occupational comparison if it is occupation-specific in its incidence. Such might be the case if, as is likely, the chance of forgetting at least one child – resulting in understatement – is broadly a direct function of the number of children everborn, i.e. the more children parents had, the greater the chance or opportunity to forget one. In that case more fertile occupations would be differentially affected because such memory loss would most depress the retrospectively recorded fertility in occupations where largest families were most common. However, this is not a problem for a study which only seeks to rank occupations cross-sectionally, according to their relative fertility level at a given point in time. Indeed, we may have confidence that to the extent that occupational fertility differentials are found to exist in a cross-sectional analysis from this data source, they are *a fortiori* robust, despite the effect of memory loss in compressing such differentials.

It may be noted that a selection feature, which reduced the likelihood of memory loss, was the fact that couples were excluded from the analysis unless both were returned on the same household schedule.[8] To a certain extent, then, the spouses would act as a mutual check on each other's memories (provided both participated in completing the form, of course). Nearly half a million women returning themselves as married were excluded from the fertility analysis because of their husband's absence on census night. Stevenson was attempting to exclude these women because of their lower exposure to the chance of pregnancy within marriage and in particular because they may not have been part of a continuing

[5] *FMR* Pt 2, p. xvi. [6] *FMR* Pt 2, p. vii.
[7] *FMR* Pt 2, pp. vii–xiv, for discussion of these effects. [8] *FMR* Pt 2, p. vii.

sexually active relationship. Certainly a proportion of the 493,679 absent husbands would have been only temporarily absent, and therefore part of a continuing marriage where the wife had spent all of her fecund married life genuinely at risk to the chance of conception. It is not possible to estimate accurately how many of these half a million absences on census night represented real *de facto* separations. It is known that Magistrates Court Maintenance and Separation applications were running at about 10,000 per annum in the period 1897–1906, whilst actions against absent husbands by the Poor Law accounted for a further 4,000 cases per annum.[9] These figures, along with the much smaller number of divorces each year, would suggest that very approximately half of the half million absent husbands can be attributed to formally broken marriages.

The occupations of the 1911 census Fertility of Marriage Report

Volume X, *Occupations and industries*, of the 1911 census, distinguished 465 occupational categories for the enumerated population. These were marshalled into twenty-three industrial 'Orders' identified by Roman numerals from I to XXII (plus Order XXIII, a miscellaneous residual for those 'Without Specified Occupations or Unoccupied'). These Orders corresponded more or less to functional subsectors of the economy: Order I was 'General or Local Government of the Country'; Order II 'Defence of the Country'; Order V 'Commercial Occupations'; Order XII 'Building and Works of Construction'; etc. These were in turn differentiated into branching suborders depending on the extent of diversity within an Order. Order I contained only two suborders, 'I.1 National government' and 'I.2 Local government' whereas Order X, 'Metals, Machines, Implements and Conveyances', was divided into eleven suborders, such as 'X.1 Iron and steel manufacture', 'X.4 Electrical apparatus' or 'X.10 Vehicles'. Finally these suborders were composed of the 465 individual occupations of the entire nomenclature. Thus, in taxonomic terms, the *social* classification supplied by the professional model was an alternative reclassification of these same 465 units according to different principles from those used to assemble them into the twenty-three industrial orders. Occupations assigned to the same industrial order could be allocated to different social classes (information on the industrial Order and suborder in which each occupation was placed is given in columns 'Order' and 'Suborder', Appendix D).[10]

[9] Evidence presented by J. E. Simon to the Royal Commission on Marriage and Divorce (1952), cited in McGregor, *Divorce in England*, ch. 2, Table XIII.

[10] As is well known, it was not until the thorough reorganisation of the GRO's nomenclature of occupations in preparation for the 1921 census that a truly occupational classification was perfected, by creating a distinct and separate industrial classification (see pp. 323–4). From the 1921 census onwards the GRO published a parallel dual classification of all employments in the economy. One classification was for economists, distinguishing industrial sector and function; the other distinguished personal occupation and social status. See *Guides to official sources*, 'No.2. Census Reports of Great Britain 1801–1931', 1st edition (HMSO 1951), pp. 37–9; and see above, ch. 5, n. 140, on the contribution of A. L. Bowley to this change in classification procedures.

The published tables in the *FMR* Pt 2 contain information for 206 occupational groupings. Most of these 206 fertility occupations correspond to individual occupational categories from the original 465, apparently chosen for a combination of their quantitative importance and their specificity of occupational description.[11] Thus, although fewer than half the total number of 465 occupational divisions were utilised in Table 35, we are told that those appearing represented fully 87.5% of all couples enumerated together on census night.[12] The numbers in front of the occupational titles or in brackets after them are a simple numerical identity series (ID) created for various data handling purposes in this study, and do not correspond to any original information in the census volumes. The ID sequence simply follows the order in which the occupations appear in Table 35.

Of the 206 'fertility occupations', 18 are in fact combinations of several of the 465 original categories. One reason for such amalgamations, which is not, however, referred to directly in the 1923 Report, can be found on inspecting the first publication in which the GRO produced indices for occupational fertility, the 75th ARRG (published in 1914). Table XVI gave fertility figures in which the number of births attributed to each occupation was derived from the GRO's vital registration system: the legitimate births registered in 1911 to each occupational aggregation of fathers. The number of fathers in each occupation was still derived from the number enumerated in the census of 1911, crudely age standardised by counting only occupied males under the age of 55 at census as the number of potential fathers in each occupation. This combined utilisation of data from both census and vital registration created problems, however. It meant that:

> In many cases . . . the fertility of the single occupational groups . . . is misleading, owing to certain characteristic differences in the return of occupations at the census and in the birth registers. As there is on the whole more precision of statement at the census, the numbers tabulated to such indefinite headings as 'general labourer' are relatively greater in the case of births, than of population and the fertility of such occupations is correspondingly overstated, . . . This difficulty has been overcome as far as possible by grouping together, in Table XVII, those headings which experience shows to be liable to confusion entailing overstatement of the fertility of some of them and corresponding understatement of that of others.[13]

[11] For instance, in the large suborder 8 'miscellaneous trades', of Order X 'Metals, Machines, Implements and Conveyances', there are eighteen different occupational categories distinguished, of which only three appear in the *FMR* tables: '106 wire-drawers, makers, workers, weavers'; '107 tinplate goods makers'; '108 brass, bronze makers'. On inspection of Volume X of the 1911 census, it is found that these three occupations are those with the largest numbers of workers in this particular suborder, excepting two others not appearing in the *FMR* tables: 'other iron goods makers'; and 'other metal workers'. It seems reasonable to conclude that these last two were omitted from the *FMR* tables, despite their numerical size because of the imprecise, residual nature of their contents. 1911 Census, Volume X *Occupations and industries*, Table 7 'Occupations of married males at nine groups of ages', pp. 68–74.

[12] *FMR* Pt 2, p. cxvii. Of course, a small number of the 465 occupational categories in Volume X were inappropriate for the construction of fertility tables by male occupation, such as 'Roman Catholic Priests', 'Charwomen' or 'Nuns'.

[13] 75th ARRG, p. xxii.

Table XVII in the 75th ARRG listed 56 such composite occupational categories, containing between them 223 – about half – of the individual occupations (which had all been listed separately in Table XVI).

It seems most likely, therefore, that these eighteen groupings of occupations retained in the *FMR* were occupational titles which Stevenson believed that even the census had failed to separate properly, following the same reasoning outlined in the 75th ARRG.[14] However, Stevenson's judgement of whether or not an occupation had been properly distinguished depended considerably on whether its reported fertility corresponded to that which he expected of it, given his assessment of its social position. In some cases the source data in Table 35 did include separate information for one or more of the occupations contained within such an amalgamation. For instance, as can be seen from inspection of Appendix B 'Civil Service Officers and Clerks' (ID 1) combines three occupations from suborder 1 'National Government' of Order I 'General or Local Government of the Country'. These three are: I.1.i. 'Post Office – Telegraphists, Telephone Operators'; I.1.ii. 'Other Post Office Officers and Clerks'; I.1.v. 'Other Civil Service Officers and Clerks'. But the last two occupations also appear separately in Table 35, as 'Post Office Officers and Clerks (other than Telegraphists and Telephone Operators)' (ID 2) and 'Civil Service Officers and Clerks – not Post Office' (ID 5).[15]

As a result it has been necessary to ensure that there would be no double counting of any couples in the ensuing analysis through their appearance in more than one occupational category (i.e. in the above example *either* ID 1 *or* IDs 2 and 5 could be included in the analysis but not both options together). Each of the eighteen composite occupations was therefore considered, to decide whether it should be retained in the analysis or dropped in preference to the more precise information available where some of its component units were tabulated independently. Consequently eleven occupational amalgamations were retained in unmodified form: IDs 4, 9, 11, 12, 34, 95, 102, 146, 150, 152, 155. Four composite occupations were omitted either wholly or partially (the above case being an example of the latter, hence there is no occupation bearing ID number 1 in all the following text and tables).[16] In the three remaining cases, which were all composites of textiles workers, it was found possible to retain and modify the

[14] Indeed, many of the individual 'fertility occupations' in Table 35 are those which Stevenson had previously thought it best to amalgamate when combining census and vital registration data. For instance, all seven shipbuilding occupations of Order X, suborder 9, were contained in group number 26 of Table XVII in the 75th ARRG, whereas Table 35 distinguishes three of them as separate occupations: IDs 109 (ship platers, riveters), 110 (shipwrights), 111 (shipyard labourers).

[15] The prefix 'Other' has been dropped in both cases because it only has relevance in the context of the original list, in Volume X of the 1911 census reports, where there are six occupations in suborder I.1, and where PO and non-PO workers had to be distinguished from each other, and also functions within the PO.

[16] The other three composites omitted for the same reason were IDs: 65, an amalgamation of merchant seamen; 118, which included together all the occupations concerned with precious metals; and 206, a residual of 'students', 'scholars' and 'others'.

composite satisfactorily by subtracting out some of the more precisely defined component occupations, whose fertility information was also tabulated separately in Table 35 (categories of spinners and weavers). The three original textiles composites (IDs 156, 160, 165) were thereby modified to produce three new IDs in their place:

207 'cotton – card room, others, undefined'
208 'wool, worsted – carding, others, undefined'
209 'textiles – bleachers, printers'.

These various decisions for composites therefore reduced the maximum possible number of male occupational categories to 202, whose ID numbers run from 2 through to 209. From this total of 202 occupational categories, 7 more have been excluded because it was judged that there were insufficient numbers of couples (fewer than thirty) to calculate each of the three comparative fertility indices used in the ensuing statistical analysis.[17] Thus, a total of 195 occupations are deployed in the ensuing test of the class-differential model of fertility decline.[18]

The possible fertility–longevity association

The population whose completed fertility is observed through the census inquiries in 1911 were married anything up to fifty or even sixty years previously.

[17] These seven omitted occupations were IDs: 10, soldiers, NCOs; 33, domestic motor car drivers, attendants; 60, motor car and cab drivers (not domestic); 63, tram service – conductors; 74, farmers, graziers – sons, relatives; 203, OAPs (former occupation not stated); 205, students. The minimum number of couples required for calculation of an occupational subgroup's mean fertility inevitably remains largely a matter of subjective judgement. It is relevant to note that the groups of couples in each age at marriage subgroup of each occupation do not, in fact, represent samples from a larger population but constitute a complete enumeration of the population in question in 1911. D. N. McCloskey suggests 30 as a reasonable minimum size for estimating averages from relatively culturally homogenous populations such as this: *Econometric history*, p. 49. Clearly, it is a primary methodological assumption of this study that these age at marriage subgroups of each of the 200 or so occupations do, in fact, correspond to relatively homogenous social units. This assumption is subject to testing on pp. 330–5 and 371–7 below, and is broadly upheld.

[18] As has been noted above (p. 291), the total number of married couples included in the *Fertility of Marriage Report*'s detailed tabulation of 206 male occupational categories (Tables 30 and 35) represented 87.5% of the entire universe of all married couples enumerated at the 1911 census. The 195 occupations used in this chapter to assess the professional model comprised 5,622,096 married males, equal to 86.5% of married males enumerated in 1911, reflecting the fact that the eleven excluded occupational categories accounted for only 1% of the married male workforce. It is possible to ascertain the class affiliation which Stevenson gave to most of the remaining occupational categories not listed separately in Tables 30 and 35 by consulting Table 28A in 74th ARRG. From this information it can be calculated that the remaining 13.5% of married couples not represented by the 195 occupations used here would have been allocated to social classes in the following way: 0.21% to class I; 2.05% to class II; 3.16% to class III; 5.40% to class IV; 1.12% to class V; 0.32% to class VI; 0.15% to class VII; 0% to class VIII; 1.09% unallocated. It is classes II, III and IV, therefore, which are somewhat quantitatively under-represented by the sample of occupations which Stevenson selected for use in the fertility tables. This is, perhaps, not surprising if it was only the most clearly defined categories which Stevenson deemed worthy of individual tabulation.

Those couples whose everborn completed fertility is recorded in the AM/DM cells of Table 35 are, in statistical terms, a sample of an original marrying 'population'. They have been selected by mortality, in fact double selected for the chance of dying, since the marriage will not appear in Table 35 if either spouse had died prior to 1911. Stevenson's calculations of this selection effect show, for instance, that while nearly 70% of marriages contracted twenty years previously had 'survived' to be enumerated in 1911, this proportion dropped to 30% at thirty-five years' duration and to less than 10% at forty-seven years' duration.[19] Furthermore, it must be remembered that these composite percentages hide considerable differences between the different AM (age at marriage) subgroups, holding DM (duration of marriage) constant. For instance, at thirty-five years' duration of marriage the proportion of those couples surviving to 1911 would be between 30% and 70% where wives had married between ages 15 and 19; while for those in which wives had originally married thirty-five years previously at ages 30 to 34, the survival rate would be only between 10% and 30%. The gross selection effects of mortality are, then, not inconsiderable. But this in itself is not necessarily a problem for the present study, unless the surviving sample population, as tabulated in Table 35, is subject to associated fertility-specific selection effects which are also occupation-specific.

The particular consideration, in this respect, which has occupied the limelight in past discussion of the 1911 fertility data, is the intuitively obvious speculation that there may be a statistical association – in either direction – between couples exhibiting longevity and their past fertility record. In the original *Report*, Stevenson had dropped the issue for lack of any clear evidence of a relationship in the findings of the early studies available to him.[20] Several years later R. R. Kuczynski published a study in which he claimed that a comparison of the 1911 census data, itself, with the birth registration records for the same period covered retrospectively by the census inquiry, constituted the strongest evidence yet available that longevity and fertility must be positively correlated.[21] However, J. W. Innes's subsequent work contained a comprehensive exposure of the fallacies in Kuczynski's reasoning when comparing the two sources.[22] After a test which Glass and Grebenik were able to make in their Report for the Royal Commission on Population on the Family Census of 1946, they admitted, somewhat reluctantly, that the fertility of those still alive at this time from the cohorts already measured once at the 1911 census 'do not suggest a correlation between longevity (beyond the end of the reproductive period) and fertility', adding sceptically 'though they do not disprove the hypothesis'.[23]

R. D. Retherford's more recent work on this subject also used data for England and Wales during the relevant period 1861–1911 (in addition to later material for

[19] *FMR* Pt 2, p. ix. Table 1. [20] *FMR* Pt 2, pp. xxx–xxxvii.

[21] Kuczynski, *The measurement*, pp. 93–6. [22] Innes, *Class fertility trends*, p. 22 n. 1.

[23] Glass and Grebenik, *The trend and pattern of fertility*, ch. 6, Appendix 1, comments in reference to Table 4.

the USA and New Zealand).[24] Retherford usefully distinguishes between the possible *direct* negative effects of fertility on average female longevity, in causing death through maternal mortality; and other *indirect* effects of the burdens of childbearing, in somehow shortening the mother's life-span.[25] He notes that most studies have investigated only the latter, producing contradictory results and very weak associations.[26] His analysis of the other, direct effects of fertility change on female longevity, during this period of relatively ineffective medical intervention, is particularly relevant to the present study, since it is fertility-specific effects which are most important for us to assess. He finds that age-specific maternal mortality rates in this country rose between 1861 and 1911, when measured in terms of deaths per 100,000 births; but fell if measured as deaths per 100,000 female population. That is to say that the risk of dying in childbirth was increasing, but since the average number of confinements per woman was falling, the net result was decreasing numbers of women dying from this cause.

These findings dovetail nicely with those of McKeown and Brown, and, more recently, Brian Benson and Irvine Loudon. The increased risk of dying in childbirth could be attributed to the appalling standards of hospital hygiene in the latter half of the nineteenth century, which, according to McKeown and Brown, resulted in a high incidence of puerperal infection in a period when hospital deliveries were on the increase as a proportion of all births.[27] Brian Benson found for northern England that female age-specific death rates for the childbearing period (ages 25–55) peaked at 12.33 per 1,000 in the early 1860s and thereafter declined continuously down to 1911.[28] They declined considerably more rapidly than male rates for the same age group, which would suggest that maternal mortality, the major sex-specific cause of death at those ages, was largely responsible for the relative female improvement; but only, of course, by virtue of the falling number of conceptions per woman as suggested by Retherford's analysis. A further confirmation that maternal mortality was an important component of female adult mortality at these ages is provided in the 75th ARRG (for 1911), where it was noted that up to age 43 the mortality of married women was higher than that for the unmarried, but not thereafter.[29] Irvine Loudon's recent work confirms that hospital delivery and medical intervention in general continued even into the interwar period to be scandalously dangerous for the mother and that delivery at home by a well-trained midwife was a safer option. With the expenses of hospital delivery a deterrent to the less affluent mothers, the net effect according to Loudon was that it was no safer to be rich than poor in giving birth:

[24] Retherford, *The changing sex differential*, ch. 5. [25] Retherford, *The changing sex differential*, p. 57.

[26] Retherford, *The changing sex differential*, pp. 58–9. It was only this latter type of effect which was referred to by Glass and Grebenik (see n. 23).

[27] McKeown and Brown, 'Medical evidence'.

[28] Benson (unpublished PhD thesis), pp. 60ff. Benson's data uses an age period of 25–55 to represent the childbearing period, which is taken as 15–45 in this study.

[29] 75th ARRG, pp. xlix–li.

fewer births was the only general correlate of higher maternal survival throughout the period 1880–1940.[30]

How, then, does this impinge on the analysis here of occupational differentials in fertility, as recorded in Table 35? Those women at this time continuing to experience a relatively large number of births were running an increased risk of maternal mortality. Those reducing the number of confinements were successfully avoiding these increased risks and so, relatively, were much more likely to have survived to be enumerated in 1911. In that case, those occupations with the highest levels of fertility would, if anything, be registering artificially low figures of completed family size at the census of 1911 because the retrospective nature of the census fertility survey would result in disproportionate maternal mortality (lowest survivorship to 1911) among the more fertile mothers. The selection bias is therefore against high fertility in that occupations with highest fertility would be most prone to loss of their higher fertility couples. Any cross-sectional fertility differentials between occupations based on comparisons of surviving couples within a single original marriage cohort would therefore be reduced *in potentia*. Hence, once again, any positive findings of such differentials between the occupations can be considered *a fortiori* robust.

Thus, it has been established that comparative rankings of occupations according to cross-sectional differentials in their completed fertility as recorded in Table 35 are not invalidated by those distortion effects to which demographers and epidemiologists have drawn attention. Provided a synchronic comparator is used, it is therefore possible in principle to proceed to construct a reliable and robust measure of *relative* fertility levels with which to compare and classify the occupations.

Examination of the professional model of class-differential fertility decline

The professional, class-differential model of fertility decline predicts that the range of occupational variation evident in fertility behaviour will exhibit a rank ordering that follows the social class affiliation of the individual occupations. In order to offer a statistical assessment of the model's performance, robust and reliable comparative indices of occupational fertility behaviour are therefore required. It has now been shown that such measures can be constructed from a retrospective source such as the 1911 census in the form of a synchronic, comparative measure of the relative fertility levels of different occupational groupings of couples drawn from the same marriage cohort.[31] Taking the youngest such cohort of couples with completed fertility in 1911 (i.e. where wives were aged over 45 years), it is possible to compute the average number of everborn children

[30] Loudon, 'Maternal mortality 1880–1950'; Loudon, 'On maternal and infant mortality 1900–1960'; Loudon, *Death in childbirth*.

[31] For a fuller discussion of the methodological issues involved in constructing comparative occupational fertility indices, see Szreter (unpublished PhD thesis), section 5.5, pp. 192–205.

for each occupation, controlling for wife's age at marriage. The occupations can then be rank ordered and compared according to these figures.

By referring to the representation of the data in Table 35 as a matrix of cells (Figure 6.1), it is seen that the most recently married cohort couples with completed fertility histories are those in:

AM 15–19 DM 1871–80

AM 20–4 DM 1881–5

AM 25–9 DM 1886–90

This corresponds approximately to the birth cohort of women, 1855–65. The fertility indices applying to each of these three subsets of couples will henceforth be referred to, respectively, as: AM1/71–80; AM2/81–5; AM3/86–90.[32]

Most of the wives of this youngest cohort of completed fertility would have been aged 45–54 years old in 1911.[33] According to the calculations performed on the schedules in the Report, this would mean that, on average, at least 75% of their husbands would have been aged under 59 years and over 90% under 64 years of age at the point of the census in 1911.[34] This means that most of these men would not yet have been subject to the more extreme rigours of age, enforcing retirement or changes to lighter work, which could otherwise represent a distortion of the occupational structure of the population from this study's point of view. The occupations entered on the schedules by these men would have been predominantly the genuine occupation of destination, i.e. that in which the individual was engaged for most of his working life and which would, therefore, most accurately reflect his position within society when measured in this way.

Of the three quinquennial female age at marriage (AM) groupings, by far the most important is AM 20–4, on the grounds of typicality. For virtually all occupational groupings, this is the modal age at marriage group.[35] By definition, therefore, AM 15–19 and AM 25–9 contain 'selected' groups of women: those who married at relatively young and relatively old ages, respectively.[36] We would,

32 The ensuing analysis of fertility differences has been restricted to those couples where the wife's age at marriage was below 30 years, since there were insufficient numbers of couples recorded in many of the 195 occupations above this age at marriage.

33 A minority among those marrying in the 15–19 age group would have been aged slightly older (55–9 years of age) because Table 35 presented decennial groupings for all durations of marriage above thirty years (quinquennial groupings were used at lower durations). To measure the completed fertility of a group containing those marrying as young as 15 years old, it is necessary to select those having been married for no less than thirty years and so a ten-year duration band has to be used, giving a wider spread of ages.

34 Derived from *FMR* Pt 2, p. xi.

35 Of the 195 fertility occupations used here, there were sixteen where the modal female age at marriage group was 25–9 years old, rather than 20–4 years of age. These sixteen exceptions comprised twelve of the eighteen categories of professional occupations (IDs 17, 20, 18, 46, 25, 26, 21, 13, 27, 22, 148, 14). The four others were: drapers, mercers (168); domestic indoor servants (31); hospital, Poor Law, benevolent society officials (38); and police (6). See chapter 7, n. 4 for a listing of ID numbers and titles of all eighteen professional occupations.

36 This is most true of AM 15–19, as the modal age is closer to 25 than to 19 for most occupations and is, of course, slightly over 25 for the sixteen occupations mentioned in the previous footnote.

therefore, be well advised to pay most attention, in comparison and classification of the occupations, to their relative positions as measured by the fertility level of AM 20–4, DM 81–5 (hereafter AM2/81–5). This index, then, is used as the primary reference point. The fertility levels recorded by the occupations for AM 15–19, DM 71–80 (hereafter AM1/71–80) and for AM 25–9, DM 86–90 (hereafter AM3/86–90) are given the status of supplementary information, serving to corroborate or qualify the evidence of AM2/81–5.

We have now arrived at the point where a critical assessment can be made of the professional model's class-differential representation of falling fertility. We have at our disposal a three-pronged measurement tool (the three different AM subpopulations of each occupation) to compare the differences between the occupations in their fertility behaviour. The most important of the three indices is clearly that for the modal age at marriage, AM2/81–5. But before reporting the results of this statistical evaluation, it is important to be clear about relevant criteria for forming a judgement as to the professional model's performance. A simple and definitive 'pass' or 'fail' is highly unlikely to emerge from an exercise in statistical interpretation and judgement such as this. It is therefore necessary and helpful to provide a context for judgement by specifying in advance the significance (in the substantive rather than merely statistical sense) of different possible levels of performance of the professional model of fertility decline.

A strong and relatively unequivocal corroboration for a theory of class-differentials would be provided by a pattern in which the fertility levels of the component occupations within each class proved to be reasonably tightly bunched around their class mean, demonstrating that the classes approximated to both homogeneous and discrete entities. Of course, there would be some outliers in each class but a high degree of continuity in the run of occupational fertility values, without any clustering, certainly would not conform to this kind of highly positive confirmation of the class-differential model.

Secondly, it might be found that there was no bunching of occupational fertility values around their class mean and correspondingly no clear separation between the graded social classes, as each one merged into the next. But it might still be the case that the fertility levels of the individual occupations followed a rank ordering more or less in accord with their graded class affiliation: class I occupations appearing on a rank-ordered list before those of class II and so on. This would be a qualified success for the professional model: class-graded rather than class-differential fertility decline.

Thirdly, a still greater degree of overlap between the occupations of the adjacent graded classes might present itself. More than a merging at the edges, there might be such substantial overlapping of the fertility values recorded by many of the individual occupations drawn from different classes that some of the social classes could hardly be distinguished from each other in terms of their occupational contents, although still perhaps preserving some overall and very general correspondence with the professional model. This would suggest that the class-graded model was far from an accurate or useful summary of the occupational patterns revealed by the 1911 census.

Finally, it would amount to nothing less than a complete negation of the professional, graded model if the occupations within each of the classes were found to be spread across the whole range of fertility values, from high to low, to such an extent that their class allocation had no predictive power at all over their comparative fertility levels.

How, then, does the professional model perform in terms of these four kinds of outcome? First, the frequency distributions for the three different fertility variables, Figures 6.2, 6.3, 6.4 (all eight classes and 195 occupations) and Figures 6.5, 6.6, 6.7 (the five graded classes only, comprising 176 occupations) show no significant discontinuities. More complex statistical manipulations using factor, cluster and discriminant analysis confirmed this *prima facie* graphical evidence: that there is no significant bunching or clustering of the occupations into a set of groupings, either corresponding to the professional model's social classes, or to any other, alternative set of groups. The class-differential model in its true sense cannot therefore be upheld by the evidence: the model fails the test for the highest level of performance, as outlined above. Nor apparently were there any other 'natural' groupings or clusterings in the data.

But what, then, of a model of class gradations – the second level of performance, of qualified confirmation for the professional model? In order to assess this Tables 6.1 to 6.5 present the results of a method for examining the extent of discrepancy between the professional model's predictions for a rank ordering of the occupational fertility levels and the actual rankings observed, according to each of the three fertility indices. The contrast between Table 6.1 (predicted distribution) and Table 6.2 (random distribution) displays the difference between the first and fourth levels of performance identified for the professional model, as defined in the text above. Tables 6.3, 6.4, 6.5 then display the professional model's actual performance according to each of the three comparative fertility indices for the 176 occupations distributed around the five graded classes. Tables 6.3–6.5 consistently show high percentages of misclassification across the full range of fertility values and in all five of the graded social classes. Bearing in mind the frame of reference provided by Tables 6.1 and 6.2, these poor results indicate that the professional model's performance is in the region of the third level of outcome: not an outright refutation but very unimpressive.

An extremely important further exercise was completed for the primary index, AM2/81–5. Given that the occupational categories themselves vary substantially in size as sources of employment in the population as a whole, it is important to assess the effect of their relative quantitative weightings. This factor might still 'save' the validity of the graded professional model, despite the apparently

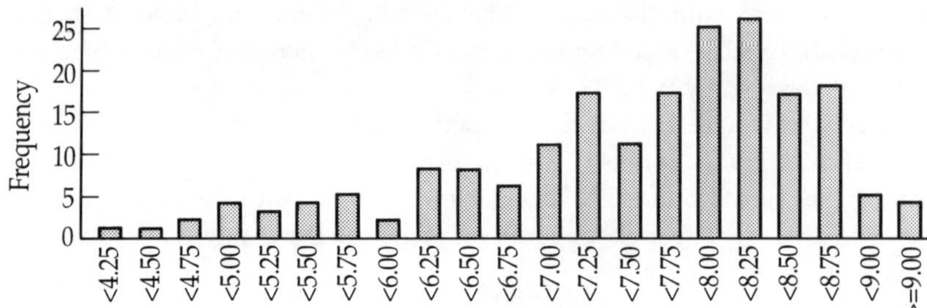

Figure 6.2 Frequency distribution of occupational fertility levels (N = 195): by AM1/71–80

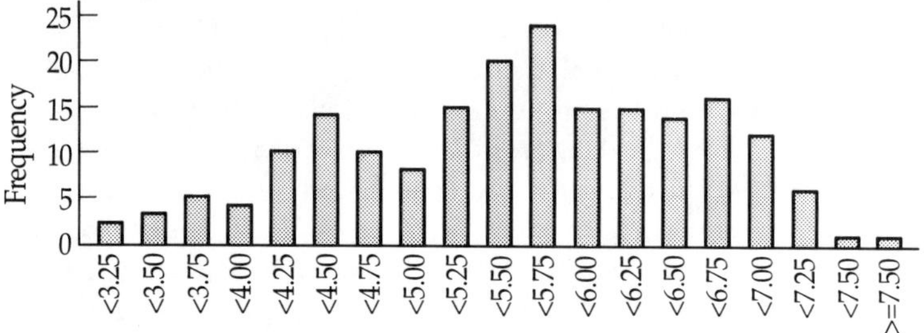

Figure 6.3 Frequency distribution of occupational fertility levels (N = 195): by AM2/81–5

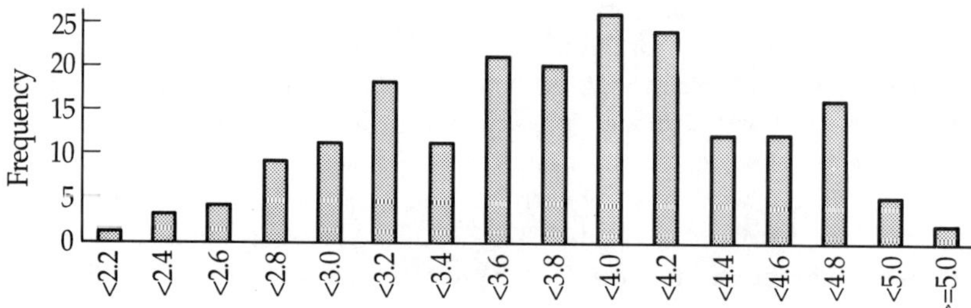

Figure 6.4 Frequency distribution of occupational fertility levels (N = 195): by AM3/86–90

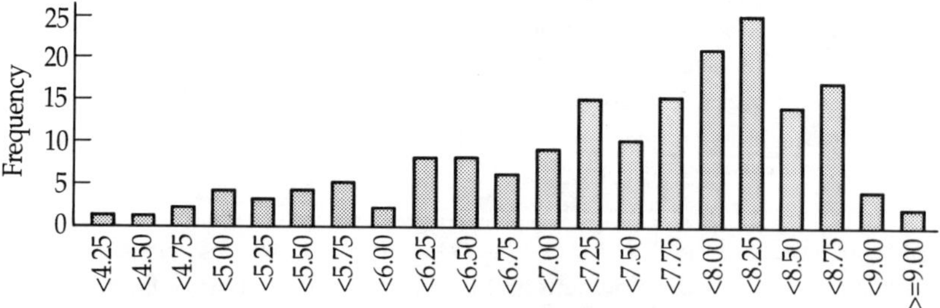

Figure 6.5 Frequency distribution of occupational fertility levels (five classes only, N = 176): by AM1/71–80

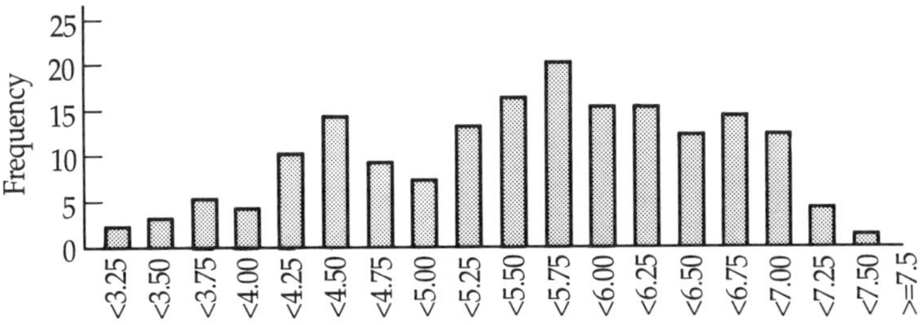

Figure 6.6 Frequency distribution of occupational fertility levels (five classes only, N = 176): by AM2/81–5

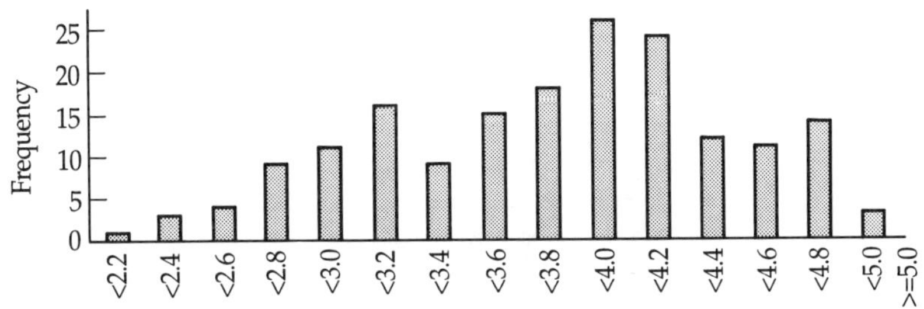

Figure 6.7 Frequency distribution of occupational fertility levels (five classes only, N = 176): by AM3/86–90

Table 6.1 *Predicted versus actual class composition of occupational rankings: predicted by the professional class model*

N	Social class	Predicted class of occupational rankings I	II	III	IV	V
31	I	31	—	—	—	—
40	II	—	40	—	—	—
44	III	—	—	44	—	—
33	IV	—	—	—	33	—
28	V	—	—	—	—	28
Total 176		31	40	44	33	28
Percentage misclassified		0	0	0	0	0

Table 6.2 *Predicted versus actual class composition of occupational rankings: completely random distribution*

N	Social class	Predicted class of occupational rankings I	II	III	IV	V
31	I	6	7	8	5	5
40	II	7	9	10	8	6
44	III	8	10	10	9	7
33	IV	5	8	9	6	5
28	V	5	6	7	5	5
Total 176		31	40	44	33	28
Percentage misclassified		81	78	77	82	82

Table 6.3 *Predicted versus actual class composition of occupational rankings: actual composition by AM1/71–80*

N	Social class	Observed occupational rankings reformed into predicted class groupings I	II	III	IV	V
31	I	23	6	1	1	—
40	II	7	20	7	6	—
44	III	—	12	18	9	5
33	IV	1	2	13	8	9
28	V	—	—	5	9	14
Total 176		31	40	44	33	28
Percentage misclassified		26	50	59	76	50

damning results of the foregoing analysis. A reprieve might, after all, appear to be warranted if those occupations within each social class which were located within the 'predicted' range of fertility values for their graded class were in fact found to be quantitatively much more significant than the discrepant occupations. This is certainly a plausible possibility: it might well be the case that those occupations composed of relatively small numbers might be exhibiting the greatest degree of variance in their recorded fertility values, straying away from their social class 'norm', and they might therefore be creating an unduly pessimistic picture of the professional model when measured in the above way.

Thus for each of the 176 fertility occupations in the five graded social classes, an index of their relative quantitative significance was derived from the 1911 census

Table 6.4 *Predicted versus actual class composition of occupational rankings: actual composition by AM2/81–5*

N	Social class	Observed occupational rankings reformed into predicted class groupings I	II	III	IV	V
31	I	23	6	2	—	—
40	II	7	21	6	6	—
44	III	1	12	18	11	2
33	IV	—	1	14	9	9
28	V	—	—	4	7	17
Total 176		31	40	44	33	28
Percentage misclassified		26	48	59	73	39

Table 6.5 *Predicted versus actual class composition of occupational rankings: actual composition by AM3/86–90*

N	Social class	Observed occupational rankings reformed into predicted class groupings I	II	III	IV	V
31	I	19	10	2	—	—
40	II	9	18	9	4	—
44	III	2	8	18	11	5
33	IV	1	4	12	10	9
28	V	—	—	3	8	17
Total 176		31	40	44	33	28
Percentage misclassified		39	55	59	70	39

data. The figure used was for all married males (all ages) enumerated in each of the 176 occupations at the 1911 census.[37] Each of these occupational totals was then expressed as a simple percentage of all married males in all 176 occupations in 1911 (a total of 4,676,717 married males, representing 72% of the entire universe of 6,495,786 married males enumerated in all 465 occupations).[38] The percentage size

[37] Table 7 of 1911 Census, Volume X.

[38] The reason for the difference between this figure of 72% and the figure of 86.5% previously mentioned in n. 18 above, is, of course, due to the removal from this particular exercise of a further nineteen occupational categories relating to the three industrial classes. The twelve occupations of class VI, textile workers, represented 3.1% of all such married males; the four occupations of class VII, miners, accounted for 7.3%; and the three agricultural labouring occupations in class VIII comprised a further 4.1%, making 14.5% in all.

Table 6.6 *Predicted class sizes and actual class composition, showing percentage of enumerated couples misclassified on a quantitative basis (by AM2/81–5)*

Percentage size	Social class	Class affiliation of occupations, weighted by size, rank ordered by comparative fertility level I	II	III	IV	V	Percentage misclassified
13.31	I	8.08	4.81	0.41	—	—	39.25
23.61	II	5.12	10.61	2.69	5.18	—	55.05
28.40	III	0.10	7.41	15.22	3.29	2.37	46.40
15.51	IV	—	0.78	6.97	2.89	4.86	81.35
19.18	V	—	—	3.10	4.13	11.94	37.72
100.00	I–V	13.31	23.61	28.40	15.51	19.18	51.72

of each of the graded social classes was then computed by summing the percentage figures for all the occupations in each class. A table of expected versus actual class percentages, analogous to the comparison mounted in Tables 6.1–6.5, could then be constructed, as Table 6.6.

In Table 6.6 the percentage size of each of the graded social classes is shown in the left hand column. If the average fertility of the married couples of the occupations in each class had corresponded to that predicted by the professional model, then the same percentage figures as those appearing down the left hand column should be recorded horizontally opposite each class in the indicated diagonal of boxes. The figure in the right hand column horizontally opposite each social class therefore expresses the percentage of its total number of couples recorded as falling outside that diagonal.

As can be seen from inspection of Table 6.6, perhaps somewhat surprisingly, the introduction of the quantitative dimension in fact only further emphasises the inadequacies of the professional model. With the quantitative dimension incorporated into the analysis even social classes I and V record almost 40% of their couples misclassified. While class IV appears completely to disintegrate as a functional part of a graded model: it actually has nearly twice as many couples with fertility typical of class II, rather than class IV; and the figure of over 80% misclassified is as bad as it possibly can be (since 20% would be classified 'correctly' on the assumption of random allocation). The figure in the bottom right corner records that 51.72% of all couples enumerated in these 176 occupations were misclassified by the professional model. To put this figure in context, a completely random distribution of couples' fertility (i.e. the fourth level of performance for the professional model, outright rejection) would have generated a figure here of approximately 80%, while an excellent to good fit with the professional model should have generated a figure ranging from close to zero up to about 20%.

Conclusion

The professional model of fertility differentials can only claim a modicum of accuracy for its predictions, even at the two extremes of the social scale. The professional model is only apparently valid in the most simple sense: that the most privileged section of the population, the couples of the model's class I (representing about 11% of all married male workers in all 195 occupations in 1911) are in the lowest fertility range and the poorest section of the community, class V (approximately 16% of all married male workers) are in the highest fertility range.[39] The professional model of class-differential fertility appears to succeed, therefore, only in discriminating between the occupational fertility behaviour of about one tenth of the population occupying the highest-status and one seventh occupying the lowest-status socio-economic employments, respectively in class I and class V.

But even this limited success is a false impression, which exaggerates the adequacy of the professional model's performance as a valid statistical summary of the whole nation's occupational fertility patterns. This is especially true if the anomalous fertility behaviour of the occupations in the three special industrial classes, created by Stevenson for the low-fertility textile workers and the high-fertility miners and agricultural workers, is brought back into the picture, as it should be if there is to be an assessment of the professional model's overall validity to represent the fertility patterns of the whole nation.[40]

Further pursuit of the quantitative dimension of analysis, as in Table 6.6, shows that it is not in fact true that social class I occupations exclusively dominate the lowest fertility tail of the distribution of fertility values, nor that social class V correspondingly dominates the highest fertility tail. When the occupational contents of the extremes are examined more closely, among the twenty occupations which compose that 5% of the married male population with lowest fertility of all, class II is actually represented in greater numbers than class I![41] At the other end of the scale, there are no class V occupations at all to be found in the highest fertility

[39] The discrepancy between these figures for the percentage size of classes I and V and those given in Table 6.6 results from the inclusion here of the occupations of classes VI, VII and VIII, which between them account for 14.5% of the married male workforce of 1911, as specified in the previous footnote.

[40] Two of the three special industrial classes, VII (miners) and VIII (agricultural labourers), were expected by Stevenson to occupy the highest fertility values; whilst the other special class, VI (textile workers), was judged by him to fall between classes II and III. *FMR* Pt 2, p. lxxvii (and see below, n. 46).

[41] Class II contributes 2.45% as against 2.34%, with the balance of 0.21% contributed by the class III occupation, ID 31 'domestic indoor servants'. These calculations can be derived by examining the 'class' and 'cum pcent' columns of the twenty lowest fertility occupations, listed at the top of Appendix C.

5% tail of the distribution for the nation as a whole. This is because the single class VII occupation, the highly paid coal-miners at the face (ID 84), which comprised fully 5.5% of the married male workforce in 1911 (by far the largest single occupational category), clearly returns the highest fertility of any occupation. In fact even among the highest fertility 10% or 15% of the population, class V occupations played only a minor role, contributing 2% and 4.64%, respectively![42]

In fact, therefore, the professional model offers little more enlightenment than the broad and heavily qualified finding that most (but not all) of the wealthiest and most educated in the nation – the professional élite – were *among* the earliest birth controllers (but certainly did not exclusively constitute the only pioneering social group in this respect), while some of the poorest in society – the unskilled labourers – were *among* the last to control their fertility (but, again, were far from alone in this). As for the vast majority of the population between these two extremes, the professional model of class-graded fertility decline would appear to be a very poor descriptive guide and heuristic framework for the study of falling fertility in British society.

The foregoing verification exercise would seem to suggest, therefore, a far from satisfactory performance by the professional model of fertility decline. The results of the test correspond most closely to the third of the four possible outcomes specified at the outset of the exercise. Although the professional model has not been completely and absolutely discredited – the fourth outcome – the performance could not have been much worse without making such a judgement unavoidable. In particular, the results of the last exercise, bringing in the quantitative dimension, come perilously close to the fourth category of complete refutation.

In drawing this substantive conclusion regarding the limitations of the professional model of fertility change, I appear to differ from the results of a different statistical test of the 1911 social classes published in 1989 by Michael Haines.[43] Haines used the same occupational fertility data for 190 of the male occupational groups from the 1911 census to perform ordinary least-squares regression analyses. His results showed that for the marriage cohorts of completed fertility from which AM1/71–80, AM2/81–5 and AM3/86–90 are drawn, 60–5% of the variance in individual occupations' fertility levels was statistically 'explained' by their social class affiliation.[44] Since this indicated that substantially more than half of the variance was attributable to social class effects, Haines suggested that his exercise showed that 'social class was a good predictor of differential fertility'.[45]

How then does this relate to the results reported here? First, it should be noted that there is not an enormous difference between Haines's figures and the final outcome of the current analysis, which showed that a little less than a half of all

[42] The figures on which this calculation is based can be found by examining the 'class' and 'cum pcent' columns of the highest fertility occupations, listed at the bottom of Appendix C.

[43] Haines, 'Social class differentials'.

[44] Haines, 'Social class differentials', Table 3.

[45] Haines, 'Social class differentials', p. 31.

couples were correctly allocated by the professional model of class-differential fertility decline. The main methodological difference, which probably arithmetically accounts for much of this discrepancy in the two sets of results, is due to the fact that Haines retained all eight classes for his statistical test. The three anomalous industrial classes do, in fact, each contain a relatively small and tightly bunched (in terms of their fertility values) set of occupations; and therefore their inclusion in an exercise of this sort will appear to boost the statistical performance of the class model.[46] Had Haines used his method to test only the five classes of the professional model, the proportion of variance explained would certainly have been lower, as reported in this exercise.[47]

However, what is most important is that it needs to be recognised that Haines's objectives and those of this study are in fact quite distinct, despite the superficial similarity of the two exercises. The present study is concerned to test the validity of the professional model of unitary fertility decline composed of the five graded classes, a scheme which has been considered for many decades to show a relationship between 'social class' and fertility. It has been found wanting. If Haines has shown that the hybrid scheme of five graded classes plus three special industrial classes performs significantly better, then this is no surprise. It is integral to the case *against* the professional model that it was incoherent because it depended on the anomalous industrial classes to deal with large chunks of the workforce which did not fit the model (particularly the highly paid miners at the high fertility extreme and the lowly paid textile workers with very low fertility).

Haines has in fact indirectly acknowledged this point in a subsequent article. *Pace* his conclusion in 1989 – claiming that his results showed that 'social class' was a good predictor of fertility differentials – Haines has now acknowledged that the eight categories of the 1911 scheme do not really correspond to a social class model: 'it must be borne in mind that these are really occupational groupings without a solid underlying theoretical rationale for a characterisation as social classes'.[48] Thus, Haines's results do not, in fact, contradict those reported here above and certainly do not constitute a statistical validation of the professional model of class-differential fertility decline.

It is, perhaps, somewhat surprising, in view of the poor statistical performance reported here, that the professional model of class-differential fertility decline should have achieved such a substantial degree of empirical credibility in the first place. How was it that a class-graded model could have appeared to be so robust?

[46] This can be verified by visually examining Appendix C, where the 'class' column shows the four mining and three agricultural occupations all falling closely together near the bottom of Appendix C, while the twelve textiles occupations (class VI) are all found between rank positions 47 and 107.

[47] Other – probably small – arithmetic sources of difference are due to Haines's selection of slightly fewer occupations and his rather mystifying decision to lump together all female ages at marriage among those marrying in the period 1881–5, thereby unnecessarily depriving his results of a certain degree of demographic rigour.

[48] Haines, 'Occupation and social class', p. 200.

The principal technical reason for this is that the *average* fertility values for the five graded classes could still exhibit the order predicted by the professional model despite all the internal variance and heterogeneity that has been demonstrated. Only in a clear case of the fourth type of outcome (as outlined in the previous section) would the average values for the social classes cease to fall into the ranked order predicted by the professional model. Students of fertility change seem to have been content to accept more or less on trust that the overall pattern of class gradations represented by the average values was a sufficient guarantee of the model's value. Therefore a rigorous test of the model and an examination of the extent and dimensions of the underlying variance within classes was never attempted independently of Stevenson's own original examination of the issue in Part 2 of the *Fertility of Marriage Report*.

In fact, when the full text of this *Report* is examined, Stevenson's detailed exploration of occupational variation in fertility and nuptiality is found to be commendably thorough and full of important insights, along with his analysis of other dimensions of variation, too (especially his treatment of issues relating to degree of urbanism and migration).[49] Nevertheless, Stevenson chose in his summary of the evidence to emphasise the pre-eminence of the overall pattern of class gradations and this was something which he became ever more certain of in his subsequent treatments of the subject. This was for the reasons which were analysed at the end of the previous chapter: his attraction to the thesis of diffusion and his confidence in the value of the professional model because of the regular grading which it also exhibited for measures of mortality.

Of course, there was some degree of association between both fertility and mortality and 'social class', as measured by the professional model. The conclusion to be drawn from the statistical analysis presented in this chapter is not that the influence of social class, as measured by the professional model with all its faults, is utterly negligible. Clearly there was a certain, highly general relationship between wealth/poverty and changing fertility behaviour. However, it has been shown that the strength of this association was unimpressive and its character very imprecise. It is not the kind of compelling correspondence between model and evidence which would seem to justify decades of acceptance as an orthodoxy and the virtual abandonment of any search for alternative approaches and analyses of the body of data which it summarises.

The key point is not so much the absolute redundancy of the professional model, but the intellectual and scientific opportunity cost of failing to explore alternatives to it and of persisting with such a poor, partial and vague model.

It would therefore seem to be high time to put on one side the presuppositions associated with this view and to initiate a new exploration of the social contours of falling fertility in modern Britain. For the present study, the obvious place to begin

[49] *FMR* Pt 2, pp. civ–clviii.

is with the detailed occupational fertility evidence from the 1911 census. So far this data has been used only to examine critically the established orthodoxy. But the same body of evidence can also be deployed for a more positive investigation of the characteristics and causes of falling fertility in Britain during the decades preceding the 1911 census. This task will now be undertaken in the remaining chapters.

7

Multiple fertility declines in Britain: occupational variation in completed fertility and nuptiality

Introduction: an alternative grouping of occupations according to fertility behaviour

The previous chapter has demonstrated that the official endorsement of the professional model of social classes has resulted in the perpetuation of a misleading summary representation of the fertility evidence collected at the 1911 census. This chapter will attempt to re-evaluate the detailed evidence on occupational variation in the fertility of marriage. Supposing Stevenson and his contemporaries had not been so predisposed towards a classification and interpretation in terms of the professional model, what, if any, alternative social patterns could have been discerned from this enormous database?

In order to investigate the socio-demographic patterns of similarity and difference exhibited by the 195 available male occupational groupings, the same indices of completed fertility from the marriage cohort of the 1870s and 1880s will initially be deployed. Later in the chapter, additional dimensions of comparison will be introduced in the attempt to build up a fuller picture of the social, economic, political and cultural sources of variation in fertility behaviour which lie behind the occupational patterns presented in this first section. This additional information includes the extent to which each occupation was composed of employers, employees and the self-employed; the degree of variation in completed fertility exhibited by the younger- and older-marrying subsets within each occupation; divergences in marriage patterns between the occupations; and an exploration of the extent to which different forms of employment entailed relative segregation of the sexes in the workplace. On this basis, various conclusions are offered regarding the overall, descriptive form of the phenomenon in question. It is suggested that the occupational evidence indicates not one, but many fertility declines occurring in England and Wales.

One obvious, alternative approach to the analysis of occupational fertility data from the 1911 census would be that of inductively allowing the data to act as the guide to classification, rather than imposing upon it an *a priori* ordering. This notion – that there might be 'natural' classes or groupings latent within the occupational data – was initially pursued. However, if there were any such clusterings or discontinuities, they were not amenable to a variety of statistical manipulations (Discriminant, Cluster, and Factor Analyses) which were applied to the data.[1] These efforts were uniformly unfruitful because of the absence of any marked discontinuities in the occupational fertility variables as implied by the frequency distributions cited above.[2]

Figure 7.1 presents an alternative systematic socio-economic grouping of most (185) of the 195 occupations according to their relative differences and similarities in completed fertility, as measured by the index, AM2/81–5. The full information upon which Figure 7.1 is based is reproduced in the large table as Appendix C, where the 195 occupations are listed in rank order according to AM2/81–5. Figure 7.1 is therefore an abstraction from Appendix C. It shows the relative position of fifty social categories (twenty are individual occupations and thirty are groupings of occupations) according to the completed fertility index, AM2/81–5. Figure 7.1 presents visual information depicting the relative quantitative importance of the various groupings of occupations. The boxed area which each named category occupies is proportional (approximately) to its relative size in the male workforce in 1911 (following the same methodology as for Table 6.6 in the last chapter, the size of each of the 195 occupations was calculated as a percentage of the figure for all married males of all ages enumerated at the 1911 census in all 195 occupations summed together).[3] All the figures cited below and in the following footnotes for percentage size of various occupations and groups of occupations are calculated on this basis.

The centres of the boxes in Figure 7.1 are placed on the vertical axis as closely as possible to the average fertility value recorded for AM2/81–5 by the occupations in question, or according to the range of average values recorded where the box refers to a group of occupations. The occupational contents of each box in Figure 7.1 correspond to those occcupations named and listed in the text and footnotes at the appropriate points in the immediately following discussion, which commences with those of lowest fertility. The discussion details the way in which the fuller list in Appendix C has been summarised into these fifty categories. Figure 7.1 in fact explicitly summarises information relating to no less than 185 of the total of 195 occupations. The ten occupations omitted, listed in footnote 3, are those whose

[1] Some of the positive results of this work will be discussed in a later section of this chapter, as it contributed to analysis of the relationship between nuptiality and fertility.

[2] See previous chapter and Figures 6.2–6.7.

[3] The total number of such married males in these 195 occupations in 1911 was 5,622,096, representing 86.5% of the entire universe of 6,495,786 married males enumerated in all 465 occupations in 1911. The following ten occupations have been omitted from Figure 7.1 (they are listed preceded by ID number and followed by fertility level, according to AM2/81–5): 29 actors 3.73; 202 pensioners 4.66; 28 musicians, music teachers 4.70; 15 itinerant preachers, missionaries 4.86; 66 merch. service/seamen–navigators 5.44; 30 performers, showmen, sportsmen 5.48; 70 harbour, dock, lighthouse officials, servants 5.75; merch. service/seamen–engineers 5.92; 198 costermongers, hawkers 6.36; 83 fishermen 6.81. Altogether these ten occupations amounted only to 2.813% of all married males enumerated in the 195 occupations.

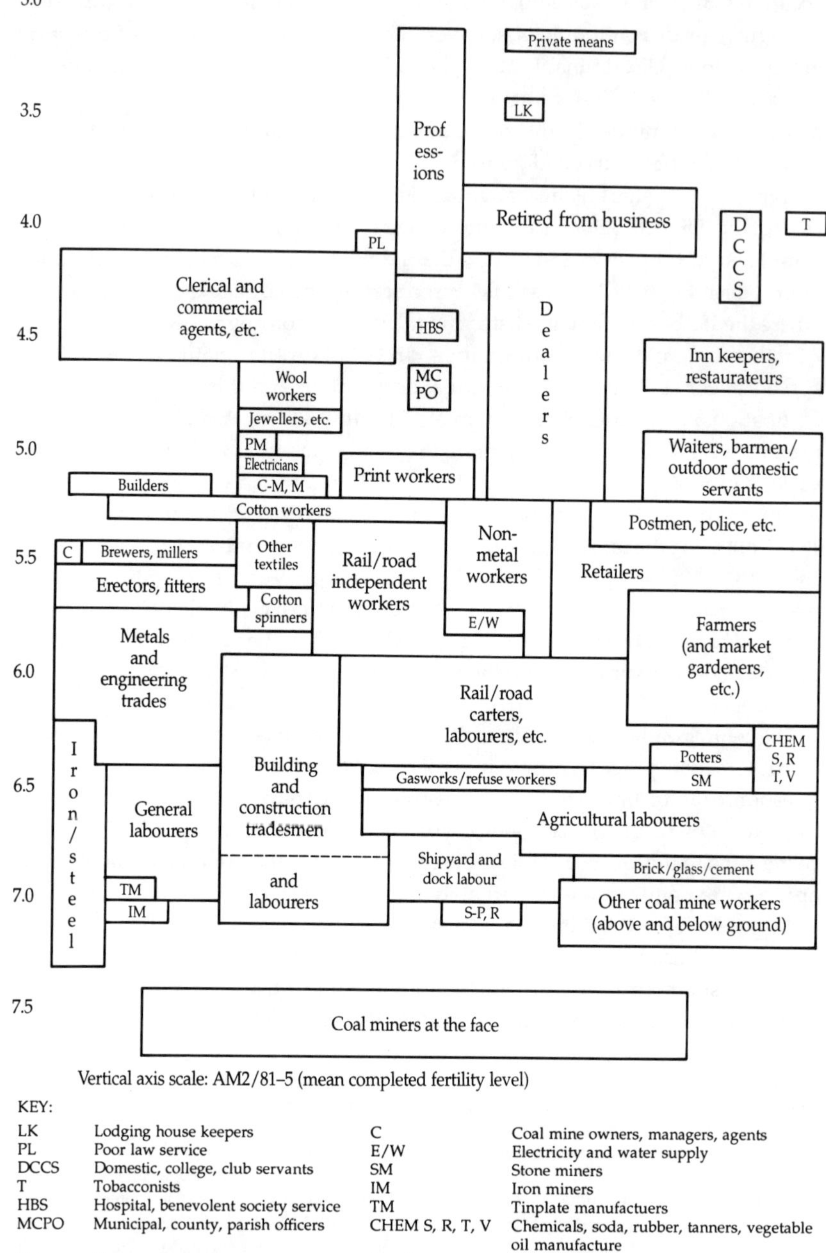

KEY:

LK	Lodging house keepers	C	Coal mine owners, managers, agents
PL	Poor law service	E/W	Electricity and water supply
DCCS	Domestic, college, club servants	SM	Stone miners
T	Tobacconists	IM	Iron miners
HBS	Hospital, benevolent society service	TM	Tinplate manufactuers
MCPO	Municipal, county, parish officers	CHEM S, R, T, V	Chemicals, soda, rubber, tanners, vegetable oil manufacture
PM	Piano, organ makers	S-P, R	Ship platers, riveters
C-M,M	Car makers, mechanics		

Figure 7.1 Summary of occupational patterns of completed fertility (as measured by AM2/81-5), showing relative sizes of groupings of occupations as sources of male employment in 1911

Table 7.1 *Spearman R^2 correlation coefficients between fertility level indices*

Fertility indices	Coeff.	Signif.	N (occs.)
AM2/81–5 with AM1/71–80	0.94164	0.0001	195
AM2/81–5 with AM3/86–90	0.95440	0.0001	195
AM1/71–80 with AM3/86–90	0.90531	0.0001	195

social or demographic characteristics are uninterpretable. Figure 7.1 includes all of the occupations of major quantitative significance, such that the 185 occupations covered comprise over 97% of the total number of couples represented by all 195 occupations. It can, therefore, be taken to show a fully representative picture of the overall social morphology of falling fertility in Britain, as captured by the most important occupational index of completed fertility, AM2/81–5.

As Table 7.1 confirms, the rank position which an occupation holds according to AM2/81–5 is generally highly correlated as an indicator of its rank position with either of the other two fertility measures for the younger- and older-marrying subsets in each occupation, AM1/71–80 and AM3/86–90, respectively. The interesting exceptions to this will be discussed at length below in the section on fertility variance within occupations. The individual occupational values for AM1/71–80 and AM3/86–90 and for their ranked equivalents (RANK/AM1 and RANK/AM3), used in the calculations for Table 7.1, can be found in the appropriate columns of Appendix C.

The first panel of Appendix C, containing the occupations of lowest fertility, shows that the ancient professions of the law, of arms and of the church, along with medicine and a range of 'newer' professions such as civil engineers, architects and accountants are, indeed, to be found among the leaders of the trend towards smaller families, as reflected in Figure 7.1.[4] Secondly, the aristocratic and independently wealthy are also to be found here, best represented by the occupational category of 'private means' (204).[5] Thirdly in the lower half of the panel and at the top of the

[4] Together these comprise the liberal professions, which are here defined as the following eighteen occupational categories (IDs in brackets): barristers (17); army officers (9); officers of the navy, marine (11); physicians, surgeons (20); solicitors (18); banks – officials, clerks (46); civil, mining – engineers (25); painters, sculptors (26); scientific pursuits (24); dentists (21); Anglican clergy (13); architects (27); accountants (43); teachers (22); civil service – officers, clerks (5); authors, editors, journalists (23); chemists, druggists (148); nonconformist clergy (14). These represented 3.25% of all married males in the 195 occupations.

[5] Numbers before occupational names, or in brackets afterwards, are ID numbers for the occupations and do not refer to variable values. Wherever there is more than one ID listed together in the text or footnotes, the order in which they are listed is that in which they occur in the relevant Table or Appendix under discussion at the time.

second panel can be found most of the nine clerical and commercial categories.[6]

Fourthly, as can be seen from Figure 7.1, 'retired from business' (201) was particularly important because of its numerical size, comprising no less than 3% of the total of all married males (it was the third largest occupational category after ID 84, coal hewers, and ID 61, carmen, carters). Indeed, this single occupation contained almost as many married couples as all the eighteen categories of liberal professions put together. Thus, 'retired from business' was at the core of an important set of commercial and business occupations with extremely low fertility. This was a social group which was quite distinct from the professions, and whose significance as early birth controllers has been somewhat obliterated from consideration by the professional model of fertility decline.

Among the leading ranks of birth controllers (the first twenty or so occupations listed in Appendix C) there can also be found a number of occupations from the official class II. These anomalous class II occupations are mostly categories of proprietors drawn from the business sector. Although Stevenson was prepared to accept into social class I a few occupations drawn from the business community, most were allocated to class II and he does not necessarily seem to have selected those exhibiting the lowest fertility for class I status. Builders (123) and coal mineowners (87) were both included by Stevenson in class I but their fertility levels seem quite out of place for such a designation (they are to be found towards the bottom of the second and third panels of Appendix C, respectively). Coal (and metal) mineowners, agents, managers (87) is consistently the lowest placed (i.e. highest fertility) occupation in class I, according to all three fertility indices. Indeed, according to the index for the youngest marrying, AM1/71–80, the fertility level of this occupation was actually typical of class V![7] While including these two categories from the business community in class I, several other much lower fertility business categories were excluded by Stevenson, such as lodging, boarding house keepers (188), tobacconists (185) and, especially, 'retired from business' (201). Although the single category 'merchants (commodity undefined)' (40) was justifiably (according to its low fertility) included in class I, other 'merchants' of the business community were consigned to class II despite their similarly low fertility. The latter included the more capitalised among the various categories of wholesale dealers: those in jewellery (122), two in textiles (169, 168), and one in footwear (173).

Stevenson's tendency to define only the liberal professions – even including their junior and clerical staffs – as being of highest status in his social class I, while relegating almost all of those involved in commerce to a lower social position may,

6 Counting such clerical and commercial occupations as the following nine categories: PO officers and clerks (2); law clerks (19); auctioneers, etc. (44); commercial travellers (42); brokers, agents, factors (41); commercial, business clerks (45); insurance – officials, clerks (47); railway – officials, clerks (49); insurance – agents (48). Together these represented 6.6% of all married males in the 195 occupations.

7 Yet, Stevenson was sufficiently certain of their elevated status to include this occupational group, with a dozen other class I occupations, in an élite 'class Ia', those which he considered most definitely composed of 'the middle or upper classes'. *FMR* Pt 2, p. xvi.

indeed, have accurately reflected a genuine contemporary assessment of social status differences. In that case, however, the low fertility of the business community simply constitutes further evidence, along with that of the textile workers, that the chronological order of precedence in the social pattern of changing fertility behaviour in British society did not conform to the conventional status hierarchy, as claimed by the professional model. (But it may alternatively be interpreted as indicating an imprecise knowledge of the business community on the part of Stevenson and his officials, probably due to, and compounded by, a biased assessment of such commercial occupations' social standing, relative to that of the professions. The latter seems eminently likely: chapter 3, above, has given an account of the historical origins of this ideological bias in official thinking.)

It should not escape attention that there are three occupations among this first panel in Appendix C, the lowest-fertility occupations, which Stevenson assigned neither to his class I nor even to class II. These are: domestic indoor servants (31), college, club–service (37) and caretakers (not government) (39). All three of these male occupations are predominantly composed of couples who lived in the direct employ and in close social contact with the most wealthy part of society, being their personal servants.[8]

Lodging house keepers have already been mentioned in the leading group of low fertility occupations and are indicated as such in Figure 7.1. They are also joined there by restaurateurs and café owners (187), and hoteliers and inn-keepers (189), both of which are found in the uppermost quarter of the second panel of Appendix C. Some at least of the latter category, which includes publicans, would have had unequivocally working-class origins and associates. It is interesting to note that all three of these categories, along with tobacconists (185), were exceptional in the degree to which females were employed in their industries: approaching equal numbers in three cases and actually massively exceeding males by a factor of eight to one in the case of lodging house keepers.[9] These occupations were also similar to each other in that they married at unusually young ages considering their low completed fertility. Nuptiality patterns are discussed at length below on pp. 335–50, where it is shown that in general there was a strong correlation between occupations with low fertility and late age at marriage; and the significance for fertility behaviour of substantial differences between sectors of employment in the sex ratios at work is a theme which will be further discussed below in the final section of this chapter.

Also in the second panel of Appendix C there are found the remaining

[8] These three occupations amounted to 0.7% of married males in the 195 occupations. There were separate categories in the full occupational classification of the census for 'Warehousemen' and for 'Messengers, Porters, Watchmen (not Rail or Gov't)', both of which were classified into Order II, suborder 5. It therefore seems reasonable to assume that ID 39 'caretakers (not gov't)', which derives from suborder 3 of Order IV 'Domestic Offices or Services', related to domestic or club caretakers and porters, and not to those employed in industrial or commercial establishments.

[9] Calculations from Census 1911, Volume X, Tables 3, 8.

occupations connected with personal service upon the propertied classes: domestic coachmen, grooms (32); domestic gardeners (35); and barmen (190), and waiters (not domestic) (191).[10] This second set of servants differs from those in the first panel in that their contact with their employers was less intimate, being either outdoor servants or employees of independent commercial establishments catering to the upper and middle classes; they are therefore grouped separately in Figure 7.1. There is, then, a quite well-defined effect on fertility levels, whereby couples working in the deferential, personal service occupations returned fertility levels significantly below that associated with their social class allocation in 1911 by Stevenson. Further evidence for the importance of this effect is provided by all of the other class IV occupations which record extraordinarily low fertility levels for an occupation so classed: men of the navy (12); civil service messengers (incl. PO) (4); postmen (3); police (6).[11] These, too, are occupations of petty officialdom intimately associated with the institutions of deference in Victorian and Edwardian society, to which should also be added 'church, chapel, cemetery officers' (16). These five categories are therefore grouped together in Figure 7.1.[12]

The second panel of occupations additionally contains all the remaining nine categories of 'dealers' – those in foodstuffs, hardware, clothing and household materials – to add to those merchants and dealers already mentioned above (in jewellery, fabrics and clothing).[13] Within the distibution sector, there is a clear split between the categories of dealers and those of retailers in their recorded

[10] These four occupations comprised 2.25% of married males in the 195 occupations. At this time most waiters (191) would, of course, be waiting on the upper classes. It is assumed here that those returning themselves as barmen (190) would also have comprised mostly those working in establishments similar to the waiters. Of course, it is certainly the case that 'barmen' was an occupation of somewhat mixed social composition, requiring a judgement to be made. It seems unlikely that very many married men aged in their forties and fifties would have found primary employment as non-proprietorial barmen in working-class public houses at this time: this would more likely have been an occupation of younger working-class men. Although the latter would have returned themselves as 'barmen' in the census, they would not in general have been married to women aged 45–58 years old, who were the subject of this analysis. The occupation's extremely low completed fertility, as measured here, indicates that this reasoning is probably correct: most older male barmen, married to women of this age, were probably working in genteel establishments.

[11] ID 10 'soldiers and NCOs' is not available for fertility analysis because of the small numbers of married couples.

[12] These five occupations totalled almost exactly 2.0% of all married males in the 195 occupations.

[13] In rank order of their fertility levels, these nine categories of dealers were: ironmongers/hardware merchants (117); grocers, dealers in beverages (183); clothiers, outfitters (171); pawnbrokers (197); cheesemongers, provision dealers (176); bakers, confectioners (dealers) (182); furniture dealers (139); corn, flour, seed–merchants, dealers (180); coal, coke – merchants, dealers (90). 'Clothiers, outfitters' (171) and pawnbrokers (197) may both seem marginal cases for allocation to the category of dealers, rather than retailers. However, given the much greater amount of capital tied up in stock which was required in order to operate as a clothier or pawnbroker relative to any of the food retailers discussed below, it seems reasonable to retain them with the 'dealers'. Pawnbrokers are referred to by Winstanley as 'the working man's bankers': *The shopkeeper's world*, ch. 12. Certainly their fertility behaviour is typical of dealers and much lower than all retailers. Altogether the fourteen kinds of dealer, including the five previously mentioned in the text (IDs 40, 122, 169, 168, 173), represented 5.0% of all married males enumerated in the 195 occupations.

fertility behaviour. While the former predominantly share the low fertility levels associated with the non-manual occupations mentioned so far, the latter exhibit fertility levels more typical of the manual working-class occupations. Yet, according to the professional model's classification, dealers and shopkeepers were simply lumped together within class II. This has entirely obscured the possibility of discerning this marked difference in the fertility patterns of these two different social groups.

Inspection of the second panel also reveals that there is an interesting split visible within the textiles sector of industry. Of the twelve constituent occupations of class VI, the three relating to the West Riding wool and worsted industry are quite distinctive in returning the lowest fertility levels: spinners, weavers and others in wool are all clustered together in the upper half of the second panel of Appendix C. Two of the four Lancashire-based cotton occupations then follow in the bottom quarter of the panel plus a third at the very top of the third panel. Here, among the middle quintile of thirty-nine occupations, there are the remaining half dozen textiles occupations. But the fourth cotton category, spinning processes (157), in fact records the highest fertility of any of these twelve textiles occupations, hence its separate location in Figure 7.1.

This points to a yet further degree of demographic differentiation within the textiles sector. Not only were there apparently quite distinct fertility régimes in West Yorkshire and in Lancashire and not only were these two localities somewhat different from those engaged in other branches of the textiles industry, but also within the Lancashire cotton industry there seems to have been a sufficiently systematic divergence between the families of the male spinners and those of other categories of male employment to show up as a marked fertility difference in this nationally aggregated data. Furthermore, all this variance *within* the textiles industry is despite the shared characteristic of the industrial sector as a whole: that of being in the van of the fertility decline among the manual working classes of the country. Thus, even among this relatively tightly defined socio-economic group with distinctively similar fertility behaviour – when viewed from afar with such a cumbersome measuring instrument as the official classification scheme – it is still the case that socially significant differentiation in fertility behaviour appears as soon as a more discerning inspection is made.

It is also obvious from Appendix C that this reputation for low fertility in the late nineteenth century, which textiles workers have long had, should be shared with certain other manual occupations. Apart from the wool operatives of West Yorkshire, one of the other leading low-fertility sectors of the manual working population appears to have been the skilled men in the jewellery and precious metals trades (IDs 119, 120), geographically concentrated mostly in the metropolis and in the Hockley district of Birmingham. This was evidently no surprise to Stevenson who placed them – uniquely for manual occupations – in his class II. Doubtless this was due to the highly capitalised nature of the craft and its strong historical associations with the ultra-respectable world of banking.[14] As can be seen from Figure 7.1 other working-class occupations which exhibited very low fertility (but were not explicitly recognised as such by receiving class II status in Stevenson's scheme) included those in the printing trades (IDs 154, 155); piano, organ makers (121); and two relatively new occupations: electricians (103) and 'motor car–chassis makers and mechanics' (114).[15]

Turning to the middle panel of Appendix C,there are found all but one of the eight smaller scale shopkeeping and retailing businesses: general shopkeepers, dealers (196), nursery, seedsmen, florists (80), hairdressers, wig makers (174), milksellers, dairymen (175), greengrocers, fruiterers (184), fishmongers, poulterers (178), butchers (177), and bakers – biscuits, cakes (181) (the last in the next panel).[16] Secondly, there are workers in brewing (186) and cereal milling (179), who should probably be counted as a distinct social grouping from that of retailers, given the rather different working environments, though they appear to record very similar fertility levels. Thirdly, there are also several further categories of skilled manual workers, tending to be those artisan craftsmen who did not work primarily in metals and these are collected together in Figure 7.1 as 'Non-metal workers'.[17]

The relatively large occupation of 'erectors, fitters and turners' (98) is also found in this middle panel. This comprised a variety of relatively well-paid and independent artisans with general mechanical and engineering skills found in substantial numbers in almost every branch of industry. They traced their ancestry to the breed of millwrights who installed and maintained the first generations of factory machinery and were often referred to by their contemporaries as 'engineers', to the institutional chagrin of those who had qualified into the engineering profession. They are dealt with in Figure 7.1 as a social category in their own right, though no doubt one of rather mixed provenance.

Finally, there is also very noticeable in this middle panel of Appendix C a group of manual occupations which represent the main core of those employed with particular responsibilities in the rail and road transport industries (i.e. excluding general labouring and messenger categories which are found further down Appendix C).[18]

14 Wilson, *England's apprenticeship*, ch. 10.

15 These seven categories of low-fertility manual occupations between them accounted for just over 2% of the married male workforce in the 195 occupations.

16 Between them, these eight retailing occupations comprise 4.2% of married males in the 195 occupations.

17 There are eight categories of non-metal artisans: upholsterers (138); and tailors (170) were, of course, both connected with the textiles industry. Other such crafts found here were: coach, carriage makers (115); saddlers, harness makers (153); and wheelwrights (116). However, cabinet makers (136), boot, shoe makers (172) and sawyers, wood-cutting machinists (140) all recorded a slightly higher fertility, overlapping with some of the metal-handling artisans. Plumbers (132) and carpenters (125) are not included because they belong to the building trades discussed below. Altogether the eight categories of non-metal craftsmen totalled 2.6% of the married males in the 195 fertility occupations.

18 Signalmen (52); motor car drivers (domestic and non-domestic) (34); railway guards (51); stable

Across this central range of the frequency distribution, where there is little absolute difference between the recorded fertility levels of the thirty-nine occupations listed, there are, then, half a dozen distinguishable types of occupation and each type is associated with radically different kinds of working conditions and degree of control or authority over its work processes. Stevenson's classes I, II, III, IV and VI all have their representatives among the occupations collected here in the third panel of Appendix C, underlining, once more, the limitations of the professional model's graded hierarchy as an informative summary of the patterns of occupational fertility variation.

Turning to the fourth panel of somewhat higher fertility occupations in Appendix C, there is first a group of relatively independent or petty bourgeois occupations connected with the agricultural sector: other gardeners (not domestic) (82); market gardeners (including labourers) (81); farm–bailiffs, foremen (75); and gamekeepers (36). In Figure 7.1 these have been added to the substantial category of farmers (73) found in the previous panel of Appendix C.[19] Although recording somewhat higher fertility than most other petty bourgeois occupations such as those in retailing, their fertility is distinctly lower than that of the three categories of agricultural labourers, which Stevenson assigned to the special class VIII. This difference is no surprise. Apart from the social distinction between the two, market gardening was experiencing a substantial expansion in prosperity and numbers during the four decades before 1911, contrary to the more general trend of depression and falling employment in the agricultural sector.[20] The agricultural labourers are found tightly bunched together in the middle of the final panel of Appendix C, along with shepherds (76), who were not included in class VIII by Stevenson for some reason which remains obscure. These observations on the fertility of agricultural workers provide further testimony, in two different ways, to the relatively powerful effect of economic sector upon occupational fertility levels. On the one hand the generally high fertility of the agricultural sector appears to influence even those working relatively independently in its more commercial branches, such that their fertility is the highest among petty bourgeois

keepers/coach, cab proprietors (57); railway engine – drivers, stokers, cleaners (50); rail – pointsmen (53); coach, cabmen (58); rail – porters (56); and tram – drivers (62). Note that although included here with the more highly trained or responsible group of rail/road workers, the tram-drivers record a significantly higher fertility, indicating that they were less clearly differentiated from the labouring categories of the transport sector, which are found in the next panel, with higher fertility. These seven labouring categories within the transport industry are: trams – others (64); messengers, watchmen (not rail or government) (72); horsekeepers (59); rail – platelayers (54); engine-drivers (miscellaneous – not rail) (200); carmen, carters (61); and rail – labourers (55). Altogether the first group, of lower fertility transit occupations, comprised 3.3% of the married males in the 195 fertility occupations; while the seven labouring occupations amounted to 6.5%

19 These five categories of agriculturalist comprise 4.5% of married males in the 195 occupations.

20 Alun Howkins has estimated that, including women workers, there was as much as a 75% rise in the numbers in market gardening and nurserying, 1871–1911 (to a total of 140,000 in 1911). According to Howkins there was a 44% fall in the agricultural sector's total employment over the same period (from a figure of 1.61 million in 1871). Howkins, *Reshaping rural England*, pp. 171, 211.

employments. Secondly, although the four different kinds of agricultural labourer (i.e. including shepherds) were employed in a diversity of farming régimes in different parts of the country, their averaged fertility behaviour was almost identical.

A great many of the occupations in the penultimate panel of Appendix C comprise the remainder of the skilled manual workers, these being mostly fifteen categories associated with metalliferous products, which are collected together in Figure 7.1 as 'Metals and engineering trades'.[21] Those in the building and construction industry are also principally contained within this and the final panel. They show the expected separation between slightly lower fertility tradesmen and the higher fertility of their respective labourers.[22]

However, it was certainly not universally the case that the more highly paid and skilled workers within a given industrial sector always recorded lower fertility than the labourers, a notion which has, of course, been raised to the level of a dogma as a result of the long-standing acceptance of the professional model of fertility decline. The best known and quantitatively most significant example of the inverse was in the coal-mining industry where the high-earning and higher-status hewers at the coal face recorded highest fertility, as can be seen from Figure 7.1. It has been pointed out that this was also true of cotton spinners and it can be seen from the final panel of Appendix C that this pattern additionally applied in the shipbuilding sector. The more skilled and highly paid ship platers and riveters (109) record higher fertility than shipyard labourers (undefined) (111).

Within the iron and steel industry there seems to have been no straightforward relationship between skill and lower fertility: blast-furnacemen (91) and puddlers (92) in iron and steel production both recorded much higher fertility than either ironfoundry labourers (96) or undifferentiated workers in steel manufacture smelting and founding (93), although the most skilled category of all, moulders

[21] These fifteen predominantly metals-handling tradesmen represented 4.9% of the married male workforce in the 195 occupations. They comprised the following: gasfitters (133); rail – coach, wagon makers (112); shipwrights (110); cutlers, scissors makers (105); electrical apparatus makers, fitters (102); cycle makers (113); tool makers (104); metal machinists (99); tinplate goods makers (107); blacksmiths, strikers (97); wire workers (106); engineering – undefined labourers (100); coopers (141); boilermakers (101); brass, bronze workers (108).

[22] The rank order from low to high fertility is as follows: builders (123); timber merchants (142); plumbers (132); carpenters (125); painters, decorators (131); masons (128); plasterers (130); french polishers (137); bricklayers (126); followed by five categories of labourers: road labourers (135); navvies (134); builders' labourers (124); masons' labourers (129); bricklayers' labourers (127). In the 1911 census, Volume X, using information from column 11 on the household schedule ('Industry or Service with which worker is connected'), it is stated that 57% of a total of 17,116 gasfitters enumerated were *not* employed in the Housebuilding sector of the economy; and therefore the occupation of gasfitters is not included in this list of building tradesmen but in the previous grouping of metals-handling tradesmen. (For comparison only 15.5% of carpenters and 13% of plumbers were employed outside the Housebuilding sector.) The numbers employed in the housebuilding sector as a whole had actually fallen by 9% since the 1901 census, with the tailing off of a long housebuilding boom which had lasted from 1897 to 1907. Nevertherless, this sector was still a large employer: the building tradesmen listed above represented 4.3% of all married males in the 195 occupations; and the building labourers counted for a further 2.3%.

and fettlers (95), did, indeed, record the lowest fertility in the industry. However, for a 'skilled' occupation which Stevenson assigned to class III, moulders and fettlers recorded an extremely high fertility, much closer to the average class V fertility level than that for class III. There is, of course, the perhaps significant difference that whereas the higher-paid building tradesmen such as plasterers and bricklayers could perhaps realistically aspire to the independent status of becoming self-employed (if not actual small-scale employers), this was a comparatively rare form of independence for coal miners and ship-riveters and especially for skilled workers in iron foundries and steel mills, for all their higher skills and earnings.[23] The influence of proprietorship upon fertility behaviour will be addressed in detail in the next section.

Among the highest fertility occupations there are still important patterns of occupational variation to be observed, which are reflected in the groupings in Figure 7.1. An instance of this is the 10% difference in recorded fertility levels within the chemicals industry between those employed in manufacturing chemicals and in rubber, grease, soap and manure producing plants (IDs 147, 150, 151 at the bottom of the previous panel of Appendix C), as against workers in the same sector of the economy producing brick and glass (IDs 143, 146), with tanners and vegetable oil refiners (IDs 152, 149) falling between the two. These may reflect regional as well as income or workplace differences. Among the growing numbers of municipal employees spread around the nation's towns and cities, specifically regional or local differences cannot, of course, be addressed with nationally aggregated data of this sort. But there is a marked difference in recorded fertility between those in electricity and water supply (IDs 194, 193), and those with higher fertility employed in refuse disposal and the gas works (IDs 195, 192). As one might imagine, the last two were considered far less desirable and were lower-paid forms of municipal employment.[24]

The three kinds of mining occupation exhibit considerable variation in their fertility behaviour, though all are contained within the final panel of Appendix C. Coal miners at the face (84) record, quite clearly, the highest fertility of any occupation, nearly 17% greater than the figure for stone miners (89); whilst iron miners (88) fall exactly between the two. By contrast, the three occupations

[23] Unfortunately, the census volumes do not give information, as they do for many other occupations, regarding the proportion of coal miners who were either self-employed, or even employers. It seems to have been assumed that all those enumerated were employees. The small number of self-employed miners probably therefore appeared under ID 87 coal – mineowners, which may therefore explain its high fertility. As for riveters in shipbuilding, the census shows that, amongst married men, there were 130.62 employees above age 44 for every non-employee in this occupation, as against the comparable figures of 3.068 and 5.679 for plasterers and bricklayers, respectively. Calculations from Census 1911, Volume X, Table 7. See below, next section, for further analysis of this dimension of information on 'industrial status' (i.e. employership status).

[24] For instance Charles Booth, writing of employment in the metropolis in the 1890s, found the lowest paid in-migrants from the countryside working in the gasworks and as railway labourers. Booth, *Life and labour*, ser. 2, Vol. V, p. 33.

connected with seaport labouring (IDs 68, 69, 71) all record very similar fertility levels, suggesting that, like the tightly bunched agricultural labouring occupations, they are recruited from a single population as regards fertility behaviour and its determinants – and, again, despite great differences in geographical location. Were, then, docklands another distinctive form of generic community from a socio-economic and demographic point of view, similar to that of the better documented cases of coal-mining villages?[25]

Finally, it seems well worthwhile to comment on the appearance of 'china, pottery manufacture' (145) in the last panel of high-fertility occupations, despite the fact that this was largely an industry where there was abundant opportunity for participation in paid employment outside the home on the part of women, both before and after marriage. It is this aspect of the textiles communities which has always been considered a key to the explanation of their unique, low-fertility demographic régime, which included a peculiarly early adoption of birth controlling practices and the continuation of excessive infant mortality in spite of these smaller families. But it would seem from this control comparison with the earthenware industry of the Potteries that the employment of married women away from the home may only be a part of a satisfactory explanation of the unusually low fertility of the textiles communities, and not, alone, a sufficient explanation.[26]

Variation in composition of occupations by employment status

Contrary to Stevenson's belief at the time, the system of occupational classification used by the GRO for the 1911 census did not always succeed in distinguishing adequately between the individuals' personal occupations, as distinct from their industrial functions.[27] Columns 10 and 11 on the census schedule did provide for the collection of separate details regarding 'Personal Occupation' and 'Industry or Service with which worker is connected', respectively (see Appendix A). But the single scheme of occupational definition used for collation and tabulation of this data could not cope with the demands of what were, in effect, two independent dimensions of information on each individual.

[25] Haines, *Fertility and occupation* (a study of British and US mining communities); Mosk, 'Fertility and occupation'.

[26] It should, however, be noted that there were significant differences between the two industries in the relevant characteristics. First, the Potteries employed only about one third the total workforce of the woollen, and one fifth that of the cotton industries. Secondly, among the working population, the number of married or widowed women aged 45–54 at the 1911 census, expressed as a proportion of the number of married men of the same age, was only 23% for the Potteries, as against 37% for the wool and 55% for the cotton industries. Calculations from Tables 3, 7, 8 of Volume X of the 1911 census. It is not, however, intended to suggest that these differences are in themselves a sufficient explanation for the anomaly noted in the text, especially in view of the fact that it was the wool and not the cotton industry which exhibited lowest fertility of all. For further, extensive discussion of the reasons for differences between the Potteries and the textiles communities, see below, pp. 496–8.

[27] Stevenson, 'Suggested lines of advance', p. 701.

Stevenson was certainly in good company at this time in overestimating the coherence of the census's occupational nomenclature. His remarks on the subject closely resemble the contemporaneous views of A. L. Bowley, the most methodologically sophisticated and articulate quantitative empirical investigator of the period.[28] Bowley's ideas were important in the eventual resolution of this problem, culminating in the vastly improved official system of dual occupational and industrial classification adopted at the British Empire Statistical Conference in 1920 and operated from the 1921 census onwards.[29] Yet even Bowley had not yet realised what the true requirements were, as an article of his in 1908 demonstrates (it was not until the publication of his important *The nature and purpose of the measurement of social phenomena* in 1915 that this advance in his understanding of the problem is evident).[30]

The main shortcoming of the occupational nomenclature used to tabulate the results of the 1911 census was that many categories of industrial employment contained a mixture of employers and the self-employed along with the larger bulk of employees. Stevenson particularly came to appreciate this drawback when he attempted to place the occupations into his graded scheme of social classification.[31] Yet, the information collected at the census in 1911 did contain a means by which this problem could have been largely solved: the returns as to employment status in column 12 of the census schedule, which allowed the individuals within an occupation to be classified into employers, self-employed and employees. However, Stevenson refused to utilise this data to help to refine the occupational definitions employed.

Part of the reason for this lay in Stevenson's early application of the social classification system to the illustration of class-differential mortality calculated from vital registration and census data combined. It had therefore been necessary, when first constructing a published version of the social classification scheme, to be governed by the limitations on occupational information available in the less discerning occupational description given on death registration forms, where there were no details as to employment status. Hence much of the original need for the indeterminate class II. However, in the 1923 *Report*, which was based on census data alone, Stevenson could have divided up many occupations according to the employment status information on the household schedules. The reason why he did not do so appears to hark back to the long-established distrust which the

28 See ch. 5, n. 140. Bowley was a key member of the Royal Statistical Society's Census Committee. Bowley's article of 1908 was far more detailed and rigorous than the collective deliberations of the Committee itself, whose recommendations were, nevertheless, very important. On the latter, see *JRRS* 71 (1908), pp. 496–9; *JRRS* 72 (1909), pp. 574–93.

29 For an illuminating account of these issues at the 1920 conference, see Beaud and Prévost 'La Classification canadienne'.

30 This was probably the most sophisticated treatment of the subjects of social classification and occupation-related measurement until the post-Second World War work on social mobility under D. V. Glass.

31 74th ARRG, p. xli. Cited above, pp. 258–9.

medical statisticians of the GRO held for the employment status information, an innovation which had originally been forced upon them as the one concession to the pressure mounted at the Treasury inquiry in 1890 by Marshall and Booth.[32]

It was claimed repeatedly at the GRO that it was a question never answered accurately, and therefore merely a superfluous addition to the overburdened census schedule and an onerous extra task in tabulation.[33] Representatives of the Home Office and the Labour Department of the Board of Trade continually had to defend inclusion of this question on the census schedule against attempts by the GRO to have it removed. One of the interesting by-products of this long wrangle was the recommendation in 1900 – which was duly taken up by the GRO – that the wording on the 1901 census schedule be changed from 'Master' to 'Employer', 'because many workmen appear to dislike the former term'.[34] Nevertheless, Stevenson seems to have had no faith in the efficacy of this alteration, and continued virtually to ignore the variable in any serious analysis. In 1927 he was to be found still attempting to persuade the civil service Committee on the 1931 census to have the column dropped from the schedule.[35] He was forced to declare himself 'surprised' when presented with the results of a recent investigation conducted by the Ministry of Labour, a follow-up exercise on the responses given at the previous census which proved that there was almost no mis-reportage among a sample of 80,000 men who had returned themselves as foremen at the 1921 census.[36] This, the only rigorous test of the suspicions expressed by the medical statisticians, suggests that they were probably wrong, and that the information as to employment status returned at the census was generally *bona fide*, and could, therefore, have been utilised to refine the occupational classification.

This is an important practical conclusion for present purposes. The availability of this information on employment status in tabulated form means that it may at least be worthwhile undertaking some form of statistical assessment of the scale of effect of this factor on the recorded fertility levels of those occupations of variable composition by employment status. This consideration particularly affects the somewhat disparate and varied set of occupations which are subsumed within the categories of the skilled and semi-skilled manual workers, which Stevenson tended to allocate to the official social classes III, IV and VI.

Although a breakdown by employment status is not available in the fertility tables published in 1923, there do exist published tables in Volume X of the 1911 census, which give the numbers returning themselves as employers or workers on

[32] See pp. 115–16.

[33] See the comments made by W. Ogle in: 'Discussion' (1886), p. 438; and 'Discussion' (1894), p. 683. Additionally, there are the critical comments of A. Bellingham (Secretary at the GRO) recorded in an extensive GRO internal 'Memorandum in Reference to the next census of England and Wales in March 1911', dated July 1908 (PRO RG 19/45, pp. 26–7).

[34] H. Llewellyn Smith, Labour Dept to GRO, dated 21 November 1900 (PRO RG 19/10, Item 11).

[35] Meeting of 21 November 1927 (PRO RG 19/120, p. 1).

[36] PRO RG 19/120, p. 16. Report by Mr Ramsbottom of the Ministry of Labour to meeting of 20 February 1928.

own account in each occupation.[37] This makes it possible to conduct a statistical assessment of the extent to which differential levels of fertility among these occupations were associated with co-variations in their proportional composition as between employers, the self-employed and employees. Unfortunately, Volume X does not give age-specific information on employment status, although it does so for the distinction by marital status. It therefore seemed that the best index to take would be one expressing the ratio of all married employers plus all married own account workers to all those married males in the occupation aged over 44 years. This is the ratio index R/OWNEMP.[38] Similarly an index expressing the ratio of employers only to all those married males over 44 years old (R/EMPLOY) was computed; and one for the ratio of self-employed only (R/OWNACC). In Appendix D, they are also rank-scored as: RANK/OEMP; RANK/EMPLOY; RANK/OWNACC.

The Spearman rank-order correlation coefficients for these three ratio indices when correlated with each other and, more importantly, with the three fertility level indices are given in Table 7.2A.[39]

These three indices all consistently show the expected positive correlations with the fertility level indices, the ratio of employers rather than of self-employed clearly being the more significant correlate (since the smallest ratios indicate the highest proportions of employers to employees, this is therefore reflected in a positive correlation between low fertility and low ratio figures). The other positive correlations are reasonably strong across the dataset as a whole and suggest that it may be well worth while examining the data in more detail. In Appendix D the fertility occupations are again listed in order according to AM2/81–5, and the figures for the three significantly correlated employment status indices are displayed (for the 110 occupations for which employment status information is available). A number of further, detailed points emerge from this tabulation.

37 Census 1911, Volume X, Tables 3, 7.

38 There are two reasons for constructing the ratio index in this way. If a ratio is based on all married workers of all ages in the occupation, then systematic distortion will occur where occupations differ in the proportion of younger workers they contain. This differential property is of no direct interest to the attempt to obtain a comparative indicator of the employment status mix amongst men married to women aged 45–54; and it would therefore constitute an unwanted distortion. On the other hand, it is desirable to include all married men above age 44 (and not merely those aged 45–54) as the base number for the ratio, in recognition of the fact that the employers and self-employed would tend to be most concentrated at the highest ages in any given occupation, and so differences in the age structure at these higher ages should be taken into account. It should be noted that the indices are only available for 110 of the 195 fertility occupations, since there were many for which the employment status distinction was inapplicable (e.g. independent professionals, clerks of all forms, labourers of all forms, municipal or railway employees). There is one less occupation for indices using the self-employed figure because ID 94, tinplate manufacture, uniquely returned no self-employed workers in 1911.

39 The fourth new index in Table 7.2, RATIO/OE, measured the ratio of own account workers to employers in each occupation, regardless of the number of employees. As might be expected, this ratio is completely uncorrelated with differential fertility behaviour and the detailed results are not, therefore, reproduced in Appendix D.

Table 7.2 *Spearman R^2 correlation coefficients between employment status and fertility level indices*

	R/OWNEMP	R/EMPLOY	R/OWNACC	RATIO/OE
A. Whole sample (N=110)				
AM2/81–5	0.54811	0.63331	0.45709	−0.00805
	0.0001	0.0001	0.0001	0.9335
AM1/71–80	0.52300	0.58396	0.45460	−0.07597
	0.0001	0.0001	0.0001	0.4302
AM3/86–90	0.44550	0.54010	0.36874	0.04667
	0.0001	0.0001	0.0001	0.6282
B. All occupations except dealing, retailing and textiles (N=74)				
AM2/81–5	0.52634	0.55633	0.48541	−0.17037
	0.0001	0.0001	0.0001	0.1467
AM1/71–80	0.51639	0.48882	0.51334	−0.29383
	0.0001	0.0001	0.0001	0.0111
AM3/86–90	0.42620	0.47886	0.40748	−0.11775
	0.0002	0.0001	0.0003	0.3177
C. 'Skilled' occupations only (N=45)				
AM2/81–5	0.52925	0.62477	0.44440	0.07128
	0.0002	0.0001	0.0022	0.6417
AM1/71–80	0.48696	0.47958	0.45389	−0.04071
	0.0007	0.0009	0.0017	0.7906
AM3/86–90	0.31726	0.40975	0.28327	0.07339
	0.0337	0.0052	0.0594	0.6319

Note: statistical significance levels underneath.

First, it is remarkable that all those commercial occupations recording low fertility do so despite often containing a substantial admixture of employees, which in the case of '188 lodging house keepers' and '169 dealers in textiles fabrics' amounts to half or more of the number enumerated above the age of 44. Either this means that those within the occupation who *were* employers must have been recording extremely low fertility – probably even lower than most professionals; or it simply means that the relatively low fertility of these occupations was not confined only to those drawn from the class of employers.

Secondly, there is confirmation of the extraordinary behaviour of the textiles operatives. Their low fertility is achieved despite the virtual absence of workers on own account or employers from their ranks.

Thirdly, the marked difference in fertility behaviour between dealers and retailers, many of them handling similar products (often foodstuffs), is all the more intriguing on inspecting their composition by employment status. For, if anything, the retailers (who have higher fertility) are constituted from a greater proportion of independent, capital-owning proprietors (employers plus self-employed) than are the dealing occupations. In fact, all the retailing occupations are drawn from among those occupations containing the greatest concentration of proprietors (and therefore the smallest proportion of employees).[40] Thus, the dealer categories record their lower fertility in spite of considerable dilution by their own employees, whereas the retailers return a higher fertility even though proportionately more of them are independent, autonomous proprietors.

There are several possible reasons for this. In their cross-national historical studies of shopkeepers and artisans, Crossick and Haupt note that there was a fundamental social difference among shopkeepers between those families which comprised the well-established, geographically stable, ratepaying shopocracy of each town, as against a large group of more transient traders.[41] As described in John Benson's study of *Penny capitalists*, some of the latter could be little more than stall-keepers who only took up selling during times of hardship due to unemployment, disability or old age.[42] Probably most of these rather marginal, small traders would have returned themselves as self-employed retailers rather than as self-employed dealers, thereby especially inflating the number of apparent 'proprietors' among the retailers. This distinction in the fertility behaviour of dealers and retailers tallies with the views of C. P. Hosgood, based on detailed local research, who has argued that in the Edwardian period the 3,300 shopkeepers of Leicester 'comprised two distinct factions – "domestic" or small shopkeepers, who were firmly grounded within the working-class community, and "principal" or large shopkeepers, who participated fully in the middle-class world'.[43]

It may also be the case that those who were employees in the more substantial enterprises typically owned by dealers were more likely to restrict their fertility at this time than the independent small shopkeepers. Dealers' assistants and shop-workers in large stores may well have been somewhat akin in their aspirations and economic position to another low-fertility social group at this time: office workers. Like 'white-collar' office jobs, these were positions where the remuneration fell substantially below the level required to maintain the high standards of appearance set for the workers and assumed to be desirable by the social superiors who were their bosses and clients at the place of work, creating for this group a particularly extreme discrepancy between aspirational and actual living standards.[44] All this only underlines and enlarges upon the important differences between the two types of proprietary selling occupation, retailers and

[40] On this criterion of composition by employment status two marginal occupations, '197 pawnbrokers' and '174 hairdressers, wig makers', classify themselves as 'dealers' and 'retailers', respectively.

[41] Crossick and Haupt (eds.), *Shopkeepers and master artisans*, p. 7.

[42] Benson, *The penny capitalists*. This was a variant of the modest, semi-domestic trading activities pursued on and off by many working-class wives to supplement family incomes and mostly not recorded at all by the census.

[43] Hosgood, 'The "pigmies of commerce"', pp. 439–40.

[44] For extended discussion of this, see below, pp. 476–8.

dealers, which the official classification simply lumped together in class II. It appears that there was also an important social discontinuity between employees in dealing and those in mere retailing. This distinction was in terms of their social recruitment, their scale of economic activity, their aspirations, their working conditions and the extent to which they were likely to be integrated into the working-class or the middle-class 'worlds'; and this was apparently paralleled by a considerable divergence in fertility behaviour. In this particular branch of the service sector of the economy, it may be, therefore, that independent and proprietorial status *per se* was *less* likely to be correlated with fertility controlling behaviour than was association, even only as an employee, with the genteel milieu of the larger stores and enterprises which were increasingly appearing during the three decades prior to 1911.[45]

There are, then, at least three sets of occupations – dealers, retailers and textiles workers – whose fertility behaviour in relation to their relative composition by employment status is at variance with the expected positive relationship which has been found to obtain generally across the dataset of all 110 occupations.

It has already been mentioned that information on employment status might be especially relevant to the differences in fertility behaviour evident within the various categories of skilled and partly skilled manual workers. Does the proportion of employers or self-employed within each skilled manual occupation have a significant impact on their relative fertility behaviour?

In carrying out such an analysis of 'skilled' occupations, the definition of skill is itself highly problematic and whichever occupations are chosen for a statistical treatment, they will remain a disputed selection.[46] Both an inclusive and an exclusive approach to selection was therefore adopted. First, a statistical analysis was performed on all occupations except those in dealing, retailing and textiles occupations. Excluding the 36 occupations relating to these three sectors leaves a somewhat eclectic collection of 74 occupations. An additional analysis was therefore also performed on a restricted selection of just 45 occupations by further excluding, first, those occupations which contained only a very small proportion of employers plus self-employed relative to employees and, secondly, those where the ratio of employers to self-employed was very high. This was done on the grounds that these were two sets of occupations exhibiting an extreme degree of discontinuity between employers and employees, something relatively unusual for a skilled, craft or artisanal form of employment.[47]

45 Winstanley, *The shopkeeper's world*; Jeffreys, *Retail trading in Britain*; and see below, ch. 9, n. 98.

46 For a helpful discussion of the complex issue of skill in this period of British industrial history, see More, *Skill and the English working class*, especially chs. 1, 7–11. See also Savage, *The dynamics*, pp. 41–51, on craft apprenticeship skills and 'factory skills'; and Reid, *Social classes and social relations*, pp. 33–4, on apprenticeship training versus time-serving 'seniority', as different methods for acquiring skilled status in different industries.

47 All occupations in the uppermost quartile of values of R/OWNEMP (taking the distribution for the total of 110 cases) were omitted. This excluded occupations with more than 9.345 employees per

The results for each of these two analyses are presented in Table 7.2B and Table 7.2C. They show a broadly similar result to the original analysis for all 110 occupations. The only noteworthy difference was a strengthening in the positive correlation with fertility levels of the self-employed ratio index and a slight worsening of the employer ratio index for the larger selection of 74 occupations; however the more restricted subset of only 45 occupations shows a return to an almost identical correlation pattern to that for the overall set of 110 occupations. Differences between occupations in their proportional composition from the three different types of employment status – particularly the proportions of employers – was, therefore, of considerable importance in accounting for differentials in recorded fertility levels between the occupations of skilled and semi-skilled categories. (However, as with the whole sample, this still only explained less than half of the overall statistical variance.)

A major part of the reason for the very imperfect correlation between fertility levels and employment status may be that, as was found with the analysis of fertility and skill level, different industrial sectors or localities exerted their own strong and independent influences on the fertility behaviour of workers and their families. For instance, as Figure 7.1 shows, although skilled tradesmen in the building and construction sector tend to record lower fertility than the unskilled labourers in their own sector of industry, nevertheless their fertility is higher than the *unskilled* workers of many other industrial sectors, such as textiles, printing, non-metal trades; their fertility is also somewhat nearer to the levels recorded by their own labourers than to the fertility levels of many categories of skilled workers employed in other sectors of the economy.

What conclusions can be drawn from the mixed results of this exercise? It appears that those occupations where the proportion of self-employed and employer craftsmen was highest tended also to be those in which the practice of fertility controlling behaviour was more pronounced, indicated by the moderately strong positive correlation between fertility levels and the employment status indices. To risk the ecological fallacy, one might make the inference that amongst these men, predominantly aged 45–55, the results suggest that family limitation was mainly practised by the subset within each category of skilled workers who were independent masters while the remainder, who were still employees at this relatively senior stage of their working lives, would in that case have been returning the much higher fertility levels more typical of the manual working-class occupations composed entirely of employees: the various categories of labourers. However, there are certainly enough exceptions, in particular textiles workers and retailers, to warn against the premature acceptance of such an inference. This

non-employee. Secondly, all those from the lowest quartile of RATIO/OE were omitted, which excluded occupations where employers outnumbered own account workers by more than 3.73 to 1 (RATIO/OE less than 0.268).

hypothesis can in any case be directly investigated through an analysis of fertility variance within occupations.

Variance in fertility control within occupations

It is possible to make an assessment of the dispersion about the mean fertility level within the occupational divisions of the 1911 census. It will be recalled that it was argued at the commencement of the statistical analysis in the last chapter that the most significant single indicator of an occupation's fertility behaviour was the fertility level recorded for that subsection of each occupation whose wives married between the age of 20 and 24 because this was the modal or typical age at marriage in the great majority of occupations. By the same argument, there is available here information for the unusually early marrying (age 15–19) and the unusually late marrying (age 25–9) 'tails' of the normal distribution of age at marriage within each occupational category. In effect there are three distinct subpopulations for each occupation, according to their differing nuptiality behaviour. If these subpopulations all exhibit similar comparative fertility levels, this would be strong evidence against any significant degree of dispersion or variance in fertility behaviour within the occupational group. Indeed, differentiation according to marriage age is a particularly appropriate instrument for probing the extent to which the employer and employee components of skilled manual occupations might have represented socially distinct constituencies. Ogle's study of social variation in marriage ages and practices during the 1880s concluded that there was a marked correlation between low age at marriage and proletarian occupational status: those marrying late within each occupation might therefore be disproportionately represented among the employers and self-employed.[48]

Table 7.3 lists all those individual occupations, drawn from the whole set of 195 male occupations, which exhibit a significant degree of such variance in their relative fertility levels, as recorded for their three different nuptiality differentiated subpopulations.[49] The table presents a typology of six different manifestations of such variance. The six types really represent two major forms of variance, each form taking three statistical manifestations. In Group A, types 1, 3 and 5 comprise those occupations in which the tendency is for the elder-marrying to exhibit relatively higher fertility than the younger-marrying subpopulation. The opposite tendency obtains for Group B: types 2, 4 and 6. Overall, it should first be noted that there are in fact relatively few occupations listed in the six panels of Table 7.3. Of the total of 195 occupations, 164 do not exhibit any substantial internal variance in

[48] 48th ARRG, p. ix. See above, p. 82, for further details.

[49] An occupation appears in Table 7.3 if any one of the three fertility indices scored a rank position more than thirty-nine ranks (one fifth of the total number of rank positions) different from either of the other two. Obviously, this is an arbitrary criterion, which is simply intended to exclude a profusion of minor differences and to focus attention upon the most substantial cases.

Table 7.3 *Occupations displaying internal variance in their fertility levels according to wife's age at marriage*

Group A Fertility **increasing** with increasing age at marriage

Type 1: younger-marrying subset distinguished by low relative fertility

12 men of the navy
62 trams – drivers
113 cycle makers
58 coach, cabmen
67 merchant service – engineers
147 manufacturing chemists

Type 3: elder-marrying subset distinguished by high relative fertility

53 pointsmen, level crossing operators
51 railway – guards
66 merchant service – navigators

Type 5: gradient from elder to younger of high to low fertility

6 police
15 itinerant preachers
54 rail – platelayers
56 rail porters
73 farmers, graziers
181 bakers – biscuits, cakes
190 barmen
195 refuse disposal

Group B Fertility **decreasing** with increasing age at marriage

Type 2: younger-marrying subset distinguished by high relative fertility

142 timber merchants
184 greengrocers
87 coal mineowners, managers
90 coal, coke dealers
114 motor car – chassis makers, mechanics
115 coach, carriage makers
196 general shopkeepers, dealers

Type 4: elder-marrying subset distinguished by low relative fertility

136 cabinet makers
149 oil (vegetable) – millers, refiners
146 glass manufacture

Type 6: gradient from elder to younger of low to high fertility

163 hosiery
167 textiles – calenderers, finishers
187 cafe – owners, restaurateurs
207 cotton – cardroom, others

Note: see n. 49.

their fertility behaviour when measured in this way. In Group A there are 17 occupations and 14 in Group B. In Group A there was a tendency for the elder marrying to return a higher fertility level than the younger marrying. It is probably safe to assume that the appearance of the sea-faring occupations, IDs 12, 67, 66, is principally the result of the involuntary separation between spouses which is implied by pursuit of these occupations (something which may well apply also to ID 15).[50] 'Farmers, graziers' (73) might be an analogous case. If late age at marriage was forced upon certain individuals because they were waiting to 'inherit' a farm, rather than this reflecting any particular motivation to restrict family size, then once having acquired the farm and married, this would explain the unusually high relative fertility of those who married latest. On the other hand there may be some evidence here of farmers aiming at a particular family size but one which was sufficently large that only the younger-marrying farmers faced the need to restrain their fertility.[51]

Many of the other occupations in Group A may be those to which rural, Irish or overseas migrants to the towns tended to gravitate: these were all social groups often treated as ethnic aliens by the resident urbanites. Due to their rural origins, such migrants would typically have failed to establish themselves with an urban trade or industrial skill. It is a well-attested phenomenon of settled and established urban populations, certainly true of late nineteenth-century Britain, that the already-resident urbanites tended to monopolise the more lucrative sources of employment.[52] New arrivals therefore turned to these lower-paid service sector occupations, which required no apprenticeship, no 'contacts' and little, if any, special training (IDs 62, 58, 6, 190, 195). One hypothesis might, therefore, be that these occupations contained a high proportion of such migrants. Their nuptiality norms and fertility expectations may well have been somewhat different from those of the urban born and bred, and more typical of the four categories of agricultural labourers with their relatively late age at marriage and unrestrained high fertility. This supposition is also supported by the appearance here of half of the eight occupations associated with the

50 An equal degree of separation at all ages would depress the fertility of those marrying at younger ages disproportionately more than those marrying later. This is first because of the greater average fecundity of groups of women in their late teens, early and mid-twenties than at any other age. Hence, interruption of normal exposure to the risk of conception will have a greater relative effect, in terms of fertility foregone, at those ages than at later ones. Secondly, it is also the case that there is an independent effect due to the tendency for age-specific fertility to decline faster at successive ages for those groups of women married longest. On average repeated periods of involuntary abstinence would act to amplify this fertility-depressing effect all the more among those married earliest. On the latter effect, see Page, 'Patterns underlying fertility schedules'.

51 For further support for this latter hypothesis, see p. 376.

52 Hence Eric Hobsbawm has written that 'The right to a trade was not only a right of the duly qualified tradesman, but also a family heritage . . . for their sons . . . fathers insisted on privileged access': *Worlds of labour*, pp. 264–5. For additional evidence to that cited by Hobsbawm, see Crozier, 'Kinship and occupational succession'. Also, for independent evidence of the reciprocal process of in-migrants having to turn to the less desirable employments, see above, n. 24.

railways (IDs 53, 51, 54, 56). Three of the four *other* rail occupations are those which required a period of training to be successfully completed, and they show no sign of this fertility gradient by age of wife at marriage. The shared characteristic of most of these occupations in Group A, then, is that delayed female age at marriage is far from being part of a conscious low fertility strategy, either in combination with, or as an alternative to, birth control within marriage. It simply reflects the imposition of an 'exogenous', unwanted, labour market-induced restraint on marriage due to relative poverty among couples whose fertility was otherwise unrestrained.

Turning now to Group B, here are found those occupations in which the elder marrying were controlling their fertility within marriage considerably more than the younger subset. The presence in Group B of coal, coke dealers (90) and coal mineowners, managers (87) among the fourteen occupations with differentially high fertility among their young marriers may indicate that many of the employers and own account workers returned under these headings were men who had risen out of the local mining community to their positions of responsibility in the industry, and so exhibited similar high fertility to those among whom they had been brought up.[53] This would tally with the fact that it was the youngest-marrying subset of this occupation which was divergent, in the sense of recording fertility levels at odds with the occupation as a whole. Miners were typically very young marrying and therefore those who had risen from the ranks into the self-employed or even managerial class would be disproportionately represented among the youngest-marrying sections of IDs 87 and 90. It is hypothesised that a substantial proportion of the young-marrying within each of these two occupations had changed their employment status during the course of their lives and so these two occupations were composed of two types of recruit: those who inherited the (usually larger) businesses; and those who rose to the position of employer from among the workers.

It may be that this hypothesis would be valid in relation to several of the other occupations, mainly covering small-scale traders and craftsmen, appearing in Group B, such as: IDs 142, 184, 114, 115, 196, 136, 149, 146 and 187. However, it seems more likely, on balance, that in most of these cases the difference between the less fertile elder-marrying and the more fertile younger-marrying subsets reflects the difference between the proprietors or master artisans, concentrated

53 Alternatively, this could simply be caused by false or misinterpreted information entered on the census schedule, whereby these ostensible categories of employers and managers might have been diluted by accidental inclusion of a number of their employees and workers. This would be consistent with the fact that the average fertility *level* of those marrying youngest within the occupation was so high that it was approaching the typical fertility levels of employees. However, this would also have required the consistent falsification of information in three separate columns on the census schedule (columns 10, 11 and 12 – see specimen in Appendix A), as well as the negligence of the local enumerator in not spotting the inaccuracy; or else similarly consistent misinterpretation of the information by the schedule's processors in London. It therefore seems more likely that this was a genuine feature of these two occupations.

more among the late-marrying subsets, and their employees, disproportionately represented among the younger marriers.

The remaining occupations of Group B are all connected with the textiles industry: IDs 163, 167, 207. In fact, almost all the textiles occupations of Stevenson's class VI exhibit this same pattern to a less pronounced extent: a relatively greater degree of fertility control among those couples marrying at higher ages.[54] As will become apparent in the next chapter, this seems to have been a particularly marked characteristic of the textiles occupations, with respect to incomplete as well as completed fertility. In view of this consistency of pattern across the industry, it is very unlikely only to be a reflection of differences in social composition and recruitment within individual occupations (greater concentration of employers among the older marriers). It most probably represents a genuine and significant feature of these communities and the way in which fertility was controlled in them, as will be discussed in the next chapter when 'stopping' and 'spacing' is considered.

Overall it is the absences from either part of Table 7.3 which are most significant. None of the dealing occupations and only three of the eight retailing occupations appear (IDs 181, 184, 196). Only a few of the two or three dozen artisanal and skilled manual occupations from factory or small workshops are to be found here.[55] Some of the occupations which do appear are those which were composed of particularly polarised mixes of employers and employees, where the former were owners of relatively large-scale enterprises and there were relatively few intermediary individuals within the occupation, returning themselves as own account workers. This applies to oil (vegetable) – millers, refiners (149), coach, carriage makers (115), and glass manufacture (146). (But of course there are also several such 'polarised' occupations which do not appear here, for instance from the iron and steel industry.)

However, the vast bulk of occupations containing skilled tradesmen do not show a significant degree of internal heterogeneity in their fertility behaviour. This would strongly imply that the tentative hypothesis offered at the end of the last section would not be justified. There is no evidence here to support the speculation

54 With the exceptions of: cotton – winding processes (158), where the relationship is reversed; and lace manufacture (164), where both younger and elder marrying have lower relative fertility than the typical age at marriage subgroup.

55 There would seem to be just four exceptions in the former category: cycle makers (113); motor car chassis makers (114); coach, wagon makers (115); and cabinet makers (136). Cabinet makers were the only traditional craft which Hobsbawm included in his 'labour aristocracy', on the strength of the evidence of their high pay from the 1906 wage census data. Though he noted that as a craft it contained an abnormally high percentage of low-paid males (22.7% earned less than 25 shillings per week). See Hobsbawm, 'The labour aristocracy', tables II, III, IV. This may help to explain the heterogeneity of behaviour in this one case. It may perhaps be that each of the other three categories also contained a particularly heterogenous mix of a core of high-status and highly paid workers along with a group of much lower paid workers. Hobsbawm does not give information on any of these other three categories. For further discussion of Hobsbawm's analysis, see below, pp. 355–7.

that within these skilled manual occupational categories, individuals' status as employer, self-employed or employee further differentiated the degree of birth control likely to be practised. The evidence suggests, rather, that for these occupations there was no subset of independent masters among the skilled artisans, whose fertility was lower than that recorded for the occupational category as a whole.

A more significant distinction within the ranks of such artisans and skilled categories may, indeed, be that which was originally suggested and which is illustrated in Figure 7.1: differences between industries and communities. It seems that, independent of *skill* or *proprietorship*, workers in textiles and artisan manufacturers of luxury goods recorded lowest fertility, followed by non-metal craftsmen and their assistants, in turn followed by metal-working artisans; and then, finally, the building tradesmen and their assistants.

Occupational differences in nuptiality

No account of the fertility characteristics of occupations would be satisfactory without discussion of the relationship between varying fertility levels and nuptiality behaviour. Of course, demographically it is information on *female* age at marriage that is most valuable for drawing inferences about the degree of birth regulation practised by different occupations. The only comprehensive source for such occupationally specific information on female age at marriage is, again, Table 35 of the *FMR*, Pt 2.

The only way in which the data in Table 35 can be used to measure occupational variation in age at marriage is by expressing the number of men, in any given occupation, recorded as marrying women in one of the three age groups, 15–19, 20–4 or 25–9, as a proportion of the total number marrying in that occupation, for all the three age groups together; or by some mathematical derivative of that procedure. However, quite clearly, the many occupations were subject to widely varying rates of mortality, which will considerably distort the capacity of such a measurement to record accurately the differences between occupations in the proportions *originally* marrying at the three different ages, up to forty years previously. A satisfactory solution to this measurement problem can, however, be achieved.[56]

[56] An avenue initially explored to deal with this problem was that of reinflating the 1911 figures by a factor appropriate to the differential degree of mortality which the couples in each occupation had suffered over the previous decades. However, this was confounded first by the lack of consistency of occupational definitions between censuses over the previous forty years, and secondly by the associated lack of consistency in the mortality experience of those seventy to eighty occupational groups which could be traced back to 1881 in the decennial supplements of the RG, where information on occupational mortality is given. The rank positions of these eighty or so occupations, from one decade to the next, were too variable to permit a relative inflation factor to be assigned to them for the period as a whole.

Those surviving couples, from which the three occupational fertility indices used so far have been calculated, represent a single birth cohort of females who married at three different average ages.[57] Since they were born over the same period (1852–65) then, for any given occupational category, these three subgroups will have been subject to equal mortality depletion (because they are all, on average, the same age in 1911). The ratio between the number surviving to 1911 in any one of the three age at marriage subsets to that for either of the other two should therefore faithfully reflect the ratio between their numbers when they *originally* married, regardless of the intervening depletions of mortality. Since the modal age at marriage group for virtually all occupations is 20–4, the number married at each of the other two age groups, younger (15–19) and elder (25–9), can therefore be expressed as a proportion, less than unity in both cases, of the larger number of couples in the modal age at marriage group (20–4). If this derivative proportionate figure for those marrying young is then divided by that for those marrying late, then a single ratio figure results. This is an index which assumes a value of unity (i.e. a value of 1.0) when the proportion of young marriages exactly equals the proportion of late ones. The value varies from unity down to zero for occupations with a greater preponderance of late marriage; and it varies from one to infinity for those with the opposite tendency. Given that occupations are only used in this analysis where at least thirty couples were enumerated in each of the three age at marriage subgroups, the values of the resulting indices vary, in practice, between approximately 0.5 and 2.5, for occupations with relatively large proportions of late marriers, and of young marriers, respectively.

Although this index does not provide a linear scale or an interval level of comparison between the occupations, it does nevertheless provide a reliable basis for rank ordering the occupations with respect to their female age at marriage strategies: one which avoids the distorting influence of differential mortality effects. The resulting index ratio effectively indicates the relative degree to which the couples in the 195 different male occupations delayed marriage; it appears in various tables below as 'PRUDMARR' (prudential marriage index).[58] In Appendix C the column RANK/PRUDMARR shows the rankings of each occupation according to PRUDMARR, with lowest rank scored by the occupation with the largest proportions marrying at older ages: greatest propensity to prudential, late marriage.

Table 7.4 records the nature of the overall correlation, across all 195 occupations, between occupational fertility level (for the three fertility indices), and PRUDMARR,

[57] See above, pp. 287–8.

[58] To check whether omission of couples marrying above the age of 29 might alter the ratio index significantly, a second shadow variable, 'AMPRPN3B', was also constructed, by including those marrying between the ages 30–4 with those aged 25–9, as the older marrying subpopulation. The Spearman correlation coefficient between these two variables, PRUDMARR and AMPRPN3B, was 0.99573 for the dataset of 195 occupations, indicating that the addition of those marrying above the age of 30 had no significant effect on the rank position of the occupations.

Table 7.4 *Spearman R^2 correlation coefficients between prudential marriage and fertility level indices*

	PRUDMARR
AM1/71–80	0.81275 (0.0001)
AM2/81–5	0.79937 (0.0001)
AM3/86–90	0.72995 (0.0001)

Note: statistical significance levels in brackets, N = 195.

the index measuring age at marriage. The most important general finding is the strong positive correlation between low levels of completed fertility and late age at marriage. This suggests that, as a general rule, those occupations where couples exhibited the greatest degree of fertility control *within* marriage were also those in which there was the highest proportion of couples marrying relatively late. This would imply that both late marriage and birth control within marriage were being employed simultaneously by couples in those occupations recording low completed fertility in 1911, as alternative or joint means to the same end: regulation of family size.

However, this general inference appears to be somewhat contradicted by the fact that the coefficient of correlation is significantly *weaker* for the elder-marrying subset among the occupations (the correlation of PRUDMARR with AM3/86–90). In pursuing this qualification a particularly interesting result emerged from the consequent analysis. In order to assess whether this overall positive correlation was relatively uniform throughout the range of fertility values for all 195 occupations, they were divided into five equal quintile groups (ranked according to their value for the main fertility index, AM2/81–5). This produced something of a surprise, as can be seen from the results in Table 7.5.

It would be expected that the values for the correlation coefficients would be less impressive for a smaller run of values, as is indeed the case for the two quintiles of highest fertility occupations. However, the almost complete lack of a relationship between age at marriage and fertility level in the three *lower fertility* quintile groups is somewhat unexpected. On the hypothesis that late marriage was either a joint or alternative means to birth control within marriage to achieve smaller families, it is among the lowest fertility part of the nation that the relationship should be strongest, and not vice versa.

Figures 7.2, 7.3 and 7.4 graphically display the relationship between age at marriage (PRUDMARR) and fertility levels for all 195 occupations (AM1/71–80, AM2/81–5 and AM3/86–90, respectively). It can be seen that although that half of the total number of occupations falling in the lower fertility range of the distribution do, indeed, exhibit a distinctly later age at marriage strategy than the half with higher fertility, nevertheless there is virtually no clear trend relationship between the two variables (PRUDMARR and AM2/81–5) *within* that half of the

Table 7.5 *Spearman R^2 correlation coefficients between prudential marriage and fertility level indices: quintile groupings of occupations ordered by AM2/81–5*

	PRUDMARR
1st quintile (N=39)	
AMI/71–80	−0.01174
	0.9434
AM2/81–5	−0.06417
	0.6979
AM3/86–90	−0.35283
	0.0276
2nd quintile (N=39)	
AMI/71–80	0.29236
	0.0672
AM2/81–5	0.18368
	0.2566
AM3/86–90	−0.04484
	0.7835
3rd quintile (N=39)	
AM1/71–80	0.36194
	0.0236
AM2/81–5	−0.00304
	0.9854
AM3/86–90	−0.21862
	0.1812
4th quintile (N=39)	
AM1/71–80	0.58424
	0.0001
AM2/81–5	0.57036
	0.0001
AM3/86–90	0.26811
	0.0944
5th quintile (N=39)	
AM1/71–80	0.45729
	0.0034
AM2/81–5	0.43279
	0.0059
AM3/86–90	0.33279
	0.0384

Note: statistical significance levels underneath.

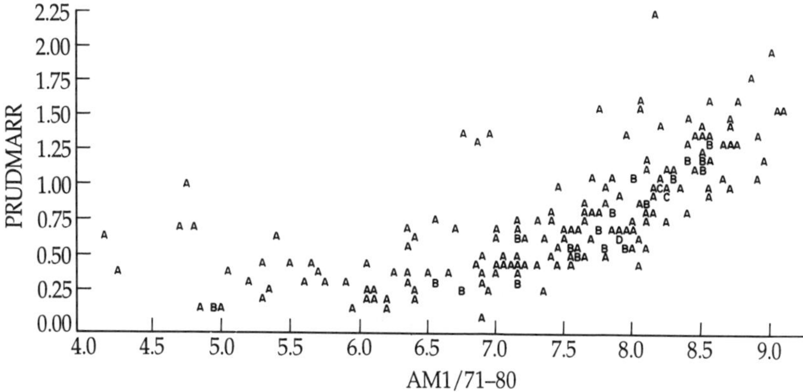

Figure 7.2 Frequency cross-tabulation plot of the relationship between delayed marriage (PRUDMARR) and completed fertility: by AM1/71–80

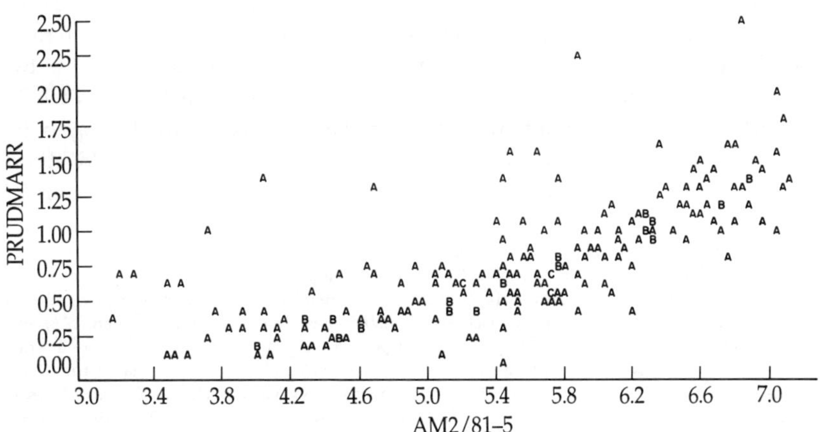

Figure 7.3 Frequency cross-tabulation plot of the relationship between delayed marriage (PRUDMARR) and completed fertility: by AM2/81–5

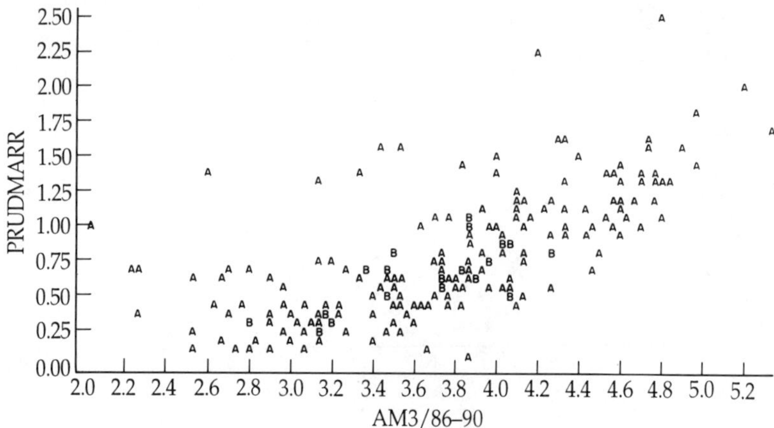

Figure 7.4 Frequency cross-tabulation plot of the relationship between delayed marriage (PRUDMARR) and completed fertility: by AM3/86–90

occupations recording lower fertility. This is despite the fact that there is a positive relationship visible in the slope among that half of the occupations with higher fertility.

The reason for all this is graphically illustrated by Figure 7.5. This shows the results of applying a principal components factor analysis to the four demographic variables for the 195 occupations.[59] Of course, the three fertility level variables are all strongly correlated, and so these four variables are mainly measuring just two dimensions of variation between the occupations: first, their combined fertility levels; and secondly their varying age at marriage strategies. Even these two dimensions are quite strongly correlated for many of the occupations, as Table 7.4 reported. If there were a uniform strong correlation across the whole range of the 195 occupations then the first principal component, factor 1, would absorb virtually all statistical variance within the data, and the observations of Figure 7.5

[59] The function of principal components analysis is to form a smaller set of artificial variables out of a number of empirical variables, such that the artificial variables are orthogonal (entirely uncorrelated) and such that the first artificial variable (principal component) absorbs the maximum possible of the total statistical variation in the dataset. See Koutsoyiannis, *Theory of econometrics*, ch. 17.6, for a general account of the method of principal components. The data for two of the four empirical variables used here were transformed so that they would approximate to a normal distribution, a necessary prerequisite for this form of principal components analysis. Whereas the data values for AM2/81–5 and AM3/86–90 were adequate in their raw state, AM1/71–80 required a slight transformation, by the positive exponential, 1.063. The variable PRUDMARR also required transformation, by the negative exponential, −1.10. These transformation values were attained by a process of trial and error, using the formulae for computing coefficients of skewness and kurtosis in Snedecor and Cochran, *Statistical methods*, pp. 84–9; and Table A6, parts I and II, p. 552, which gives values for these coefficients for judging when the data has been transformed sufficiently. This resulted in four variables each of which was normally distributed by the criteria of skewness and kurtosis, at the 5% level of significance, for a sample of 200 cases, according to Table A6 in Snedecor and Cochran.

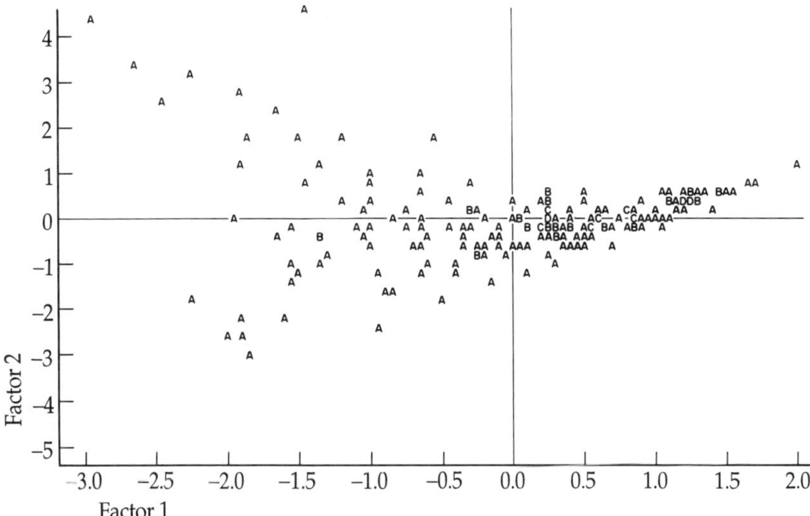

Figure 7.5 Principal components (factor analysis) for four demographic indices: AM1/71–80; AM2/81–5; AM3/86–90; PRUDMARR

would then simply align themselves on a single axis (factor 1). This is, in fact, the dominant pattern among approximately three-fifths of the occupations – those with highest fertility. However, Figure 7.5 shows that as the factor loading on the first principal component (which primarily reflects the combined values of the occupational fertility level indices) decreases further, so the degree of significant independent variation around the orthogonal axis, factor 2, increases in *both* directions simultaneously, giving the funnel-shaped effect to the figure's appearance.

Figure 7.5 shows that among those eighty or so occupations recording the lowest completed fertility levels in 1911, there is very great and *bi-directional* variation in their age at marriage strategies, relative to the *general* trend of a strong degree of positive correlation between low fertility and delayed nuptiality found in the dataset of all 195 occupations.

Indeed, the really interesting finding which this figure illustrates is that there are three distinct marriage strategies evident among those controlling their fertility most effectively. One set of these occupations appears to achieve its low level of marital fertility in combination with a particularly high age at marriage strategy (a relatively high positive loading on factor 2). At the opposite extreme, there is the most unusual group of occupations. These record their very low marital fertility despite also exhibiting an age at marriage pattern which is relatively *young*. Between these two lies the third, more normal group of low-fertility occupations, those closer to the principal component axis. They regulate their fertility in association with the kind of relatively high age at marriage strategy that would be predicted by the positive correlation which exists between the two variables across the dataset as a whole.

Table 7.6 shows the eighty-two occupations of lowest fertility divided into three equal groups (A, B and C) according to whether they exhibit relatively young (A), relatively old (B) or 'normal' (C) age at marriage characteristics. Within each of the three panels of Table 7.6 the occupations are listed in order by fertility level, according to AM2/81–5. The occupations in emboldened type are those exhibiting the most extreme divergences in their nuptiality behaviour. Between the emboldened occupations listed in panel A and those listed in panel B there is a more than eightfold difference in the extent to which older marriers outnumbered younger marriers, despite their similar fertility levels.[60]

One fascinating aspect of this analysis is the clear form of socio-demographic discrimination which it presents, even among the few occupations recording the very lowest values for AM2/81–5. These are the first half-dozen or so occupations on each of the three lists for Table 7.6. Among the relatively young marrying at the head of list A are to be found all three occupations which most unequivocally represented the exclusive preserve of those born into inherited wealth: those living off private means and the two categories of military officers. Among the professions it was these two military careers which had been the least reformed, least meritocratic and least subject to market pressures in the performance of their services, especially when those in this marriage cohort had first entered these careers in the 1860s, 1870s or 1880s.[61]

By contrast at the head of list B, those delaying marriage most rigorously, are to be found many of the other liberal professions. These were the bulk of the recently formed or reformed professions which had all been made more meritocratic through examinable recruitment.[62] These were clearly exhibiting a quite different set of marriage expectations and practices.

60 With modal age at marriage for all occupations in this marriage cohort lying nearer to age 25 than to age 19, the difference between relatively young- and relatively old-marrying occupations can be measured by comparing the extent to which the numbers marrying at 25–9 exceeded those at 15–19. All occupations in panel B of Table 7.6, the older-marrying list, returned at least three times as many couples married at age 25–9 as at age 15–19. All occupations in panel A, the young-marrying list, returned significantly less than twice as many couples marrying at 25–9 than at 15–19. Occupations in emboldened type in panel B are those where more than four times as many married at 25–9 as at 15–19. On the young-marrying list, panel A, emboldened occupations are those where the number marrying at 25–9 was less than half as high again than the number marrying at 15–19.

61 The practice of obtaining army commissions by purchase had only finally been abolished by Gladstone in 1871 but, as W. J. Reader points out, this did not prevent the military career from remaining predominantly an exclusive preserve for the sons of the wealthy. This was due to the combination of low pay alongside a particularly high-cost lifestyle, which continued to be considered *de rigueur* by the officer class. Reader, *Professional men*, p. 98.

62 Apart from barristers the only other major professional category on the third list, dentists (21), only narrowly missed inclusion with the other liberal professions in the second list. Indeed, the

This manifest difference in the strategies of family formation and family planning is plausibly and systematically related to differences which existed within the nation's upper and middle classes, in terms of family background and dynastic aims, financial means, relative security of income and career structure.[63] The period 1870–1914 witnessed the consolidation of a relatively large metropolitan, rentier class. Company directorships in the City became increasingly desirable in the eyes of the landowning élite, as they increasingly came to appreciate the financial importance of direct access to the best information on the most lucrative overseas investments – which they actively sought in order to avoid the financial consequences of falling domestic rents due to the prolonged agricultural depression from the 1870s. Accumulation and inheritance of wealth continued to be the primary dynastic strategy of this landed and financial élite, who predominantly lived in the Home Counties and educated their sons and daughters in the nation's most exclusive and expensive public schools. Indeed, the latter had now become the major formative institution for socialisation into and membership of this 'class', or social status group. The significantly less wealthy, commercially active, professional and managerial middle class, by contrast, necessarily consumed, rather than accumulated, most of its income in order to enjoy the comfortable standard of living to which it aspired. As likely to be provincially located as metropolitan, the members of this social group could only hope to pass on to their children a primarily cultural (rather than cultural *and* material) inheritance, sufficient to ensure a well-rewarded but necessarily busy, working life: secondary education was typically at one of the reformed, grammar day-schools in the towns or at one of the less expensive public schools. These two social constellations, the rentier-financial and the professional-commercial, exhibited very low completed fertility in 1911 but, as has been shown, this was in the context of very different marriage strategies.

This discovery of considerable heterogeneity in nuptiality patterns among the leading birth controllers in British society is a significant embarrassment for any theory which envisages fertility decline as a single unitary process. Even among the numerically small and precisely defined group of occupations which 'led' the fall in the nation's fertility, there was substantial variation in the age at which they married and (therefore) in the extent to which they actually practised some form of

appearance of barristers (17) at the head of list C may well result from its being the most 'aristocratic' and expensive to enter of these more genuinely competitive and market-oriented professions. Its in-between nuptiality pattern therefore resulted from its recruitment from a relatively equal mix of the diametrically opposed characteristics of the two distinct social constituencies, which head each of the other two lists. This is supported by Daniel Duman's research on the social and occupational origins of the Bar. Duman shows that in 1885, 36% had professional fathers (including civil servants as professionals) and 32% had gentry or landed origins; of the remainder 15% had fathers in business and 11% were themselves barristers; leaving 6% 'other' or 'unknown'. Duman, *The English and colonial bars*, Table 1.6.

[63] On this widening cultural division within the propertied class during this period, see Harris, *Private lives*, pp. 69–70, 103–10. For further amplification of these themes, see below, pp. 468–77.

Table 7.6 *Variation in proportions marrying younger and older wives among occupations with low completed fertility*

A Those low-fertility occupations marrying a relatively high proportion of **young** *wives*

204 private means
9 army officers (incl. retired)
11 officers of navy, marine (incl. retired)
188 lodging, boarding house keepers
29 actors
201 retired from business
39 caretakers, not govt
189 hotel and inn keepers, publicans
202 pensioners
28 musicians, music teachers
187 cafes, restaurants – keepers
119 goldsmiths, silversmiths
208 wool, worsted – carding, others
139 furniture dealers
120 watchmakers, clockmakers
121 piano, organ makers
190 barmen
114 motor car – chassis makers, mechanics
158 cotton – winding
90 coal, coke – merchants, dealers
123 builders
155 others in printing
16 church, chapel, cemetery officers
159 cotton – weaving
196 general shopkeepers, dealers
207 cotton – card room, others
164 lace manufacture

B Those low-fertility occupations marrying a relatively high proportion of **older** *wives*

20 physicians, GPs
18 solicitors
46 banks – officials, clerks
25 civil, mining engineers
24 scientific pursuits
13 clergy (C of E)
31 dom. indoor servants
27 architects
43 accountants
22 teachers
7 Poor Law service
5 civil service officers and clerks
2 PO officers and clerks
19 law clerks

Table 7.6 *continued*

148 chemists, druggists
42 commercial travellers
14 clergy (nonconf.)
45 commercial, business clerks
38 hospital, benevolent service
168 drapers, linen mercers
47 insurance officials, clerks
117 ironmongers
49 rail – officials, clerks
197 pawnbrokers
12 men of the navy
191 waiters (not domestic)
3 postmen
6 police

C *All other low-fertility occupations*

17 barristers
26 painters, sculptors, artists
185 tobacconists
40 merchants (commodity undefined)
21 dentists
122 dealers in jewellery, gold
23 authors, editors, journalists
44 auctioneers, valuers
37 college, club service
41 brokers, agents, factors
169 textiles, fabrics – other dealers
173 boot, shoe, clog dealers
183 grocers, dealers in beverages
162 wool, worsted – weaving
171 clothiers, outfitters
161 wool, worsted – spinning
8 municipal, parish, county officers
15 itinerant preachers
176 cheesemongers, provision dealers
182 bakers, confectioners (dealers)
32 dom. coachmen, grooms
180 corn, flour dealers
154 printers – hand compositors
48 insurance agents
103 electricians
35 dom. gardeners
4 civil service messengers

birth control. If such variation in patterns of family formation exists just within that part of the population represented by these few élite occupational groups, this is strong testimony in favour of the existence of a wide variety of family-building forms changing alongside each other across the diverse social groups and communities of the nation, rather than the diffusion of a single new norm or the operation of a single process.

The evidence in Table 7.6 also indicates a number of further social distinctions behind the pattern of falling fertility at this time. Clearly a second distinct social group who shared with the established competitive professions – to only a slightly lesser extent – a tendency to late marriage was that comprised by six of the nine categories of clerical and commerical workers (IDs 5, 2, 19, 45, 47, 49), including the quantitatively most important one (by far), 'commercial and business clerks' (45). The late-marrying pattern is also evident among a third group, which can be characterised as 'deferential' occupations, those on the receiving end of the structures of authority and status in British society at this time (IDs 31, 12, 191, 3, 6).[64]

On the other hand, the list of young-marrying, low fertility occupations presents an altogether different complexion from that of the professional, white-collar and deferential late marriers. Those with inherited wealth have already been mentioned. A second distinct type of low-fertility, early marrier is found in a set of independent proprietors of businesses and commercial concerns, of which 'retired from business' (201) forms quantitatively the most significant example (IDs 188, 201, 189, 187, 123).[65]

Thirdly, there are various categories of working-class occupations. These represent some, but by no means all of the low-fertility manual occupations. The divisions within the textiles industry are again confirmed. Cotton textile workers and lace workers are found among these relatively young marriers but not, on the whole, the wool workers (with the exception of ID 208).[66] The previously identified set of low-fertility manual trades involved in manufacturing jewellery and other high-value luxury goods are also found here among the relatively young marriers (IDs 119, 120, 121, 114).

Thus, one broad socio-cultural distinction which appears to emerge from the foregoing lies between the professional, clerical and most of the deferential occupations on the one hand, and on the other hand all the other occupational groups already embracing low completed fertility in 1911. The distinction lies not

64 Although there were also three other 'deferential' occupations to be found in the third list: IDs 37, 32, 35.

65 The numerically extremely large category, 'retired from business' (201), no doubt contained elements of both the two main groups: those with inherited family wealth, and those of more humble origins who had only achieved sufficient commercial success in their own lifetimes to retire in their late forties and fifties (the probable age of most of the husbands in this dataset). Although some dealers are also found here (IDs 139, 90, 196), it must be pointed out that the majority of dealers did not marry particularly young wives and so are found on the third list.

66 The fourth cotton occupation, the spinners (157), recorded too high a fertility to be included in Table 7.6. They also married relatively young.

in any substantial differences between the two in their fertility levels, which were equally low, but rather in their divergent associated nuptiality patterns. No manual working-class and hardly any proprietary commercial occupation, however low its fertility level, postponed and deferred marriage to the same extent as the professional, clerical and 'deferential' social groups of this generation.

This finding is particularly at variance with the notion that the professional class, above all, were in the vanguard of a national movement towards the adoption of more rational means to control fertility within marriage, closely followed by the 'lower middle-class' clerical workers. Since both of these groups tended to marry significantly older wives than other social groups recording similarly low fertility levels, this means that *on average* it was couples in the *other*, younger-marrying social groups identified here – those with inherited wealth, businessmen and commercial proprietors, certain textiles workers and luxury goods makers – who would have been practising, if anything, a slightly greater degree of birth control *within marriage*.

Figures 7.2–7.5 all showed that the nuptiality patterns among the higher fertility occupations (the 113 not listed in Table 7.6) conformed to the more straightforward and simple, graded pattern of the sort one might broadly expect, where the lower the completed fertility recorded by an occupation, the higher was the proportion marrying wives at older ages. This more simple pattern of correlation raises the possibility, which should be tested for, that much of the variation, in both relative fertility and nuptiality characteristics, between occupations within this group of higher fertility occupations may be the product of a compositional effect, arising from variations between the occupations in the proportions of employees they contain.

As reported in the first panel of Table 7.7, the overall relationship between age at marriage strategy and the three industrial status variables is remarkably similar to the relationship reported with the three fertility level indices (see above, Table 7.2).[67] Again, it is R/EMPLOY, the index measuring the ratio of *employers* to all others enumerated in the occupation, which shows the strongest positive correlation – in this case with late age at marriage. The same pair of further analyses, as in Table 7.2, were performed: first the number of occupations was reduced to 74 by excluding textiles operatives, dealers and retailers; and then reduced still further to 45 occupations in the same way as previously. As can be seen from the lower panels of Table 7.7, the effect was again similar: the first stage tended to dilute the positive correlations, whereas the second stage returned that for R/EMPLOY almost back to its original score. However, in this case the other two employment status indices continued to deteriorate, to a score lacking statistical significance in the case of R/OWNACC, the ratio for self-employed workers.

[67] Although all 110 occupations for which employment status information is available are included in Table 7.7, in practice most of them do, indeed, represent the 110 or so occupations with higher fertility (the main exception being a dozen or so occupations of various types of 'dealers').

Table 7.7 *Spearman R^2 correlation coefficients between prudential marriage and employment status*

	PRUDMARR	
A. Whole sample (N = 110)		
R/OWNEMP	0.41597	(0.0001)
R/EMPLOY	0.52075	(0.0001)
R/OWNACC	0.31447	(0.0008)
RATIO/OE	0.08447	(0.3803)
B. All occupations except dealing, retailing and textiles (N = 74)		
R/OWNEMP	0.37194	(0.0011)
R/EMPLOY	0.42583	(0.0001)
R/OWNACC	0.32315	(0.0050)
RATIO/OE	−0.03308	(0.7796)
C. 'Skilled' occupations only (N = 45)		
R/OWNEMP	0.31818	(0.0332)
R/EMPLOY	0.49144	(0.0006)
R/OWNACC	0.18933	(0.2129)
RATIO/OE	0.22055	(0.1454)

Note: statistical significance levels in brackets.

Thus, it is the proportion of employers, rather than self-employed, which appears to be most positively associated with varying age at marriage strategy (as was also the case with varying fertility levels). Occupations exhibiting prudential nuptial behaviour, through postponement of marriage, tend to be those in which employers are to be found proportionately more. Unfortunately, the information collected in 1911 on employment status is nowhere tabulated in such a way as to render this hypothesis conclusively testable. Nor is it possible to confirm whether this association represents a causal or a selective effect. Were those who married relatively late born into the employer class and, hence, postponing marriage from within the cultural mores of that social group; or was it the case that, on average, it was those who married older wives who were thereby assisted in rising to employer status because of the lesser burdens which their consequently smaller families placed upon their energies and resources? (Although, it might be expected that this kind of selection effect should be even stronger with respect to the proportion of self-employed in each occupation. But the proportion of own account workers in an occupation, regardless of employers, is considerably less strongly correlated with relatively late marriage, especially in the case of skilled manual and artisan occupations.)

It is, then, the division between employer and employee, which is once again confirmed as tending to produce distinctive forms of demographic (fertility and nuptiality) behaviour, rather than any distinction between self-employed and employee. This would tend to qualify an observation made by the political historian, J. R. Vincent, when discussing characteristics of late nineteenth-century poll-books shared in common with census returns at that time: their apparent failure to distinguish the different grades of 'employment status', especially the supposed separation between independent masters and employee journeymen in skilled trades.[68] Vincent questioned whether the vexation shown by Dr Ogle, the census statistician, at respondents' imprecision in their returns was in fact justified. Vincent instead suggested that this might well indicate a real contemporary 'feeling that people engaged in making the same kind of thing were the same kind of people'. Vincent concluded that 'if in the nineteenth century the pattern of self description implies that the social distance between masters and journeymen was not important to them, then probably it was not objectively important either'.[69]

The evidence of demographic behaviour analysed here seems to suggest that by the end of the first decade of the twentieth century, there was some degree of social discontinuity within the manual working class between those artisans or manufacturing craftsmen who were themselves employers of others (a position they had achieved by the age of fifty years old or so – the typical age of the husbands of this cohort of women), and all others of comparable mature age in the same trade. But the difference between self-employed masters and employee tradesmen was apparently much less significant. The inference is that it was not so much 'skill' or craftsmanship that was the socially differentiating factor among manual workers, at least with respect to demographic behaviour, but proprietorship and especially employership status.

Employership entailed not only authority over others and the responsibility which this confers. It may also have represented for many employers (though by no means all) a somewhat greater degree of security through insulation against the immediate problems attendant on any kind of physical impairment through injury or illness. This was the much-feared sword of Damocles hanging over all those who relied upon their physical fitness to earn a living in an era before national insurance (which did not come into operation until the 1911 National Insurance Act). Of course, the employer and his family were far from absolutely secure. But the forms of insecurity suffered by employed workers and by employers were importantly different. The anxiety of business failure hung over employers and they had further to fall socially than their employees if they did get into difficulty. But this threat was in their case all the more a spur to the exercise of their prudential reflexes and the predicament presented itself to them as a test of their forethought and diligence. The non-unionised employee (still most of the workforce throughout this period – see below, p. 355) was, by contrast, both acutely vulnerable to redundancy or physical incapacity and also frequently in no position to do anything about these problems before or when they struck.

68 Vincent, *Pollbooks*, pp. 51–4. 69 Vincent, *Pollbooks*, p. 53.

In other words, the control of family size, the postponement of marriage and the acquisition of a position of employership status, which guaranteed the family's weekly income relatively independently of the breadwinner's state of health and physical efficiency, appear to have been strongly associated patterns of prudential behaviour at this time characterising a certain section within that larger part of the population directly dependent on the industrial and commercial market place for making a living. However, as stated above, it is not possible with national aggregate data of the sort analysed here to investigate further the possible direction of causation within this bundle of associations.

Furthermore, the overall picture regarding these patterns of association between proprietorship or employership status and nuptiality is, once again, as with the fertility evidence, made less straightforward by examination of the occupations involved in the retailing and dealing sector of the economy.[70] For these social groups a quite different relationship prevailed from that found among the manufacturing workers. As noted above, the eight retailing occupations tend to contain the smallest proportions of employees found among any of the 1911 occupational categories and, consequently, a relatively large proportion of independent, small proprietors. On the other hand the fourteen categories of dealers contain significantly larger proportions of employees. Yet it is the occupations of dealers, and not the retailers, which exhibit the most marked tendency to prudential, late marriage.[71] This, therefore, once again, underlines the point that the influences upon occupational variations in family building behaviour were highly variable, such that the same 'factor', such as in this case employment status, might have quite different demographic effects and implications for different social groups in different sectors of the economy.

Segregation of the sexes at work – and in the home?

In the foregoing discussion it has frequently been inferred that, apart from proprietorship or employership status, industrial sector or affiliation seems to have exerted a particularly marked effect on the patterns of occupational fertility and nuptiality. This seems to have been especially the case where such industrial affiliation simultaneously implied probable residence in an all-embracing industrial community and where it was also associated with a particularly strongly established and engrained set of gender roles, *vis-à-vis* the workplace (and therefore in the local culture of the encompassing community, too).

Indeed, those occupations recording the highest fertility of all (at the bottom of Appendix C) appear to have in common neither especially urban nor rural location, nor low level of skill required, nor low remuneration (in view of the

70 See the above discussion of dealers and retailers, pp. 326–8.

71 The only exceptions are furniture dealers (139) and coal, coke dealers (90) and, possibly, cheesemongers, provision dealers (176).

presence among them of highly paid coal hewers and ship platers and riveters, for instance). They have in common simply the extremely heavy physical nature of the work involved. This went alongside a set of collateral characteristics of the working environment of such occupations: a tendency for the work to be performed in the company of large numbers of other male wage-labourers who were equals, and with relatively few supervisors or employers present, certainly compared to most workshop or factory environments.[72] Typically there would be virtually no women at all in the place of work. These might in some sense be described as conditions of work most likely to breed a 'machismo' culture among the men involved. The men shared together, as a group of wage-labourer equals, an arduous daily work experience; their womenfolk, meanwhile, were almost completely excluded from this dangerous, exhausting and dramatic world in which the men's emotional, as much as their physical, energies were so thoroughly absorbed.[73] All this was often compounded, certainly in the case of many colliery villages and iron- and steel-making localities, by an almost complete absence of any employment opportunities at all for women, which further polarised the range of possible gender roles available for individuals in such communities.

Table 7.8 gives simple summary figures for the ratio of all males to all females working in eighteen of the twenty-three 'Industrial Orders', the large economic categories into which occupations were classified at the 1911 census.[74] The ratios for each industrial order are emboldened and are followed in several cases by ratios for certain individual occupations. All occupations within an Order are individually listed where their sex ratios differed significantly from the average figure for the Order to which they belong. Also a small number of other occupations are listed individually, where their fertility behaviour has already been remarked upon as being of particular interest in its own right. Overall the table is laid out with the eighteen Industrial Orders ranked according to the gender ratio and grouped into three equal divisions: the six Orders with the

72 These physically demanding occupations comprise most of those occupations with the lowest proportion of employers or own account workers. Of course, in branches of industry where large amounts of human labour, rather than machinery, were performing most of the work done, the employers had a diminished requirement for setting up a dense and substantial hierarchy of interlocking supervisory positions to ensure responsible and efficient working of their mechanised plant than in those sectors where such expensive capital assets were involved.

73 On the limited female presence in the mining industry – above ground as pit-brow lasses – see John, *By the sweat of their brow*. On the distinctive cultures of coal-mining communities, see the ethnographic classic by Dennis, Henriques and Slaughter, *Coal is our life*; also Moore, *Pit-men, preachers and politics*; Harrison (ed.), *The independent collier*; Bulmer (ed.), *Mining and social change*; Benson, *British coalminers in the nineteenth century*.

74 See Appendix D for a full listing of the Orders and suborders in which each occupation was placed in 1911. The information is drawn from Census 1911, Volume X, Table 3. The ratios simply reflect the number of all enumerated female workers above age 10 to all male workers above age 10. It is, of course, the case that many female workers were not properly recorded by the census, and the figures therefore have to be treated only as indicative.

Table 7.8 *Gross sex ratios of employment in selected Industrial Orders and some occupations*

Industrial Order or occname		Ratio M:F
XII	**Building and Construction**	1,500:1
XXI	**Municipal Services (all)**	1,000:1
IX	**Mining**	200:1
VI	**Conveyance (i.e. Transport Sector)**	56:1
X	**Metals, Machines, Implements**	15:1
X.2	Tinplate manufacture	7:1
X.3	Boilermakers	1:0
X.4	Electricians	450:1
X.4	Elec. apparatus makers	6:1
X.5	Cutlers, scissors makers	5:1
X.6	Tinplate goods makers	2:1
X.6	Wireworkers	7:1
X.6	Brass, bronze workers	3:1
X.6	Cycle makers	6:1
X.9	Shipbuilding	450:1
X.10	Car mechanics, makers	85:1
VII	Agriculture	12:1
XIII	**Wood, Furniture, Decor'ns**	8:1
XIII.2	Sawyers, wood machinists	1,300:1
XIII.2	Coopers	400:1
I	**General or Local Gov't**	5:1
V	**Commercial**	5:1
XI	**Precious Metals, instruments**	4:1
XI.1	Goldsmiths, silversmiths	3:1
XI.2	Watchmakers	15:1
XI.3	Piano, organ makers	50:1
XV	**Chemicals**	4:1
XIV	**Brick, cement, pottery, glass**	3:1
XIV.1	Potteries	3:2
XIV.1	Brick, glasss	15:1
XVII	**Paper, print**	2:1
XVII.2	Printmakers	5:1
XX	**Food, Tobacco, Drink and Lodging**	2:1
XX.1	Retailers – food	3:1
XX.1	Butchers	11:1
XX.1	Bakers, confectioners (dealers)	2:3
XX.2	Tobacconists	6:5
XX.4	Lodging, boarding house keepers	1:8
XX.4	Inn keepers	3:2
XVIII	**Textiles**	3:2
XVIII.2	Textiles – wool and worsted	4:5
XVIII.1	Textiles – cotton	2:3
XVIII.1	Textiles – cotton spinning	3:2
XVIII.5	Textiles – hosiery	1:3
XVIII.5	Textiles – lace	1:2
III	**Professional Occs. and their Subords.**	1:1
XIX	**Dress**	1:2
IV	**Domestic Service**	1:4

Note: Industrial Orders which were omitted from the table: II **Defence**; VIII **Fishing**; XVI **Skins, etc.**; XXII **Others**; XXIII **Unspecified**.

greatest preponderance of males in the first grouping and the six Orders with the highest proportions of females in the last grouping.

As can be readily appreciated there is overall a substantial degree of correspondence between Table 7.8 and Figure 7.1. Industrial sectors where women's work was virtually unknown correspond remarkably well with the higher fertility occupations, and vice versa. The peculiar property remarked upon above, whereby metal-working tradesmen were associated with higher fertility than craftsmen not handling metals, has its correlate in the gender ratios reported here: namely a far higher rate of male to female workers in the engineering industries than elsewhere. The correlation is suggestive of the possible reasons for this difference, as being something associated with the factors producing this divergent sex ratio in the respective workforces of these two distinct branches of industry. (This will be pursued immediately below in the discussion of trade unionism and sex ratios in the workforce.)

The exceptional nature of the relatively high fertility of the North Staffordshire Potteries is once again confirmed by Table 7.8. The proportion of women workers is one of the highest, only a little less than all the textiles operatives categories, and yet this was one of the higher fertility occupations. (The explanation for this anomaly will be taken up in chapter 9, when the issues raised here regarding the gendering of labour markets and communities' cultures will be discussed in much greater detail.) Conversely, among those few non-textiles, manual occupations of very low fertility, there were one or two other specific exceptions to the general association between low fertility and relatively high rates of female employment. While goldsmiths, silversmiths and printworkers tended to confirm the relationship, with as many as one quarter to one fifth of those returned in these occupations being female, there was an almost complete absence of females in the relatively new employments of electricians and car mechanics.

Finally, in several cases it is worth noting that unusually late or early ages at marriage (Table 7.6) seem in some cases to be associated with a relative lack of, or abundance of opportunity to meet a partner at work. Certainly, as previously mentioned, tobacconists, lodging house keepers and innkeepers all contain very large proportions of female workers, as do lace makers, and especially hosiery manufacture. All of these were relatively young-marrying occupations despite their low fertility. This hypothesis certainly also works well in reverse with regard to the relatively late-marrying railways occupations, the municipal workers (including tramworkers), and also the deferential occupations: waiters, postmen and police. In all these late-marrying cases there were virtually no women at work. It is also true that butchers are an unusually male-dominated occupation among the retailers and they are both relatively late marrying and the highest fertility retailing occupation. The major exceptions to this also seem explicable. The late-marrying habits of domestic servants, despite abundance of females in the workplace, can, of course, be attributed to the special residential requirements of the job. The young age at marriage of wives of coal miners, despite absence of women at work, is also easily explained in the conditions of unusually high earnings for young males combined with considerable competition to secure a wife, since the almost complete absence of gainful employment for young women in many colliery communities often led to imbalances in the sex ratio. The same labour market characteristics which attracted young men to the coalfields were responsible for a flight from them of independent young women.

It seems likely that this factor – the degree of participation of females in the workplace – was most important as an influence on occupational differentials in fertility control or nuptiality behaviour in those cases where the occupations in question would have constituted the major form of employment for an entire town or urban community (which could be a district in a larger city). In other words, this influence was important where social relations (or their relative absence) between the sexes in the workplace constituted a major structuring force on relationships between *most* men and *most* women in the overall community concerned, not just affecting a fraction of the local population. In this connection it is interesting to note the results of one of the most enterprising exercises in Stevenson's official *Report* of 1923. This was an assessment of the extent to which the characteristic unusual fertility behaviour of the three special industrial classes was shared by other occupations in their localities.[75] He found that 'the high fertility attaching to mining and agriculture is largely or altogether peculiar to these industries . . . On the other hand, the low fertility of the textile industry is very largely shared by the general population of the areas in which it is carried on.'[76] Most significantly, he went on to conclude that: 'Where the wife works little, as in agriculture, or not at all, as in coal mining, the husband's occupation alone can influence fertility; but where the wife works much, as in textile production, it may be that her work largely or even mainly governs the situation.'[77] Stevenson did not, however, pursue further the implications of these inferences when it came to formulating his summary interpretation of the most important influences upon the occupational patterns of falling fertility, choosing instead to opt for the general explanatory notion of diffusion, as has been shown in chapter 5.

Of course, patterns of female employment, in different industrial sectors and communities, were far from a matter of random chance at this time. This had been for decades an area of intense political negotiation between the organisations of working men and the local employers concerned, as well as being the subject of some early interventions on the part of the central state in the form of legislation restricting the hours and conditions of juvenile and female workers (and subsequently adult males, too) in certain industries, notably in textile factories and in coal mining. Before undertaking a more extended examination of these issues in chapter 9 a brief exercise can be engaged in here, to assess at least the *prima facie*

[75] *FMR* Pt 2, pp. cxvi–cxvii, and Tables 42 and 43. [76] *FMR* Pt 2, p. cxvii. [77] *FMR* Pt 2, p. cxvii.

evidence for or against the general hypothesis that the relative success of patriarchal, 'exclusionist' collective bargaining tactics by male workers and employers may have been an important contributory factor to patterns of sexual segregation at work and so may also be an integral part of the explanation of occupational fertility differentials. This can be done, crudely, by comparing both the occupational fertility differentials and the related sex ratio differences with the degree of likely effective male trade union activity in different occupations and branches of industry.

However, trade unionism in this period is an extremely complex issue. Trade unions were undergoing their most dramatic phase of transformation and growth, with total membership rising from just three-quarters of a million workers in 1888 to over 4 million by 1914, as the new, amalgamated, 'all-grades' unions expanded.[78] To attempt to use an index of trade union affiliation for individual occupations would be extremely misleading at a time when figures were changing so dramatically and since unions varied so greatly in their effectiveness. What is really required, to assess the significance and impact of unionism on sex-specific employment and remuneration levels, and consequently on power relations between the sexes in communities, is an index of 'successful unionism'. This relates to effective male worker bargaining power in the industry concerned, as measured by achieved differentials of security and remuneration between the core of established male workers and the peripheral area of unskilled labour, which was the part of the labour market available to females.

Probably still the best available data of this kind for a brief, general assessment of this effect is provided by Eric Hobsbawm's categorisation of the results of the 1906 wage census, carried out by the Board of Trade's Labour Department. Incidentally, such an exercise would be interesting in its own right, simply for the opportunity afforded to assess the fertility behaviour of the occupational categories which actually composed Hobsbawm's much-disputed 'labour aristocracy', an independent and alternative but analogous concept to that of class III of the official, professional model, relating to a privileged stratum within the manual labour force.

Hobsbawm claimed that this stratum corresponded to about 15% of the labouring population in the period *c.* 1890–1914.[79] He defined the labour aristocracy at this time in terms of those industries containing the highest proportions of workers with weekly earnings above both 40 shillings (£2) and 45 shillings; and

[78] According to the 1911 census results, the total male workforce above age 15 in 1911 was 11.1 million, of which approximately 9.3 million were working-class employees (the total female workforce above age 15 enumerated in 1911 was 4.6 million). Census 1911, Volume X, Tables 3, 8. On the changing pattern of industrial relations in Britain during this period, see Phelps Brown, *The growth*; Clegg *et al.*, *A history of British trade unions since 1889*, Vol. I; Mommsen and Husung (eds.), *The development of trade unionism*; also Hunt, *Regional wage variations*, ch. 9. For more general surveys: Pelling, *A history*; Lovell, *British trade unions*; Hunt, *British labour history*.

[79] Hobsbawm, 'The labour aristocracy', p. 285.

with the lowest proportions below 25 shillings.[80] Within these sectors, he further distinguished a 'Super Aristocracy' of more specific occupations, in which over 40% of the male workers earned over 40 shillings in the week of the census.[81] A comparison of these groupings with the fertility evidence is intriguing, given the predictions of the professional model, for the almost complete lack of correspondence between this 'labour aristocracy' and the leaders of fertility restriction among the working classes.

Hobsbawm's aristocracy was concentrated in various industrial sectors, where unionism was strongest: Iron and Steel; Shipbuilding; Engineering and Boilermaking; Metalworking; and Building; along with the occupations of cabinet making, printing and hosiery.[82] Of all these various groups of workers, only printing and hosiery can be considered to correspond with those occupations which have been identified as leading practitioners of fertility restraint among the ranks of manual workers. All the metal-related and building sector occupations, which form the bulk of Hobsbawm's aristocracy, are certainly *not* found amongst these leading birth controllers. This would also seem to be true of Hobsbawm's 'Super Aristocracy', which consisted of certain piece-rate workers: a sizeable section of the cotton spinners; lace makers '(Lever branch)'; railway engine drivers; puddlers and rollers in the steel industry; platers, caulkers and riveters in shipbuilding and engineering; along with fitters and turners in the last-named industry. Even the two textiles occupations included by Hobsbawm were not those of lowest fertility. Indeed, 'cotton spinners' (158) was the highest completed fertility occupation among those representing the textiles industry.

By contrast the wool industry (alongside another low fertility sector, 'Food, Drink, Tobacco', i.e. retailers), actually fell into Hobsbawm's low-paid category, with only 5.7% earning above 40 shillings, and 50% earning below 25 shillings per week. The higher fertility sectors of 'Clothing', 'Pottery', 'Chemicals', 'Railways' and 'Public Utilities' all fell into Hobsbawm's 'Medium' category, containing 8–10% high-paid and 35–50% low-paid workers.[83]

Thus, among these sectors and occupations – those for which appropriate information is available – there is no contradiction of the hypothesised inverse relationship between fertility restriction and 'successful male unionism', as measured in this manner by Hobsbawm. With the exceptions of the printing and hosiery industries, it is also true that the well-organised and well-paid sectors and occupations, as identified by Hobsbawm, are ones which correspond to those with relatively few women at work, according to Table 7.8 (the cotton spinners are the

80 Hobsbawm, 'The labour aristocracy', Tables III and IV.

81 Hobsbawm, 'The labour aristocracy', Table V.

82 These are the sectors in Hobsbawm's Tables III and IV, which return *both* over 18% earning more than 40 shillings, and also less than 35% earning less than 25 shillings. Cotton returned 18.6% in the former category but 40.6% in the latter, and is therefore not counted as an 'aristocratic' sector here.

83 Unfortunately, the 1906 survey was not a complete one, and there appears to be no information for either the jewellery and precious metals sector or for mining.

only specific textile occupation to record a great preponderance of males, 2:1, relative to the sectoral norm for textiles of approximately even numbers between the sexes).[84] This suggests that localised political and social factors, related to workplace practices and relative trade union power, may well have played a significant part in accounting for the apparent influence of industrial sectors over the recorded patterns of occupational fertility differentials.

The incidence of female employment was strongly a function of the combination of industrial employment structure and the related degree of unionisation, or bargaining power of the male workers that had historically evolved in a particular industry. It appears therefore to be a promising general hypothesis that, *if* sufficiently concentrated within any given locality or community, these factors could interact to exert relatively strong influences over the fertility behaviour of some occupational categories. This would work well in explanation of the differential patterns of occupational fertility behaviour in mining, textiles, the iron and steel industry, metals versus non-metal crafts, and shipbuilding. It would not necessarily be inconsistent with the fertility levels of those occupations in the building sector, municipal services, retailing and transport sectors, since workers in all of these sectors were distributed relatively evenly and in relatively small numbers across all working-class communities. None of these sectors was sufficiently geographically concentrated in its incidence to have exerted strongly determinative influences over the sex-specific employment patterns of entire towns or districts (with the possible exception of railway workers who often formed small residential ghettoes near the main stations in many towns). However, the cases both of pottery workers and of the agricultural labourers are not so obviously in agreement with such a general hypothesis. It does not, for instance, seem that the potteries dominated their local labour market any less so than was the case in the textiles industry.[85] There may, however, be an explanation for both of these groups, potters and agricultural workers, in terms of the relationship between male and female working patterns, something which is addressed in more detail below in chapter 9.

Overall, these findings broadly indicate the existence of two polar types of 'working-class' community, and associated family households. First, that of the

[84] However, as the detailed studies of hosiery and printing make clear, the substantial presence of female workers in each of these industries was not the sign of male trade union weakness which it tended to represent in many other contexts. In both cases detailed studies have shown that organised male workers managed to maintain and even extend their relative powers and privileges during the latter nineteenth century: Osterud, 'Gender divisions'; Cockburn, *Brothers*, especially pp. 151–9.

[85] In the county borough of Stoke-on-Trent, over 40% of the total enumerated workforce of 111,806 in 1911 (74,550 males and 37,256 females) were employed in the Potteries (just over 23,000 of each sex). This percentage is very similar to that for those occupied in the textiles industry in such Lancashire boroughs as Burnley, Oldham and Preston, and such Yorkshire ones as Bradford, Halifax and Huddersfield. The only difference was a slightly greater preponderance of female workers in the textiles factories. Calculations from Census 1911, Volume X, Table 13.

politically incorporated unionised male breadwinner, with a financially entirely dependent, socially segregated and domesticated wife, fully engaged in bringing up a large, unrestricted family, for whom there was no substantial alternative economic role outside the home locally available. At the opposite extreme, there was the somewhat lower-paid male worker without a union, or in an industry where unions were without strong bargaining power, with an economically active working wife. In the latter case spouses shared the experience of the world of work and its particular cares and they jointly contributed to the household's exchequer. To balance their precarious family budget required the wife's earnings, and so her absences from the labour market for childbearing would produce evident short-term financial problems, which would grow into chronic and long-term deficits if too many small children appeared one after another, requiring her permanently to devote herself to full-time domestic duties. These are far from being fictional abstractions, as the well-researched examples of coal-mining and cotton textiles communities illustrate.[86] However, they are also ideal types in a Weberian sense: the couples in most occupations or communities would fall somewhere between these two poles, along the various, relatively independent dimensions of variability: degree of male political organisation; gendered role division; relative co-operation and communication in sexual and reproductive behaviour; degree of mutual responsibility for the domestic budget.

It should, however, be noted that Jona Schellekens has recently offered an alternative interpretation of some of the evidence discussed in this section, also relating the results of the 1906 wage census to some of the occupational fertility differentials from the 1911 census.[87] Following up an approach pioneered by Michael Haines in 1979, Schellekens has argued that the main reason why male occupations involved in physically heavy work recorded the highest fertility in 1911 was due to the fact that workers in such industries experienced a steep decline in earnings after a peak when aged in their thirties or even younger. This created a particularly pronounced need for additional income at later stages of the family life-cycle to be provided by children and adolescents, providing a rationale for high fertility.

Although the reasoning is plausible, Schellekens does not in fact offer any independent or verifiable evidence in favour of his hypothesis. This is because when comparing the fertility of forty or so occupational categories from the 1911 census the values for the variable supposed to measure steepness of income decline are no more than hypothetical estimates which Schellekens himself devised; furthermore the reader is not informed of the actual values assigned. Schellekens's description of his methodology is as follows: 'There are no exact data on steepness of the life-cycle drop-off in adult wages by occupation. It is known,

[86] On mining communities, see above, n. 73. On cotton communities, see Anderson, *Family structure*; White, *The limits of trade union militancy*; Joyce, *Work, society and politics*; Savage, *The dynamics*.

[87] Schellekens, 'Wages, secondary workers'.

however, approximately which occupations were characterized by a relatively steep decline. These were the occupations which demanded physical strength, such as mining and metallurgy.'[88]

However, this would not be a correct reading of the historical evidence presented by Michael Haines in 1979, which is the only such evidence referred to in Schellekens's article. Haines's evidence was based on information collected in 1889–90 for a comparative study conducted by Carroll D. Wright, US Commissioner of Labor. There were income statements from 1,024 British families relating to four industrial sectors: iron and steel; mining; textiles; glass. The evidence showed that in addition to iron and steel workers, it was glass workers and *textiles* workers whose adult male earnings peaked early at 30–9 years of age; whereas, quite to the contrary, peak mining wages did not tail off until unusually late, after age 50–9.[89] Haines himself interestingly speculated that the causes of these different age-earnings profiles in different industries (both in Britain and in the USA, where Carroll Wright provided a somewhat wider range of information) might be related to strength of trade union organisation, with strong unions able to maintain the privileges and income of their senior members (trade unions were insistent that older workers should not undercut those in their prime by accepting lower rates).[90]

It is this interpretation which has been argued for here, above, and which fits much better the actual evidence of relationships between adult male age-earnings profiles and child participation in the labour market than Schellekens's emphasis purely on the physical demands of different industries. Where male trade unionism was notoriously weak as in the textiles sector, the potteries and the agricultural sector, adult earnings were generally low and employers were free to employ older, more vulnerable workers at lower rates. Hence, also, the families' need for income from their children and the relative inability of the workers to deny employers access to this source of cheap, undercutting labour. As a result, juvenile labour was most common in textiles and the potteries.[91] Child employment was lowest of all in the more unionised coal, iron and metallurgy industries, as Haines noted.[92] The causation behind these patterns flows from the relative strength of trade unions in different sectors and their capacity to structure the labour market in the interests of the industry's adult males, and not directly from the relative physical demands of each kind of work.

To summarise: the relative non-correspondence between Hobsbawm's unionised, more highly paid and regularly employed occupations and those exhibiting the

[88] Schellekens, 'Wages, secondary workers', p. 7.

[89] Haines, *Fertility and occupation*, Table II-1, p. 45. Note that according to this Table, in Carroll Wright's data this was also true of miners in other European countries while the earnings of miners in the USA declined significantly only after age 40–9, still relatively late by comparison with other industries in the USA. See also Haines, 'Industrial work'.

[90] Haines, *Fertility and occupation*, p. 43.

[91] Whipp, *Patterns of labour*, pp. 76–7.

[92] Haines, 'Industrial work', p. 309.

greatest degree of fertility control is an extremely significant finding, albeit only a provisional one given the somewhat undifferentiated state of the evidence used here. It is important to acknowledge the likely conceptual link between patterns of public, formal political organisation and workplace activity, and patterns of domestic relations between spouses, and also of community attitudes towards family and parental responsibilities – the informal politics of everyday life. Both of these were affecting nuptiality and fertility behaviour in this period. This recognition brings together the narrative of politically mediated change in industrial practices in any given community and the structure of domestic roles and household consumption and production patterns, as intimately related processes. As the distinctive community cultures of the mining villages and the mill towns have long been known to demonstrate, it seems probable that wherever large proportions of the family households in a locality experienced similar workplace and domestic arrangements these inter-related forces could create and maintain strongly pronounced local customs and rules governing the principles on which fertility and nuptiality behaviour was decided. This theme will be explored further in chapter 9.

Conclusions: multiple fertility declines

The misleading abbreviation of the range and complexity of social variation exhibited by the empirical data collected at the 1911 census, which occurred as a result of the superimposition upon it of the unitary, graded professional model of social classes was demonstrated in the previous chapter. It remains to summarise the alternative patterns and conclusions which have emerged from the exploratory analysis and discussion presented in this chapter.

First, the socio-economic complexion of the 'top' and the 'tail' of the distribution of completed fertility levels in 1911 – the least fertile and most fertile 5 or 10%, respectively – is clear and is contrary on both counts to the main thrust of the professional model of fertility decline. The tail is composed almost exclusively of the highly paid hewers of the coal-mining industry and not the 'unskilled labourers' of class V, as in the professional model.

The top is much more varied in its occupational composition, comprising four distinct social groups. Two of these were of approximately equal quantitative importance: the late-marrying liberal professions on the one hand and, on the other hand, those who had achieved sufficient success through their own business and commercial activities to have been able to retire while still aged in their late forties or early fifties. The third category were those declared to be of private means, which has been interpreted here to denote principally the privileged rentier élite with inherited wealth. This would, of course, be a mixture of the longer-established landed families and those whose inherited wealth was of more recent industrial or commercial origins, perhaps only created by the preceding generation.[93] The fourth social group exhibiting extremely low fertility was composed of domestic indoor and college or club servants.

If any one specific social group of any size can be identified as controlling their fertility to the greatest extent then it is the third of these, those of private means. Although both this category and those 'retired from business' share the characteristic of marrying relatively young wives, by contradistinction with most of the established professions, it seems unhelpful to classify them together as a single socio-demographic group, given the considerable difference between their recorded average fertility levels.

The second general point relates to that great majority of the population who are found in the many categories of 'manual' occupations. It is quite misleading to claim, as the official classification does, that it is either accurate or helpful to reduce all the dimensions of fertility variation visible there to a single nationally applicable distinction: as between low-fertility skilled and high-fertility unskilled occupations. This does not accord well with either the general patterns found here or with the specific relationship between skill and fertility found within several industries. In fact where the possession of 'skill' was associated with strong unionisation, it appears that the relationship with low fertility was likely to be an inverse one, *pace* the implications of the received wisdom of the professional model of fertility decline.

Thirdly, the quite distinct factors of either employership or propietorship status, only partially recognised in the occupational classification scheme used in 1911 and entirely ignored by the professional model, were probably more important than the possession of a skill in influencing and differentiating fertility and nuptiality behaviour among that large majority living and working in the many working-class and provincial, industrial communities all around the country. Although these two aspects might have been correlates of each other in some cases, such as in the case of independent master-craftsmen, they were certainly not *necessarily* so. Railway engine drivers were skilled but could never, of course, have been proprietors or employers. It was, then, proprietorship and employership, rather than simply skilled status – even as a self-employed (as opposed to an employing) craftsman – which seems to have been most reliably correlated with a greater propensity both to marry later and to control fertility within marriage, among the industrial working and bourgeois class.

93 There is a lively continuing debate on the characteristics and sources of wealth of the socio-economic élite in Victorian and Edwardian Britain. See Rubinstein, *Men of property* and 'New men of wealth'; Stone and Stone, *An open élite?*; Thompson, 'Life after death'; Rubinstein, 'Cutting up rich'; Thompson, 'Stitching it together again'. The latter two contributions appear to have established, first, that three-quarters of the exclusive club of entrepreneurs (111 in total) who became attested millionaires or half-millionaires during the nineteenth century acquired substantial landed estates for themselves or their offspring (Thompson). But, secondly, that this was not a form of social assimilation nor an economic strategy displayed by a wider group of the 'lesser wealthy' – according to a 100% sample of 337 individuals leaving between £100,000 and £500,000 at death during the years 1873–5 (Rubinstein).

Indeed, there is suggestive evidence from the statistical analysis that in many industrial trades skill may only be related to lower fertility in functioning as a necessary but not sufficient entry qualification for eventual attainment of proprietorship status. However, the causation lying behind these observations cannot be conclusively teased out with this data. It may be that it was those men who had by their late forties and early fifties achieved and successfully maintained the status of employer or self-employed within any occupational category who were on average self-selected as those who had opted – voluntarily *or not* (i.e. the accident of relative sterility may have promoted their economic success) – for small families and the husbanding of their resources.

Fourthly, in addition to this employership and proprietorship aspect, there is visible within the larger body of data relating to the working classes another equal if not more important influence on differential fertility behaviour: that of affiliation to a given industrial sector and the likely local differences in the structure of gender relations at work and at home which this frequently entailed. This appears to exert a strong determining effect on fertility behaviour quite independent of – and cutting across – both skill and 'employment status' or proprietorship factors. It is illustrated, for instance, by the distinctions between the different branches of the textiles industry (wool and worsted as against cotton; cotton spinning as against the rest of the cotton industry), or by the uniformity of the transport sector, or by the different types of mining (coal, iron, stone) or by the split betweeen craftsmen of the metals industries and those of the wood-working and textiles sectors. Overall there was, therefore, much variation manifest in the fertility behaviour of working-class occupations, but not such as to follow a single, comprehensive dimension of a nationally applicable factor, such as 'skill' level.

Figure 7.1 suggests instead that the patterns discernible in the occupational fertility levels of the manual division of the nation attest to the existence of a set of relatively distinctive fertility régimes based around industrial sectors. This seems especially true where industries were regionally or locally concentrated into a number of relatively discrete locations, such that affiliation to the industrial sector simultaneously implied for the workers contained within it a distinctive encompassing economic and cultural environment. This typically included a set of politico-economic forces reflecting relative trade union bargaining power, gendering the local labour market and domestic roles in certain specific ways. These amount to distinctions of 'community', in the political and cultural sense of the term defined by C. J. Calhoun.[94]

[94] In 1980 C. J. Calhoun published a helpful, revisionist treatment of the concept of 'community', and its place within the history of industrialising societies. Calhoun's 'community' is entirely distinct from the classical sociological usage, which was used to denote essentially conservative, hierarchical, organic and static social entities, which were supposedly characteristic of the pre-industrial period in contrast to the politically antagonistic class relations of post-industrial, urban society. The origins of this oppositional pairing lie in the famous dichotomy of *Gemeinschaft und Gesellschaft*, the title of Ferdinand Tönnies's seminal work of synthesis published in 1887. This was also a

Hence, there appears to be a reasonably clear order in which the industrial sectors appear when ranked according to their fertility behaviour in Figure 7.1. Among the working classes twenty or more distinct fertility régimes can be distinguished, even at this national scale of aggregation of the occupational evidence. It is not only the case that each of these twenty or more industrial sectors exhibits its own distinctive range of fertility levels but also that each exhibits its own specific relationship between completed fertility, nuptiality and employment status, skill or pay. For instance, in some the relationship between fertility and 'skill' is strongly positive, in some strongly negative and in some apparently absent. It has been particularly suggested that systematic differences between industries and communities in the politically mediated issue of the extent to which women and children were able to participate in the labour market may be strongly related to these varying relationships observed between male occupation, fertility and nuptiality.

To summarise, therefore, the occupational fertility evidence displayed in Figure 7.1 seems to reveal neither two opposed relational classes in a straightforward Marxian sense, nor a nationally coherent, hierarchical pattern of status stratification in a broadly Weberian sense, as expounded by the professional model. The demographic indices are continuous variables. Nevertheless, a primary division into two relatively discrete groupings of occupations of lower and higher fertility is visible. The numerically smaller of these two segments contained the non-manual occupational categories of wealth and privilege plus those who served them most closely both at work and in the home, that is, in their roles as producers and consumers. These social groups tended to be geographically heavily concentrated in the most salubrious residential districts of the metropolis and the country's dozen or so other major cities (and in the favourite resort and spa towns). This was an inevitable spatial correlate of these occupations' economic functions, which were primarily those of administration, professional service, business management and their clerical and domestic assistants.

However, in the second, numerically much larger section of the nation, there are

conceptualisation endorsed by Max Weber. Calhoun's thesis is that 'community' represents the kind of politically significant relations, forms of authority and modes of consciousness which are formed out of those moral commitments between individuals which can only occur where relationships are predominantly face to face. This is in contrast to those forms of regulated behaviour and formal authority relations which result from merely following rules and legal obligations to relatively abstract and remote entities, enforced where necessary by non-local agencies and visitations. Calhoun points out that 'community' relations may as likely form in post-industrial as in pre-industrial settings: urban ghettoes, factory towns or even affluent suburbs. They are equally as likely to produce hierarchical, deferential relations as revolutionary, 'class' sentiments and values. According to Calhoun 'community' refers to the quality of the social relations involved and how they are formed. 'Community' is in principle entirely historically variable in its political manifestations and results: these are the consequence of other, contingent events and forces. Calhoun, 'Community', especially pp. 107–9. See below, pp. 546–58, for a further and fuller discussion of class, community and fertility, invoking the novel concept of 'communication communities'.

subdivisions and patterns of recorded fertility behaviour which are more strongly marked by a variety of regional, local and industrial sectoral variations. The evidence presented here suggests that falling fertility among this part of the nation was far from a process graded by neat and identifiable, nationally applicable status or social class patterns. It was the relatively massive, and highly localised variations between communities, especially in the degree to which their labour markets were sexually segregated and divided, which may well largely account for occupational fertility differentials during this period of falling fertilities. This was something which was integrally linked to the history of local industrial relations and work practices in each of these places.

Thus, the principal positive conclusion to emerge from all the foregoing analysis is an alternative overall view of the socio-morphological *form* of the historical process whereby fertility declined in Britain. The occupational data of 1911 has conventionally been considered to support the notion of a single, socially graded and unified national event, '*the* fertility decline'. However, the patterns actually revealed by the 1911 census, as explored here, are much more complex and less clear-cut than that. The overall picture to emerge is one of multiple falling fertilities in Britain: an essentially fractured and fissured set of relatively independent processes, occurring in different ways over a period of nearly a century in different locations and communities. It is certainly quite possible that if sufficiently detailed data were available it would even show some social groups or communities exhibiting important counter-trends of rising marital fertility and/or decreasing age at marriage during parts of the period, 1860–1940. The work of Woods and Smith, on fertility and nuptiality variation in the 630 or so registration districts of England and Wales, is certainly suggestive of this. Their estimates indicate that from 1861 to 1891 both marital fertility and nuptiality in many of the country's mining districts may have increased substantially.[95]

The idea of a neatly socially graded single event should be replaced by the picture of many geographically and chronologically disparate processes occurring in distinct contexts and for different reasons. It is because these have formed, overall, a chronologically overlapping sequence of such changes that this has produced the illusion at an aggregate, national level of a relatively smooth unitary process. This misapprehension needs to be recognised for what it is: an elementary statistical fallacy, an artefact created by aggregation. The plausibility of this illusion has been maintained by and has in turn reciprocally supported the

[95] Woods and Smith, 'The decline of marital fertility', Figures 6 and 7; Woods, 'The fertility transition', Figure 6. Note, however, that the interesting results for enumeration districts reported by Smith and Woods can only be treated as suggestive rather than as rigorous findings, given the nature of their sources. This is because sex- and age-differential migration causes significant but unfortunately unmeasurable biases in calculations of this sort, where the age-specific female census population of each district in 1861 and 1891 provides the denominator and the averaged number of births registered from 1861–3 and 1891–3, respectively, provides the numerator.

professional model of fertility decline, the classification scheme which has structured the official statistics from the day in February 1910 when, behind the scenes at the GRO, a national fertility inquiry was first seriously mooted by T. H. C. Stevenson.

Finally, the evidence afforded by the occupational fertility differentials might itself help to reveal the very reasons for its own historiographical misinterpretation: the reasons for the *a priori* application of the professional model of hierarchical relationships to the empirical data from 1911. It was the predominantly metropolitan-dwelling status group of professional, liberal intellectuals who constituted that part of society which framed, discussed and investigated the issues of fertility and mortality in terms of class and social position, as has been shown at length in Part II above. It is primarily their cultural artefacts which remain to posterity as the main forms of historical evidence, both qualitative and quantitative. This is especially true in such a poorly documented area of behaviour as that of family life and reproductive and sexual behaviour, and the changes that were dimly perceived to be occurring.

The official census report on the fertility of marriage in 1911 is a paradigm example of this. The model of British society as a unitary status-differentiated hierarchy which it contained may not only have been an ideologically appropriate one for this social group. It may also have accurately reflected their perceptions of their daily experience in the metropolis of London, surrounded by deferential servants in the home and by junior clerical staff at work. This professional and administrative class interacted at a greater social distance with the many petty bourgeois and artisanal occupations of the capital – those who came by the tradesmen's entrance to sell, install and maintain. 'Beyond' this social pale were the municipal workers operating the trams, the staff at railway stations and finally – culturally and economically furthest away from them of all – the labourers, such as those at the docks or on building sites, with whom they would rarely have come into any spoken contact at all. Excluded almost altogether from this official, administrative and metropolitan, professional representation of society were the industrial and commercial employers and employees, whose activities so influenced provincial, urban Britain.[96]

The conceptual problem which has ever since bedevilled the analysis of changing fertility behaviour occurred when this geographically and socially specific perspective, reflecting the personal views, the commonsense inferences drawn from daily experience, and the institutional interests of the professional officials of the GRO, was naïvely assumed to be an accurate single representation of social relations throughout all of Britain in every town and district. Whereas, in

[96] As the penultimate section of chapter 2 demonstrated, the relative exclusion of business employers from the GRO's classification scheme up to and including the 1911 census was also partly the result of its need to protect its institutional and cognitive interests against the 'Marshallian' claims of the Labour Department.

fact, the metropolis was only one among many different and changing regional communities throughout the land. Admittedly it was the largest and culturally the most influential; but it was also the most complex and varied in its economic life, although this is not something conveyed at all by the Olympian perspective of the professional model. Indeed, it was probably in many ways most atypical of the rest of the nation. Most of the country's provincial cities and communities each possessed their own distinct socio-economic character tied to a specific base of one or two or a small number of specific industries and employers, associated with a local political history and culture which had produced a unique configuration of social relations.

With the invention of the professional model of social structure, a specific, rationalised and simplified *model* of the world inhabited by the Edwardian metropolitan professional middle class was transposed into a unitary hierarchical representation of the whole of British society generally, as it supposedly existed throughout the country. This was then used as a tool for the ostensibly scientific analysis of a particularly complex and changing form of social behaviour. Practices of family formation in fact changed in a variety of ways and according to divergent chronologies under all the varied cultural, political and economic conditions prevailing in the scores of different communities all over the country. But all this variety was simply expunged from the record by being pressed into a single conceptual and statistical mould – the professional model.

How was fertility controlled? The spacing versus stopping debate and the culture of abstinence

The spacing versus stopping debate

The previous chapter has explored the pattern of falling fertility evident in the detailed occupational data derived from the 1911 census; and it sought to offer some preliminary analysis to account for the social diversity that was found. Before further intellectual progress can be made with the most fundamental questions of *why* different sections of society began to change their fertility behaviour so dramatically during this particular period, it will be of great assistance first to investigate *how* the regulation of births within marriage was achieved.

In this area of intimate behaviour, direct testimony of a representative kind, on any scale, on reasons for birth control or techniques employed is virtually absent from the historical record of Victorian and Edwardian Britain. It has therefore proved equally as difficult for historians and demographers to discover which were the most important methods used to control births as it has been to reconstruct the principal motives involved. To establish with some confidence how birth regulation within marriage was achieved during the decades before the Great War would, therefore, in itself be an important advance in our knowledge. In this chapter the 1911 census data is further explored, alongside other relevant primary sources from the period, in an attempt to provide an answer to this question.

There are two related, but formally and empirically independent, kinds of questions regarding how birth control was achieved. There is the question of what methods were employed (withdrawal, condoms, caps, rhythm, abstinence, etc.); and there is the question of what, if any, strategy of family building was deployed. This chapter will therefore seek to address both questions, starting with the latter issue.

Where the question of family-building strategy is concerned, the well-established debate over 'stopping' versus 'spacing' provides the central focus of inquiry and point of departure. Under a 'stopping' regime of 'parity-specific' control, births ('parities' in the demographic terminology) are allowed to arrive without any particular attention to timing until a maximum sustainable number has been reached (which is usually held to reflect a 'target', or norm-related ideal of family size), at which (parity-specific) point there is an absolute cessation of childbearing. 'Spacing', by contrast, is manifest in attention to slowing the rate at which births arrive throughout much, if not all, of the reproductive union, but without there being a particular cut-off point at a certain family size or after a specific number of parities.

As a result of the salience of this debate, the effort in this chapter to establish empirically whether stopping or spacing behaviour was primarily responsible for falling fertility in Britain before the First World War is far more than a mere semantic or logical quibble. As was made abundantly clear in the seminal exchange in this debate, between J. Dupâquier, M. Lachiver and John Knodel, the spacing versus stopping debate goes to the heart of the central causal questions and the policy issues relating to fertility change.[1] Historical evidence in favour of 'stopping' has been seen as implying that systematic birth control arrived in the recent past as an absolutely novel and revolutionary form of behavioural change, with all that that implies socially and culturally: *La Révolution démographique*, as Adolphe Landry hailed it.[2] 'Spacing' would be more consistent with a more gradual process of change, perhaps merely an intensification of practices, habits of calculation and motives long in evidence already. Was the mass adoption of some form of family planning an innovation or merely an adjustment, to use Gösta Carlsson's oft-repeated formulation of the main conceptual alternatives?[3] If birth control was previously outside the cultural frame of reference for calculative behaviour, then its spectacular spread in recent times should be more accurately characterised as an absolute innovation of a particularly dramatic kind.

Throughout most of the postwar period demographers have attempted to resolve this issue with the aid of a measuring instrument supposedly designed to discriminate between uncontrolled and controlled fertility: the Coale–Trussell Princeton models for studying the empirical data of human fertility variation, adapted from the original work of Louis Henry. However, as was discussed in the introductory chapter, there are serious conceptual caveats concerning the validity of the mutually exclusive dichotomisation of all fertility behaviour as either 'natural' or 'planned', as defined by this methodology. Demographers themselves have now become concerned that a measuring technology originally designed to detect as precisely and unequivocally as possible the presence or absence of fertility-controlling behaviour in any given community may in fact have systematically hidden the existence of such behaviour and distorted our understanding of this phenomenon.

1 Knodel, 'Espacement des naissances' (including debate with Dupâquier and Lachiver). The original article outlining the Dupâquier–Lachiver method was Dupâquier and Lachiver, 'Sur les débuts de la contraception'.

2 Landry, *La Révolution démographique*.

3 Carlsson, 'The decline of fertility'.

How can this have happened? First, by fixing itself according to the schedule of 'Hutterite' age-specific fertility rates, the functional form of 'natural fertility' was unwittingly tied to that particular community's pattern of marriage-duration specific sexual activity. It was not originally appreciated by Louis Henry that the pattern of age-specific fertility might be significantly affected at longer marriage durations by variations in norms of frequency of sexual activity, something which he has subsequently acknowledged.[4] The Hutterites have in fact proved to be somewhat unusual in demographic terms in the extent to which their extremely distinctive beliefs, practices and supporting social system positively enjoined couples to continue sexually active and child-bearing lives as long as possible, thereby resulting in relatively high fertility at long durations of marriage, over the latter part of the female fecund period.[5] Hutterite fertility was not simply generally high, therefore, but differentially high over the later part of the fecund age range. This is a particularly unfortunate property for a schedule supposed to represent a standard functional form and against which the deviation towards controlled fertility was specifically measured by a supposed shortfall in births at the higher parities, precisely that age range where Hutterite culture produced its unusually enhanced 'natural fertility' characteristics.

Secondly, and even more importantly, it has come to be appreciated that by directing attention too exclusively to the identification of one particular kind of fertility control – parity-specific 'stopping' – other strategies of birth control have not been properly assessed. By far the most important of these is likely to have been 'spacing'. The Princeton measurement technology, as currently constructed, does not enable the positive identification of moderate degrees of this kind of spacing behaviour as deliberate control if, as is likely, there is an absence of any age-specific or parity-specific interference with the overall fertility schedule.[6] Such spacing corresponds to steady restriction across the age range and would therefore merely be recorded by the Princeton measures as natural fertility at a low absolute level relative to the Hutterite standard.[7] Equally, 'starting', which is a particular form of spacing involving a delay before the first birth only, is also unlikely to be detected by the Princeton measures. Moreover, the problem of

[4] See Henry, 'Some remarks', p. 564. The contribution which first demonstrated the important general point that duration of marriage caused independent sources of variation in age-specific fertility rates was: Page, 'Patterns underlying fertility schedules'; and see above, pp. 26–7.

[5] Ericksen *et al.*, 'Fertility patterns and trends'; and Ericksen *et al.*, 'Response to Louis Henry', p. 565. For a brief introduction to the extraordinary and peripatetic history of the Hutterite community before settling in North America, and an enlightening analysis of the relationship between their theology and social practices, see Peter, 'The certainty of salvation'. Also, more generally, Hostetler, *Hutterite society*.

[6] Wilson, Oeppen and Pardoe, 'What is natural fertility?', pp. 5–6; Okun, 'Evaluating methods'. This applies to the measures specified in Coale and Trussell, 'Model fertility schedules'; and Coale and Trussell, 'Technical note'.

[7] Bean, Mineau and Anderton, *Fertility change on the American frontier*, p. 198.

interpretation is further compounded by the well-established effect of lactational post-partum amenorrhoea, whereby 'spacing' patterns can be observed because of a community's practice of prolonged breast-feeding, something which may or may not be done deliberately to achieve this spacing effect.[8]

Judith Blake has most clearly and forcefully summarised the central conceptual problem with the Henry–Coale–Trussell methodology and its consequent limitations as a technical means for studying changes in the extent of birth control practised by any population.[9] Through inference from an elaborate and sophisticated apparatus for measuring behavioural outcomes it seeks to provide a supposedly unambiguous empirical marker, tracking fundamental change over time in individuals' reproductive *intentions*: from 'natural', uncontrolled to controlled fertility. But it is now known that the 'natural' category can contain any admixture of purposive controllers mixed in with the non-controllers, provided the former are predominantly 'spacing' or 'starting' rather than 'stopping'. At best, therefore, the Henry–Coale–Trussell methodology can only show when such intentions became translated into the 'stopping' form of control. This is a particularly incapacitating limitation for a methodology which has been deployed (as in the Princeton European Fertility Project) supposedly to reveal exactly the geographical and social dimensions of the first historical appearance of deliberate birth controlling behaviour in different nations and populations around the world. Indeed, it has now been conclusively established that at least in some historical communities, where research has been carried out without exclusive reliance on the Princeton 'natural fertility' measurement apparatus, spacing as a method of birth control anterior to or combined with stopping has played an integral role during the recent historical episodes of fertility decline in a number of countries.[10] This is conceptually a crucial finding for our understanding of how it is that populations come to control their fertility and it is a discovery which exclusive reliance on the Princeton armoury of fertility indices had previously obscured.

On reflection, this historical finding is hardly surprising. In a relatively low-income context where effective forms of contraception were lacking, infant mortality high, margins above material subsistence relatively narrow, maternal health likely to be poor and endangered by confinements, and with illness or temporary disablement of either or both spouses a frequent occurrence, 'spacing'

[8] Knodel, 'Starting, stopping and spacing'. 'Starting' was coined by Lesthaeghe to refer to the extent of fertility control in a community due to practices which delay the normal age at which childbearing commences: Lesthaeghe, 'On the social control of human reproduction'.

[9] Blake, 'The fertility transition'.

[10] Two groups of researchers first identified such spacing behaviour as a significant practice in the US fertility decline: Anderton and Bean, 'Birth spacing and fertility limitation' (with respect to the Mormon community); and David and Sanderson, 'Rudimentary contraceptive methods'. The importance of such behaviour among at least some groups in France's, Italy's and Britain's fertility declines has also now been demonstrated using three different methods: David and Mroz, 'Evidence of fertility regulation'; Kertzer and Hogan, *Family, political economy and demographic change*, pp. 171–2; Crafts, 'Duration of marriage, fertility and women's employment opportunities'.

would have been an obvious – perhaps the only obvious – way for a couple to exert some helpful control over their personal Malthusian predicament. Margaret Hewitt long ago argued that industrially employed Victorian mothers would have spaced their births both to keep in employment and to maintain their own strength.[11] Hence, the notion that parity-specific 'stopping' is the only form of aspirational, target-oriented fertility control has been rightly questioned. Spacing may be just as much part of a planned strategy, but one aimed at maintaining a target living standard, rather than an ideal family size.[12] Indeed, it has been acutely pointed out that the 'stopping' strategy would itself only become 'rational' – an obvious and logical way of implementing family planning intentions – once a highly dependable contraceptive means was both available and acceptable.[13] This logical condition is something which did not apply for the vast majority of married couples in British society until well into the twentieth century.[14]

What light, then, can the 1911 fertility evidence throw on these questions? In fact, by turning to the occupational evidence on *incomplete* fertility, it is possible to establish quite conclusively the relative extent to which those marrying before 1911 were deploying spacing as against stopping forms of birth control.

The incomplete and completed fertility of occupations compared

The principal source of information from the 1911 census on male occupational differentials in *incomplete* fertility is Table 30 of the *Fertility of Marriage Report*, Part 2. This presents information on the same 206 occupational categories as Table 35 (used for the analysis of completed fertility in the previous chapter). Once again the data has been cross-classified according to the same female age at marriage subdivisions and the familiar principle of quinquennia of marriage duration. However, in the available tables the first quinquennium of marriage duration was additionally split into two duration periods, relating to those marriages of up to two years' duration and, separately, the next three years of marriage duration.[15] As a result, there were substantially fewer couples in each of these two categories, covering marriages of shortest duration before 1911. It was therefore decided to use the third marriage duration period of Table 30, relating to those married for between five and ten years in 1911, as the basis for a statistical analysis of comparative incomplete fertility levels. This enabled the analysis to be performed

[11] Hewitt, *Wives and mothers in Victorian industry*, p. 95. For a recent contribution also arguing in favour of spacing on these grounds among some of the textiles workers of Keighley in West Yorkshire, see Garrett, 'The trials of labour'.

[12] Landers, 'Fertility decline and birth spacing', p. 107.

[13] David and Sanderson, 'Rudimentary contraceptive methods', p. 314.

[14] For extensive further discussion and support for this viewpoint, see below, pp. 389–424, 558–78.

[15] According to the instruction on the census schedule, only the completed number of years married was to be entered. The first duration period therefore covers marriages from one day to one year and 364 days; the second period covers those from two years exactly up to four years and 364 days, etc.

on the same 195 occupational categories used in the previous chapters. As a result of the smaller numbers of women marrying under 20 years old in this more recent marriage cohort, only the two most frequent female age at marriage categories are deployed in the following analysis: for those marrying at age 20–4 (AM2/01–5) and at age 25–9 (AM3/01–5).[16] Appendix E gives all the values and occupational rankings for both of these incomplete fertility variables.

Before turning to an examination of the spacing versus stopping debate in the light of this evidence, it is a helpful preliminary exercise to assess how the occupational patterns for incomplete fertility compare with the positive findings reported in the previous chapter relating to completed fertility. Of course, those married in the 1880s had had a different and longer historical experience before 1911 than those married in the 1900s and significantly different patterns can therefore be expected in the occupations' fertility and nuptiality behaviour.

Table 8.1 shows that across the dataset of 195 occupations there was a surprisingly high degree of correlation between the rank position scored by an occupation according to the two pairs of fertility indices for the 1880s marriage cohort (AM2/81–5 and AM3/86–90) and for the 1900s cohort (AM2/01–5 and AM3/01–5). As well as these two sets of correlations, Table 8.1 includes, for comparison, the equivalent correlation coeffficients for those married ten to fifteen years (AM2/96–00, AM3/96–00) and for those married just two to five years (AM2/06–9, AM3/06–9), which confirm the same pattern of strong correlation.

The high values of these correlation coefficients indicate that in general the patterns of occupational differentials in completed fertility, as summarised in Figure 7.1, were remarkably similar to those generated by the incomplete fertility evidence among those marrying in the 1900s. In general, there was a close match in 1911 between the extent to which couples in a given occupational category then aged in their late forties and fifties had regulated fertility across the previous twenty to thirty years of their marriages and the extent to which much younger couples in the same occupation, mostly in their thirties, were now regulating their fertility during the first five to ten years of their marriages.

This point is further amplified by Table 8.2, which gives details of the minority of occupations which did exhibit significant changes in rank positions, based on a comparison of individual occupations' rankings for the two matched pairs of age at marriage indices: AM2/81–5 with AM2/01–5; and AM3/86–90 with AM3/01–5. When comparing AM2/81–5, the basis for Figure 7.1, with AM2/01–5, Parts A and B of Table 8.2 show that only thirteen individual occupations were found to have

[16] By the turn of the new century the gradual general trend towards later marriage which had been in train since the 1870s had resulted in 12 of the 195 occupational categories registering fewer than thirty couples in the youngest-marrying (age 15–19) subdivisions of this marriage cohort. In all but 31 of the 195 occupations, the *modal* female age at marriage in this cohort continued to be 20–4 years old (see below, p. 393).

Table 8.1 *Spearman R^2 correlation coefficients between completed and incomplete fertility level indices*

Fertility indices	Coeff.	Signif.	N (occs.)
AM2/81–5 with AM2/01–5	0.95675	0.0001	195
AM3/86–90 with AM3/01–5	0.91442	0.0001	195
AM2/01–5 with AM3/01–5	0.94382	0.0001	195
AM2/81–5 with AM2/96–00	0.96681	0.0001	195
AM3/86–90 with AM3/96–00	0.94952	0.0001	195
AM2/96–00 with AM3/96–00	0.96138	0.0001	195
AM2/81–5 with AM2/06–9	0.90778	0.0001	195
AM3/86–90 with AM3/06–9	0.89044	0.0001	195
AM2/06–09 with AM3/06–9	0.90048	0.0001	195
AM2/01–5 with AM2/96–00	0.98197	0.0001	195
AM2/01–5 with AM2/06–9	0.96127	0.0001	195
AM2/96–00 with AM2/06–9	0.94870	0.0001	195
AM3/01–5 with AM3/96–00	0.96055	0.0001	195
AM3/01–5 with AM3/06–9	0.94572	0.0001	195
AM3/96–00 with AM3/06–9	0.93813	0.0001	195

moved rank position significantly (readers are reminded that in Table 8.2 a lower rank position signifies lower fertility).[17]

Although in some cases these discrepancies in rank position may reflect genuine differences in fertility behaviour between similar socio-occupational groups drawn from the two marriage cohorts, the effects of differential occupational composition and recruitment need to be borne in mind as the most probable source of differences. In other words a comparison of this sort, involving occupational groupings of men of different ages, is not really comparing like with like, even when made at the same point in time. Despite the fact that the two groups of men are recorded in 1911 as pursuing exactly the same occupation, there must still be some socio-economic differences between the two generations in certain occupations, since one group was aged approximately 45–60 years old, whereas the other group was typically 30–40 years old. Indeed, in view of this the high degree of overall correlation found across the two cohorts is all the more surprising and is, perhaps, testimony to the robustness and utility of occupation as a particularly appropriate social unit, at the national aggregate level, for the analysis of fertility and nuptiality change in British society at this time. In many of

[17] The necessarily arbitrary criterion adopted for defining significant difference in rank position was that of only thirty rank positions up or down. It was decided to use this rather overgenerous criterion because there was such consistency in the data that there would have been very few occupations at all in Table 8.2 on the more exacting criterion of forty rank positions' difference, as was used above in chapter 7 for Table 7.3.

Table 8.2 *Occupations differing by at least thirty rank positions according to completed and incomplete fertility level indices*

ID Occupation	Size	Rankings	
		Completed	Incomplete
A Incomplete fertility ranking **lower** *than completed, AM 20–4*			
62 trams – drivers	0.209	142	106
157 cotton – spinning	0.578	107	66
158 cotton – winding	0.200	69	34
159 cotton – weaving	0.687	78	25
163 hosiery man'fre	0.145	100	68
B Incomplete fertility ranking **higher** *than completed, AM 20–4*			
38 hospital, benevolent society	0.170	36	77
70 harbour, dock, lighthouse official	0.265	114	156
73 farmers, graziers	2.879	104	148
80 nursery, seedsmen, florists	0.258	88	118
186 brewers	0.310	95	134
188 lodging, boarding house keepers	0.132	7	58
190 barmen	0.151	67	133
196 general shopkeepers, dealers	0.409	79	111
C Incomplete fertility ranking **lower** *than completed, AM 25–9*			
51 rail guards	0.315	135	100
53 rail pointsmen	0.184	165	103
87 coal mineowners	0.084	112	52
90 coal, coke merchants	0.341	98	68
104 tool makers	0.247	118	70
106 wire workers	0.181	140	94
115 coach, carriage makers	0.251	115	71
157 cotton – spinning	0.578	91	46
158 cotton – winding	0.200	73	10
159 cotton – weaving	0.687	59	7
162 wool – weaving	0.242	42	9
172 boot, shoe makers	1.595	143	112
178 fishmongers	0.409	123	89
181 bakers – biscuits, cakes	0.651	153	107
195 refuse disposal	0.188	193	162
D Incomplete fertility ranking **higher** *than completed, AM 25–9*			
13 clergy (C of E)	0.277	31	83
16 church, chapel, cemetery officers	0.108	55	146
17 barristers	0.044	4	75
20 physicians, surgeons	0.278	14	55
30 performers, showmen	0.247	66	108
32 domestic coachmen, grooms	0.696	77	114
36 gamekeepers	0.201	144	175
40 merchants (commodity undefined)	0.064	26	61
58 coach, cabmen	0.377	119	153
64 trams – others	0.150	98	130
70 harbour, dock, lighthouse officials	0.265	109	156
146 glass manufacture	0.238	125	171
149 oil (vegetable) – millers, refiners	0.105	103	164
180 corn, flour merchants, dealers	0.202	78	127
190 barmen	0.151	88	152
191 waiters	0.177	65	110
194 electricity supply	0.173	96	141

the individual cases where substantial fertility differences emerge, it is probable that it is these generational differences in experience and in the social recruitment and status of workers of varying ages which primarily explain the observed demographic differences.[18]

There are, however, two somewhat more systematic divergences clearly visible in Table 8.2, which may indicate genuine differences between the two cohorts in fertility behaviour. One of these relates to the textiles industry. Three of the four occupations representing Lancashire cotton operatives (159 weavers, 158 winders, 157 spinners) are among the five occupations listed in Part A. This finding for the textile industry is confirmed by the figures in Part C for those marrying wives aged 25–9, where the same three cotton occupations are found with much lower rank positions; and this time joined by the wool weavers, too. Among this elder-marrying section of those with incomplete fertility, cotton weavers (159), wool weavers (162), and cotton winders (158) were among the ten least fertile occupations from the entire total of 195 (seventh, ninth and tenth, respectively); and they were joined in this extremely low fertility by wool spinners (161), who were the seventeenth least fertile occupation, according to AM3/01–5. It is certainly noteworthy that among those marrying slightly older than average wives, these four proletarian occupations from the wool and cotton sectors of the textile industry were controlling their marital fertility more rigorously over the first five to ten years of marriage than almost any other occupations in the population.[19]

This shows that textile workers in 1911, especially those in the Lancashire cotton industry, were particularly assiduous in spacing births over the first five to ten years of marriage (and quite possibly also delayed the first birth after marriage, i.e. practised 'starting', too). This is, of course, what would be expected if it was an aim of textile workers to try to avoid having so many young, dependent children that their mother had to retire altogether from the workforce before the eldest child could begin to earn. Whether this characteristic of pronounced spacing in the early years of marriage was a relatively new development cannot, unfortunately, be answered conclusively with the kind of data available here. Also, the fact that spacing from early in marriage was so particularly marked among those textiles couples who married latest hints at further, fine-grained differences of family-building strategy and of birth control methods and motives, which can only be explored with much higher quality data than is available here.

Of the eight occupations listed in Part B of Table 8.2, the two most important are farmers, graziers (73) and lodging, boarding house keepers (188). The former was important because of its quantitative size and the latter because it was the seventh

[18] See n. 33 below, for discussion of several examples of the latter.

[19] The remaining eleven cases listed in Part C, where the rank position for those marrying at 25–9 was much lower for incomplete than for completed fertility, are of much less substantive significance, in that there is no corresponding movement in the other incomplete fertility index for those aged 20–4 at marriage; nor do they imply a different position in Figure 7.1 for any of the social groups identified there.

least fertile occupation when measured by completed fertility (AM2/81–5) but only the fifty-eighth in terms of incomplete fertility (AM2/01–5), a relatively large discrepancy. In the case of farmers, this is an unambiguous occupational title and it is unlikely that the fertility difference between the younger and the older generations (those of incomplete and completed fertility, respectively) can be simply ascribed to a socio-economic difference between the two. This may, therefore, accurately reflect the fact that farming couples hardly restricted their fertility at all during the first ten years of marriage but thereafter did so to a significantly greater extent. This is also consistent with the finding reported in the previous chapter that among the 1880s marriage cohort, farmers were unusual in that those who married youngest exhibited relatively low fertility compared to those who married latest.[20] The suggestion made there that the fertility of this occupational group may, therefore, have been influenced by a target family size (but a target size which was quite large), would seem to gain some further support from these results. Of course, this form of parity-specific control is supposed to characterise the whole population during fertility transition according to the proponents of the 'stopping' thesis. However, the evidence here suggests that social groups such as farming couples were unusual and it was rare to find an occupation which exhibited a much greater relative degree of fertility restriction over the last half of the wife's fecund period, compared with the first five to ten years.[21]

In the other case of this sort, the socially composite nature of ID 188, 'lodging, boarding house keepers', suggests that there may be two different social constituencies being measured here. The younger couples in their twenties and thirties in 1911 may have been disproportionately composed of those running small, low-rent urban lodging houses for working men, whereas the older couples in their late forties and fifties may contain a much higher proportion of those managing substantial establishments, including those boarding houses in resort towns catering for the leisured classes. A similar age-related difference in the social composition of the occupation would also seem to be the obvious explanation for the appearance in Part B of: general shopkeepers, dealers (196);

[20] Chapter 7, p. 332

[21] An alternative interpretation is that the incomplete fertility figure represents the unrestrained fertility of only a selected set of relatively young farmers who had 'inherited' their farms relatively early, whereas the completed fertility figure, representing a group of much older men, includes all those other farmers who had had long waits before inheriting and may, therefore, have been more inclined to regulate their fertility while waiting. However, this thesis does not appear to gain any circumstantial support from the nuptiality indices in Appendix C (RANK/PRUDMARR) and Appendix F (RANK/AMRAT2). These show that while farmers marrying in the 1880s married relatively late (rank 58), those marrying in the 1900s postponed marriage to an even greater extent (rank 22). This suggests no easier access to farms among this younger cohort. This would be consistent with the well-known increasing difficulties faced by the agricultural sector during this period of rising imports and falling rents.

hospital, benevolent society service (38); and barmen (190) which appears in both Part B and Part D.[22]

Finally, in Part D of Table 8.2 the second of the two more systematic divergences in occupational rankings is found. Here, the older-marrying subsets of three of the most established professions (Anglican clergy; barristers; and physicians, surgeons) all appear to be exhibiting much less control over their marital fertility during the first five to ten years of marriage than would be predicted from the very substantial limitation displayed by the completed fertility of those in the same occupations who had married twenty years earlier. This, then, is intriguingly the opposite pattern to that of the older-marrying subset of cotton and wool operatives. Whereas the latter appear to be limiting fertility even more stringently from the start of their marriages, these three professional groups show relatively less family limitation initially, leaving open the implication that the professionals' birth control was practised all the more rigorously during the later stages of the marriage. This, therefore, returns us to the central issue of spacing versus stopping behaviour. The textile couples tend to exhibit a pattern of birth control consistent with a marked degree of spacing from the start of their married lives. These three categories of professionals were, by contrast, apparently displaying somewhat less spacing if they married relatively late, possibly a pattern more consistent with a greater resort to stopping behaviour. However, these are merely faint signs, difficult to interpret. In the next sections a much more systematic assessment will now be made of the important issue of the relative incidence and significance of these different forms of family planning in Britain before the Great War.

Spacing, stopping and the occupational evidence of incomplete fertility

How, then, does the occupational evidence of incomplete fertility in 1911 relate to the spacing versus stopping debate? Appendix E presents a listing of the 195 male occupations ranked according to the fertility index, AM2/01–5: the mean number of children born to those couples in each occupation where wives were aged 20–4 at marriage (AM2), who married during the years 1901–5. This therefore represents each occupation's average fertility during the first five to ten years of marriage (i.e. after an average of 7.5 years' duration of marriage).

The information in Appendix E has very considerable significance for the stopping versus spacing debate. As can be readily appreciated, there is an extremely wide degree of variation in the fertility levels recorded by the different

[22] See ch. 7, n. 10, on the uncertainties of the social composition of barmen. One other occupation was found in both Parts B and D: 'harbour, dock, lighthouse officials, servants' (70). This was one of the few occupations omitted from Figure 7.1 because, like fishermen and merchant seamen (though to a lesser extent), there is an unmeasurable degree of reduction in wives' exposure to the risk of fertility because of husbands' occupational absences (the lighthousemen).

occupational groups. Couples in the highest fertility occupations had already experienced almost twice as many births as those in the occupations of lowest fertility. This is a scale of difference not much less than that reported in Appendix C and Figure 7.1, showing variation in completed fertility after a full twenty-five to thirty years of marriage for those marrying wives aged 20–4 in the early 1880s. Appendix E also shows that this degree of variation is almost exactly the same where wives married at 25–9 (AM3/01–5).

The most significant finding, therefore, is that couples in England and Wales in those many occupations recording relatively low fertility in 1911 must have been restricting themselves to an extremely low birth rate from very early on in marriage, during the first five to ten years. This indicates a great deal of spacing.

In order to assess and evaluate the extent of fertility reduction indicated by the data in Appendix E, it is possible to make a rigorous comparison with the high-quality age-specific fertility information available in the Cambridge Group's body of family reconstitution data, which is derived from twenty-six parish registers during the period 1538–1837. This data can be used to establish a benchmark, showing the typical fertility of English couples after an average of 7.5 years' marriage during the period definitely before that of dramatically falling fertility. Following the critique that has been mounted (here above and elsewhere) of the concept of natural fertility, it is *not* being claimed that the difference between this figure for the period 1538–1837 and the values recorded for the occupational groupings in Appendix E can be regarded as a precise, interval-scale measure of the extent of fertility control being practised in 1911.[23] The comparison does, however, provide a robust general indicator of the extent to which married couples in 1911 were having significantly fewer births over the first five to ten years of marriage than had been the norm in English society during earlier centuries.

The most rigorous standard against which to make a judgement of this sort is to compare the occupational fertilities in 1911 with a similarly constituted sample of couples drawn from the pre-1837 reconstitution data from which all prenuptially pregnant women have been deliberately excluded.[24] This deals with the possible objection that the low incomplete fertility of some occupations in 1911 might be partly attributed to unusually low proportions of prenuptial pregnancies (an important potential source of bias, given that approximately 20.7% of all first brides aged 20–4 were prenuptially pregnant in the pre-1837 data and as much as 28.6% among those married at age 20–4 in 1911).[25] Clearly, this objection could

[23] See above, pp. 368–70.

[24] This can be done because the reconstituted parish register data gives sufficiently detailed information so that women can be defined as prenuptially pregnant if the record of their first child's baptism in the parish registers indicated a birthdate less than eight months after the date of their marriage (the extra month is to allow for non-prenuptially conceived premature births). According to this definition, an estimated 20.7% of all wives married at 20–4 in the pre-1837 dataset were prenuptially pregnant and were therefore excluded from the ensuing calculation.

[25] T. H. C. Stevenson showed that in the 1911 census returns there was a very marked general relationship across all social groups between female age at marriage and prenuptial pregnancy, such that the percentage of prenuptially pregnant brides declined rapidly from an estimate of about 75%

have little force if the low-fertility 1911 occupational groups (all of which would include a certain proportion of the prenuptially pregnant) exhibited even lower fertility than a pre-1837 sample whose fertility had already been artificially reduced to a minimum by the deliberate removal of all prenuptial pregnancies.

Accordingly, the average number of live births over the first five to ten years of marriage born to these non-prenuptially pregnant wives marrying at 20–4 before 1837 was calculated and found to be 2.71.[26] As can be seen from Appendix E, all but 27 of the 195 occupations of 1911 in fact recorded an even lower level of average fertility than 2.71 for AM2/01–5. Indeed, as many as 45 of them record a value of less than 2.0, which is over 25% lower. Clearly, then, differences between the occupational groupings in the extent to which they do or do not contain prenuptially pregnant women is a factor quite inadequate to explain the scale of the relatively low fertility of so many of the 1911 occupational groups over their first five to ten years of marriage.

However, before conclusions can firmly be drawn from the evidence displayed in Appendix E, mention should also be made of the possible disturbing influence of infant mortality. Assuming no substantial difference in breast-feeding habits, a population with a lower rate of infant mortality will, on average, exhibit slightly lower fertility because of longer intergenesic intervals due to increased lactational amenorrhoea, whereby breast-feeding delays the return of ovulatory menstrual cycles. Mothers whose infants die will not breast-feed for as long as those whose infants survive, and so they will be susceptible to pregnancy slightly earlier. There was certainly a significant difference between the infant mortality levels of the Edwardian period and those typical of the pre-1837 parish register population.[27]

at age 15 to 37% by age 20, and to 22% by age 25, staying roughly constant thereafter at about 20% throughout the rest of the age range: *FMR* Pt 2, Table II, pp. x–xi; lxxxix–xci. (See below, n. 37, for details of the estimation method and note that Stevenson advised that these percentages, which are somewhat higher than those for the pre-1837 population, are to be treated as maximum estimates, since a certain, unmeasurable fraction were the result of simple misstatement on the census schedules.) Most interestingly, Stevenson found a lower than average incidence of prenuptial pregnancy at the most sensitive ages of 15–19 *not* among the professionals of his social class I but among each of the three special industrial classes (textiles workers, miners and agricultural workers). Only at marriage ages above 24 did social class I exhibit the lowest rates of prenuptial pregnancy. Apart from Stevenson's treatment, see also the discussion of the issue by Glass and Grebenik in *The trend and pattern of fertility*, Appendix 3.

26 This exercise was kindly performed for me by Jim Oeppen of the Cambridge Group, modifying a programme originally devised by Chris Wilson, to both of whom I am most grateful. The wives from the parish reconstitution data were classified into exactly the same age at marriage and duration of marriage divisions as those used at the 1911 census and the reconstitution data was also modified appropriately to take into account the small differences which would result from the fact that the 1911 data was compiled from a retrospective survey, rather than collated continuously as with the parish registration system.

27 The infant mortality rates of the occupational groups drawn from the 1911 census data are shown in the column 'IMR' in Appendix E. These figures for infant mortality by male occupation are drawn from Table 28A of the 74th ARRG (for the year of 1911) and therefore relate as nearly as is possible to exactly the same population as covered in the 1911 census occupational fertility tables. As the blanks for the IMR column in Appendix E indicate, in thirty-nine cases there was no exact equivalence between the two sources in the occupational information on infant mortality. Note, also, that 1911 was

However, a simple hypothetical calculation, reproduced in Appendix H, shows that the scale of this effect is relatively small. Even when comparing the 40 or 50 occupations with lowest infant mortality rates in 1911 with the pre-1837 population, this effect can at most account for only a 3-4% difference in the recorded fertility levels.

Thus, the comparison with the pre-1837 parish data does, indeed, support the initial interpretation of the information displayed in Appendix E. Many occupational categories were spacing births very substantially during the first five to ten years of their marriage. The occupational categories which were showing the highest degree of fertility control – those listed in the first panel of Appendix E – were spacing to such an extent over these first years of marriage that their fertility was already at least one quarter and probably about one third lower than the typical fertility of demographically comparable English populations before 1837.[28]

It is additionally possible for this marriage cohort of the first decade of the twentieth century to make a very rough comparison between the degree of occupational dispersion in fertility rates after just 7.5 years of marriage, as reported in Appendix E, and the same cohort's dispersion after a further fifteen years of marriage when fertility had been completed. This is because the completed fertility of a sample of the surviving couples of this marriage cohort were included as part of the 1946 family census, the sample survey which formed the demographic centrepiece for the Royal Commission on Population appointed in 1944. The data from that survey were analysed by D. V. Glass and E. Grebenik and are presented in a form sufficiently similar to the tables of the 1911 census *Report* to make a comparison of sorts possible.[29] For wives married at 20–4 in

a year in which infant mortality was particularly high all over the country because of the combination of a harsh winter and a long hot summer. This has been taken into account in the exercise reported in Appendix H, where an infant mortality rate of fifty per thousand has been used to represent the low-fertility occupations of 1911, a figure somewhat lower than most of those shown in Appendix E.

[28] If the comparison had been made with the pre-1837 population containing its full complement of the prenuptially pregnant wives, the benchmark comparison figure would have been 2.91 and not the more conservative figure of 2.71, as in the text. On the basis of this more realistic comparison, the forty-five occupations recording AM2/01–5 values below 2.0 exhibit fertility levels about one third lower than that recorded for the pre-1837 population. Furthermore only the six occupations at the bottom of Appendix E recorded a higher figure than 2.91, suggesting that the complete absence of any birth control through spacing was confined to relatively few occupational groups by 1911.

[29] Glass and Grebenik, *The trend and pattern of fertility*, Table 44, gives the completed fertility for the marriage cohort of 1900–9, distinguishing age of wife at marriage by the same quinquennia as in the 1911 census *Report*. The whole sample population of 1946 was divided by Glass and Grebenik into nine 'social status categories' according to male occupation. However, due to differences in the principles of occupational definition and classification only five of these categories can in any way be compared with analogous sets of occupations from the fertility tables of the 1911 *Report*. Fortunately, two of these roughly comparable 'social status categories' from the 1946 study comprise the least and the most fertile social categories from the 1900–9 marriage cohort: category 1, Professions; and category 9, Labourers. Of course, this can provide only a very approximate comparison. Given both age-related and fertility-related occupational mobility in the intervening period, as well as the significant changes in the way each set of occupations was recruited and defined during the intervening decades, these comparisons should certainly not be taken as literal and precise comparisons of exactly the same couples over time. They are merely an indication, in place of such an

1900–9 with professional husbands, a completed fertility of 2.66 livebirths was recorded in 1946; whereas labourers' wives had had an average of 4.78 children by 1946. This is a 79.7% difference, somewhat greater than the 61.7% fertility differential which had already been established between these two social groups of this same marriage cohort according to the 1911 census, taken after an average of just 7.5 years of their marriages had elapsed.[30] There was, then, some further relative intensification of the extent to which fertility was controlled at the higher parities by the couples in the professional occupations. However, it remains true that over three-quarters of the extent of difference in fertility restraint between this, one of the lowest fertility groups, and those exibiting very high fertility, had apparently already been established as a differential during the first few years of marriage. This is an indication that the professional middle classes of this generation, marrying in Edwardian times, were *both* 'spacing' early in their marriages and also 'stopping' (or else increasing the rigour of their spacing strategy later in their marriages as well).

This, then, somewhat supports and adds to the inferences drawn from Table 8.2 at the end of the previous section. Professionals exhibit distinctive fertility controlling patterns, compared with textile workers, the proletarian group with lowest fertility. All the signs are that textile workers *only* (or primarily) spaced births, that they probably did so from the beginning of marriage (i.e. that this embraced 'starting', too) and they did so even more rigorously when marrying late. The professionals, on the other hand, appear to exhibit more of a mixture of both spacing and stopping but not as alternatives to each other. Spacing was very much the norm from early in marriage for them, too. But spacing among professionals was apparently augmented by stopping – or perhaps by 'enhanced spacing' – at longer marriage durations and higher parities. It could be that the behaviour of this last generation of professionals to marry before the Great War is exhibiting the earliest signs of a further shift from spacing only towards the target-related pattern of stopping, as well. Of course, it has been the combination of both spacing (including 'starting') and stopping which has, ultimately, become established as the typical form of fertility behaviour throughout the population today.

ideal of comparison. The three other categories from the Royal Commission Report which can be broadly compared with occupational categories from the 1911 census *Report* were: 4, Salaried employees; 7, Farmers and farm managers; and 8, Agricultural workers. The four remaining status categories, which cannot be easily compared with any of the 1911 occupational groups were: 2, Employers; 3, Own account workers; 5, Non-manual wage-earners; 6, Manual wage-earners. On the classification principles adopted by the Royal Commission, see *ibid.*, pp. 18–23.

[30] This is based on the estimate that in the 1911 census Report the eighteen professional occupations recorded values for AM2/01–5 of approximately 1.75; while the ten occupational categories relating to non-agricultural labourers recorded values of approximately 2.83, a difference of 61.7%. As can be seen from Appendix E, the figure of 1.75 for the eighteen professions is simply the mid-point of the range from 1.57 for army officers to 1.93 for nonconformist clergy. Similarly, the labourers' figure of 2.83 bisects the range from rail labourers at 2.66 to dock labourers at 3.00. No greater degree of precision is merited because of the very approximate nature of the comparison being made here (see previous footnote).

Overall, however, it should be emphasised that the most important summary finding to emerge here is the prevalance of spacing from very early in marriage as the method generally adopted by those couples who were regulating their fertility in England and Wales in the period before the First World War. This is the first time that comprehensive evidence of this sort has been considered to demonstrate that spacing and not stopping was the typical, primary method of birth control throughout a European nation during its initial stages of falling fertility. J. C. Caldwell *et al.* have recently presented evidence of such spacing among young married women in sub-Saharan Africa, suggesting that this may constitute a 'new type of transition'.[31] But this newly interpreted historical evidence from England and Wales indicates, on the contrary, that this was exactly the main method deployed at least in one part of Europe in the past.

The timing of marriage and the regulation of fertility, 1901–11

In the previous chapter it was shown that there was generally a strong positive relationship between marital fertility control and delayed marriage among those marrying in the 1870s and 1880s. Certain significant exceptions were found when the data were inspected in detail, particularly among the least fertile social groups. But in general there was a marked overall pattern, such that those male occupations recording lower completed family sizes in 1911 were also those which had married a greater proportion of older wives approximately three decades earlier. Was this positive correlation also found among the cohort marrying in the 1900s? And, if so, were the same detailed differences visible among the lowest fertility occupations (the very late-marrying middle-class professions as against the relatively younger-marrying occupations representing those of independent means and those 'retired from business')?

As the high positive correlation coefficients reported in Table 8.3 show, the strong general relationship did, indeed, continue to hold true for the younger cohort of couples who had married between 1901 and 1905. Those occupations recording relatively low incomplete fertility in 1911 (AM2/01–5 and AM3/01–5) were also those in which high proportions married relatively late (AMRATIO2) and low proportions married young (AMRATIO3).[32] The bottom part of Table 8.3

[31] Caldwell, Orubuloye, and Caldwell, 'Fertility decline in Africa'.

[32] The two comparative occupational nuptiality indices for the twentieth-century cohort, marrying 1901–5, AMRATIO2 and AMRATIO3, are constructed in a slightly different way from PRUDMARR in the previous chapter, since the need to devise a mortality-free measure is not paramount for this cohort marrying just before the 1911 census. AMRATIO2 is based on the ratio of the number of couples where wife's age at marriage had been 25–9 divided by the (usually larger) number for those marrying at age 20–4. AMRATIO3 represents the number marrying at 15–19 divided by the (always greater) number at 20–4. AMRATIO2 is the more important of the two indices because the majority of couples in all occupations married at these ages (in 12 of the 195 occupations fewer than 30 couples married wives under age 20). The two indices are, of course, strongly correlated, as Table 8.3 shows. The values for AMRATIO2 and the rank positions of each occupation according to AMRATIO2 (RANK/AMRAT2) are listed in full in Appendix F.

Table 8.3 *Spearman R^2 correlation coefficients between occupational age at marriage and fertility indices, 1901–5; and comparison with 1880s*

	AMRATIO2	AMRATIO3
AM2/01–5	0.84838 (0.0001)	0.79678 (0.0001)
AM3/01–5	0.76512 (0.0001)	0.71638 (0.0001)
AMRATIO2		0.87362 (0.0001)
AM2/81–5	0.87265 (0.0001)	0.76593 (0.0001)
PRUDMARR	0.82116 (0.0001)	0.79486 (0.0001)
N (Occs.)	195	195

Note: statistical significance levels in brackets. For method of constructing AMRATIOs, see n. 32.

also confirms that these were predominantly the same occupations which recorded low completed fertility and late marriage in the 1880s marriage cohort.[33]

What, if anything, was the relationship between delayed marriage and spacing after marriage among the cohort marrying in the first years of the new century? Were there systematic differences between the younger- and elder-marrying subsets in the extent of spacing practised over the first five to ten years of marriage? In order to provide answers to these questions, it is first necessary once again to have recourse to the Cambridge Group's pre-1837 reconstituted parish data, to assess the proportion of the difference between the rates which is attributable to the varying fecundity properties and to the different prenuptial pregnancy rates of groups of women marrying at the two different quinquennial ages, above and below age 25.[34]

Analysis of the Cambridge Group dataset (as specified in n. 26) showed that after 7.5 years' marriage women marrying at 20–4 had produced an average of 2.91

[33] Only a few occupations showed major differences in nuptiality behaviour between the two cohorts. Most of these were probably the result of age-related selection effects altering the social composition of the occupations. Those which apparently married relatively young in the 1880s but delayed marriage much more in the 1900s were: retired from business (201); pensioners (202); army officers (9); coal – mineowners (87); and hosiery workers (163). The reverse was true of: police (6); postmen (3); waiters (191); men of the navy (12); domestic and non-domestic motor-car drivers (34); car, chassis-makers, mechanics (114); barmen (190); and cycle makers (113). In the cases of cycle makers, car makers and car drivers, it seems probable that the younger members of the occupation, those marrying in the 1900s, were recruited into a significantly lower-status occupation than had been the case ten to twenty years earlier, when most of those aged in their forties and fifties in 1911 had probably entered these occupations. In all other cases, except perhaps 'army officers', it seems most probable that, given the nature of the occupations concerned, the younger cohort represent a selected subset of higher status (in the case of the first group) or lower status (in the case of the second group as in the example of barmen, see ch. 7, n. 10) occupations.

[34] The lower effective fecundability of women after age 25 is mainly due to a rising risk of intra-uterine mortality after that age: Weinstein *et al.*, 'Components of age-specific fecundability', pp. 458–9.

livebirths and those marrying at 25–9 had produced 2.76, a difference of just over 5% (the latter figure being 0.94845 of the former, but requiring adjusting to 0.94456 before application to the 1911 population).[35] It therefore follows that in 1911 if those couples in each occupation where wives married at 25–9 were practising the same degree of spacing as their younger-marrying peers, their average incomplete fertility values at five to ten years' marriage duration should be just under 95% of the figure recorded for those marrying at 20–4.

Appendix F shows that there is an almost universal pattern of behaviour, whereby the older-marrying subsets within each occupation were apparently spacing their births over the first five to ten years of marriage to a greater extent than those marrying at 20–4. The 195 occupations are rank ordered in Appendix F according to the variable AM25PC20, which expresses the incomplete fertility value for those marrying at 25–9 as a percentage of the figure for those marrying at 20–4, comparable to the corrected figure of 0.94456 cited immediately above, derived from the exercise using the Cambridge Group pre-1837 reconstitution data. As can be seen, all but 10 of the 195 occupations record a lower value than 0.94456. In exactly half of the occupations, the figure is over 10% lower in real terms (a value for AM25PC20 of 0.844 or less).[36]

[35] In this case the prenuptially pregnant women were *not* artificially removed from the pre-1837 dataset, since it was important to preserve their effect for the purposes of a realistic comparison of the two different female age at marriage groups, to simulate as closely as possible the characteristics of the 1911 census population, which included prenuptially pregnant brides. It is, of course, for this reason that the figure of 2.91 livebirths differs from the figure of 2.71 cited previously, in the text above. There was some difference between the two populations (pre-1837 versus 1911) in the extent to which those marrying at 20–4 exhibited a greater degree of prenuptial pregnancy than those married at 25–9, the effect of which needs to be taken into account. In the pre-1837 population it can be estimated that 20.7% of first marriages at age 20–4 were prenuptially pregnant and 20.3% at age 25–9 (see above, p. 378). In the 1911 population the comparable estimates were 28.6% and 20.0%, respectively (see above, p. 378). This means that the extent to which the fertility of those marrying at 25–9 was lower than those marrying at 20–4 would be slightly greater in the 1911 population than in the reconstitution population because there were, in effect, a net 8.2% fewer prenuptially pregnant wives among the older marriers (relative to the younger marriers) in 1911 than in the pre-1837 population. This means that as well as the 20% exposed to prenuptial pregnancy among the older marryers in each population, an extra one twelfth (8.2%) of the older wives in the pre-1837 population were also exposed to the risk of prenuptial pregnancy. Assuming that each prenuptially pregnant wife represents an extra 4.5 months' exposure to intercourse before marriage, this represents an additional 5% exposure in each case (4.5 months is exactly 5% of 7.5 years – 90 months). If the differential of 94.845% were therefore adjusted downwards by the full amount of 0.41% (5% multiplied by 8.2%), this would produce a figure of 94.456%, the adjusted figure used here in the text. To summarise: this calculation shows that the difference of differentials in prenuptial pregnancy between the two age at marriage groups between the two populations (pre-1837 versus 1911) does not significantly alter the main result, based on using the pre-1837 population as a guide for the 1911 population. This indicates that in the 1911 population, the expectation would be that after 7.5 years of marriage the fertility of those marrying at 25–9 would be just under 95% of the fertility of those marrying at 20–4, as a result of differences in fecundability and differing propensities to prenuptial pregnancy.

[36] Note that the order of their listing in Appendix F does not, therefore, necessarily correspond to any ranking of the extent to which each category exhibited birth controlling behaviour. Appendix F therefore needs to be interpreted with care, as it is unlike previous displays and tables. Occupations at the bottom of the table are not necessarily those exhibiting the highest fertility and the least

In order to make one further, approximate test against the possibility that these results might be due to a greater proportion of prenuptial pregnancy among the younger-marrying subgroups, a variable was created giving an indication of the relative propensity towards prenuptial pregnancy in each occupation.[37] No

spacing in an absolute sense; nor do those heading the table necessarily record the greatest degree of spacing. For instance, 'indoor domestic servants' (ID 31) recorded the sixth lowest incomplete fertility of any occupation among those marrying at 20–4 and the second lowest for those marrying at 25–9; but the occupation is found exactly in the middle of Appendix F, with a value for AM25PC20 of 0.8444. This figure simply shows that the elder-marrying subset (wives marrying at 25–9) recorded 15.56% (1 – 0.8444 x 100) fewer births than the younger-marrying subset (wives marrying at 20–4). The occupation is ranked in the middle of Appendix F because this happens to be almost exactly the typical or average percentage amount by which elder marriers spaced their fertility more than the younger marriers in each occupation. Hence 133 occupations (two-thirds of the total), occupying the middle rankings in Table 9.5, exhibit AM25PC20 values ranging from 0.80 to 0.90, reflecting this 'normal' or typical tendency of most occupations to show a 10–20% deficit in the average number of births to those couples where wives married at 25–9 years of age, relative to those marrying at 20–4.

37 The method used for calculating this occupation-specific estimate of propensity towards prenuptial pregnancy was an adaptation of the ingenious calculation which Stevenson devised to compare his social classes for the same purpose (the main difference is that Stevenson compared the number married at 0–1 year's duration with those married at 1–2 years' duration). For each occupation the number of marriages recorded as of 3–5 years' duration was expressed as a ratio, relative to the smaller number returned as of 0–2 years' duration. Theoretically, a ratio figure of 1.5 should result from such a calculation, *ceteris paribus*, given that the former covers three years' worth of marriages and the latter only two years'. Stevenson noted that this ratio would be altered by two small disturbing effects but concluded that these two cancelled each other out: the marriage rate during the two years preceding the census was slightly lower than that of the three previous years but the higher numbers in the latter category were subject to greater depletion from exposure to the chances of mortality and separation. In fact all but five of the 195 occupations produced ratio figures above 1.5, indicating an excess of marriages at 3–5 years', relative to the number at 0–2 years' duration. Stevenson was able to show that this discrepancy, which also occurred among all his eight social classes where women married at 20–4, was principally due to the fact that on the self-returned census schedule couples were free to overestimate their marriage durations so as to appear compatible with the age of their eldest child. Marriages of 3–5 years' duration were, of course, also vulnerable to overstatement (and so depletion) on this account; but this category compensatingly 'received' the overstated marriages from the 0–2 category whereas the latter, being the shortest duration category, could not benefit from such a compensatory addition to its depleted numbers. Hence the shortfall in number of marriages reported at 0–2 years' duration relative to the number at 3–5 years' duration was the key inferential statistic indicating the extent of prenuptial pregnancy in each occupation. As an estimate for such a relatively precise social category as an individual occupation, this statistic does, however, have to be treated with great care. It is perfectly possible, for instance, that some occupations experienced genuine trade-related or other relatively random fluctuations in the marriage rate (in either direction) during the two years preceding the census, as against the previous three years, which would create distortions in such a detailed comparison. The figure derived from this exercise can therefore only be treated as very broadly indicative of the relative tendency to prenuptial pregnancy of each occupation and can in no way furnish a meaningful absolute figure of percentages premaritally pregnant. Hence the figures, once calculated, were rank-scored for presentation in Appendix E (as column, PRNUPREG) and have not been used for any more exacting form of analysis or correlation with other variables. It is also for these reasons that there has been no attempt to construct more precise estimates of prenuptial pregnancy for age-specific subsets of occupations. Although these would in theory constitute a more exact measure for present purposes, given the nature of the above methodological reservations such an exercise would be statistically spurious and substantively uninterpretable. For Stevenson's original method and calculations, see *FMR* Pt 2, pp.viii–xi; lxxxix–xci. Also on marriage rates during the period, see 74th ARRG, pp. xii-xiii.

positive correlation was found between this indicator for prenuptial pregnancy and the variable AM25PC20.[38] This confirms therefore that the marked general difference between the fertility of those marrying at 20–4 and those marrying at 25–9 cannot be attributed to differences between the two sets of wives in the proportions pregnant at marriage and must therefore be primarily attributable to greater birth control through more spacing among the later marriers.

The statistic AM25PC20, in effect, measures the extent to which an occupation contains a substantial subset of late-marrying couples whose births are spaced to a significantly greater extent than their younger-marrying peers in the same occupation. That this was, indeed, generally the case is undoubtedly the most significant single finding to emerge from this part of the analysis: however much couples spaced births over the early years where wives had been aged 20–4 at marriage, in most occupations there was an additional, independent age effect. It was those marrying at 25–9 who spaced to an even greater extent, typically producing 5–15% fewer births (in real terms, after allowing for the 5% due to the involuntary, lower fecundity and lower propensity to be prenuptially pregnant among these older women).[39]

The occupations heading Appendix F are those where elder-marrying couples restricted their fertility during the first 7.5 years to such an extent that the average number of births was fully 20–30% less than the average for those marrying at 20–4 (this applies to the first thirty-four occupations listed). Most of the occupations appearing here are drawn from the manual working classes. It has already been noticed, in Table 8.2, that among the later-marrying subsets, some of the most important textiles occupations were among those exhibiting the greatest degree of spacing over this initial period of marriage. By contrast, several of the established professions were relatively fertile among this older-marrying subset. This is corroborated here, in that none of the professions are found in the upper half of Appendix F. Indeed, most are found at the opposite extreme. On the other hand the textiles industry is clearly prominent at the very top of Appendix F, with nine of its twelve occupations present, including lace and hosiery workers.

[38] The relevant Spearman R^2 correlation coefficient between AM25PC20 and PRNUPREG (rank scores for each occupation are given in Appendix E) for the whole dataset of 195 occupations is −0.11919 (0.0970 significance level).

[39] It is interesting to note that although the two relevant fertility indices, AM2/01–5 and AM3/01–5, are strongly positively correlated with each other, they are virtually uncorrelated with AM25PC20. Spearman R^2 correlation coefficients with AM25PC20 across the 195 occupations are: −0.11055 (significance level 0.1239) for AM2/01–5 and +0.17871 (significance level 0.0124) for AM3/01–5. Hence, low-, medium- and high-fertility occupations are found all mixed together in the top, middle and bottom panels of Appendix F. This, then, is mathematical testimony to the substantive independence (from the purely 'occupational' sources of fertility differentials) of the association between delayed marriage and enhanced spacing. Formally, this results from the fact that AM25PC20 is, in effect, measuring something analogous to an independent, second-order differential in calculus: the degree of difference between the differences in spacing practised by the younger- and older-marrying subsets in each occupation.

Several of the other low-fertility proletarian occupations are to be found at the top of Appendix F: cabinet makers; coach and carriage makers; piano makers; goldsmiths; and 'others in printing'. However, some of the higher-fertility proletarian occupations are also found near the top of Appendix F, including pottery workers; manufacturing chemists; refuse disposal; vegetable oil millers; and costermongers. Additionally, there are several categories of metal workers: wire workers; tool makers; brass workers; tinplate goods makers; metal machinists; one dealing occupation – in textiles and fabrics – and two retailers, fishmongers and florists.

In general this shows that variation in fertility and nuptiality practices was increasing in proletarian communities before the Great War. *Some* prudential sub-sections – even of some of the higher fertility occupations – were becoming more conscious of the problems of large families by the Edwardian period. These especially prudential couples were marrying late and spacing births significantly more than others, even in the same occupations and communities, the younger marriers. The latter may have been continuing to adhere to a more traditional, plebeian pattern of courtship and nuptiality behaviour, where marriage tended to be triggered by commencement of sexual relations (especially if pregnancy occurred), rather than vice versa. These possible differences within working-class communities may well repay further research.

Almost all of the professional occupations (fifteen out of a total of eighteen), as well as that of 'private means', are in fact found among the forty or so occupations at the bottom of Appendix F; also five of the fifteen dealing occupations and two of the nine white collar occupations.[40] Among these occupations at the foot of Appendix F, the incomplete fertility of the late marriers differs from the young marriers by less than 7% in 'real' terms. Indeed, ten of these occupations record a figure of AM25PC20 somewhat above 0.94456, actually indicating slightly *less* birth control among the elder-marrying subset. These ten occupations are: merchants (commodity undefined); barristers; itinerant preachers; Anglican clergy; physicians; church and chapel officers; army officers; auctioneers and valuers; dealers in jewellery; and architects. For these predominantly professional occupations, therefore, those couples who waited to marry apparently felt no *greater* urgency or desirability to space births over the early years of marriage than did those marrying at 20–4. *Whereas* the norm in the great majority of other occupations was for older marriers to perceive an even greater need to space their births than those marrying at younger ages.

In explaining this it may well be relevant to note that twelve of the professions, including ten of the fifteen found at the bottom of Appendix F, were among the minority of thirty-one occupations in which the modal age at marriage among the

[40] The three professional exceptions were: banks – officials, clerks (46); accountants (43); chemists, druggists (148). See chapter 7, n. 4 for the full list of professional occupations; nn. 6, 13 for the lists of white collar and dealing occupations, respectively.

1901–5 marriage cohort was actually the 25–9 age range, rather than the 20–4 grouping as in all other occupations.[41] In other words the unusual feature displayed by these occupations at the bottom of Appendix F may simply follow from the fact that it was normal for most of these occupations to marry relatively late. Therefore the method of comparison used here, which divides the marriers in each occupation at age 25, fails to discriminate two socio-demographically, prudentially distinct subsets within these particular, very late-marrying occupations; and hence the amount of spacing practised by each subset is about equal.

However, while this kind of statistical, selectionist argument may provide the particular reason for the appearance of these low-fertility, high age at marriage occupations at the bottom of the listing, it does not explain the overall pattern presented in Appendix F. Thus, examining the opposite end of the listing, it is not simply the case that those occupations in which it was most *unusual* to marry relatively late exhibit the greatest degree of difference in spacing between the two age at marriage subsets. The textiles workers, for instance, were relatively late marrying (with the conspicuous exception of lace workers), while here exhibiting the widest of fertility differentials between their younger and later marriers. A systematic statistical analysis for the whole dataset of 195 occupations confirms that this selectionist hypothesis cannot account at all for the overall pattern of spacing differentials between younger- and older-marrying subsets.[42]

Returning to the bottom of Appendix F, most of the remaining categories found there comprise a set of occupations which exhibit the least spacing of all. This includes two of the four categories of agricultural labourers: agricultural labourers with undefined duties; and shepherds. There are also seven other high-fertility occupations: shipyard labourers; plaster, cement manufacture; tinplate manufacture; bargemen and lightermen; iron miners; coal hewers; and builders' labourers. These nine high-fertility occupations at the bottom of Appendix F are, indeed, unusual in that they appear to be composed relatively uniformly of couples who did not regulate their births, regardless of the age at which they chose (or were constrained) to marry. All other high-fertility occupations at least exhibit some tendency for the older-marrying subset to space their births more than the younger marriers.

Thus, it is these nine occupational categories which show the most consistent evidence of almost complete absence of any birth spacing over the first five to ten years of marriage in the period before 1911. Of course, this certainly does not mean that couples of this marriage cohort in these occupations did not *subsequently*

[41] The identities of the thirty-one occupations can be easily seen from Appendix F, where they score a value below unity in column AMRATIO2. (Also see above, n. 16.)

[42] The Spearman R^2 correlation coefficients are actually mildly negative between AM25PC20 and both measures of nuptiality: −0.21002 (0.0032 significance level) with AMRATIO2; and −0.17867 (0.0125 significance level) with AMRATIO3.

restrict their fertility – at higher parities – later in their marriages. Indeed, the evidence of the 1946 family census, already mentioned above, certainly suggests that many couples drawn from these occupations in this marriage cohort did eventually restrict their fertility to some extent later in their marriages.[43] This means that among this Edwardian marriage cohort those confining their birth control to the later stages of marriage only and to higher parities only – the classic 'stopping' pattern of fertility control – were in fact precisely those elements of the population who controlled their fertility the least and the latest. This again suggests that 'stopping' did not necessarily play a leading, early role as the principal strategy of fertility regulation in British society, but may have been more associated with a later stage of the process.

The continuing significance of late marriage: a culture of sexual abstinence

What, then, has been learned from this further consideration of the relationship between incomplete fertility and nuptiality patterns in the cohort marrying before the Great War? First, that spacing over the early years of marriage was a widespread practice among many couples, especially those occupational groups who controlled their fertility most rigorously. Secondly, there appears to be a continuing central significance for the timing of marriage as an integral part of the populace's family planning tactics.

Delayed marriage was particularly marked as a complementary characteristic of those groups of couples within most occupations who regulated fertility most carefully after marriage: in other words, those marrying older wives spaced their early births the most. In this section it will be argued that these findings have far-reaching interpretative implications, both for our evaluation of the main methods used to control births during this period and also for our overall conceptualisation of the form taken by the long-term demographic changes which have occurred in Britain during the modern and early modern periods.

It is now a well-established commonplace of the social and economic history of early modern England that this society was the classic exemplar of the 'North-west European' pattern of 'late marriage', first delineated by John Hajnal.[44] English society was at this time characterised by strict observance of the taboo against

[43] Even the highest fertility social status category used by Glass and Grebenik, 'Category 9. Labourers', recorded an average completed fertility in 1946 of 4.78 and of 3.36 livebirths for those marrying wives in 1900–9, aged 20–4 and 25–9, respectively. This was at least 30% below the comparable range of completed fertility levels for occupations of labourers marrying in the 1880s, as recorded in the 1911 census and reproduced here in Appendix C. Glass and Grebenik, *The trend and pattern of fertility*, Table 44. See above, n. 29, on the definition of the Royal Commission's social categories and their comparability with the 1911 census data.

[44] Hajnal, 'European marriage patterns in perspective'; and Hajnal, 'Two kinds of preindustrial household formation system'.

household co-residence of closely related reproducing couples. This ensured that fertility was for centuries broadly homeostatically regulated through variations in the percentage of each female birth cohort enabled to become reproductively active through entering marriage, which was in turn dependent on a young couple's securing access to an adequate flow of income to acquire and maintain an independent household unit. This was a régime of effective social regulation over 'starting' (to reproduce), as Lesthaeghe has termed it.[45] This was achieved more or less in the manner first described and prescribed as the 'preventive check' of 'moral restraint' by Malthus in 1803 in the second edition of *An essay on the principle of population*. The changing proportion of couples in each cohort able to enter marriage, and the average age at which they did so, was governed by the varying economic prospects each succeeding generation faced in its struggle for access to the independent economic units which nuclear family households represented.

However, the era of industrial and urban transformation, 1750–1870, is considered so to have altered society and economy as to have caused the demise of this long-functioning régime. Michael Anderson long ago showed that by the mid-nineteenth century growing industrial centres such as Preston were characterised by all kinds of complex and extended family households as lodgers, immigrant cousins and adult sons and daughters – some married even – all crowded together, sharing households in towns full of work and short of cheap housing.[46] Wrigley and Schofield argue that the 'Malthusian' demographic *ancien régime* finally came to an end after the third quarter of the nineteenth century when, for the first time, national marriage and fertility rates did not continue to follow the upward and downward secular trends in the national aggregate real wage index, a continuing upward trend in the latter being accompanied by an actual downturn in both the demographic indices from the 1870s.[47]

[45] Lesthaeghe, 'On the social control of human reproduction'. See above, n. 8.

[46] Anderson, *Family structure*.

[47] Wrigley and Schofield *The population history*, pp.435–6. This interpretation has since been reasserted by Roger Schofield in the course of an important debate generated by Jack Goldstone. Goldstone refined the Wrigley and Schofield measuring method, for both the demographic and real wage data which they had presented, to argue that the essential revolution in nuptiality behaviour was already taking place as early as the second half of the eighteenth century. Goldstone argued that whereas formerly the main way in which nuptiality affected fertility was only through shifts in the proportions of each female birth cohort entering marriage, it was changes in the age at marriage that became an important variable in the eighteenth century. From the mid-eighteenth century a distinctively new and growing element of the workforce – proletarianised wage-workers in both rural and urban sectors of the economy – was actually marrying much earlier than ever before. This was due to the buoyant and rising demand which the economic growth associated with industrialisation created for their own and their children's labour. This held out a sufficiently secure prospect of a future stream of regular earnings for the proletarian family and its members – however modest the wage-payments involved – so as to satisfy from relatively early in adulthood the traditional, engrained prudential marriage requirement that the couple could reasonably expect to support themselves as an economically independent household. A debate is now in progress, as Schofield has responded by arguing that the greater importance of age at marriage over proportions marrying was only a temporary interlude during the eighteenth century. It was due to two

There has, therefore, been a strong tendency among demographic historians confidently to demarcate modern English fertility history into two distinct epochs, one in which nuptiality alone was the main variable of interest and a subsequent, post-industrial period in which contraceptive marital fertility control has eventually become the principal regulating mechanism.[48] But the foregoing analysis would suggest that this distinction may not be entirely helpful in aiding our understanding of the causation entailed in the key process which produced the shift from one to the other régime: the onset of widespread marital fertility control from the 1870s. It is, of course, broadly descriptively accurate that a shift of this sort occurred; and with hindsight it can be seen that in the long run birth control within marriage has functionally replaced and rendered redundant the fertility-regulating aspect of prudential marriage behaviour. But it may nevertheless be fundamentally misleading for our understanding of the way in which marital fertility control was first taken up within English society to draw from these observations the apparently logical inference that the two are in some sense mutually exclusive, chronological alternatives to each other and can therefore be treated separately in terms of their historical provenance and causation.

It may be more helpful to recognise the significance of the fact that delayed marriage apparently co-existed as a practice and formed part of an integrated field of options for those considering how and when to build a family *throughout* the protracted period during which the planned control of fertility within marriage became established as a behavioural norm. Indeed, it is salutary to return to the first sentence of John Hajnal's seminal paper on the 'European marriage pattern' published in 1965, in which he dated the pattern's demise, particularly in Britain's case, to the year 1940.[49] Perhaps, then, the epitaph on

contingent factors, a rise in cottage industry and increasing generosity of the Poor Law, both of which subsequently declined during the second quarter of the nineteenth century, at which point the demographic *ancien régime* re-emerged for two or three decades, if in somewhat attenuated form. This, therefore, would still leave the 1870s as the point at which Britain's demography and nuptiality altered fundamentally. Note that whatever the differences between Goldstone and Schofield concerning a possible nuptiality revolution in the eighteenth century, they would both concur that there was one (a second one for Goldstone) in the late nineteenth century. Goldstone, 'The demographic revolution in England'; Schofield, 'Family structure, demographic behaviour and economic growth', especially pp. 298–303.

48 For a recent recapitulation of this theme, see Wilson and Woods, 'Fertility in England: a long-term perspective'. Unfortunately, the Coale–Trussell methodology has incidentally formally encouraged this tendency among demographers, through its development (for perfectly understandable reasons) of the conceptual and arithmetic distinction between nuptiality and fertility components of a populations's overall fertility and the insistence that only a certain kind of modification in the latter can be construed as the essential component which signifies completion of the process of demographic or fertility transition: Coale, 'The demographic transition'. However, note that A. J. Coale himself has recognised that fertility-restraining changes in nuptiality behaviour did apparently have significant effects in the developing countries during the 1960s and 1970s: 'T. R. Malthus and the population trend of his day and ours', cited in Macfarlane, *Marriage and love in England 1300–1840*, p. 32.

49 Hajnal, 'European marriage patterns in perspective', p. 101. This statement was firmly based on Hajnal's earlier cross-national research, which had pioneered the method of calculating singulate

nuptiality as a major fertility regulator in English society has been written for a period too early?

All commentators are, of course, well aware that the national trend of a fall in marital fertility from the late 1870s was also accompanied by a gradual decline in nuptiality. But in the same breath it is always – quite correctly – pointed out that the restriction on fertility through nuptiality was of much less quantitative significance than the novel development of widespread control of births within marriage. This emphasis on controlled fertility within marriage as a new and distinct phenomenon surpassing the tired, old inefficient ways of delayed prudential marriage has perhaps distracted us and disabled us from being able to see the important similarities between the two kinds of behaviour as these must have appeared to the historical agents themselves at the time: in terms of the motives, methods and outcomes involved. It has already been noted that the occupational data, both for the marriage cohort of the 1870s and 1880s and for that of the 1900s, shows a very strong overall positive correlation between delayed marriage and fertility control within marriage. In general, the same occupational groups of couples apparently tended to deploy both methods together. Perhaps there is a powerful clue in all this to the nature of the methods normally used to achieve birth control within marriage? And, perhaps, from this we can in turn infer the probable motives involved?

It needs to be recognised that the cultural norm of prudential marriage had provided for centuries not simply a set of sanctions 'imposed upon' individuals – regarding the appropriate future flow of income and the desirable standard of living to be reasonably expected in order for a couple to get married and set up house. More than this, it was the manifestation of a culturally engrained framework of thinking, both about marriage and family formation and about sexual relations and reproduction, which individuals believed in and endorsed. It placed this process within an essentially economic calculus for the young individuals concerned: the direct link with independent householding and with making a livelihood was there for all to see and think upon.[50] As even Goldstone acknowledges, this way of thinking was by no means demolished by the vicissitudes of the industrial revolution era: in the eighteenth century some couples married earlier than ever before because in a fast-growing economy they could satisfy their own consciences regarding the prudential criteria for marriage and family building at an earlier age than was possible for previous generations.

For all individuals brought up in British society over many centuries, to delay marriage and therefore to submit to sexual (coital) abstinence as young adults was

mean age at marriage (SMAMs). Hajnal showed that a marked decline in the mean age at marriage and in the proportions of women in each cohort remaining unmarried was an historically recent event, which in Britain's case dated from the mid-1930s (though interrupted by the war): 'Age at marriage and proportions marrying', especially Tables 3–6.

[50] For a full exposition of this thesis, see Macfarlane, *Marriage and love in England 1300–1840*; and Kussmaul, 'When shall we marry?'.

a long-accepted and established indigenous practice.[51] The fact that this was done for evidently economic and reproductive reasons is highly relevant, although it is not the primary point being made here. The main point is that for generations sexual self-denial had been the institutionalised norm for young unmarried adults in Britain's culture, necessarily associated with the 'peculiar institution' of late marriage. This, then, was a population that had been thoroughly schooled over centuries in the attitudes and expectations required for acceptance of this form of self-restraint. Although mean age at first marriage had, of course, fallen somewhat since the early eighteenth century, Britain in the late nineteenth century was still very much a 'late marriage' régime, according to the criteria proposed by John Hajnal.[52] Much routine sexual abstinence was still required from its young adults, as average age at first marriage (singulate mean age at marriage) remained above 25 years throughout the period, even for women, with 10% or more remaining celibate beyond age 45; illegitimacy was still running at relatively low levels (in international comparative terms) and had fallen to an exceedingly low rate by the Edwardian period.[53]

This long-term historical conditioning may be relevant for interpretation of the occupational demographic evidence from 1911. This has shown a close continuing relationship between delayed marriage and both restricted completed family size and the spacing of births from early on in marriage. It may therefore be arguable that these findings strongly suggest that during the initial period of rapidly falling fertility before the Great War the practice of 'attempted abstinence' – reduction in the frequency of intercourse – may have provided the populace at large with its principal means to restrain fertility once married.

For the late Victorians and Edwardians control of marital fertility could be achieved through three possible methods: effective contraception; non-coital sexual relations between spouses; or sexual abstinence with the marriage partner (the third of these methods may well have been associated with keeping mistresses or with the sexual exploitation of servants or prostitutes on the part of some males, especially those of the most privileged class).[54] It is only in a society

51 Peter Laslett's thesis that non-marital and illicit sexual activity was not widespread (though, of course, it certainly existed – see Quaife, *Wanton wenches*) in pre-industrial English society remains as yet unchallenged: Laslett, *Family life and illicit love*.

52 Hajnal, 'Two kinds of preindustrial household'.

53 On the difference between modal and mean age at marriage, see above, n. 16. Figures for singulate mean age at marriage and proportions single at ages 45–54 for the period 1851–1911 are from: Wrigley and Schofield *The population history*, Tables 10.3 and 10.4, p. 437. On illegitimacy, see Laslett and Oostereven, 'Long-term trends in bastardy'; and Teitelbaum, *The British fertility decline*, Table 6.10a. Even when illegitimate births in England had represented approximately 7–10% of all births during the first half of the nineteenth century, this was still only moderate in international, comparative terms. By the Edwardian years illegitimate births represented fewer than 4% of all births (Wrigley and Schofield *The population history*, p. 438).

54 As one would expect given their essentially surreptitious nature, there is no firm historical evidence with which to estimate the true extents to which mistresses were kept or adultery occurred at this time, for all that it provides a theme in some novels of the period. There is certainly robust evidence

which has thoroughly mastered and socially assimilated either or both of the first or second of these methods as common practice and public knowledge (that is, something well known among all young adults contemplating marriage and not just an esoteric practice experimented with in private after marriage by a few; or knowledge passing clandestinely by word of mouth among certain older adults) that there would be no expected positive statistical correlation between the incidence of delayed marriage and of restricted fertility within marriage. For it is only in either of these circumstances that there will cease to be a general perception by the young adults of the society of a continuing need to delay marriage as an essential part of a prudential strategy to restrict the number of dependants to a manageable number.

Hence, so long as the incidence of delayed marriage continues to be positively correlated with limitation of births within marriage, as has been found to be the case in the 1911 occupational data analysed here, this is extremely strong *prima facie* evidence that the principal method of birth control known and being deployed by this population was some form(s) of sexual abstinence within marriage. No doubt for most couples 'attempted abstinence' or 'coital spacing' would be the most accurate description. A regimen of abstinence punctuated by lapses on either or both sides was probably typical. However, it is now known that any form of such behaviour significantly reducing the frequency of intercourse

of a general kind on the use of prostitutes, although it is not possible to estimate how frequently married, as against unmarried, men were employing prostitutes. For a helpful review of the bewildering range of estimates on the prevalence of prostitution in London during the nineteenth century, see Mason, *The making of Victorian sexuality*, pp. 72–103. Mason concludes that there were many thousands, but not many scores of thousands, of prostitutes working in London in the second half of the century; furthermore, the definition of a prostitute is intrinsically problematic and it must be borne in mind that the figures relate to a transient source of employment for many of the individuals involved. The Royal Commission on Venereal Diseases of 1913–16 presented a report by T. H. C. Stevenson on 'Statistics of mortality from venereal diseases in England and Wales'. Despite the stigma surrounding the disease, Stevenson considered it possible to provide the Commission with estimates of the relative incidence (over time, between localities and social classes) of syphilis, by including in the analysis three other causes of death which were often used by certifying doctors as euphemisms (locomotor ataxy, general paralysis of the insane, and aneurysm). Although, as Stevenson insisted, no confidence can be placed in the absolute values exhibited by this evidence, the relative social patterns were clear: the highest (age-standardised) rates of incidence were recorded among the wealthiest males of social class I and the poorest of social classes IV and V; and clearly the lowest rates (approximately one-half lower) were recorded among classes VI, VII and VIII, i.e. the textile, the mining and the agricultural communities. *Final Report of the Royal Commission on Venereal Diseases*, PP XVI 1916, Cd 8189, p.19 and Appendix I, Table 3. The Commission ventured the cautious summary estimate (p. 22) that probably no less than 10% of the population was infected with syphilis in the largest cities (bearing in mind that typical age of infection was in the twenties and thereafter the infection would remain in the body for decades). The Commission concluded (p. 7) that it was quite impossible to tell whether there had been any real increase or decrease in incidence during the previous fifty years. On prostitution and children in sexual slavery in Victorian Britain see also Walkowitz, *Prostitution and Victorian society*; McHugh, *Prostitution and Victorian social reform*; Finnegan, *Poverty and prostitution*. On sexual exploitation of servants, see Gillis, 'Servants, sexual relations'; and Barret-Ducrocq, *Love in the time of Victoria*. See also Banks, *Victorian values*, pp. 85–96.

could have very considerable fertility-reducing effects, through much increased spacing between pregnancies.[55]

Bongaarts's work indicates that even if 'attempted abstinence' meant no more than that couples were restricting themselves to intercourse once every week, a definite spacing effect of about eight months would accrue (i.e. eight months additional to the average time of three to four months taken to get pregnant under a fertility-maximising régime of fifteen to twenty acts of intercourse per menstrual cycle).[56] More sustained efforts at abstinence would have proportionately greater effects. A reduction to once a fortnight would result in an average additional spacing effect of eighteen months, while an average frequency of only one act of intercourse per month would in itself result in an average additional wait of over three and a half years according to Bongaarts (this would therefore account for a total of approximately four and a half to five years' spacing between births in a population with a breast-feeding norm of, say, six months).[57]

To claim that attempted abstinence or coital spacing was the most quantitatively important way in which fertility was restricted during this period, 1860–1914, does not, of course, mean that many in such a population would not also have been very interested in discovering more efficient or less ascetic, alternative forms of contraception; nor that examples could not readily be found of some couples in some social groups and communities experimenting with these alternatives.

[55] Ironically in the present context, one of the first studies to indicate the importance of coital frequency on a large scale was the work of Rindfuss and Morgan, reporting a *rise* in fertility. They pointed out that the proportion of early marital conceptions had risen remarkably in a number of Asian societies because of much higher rates of intercourse early in marriage consequent on the abandonment of the practice of arranged marriages and the increase in marriages of mutual attraction. They rightly concluded: 'All this suggests that coital frequency may be more important than demographers have heretofore thought.' Rindfuss and Morgan, 'Marriage, sex, and the first birth interval'.

[56] Bongaarts, 'The proximate determinants', p. 116, Table 4. This indicates that a reduction from fifteen to twenty acts of intercourse to four per menstrual cycle would extend the average length of time taken for pregnancy to occur from just three to four months to eleven to twelve months. This is additional to the independent effects of lactational amenorrhoea (see next footnote). Note that exact specification of the physiological parameters determining human fecundity remains a matter of scientific debate, primarily because both the duration and the exact characteristics of the fertile period remain the subjects of research, with most estimates varying between two and six days. For a helpful recent review and contribution, see Weinstein *et al.*, 'Components of age-specific fecundability'. Weinstein *et al.*'s model is broadly consistent with the Bongaarts figures reported in the text here, in that their Figures 5 and 6 indicate that for women aged 20–30 years maximum 'effective fecundability' is approximately halved if coital frequency falls from a maximum (twenty-five to thirty times per month in their model) to five times per month; it is further reduced to an eighth at a coital frequency of once per month. Note that Weinstein *et al.* particularly observe (p.462) that 'At low frequencies (below five per month) small increases [in coital frequency] result in substantial gains in predicted effective fecundability.' The inverse of this observation is particularly significant in the present context: reductions of average coital frequency below five times per cycle have very substantial spacing effects.

[57] Bongaarts, 'The proximate determinants', Table 4. Bongaarts's Figure 1, p. 109, shows that empirical observation has found that while a norm of six months' breast-feeding produces approximately three months' average amenorrhea, twelve months' breast-feeding results in a mean of eight months' amenorrhea.

Hence the available evidence of increased public interest in contraceptive literature, devices and techniques during and after the Bradlaugh–Besant trial, 1876–9.[58] But this growing curiosity on the part of *some* does not equate to conclusive evidence for a popular culture which has generally mastered such alternative techniques as a normal part of its repertoire and therefore no longer thinks in terms of abstinence and sexual continence as its principal means to restrain births. Indeed, the demand for this information is itself powerful evidence of a generally prevailing state of relative ignorance on matters sexual and contraceptive at this time, something confirmed by qualitative evidence still well into the twentieth century.[59]

Basic sex education could be and was viewed highly negatively in a culture which so prized female 'purity': 'when in my own youth, I discovered how girls were sent ignorant through life into marriage . . . I was told by one, who herself had the care of daughters, that the ignorance formed too valuable an addition to the virginal charm of womanhood in the marriage market'.[60] Although birth control itself may have become a more permissible topic for private discussion after the Bradlaugh–Besant trial, nevertheless public attitudes towards most of the possible techniques remained those of suspicion if not scandal, involving a set of stigmatising moral associations.[61] While 'sexual continence' was considered the only respectable and moral method of birth control which could command assent in any public statements, religious and medical opinion was divided even on this; it was suspected that it resulted in the resort to prostitution where the virtues of true self-control failed. Prostitution bred the evil of venereal disease and the use of condoms was associated with this traffic. Other female preventives such as plugs and pessaries were equally associated with the business of the prostitute. All forms of preventive were viewed as dangerous if allowing sensual self-indulgence and discouraging habits of personal self-discipline, especially in the lower orders. Finally, the prevention of births in general was associated with the most un-Christian activities of prostitutes and fallen women: abortion and infanticide.

Hence Peter Gay, in his magisterial survey of the emotional life of the Victorian bourgeoisie, speaks of 'a certain half-knowledge about sexuality, an atmosphere of mystery'.[62] Mystery was institutionalised in a society which strove to protect the market value of innocent brides by keeping from them knowledge which could

[58] The first historical account of this surge in public interest was: Himes, *Medical history*.

[59] Over thirty years after the Bradlaugh–Besant trial, 12% of the 160 working-class letters collected in M. Llewellyn Davies's *Maternity* (published 1915), still professed complete ignorance on sexual matters at the time of marriage (those claiming ignorance were letters 11, 21, 24, 28, 29, 37, 45, 72, 81, 84, 88, 90, 91, 92, 95, 127, 146, 156, 160). On middle-class ignorance around the turn of the century, see Jalland and Hooper, *Women from birth to death*, section 4.1 'Sex education for females'. Also, see pp. 413–17, 560–6, below.

[60] Laurence Housman, *The immoral effects of ignorance in sex relations* (1911): extract reproduced in Jalland and Hooper, *Women from birth to death*, p. 228.

[61] This paragraph summarises the more extended treatment of this theme on pp. 409–13, below.

[62] Gay, *The bourgeois experience*, Vol. I, p. 257.

lead to degrading thoughts or, worse still, urges.[63] Gay confesses he has been able to glean little from bourgeois diaries and letters, so that 'The evidence is notoriously fragmentary, but there were scattered incidents – little more – of bourgeois wives locking the bedroom door on their husbands, of bourgeois husbands thoughtfully protecting their wives from unwanted pregnancies, and of shamefaced discussions about limiting the number of offspring. These discussions became more frequent and less shamefaced as the century went on'.[64] And Gay, himself, is unable to offer the reader almost any documented evidence for this. This was not, then, a culture which was at home with its sexuality. Thus, Gay contrasts the Anglo-Saxons and the French at this time: 'to judge by the contemporary literature, the French practised birth control without writing about it; the English and the Americans wrote about it [in medical articles and propagandist pamphlets] without practising it'.[65] All this is despite Gay's professed intention to offer a self-consciously revisionist interpretation of proverbially 'Victorian' attitudes to sex and sexuality in the nineteenth century. Gay's is one of a number of such studies which have provided an important corrective to monolithic caricatures of 'repression'. However, the net outcome of this historiography is not, in fact, a demolition of Victorian prudishness, sentimentality and hypocrisy but a more sophisticated and constructive understanding of it.[66]

While many Victorian women and men were explicit – indeed could be positively pretentious and mawkish – in their expressions of love and emotionality, wives and lovers were on a pedestal of emotional spirituality which could leave the physical and practical aspect of sexual expression unarticulated and *infra dignitatem*.[67] The capacity of some individuals and couples to achieve sexually

[63] For evidence of the Victorian concern with and attempts to police female masturbation (extending to the barbarity of medical clitoridectomy), see the various extracts from throughout the period 1860–1914 collected in Jalland and Hooper, *Women from birth to death*, section 4.3 'The secret sin of self-abuse'.

[64] Gay, *The bourgeois experience*, Vol. I, pp. 243–4, 272.

[65] Gay, *The bourgeois experience*, Vol. I, p. 259.

[66] Cominos, 'Late-Victorian sexual respectability'. See Marcus, *The other Victorians*, chs. 3–4, on the pseudonymously authored ('Walter'), 11-volume 'Erotic grand tour', *My secret life*, privately published in 1888; on the less explicit diaries generated by the unusual Arthur Munby-Hannah Cullwick relationship, see Hudson, *Munby*; Stanley, *The diaries of Hannah Cullwick*. More generally, see: Foucault, *The history of sexuality*; Weeks, *Sex, politics and society*; Walkowitz, *Prostitution and Victorian society; Gay, The bourgeois experience*; and Maynard, *Victorian discourses on sexuality and religion*; Porter and Hall, *The facts of life*. One recent study documenting more open, less 'Victorian' attitudes to sex and sexual morality in the behaviour of at least some proletarians and patricians is: Barret-Ducrocq, *Love in the time of Victoria*. Nevertheless, other sources document the pervasive force of repressive sexual attitudes and laws in the lives of the majority throughout the first half of the twentieth century, at the point where the testimony of oral history has become available: Thompson, 'Courtship and marriage in Preston'; Crook, 'Tidy women'; Roberts, *A woman's place*, pp. 84–6; Humphries, *A secret world of sex*; Cohen, 'Private lives in public spaces'. For evidence of both inhibitions and the wish to surmount them, see Hall, *Hidden anxieties*.

[67] There has been much more research on this in the USA than in Britain and it is possible that the British were somewhat less forthcoming in this vein than the Americans. On Victorian men's and women's emotionalism in the USA, see Rothman, *Hands and hearts*; Lystra, *Searching the heart*; Seidman, *Romantic longings*. On Britain, see Maynard, *Victorian discourses on sexuality and religion*.

satisfying or mutually rewarding relationships was in despite of, not because of, the standards of 'respectable', *public* discourse on the subject. Public silence on the supposedly sordid details of physical expression remained conducive principally to ignorance and its twin, fear, long after the Bradlaugh–Besant trial. For instance, Annie Besant herself lost custody of her children because her public advocacy of detailed methods of birth control for women was deemed unfitting for a mother; while the proclaimed secularist and neo-Malthusian, George Drysdale, long continued to find it desirable to retain his anonymity as the author of a libertarian text which dared to discuss physical sexuality, *Physical, sexual and natural religion* (originally published in the 1850s).[68]

All this serves to strengthen the argument that mass contraception was not being practised as the principal form of birth control in this period. It may well be, therefore, that the key behavioural and cultural innovation, which accounts for the early stages of falling fertility in Britain after the mid-nineteenth century lay in the increasing extension of the long-established, indigenous practice of sexual abstinence among young adults into married life (albeit that such abstinence would in many cases have been of a relative, rather than an absolute kind).[69]

Indeed, as the extract cited above on the title page of Part III records, in 1848 on the eve of this posited change in marital behaviour, that most percipient of middle-class contemporaries, John Stuart Mill, was publicly advocating such a move towards abstinence within marriage as a birth controlling strategy.

A re-examination of the historical evidence for and against the practice of attempted abstinence in Britain before 1940

What additional evidence can be examined for or against this putative thesis that attempted abstinence played a much more important role in restricting marital fertility in Britain before the Great War than has previously been appreciated? It is obviously essential to consult and interrogate the available alternative primary sources of historical evidence, other than the 1911 fertility census.

Any direct evidence at all on methods of birth control used in British society *before* the Great War remains a rarity and has to be treated with caution. However, some evidence does exist. The following reappraisal will argue that, contrary to the conclusions which have previously been drawn by other historians, a careful scrutiny of this body of evidence in fact supports the view that attempted

[68] On Besant and the trial – one of many colourful episodes in the life of a committed maverick, see Taylor, *Annie Besant*. For a study of the secularist birth controllers, George and Charles Drysdale and their respective mistresses, Letitia Ridley and Alice Vickery, see Benn, *The predicaments of love*. George Drysdale's *Physical, sexual and natural religion* (published 'by a Student of Medicine' in 1854) is better known by its reissued title of 1859 (also anonymously authored 'by a Graduate of Medicine') as *The elements of social science*.

[69] Recent detailed studies of sections of other national populations have also presented evidence that periodic sexual abstinence was the principal method of fertility regulation being employed by early family planners: Lewis and Lockridge, '"Sally has been sick"'; Kemmer (unpublished PhD thesis).

abstinence within marriage was the single most widespread and frequently used method of birth control during the period before the First World War.

Of course, there can be no doubt that a range of other methods of controlling fertility was also employed during this period: condoms; coitus interruptus and reservatus; non-coital sexual gratification; attempts at a rhythm method; abortion, both surgical and self-induced through taking (often ineffective) abortifacients or violent exercise; sponges, pessaries, plugs and pills; spermicidal sprays and foams; douching; early diaphragms and caps; prolonged breast-feeding; and even occasionally infanticide.[70] It is also true that there is considerable evidence available that several of these other contraceptive methods did indeed become increasingly popular in the interwar period.[71] This has perhaps tended to encourage the view that the same must have been true before the 1920s.

However, as the ensuing analysis will show, it is an illusion to suppose that there is any robust, positive historical evidence – quantitative or qualitative – in favour of such a view. It will be shown that the proposition that any of these alternative means, including even coitus interruptus, was the *principal* method used in the late Victorian and Edwardian era, rather than attempted abstinence, rests on virtually no verifiable evidence. Indeed, quite to the contrary, the substantial positive evidence from this period, such as it is, indicates both that attempted abstinence was the main method deployed before the First World War and that it was of continuing importance into the interwar period, at least throughout the 1920s.[72]

There appear to be only four sources of systematic positive direct testimony on contraceptive practice in Britain before the Great War (i.e. sources which purport to be something more than merely the idiosyncratic reportage of what a single individual did or believes others to have done): Ethel Elderton's birth control survey published in 1914; the retrospective interviews conducted for the Royal Commission on Population of 1944–9; the collection of letters on maternity sent to the Women's Cooperative Guild in 1913; and the National Birth Rate Commission's fertility survey of 1914.

[70] Infanticide undoubtedly existed in various forms in nineteenth-century Britain, from the simple abandonment and exposure of unwanted children to commercially motivated acts related to burial insurance and 'baby farming' (see Rose, *Massacre of the innocents*). However, as Ann Higginbotham effectively demonstrates, Victorian moral panic over the prevalence of infanticide was never based on a statistically significant practice. The panic was itself, of course, culturally highly significant: a conservative collective response to the problem of impoverished (often illiterate) unmarried mothers, which operated through social condemnation of individuals rather than an attempt to change the difficult conditions of their lives, which would have entailed countenancing major, redistributive social change. Higginbotham, '"Sin of the age"', pp. 324, 325–6, 328, 336–7. On the quantitative aspect of infanticide, see also Behlmer, *Child abuse*, p. 18.

[71] Apart from the influential findings of the Royal Commission on Population, 1944–9, discussed in detail below, Himes found that the somewhat inefficient methods of coitus interruptus and abortifacient pills had been most frequently used among those sufficiently dissatisfied with the results to attend a birth control clinic in interwar Liverpool: 'British birth control clinics'. Enid Charles found the sheath (condom) to be favoured as the most reliable method among 420 mainly middle-class birth controllers in the early 1930s; she also found that coitus interruptus and the cap were extensively used: *The practice of birth control*, p. 50 (see below, n. 96).

[72] See below, p. 408 and n. 119.

Given the contentious and clandestine nature of birth control throughout the pre-Great War era, it is vital to pay much more attention to direct testimonies from individuals regarding what they themselves did, rather than taking on trust the indirect testimony of contemporaries regarding what they claim *other* persons were doing. In this regard the first of these four sources is to be treated with particular circumspection, though it has often been cited uncritically. Ethel Elderton's account consisted of a selective summary (in fact selected by Karl Pearson) of the reported opinions of a large number of anonymous local correspondents on birth control practices in the 104 registration districts of the northern counties (Lancashire, Cheshire, Yorkshire, Cumberland and Westmorland, Durham and Northumberland). As far as is known, none of these informants were themselves working class.[73] They were not reporting on their own behaviour but on that of unidentified others and they frequently invoked hearsay or illustrative anecdote; also they often tended to mention events in the quite distant past, such as the visit of Bradlaugh or Besant to the area, rather than deploying more recent and direct evidence (on the number and location of retailing outlets for contraceptives, for instance).

Furthermore, once the provenance of this survey of local opinion and its methodology are investigated in more detail, the validity of its findings becomes even more questionable and their interpretation all the more difficult. The local correspondents were responding to a standard format of three leading questions.[74] The first two asked about social and economic conditions (wages and unemployment) and changes in the chief industries and occupations over the last fifty years. The third question was the critical one and itself comprised three dimensions: the extent, character and date of arrival of birth control propaganda in their area; whether in their opinion this was responsible for a fall in the birth rate locally; and whether that fall was equal among all social classes. Despite Elderton's authorship of the Report, both the formulation of the third question and the form in which the resulting responses were published were in fact the sole responsibility of Karl Pearson.[75] There was a clear methodological 'health warning', prominently

[73] From internal evidence in the published Report it is evident that most of the correspondents were local medical men, along with some chemists and philanthropic workers. I have been unable to discover hardly any of the papers or original correspondence relating to the project or to establish the identity of any of the correspondents from consulting the relevant archival holdings of University College, London, where the Biometric Laboratory was located. An exceptional survival (see n. 75) shows that local medical men were sought as correspondents and that they were given an undertaking that the information supplied would be 'strictly confidential', hence the anonymity in the published report. This is also confirmed by a letter from Elderton to Pearson dated 12 April 1911, where she reports that 214 MOHs had not answered their request for information, while 169 returns had been received (Pearson Papers 682/7).

[74] Elderton, 'Report of the English birth rate', pp. 8–9.

[75] The evidence that the third question was originally formulated in this way by Karl Pearson is in the Pearson Papers, where there is a handwritten draft for a letter, dated 24 January 1910, seeking the co-operation of a medical professional in Congleton for Elderton's project. The first two questions are posed and are then followed by an additional section at the end of the letter in a different hand:

appended in the Report to the description of these three questions: 'It is obvious that no direct facts or statistics can be available for answering the third question as to the influence of deliberate limitation of the family, and it must be emphasised that the statements made by our correspondents are in most cases only opinions and they themselves have insisted on that fact.'[76]

Despite this some historians have uncritically cited this source to give the impression that the impact of the propaganda campaign of the Malthusian League was widespread and that contraceptive knowledge and use of devices, including sheaths, may have been almost ubiquitous in some parts of the north of England at this time, along with the practice of abortion.[77] This is easily done, by simple selective citation. Fryer cites the opinions of the twenty-seven correspondents (drawn from twenty-six different registration districts), whose reports contained the most positive and convincing testimony to the impact of birth control propaganda and the use of birth control appliances.[78] He does not explain that these are a selection from several hundred reported sets of opinions (because most of the 104 registration districts contained several distinct communities and Elderton often obtained a report from each community) and that in fact only a minority of the correspondents offered the opinion that birth control information or devices existed in their district.[79] It is quite impossible from this kind of evidence

this is Pearson's handwriting (and it is his signature on the letter), adding the three clauses of the third question: Pearson Papers, 912. In the published Report's 'Prefatory Note' it is stated on p. viii that all the selections for publication from among the responses of the local correspondents were made by Karl Pearson. The large amount of work which both Pearson and his Assistant Director, David Heron, put in on the Elderton Report is confirmed in the confidential *Journal of the Galton Laboratory*, p. 8 (Pearson Papers 246).

[76] Elderton, 'Report of the English birth rate', p. 9.

[77] For an uncritical reading of this sort, see Fryer, *The birth controllers*, pp. 205–10; Mason, *The making of Victorian sexuality*, pp. 60–4; and on abortion see below, pp. 428–9.

[78] Fryer, *The birth controllers*, pp. 205–10.

[79] For instance, to take as a crude sample the information presented on pp. 28–33, covering the first three of the 104 registration districts in Elderton's Report (the Lancashire districts of Ulverston, Blackburn and Fylde). Reports were received from separate correspondents in all but one of seventeen distinct communities in these three districts. In four cases (Church, Ostwaldtwistle, Fylde, Fleetwood) the summary of each correspondent's information indicates that no reference at all had been made to birth control (the content of a methodological footnote on pp. 30–1 and the fact that it was stated in the 'Prefatory Note' that Pearson was intent on presenting as much positive material on birth control as possible from his correspondents' opinions, means that it is safe to conclude that there was no information in the original return where it is not mentioned in the published report). In the remaining twelve communities it was positively stated in five cases (Ulverston, Darwen, Great Harwood, Rishton, Blackpool) that no propagandism for birth control had come to the correspondent's attention; and in five cases (Blackburn, Clayton-le-Moor, St Anne's-on-Sea, Thornton, Poulton-le-Fylde) the local respondents were of the opinion that advertisements or local knowledge of contraceptives did exist. In one case (Darwen), there was a hearsay reference to the practice of abortion; and in Lytham it was stated that limitation of births occurred but that this was not due to 'propagandism' but to discussion among those who 'determine to keep down the size of the family' (the method was unspecified and this might, therefore, have been an allusion to abortion, coitus interruptus or abstinence). In this small test sample from Lancashire, therefore, there was positive opinion expressed by the correspondents in only a maximum of seven out of seventeen communities.

to form any independent assessment as to whether large or small proportions of the district's population are implicated even in the minority of places where correspondents did mention birth control. Finally, any impression gained of a truly extensive use of appliance methods of contraception in the population at large would appear to be heavily qualified, if not flatly contradicted, by the three other contemporary sources which do, at least, record direct testimonies.

Of these three by far the most technically rigorous source of systematic information available on contraceptive practices throughout the first half of the twentieth century is the impressive Lewis-Faning survey conducted for the Royal Commission on Population. This was an extremely detailed interview-based questionnaire administered to a sample of 3,281 women of all ages between August 1946 and June 1947.[80] It is this inquiry which has been understood to have authoritatively tracked the wide spread throughout the population of various appliance methods of contraception during the interwar period. But – of great relevance to the interpretation being offered here – it also simultaneously indicates exceedingly little use of any of this range of 'appliance methods' of contraception in the period before the Great War.

Only 2% and 9% of respondents, respectively from the two marriage cohorts of 1900–9 and 1910–19, acknowledged use of any form of 'appliance methods' of contraception – *at any time during their married lives* (i.e. including the interwar period). By contrast a further 13% and 31%, respectively, reported using *only* 'non-appliance methods'.[81] Almost a half of those who regulated their births by non-appliance methods gave 'lack of knowledge' as their reason for not using appliance techniques.[82] The Royal Commission's findings, therefore, directly contradict the general inference which might be drawn from the Elderton Report. The use of condoms or any appliance methods of contraception before the Great War was found to be minimal and there seems to have been widespread ignorance of these methods even among those who were controlling their fertility.

However, the Royal Commission survey poses its own problems for the interpretation of the 1911 census evidence which has been presented so far in this chapter. It appears to show that while non-appliance techniques were much the more frequently used method before the interwar period, this related primarily to coitus interruptus. Contrary to the argument which has been presented above, the

80 A total of 10,297 women attending hospital in 1946 and 1947 were interviewed and the figure of 3,281 represents those who were not attending hospital for maternity-related reasons (because of the obvious fertility bias this would introduce). The sample was primarily drawn from London (42%), Glasgow (22%) and the West Riding of Yorshire (16%). Lewis-Faning, *Report on an Enquiry into Family Limitation and its Influence on Human Fertility during the Past Fifty Years*, Papers of the Royal Commission on Population, pp. 3–5 and Table 21, p. 35.

81 *Report on an Enquiry into Family Limitation*, Tables 2 and 5. The note on p. 53 of the Report, regarding the definitions used, explains that those returned in the tables as using appliance methods could have done so at any time in their marriage, whereas those returned as using non-appliance methods were those who had never used any appliance method at any time.

82 *Report on an Enquiry into Family Limitation*, Table 126.

Lewis-Faning survey unequivocally reported that there was very little abstinence of any form being practised at any time among its respondents.

How well does this claim stand up to scrutiny? Despite the impressive methodology of the Royal Commission's survey, it was recognised by its own author at the time that there were flaws in the results obtained from the questionnaires and interviews and that there must have been some substantial concealment of birth control.[83] The fact that only 15% of the women questioned from the 1900–9 marriage cohort acknowledged regulating their fertility at any time during their marriage (by either appliance or non-appliance methods) was far too low. Even the figure of 40% for the marriage cohort of 1910–19 must be a very considerable underestimate as the true figure is likely to be much closer to 100%. Could these large discrepancies and missing birth controllers be relevant to the Royal Commission's categorical findings against any form of abstinence? To pursue this, it is necessary to examine in detail the methodology used by the survey.

Developed from earlier, predominantly American survey work of this sort, the interview was specifically and adroitly designed to deal with respondents' predictable reticence in discussing their sexual practices.[84] But of course reluctance to divulge information, despite assured anonymity, must account for some part of the shortfall in these self-reported birth controllers. Ingenious inferential estimations in the Report itself were able to show that, at the minimum, approximately 17% of the 838 women questioned from the three earliest marriage cohorts combined (1900–9, 1910–19, 1920–4) must have been concealing the use of birth control.[85] The Report was also well aware that unwillingness to give full information was likely to be particularly marked where abortion had been used.[86] But this factor alone could not account for more than a part of the large scale of the discrepancy between reported behaviour and actual fertility.[87] It was obvious, just from the national aggregate fertility rates, that the majority of couples, even of the earliest marriage cohort of 1900–9, must have restricted their fertility quite considerably at some point during their marriages.

Could there, then, be a further, undetected and important flaw in the methods used for eliciting the information on people's contraceptive practices during the previous fifty years, which particularly affected the responses from the earliest cohorts? A close inspection of the reported interviewing questions and techniques used in 1946–7 indicates that this may well be the case. The procedures adopted would appear to have had the effect of positively excluding virtually all of those practising attempted abstinence.

A detailed account of the relevant questions and procedures used in the

[83] *Report on an Enquiry into Family Limitation*, ch. VII, pp. 89–90, 92.
[84] *Report on an Enquiry into Family Limitation*, chs. V, XI.
[85] *Report on an Enquiry into Family Limitation*, ch. VII.
[86] *Report on an Enquiry into Family Limitation*, ch. XI.
[87] See below, pp. 424–31, for a full discussion of the relative prevalence of abortion.

interviews is given in chapter V of the Lewis-Faning Report. Here it is recorded that the crucial question asked in the survey was:

Q.5: – Has abstinence or birth control been used to space or avoid pregnancies at any time?[88]

While this would seem straightforward and comprehensive, it was wisely anticipated that many of the survey respondents would not know exactly what the terms 'abstinence' and 'birth control' meant.[89] To assist the interviewer in explaining precisely what information was required the Report records that:

A definition of birth control together with some guidance was printed in apposition to the question, viz:-

'Contraception (Birth Control) is the use by either sex of any means whatsoever whereby coitus (the act of union between man and woman) may be experienced while at the same time the fusion of the ovum with the spermatozoon may be averted so that conception does not take place.' It will be seen to include all chemical and mechanical methods (here called the 'appliance methods'), coitus interruptus and the use of the 'safe period'. *For the purpose of the enquiry abstinence of periods of less than 6 months need not be considered* [emphasis added].[90]

Finally, in addition to these instructions, interviewers were advised that: 'Before recording a *negative* answer the woman must be questioned as to whether her husband had been "Careful"– the term by which coitus interruptus is frequently known – and as to whether intercourse had ever been restricted to particular periods of the menstrual cycle' (original emphasis).[91]

Hence, as can be seen from the guidance instructions, whereas the interviewer was asked to search thoroughly for any signs of coitus interruptus or the safe period, all forms of short-term (less than six months at a time) and relative abstinence were to be ignored. The importance of all but the most ascetic regimens of abstinence was thereby positively excluded by design from the survey's findings. However, as stated above, research has now shown that much less dramatic reductions in coital frequency than those ruled out from consideration in the Royal Commission's survey can have very substantial effects upon birth spacing.[92]

These procedures would seem to explain, therefore, the curious result recorded by Lewis-Faning when first presenting the overall results of the percentages of

[88] *Report on an Enquiry into Family Limitation*, p. 48.

[89] As even the recent National Survey of Sexual Attitudes and Lifestyles found (the most important detailed survey of sexual behaviour ever mounted in Britain, based on a random sample of 18,876 interviews, conducted from May 1990 to November 1991), this problem is still to the fore today. 'Sexual behaviour is rarely spoken about publicly and as a result the language used to describe it is inadequate and inappropriate. . . . there was wide variation in the meaning attached to crucial variables such as "sexual partner" and "having sex".' Wellings *et al.*, *Sexual behaviour*, pp. 12, 18–19.

[90] *Report on an Enquiry into Family Limitation*, p. 49. Since identifying this significant limitation in the instructions of the questionnaire, it has been brought to my attention that it has also previously been pointed out by: Kemmer (unpublished PhD thesis), p. 94; and by Langford, 'Birth control practice', Appendix 3.1, p. 63.

[91] *Report on an Enquiry into Family Limitation*, p. 49.

[92] See above, p. 395.

each marriage cohort using appliance and non-appliance methods: 'Non-appliance methods were taken to include Coitus Interruptus (CI), abstinence and "safe period", but in fact the amount of reported use of abstinence and "safe period" was trivial and non-appliance methods may be taken throughout to refer to Coitus Interrruptus' (*sic*).[93] It is this summary statement which has consistently misled historians, such as most recently Wally Seccombe, in appearing to be an authoritative finding against abstinence.[94]

It seems highly probable, therefore, that in addition to the depletions caused by simple reticence and by respondents' wishes to avoid mentioning abortions, a large part of the reason for the implausibly low proportions of birth controllers returned among the 1900–9 and 1910–19 marriage cohorts of the Royal Commission study was that many – probably still the majority among these two cohorts – achieved their birth spacing primarily through attempted abstinence, which went unrecorded. It has been suggested that in most cases such attempted abstinence, although taking place on a relatively long-term basis (for several months or perhaps even years at a time) was probably characterised by intermittence and many lapses. In fact it was little more than 'coital spacing'. Intercourse may, then, have generally taken place among such couples much more frequently than once in six months and yet a major birth spacing effect would still have resulted, as shown by the calculations of Bongaarts cited above. However, Lewis-Faning's survey would have positively excluded all such coital spacers from the ranks of reported birth controllers.

It does seem a little strange that their findings did not give Lewis-Faning and his associates greater pause for thought. In general the Report was a model of thoroughness and rigour in its careful and probing examination of the data collected. The probable reason for this 'blind spot' was a misplaced confidence that only the most gross interference with coital frequency could significantly affect the birth rate. This reflected the unfortunately quite incorrect prevailing scientific understanding of the relationship between coital frequency and the chances of conception, something which only became the subject of scientific study in the 1960s.[95] Hence, other, small-scale surveys from the interwar period, which have sometimes been cited as providing evidence regarding the frequency of different methods of birth control, also turn out on closer inspection to suffer from this same blind spot, typically excluding proper consideration of abstinence

93 *Report on an Enquiry into Family Limitation*, p. 8.

94 Seccombe, 'Starting to stop', pp. 159–60; Seccombe, *Weathering the storm*, p. 160 and n. 21.

95 The specialist journal *Fertility and Sterility* commenced publication in 1949. However, much of the most important early empirical research on the effect of coital frequency on conception was not published until the 1960s: Lachenbruch, 'Frequency and timing of intercourse'; Barrett and Marshall, 'The risk of conception'. Ironically, it was a later contribution to the Royal Commission's work, which is considered to have been an important pioneering effort, defining the most important parameters and relationships: Glass and Grebenik's analysis of the 1946 sample family census, published in 1954 as *The trend and pattern of fertility in Great Britain*.

as a possibility.[96] Furthermore, as Chris Langford has documented, the exclusion of abstinence for periods of less than six months was a mistake repeated in the next social scientific survey of British sexual practices and birth control, mounted by the Population Investigation Committee (PIC) in 1959–60.[97] By the time that a more appropriately formulated question appeared, in the subsequent PIC survey of 1967–8, the earliest marriages questioned were those contracted between 1926 and 1930, which were too late for abstinence to have played a major role in their birth controlling behaviour. Thus, has been accomplished the virtual 'disappearance' of any substantial record of attempted abstinence from the British survey record.[98]

However, when the results of these more recent surveys are reassessed in this light, they do provide some positive evidence for the continuing practice of attempted abstinence by a significant minority, even into the 1950s and 1960s, which is at least suggestive of its greater importance earlier in the century. In the responses to both the 1959–60 and 1967–8 PIC surveys, just under 3% of men (1959–60) and of women (1967–8) from all marriage cohorts between 1926 and 1950, reported having at some point abstained, for periods of at least six months (the 1959–60 question to men) or for only one month at a time (the 1967–8 question to women).[99] In the 1970 Office of Population Censuses and Surveys (OPCS) inquiry, where the question was widened still further to that of 'going without sexual intercourse', without specifying any minimum time limit at all (and therefore represented a true question asking about reduced coital frequency although unfortunately it was asked only of women), consistently 5–6% of all marriage cohorts (1946–50 to 1966–70) reported having reduced coital frequency at some time; and 3–5% of all cohorts reported it as their current method of birth control in 1970.[100] Interestingly, the figures for these same marriage cohorts for

[96] For instance Charles, *The practice of birth control*. On p. 22 Charles reproduces a copy of the form used to elicit the positive information from 420 women on their methods of birth control, which is the database for her study. This included a long list of eight specific techniques but did not mention abstinence. Nevertheless sixteen of the respondents registered use of this method (Table X, p. 50). Similarly, Florence, *Birth control*, produced a table (p. 97) of the methods previously tried by 265 of the first 300 patients who came to the Cambridge Birth Control Clinic from 1925 to 1927. This showed that 76 professed never to have tried any form of contraception; 118 had practised coitus interruptus at some time; and 86 had tried some other method (including, therefore, 15 who had also tried interruptus). Of the 86, the sheath had been tried by 31; 19 used the cap; 15 used the soluble pessary and only 6 had practised abstinence. Yet, Florence also volunteered the information that 'many more than the six patients listed in the table had abstained from intercourse for weeks or even months at a time because of illness or absence or following the birth of a child. But only these six had deliberately chosen this method to prevent conception' (p. 95). Additionally see below, p. 413 for Florence's evidence on generally low rates of coital frequency among this same sample.

[97] Langford, 'Birth control practice in Great Britain', Appendix 3.1.

[98] Indeed Douglas Sloan would see this as part of a more general bias, which he has discerned in the procedures of most postwar contraceptive surveys, which have had the effect of enhancing the number of respondents who can be classified as positive users of contraceptives and minimising the number of respondents whose fertility may be low for other reasons: Sloan, 'The extent of contraceptive use'.

[99] Langford, 'Birth control practice', Table 3.3 and p. 64.

[100] Langford, 'Birth control practice', Tables 3.3 and 3.5, and pp. 64–5.

both current and ever use of abstinence fell back to a negligible 1% at the next OPCS survey of 1976, where the question was once again extremely restrictive, specifying abstinence as 'not having intercourse/sex for several months, to avoid getting pregnant'.[101]

Furthermore, despite the methodology of the Royal Commission's survey and its successors having almost succeeded in entirely expunging from the historical record any substantial evidence of attempted abstinence, especially from the pre-Great War period, the two remaining major contemporary sources of direct testimony from before 1914 do refer unequivocally to this form of behaviour. First, there are the letters written to the Women's Cooperative Guild in 1913 in support of the maternity scheme, for which they were campaigning. These are strongly representative of the working classes, mainly the better-off but including a considerable number of the least fortunate (i.e. their husbands are recorded as low-paid, unemployed, physically debilitated or alcoholics).

Unlike the other three sources, this was not an inquiry explicitly aimed at eliciting information on birth control and so most of the letters make no direct or indirect mention of any form of contraception, though it is clear from the birth histories in many of these letters that they had restricted their fertility somehow. For those letters from which some knowledge or use of some form of birth control can be inferred, content analysis shows the following:[102]

(i) 2.5% (4) of the writers explicitly mention 'preventives', though not necessarily claiming to have used them themselves;
(ii) 7.5% (12) directly mention spacing their births or directly imply the use of periods of abstinence or else explicitly advocate the desirability of sexual continence on the part of husbands;
(iii) 7% (11) directly imply the regulation of births in their own case through some unspecified means or explicitly discuss birth control, but in the abstract and without giving any clue as to the means envisaged;
(iv) 5% (8) discuss abortion (not usually as something they have done themselves but as something which women might consider when they are feeling particularly desperate or depressed).

The relatively small number exhibiting any positive knowledge of appliance methods does broadly tally with the findings of the Lewis-Faning survey for the earliest marriage cohort;[103] as does the large number (19) confessing great ignorance of sexual matters at marriage.[104] Among these working-class women, therefore, the available positive evidence indicates that some form of abstinence

[101] Langford, 'Birth control practice', Tables 3.3 and 3.5, and pp. 65, 67.

[102] According to Margaret Llewellyn Davies's 'Introduction', the 160 letters published were representative of all 400 or so originally received: *Maternity*, p. 3. The letters found in each of the four categories in the text are as follows (i) 20, 33, 62, 69; (ii) 8, 15, 21, 24, 37, 41, 54, 73, 84, 101, 120, 123; (iii) 19, 47, 78, 91, 102, 114, 129, 130, 139, 145, 150; (iv) 5, 12, 15, 16, 17, 20, 32, 139. (NB some letters occur in category (iv) and another category, too.)

[103] See above, p. 402. [104] See above, n. 59, and below, n. 163.

was the most commonly understood means to avoid births, with abortion as the second most frequently mentioned expedient.

Intriguingly this corresponds closely to the picture revealed by the most comparable source for the immediately postwar period, the Stopes correspondence from the 1920s. From an analysis of the 10,000 or so letters written to Marie Stopes, mostly between 1919 and 1927, Claire Davey was able to present an analysis of 1,659 in which sufficient details were given as to contraceptive methods. This showed that among the 788 'working-class' respondents, abstinence was the single most frequently cited method (28%); followed by coitus interruptus (16%), attempted abortion (16%), the cap, with or without pessaries (11%), and prolonged breast-feeding (7%). Among 788 'middle-class' respondents the cap/cap with pessary was most frequently used (33%); followed by coitus interruptus (15%), sheath (12%), douche (10%), attempted abortion (10%), abstinence (8%) and quinine pessaries alone (6.5%). Note that Davey herself cautioned that these results almost certainly represent an underestimate of the extent of abstinence and an overestimate of the use of caps and pessaries. The latter effect was due to Stopes's own strongly expressed preference for this method, which would be known to her correspondents; while Davey advises that her own methodology underestimates the extent of abstinence because she excluded all indications of abstinence in the letters, except where it was explicitly stated that all sexual contact was avoided in order to control fertility.[105]

Fourthly, probably the most important single source of direct testimony for the period before the Great War, because of the numbers involved and the detailed information elicited (although related to the middle classes only), is the National Birth Rate Commission's 'voluntary census' of 1914. This was a survey in which questionnaires were despatched to as many women graduates as could be located in order to assess the possibility of differences in fertility and contraceptive practices between university-educated, middle-class women and their non-university-educated sisters or cousins (the results showed no significant difference between the two).[106] A total of 634 schedules were returned in a usable form from women of all ages and marriage durations. Of these, 289 (45.6%) positively acknowledged restricting their fertility; 189 (29.8%) denied having done so; and the remaining replies were apparently unclear on this point. Of the 289 birth controllers, 30% (86) failed to specify the means employed. Of the remaining 203 cases:

13% (26) specified coitus interruptus;
10% (20) specified condoms;

[105] Davey, 'Birth control in Britain during the interwar years', Table 3, p. 336; and pp. 332–4 for methodological reservations.

[106] Brown, *et al.*, 'The fertility of the English middle classes', p. 179. A preliminary version of the results was also presented by Major Greenwood in his evidence to the National Birth Rate Commission: *The declining birth-rate*, pp. 322–34 (evidence presented 4 December 1914). Apparently the initial inquiry had been administered by Dr Agnes Savill, another member of the Commission.

16% (32) specified pessaries and douches;
10% (20) simply referred to 'artificial means';
52% (105) stated that 'continence' was the method used.[107]

It is also illuminating to take into account the accompanying detailed interpretative comments of the authors on these statistics. These would seem to suggest that, overall, there was probably a small understatement of the incidence of coitus interruptus and a substantial underestimate of the prevalence of attempted abstinence or 'continence'. First, it is stated that the category of 'continence' included both attempted abstinence and the rhythm method (in the entirely mistaken form in which it was at this time generally practised).[108] Although the number of each is not given, the presentation implies that the latter is a minor feature of the replies.[109] Secondly, it is noted that 'artificial limitation' can in fact include coitus interruptus, according to the current idiom.[110] Thirdly, and most significantly, the authors state that they strongly suspect that a large number of couples where fertility was in fact being restricted through abstinence had returned themselves among the 189 persons in the category stating that they practised no restriction at all.

Their reasons for this last suspicion derived in the first place from the startling result which they found in their data, whereby, even after excluding all childless marriages from the comparison, 'we can demonstrate no sensible difference between the size of family in "limited" and "unlimited" marriages'.[111] In other words the average family size of those women who claimed to have limited their fertility in some way was little different from those who claimed not to have done so. To explain this the authors then argued that because of prevailing religious and moral scruples, whereby the positive restriction of births was still considered as sinful in principle and contrary to the sacrament of marriage, it was common practice among their middle-class contemporaries only to equate family limitation with active interference with coitus through either appliance methods or interruptus (conjugal Onanism as it was often pejoratively termed in reference to the biblical

[107] Brown *et al.*, 'The fertility of the English middle classes', Table XLVI.

[108] Until the discoveries by K. Ogino and H. Knaus, first published in 1929 and 1930 respectively, it was wrongly believed that the middle of the cycle between periods was least fertile. See Barrett and Marshall, 'The risk of conception', p. 455. It was only during these same years that the role of the reproductive hormones of the ovary and the pituitary were first understood: see Laqueur, 'Orgasm, generation', p. 27. More generally, see: Borell, 'Biologists and the promotion of birth control research'; and Pfeffer, *The stork and the syringe*. Note, however, that as early as 1922 A. M. Carr-Saunders had been able to report the results of some remarkable wartime research in Germany, which had shown that fertilisation was most likely from six to thirteen days after menstruation: Carr-Saunders, *The population problem*, Appendix II, reporting the work of 'Siegel' (no initials given) published in *Münchener Medizinische Wochenshrift* in 1916.

[109] Brown *et al.*, 'The fertility of the English middle classes', p. 201.

[110] Brown *et al.*, 'The fertility of the English middle classes', p. 203.

[111] Brown *et al.*, 'The fertility of the English middle classes', p. 199.

passage).[112] Abstinence or sexual continence was therefore the preferred method for those of tender conscience to achieve the goal of birth control, while enabling themselves to continue to believe they had not broken any religious or moral precepts (something of a parallel to the present-day Roman Catholic attitude towards the rhythm method).

For instance, it seems extremely likely, given the Anglican Church's formal opposition to contraception in any circumstances until the 1930 Lambeth conference, that abstinence must have been the method adopted by most Anglican clergymen and their wives for many decades – apparently to great effect, as they were one of the occupational categories recording the smallest average family size at the 1911 census. The strict attitudes on such matters of another professional body as late as 1929 can be gauged from the extraordinary dismissal of the young (later Sir) William Empson from his Fellowship at Magdalene College, Cambridge, because college servants had discovered him to be in possession of 'various birth control mechanisms'.[113] Empson was unlucky: perhaps one year too early. At the Lambeth conference in 1930 it was acknowledged that artificial contraception could be acceptable 'where there is a morally sound reason for avoiding complete abstinence . . . provided this is done in the light of . . . Christian principles'.[114] Note the direct acknowledgement in this statement by the Anglican hierarchy that abstinence was presumed to be the extant method practised by its flock.

Additionally, it may be pointed out that because the National Birth Rate Commission's survey, like the Royal Commission's questionnaire of 1946, was addressed exclusively to wives, a considerable proportion of them may simply have been unaware of the extent to which their husbands were in fact practising sexual continence and radically reducing the frequency of sexual advances within the marriage (this, of course, assumes that males were usually expected to take the sexual initiative in most marriages at this time, which seems indisputable as a generalisation, though, no doubt, exceptions existed). This point is in fact amplified in an intriguing footnote added by the medically trained Major Greenwood to the National Birth Rate study, where, invoking Freud's work, he briefly discusses the possibility that the statistics he has presented may to some extent reflect the phenomenon of 'abnormal sexual life' among some British middle-class males, in the form of 'quite frequently an absence of conscious sexual desire due to "unconscious" determinants'.[115]

While this may be a reference to homosexuality, I think it more likely, given the context and the exact words used, that Greenwood is suggesting that there exists a syndrome of self-imposed male frigidity or even impotence for some middle-class men which was referred to in the specialist medical literature as sexual

[112] Brown *et al.*, 'The fertility of the English middle classes', pp. 201–3.
[113] R. Luckett and R. Hyam, *Magdalene College Magazine and Record* (1991).
[114] Cited in Soloway, *Demography and degeneration*, p. 193.
[115] Brown *et al.*, 'The fertility of the English middle classes', p. 203.

neurasthenia.[116] Presumably this was substantially caused by finding themselves caught in the vice-like grip of an economic and social requirement to restrict family size while being denied by their religious conscience the use of all but the most ascetic of means to this end.[117] L. A. Hall has shown that there are many distinct echoes of this attitude and perceived predicament in the letters asking for advice, written by men of all classes to Marie Stopes in the 1920s.[118] As over 40% of the thousands of letters received by Stopes were from men, this is probably the most important and extensive source of direct evidence on male attitudes to reproduction and sexuality in the early twentieth century, albeit for the post-Great War period. It also, incidentally, provides plenty of further testimony to the continuing practice of abstinence in the 1920s.[119]

If unilateral male abstinence were a significant component of the birth controlling practices in British society throughout this period, it would certainly further help to explain the generally low levels of family limitation consistently reported in all of the above three sources of direct testimony. This is because they all addressed their inquiry exclusively to wives, a methodological limitation which has apparently been repeated in all but one of the subsequent major demographic surveys of birth control and reproductive behaviour until the most recent inquiry, which was motivated by the AIDS outbreak.[120]

Not until the marriage cohorts of the 1930s did the proportions of birth controllers reporting themselves to the Lewis-Faning survey rise to credible levels, replacing the unrealistically low proportions self-reported in the earlier marriage

116 On the construction of homosexuality in Victorian Britain, see Weeks, *Coming out*; Weeks, *Sex, politics and society*, ch. 6. Kevin Mumford has argued that the discourse on sexual neurasthenia in transatlantic medical psychology from the 1880s through to the 1920s is symptomatic of a crisis of confidence in male middle-class sexuality at this time: Mumford, 'Lost manhood found', especially pp. 89–90. Also see below, pp. 558–66.

117 Michael Mason has argued that despite clear medical evidence of spontaneous ovulation since the 1840s, the belief continued to be relatively universal in British educated society until the 1870s and 1880s that ovulation occurred only with female orgasm (on analogy with the male ejaculation of sperm). However, the fact that this belief was thereafter no longer credible left males with no alternative but to abstain from coital sexual pleasure themselves, rather than rely on their wives' self-control, if they wished to avoid conception. This, then, simply transferred the onus of self-denial and sexual frustration from one gender to the other within the Victorian marriage bed. Mason, *Victorian sexuality*, pp. 201–3. Gigi Santow has noted evidence that this belief has continued to exist occasionally among the poor in the twentieth century: 'Coitus interruptus', p. 17.

118 Hall, *Hidden anxieties*, ch. 4.

119 Hall, *Hidden anxieties*, ch. 4, *passim*, which, *inter alia*, includes a dozen or so direct references to abstinence – more than any other specific method mentioned.

120 Langford, 'Birth control practice', Table 3.1 and pp. 60–1. The exception was the PIC survey of 1959–60, which unfortunately specified abstinence extremely restrictively as avoiding intercourse for six months or more. There was a slight but statistically insignificant tendency apparent for men to report such abstinence more than women. See also pp. 406–7, above. Three other surveyors of sexual behaviour did interview men as well as women; but they did not produce comparable data on methods of birth control within marriage. Slater and Woodside, *Patterns of marriage*; Schofield, *The sexual behaviour of young people* and *The sexual behaviour of young adults*; Gorer, *Exploring English character* and *Sex and marriage*.

cohorts. This may, then, reflect two related occurrences, producing statistical effects in the survey's results. First, as appliance methods were increasingly becoming acceptable and respectable, there was a declining proportion of married couples in each successive marriage cohort who were practising attempted abstinence as a mutually acknowledged method of birth control but one which was not reported to the Royal Commission because of the flaw in the questionnaire. Secondly, there was a declining proportion of husbands having to endure a solitary, unilateral form of sexual continence (whose true extent was unknown to their wives), because it was also now superseded by the mutually acceptable forms of contraception which were now increasingly available.

To be able to assess this hypothesis, it would be ideal if substantial evidence existed on typical frequencies of sexual intercourse in the past. It does not. Indeed, until the publication of the results of the most recent national survey of sexual behaviour, conducted in 1990–1, there was virtually no representative information of this sort available.[121] The new survey has found that among the 3,548 married and 445 cohabiting women, aged 25–44, in the random sample interviewed, the median frequency of intercourse was 5 times per month (four weeks).[122] The results of this survey can be compared only with a single, much smaller source of quantitative information from the period before the Second World War, a study undertaken in 1929–30 but only published in 1937.[123] The records of coital frequency were based on the diaries kept by fifty-six women (51 of whom were married) aged from 23 to 45 (average age 30.6) cohabiting with a partner throughout the period of the study. The median frequency of intercourse among this sample was four (in fact 3.7) times per month (menstrual cycle).[124] Both the 1990–1 and the interwar coital frequency distributions exhibit similar, highly skewed functional forms (hence the use of the median value because a small number of women recorded very high frequencies of intercourse during some of their cycles). The prewar sample does, therefore, appear consistently to have the

[121] Wellings *et al.*, *Sexual behaviour*, pp. 3–4, on the problems of many of the previous investigations, including even Kinsey's work, based as it was on voluntary, self-selected samples.

[122] Wellings *et al.*, *Sexual behaviour*, Table 4.1, p. 140.

[123] McCance *et al.*, 'Physical and emotional periodicity'. This was a study of physical and emotional correlates of the menstrual cycle, which fortunately included observations on the incidence of sexual intercourse during a six-month period when diaries were kept by the study's participants. The researchers aquired their small sample haphazardly, mostly through snowballing personal contacts and therefore the participants were mostly drawn from the educated middle classes (pp. 572–5, 581–2). I am extremely grateful to Lesley Hall for alerting me to the existence of this study: on the trouble which McCance and his colleagues had in getting such a study published even in a purely scientific context (twice rejected by the Royal Society), see Porter and Hall, *The facts of life*, pp. 175–6, 191–2.

[124] McCance *et al.*, 'Physical and emotional periodicity', Figure 10, p. 608; according to the information on p. 581, sixteen further women in the study were excluded fom this analysis because of incomplete records or because they were menopausal, and one because she became pregnant during the study period.

properties of a significantly lower coital frequency version of the 1990s population.[125]

Given the singular nature of this early source on coital frequency, it can be treated as no more than suggestive in its support for the thesis of reduced coital frequency during the period of falling fertilities. However, it does record the kind of partially abstemious pattern of intercourse which, according to Bongaarts, would be sufficient to exert a significant spacing effect on fertility. In this interwar sample the fifty-six women gave evidence on coital frequency over six months, hence covering a total of 237 cycles: 7% (17) of these cycles were completely abstinent; in a further 11% (24) intercourse occurred only once during the month; additionally in another 14% (33) of the cycles intercourse took place only twice. Altogether, in 60% (142) of these 237 cycles intercourse occurred no more than once per week.[126]

One other source from this period which does comment on coital frequency is the Lella Florence survey of Cambridge couples. Unfortunately the information is not expressed in a precisely quantitative manner and it is based on a highly selected sample (those voluntarily attending an early birth control clinic). For what it is worth, Florence states that, '*The great majority* of men whose wives have visited our Clinic are extremely moderate and self-controlled'[127] (emphasis added). Having noted that 'There are a few who indulge in nightly *coitus* – one or two so abnormal that an even more frequent demand is sometimes made', Florence then offers a definition of what she means by 'moderate':

> But it was a genuine surprise to me to find how many couples indulge only moderately: how many habitually leave intervals of two, four, or six weeks; how many, in reply to my question, answered 'Oh, three or four times a year'; how many others practise abstinence over long periods – six months or a year, after the birth of a child; and how many others have adopted abstinence permanently.[128]

This quotation raises the possible importance of one other kind of explanation which should be considered to account for the generally low proportions of women reporting themselves as practising birth control in the survey sources. Relatively low rates of coital frequency sufficient to reduce fertility – amounting even to virtual abstinence in some cases as in this quotation – may simply have been viewed as normal or natural behaviour by respondents. Before the public discourse triggered by Marie Stopes there was certainly precious little information available to individuals with which to assess what was normal, if they ever considered the matter. Coital frequency may have fallen quite significantly during

125 At the 75th centile of each distribution, women aged 25–44 who were married or cohabiting in the 1990s were experiencing ten acts of intercourse per month, as against six acts in the prewar sample; and at the 25th centile the respective figures were 2.5 acts in the 1990s and 1.65 acts before the war. McCance *et al.*, 'Physical and emotional periodicity', Figure 10, p. 608; Wellings *et al.*, *Sexual behaviour*, Table 4.1, p. 140.

126 All calculations derived from data in McCance *et al.*, 'Physical and emotional periodicity', Figure 10, p. 608.

127 Florence, *Birth control*, p. 119.

128 Florence, *Birth control*, p. 119.

the late nineteenth century without many couples necessarily being aware of this, nor even of the effect it was having in reducing their family size. It is certainly a rationalist fallacy simply to assume a willed purpose and a conscious intention behind all forms of behavioural change.

There is of course copious anthropological evidence that the passion between the sexes is not as constant as Malthus's first *Essay on Population* axiomatically stated (and as Malthus himself in fact fully recognised in his second *Essay*, through the concept of 'moral restraint').[129] Just as with the attested effects of age and duration of marriage, changing cultural and ideological norms of sexual activity might then be posited as a major influence reducing coital frequency and so also reducing the birth rate.[130] Within living memory there have been remarkable shifts in norms relating to sexuality in Britain, while surveys have shown significant behavioural change over the same period and also considerable international variation in sexual practices.[131] In the 1960s there was the popular endorsement of so-called sexual liberation consequent on a general appreciation of the contraceptive virtues of the oral pill. In the 1980s there was the move towards 'safe sex' with the cultural impact of the AIDS epidemic.[132] These episodes clearly show that the codes and the character of sexual behaviour can vary quite rapidly in response to private or collective rationalisations of perceived change in the conditions under which sexual activity can be enjoyed.

It is also of relevance that there is something of a cultural parallel with the AIDS threat, in that throughout the period during which fertility fell the venereal diseases of gonorrhoea and, especially, syphilis were greatly feared and a source of shame for victims. Each of these periods of threat has, for instance, elicited a well-publicised feminist call for celibacy as a solution to women's predicament.[133] In Britain, Davenport-Hines inclines towards the view that it was only in the 1920s that there was a decline in public interest in and fear of venereal disease.[134] This is

[129] Ford, *A comparative study of human reproduction*; Ford and Beach, *Patterns of sexual behaviour*.

[130] On the former, see, for instance, Weinstein *et al.*, 'Components of age-specific fecundability'.

[131] Carballo *et al.*, 'A cross national study'.

[132] For instance, Germaine Greer's *Sex and destiny* was a popular publication from this period advocating the virtues of celibacy, at least for women.

[133] Hamilton, *Marriage as a trade*, pp. 37–8; Germaine Greer (previous footnote). For an explicit study of the similarities in these respects between the Victorian *Fin de siècle* and the present one, see Showalter, *Sexual anarchy*.

[134] Although his evidence makes it clear that this was a relative decline with subsequent outbursts of anxiety: Davenport-Hines, *Sex, death and punishment*, p. 247. Chapters 2 and 5–7 of Davenport-Hines's study in effect comprise the nearest there is to a history of venereal diseases in Britain to parallel Quétel's account for France. Davenport-Hines gives evidence on public, official, military, ecclesiastical, feminist and medical attitudes to venereal diseases. Quétel has argued that in France the interwar era 'was literally obsessed with the fear of syphilis' (pp. 135–6). Quétel attributes this to the zealous moralising preventive propaganda effort of the French movement for social and moral hygiene sanctioned by the medical establishment. Even though relatively effective treatments for syphilis were developed during the second decade of the twentieth century with Salvarsan, Neosalvarsan and the Bordet–Wassermann test, the French movement continued to follow the principles laid

consistent with Frank Mort's argument that the late nineteenth century witnessed a clearly defined middle-class and feminist crusade for moral reform in sexual behaviour as the answer to the related problems of prostitution and venereal disease.[135]

It had been an earlier, exclusively male, medico-scientific discourse which had resulted in the Contagious Diseases Acts of 1864, 1866 and 1869, which in themselves provoked the subsequent feminist reaction. The Acts were ostensibly brought in to control the health problems associated with prostitution in barracks and port towns. In thereby implicitly legalising an institution considered to be the antithesis of Christian marriage, the wrath of both the Evangelical conscience and the feminist movement was aroused. The National Association for the Repeal of the Contagious Diseases Acts commenced its campaign in 1869 and later in the same year a separate feminist Ladies National Association also formed. It emphasised the illogicality and ineffectiveness of the laws, as preventive health measures, in giving powers of detention and medical inspection over women while failing to do so for their male clients. The eventual success of the campaign in the mid-1880s was complete. It secured not only repeal but also the strictest rules against sex in the world at that time, in the form of the 1885 Criminal Law Amendment Act, raising the female age of sexual consent from 13 to 16 years (it having been raised in 1875 from 12 to 13).[136]

By the 1880s this was part of a wider, burgeoning moral 'Purity Campaign', whose works were to engender an increasingly strict formal regulation of various dimensions of sexuality, constraining its legal and public expression into a heterosexual, monogamous straitjacket. Since the formation in 1863 by the Metropolitan Police of a department to deal with Obscene Publications, laws against pornography were progressively tightened including, of course, the censorship system which was ultimately to catch *Ulysses* (1923) and *Lady Chatterley's lover* (1928) in its net.[137] All forms of homosexual activity were, at a stroke, criminalised by the Labouchere amendment to the 1885 Criminal Law Amendment Act.[138] The police were zealously assisted in enforcing these laws by

down at the turn of the century by its pre-Salvarsan founder, the eminent syphologist Alfred Fournier, in stressing the need for a behavioural reform and the crusade for a chaste nation. Quétel, *History of syphilis*, p. 192, and see especially chapters 6, 8–9. On venereal diseases in the USA, see Brandt, *No magic bullet*.

135 Frank Mort, *Dangerous sexualities*. Mort argues that earlier in the century prostitution had been seen initially as simply a 'class' problem, reflecting the unruliness of the lower orders; and subsequently as a technical, medico-scientific problem. See also Davenport-Hines, *Sex, death and punishment*, chs. 5–6. For more on the significance of the feminist role in the social purity movement, see below, pp. 566–70.

136 The Act was passed in the wake of the famous 'Maiden tribute of modern Babylon' scandal, a successful sensationalist newspaper exposure of child slavery and prostitution in the West End: Walkowitz, *Prostitution and Victorian society*, pp. 246–7.

137 Hyam, *Empire and sexuality*, ch. 3, pp. 65–71.

138 Weeks, *Sex, politics and society*, p. 102.

the local branches of such voluntary bodies as the Vice Society (active from the late 1860s) and the National Vigilance Association (active from the mid-1880s).[139]

The available evidence on such matters as attitudes surrounding venereal disease, homosexuality and prostitution might, therefore, be taken as indicative that sexual behaviour was increasingly cast in a negative light by the late Victorians, as a source of problems and anxieties and as something requiring ever more stringent self-regulation and formal controls. This is closely related to the class-inflected public opprobrium reserved for the condom and for other forms of efficient contraceptive. Davenport-Hines has helpfully shown how this was essentially similar to the ambivalent official, medical and ecclesiastical attitudes subsequently expressed towards the possibility that calomel cream could be an effective preventive against venereal disease.[140] The same views were repeatedly articulated in the 1880s, to the Royal Commission on Venereal Diseases of 1916, and beyond into the early 1920s: that the real source of disease was the lamentable lack of self-control on the part of the lower orders; that any invention such as the condom or calomel which permitted absence of self-restraint to go unpunished would only exacerbate the root problem; and that sexual continence was the only true and moral answer to the problem.[141] As Ronald Hyam has put it (somewhat categorically): 'The worst result of the late-Victorian campaign was the silence which descended over all aspects of sex, producing the most appalling ignorance . . . Real sexual activity receded so far into the background that according to Larkin's famous poem it was not rediscovered again "until 1963".'[142]

Many individuals in many communities during the late Victorian era and after may, then, have come to entertain quite strongly negative or at best guilty and ambivalent feelings towards sex, as something animal-like and base, associated with life-threatening and dishonouring disease and with the literally dirty parts of the body.[143] Added to this, there were the well-known hazards to the health and even the life of the woman if pregnancy ensued. This was almost certainly a fear which was quite rationally on the increase in this period because the risks of death in childbed remained as high as ever, whereas *other* causes of premature death among women of childbearing age (notably tuberculosis) were finally beginning to abate.[144] All this would be conducive to a régime of low coital frequency

[139] See Weeks, *Sex, politics and society*, ch. 5; also Bland, 'Feminist vigilantes'; Bristow, *Vice and vigilance*. Furthermore, all this should be placed in the exactly contemporaneous context of the developments discussed in chapter 4, whereby the more anarchic aspects of the proletarian environment were increasingly brought to order under the supervisory purview of an expanding range of public service educational professionals and health officials: chapter 4, especially pp. 190–7 and 203–7.

[140] Davenport-Hines, *Sex, death and punishment*, pp. 223–6.

[141] For numerous examples of these views, see Davenport-Hines, *Sex, death and punishment*, pp. 195–6, 197–8, 199–200, 220, 221, 237, 241–2, 243.

[142] Hyam, *Empire and sexuality*, p. 71.

[143] On the complex social and moral associations between class, gender and sexuality in Victorian bourgeois ideology and socialisation, see below, pp. 450–60, and especially pp. 467–9.

[144] See above, pp. 295–6.

voluntarily adopted by both partners and therefore seen by them as merely normal and 'civilised' behaviour, rather than as necessarily a deliberate form of birth control. Such a framework of beliefs, including concerns for maternal health, would also provide the rationale for investing abstinence itself and the practice of conscious self-restraint with a positive evaluation – quite independently of any possible birth controlling motives.

This cultural explanation for reduced coital frequency might, therefore, short circuit the sphere of personal, conscious *choice*, as far as the relationship between reduced coital frequency and reduced fertility is concerned. According to this view it would be individuals' negative emotional dispositions towards sexuality or their evaluative premises regarding sexual behaviour (derived from the norms of their peer groups) which would have changed, with coital frequency and fertility both diminishing as an unintended, but direct consequence. From the point of view of accounting for the substantial momentum of falling fertility which took place in so many different social groups, the question is whether this explanation – falling coital frequency merely as a by-product of a culture of sexual disinclination – is in itself plausible as a sufficient explanation. While it is almost certainly a part of the story, it seems to me that the balance of the demographic and cultural evidence appears to point to the greater importance of deliberate, negotiated birth regulation as a positive motive, albeit one that was mediated through a culture of anti-sexuality.

There are three principal reasons for this judgement. First, the strong statistical association in the 1911 occupational data between delayed marriage and reduced completed and incomplete marital fertility bespeaks a consistency of purpose on the part of couples consciously aiming at restricting family size. Secondly, there is substantial evidence in the published analysis of the Cambridge Group's aggregative parish data, to provide grounds for believing that moderate degrees of marital fertility control – presumably through abstinence – had been a normal practice in British society throughout the early modern period.

This is based on the evidence, first, of short-term variation in fertility across the period 1548–1834, analysed by Ron Lee in chapter 9 of Wrigley and Schofield's *Population history of England*, using the Cambridge Group's aggregative parish register data.[145] Lee's time-series analysis found that throughout these three centuries marital fertility was quite markedly responsive to rises in wheat prices, with marital fertility depressed six to fourteen months after a price rise (after allowing for the additional, small short-term effect attributable to nuptiality variation).[146] Although Lee tended to emphasise foetal loss as a possible cause, he did at one point speculate that 'Couples might consciously restrict their fertility in hard times'.[147] Most intriguingly, Lee also noted in his conclusions that

[145] I am grateful to Tony Wrigley for drawing my attention to the significance of this evidence.
[146] Wrigley and Schofield, *The population history*, pp. 370–1, 375, 383, 397.
[147] Wrigley and Schofield, *The population history*, p. 370.

'Responses to increases and decreases in prices were *symmetric*' (emphasis added).[148] He did not apparently pursue the implications of this observation: that marital fertility actually *rose* above trend when the price of wheat was low, as well as vice versa. This release of fertility within marriage during periods of unusual prosperity strongly suggests that couples were deliberately moderating their fertility – albeit only slightly – most of the rest of the time: when prices were at their normal level. This would have been most obviously possible through self-imposed restraints on intercourse or, in other words, via a modest degree of occasional abstinence.

This, therefore, would amplify the earlier analysis and observations made by Chris Wilson, whose research showed that the relatively low marital fertility of sixteen reconstituted English parishes in the seventeenth and eighteenth centuries was partly explicable through lower 'fecundability', associated with a probable rate of coital frequency which was well below the highest rates apparent in the range of comparisons available to him for pre-industrial populations of European extraction.[149] The significance of the foregoing interpretation of Lee's analysis, regarding cost-of-living-related, short-term fluctuations in marital fertility in *both* directions would suggest that this modest coital frequency in England reflected a conscious and deliberate form of marginal abstinence, rather than something primarily culturally determined and largely beyond individuals' calculus of conscious rationality. It is interesting to note in this context that Barry Reay has recently produced evidence from nineteenth-century parish reconstitutions, which indicates some marital fertility regulation in rural communities in Kent in the 1830s and 1840s. Reay argues this may have been a direct short-term fertility response to the more draconian provisions of the New Poor Law, suddenly reducing outdoor relief for those with large families.[150]

Furthermore, the findings of the Cambridge Group's new family reconstitution volume are highly suggestive, with respect to this hypothesis. One of the most significant new findings to emerge is that the important rise in the nation's fertility after 1750 was due to rising marital fertility, and not just to increasing frequency of marriage, as previously thought. The average number of births occurring within any given period of marriage increased after 1750; and it did so in an especially marked fashion among married women above age 35, in the latter part of their

[148] Wrigley and Schofield, *The population history*, p. 400.

[149] Wilson, 'The proximate determinants of marital fertility', pp. 218–19. Wilson found that the English data were consistent with an average coital rate of 0.25 (intercourse once every four days; i.e. 1.0 equates to intercourse every day), which compared with a maximum average rate of 0.31 (intercourse once every 2.5 days) for the married couples of French Canada. The lowest coital rates estimated by Wilson were 0.18 (intercourse once every 5.5 days) for the individual villages of Middels in Ostfriesland and for Crulai in Normandy. Apparently, the concept of 'fecundability', as the probability of a married woman conceiving during a menstrual cycle in the absence of any deliberate birth control, was first introduced by Corrado Gini: 'Premières recherches'.

[150] Reay, 'Before the transition'.

childbearing careers.[151] This strongly implies that married couples, especially where women were above age 35, had previously, before 1750, been restraining their fertility somewhat at higher parities – in a manner which they apparently then relaxed at a time of generally rising labour demands, during the second half of the eighteenth century.

This English evidence of marital fertility variation in the early modern period appears to be susceptible to a more definite interpretation of conscious regulation than that which was presented for pre-industrial German villages by Knodel and Wilson. In a meticulous examination of fertility patterns in fourteen German villages during the eighteenth and nineteenth centuries they showed that after the first quarter of the nineteenth century there was a secular trend of an increasing rate of conception within marriage.[152] To explain this, Knodel and Wilson opted for a primary emphasis on the possibility that changing breast-feeding habits, associated with changed female work patterns, had shortened the period of lactational amenorrhoea.[153] But they also showed a keen awareness that a possible alternative explanation was that there may well have been changes in coital frequency (towards greater frequency, implying that German couples had previously been practising a relative abstinence); furthermore some of their most detailed evidence suggested the intriguing possibility that 'a period of reduced frequency of intercourse or of abstinence following a birth was developing, perhaps as the concomitant of greater concern for maternal health'.[154] The key difference between this German evidence for (possible) changes in the frequency of intercourse and its permitted periods as a long-term trend over time, and the English pattern, is that without Lee's accompanying evidence of upward and downward fluctuation from year to year, long-term secular trends could be interpreted as the consequence of largely unconscious, cultural or economic forces altering couples' expectations or behaviour without their being fully aware of it. The English evidence, however, is much stronger, positive and unambiguous testimony to the existence of a conscious culture of fertility control, albeit only at the margins, which may well have been achieved through occasional, periodic or temporary abstinence.[155]

[151] Wrigley, *et al.*, *English population history*, ch. 7, 'Fertility', Tables 7.12 and 7.37. This, therefore, confirms for the English population generally the findings previously reported for Quakers: Vann and Eversley, *Friends in life and death*, p. 251.

[152] Knodel and Wilson, 'The secular increase'.

[153] Knodel and Wilson, 'The secular increase', pp. 78–9.

[154] Knodel and Wilson, 'The secular increase', p. 73 and p. 71. See also below, p. 562, for independent evidence of the related practice of *Schonjahre* in Germany towards the end of the nineteenth century.

[155] In a recent survey examining the early modern cultural and literary evidence for references to coitus interruptus, Gigi Santow has pointed to the possible importance of post-partum sexual abstinence within marriage in early modern Europe. The church's long-established view was that breast-feeding should not be disrupted by a new pregnancy, though it varied in its opinion as to when maternal weaning and resumption of sexual activities should occur (with wet-nursing adopted by some, such as among the French and English upper and middle classes, as a way to continue the infant's breast-feeding while the spouses were thereby enabled to resume sexual relations without flouting

Marital fertility may then, in fact, have been subject to regulation throughout the early modern period in England but at a relatively low level of intervention most of the time. With the fertility-depressing and standard-of-living enhancing effects of the institution of late age at marriage, there was little call for any radical restriction on sexual intercourse within marriage. But this does not mean that fertility was not in fact regulated.

These two dimensions of demographic evidence, from the 1911 census and from the early modern period, would seem, therefore, to tip the balance of probability firmly in favour of conscious, attempted abstinence to restrict births as the main cause of reduced coital frequency in the late Victorian and Edwardian period. But there is a third reason for arguing that attempted abstinence was a consciously negotiated development. This lies with the cultural and socio-political evidence from the period. As will be argued below, when the role of organised feminism is re-evaluated, a public discourse explicitly promoting the virtues of sexual continence, primarily on moral and on health grounds, was, in fact, consciously developed and elaborated in this period. This was promoted principally through the literary genre of the 'New Woman' novels, which enjoyed quite a popular readership, through certain forms of medical advice literature, and also in the writings of the ideologists and campaigners of the late Victorian and Edwardian feminist movement.[156]

Finally, the importance of 'a culture of abstinence' in providing the principal means for birth control in British society throughout the period in which fertility fell is further confirmed by reconsideration of the relationship between attempted abstinence and the practice of coitus interruptus, the principal contraceptive method positively identified in the Royal Commission's findings. In the absence of much other positive evidence, most historians, including for instance J. A. Banks and Angus McLaren, have concluded that it is most probable that coitus interruptus was the principal method of birth control used before appliance methods became more widespread. But are coitus interruptus and abstinence really the distinct and separable – alternative – practices which they have been assumed to be? As a result of the considerations in the ensuing paragraphs, it will be concluded that in the British context coitus interruptus in fact represents a species of sexual abstinence. And hence, positive evidence for the practice of withdrawal is in fact further evidence both for the culture of abstinence, and, it will be argued, also for the existence, alongside withdrawal, of the practice of attempted abstinence, itself.

As has already been indicated the concept of 'abstinence' *tout court* is too simple

the letter of the 'law'). Santow, 'Coitus interruptus', pp. 32–5. However, note that there is reason to believe that any prohibition on intercourse during lactation was not generally observed in Britain: Fildes, *Breasts, bottles and babies*, pp. 60–4, 105.

156 See below, pp. 566–74, for the evidence in favour of this argument.

and undifferentiated: its historical manifestations have been manifold. Pure or strict abstinence should be distinguished from attempted, from occasional and from periodic forms of abstinence; and mutually agreed abstinence should be distinguished from unilateral abstinence; this in turn might be imposed either by husband or by wife; with the further distinction that one or both spouses might or might not be engaged in sexual activity with third parties. There is additionally the dimension considered in the previous section: conscious and unconscious forms of abstinence. Strictly speaking abstinence implies conscious intentionality. But in the context of socialisation into a culture where 'continence' is considered a positive and noble virtue, it can be appreciated that the question is not quite so straightforward.[157]

Furthermore, it follows from consideration of the range of forms of *conscious* abstinence, that in terms of intentions – means and ends – there might, after all, be very little distinction between attempted abstinence and coitus interruptus. The essential character of conscious, attempted abstinence in British society at this time lay in the denial, to oneself or to one's partner, of sexual gratification (for the ulterior purpose of avoiding another birth or protecting a partner's health). Coitus interruptus, like abstinence, represented a voluntary, private act of renunciation by husband, by wife or by both together (for the same ulterior reasons) of the unrestricted expression of their sexual inclinations: it is an obvious form of self-censorship or delimitation of the range of sexual activity permissible (in that completed coitus is to be avoided).

There is, therefore, a genuine sense in which, for all the very obvious difference in behavioural manifestation, couples in British society who engaged in a régime of coitus interruptus were involved in essentially the same 'game' of sexual self-restraint as those practising the various forms of conscious abstinence. Indeed, it is quite implausible, and an artificially compartmentalising approach to human behaviour, to suppose that coitus interruptus as a regular practice in marriage in British society at this time can be clearly separated from a more general tendency to reduce the frequency of initiation of sexual activity. This is at

[157] Consider, for instance, the question: to what extent, in these circumstances, would a lower frequency of initiation of sexual activity represent a conscious act of 'restraint' (upon something which the individual would otherwise have wanted to engage in)? Or, there is the possibility that the culture of continence might be so pervasive that a low frequency of sexual activity unconsciously occurred without it being willed; this is the hypothesis which has been considered and rejected for modern and early modern British society in the preceding paragraphs. There is also the important distinction between restraint in sexual behaviour and the different, albeit closely related, question of perceived sensual and emotional restraint. As Malthus, himself, pointed out, the latter did not *necessarily* follow from the former. Malthus argued that individuals' passion might even be enhanced in countries where constraints on gratification existed and many Victorians may have believed this. (This foreshadowed Freudian notions of repression and sublimation as different possible outcomes of the rechannelling of sexual or erotic energy, since Malthus's view, like Freud's, was premised on a notion of the libido or sex drive as in some sense an invariant of nature, and therefore requiring its manifestation in one form or another.) On Malthus, see Mason, *The making of Victorian sexuality*, p. 268.

least obvious in the form of the reductionist argument: that if the tautology is granted that restricted sexual behaviour (of which coitus interruptus is an example) is less satisfactory than unrestricted sexual behaviour (where full coitus may take place – and anything else, of course), then, at the margins, a couple will more often refrain from sexual activity (when tired, suffering from a headache, etc.) under a regime of restricted sexual behaviour, than if they were not so restricted. Coitus interruptus and attempted abstinence were, then, part of a continuum of forms of contraceptive behaviour in British society, which flowed from the same strategy of sexual self-censorship.[158]

Since the relationship between the spouses was the forum in which this repertoire of forms of sexual self-negation and mutual denial was acted out, it is likely that in many cases the two individuals were driven towards ritualised and formulaic patterns of sexual interaction, in order to deal with the problem which they now faced in their relationship, of chronic uncertainty over their own and over each other's genuine sexual wishes and motives: sexual 'bad faith' (in Sartre's existentialist sense) is endemic in such a culture. Such couples are now in the land of sexual 'doublespeak': it is telling that George Orwell, in *Nineteen eighty-four*, a literary product of the latter part of this era in British society, was drawn to dwell on the question of the relationship between the public dishonesty in human relations of totalitarian political régimes and the poor quality of the personal and sexual relations of its citizens, the fictional Winston Smith and Julia.

The extensive practice of abstinence in Britain can therefore be recovered by inference from the historical record of withdrawal, if the above chain of argument is accepted. Its implication is that the positive recollection of coitus interruptus can properly be taken as indicative of the existence of a larger and encompassing 'world' of self-imposed sexual restraint in the society in question. The silent and invisible record of the awkward necessity of attempted abstinence, suppressed from the individual and collective memory, can be indirectly recovered from the visible, voiced acknowledgement of the positive act of coitus interruptus.

Previously, contemporary investigators and historians have tended to interpret statements from couples or individuals that they practised coitus interruptus as representing an alternative to the practice of abstinence; and therefore as so much evidence *against* the prevalence of abstinence. But, if the above considerations and arguments are valid, then individuals and couples who, in response to social

[158] Note that the sexual meaning and the social significance which can be attributed by us, as historians, to the act of coitus interruptus depends utterly on the cultural context in which it occurred, rather than on the activity itself. It is argued throughout this section that in a British 'culture of abstinence', coitus interruptus was an integral part of a range of sexually abstinent and inhibitory behaviours. However, it is perfectly possible that in the entirely different cultural context of a relatively uninhibited, positively pro-sensual popular culture, as may have been more the case in France, for instance, coitus interruptus would have been understood by its practitioners – and therefore should be interpreted by historians – as an integral part of a range of behaviours intended either to facilitate the increase of sexual activity or to enhance the sensual pleasures involved, or both.

surveys and oral historians, recall the practice of coitus interruptus in their marriages can also be counted as individuals and couples who were practising a generalised form of abstinence – sexual self-restraint – in their marriages. Couples retrospectively acknowledging their practice of withdrawal were acknowledging that they voluntarily delimited their sexual encounters with each other in a purposive, systematic way.

The argument here, therefore, is that the historical record of the practice of withdrawal is an indicator of the more general disposition of a perceived necessity among a given generation in Britain for self-denial in sexual relations between spouses. It is an indicator of an encompassing sexual culture of attempted abstinence and restraint, practised both by those couples who positively acknowledged to investigators their practice of interruptus, and also by a wider constituency of couples who had failed to negotiate the practice of withdrawal with each other and who may or may not have acknowledged (publicly or even to themselves) that their low frequency of intercourse was a form of sexual abstinence.

Furthermore, this is of great significance to the attempt to explain how fertility was brought under such effective control by the pre-Great War marriage cohorts; and in a way which might, to some extent, square with the qualitative evidence presented above, particularly the retrospective findings of the Royal Commission. This only found evidence of withdrawal, and even that at only modest levels, as a substantial practice among these cohorts. It would explain the conundrum whereby relatively small percentages of the surveyed couples recorded exclusive reliance upon abstinence, whereas the indications from independent evidence from the period (from Lella Florence and the McCance study) do suggest relatively low rates of coitus among many couples. Couples who had sex only a few times a month and tended to practise coitus interruptus when they did, would not report themselves as having practised abstinence, but interruptus, only.[159] But in reality

[159] Those practising the combination of coitus interruptus and reduced coital frequency would not necessarily acknowledge the latter as abstinence, because of its insidious, supplementary aspect and because they may not even have properly acknowledged it at the time, to each other or even to themselves as individuals. It is much more likely that an individual will remember and publicly acknowledge a category of activities which positively did occur (interruptus, especially since it involves another person, their partner), than a category which, in a sense, never existed (abstaining from more frequent sexual intercourse than they would otherwise have liked). This is especially likely when it is considered that the internal decision to deny or to defer sexual gratification on any specific occasion simultaneously involves willing the suppression and the denial of the existence – the force – of the desire which prompts the inclination towards sexual initiation. In a conjugal régime of attempted abstinence, this would tend to become a quasi-reflex, to which the practitioners habituate and become inured. As a result the memory, especially in hindsight, is more likely to be one primarily of simple disinclination – the absence most of the time of a willed desire to have sexual relations – than a positive memory of all the sexual events which never occurred. And even where the latter does exist as the memory's interpretation of what transpired, it is likely to be a negative and unwanted memory, which in itself is therefore likely to be emotionally suppressed and unlikely to be volunteered, with relative indifference, to investigators conducting broadcast surveys. (Whereas, it is precisely the suppressed nature of such problems of sexual self-denial and maladjustment between partners which created one section of the market demand for psychiatrists,

this was a combined mix of the two and, as a contraceptive method, a very 'potent' one. The combination of coitus interruptus with abstinence (reduced coital frequency) would, in fact, be extremely effective as a birth controlling method (all the more so where the resolve existed to procure an abortion where, occasionally, this combined method failed).[160]

An evaluation of the incidence of abortion in Britain before 1940

Before coming to a balanced judgement of the relative importance of the various possible methods for curtailing fertility in Britain before the First World War, a final thorough consideration must be given to the question of abortion. As mentioned in the historiographical survey in Part I, there is an important line of thought, chiefly represented by the work of Angus McLaren and Diana Gittins, which has argued forcefully that abortion was an important method of fertility regulation, at least among the working class. According to McLaren abortion was a major form of birth control among the needy poor, reflecting the tactics of sporadic desperation, rather than any form of aspirational behaviour.[161]

Gittins has if anything gone even further than McLaren and has argued that, in contrast to the male-initiated methods of coitus interruptus and the condom which, according to her were more prevalent among the middle classes, most working-class family limitation was achieved through exclusively female methods, particularly abortion.[162] The necessary contacts and knowledge for this were acquired by women during the periods of factory, shop or office work which many working-class women undertook before marriage. Gittins has suggested that such proletarian women were therefore more independent and more in control of their destinies in this crucial respect than the comfortable and cosseted women of the middle classes, who remained contraceptively dependent, as in so much else else, on their husbands. This would leave male working-class attitudes to birth control virtually irrelevant, because of their relative ignorance or disinclination to know about what their womenfolk did in these matters.

There are a number of problems with this interpretation, however. If abortion was the main means of plebeian birth control, as Gittins has suggested, and was employed only as a desperate expedient, as McLaren has argued, this would tend to predict a falling fertility to be recorded first and most markedly for those

of which Freud's career was an early example.) On Freud, see below, pp. 561–2. For testimony on the pains of self-restraint, see below, pp. 562–3.

160 This important point has been empirically demonstrated with statistical evidence of a multiplicative 'interaction effect', whereby two or more relatively inefficient methods of contraception were shown to be more effective than the sum of their parts would have predicted, when combined together as a joint set of contraceptive practices: David and Sanderson, 'Rudimentary contraceptive methods'.

161 McLaren, 'A woman's work'; McLaren, *Birth control*, especially ch. 13; see also Knight, 'Women and abortion'.

162 Gittins, *Fair sex*, pp. 160–4; and see above, pp. 52–4.

occupations with the most insecure and low-paid sources of income. In general, however, within any given industrial sector, this is not the case. Although, as has been shown, skilled workers as defined by Hobsbawm are conspicuous by their absence from the ranks of the proletarian pioneers of family planning, it is still various types of unskilled labourer, representing those with the most precarious and lowest paid forms of employment, who are well represented among those with the highest completed and incomplete fertility recorded in 1911. The general validity of a strong version of the Gittins–McLaren interpretation is, therefore, highly dubious (though it may still be valid in restricted cases, for proof of which more precise research would be necessary).

On the other hand, one aspect of the hypothesis put forward by Gittins receives some qualified support from the occupational fertility evidence. It seems to be the case that in those communities where there was relatively rigid role segregation between working men and their non-working wives (in mining, heavy industry and the most effectively and successfully unionised categories of employment) there was relatively much less spacing of births than in those occupations carried out in communities where female participation was more the norm, such as textiles and retailing. However, whether this supports Gittins's contention that working women in these latter communities were collectively, almost conspiratorially, responsible for their birth controlling activities, in the face of their husbands' ignorance or even disapproval, is another matter altogether.

It is maintained here that a strong version of Gittins's thesis, that working-class women such as textiles operatives controlled their births unilaterally and collusively as a group but without reference to their husbands, is improbable as a general interpretation because it remains inconsistent with other relevant evidence. One of the most consistent themes emanating from the sources of direct testimony from women of all classes for the entire period to the 1920s is their profound ignorance of reproductive biology at marriage, absence of the most rudimentary instruction from their own mothers, and often innocence, or fear and distaste at their own bodies' sexual functioning.[163] This sits uneasily with the view that a shared knowledge of and control over reproduction was one of the main power bases of proletarian women.

It therefore seems more consistent with the occupational fertility data from

[163] Marie Stopes was, of course, herself a classic example with her unconsummated first marriage. One of the chief reasons for the great success of her publications after the Great War was that they answered people's questions. Other evidence of popular ignorance on sexual matters is contained in many of the letters published by Llewellyn Davies in *Maternity* (see above, n. 59); in the accounts by the staff of Marie Stopes Mothers' Clinics of working women's reluctance to be examined or even to touch themselves (Cohen, 'Private lives in public spaces'; Florence, *Birth control*, pp. 123–4); and in the findings of oral historians: Roberts, *A woman's place*, pp. 15–18; Chinn, *They worked all their lives*, pp. 143–4. Steve Humphries cites the unpublished Mass-Observation sex survey (England, 'Little Kinsey'), which found as late as 1949 that only 11% of respondents had received sex education from their mothers and only 6% from their fathers: Humphries, *A secret world*, p. 40.

before the Great War to infer that those groups within the working classes limiting their families' size most effectively were not those in which the 'battle of the sexes' had led to such a stand off between husbands and wives that the latter were driven surreptitiously to attempt to control their fertility through repeatedly exposing themselves to the dangers of illegal abortion. It seems more likely that the enhanced bargaining powers of women and wives in circumstances such as in the textiles communities, where they had significant earning power, would have resulted in their successful negotiation and enlistment of an adequate degree of co-operation from husbands, such that they did not have to run the health risks of abortion.[164]

In the letters published by Margaret Llewellyn Davies in *Maternity* there are frequent comments on whether or not husbands were 'good', 'co-operative', 'loving', or else 'bad', 'worrying' and even 'brutal'. Whether or not all these statements can be taken as applying to sexual behaviour (and in many cases they clearly do), they demonstrate that the general *issue* of the extent of both economic support and emotional co-operation forthcoming from husbands was considered to be something very variable and something of great importance by most of these women. Time and again in the letters, women comment on the persistent low state of health or permanent infirmity which they were left with after a difficult, sometimes life-threatening confinement.[165] It is clear that for many of them, in a physically weakened or mentally depressed state for long periods of months or even years, the sexual attentions of their partners could be an unwelcome further 'worry'. In these circumstances 'good', 'loving' partners were those who did not express themselves sensually and who were sufficiently concerned with their wives' health that they did not insist on their 'conjugal rights'; while 'brutal husbands' carried on regardless. This is also the conclusion which Wally Seccombe has drawn from his systematic reading of the 200 letters published by Marie Stopes in *Mother England*, a random sample of those written to her in the year 1926.[166]

Sex was undoubtedly a problem and subject to intense negotiation between spouses because childbirth was so clearly a source of ill health and even mortal

164 As detailed below (p. 430), Coleman's study of Japanese society identified abortion as a method specifically favoured by an extremely male-dominant culture, rather than as something necessarily associated with the assertion of female powers. Furthermore, Barret-Ducrocq concluded from her reading of a sample of unmarried mothers' depositions to the Thomas Coram Foundling Hospital in London between 1851 and 1879 that 'it was men . . . who generally proposed abortion . . . Women, on the other hand usually had to be persuaded, almost compelled . . . we should also remember that abortion in the nineteenth century was an alarming and dangerous experience.' Barret-Ducrocq, *Love in the time of Victoria*, p. 130. See also Ottosson, 'Legal abortion in Sweden', who found few women inclined to seek illegal abortion, even when refused a legal one.

165 Llewellyn Davies, *Maternity*, *passim*.

166 Stopes (ed.), *Mother England*. Apparently the 200 letters were drawn from her files according to surnames beginning A–H. Seccombe observes that 'Men who are portrayed as being co-operative outnumber unco-operative males two to one, with the former constituting a clear majority even in the letters of female respondents.' Seccombe, 'Starting to stop', p. 177.

danger for women. No doubt some husbands' acquiescence in the avoidance of further births was only in the passive form of studied ignorance, leaving the details of contraception and the responsibility for any abortions when methods failed to their wives.[167] However, writing of the 43,000 interwar women who came to the Marie Stopes Mothers' Clinics and were mostly fitted with their *own* caps or diaphragms, for which they paid the not inconsiderable sums of 4–6 shillings, Deborah Cohen has noted that even for these women, 'it was often nearly impossible for a woman to practise birth control without her husband's knowledge . . . if a man wanted to prevent his wife from using birth control he was likely to succeed'.[168] Given the expense and impracticality of purely female methods of contraception, such as douches, pessaries, caps and diaphragms, in the crowded, unplumbed working-class houses typical before the later interwar period, a more active male co-operation, in the form of voluntary abstinence, reduced coital frequency, coitus interruptus, non-coital sex and the positive *acceptance* of the use of diaphragms, pessaries and condoms, seems much more likely to have been the most effective method of birth control actively sought by women, rather than the 'independent' resort to abortion.

In support of this viewpoint, there is, finally, some relevant evidence reported by T. H. C. Stevenson in his analysis of the 1911 census data. Stevenson was able to show that the fertility of Irish-born (mostly Catholic) men married to English-born wives was significantly higher than that of English-born men married to Irish-born wives. From this (and some other, supporting evidence on the sex-differential fertility of rural–urban migrants) Stevenson concluded that there was a general pattern evident, whereby the birthplace of the husband seemed to have more influence on family size than that of the wife. He reasoned that if the fertility differentials were themselves due to 'restraint' that the reason for these findings must be that, in general 'discretion in exercise of this policy of restraint rests in practice more with the husband than the wife'.[169]

Of course, abortion would still have played its part, but the foregoing interpretation would cast it very much in a secondary role, as a back-up. This would entirely tally with the statistically based estimates that have been made of the quantitative incidence of induced abortion. These are principally derived from official work done by various inquiries during the 1930s. These estimates have been summarised by Glass and by McLaren: they range from a minimum of about 60,000 to an extreme maximum of 125,000 per annum, with 90,000 per annum being the most widely cited maximum estimate.[170] Although there are no statistical

[167] Hoggart, *The uses of literacy*, p. 41.

[168] Cohen, 'Private lives in public spaces', pp. 110–11.

[169] *FMR* Pt 2, p. cliii.

[170] Glass, *Population policies*, pp. 50–5, 427–9; McLaren, 'The sexual politics of reproduction', pp. 96–7. The figure of 90,000 per annum was the figure arrived at by the Abortion Law Reform Association from the estimates prepared by the BMA's *Report of the Committee on Medical Aspects of Abortion* (1936). It was also a figure endorsed by D. V. Glass in *Population policies* (pp. 54–5) in his own

estimates available for earlier decades it is considered by these authorities that induced abortion rates were higher in the 1930s than at any previous time.[171] But abortion rates even on the scale of 125,000 per annum can only account for a fraction of the conceptions foregone. If the married women of the 1930s had still been conceiving at the same rate as married women in the 1870s, they would not have been producing 600,000 livebirths each year, as they did in the 1930s, but well over one and a half million (this includes the fertility-depressing effect of their later average age at marriage).[172] Married women in the 1930s were evading over 900,000 livebirths per year, of which the most extreme estimate would suggest that only up to 15% (125,000) could be attributed to abortions, (while the most likely maximum estimate would indicate 10%). Only dramatically higher levels of abortion than this, by a factor of about three to four times, would substantially alter the conclusion that abortion was only a birth controlling method of secondary importance in a quantitative sense.[173]

Furthermore it is noticeable that, although several *other* towns are mentioned, contemporary reports from before the Great War of the prevalence of abortion, based on the clinical experience of medical practitioners, do not refer to its existence in either the Lancashire or the West Yorkshire textiles towns in the period before the 1911 census, precisely the places where proletarian birth regulation was most firmly established.[174] This tends to suggest that the resort to

independent consideration of the BMA Report in conjunction with the Ministry of Health's *Report of an Investigation into Maternal Mortality* (1937) and the Birkett Committee's *Report of the Inter-departmental Committee on Abortion* (1939). For further information on the study of abortion rates in the 1930s, see Brookes, *Abortion in England*, especially ch. 5 and p. 111.

171 *Report of the Royal Commission on Population*, ch. 4, paragraph 82; Lewis-Faning, *Report on an Enquiry into Family Limitation*, ch. XI, especially pp. 167, 170–1. Neither McLaren nor Glass (n. 170) has entertained the possibility that a higher rate of abortion might have applied in any earlier period.

172 These figures are derived from information in *The Registrar-General's Statistical Review of England and Wales for 1938 and 1939, Text Volume*, New Annual Series Nos. 18 and 19 (HMSO 1947), Appendix, Table I, p. 232.

173 Abortion would, of course, have had some further effect in reducing fertility as a result of consequent sterility among a certain proportion of those undergoing abortions. The various possible sources of increased involuntary sterility, including also venereal disease, were minutely examined in the investigations carried out for the Royal Commission on Population by E. Lewis-Faning and also in the *Report of the Biological and Medical Committee* (Papers of the Royal Commission on Population, Vol. IV). From these researches it was concluded that the combined effects of all these various sources of involuntary sterility were relatively negligible in accounting for the national fall in fertility which had been experienced. For a summary of their conclusions, see *Report of the Royal Commission on Population*, ch. 4, especially paragraphs 76–9.

174 McLaren, *Birth control*, ch. 10, especially pp. 242, 248. McLaren's information is principally based on what is by far the most comprehensive and careful discussion of the available, verifiable historical evidence on the incidence of abortion in Britain. This is contained in Glass, *Population policies*, pp. 50–5 and 427–9. Glass notes that the existence of medical evidence for the use of diachylon is specified for Sheffield, Barnsley, Doncaster, Leicester, Nottingham, Bedford and Birmingham before 1906, spreading by 1913 to Leeds, Manchester, London, Bristol, Hull, Newcastle-upon-Tyne, Glasgow, Aberdeen and Cardiff. The textiles towns of West Yorkshire and Lancashire are conspicuous by their absence from this list, until midwives reported its use (but only in Nelson and Burnley) to a 1914 official inquiry on 'Infant Mortality in Lancashire', PP XXXIX 1914, p. 70. By

abortion, where it occurred, may have been most common in those communities where the practice of effective birth spacing by co-operating married couples was *least* well established. Rather, then, than representing the main proletarian method of systematic birth control organised by collusive female networks, abortion in this period may have been most frequently found necessary by relatively isolated women living in those communities where regulation of family size was not recognised by couples as a common goal.

Thus, birth spacing occurred earliest in those working-class communities in which husbands and wives were most likely to function more equally as joint economic providers for the home and where a work role induced division in the culture, priorities and ways of thought of the two sexes was likely to be least pronounced. Among these social groups men and women were most likely to share priorities in their approach to the family's economy and to the costs represented by a large or fast-growing family: they spoke the same language in these matters. They were therefore more likely, on average, to be actively co-operative with each other with respect to identifying and acting upon the problem of a fast-growing family than men and women in those communities where a workplace-induced, gendered segregation of culture, roles and language prevailed.[175] Hence, apart from textiles workers in both Lancashire and West

contrast, as P. Knight has observed, the opinions from some of the correspondents in northern districts reported by Ethel Elderton in 1914 do, indeed, make claims that abortion was practised in several textiles towns: Knight, 'Women and abortion', p. 58; and see Glass, *Population policies and movements*, p. 52 n. 1. for exact references to abortion in Elderton, *Report on the English birth rate*. However, the same important cautions apply to the reliability of these unattributed, second-hand reports as were raised in the previous section regarding the prevalence of appliance forms of contraception (see p. 401). While Knight points out that in 26 of the 104 registration districts of England north of the Humber, at least one of the correspondents believed abortion to be significant, she fails to make explicit the balancing observation that in 78 of the districts none of the correspondents mentioned it.

175 This formulation does not necessarily entail the proposition that communities of textile mill workers be considered, in some Whiggish sense, to have been proletarian 'pioneers' of a more companionate form of marriage than that which existed elsewhere in the working classes. It is merely asserted here that major differences between communities in the extent to which women's work was acceptable and financially advantageous produced differences in overall bargaining power between the sexes, and associated differences in the linguistic resources available to the two spouses to negotiate with each other – from something more like the same premises – over the difficult issues of sex, fertility and family size. It is perfectly feasible that for all their income-earning inequalities and even regardless of their posited lack of communication on matters of childbearing, husbands and wives in mining communities may, on average, have been more content with their reciprocal, sex-typed roles and even may have have had warmer relationships with each other than couples in textiles towns. They may even have perceived themselves as more equal, although today's observers would not necessarily concur. For instance, in M. Llewellyn Davies's *Maternity*, there are at least two examples where a husband's *not* confiding and sharing with his wife some vitally important problem (including, in one case, his intention to end the lives of the whole family) is reported by the wife in her letter as a positive illustration of her husband's caring and loving relationship (letters 88 and 134). All this is, of course, quite another matter, relating to the perhaps ultimately unanswerable question of the emotional quality of marital relationships. While not entirely unaffected by the gendering of the labour market, this is a distinct matter, subject to a complex range of additional social, cultural and personal influences and is not to be confused with

Yorkshire, the other quantitatively most significant sections of the working classes exhibiting relatively low fertility before the Great War were the various categories of retailing shopkeepers: those small proprietorial businesses typified by husband and wife teams behind the counter, which often survived in working-class areas only on the narrowest of profit margins and through the careful husbanding of resources by the two partners.

Indeed, it is to be noted that this general point, regarding the importance of gender and spouse relations, would still be valid even if contraceptive techniques other than attempted abstinence were playing a leading role in late nineteenth-century working-class communities. The main possible alternatives (abortion not being a contraceptive) at this time were: coitus interruptus and other forms of non-coital sexual gratification; or 'appliance methods' (i.e. condoms, caps, home-made pessaries or occlusions, sponges, douching and sprays). To be used effectively in the working-class marriage bed ('bedroom' being something of a luxury in many cases) all such alternatives typically would have also required an adequate communicative relationship between the spouses and, at the least, an acceptance if not positive endorsement of the methods on the part of husbands. The importance of the latter point is suggested, for instance, by the remarkable findings of Samuel Coleman's study of birth control in postwar Japanese society. Coleman's research showed that the reason for the much-remarked peculiarity, whereby the principal means of birth control in modern Japan has long continued to consist of the rather antiquated technology of condoms, the rhythm method and induced abortion, lay in this strongly male-dominated society's history of powerfully institutionalised male hostility to the main alternative forms of contraception (the oral pill, diaphragms and sterilisation) because of the greater control and potential sexual autonomy which these methods give to women.[176]

While it is not intended to suggest that British working-class mores were exactly similar to those in modern Japan, oral history confirms a culture of profound female deference (no doubt flouted on occasion – no norms are absolute) to husbands' 'conjugal rights' in the period before the Great War, even where the same sources of evidence have been deployed to demonstrate convincingly the great powers of matriarchy in many other domestic matters. For instance, Carl Chinn writes that 'not even the strongest and most assertive matriarch would believe it correct to acknowledge, at least publicly, that she refused her husband his marital rights'.[177] However he also detects a subsequent shift among his respondents later in the interwar era when 'A man's right to have sex whenever he demanded it was questioned more and more by many of the new generation of

the question of community norms relating to relative bargaining power between the sexes and relative perceptions of child costs, which are the critical issues addressed here regarding the elucidation of social patterns of fertility change.

176 Coleman, *Family planning in Japanese society*.

177 Chinn, *They worked all their lives*, p. 142. This is a study based on oral history conducted in a poor area of Birmingham, which has particularly emphasised the powers of a working-class matriarchy. See also Roberts, *A woman's place*, pp. 84–6.

women (although not all).'[178] The obverse of Gittins's thesis may well therefore be correct: that as well as, and apart from, the effects of the quite different economic relationships involved, the culture and values of communities with strongly male-dominated labour markets may have particularly obstructed the emergence of an effective form of birth-controlling behaviour in the form of male 'continence'. This would not be dissimilar to the documented effects of a particularly male-dominant culture, as in Japan or as with the *respeto* ethic in Puerto Rico, in reducing effective communication between spouses on such matters.[179]

Furthermore, as the modern Japanese case documented by Coleman suggests, a relatively high incidence of abortion does not necessarily indicate female control over contraception nor does it necessarily function as an alternative to other forms of contraception.[180] It may well be, then, that the probable rise in abortion which occurred in Britain during the later period, after the Great War and on into the post-Second World War era, reflects the increasing frequency of sporadic incidents of failure of communication, intent, resolve or technique among couples who were more generally utilising *other* methods to restrain the formidable powers of 'the passion between the sexes' – but methods which were intrinsically unreliable and experimental.[181]

In summary, while some women may have used abortion as an independent means to limit their fertility because of the lack of a satisfactory understanding with their husbands, the argument put forward, principally by Gittins, that this represented the major method of proletarian contraception, preferred by women in those communities where birth control was most marked, would seem highly unlikely. It discounts far too lightly the moral qualms, the ignorance and fears and the genuine health risks involved. Furthermore, even the highest statistically based contemporary estimates of an abortion rate of 15–20% of current births actually occurring (suggested for the 1930s) was not on a scale sufficient to account for more than a small part (10–15%) of the overall massive shortfall in the number of livebirths *not* occurring.[182]

[178] Chinn, *They worked all their lives*, p. 148.

[179] Stycos, Back and Hill, 'Problems of communication between husband and wife'. See above, p. 34, for mention of this anthropological work.

[180] Of course, there was a major difference between Japan and Britain in the general aceptability of abortion to each society's patriarchs, given the latter's Christian tradition of abhorrence of abortion.

[181] Hence Chesser found in the early 1950s that as much as one quarter of those interviewees who answered the relevant question admitted to trying to terminate a pregnancy on an occasion when they thought they might be pregnant; and that this was most marked among those women most in control of their own contraception or in joint control of it with their husbands, rather than among those where the husband only was in control. Chesser, *The sexual, marital and family relationships*, p. 470.

[182] Note also that David and Sanderson's re-examination of the primary sources for the USA have uncovered serious errors in the transcription and interpretation of the results of contemporary studies of the quantitative incidence of abortion: 'Rudimentary contraceptive methods', pp. 332–4. They show that these errors have led the authors of a number of influential historical studies seriously to overestimate the incidence of abortion in the USA. This applies, for instance, to: Mohr, *Abortion in America*; and Reed, *From private vice to public virtue*.

Conclusion: a variety of methods within a culture of abstinence

The foregoing analysis has shown, therefore, that the data on incomplete fertility collected at the 1911 census is strongly and unconditionally in favour of the proposition that the great majority of couples who were limiting their fertility in Britain in 1911 were generally doing so through the practice of spacing rather than stopping.

Of course, these findings cannot be construed as positive evidence that parity-specific stopping behaviour was not being practised at all before the Great War. But they do strongly indicate that the prevailing assessment of the relative quantitative importance and conceptual significance of each of these two very different methods should be entirely reversed for this period of British demographic history. Although some scholars, such as P. A. David, have already begun to question it, the long-prevailing orthodoxy apparently remains at present intact: that the modern phenomenon of secular fertility decline has been principally characterised throughout its duration by the emergence of parity-specific forms of birth-controlling behaviour.[183]

But the evidence presented here from the 1911 census seems to be quite unequivocal in showing that spacing was the principal form of family limitation practised by those who controlled their fertility most systematically during the period before the First World War. Ironically, the only occupational categories from this generation whose fertility behaviour might appear to be consistent with the hypothesis of birth control at high parities *only* – the classic 'stopping' form of behaviour – would be those controlling their fertility the least. This would relate to the occupations found towards the bottom of Appendix E, recording relatively high and unlimited incomplete fertility over the first five to ten years of marriage. In fact, the Royal Commission's 1946 survey independently confirms this general interpretation of the primary significance of spacing from early on in marriage. The survey found that among those marrying in both the 1900s and the 1910s, of those who acknowledged the use of any birth control methods over 70% had apparently done so from within the first five years of marriage.[184]

Therefore in Britain, at least, if not elsewhere, too, the formation of public socio-cultural norms defining particular sizes of family as desirable ideals or targets only emerged *subsequent* to the initial period of falling fertility and not as an integral part of its early causation. It would certainly be an interpretation consistent with what is known of the condemnatory nature of public discourse on the subject of birth control throughout the period until well after the Great War. This is something which would have strongly inhibited the cultural formation and

[183] For instance, in two recent independent statements on the nature of Britain's fertility decline, Robert Woods and Wally Seccombe found themselves quite able to concur with each other on this, despite their differences in methodological approach: Woods, 'Debate'.

[184] *Report on an Enquiry into Family Limitation*, Table 67, p. 93.

ideological articulation of explicit *public* norms and ideals of small family sizes.[185]

During its first few decades the secular decline in national fertility rates from the 1870s may well have been due to ever greater proportions of the population taking up the practice of spacing their births, possibly from quite early in marriage. With the evidence available from the published tables of the 1911 census, there is no way of showing conclusively with completed fertility indices whether spacing initially began among the earlier marriage cohorts at relatively high or low parities (the extreme version of the latter being 'starting') or possibly somewhere in between. It may well be the case that in some communities or social groups spacing typically had begun early in marriage and in others at a later stage. This will be an important task for future research to establish.

However, it should be noted that if it does prove to be the case that other research in due course demonstrates that it was the higher birth parities where fertility was reduced first among the earliest birth controllers marrying in the 1850s and 1860s, the results reported here would now counsel against acceptance of such findings as straightforward evidence in favour of stopping rather than spacing. It may well be that the earliest detectable form of family limitation in the nineteenth century will prove to exhibit an apparent pattern of 'stopping' rather than 'spacing' behaviour – by which is meant the curtailment of births relatively late in the marriage rather than from early on in marriage. The key question is whether this kind of limitation of high parities really equates to 'stopping', as opposed to 'late spacing', in the conceptual spirit in which these two terms are used as opposites. If the identification of a pattern of 'stopping' is to mean anything substantively distinct from 'late spacing', it must imply that the birth controlling behaviour in question was guided by some kind of target or ideal family size, whereas late spacing makes no such necessary assertion.

Since it has been shown here that spacing from early on in marriage, rather than stopping, was *the* predominant form which family limitation took throughout most of British society by the Edwardian period, evidence from earlier decades should be interpreted very carefully in this light. For instance, a woman delaying or spacing her births towards the end of her reproductive span may well produce a 'stopping' pattern of relatively early age at last birth. This and other demographic patterns, such as lengthening intergenesic intervals at highest parities, which might otherwise be seen as straightforward signs of 'pioneering' couples or groups exhibiting *apparent* 'stopping' behaviour, might in fact more correctly be understood as evidence for late spacing and *not* for stopping. In other words, the spacing behaviour which can be observed in full force from early in marriage in

185 McLaren, *Birth control*; Soloway, *Birth control*, p. 193. Soloway has also pointed out that, along with the Anglican Church itself, the majority of contemporaries considered that it was not until 1930 that birth control formally became a 'decent' public subject in British society. This was also the year in which the government permitted public welfare centres to disseminate contraceptive information. See above, p. 410.

the Edwardian period may well have initially begun at higher parities only. The key point is that evidence of regulation at high parities or among older married women only cannot now be treated as an unequivocal sign of stopping behaviour, at least in the British case.[186]

Of relevance to this argument, as has been noted above, is the important point made by John Landers that spacing can itself be understood as an aspirational and target-related form of birth control, where the goal is not to attain a specific or ideal family size but to maintain, defend or enhance a specific standard of living.[187] Hence, evidence of birth control among some pre-industrial communities and social groups may also be interpreted as 'late spacing'.[188] It may well be that in previous centuries there have been couples who have deliberately attempted to avoid another birth at some point in their family building in order to defend their standard of living. *Ceteris paribus*, this is more likely to have been attempted at relatively higher parities, but this should be interpreted as 'late spacing' and not 'stopping'. As noted above, there is evidence of precisely this pattern, especially during the somewhat economically difficult period 1650–1749, in the family reconstitution data for England.[189] Obviously, spacing and attempted abstinence within marriage were being practised during the late nineteenth century on a much more extensive scale than ever before, but whether they were entirely new forms of behaviour or not remains an issue for future resolution (I suspect not).

Parity-specific family limitation aimed at a target family size may only have appeared as a general practice throughout British society rather late in the day: as a *consequent*, second-phase phenomenon some time during the interwar era, and therefore *after* the period which has been classically considered to encompass initial onset of 'the fertility decline' in British society. The new norm in favour of the small family may well have initially emerged in many communities or social groups as a *de facto*, rather than *de jure* cultural form. In other words it became established as the highly visible *result* of the private decision-making and spacing behaviour of a large and increasing number of couples, who initially behaved in this way regardless of publicly accepted norms articulated by churchmen, politicians (both those who saw themselves as representing the middle class and many working-class representatives, too), and the medical establishment.[190] The

[186] For an example of a detailed British study which has apparently uncovered such a pattern among worsted workers in Bradford (subject to the technical limitations of the 'own-child method', which is necessary for estimating age-specific fertility values from manuscript census sources), see Ittmann, 'Family limitation and family economy in Bradford', Table 1 (though see ch. 9 n. 139 for reservations on Ittmann's wider interpretation).

[187] See above, n. 12.

[188] For a helpful and balanced summary of the rest of this range of evidence, see Vann and Eversley, *Friends in life and death*, ch. 4.

[189] See above, pp. 418–19.

[190] On working-class political figures' predominantly negative attitudes towards birth control before the First World War, see McLaren, *Birth control*, chs. 3, 9–13; on the church and the medical establishment, see Soloway, *Birth control*; and Soloway, *Demography and degeneration*.

blatant evidence before their eyes of the various benefits of such smaller families, alongside the increased provision of voluntary and governmental information and facilities for contraception in the interwar period, may then have produced a secondary wave of stopping behaviour (including among them those who had not previously found any reason to space their fertility – couples in the higher fertility occupations, as of 1911).[191]

Meanwhile, by the beginning of the interwar era those many other members of society whose own parents' generation had already achieved relatively small families through spacing would, by this time, have become so accustomed to the 'norm' of smaller families, in which they had themselves been brought up, that notions of a specific target size of family – 'the' small family of two or three children – could become lodged in their daily discourse and popular culture, as reflections and rationalisations of the predominant family patterns which they perceived around them. This view gains some independent support from the Lewis-Faning survey for the Royal Commission on Population. This found, first, that only among the non-manual classes were there significant percentages of couples already regarding third and fourth parities as 'unwanted' births from among the earliest cohorts questioned (those marrying before 1920). Secondly, there was a marked general development in that the first postwar marriage cohort of 1920–4 showed a sharp increase over earlier cohorts – across all social classes – in the percentage of couples identifying the fourth child and upwards as 'unwanted'.[192] Only once such ideals were in common currency as practical targets, combined with the greater acceptability and lower cost of the most efficient forms of contraception, could it have made sense for couples to have all the children which they intended to have in relatively rapid succession and early in their marriage, discounting the risk of subsequent contraceptive lapses, which remained a chronic problem where attempted abstinence or coitus interruptus were the principal methods used.

It is highly relevant to this consideration that it has long been known that the rapid rise in production of cheap and easy-to-use condoms did not occur until the 1930s when the previous, rather aptly-named 'cement' process of manufacture was replaced by the liquid latex process, resulting in cheaper and much lighter, more comfortable prophylactics.[193] The thick rubber condoms made by the 'cement' process were expensive for the working classes, morally tainted in the eyes of middle and working classes alike, and extremely undelectable for all

[191] Some corroboration for this viewpoint is contained in the analysis presented in *Report on an Enquiry into Family Limitation*, ch. VI. This found evidence to suggest that among cohorts marrying in the 1910s and 1920s the non-manual classes were actively regulating and planning births from the very start of marriage, whereas there was a tendency among manual workers and their wives only to turn to effective contraception after they found their families had grown too fast (which could also be quite early on in their marriages).

[192] *Report on an Enquiry into Family Limitation*, ch. X., especially Tables 97 and 99.

[193] Peel, 'The manufacture and retailing', p.122.

concerned – sometimes requiring soaking in hot water to render pliable.[194] The greater familiarity which men had had with the old-style condoms because of their utilisation during the Great War probably did not produce any immediate dramatic rise in their use in the marriage bed in the 1920s because the context had only further emphasised their long-standing unsavoury associations with prostitution and disease. As Deborah Cohen has shown, one of Marie Stopes's prime aims and achievements was to combat these associations, using her interwar clinics to counter the disreputable image of contraception and to convince working-class women that they could discuss their bodies and their sexual functions as a respectable matter.[195] Hence, the increased take up of appliance methods in the 1930s also coincided with birth control emerging as a more acceptable topic of public and private discourse, symbolised by the Anglican Church's, the BMA's, and the government's relaxation of their strictures from 1930.

Finally, it should be underlined that the overall interpretation offered here is certainly not intended to contradict all the emphasis that has been laid in the previous chapter on the importance of variations in fertility behaviour between different social groups and different communities around the country. Many possible methods of birth control were no doubt used in Britain in varying degrees by couples finding themselves in widely differing socio-economic and cultural contexts during this period. There is some contemporary testimony, for instance, to the effect that lead-based abortifacients may have been more commonly used where its industrial application brought its effects to women's notice, as in Newcastle, home of the white lead industry, and Stoke, where lead was used in glazes.[196] If they can be relied upon at all, the reports sent to Elderton just before the Great War at the least suggest very considerable variation from one northern town to another in the extent and use of different methods of birth control. It is integral to the concept of a common culture of abstinence, as formulated above, that attempted abstinence and reduced coital frequency be seen as a central part of a varying mix of integrated birth controlling practices through sexual restraint, notably including coitus interruptus, as argued above.

Moreover, the fact that the central method employed was in most cases the same

194 On production and price, see Peel, 'The manufacture and retailing', p. 116. On soaking in hot water, see the instructions for use cited in Branca, *Silent sisterhood*, p. 137. For several contemporaries' expression of the unsatisfactory nature of 'thick preventatives' as late as the 1920s, see Hall, *Hidden anxieties*, pp. 92, 95.

195 Cohen, 'Private lives in public spaces', pp. 103–8.

196 NBRC, *The declining birth-rate*, pp. 313–21, 298–312. On Newcastle, evidence of Professor Sir Thomas Oliver (a pioneer public health investigator in the field of industrial diseases), presented 20 November 1914. On Stoke, evidence of Dr George Reid (Staffordshire County MOH), presented 13 November 1914. Note that Oliver's research showed that while female work with lead in factories substantially raised the frequency of stillbirths they experienced and so brought lead's powers to their attention, individual women seeking to bring on an abortion did this by swallowing a combination of aloes and diachylon plasters (containing lead), which were bought from chemists. Reid also stressed the latter method in the Potteries.

– attempted abstinence – does not mean that the motivations and reasons for its use did not vary. As the important study by J. and P. Schneider has documented, the same contraceptive technique (which they found to be 'coitus interruptus' but which, I would argue, may qualify as part of a 'culture of abstinence') was deployed with the same successful effect by three different social groups in the same community in Sicily. But, as the Schneiders carefully show, the reasons for adopting the method, and its social and cultural significance to the practitioners in each of the three different groups, was quite distinct.[197]

It may well also be the case, as Debbie Kemmer has most persuasively argued, on the evidence of the relevant contemporary public statements which professionals (mostly medical) published, and as Major Greenwood's aside might seem to suggest, that although they were one of the few social groups who possessed the means and the household amenities to experiment with the expensive and cumbersome appliance methods, the most rigorous practitioners of abstinence

[197] Superficially this looks like a textbook example of the diffusion down the social hierarchy of new ideas and techniques but the Schneiders have shown in detail that there were three separate fertility declines occurring in the same place, clearly distinct in terms of the social constituency involved, the timing, the direct politico-economic causes and the aims involved. The landowning gentry élite had already become family planners during the period before the First World War, in response to the Prairie wheat-induced European depression in agricultural prices and the perception of a new need to provide their children with expensive educations as an alternative source of élite status and income security. The methods used by this élite were a combination of withdrawal and long periods of abstinence among wives, who turned a blind eye to their husbands' not infrequent violations of the peasant girls among their household servants (resulting in resort to clandestine abortion in Palermo when necessary). This practice engendered a chilling 'brutalisation' of gender relations not only between the spouses of the landowning class itself but also within the class of their victims, because the poor labourers, who were the husbands and fathers of the systematically abused and 'dishonoured' women, suffered chronic low self-esteem, seeing themselves as 'the beaten-down cuckold' (*cornutu bastonatu*). The landless peasantry did not curtail their fertility until after the Second World War, when land reform and the introduction of compulsory elementary education finally removed the patron class from their backs and transformed their working and domestic lives, so that a 'decent' and 'honourable' home became an attainable possibility. At the time of the Schneiders' interviews in the mid-1960s, three or four well-spaced children – and not just two – seemed to have become the norm for this class. Meanwhile, birth control had come to the relatively independent third section of the same community, the artisan class, in the interwar decades, when the strict quotas introduced by the new US immigration laws were perceived by this group as a serious restriction on their employment and income-earning opportunities, as there had been a well-established flow of emigration. By contrast with the landowning gentry this fully politicised, socialist and anti-clerical artisanate, with many occupational and political links abroad, were characterised by the Schneiders as having a highly articulate 'contraceptive culture' both in public and private. There was much discussion among them of the 'proper' family size and of the 'French' family model, resulting in rapid adoption of a two-child family norm. The interviews (with both husbands and wives) showed much more companionate relations between spouses in this class than in either of the other two. Withdrawal seems to have been the general method used, with couples having particularly prided themselves on their controlled family formation as the manifestation of their successful exercise of *volontà* (will power). In the interwar period they saw this in socio-political class terms, as distinguishing themselves from the prolific *bestie* (animals) around them, including in this category, of course, the philandering gentry. See Schneider and Schneider, *Culture and political economy in western Sicily*; Schneider and Schneider, 'Demographic transitions'; Schneider and Schneider, 'Going forward in reverse gear'.

during the Victorian and Edwardian period were in fact to be found among the professional middle class with their highly developed ideology of rational self control.[198]

For the upper classes, there is a sliver of fascinating complementary evidence, taken from the private correspondence in 1901 of the upper-class fiancée of a young military officer, which unequivocally records a very candid, confident and amused attitude towards sex, at least on her part.[199] In fact, although relatively brief, this is an extremely rich and complex piece of evidence, valuable for casting light on many of the issues addressed here. It shows a young fiancée quite clear in her own mind that 'I love babies but I do so want to enjoy my married life . . . without being ill or miserable'. She points out that 'we can afford to wait being both young' (which would not be the case for many professional couples at this time who married much later than those of 'private means', as we have seen). She also cracks jokes about the number of condoms she has ordered (six dozen) and the – serious – request from her supplying agent for her husband's 'size'! Although in many ways demonstrating a remarkably comfortable and relaxed relationship and set of private sexual attitudes, the correspondence interestingly confirms the force of more recognisably 'Victorian' aspects of their society. Even for this class, the simple issue of access to condoms was apparently far from straightforward: they were ordered in bulk by post from Paris through the intermediary services of the masseuse of a female friend of the fiancée's. There was also concern expressed, twice, that their possession of the 'FL' (French letters) must not become public knowledge (while their acquisition had, therefore, already compromised the two spouses, in that third parties from the servant class had had to be involved). There was also a need to assure her future husband that they were absolutely safe, and some uncertainty expressed as to their correct method of use.[200]

Although, alone, this cannot legitimately be interpreted as representative of the practices and attitudes of a wider social group, it is tantalisingly suggestive of exactly the kinds of social differences in sexual attitudes and contraceptive behaviour indicated by the foregoing analysis of the detailed demographic evidence in this and the previous chapter: the differences in nuptiality strategy between the unusually young marrying, rentier, upper class and the late marrying professions. It has been argued that the strong and long-continuing general association between late marriage and birth control after marriage indicates the importance of a sexual culture of abstinence in Britain, especially among the highly prudential professionals, who delayed marriage the most. By the inverse of the same argument, a different and more positive culture of contraception might be found most frequently (though even here, by no means ubiquitously) among

[198] Kemmer, (unpublished PhD thesis).

[199] Jalland and Hooper, *Women from birth to death*, p. 278: short extracts from four letters from an upper-class lady to her fiancé, written 8, 9, 10, 19 September 1901.

[200] All quotations from Jalland and Hooper, *Women from birth to death*, p. 278.

the couples in that one section of society, those of private means, which has been identified as most obviously bucking the nuptiality trend. The extract also illustrates the general point that a fairly positive and uninhibited attitude towards their sexuality was probably important for a couple to practise effective contraception (as opposed to abstinence), given the limitations of the methods available.

It is certainly also likely that before the Great War 'sexual continence' was rarely as rigorously practised among working class communities as it was among some groups in the professions and the middle classes. The low fertility of the textiles towns in this period may well have been achieved with a greater admixture of other methods, such as home-made sponge plugs (particularly recalled by Robert Roberts in *The classic slum*), pessaries, sheaths, prolonged lactation and, of course, abortion, than was the case elsewhere. Even here, however, the interpretation offered above would indicate that a 'culture of abstinence' – including withdrawal – which resulted in reduced coital frequency within marriages, would have been a central feature of such contraceptive behaviour; and it has been pointed out that abortion is a complementary accompaniment to such low-cost methods of birth control.

Thus, to conclude that attempted abstinence, embracing coitus interruptus, was, overall, the single most important form of birth control before the Great War in Britain is not mutually exclusive with the argument that considerable variation in the cultures of contraception was also to be found at this time in different localities and among different social groups. From his historical research and cross-cultural studies of varying fertility practices in the past, Angus McLaren has demonstrated the existence of a multitude of 'cultures of contraception', as Gillis, Tilly and Levine have termed it.[201] It seems most helpful, therefore, to envisage this period of greatest historical change in the fertility of British society as one in which multiple cultures of contraception were changing and adapting alongside each other within the different social groups and communities identified above. But all this happened within the general context of a culture of abstinence, which meant that the reduced coital frequency resulting from attempted abstinence was the principal common denominator among all these mixes of practices.

201 In their introduction to Gillis *et al.*, *The European experience*, p. 5; McLaren's work has been principally reported in his *Reproductive rituals* and *A history of contraception*.

PART IV

Conceptions and refutations

Socrates: So the work of midwives is a highly important one; but it is not so important as my own performance. And for this reason, that there is not in midwifery the further complication, that the patients are sometimes delivered of phantoms and sometimes of realities, and that the two are hard to distinguish. If there were, then the midwife's greatest and noblest function would be to distinguish the true from the false offspring – don't you agree?

The Theaetetus of Plato, 150b, translated by M. J. Levett and revised by Myles Burnyeat (Indianapolis 1990)

9

A general approach to fertility change and the history of falling fertilities in England and Wales

Parts I and II of this study have provided an extended critique of the orthodox representation of falling fertility in Britain before 1911. In the course of the exploratory statistical analysis in Part III a number of specific new findings have emerged. It is now time to draw all these together and to attempt to produce a coherent, general alternative to the old orthodoxies. First, a new general framework for approaching the study of fertility change will be suggested. Secondly, this will be used as the basis for a new interpretation of the history of falling fertilities in modern Britain which is consistent both with the 1911 evidence of occupational variation and with the wider context of modern Britain's social history and its current historiography.

The perceived relative costs of childrearing: a general heuristic framework for studying fertility change

At the outset of his celebrated article published in 1966 Gösta Carlsson elegantly expressed the enigma which lies at the heart of explaining the phenomenon of fertility change: 'It is an instance of highly significant social change through individual or at least decentralised decision.'[1] There is apparently something very general involved in the episodes of secular falls in fertility which have occurred in so many societies in different parts of the globe and at different points in their respective trajectories of economic development. This generality inheres both in the sense that the phenomenon has occurred repeatedly in many different nations' histories and in the sense that within each of these countries virtually all geographical parts and communities have eventually been affected, although requiring two or three generations for this to occur in many cases. Yet, in addition to accounting for this international and cross-cultural aspect, a truly satisfactory explanatory framework has to be sufficiently flexible to accommodate the great

[1] Carlsson, 'The decline of fertility: innovation or adjustment process', p. 149.

diversity of cultural and economic circumstances under which different individuals and couples have apparently been moved to restrict their fertility and to 'plan' their families.

In the most general of senses it may appear that a single straightforward cause can be found in the fact that the normatively sanctioned costs of childrearing must rise very considerably in any society experiencing economic development, a thesis finding favour in the recent synthesis offered by David Levine.[2] This is entailed in the conventional definition of economic development, which requires a pronounced overall rise in the quality of human capital inputs in order to sustain an economy's transformation towards an increasing preponderance of high-value secondary and tertiary (service) sector activities. It is also an explanation favoured by neoclassical micro-economists, who have additionally argued that another entailment of economic development is that rising consumption opportunities result in increasingly competitive allocation of scarce parental resources of time and money between childrearing and consumption activities, thereby driving fertility down.[3] Hence the apparent universality of the general historical association observable between successful economic development and the adoption of family planning throughout a society.

Such a perspective is certainly helpful in directing attention towards the central issue of the perceived costs and benefits of children. But it remains at a somewhat abstract level of analysis. It does not distinguish, for instance, between individual and collective definitions of such costs and benefits. More importantly this is not in fact the general *causal* proposition which it may superficially appear to be. It is essentially a *post hoc* observation of the minimum changes in human capital formation and consumer expenditure necessary for a particular conventional definition of economic development to occur. It is therefore primarily a statement concerning the necessary causation involved in economic development, rather than one specifying something essential for falling fertility. The historical cases of widespread fertility control in late eighteenth- and early nineteenth-century rural France and Hungary empirically confirm this logical point: that the attainment of low fertility has apparently been a precondition for sustained economic development over the long term, but economic growth and its entailments are not a necessary part of a general explanation for widespread falling fertility in a society.[4]

A genuinely satisfactory, comprehensive explanation of fertility change has to refer directly to the concrete concerns and perceptions of historical individuals, properly contextualised in their households and varying social environments. Simply to invoke large-scale, impersonal economic forces or cultural change is to

[2] Levine, *Reproducing families*, pp. 173, 192.

[3] On neoclassical micro-economics and fertility see pp. 37–45.

[4] Bourgeois-Pichat, 'The general development of the population of France'; Andorka, 'La Prévention des naissances en Hongrie'; Andorka, 'Family reconstitution'.

remain at an unconvincing distance from the phenomenon and to fail to take into account the significant historical and intra-national variation that is everywhere evident, as this study has demonstrated in the British case. The direct agency of change was each set of potential parents and the locus of change was each family household in its local context.

Yet transindividual forces were, clearly, of significance, too. To convince and be useful, a theory of falling fertilities needs also correctly to identify what it is that is so general about the phenomenon while being formulated in such a way that in principle, at least, it can embrace all of the variety of concrete historical circumstances in which actual individuals and households have been documented to have changed their fertility. Finally, the explanatory theory has to be conceived in such a way that it is no mere tautology but an empirically testable, refutable set of propositions. Indeed, the ultimate test for any such theoretical framework in this particular field of study could be said to lie in the future rather than the past, since there are still many societies and communities around the world in which fertility remains relatively high or relatively unrestricted.

What kind of general explanatory framework can simultaneously identify a quasi-universal cause of mass change in fertility behaviour whilst also providing the almost infinite flexibility necessary to encompass all the divergent contexts in which different nations, social groups, communities, couples and individual women have been moved to regulate their fertility? The answer to this conundrum would seem to be simply to focus unequivocally upon the central issue: change in the relationship between children and their carers. The general common factor which explains the fall in average family size in so many different communities over the last two to three centuries can be formulated as: a change in the *perceived relative costs of childrearing*.

This beguilingly straightforward formulation in fact provides a much more comprehensive heuristic framework for inquiry into the causes of changing fertility than may at first sight appear to be the case. Note that, regardless of first impressions, this formulation – the perceived relative costs of childrearing – does *not* in fact refer primarily to economic considerations. That is only one among a rich range of meanings for the term 'relative costs'. Within this putative research programme, the 'costs' of children are, therefore, to be explored in their widest senses and, being 'relative', entail consideration of all forms of benefits, too – whether economic, social, cultural or emotional. Secondly, as these costs and benefits are 'perceived', this approach critically involves the identification of the perceiving agents and their inter-relationships with the infants and children in question. Obviously this means parents, but also other kin and guardians in many cultures: siblings, neighbours, others in the community and, ultimately, all interested political institutions and figures including the state. Indeed, focus on the sources of change in these agents' perceptions potentially involves the researcher in careful consideration of the full range of ideological, cultural, political and social forces and events in the histories of the national and local communities concerned: all the diverse, changing information contexts (see pp. 39–41).

Thirdly, childrearing refers to the full gamut of requirements for reproducing the next generation, starting with the pleasures of conception (for some only – endured on sufferance by many women throughout this period in Britain's history), the pains of childbirth, and including all forms of socialisation – training and education – up to and including the point of entry into independent adulthood, however that may be variously defined. According to the proposed framework, changing social and cultural definitions of the tasks involved in childrearing or of the state and duration of childhood (including the duties of children to parents, which may be long continuing in some cultures) exert a strong influence on fertility behaviour. It can be seen that the processes of industrialisation and urbanisation have invariably been associated with falling fertility because significant shifts in perceived relative childrearing costs and reciprocal duties of this sort have always been involved under these circumstances. However, significant shifts can occur in a variety of other circumstances, too, as the examples of pre-industrial, rural France and Hungary demonstrate.

This apparently simple formula – perceived relative costs of childrearing – therefore has the capacity to identify both the general and the particular aspects of the central, historically changing relationship involved in the study of falling fertility. It defines why it has occurred repeatedly in so many different contexts while at the same time indicating the enormous variability of potential forces and events involved in any particular historical case. However, it is only empirical research, within this interpretative framework, which can convincingly reconstruct how fertility changed in any given place and time; and what the most important configuration of influences were in any particular case.

There is, finally, one potentially important range of causal influences which may appear to be omitted by adoption of this framework. By use of the term 'perceived' it is not intended to delimit the range of considerations only to those forces of which contemporaries were consciously aware. It is not necessary to posit that individuals in the past (or in the present) must be aware of either the nature or the provenance of changes that occur in their environment in order for such changes to influence their perceptions and cause them to change their behaviour. While remaining unremarkable and unremarked upon, gradual and imperceptible changes in circumstance may nevertheless elicit acts of accommodation and adaptation on the part of individuals, which amount over time to significant social or, in this case, fertility change.

Thus, a response to the explanatory predicament outlined by Carlsson has been formulated. It is proposed that study of changes in perceived relative costs of childrearing be considered as a general analytical framework for understanding the diverse causation involved throughout the many constituencies of British society in bringing about the national phenomenon conventionally referred to as 'the fertility decline'. Focus upon the variable relationship of perceived relative childrearing costs provides a single, clearly defined route of causation. To be accounted an important cause of changing fertility, any hypothesised factor must be shown to have influenced significantly parental and other relevant carers' perceptions of the emotional, social, cultural, health-related or financial costs and benefits of childbearing and childrearing. This provides a strict heuristic framework to evaluate the possible power and relevance of hypothesised explanations, but it does not in advance limit in any way the number or kind of hypotheses or the range of evidence that can be deemed potentially valid or important, nor does it constrain towards a single, national, unitary explanation for the phenomena.

The general framework and falling fertilities: childrearing, gendered roles and identities

If the foregoing statistical analysis in Part III and the interpretation of evidence at the end of the previous chapter are substantially correct, this would significantly redefine the nature of the problem involved in explaining the onset of falling fertilities, at least in Britain. It was argued in chapter 8 that the sexual abstinence which had always been practised by most young adults in Britain before entering into the responsibilities of marriage and undertaking to start a family was now increasingly extended by some couples beyond the wedding day, in order to maintain some control over the rate at which the ensuing family responsibilities grew. It was the systematic deployment of abstinence in this new context which was novel.

According to this interpretation, therefore, it would no longer be necessary to postulate that the onset of falling fertility must have been due to large proportions of the population suddenly beginning to take up radically new forms of behaviour, undergoing some form of dramatic transformation in *mentalité*.[5] The reimposition upon themselves of sexual abstinence *after* marriage by certain groups within the population represents the most important innovation, which accounts for the beginnings of the national trend towards generally lower marital fertility. Efforts at causal exegesis do not therefore need to be premised on the idea that some kind of absolute metastasis needs to be explained, in terms *either* of the general goal of controlling family size *per se or* the novelty of the methods employed to execute this aim. Both are now seen as no more than extensions of already extant ways of thought and practices.

The key problem of historical explanation resolves instead into the single issue of identifying why it was that couples wanted to control their family-building to

[5] As Part I has documented, this viewpoint has always dominated the historiography on 'fertility decline' and is not exclusively associated with the postwar modernisation/demographic transition consensus. For a recent restatement, in an article which otherwise claims to be distancing itself from the notion of 'demographic transition' as an outdated framework, see van de Walle, 'Fertility transition, conscious choice', p. 489.

such an extent or in such a way that delayed marriage *alone* was no longer perceived as an adequate form of regulation to achieve this goal *even though* it continued to be practised *as well* by those occupational groups who were controlling their fertility most systematically in 1911. There must therefore have been historically new considerations and factors influencing many married couples *after* their deferred marriages. Apparently quite soon after marriage in many cases.

What new or changed circumstance in the lives of increasing numbers of married couples in Britain, drawn from several different social groups and communities, could have affected them sufficiently to produce this innovative extension of abstinent behaviour at this specific point in their lives, soon after marriage? A satisfactory and full answer to this question would explain how and why 'the fertility decline' originally *began* to occur.[6] There is, in fact, an obvious general form of answer to this question, which leads straight back to the proposed heuristic framework. The type of new consideration which would act to influence couples with precisely the kind of timing specified – only after the point of marriage – is, of course, significant changes in the perceived relative costs of children themselves.

A new need to space the rate at which births occurred after marriage would particularly arise as an additional or separate expedient to that of an already established practice of prudential marriage (which, of course, only restrained the commencement of family growth, not its pace) under any of several possible circumstances of ideological or material change. For instance, if the perceived unit 'costs' (in emotional, health or economic terms) of additional children proved to be significantly higher than customary wisdom and previous practice foretold for those anticipating marriage. This could presumably happen because of intervening or novel (and therefore inadequately anticipated) historical changes in norms, in tastes or in relative prices occurring in the interval between the period of childhood and adolescence – during which individuals formed their relevant expectations – and the point in their lives after marriage at which they began to shoulder these childrearing responsibilities.[7] Secondly, it might, for instance, be

[6] Questions such as how, once some groups began to control their marital fertility, they then came to do so more and more, or how it was that others not at first affected subsequently also began to practise birth control are separate, if related, issues. It is not intended to imply that it can be assumed that the answers to these questions follow from some form of automatic momentum in the phenomenon of falling fertility, such that once the first stages of falling fertility have been explained so all else simply falls into place. Indeed, this would be contrary to the developmentalist view of falling fertility presented below on pp. 534–46. But the specific intellectual task being addressed at this point in the text is only to explain the first stages of marital fertility control.

[7] In terms of the purely budgetary aspects of children's costs to the household, a transformation of this type in the unit costs of childrearing could happen if it was increasingly found that the basic costs required to clothe, house and feed each additional child shifted from a declining marginal function to an additive one. This would, for instance, occur if tastes and normative standards in a given community changed such that each additional child was no longer expected to take up its siblings' cast-off clothes but to be bought its own; no longer to sleep and play alongside other family members

the case that marriage or the married state was becoming more favoured – for either cultural or economic reasons, or both – while having children, or having the larger families which would result from this greater popularity of marriage, had not experienced any corresponding enhancement in its value, or possibly even the opposite.

Thirdly, it may have been that the relative costs associated with having children came to be perceived as less a function of the overall number of children produced across the lifetime of the marriage (which the device of delayed marriage could deal with to a considerable extent), and rather more as being due to the family's rate of growth or its absolute size during its earlier stages. If it was increasingly becoming evident to people in various socio-economic circumstances that presiding over a fast-growing family was a difficult and burdensome undertaking, for reasons which had not previously been perceived to be the case, then the extension within marriage of the tried and tested method of sexual abstinence would be the most obvious response for them to make. In drawing on their own premarital experience, only recently renounced, and on their culture's long-established mores, this required no additional technical knowledge nor presupposed any fundamental revolution in *mentalité*. As has been shown (pp. 417–19), there is sufficient evidence in the pre-industrial English record strongly to suggest that a pattern whereby couples occasionally resorted to post-marital temporary abstinence was a reasonably well-established part of the repertoire for dealing with fluctuations in prosperity from the mid-sixteenth century onwards.

The difference in the late nineteenth century, therefore, was that protracted periods of abstinence, low coital frequency or coitus interruptus were practices now adopted by many couples as a semi-permanent feature of marriage throughout its course, in good times and bad, rather than as something conventionally observed during lactation or resorted to in times of hardship and anxiety. This may possibly signify something of the motivation involved. Since the justification for postpartum abstinence had always been in the health concerns for the child and the mother, this may reflect an enhancement of collective sensitivities to these issues; and it may indicate a related downgrading in the importance accorded to the husband's 'conjugal rights'.

Alternatively (or additionally), it may indicate that an increasing number of couples were perceiving themselves to be in a chronic and semi-permanent predicament in which outgoings, needs and wants were outrunning income and resources (or, conversely, that for the first time many believed a permanent

in the same space but to have its own space; to be fed entirely from foods purchased on the urban market rather than those grown on the family smallholding, garden or allotment. Obviously changes of these sorts and on this scale did not happen overnight to families in Britain during the period 1860–1940. But this briefly illustrates several of the kinds of changes in unit budgetary costs, associated with the shift from a predominantly rural to an urban environment, which the average ideal typical working-class family experienced during this period as a result of changing norms (i.e. cultural as much as economic change).

improvement in their living standards was within their grasp if they could control their expenditure sufficiently). Studies of wages and incomes have shown that this increasingly urban population was, from a purely financial point of view, receiving on average a greater margin of disposable income than ever before, although there were certainly at least two distinct periods, during the 1870s and during the 1900s, when the longer-term general trend rise in national aggregate real wages faltered (while the 1880s and 1900s also included periods of serious mass unemployment).[8] Given, however, that earnings had been, in general, rising across most of the nineteenth century, for this thesis to explain restricted fertility it would indicate a primary role either for new, increasing consumer aspirations or for rising standards of expenditure on children (or both) outrunning the more modest rises in incomes, thereby creating the common perception of a narrower margin between desired outlays and means.

Investigation of the historical causation involved therefore rests on an inquiry into the sources of such changes in spouses' perceptions of the relative costs of childrearing, with the available data of occupational variation providing the detailed evidence against which the plausibility of different hypotheses can be assessed. The potential historical causes of such changes in perceived relative costs are extremely diverse and depend critically on the changing, ideologically negotiated values and norms defining the roles of child and parent, including, in the latter case, the extent to which gender relations created different, conflicting or complementary perspectives between husbands and wives.[9] To raise the issue of changes in gendered, familial roles and social identities as a possible important influence upon falling fertilities entails an evaluation of the research that has been published on 'separate spheres' and patriarchy, the concepts which dominate the nineteenth-century historiography of gender relations.

The question of the historical formation and significance of the 'Victorian' ideology of 'separate spheres' is one of the most contentious and potentially fruitful areas of current historical research, from which only a provisional summary account of the relevant aspects can be constructed here. It seems likely that not only the commercial and professional, as once thought, but also the landed and aristocratic classes played a full role in British society in promoting this powerful moral model of public and familial, political and domestic gender identities.[10] The patriarchal, male sphere was held to be that of the public world of activity: commerce, politics, the arts and sciences. The female, maternal sphere was its passive, domestic, private complement, centred on a moral, nurturing role.

[8] For the latest reworking of real wage trends in this period, based on a new index of average money earnings, see Feinstein, 'What really happened to real wages?'.

[9] For an accessible general introduction to these issues, see Gillis *et al.* (eds.), *The European experience*, Part II, especially contributions by J. R. Gillis on the changing meaning of motherhood, and by E. Ross, and M. J. Maynes.

[10] On the commercial middle classes, see: Davidoff and Hall, *Family fortunes*; and on the upper classes, see Colley, *Britons*, chs. 4 and 6.

The patriarch was the family's legal representative and secular protector, the matriarch was her husband's and her family's spiritual guardian. Of course, 'separate spheres' did not constitute a monolithic, universally observed and invariant pattern of behaviour: it was an ascendant, wide-ranging code, constantly subject to negotiation and review, interpreted variously and flouted by some.[11] The mid-century decades probably witnessed the high noon of this inegalitarian code, symbolised in the Matrimonial Causes Act of 1857 which enshrined in statute the Victorian sexual 'double standard': that female infidelity alone was sufficient grounds for divorce whereas mere infidelity on a husband's part was not.[12] Slowly at first, but gathering momentum during the last two decades of the century, a movement ensued both in public and in private to redress the imbalance in women's conjugal and legal powers, exploiting to considerable effect the contradictory tension within the gendered ideology between the acknowledged position of moral authority which a model matriarch embodied and her subordination in law and politics to a somewhat lesser mortal.[13]

'Separate spheres' might, perhaps, be best understood as the Evangelically inflected, gendering aspect of the more general, mid-Victorian, liberal, Evolutionary consensus of the governing and propertied classes. This was the ideology which emerged as dominant from the intellectual ferment and political flux of the first

[11] Many married women out of necessity – and even many middle-class matrons out of choice – did in fact have occupations outside the home in the nineteenth century. However, these were mostly a subset of relatively demarcated forms of employment: unpaid philanthropic or 'caring' roles in the latter case; extremely badly paid jobs in the former case. Teachers and textile workers were the two numerically most significant exceptions to this state of affairs, but there were several others, such as lodging house keepers. See, for instance, Prochaska, *Women and philanthropy*; Burman (ed.), *Fit work for women*. Research will no doubt continue to produce ever more examples of both married and unmarried nineteenth-century women whose individual activities were at variance with the 'separate spheres' code, following the lead of Hollis, *Ladies elect* (on women in local government from 1869 onwards); Peterson, *Family, love and work* (on the women of the upper middle-class Paget family and their acquaintances); and Guest and John, *Lady Charlotte*.

[12] Thomas, 'The double standard', provided the classic account of the parliamentary debates surrounding the 1857 Act. For an important recent analysis within a wider context, see Poovey, *Uneven developments*, especially pp. 51–88.

[13] The private stresses and strains of this renegotiation of marital relationships within the Victorian bourgeoisie is the principal thesis of A. J. Hammerton's *Cruelty and companionship*, especially Part II. For a stimulating, semi-fictional reconstruction of the marriages of several eminent Victorians (including Harriet Taylor and J. S. Mill, George Eliot and G. H. Lewes), see Phyllis Rose's *Parallel lives*. The public political movement truly began with the formation of the first Women's Suffrage Committee in London in the year of the 1867 Reform Act, to fight the continued exclusion of women from the franchise. An early success was won in securing the vote in local elections in 1869. Significant expansion of female secondary and higher education, especially from 1869 through to the end of the 1880s, was also won, following in the wake of the revival of élite schools and university provision for males, which had already occurred earlier in the century (see ch. 10, nn. 46, 48). Other campaigns took over a decade to make genuine legislative headway, initially signalled with the passing of the second Married Women's Property Act in 1882 and the suspension of the Contagious Diseases Acts the following year. See Sutherland, 'The movement for higher education of women', especially, pp. 92–3, 106; Holcombe, *Wives and property*; Walkowitz, *Prostitution and Victorian society*. For more on the feminist movement, see below, pp. 566–74.

half of the nineteenth century and whose intellectual and institutional characteristics have been discussed in some detail in chapter 3, when dealing with the deeper ideological origins of the 'professional model' of society. The related notion of 'separate spheres' has a complex historical sequence of ideological and social origins, which historians are continuing to discover: in Puritan biblical exegesis on marriage traceable to the Reformation century; in Lockean constitutional assumptions that political activity and economic responsibility was the province of male heads of household only; in Rousseau's notion of ideal womanhood as the moral and therefore necessarily (according to Rousseau) private tutor of children and husbands; in the status aspirations of the commercial classes, which entailed the separation of their homes from their businesses and the 'retirement' of their wives to the home; in the classical education glorifying the patriarchal *polis* of Greece, an education which the scions of the aristocracy and other young gentlemen received from the clergymen who taught them in their public schools and the bachelors in their universities; and in the self-reformatory political instincts of the British upper classes, seeking to project a worthy and meritorious image in the wake of the disasters in America and the menacing spectre of revolution in France.[14]

How, then, might this post-Enlightenment, emerging evangelical and liberal consensus on gender roles and associated sexual codes have any specific relevance to the historical explanation of changing fertility behaviour in Britain? It was in particular the obsessional cultural preoccupation with rational self-control in the individual as the key to both personal achievement of and public acknowledgement of the prized political virtues of 'independence' and 'manliness' (and the reciprocal female virtues of humility and domesticity) which was of central significance to the subsequent history of fertility and sexuality.[15] This was in turn related to the political and ideological priority for establishing principles of 'order' and stability in a novel, shifting and threatening world.

The last generation of the eighteenth and first generation of the nineteenth centuries lived through an unprecedentedly intense sequence of challenges and threats to their beliefs, to the nation's survival and to their own personal capacities. They witnessed a stupefying succession of events, including the separation of the American colonies, the ideological challenge of the French Revolution, the military threat of Napoleon and the nation called to arms, and all the while the unfolding social upheavals of an industrial revolution changing the landscape and townscape. Gone were the unquestioned moral and social certainties of revealed religion and a landed hierarchy. In this context the development in polite

[14] For a general introduction, though already somewhat dated in this fast-moving field, see Rendall, *The origins of modern feminism*, chs. 1–3; and Pahl, *Divisions of labour*, chs. 1–3. See also Davidoff and Hall, *Family fortunes*; Pateman, *The sexual contract*; Newsome, *Godliness and good learning*; Honey, *Tom Brown's universe*; Roach, *Public examinations*; Jenkyns, *The Victorians and Ancient Greece*; Colley, *Britons*, chs. 4–6.

[15] The argument in this paragraph is an interpretation derived principally from Porter, 'Mixed feelings'; Mintz, *A prison of expectations*; Weeks, *Coming out*; and Sedgwick, *Between men*.

society of a preoccupation with rational, social order, in both public and private life, is understandable. Steven Mintz has documented this in Anglo-Saxon polite culture on both sides of the Atlantic. He shows a growing focus on the goal of intimate self-control in childhood training and in relations between family members in early nineteenth-century advice manuals on 'the art and responsibility of family government' and in the family letters and literature of the individuals he studied.[16]

According to Mintz, emphasis on the art of 'self-government' satisfied this transitional age's great socialising predicament: a patriarchal, hierarchical, deferential society needing to adapt to the requirements and opportunities (for individuals with initiative) of a contractual, individualistic dynamic economy.[17] In earlier centuries there had necessarily been more emphasis in childhood training on breaking the will of the child, obedience to God and to his representatives in this world – the lords temporal as well as spiritual – and respect for parents, particularly fathers.[18] There was a clear rationale in this: it was an entirely appropriate and caring way for parents to prepare the vast majority of individuals for their lives of toil and service in a relatively static, deferential, divinely authorised hierarchy, in which fathers and men were the principal controllers of access to the skills, patronage and resources necessary to make a living.[19] The social and employment lessons of the industrial revolution, however, were those of new market opportunities for commercially able and self-confident individuals: those who were prepared to innovate and not necessarily follow their fathers' ways of doing things; and there was the availability for allcomers, including those with less acumen, of well-paid (relative to the traditional alternatives of farm service and apprenticeship) wage-labour in the new factory towns for the young sons and daughters of the poor. The transmission by parents of their own specific skills and knowledge and the value of patriarchal contacts and financial assistance was at a discount in this society of change.

It came to be understood, therefore, that the best that parents could now do for their children in a more liberal and open world of new opportunities was to encourage the development of their general intelligence and resourcefulness.[20]

16 Mintz, *A prison of expectations*, p. 28 and *passim*. The individuals were: Robert Louis Stevenson, George Eliot, Harriet Beecher Stowe, Catherine Sedgwick and Samuel Butler. See also Gay, *The bourgeois experience I*, pp. 260–3. As the journal *Victorian Studies* has long exemplified, regardless of the political break in 1783, in many respects there was an Anglo-American religious, literary and scientific, and consumer culture throughout the nineteenth century, indexed in the continual flow of people and goods between the two countries.

17 Mintz, *A prison of expectations*, ch. 3.

18 Greven, *The Protestant temperament*; Morgan, *The Puritan family*.

19 Wrightson, *English society*, chs. 4, 6–7; Pollock: *Forgotten children*; Houlbrooke, *The English family 1450–1700*; Houlbrooke, *English family life 1576–1716*.

20 Hence, the third section of chapter 3, above, has shown how it was during this period that T. B. Macaulay and others found it so important to develop the practice of open examination for the nation's educational institutions, a related recruitment system for the government civil service and, indeed, an entire ideological edifice of 'meritocracy', which represented an accommodation with and rationalisation of these new developments.

Increasingly, the aim of childrearing came to be seen as imparting the capacity for self-guidance in the unknown life ahead, through instilling qualities of independence, honesty, self-control, perseverance and diligence: what the liberal middle-class Victorians called 'character' and the working class revered as 'independence'.[21] Both were quintessentially male in their meaning: 'manliness' was a central term of approbation and legitimation, recognised by both patricians and proletarians. Research has shown its crucial rhetorical deployment in political and legal contexts at this time to win important public arguments.[22]

Where fertility and abstinence are concerned, the important aspects of this pedagogy of primarily masculine self-control was, of course, in relation to codes of sexuality and practices of sexual behaviour. Under the influence of the Enlightenment's emancipatory, anti-clerical, pro-sensual celebration of the virtues of nature and natural processes, manliness in the eighteenth century had come to be equated with both political and sexual independence (only a few of the most radical Enlightenment thinkers, notably Jeremy Bentham, conceived of such freedoms for women as well; notoriously Rousseau did not). However, in the course of the first half of the nineteenth century, manly independence as self-control came to be re-interpreted to include sexual self-control. The perceived godlessness and sexual anarchy of the previous century was considered to have issued in a fateful, admonitory dénouement in France's case. The catastrophe of the French Revolution had occurred because an effeminate society had allowed disorder to prevail. Sexual and political dissolution went hand in hand, exemplified in the granting of too much political power at the French court to members of the dependent sex.[23]

During the first decades of the nineteenth century a personally restrictive, politically 'safe' sexual code was promoted in British society, by both the Evangelical, theological and the Romantic, secular discourses of popular reaction to French revolutionary excesses.[24] It was increasingly emphasised that sex was purposive – for procreation – and it was therefore spiritually sacrosanct; it should be conjugal only and indulged in by both partners to create children and not merely for pleasure. An extant eighteenth-century preoccupation with the

21 Collini, *Public moralists*, ch. 3; Mason, *The making of Victorian sexuality*, pp. 20–35; Mason, *The making of Victorian attitudes*, ch. 3.

22 Fulcher, 'Gender, politics and class'; Collini, *Public moralists*, ch. 5.

23 On this diagnosis of France's weaknesses in British polite culture, see Colley, *Britons*, ch. 6, especially pp. 250–2.

24 Roy Porter long ago identified the last decades of the Georgian era as a period in which a reaction was setting in within polite society against the Enlightenment's glorification of sensuality, which was coming to be denigrated as vulgar, passé, mechanistic and materialist: first, by those seeking in love more Romantic, transcendental meanings (most fully expressed subsequently in the works of Kingsley, Patmore and Clough); secondly, the increasingly influential Evangelicals were also hostile to the public celebration of a sensualist hedonism. Porter, 'Mixed feelings', pp. 20–1; and for confirmation of this perspective in a recent collection of empirical studies on a related theme, see Hunt (ed.), *The invention of pornography*; and see McCalman, *Radical underworld*, Pt III.

undesirability of masturbation in children (paradoxically because of the 'liberal', Enlightenment view of children as malleable 'innocents', rather than as the Fallen of the bible) was now enjoined with earnest prohibitions on 'conjugal Onanism' – the sin of sex for mere pleasure's sake in marriage.[25] Since 'public' displays of sensuality and non-procreative sexuality were increasingly frowned upon, the entire range of other sexual practices, incidentally including sensual expression and sexuality between men, was swept out of sight and into 'the closet', where much of it has since remained for well over a century.[26] By the mid-century decades there is abundant evidence that this cultural development had generated a consequent preoccupation among the élite with the intrinsically problematic business of the battle for sexual self-control. The evidence is in the pathological medical discourse and 'scientific' technology of bodily and sexual regulation prescribed for deviants, including the well-known concerns with masturbation in both sexes, spermatorrhoea (wet dreams), and female sexual anatomy and functioning.[27]

Where the relationship between this changing sexual code of self-restraint and moderation and the history of fertility behaviour is concerned, the central relevant influence can be located, not surprisingly, in the writings of the Reverend Thomas Malthus and the ensuing discussion of his ideas within mainstream, liberal and conservative British culture. Previously, following Christian religious principles based on an amalgam of the Pauline view of marriage and other bibilical precepts, notably including the prohibition on infanticide, the conventional theological

[25] Neuman, 'Masturbation, madness'.

[26] Sedgwick, *Between men*; Weeks, *Coming out*. This, of course, resulted in the growth of a sexual 'underworld' and counter-culture of illicit sexuality, whose existence has been cleverly recovered by F. Barret-Ducrocq (*Love in the time of Victoria*), and which was also attested to in Steven Marcus's *The other Victorians*. Even 'normal' sexual expression was increasingly manifested in a variety of indirect forms of articulation in this era of Bowdlerisation (Thomas Bowdler's expurgated *Family Shakespeare* was published in 1818). The coded language of sensuality in Victorian novels is still being unpicked in order to be understood by historians: John Maynard, *Victorian discourses* (see below, pp. 458–9). There is also the related phenomenon of 'parasexuality', a term which Peter Bailey has coined to apply to Victorian barmaids' deliberate eroticism of demeanour in a context where actual sexual relations were not on offer (unlike the prostitutes on the streets outside): 'Parasexuality and glamour'. Michael Mason has noted contemporaries' remarks on the convergence between the attire of the higher-class prostitutes plying their trade at the theatre and the respectable ladies' full evening dress décolletage: *Victorian sexuality*, pp. 98–9. The strategic and tactical use of parasexual dress – and demeanour – by women (and, of course, men) to assert individually or collectively their powers, practically or symbolically, is a fascinating area for further research, indicative of the enormous flexibility of manifestation in sexual and gender relations and behaviour; it is certainly of great significance in the social history of sexuality in the twentieth century. For, perhaps, the ultimate development in 'barmaid' parasexuality, there is the recent phenomenon of table-dancing clubs in the USA, where women perform naked for individual male clients while conversing with them, but under strict rules that no physical contact or sex is permitted for the clients (*Choice: Men only – the girl club* broadcast on Channel 4, 27 June 1994).

[27] Banks, *Victorian values*, pp. 89–93; Gay, *The bourgeois experience I*, pp. 145–68, 294–327; Barker Benfield, 'The spermatic economy'; Barker Benfield, *The horror of the half-known life*; Mason, *Victorian sexuality*, pp. 205–15; Jalland and Hooper, *Women from birth to death*, section 4.3 'The secret sin of self-abuse'; Moscucci, *The science of woman*.

position had been that after marriage untrammelled sexual relations and reproduction should be allowed to take their course, while trusting in divine providence to look after the fate of the growing family. First enunciated in 1803 in the second edition of his famous *Essay*, Malthus's thesis of 'moral restraint' stimulated an intense debate across the secular and theological spectrum, as to its morality or even feasibility.

The most influential theological support for 'moral restraint' came from the Evangelical future Archbishop of Canterbury (1848–62), John Bird Sumner, in his two-volume *A treatise on the records of Creation*, published in 1816.[28] Although in propounding 'moral restraint' Malthus and Sumner were primarily endorsing the notion of sexual restraint through delayed marriage, this involved explicit discussion of the desirability of sexual self-restraint *per se*, at least in the ecologically crowded conditions prevailing in contemporary Europe.[29] Boyd Hilton has identifed the Reverend Thomas Chalmers (1780–1847), the archetypical Evangelical, as the principal ideologist who went beyond Sumner's and Whately's support for Malthus, by thoroughly integrating in his teachings the moral, spiritual and practical, economic dimensions of the notion of self-restraint: 'It was Chalmers who erected the "preventive check" into a system of moral theology, in which prudence and chastity were not merely rational responses to a crisis, but spiritual imperatives in their own right.'[30]

Hence, Michael Mason has argued that from the post-Malthusian discussion there had emerged – though not until the 1830s and 1840s – an Anglican and Evangelical consensus regarding the *normality* of self-control and moderation in sex as the sign of the properly adjusted, spiritually healthy and civilised individual.[31] In fact the new 'doctrine' of 'moral restraint' of Malthus's second *Essay* of 1803 can be seen as a dialectical prime mover of a wider-ranging, fundamental shift in social thought which subsequently occurred in Britain, of which this emphasis on sexual self-restraint was a part.[32] This was a shift away from the theological, conservative view of humanity as forever fixed in its fallen nature, which, paradoxically, Malthus initially saw himself as defending against the utopians, Condorcet and Godwin. 'Moral restraint' opened up the possibility of envisaging a practical means to the progressive moral reform and self-reform of human nature, containing the seed of the various ensuing evangelical, ameliorationist and environmentalist movements and programmes which characterised the

[28] Soloway, *Prelates and people*, ch. III, especially pp. 95, 101.

[29] See the passage from Sumner's *Treatise* cited by R. A. Soloway, where Sumner contrasts the reasonableness of allowing the unlimited expression of natural desire in 'the empty wastes of America', whereas 'under the different appearance which most European countries present, rational prudence interferes as a check to the natural desire': Soloway, *Prelates and people*, p. 100.

[30] Hilton, *The age of atonement*, p. 79. Richard Whately was Drummond Professor of Political Economy in Oxford, 1829–31, before becoming Archbishop of Dublin, 1831–63.

[31] Mason, *The making of Victorian sexuality*, ch. 4.

[32] Boner, *Hungry generations*.

remainder of the century (including the public health 'programme' of the GRO).[33] Sexual self-control and sexual continence were now viewed as spiritually correct forms of conjugal behaviour which, incidentally, implemented Malthusian prudence. Indeed, this was something which later in the century could come to assume the status of a grand social evolutionary goal, for instance in the work of the atheist liberal thinker, Herbert Spencer, or the Victorian anthropologist C. S. Wake.[34]

St Paul was, thus, reinterpreted during the course of the first half of the century, in view of the Malthusian focus on the threat which unbridled fertility represented for a family's financial independence. As a result it began to be arguable among those of tender conscience that it was spiritually more respectable *not* to abandon one's children and the health of one's wife to the vagaries of chance, and to take personal responsibility for one's family's reproductive fate throughout its life-cycle through the regulation of sexual inclination. Malthus's concept of 'moral restraint' could be understood, therefore, as extending further the traditional Protestant virtue of prudence beyond merely consideration of when was the 'proper' time to marry.[35] Once systematic birth control within marriage, as opposed to the traditional method of birth control through avoidance of early marriage, had come to be appreciated as a thinkable option, by at least some sections of opinion within British society, sexuality within marriage now became, in principle, a matter for more intense social and ideological negotiation than ever before.

From this perspective the alternative option of mechanical, contraceptive methods of birth control was considered morally debasing in its aim of non-procreative, sensual self-indulgence. This was inimical to the sacrament of marriage, subversive of manliness, and of the role and health of women as mothers and wives. Hence, it has often been remarked that in Britain the appearance of birth control pamphlets and propaganda started with a spate as early as the 1820s but appears to have had virtually no perceptible public impact in the ensuing decades, diminishing to a trickle until the last quarter of the century.[36] The pamphlets appeared in the period of experimentation and negotiation of public codes of sexual expression, which preceded the establishment of the 'Malthusian' orthodoxy, of conjugal continence.[37] They then diminished because contraception had become an intrinsically indelicate, vulgarly sensualist and materialist, and therefore unrespectable, subject: the province of irreligious secularists.[38]

33 See above, pp. 85–93.

34 C. Staniland Wake's ethnographically grounded *Development of marriage and kinship* (1889) envisaged a state of sexual abstinence practised by a social élite as the culmination of human development: Weber, 'Science and society', p. 278. Regarding Spencer's thesis of individuation and the so-called 'spermatic economy' see above, ch. 5, n. 101.

35 Banks, *Victorian values*, chs. 2 and 4.

36 Himes, 'Editor's introduction'.

37 Mason, *The making of Victorian sexuality*, chs. 1–2. On the disruptions of regulated gender roles and demarcations during the Napoleonic Wars, see Colley, *Britons*, ch. 6.

38 Banks, *Victorian values*, chs. 2–3.

Thus, it has been shown by other scholars that the Victorians did not simply deny the power of sexuality in their lives. Influenced by the transcendental, Romantic and Evangelical, theological reactions of the first half of the century, they sought to spin an elaborate web of spiritual and social control around it (as, indeed, does every culture), sanctifying only responsible, prudent heterosexual relations within marriage.[39] In Steven Seidman's words:

Their strategy involved compartmentalising sex or cordoning it off from other spheres of life. Sex was to be restricted to heterosexual marriage and, within that domain, it was centred on coitus. Since sexual intercourse within marriage was no protection against sensuality, an ethic of self-control enjoining the individual to extinguish all carnal thoughts and desires became necessary. Ultimately, sexual desire had to be transfigured into an ideal of spiritual love in order to render it a benevolent power. Proposing to make love the basis of marriage may have allowed Victorians to control sexual desire but it also demanded the de-eroticization of sex.[40]

There is certainly evidence that the mid-Victorian middle classes were becoming increasingly preoccupied with the problems of sexual relations within marriage as a negotiable area. John Maynard's stimulating study of the relationship between religious and sexual prescriptions in the work of certain popular Victorian literary figures (Arthur Hugh Clough, Charles Kingsley and Coventry Patmore) focuses particularly on the centrality of issues of sexual regulation and marriage for them.[41] Thus, whereas sexual behaviour outside and before marriage had always been subject to prescriptive norms, it is significant that from the early to mid-nineteenth century onwards the question of the character of sexual relationships *within* marriage now gradually became the subject of public, ideological re-working and debate. This appeared first in explicit form, on both sides of the Atlantic, in the exhortations and advice of secular rationalists such as Jeremy Bentham and John Stuart Mill and Freethinkers such as Francis Place, Richard Carlile, Robert Dale Owen and Charles Knowlton. But similar themes were also appearing in the more coded language of the popular novels devoured by respectable opinion, such as those of Jane Austen, Charlotte Brontë, George Meredith and Charles Kingsley (although much earlier novels, such as Samuel Richardson's *Pamela, or virtue rewarded*, did deal with sexual and power relations, this was primarily in courtship and outside marriage).[42] A growing preoccupation in the second quarter of the

39 Porter, 'Mixed feelings', pp. 20–1.

40 Seidman, 'The power of desire', p. 62.

41 Maynard depicts an obsessive struggle between, on the one hand, the Tractarian, Newmanite and Puseyite 'Roman' tendency to equate only celibacy with piety, as against, on the other hand, the attempt to construct a carefully demarcated and regulated, exclusively marital, heterosexuality as an alternative, Protestant and Puritan model for the spiritual salvation of the two marriage partners. This was particularly clearly elaborated in Charles Kingsley's case, where he denounced Catholic asceticism as a false turning taken by the early third-century Church Fathers. Maynard, *Victorian discourses*, especially ch. 3, and pp. 93–4. See also Brown, *The body and society*.

42 Maynard, *Charlotte Brontë*; Maynard, *Victorian discourses*. Note Maynard's comments on the euphemistic language with which Victorian novelists addressed sexual issues: 'Before we sneer too easily at Victorianism we should consider that the novel was as much in the Victorian public realm

nineteenth century with 'Careful love', as the renegotiation of sexuality within genteel marriage, has similarly been demonstrated for polite society in north-eastern USA and also in the south.[43] Of course, there can be no doubt that in certain sections of society (the less earnest-minded within the aristocratic set being a prominent example), among some individuals and some couples, sensuality continued to be prized, adultery schemed and mistresses kept. However, in an urban culture of competing status groups, whose public codes of moral and political respectability were becoming synonymous with the virtues of sexual self-control, in order to retain a reputation for gentility this sexual activism now necessarily became a private and clandestine matter.[44]

Furthermore, it is Michael Mason's contention that this Victorian anti-sensualist code of self-control, emerging as dominant during the three decades following the end of the Napoleonic Wars, was in fact socially rather broadly based.[45] Following the contemporary testimony of Francis Place, regarding the London radical culture which he knew well, Mason argues that this code was rooted as much in the plebeian ideology of independent self-improvement – 'radical genteelness' – as it was in the prudishness of the bourgeoisie.[46] There is also corroborating evidence in other historians' work, for instance on the independent plebeian support for the Queen in the Queen Caroline affair of 1820, a formative political event in the process of cultural renegotiation of gender roles and sexual proprieties towards a more 'domesticated' morality.[47] Although proletarian communities outside London would no doubt have varied enormously in this respect, it is noticeable that after

as television has been in the last half of the twentieth century and probably subject to the same degree of control of expression in sexual matters, at least during hours when children watch – also the controlling audience imagined by censors of novels.' Maynard asserts that 'Kingsley probably managed to communicate the gist of his sexual vision to his age. Only the succeeding age was blind to it because of its presuppositions concerning the ubiquity of sexual repression among eminent Victorians' (*ibid.*, p. 101). See also Caine, *Victorian feminists*, ch. 2.

43 David and Sanderson, 'Rudimentary contraceptive methods', n. 20, citing the unpublished research of Nissenbaum, 'Careful love: Sylvester Graham and the emergence of Victorian sexuality in America, 1830–1840' (unpublished PhD thesis). This has now been revised and published as Nissenbaum, *Sex, diet, and debility*. See also David and Sanderson, 'The emergence of a two-child norm'; and Seidman, 'The power of desire', especially pp. 51–9. On the south, see Lewis and Lockridge, '"Sally has been sick"' (discussed on p. 571, below).

44 Hence, Michael Mason has found examples in this period of the town-dwelling upper classes finding that they had to observe this code and so becoming intensely preoccupied with maintaining the *appearances* of sexual decorum before their social inferiors. This was something which others of their social group were still free to ignore in their country seats, where socially they still ruled the roost undisputed. Mason, *The making of Victorian sexuality*, pp. 110–15. For another, well-documented non-aristocratic example from the USA, see Peter Gay's account of the sex life of Mabel Loomis Todd: *The bourgeois experience I*, pp. 71–108. Carl Degler long ago made the sensible, general point that public norms, documented in prescriptive literature, may bear only a loose relationship to the variety of beliefs and behaviour practised in private: Degler, 'What ought to be and what was'.

45 Mason, *The making of Victorian sexuality*, pp. 133–73; and, more generally, Mason, *The making of Victorian sexual attitudes*, *passim*. On its dialectical foil, see McCalman, *Radical underworld*, *passim*.

46 Mason, *The making of Victorian sexuality*, pp. 20–35 and ch. 3.

47 Wahrman, '"Middle-class" domesticity', especially pp. 402–7.

an historical peak in the mid-century decades, illegitimacy rates – a gross measure of plebeian sexual 'respectability' – did, indeed, fall substantially throughout the latter half of the century, while religious attendance and the celebration of marriage became more popular; and crime and drunkenness less common.[48] This late nineteenth-century development was something different from, but parallel with, the bourgeois social purity movement of the same period.[49]

In addition to the emergence of 'self-government' as a cultural norm in the first half of the nineteenth century, it is important also to examine concomitant changes in familial roles and social identities, and the influence that these had on perceived relative childrearing costs. Where fatherhood is concerned Victorian society is, of course, considered to have been one in which patriarchal authority was highly emphasised: the era of the 'paterfamilias' leading family prayers by the hearthside. However, it is also true that this process of cultural and symbolic assertion was occurring in the context of a practical withdrawal from childrearing and a physical absence of the father from the family household. The general cause of this was the separation of home and workplace, which was becoming the norm by the mid-nineteenth century. The commercial and professional middle classes moved to the salubrious suburbs being built on the upwind, western side of most of the city centres where they earned their livings. Men of the labouring class, although they generally continued to live near their work until the tramways were built in the last quarter of the century, were increasingly away from the home, drafted into the factory in relatively inflexible shifts for ten hours or more per day, six days a week: 'Saint Monday' and its decline records both the resentment of this unfreedom and its increasing imposition.[50] Fathers' presence in the home was increasingly confined only to the beginning and ends of the day plus Sunday.

Hence, the practice of the 'nursing father', depicted in early modern sources and in Davidoff and Hall's portrait of the middle classes in the late eighteenth and early nineteenth centuries appears to have declined.[51] In its place John Tosh has argued that the research of those historians who have addressed fatherhood in the nineteenth century, such as his own and that of David Roberts and A. J. Hammerton, shows three other, documented images of fatherhood becoming predominant in the remainder of the century: the absent father; the tyrannical father; and the anxious father.[52] These were the various manifestations of a reality in which Victorian fathers, despite the culturally induced expectation of a leading familial role, actually found themselves increasingly powerless to control and

[48] Harris, *Private lives*, pp. 153–4, 158–9, 209–10. On illegitimacy rates, see ch. 8, n. 53.

[49] See pp. 415–16 and 568–70 for more on the British purity movement. On social purity and the Comstock laws in the USA, see Pivar, *Purity crusade*.

[50] Reid, 'The decline of Saint Monday 1766–1876': charting the disappearance of workmen's optional habit of not turning up for work on the day after Sunday.

[51] Davidoff and Hall, *Family fortunes*, ch. 7.

[52] Tosh (unpublished paper), referring to Roberts, 'The paterfamilias'; Hammerton, *Cruelty and companionship*; Tosh, 'Domesticity and manliness'.

supervise in detail their families' lives and their sons' and daughters' fates. This was because of their physical absence and, as explained by Mintz, the decreasing significance of their social role in the transmission of skills and training to children, whether middle or working class. Middle-class children increasingly acquired their formal education in schools and through the attainment of examinable credentials. Among the working classses during the second half of the century on-the-job training in factories, at no cost to parents, was tending to supersede parental training or parentally mediated apprenticeship placement in a small workshop.[53]

It has been argued by historians that among both the middle and the working classes, the meaning of the key manly virtue of 'independence' was transformed during the 1830s, 1840s and 1850s. Instead of referring to a political aspiration, it came to mean more exclusively the desirable occupational capacity of a household head to earn an adequate family income. Adequate meant enough to keep his family in a state of 'comfort' if he was middle class or 'respectability' (i.e. safe from the Poor Law and free from the debt collector) if he was working class. In the case of the propertied middle classes, this was partly because their political demands had been substantially met in 1832. Incorporated within a reformed electoral constitution, though they continued to pride themselves on their 'independence' this had lost its radical, reform meaning for them. Politics came to mean 'the office'; and the male middle classes increasingly devoted themselves to building professional associations and joining other club-like societies as the sources of respectable identity, status and security.[54]

It seems likely that the Chartist movement was important in emphasising, primarily for political reasons relating to its campaign for manhood suffrage, the virtues of male independence and breadwinning among the working classes and the corresponding female virtues of 'domesticity' (as will be discussed in detail further below, on pp. 484–8). This spawned the subsequent rather divisive and sectional strategy of craft unionism as the principal form of working-class self-organisation until near the end of the century – the poor man's professional association; male clubs also proliferated among this group.[55] Successful breadwinning outside the home, in competition with his male peers, thus became for the Victorian male, of patrician or proletarian status, the primary activity, aspiration and source of identity. This was to the relative exclusion of both a larger political agenda and an emotional investment in active fathering and nurturing of his children. Childrearing was more exclusively than ever before identified as mothering only – assisted by elder siblings, grandparents and female neighbours, but less by nursing fathers.

The point of all this, with regard to the historical explanation of falling fertility,

[53] More, *Skill and the English working class.*

[54] Reader, *Professional men*; Bourne, *Patronage and society*; Morris, 'Voluntary societies and British urban elites'.

[55] Morris, 'Clubs, societies and associations'.

is that having children and paternity, although of continuing symbolic significance as the ultimate rationale for the patriarchal devotion to income-earning, was of decreasing importance as a practical activity and, therefore, as a source of identity, collective expertise and pride to men. For the typical Victorian head of household it was important to have a family and to feed, house, clothe it succesfully.[56] But it was decreasingly possible to participate fully in the activity of rearing children and it was decreasingly seen as an appropriate source of adult, *male* personal development and social identity, which was instead focused on the world of work outside the home. It has also been cogently argued by John Tosh that among the middle classes, who could afford it, this polarisation of gender roles created a powerful logic for the move towards socialising boys in 'public', boarding schools, away from the 'private', maternal, female home.[57] The latter was now seen as as an inappropriate socialising environment for the world of competition, work and male associations, which lay ahead of the middle-class male. It was better for him to join his first club – the old school tie – as early as possible and become adept in the public world of male rivalry, co-operation and competition.

As a result adult male resources for emotional involvement with the rearing of children declined: the family was important, but a small number of children constituted; a family and its father was more likely to have a more developed relationship with each of them in the small amount of domestic time available to him if there were fewer, rather than more of them. After the first couple of children, each additional child did not so much represent to the father the company of a new personality, a fresh affirmation of parental identity and a further opportunity to deploy and develop the proud skills of parenting, as it did for his partner. Rather, it primarily represented greater responsibilities and demands on his precarious income-earning capacities, less pocket-money left for cultivating the company of his peers and developing with them the social skills which mattered to his identity, occupational efficacity and sense of self-esteem, less respite at home from the working-day, and less time with his partner and with each of the other children. The argument, therefore, is that in both patrician and proletarian worlds (for distinct historical reasons) the increasing bifurcation of parental roles, along with related developments in the ideology of gender difference, created the cultural conditions in which it was possible for men to see large numbers of children less as an act of god, less as individual persons whose rearing was constitutive of their own identity, and more as emotionally problematic and economically burdensome.

When the question of mothering is addressed, obviously the foregoing entails a set of reciprocal changes envisaging the intensification of 'mothering' as a practical activity in Victorian Britain and as a source of gendered identity.

[56] In discussing broad cultural shifts at this somewhat abstract level it is easy to lose sight of all the variation in actual behaviour always present, which will be discussed throughout the remainder of this chapter. [57] Tosh (unpublished paper).

However, even at this level of abstraction there is need to distinguish at least three kinds of economic and 'classed' cultural contexts, in each of which the formation of gender roles and mother–child relationships within the home would have developed quite differently. First, as indicated by McBride's work, in wealthy households with multiple servants and nannies, a relatively distant relationship may typically have prevailed between children and parents, including mothers. Many young children in this class formed their most intimate bonds when young with those whom they also came to see as their servants; and they subsequently spent a large proportion of their later childhood away from home at preparatory and boarding schools.[58] For entirely different reasons, children among the urban poor may also have been brought up without particularly exclusive contact with their own mothers (though that contact would have been very intimate when it occurred), as a régime of 'shared mothering' among the neighbourhood matriarchy, grandmothers and elder sisters seems often to have prevailed in such communities.[59]

Between these two extremes of wealth and poverty there was a varied middle ground, which included both moderately comfortable middle-class and petty bourgeois households as well as the more secure and independent of the working class. In these households some domestic assistance could be afforded but not a lot: enough to deal with the most physically onerous and time-consuming chores (which were many in the pre-consumer durables household). Among this category a more intensive and continuous contact between mothers and their own children was both practicable and deemed desirable by the dictates of respectability, both in its genteel and its proletarian variants (although great variability no doubt occurred here, depending on maternal personality and relative inclination towards physical closeness). Clearly, these three ideal-types of mothering and parenting are no more than helpful illustrations of the range of different conventional definitions of the reciprocal roles of motherhood and childhood that could be found in different social groups and communities in Britain during this period. For effective, empirically engaged analysis of the changes in perceived relative childrearing costs which were actually experienced in British society during this period, it is necessary to leave behind the armchair typologies and inquire further into the quite distinct constellations of cultural and political forces shaping the circumstances of the many differently constituted social groups and communities which are clumsily amalgamated in such a typology.

Consideration of these wider cultural developments in definitions of childhood, fathering and mothering is important, however, and helpful in providing a general historical explanation for the grand social shifts in perceived relative costs

[58] McBride, 'As the twig is bent'. See below, next section, for a full discussion.

[59] On motherhood as a shared role involving a set of women and children, rather than the specific individual relationship of a mother and her own child, see Gillis, 'Gender and fertility decline'; Chinn, *They worked all their lives*.

of childrearing which lie behind falling fertility. But this offers only a necessary and not a sufficient explanation: predisposing, not exciting causes. The account offered in this section can explain why a dramatic general fall in fertility occurred in Britain in the post- rather than pre-Enlightenment period. It can perhaps suggest why it occurred after 1832 in the middle classes or after the 1840s in the working classes. But, of course, the most dramatic changes occurred some time after either of these dates and in quite varied ways in different social groups, as the previous chapters have shown. To provide the more discriminating degree of explanation required to show how and why fertility and nuptiality changed in the specific way that they did and at the time that they did in different sections within British society, it is necessary to turn to a more detailed consideration of the changing social and economic context of each of the various groups and divergent communities.

The remainder of the chapter will therefore attempt to offer an account of the 1911 census occupational fertility evidence, in terms of the heuristic framework of changes in the perceived relative costs and benefits of childrearing. Since the social, cultural and economic world of the middle classes (broadly defined), on the one hand, and the working classes, on the other, were so profoundly dissimilar, it is necessary in the following sections to offer separate discussions of the sources of fertility variation within each of these two divisions of society. The enormous disparity between these two, in terms of typical wealth and income, combined with their quite disparate cultural heritages, ensured that both their perceptions of relative costs and their definitions of parental and childhood roles and identities differed fundamentally from each other.

Of course, there was certainly no absolute socio-demographic boundary between these two social constellations and the border area between them is inherently contentious. It is not intended that the division operated in the next sections be considered to imply a definitive final statement on the nature of the nation's class relations. The main source of statistical evidence used here imposes its own constraints and the justification for the kind of distinction adopted here is partly that it makes most sense of this particular body of evidence on occupational patterns in demographic behaviour. The 1911 census specifically delimits the possibilities for a satisfactory treatment of large- and medium-scale industrial employers and managers; and also the smallest-scale proprietors: retail shopkeepers and independent craftsmen and artisans. While discussions of the former two categories are included here within the bourgeoisie, the latter two are treated below as part of the working classes, despite constituting the classic forms of petty bourgeoisie. It is acknowledged that understanding the fertility behaviour of these groups would particularly benefit from appropriate further research, since they are poorly defined in the sources used here. The proposed distinction might more accurately be described as being between the patrician and the plebeian 'worlds', to avoid any confusions that the Marxist pair of classes are implied. The broad division into these two social constellations is, then, no more than a first approximation and is primarily required to facilitate a manageable presentation.

The historical causes of falling fertility and nuptiality variation within the upper- and middle-class milieu

The analysis presented in the previous chapters indicated that interpretation of changing fertility and nuptiality within the patrician world resolves into examination of the occupational evidence for six distinct social groups: the professions; those of inherited private means; those of substantial wealth generated from their own business activities; more modest, medium-sized business proprietors; clerical and commercial 'white-collar' workers; and indoor domestic servants.

The rationale in putting together these six social groupings as 'the middle classes' (more accurately 'the upper and middle classes') was broadly indicated at the end of chapter 7 but can now be further amplified. Apart from having in common the fact that they recorded among the lowest fertilities in 1911 (they are joined in this by most categories of wool and cotton textiles workers), it was pointed out that these were groups who, by definition of their economic functions, lived or worked together closely and their daily experience was therefore strongly shared, if by no means identical. They comprise the nation's landed, commercial and professional élites, plus their entourages of servants and employees, at home and in the office.

By contrast the majority of those in all the other occupational categories, placed here in the plebeian division of the population and dealt with separately in the following sections, would have had relatively little contact with the genteel classes. By virtue of their modest capital, the self-employed artisans, shopkeepers and small businesses of the petty bourgeoisie were, both functionally and socially, formally independent of their social superiors, unlike either domestic servants or white-collar office workers. The petty bourgeoisie predominantly lived out their lives in a plebeian milieu, for all that many of them may have cherished somewhat distinct aspirations from their proletarian neighbours and for all that their experience of this potentially harsh environment was alleviated by their superior resources. Indeed, Crossick and Haupt have written of the petty bourgeois shopkeepers and the manual workers as the two complementary halves of the working-class 'world', rather as J. F. C. Harrison has argued that servants and the served constituted the essential reciprocal halves of the middle-class 'world'.[60]

In the spirit of Hegel's classic dissection of the nature of the master–slave relationship, J. F. C. Harrison has perceptively written of the Victorian middle class and its social relations:

The keeping of servants was for the middle classes more than just a matter of living comfortably or defining one's status within the ranks of superior persons. It went to the very

[60] Crossick and Haupt (eds.), *Shopkeepers and master artisans*, p. 19.

heart of the idea of class itself. . . . The essence of middle classness was the experience of relating to other classes or orders in society. With one group, domestic servants, the middle classes stood in a very special and intimate relationship; the one in fact played an essential part in defining the identity of the other. Domestic servants were members of the household, with all the intimate relationships that living closely with other people entails. Yet they were excluded from the privileges of kinship and were always in a position of economic and social inferiority.[61]

As Erving Goffman has put it, 'Deference must actively be sought, it cannot be given to oneself.'[62] For all their wide divergences in wealth and status, the servant-employing class and the class of servants were, culturally, mutually dependent through and through. Thus, when it comes to analysing the causes of changing fertility and sexual behaviour, these six social groupings of occupations form an integrated cultural constellation, corresponding to the 'middle-class' or patrician world, more intimately inter-related than may at first sight appear to be the case.

What, then, were the aspects of this bourgeois, servant-centred world of class and status relations which were so significant to the history of changing nuptiality and fertility behaviour? Of particular relevance was the dramaturgical creation by the socially unequal protagonists, servants and served, of the characteristic Victorian upper- and middle-class set of familial relationships, especially the conception and practice of motherhood. The practical class privileges of middle-class wives were of relevance here. As the managers of substantial households, few upper- and middle-class women can be considered to have been economically inactive.[63] A glance at the duties and responsibilities prescribed in Mrs Beeton's famous *Book of household management* confirms this.[64] Their substantial powers expressed themselves most obviously in their management of a retinue of domestic servants, often including men. As Theresa McBride and Leonore Davidoff have each shown, as a result of the wife's social engagements and busy, managerial role, the nanny and nurse-maid was of central significance in upper middle-class 'mothering'. She imparted a very particular twist to the socialisation into their classed and gendered worlds of these upper-class children.[65] It is this

61 Harrison, *The early Victorians*, pp. 109–10. Note that Harrison's observations on the centrality of relationships with servants as formative of the self-consciousness of the middle class is in no way contradicted by the important finding by E. Higgs that a substantial minority of mid-nineteenth-century proletarian households contained a domestic servant, too: 'Domestic service', Table 4.1 (see below, n. 106). This does not detract from Harrison's analysis but merely establishes that domestic service took different forms. For Harrison it is not the presence or absence of a domestic servant that is significant in itself but the fact that in middle-class households the intimate contact with and formal control over such domestic servants provided the principal forum in which class relations were learned, elaborated and internalised on both sides.

62 Goffman, 'The nature of deference and demeanour'; and see also, on the socio-cultural and political complexities of deference and other forms of domination and resistance, Newby, *The deferential worker*; and Scott, *Domination and the arts of resistance*.

63 This is still a rather under-researched area, but see Davidoff, *The best circles*, ch. VI.

64 Beeton, *The book of household management*.

65 McBride, 'As the twig is bent'; Davidoff, 'Class and gender'.

aspect of the general relationship of servants and served which is perhaps of most direct significance to the discussion of changing fertility and associated sexual behaviour within the upper middle-class world.

In a highly compressed account, following Max Weber's original analysis of the phenomenon of eroticised sexuality in a rationalised society, Leonore Davidoff has elucidated the relevant set of logical and psychological relationships which were culturally engendered and reinforced through the nanny system of upbringing.[66] Davidoff shows its integral role in reproducing and colouring both the practice of separate spheres and the related Victorian 'double standard' of sexual morality. In seeking to define themselves exclusively as the active, rational, controlling, planning class, adult males of the governing élite simultaneously created their own moral and intellectual prison: an over-riding preoccupation with self-control and a shaming fear of vulnerability to the disordered and uncontrolled nature of their emotional and sexual feelings.[67] At its most extreme in individual cases this could result in a complete repression of open, sexual expression. Victorian moral discourse increasingly stigmatised sexuality through a set of negative symbolic associations: that it was animal, dark, irreligious, polluting, unclean and unhygienic, corrupting and criminal. Sensuality was irrational and therefore female. It was primitive and irresponsible and therefore associated with lesser peoples: uncivilised natives, the lower social classes, children and, of course, again, women.

However, the female valency was also required by separate spheres ideology to symbolise the genteel flame of spiritual purity, never extinguished in the domestic hearth. As expressed in the House of Commons in 1923, during the course of the debate on the Act which finally rescinded the inegalitarian aspects of the 1857 Matrimonial Causes Act: 'chastity in women is a star that has guided human nature since the world began, and teaches us of the other sex things which we could not otherwise know. We bow in humble reverence to that high star of chastity.'[68] This must be counted a distinctly old-fashioned attitude by this date, since both the 1890s and the 1920s witnessed important realignments of the prevailing sexual codes away from the mid-Victorian Madonna or Magdalene syndrome, with its polarised class connotations.[69] According to this mid-Victorian code for polite society, a true lady had risked not only her personal reputation but, by definition, also her social position if appearing too publicly to harbour sexual inclinations. Whereas a working woman of the labouring poor was stereotypically expected to be irredeemably sensual and barely in control of herself. As a result she was a figure of guilty fascination as well as condemnation for the genteel male, as W.E. Gladstone so memorably illustrated with his compulsive nocturnal missions to attractive fallen women, followed by bouts of self-flagellation.[70]

66 Davidoff, 'Class and gender', especially pp. 17–30, citing Max Weber, 'Religious ethics and the world'.

67 See also Mintz, *A prison of expectations.*

68 Sir Henry Chaik, cited in Phillips, *Untying the knot*, p. 192.

69 See pp. 569–72.

70 Matthew, *Gladstone 1809–74*, pp. 92–5, 156–7.

The mid-Victorian nanny, unlike the more highly paid governess, was typically drawn from relatively lower-class origins. Nannies critically intervened between young children of the patrician class and their mothers, as the principal persons involved in early socialisation. Many upper middle-class mothers thereby remained relatively remote, idealised figures with whom physical and emotional contact was strictly rationed, certainly by comparison with the availability of the nanny who was intimately and intensively involved with the children's daily physical and emotional needs. When older the child learned that nanny was one of a class of servants all of whom were involved with the dirty and menial work of the household. As Davidoff shows, here in the nursery the entwined symbols and habitus of class and gender relations were enacted out and insidiously imbibed:[71]

For middle-class children, these social divisions and their erotic overtones were also reflected in a spatial view of their world – a view which started with their own bodies, extended to the houses where they lived and eventually to their village, town, or city. . . . The servants . . . lived and worked in the dark underground parts of the house. Their territory was the 'back passages' (nursery euphemism for anus) . . . where waste and rubbish were removed. . . .

Little ladies and gentlemen did not sit on steps; they stood absolutely straight; they did not whistle, scuff, or slouch. By imitating middle-class adults they learned habits of command through silent body language, through the way they looked at people, through tone of voice as well as accent.

Servants in return showed deference in the way they used their bodies, a point also observed by the children of the house. Servants stood when spoken to and kept their eyes cast down.[72]

Thus, were created and reproduced the distinctive inhibitions and class-inflected sexual attitudes and gender relations of the Victorian upper middle classes, as documented in Jeanette Marshall's diary.[73] Warmth and sensuality was something associated less with their distant, idealised mothers, and more with the women of the lower classes, as embodied by their nannies. Hence, just as little children slept away from their parents and were tended in the night by nannies, so, too, it was quite conventional for some spouses, with their busy and rather independent social and professional lives, to sleep apart in this class – a 'luxury' which only they could afford.[74] In this context it becomes more understandable, therefore, that many in this class could have practised sexual abstinence within marriage, either ascetic or associated with extra-marital affairs or other 'lapses' with prostitutes and servants. Given this upbringing, with its projection of the lady of the house as

71 As the following quotation illustrates, 'habitus' refers to the socially engendered and differentiating aspects of body language, demeanour and manners. It therefore has strong affinities with Goffman's notion of the dramaturgical production of individuals' identities and of their social relations (see above, p. 466). Habitus is a sociological concept coined by Pierre Bourdieu: *Outline of a theory of practice, passim.*

72 Davidoff, 'Class and gender', p. 27.

73 For Jeannette Marshall's (1855–1935) diary, see Shonfield, *The precariously privileged*. This closely confirms Davidoff's analysis: especially pp. 229–35 on the nanny's intervening role between mother and infant and Jeannette's dependence on her nanny's expertise rather than her own or her mother's; and pp. 197–210 on male sexuality.

74 On the social round of the upper middle class, see Davidoff, *The best circles*, chs. II–III.

an 'idealised', almost asexual being, it would not be surprising if abstinence were among the principal methods of birth control which suggested themselves to patrician males, once motivated to regulate the number of their dependants.

Theresa McBride's research shows that 'the nanny-state' was a form of upbringing primarily restricted to the upper middle classes only (including the most successful among the professional and commercial classes, as Jeanette Marshall's diary confirms) because they alone could afford the kind of establishment which supported multiple servants. The bulk of other, less exalted middle-class households employed only one or two servants, primarily to perform all manner of household drudgery, which thereby freed mothers for greater attention to their children (their principal activity, since respectability required that they did not go out to earn a living, although philanthropic work was of course permissible and significant in their lives).[75] McBride argues that consequently this less affluent section of the middle class experienced a significantly different and closer relationship between mothers and their nursery children.[76] Relations between spouses within these middle middle-class marriages were almost certainly different in quality and may have been more confiding than among the upper middle class; although there can be no certainty, without further research, that this resulted in more equal relationships, especially where the difficult questions of birth control were concerned.[77] Certainly it is very plausible that among this hard-working, aspirant section of society, paternal absence from the home may have been even more pronounced than among the upper classes; moreover the socialisation of boys outside the maternal home was equally practised in both social groups.

Among the six social groups within the middle classes, it has been the professions who have attracted by far the most attention in previous studies of falling fertility. By the 1920s when the first thorough and systematic analyses of Britain's fertility decline appeared, with Stevenson and Beveridge proudly emphasising the 'leading' role of the professions in the 'diffusion' of the new behaviour, they were already a firmly established social group and source of identity. Indeed, they were so powerfully institutionalised that most of the

[75] McBride, 'As the twig is bent', p. 48. On female philanthropic work throughout the century, see Prochaska, *Women and philanthropy*.

[76] McBride, 'As the twig is bent', p. 48.

[77] The influence of the subsequent school and work environment of middle, middle-class men would certainly militate against the model of a more equal wife–husband relationship than among the upper class. Both secondary schools and work were notoriously misogynist and élitist environments, taking their social cue from the values of the upper-class males who typically ran them. Before their professional or commercial training boys of all ranks of the aspirant middle class were sent either to the less exclusive boarding public schools or to the better, reformed grammar schools. Enough Latin was imbibed at these second rank educational institutions to ensure the lifelong deference of their *alumni* to their social superiors, who had received the full classical training at the most expensive public schools. The symbols and habitus of class and gender relations, inculcated in the upper middle class, thereby cast their pervasive influence and shadow much wider, throughout the middle-class 'world'.

academics and officials participating in the debate at that time unhesitatingly identified themselves with the liberal professions as their own social status group.

However, the very success of their nineteenth-century campaigns for recognition, autonomy and influence is in danger of obscuring the essential precariousness which most individual 'professionals' perceived to be their social predicament throughout most of that period of struggle for institutional recognition. In order to help to explain the professions' full-fledged early endorsement of family planning, and hence the timing of the commencement of falling fertility among the middle classes, it has to be appreciated that throughout the Victorian and Edwardian periods the professions as a social group and the majority of individuals pursuing 'professional' occupations persistently perceived themselves to be in a marginal social and economic position (relative to the far from modest aspirations which they collectively and individually entertained for a certain socio-economic pre-eminence).

This was the classic period in which the professions institutionalised themselves politically in British society as qualifying associations (although the so-called 'status' professions of arms, the law, the church and medicine had existed in rudimentary form since long before the nineteenth century).[78] Driven, of course, by the vigorous economy's growing demand for a proliferating range of professional and commercial services, virtually all of the eighteen occupational categories from the 1911 fertility census which are defined here as 'professional' incorporated themselves by statute or royal charter during the Victorian period.[79] But the very fact that this was a period of continuous expansion in the professionalising of services means that at any time throughout the second half of the nineteenth century it was statistically true that the majority of men pursuing any profession would have been relatively young (as each suceeding cohort was increasing in numbers). The majority would have perceived themselves as the junior and insecure members of a trade which offered a promising but rather precarious way of attaining the high rewards of social respectability and a comfortable standard of living, for which they were striving.

But all of this was dependent on the proof of their own abilities. Hence, it is predictable that among all the occupational categories, it should have been professionals, as a group, who showed the greatest *sensitivity* to the fragility of their financial position during this period.[80] However, it needs to be further

[78] Twenty professions came into existence 1800–80 and a further thirty-nine 1880–1914: Perkin, *The rise of professional society*, pp. 85–6. See also Reader, *Professional men*; and, on the earlier history of the professions, see Prest (ed.), *The professions*.

[79] Millerson, *The qualifying associations*, Appendices I and II.

[80] Anne Digby notes that whereas the insecurity of the legal profession tended to manifest itself in higher rates of bankruptcy, the medical profession exhibited a particularly high rate of suicide in the late nineteenth century (though barristers, solicitors and their clerks also exhibited suicide rates well above average). Digby, *Making a medical living*, pp. 155–62. On occupational suicide, see Anderson, *Suicide*, pp. 93–7.

explained why, in so doing, they should have paid particular heed to the deferral of marriage as a solution to these anxieties; and additionally why they were particularly cautious about the rate at which their families and consequent domestic outlays grew after marriage. Applying the heuristic framework of relative perceived childrearing costs identifies this as the key development requiring explanation: but how and why were the professions particularly vulnerable to these considerations?

J. A. Banks has provided the pioneering attempt to document and analyse the historical escalation in the Victorian middle classes' 'standard of living': the minimum material domestic comforts and household services deemed necessary by this status group to maintain 'a due social position'.[81] His is the original account of rising perceived relative childrearing costs, for this particular class, in an age when a well-entrenched and resourceful, still-landed, upper class faced the phenomenon of the mass parvenus created by economic growth. In the ensuing competition for status through social differentiation Banks noted as particularly significant the emergence of an intrinsically escalatory expectation identified by contemporaries at mid-century, whereby 'newly married couples expect to begin where their fathers and mothers ended'.[82]

Banks demonstrated the way in which this aspiration consequently led to the perceived need for an expensive education for all children as an integral part of the middle-class way of life because it was the only safe way to ensure the dynasty's continuing high status.[83] This class maintained its privileged position, first, through the capacities of its sons to command entry to the high-earning service sector of professional, administrative and financial jobs and, secondly, through its ability to avoid the costs of maintaining non-earning daughters through successfully marrying them off.[84] It was recognised that success in both of these aims required as great an outlay on secondary education as the parents could afford: for the sons to compete in the job market and for the daughters to win through in the even more competitive marriage market. Such heavy financial investment in each child necessarily focused the middle-class mind upon late marriage as a means to amass the required resources and to minimise the number of dependants.[85] But in this competitive environment the unit expenditure on children continued to rise relentlessly for this class: for instance, tuition fees in public schools approximately doubled from 1870 to 1900 and the additional costs of a university education were even becoming a requisite for the ambitious by the end of the century. Banks argues that the traditional prudential restraint of late marriage became unequal to the requirement for stringent family limitation needed by this class and so the

[81] Banks, *Victorian values*, p. 47. See in particular Banks, *Prosperity and parenthood*, chs. IV–VIII.

[82] Banks, *Prosperity and parenthood*, p. 45, citing the *Times* on 2 July 1861.

[83] Banks, *Prosperity and parenthood*, chs. IX–XII.

[84] For a case study of the Victorian professional middle class precisely exemplifying these considerations regarding sons and daughters, see Shonfield, *The precariously privileged*, pp. vi, 14, 123–32, 134, 143–4.

[85] Banks, *Prosperity and parenthood*, ch. III.

restriction of fertility within marriage itself came to be practised, once religious scruples had been circumvented.[86]

What can perhaps be added to Banks's richly informative work is an additional explanation of why the professional elements of the middle class should have been particularly susceptible to participation in the attritional status war of domestic consumption.[87] Indeed, if the analysis below is correct, their historical expansion as a group may perhaps be justifiably looked upon as having provided the primary motor force driving this important dynamic of spiralling inflation of domestic conspicuous consumption during the Victorian period.[88]

This analysis flows from an emergent property resulting from the peculiar nature of the market for professional services. The chartered profession, once successfully institutionalised, constituted a 'market shelter' by juridically fixing the minimum price and the supposed quality of services offered (through the process of licensing to practise only those having passed the approved exams).[89] There is, by design therefore, a lack of the usual kinds of discriminatory information available for a competitive market to function (differential pricing and some understanding on the part of the buyers of the different qualities of the goods available from the sellers). But individual professionals within their sheltered market still competed with each other for the limited custom available, while the customer's interest was, as ever, to discern the best value for money.[90] This necessarily created functional alternatives to the conventional market signals (formal advertising was banned as professionally unethical). Since individual clients could hardly judge for themselves the quality of the service offered, the main possibilities were reliance on personal recommendation or on metonymic signalling.[91] In an increasingly urban culture it was the latter method of judgement which was becoming more important: the potential consumers made a judgement of the value of the service offered by a particular professional from their ability to

[86] Banks, *Prosperity and parenthood*, ch. XI, especially pp. 187–9; and Banks, *Victorian values, passim.*

[87] The following argument, regarding the critical economic function of conspicuous consumption for professionals operating in a free market, in signalling the individual's professional worth and 'honour' to the lay market, is particularly effectively expressed in the excellent thesis by S. P. Walker (unpublished PhD thesis). See also Walker, *The Society of Accountants in Edinburgh.*

[88] Of course, this is not to assert that rising standards of domestic consumption and consumer aspirations were historically novel phenomena. It is merely being argued that professionalisation imparted a particular character to the phenomena in the Victorian era. On consumerism before the nineteenth century see, for instance, McKendrick, Brewer and Plumb, *The birth of a consumer society*; Brewer and Porter (eds.), *Consumption and the world of goods*; Weatherill, *Consumer behaviour*; Thirsk, *Economic policy and projects.*

[89] The notion of professions as exclusionary shelters from the market comes from the pre-eminent American sociologist of the professions, Eliot Friedson: *Professional powers.*

[90] On the economic dimensions of medical practice, see Digby, *Making a medical living*, Part II.

[91] The term, metonymic signalling, has been coined by Stephen P. Turner, referring to the general process, in a complex economy with much functional division of labour, whereby a lay audience of 'consumers' seeks to judge the value and quality of the product offered to them by a specialist set of 'producers'. Turner, 'Forms of patronage'; Turner, 'The survey in nineteenth-century American geology'.

decode the probable meaning of some associated signals. Hence, the particular importance for the professional to exhibit as convincingly as possible all the trappings of success: high-rent premises; expensively equipped offices; membership of status-conferring clubs; residence in a desirable neighbourhood, and so on.

Here, then, there was a fundamental difference within the middle classes between the commercial, market position of the producer of professional services and the manufacturer or distributor of industrial or consumer goods. The value and success of the latter was in principle judged more directly by the consumers through their personal handling and use of the goods produced and the relative ease of price comparison with alternative products (although the power of advertising, marketing, packaging, etc., to influence perceptions of such comparisons must, of course, be acknowledged even in the nineteenth century). By contrast, in the professional market consumers had to deploy inferences relating to the characteristics of the person offering the service in place of direct knowledge of the product, as the basis for their market choice. Industrial producers and commercial distributors only had to *make* money, through the success of their products in the market place. They had no pressing commercial need additionally to spend money in conspicuous consumption, to involve their domestic budgets and personal life-styles directly in the business of earning a living. By contrast the professional was judged directly on his office's appearance, his personality, manners, values, pastimes, district of residence, life-style and the quality of his social entertaining. Judgement was both by his prospective clients and by his professional peers and superiors in the same firm or elsewhere, from whom came business and referrals. To make money, therefore, the professional also had to *spend* money on his domestic budget, to 'keep up appearances' preferably on as grand a scale as possible.[92]

The timing of the enormous outlay which marriage and the establishment of a family household involved, and also the scale of subsequent expenditure on children, was therefore a critical matter for the professional by virtue of these special characteristics of his market position. Furthermore, the outlays on conspicuous consumption were particularly crucial as well as particularly onerous precisely for those struggling most for professional business, the young and the marginal. As has been argued, they probably comprised the numerical majority of all professional individuals throughout this period of nascent expansion

[92] The case of John Marshall (1818–91), FRCS, recorded through the diary of his eldest daughter (Ellen) Jeanette, exemplifies the salience of these considerations, even for one who had risen to the peak of the medical profession (Marshall became Professor of Anatomy at the Royal Academy in 1873 and was thereafter earning £4,000–5,000 per annum). Although, in employing only three domestic servants and possessing no second home in the country, he was more frugal than some of the select group of his professional peers, he left relatively little at death (£21,800 gross). His main items of conspicuous consumption were the sumptuous residences he rented for his family in Savile Row and Cheyne Walk, where parties were thrown for his medical colleagues and artistic friends (the pre-Raphaelites), the status symbol of a two-horse brougham, and regular long foreign holidays for the family. Shonfield, *The precariously privileged*, pp. 1, 133–7, 186.

of the professions. Hence, for these reasons, the historical process of professionalisation itself may well have provided the true motive force behind the emergence of the particularly intense battle of conspicuous consumption charted by J. A. Banks from mid-Victorian times onwards, and hence the professionals' pre-eminent place as late marriers and among the instigators of family planning.

The particular characteristics of the professional predicament can also be illustrated by the differences encountered when turning to consideration of other elements of the patrician world. It will be recalled that 'private means' and 'retired from business' were the two most quantitatively significant categories of that set of upper- and middle-class, low-fertility occupations which were identified by the principal components analysis reported in chapter 7 as most *unlike* the professions. They combined very low completed fertility with a relatively young nuptiality régime. Three other professions, however, also stood out at that time – among those entering them in the 1860s and 1870s – as more like 'private means' in this respect: army officers, navy officers and, to a lesser extent, barristers. It was argued in chapter 7 that this was because these three vocations had remained the least reformed of the professions, still requiring considerable independent means and patronage for successful entry into their ranks. They were therefore composed of individuals born into the ranks of the independently wealthy to a greater extent than any of the other professional categories at that time and, unlike other professionals, had the financial security to contemplate marriage early. But according to Appendix F the nuptiality behaviour (indicated in the columns AMRATIO2 and RANK/AMRAT2) of those entering the bar and the army officer class had, by the 1890s and 1900s, ceased to resemble those of private means and had become almost indistinguishable from the other competitive professions (sharing the lowest rank values of RANK/AMRAT2). This would seem to reflect the eventual influence upon even these two careers of the professional reforms of the nineteenth century.[93]

Furthermore, Appendix F reveals that, in terms of their incomplete fertility, significant differences between the two occupational categories representing the very wealthy had also appeared by the Edwardian period. Those of 'private means' and those 'retired from business' had exhibited great similarities in their patterns of completed fertility among the earlier marriage cohorts of the 1870s and 1880s and they had been quite different from the liberal professions. But among those marrying in the 1900s the degree of additional birth spacing practised by those who married at older ages differed considerably between these two occupational categories. Those 'retired from business' who deferred marriage to

[93] On the military professions, see Reader, *Professional men*, p. 98. On the Bar, Daniel Duman's research has demonstrated that a marked trend away from landed and gentry recruitment and towards recruitment from within the ranks of the professions was already in train across the period 1835–85, although still not having decisively tipped the balance in favour of the latter by 1885: Duman, *The English and colonial bars*, Table 1.6. See ch. 7, n. 62 for further details.

25–9 produced 20% fewer births over the first 7.5 years than those marrying at 20–4, a large differential which placed this occupation in thirty-second place in Appendix F. However, those returned as of 'private means' were quite different, sharing with the liberal professions the rather unusual characteristic of exhibiting little difference at all in spacing between the older- and younger-marrying subsets (and the occupation is therefore found at the bottom of Appendix F). However, 'private means' and officers of the navy still exhibited a slight tendency to marry relatively young for such low-fertility occupations, whereas 'retired from business' and army officers were now, among the 1900s marriage cohort, as likely to defer marriage as any of the prudential professions.

Is this difference, perhaps, testimony to the effect of a much greater degree of certainty of knowledge as to their future economic security enjoyed from the start of their adult lives by those fortunate enough to be of 'private means', relative to those returning themselves as 'retired from business' (and, of course, relative also to the liberal professions)? Clearly for businessmen to be already retired while aged in their thirties or forties (the probable age in 1911 of most of the husbands of the marriage cohort of 1901–5, which provides the data for the incomplete fertility presented in Appendices E and F) they must have been extremely successful businessmen. But for many this would not have been a success they could have counted on when younger, before marriage and during its early stages. Hence, then, the delayed marriage for most in this occupation and the extremely careful control of fertility even after marriage had been deferred. By contrast for those born into 'private means' among this first twentieth-century marriage cohort the choice of whether to marry a relatively young wife at 20–4 or an older one at 25–9 was, almost uniquely among the low-fertility occupational categories distinguished at the 1911 census (they were joined in this only by navy officers), a matter of relative indifference in terms of its fertility or economic implications.

There is some further corroboration for this interpretation from the parallel evidence that is available from the 1911 census for the incomplete fertility of female occupational categories, which is analysed in detail below (pp. 503–13). The numerically large female occupation of 'private means' may well provide an opportunity for observation of the most exclusive reaches of the upper classes. This would apply if it can be assumed that most of those young married women taking the trouble to return themselves on the 1911 census schedules as possessed of private means, independently of their husbands' occupational return, represent the very wealthiest subset of the much larger group of married couples returned under this title in the male occupational tables, on the grounds that this female occupational category represents couples where both man and wife had brought significant assets into the marriage and were very much aware of this. Uniquely among the sixty-six female occupations, 'private means' showed, exactly like its male counterpart, almost no difference in fertility control over the first 7.5 years of marriage when comparing those marrying at 20–4 as against those marrying at 25–9.

The only other male occupations which show some signs of sharing with 'private means' and navy officers this unusual characteristic (though to a lesser extent) are the five distinct dealing occupations, which appear towards the bottom of Appendix F: merchants (commodity undefined); dealers in jewellery; dealers in boots and shoes; corn merchants, dealers; and clothiers, outfitters. In differing in this way from the ten other types of dealers (such as drapers, ironmongers, grocers, pawnbrokers, furniture dealers), it may be that those men aged only in their thirties in these five categories of dealers were composed much more consistently of a relative economic élite of larger and more secure family enterprises. It is certainly the case that many merchant bankers and other general financiers and entrepreneurs returned themselves under the first of these categories, as 'merchants (commodity undefined)'. Indeed, given that there are no pure categories of major business proprietors or industrial employers available from the 1911 census, it may be that these five categories of dealers from this marriage cohort of young men are the nearest approximations available to the employer business élite. The point about security and certainty from early on in their lives may, then, apply to these five occupations, as well as to 'private means'. By contrast, those who had 'retired from business' may represent a group experiencing relatively spectacular and unexpected business success, whereas these categories of dealers may principally represent those brought up to manage substantial and established, but more steadily growing, family businesses.

As has been discussed in chapter 7, the 1911 census data is not at all well-constructed for analysing in any detail the fertility and nuptiality behaviour of large or small business proprietors or industrialists. Such behaviour has had to be inferred from the 'retired from business' occupation, from categories of dealers and from the correlations for the employment status variables reported in chapter 7. However, the remaining categories of dealers after the five mentioned in the previous paragraph, along with innkeepers and restaurateurs, may perhaps be taken to represent the fourth element of the middle classes: an intermediary grade of medium-sized businesses (acknowledging that some of the latter should be included under the petty bourgeoisie to be dealt with separately below). This group of occupations, representing medium-sized businesses, showed a consistent set of demographic signs indicating self-perceptions of marginalism and economic striving: relatively late marriages, low completed fertility, considerable practice of spacing and more marked spacing when marrying later. While it appears that their self-restraint in all these respects was not as pronounced as that of the majority of professional occupations, this remains a conditional observation, since the behaviour of the employers in each category is somewhat clouded by admixture with their own employees. Future research may well show that business proprietors were every bit as assiduous as the professionals in their family limitation, despite (or because of) their tendency to marry somewhat younger.

The fifth social group within the middle-class constellation, the white-collar workers, were a set of occupations all of which worked in subsidiary roles supervised by their superiors in business and professional occupations. Some of these arguably enjoyed a social and economic position little different from that of the professional and business classes. In the important respect of self-organisation, 'auctioneers, valuers, house agents' differs from the eight other commercial and clerical occupations and it is arguably closer at this time to a professional than a commercial occupation.[94] Hence, unusually for a commercial occupation, it is found at the foot of Appendix F. In general, however, these commercial and clerical occupations commanded a distinctly lower status and level of remuneration than was achieved by those having qualified into one of the eighteen professional categories.

The disposable incomes of white-collar workers were typically less than professionals' but the demands on their incomes were less, too. While a certain minimum of attention to his personal presentation and expenditure on his appearance was important for a clerk or salesman, his domestic expenditure and any conspicuous consumption he indulged in had very little power to influence the scale of his earnings in the way that it could so critically for young professionals seeking to establish themselves.[95] Clerical and commercial salaries were relatively modest and fixed in relation to the possibilities open to professionals and businessmen.[96] However, with an ever increasing proportion of the population acquiring the skills of literacy, there was a tendency to oversupply, despite the rising demand reflected in continuing disproportionate expansion in the numbers employed.[97] Clerical and junior commercial workers and their families therefore faced their own kind of insecurities, if the head of household should lose his

[94] It was at this time a more nationally organised occupation with more serious professional pretensions than accountancy, notwithstanding the fact that in the longer term it was accountancy which proceeded to establish its professional credentials more successfully. The Chartered Auctioneers' and Estate Agents' Institute was founded the year after the 1911 census by amalgamation of the two established bodies in the field, the Institute of Auctioneers and Surveyors of the UK and the Estate Agents' Institute. Accountancy, both north and south of the border, was at this time of distinctly lower status than most other professions proper, and it was still subject to a much greater degree of fragmentation and institutional competition among its various national and several regional associations. Millerson, *The qualifying associations*, pp. 27, 248. On accountancy in Scotland at this time, see Walker, *The Society of Accountants*. For a list of the nine commercial and clerical occupations, see p. ch. 7, n. 6.

[95] For instance, Mrs Layton remembers of her father, a government clerk in the 1860s and 1870s: 'My father's position compelled him to keep up an appearance . . . quite out of keeping with the neighbourhood we lived in' (which was Bethnal Green). Llewellyn Davies, *Life as we have known it*, p. 6. An aspirant professional would have wished to be able to entertain his colleagues in a more elevated neighbourhood than this.

[96] In the example of Mrs Layton's father (previous footnote), as his family grew he supplemented his fixed clerical income with the tailoring work that was plentiful in London's East End.

[97] Male commercial clerks increased by 17.1%, to 360,478 between 1901 and 1911 (the national average increase in the male workforce was 10.9%). They were still a very young occupation, with 72% below age 35 (the national average figure was 54%). Females in this sector had meanwhile more than doubled to 117,057, but were, of course, almost all unmarried because of the employers' convention of the marriage bar. Census 1911, Volume X, Tables 3, 8.

position – the social and moral calamity which animated the plot of E. M. Forster's *Howards End*. This threatened the clerk and his family with a calamitous fall into the ranks of manual work, without possession of an apprenticed trade.

The lot of the manual worker's family was the childhood background which most of the men and their wives in this social group fervently hoped they had left behind them, as a self-selected group of those who had chosen to leave the ranks of manual labour. In these circumstances of abiding insecurity of tenure in their new-found social destination, the most prized jobs were those in the most secure organisations, especially government departments where the hours remained somewhat gentlemanly; also those with large railway companies, major banks and the new chain stores and multiples.[98] Many in this group were no doubt especially prey to the desire to identify as closely as possible with the culture and living standards maintained by the supervisory professionals and managers with whom they were in relatively close contact in the workplace and who controlled their destinies, through the power of hiring, firing and providing character-references. Those who were tempted to emulate the living standards of others on far superior incomes were drawn inexorably in, at a lower level of financial outlay, to an analogous vortex of spiralling conspicuous consumption. As a result, in the 1911 census evidence these occupations show all the consistent signs of fertility control in only slightly less pronounced fashion than the professions: prudential marriage, birth spacing immediately after marriage and low completed family size. But note that this was entered into for their own cultural and economic reasons, quite distinct from those of the qualified professionals and employers whose economic predicaments and cultural reasons for conspicuous consumption were substantively different. Neither does this group's low fertility and late marriage necessarily represent an imitation of professional models of behaviour: they had their own reasons for such behaviour.

Finally, the dramatically low completed fertility and late marriage of indoor servants, originally noted when discussing completed fertility in Figure 7.1, is if anything even more pronounced in the record of their spacing behaviour in Appendix E. Within the confines of the hierarchical, professional model of fertility decline this would, of course, be interpreted as classic evidence of cultural mimesis and 'diffusion'. According to this view, through the learning process of living in such close proximity to their social superiors, domestic servants would be expected to be among the first of the lower orders to imitate the pioneering family planning behaviour and values of their masters, the servant-employing upper class and the professional and commercial bourgeoisie. But it would seem more

[98] On the growth of the larger retail and chain stores, see Mathias, *The retailing revolution*. The working environment and status of shop assistants was changing significantly as these stores expanded while practices associated with traditional smaller retailers declined, particularly the exploitative 'living-in' system, whereby shopkeepers supposedly acted *in loco parentis* to their young assistants. On the outmoded living-in system for shop assistants in Edwardian England, see C. F. G. Masterman's attack upon it in *The condition of England*, ch. 5; and see above, p. 328.

obvious to note that the low fertility of this male occupational category was likely to have been directly due to the threat which unrestrained fertility would represent to their capacity to continue in such a livelihood. Large families were seldom welcomed by employers as part of the living-in arrangement which usually went with the job. In consequence, those with uncontrolled fertility would on average be selected out of this occupation. The potential costs to the family's livelihood of too many children were, therefore, nowhere more clear than to this group of workers.

However, in order to explain why the perception of such costs should have significantly risen after 1860, *pari passu* with the perceptions and changed practices of their employers, a more convincing argument than simple automatic emulation on the part of servants might refer instead to the pressure put upon them by a downward revision in their employers' conventional standards and definitions of a large family. As the servant-employing class itself found it increasingly necessary to restrict its own family size for the various reasons discussed above, it may well have adjusted downwards, either consciously or not, its tolerance for large families among its resident servants. Indeed, this development, and servants' resentments of the further restrictions on their latitude which this represented, may well have been one of the unspoken reasons for the as yet rather imperfectly explained flight from service across this period, with a markedly declining availability of male domestic servants and steeply rising costs of female domestics after the 1870s.[99] To look upon such male service occupations as in some sense a bridge to the working classes, or as an agency of diffusion for the birth controlling values and behaviour supposedly uniquely innovated by the middle classes, is to ignore the extent to which male servants and their families typically lived in entirely separate physical and cultural environments from the communities in which most of the manual labouring population lived. Hence, their treatment here as part of the patrician division of the nation. They were an integral part, albeit cast in the subordinate role, of the middle-class 'world' and were simply not present, by definition, in the social relationships which structured most working-class communities.

It might, however, be additionally or alternatively inferred from this evidence – the low fertility of male servants and deferential occupations – that the distinct

[99] Banks, *Victorian values*, pp. 108, 183. In accounting for this over the long term, Banks must be correct in pointing to the shrinking pool (as a proportion of the total population) of rural labourers, whose sons and daughters had always supplied the wealthy with their most compliant source of cheap, resident domestic labour. This is confirmed by E. Higgs, who shows that a rising proportion of rural-born, in-migrant domestic servants in mid-century Rochdale reflected the positive disinclination of urban-born girls to submit to the limitations on personal freedom which domestic service entailed, even though wage-levels were surprisingly close to factory wages once board and lodging was included: 'Domestic service', pp. 139–45. Additionally, Ebery and Preston have argued for the importance of the late Victorian service sector expansion of alternative, more attractive and well-remunerated employment for young unmarried, relatively independent urban females: in shops, catering, teaching and clerical work. Ebery and Preston, *Domestic service*.

institution of *female* domestic service may have been a major agency of diffusion of birth controlling techniques and values to the working classes, even if that of male domestic service was not. This is, for instance, an hypothesis which has been entertained on a speculative basis by both J. A. Banks and Leonore Davidoff.[100] However, both the statistical evidence and the direct testimony that is available strongly contradict this supposition. Based on her questioning of thirty women born between 1890 and 1914, Gittins concluded that those in domestic service were by far the least likely to acquire any knowledge at all of sexual and reproductive matters prior to marriage, whereas it was those in factory and office work who were relatively well informed.[101] The loneliness and isolation which domestic servants could experience is independently confirmed for the late-Victorian period by some of the memoirs collected in *Life as we have known it*.[102] Neither does Pamela Horn, in her much-cited study of Victorian servants, suggest that confidences on these matters flowed at all freely between servants and employers.[103]

Furthermore, the statistical evidence is against this hypothesis on several counts. First, the incidence of such domestic employment for young girls was least common, while *other* kinds of industrial female employment were *most* common, in precisely those parts of the country where birth control was adopted earliest by working people: in Lancashire and the West Riding of Yorkshire, as Davidoff's own figures show.[104] Secondly, Edward Higgs's important revisionist work on the census figures themselves, interpreted in the light of his detailed research on the changing methods of official collection and tabulation of the information, has suggested that the number of girls and young women employed as domestic servants has probably been substantially overestimated by previous students, principally at the expense of an underenumeration of female agricultural workers.[105]

100 Banks, *Victorian values*, pp. 107–8. Banks, however, notes the importance of Gittins's evidence (see next footnote), to the effect that there was a strong taboo against any explicit discussion of sexual and related matters between the mistress and her servants. Davidoff, 'Mastered for life', n. 81. Davidoff calculated that in 1881 one third of all girls aged 15–20 were employed in domestic service. *Ibid.*, p. 410. But see E. Higgs's 'Women, occupations and work', which radically revises these figures downwards (footnote 105, below).

101 Gittins, *Fair sex*, ch. 3. See also Gittins (unpublished MA dissertation); and Gittins, 'Married life'.

102 Llewellyn Davies, *Life as we have known it*, pp. 24–33 (Mrs Layton), 58–60 (Mrs Wrigley).

103 Horn, *The rise and fall of the Victorian servant*, especially chs. 7–8.

104 Davidoff, 'Mastered for life', p. 410. For illustrative statistics on female employment for several mill towns in 1861, see Joyce, *Work, society and politics*, Table 3, pp. 108–9. For the distribution of female domestic servants by counties and London boroughs, see Board of Trade, Labour Department, *Labour Gazette* 10 (1911), Table VIII, p. xxvii.

105 Higgs, 'Women, occupations and work', Tables 4 and 5 suggest that throughout the period 1841–91, inclusive, the number of female domestic servants, as shown by the published reports of the census, has been overestimated by as much as 100%! Even if this bold claim is not subsequently upheld fully, Higgs's article has done enough to indicate a substantial overestimation in this category, primarily because many women working as agricultural workers have been wrongly classified as domestic servants. It is, of course, true that female participation in various other categories of employment, as well as agriculture, has almost certainly been seriously underestimated in official sources from this period. See above, p. 123; below, pp. 504–5, 576.

Thirdly, Higgs has also, separately, shown that a large proportion of female domestic servants, perhaps approaching one half in many towns, were in fact employed in working-class homes (but note that this finding has no application to male domestics).[106] This further detracts from the hypothesis that female domestic service was instrumental in spreading family planning down a putative social hierarchy, since for female domestics to have performed the posited role in imbibing and disseminating middle-class attitudes and behaviour, they would have to have been employed in middle-class homes.

The gendered, patriarchal labour market and the working-class family

The plebeian section of the nation was, of course, numerically much larger than the patrician constellation. It was distinguished from the latter, above all, by the fact that in an era before any form of national social security, accident and illness insurance, old-age pensions or minimum wage legislation (all of which only first appeared between 1908 and 1911), the vast majority of the working class lived in a régime of chronic inadequacy and insecurity of family income of a form which ensured recurrent deprivations and which could threaten the integrity and survival of the family. Whereas the principal socio-economic force influencing changes in perceived relative childrearing costs among the various social groups of the middle classes can be characterised as that of social status aspiration, it was considerations of sheer economic necessity which tended to be much more directly influential in altering perceived relative costs of childrearing among the divers communities of the proletariat. It also inevitably followed that under these circumstances, quite different – and widely varying – understandings prevailed, regarding childhood and childrearing and the roles of parenthood, motherhood and of spouses.

Seebohm Rowntree's pioneering analysis of working-class families in York at the end of the century graphically revealed the fundamental problem of life-cycle impoverishment which all working-class families faced. The power of Rowntree's analysis was in demonstrating the generality of the problem, for all but the most fortunate of proletarian families – those where the male breadwinner enjoyed an accident-free working life of regular, high earnings. The income of all other families inevitably fell below subsistence during two phases in the life-cycle, as measured by the famous 'poverty line', based on the market cost of maintaining mere physical efficiency.[107] This happened first and most universally from five to fifteen years after marriage, under the usual conditions where there were an increasing number of young children who had not yet begun to earn. Secondly a

[106] Higgs, 'Domestic service', Table 4.1, which indicates that over 40% of those households employing domestic servants in Rochdale, 1851–71, were 'working class' (293 out of the 697 households in Higgs's sample where the household head's occupation could be positively determined).

[107] Rowntree, *Poverty*, ch. IV and Appendices C, G, H.

couple was often struck again in old age after about forty years of marriage, when a husband's physical powers began to wane and children had left home and had their own growing families to support.[108] It is not so surprising, in view of Rowntree's analysis, that recent anthropometric research has shown that despite a century-long, fluctuating national trend of rising real wages since the 1810s, the overall health and viability of the typical labouring family, as measured by the age-specific growth profiles and height attainments of its children, was no better in the decade before the Great War than it had been in the decade following the Napoleonic Wars.[109]

There were a number of collective and institutional strategies, in which a few of the more fortunate among the working class were able to participate, which attempted to deal with the chronic and acute problem of income insecurity.[110] The protection of trade union organisation was an option successfully pursued by a small minority while membership of Friendly and other mutual provident associations was taken out by many others. There was the possibility for some of employment in the Co-operative movement's businesses and in certain other proletarian institutions such as Friendly Societies. Employment in the large railway companies was eagerly sought despite the modest pay because of the perceived security in working for such large organisations; employment in municipal, county and central government, including the public utilities, and as policemen and postmen was also prized because of the relative security of the income.[111]

But for the majority of workers, who did not enjoy such institutional sources of security – and even for those who did (because of their low pay) – it was still necessary to resort to a wide range of household survival strategies to deal with their predicament. Lodgers were taken; items pawned; neighbours and kin might give childcare one year, perhaps in return for the same the next; elder daughters frequently became deputy-mothers at young ages, something to which school attendance committees were still prepared to turn a blind eye at the end of the century;[112] washing, clothes making, keeping a small shop, an allotment or a pig could all help.[113] In addition to recognised part-time factory work and sweated outwork, there was a large range of casual child employment for pennies, such as

108 Rowntree, *Poverty*, ch. V.

109 Floud *et al.*, *Height, health and history*, p. 319. Of course, much of this was also to do with the fact that whereas the typical labouring family in 1820 still lived in the countryside, by 1900 its environment was unrelievedly urban and industrial.

110 See below, pp. 509–11, for Mike Savage's conceptual approach to the range of possible strategies.

111 Hence, 'a widespread perception in the entire period 1875–1914 held that government employees in general and Post Office employees in particular were better paid and enjoyed more job security than comparable workers in private employment.' Perry, *The Victorian Post Office*, p. 46. Uniquely among such workers during this period they enjoyed the benefits of a non-contributory pension plan: Daunton, *Royal Mail*, pp. 246–7.

112 See below, n. 204, for evidence of this.

113 See Davidoff, 'The separation of home and work?'.

errand running and parcel carrying, lather-boys for barbers, working for small-scale milksellers, greengrocers, firewood hawkers, newspaper sellers and, of course, all kinds of domestic chores for girls.[114] Finally, there were more desperate expedients still, of which stealing for food, a wife's temporary resort to prostitution, or a single mother's permanent employment in this way were probably all considered a lesser evil than the family's surrender to the icy mercies of the Poor Law.[115]

Thus, the fight against income insecurity, poverty and the workhouse was the fundamental condition of existence for working people throughout this period. The best way to wage this war changed as the family's circumstances altered. But it also varied significantly because of the different characteristics of proletarian communities: the divergent range of local resource options that were available to the household. Evidently, there were topographical and geological reasons for variations in the kinds of employment available in different parts of the country. But equally there were significant divergences in the politically mediated histories of industrial relations in different industries and towns; and this critically differentiated the character of their labour markets. To explain the diverse working-class occupational fertility patterns observed in 1911, it is therefore necessary to relate them to these locally varied histories of labour relations.

This is principally for two mutually reinforcing reasons. First, substantial variations between occupational groups in the extent to which women and children worked in the formal economy directly affected the household economics of relative childrearing costs and benefits. This is especially true when it is borne in mind that typically those communities where female and child employment was more common were also likely to be those where male earnings were least satisfactory, because the two local labour market characteristics were often joint outcomes of the same historical factors: the relative effectiveness or weakness of male trade union bargaining power, as suggested by the evidence presented above (pp. 350–60).

Secondly, this effect of a strong internal relationship between local labour market characteristics and the relative costs of childrearing was further reinforced by the equally important social and cultural consequences of labour market gendering, influencing the crucial dimension of gendered perceptions of these costs and benefits. The more extreme the dichotomy between male and female economic roles prevailing in a community, the more likely that the costs and benefits of fertility would fall unevenly on the two sexes and that communication between spouses on matters of fertility and sexual behaviour would be rigidified according to ritualised public conventions – the 'machismo' pole of the continuum

[114] Keeling, *Child labour*, see p. 251. See below, p. 526, for the statistical incidence of these casual activities. On child sweated labour, see Sherard *The child slaves*.

[115] For personal testimony of boys stealing for food and of a single mother's maintenance of her independence through prostitution, see Ray Rochford and Maria Davis, respectively, in Humphries and Gordon, *A labour of love*, pp. 150–1, 142–5; Humphries, 'Steal to survive'. More generally, see Finnegan, *Poverty and prostitution*; Crowther, *The workhouse system*, Part II.

proposed above, on pp. 350–1, 357–8. This would be more likely to impede the private evolution of the flexible attitudes towards a husband's 'conjugal rights' and the novel forms of sexual behaviour within marriage, including periods of abstinence and coitus interruptus, which the above account has identified as the principal means of birth control accessible and available to the British working population at this time.

It might be added, thirdly, that in those areas where relatively exclusive male access to the local labour market had been successfully negotiated with employers and where there was least opportunity for adult females to earn any form of income, the social role of an adult female would have become relatively confined to that of a wife and mother, resulting in the necessary emigration of those not so employed and a related tendency towards early marriage for all who remained. Given that extension of 'learned' premarital abstinence has been identified as a major method of birth spacing at this time, the minimising of any period of delay before marriage would tend to militate against couples in these communities adopting such behaviour after marriage. Note that all of these three factors are mutually reinforcing, acting in the same direction upon the critical variable of perceived relative childrearing costs.

The nineteenth-century history of labour market negotiation between workers, employers and – on important occasions – the state is, therefore, extremely relevant for an understanding of occupational fertility patterns. By influencing the differential earning capacities of fathers, mothers, sons and daughters, the shifting bargains which were struck in different industries and communities over wages and working conditions vitally affected the central fertility variable of perceived relative childrearing costs. This varied history of labour relations in each of Britain's proliferating sectors of industry is, of course, far too complex and varied for a comprehensive account of each sector to be offered here. It is also still too under-researched in many respects. The following analysis will therefore be restricted to a brief survey of the provisional knowledge available regarding general developments during the important formative period in the first half of the nineteenth century, followed by more detailed attention to those industrial sectors which have emerged from the foregoing account as of particular interest where the history of fertility change is concerned.

There is something of a consensus beginning to emerge among social historians of labour and gender that it was through the evolving language and rhetoric of the Chartist movement in the course of its most dynamic phase, 1837–48, that the dominant political forces and institutions within the organised working class came to endorse an unequivocally patriarchal ideology.[116] The preceding decades

[116] These developments have been analysed by a number of scholars, including Thompson, *The Chartists*, who traced the early female participation in Chartism, but later withdrawal from its leadership; Valverde, '"Giving the female a domestic turn"', on the Ten Hours Movement's discrimination against women as 'unfree' agents. See also Land, 'The family wage'; Alexander, 'Women, class and sexual differences'; Clark, 'The rhetoric of Chartist domesticity'; and, more generally, see Scott, *Gender and the politics of history*, ch 3.

of unprecedented economic change and political challenges had witnessed intense debate on both sides of the English Channel over the propriety of traditional patriarchal forms of authority within the polity and the family.[117] During these decades – which witnessed the revolution in France, the perceived threat of the British Jacobins at home, the French Wars, the Queen Caroline Affair, primitive socialism and Owenite communes – gender and familial roles, marriage and sexual codes were in the ideological melting pot, within both polite and plebeian cultures.[118] Bearing in mind Chodorow's thesis of the reproduction of gender roles through the reproduction of mothering and Judith Bennett's unarguable point that 'Patriarchy has clearly existed in many different manifestations in many past societies', this should be seen as a protracted period of patriarchal adaptation and reconstruction of gender roles in the labour market, under transformative social and economic conditions, rather than as 'the' origin of 'modern' gender inequalities (replacing an implied previous 'golden age').[119]

The proletarian reconstitution of patriarchal relations was in no sense a simple mimesis of the 'separate spheres' ideology of the propertied upper and middle classes; but it was a political and ideological response to it. The adoption by working-class political institutions of their own proletarian notion of the virtues of 'domesticity' and of the symbol of the male breadwinner as exclusive earner of the family wage were both expedients generated by the dialectical needs of Chartist politics. Initially, Chartism was ambivalent on gender issues, reflecting the disagreements of contemporary debate. As Catherine Hall has pointed out, William Cobbett, the single most important influence on working class Radicalism according to E. P. Thompson, was a major disseminator from the 1820s onwards of a companionate but relentlessly patriarchal model of conjugal life to the literate working-class.[120] On the other hand, there was William Thompson and Anna Wheeler's *Appeal on behalf of one-half of the human race, women, against the pretensions of the other half, men, to retain them in political, and thence in civil and domestic slavery*, published in 1825. And, of course, the Owenite socialist movement spawned a number of important, sexually egalitarian social initiatives (such as the industrial communes of New Lanark and Queenswood), though these did not survive beyond the early 1840s; and there were trade unions for both sexes (culminating in the short-lived Grand National Consolidated Trade Union of 1834).[121]

Partly as a result of the perceived practical failings of the Owenite experiments, the patriarchal position gradually became more dominant among the Chartists,

117 Hunt, *The family romance*; Mintz, *A prison of expectations*.

118 Taylor, *Eve and the New Jerusalem*; Laqueur, 'The Queen Caroline Affair'; Colley, *Britons*, chs. 4–7; Mason, *The making of Victorian sexuality*.

119 Chodorow, *The reproduction of mothering*; Bennett, 'Feminism and history', pp. 262–3; see also Erickson, 'Introduction', on the mythic golden age of gender equality.

120 Hall, 'The tale of Samuel and Jemima', pp. 92–4.

121 Taylor, *Eve and the New Jerusalem*, provides a most stimulating treatment of the gender issues posed by the Owenite movement.

particularly when defending themselves against the assertions of the propertied class that their dissolute homes and domestic conduct proved their continuing unworthiness for the vote.[122] Both moderate ('moral force') and, subsequently, militant ('physical force') wings of the Chartist movement began to argue that their womenfolk should be excluded from factory work so that they could devote themselves to the creation of virtuous and ordered homes.[123] This was, in effect, to call the bluff of the charge levelled by the propertied governing and employer class. It was a strategy which produced rapid parliamentary dividends, resulting, for instance, in the protective Mines and Factory Acts and a Public Health Act. Though the latter proved far from effective, this legislation was understood to be sincerely designed to provide the manufacturing districts with healthier homes presided over by full-time mothers. Indeed, Gareth Stedman Jones has attributed the deflation of the Chartist movement after 1848 in part to the fulsome response by the state to this aspect of its agenda.[124]

A patriarchal model of family structure and authority was also entailed in the case put forward by the Chartist movement in developing the novel argument that labouring men should qualify for the vote by virtue of their wage-labour.[125] The Lockean constitutional orthodoxy held that only the independent possession of personal property could guarantee an individual's independence of political judgement and therefore justify the right to vote. The Chartists argued that since, according to Locke himself, property only ultimately represented the fruits of labour, working men's rights to vote followed directly, in principle, from the value of their labour. Provided only that this labour was remunerated fairly, as a 'family wage' sufficient to maintain himself and his family without reliance on others, the working man's labour therefore provided him with the necessary Lockean independence which justifed his right to vote. Hence, the political imperative of campaigning for the male breadwinner's 'family wage'. Furthermore, commitment to this ideological programme entailed the proposition that women and children should not earn income, since this would abrogate the patriarch's claim to independence.

[122] On the sensitivity of Francis Place, the draughtsman of the People's Charter, to this charge, see Mason, *The making of Victorian sexuality*, pp. 22–3, 29.

[123] Clark, 'The rhetoric of Chartist domesticity', especially pp. 65–77.

[124] Stedman Jones, 'Rethinking Chartism', p. 177: this was alongside the popular repeal of the Corn Laws, the Bank Charter Act and the Joint Stock Company Act, all of which were popularly understood to be attacks on the vested interests of various factions of the propertied élite.

[125] Scott, *Gender and the politics of history*, pp. 62–5; Sewell, Jr, 'How classes are made', pp. 68–71. The extent of this novelty can only be fully appreciated when it is understood that to be entirely dependent on the wages of a master was deemed in popular culture to be the very antithesis of freedom according to traditions dating back to the sixteenth and seventeenth centuries. Independence was considered to reside in land holding, at least as a tenant. Wage-labour was generally seen merely as an apprenticed, junior or supplemental activity, demeaning for a grown man as head of household. Apparently even the radical Levellers of the Commonwealth era considered that landless wage-labourers had forfeited their status as 'freeborn Englishmen' and could not be enfranchised. Hill, 'Pottage for freeborn Englishmen'.

James Cronin has argued that the heavy ideological commitment which the state made to the economic and fiscal policies of *laissez-faire* at this historical juncture, in response to the combined political demands of popular radicalism and bourgeois liberalism, had important long-term patriarchal implications for the future social policies of the state.[126] Since the political nation thereby became constituted as propertied and male, 'feminine' social policy issues relating to family health, household conditions and welfare became marginalised at the level of national politics; while the male political organisations of the working class focused their energies on the workplace contest for control with employers and the issue of male citizenship. In consequence, the bargaining powers and rights of women and children, relative to patriarchs, were down-graded.

This distinctively proletarian patriarchal ideology was premised on the notion that a male head of household should be legally and economically responsible for 'his' family, and that, having achieved this, he should then be a full constitutional member of the polity. The ideology was developed outside Chartism as well, elaborated through the Ten Hours Movement, which drew support to its cause from the Evangelical, philanthropic and Tory constituencies in Parliament because of its willingness to equate women with children as 'unfree' legal minors in need of patriarchal protection.[127] Furthermore, such gendered rhetoric was subsequently institutionalised in the political practice of the craft unions.[128] It was an effective bargaining ploy because employers found it difficult to deny the justice of arguments in favour of 'male breadwinners' being paid 'family wages', consistent as this was with the moral code of 'separate spheres'.[129]

Thus, the eventual outcome of the ideological and political manoeuvrings of workers, employers and the state during the first half of the nineteenth century was the reconstruction and adoption by the dominant institutions of organised labour of a patriarchal ideology, defining waged work as the primary social role

[126] Cronin, *The politics of state expansion*, pp. 19–26. See above, n. 124, regarding the principal legislative commitments to *laissez-faire*.

[127] Rose, *Limited livelihoods*, p. 146.

[128] According to the Webbs' classic historical interpretation, the exclusionist New Model Unions emerged from Friendly Societies and other associations during and after the 1850s along the lines pioneered by the Amalgamated Society of Engineers (ASE). They each delimited their membership to a particular sector of industry and deliberately excluded unskilled males and females. Having read their political economy and absorbed its immutable laws, as urged upon them by their social superiors since the early years of the century, male trade union organisers were now intent upon the strategy of long-term control over the supply of specialised labour as the key to raising its price – their wages. They explicitly aspired, via control over the terms and conditions of apprenticeship, to a similar degree of power over recruitment to specific areas of the labour market as that which was being contemporaneously won by the middle-class male professionals. Webb and Webb, *The history of trade unionism*, pp. 218–220.

[129] Thus, for instance, Sonya Rose's careful analysis of industrial relations in the Kidderminster carpet-making industry shows that 'To vindicate their employment practices employers in the last quarter of the century might have argued a women's rights position or that the work was particularly suited to women's natures. Instead, they were careful to state that although women had a right to employment, men should be the breadwinners.' Rose, *Limited livelihoods*, pp. 133–4.

and source of identity for the male household head; and domestic, maternal care as the principal female role. A parallel development had occurred within polite society but there was an enormous difference between the two social worlds in the practical implications of their ideologies. For the working classes, this represented no more than an aspiration: the guiding outlines for a political programme, rather than an attainable (and, to some middle-class women, an irksome) reality. In most working-class communities throughout the remainder of the century the majority of proletarian patriarchs were non-unionised, bringing home insecure, inadequate and irregular earnings. As a result the household's prosperity and sometimes its survival depended on the economic activities of those 'junior' members, whose capacity to earn was minimalised by the exclusionary ideology and tactics of the negotiations taking place between patriarchal employers and workmen's representatives.[130]

Thus, working-class men and women (and their children) were in a predicament of 'competitive interdependence' in the labour market, which caught them in a chronic mutual conflict of interests.[131] The interests of skilled were pitted against unskilled, residents against immigrants, men against boys, males against females.[132] It was subject to these conditions that growing proletarian families in most industrial communities had to adapt their household survival strategies.

Fertility and nuptiality variation between the communities of the working classes

How, then, does the explanatory role of negotiated gender and age discrimination in local labour markets (in terms of both job availability and pay levels) apply in practice to the main patterns of occupational fertility differentials among the working class which have been described and analysed above? Although every locality and branch of industry was in principle subject to its own distinct course of events in these terms, nevertheless certain general observations are justifiable. In

130 The extent to which the male breadwinner was established as a reality in some areas of industry was as much to do with its acceptability to the employers as it was the product simply of trade union muscle. As Harriet Bradley has remarked, in many sectors of industry where expensive machinery and remote delegation of decision-making was unavoidable, it was in employers' interests to recruit a core workforce of responsible supervisory workers whom they felt could be trusted (typically mature patriarchs like themselves), while having access to a reserve army of cheap female and young male labour to be hired and fired as fluctuations in trading conditions demanded. Bradley, *Men's work, women's work*, p. 171.

131 The notion of the 'competitive interdependence' of men and women in the labour market has been conceived by analogy from the more general predicament of capital and labour. According to Patrick Joyce, it was the work of M. Burawoy which was important in drawing attention to the interdependence of capital and labour, as a complementary perspective to the traditional Marxist emphasis simply on their relationship of conflict: Joyce, *Visions of the people*, p. 406, referring to Burawoy, *Manufacturing consent*; and Burawoy, *The politics of production*.

132 For two important articles, each exploring the gendered aspects of these social and political divisions within the working classes, including those between skilled and unskilled, see McClelland, 'Some thoughts on masculinity and the "Representative Artisan"'; and Sonya Rose, 'Respectable men, disorderly others'.

many cases the playing out of various important local and national developments during the first half of the nineteenth century was responsible for setting the seal on a number of significant large-scale regional and sectoral distinctions in the gendering of labour markets, which continued to prevail throughout the period 1870–1914.

Notable among these enduring developments were the extreme differences which emerged in the gendering of labour markets in the textiles and the coal-mining industries, which can be traced to the Factory and Mines Acts of the 1830s, 1840s and 1850s. These innovatory statutory controls were in no sense the only cause of these differences. In both cases they codified already extant tendencies in the respective labour markets. The effect of the legislation was to constrain within juridical bounds the potential for further historical change in the labour market characteristics of each of the two industries and to confirm that they would develop along rather different lines.

By the 1830s the textiles industry was already, on both sides of the Pennines, a sector in which the waged factory workforce was recruited from relatively large proportions of women and children.[133] The early Factory Acts, notably 1833, 1844 and 1853, applied exclusively to textiles, placing certain restrictions on the hours and conditions of employment for women and children. It is well known that such was the established and integrated role of the relatively cheap labour of women and children in the factory workforce that by carefully delimiting their working day to a maximum of ten and a half hours between 6 a.m. and 6 p.m. the 1853 Act effectively simultaneously so limited the male working day, too. The early Acts in fact placed the greatest burdens on employers with respect to young children. Age 13 was established as the minimum for full-time employment and age 8 as the minimum for part-time employment (six and a half hours per day). In the latter case employers were responsible for ensuring that their juvenile employees were receiving an education (minimum three hours per day). It was, of course, still worthwhile for employers to take on children provided their wage-rates remained very low, relative to those for adults of either sex.

These specific labour market features of the textiles industry, juridically

133 The textiles industry had been the classic locus for the early history of factory growth. Adult male householders, used to the independence they enjoyed as workers in their own homes (such as the many handloom weavers), had initially proved extremely reluctant to give up this freedom and to enter the employers' mills to work on powered machines. This had allowed the employers to recruit a largely female and juvenile workforce during the early decades from the end of the eighteenth century, when they became a firmly established presence in the new working environment of mass production. For a full account of this see Joyce, *Work, society and politics*. The Factory Inspectors' returns used by Mitchell and Deane show that in the cotton industry in 1838, of 259,000 workers employed in factories, 141,000 were females above age 13 and 12,000 were children of either sex below age 13, leaving 106,000 males above age 13. The same source shows a workforce that had more than doubled to 577,000 by 1907, composed of 359,000 females and 218,000 males while 19,000 of the total were half-time workers under age 14. Mitchell and Deane, *Abstract of British historical statistics*, p. 188.

cemented into place by the early Victorian statutes, resulted in the establishment of a very clear and distinctive economic logic of family formation for working-class households in these communities, with certain consequences for perceived relative childrearing costs and benefits. With the institutionalised abundance of female and juvenile labour, adult male bargaining power to hold out for differentially high rates of pay was not strong (though they did achieve some success, notably in the higher rates paid to mule spinners in the cotton industry and to overlookers in the worsted industry). Waged work was therefore available for wives at very reasonable rates of pay by contemporary standards (generally somewhat below the rates earned by males but the difference was narrow by comparison with the wide sex-differentials in pay in most other sectors of the economy). As juvenile earnings were significantly lower than those of either parent (they were not only lower *pro rata* but also only based on part-time work until age 13), it was most lucrative for a couple to try so to arrange their childbearing as to maximise both spouses' ability to earn or at least not to have so many children so quickly that the wife was taken out of the workforce before the first child reached the more substantial earning capacities of teenage. If the children arrived too fast and no childcare could be found then it would be vital for the husband to find a higher paying job than those generally available in the textiles industry (apart from mule spinners). In one of the few rigorous studies of the relationship between employment and the family life-cycle, R. Burr Litchfield found that in Stockport between 1841 and 1861, mothers with children often initially continued to work: 'The return from the mill to the family appears to have been an event less related to the nurturing of small children than to the moment . . . when children were beginning to be old enough to contribute independently to family support.'[134] It could pay a mother to stay in work while utilising a range of childcare arrangements, which included eldest daughters, grandmothers or aunts, neighbours or minders. In mid-nineteenth-century Preston, Stockport, Oldham and Bradford high proportions of grandparents have been found co-residing in their children's households, providing childcare services for working parents.[135]

Subsequent education and factory legislation, from 1870 onwards, further reinforced these effects in textiles regions by restricting child labour ever more rigorously.[136] As a result employers turned increasingly to their principal low-cost

134 Litchfield, 'The family and the mill', p. 191.

135 For Preston, Stockport and Oldham: Anderson, 'Household structure and the industrial revolution', pp. 224, 230–1. On Bradford: Ittmann, 'Family limitation and family economy in Bradford', p. 556.

136 Apart from the highly significant effects of successive Education Acts (see below, pp. 516–17), the consolidating Factory and Workshops Act of 1878 confirmed the important extensions of the 1874 Factory Act, whereby the ten-hour day became the new maximum, with minimum age for full-time employment raised to 14 and minimum part-time age raised to 10 years old. This later industrial legislation, incidentally, applied in principle to all workplaces with more than fifty employees, and not just to the textiles industry. However, note that its potential fertility effects, in being conducive towards the adoption of birth spacing, would only be likely to apply strongly in those communities

alternative: adult female labour. And, perhaps more to the point, married women found it necessary to return to, or to stay in the workforce longer because of the further restriction on their children's earning capacity. There is a clear overall pattern of substitution between these two sources of cheap labour (women and children) visible across the period 1835–1911 in the textiles industry, with the turning-points closely following the effects of the relevant Acts, *pace* the interpretation of these same events offered by Clark Nardinelli.[137] Karl Ittmann's local study of Bradford has also confirmed this relationship in more detail. He found rising participation rates of married women aged 30–49 in Bradford across the period 1851–81, while there was a pronounced fall in child labour under age 14.[138]

Thus, legislation effectively preserved, institutionalised and then in the 1870s amplified the key effects, in terms of the perceived opportunity costs of childrearing, of the unusual, relatively ungendered labour market conditions which had originally developed of their own accord in the two large branches of the textiles industry. It was the timing of this increased turning of the screw, through Factory and Education Acts, which elicited the intensifying fertility controlling response from the 1870s onwards. This thesis is supported by the strong statistical relationship found between the fall in income-earning activities by young children and the compensating rise in their mothers' participation in the labour market, especially when placed alongside Burr Litchfield's evidence of mothers' quitting the workplace earlier in the century as and when their children could earn.[139]

where there was already a relatively non-gendered labour market, with relatively high earnings available for married females, as in the textiles industry.

137 In the face of his own evidence, C. Nardinelli has perversely insisted on arguing that it was not statutory restrictions but the effects of technological developments in the textiles industry – supposedly rendering child labour less usable – which were primarily responsible for decline in child employment during the nineteenth century. Yet the most important evidence presented by Nardinelli, a table on p. 746 of his article derived from the data published in the annual reports of the Factory Inspectorate and displaying percentages of males and females above and below age 13 employed in textiles factories, clearly supports quite the opposite set of conclusions. A dramatic fall in child labour and a compensating rise in female labour occurred in the 1830s, 1840s and early 1850s, with the impact of the first round of factory legislation. But the ensuing decades of legislative and administrative quiescence were characterised by a gradual creep back toward increasing child employment in place of older females. This occurred from the later 1850s until the mid-1870s, regardless of the steady continuing spread of the principal 'child-saving' technological innovation (according to Nardinelli), the Roberts 'self-actor'. In Nardinelli's table, this temporary trend was reversed, however, after 1874. This was the year of the important Factory and Workshops Act which raised minimum ages for both full- and part-time child employment for the first time since the 1840s (see previous footnote). Thereafter, the period down to the Great War was one of ever-tightening control over the child labour market through the combined effects of Factory and Education Acts, allied to the school attendance administration (see below, pp. 516–17). In Nardinelli's table this later period shows a trend fall in child labour accompanied once again by increasing female participation. Nardinelli, 'Child labor', pp. 746–8. For a thorough study of this subject, which unfortunately came to hand too late for inclusion here, see Bolin-Hort, *Work, family*.

138 Ittmann, 'Family limitation', pp. 555–6, 570.

139 In placing primary emphasis for the general explanation of falling fertility among textile workers upon the parental response to legislative tightening of juvenile labour market conditions, I am offering a very different analysis to that which has been proposed by Ittmann, based on his detailed

By contrast, in the coal-mining industry, which was of course the only other major sector of industry to receive such general statutory regulation of its labour market so early in the century, the principal effect of the 1842 Mines Act was to enforce an absolute prohibition on underground work by the female sex and by boys under age 10. In terms of its influence on perceived relative childrearing costs this prohibition had quite the opposite influence upon the logic of family formation to that of the early Factory Acts in the textiles industry. In the many pit towns in the coal industry, where there was little alternative employment for women, the opportunity costs of frequent childbearing in affecting a mother's income-earning capacities were negligible following the Mines Acts. Miners could, of course, already earn high wages when relatively young, encouraging their early marriage. Their sisters, if they did not leave the community, were also best off married as soon as possible to escape, if only temporarily, the crowded parental home and its never-ending chores.

As pointed out above, proletarian families were faced throughout this period with the chronic working-class problems of poverty and insecurity of income. Even if they escaped bouts of unemployment and injury to the principal breadwinner, the phenomenon of life-cycle poverty ensured that periods of serious hardship were a universal experience. In most communities each individual family and household as it grew and expanded might come to any one of a range of shifting arrangements and adaptations in order to survive. But in typical mill towns and in many colliery communities the range of feasible adaptive strategies was much less variable and more clearly delimited for all families concerned. In the one case, this was because of the unusual availability of well-paid adult female work and low-paid (but regular) juvenile work for both sexes. In the other case it was because of the equally clear absence of earning capacities for all females, young and old, allied to unusually high earning power for young adult males, and to reasonable job security (accidents apart) especially later in the century because of the strength of unions.[140] These prevailing labour market conditions imposed

and stimulating study of Bradford: Ittmann, 'Family limitation'. Ittmann chooses to emphasise cyclical trading conditions and particularly the impact on family budgets of difficulties experienced by the worsted industry for a decade or so after 1873. However, there are a number of problems with this as a convincing, general explanation. First, as Ittmann himself acknowledges (p. 561), fortunes varied during the 1870s and 1880s in different branches of the textiles industries of Lancashire and Yorkshire and yet falling fertility was a general phenomenon. Secondly, there had been severe trade depressions in different parts of the industry before (including, for instance, the widespread cotton famine due to the American Civil War in the early 1860s) without this 'triggering' a secular trend of falling fertility. Ittmann seems to have wandered away from an analysis more like that offered here because of his rather ill-judged assertion that young children's labour could not have made a significant contribution to family income (p. 555). To families consistently struggling to survive (a point Ittmann himself makes on the same page), a child's earnings of approximately 2 to 4 shillings per week was far from insignificant, representing up to 25% of a mother's likely earnings. In many cases, the 5–10% of the family's income brought in by a young child probably was the important margin above subsistence.

140 Clegg *et al.*, *A history*, ch. 3.

therefore rather strong and general economic and logistical 'rules' upon expanding proletarian families playing the survival game, leading to somewhat similar and uniform optimal strategic 'solutions' being adopted by most families in each community. Thus the textiles occupations and the coal-mining occupations show up in 1911 as the two working-class extremes in the national tables of occupational fertility and nuptiality because they each contain a vast majority of couples resident in one of these two quite distinct and different forms of community, where in each case most families tended towards the same kind of survival strategy with a characteristic (and contrasting) fertility implication in each case.

Similarly to mining districts, where iron and steel or heavy engineering comprised the primary sources of employment on offer, the rigorously gendered labour market virtually forced all men and women into a tightly constrained pair of reciprocal, extremely unequal and opposite gender roles, as providing 'breadwinner' and dependent homekeeper, respectively. In some other sectors of the economy, by contrast, the availability of significant, independent wage-earning opportunities for women and wives both raised the direct opportunity costs of each child to the married couple and simultaneously tended to enhance the bargaining position and status of women in general, as in many textiles communities. For instance, in the case of plebeian shopkeepers, but for somewhat different economic reasons than in the textiles industry, this also produced the negotiation between spouses of quite *similar* and shared roles – both before and after marriage and inside and outside the home.

Sylvia Walby and Ellen Jordan have drawn a broad distinction between 'old' manufacturing industries and 'new' or 'radically reorganised' ones, which may be helpful in relating industries' broad differences in gender relations to their varying fertility patterns in 1911.[141] 'Old' industries constituted, by 1911, a set of industries including textiles, earthenware, tailoring, clothes manufacture and dress making, boot and shoe making, the production of certain staple metal goods (tinplate, brass, wire, and cutlery), jewellery making, Black Country nail and chain making. In all these cases a female workforce had firmly established itself before the 1830s and 1840s, that is to say before the era of Chartism and the ideology of 'the male breadwinner'. As with the textiles industry, the typical pattern of industrial relations in these 'old' industries was that of 'job segregation'. The female workforce, while tolerated as a continuing presence in the workplace, tended to be confined where possible to lower-paid, supposedly lower-skilled jobs. By contrast the 'new' branches of industry were those which had only first emerged since the 1840s or else had experienced a transformative radical reorganisation and capitalisation since the decade of Chartism. Wholesale 'industrial segregation' was the more common industrial relations strategy in these cases, as male workers often successfully campaigned for (or employers actively promoted) the complete

[141] Walby, *Patriarchy at work*, ch. 5; Jordan, 'The exclusion of women from industry'.

exclusion of women from the workplace. This would seem to apply quite accurately to most branches of the transport industry, especially the railways, and to workers in utilities and municipal services; also to the iron and steel, heavy engineering and shipbuilding industries, and partly to the chemicals industry.[142]

Obviously, the correlation between old and new industries and the evidence of occupational fertility differentials is likely to be a far from perfect one, given that many of the men pursuing any given occupation typically lived in large urban communities where women's labour market opportunities were not determined solely by the characteristics of any single sector of industry, whether it be old or new. Large towns like Middlesbrough, where the iron and steel industry dominated the labour market of the entire community, were the exception, not the rule.[143] Nevertheless those occupational groupings drawn principally from 'new' sectors of industry, where the post-1840s ideology of the 'male breadwinner' had largely succeeded in creating a single-sex workplace, were predominantly those exhibiting higher completed and incomplete fertility and an earlier age at marriage. Conversely, occupations drawn more from 'old' branches of industry, which had experienced no transforming change in scale or technology of production since 'the gender ideology watershed' of the 1830s and 1840s, tended to exhibit lower fertility and later marriage. The analysis of Walby and Jordan therefore seems helpful in accounting for the occupational patterns evident in Figure 7.1 and in particular for the relationship between gross sex ratios of employment and different industries' fertility levels, discussed on pp. 351–4 and indicated by Table 7.8. The 'new' industries were those in which the effective trade unions of Hobsbawm's 'labour aristocracy' were most likely to be found.

However, there was one generic type of strategy available to some of the more fortunate and capable proletarian couples and their families, which offered the possibility of evading some of the conflicts of interest generated by the predicament of competitive interdependence in the patriarchal labour market. This was to opt for self-employment, so that the spouses could in principle determine their own pattern of deployment of their family's available labour resources, as between income-earning and domestic production.[144] Although in fact accompanied by its

142 The mining industry has already been dealt with as a special case, where such industrial segregation was enshrined in law as an early victory for the 'male breadwinner' movement (primarily as a result of MPs' sensitivity to the impropriety of the two sexes mixing underground in the state of undress necessary to do the work of coal-getting). The course of gender relations in other *non-manufacturing* sectors of the economy, such as the (non-transport) service sector, agriculture, fishing and the building trades, are not explicitly covered in the analyses offered by Walby and Jordan. Although by no means new industries, exclusion was certainly the pattern in the last two cases, while segregation was more the rule in the other two.

143 On Edwardian Middlesbrough, see Lady Florence Bell's contemporary testimony, *At the works*.

144 On the notion of domestic production and the reasons why it is misleading to define activities within the home as less productive than those performed outside it in the wage-labour market, see Pahl, *Divisions of labour* chs. 1–2.

own serious risks of bankruptcy, this was certainly seen by many proletarians as a beckoning pathway to much-prized independence. They required either capital or literacy or both. For most labouring parents this opportunity was something to be attained by saving so as to start a shop or other small business later in life. As Robert Roberts has intimated in his memoirs of the Edwardian period in his childhood home of Salford:

> That wide section beyond the purely manual castes . . . was considered by many to be no more than 'jumped-up working class', not to be confused with the true order above: but the striving sought it nevertheless, if not for themselves, at least for their children. The real social divide existed between those who, in earning daily bread, dirtied hands and face and those who did not.[145]

Increasingly during the period before the First World War, the more fortunate members of the working class were finding themselves able to to fulfil this dream. The 1911 census recorded a marked decennial increase (well above the national average increase) in retailers and noted that it was becoming a popular employment to adopt in middle age.[146]

Shopkeeping in particular often involved both spouses working together in the business. Indeed, such businesses were sometimes run by wives on their own, as also were many clothes-making small firms, such as milliners and drapers (though the latter may have been somewhat less plebeian in their origins). In a large range of other self-employed businesses, such as proprietorial artisans and craftsmen of all kinds, those running small transport firms, or market gardeners, direct female participation was less likely, according to the census returns. However, the latter certainly underestimate the true extent to which wives actually participated in even these concerns by, for instance, doing the books and paperwork, or acting as unpaid buying and selling agents. Of course, couples able to opt for the strategy of self-employment were not thereby immune from the wider patriarchal conventions and practices of the time. But the two spouses concerned did create for themselves the possibility of a somewhat distinct set of options and bargaining positions. In the case of small-scale shopkeeping Christopher Hosgood has additionally emphasised the extemely interesting point that there was a sense in which such

145 Roberts, *The classic slum*, p. 19.

146 1911 Census, Volume X. In the preliminary discussion it is observed that in 'Order XX, Food, Tobacco, Drink, Lodging', virtually all occupations selling foods registered an increase in males since the last census of from one and a half to three times the national average male increase in numbers occupied (the national average figure was 10.9%). Furthermore, it was noted that this increase was especially marked in the age range 35–65. Increased male employment in the sector as a whole (Order XX) was up by 18% on the 1901 figures. The total of 474,683 females was up by 58.5%; but the female figures for 1901 and 1911 were not comparable because relatives helping out were now classified to the occupation, whereas they had been excluded in 1901 (when they were simply defined as 'unoccupied'). The sector as a whole now employed 913,565 males, 8% of the total occupied male population in 1911. This was, for instance, about equal to 'Order XII, Building and Works of Construction'. Source: Census 1911, Volume X, Table 3.

'domestic shops' and the activity of shopkeeping crossed the gender divide, which characterised much working-class culture. Not only were corner shops 'the housewives' pub' and a major conduit for community gossip, but Hosgood has found among his male Leicester shopkeepers that 'whereas shopkeepers were an integral part of women's informal domestic culture, they were seldom active in male institutions, such as the working men's club and the friendly society'.[147] This is an example of the way in which gendered working practices in different industries could strongly influence the general pattern of associations and quality of communications between the sexes and therefore between spouses, something of great importance in determining the capacity of spouses to negotiate birth control together.

Most couples in a working-class community were primarily influenced by the prevailing gendered labour market conditions, relative wage-levels and consequent 'resource options' of their neighbourhood and had to fit their family roles around this, often primarily governed by the differentially high adult male wage-rates that were attainable.[148] However, the petty bourgeoisie, in having some autonomy and discretion over the way in which the family's labour was expended, between its income-earning and its domestic production activities, could, in theory at least, fit work and family roles more flexibly around each other to suit the growing family's shifting requirements. No doubt in the case of exclusively male-operated small businesses, such as many of the artisan craftsmen, this may hardly have resulted in a greater similarity of roles between husband and wife and may even have been conducive to some of the most relentlessly patriarchal situations, where the couple's aspirations for upward mobility through business success may have led to entirely domesticated and socially isolated wives.[149] But in other cases, where wives could and did participate fully or partially in the business, this would have set up a more equal perspective and bargaining position between the two spouses, conducive to greater communication and co-operation over the issues of perceived relative costs of childrearing.

Historical explanations have now been offered for the fertility differentials exhibited by many working-class occupations and industrial communities, which are consistent with the perceived relative childrearing costs framework. However, there is one obvious occupational category and industry which would seem to present something of a difficulty to the analysis that has been offered so far. Alongside the textiles industry, the earthenware industry of North Staffordshire was also unusual in its association with large-scale female labour market participation and yet, unlike the categories of wool and cotton workers, it apparently did not return evidence of unusually low completed or incomplete

147 Hosgood, 'The "pigmies of commerce"', p. 448.

148 On 'resource options', see Pahl, *Divisions of labour*, p. 21.

149 For contemporary evidence on this syndrome in some artisans' marriages, see Hammerton, *Cruelty and companionship*, pp. 50–2.

fertility in 1911. If anything, quite the opposite. Yet it can reasonably be claimed that this industry was sufficiently geographically concentrated that its relatively ungendered labour market must have exerted strong community-wide influences upon the culture and economy of family formation throughout the six towns of the Potteries, comparable to that posited for the textiles industries in Lancashire and West Yorkshire. As will become clear, examination of the reasons for this anomaly leads to a general consideration of the phenomenon of homeworking among female workers during this period, 1870–1914. In fact, as will be seen, this provides a highly significant explanation, consistent with the perceived relative childrearing costs framework, for the high fertility of various remaining social groups within the working classes, and not just the Potteries workers.

The explanation for the fertility behaviour of the Potteries may lie in a combination of several reasons. First, it has been noted that the Potteries was a region with a considerable coal-mining presence, although it did not dominate the occupational structure as much as pot making. The relatively high fertility of potters' wives might partly reflect this influence, although it seems the weakest hypothesis. Secondly, and more importantly, there was an important divergence between the textiles and the earthenware industries in the historical development of their typical working practices and the way in which these were integrated with the proletarian family economy. The common practice in many forms of manufacturing before the mid-nineteenth century had been that employers and putters-out paid a joint family wage to household heads in return for work performed under their supervision. This was essentially a form of subcontracting, typically by the male household head to a team of junior members under his care, often including his wife. Although this pattern was almost completely replaced by the rise of a general market in the labour of individuals who were paid individuated wages, historians of gender relations and the family have shown that the extension of this new pattern of remuneration did not proceed in any nationally uniform manner, as a simple correlate of industrialisation, mass production or the expansion of the factory system.[150]

The textiles and earthenware industries differed considerably from each other in this respect by the late nineteenth and early twentieth centuries. In the textiles industry continuation of the family wage form had initially been encouraged in the factories, especially by employers. But by the last quarter of the century this had generally been replaced by individual wages for each worker (although family contacts remained important modes of recruitment in some, but by no means all, towns).[151] This was partly because during the third quarter of the nineteenth century adult male employees had successfully negotiated with the male employers to establish the principle of job segregation throughout the industry so that the higher paid forms of work and more supervisory posts were

150 Seccombe, 'Patriarchy stabilised'.

151 Joyce, *Work, society and politics*; Savage, 'Women and work in the Lancashire cotton industry'.

deemed to be the exclusive preserve of adult males, sometimes physically and logistically separated from the other tasks performed by women and children. Somewhat unusually, historical developments had gone in the opposite direction in the Potteries. The industry was characterised at the end of the century by hundreds of small-scale units of production, the pot-banks. In this relatively informal and intimate set-up, the family and its close kin often acted as self-recruiting work-groups or small teams with a joint income derived from their activities.[152] As a result of this arrangement, there was an economic perception for these households that the more children they had, the more hands were available and the greater was the family's overall earning power in the local economy.[153]

Finally, a third, closely related and important factor was that the detailed working practices in the many small workshops of the earthenware industry, with its enormous range of highly differentiated, hand-thrown and hand-painted products, were entirely different from the rigorous shift-working régime required by the mass-production techniques in the larger, powered textiles factories. Hence, there was great time flexibility generally available for the individual members of the hundreds of small, self-determining work-groups in the Potteries. Along with the close residential proximity of most workers to their scores of small workplaces, Richard Whipp has argued that this much facilitated parents' (mainly mothers') capacity to fit in their domestic duties around their working-day.[154] Thus, notwithstanding the similarity that in both textiles and earthenware manufacturing communities married women had an unusual degree of access to the formal labour market outside the home, the context in which this participation occurred was quite different. In the textiles regions married women's income-earning activities directly raised the opportunity costs of childrearing, whereas the entirely different working practices in the Potteries meant that this was not necessarily the case there.

Whipp is, in effect, arguing that the pattern of work in the late nineteenth-century Potteries was in certain key respects similar to that which had encouraged such high fertility among homeworking cottage industry workers a century before: domestic family work-teams in which work and childcare were relatively easily combined. It is particularly significant, therefore, that this pattern was also

[152] Richard Whipp's work emphasises the family team as a well-established feature of the industry during the period 1875–1914: Whipp, 'Women and the social organisation'; Whipp, *Patterns of labour*, ch. 2. This pattern was not a 'survival' of earlier practices but resulted from the revolutionary introduction into the pot banks in the 1870s of the 'jolly' and the 'jigger', permitting the substitution of unskilled female for skilled male labour. Hence M. Dupree found little evidence for family teams at mid-century but an increasing presence of young girls and wives from the 1870s. Dupree, (unpublished DPhil thesis) pp. 336–8 (the revised version of this study is now published as: Dupree, *Family structure*). Jacqueline Sarsby's oral testimonies suggest a subsequent weakening of the pattern of family teams during the interwar period: *Missuses and mouldrunners*.

[153] Whipp, 'Women and the social organisation', pp. 108–9.

[154] Whipp, 'Women and the social organisation', pp. 111–14.

restimulated in other branches of industry during the last third of the nineteenth century as a consequence of the series of regulatory Acts from the mid-1860s onwards, associated with the Nine Hours campaign, which culminated in the Factory and Workshops Consolidation Act of 1878.[155] As Sonya Rose has comprehensively demonstrated, the legislation of the 1870s had the unintended consequences of reinvigorating low-wage homeworking among the wives of the labouring poor, directly due to the thoroughgoing patriarchal assumptions on which the protective legislation was premised.[156] Such patriarchal policies had, by then, a long history in the country's social legislation, dating back to the Factory Acts of the 1830s and, especially, the 1834 New Poor Law, as Pat Thane long ago pointed out.[157] Although challenged by some, it was this perspective which was reasserted and which informed the position taken up both by employers and trade unionists and government health officials during the 1870s debates generated by the Nine Hours campaign and the associated factory and workshops legislation.

Ignoring the potential benefits to poor families of a higher family income through higher maternal earnings, concern was instead focused in these debates, which framed the legislation of the 1870s, on the possible child health implications of a mother's absence from the home by going out to work.[158] The justifying premise from the trade union side was that in competing for work with men, women were undermining their own husbands' wage-levels. (The problem, of course, for poor families was that they needed the higher incomes immediately and could not afford to wait for females' withholding of their labour to lead eventually to the hoped-for rise in the marginal rates of pay for unskilled male labour.) This negative attitude towards working mothers was still predominant among employers, working-class leaders and health officials themselves at the beginning of the next century. Only at that time did it at last begin to be accepted that careful research, of the sort conducted in Birmingham by Dr Jessie Duncan and Dr John Robertson (see pp. 244–5), showed that for poor families the much-needed health gains of higher family income could outweigh whatever costs were incurred in lost maternal time in the home.

By putting their work out to private households after the 1870s, employers could continue to avoid the costs involved in complying with the stricter regulations on working conditions in designated factories and workshops. They reaped the additional economic advantage of being able to pay as little as they could get away with, to a fragmented workforce of isolated outworkers. Hence, in

155 Pennington and Westover *A hidden workforce*; Rose, *Limited livelihoods*, p. 74.

156 Rose, *Limited livelihoods*, pp. 53–74, 90–9.

157 Thane, 'Women and the Poor Law'.

158 Charles Roberts's original involvement in the anthropometric research reported in detail in chapter 3, above, came about as a result of his participation in the government research under J. H. Bridges generated by these debates. As an individual official intimately involved in the creation of this legislation, his social evolutionary views (cited on pp. 143–5) provide particularly graphic testimony to the patriarchal perspective, with which employment issues were addressed at this time.

this period the subcontracted homeworker was once more on the increase in certain non-mechanised, labour-intensive branches of manufacturing, the notorious sweated trades. This did not begin to come under effective regulation until the trade boards were first established by the young Winston Churchill in 1909, the first four of which set minimum wages for chain making in the Black Country, and for cardboard-box, cheap clothing and lacemaking and finishing in London's East End.

There are no truly reliable estimates of the extent of such homeworking in this period because employers only began reluctantly and patchily to keep lists of their outworkers after the 1901 Factory and Workshop Act; while many mothers and children did not acknowledge their homework when census returns were filled out. Earlier historians have emphasised a decline in homeworking during the later nineteenth century.[159] But Schmeichen's research indicates that in London outworking was actually on the increase until 1911; and in view of the recent work of other historians such as Pennington and Westover, and Sonya Rose, this may be more generally true of the period after the 1870s Factory and Workshops Acts than has previously been suspected.[160] If Schmeichen is right that approximately one third to one half of outworkers went unreported in the census, then this would imply that as late as 1911 there were about 500,000 females above age 10 engaged in homeworking in England and Wales, which would have represented 10% of the entire female workforce above age 10.[161]

This is extremely significant for analysis of the socially differentiated patterns in fertility recorded in the occupational evidence in 1911. The availability of such homework encouraged the poorest working-class families to continue with their early marriage and high-fertility practices as a viable method of apparently maximising income (within the very limited opportunities that such families perceived as open to them). It was predominantly those women who were in the most difficult financial positions who took on outwork, often having to enrol their children, too, because of the extortionately low piece-rates offered by the putters-out. As Sonya Rose's detailed research has shown, women working at home as lace clippers in Nottinghamshire were likely to be under age 35 with small children, whereas once their children were older they tended to return to the local factories for the much higher wages available there.[162]

Similarly in London's East End many of those involved in the cheap clothing sweated trades were the wives and children of construction and dock labourers, whose low and irregular earnings were famously documented in Charles Booth's survey.[163] For these women the paltry sums they could earn were desperately

[159] Bythell, *The sweated trades*; Treble, *Urban poverty*.

[160] Harris, *Private lives*, p. 67, points out that a major facilitator of rising home-working in this period in the clothing industry was the arrival of the cheap domestic sewing-machine, a kind of latterday loom.

[161] Schmeichen, *Sweated industries*, Appendix A. Estmated figures on female workforce from Census 1911, Volume X, Table 3. [162] Rose, *Limited livelihoods*, pp. 85–90.

[163] Rose, *Limited livelihoods*, pp. 82–3.

needed, while homeworking had the vital advantage that it could be fitted in around the demands of childcare or even temporarily dropped altogether if necessary. It also enabled them to avoid additional costs which would be incurred if they went out to work, such as infant feeds and payment for childminding.

Thus, this would help to explain why high fertility characterised two such different types of working-class family in Britain at this time. First, among those social groups in which husbands' work was chronically inadequate or irregular, it had a clear positive rationale in terms of the family's survival strategy. This was because outwork for mothers and children, despite its extortionately low rates of pay, seemed a godsend if nothing better was on offer. The availability in many communities of such labour-intensive homeworking for mothers and children during the last quarter of the nineteenth century positively encouraged and facilitated large families and rapid childbearing among this group. Secondly, in the very different circumstances of the many coal-mining communities and centres of heavy industry, attention to the same kinds of consideration, emphasised by the heuristic framework of perceived relative childrearing costs, shows how they may also all have operated to sustain or even increase high marital fertility during the close of the Victorian period. For coal miners, iron and steel and engineering workers, such as ship platers and riveters, the period 1881–1911 was one of buoyant labour demand and exceptionally strongly rising real wages for male heads of household. According to Routh's careful analysis of the 1906 Board of Trade wage inquiry and other contemporary sources, these two categories of worker were among the most highly paid in the working classes, recording over twice the earnings of the lowest paid, who were primarily the agricultural labourers.[164] This would, if anything, have reduced the perceived relative costs of a large family for such workers, *ceteris paribus*, because a larger family did not imply less income per head if the breadwinner's real wages were rising over time. Hence, it is these two groups of proletarian occupations, the extremely high paid and the chronically low paid, which are predominantly found at the bottom of Figure 7.1.

These two examples show that differentially high fertility of certain occupational categories during this period, when others alongside them were experiencing falling fertility, is not necessarily to be explained simply by their relative ignorance or imperviousness to those stimuli which were apparently influencing couples in other communities to adopt forms of birth control. Once the economic circumstances of different types of family and community are more fully understood, the positive rationale behind high fertility becomes apparent. One of the great fallacies underlying the myth of the single unitary 'fertility decline' is that all in society are conceived as moving in the same direction, though at different speeds. But not all sections of the population were propelled in the same broad direction at this time,

164 Routh, *Occupation and pay*, table on pp. 86–7 shows average earnings for coalface workers in 1906 at £112 per annum with ship platers and riveters at £128; tables on pp. 91–2 show agricultural labourers earning an average of just £48 in 1906.

as these two cases illustrate. Household strategies entailing high fertility are much more satisfactorily explained, with reference to the heuristic framework of perceived relative childrearing costs, in terms of the positive reasons – the perceived childrearing benefits – whereby some social groups found high fertility to be in their interests, rather than through a neo-evolutionary and implicitly teleological explanation which merely envisages differentially high fertility as an historical 'survival' from an earlier world.

There is, finally, one other distinctive high-fertility group which has been little discussed so far and to which the present considerations may have some relevance. These are the various categories of agricultural workers. It is this group, above all, which has always appeared to support most obviously the notion of high fertility as a 'survival' of 'natural fertility' in those dwindling rural backwaters supposedly untouched by 'modernisation'. However, with the concept of natural fertility itself disintegrated (as discussed in the opening section of the previous chapter) and with the evidence noted in chapter 8 (pp. 417–20), that low-level fertility regulation may have been the norm in pre-industrial agrarian British society, there is a more obvious need for positive reasons to explain high fertility among rural workers in this period. It may be that a version of the homeworking argument has some application here, too.

The ideology that excluded women from unions and argued that they should be out of the fields and 'minding their houses' was as prominent from the 1870s in Joseph Arch's Agricultural Labourers' Union as it was elsewhere in the labour movement.[165] A similar ideology predominated among paternalist landholders in those large stretches of the countryside, including most of the north, where agricultural trade unionism was a dead letter. Nevertheless, throughout the many different agricultural régimes of the country women and wives continued to play a vital, if subsidiary and low-paid, labouring role, even if this was not everywhere as clearly manifested as in the Northumberland 'bondager' system, whereby every hired male was expected to provide a female worker alongside himself.[166] It may be, therefore, that in this notoriously low-paid sector of the economy, early marriage and high fertility made economic sense for reasons similar to those analysed above for homeworking mothers and their low-paid husbands. For those on such low incomes, the tiny amounts of supplementary income that could be gained from work done by wives and children in and around the cottage home and garden and in the busy seasons of the year might well seem all to the good and quite vital to the family's livelihood, justifying as large a family of helpers as possible.[167]

This phenomenon of the wives of the very poor working at home as outworkers may, then, provide an extremely important part of the explanation for some of the

165 Howkins, *Reshaping rural England*, p. 189.

166 Howkins, *Reshaping rural England*, p. 50; see also pp. 101–8, 204–5.

167 See the 1912 survey of rural poverty: Rowntree and Kendall, *How the labourer lives.*

occupational fertility differentials as recorded in the 1911 census because of its implications for the central variable of perceived relative costs of childrearing. As the following section will show, it may also offer an important general guide for interpretation of the fertility differentials which were recorded among *female* occupational categories in 1911, also using information which can be gleaned from the published tables of the 1911 census.

Fertility and married female employment

Table 37 of the *Fertility of Marriage Report* (Part 2) gives details for sixty-six female occupational categories of children everborn, cross-classified by the same age at marriage and duration of marriage subdivisions as for the male occupations in Table 30.[168] Where these occupations related to the same title as a male occupation, that title and ID number were retained. In thirty-one cases, there was no equivalent occupation listed in the male occupational fertility tables and so new titles and ID numbers (running from 210 to 240 inclusive) were allocated.

The sixty-six occupations used in the ensuing analysis in fact represent 87.37% of the 680,191 married women enumerated as in employment at the 1911 census.[169] However, despite this impressive figure it is important to be clear that those appearing in this table still represent a much-restricted subset of all working women. Paid employment was the norm for unmarried women: 69.61% of all unmarried women over age 15 (3,557,039 individuals) and 43.1% of all widows (411,011 persons) were recorded in the census as in employment; but working wives comprised only 10.25% of all married women enumerated in 1911.[170] On average an enumerated female occupation was composed of 76.6% unmarried women, 8.8% widowed women and 14.6% married women.[171]

Across different industrial sectors and in certain specific occupations, the proportionate distribution of married women varied quite substantially. Most notably in Order V (Commercial Occupations) they formed only 2.6% of the female total; in the quantitatively most important single occupation within that Order there were 114,943 female 'Commercial and business clerks' (ID 45) over age 15, but only 1.5% were married.[172] In Order III (Professional and Subordinate

168 There are in fact seventy occupational subdivisions in Table 37 but four of these were not used in the ensuing analysis here because they were superfluous conglomerates, relating to the textiles and retailing industry, combining together individual occupations which were also tabulated separately in Table 37 among the other sixty-six occupations.

169 Census 1911, Volume X, Table 8.

170 Census 1911, Volume X, Table 8. Married women comprised one half (50.06%) of all women over 15 years old in 1911 (of the remainder, 39.53% were unmarried and 10.41% were widows). Thus, instead of forming their proportionate one half of the enumerated workforce, married women comprised only one seventh (14.6%) of the female workforce aged over 15.

171 Census 1911, Volume X, Table 8: percentages of the 4,648,241 women engaged in occupations in Orders I–XXII, who were above age 15 in 1911.

172 Census 1911, Volume X, Table 8.

Occupations) 11.4% of employed women were married; but in the quantitatively most significant single occupation, 'Schoolmistresses, teachers' (ID 22), which contained a total of 182,945 women workers, only 6.3% were married.[173] Conversely, married women were over-represented in two other sectors employing relatively large numbers of women. Of the 683,781 employed females above age 15 in Order XVIII (Textile Fabrics), 22.6% were married; and in Order XX (Food, Tobacco and Lodging) 30.1% of the 466,872 employed females were married.[174]

Hence, in giving the figure for the number of *married* females (of all ages) recorded in each of the sixty-six occupational categories in 1911, the information in the 'Size' column in Appendix G does not necessarily reflect at all accurately the relative importance of each occupation as an overall employer of female labour. Married women who worked in the paid labour market were an unusual and selected subset of all employed women and also of all married women. Furthermore, the sources and rigour of these selective forces varied enormously in different industries and in different communities. As a result great caution is called for in interpreting this data. In particular, there is a very strong likelihood that women who continued to work after marriage were able to do so because of low fertility.[175] This could be because they were deliberately restricting their fertility, but it may also represent the involuntary selection effects of infertile couples or postpartum sterility. For these reasons, consideration of this female occupational fertility data has been delayed to this late stage and given only a supplementary role in this study. While the subject could hardly be more important and interesting, the nature of the statistical evidence available from the 1911 census is such that only a limited range of inferences can safely be drawn from it. This judgement is all the more compelling if consideration is given to the inadequacies of the initial recording by enumerators of female paid occupations because of the frequently informal or part-time nature of their employment, and the compounding problems of the changing classification policies operated by the census officials.[176] In short, the census has serious limitations as a source for the study of female employment at this time, although there is a paucity of alternatives for large-scale analysis.[177]

173 Census 1911, Volume X, Table 8.

174 Census 1911, Volume X, Table 8. Of the 411,011 widows in employment, 173,736 (42.2%) were found in Order IV (Domestic offices or services): about one half listed as domestic indoor servants and the other half working as charwomen or laundry workers. A further 73,710 (17.8%) were in Order XX (Food, tobacco, lodging): over one half of these being proprietors of lodging and boarding houses or inns and hotels. Another 49,626 (12%) were in Order XIX (Dress), almost half of whom were dressmakers. Most of the remainder were distributed between Orders XVIII (Textiles), III (Professional and subordinate services) and VII (Agriculture).

175 For an empirical demonstration of this among textile workers, see Garrett and Reid, 'Satanic mills, pleasant lands'.

176 On sources of probable underenumeration with regard to female employments and on changing classification policies, see Higgs, 'Women, occupations and work' (n. 105, above); and chapter 2, p. 123. For a specific example of the latter effect on the number of female shopkeepers recorded in the census, see above n. 146.

177 For the argument that the census figures on female employment do, for all their problems, have

In Appendix G the sixty-six female occupations are rank ordered according to the incomplete fertility level recorded for those married at age 20–4 after five to ten years of marriage (AM2/01–5). As well as 'Size', the additional columns in Appendix G give the fertility level and ranking for those married at 25–9 (AM3/01–5 and RANK/AM3, respectively). For the thirty-five female occupations which have male equivalents in Table 30, the two columns PC2/01–5 and PC3/01–5 show the female occupational fertility value as a percentage of the male value for the same occupational title.

The first and most obvious conclusion which can be drawn from Appendix G is that the incomplete fertility of couples with enumerated working wives was in general markedly lower than was recorded among the generality of male occupations; and in some cases fertility was extremely low for this period.[178] All but a dozen female occupations record a value for AM2/01–5 lower than fully one half of the 195 male occupations. If, therefore, the previous section has established that the spacing of births from early on in marriage was the chief method of family planning and was a widespread practice among married couples before the Great War, this evidence shows that such spacing was practised most rigorously among that relatively small minority of couples where a wife was enumerated as in employment. This seems to have been true across all social classes and groups, from 'private means' to hawkers and costermongers.

This general observation is strongly confirmed by the percentage figures in the last two columns of Appendix G, which show that where a wife was in paid work the average number of children born over the first 7.5 years of marriage was only 60–95% of the number born to couples where the husband was recorded as ostensibly employed in the same kind of work. Of course, the degree to which these percentages represent comparisons of like with like should not be overemphasised. In many cases women with the same job title were performing different jobs, certainly receiving less pay, and almost invariably accorded less status than the male equivalents. Nevertheless while taking this into account there are still several cases where a comparison across the gendered labour market can be illuminating, especially where the character of the occupation is well defined (even though it may have had somewhat distinct meanings for each of the sexes). Teachers (22), private means (204), and wool weavers (162) are all quantitatively important married female categories where male occupations of the same title have already been shown to have recorded very low fertility over these first years of marriage. Yet couples where women had married at 20–4 and were employed in these occupations had evidently restricted their fertility to an even greater extent,

considerable value for the historian, and a study which puts them to good use, see Jordan, 'Female unemployment in England and Wales 1851–1911'.

[178] The lowest-fertility male occupation is that of 'actors' (ID 29) with a value of 1.3995 (Appendix E); but there is little demographic value in the figures for this occupation because of the peripatetic and irregular lifestyle involved. The second lowest fertility male occupation is that of 'army officers' (ID 9) with a value of 1.5758; seven of the female occupations record a lower value than this.

having had on average little more than a single birth over the first seven and a half years of marriage.

There is also a significant observation to be made on the difference between male and female occupations in the extent to which those couples where the wife was aged 25–9 at marriage were restricting their fertility *more* over the first five to ten years than those marrying at 20–4. Among the male occupations there was a fairly constant relationship across the whole dataset of 195 occupations whereby the figure for average number of children born to those marrying at 25–9 was 85–90% of the figure for an occupation holding the same rank position among those marrying women aged 20–4. However, the divergence between the two age at marriage subsets among the set of female occupations was still more marked, with the incomplete fertility of the older-marrying working wives averaging only 70–80% of that of those marrying at 20–4.[179] Women who married late and continued in paid work were, with their partners, among the most rigorous birth controllers in the population.

Most of the female occupations at the bottom of Appendix G, unusually exhibiting relatively high incomplete fertility, are occupations pursued either at home or on an irregular and almost casual basis (which would therefore not interfere with childrearing) by wives of the poor. Several of these contain very high proportions of homeworkers, including the lace workers investigated by Sonya Rose, who stand out among all the categories of textiles workers with uniquely high fertility. Indeed, the lace industry is very similar to the earthenware industry in its socio-demographic features. Both are exceptions to the general rule that industries which generate communities with relatively high proportions of females in paid work exhibit the lowest fertility among the working classes. In both cases, more detailed research shows that this was because the detailed context in which female participation took place in each of these two cases was in fact conducive (for different reasons) to high fertility, rather than creating direct opportunity costs in childrearing. This is further confirmed in Appendix G by the unusual feature of these two occupations: that the fertility rates of couples with working wives in these two industries are every bit as high as the rates generated by the male occupational groupings.

It is, however, true that certain other female occupational categories also show very high proportions of homeworkers and yet return relatively low fertility. Milliners and tobacconists are good examples of this. However, these occupations' working environments were almost the antithesis of homeworking lace makers, glove makers or cardboard box makers. This can be demonstrated by reference to the census tabulations of the information that is available regarding the proportions of these married women who were own account workers or employers in their own right, as opposed to mere outworking employees. In lace manufacture, of

[179] The single outstanding exception to this, 'Private means' (ID 204), has already been mentioned above, p. 475.

6,265 married female workers, 3,199 worked at home, of which only 261 identified themselves as either employers or working on their own account.[180] By comparison, of 3,501 married female milliners, 1,927 worked at home and 1,486 of these did so as employers or on their own account.[181] This indicates that whereas home working for lace-working wives was a correlate of poverty and dependence as outworkers, many married milliners worked at home on their own terms, or even as employers. These were businesswomen in an entirely different market position and probably enjoying a situation of relative economic equality *vis-à-vis* their husbands. For them, too rapid childbearing would disrupt their relatively lucrative economic activities. Married, homeworking lace workers and those in the sweated trades, such as cardboard box makers, by contrast endured a predicament of equality of poverty with their husbands, which, it has been suggested, was positively conducive to high fertility.

These examples illustrate that the extent and ways in which working-class women and wives participated, along with their husbands, in earning the family's income varied across a spectrum of possible arrangements. It is vitally necessary to understand the meaning and significance of wives' participation to the couples concerned in these different contexts before the full implications for fertility behaviour can be assessed. In these terms a set of distinct ideal types of spouse and gender relations, with respect to female labour market participation, can be discerned from the foregoing discussion.

In the first type there was relatively full-scale participation by wives in the formal wage economy of factories and workshops exclusively outside the home in communities in which this was deemed thoroughly acceptable, was sanctioned in community norms and was not considered to impugn in any way the respectability of the family. This corresponds to the mill town experience typical of Lancashire and West Yorkshire with its pronounced fertility-regulating implications. But there were also significant variants on this. It was considered perfectly acceptable for wives to work in the Potteries, without any perceptible fertility-diminishing effects, for the reasons discussed above.

The high-fertility families of pit villages were the paradigm of a second type, in which female participation in the formal labour market was taboo and a slur on a man's reputation in the community and in which there was very little scope in any case for such female participation. In a third type the male household head's wages were not sufficient to maintain his family, as was the case in the textiles towns and the Potteries, but wider community support for the acceptability of a wife going out to work was lacking. Hence female participation, though vital for the family's welfare, was viewed negatively by the two spouses themselves in accordance with their community's norms, and was undertaken at some cost to the husband's pride and to the family's status in their neighbourhood. In a fourth

[180] Census 1911, Volume X, Table 8. [181] Census 1911, Volume X, Table 8.

and a fifth type, the same conditions might apply as in the third type but the wife's participation would be in the form of homeworking from putting-out employers, either because formal wage-work was not available (type four) or as a choice to avoid the shame of being seen to have to go out to work in public (type five). In a sixth ideal type, a wife's participation might be in the form of running her own shop or small business which, depending on its scale and trade, might add to or detract from the family's social position. Furthermore, if an independent employer, such as in the example of the milliner or tobacconist discussed above, this might be felt by her husband to augment or to threaten his own status. A seventh important type occurred where husband and wife were self-employed in business together, as in many small shopkeeping concerns. This was an arrangement which generally carried considerable prestige for the family and was the dream of many working-class couples, although chronic risks of bankruptcy and bad debts, of course, had to be reckoned with. Finally, an eighth type occurred where a wife's status and income as an employee was clearly more important than her husband's, such as where a female teacher or clerk might be married to a labourer. However, because of employers' voluntary but assiduous operation of the marriage bar, these cases were probably rather rare, as is confirmed by the relatively small numbers of married women returned within these occupations at the 1911 census.

As can be seen from consideration of these eight types, all of which existed in varying numbers in different places, the implications of female employment – in terms of perceived relative childrearing costs – could vary substantially. So, too could its probable impact upon the bargaining positions of the two spouses and their capacity to co-operate in sexual and reproductive matters. In those contexts, such as in types two to five and eight, where a wife's income-earning activities tended to challenge the self-respect of husbands, this may have tended to complicate negotiations between spouses, whether explicit or implicit (i.e. articulated or not), over the intrinsically difficult issue (for this generation) of 'conjugal rights'. In these cases female employment might actually have impeded spouses' capacity to develop an effective birth-regulating response to their predicament, since it has been argued that in general the most effective techniques of limitation required full male co-operation (especially where abstinence was being attempted). Whereas, in the different contexts of types one, six and seven, the wife's joint participation in generating the family's income was probably not perceived as threatening to her husband. Instead, it was simply seen as an integral part of a wider set of practices in which the couple necessarily shared the responsibilities for the household's survival strategy, associated with a similar viewpoint as joint earners. This may then – on average – have been conducive to their viewing their sexual behaviour and family building from a similar standpoint.

These ideal-types are, of course, only heuristic devices to illustrate the nature of the work-related forces in the community affecting conjugal relations and they are not to be construed as blanket descriptions of different industries. For instance, although, as a result of husbands' absences, fishing communities the world over are similar in the extent to which they acknowledge and rely upon wives' relative autonomy in the home community and often on their earning roles, yet the recognised authority which women enjoy by virtue of this varies enormously. In a fine, penetrating study of the fishing industry in Britain by Paul Thompson, he has shown how specific historical changes in the conditions of work in different places within the same industry generated sharply divergent outcomes for conjugal relations.[182] Thompson was able to identify a precise historical episode in which the 'brutalisation' of gender and spouse relations occurred within the inshore fishing communities of North-east Scotland after the 1880s. By comparison the relatively egalitarian Shetlands communities, for instance, remained unaffected. This was traced by Thompson to the enforced proletarianisation of the independent fishermen boat-owners, who were reluctantly turned into dependent wage-earners on the new Aberdeen trawler fleets. In 1919 the employers successfully resisted, through the aggressive tactic of an eleven-week lockout, the trawlermen's attempts at least to establish a right to a twenty-four-hour leave between the long trips at sea.[183] The employers' response to the men's plight was simply to supply them with free whisky when they were at sea. Thompson concluded:

> It seems that family relationships are likely to be much more seriously affected when working conditions are not only especially bitter and far more distant from home, but the men sense the degree of their own exploitation by merchants or employers. Such experiences may harden them and drive them towards self-indulgence and assertion of their own male authority when they return home.[184]

In the Aberdeen trawling communities, the sad outcome of this development was a marked deterioration in relations between spouses. As the typology indicates, therefore, the culturally and historically refracted attitude towards work, as well as the conditions of work, were important in influencing the quality of conjugal relations in different parts of the country.

Mike Savage's work has been particularly stimulating in suggesting an approach to the analysis of these differences in the historical development of gender relations, which illuminates their systematic relationship with local politics and industrial relations practices. Savage has developed a typology of three different collectivist political strategies of working-class political behaviour each aimed at reducing or removing the fundamental problem of income insecurity: detaching the rate of remuneration from the laws of the market; ensuring job security; or detaching essential consumption services, such as housing costs, health costs, domestic services, perhaps even food costs, from the laws of the market.[185] According to Savage's terminology, these correspond, respectively, to an economistic, a mutualist and a statist political strategy. In the

[182] Thompson, 'Women in the fishing', p. 3.
[183] Thompson, 'Women in the fishing', p. 23.
[184] Thompson, 'Women in the fishing', p. 22.
[185] Savage, *The dynamics*, p. 15.

first strategy, trade unions mobilise the power of collective bargaining to enforce non-market wage-rates upon employers. In the second, workers form their own co-operative businesses guaranteeing employees their livelihoods. In the third, they campaign for the agencies of the local or central state to provide essential household services as of right.

Alongside the genuinely collectivist, egalitarian variant of each of these strategies, Savage argues that there is also a 'sectionalist' ('individualist' or 'patriarchal') version of each of these methods for abrogating the labour market, which results in the emancipation of only one set of workers at the expense of others; and historically, these have been the more usual kinds of strategy adopted. The most common strategy has been the sectional pursuit of their own enhanced wage-levels by unionised, skilled or supervisory adult males, at the expense of employment opportunities for women and junior males. This enabled male trade unionists to 'capture' adult female labour for the free (non-market) provision of necessary domestic services for their households.[186] Savage has demonstrated empirically that where this patriarchal strategy developed most strongly, such as in the South Wales coal-mining industry, the Barrow-in-Furness shipbuilding industry or the steel and cutlery town of Sheffield, there was only weak support from working-class organisations for the provision by municipal or central government of domestic welfare and health services.[187] Men in these communities perceived the collective provision on the rates of services which they received for free from their wives and daughters as financially burdensome and unnecessary, while the women tended to resent an encroachment on their own domestic roles, the sources of their pride and identity.

However, Savage points out that on the basis of this kind of evidence some historians have mistakenly written of a general working-class hostility to the state and even to welfare provision. He shows that there was a different outcome in those – admittedly fewer – communities, such as most of the weaving towns of north-east Lancashire or wool towns such as Huddersfield, where male and female participation and wage-rates were more equal.[188] Huddersfield, for instance, was a major pioneer of infant welfare schemes.[189] The patriarchal, sectionalist economistic strategy had never made sense here because male and

[186] This was a point which Jane Humphries also made with reference to the earlier nineteenth century: Humphries, 'Class struggle and the persistence'; Humphries, 'Protective legislation'; Humphries and Rubery, 'The reconstitution of the supply side'.

[187] Savage *The dynamics*, pp. 52–3.

[188] There has generally been more detailed research published on Lancashire of a form which can helpfully be matched up with this study's fertility preoccupations. But certainly there is evidence of similar variation within the West Yorkshire wool industry. Joanna Bornat, for instance, has noted that larger proportions of women were employed in the low-value shoddy industry of Batley and Dewsbury as well as in Huddersfield, where the wage-differential between men and women was only 10–15%. Whereas in Bradford, for instance, relatively more men were employed and the male rates of pay were significantly higher. Bornat, 'Lost leaders', p. 210.

[189] Parton, 'The infant welfare movement'.

female labour market participation had always been much more equal as had wage-rates.[190] As a result males had more of a direct interest in the collective provision of services, whose domestic burdens they shared with their wives. Correspondingly, women's status did not depend solely on their domestic roles and so they did not feel threatened but assisted by collective provision. Savage is able to show that much stronger collectivist versions of mutualist and statist political strategies developed here than in Preston, including popular support for welfare measures and extending even to early support in the interwar period for such radical, full statist measures as nationalisation of the means of production.[191] Thus, politically mediated gender relations – so important an influence on fertility strategies – varied locally in complex but, ultimately, discernible ways; they are something which would repay future research.

Savage has particularly identified the question of control over mode of recruitment and training as a key issue in determining the divergences in gendered labour markets between different towns. Some employers were content to recruit informally through relying on their employees' contacts, as in Preston, Blackburn and Burnley. By contrast the big employers in Bolton and Ashton were much more systematically interventionist and paternalist in personally overseeing the selection and, indeed, socialisation of their workforce. The 'Bolton model' recruited through the employer-subsidised institutions of school and church, and required a girl's name to be put forward as prospective employee at the age of 13. But even within the first category of employee self-recruitment, there were further differences, highly significant for our concerns with the relationship between fertility behaviour and gender relations. In Preston the more highly paid adult male overlookers were exclusively entrusted with recruitment. Whereas in Blackburn and Burnley, where there was a much nearer equality of pay between the sexes, general family contacts via either sex were the recognised mode of recommendation and recruitment. These differences partly stemmed from the fact that the goods produced in Preston were a higher quality, high-value product. Employers were therefore more anxious to establish some hierarchy of responsible accountability among their workers to prevent expensive mistakes. As a result low unit cost was not the only criterion applied to labour recruitment in Preston, as employers looked to mature male heads of families, like themselves, to take on these responsibilities. It was this which enabled the adult males to monopolise the higher paid supervisory functions and to arrogate to themselves exclusive control over recruitment. They thereby became respected figures in the local community, whose grace and favour was to be cultivated.

Important socio-cultural and fertility consequences flowed from these highly localised differences between the labour market practices of firms and sub-branches of the industry. For instance, according to contemporary and oral history

190 On wage-rates in Huddersfield, see Joanna Bornat's research, cited in n. 188.

191 Savage *The dynamics*, pp. 53–4.

testimony Burnley was a community of much greater genuine gender and spouse equality than Preston, in terms both of the patterns of domestic responsibilities and the 'public' sphere of a high degree of political self-organisation.[192] In Preston the male working-class overlookers actually themselves discouraged unionisation of the weaving workforce, fearing this would lead to loss of their own privileged positions; they were also reluctant to recruit other males because they were possible future competitors for their own jobs and so they preferred to take on their own and their friends' daughters and wives.[193] Unlike many of the other, more gender-egalitarian textile towns of Lancashire, the male working class in Preston were initially opposed to the collective provision of welfare and health services.[194] For a Lancashire textiles town Preston was, therefore, rather unusual, with its aggressively patriarchal norms of authority and control among a workforce that nevertheless contained many females as in all other mill towns. In this context, its anomalous fertility perhaps becomes more understandable. In his official *Report* on the 1911 census, Stevenson singled out Preston as an exception among all the Lancashire textiles towns in recording fertility higher than the national average, even. This was something which Stevenson was unable at that time to explain. But it becomes more understandable from within the perceived relative childrearing costs approach, which directs attention towards investigating the local configuration of gender relations, which is in turn related to authority and recruitment in the labour market.[195]

The eight ideal types of spouse relations, outlined above, are illustrative and certainly do not exhaust the range of possible permutations. As the cases of the female workers in the Potteries and the exceptional textiles workers in Preston both demonstrate, further detailed local research is necessary to elucidate precisely the full complexities of the relationship between female labour market participation, community gender relations and fertility behaviour. But the most penetrating research available so far, including that which relates to these two unusual cases, gives some grounds for confidence that the general methodological approach advocated here is a helpful one for understanding this relationship and for analysing the historical variability of fertility behaviour. This approach has

192 Savage, 'Women and work', p. 211.

193 Savage, 'Women and work', p. 213; Savage, *The dynamics*, pp. 78–80.

194 Savage, *The dynamics*, chs. 4–5.

195 *FMR* Pt 2, p. cxxxv. Note that although Preston had a significant community of Irish Roman Catholics, this would not seem to be a convincing explanation for its high fertility since it was by no means alone in this feature among the Lancashire textiles towns. For comparative figures on the Catholic, Irish presence in various towns see, for instance, Joyce, *Work, society and politics*, pp. 251–2; Savage, *The dynamics*, pp. 110–12; and Dennis, *English industrial cities*, especially Table 2.3, which shows Preston with no greater proportions of Irish-born in 1851 or in 1901 than either Bolton or Stockport. Henry Pelling noted that there was also a British Catholic presence in the Preston area and he also found that Preston exhibited a particular adherence to the Conservative party in its electoral behaviour throughout this period. However, in the latter characteristic, it was little different from Blackburn, which also had a substantial Catholic minority: Pelling, *Social geography*, pp. 260–2.

been derived by following through the interpretative implications of the heuristic framework of perceived relative childrearing costs and benefits in terms of different household survival strategies.

Indeed, if the foregoing analysis is broadly correct, then this would indicate one of the means by which the unusual labour market conditions of radically increased female participation rates during the First World War may well have provided an important 'learning experience' for several of those sections of the population which had not previously been particularly susceptible to the logic of family limitation. The Great War has been considered of possible importance in spreading the practice of family limitation because of the greater usage of prophylactics against venereal disease. In fact this association probably only increased the general unacceptability of condoms. However, it may well be that the war's greater significance was in drafting into the more highly paid waged workforce, outside the home, a large proportion of the nation's young, unmarried and poor, married women, who had not before been in a position to appreciate the scope for personal consumption which such relative economic independence conferred. They may therefore have gained, for the first time, a practical and personal appreciation of the consumer and leisure opportunity costs which repeated and uncontrolled childbearing entailed for them.[196] This may then have stiffened the resolve of this generation to reap the benefits of fewer confinements when their menfolk returned home.

Thus, the gender- and age-related (to be discussed more in the next section) characteristics of local labour markets, reflecting a long, negotiated history in each industry and town, were likely to have had a particularly powerful potential to influence fertility patterns in a working-class community, often compounded and reinforced by the character of its prevailing political organisations. These factors tended to exert a set of consistently mutually reinforcing influences upon perceptions of changing relative childrearing costs. They acted simultaneously both on the economics of childrearing and on the formative and gendered *perceptions* of relative costs and benefits determined by the relative bargaining positions and powers of husbands and wives.

The state, the community and normative change in childhood dependency and fertility

While the previous section has provided an explanation for the observed fertility differences between industries and occupations, it has only incompletely addressed the problem of explaining the widespread *change* in fertility behaviour experienced

[196] Certainly, two of the principal changes in working-class cultural practices which Elizabeth Roberts attributes to wartime experience, on the basis of her oral history evidence, were: that women increasingly joined their husbands in visiting the pub; and that all the family were making a habit of visiting the cinema. Roberts, *A woman's place*, pp. 122–3.

by most communities of the working population, beginning with the textiles workers in the 1860s and 1870s and ending with the colliery communities in the 1920s and 1930s. Only in the specific and unusual labour market conditions of the two major textiles regions has a genuinely sufficient historical explanation for the falling fertility already been given, in terms of the tightening restrictions on the child labour market from the 1870s.

In order to explain fertility change elsewhere, in terms of the perceived relative costs and benefits of childrearing, it is necessary to examine the course of certain politically engendered cultural and economic changes affecting working-class communities across the last quarter of the nineteenth and first quarter of the twentieth centuries. These relate to the processes whereby the dependent character of childhood and the social and legal burdens of parenting were redefined and extended among the working classes. If the previous section focused on the gendering of local labour markets, here the emphasis is more on change in its age-related aspects. Parental perceptions of relative childrearing costs were thereby altered because the meanings and the responsibilities of parenting and of childrearing altered. Associated with this, from the 1870s onwards the precarious budgetary balance of the vast mass of working-class families in most towns and industries all around the country was being forcefully disturbed. Household survival strategies were being repeatedly and cumulatively pushed in a direction which militated against placing any great reliance on significant contributions from young children, in terms either of income or domestic assistance.

On pp. 452–61 and 485–8 above, it was shown that during the 1830s and 1840s the working classes (like the middle classes but for distinct reasons) became committed to a strongly gendered ideology of familial and working roles. It was argued that in Britain this was a necessary condition, albeit of a general kind, for a widespread reduction in marital fertility to occur. This was because it altered men's involvement in childrearing, as argued on pp. 460–2, and was conducive to their more economic assessment of the meaning of having children. In the closing decades of the century this necessary condition was now transmuting into a sufficient explanation for falling marital fertility among the labouring poor through the catalyst of further political events, in the form of the state's insistence, albeit locally mediated and negotiated, on expanding and enforcing the dependent nature of childhood.

There were, broadly, three general forces involved. First, there was the province of ideological debate, in which the contested scientific study of child development in early educational psychology, eugenics and the public health field was vying with longer-established religious, humanist and economic perspectives to determine the collective definition of childhood and the character of the social institutions most appropriate for it.[197] Secondly (in fact historically predating this unfolding

[197] This was discussed in detail on pp. 204–16, above. For a detailed case study of the way in which the new scientifically produced knowledge of childhood was influencing the pedagogic approach of a religious community in this period, see Green, 'The religion of the child'.

debate and in many ways the source and stimulus of it), there was the brute fact of the juridical state offensive to extend elementary education, via the combined effects of the Factory and Education Acts.[198] These were enacted for a complicated and varying mix of political reasons, relating to the extension of the franchise and class anxieties over the electorate's character, the perceived need to emulate other states' initiatives in this direction, such as those of France and Prussia, the performance of the economy, and TUC pressure for restrictions in the labour market. But, whatever the motives, this evolving combination of legislative acts was having the direct effect of practically redefining childhood as a period of training and financial dependence, ultimately to age 14, by 1918.

Thirdly, in association with this, a combination of official and voluntary agencies were increasingly brought into existence endowed with quite novel powers for detailed interference in the working-class home in order to ensure that parental responsibilities were being discharged. Initially in mid-Victorian Britain these agencies had comprised a scattering of evangelical bible missionaries, organised mothers' meetings, lady health visitors and a few officials trying to enforce the early factory, industrial schools and health acts. However, as has been documented at length above (in chapters 4 and 5), by the beginning of the new century the imperial state's growing concern with the health and 'National Efficiency' of its citizenry had resulted in much increased efforts to advise and guide the lives of the poor, though generally stopping short of providing them with material assistance. Furthermore, it seems that this increasingly close supervision of the proletarian family inside its domestic space was gradually being received with an acknowledged legitimacy in many working-class communities (see below p. 520).

As Sheila Ryan Johansson has correctly pointed out the policies and provisions of the central and local state – or their absence – should always be considered as potential influences upon fertility behaviour, whether they were explicitly designed to be or not.[199] They provide an important set of institutional rules within which childrearing costs and benefits are defined and perceived. In Britain, of course, it is not necessary to look hard to find explicit policy designed to influence fertility. The (in)famous Poor Law (Amendment) Act of 1834 had been explicitly devised by the central state to rewrite the existing 'Speenhamland' rules governing the provision of welfare support in such a way as radically to discourage the labouring poor, who comprised the vast majority of the population, from early marriage, high fertility and premarital sex (by including punitive bastardy clauses). After the turn of the new century, despite the counter-arguments of eugenicists, the overall thrust of government policy was designed to preserve and enhance infant and child life (and survival chances) among the working class and so to raise the effective fertility of the imperial nation. Ironically, each of these phases of explicit state policy was, in fact, followed by trends in national fertility

[198] See pp. 204–7 on the way in which the health problems of the newly enrolled school children stimulated study and policy. [199] Johansson, '"Implicit" policy'.

and nuptiality which were the opposite to that sought. However, Johansson's point is that the consequences of all central and local government policies and activities, whether intended or not, are an important part of the explanation of fertility change and this is certainly demonstrable in late nineteenth-century Britain, where there was a great deal of government activity influencing the family. In Britain's case the role of voluntary and charity associations must also be acknowledged as a third agency, of roughly equivalent importance to local government institutions throughout much of the nineteenth century, again because of the merely supervisory and delegatory role accorded to the central state and its officials, a political legacy of the Glorious Revolution.[200]

From the edicts of the central state and from the agencies of local government there was a relentlessly and progressively increasing pressure upon parents and employers to ensure that children under the minimum school-leaving age were in full-time education and that they were therefore ineligible for any significant form of income earning and also less available for domestic chores. After decades of parliamentary hesitation, the Forster Education Act of 1870 finally laid down the principle that all should receive and pay for elementary education, subject to the remission of fees for poor parents.[201] However, it was not till the end of the following decade that this principle was made more truly effective: the Sandon Act (1876) created an enforcing machinery of school attendance committees and the Mundella Act (1880) ensured that the relevant local authorities were actually *compelled* to pass the bye-laws necessary to make such elementary education a universal reality. The national minimum age at which children could be exempted from school attendance on passing the highest grade exam, set at age 10 in 1876, was raised to 11 in 1890 and to 12 in 1899 (and finally to 14 by the Fisher Act of 1918).[202]

200 Dyson, *The state tradition*, pp. 39–40. The fact that Britain's central state ruled through delegation did not, of course, mean that it was weak. Indeed, the consensual nature of its power had quite the contrary effects, as John Brewer has shown for the eighteenth century: *The sinews of power*.

201 The history of a wary Parliament's insistence on national elementary educational provision had begun with the first state grants for education in 1833 and with the educational clauses of the early Factory Acts. Thereafter it remained bogged down for a quarter of a century in the interminable wrangling between Anglican and nonconformist denominations, jealous to protect their vested financial and pedagogic interests in the approximately 20,000 voluntary schools which they ran. The 1870 Forster Act was administratively and financially a compromise to placate these feuding religious factions. Not till the Balfour Education Act of 1902 was the religious influence formally removed, with the creation of a comprehensive national network of entirely secular local education authorities (tied to the existing set of elected county and county borough councils), with powerful co-ordinating responsibilities for the provision of virtually all forms of education in their area. See Laqueur, *Religion and respectability*; Sutherland, *Policy-making*; Simon, *Education and the labour movement*; also Pelling, *Social geography*, *passim*, for the importance of the politics of education at the constituency level in influencing voting patterns throughout the period 1870–1914.

202 From 1906 onwards the Board of Education also revised the minimum initial period of dependency at home upwards to age 5 before school could be started, age 3 having been the previous permitted practice: Thane, *The foundations*, p. 76. For further details on the tortuous pre-history, from the 1860s, of fixing the statutory age for starting school at 5, see Szreter, 'The origins of full-time compulsory education'.

It was not until the early and mid-1890s, with gradual implementation of the Assisted Education Act of 1891, that fees finally disappeared, so that elementary education at last became genuinely universal and free.[203] Thus, throughout the last quarter of the century most working-class parents were finding themselves faced with an increasingly unavoidable set of educational expenses and inconveniences in having children.[204] Although many working-class parents were in favour of educating their children to at least some extent whenever possible, it was the inflexibility and universality of the demands on all their children's time all of the time which was a new burden.[205] The fact that most localities found that they needed to create and expand a well-worked administrative machinery of officers and visitors for the enforcement of school attendance, the payment of fees and arrears, and the organisation of remittances for the needy, unequivocally demonstrates that the nation's compulsory education programme was, indeed, registering an unwanted impact upon the precarious budgetary balance of many working-class families.[206] Through these officials' unceasing efforts, regular attendance at elementary school among the working classes had been slowly pushed up from 68% in 1870 to 82% by 1895.[207]

After the early 1890s the ignominy of repeated appearances at tribunals for the remission or non-payment of fees was no longer part of the working-class experience of schooling their children. But this by no means meant that poor working-class families were now left to their own devices. While school pence disappeared, the house visitations of the school attendance officers continued; and were accompanied by a steadily accumulating range of other policing interventions in the working-class home and community.[208] Of course, the streets had long been

203 Sutherland, *Policy-making*, chs. 10–11.

204 There was certainly much local variation in this: different local school boards interpreted their important powers to remit school fees and to harass parents for arrears quite differently; local magistrates were more or less lenient in excusing non-attendance on grounds of poverty; and schools themselves often turned a blind eye at regular non-attendance by an older girl if it was known she was needed at home. Lewis, 'Parents, school fees', p. 308, notes, for instance, that in 1884 the London School Board was remitting only 4–5% of fees at a time when the Manchester Board was remitting 12%. Marsden, *Unequal educational provision*, provides the most general account of the continuing local variation in the early period of 'universal education' after 1870. On toleration of older daughters' absences for domestic duties, see Davin, *Little women*, ch. 10; also Booth, *Life and labour* ser. 1, vol. III, p. 230. Also, see above, ch. 4, n. 117.

205 For the latest attempt to assess rigorously the influence of the state's educational legislation, as against voluntary participation, on the nation's rising literacy rates, see Mitch, *The rise of popular literacy*, who judiciously (given the difficulties of the statistical evidence) comes to an open-ended conclusion. On the earlier nineteenth-century history of autonomous working-class educational provision, see Gardner, *The lost elementary schools*.

206 For documented proof of this, see Belfiore, (unpublished DPhil thesis). On the establishment of attendance committees and officers under the Sandon (1876) and Mundella (1880) Education Acts, see Sutherland, *Policy-making*, chs. 4–5. The only full, published historical account of the operation of the attendance enforcement system is that for London by D. Rubinstein: *School attendance*; see also Lewis, 'Parents, school fees'.

207 Sutherland, 'Education', p. 145.

208 Such was the extensive nature of systematic contact between the network of school attendance officers and the families of the working classes whom they chivvied and cajoled, that when Charles Booth conducted his famous street survey of London in the late 1880s it was to these officers that he

subjected to an increasingly effective surveillance by the steadily learning provincial police forces, formed by the County Constabulary Act of 1839 and the County Borough Police Act of 1856.[209] But it was the working-class home itself which became more and more the target of attention during the last quarter of the century.

Housing and overcrowding inspections were more frequent, sanctioned under a range of statutory and bye-law regulations. Preventive health laws justified the destructive fumigation of rooms, clothes and belongings, the quarantining of individuals and sometimes finally resulted in the demolition of whole courts and neighbourhoods.[210] By the 1900s housing, sanitary and nuisance inspectors working under the local MOH, had been joined by female Health Visitors, who visited homes following up tip-offs from teachers (or as the result of formal school medical inspections operated by some local authorities in advance of the state-funded system inaugurated in 1907 by the Progressive Liberal administration). Compulsory schooling for the poor had revealed verminous or inadequately fed or clothed children, whose parents were clearly in need of advice – at the least. The innovation of free school meals, initially by charities and after 1907 by local education authorities, required the identification of those truly meriting this handout. This, of course, meant another intrusive visit from an official and a form of means test, however benevolent the intention.[211] Finally, in the Edwardian period, with the Midwives Act of 1902 and the provisions for post-natal visiting facilitated by the Notification of Births Act 1907, the occasion of giving birth itself was put firmly within the control of a nexus of local officials.[212]

All this established for working-class parents a clear, repetitively reinforced practical association between childrearing and responsibilities to official and voluntary philanthropic agencies from the moment of birth onwards and throughout school age.[213] Indeed, the expansion of local maternal health centres from 1906, formally endorsed by the state as a national network of 2,000 such centres with the Maternity and Child Welfare Act of 1918, eventually encouraged the notion that this responsibility extended to the months before birth, too. As Ellen Ross has pointed out, the net outcome of all this was to engender in working-class mothers the perception of a much-expanded range of personal responsibility for the health of their children: 'The Infant Welfare movement's proposition that mothers did, if

successfully turned for assistance. This was following a suggestion made to him by Joseph Chamberlain, who was impressed with Birmingham's attendance officers' unparalleled knowledge of the urban poor from their house to house visitations: Simey and Simey, *Charles Booth*, p. 80. See above, pp. 190–207 and 243–6, for a much fuller account of the developments mentioned here in the next two paragraphs.

209 Gatrell, 'The decline of theft and violence'.

210 Wohl, *Endangered lives;* Hardy, *The epidemic streets.*

211 By 1911–12, 131 out of the 322 education authorities in England and Wales had taken up these powers following the permissive Education (Provision of Meals) Act 1906: Thane, *The foundations*, p. 75.

212 For a full exposition of these developments, see Dwork, *War is good for babies.*

213 For an interpretation including similar developments in France, see Donzelot, *The policing of families.*

they carefully enough followed the instructions of health visitors or doctors, have full power over child life and death was presented to a female working-class public accustomed to toil and worry over sick children, mourning and regret over dead ones, but not to *self-blame*' (emphasis added).[214]

Internalisation and acceptance of this proposition and its potential for self-blame was an enormous motivator, which massively enhanced the emotionally generated perceived costs of children. Note that there is no claim here that mothers now began to love or care for their children 'more' in any absolute sense (the crude, evolutionary 'modernisation' thesis, which has been so convincingly demolished by Linda Pollock).[215] The point is that in continuing to care for them to the limits of their emotional and material capacities as they always had, mothers were now coming to see and to believe that there was a much enhanced range of actions which they could take which were effective in preserving their infants' lives and welfare. This implied the emergence in each community's norms of more exacting standards of the time-, energy- and resource-consuming activities and anxieties necessary for mothers (and fathers) to undertake in order to continue to satisfy themselves that they had done as much as was within their powers to enhance their child's well-being: 'a revolution of rising expectations about the maternal role'.[216] This is not, then, an argument that the strength of the maternal imperative and the emotional relationship towards her children changed absolutely, but that the behaviour and 'costs' which it implied did so, because of changed perceptions and norms: new understandings of good mothering and upbringing.[217]

During this period the paternal role was, if anything, being subject to even more radical, formal redefinition. The general social psychological implications of fathers' separation from the home and from childrearing have already been discussed, above. In the later nineteenth century there was an important sequence of fundamental legal modifications to the centuries-old presumption in law of virtually absolute patriarchal control over children and wives.[218] This process has often been considered to be symbolised by the various duties and sanctions

214 Ross 'Mothers and the state', pp. 53–4.

215 Pollock, *Forgotten children*.

216 José Harris's phrase: *Private lives*, p. 80.

217 This is in line with the interpretative approach of historians of parenting and motherhood in early modern Britain, such as Pollock: *Forgotten children*; and *A lasting relationship*; Fildes (ed.), *Women as mothers*.

218 Custody of Infants Acts of 1839 and 1873 had already granted judges the discretion to abrogate paternal rights in favour of maternal custody for young children under certain limited conditions. The 1886 Guardianship of Infants Act first required courts to have 'regard to the welfare of infants'. By 1925 the continuing process whereby paternal claims were diminished by recognition of children's rights, was formalised in a further Guardianship of Infants Act, requiring all courts to regard the welfare of the child as the first and paramount consideration in custody cases. Lowe, 'The legal status of fathers'. On the legal emancipation of wives, see Holcombe, *Wives and property*; and see ch. 5, n. 14, where it is noted that Behlmer lists seventy-nine acts passed between 1870 and 1908 successively restricting patriarchal rights and enhancing those of children.

laid upon parents by the famous Children Act of 1908.[219] As G. K. Behlmer's important study of the work of the NSPCC (National Society for the Prevention of Cruelty to Children) has shown, alongside these legislative developments there was also significant practical pressure being exerted in this direction on the ground in working-class communities. The NSPCC developed unparalleled expertise in detailed case work throughout the country. Behlmer and Ferguson have shown how the effectiveness of the NSPCC derived from its informal but comprehensive and effective links with the full range of local official and voluntary agencies of social regulation – the police, the schools, the Poor Law, the MOHs, and the COS – while at the same time successfully cultivating the trust of the working-class communities themselves.[220] The 'cruelty men' were typically retired policemen (no women were employed) and Behlmer argues that the three-quarters of a million children assisted during the period 1889–1903 is testimony to the fact that in many communities they were welcomed. They could be the means for anonymous restraint of the neighbourhood's rougher elements, in a period when more traditional collective controls (rough music) had themselves been suppressed by the police.[221]

Thus, fathers, as well as mothers, were subject to a related battery of juridical and economic, social and practical influences upon their perceptions of childrearing, rendering it a more responsible, expensive and potentially troublesome business.

However, popular, publicly articulated norms regarding childrearing and fertility seem only to have eventually changed during the second quarter of the twentieth century. Carl Chinn states that his oral evidence from the Birmingham poor in the first three decades of the century indicates that 'many men regarded a large family as a public display of their manhood'.[222] Elizabeth Roberts also found in Barrow and Preston that community norms in favour of large families continued to be invoked until the eve of the Second World War.[223] The nature of the eventual transformation in popular norms, which probably occurred in most places at some point between the 1920s and the 1940s, was encapsulated by the authors of a Mass-Observation Report published in 1945 who found that 'The old social attitude which considered it immoral to restrict families is giving place to an attitude which considers it immoral *not* to restrict them' (original emphasis).[224]

Mass-Observation collected an abundance of evidence colourfully recording the functioning of powerful norms in the mid-1940s, both positively enjoining

[219] Behlmer, *Child abuse*, pp. 198, 220. See also the important article by Deborah Gorham: 'The "Maiden tribute"'. The 1908 Act was a consolidation of a series of anti-cruelty statutes successfully lobbied for by the NSPCC, from the mid-1880s: an Act of 1889 had been their first success, restricting parents from profiting from selling and begging by children.

[220] For a detailed account of the NSPCC's mode of operation on the ground at this time, see Ferguson, 'Cleveland in history'.

[221] Behlmer, *Child abuse*, pp. 162–75, 219–22.

[222] Chinn, *They worked all their lives*, p. 141.

[223] Roberts, *A woman's place*, pp. 85–6.

[224] Mass-Observation, *Britain and her birth-rate*, p. 75.

small families and proscribing large ones of more than just two children. For instance, a Lancashire housewife of 53 years old was reported as writing:

My own opinion is that people wish to have a small family on account of public opinion which has now hardened into custom. It is customary – and has become so during the last twenty-five years or so – to have two children and no more if you can avoid it. A family of five or six children loses in prestige and, some think, in respectability. . . . If anyone doubts this let him walk along a seaside promenade with five or six children of varying ages and see the attention they attract.

. . . I know of only five families with three children. One of these mothers, said to me: 'I was so ashamed when the third was expected. I wouldn't go out if I could help it.'[225]

A secretary aged 41 corroborated that there was: 'An idea that has been about for, say, twenty-five years that one child (possibly two children) is/are enough, with the result that people are afraid of their neighbours' criticisms if they have long families' *(sic)*.[226]And from the other side of the fence, a father of five whose wife was expecting a sixth wrote of 'what misery the wife suffers by those nasty loud remarks, not to her, but at her, concerning rabbits and their habits etc.'.[227] And from the wife of another persecuted couple, a defensive but resolute stand:

I am the mother of four young children and I might add that they are all very bonny infants, and therefore in no way to be deplored. *But* if you could only *see and hear* how we, their parents, are condemned, pitied and ignored in turn by worthy(?) [*sic*] citizens, and even our own relatives. We have been called lustful and irresponsible producers, . . . We cannot, by many standards, afford these children at all, but then I, for one, believe that courage and self-sacrifice are more important by far than wealth. . . . How I smile when young women friends pity me my lost figure, and deplore the fact that I never go out in the evenings [original emphasis].[228]

This evidence clearly suggests that by the mid-1940s the small family norms were underpinned by a set of closely related negative moral judgements, which acted to identify, label and stigmatise parents of large families as sexually undisciplined, socially unrespectable and liable to be bringing up unhealthy citizens. The charge of bestial 'lustfulness' levelled at these parents of large families and the feelings of 'shame' reported by one are interesting indications of startlingly negative, anti-sensual attitudes, which seem to imply that sexual behaviour in itself, even between husband and wife, was considered a morally tainted activity apparently to be avoided if at all possible. Any unequivocal public signs of actually enjoying sex or indulging in it, such as the proof of a large family, were apparently to be condemned. Thus, incidentally, these extracts are further testimony to the pervasiveness of the 'culture of abstinence', argued for in the previous chapter, demonstrating the tensions and even anger that existed in

225 Mass-Observation, *Britain and her birth-rate*, pp. 74–5.
226 Mass-Observation, *Britain and her birth-rate*, p. 75.
227 Mass-Observation, *Britain and her birth-rate*, p. 75.
228 Mass-Observation, *Britain and her birth-rate*, p. 75.

British popular culture in the 1940s over sexual behaviour, which was, clearly, still seen by many as intimately linked to reproduction.

The process and timing whereby this shift in norms occurred probably varied in each working-class community, depending on its character. It cannot simply be seen as a cultural response to the badgering and didactic activities of the growing army of local authority officials and volunteer social workers, creating an unfavourable climate of opinion towards large families. As has been suggested by the above account, their activities probably intensified most substantially during the late Victorian and Edwardian periods, *pari passu* with the onset of falling fertility in many communities. But it seems likely that shifts in working-class communities' norms and collective ideals regarding small families did not occur until some time during the interwar period. How such norms changed, and the possible role of officials and social workers, in catalysing such change, must inevitably remain a somewhat speculative issue, given the present lack of detailed evidence. However, some relevant findings can be adduced and a number of relevant points can be made.

First, the transaction between voluntary and local authority officials and the working-class subjects of their activities has to be understood as a relationship, influenced by the class, gender and social roles of the participants. Where the object was to alter behaviour and attitudes through learning, as with the midwifery, mothers' meetings and health visiting efforts, aimed at inculcating more hygienic practices among working-class women, it seems probable that the transaction was most effective where a particular balance of social considerations was met. Communication across the class divide between highly educated, middle-class, professionals and highly stressed, working-class mothers was particularly problematic. These cross-class transactions were most popular and effective where the relationship was also economically functional for the working-class women, and not simply didactic.[229] Certainly the recipients had to respect the advice-givers, but the advice-givers had to reciprocate this respect and be able to deliver the information in a way that made sense to the recipients, without asking them – explicitly and implicitly – to change too many of their ideas at once. Thus, George Reid, County MOH for Staffordshire, believed in 1914 that the infant health threat posed by artificial feeding among working women in the Potteries had not been seriously redressed in his area until the expansion of female health visiting following the 1902 Midwives Act. Reid stated this was specifically because, 'A woman will pay more attention to another mother, ignorant though she may be, than to a doctor' (doctors were of course predominantly male at this time).[230]

Margaret Loane, working at exactly this time as a district nurse (though she was

[229] Davies, 'The health visitor as mother's friend'; Prochaska, 'A mother's country'; Marks, '"Dear old mother Levy's"'.

[230] NBRC, *The declining birth rate*, p. 312; and for more on Reid's research, see pp. 245–6.

not a mother), focused on the importance of these problems of communication across the classes in many of her publications, including detailed advice in her nursing manual.[231] As Ross McKibbin has pointed out, there was considerable ambiguity in her views. These both encompassed a vocational belief that through her improving agency (though not solely through this means – she also considered important the power of education and of wider social and economic forces) significant cultural transmission of values and practices would eventually occur. Yet, ultimately, from reflection on her widespread experience Loane also concluded, 'I doubt if any real conversation between members of two classes is possible. All my conversations with my patients and their friends have been of an exceedingly one-sided character.'[232]

These conclusions have been confirmed more rigorously in Anders Brändström's detailed research on infant mortality in Sweden's northernmost parishes in Nedertorneå. Brändström found the most significant factor accounting for the timing of falling infant mortality there to have been

> the introduction of the licensed midwife in the countryside. . . . they often also functioned as local 'medical officers' in rural Sweden. Contrary to the physicians, they were often recruited from the ranks of the local farmers and were more familiar with their ways of thinking and acting. Therefore, they could bridge the gap between scientific medicine and popular culture. There are frequent reports from provincial physicians all over the country during this period to support this.[233]

These licensed midwives, drawn from the same social origins as their clients, were probably the perfect agency for the job. As Brändström observes, their specialised training 'gave them a unique position in society. In the eyes of the public they stood for something "scientific" or had in some sense a higher status which distinguished them from the unlicensed midwives. . . . The result was a very quick acceptance of their services by the public.'[234] This evidence suggests that in attempting to explain how childrearing norms changed in working-class communities and what contribution was made by the 'policing agencies' of local officialdoms and middle-class voluntary workers, it is not enough simply to examine the aims of the agencies or the number of qualified personnel deployed in any area. According to Dr Reid it was quite easy to be overqualified.

Attention needs to be paid to local class relations and recruitment policies regarding the social origins, degree of training and gender of the officials concerned, as well as, ideally, their practices. This links up with the anthropologist, Eric Wolf's, seminal emphasis on the importance of what he termed 'brokers', as facilitating and determining the character of communication between localities

231 Loane, *Outlines of routine.*

232 Loane, *From their point of view*, p. 231. Cited in McKibbin, 'Class and poverty in Edwardian England', p. 181. McKibbin, especially pp. 179–85, provides a highly stimulating examination of this aspect of Loane's work.

233 Brändström, (unpublished conference paper), p. 13.

234 Brändström, (unpublished conference paper), pp. 18–19.

and the larger polities of which they form a part.[235] These key agents are Janus-faced, marginal and mobile individuals, who, like the midwives of Nedertorneå, speak the language both of their own localities and of the state: they make their living from this translation and articulation function which they perform.

A second important development at this time in British society, which effectively embodied and transmitted shifts in community norms of acceptable family size and rates of family growth, occurred through the distinct medium of transactions between landlords and tenants in the housing market.[236] There is sufficient evidence from the witnesses to the 1914 National Birth Rate Commission to show that family size and number of dependants had become a major consideration in the urban housing market. Landlords and their agents were apparently coming to look upon large families as a nuisance and a sign of likely trouble ahead. The Commission specified that more than four or five children seemed the number that was commonly deemed too large.[237] A *de facto* equation of respectability with smaller families was apparently now in operation, especially among private landlords.[238] Clearly such discrimination on these grounds reflects assumptions that regulation of family size, through whatever means, was not only a possibility but a not unreasonable expectation from the respectable poor. In looking for signs by which to judge the character and reliability of a prospective tenant family size was coming to be seen as a useful indicator: a large family was a negative signal.

Meanwhile public and philanthropic bodies, such as the LCC or the Guinness Trust, though equipped to accommodate larger families, also effectively discouraged their growth through their careful monitoring of crowding levels in annual censuses and their rules that expanding families move to larger and therefore more expensive units of accommodation.[239] The signs of the evolution of such practices among both private and institutional landlords, caught in the evidence of the National Birth Rate Commission on the eve of the Great War, attest to one of the important social forces involved in the process of change in a community's fertility norms.

Transformation in collective norms regarding the perceived relative costs of

235 Wolf, 'Aspects of group relations'.

236 Of course, this was not entirely independent of the 'policing' activities of local authorities. It reflected another aspect of encroaching local authority control over the conditions of working-class life; moves against the worst excesses of overcrowding and rack-renting by slum landlords have a long history. Both local and then central government undoubtedly inaugurated a new phase of more serious and ambitious schemes of slum demolition and more persistent regulation of overcrowding from the 1870s onwards, symbolised by Chamberlain's New Street reconstruction scheme in Birmingham's city centre and the subsequent Artisans' and Labourers' Dwellings Act of 1875, which it inspired. The scale of activities was initially very slow in gathering momentum, so that a serious town planning movement and large numbers of tenancies in local authority control did not become a reality until the Edwardian period and after. See Wohl, *Endangered lives*, chs. 11–12.

237 NBRC, *The declining birth rate*, p. 51.

238 NBRC, *The declining birth rate*, pp. 195–6, 199, 275, 283.

239 NBRC, *The declining birth rate*, pp. 188–95, 219, 236.

childrearing is certainly one of the most powerful factors explaining the relative universality of change in family sizes in any community. It is in the nature of explicitly articulated norms, which reflect collective moral evaluations, that if they are to change at all then this will be a relatively rapid and all-encompassing process. As the balance of a community's collective judgement and wisdom on a matter of crucial importance such as this tips across from the positive to the negative (in respect of large families in this particular case), it is important to individuals' self-esteem and status within the community not to be left behind.[240] Thus norms function in such a way as to produce a social pattern of historical change analogous to that of the 'punctuated equilibrium', which evolutionary zoologists have discerned in the palaeontological record of species origination.[241] In most communities and in most social status groups within British society the balance tipped at some point during the period 1900–50, but this occurred at different points in time in different places and among different groups.

Conclusions

It has been shown that during the late Victorian and Edwardian period, proletarian families in many towns were being subjected to a cumulation of legal, social and economic pressures favouring small families from several sides simultaneously. Broadly speaking, these can be characterised as activities of 'the state'; and in that sense 'the state' can be considered very important in contributing to the creation of the economic and cultural conditions in which couples conspired to change their fertility behaviour and which, eventually, shifted the fertility norms of whole communities. However, it is to be noted that this reflects a complex and inclusive understanding of 'the state', which encompasses much more than Westminster and Whitehall: all the varied kinds of local government officials and the full range of local voluntary association agencies, all acting as 'brokers' of different sorts. It was their interaction with local communities which was integral in determining the course of demographic change, rather than any identifiable *fiat* from the centre, and this crucially qualifies the sense in which 'the state' is deemed important.[242]

Even after school pence were finally abolished in the 1890s, the poor working-class family was still left with the permanent loss of labour and earnings

240 On a related issue of 'tipping models' of behavioural change, see Schelling, *Micromotives and macrobehaviour*. I am grateful to Partha Dasgupta for this reference.

241 'Punctuated equilibrium' was first enunciated as a theory by Niles Eldridge and Stephen Jay Gould in 1972: Bowler, *Evolution*, pp. 336–7. According to this thesis sudden periods of intense change sweep through a social or animal system as an important new idea or a mutational form with superior adaptational characteristics becomes established. But between these spasms of change there may be long periods of relative stasis during which the ecological balance established among the competing species remains self-equilibriating.

242 See below, pp. 588–9, for further discussion of the nature of 'the state', in the light of Michael Mann's theoretical work.

from its younger members. The fact that this was still experienced as an important source of financial discomfort by many working-class families is attested by the continuing resort to casual forms of labour for their children out of school hours, the so-called 'boy labour problem' identified by Edwardian middle-class reformers.[243] A thorough local survey of the phenomenon, carried out in Leeds in 1902 and 1910, indicated that about 7% of all school-age children (and therefore quite probably as much as 20% of those aged over 10 years) were involved in these activities in the Edwardian period.[244] Of course, the fact that this evidence indicates that substantial numbers of poor urban families were still in the Edwardian years able to derive some income from their young and teenage children also demonstrates that there were social and economic limits to the budgetary impact upon them of state education and employment legislation. Also, as has been discussed at length above, contributions by low-paid, homeworking children were another continuing source of earnings. For families existing on low and irregular incomes even small gleanings from children, before and after school, may have continued to be perceived as a significant contribution.

Paradoxically, it was also at the other extreme of proletarian experience that the effect of marginal changes in the earning capacities of children would have had least influence over perceived relative child costs. This was that minority of working-class families in which the male breadwinner's wage was considered to be genuinely adequate for all needs and aspirations, since these families had never relied on this form of income anyway. Hence those occupations containing couples with unregulated fertility in 1911 comprised not only various categories of the lowest-paid (unskilled industrial workers and agricultural labourers) but also certain relatively well-paid categories of manual workers: notably coal miners and ship platers and riveters.

Coal miners and ship riveters perceived their incomes to be high and rising throughout most of this period, in terms of their own communities' rather sharply delimited aspirations. They were occupations performed predominantly in fiercely exclusive proletarian communities. In these culturally autarkic enclaves such workers and their families perceived themselves to be doing very well in relation to the main relevant comparators, which was their own previous experience and that of any of their neighbours who were employed in other, less remunerative forms of work. Thus, it was within these locally circumscribed terms that shipbuilding workers' and miners' expectations, closely tied only to their own

[243] Hendrick, *Images of youth*; but note that Michael Childs offers a rather different interpretation of contemporaries' concerns, arguing that there was also an anxiety as to the extent to which slightly older youths' access to employment was rendering them independent of parental control: *Labour's apprentices*.

[244] Keeling, *Child labour*, p. 251. See above, pp. 482–3, for the kinds of activities involved. Carl Chinn cites a national study in 1908 by Nettie Adler which came to similar conclusions, finding that on average 9% of schoolchildren worked outside school hours. Chinn, *They worked all their lives*, p. 68. See also Thane, *The foundations*, p. 41.

industry's fortunes, were only finally rudely disappointed in the severe recessionary conditions of the 1920s. For coal miners the trend of increasing prosperity, which they had become accustomed to over several decades, not only ceased but was dramatically reversed, as real wages were cut by up to 50% and working hours were raised following the miners' defeats in the strikes of 1921 and 1926.[245] It was probably sheer economic shock, on this scale, which was primarily responsible for mining communities' reconsideration of their relative childrearing costs at this time and the subsequent fertility decline which ensued within the mining industry.

To argue that a rise in perceived relative costs of childrearing was the most important cause of changing fertility among the working classes is, in a sense, to follow the general lead of J. A. Banks. Banks most thoroughly documented rising perceived relative costs among the professional and commercial middle classes. However, it is also to insist on paying full attention to the particular social reference framework within which different social groups and communities defined their childrearing costs and benefits. This entails recognition of the importance of the changing ideological, political and juridical context in which such evaluations were constrained and constructed. Hence, Banks devoted much of his 1981 contribution to examining the shifting moral and religious beliefs within the middle classes.[246] The motivations involved and the relevant, politically mediated changes in the law, in the local economy and in family roles were, therefore, the result of quite different forces within the middle-class world and in each of the diverse communities of the working classes. An obvious source of fundamental difference between the middle-class world and that of working people was in the maternal income-earning role. This was a non-variable in respectable 'middle-class' circumstances because it was definitionally absent. By contrast, the manner and extent to which working-class families relied upon mothers' and children's independent, paid work outside and inside the home was one of the principal variables of crucial significance in accounting for varying fertility patterns among proletarian households and communities.

A key part of Banks's analysis for the middle classes was their susceptibility to rising aspirations born from their 'openness' to the daily observation of those with greater material and cultural resources. The social and cultural formation of this open disposition among the professional and commercial bourgeosie no doubt lay in the collective psychology of those who, as employers or self-employed, were in a common position of complete responsibility for their own survival in the selling of goods and services in the market place. In this context aspirational behaviour is born as an emergent property out of the more obvious defensive motivation of the imperative of avoiding bankruptcy or indigence. For people in this position of both vulnerability to the vagaries of the market and yet perceiving themselves as possessing the capacity to act against that vulnerability, the most urgent requirement

[245] Supple, *The history of the British coal industry, 1870–1946.*
[246] Banks, *Victorian values.*

presents itself as the goal of building up a protective cushion against potentially disastrous temporary shortages of trade. This translates socially and culturally into respect for and emulation of those who show themselves to be in this protected position, the desire and the utility of displaying one's own success in pursuit of this goal, and so imperceptibly this translates into acquisitiveness for its own sake and conspicuous consumption. It is precisely the significance of this relatively 'open' reference framework, governing middle-class Victorians' perceptions of their changing living standards, which was central to J. A. Banks's pioneering analysis of their fertility behaviour.[247]

It is this, the proper sociological conceptualisation of historical actors' and communities' comparative reference frameworks, which has been omitted from almost all the too exclusively materialist work done by economic historians within the 'standard of living debate'.[248] Broadly speaking such reference frameworks, whereby individuals and families have evaluated their standard of living, have historically varied from the exclusively 'insular' to the radically 'open'. In these terms working-class communities were a world away from the aspirational striving of the middle classes. For most working-class communities the fundamental notion of 'respectability' throughout the period before the Great War was that of living within one's means and not aspiring to live beyond them. Compared with competitive and aspirational bourgeois aims and motives, this bred an economically conservative and culturally static set of values, so that working-class communities were much less 'open' and were each a law unto themselves.

Proletarian communities, even if not generally as doggedly culturally myopic as some mining villages could be, tended therefore to operate an insular, self-denying ordinance for their inhabitants. Ambitions for social status and consumer aspirations were contained within the very modest limits which were appropriate to the circumstances of the great majority of the community. As discussed above, the nation's system of educational provision had been effectively designed by the Royal Commissioners of the 1860s to keep working-class children permanently within the working-class communities where they were born.[249] The 'scholarship ladder' erected by the Board of Education's Free Place Regulations of 1907 began to provide the working masses with a trickle of free places to grammar schools for a select few. But before this there was no realistic, institutional means of social mobility visible to proletarian parents. It was simply unrealistic for the vast majority of manual workers, and an irrelevancy to them, to attempt to equip their children with the luxury of a secondary education. Hence, the preliminary studies

247 Banks, *Prosperity and parenthood*.

248 For an important exception, focusing on different generations of workers' perceptions of their changing standard of living, see Neale, 'The standard of living 1780–1844'; and for a recent call for 'an economic and social history of expectations', see Supple, 'Fear of failing', p. 456.

249 See pp. 149–51.

that have been completed of social mobility (measured by inter- and intra-generational occupational change) in the nineteenth century have confirmed that, despite the Smilesian rhetoric of the self-made man, the great majority of those born into the working class stayed within it.[250] While a large proportion of the clerical, white-collar class was recruited from working-class backgrounds, the small number of such positions available, even by 1911, in relation to the vast numbers in the industrial proletariat meant that this was still a form of social mobility experienced by a tiny fraction of the working class. Throughout this period, therefore, the culture of the working-class community predominantly supplied the limits to its members' social world and aspirations.

This interpretation is consistent with the theoretical work of Frank Parkin on the principles of 'exclusion' and 'solidarism' in class and status relations, a conceptual extension of the Weberian idea of the importance of different strategies of social closure.[251] Social closure refers to the means by which social collectivities ('communication communities', as they are defined, below, pp. 546–58) exclude others, usually on the basis of physical or social attributes, and so attempt to maximise the rewards available to the eligible in-group by restricting the access of others. Parkin has pointed out that Weber's notion of social closure generally implies a pair of reciprocal strategies, those of the excluding and of the excluded, those of the dominant and those of the resisting sections of society. The two reciprocal strategies are 'those based on the power of exclusion and those based upon the power of solidarism. These may be thought of as the two main generic forms of social closure.'[252] In strategies of exclusion, the dominant communication community seeks

> to maintain or enhance its privileges by the process of subordination – i.e. the creation of another group or stratum of ineligibles beneath it. Where the latter in their turn also succeed in closing off access to remaining rewards and opportunities, so multiplying the number of sub-strata, the stratification order approaches that condition of political defusion that represents the furthest point of contrast to the Marxist model of class polarisation.[253]

In politically stable, historical societies solidaristic strategies are typically found in a less complete form: almost definitionally, fully formed solidarism on the part of the excluded class corresponds closely with the revolutionary conditions of class consciousness, which is politically destabilising and therefore not a persistent historical condition. This is also because of the 'free rider' problem, which Olson identified, as a result of which the power of solidarism is more difficult to organise and mobilise, whereas élite groups within society are able to deploy the powers of the state to organise and bear the costs of the exclusionary credentialling system

250 Kaelble, *Social mobility;* Miles and Vincent, 'A land of "boundless opportunity"?'.

251 Parkin, 'Strategies of social closure'.

252 Parkin, 'Strategies of social closure', p. 4.

253 Parkin, 'Strategies of social closure', p. 5.

from which they benefit.[254] Exclusionary forms of closure therefore tend to be the preferred tactic, so that solidarism tends to be adopted *faute de mieux* by the relatively powerless and is usually admixed with a degree of internally divisive exclusionism, too. Nevertheless, Parkin argues that 'the main structural fault line in any stratification system falls along the line where power undergoes change in its organising principles [from exclusionary to solidaristic]'.[255]

This would seem accurately to characterise the situation found in late Victorian and Edwardian Britain, differentiating the 'open' but exclusively middle-class world from the 'closed' solidaristic communities of the working classes. Parkin specifically notes that the finely differentiated credentials gained from a graded national education system, alongside those authorised by professional and semi-professional bodies, represent the apogee of such an exclusionist social stratification system for the social groups involved in it.[256] On the other hand, on the other side of the fault line proletarian communication communities were each relatively self-sufficient and solidaristic in their locally rooted dialect and their refusal to engage with the aspirational culture of the exclusionary status groups of the middle-class citizens, even when resident among them; but they were also riven with the problems of competitive interdependence due to patriarchal and 'ethnic' dimensions of exclusionism, compromising their potential for a fully formed solidarism.

It has been shown that during the period 1870–1914 childrearing for most working-class families, with the principal exception (even until the 1920s) of the highly paid wage-earners in coal mining, was increasingly subject to a battery of rising perceived relative 'costs', most of which were politically created through innovations in the law, increasingly effectively implemented by a proliferating range of voluntary and official agencies. However, there was a great range in both the local incidence of and the local response to these pressures. Social shifts in definitions of childhood, motherhood and fatherhood no doubt played an important role in accounting for the ubiquity of new ideals of family life, which had emerged by the end of the interwar period. But attention to chronology suggests that these widespread cultural changes towards norms associated with small families cannot be allotted the prime-moving, causal role which it may be tempting to invoke for them.[257] The workforce in the textiles regions was

254 Parkin, 'Strategies of social closure', pp. 9–10, referring to Olson, *The logic of collective action*. Olson pointed out that where association is voluntary, it is rational for individuals to allow others around them to incur the various costs involved in collective mobilisation in order to pursue common goals.

255 Parkin, 'Strategies of social closure', p. 5.

256 Parkin, 'Strategies of social closure', p. 7; and see above, pp. 160, 164–5.

257 Viviana Zelizer's stimulating thesis of the simultaneous commercialisation and 'sacralisation' of childhood through 'The social construction of the economically "useless" but emotionally "priceless" child' could be misread in this way: Zelizer, *Pricing the priceless child*, p. 21. However, most of the interesting historical evidence presented by Zelizer, regarding developments in the USA in child labour legislation, child life insurance, compensation for accidental child death, and adoption and fostering, relates to the period from the 1890s onwards, whereas fertility in the USA

restricting its fertility long before it can be said to have endorsed a commitment to the new evaluations of childhood and parenting.[258]

Perhaps the most satisfactory way of conceptualising the relative causal significance, in accounting for changing fertility, of such cultural shifts in the set of familial roles (principally childhood, adolescence, motherhood and fatherhood) and associated responsibilities, is to see these developments as not sufficient but necessary; and furthermore as necessary in a consolidatory and chronologically posterior sense. The evidence indicates that such shifts do not appear to cause changes in fertility to begin. Changes in family size are intitiated by a minority and in despite of the prevailing norms regarding family roles and appropriate family sizes or rates of childbearing. These collective values and norms change subsequently in public recognition of the community's altering fertility, though they may change quite rapidly at that point. Although not a causal prime mover, the shift in familial roles and norms is important in consolidating – making general and relatively stable throughout the community – the new fertility régime, whatever it may be.

Probably the single factor most consistently and thoroughly related to the range of fertility variation found in 1911 was the way in which local labour markets were age and gender structured. For proletarians this strongly affected the opportunity costs of rapid child-bearing in a number of reinforcing ways. As has been shown at length above the comparative wage-levels and participation rates of males, females and minors in each branch of industry were the historical product of a nexus of continually negotiated political and ideological forces, involving bargaining between the employers, the state and workers of varying degrees of organisation. This, in turn, influenced the relative bargaining power of the two sexes in each

had been falling for decades before this. As in the case of Britain, therefore, careful attention to the chronology of these changes in popular cultural evaluations of childhood and familial roles suggests that they cannot be envisaged as performing a causal role in changing fertility behaviour in any straightforward sense.

258 As Carolyn Steedman has argued, the essence of Zelizer's transformation in childhood, insofar as the working classes were concerned, was a changed perception from the child as labourer to the child as scholar, associated with the expansion of national compulsory education. Steedman, 'Bodies, figures', pp. 22–3. However, it was in the textiles communities, where fertility was controlled first and most effectively in the nineteenth century, that there was the most sustained resistance to the full-time schooling of children and where there was the most intense conflict within the labour movement over the adoption of child welfare policies, a battle only finally laid to rest in the 1920s. See above, p. 54, on school attendance in textile areas; and on the resistance in textile areas to child welfare, see Howell, *British workers and the Independent Labour Party*, pp. 343–85; and Steedman, *Childhood, culture and class*, especially ch. 8. Note that John Stewart dates the explicit commitment of the labour movement's national leadership – specifically Ramsay MacDonald – to the positive promotion of child welfare, as against unfettered parental control within the working-class family, as late as the period 1904–9. Stewart argues that this development was considerably influenced by the findings and proposals of the Physical Deterioration Committee: 'Ramsay MacDonald', especially pp. 117–18. For a different kind of evidence that textile communities in the West Riding were not re-evaluating childhood until the Edwardian era, see Green, 'The religion of the child'.

community. This was all the more important in accounting for the occupational fertility patterns because of the technical limitations of the available methods of birth control, among which, it has been argued, the long-standing English practice of attempted abstinence played a primary role. A minimum degree of co-operation between spouses was therefore usually essential for the effective spacing of births, which the previous chapter has shown was the main form of fertility regulation practised before the Great War.

10

Social class, communities, gender and nationalism in the study of fertility change

The sections of this final chapter offer a series of summary discussions of the wider implications of the foregoing new interpretation of fertility change in modern Britain.

In the first section there is a consideration of how to envisage the general form of the historical process of falling fertilities in a way which is compatible with the variation found between different communities and social groups in Britain. This discussion is in three parts. First, it is argued that the processes of change, far from being a unitary and unifying event, should be understood as socially divisive. Fertility changed through a developmental sequence of contingent phases, rather than comprising a single, smooth 'transition'. Secondly, it is pointed out that this crucially means that descriptions and explanations which are accurate for one part of the process – the final stages after the Great War, for instance – do not necessarily provide helpful leads for understanding the origins and earlier stages of the processes of change. The opposite assumption is a fallacy that has informed the established demographic approach. Thirdly, the section concludes with a consideration of the extent to which the history of fertility control in Britain may represent an unusual or unique course of events, compared with other European countries at the time.

In the second section of the chapter there follows a discussion of historians' current understandings of class relations in modern British society. From these considerations the argument is developed that Britain during this period should be seen as fissured by a considerable number of competing and overlapping 'communication communities'. This, to some extent, innovatory view of social and class relations is designed to be compatible with the foregoing interpretation of the demographic evidence: many distinct fertility régimes changing alongside each other.

In the third section there is a discussion of the implications of the new view developed here of the methods of fertility control, as something achieved primarily through spacing and attempted abstinence, for the fast-developing fields of the history of sexual and gender relations in British society. This is a necessarily long section as it leads on to a re-examination of the relationship between the feminist political and ideological movement of the period and changing fertility. This presents a substantially new and positive estimate of its importance in contributing to falling fertility in British society.

In the fourth section there is a consideration of some directions for future research on falling fertilities, suggested by the current study. It is noted that something like an observational revolution is awaiting those studying this phenomenon, since exceedingly high-quality historical demographic records exist for every individual in the population of England and Wales in the relevant period; but at present access to this evidence is unfortunately denied by government regulations.

The penultimate section suggests the possible lessons which may be drawn from an historical study of fertility change such as this for policy applications in different contemporary contexts, referring particularly to the general heuristic framework of perceived relative childrearing costs presented in chapter 9.

Finally, there is a brief reflection on the varying conceptions of explanation and understanding that are prevalent in the historical, social and natural sciences. This is by way of a critical consideration of the relative intellectual influence which these different approaches have historically exerted on the study of fertility change in Britain, linking up with some of the themes raised at the outset in the historiographical critique presented in Part I of this study.

A new conception of fertility change in modern Britain: multiple fertility declines and a developmental sequence

A new overall picture of the fall in fertility in modern British history emerges from the detailed analysis of the occupational evidence presented in this study. Multiple fertility declines were occurring throughout the many and varied social groups and communities of Britain during the period 1860–1940. These were often overlapping each other chronologically but were largely distinct developments. Indeed, the era of falling fertilities in British society could be said to encompass the entire period from the second quarter of the nineteenth century to the present day (the latter would apply if the distinctive fertility patterns of Britain's ethnic minorities were accorded their place in the account).[1]

National aggregate occupational data of the kind analysed in Part III of this book clearly cannot do justice to the true extent of variety in fertility and nuptiality behaviour during this period. But the evidence presented here does at least indicate the scale of intellectual impoverishment which necessarily accompanies any continued refusal to explore further the political, cultural, ideological and economic forces which lie behind this semi-visible state of great variability. The

[1] For evidence of birth spacing among the Quakers in southern England from the the second quarter of the nineteenth century, see Vann and Eversley, *Friends in life and death*, ch. 4. On ethnic fertility variation in the 1980s, see Diamond and Clarke, 'Demographic patterns', pp. 190–4.

professional model has effectively drawn a veil over this more complex picture for well over half a century. It has thereby obscured the detail almost entirely from view and given the false impression of a simple and straightforward unitary national pattern, thereby soliciting and eliciting relatively simple and general forms of explanation.

The perspective on secular trends that is visible with hindsight can be extraordinarily misleading in its foreshortening tendency, which concatenates and hides significant processes running counter to the longer-term trend. Hence, as was argued in chapter 8, because in the long run in Britain contraception within marriage has replaced late marriage entirely as the principal method of family limitation, the importance of the intimate relationship of these two practices during the period in which fertility fell most dramatically had previously been lost to (hind)sight. Over the long run it can appear as if falling fertility and the emergence of 'the small family' norm has been a nationally unifying process generating uniformity, in the sense that by the 1940s and 1950s virtually all sections of the nation had adopted in common an historically new form of very low fertility (though this was not, of course, a lasting endpoint of demographic change in modern society).[2] But, despite this net outcome of temporary, relative national uniformity during the mid-twentieth century decades, it is important to realise that the historical process of fertility change itself was quintessentially characterised and driven by divisiveness and social conflicts.

This does not simply refer to the well-known fact that until the 1910s in Britain there was a generally widening gap between the rapidly falling fertility of the middle classes and that of large sections of the manual working classes, including even a possible rise in the marital fertility of some groups such as miners.[3] It refers also to the character of the intentional motivations of those involved and the impersonal forces causing such fertility change, as well as the immediate effects of such demographic change.

The work of the Schneiders (see p. 437) documents the significance of local socio-political power relations of class and gender, of international economic forces and of national politico-legislative initiatives as major contingent, non-generalisable components of a satisfactory explanation of the multiple fertility declines evident in modern Sicily. Thus, once a high degree of detailed and properly contextualised empirical knowledge has been achieved, as in this study by the Schneiders, the notion of a single unitary process of fertility decline appears crude and implausible.

Kertzer and Hogan's study of Casalecchio, a north Italian community in the lower Po valley, broadly confirms the Schneiders' findings.[4] They also find quite distinct patterns of fertility behaviour and trajectories of decline for Casalecchio's four major social groupings, the *padrone* landholders, the town-dwelling artisans

[2] See the critique of Susan Watkins's thesis on pp. 28–9. [3] See p. 364.

[4] Kertzer and Hogan, *Family, political economy and demographic change.*

and merchants, the wage-labourers (both manufacturing and agricultural) and the sharecroppers contractually tied to the *padrones* until after the Second World War. Kertzer and Hogan's evidence shows that the rural sharecropping class of poor, extended family households in Casalecchio did not significantly alter its nuptiality and fertility practices until the encompassing context – their legally institutionalised poverty – was legislatively broken apart after the Second World War, as also documented by the Schneiders in Sicily. At this point rural sharecroppers rapidly dwindled as a social formation, as did the reciprocal exploitative *padrone* way of life, too. The authors point out that

> their declining share of the population meant that their behaviour became increasingly unimportant for the character of Casalecchio as a whole . . .
>
> Thus, the growing percentage of the population in the proletariat and artisan and merchant classes increasingly meant that the behaviours of these groups, rather than those of the traditional elite and sharecropper classes, came to define life in Casalecchio.[5]

This could be read simply as a 'modernisation' style statement of uni-directional transition from 'traditional' to 'modern' social forms (and it is not in fact clear whether the authors do not entertain some residual sympathies with this viewpoint). However, there is also here the kernel of an altogether more penetrating, alternative conceptualisation of social change, which would be consonant with the concept of 'multiple fertility declines' found in Britain. In this view, individuals are not conceived as atomistic agents, being changed from a 'traditional' to a 'modern', from a non-controlling to a controlling disposition towards fertility, as a result of the impression upon them of 'modernising' forces of education, mobility and so on. Rather, the individual agents are first defined and given their identities as participants in the shared (and mutually related) cultural forms of specific, historical social groups, such as the sharecroppers, the *padrones*, the artisanate. Such agents are conceptualised as typically 'carrying' the kinds of ideological rationalisations which are culturally sanctioned as functional for the specific politico-economic context in which their primary social group or community historically finds and sees itself, having to negotiate its interests *vis-à-vis* other impinging social groups.

To some extent economic forces determine the varying proportions of a local or national population which are born into the different possible social status groups and communities and, in the very long run, sheer numbers – and compositional shifts in those numbers – probably count for a lot. But such large-scale trends of economic and social change are, of course, themselves strongly politically influenced and produced. The *longue durée* of secular change is in fact itself composed of and determined by the chronologically prior influence of a developmental sequence of much shorter-run, socio-political encounters among the jostling social groups within communities. They competitively deploy their

[5] Kertzer and Hogan, *Family, political economy and demographic change*, pp. 182–3.

unequal and varying resources of culture, ideology, and organisational capacity in the political struggle to maintain and further their respective interests.

Thus Kertzer and Hogan see Casalecchio and its predominant fertility patterns not simply changing because of an arithmetic shift in the balance of the social groups, read off as a correlate of economic growth. Such change is also contingent on the outcome of politico-ideological and cultural conflicts between the vying social groups. It is this which determines the enhanced 'carrying power' of a social group, particularly in this case that of the urban wage-labour proletariat of Casalecchio, whose presence and powers had previously been only modest:

> Improvements in public health in the late nineteenth century (inoculation programs, improved disposal of sewage, and the provision of safe drinking water) were among the most important sources of change in life chances. . . .
>
> It is noteworthy that these changes did not occur automatically as a feature of modernisation. Rather, they were the results of the demands of an increasingly vocal and radicalised proletariat, a proletariat that was also seeking improved wages for its labour. It is important, then, to view the declining fertility of the proletariat as but one part of the response of that class to its harsh economic circumstances. At the same time that individual proletarian couples were acting to improve their personal economic chances by limiting fertility, they were demanding government actions to advance their life chances and those of their children, and they were organising to demand better wages and working conditions from their employers.[6]

This, then, provides a sociologically and politically fruitful contribution, which helps with understanding the many forces of historical change involved in the process of falling fertility. Changing fertility should be related, as in this case, to the local politics and social divisions within specific communities. Kertzer and Hogan's account provides a well-documented example and model of the way in which it is the narrative history of social and political conflict between different social groups in communities, which explains how and why the potential for fertility change manifests itself in different localities and contexts.

In Britain, too, both within the middle classes and, separately, within the working classes falling fertility behaviour was caused and motivated by social and economic forces of competition and differentiation. Enough has been written in the last chapter – and more extensively by J. A. Banks – on the character of this aspirational war of status conflict within the upper, middle and lower middle classes. Within the working classes, too, differentially changing fertility behaviour, as reflected in the occupational data from 1911, was part and parcel of powerfully polarising forces, but of quite distinct kinds from those ruling the passions of the middle classes.

The fundamental divisions of interest within the industrial labour market have been discussed in previous chapters, focusing in particular on the predicament of 'competitive interdependence' between the sexes and the generations and the

[6] Kertzer and Hogan, *Family, political economy and demographic change*, pp. 181–2.

significance of the exclusionary, patriarchal bargains struck between employers and some of their adult male employees in many of the sectors of industry often with the blessing of the state. The poorly remunerated, irregularly employed, trade-less labourer, whose wife and children worked as exploited outworkers, was the reciprocal creation, entailed by the relative success of this patriarchal industrial relations strategy for the minority of adult males with apprenticed trades or strong unions. However, there was also a whole host of associated self-reinforcing, inter-related forces of differentiation involved in this divisive outcome, which included a fertility dimension.

It has to be remembered that virtually all urban working-class neighbourhoods throughout this period were continuing to receive substantial proportions of in-migrants and continued to experience high rates of residential turnover. Social historians have written of the period from the 1870s onwards as one in which the classic urban working-class communities constituted and identified themselves, as second-generation born-and-bred urbanites claimed their streets as their own.[7] Certainly the last quarter of the nineteenth century was relatively stable by comparison with all the previous decades of rapid urban growth throughout the country. But urban working-class communities in this later period were also ones in which a significant flow of in-migrants continued to arrive, even if it was now in many cases a minority rather than the majority who were new to the city.[8]

Furthermore, in the mature, slower-growing late Victorian economy there was, if anything, intensifying competition for the most secure and well-paid sources of livelihood. In this contest the sitting tenants and those able to remain stable within the urban neighbourhood networks of information and support into which they had grown up and been socialised, reaped massive advantages over the newcomers, whether these be rural in-migrants, arrivals from another city or simply those from the other side of town. As Hobsbawm has remarked, many trades, especially in the long-urbanised London environment, were practically hereditary castes.[9] And, of course, bottom of the rung, initially at least, were the ethnic in-migrants from overseas, who had come in numbers from Ireland throughout the century and were also joined in this period by Jewish refugees from the Pogroms in eastern Europe.[10]

J. C. Holley has demonstrated the nature of these forces in an important, thoroughly documented local study based on record linkage in two Scottish

[7] The seminal article was Stedman Jones, 'Working class culture and working class politics'.

[8] Census of England and Wales, 1911, Vol. IX, Table 12, shows that in London, Birmingham and Liverpool, for instance, as late as 1911 still only 55% of those aged over 25 years old were born in their area of enumeration. On the surprisingly high extent of residential mobility and in-migration in Scottish cities still at the end of the nineteenth century, see Anderson and Morse, 'High fertility, high emigration, low nuptiality'.

[9] See ch. 7, n. 52.

[10] For an examination of relations between Irish and English in the slum area known as the Kensington Potteries, see Davis, 'Jennings' Buildings'; and for the subsequent situation of the Jews, see Garrard, *The English and immigration;* Feldman, *Englishmen and Jews.*

Borders communities (Penicuik and Walkerburn).[11] It was those families with the greatest proportion of high-earning and skilled household heads who remained geographically stable over time. This was both cause and effect. Many young males acquired the opportunity to obtain their skills and apprenticeships in the first place through recommendation by parents, uncles, grandfathers or other well-disposed senior figures in their neighbourhood. The children of lower-earning males were less likely to have these local patrons because their families frequently had to move, in search of work or to avoid the rent-collector. Such families as these were locked into a chronically peripatetic syndrome, the 'unrespectable life course' as Holley puts it. This comprised low and irregular pay for the male household head, from which followed the need to change employers and homes repeatedly, in pursuit of waged work for himself or any other family members who could get it. Wives were typically employed and sometimes out of the home; and children were not in school but wherever possible earning pennies in formal, or more likely informal, work in the streets. The work which these families' members were able to find for themselves was likely to be the least financially attractive because of the family's lack of an established neighbourhood support network.

Hence, such families of low-paid males were disproportionately represented among those attracted to homeworking despite its exploitative labour intensity. As discussed in the previous chapter, the resulting encouragement to high fertility was a by-product of this; and it was also shown that this, in turn, could involve growing families with the problems in the housing market created by overcrowding, which once again led to them being moved on by landlords, perpetuating their problems. Thus, in many communities the differential fertility of working-class families was intimately related to deeply divisive polarising forces, governing patterns of residential stability, associated differential access to higher paying, (predominantly male) jobs, and self-fulfilling definitions of respectability and attributions of non-respectability.[12]

Once the picture of the nation as a unified hierarchy and the associated representation of fertility decline as a unitary process have each been replaced by a

[11] Holley, 'The two family economies'.

[12] Note, however, that there was one set of circumstances – not infrequently occurring – which the tradeless, casualised, in-migrant worker and his family were potentially better adapted to face than the household of the born-and-bred, resident apprenticed employee. The former could escape a severe locally concentrated trade depression by returning, perhaps temporarily, to their place of origin or simply moving on without any great loss of resources and contacts. Whereas the latter would be tempted to sit out a trade depression in the hope of improvement and could thereby become trapped in a seriously deteriorating situation if the industry to which he belonged was suffering permanent problems. See the description of this difference in fates in Wright, *Some habits and customs*, pp. 258–9. There is a sense, therefore, in which the flexibility of the low paid, with their casualisation, multiple side-employments and peripatetic pattern may not simply have been a worst option adopted by the footloose, but can be viewed as a rational and positive form of adaptation to the general problem of insecurity of livelihood, which they faced more frequently than anybody else.

picture of fundamental cultural and socio-demographic diversity, the search for single, uniformly applicable, causal processes to account for a national fertility decline ceases to hold its peculiar attraction. One of the most consistent findings to emerge from the Cambridge Group's study of fertility patterns and trends in England before 1837 has been their apparent national uniformity, compared with Germany or France, for instance.[13] In this historical perspective, one of the key features of the succeeding era is the dramatic increase in regional and local heterogeneity in fertility, reflecting the enormous diversity of economic and cultural contexts created by the growth of Britain's many different industries and cities. Too exclusive a focus on the falling fertility of this period has, perhaps, distracted attention from the significance of the novelty of massive variation in fertility behaviour.

The replacement of a unitary, national secular fall in fertility with the conception of 'multiple fertility declines' is wholly compatible with a separate interpretative suggestion first raised some years ago by E. A. Wrigley.[14] In the course of his scrutiny of the evidence regarding France's early and protracted fertility decline, Wrigley concluded that falling fertility there should not necessarily be seen as a single undifferentiated process of adjustment or change but may have consisted of a series of distinct developmental stages. Fertility behaviours may have shifted and changed in phases, as a sequence of deepening demographic responses to the changing socio-economic contexts, partly created by the results of the earlier steps towards fertility control.

Such a developmental process may or may not be strongly self-sustaining once under way. It certainly seems plausible that within the middle-class socio-cultural constellation the social battle for status differentiation waged through family planning tended to feed the conditions for its own perpetuation and could easily create a form of historical momentum driving family sizes downwards towards a minimum. Couples restricting their own reproduction as a means to generate a margin of resources for status differentation through conspicuous consumption and expensive cultural investments thereby unwittingly also created more 'room at the top' for the progeny of their competitors, so exacerbating the status competition for the subsequent generation and thereby producing a self-sustaining and self-fuelling phenomenon. This was first pointed out by the political sociologist, Roberto Michels, who observed that opportunities for upward mobility, as well as being affected by the cultural variable of the degree of 'openness' of a community or society, were, during the late nineteenth and early twentieth centuries, facilitated absolutely by two simultaneous 'structural' socio-economic changes.[15] First, due to economic development there was a

[13] Wrigley *et al.*, *English population history*, Table 7.44.

[14] Wrigley, 'The fall of marital fertility in nineteenth-century France'.

[15] This aspect of Michels's work is noted in Goldthorpe *et al.*, *Social mobility*, p. 11. Goldthorpe refers to:

disproportionate expansion of non-manual, service sector jobs of higher status and pay. Secondly, and equally importantly, there was the similarly disproportionate decline in the effective fertility (i.e. including an offsetting mortality decline) of those who currently held these privileged positions in the labour market.

Falling fertility was, therefore, alongside the expansion of the service sector entailed in economic growth itself, responsible for creating the socio-demographic conditions conducive to aspirational behaviour and the feasibility of upward social mobility. However, simultaneously, it was itself the manifestation of the very aspirational behaviour and ideological outlook on the part of a significantly large number of individuals within the middle classes which led to those opportunities for upward mobility being taken up and fought for. But, while valid for one section of society, this cannot necessarily provide a general explanation for falling fertility throughout society, since it was principally only the 'middle-class' world which was open to these forces. As the foregoing has shown at length, the changing fertility behaviours of the much greater proportion of the population – those living in the many, varied and relatively 'closed' plebeian communities – were subject to a range of rather different considerations.

However, it is also true for these plebeian communities that once fertility had fallen to a certain critical point, the fall may itself have become self-perpetuating and irreversible. One plausible reason for this would be in the possible effect that falling infant and child mortality would have had upon fertility at later stages of the process. It has been shown that child mortality did not fall before fertility in England and Wales and it has been shown that in most places fertility also fell before infant mortality.[16] Indeed, there are obvious reasons why more widely spaced births and smaller families should be expected to assist with reducing infant mortality.[17] But this finding, that reduced mortality among the young was not so much a cause as a consequence of the initial reductions in fertility, seems to have distracted historians from appreciation of the possibility that reduced infant and child mortality might still be important at a later stage in stimulating *further*, continuing falls in fertility. Once the process of falling fertilities is reconceptualised into a sequence of contingent stages, causation is no longer reduced only to those 'factors' which can be shown to antedate the earliest changes in fertility behaviour. In this case, then, the dramatically improving chances of infant survival registered on a national scale after 1900 may have exerted a powerful reinforcing effect on changing fertility practices, even though the latter may themselves have been partly responsible for the trend towards enhanced life expectancy in the first place.

Michels, *First lectures in political sociology*, pp. 80–2, 103–4 (originally published in German in 1927), and, more generally, to his *Umschichtungen in dem Herrschenden Klassen nach dem Kriege* (Stuttgart and Berlin 1934).

16 This was most thoroughly demonstrated in: Kabir (unpublished PhD thesis).

17 For an important recent study of infant mortality decline in England and Wales, which concurs in seeing falling fertility as one of the causes of falling infant mortality, see Woods, Watterson and Woodward, 'The causes of rapid infant mortality decline', especially Part II, p. 130.

But probably an even more important general historical reason why falling fertility might become a self-reinforcing process once past a certain point would be due to the effect of changing community norms, operating in the manner outlined on pp. 524–5, 530–1. It may both be true that the falling fertilities of European nations have been characterised by processes which in their origins were socially fractured and divisive, contingent and diverse throughout an initial and often protracted period (which may have lasted over a century in the French case according to Wrigley). Yet at the same time falling fertility may also comprise a set of phenomena which, once sufficiently underway, have tended to exhibit the characteristics of an unfolding and irreversible developmental process, because of the powerfully self-reinforcing influence of changing norms. The problem has been that demographic analysts of the causation involved have tended to see the whole process only in the latter guise, failing to examine the perfectly logical possibility that a set of similar and repeated final outcomes (the emergence of parity-specific family planning, premised on ideal family sizes) may result from many diverse origins, which may each have developed in distinctive ways prior to the 'final' outcome.

Indeed, if this contingent and developmental conceptualisation of fertility change is chronologically correct, then it can simultaneously contribute further to the historiographical explanation of its own misinterpretation. It was the construction of the Princeton fertility indices framework from the 1950s to the 1970s which obscured the possibility of discerning a picture of falling fertilities as a process with distinct stages. In the 'Princeton' approach the process of fertility change was foreshortened into a single, essential transition from 'natural' to parity-specific, controlled fertility (stopping behaviour). The methodology that was developed radically reduced the process of fertility change to the search for the origins and subsequent expansion of a single form of fertility regulation, the form which appeared to these researchers to be most common in their own times and most distinct from that of earlier periods. By methodologically excluding from observation the consideration of other possible forms of fertility regulation, this approach has produced a fundamentally misleading representation of the way in which regulated fertilities have historically evolved. In Britain, at least, parity-specific family planning appears to have emerged relatively late, from a matrix of various earlier forms of birth control. It is also worth pointing out that even as a characterisation of 'modern' fertility control, an exclusive focus on stopping is a misleading and inaccurate abstraction, since it is stopping *and* spacing (and, indeed, starting) which has been practised since the 1950s, in the sense that couples typically choose not only how many children to have but when to have them.

It is equally unnecessary to claim that any one specific form of restraint on sexual behaviour or on fertility has accounted for falling fertilities in different countries. It has been argued here that attempted abstinence was the principal method used in

British society before the interwar period. It has also been pointed out that there is really no necessary, absolute distinction between attempted abstinence and coitus interrruptus (widely defined) and therefore there may well have been considerable admixture of these two methods. The major empirical support for this particular interpretation was the demographic evidence for England and Wales. This showed, first, that spacing was already being practised extensively from early in marriage during the Edwardian period. Secondly, that there was an unusual and persistent relationship, down to the generation marrying before the Great War, such that those delaying marriage the most were also those who restricted fertility after marriage the most, indicating the absence of a 'culture of contraception' and implying a culture of abstinence, instead. It was also shown that the available contemporary qualitative evidence, such as it is, offers positive support for this interpretation; and certainly does not contradict it in the way which has previously been assumed to be the case.

Although detailed historical evidence for other countries is not abundant, there is some relevant comparative information available from the Princeton European Fertility Project on the broad chronological relationship between falling fertility and nuptiality patterns.[18] This suggests that British society was probably rather unusual in this respect. The Princeton evidence indicates that only Finland, Greece, Italy and Spain exhibit, at the national level of aggregation, a similar pattern to England and Wales of a continuing move to defer marriage for three or four decades after the initial fall in fertility, although probably only the case of Finland is genuinely comparable.[19] By contrast, in the majority of cases the overall relationship is in the opposite direction: Austria, Belgium, Denmark, France, Germany, Ireland, Portugal, Sweden, Switzerland. In five countries the evidence shows no clear relationship either way: Hungary, Iceland, Netherlands, Norway and Scotland.[20] Of course, the burden of the present study would be to suggest that considerable further variations would be expected among the social groups and communities of each of these national populations if they could be studied in sufficient detail. This superfical survey of the national level data has been conducted simply in order to show that there is strong *prima facie* evidence to indicate that the processes of falling fertilities occurred in quite distinct ways in different countries, at least with respect to the relationship between restricted marital fertility and delayed marriage, which has been identified as so important in the case of England and Wales.

In the majority of countries in which the relationship at the national level of

[18] Coale and Watkins, *The decline of fertility in Europe*, ch. 2, Appendix A.

[19] In the cases of the three Mediterranean countries this pattern is partly due to the somewhat independent social and cultural change which was occurring during this period, whereby the long-standing pattern of a wide gap between the typical ages of husbands and wives was closing, with the result that average female ages at marriage were rising.

[20] Data for Albania, Bulgaria, Czechoslovakia, Luxemburg, Poland, Rumania, Russia and Yugoslavia was insufficient to make a judgement.

aggregation was the reverse of the English case, it would be reasonable to argue that there may have been no significant stage in which fertility was restrained through the operation either of attempted abstinence or of other involuntary inhibitions on sexual intercourse. These are societies in which, by contrast with England and Wales, the national trends in marital fertility and nuptiality suggest that the population in question consciously appreciated from the start that the control which they were newly exercising over their marital fertility meant that earlier marriage was now feasible. Certainly, one of the most robust findings to emerge from Etienne van de Walle's more detailed and disaggregated study of fertility and nuptiality in nineteenth-century France was that nuptiality always rose in those *départements* where marital fertility was falling.[21]

Thus, by virtue of the inverse of the arguments made above to support the thesis of attempted abstinence as the dominant method in the British context, it is only consistent to point out that van de Walle's evidence would indicate that it is likely that the culture of abstinence was much less important in France. Indeed, both this quantitative, and other literary, evidence interpreted by J.-L. Flandrin indicates that the French were a population in which knowledge of and expertise in a repertoire of relatively uninhibited, non-coital activities, summarised as 'coitus interruptus', were relatively widespread.[22] This was the method of *marcia in dietro* ('reverse gear') which, in the next century, Sicilian artisans prided themselves on having mastered from the *più evoluto* ('more evolved') French.[23]

It certainly seems eminently plausible that sexual culture in much of France in the nineteenth century was governed by a quite different set of norms from those in Britain and that differences in methods of birth control should be seen within these different contexts. The divergence between the two in their popular attitudes towards prostitution by the late nineteenth century is highly symptomatic of this. Whereas, in Britain prostitution was primarily viewed from within bourgeois culture as a sordid and clandestine, quintessentially 'underworld' and 'deviant' activity, according to Theodore Zeldin prostitution in France was sufficiently 'normal' that French schoolboys were routinely expected to gain their sexual initiation in this way, as demonstrated in the research of Alain Corbin.[24]

[21] Van de Walle, *The female population of France*, ch. 7, especially section IV. This finding has recently been confirmed with a different methodology by David Weir, 'New estimates', pp. 322–3: 'The new estimates . . . only reinforce the general conclusions advanced long ago by van de Walle: as the control of fertility within marriage advanced, the control of fertility by (non-) marriage retreated.'

[22] Flandrin, *Families in former times*, especially ch. 4. This is one of the most illuminating and sophisticated discussions available in English of the historical evidence relating to changing social and sexual relations in this period. It should be compulsory reading for all who study fertility change. See also Flandrin, 'Contraception, marriage and sexual relations', especially n. 68. There is now a collection of Flandrin's articles available in translation: Flandrin, *Sex in the western world*. On the quite different significance of coitus interruptus in a culture of abstinence, see pp. 420–4, esp. n. 158.

[23] Schneider and Schneider, 'Going forward in reverse gear', pp. 157–61.

[24] Zeldin, *France, 1848–1945* I, pp. 305–9; Corbin, *Women for hire*.

Comparing his own clinical experience with that of his French peers, in 1879 the gynaecologist C. H. F. Routh proffered his belief that it was inevitable that a culture as tolerant of commercial sex as the French would also be one in which 'conjugal onanism' (meaning any of a range of sexual practices by married couples where sexual gratification and not conception were the aim) was prevalent. By contrast, 'as conjugal onanism is at present practised very rarely, I believe, in this country [England], we are not, as professional men, open to receive the confessions of the unfortunate victimised women as the doctors are in France'.[25] While there is an abundance of literature throughout the Victorian and Edwardian era urging the virtues of sexual self-control upon the British nation (something also found in America), it is my impression that there is no equivalent salience of this theme in French nineteenth-century culture.[26]

Thus, the predominant forms and social significance which marital fertility control assumed probably varied greatly in different cultural contexts, both in terms of spacing as against stopping and in terms of the techniques employed: voluntary or involuntary abstinence, withdrawal and so on. There is no sound reason to assume that simply because fertility was falling across broadly the same period of time in so many different parts of Europe and among European settlers overseas it must reflect a common practice or even a single, common understanding of the same practice. In fact even the simultaneity is largely illusionary, since the processes whereby fertilities fell took almost a century in many countries, lasted well over a century if all countries of Europe are reviewed together and took almost two centuries if France is included.

There is something of a salutary analogy in the field of historical study which addresses the processes of economic transformation involved in industrialisation. Although industrialisation happened in all European societies over more or less the same period of time as that of the fall in European fertilities (with England, and not France, playing the role of precocious, early leader in this case), it has not, since W. W. Rostow's theory of 'take-off' was fashionable in the 1960s, been seriously suggested by economic historians that essentially the same historical process unfolded in each case.[27] Economic historians are well aware that there have been many and varied historical trajectories of economic growth and many distinct routes to full industrialisation. Different countries and regions have engendered this common process from and with a great diversity of natural resources, different degrees of state involvement, varying military commitments, some with and some without the costs or benefits of imperial possessions. All this has occurred alongside considerable differences of cultural and political ideology and

[25] Routh, *The moral and physical evils likely to follow practices intended as checks to population* (1879): extract as reproduced in Jalland and Hooper, *Women from birth to death*, pp. 268–9.

[26] For more on the increasing emphasis on sexual self-control in British and American polite culture during the second quarter of the nineteenth century, see below, pp. 454–60.

[27] Rostow, *The stages of economic growth.*

involving quite a variety of technical and economic means.[28] Why should it continue to be assumed that there is an essential similarity in the history of 'fertility decline' in each of these different contexts?

A new conception of the relation between fertility and social class: languages, social identities and communication communities

The general heuristic framework proposed at the outset of the last chapter envisaged fertility and nuptiality behaviour in Britain varying and changing as a result of changes in the perceived relative costs and benefits of childrearing. The ensuing presentation identified a number of ideological, cultural and political developments as important. These were responsible in various ways for influencing and altering certain social groups' and communities' norms and expectations, regarding the roles and responsibilities of childhood, motherhood, parenthood, fatherhood and the respective conjugal duties within and without the home. Perceived relative costs of childrearing shifted primarily because the gendered and generational roles and norms, upon which this variable equation was premised, were themselves altered. It was not really the quantities in the equation which changed (a primarily economic issue) but the qualities: the identities of the terms themselves. The implications of childrearing and the perceptions of parental roles and responsibilities were shifting, because of transpositions in social identities and, therefore, in the information contexts (see pp. 39–41).

It is because fertility change was mediated in this way, by shifting roles and norms, that it principally occurred not to whole social classes or to individual occupations but to social groups and communities. This is because roles, norms and social identities are essential elements of the shared language of any mutually recognising, communicating human group. They are constructed by and embodied in the shared social practices and values of social groups or what might more accurately be termed 'communication communities'.

At this time in British history such communication communities predominantly took the form of neighbourhoods or street communities among the working classes; and where the middle classes were concerned, they comprised social status groups (in the Weberian sense of interdining and intermarrying networks). Both of these were also often reflected, physically, in residential patterns. But communication communities did not necessarily depend upon residential propinquity. Individuals and couples living in different towns, but striving after similar social and cultural goals and adopting similar gender and work roles and sharing a similar language, could be considered as participants in the same

[28] Indeed, N. F. R. Crafts has argued with great cogency that the successive industrialisations which have occurred over the last two centuries in so many different countries have precisely been characterised by their ever-differentiating forms of specialisation into distinct industries or novel configurations of the factors of production, according to the logic and principle of comparative advantage: 'British industrialisation in international context'.

communication community, though they would never meet or know of each other's existence.

Individuals become members of various communication communities during their lifetimes. They learn their complex codes principally through their childhood and early adulthood upbringing, in which they are socialised into at least a minimum of two such communities: that of their family (or institutional) home and that of the streets outside it, their neighbourhood. In some cases these two may be culturally almost identical and strongly reinforcing; but in others they are not. For instance, Robert Roberts's memoirs attest to his keen childhood consciousness of a difference between his own family's status code and that of the Salford working-class neighbourhood of streets which his parents' corner shop served.[29] Social identities formed through participation in and choice of communication communities.

It is tempting to assert that of these two primary communication communities it is the family home which is the more fundamental source of the identity and loyalties which characterise a communication community, as is apparently exemplified in Robert Roberts's case. However, this is to prejudge the issue. Research undertaken in Britain in the 1950s demonstrated that relatively exclusive devotion to the values of the nuclear family, as opposed to those of the immediate community of neighbours, is itself an extremely 'middle-class' trait.[30] It may well be that one of the main reasons for the historical structural fault line running between the middle-class and the working-class 'worlds' lies precisely in this difference. This may be one of the main reasons why the fertility patterns of the working-class division of the nation reflect a diversity of local occupational-industrial régimes, whereas the variation found within the middle classes presents itself more as a national set of hierarchically graded status groups, less tied to any specific locality.

For most individuals brought up in British society since the mid-nineteenth century, the church or chapel, the school, the local forum and the national mass media (pub, club, local and national newspapers, radio, then television) and, later in their lives, the place of work, have each been categories of institution which are the sites for a number of further important communication communities requiring participation. These latter institutions may or may not be relatively similar in their 'languages' to the individual's two primary communities, the family and the immediate neighbourhood.[31] In fact most individuals 'belong' to, or at least

[29] Roberts, *The classic slum.* [30] Bott, *Family and social network.*

[31] The pioneering work of the educational and linguistic sociologist, Basil Bernstein, focused precisely on this issue in his exposition of the formation of cultural capital, in Bourdieu and Passeron's sense (as expounded by Bourdieu, 'Cultural reproduction and social reproduction'). Bernstein identified the disjuncture between the culture and language of the home and that of the school as a critical source of educational difficulty for working-class children, an obstacle which was encountered in a much less extreme form by the children of middle-class parents. The latter were, by definition of their parents' occupational roles in society (which required a record of relative success in the credentialling institutions of the nation's educational system, in order to gain entry to the middle-class jobs which they held), more assimilated to the distinctive culture and language codes of

participate in, several communication communities, providing them with various, potentially conflicting loyalties and values. In any town or neighbourhood there will be a number of such communities of varying social extents and powers overlaid upon each other: both plebeian and patrician co-existing, competing and conflicting with each other. This depends on the unique local, contingent conditions of employment, the prior political history of the significant social groups in the community and other related historical factors. In particular, religious beliefs and institutions and ethnic divisions related to population movements (as occurred on a substantial scale in Liverpool, Glasgow, Manchester or in London's East End, for instance) would further multiply or strongly influence the character of the competing communication communities and available sources of social identities in any town or city.[32]

This recognition that the differing languages of different communities and social status groups critically mediated the ways in which fertility behaviour changed during this period is consistent with the new linguistic understanding of the phenomenon of social class and class relations that has been emerging among historians of modern Britain of various persuasions.[33] Hence, W. H. Sewell has offered an important recasting of E. P. Thompson's seminal historicist definition of social class: as a relationship which is experienced.[34] Sewell has argued that class relationships are to be reformulated as being composed of particular linguistic discourses, shared by a community or social group.[35] Thus, it is still being argued, here, that fertility patterns were related to the complex set of phenomena which has been previously subsumed under the contested concept of 'class', but 'class' is to be understood in the light of a new, more discriminating and disaggregated conception of its meanings.

This new view of class relations means that gender is inextricably part of any class discourse and class analysis.[36] This is because gender enters in at the most fundamental level of the language of any community since gender is – exactly like language and a part of it – a symbolic system for representing differences. Nobody is neuter! The signifiers of difference which are related to gender are therefore manifold in any human group. They constitute a compulsory component both of

schools. Bernstein, 'Class and pedagogies'; Bernstein, 'Social class, language and socialisation'. For an important ethnographic study in postwar Britain further illustrating these insights, see Willis, *Learning to labour*.

32 The literature on religion, identity, schooling, class and politics in the nineteenth and early twentieth centuries is a vast and rich one. Two helpful introductions are: McLeod, *Religion and the working class*; and Parsons (ed.), *Religion in Victorian Britain*. On religion and schooling, see above, ch. 9, n. 201. For three detailed and different studies of the additional interplay between immigration, ethnicity and what I have termed 'communication communities' see, for instance, Clarke, *Lancashire and the New Liberalism*; Waller, *Democracy and sectarianism*; Feldman, *Englishmen and Jews*.

33 Stedman Jones, *Languages of class*, was an important early statement.

34 Thompson, *The making*, pp. 9–11.

35 Sewell, 'How classes are made', pp. 68–72.

36 Rose, *Limited livelihoods*, p. 16; and, more generally, Scott, *Gender and the politics of history*, ch. 3.

every individual's identity and also of the shared language in every communication community. But exactly how the differences related to gender, in all their varied registers – the essential and the peripheral – are construed and constructed in the discourse of each community, can vary almost infinitely and is continually subject to re-interpretation.[37] Class is, therefore, gendered in modern British history. However, gender is also classed.

Similarly, in this intensely patriarchal culture, relations within communication communities were also structurated by age: generational attributions of seniority and juniority.[38] Anybody who doubts for a moment the equal significance of this force, alongside class and gender in Victorian language and ideology, should reflect on the ubiquitous extent to which both the rhetorical (in either its Evangelical or its 'scientific' forms), and the legal justifications for the privileged position of the white middle-class adult male revolved around defining all other subject groups – women, the working class and 'primitive' peoples – as equivalents to children – both culturally and formally in law (see above, pp. 155–9, for a fuller account of this ideology).

Thus, in the light of a post-Wittgensteinian acceptance that language is fundamentally constitutive of all social relations because of its prior mediating role in social cognition and perception, historians have been scrutinising and dismantling the notion of class in their detailed studies. In his most recent study of class relations in England during this period, 1848–1914, Patrick Joyce has argued that the potential for 'class consciousness' resolves into a set of questions relating to the way in which people's locally created languages, ideologies and identities do or do not relate to each other.[39] It is these which are constitutive of people's 'experience', as Thompson put it, or of their competing discourses, as Sewell has reformulated it.

Both Joyce's research and that of David Vincent have demonstrated that the local communication communities which shared the same, primarily oral and body-language dialects, constituted the fundamental social divisions of relevance to questions of social identity and class formation in the late nineteenth century.[40]

[37] For an important study focusing explicitly on the many local and regional dialect variants of the languages of class, see Joyce, *Visions of the people*. Also note the recent comment by E. P. Thompson that 'Social historians have made too little use of dialect studies, including Joseph Wright's *English dialect dictionary*, 6 volumes (1898–1905)': *Customs in common*, p. 10.

[38] Structuration is a concept formulated by Anthony Giddens. It refers to the defining historical activity of human individuals, whereby they act purposefully to bring about desired goals and social change (or to prevent it). But they do this on the basis of their previous experience and therefore within the constraints this imposes upon perceptions of their options. This formulation helpfully dissolves the artificial notion previously prevalent within liberal sociological theory, as a result of Talcott Parsons's influence, of a distinction between 'action' and 'structures'. For Giddens the latter are created by and reflected in the former. Those forces of structuration which individuals are socialised into constrain the limits of their imagination and freedom to act but at the same time constitute the resources which they deploy to effect change. Giddens, *The constitution of society*, esp ch. 1.

[39] Joyce, *Visions of the people*, p. 9.

[40] Joyce, *Visions of the people*; Vincent, *Literacy and popular culture*.

In this they are following the implications of the empirical work of linguistic sociologists and anthropologists, such as the Opies' study of children's playground games and language, Labov's research on the street argot of New York and Bernice Martin's work on popular cultures in postwar Britain.[41] These have all shown the positive functions of such oral dialect cultures in simultaneously providing their users with the means to create their own distinctive identity as a group and also acting as a repository of the most useful and up-to-date practical knowledge and insights for manipulating their environment in their own interests.

Vincent has demonstrated the historical importance of such oral dialect communities by showing that it was their vigour and vitality which was chiefly responsible for the relatively superficial cultural impact of the late nineteenth-century liberal middle-class project of universal elementary education. With the best of intentions, this was an attempt to supplant and downgrade the oral, demotic knowledge from the home and the streets, which the children brought with them into the classroom.[42] Vincent argues that the middle-class project could not succeed in the proletarian conditions of relative poverty and material uncertainty, precisely because its technology of the written word and its ideology of the power of a universal, standard knowledge, comprising facts and figures relating to bygone ages and faraway places, was, for the vast majority of these children, cumbersome and inappropriate. (Note that it is not necessary to this thesis to posit that school and learning was disliked by or unattractive to working-class children; indeed, it may well have been attractive in a diversionary way because of its exotic, escapist character.)[43] The reception of formal education was partial and relatively superficial among children growing up in urban streets and courts. They needed most a practical, memory-based, dialect knowledge of their locality and its peculiarities and they found, as a matter of experience, that it was this form of knowledge which paid off best.

The norms, roles and values of each proletarian communication community were defined through the linguistic medium of its oral dialect. However, by the mid-nineteenth century it had become conventional among the status groups of the middle classes to insist that mastery of a written, literacy-based 'language' was additionally essential for participation in their particular communication communities.[44] The model here was derived from English polite society, where what was required was more than merely the mechanical ability to read. The ideal was to be able to write and to articulate elegantly a cultural code based on a body of knowledge derived from reading the classical literature and liberal learning, ancient and modern, now available through the mass medium of vernacular,

[41] Opie and Opie, *The language and lore of school children*; Labov, *The social stratification of English*; Martin, *A sociology of contemporary cultural change*.

[42] Vincent, *Literacy and popular culture, passim*.

[43] For a reinterpretation of oral history evidence to show that school was liked as much as, if not more than, it was disliked by working-class children, see Rose, 'Willingly to school'.

[44] Anderson, *Imagined communities*, ch. 5, especially p. 77.

commercial print. By the mid-nineteenth century illiteracy (and, with it innumeracy) was not only a bar to any kind of role in government and public life, it was quite unthinkable within the secular, patrician world because of the cultural reference framework an individual would thereby lack.[45]

Hence, the urgent attention given to the renovation of the nation's male public schools and universities during the middle decades of the nineteenth century, as demand for a classical and liberal education soared among those classes who could not afford personal tutors and even among those who could.[46] As the Royal Commissioners of the 1860s well knew, with their careful design for a graded national educational system giving differential access to this culture for different social classes, not all were to be permitted to participate as effectively as others within the literacy-based shared liberal culture. And the justification, of course, was that not all *could* participate as ably as each other: verifiable inequality of educational achievement could itself provide an important source of legitimacy for status gradings of occupations, social groups and individuals.[47] But for a communication community to exist and reproduce itself, which occurred primarily through the medium of the family home, it was essential that the female sex be able to participate fully, albeit within the limits of their supposedly feebler powers. Hence, the relatively rapid attention given by the mid-Victorian middle classes to the provision of a respectable degree of female secondary and higher education for their future wives and mothers.[48]

[45] The argument here links, of course, to much broader historical themes, regarding the changing character of politics, government and the institutions of the state in Britain during the period of transformative economic growth, *c.* 1770–1850. Growing cohorts of those – many of them nonconformists – whose wealth and power derived from commercial, professional and industrial activities increasingly challenged the political monopoly founded on personal connection, which existed for the benefit of the families of the Anglican, landed, leisured élite or Old Corruption to its enemies. Espousing an earnest Evangelical commitment to better all they found around them, the intellectual vanguard of the middle classes deployed the impressive liberal ideologies of political economy and utilitarianism, with which to justify the superiority and virtues of diligence, efficiency and talent as guides for government and civil society. Facility in literacy and numeracy were the essential administrative tools for communication between impersonally, meritocratically elected individuals, rationally directing the society and economy on its path to Progress. For an early exposition along these lines, see Polanyi, *The great transformation*; for a more recent amplification, see Corrigan and Sayer, *The great arch*, especially ch. 6. For examinations of various aspects of the ideological negotiation and compromise between aristocratic and parvenu ethos, see: Hilton, *The age of atonement*; Desmond, *The politics of evolution*; Mandler, *Aristocratic government*; Turner, *Contesting cultural authority*. For a more extended discussion of the nature of the liberal, rationalist consensus which emerged in the mid-Victorian decades and after, see above, pp. 148–65.

[46] Bamford, *The rise of the public schools*; the lists in Banks, *Prosperity and parenthood*, pp. 228–30, show forty-nine male public schools founded or rebuilt between 1840 and 1870 (additional to the reformed Clarendon schools). Rothblatt, *The revolution of the dons*; Bill and Mason, *Christ Church and Reform*.

[47] See above, pp. 149–51, 164–5.

[48] Harvie, *The lights of Liberalism*; Sutherland, 'The movement for higher education of women'. Of course, many of the leading liberal and feminist campaigners believed that the provision of female higher education was a fundamental right. The lists in Banks, *Prosperity and parenthood*, pp. 228–30, show that while only ten female public schools were opened before 1870, a further sixty-eight were opened over the following twenty years.

Thus, by the second half of the nineteenth century the language of the upper and middle classes had become distinct from that of the plebeian communities, in that it was closely tied to the personal possession in common throughout the land of a culture of vernacular literacy which was national in its remit.[49] Participation in the literacy-based cultures of these communication communities could therefore transcend locality of residence into genuinely national social formations, in a way which had only been possible for the nobility of an earlier age via the Court. Schooled in similar institutions, reading the same national newspapers which now became a possibility in the railway age, absorbed in the same serialised novels of a Dickens or a Thackeray, and communicating their shared culture to each other through the Steam Age's penny post, those whose 'dialect' was literate now had a national horizon and community. It is therefore meaningful to discern in the occupational fertility and nuptiality patterns of the middle-class 'world' a set of communication communities which were national in their presence, spread out across many towns and cities, and which related to each other as competitive, graded 'status groups'. These groups did, indeed, perceive each other to a considerable extent through the graded, if contested, relationships of a status hierarchy.

However, as was stated at the end of chapter 7, although the communicating communities of the middle-class 'world' ordered themselves into a 'national' cultural hierarchy, it was and is misleading and inappropriate also to interpret the varied fertility régimes of the working classes as the product of similar communication communities, national in their extent and conforming to some form of graded status hierarchy. As was discussed in the concluding section to chapter 9, Frank Parkin's theoretical work suggests the socio-political reasons why there was something of a fault line running between the middle-class hierarchy of exclusionary status groups, and the disparate, solidaristic communities of the working classes.

The numerous plebeian, oral dialect communication communities of late nineteenth- and early twentieth-century Britain were social groups necessarily based on shared locality and a good deal of face-to-face contact. The two principal sites where this kind of personal communication could develop and flourish were the neighbourhood and the workplace. The territorial extent of such dialect communities was, therefore, only partly governed by close residential propinquity, since a population sharing a common 'travel to work' catchment area could also form the basis for such a communication community, if sufficiently in contact with each other in and around the workplace. The changing scale of industry, the layout

[49] Hence, this was the period which witnessed the related projects of creating a canon of English literature and of 'standard' English. The latter began with a proposal by the Philological Society in 1857 and culminated in the *New English Dictionary* (popularly known from 1895 as the *Oxford English Dictionary*), whose volumes from A to Z were published from 1884 to 1928. See Waller, 'Democracy and dialect', pp. 3, 26; and Collini, *Public moralists*, pp. 352–61.

of workplaces, migration patterns and the technology of urban transport systems could, therefore, all influence the character and size of such linguistic communities.

During the period in which proletarian fertility was falling fast the typical scale of the unit of production expanded considerably in many industries, while tramways completely altered urban transport systems. This was also the period during which populations and neighbourhoods stabilised in most of the new urban environments created over the previous century. In many cases, mere neighbourhood communities coalesced into standardised regional dialects centred on the large city of which they formed a part, such as in Manchester, Liverpool, Sheffield or Birmingham.[50] But elsewhere communication communities might remain much smaller. Outside the metropolis of Manchester, for instance, there were twenty different dialects to be found characterising each one of the satellite Lancashire cotton textiles towns despite their proximity and their being part of the same regional industry.[51] Indeed, in some cases, districts within a single industrial conurbation remained relatively independent in their dialect and customs, as in each of the six towns of the North Staffordshire Potteries or the many industrial villages of the South Staffordshire coalfield, the Black Country. In both these last two cases of long-established industrial regions, workshops typically remained small, workers lived around their workplaces and transport links between the different constituent communities were relatively undeveloped, leaving them quite insulated from each other.

The focus on the linguistic basis of class relations has additionally opened up a further complication in assessing the relationship between changing fertility behaviour and the range of social and political forces, formerly subsumed under the term 'class'. In his study, Joyce has carefully distinguished between two senses in which language mediated class relations:

> [language] . . . in the sense of the 'discourses' which pertained at the time to popular politics and to labour, especially to trade unions . . . relatively formal, public . . . often associated with institutions . . . is to be differentiated from the symbolic, less formal and public, often assumed and unspoken, ways in which the social world is given form by people. . . . custom, and the symbolic structure of 'everyday', community life (a structure seen in dress, gesture, the built environment for example, in non-verbal as well as verbal forms).[52]

Joyce noted that the necessity for making this distinction followed from the research findings of W. H. Sewell and W. M. Reddy on nineteenth-century French workers' notions of work, family and community. They had found that workers' understandings of these fundamental aspects of their lives differed not only from those which middle-class observers supposed they had but also from those of their own proletarian leaders, as expressed in the latter's political statements and rhetoric.[53]

[50] Waller, 'Democracy and dialect'.

[51] Joyce, *Visions of the people*, p. 198.

[52] Joyce, *Visions of the people*, p. 17.

[53] Joyce, *Visions of the people*, p. 10, referring to Sewell, *Work and revolution in France*; and Reddy, *The rise of market culture*.

This closely relates to the important distinction between 'formal' and 'practical' politics, which Michael Savage introduced in his monograph on working-class politics in Preston, 1880–1940. Derived from the empirical insights of M. Burawoy and H. Newby and the theoretical insights of Gramsci and of Giddens, Savage pointed out that there was no necessary or straightforward correspondence between the political attitudes and moral beliefs which people held by virtue of their work-related and industrial relations experiences and those of their non-work lives pursued elsewhere in their communities and homes.[54] This is related to the general point, made above, that individuals happily and normally function in command of the languages of a number of communication communities. Savage has also stressed the point that participation in these different languages frequently entails the individual holding a set of far from coherent and consistent positions. The habitus of practical politics does not map directly on to formal political dispositions.[55]

Occupational differentials in fertility change were therefore subject to the net outcome of both of these influences, practical and formal politics. The gendered definitions of familial roles and responsibilities within a community, so important in determining perceived childrearing costs and benefits, were as likely to be the product of the community's practical politics as of its formal, rhetorical discourses, espoused by predominantly male organisations. However, the interests of a community articulated through the channels of its 'formal' politics could – and in many cases did – cross-cut the 'practical' interests of the family households of its members. Hence, the resulting predicament of competitive interdependence in the local labour market between the different members of each family; and the resulting divisions of interest within the working class between unionised, geographically stable males and others. Only detailed empirical research, of the sort exemplified by Savage on Preston as discussed in the last chapter, can uncover the precise way in which 'formal' and 'practical' politics influenced gender and class relations in a particular community and can thereby show their influence on fertility behaviour.

Thus, change and variation in fertility behaviour during this period certainly was connected to class relations in British society. But such class relations are to be understood as comprehending a much more complex set of historical forces than that implied by the neo-Weberian 'professional' model of five graded social classes, or a straightforward Marxian one of propertied versus propertyless. The national occupational data that is available from the 1911 census has therefore been interpreted here as reflecting differences between 'communication communities', albeit imperfectly illustrated in many cases because of the limitations imposed by the nationally aggregated form of the occupational fertility data. The outlines of about thirty different communication communities can be identified.

[54] Savage, *The dynamics*, pp. 5–7, 10–12, 17–19, referring to Newby, *The deferential worker*. For references to Burawoy's work, see ch. 9, n. 131.

[55] On Bourdieu's concept of habitus, see ch. 9, n. 71.

Within 'the middle classes', where absolute poverty was not a threat, at least half a dozen different modes of earning a living have been discerned, each exhibiting their distinctive fertility and nuptiality régimes. The variety is greater still among the much larger number of occupational categories representing the manual 'working classes', living as they did in a host of more geographically specific communication communities. For all these different groups, patrician and plebeian, their perceived relative childrearing costs rose substantially during the period 1860–1940. But the distinctive constellations of class, status, gender and generational relations characterising each of these communication communities resulted in this happening in very different ways.

There still remain powerful sceptical objections of a general kind to the conception of fertility change as a developmental sequence, intra and internationally varied in its manifestations and diverse in its motivations and methods. How did such communication communities evolve, within themselves, towards a new pattern of family building? Furthermore, why was it that supposedly distinct communities all altered their fertility, eventually, in the same direction? And does this not, after all, imply a single nationwide process of change?

For this reason, it had originally seemed to Stevenson and to Beveridge, when studying the phenomenon in the 1920s, that the fertility decline must in some sense be a single, unified event, in which diffusion of new ideas or techniques took place. The general form of the sceptical argument against multiple fertility declines, as advocated here, is that it is implausible and theoretically cumbersome to suppose that the same kinds of novel behaviour were 'invented' independently during the same period.[56] Instead, a single process of social and geographical diffusion of new practices seems theoretically more parsimonious, argue the wielders of Occam's Razor. The response to this form of scepticism is to show why, in matters of fertility change, there might, after all, be strong reasons for supposing that multiple spontaneous 'discovery' is, in fact, *more* not less plausible on *a priori* grounds, and, therefore, equally if not more theoretically parsimonious.

In order to make out this argument, first it has to be appreciated that there has always been a wide variation of family sizes present in virtually all communities in the past, no matter how relatively high the average fertility. Variability is a general property of the fertility characteristics of all human groups at all times which, surprisingly, has not been given sufficient attention in the demographic literature

[56] The continuing intellectual debate over the notion of diffusion versus that of multiple independent discovery has a venerable history in the related disciplines of cultural anthropology, philology and archaeology, where it has formed a central focus of disagreements on questions surrounding the geographical origins and movement of early human groups and their cultural and technological characteristics. Among the most important contributions this century have been: Tarde, *The laws of imitation* (first French edition published in 1890 as *Les Lois d'imitation*); Ogburn, *Social change*; Smith, *Culture: the diffusion controversy*; Kroeber, 'Diffusionism'; Rogers, *Diffusion of innovations*; Renfrew, *Archaeology and language*. (See also ch. 5, nn. 109–10).

discussing the causes of changing fertility. Because of the universal phenomenon of the varying incidence of sterility, substantial proportions of all women and of all married couples have always produced completed family sizes of every parity from zero upwards, no matter what the average fertility level of the population in question. This would certainly have been true of all social groups and communities in Britain throughout the nineteenth century, both before and after the watershed in national fertility rates in the 1870s. For instance, calculations prepared by the Royal Commission on Population of 1944–9 (highly appropriate because they were in fact based on the 1911 census data) estimated that, solely as a result of *involuntary* sterility, 5–8% of marriages were at that time childless, a further 4–5% restricted to one child only, and another 5–6% limited to two children only.[57]

This fundamental property of variability in fertility means that couples in all communities have always been free to observe a full range of family sizes. They were therefore all free to ruminate upon the apparent practical consequences in their community of different family sizes and rates of childbearing, even if any individual woman's outcome in these terms has been generally perceived to be a matter of divine chance. After all, precepts have existed in many cultures enjoining the virtues of large families and there have been many cultures in which highly fertile females were esteemed. This is not only because this is considered advantageous in such cultures, but also precisely because it is a good fortune that many in these societies are denied.

The universal existence of a sterility-induced wide range of family sizes has meant that all communities always have many practical examples before them of the relative socio-economic advantages or disadvantages of families that are smaller or larger than the observed or ideal, culturally sanctioned norms. This means that if, for any socio-economic or political reason or combination of reasons, the balance of advantage, in terms of perceived relative childrearing costs and benefits, should shift to favour smaller or larger families than are customarily considered optimal, then there will always be available copious examples to demonstrate this discrepancy between practice and precept. There is, of course, no inevitability that an accommodating ideological shift will ensue. However, provided the extant religious or customary norms are not considered to be entirely immovable on such matters, this would provide a means for conceptualising a socio-demographic basis for the process of normative change in relation to fertility and childrearing behaviour.

Note that there is no circular argument here relying on a prior change in the relevant, extant norms of a community. A change in the relative advantages of different sized families would be open to evaluation in terms of the community's pre-existing values and preferences, through the normal process of comment, gossip and reflection on the successes and failures of different families. Whether or

[57] *Report on an Enquiry into Family Limitation*, ch. VII, p. 84, reporting the estimates prepared by the Biological and Medical Committee of the Royal Commission on Population.

not the community's norms would adapt to this by themselves shifting and, if so, how such a process of change in norms could come about, is another question requiring further research. It can be generally asserted, however, that this would probably be related to the strength and persistence of the socio-economic or politico-ideological forces rendering smaller or larger families advantageous. It is also implied by this conception of fertility change that initial responses by individuals and couples to the perceived advantages of smaller families would typically be undertaken in an independent and clandestine fashion, because of the difficulty of publicly legitimating their behaviour in the absence of supportive norms. (Whereas the diffusion thesis, at least in application to British society, has the problem of explaining how the rapid social transmission of ideals or techniques took place in a culture where the public discussion of such matters was so restricted that remarkably little evidence of any such contraceptive knowledge has survived, while oral history has consistently testified to ignorance and shame as the currency of public discourse).

According to this formulation, then, a change in collective, public norms sanctioning smaller families, as was documented on pp. 520–5 occurring in different British status groups and communities between the 1900s and the 1940s, would not have played a chronologically leading, causal role in bringing about falling fertility. Based on their reflections upon the relative advantages of the range of different family sizes visible to them among their social peers – those whose aspirations and resources were similar to their own – the married couples of any communication community initially would have begun gradually to modify their sexual and reproductive behaviour towards their new perceived optima. This occurred almost regardless of extant prescriptive norms, as a set of relatively independently taken 'private' decisions. Collective, publicly articulated norms were then renegotiated at a later stage, only when it became obvious to a sufficiently articulate and powerful proportion of the local population that the new form of privately adopted behaviour was in fact so widespread that there was a clear disparity between the communication community's professed norms and its actual beliefs and practices. (The example of the official attitudes of Roman Catholicism towards birth control interestingly shows that accommodation between professed beliefs and private practices is a culturally and politically contingent matter and in no way an automatic process).

The intense middle-class debates which erupted in the Edwardian period over the reasons for and wider implications of falling birth rates, which were analysed in chapters 4 and 5 and which generated the 1911 census itself, represent the point in time when this pass had been reached by Britain's professional and upper middle class. Many of the documents of this period, notably the reports of the National Birth Rate Commission, can be read as the public record of this renegotiation of public, social norms within this particular, highly articulate and culturally powerful communication community. Their particular concerns and the terms of their debate have left their imprint so heavily upon the historical source materials available to posterity because they were the most culturally articulate status grouping, in command of the state's intelligence instruments.[58]

Thus, the essential stochastic property of variability in human fertility in fact renders the general proposition of multiple distinct innovations by independent individual couples in different communication communities eminently plausible, where fertility change is concerned. Like the phenomenon of mutation in nature, fertility is spontaneously variable in its manifestations, thereby possessing an ever-present potential for change, which is dependent for its expression on the selection effects of the encompassing cultural environment of perceived relative childrearing costs and benefits. However, this 'environment' is politically and ideologically constructed and fully subject to the contingent forces of ideological negotiation and political contest, in both national and local contexts.

Birth control, sexual and gender relations: a reappraisal of the role of the feminist movement

The foregoing has argued that it is inaccurate and misleading to see falling fertility as essentially a singular process of transition from a society in which birth control is quite simply beyond the calculus of rational choice to one in which family planning and contraceptive practice has become the norm. This concatenates and hopelessly simplifies a more complex and varied sequence of developments. Even the summary national aggregate statistics of occupational fertility reflect a protracted and uneven set of historical processes taking place in several stages and in different ways among the varied communication communities of British society.

Historians have shown that sexual abstinence before late marriage – or even for life for a significant minority – had been common throughout the early modern period in Britain. A moderate degree of birth spacing through occasional abstinence may well also have been practised by married couples from time to time.[59] During the last half of the Victorian period spacing births seems to have become much more intensively practised in many groups so that by the Edwardian period the 1911 census shows that spacing from the start of marriage was widespread. It has been argued here that attempted abstinence was the principal means used in British society up to and including this date. Coitus interruptus and abortion were also widely practised but were of secondary importance, as were all the range of other methods.

Not until the interwar period is there positive evidence that any substantial number of people were beginning to think in terms of ideal or target family sizes. This was, in fact, entirely logical since this way of thinking and behaving required at least two premises to be met, which were probably not satisfied until this period:

[58] The work of R. A. Soloway comes closest to an interpretation in this vein: *Birth control* and *Demography and degeneration*. [59] See above, pp. 418–19.

first that the children one had were highly likely to survive; and secondly that a relatively reliable form of contraception was available (abstinence could only provide this security in its most extreme form).

It seems likely that some couples may even have continued to gravitate towards the practice of complete abstinence as their way of conforming to the small family norms established in most communities by the end of the interwar period. For this section of the population, sexual behaviour and sexuality was not generally understood as something which could be regulated and moderated at will, in conformity with the use of effective contraceptive instruments. For them it was only controllable through the most primitive means of an on–off switch, which was best kept switched off for those worried about their family size and its responsibilities. For couples of this sort, sexuality and its consequences were not something negotiable and the degree to which a person of either sex could see themselves as in control of their sexuality was limited. This would seem to be the implication of the powerful sense of shame felt by some of those with large families in the 1930s and 1940s, according to the evidence of Mass-Observation and several oral historians. Elizabeth Roberts has reported that even in the 1950s the appearance of a third child or a late addition to the family could be treated in some communities as distasteful proof of continuing sexual activity by the couple concerned. Roberts comments that 'it is interesting that at such a comparatively late date, sexual abstinence in marriage was equated with "behaving yourself"'.[60]

At the same time, for other, growing sections of society the mechanism of a reliable form of birth control was provided by the gradually increasing use of condoms, caps and diaphragms tracked, albeit imperfectly, in the results of the survey of the Royal Commission on Population. Apparently their use did not begin to become really widespread until the 1930s, when cheap and more aesthetically pleasing latex products became available for both men and women, while the Anglican Church, the government and the medical profession simultaneously relaxed their previous public opposition, which had sanctioned only abstinence. It seems probable that rates of abortion also rose to an unprecedented level at this time. The correct interpretation of this latter phenomenon may be that one result of the final emergence of a popular culture in which small families had come to be seen as both a desirable and a practically realisable goal was a much greater preparedness to take positive, evasive action (abortions) when these definite expectations and norms appeared to be threatened by an aberration, a 'mistake'.

If broadly accurate, this history of the variegated and changing mix of methods adopted by couples to regulate their fertility during the first half of the twentieth century would seem to have important implications for our understanding of the closely related parallel histories of sexuality and of wider power relations between

[60] Roberts, *A woman's place*, p. 84; and see above, pp. 520–2, evidence from Mass Observation in 1945.

men and women in society. Since gender and sexual relations are everywhere and at all times the subject of negotiation at both an individual and collective level, the dialectics of such negotiation would necessarily have been intimately involved in the processes whereby fertility was spaced and eventually planned; and also in determining the mix of methods of birth control which were used in different communication communities. It therefore follows that, having reconstructed the outlines of a history of the different and changing forms of birth controlling behaviour, certain inferences may be drawn about the likely associated history of marital sexual and gender relations. Whether or not these inferences are valid will then depend on matching them against the available historical evidence on the negotiation of gender roles, on sexual codes and sexual behaviour. However, in the present state of extremely provisional and patchy knowledge regarding the history of sexualities in Britain over the last two centuries, to assert that there must be an important relationship between that history and changing fertility does not mean that it is possible to examine that relationship in any great detail.

In seeking to draw connections between the histories of changing fertilities and sexualities, it is vital to bear in mind the helpful distinctions which Michael Mason has drawn. He has proposed that there are four categories of phenomena, which are the subject matter of the historical study of sexuality in any society: sexual activity itself; public demeanour (observable codes of behaviour and self-presentation, such as dress); professed belief and collective norms; and private belief.[61] Obviously, historical change in marital fertility is likely to be directly affected by the first of these four categories and attempted abstinence is a phenomenon of this kind. However, the practice of attempted abstinence – or any other sexual activity – occurs in the context of a (contested) culture of sexuality, which simultaneously embraces the other three categories of phenomena distinguished by Michael Mason, any of which may generate recoverable historical evidence for reconstructing relevant historical changes in sexuality.

Overall it seems most likely (though it is worth repeating that this is provisional and further research is undoubtedly required) that the *majority* experience during the period in which marital fertility was brought under control from the 1860s through to the 1930s was – paradoxically perhaps – one of increased public inhibitions and private difficulties in sexual relations between husbands and wives, men and women. This was both the cause and the effect of the fact that it was the crude and isolating method of attempted abstinence which probably remained until the 1920s the mainstay method of birth control. In this culture of abstinence (a culture of long standing although historically reconstructed and ideologically immensely enhanced during the course of the nineteenth century) birth control was achieved through attempted sexual self-control, rather than a mastery of effective, contraceptive birth control leading to greater sexual freedom.

[61] Mason, *Victorian sexuality*, p. 40.

Angus McLaren has shown in an intriguing article that this was true of Freud himself. Freud's psychoanalytic *œuvre* constitutes the quintessential artefact testifying to this period's preoccupation with sexual functioning (particularly within marriage – many of Freud's clients were married) as something problematic. McLaren pointed out that this should be related to the evidence which Freud left of his own personal experience of self-imposed abstinence after 1896 (when he was aged 39), following the rapid appearance of six children in the ten years since his marriage (which had itself been preceded by a four-year engagement – not unusual for a struggling young student of medicine).[62]

McLaren suggests that Freud's famous thesis of sexual repression and creative sublimation, which finally appeared in its fullest form in 1930 in *Civilisation and its discontents*, seems itself to be a 'sublimation' of the sexual renunciation in marriage, of which he had written both privately and publicly in a tone of candid disillusion (though not embitterment) in the 1890s and 1900s:

> It must above all be borne in mind that our cultural sexual morality restricts sexual intercourse even in marriage itself, since it imposes on married couples the necessity of contenting themselves, as a rule, with a very few procreative acts. As a consequence of this consideration, satisfying sexual intercourse in marriage takes place only for a few years; and we must subtract from this, of course, the intervals of abstention necessitated by regard for the wife's health. After these three, four or five years the marriage becomes a failure in so far as it has promised the satisfaction of sexual needs. For all devices hitherto invented for preventing conception impair sexual enjoyment, hurt the fine sensibilities of both partners and even actually cause illness. Fear of the consequences of sexual intercourse first brings the married couple's physical affection to an end; and then in a remoter result, it usually puts a stop as well to the mental sympathy between them which should have been the successor to their original passionate love.[63]

McLaren, who has championed instead coitus interruptus and abortion as the most important birth controlling methods in his work on falling fertility in Britain, comments on this passage that 'It is difficult not to believe that Freud exaggerates and presents a portrait, perhaps of his own marriage, but not that of society as a whole'; but Freud's analysis has much wider relevance than this.[64] In his study of a

[62] McLaren, 'Contraception and its discontents', pp. 524–6.

[63] McLaren, 'Contraception and its discontents', p. 523, citing Freud's *'Civilised' sexual morality*, published in 1908.

[64] McLaren, 'Contraception and its discontents', p. 523. McLaren premises his judgement on the mistaken rhetorical question: 'But can one seriously accept the notion that in most marriages at the turn of the century sexual relations were restricted to rare occasions for four to five years at best?' (*ibid.*, p. 523). In Freud's theory adult sexuality was intrinsically moral (by contrast with the unconscious impulses of the infantile mind) and health-maintaining. As McLaren notes, Freud believed that therefore the morally valid and healthy expression of sexuality required the mutually fulfilling act of spontaneous, unprotected, procreative, penetrative coitus: 'Orgasms achieved by any other means were condemned' (*ibid.*, p. 521). Although he held out hope for a future rhythm method being devised which would render such unprotected coitus non-procreative (*ibid.*, pp. 523–4), Freud considered that all currently available methods of coital contraception, including condoms and diaphragms, were not only aesthetically inadequate but also neurasthenic, i.e. productive of nervous disorders. It was the symptoms (e.g. hysteria) of these phenomena in his patients which Freud was

closely related communication community to that of Freud's Vienna, Marion Kaplan has concluded that rapidly falling fertility in the German Jewish middle class from the 1880s was achieved principally through a combination of abstinence and coitus interruptus, probably admixed in many cases.[65] Kaplan cites a set of personal memoirs (of Adolf Riesenfeld, married 1909), which, while not specifying precisely the method of contraception used, clearly reports on a husband's sense of sexual self-denial in agreeing to his wife's demands for mutually agreed periods of freedom from childbearing (*Schonjahre*), apparently a common practice.[66] It seems likely, therefore, that Freud's work can, indeed, be taken as reliable historical testimony, directly reporting on a range of contraceptive activity, including attempted abstinence, among the Viennese middle class at the turn of the century; and, of course, it attests powerfully to the associated emotional and sexual problems which some individuals and couples were experiencing as they failingly negotiated with each other and struggled with their highly imperfect techniques.

Hence, Lella Florence's description of the marital difficulties due to a régime of attempted abstinence reported to her by women attending her Cambridge birth control clinic in the mid-1920s is remarkably similar to Freud's:

> In the case of the older couples, work-weary and worn out, abstinence is apparently not a severe effort. But some of the younger women have told me what a strain is imposed upon both themselves and their husbands. The wife always felt the necessity of restraining any demonstrations of affection for her husband, and of meeting his affectionate overtures with

seeking to explain by his revolutionary link with the patient's sex life (*ibid.*, p. 517). This means that when Freud writes of 'satisfying sexual intercourse' only for a few years in marriage, this is because, as he says, couples are limited to only 'a very few [truly] procreative acts' before they find they have enough children; and so thereafter they are constrained only to non-procreative acts which, because of the inadequate nature of contraceptives, are either morally or nervously debilitating or both. Thus, Freud is not asserting that all sexual relations in most marriages are necessarily rare and limited only to the first few years of marriage. He is only asserting that fully satisfying (according to his theory), procreative coitus, is in such rare supply. Freud's valuable direct testimony to the sexual mores, motives and anxieties of his times, through the unique testimonies elicited from his couch, is not, therefore, to be dismissed on grounds of incredulity as applying only to his own marriage, as McLaren concluded in 1979.

[65] Kaplan, *The making of the Jewish middle class*, pp. 42–5. Steven Beller has argued that a defining characteristic of the Viennese Jewish middle-class identity was their enthusiasm and admiration for the liberal, emancipatory values of the post-Enlightenment German culture and language, hence it may be legitimate to treat German and Viennese middle-class Jews as part of the same communication community: Beller, *Vienna and the Jews*, esp. chs. 9–10.

[66] Adolf Riesenfeld was born in Breslau in 1884: 'Before our wedding she was able to make me agree that the first year of the marriage should be a *Schonjahr* [protected year] and sought to justify this with youth, frailty and other things.' Kaplan reports that after the birth of their first child (a daughter) his wife wanted a *Schonzeit* of at least five years, of which Riesenfeld records, 'which, alas, I had to agree to'. Kaplan comments that in his memoirs Riesenfeld 'makes much of his own frustration and his previously (premarital) passionate nature in reporting on these *Schonjahre*'; Kaplan points out that they must have been a rather common notion of the time, since Riesenfeld does not explain the term, but simply assumes the reader will recognise the concept. Kaplan, *The making of the Jewish middle class*, pp. 44–5.

coldness and rebuff, until gradually there grew up an icy barrier between them which both felt and recognised, but which they could not alter so long as abstinence was enforced. If only these couples could have known of some certain contraceptive they might have been spared much pain and much lost happiness.[67]

Other aspects of the tensions involved have also been brought out by Evelyn Faulkner in her analysis of 285 (mostly female) working-class letters written to Marie Stopes in 1925: 'Abstinence led to arguments, depression and a lack of affection . . . worry about infidelity was often a paramount consideration.'[68] Faulkner also reads the letters as evidence of a gradually shifting balance of sexual bargaining power during these decades:

Men were beginning to temper their right to incautious intercourse, but wives could only insist on restraint for a short time. . . . The women had the right to refuse sex and regulate sexual activity for a limited period of time, but the men retained the power to initiate sexual relations and to reinstate sexual activity after a lapse in time. . . . Birth control knowledge was deliberately sought to avoid pregnancies, with the intention of safeguarding their health and lives and to keep their husbands faithful. These were their personal reasons. The economic motive they shared with their husbands.[69]

Only with the growing use of cheap, efficient, comfortable and convenient contraceptives during the 1930s and after did it begin to become practical for an increasing proportion of men and women to throw off the self-denying culture of abstinence. That this was a rather gradual process during these decades was much to do with the extraordinarily high degree of confusion, ignorance and misinformation prevailing on all matters to do with the physical side of sexual relations, including therefore the uses and the relative merits of contraceptive appliances. With basic sex education in schools a discretionary rarity, even well-educated men and women were forced to experiment for the most satisfactory methods, often without a clear understanding of the relevant anatomy and physiology.[70] Hence, Claire Davey's analysis of the Stopes correspondence has confirmed the contemporary research of Enid Charles, that in the late 1920s and early 1930s 'middle-class' men and women were expressing their sexual dissatisfaction with the (pre-latex) sheath as much as with coitus interruptus; and that they apparently viewed the cap as preferable on aesthetic grounds, though remaining somewhat anxious as to its efficiency, relative to the condom.[71] Widespread ignorance and fear was hardly surprising given the extent of disagreements even among the few 'experts' of the time, frankly acknowledged by Lella S. Florence in 1930: 'The confusion existing in the field of contraceptives is nowhere more clearly demonstrated than in the conflicting views held concerning the condom, the

67 Florence, *Birth control*, pp. 119–20.

68 Faulkner, '"Powerless to prevent him"', p. 54.

69 Faulkner, '"Powerless to prevent him"', pp. 58–9.

70 On the feeble official promptings for sex education from the 1920s through to the 1940s and the inadequate results still in the 1970s, see Weekes, *Sex, politics and society*, pp. 211–12, 255.

71 Davey, 'Birth control in Britain during the interwar years', Table 4, p. 338.

necessity or advisability of douching, the necessity for removing the pessary very shortly, and the advisability of leaving it in position for some time, etc.'[72]

In Britain, only with confident and legitimate access to reliable and unobtrusive contraceptive methods could there begin to emerge a truly widespread, popular view of sexuality, its physical expression and its potentially unwanted consequences as something which was and which should be practically controllable at will. There is certainly some evidence, such as the publication of marriage and sex manuals and responses to these as well as to popular magazines, which indicate that certain elements of the population were adopting these beliefs as their own during the 1920s and 1930s.[73] Stearns and Knapp have recently argued that in the USA, at least, 'A new tone began to penetrate widely-publicised avant-garde writing on courtship and marriage by about 1920. The importance of sexual expression gained ground.'[74] However, Stearns and Knapp also note associated misogynist leanings emerging in the less romantic attitudes towards sexual and gender relations, which they chart in the 'New Love' campaign of the innovatory popular men's magazine, *Esquire*, founded in the 1930s.[75] So that 'Victorian agreement on the importance of love for men, and on its spiritual qualities, did not survive the first half of the 20th century.'[76] Greater individual control over sexual expression among men and women could equally, therefore, either enhance or detract from the emotional and companionate quality of the marriage or other gender relationships.

Oral history and cultural evidence suggests that in Britain, at least, the process of exorcising inhibited attitudes towards physical sexuality, ingrained over the previous century or so, took even a further generation before positive values relating to sexual expression throughout marriage began to become more acceptable as norms on a truly widespread social scale.[77] Although the Second World War itself may well have been a period of novel sexual license at least for some social groups, a patriarchal mood set in during the ensuing decade of defensive reaction in popular culture to the nation's evident decline from imperial pre-eminence. The associated anxieties over the status of a British manhood still in arms (conscription and national service) but apparently powerless to prevent the nation's decline in global status resulted in a virulently machismo popular culture; homosexuality was simply beyond the pale in these immediate postwar decades.[78] Superficially socially rebellious and anarchic, the literary lions who were the Angry Young Men were also ideologically reactionary. In their own inverted way

[72] Florence, *Birth control on trial*, p. 41.

[73] On interwar sex and marriage manuals, see Weekes, *Sex, politics and society*, ch. 11; and on responses to these, especially to Stopes, see Holtzman, 'The pursuit of married love'.

[74] Stearns and Knapp, 'Men and romantic love', p. 775.

[75] Stearns and Knapp, 'Men and romantic love', pp. 777–83.

[76] Stearns and Knapp, 'Men and romantic love', p. 755.

[77] On sexual norms and behaviour from oral history, see Humphries, *A secret world of sex*; and see the various sources cited in ch. 8, nn. 66, 163.

[78] Segal, 'Look back in anger'.

they gloried in the class system, through their preoccupation with tales of cross-class miscegenation, which emphasised a subordinated sexual and social role for women as upper-class pawns in the mating game, and as flawed, overly possessive lovers. This same generation's counsellors on childrearing identified mothers as the nation's weak link, in need of (male) professional tutelage to avoid the dangers of 'maternal deprivation' (John Bowlby's key concept in his best-seller of 1953, *Child care*).[79]

It is to be noted that there is certainly no clear and consistent pattern of class-differentials in changing sexual attitudes visible in the patchy evidence that is available. Claire Davey has argued that the evidence of the Stopes correspondence in the 1920s suggests that a sample of 'middle-class' couples were more likely to emphasise pleasure in sex as a priority when selecting their method of birth control and there was more participation in contraception by husbands than among a parallel 'working-class' sample of correspondents.[80] But Mass-Observation's 'Little Kinsey' survey of sexual attitudes and behaviour in 1949 found the middle classes split along quasi-religious lines. One sample, consisting of approximately 450 replies (a 15% response rate) from the members of three professions selected on the grounds that they were vocationally 'concerned either morally or physically with the sex life of others' (doctors, clergy and schoolteachers) expressed 'more rigid' views (on matters such as prostitution, illegitimacy and adultery) than a predominantly working-class sample of 2,000 interviewed in the street (where there was only a 1% refusal rate!).[81] However, on the other hand, the 700 replies from Mass-Observation's own middle-class 'Panel' of 1,200 regular volunteer correspondents exhibited significantly more 'modern' attitudes than even the street sample. It was considered that the Panel volunteers predominantly represented that section of the middle class which was most secularised in its attitudes. This was significant, since it was noted among the street sample that, apart from class affiliation and gender, regular church attendance was the only social attribute of individuals showing some correlation with 'rigid' attitudes. This tends to suggest that individuals' changing attitudes towards sexuality during the second and third quarters of the twentieth century correlated no more with their class and status position than with the relatively independent issue of their personal disposition towards an emotional conservatism or liberalism/permissiveness (something probably also broadly associated with political sympathies as well as religiosity).

To sum up, it has been argued that the historical process through which childbearing fell to the low levels of the 1920s and 1930s, far from being in itself the

[79] Riley, *War in the nursery*.

[80] Davey, 'Birth control in Britain during the interwar years', pp. 336–9. See also above, p. 408.

[81] England, 'Little Kinsey'. The full reports of this research can also be consulted in Mass-Observation File Reports 3110, 3110A and 3110B (Mass-Observation Archives, University of Sussex, available on Microfiche, published by Harvester: Brighton).

direct source of emancipated sexual relations in marriage, was probably initially associated with intensified difficulties, tensions and sexual uncertainties for the majority in society. Female personal and bodily freedom was only achieved by many individual married women either through accepting a further degree of practical and intimate dependence on their husbands' sexual care and forbearance, or by insisting unilaterally on their own unavailability – or by some combination of the two.[82] Thus, although they had in at least a minimal sense to co-operate with each other in order successfully to limit their family size, the methods involved were often highly conducive to the creation of difficulties and resentments in sexual relations between spouses. An artifical, stressful attempt to keep a physical, emotional distance from each other within the home was often involved. Even where the more efficient methods were used, these may have tended to exacerbate inequalities in gender relations by emphasising the extent to which wives were dependent on their husbands' goodwill for their peace of mind.

Even in the early 1950s Eustace Chesser's important survey of married and single women's sexual behaviour and attitudes found that among 1,097 married women, 60% of the 425 women describing themselves as in 'exceptionally happy marriages' and 70% of the 386 women in 'very happy marriages' agreed that men wanted sex more often than women; and only 41% and 31%, respectively, claimed never to have refused their husbands sexual intercourse. The figure was only 22% for the 242 women in 'fairly happy marriages' but – very revealingly – 34% for those 44 women in marriages they themselves described as 'unhappy' or 'very unhappy' – indicating a source or correlate of their unhappiness, in their relative lack of negotiating powers over sex.[83] Furthermore, 30% of women reported that fear of pregnancy made sex less enjoyable when their husbands were mainly responsible for contraception, whereas only 17% reported this fear when they took control of their own contraception.

In arguing that there was a significant relationship between changing fertility, nuptiality and sexual practices, the above account has emphasised that all this entails the wider issues of changing gender relations. This in turn demands that consideration be given to the possible influence of the political and ideological feminist movements of the period, since these have a strong *prima facie* claim to be considered among the prime movers of change in gender relations. In their pioneering assessment of 1964, the Bankses concluded that the Victorian feminist movement was positively uninterested in the contemporary birth control movement because of its anarchic, sexually libertarian connotations in the eyes of its

[82] As has been argued at length in chapter 8, especially pp. 424–31, most methods of birth control were those in which males took primary responsibility, such as abstinence, coitus interruptus and non-coital sex and the use of condoms; and other methods still required male acquiescence, if not positive co-operation, especially in working-class homes (caps and diaphragms, pessaries, douching).

[83] Chesser, *The sexual, marital and family relationships*, pp. 472, 520, 469.

opponents.[84] The feminists shunned the neo-Malthusians because they had an over-riding political need to put as much distance as possible between themselves and the supposedly sexually disreputable historical associations of the cause of feminine equality with, first, the Republican Mary Wollstonecraft, and, secondly, the utopian communes of Owenite socialism in the 1830s and 1840s.[85]

Although historical research on the nature of feminism and gender relations has advanced enormously in the three decades since, not least through the scholarship of Olive Banks herself, there has been no formal reappraisal of this judgement on the relationship between political feminism and fertility. There has appeared a somewhat different hypothesis, that of 'domestic feminism', which is associated with the historical research of the 1970s which discovered women's friendship networks.[86] Accepting the Bankses' findings, these historians have argued that the commencement of birth control in Britain was motivated by an apolitical trend among middle-class wives, partly assisted by the medical profession, to assert the need for protection of their own health by reducing childbearing, and that this was achieved despite the frequent ignorance or indifference of their husbands.[87] But the separation between the feminist political movement and changing ideologies of domestic relations posited by this body of work would now seem unsupportable and unhelpful in the light of the most recent research on organised feminism, which has shown that 'domesticity' was a primary source of feminist ideological power. Thus, while accounts of 'domestic feminism' have accurately reported one of the important ways in which middle-class women bargained for reduced childbearing, it is too limited an interpretation.

Olive Banks's prosopographical approach has provided the essential scholarly foundation for the construction of a genealogy of feminist factions and agenda and is the basis for this new, more sophisticated history of feminism.[88] Important revisionist interpretations, such as those of Carole Pateman, Susan Kingsley Kent and Barbara Caine, have emphasised the power of a conservative, Evangelically inspired, maternal and domestic ideology as a major, autonomously female driving force within feminism throughout the Victorian period, as opposed to the celebrated liberal 'Cause' with its bevy of distinguished male allies, triumphalised by Ray Strachey in 1928, the year in which the final battle for the vote was won.[89]

Pateman pointed out that liberalism, despite the eloquence of J. S. Mill, remained blind in its economic form to the inequities arising from the sexual division of labour and blind in its political form to the legal discrimination

[84] Banks and Banks, *Feminism and family planning*.

[85] On these earlier episodes and their sexual associations, see the excellent Taylor, *Eve and the New Jerusalem*; also Caine, *Victorian feminists*, ch. 2.

[86] Smith-Rosenberg, 'The female world of love and ritual'; Branca, *Silent sisterhood*.

[87] Smith, 'Family limitation'; Branca, *Silent sisterhood*. See also the many contemporary extracts illustrating these concerns in Jalland and Hooper, *Women from birth to death*, Part 3.

[88] Banks, *Faces of feminism*; Banks, *Biographical dictionary of British feminists*.

[89] Pateman, *The sexual contract*; Kent, *Sex and suffrage*; Caine, *Victorian feminists*; Strachey, *The cause*.

inherited through the patriarchal assumptions of its founding father, John Locke.[90] Pateman argued that most significant legal and social concessions won by Victorian feminists, rolling back the patriarchal powers, were won through the successful mobilisation of evangelical 'domesticity' and maternity arguments, deriving from the thesis of women's superior moral purity as mothers and from their claims to moral guidance over their children and over 'public' men.[91] Barbara Caine has documented this in a number of areas: in the case of Josephine Butler's campaign to repeal the Contagious Diseases Acts; where women successfuly claimed access to secondary and then university education; to the rights to hold their own property and income in marriage; and to guardianship of their children after separation.[92]

The power of this face of feminism could also create divisions within the feminist movement, and this occurred during the three decades before the Great War, which partly explains the halting progress of the suffrage movement. An important generational difference of perspective opened up between an eminent Old Guard of those brought up in early Victorian times, and the 'New Woman' generation, who took their right to higher education and recognised career opportunities (albeit across a more restricted range of vocations than their brothers) for granted, and were often interested in socialism and the possibilities of alliance with the organised working class (which was almost exclusively male). Furthermore, many of them had an open, inquiring mind on the question of sexuality and marrriage.[93] But Susan Kingsley Kent has importantly shown that the debilitating conflicts over tactics and strategy which fractured the suffrage movement (whether to press for votes only for the unmarried or for all women; whether to make common cause with the male leaders of the working class, and if so with which; militancy versus constitutionality) were to a considerable extent patched over and resolved by a common front among feminists of all hues – conservative and Evangelical, liberal, and socialist – on the question of sexual autonomy, especially in marriage.[94]

While this was evidently a position easily derived from liberal and socialist premises, somewhat surprisingly it was in fact the moral animus generated by the conservative evangelical position, on the high calling of women as maternal and domestic guardians of the nation's spiritual and physical security, which invested this issue with such galvanising political force in the period 1885–1914.[95] Unison

[90] Pateman, *The sexual contract*, especially ch. 4.

[91] Pateman, *The sexual contract*, p. 231.

[92] Caine, *Victorian feminists*, *passim*.

[93] Cunningham, 'The "New Woman Fiction"'; Caine, *Victorian feminists*, ch. 7. The 'New Woman' was a term of art coined in 1894 by Sarah Grand for the novels of the 1890s, where male sexuality, brutality and lack of self-control were portrayed as justifying the need for female sexual autonomy in marriage. That George Gissing's alternative soubriquet, *The odd women*, providing the title of his novel of the previous year, did not stick was, perhaps, indicative of the upper hand that the feminist position was gaining in the public debate. Rubinstein, *Before the suffragettes*, pp. 12–37.

[94] Kent, *Sex and suffrage*; see also Holton, *Feminism and democracy*.

[95] Kent, *Sex and suffrage*.

on this issue allowed liberal feminists, such as Millicent Garrett Fawcett, to join hands with conservative evangelicals such as Josephine Butler.[96] For the latter this was a natural extension of her long campaign against the most offensive aspects of the mid-Victorian 'double standard' of sexual morality represented by the Contagious Diseases Acts, whereby a system of medical regulation of female prostitutes attempted (ineffectively) to ensure freedom from venereal disease for their male clients.[97] Celibacy and spinsterhood had also long been both Evangelical and liberal feminist concerns. In public debate over the so-called 'surplus women' problem of the mid-century, the former castigated timid and materialist middle-class men for not marrying and thereby denying themselves and women a proper spiritual influence, while the latter argued that the solution was greater female access to education and independent livelihoods.[98]

These central issues of gender relations – the terms upon which marriage and sexuality were to be enjoyed (or free to be declined) – coalesced and for the first time became acknowledged matters for open public debate in the latter 1880s and 1890s: 'the very fact of male sexual expectation became an issue'.[99] The issue of male sexual restraint was pursued by feminists on both sides of the political spectrum: by the religiously inclined evangelical generation, through their almost unanimous participation in the National Vigilance Association and the associated social purity movement; and at the same time in the range of more unorthodox ideas expressed in the 'New Woman' feminist literature, drawing upon a range of secular, humanist, socialist and scientific sources of inspiration, such as Tolstoy and Ibsen, Edward Carpenter and Karl Pearson.[100] In feminist fiction in the 1890s and in feminist political statements during the next decade, the fear of venereal disease was now invoked as a compelling example to justify women's claim to a general right of control over the sexual relationship, within marriage as well as without.[101] Key rulings in the 1860s in divorce court cases had already established the right of individual women to divorce husbands for infecting them with venereal disease on grounds of cruelty, but no wider or more general claim to female sexual autonomy had been conceded.[102]

In her survey of the course of public debate on sexual relations, Carol Dyhouse

96 Caine, *Victorian feminists*, pp. 234–6.

97 On the repeal of the Contagious Diseases Acts, see pp. 415–16.

98 Banks and Banks, *Feminism and family planning*, ch. 3; Levine, *Victorian feminism*, ch. 4.

99 Caine, *Victorian feminists*, p. 258; see also Jeffreys, *The spinster and her enemies*.

100 Bland, 'The married woman'; Bland, 'Marriage laid bare'; Caine, *Victorian feminists*, pp. 252–8; Dyhouse, *Feminism and the family*, ch. 4, esp. pp. 146–7; Walkowitz, 'Science, feminism and Romance'.

101 Bland, '"Cleansing the portals of life"'; Dyhouse, *Feminism and the family*, ch. 4; Caine, *Victorian feminists*, pp. 253–9. The most extreme statement of this kind was Emmeline Pankhurst's polemic published in 1913 by the Women's Social and Political Union: *The great scourge and how to end it*.

102 Savage, '"The wilful communication"', p. 42. Note also that despite the judicial precedents since the 1860s, as late as 1899 in *Regina v. Clarence* a maverick jury was prepared to uphold a husband's right to sexual intercourse with his spouse without her consent and even when he was known to be suffering from syphilis: Harris, *Private lives*, p. 26. See also Shanley, *Feminism, marriage*, ch. 6, for relevant legal developments in Victorian Britain.

has suggested two distinct watersheds in this period.[103] First, in the later 1880s and 1890s the subject was opened up to explicit discussion. But at this point Dyhouse sees female participation as mainly defensive and moralistic, focusing on the problems of male 'violence' in their unilateral assertion of unlimited 'conjugal rights', premised on notions of female sexual passivity and dependence. This was contrasted with the virtues of a relationship based on emotional equality, mutual respect and, therefore, relative sexual continence for husbands (who were still presumed to have a more insistent sexual appetite). Calls for sexual continence from husbands were forthcoming in the New Woman novels and in many popular publications, where the demand was often linked to the question of maternal health and the consequent need to space births.[104]

There was a significant alliance on this issue between feminist women and a section of the medical profession, still predominantly male. For instance in the chapter on 'The question of sexual abstinence', in the 1908 English translation of the sixth edition of his pioneering textbook, the German physician and sexologist, Iwan Bloch, identified five different schools of opinion on the relative value of the practice of sexual abstinence.[105] He dismissed equally the 'apostles of absolute abstinence' (such as Tolstoy), those who doubted the possibility of abstinence, and the hypocrites who wanted a 'duplex sexual morality' – the double standard. As a medical man he advocated the spiritual and physiological virtues of relative and temporary forms of abstinence, regularly practised, and allied himself with the fifth 'school', those who advocated purity for both sexes before marriage.[106] Here he cited Sarah Grand's archetypal 'New Woman' novel, *The heavenly twins*, as the representative of this viewpoint.[107]

However, this medical and feminist alliance was also linked to the promotion of the somewhat defensive discourse of the pathology of childbirth and the need for male sexual 'continence' to protect women.[108] The emphasis on women's frailties and the pain and dangers of confinement was in order to elicit their spouses' voluntary compliance with the sexually abstemious régime necessary to protect

103 Dyhouse, *Feminism and the family*, pp. 158–93.

104 For instance: Dr Mary Scharlieb, *A woman's words to women on the care of their health in England and in India* (1895); Dr Mary Scharlieb, *The seven ages of woman* (1915): extracts cited from both in Jalland and Hooper, *Women from birth to death*, pp. 209–10, 230–1, 272–3. Francis Swiney, *The bar of Isis* (4 editions 1907–19), discussed in Dyhouse, *Feminism and the family*, pp. 168–9. See also Seccombe, 'Starting to stop'.

105 Bloch, *The sexual life of our time*, ch. XXV.

106 Bloch, *The sexual life of our time*, pp. 673–4. Bloch was in favour of periodic abstinence because of his adherence to the 'spermatic economy' view that too much dissipation of sexual energy sapped a man's intellectual and spiritual capacities, which were necessary for his self-development (Herbert Spencer's 'individuation' theory – see chapter 5, footnote 101).

107 Bloch, *The sexual life of our time*, p. 673. In the novel the heroine, 'Evade', at the last minute leaves her groom at the church door when she learns of his duplicitous 'preconjugal career'.

108 While the medicalisation of childbirth in the hands of a predominantly male profession was a longer-term outcome of the success of this discourse, the point is that its original creation was not simply a male, medical conspiracy, but as much, if not more, a female-motivated construction, for these other, 'feminist' reasons.

their wives' health. In documenting a similar development in America in the ante-bellum South, Lewis and Lockridge have perceptively written of its ambivalent effects, in the short term for spouse relations and in the longer term for gender relations:

> Family limitation . . . could be purchased only by sacrificing the physical intimacy that the nineteenth century's cult of romantic love had awakened. . . . ironically women themselves may have encouraged the belief that they were frail . . . Such a view perhaps gave them leverage over their husbands . . . but it was possibly as 'the weaker vessel', and not as autonomous equals that Virginia gentry women finally prevailed on their husbands to liberate them from the pain of childbirth.[109]

According to Dyhouse it was not until a second watershed, encompassing the interwar years, that the positive theme of sexual pleasure as something important for women entered and spread through public discourse. This was, famously, trumpeted as a right within marriage for all women by Marie Stopes: 'Self-publicist though she was, Marie Stopes's own description of her book, *Married Love*, as having "crashed English Society like a bombshell" in 1918 is probably not too much of an exaggeration. . . . The list of individuals who have testified to its impact is endless.'[110] Within the educated class the sexual mores of their parents were now seen by many in the 1920s as decidedly 'Victorian'.[111] The goal of self-control for both sexes, so noble for the late Victorians, was now dismissed as unwanted prudery by those regarding themselves as 'advanced' in this post-Freudian generation.[112] Some individual feminists from rather privileged enclaves (those who could still afford servants in the 1920s) have left records of their active pursuit of personal sexual liberation in the interwar years.[113] But this probably reflects minority behaviour even within their own class at this time.[114] Whether or not this clandestine behaviour was widespread within this communication comunity, it was certainly deliberately private, which is why the novels of D. H. Lawrence, James Joyce and H. G. Wells, daring publicly to portray this kind of behaviour,

109 Lewis and Lockridge, '"Sally has been sick"', p. 13.

110 Dyhouse, *Feminism and the family*, p. 179.

111 Mason, *The making of Victorian sexuality*, pp. 8–10.

112 Rapp, 'The early discovery of Freud'.

113 Dyhouse, *Feminism and the family*, pp. 179–82, discussing the sexual attitudes and behaviour of Naomi Mitchison, Dora Russell and Margaret Cole.

114 Hence, for instance, Z. Shonfield has concluded from her reading of the upper middle-class diaries of Jeanette Marshall (born 1855) and her daughter Rosalind Seaton (born 1892), that at the age of 29 'There is no evidence that she [Rosalind] was much more relaxed about sexual matters than Jeanette had been at a comparable age.' (Jeanette had been a virgin when married at the age of 36; Rosalind married at age 35.) This is a significant observation because Rosalind was a fashionable artistic designer, an archetypal member of south-west London's smart set in the 1920s, not averse to smoking and riding pillion on a motorbike, regular dancing into the early hours and weekend parties at friends' houses in the country: 'She flirted assiduously and somewhat indiscriminately, as her mother, too, had done in her twenties and early thirties.' Shonfield, *The precariously privileged*, pp. 197, 241–4. Shonfield is drawing a distinction between the 'parasexual' public demeanour of Rosalind Seaton in the 1920s (and her mother in the 1870s and 1880s) and the more cautious reality of her actual sexual behaviour. On parasexuality, see ch. 9, n. 26.

attracted such controversy and opprobrium even from some members of the same class. As Jane Lewis has commented of the greatest self-publicists of this set, the Bloomsbury group, 'in seeking to separate private lives from public duty it also cut off sexual behaviour from public debate. It did not seek to make personal life a public issue as [H. G.] Wells did.'[115]

Melman's valuable, systematic and sophisticated analysis of the more popular forms of relevant interwar literature, including a large number of women's fiction magazines, has concluded that the 1920s did witness a genuine period of postwar escapist experimentation and diversification in popular models of female roles, symbolised in the celebrated popular image of the decade, the non-domesticated female androgyne, the 'Flapper'.[116] Although remaining euphemistic and indirect in its allusive mode of expression, Melman shows that there was also a flourishing market in the sex novel of escapist fantasy fiction. But this widening 'plurality of discourse' seems to have suffered a pruning back in the face of the harsh realities of the recessionary 1930s, leaving the more conservative models and ideals more prominent in popular culture once again. Thus, in terms of the distinctions laid out by Michael Mason, the interwar period does not, overall, seem to experience any permanent, fundamental change in *public* ideals on a truly social scale, regarding more egalitarian gender roles or towards a generalised endorsement for the freedom of sexual expression. However, the interwar era did see a significant move by some in all classes towards the acknowledgement in *private* of sensuality within marriage, something which appeared revelatory to those affected. But even among the upper middle class, public norms and codes of practice were still in the 1930s at variance with their clandestine adventures. This did not, overall, amount to a revolution in public attitudes towards sexual behaviour.

Furthermore, all who have researched the subject have emphasised that most available evidence for other social groups and communication communities, from maternity and birth control clinics, oral history and the thousands of extant letters written to Marie Stopes, indicates that elsewhere in society there still remained a profound well of female (and male) sexual ignorance during and after the 1920s. There was a continued prevalence of what were perceived as far from satisfactory sexual relations – in both middle and working classes – during the interwar period.[117] No doubt for many women the popular and escapist romance literature made them aware of their unsatisfactory relationships without necessarily offering them any means to change them. That such issues were gradually dawning on women and that feminist ideology and politics was one of the influences bringing about this change is undeniable. The point, however, is that for the majority of the population the evidence indicates that both public discussion and private sexual behaviour and beliefs remained inhibited – albeit subject to

[115] Lewis, 'Intimate relations', p. 81. [116] Melman, *Women and the popular imagination*.

[117] See above, ch. 8, n. 66, pp. 426–7 and 562–6. Also Holtzman, 'The pursuit of married love'; Brookes, 'Women and reproduction'; Hall, *Hidden anxieties*; Cohen, 'Private lives in public spaces'.

intensifying negotiation – during this period in which marital fertility was finally brought under most rigorous control.

Thus, an era in which there existed a generalised social perception on the part of young men and women that they lived under circumstances of sexual liberation seems to have followed rather than accompanied the historical process of falling marital fertilities. According to the most authoritative research available, the recently completed National Survey of Sexual Attitudes and Lifestyles, the median age of sexual initiation for both sexes fell most markedly in Britain in the 1950s and early 1960s, a change in private behaviour that was not necessarily reflected much in the public norms of that period.[118] It seems, then, that the subsequent famous 'sexual revolution' in popular culture of the latter half of the 1960s, embracing a rapid response to the availability of the oral pill, may well have trailed behind an earlier change in private sexual practices. This represents a similar reinforcing function for public sexual norms as that envisaged in the last section of chapter 9 for community norms of family size: they follow an initial change in the private behaviour of a growing minority of individuals, publicly endorsing the new pattern and thereby stamping it as an orthodoxy.

To summarise, given the new emphasis in this study on spacing and attempted abstinence as the major method of birth control until at least the 1920s, it would seem likely that feminist ideology played a significant, if somewhat surprising, role in the process of falling fertility. The surprising aspect is in the important contribution of a strongly evangelical strain within feminism, which was insistent on exploiting to the full the moral claims of a rather conservative emphasis on women's 'domestic' and maternal virtues. This added great political weight: the Mothers' Union, founded in 1886 to extol these ostensibly conservative aims, was the largest women's organisation of the entire period.[119]

Sexual continence in husbands – and the implied field of male sexual expectations in general – became a moral battlefield in the late Victorian era open to public discussion, albeit in somewhat euphemistic terms. While this does not constitute conclusive evidence for the causal importance of political feminism in bringing about a falling birth rate, the development of a public discourse of abstinence ('continence' was the preferred term of the period) may well have been a functionally necessary rationalisation for such self-restraint to have been successfully sustained on a socially widespread scale. Given the technical difficulty of restricting fertility effectively at this time, the adoption of a strongly negative disposition towards conjugal sensuality may have been essential, at both individual and collective levels of articulation, for a régime of attempted abstinence to have worked. Such norms, encompassing a negative disposition towards sensuality, were functional in that they appealed to and assisted individuals who wished to

118 Wellings *et al.*, *Sexual behaviour*, pp. 37–9. I am grateful to Avner Offer for drawing my attention to these findings.

119 Harris, *Private lives*, p. 27.

restrain their marital fertility: by providing them with an enabling ideology and shared 'language', entailing birth controlling priorities. The importance of the feminist purity movement and the 'New Woman' ideology in contributing to falling fertility in Britain would be in the way that it provided the dialectical origins for the elaboration of this discourse. Furthermore, its existence constitutes additional cultural evidence in favour of the thesis being presented here: that attempted abstinence was, indeed, a major contemporary cultural preoccupation, primarily in the form of the exhortations to male continence and the 'New Woman' claims for female sexual autonomy in marriage.

Alongside these developments in feminist thought and politics, there were, of course, certain other social, economic and cultural changes during the first half of the twentieth century of relevance to sexual and gender relations. These were probably, overall, partially offsetting in their effects, being conducive to the continuation of a dependent role for most women, as domesticated housewives financially dependent on their salaried or wage-earning husbands. There were a number of dimensions to this. First, although recent historiography has uncovered a much more active range of feminist political associations in interwar Britain than had previously been suspected, it seems nevertheless true that during the first four decades after women's formal political emancipation in 1919, there was remarkably slow penetration by women of the more privileged end of the labour market and of the civil institutions of power: the professions, the ranks of employers, the civil service, Westminster, the City, the trade unions, the gentlemen's clubs and the workingmen's pubs were all in 1960 pretty much where they had been in 1910. This has been partly attributed to the defensive cultural reactions elicited in the wake of each of the world wars.[120] But as more research appears, demonstrating the activism of interwar feminist organisations, it is also beginning to become apparent how resourcefully and ruthlessly male interests were promoted by incumbents and how feminists were struggling to fight this.[121] A range of formal and informal techniques was deployed against women, from outright exclusion and the marriage bar to more insidious forms of marginalisation.[122]

Secondly, in those parts of the country in the south, the midlands and the south-east, where husbands were generally able to avoid mass unemployment,

[120] Pugh, *Women and the women's movement*, especially chs. 2, 5, 7, 9; Kent, 'The politics of sexual difference'; Thane, 'Towards equal opportunities?' (on Churchill's personal intervention to stymie equal pay after the Second World War); Light, *Forever England*.

[121] On interwar feminism, see Thane, 'Visions of gender'; Thane, 'Women in the British Labour party'; also the essays in Smith (ed.), *British feminism*; Graves, *Labour women*.

[122] The higher civil service, for instance, provides good examples of both. Meta Zimmeck has shown in detail how females were screened out by the introduction after the Great War of the device of the interview into the selection process, as it was found that written examinations were incapable of excluding women because many performed as well as the men: Zimmeck 'The "new woman"'. Another example, still extant to this day, is the prevalence of cricketing metaphors in civil service argot, an apparently innocuous but clearly gender marginalising practice. On the apparent statutory removal of the marriage bar by the 1919 Sex Disqualification (Removal) Act and the immediate judicial resuscitation of it, see Dyhouse, *Feminism and the family*, pp. 77–81.

adult male real wage levels in a heavily unionised workforce generally continued to rise across the interwar period.[123] In these parts of the country an ever-increasing proportion of the working class and the lower middle class were able to attain their parents' and grandparents' dream of the respectable lifestyle of a non-working wife and mother at home and children in school, based on the male breadwinner's financial ability to support the family alone.[124] Elsewhere, this outcome was forestalled by the shocking levels of redundancy, especially in communities in the north-east and north-west and in South Wales, where the declining staple industries of coal, cotton, iron and steel, engineering and shipbuilding were concentrated.

This probably wreaked havoc with gender roles and identities in the affected regions, although there is insufficient research available on the differences in working-class experiences during the 1920s and 1930s to be sure of this. Two influential studies in the 1950s both depicted gender-divided, embittered coal-mining communities at that time.[125] It has been questioned whether this validly represents the character of such communities earlier in the century.[126] The findings of the 1950s are therefore suggestive of a possible 'brutalisation' of gender relations, due to the interwar period of male employment difficulties, similar to the events carefully documented in Paul Thompson's impressive study of fishing communities in north-east Scotland and also to those which have occurred, once again, in places devastated by male unemployment in the 1980s and 1990s.[127] There was, then, considerable regional divergence in proletarian families' experience of work and relative affluence or decline in the interwar period. Only with the economy moving to a wartime footing in the late 1930s did a general pattern of widespread rising household incomes return, with full adult male employment thereafter sustained for several decades, following the wartime historic political commitment to full employment policies, alongside the newly enhanced family-supporting structures of the welfare state.[128]

From the late 1930s and on through the unemployment-free 1940s and 1950s virtually all married working-class men and women now found themselves increasingly able to enjoy the segregated work and domestic roles and the rising standard of living enjoyed in much of the south-east since the interwar period. There was almost certainly a gradual overall decline across the first half of the

123 On the geographically divided performance of the interwar economy and living standards, see, for instance, Pollard, *The development*, chs. 2–4.

124 Roberts, *A woman's place* and *Women's work*. For similar arguments, see also Bourke, *Working-class cultures*, ch. 3; Bourke, 'Housewifery'.

125 Dennis *et al.*, *Coal is our life*; Zweig, *The worker in an affluent society*.

126 Lummis, 'The historical dimensions of fatherhood', pp. 44–5.

127 Thompson, 'Women in the fishing'. See p. 509. On the 1980s and 1990s, see Rosalind Coward, 'Whipping boys', *Guardian* 3 September 1994, pp. 32–5. For documentation of 'de-brutalisation' in late nineteenth-century plebeian London, see Tomes, 'A "Torrent of abuse"'.

128 Milward, *War, economy*; Alford, *British economic performance 1945–75*; for contemporary testimony to the positive impact of the postwar Labour government's welfare state on working-class family budgets, see Rowntree and Lavers, *Poverty and the welfare state*.

century in the informal income earning by married women which was necessitated by poverty, such as homeworking (although the depressed areas would have experienced a temporary counter-trend until the late 1930s). As Ray Pahl has put it, 'Women who had previously relied on mutual aid and support from female kin and neighbours became more dependent on their husbands and state agencies.'[129] With husbands generally more able to earn a family wage and with the memory of their crowded childhood homes and harassed mothers before their eyes, it would seem plausible that many wives were becoming content with the novelty of being able to enjoy and manage 'a happy, clean home', in Diana Gittins's words.[130]

Nevertheless, the novelty could not be a lasting source of fulfilment; there were certain, more dynamic forces working both for and against segregated gender roles and greater personal liberty for women. Although the nineteenth-century statistics are extremely difficult to interpret, it seems probable, as Catherine Hakim has argued, that from the 1860s there was a substantial secular decline in the proportion of economically active *married* women to an historical low during the first quarter of the twentieth century, followed by a sustained rise to the present day, which by the 1960s probably exceeded the mid-nineteenth-century economic activity rates (notwithstanding important differences in definitions between the two dates).[131] As Wandersee has argued with respect to a similar trend in the USA, these statistics reflect an initial decline in the proportion of married women driven by poverty to work in and on the margins of the formal labour market, with a subsequent counter-trend partly chronologically superimposed, representing a secular rise in married women's voluntary participation in the labour market, for the distinctly aspirational and consumerist goal of increasing their own and their family's standard of living – rather than merely desperately defending it.[132]

If the imperative of mass consumption was legitimating increased economic activism on the part of married women (but with the important caveat that this tended to be in lower-paid and lower-status employments and therefore was not necessarily conducive to enhanced female autonomy), a yet further dimension of change during this period – the expansion of the welfare state – was probably on balance having a substantial counter-influence. This is because the welfare state's measures have been derived throughout the twentieth century from a set of quasi-official doctrines concerning the biological and psychological importance of

[129] Pahl, *Divisions of labour*, p. 75.

[130] Gittins, *Fair sex*, p. 183. See above, pp. 52–4, for Gittins's interpretation. For the sense of revival experienced by working-class slum-dwellers in the interwar period on moving into the new spacious, suburban homes, many built by councils in the 1930s, with their own garden, domestic water supply, bathrooms and electric lights, see, for instance, the memories of Rose Townsend in Humphries and Gordon, *A labour of love*, p. 157; or Margaret Perry (concerning her parents) in Burnett (ed.), *Destiny obscure*, pp. 323–4.

[131] Hakim, 'Social monitors', pp. 43–5, 48–9. Note that it has been shown that the more recent twentieth-century figures continue to contain many statistical pitfalls: Joshi and Owen, 'How long is a piece of elastic?'.

[132] Wandersee, *Women's work*.

motherhood, while also respecting the arguments of organised labour on the importance of maintaining male householders' family wages.[133] While the welfare state and its accompanying ideology has been relatively supportive of women occupying what was seen by successive governments as a conventional, maternal and economically dependent familial role, it has, therefore, inevitably created opportunity costs and sanctions against the alternatives, of female economic activism.

However, a fourth development, tending towards greater generalised female independence has been the advent and accessibility of effective, acceptable contraception. This at last broke the seemingly necessary link for all women between the activity of sex – with its possible pleasures – and the harsh realities of childbearing – with its more certain pains and threats to health. For women in general (as opposed to a few privileged individuals) to be able to view their own bodies as something potentially distinct from the childbearing function and to be able to endorse personal sexual fulfilment as an independent goal of high significance and emotional value, a collective perception of the genuine availability and accessibility of reliable contraception must probably be a necessary precondition. Hence, the findings cited above in the national survey of sexual behaviour, that age of sexual initiation was falling markedly during the 1950s. Yet it must be borne in mind that still throughout the 1950s and early 1960s an *unmarried* woman had no recognised legal right of access to contraceptives.[134] The alternative of resort to abortion was, likewise, illegal until the 1967 Abortion Act, while illegitimacy continued to carry a great stigma.[135] To a considerable extent men, therefore, retained control over the culture of contraception even in the 1950s, especially where sexual relations were occurring outside marriage, which often established formative behavioural patterns among the young of both sexes.[136] However, when in the course of the 1960s the pill was developed and then made accessible through the Family Planning Act of 1967, the opportunity finally appeared for women themselves to grasp independent control over this aspect of their lives regardless of age or marital status; and there was a rapid response.

Britain's modern history suggests, therefore (but certainly does not prove), that without accessibility to the oral pill during the 1960s, the historical process

[133] Some of the principal historiographical contributions establishing this have been: Wilson, *Women and the welfare state*; Davin, 'Imperialism and motherhood'; Lewis, *The politics of motherhood*; Macnicol, 'Family allowances and less eligibility'; Riley, *War in the nursery*; Pedersen, 'The failure of feminism'; Pedersen, *Family, dependence*; Koven and Michel, 'Womanly duties'; Koven and Michel (eds.), *Mothers of a new world*; and for a recent summary of the debates generated by comparative studies, see: Lewis, 'Gender, the family and women's agency'.

[134] There were ways around this for the determined: apparently single women who presented themselves at family planning clinics with engagement rings could often obtain their own contraceptives (source: Liz Lochead, personal communication 8 October 1994).

[135] On the stigma of illegitimacy, see Humphries, *A secret world*, ch. 3.

[136] Hence Chesser's survey of sexual behaviour in the early 1950s found higher proportions of couples (over 40%) in which husbands, only, took the birth control precautions, among those couples where women married relatively young (under age 25). Chesser, *The sexual, marital and family relationships*, p. 461.

whereby the emergence of birth control and small families has been broadly associated with the emergence of public norms and sexual codes of increased personal freedom for women, greater control over their sexuality and their bodies – and eventually increasing cultural and economic independence of a more general kind – may be more contingent and elliptical than otherwise appears to be the case. The oral pill was rapidly seized upon by women in the west as a practical method to control their own contraception entirely independently of men. This indicates a strong, long-suppressed demand for such a technology on their part. This also indicates that the unusually socially and sexually libertarian popular culture of the late 1960s may have played a particularly significant role in bringing this about, also creating sufficient political momentum to carry through Parliament the 1970 Equal Pay and 1975 Sex Discrimination Acts, which came into operation in December 1975, under the aegis of the Equal Opportunities Commission, and which remain the principal legal bastions of female economic independence.[137]

The presumed historical link between the practice of effective birth control and the personal independence of women, or indeed the emancipation of sexual relations in a more general sense, therefore appears much more tenuous and indirect in Britain's case than may have been previously appreciated. It seems likely that the period of secular fertility decline itself was characterised more by an increasing intensity of cultural negotiation and private bargaining between husbands and wives over the terms and conditions on which sexuality was enjoyed in marriage. Furthermore, the earlier part of this process before the Great War was characterised by the development of an inhibitory, anti-sensualist discourse, which, it has been argued, was functionally related to the primitive methods deployed, principally forms of abstinence. The ensuing three to four decades witnessed a socially uneven thawing in the codes of sexual continence, as a more sensualist commitment was renegotiated by individual husbands and wives – rapidly in some cases, gradually or not at all in others. But it was not until the late 1960s, some decades after fertility had completed its fall, that public discourse and sexual codes of behaviour became more explicitly sensualist and permissive. Not until this same decade did contingent developments in the technology of contraception enable women finally to acquire genuine, independent control over their own reproductive destinies, one of the necessary (but not sufficient) conditions for more egalitarian and emancipated sexual and gender relations.[138]

137 The case of contemporary Japan also supports this interpretation, in that according to Coleman's research in the 1970s the oral pill was virtually prohibited in a low-fertility culture where females nevertheless remained thoroughly subordinated in economic and political terms and where men viewed the pill as a threat to their power. Coleman, *Family planning in Japanese society*: see above, p. 430, for further details.

138 As S. Pollack has concluded from her survey of sexual behaviour in the 1980s: 'Potentially contraceptives are as coërcive as they are liberating. The gains and losses for women need to be analysed in view of the political relations into which new contraceptives are born.' Pollack, 'Sex and the contraceptive act', p. 65.

Some possibilities for future research on changing fertility and nuptiality in England and Wales

It goes without saying that it is hoped that the positive findings and interpretation to emerge from this study and the heuristic framework for the analysis of fertility change, presented in chapter 9, will stimulate further research. No doubt the testing of the arguments and hypotheses offered here will result in their modification, revision and eventually their refutation or supersession, which history shows is the healthy, mortal fate of most stimulating ideas and theories. A number of questions for further research have been raised by the foregoing account and also a number of indications for productive future approaches.

The importance of changing attitudes towards sexuality and sensuality, and changing sexual practices, have been indicated as areas of major importance. This necessarily follows from the case that has been argued that a culture of attempted abstinence within marriage, embracing the practice of coitus interruptus, was the principal means of birth control used. The concept of British – or English – society exhibiting a 'culture of abstinence' in this period, *c.* 1850–1950, raises a range of derivative questions. In particular, was Britain relatively unique in this respect and, if so, why? To what extent were there continuities between Victorian 'continence' and earlier practices, on the one hand, and earlier codes of sexual behaviour, on the other hand? Whatever the relative merits of the particular interpretation advanced here, the general issue of the relationship between changing reproductive behaviour, methods of birth control and the history of sexual attitudes and behaviour is clearly a central one for future inquiry, and something that has remained for too long scandalously under-researched.

It is possible that further sources of information on the mix of contraceptive methods used or even direct information on the sexual behaviour of different social groups may come to light and that these will enable reasonably plausible reconstructions of motives and sexual practices. A good example of this is the judicious and resourceful use by David and Sanderson of the famous Mosher survey of the sexual and reproductive behaviour of forty-five middle-class women in the USA around the turn of the century.[139] However, for the late Victorian and the Edwardian periods, as a source of detailed information this remains almost unique in the Anglophone world. Nevertheless, oral history research would be invaluable in recovering similar details, at least for the subsequent interwar and immediately postwar generations and this must now be considered an urgent research priority. Another potentially rewarding approach, although extremely labour intensive, would be an attempt systematically to analyse the details of sexual practices and attitudes contained in the large amount of personal correspondence and other private literary material surviving from the period.

[139] David and Sanderson 'Rudimentary contraceptive methods'. See also MaHood and Wenburg (eds.), *The Mosher survey*.

Relevant references would be few and far between and would, by definition, be the product of a particular and unusual type of personality. But such a form of testimony has a very high truth value when investigating a subject of this sort (since more public forms of communication were subject to the social conventions of decorum, which the historian needs to get behind and underneath) and this might, therefore, be considered to justify the effort.

The emphasis on the importance of communication communities as the socio-cultural units in which fertility change occurs points to the need for properly contextualised comparative local studies as the most important way forward for future demographic research on changing fertility and nuptiality in Britain. Only through studies of this sort can this thesis be tested and the identity and fertility of the overlapping and overlaid 'communication communities' in any locality be examined. Although a difficult task, examining fertility change through properly contextualised local studies is potentially rewarding, as has been demonstrated by Kertzer and Hogan, the Schneiders, Mike Savage and Richard Whipp.

Another, complementary focus for future research could be on the changing social roles and norms relating to childrearing and familial roles among different communication communities; and the relationship of these to a more complex understanding of the potential influence of central state policies, as mediated by local government and voluntary agencies and by officials on the ground. Certain pioneering studies have shown that collective definitions of the primary, social and familial roles of childhood, adolescence, motherhood, fatherhood and parenthood were subject to change during this period; but most of these studies have only sketched general, national trends.[140] To link these developments in any convincing way to fertility change it will be necessary to study these relationships at the local, community level. Paradoxically, perhaps it is only through such local studies that the role of the 'state', in Michael Mann's sense (see next section), can be properly investigated.

There are also a number of more specific socio-demographic questions raised by this study, surrounding the characteristics of changing fertility in England and Wales. For instance, do the relatively robust occupational patterns and rankings, as summarised in Figure 7.1, actually hold up in specific communities? Or do some towns and cities exhibit different relationships between the fertility and nuptiality of these socio-occupational groups? It has been acknowledged that the functionally interacting communication communities composing the 'middle-class' world constructed their relationships as a national, social hierarchy of aspirational status relationships. By contrast, it has been argued that the vast majority of the population lived in a large number of more locally circumscribed, proletarian

[140] See above, pp. 450–64. Other studies of relevance to this theme include: Musgrove, *Youth and the social order*; Pinchbeck and Hewitt, *Children in English society*; Thompson, *Edwardian childhoods*; Springhall, *Coming of age*; Hendrick, *Images of youth*; Gillis, *Youth and history*.

industrial communities, which were socially and culturally excluded, by Weberian 'closure', from this competitive 'national' hierarchy of polite society and its fringes. These various proletarian communication communities differed greatly in size and character, from a colliery village or a single factory town to almost an entire city such as a Middlesbrough or a Sheffield (which in turn contained distinct neighbourhoods, though many with strong similarities). It was, of course, the great diversity of extant industries in Britain at this time which determined that these communities were each distinct socio-demographic worlds in themselves, reflected in their disparate fertility and nuptiality patterns. Only comparative local studies will be able to examine further this posited discontinuity in the principles upon which 'communication communities' formed. Did professionals in heavily proletarian cities, such as Sheffield, in fact exhibit fertility and nuptiality behaviour more like their fellow-citizens, rather than like other professionals elsewhere? Did municipal, transport, retailing, labouring occupations tend to take on the demographic characteristics of whichever community in which they are found? Did coal miners' or iron and steel workers' fertility vary when they were located in communities which took their character more from another industry, as for instance in many North Staffordshire or Lancashire towns?

Proprietorship and employership have been identified as more important influences over differential fertility and nuptiality patterns than 'skill', especially among those successful enough to return themselves as 'retired from business'. Who were this last, numerically large category? Were proprietors already marrying late or exhibiting low fertility before they became employers? Did small-scale employers restrain their fertility more or less than large employers? Were industrialists similar to other kinds of employers in this respect? What about the self-employed? These are all questions for future research.

It has also been found that female employment, both inside and outside the home, has great significance. What difference did this make in different communities? Within a single town, was the fertility of textile workers with wives working in their own industry different from that of those with wives working in other employments – or not working at all? Did some sections of the population in some circumstances, such as those with homeworking wives, exhibit counter-trends of temporarily rising fertility?

The relationship between prudential, delayed marriage and fertility control within marriage has been identified as a major, and probably quite unusual, socio-demographic feature of falling fertilities in Britain. There is evidently much further research which could be undertaken to examine more fully the exact characteristics of this relationship. A marked general relationship has been found in the case of most occupational groups between deferred marriage and fertility regulation within marriage, but there were interesting variations on this theme. The implications of the difference between late-marrying professionals and younger-marrying rentiers has been considered quite fully; it is also true that the clerical and the so-called 'deferential' occupations, such as policemen and postmen, exhibited similar characteristics to the prudential, abstinent professions, while various categories of commercial proprietors align themselves more with the rentiers in this respect. These patterns might be suggesting that the markedly prudential nuptiality and fertility behaviour of clerical workers, postmen and police was the result of the unusual degree of security of income at a relatively adequate level – including pensions – enjoyed by many of them. This would have been important in empowering them to take a more planned approach to their lives than those in business, who remained more at the mercy of the market. On the other hand, it might be hypothesised that the status insecurity of the 'deferential' social groups may have rendered them particularly vulnerable to an exaggerated respect for the anti-sensualist public codes of 'Victorian' sexual respectability, which therefore committed them to a culture of abstinence as the only non-disreputable method of marital birth control, so resulting in their tendency to delay marriage, as a complementary strategy. According to this view, the propensity of independent proprietors to marry younger, while nevertheless achieving the same low fertility as the deferential occupations, might be attributed to their greater cultural 'independence' and preparedness to use appliance contraceptives or to engage in non-coital forms of sex, as may have been the case among at least a section of the rentier, upper class.

Certain aspects of some of the qualitative evidence analysed during the last three chapters have indicated that at any given point in time (and subject to the relevant shifting social norms), it may be individuals' degree of 'religiosity' which principally influences their positive or negative evaluation of sexuality, which in Britain during this period would have been associated with their preparedeness to use contraceptives or engage in non-coital sexual behaviour. Although random variations between individual personalities are evidently highly significant in determining this, it is not impossible that certain general associations might be demonstrable between certain kinds of occupational or community milieu and 'religiosity'.[141] These issues link back to the future research agenda in the history of sexuality: only further empirical research can adjudicate between the relative importance of all these various hypotheses.

It has been found that by the Edwardian period spacing from early in marriage was a generally established practice. It has not, however, been possible with the evidence available here to assess the relative importance of 'starting' (the

[141] A high degree of 'religiosity' is here intended to connote a strong commitment towards what is seen as a 'traditional' code of morality (as opposed either to the lack of such a strong commitment or else to the conscious endorsement of an alternative, 'progressive' or secular code). On religious attitudes and reproduction, see Simons, 'Reproductive behaviour'. Michael Mason's *The making of Victorian sexual attitudes* provides, throughout, copious evidence from the early and mid-nineteenth century to demonstrate empirically the significance of this link between 'religiosity' and disposition towards sensualism: among the fervent believers of various denominational sects; among categories of Freethinkers; and among the worldly and patrician, socially conservative proponents of 'classic moralism'. See also Rose, *The Edwardian temperament*, pp. 80–91, for some relevant suggestions.

particular form of spacing which involves a delay before the first birth) within the overall pattern of spacing. Nor has it been possible to examine in any detail the actual changing distributions of different family sizes (parity distributions) in different occupations. This relates to the question of how the general pattern of spacing became established among different groups over the preceding decades. Did spacing start with the last births or was it always practised from relatively early in marriage? An intriguing specific case of this is provided by the Lancashire cotton workers, who showed themselves to be exhibiting an exceptional degree of early spacing, especially among the late marriers, during the Edwardian period. Was this a relatively recent development, or had the cotton workers and their wives of the 1870s and 1880s also spaced births particularly during the early years of marriage? And how important was 'starting' within this? If spacing was so firmly established before the Great War, how and when did the parity-specific 'stopping' pattern, typical of the late interwar and postwar eras, eventually emerge alongside it? A related issue is to examine more precisely how, when and why the important, general relationship between delayed marriage and birth control within marriage eventually ceased to hold in the twentieth century.

Comprehensive evidence of exactly the right sort to answer many of these socio-demographic questions does in fact exist and its location is well known. Indeed, there is an *embarras de richesse*. There is, first, the manuscript household schedules of the 1911 census, the raw data for each household from which the occupational tables, analysed here above, were compiled as abstracts. Secondly, there is the national body of civil registration data, established in 1837 to record every birth, death and marriage in England and Wales. The problem, however, as all demographic historians will know, is *access* to each of these superb sources of historical information on changing fertility and nuptiality in England and Wales. At present this is denied by Parliament. This is particularly galling from an intellectual and scientific point of view, in that this is not the usual problem encountered by historical researchers, which frequently lies in the simple absence of certain important categories of information because of the non-survival (or in the case of pre-modern history the non-creation) of the documents giving the required type of evidence. The problems in this case are not of this absolute form but are merely, tantalisingly, administrative.[142]

[142] The Public Records Acts of 1958 and 1967 decree that the original household schedules completed in 1911 will remain under lock and key for 100 years. Higgs, *Making sense of the census*, p. 20. The hundreds of millions of vital registration records stored by the Office of Population Census and Survey at Titchfield in Hampshire are equally unavailable for systematic research because they are made accessible only for individual consultation by paying members of the public at OPCS headquarters in St Catherine's House in central London. It is vital registration sources of precisely this kind which have been successfully used in Scotland for detailed research on fertility change during this period, involving the labour-intensive reconstruction of maternity histories and the changing family structures of different social groups: for instance, Walker (unpublished PhD thesis); and Kemmer (unpublished PhD thesis). This is not possible for England and Wales because, unlike in Scotland, the present rules governing the administration and financing of the archive south of the border do not enable systematic academic searches to be mounted.

By contrast, it is possible to study fertility and nuptiality change in great detail in the modern histories of some other countries, such as in Scotland or in Sweden, because of the availability there of the appropriate information.[143] However, there are some promising rays of light on the horizon, insofar as the history of fertility change in England and Wales is concerned. First, government policy with respect to the availability of the civil registration documents for research is under review and could, conceivably, change. Secondly, in the mid-1980s, Peter Laslett was successful in encouraging the then-Registrar-General, A. R. Thatcher, to make available to the Cambridge Group for the History of Population and Social Structure a small anonymised sample of the manuscript census records from the closed censuses of 1891–1921 relating to thirteen different communities. This, therefore, includes information from the 1911 census's fertility inquiry. Unfortunately, the lack of nominal information and the relatively small sample sizes limits the extent of detailed contextual information – record linkage – that can be usefully deployed in analysing this data. Nevertheless, this concession by the Registrar-General of England and Wales does mean that some progress with providing robust answers to the kinds of socio-demographic questions outlined above can now be anticipated before 2012.[144]

History and policy implications

As Part II has shown, the study of fertility change in Britain, as elsewhere, has been motivated from the start by policy considerations. The principal historical sources of demographic evidence can only be independently examined, therefore, as in Part III, once they have been thoroughly deconstructed and once this provenance has been fully investigated, understood and intellectually discounted, the object of Part II and chapter 6, above. Part I showed, furthermore, that several generations of such policy concerns have thoroughly infiltrated the intellectual history of the field of historical and social scientific study of fertility change, setting the terms of reference for the inherited intellectual and scientific debates.

There always has been and, no doubt, always will be a dialogue between those studying historical fertility change and those engaged in policy-related work. For social and policy scientists there is no alternative but to attempt to learn from the past in such matters. The only choice is between those who act with as critical, informed and emancipated an understanding of the past as they are capable of achieving and those who act on the basis of an only half-digested or unreflecting knowledge of the past. Only the most ignorant or the deluded actually believe

[143] On the sources available for study of Sweden's fertility history, see Lockridge, *The fertility transition in Sweden*; and see ch. 1, n. 2. On Scotland, see previous footnote.

[144] The thirteen communities, from which samples were taken were: Abergavenny; Axminster; Banbury; Bethnal Green; Bolton; Earsdon (Co. Durham); Morland (Westmorland); Pinner; Saffron Walden; Stoke-on-Trent; Swansea; Walthamstow; York. The kind of analysis which is possible with this new source has been demonstrated in: Garrett and Reid, 'Satanic mills, pleasant lands'.

themselves to be acting without reference to the past or in a supposedly novel or revolutionary way. As one genuinely revolutionary thinker concluded of the field of economics and economic activity: 'Practical men, who believe themselves to be quite exempt from any intellectual influences, are usually the slaves of some defunct economist.'[145]

The foregoing account would strongly indicate, following Wrigley's suggestion, that a conception of falling fertility as a sequence of mutually dependent but by no means historically inevitable developmental stages is a much more heuristically fruitful formulation than that of the simplistic dichotomy of a transformation from traditional, natural to modern, planned fertility. Closely related to this latter perspective, there has been a consistently reiterated, pronounced historiographical tendency within the field to view human fertility change through the blinkered spectacles of a stultifying, linear, evolutionary perspective. As has been suggested, this is much to do with the fact that many of the most influential contributors to the field from earliest times (such as Malthus, Drysdale, Dumont, Pearson, Stopes, Landry, Himes and Notestein) have in fact been simultaneously wearing two hats. They have been both studying the phenomenon of human fertility and also actively attempting to influence fertility behaviour in their own or in other societies. They have all therefore, whether explicitly or only implicitly, held a strong moral position on birth control and family planning as either a good or bad thing – to be promoted or not for different sets of peoples. Moreover, both in the 1930s and again since the 1950s this has been part of a much wider and increasingly heavily resourced international movement.

When introducing the general heuristic framework of perceived relative childrearing costs and benefits at the beginning of the last chapter, it was noted that if this was a genuinely general approach, then it should be applicable in ways that are helpful and elucidatory to other historical, contemporary and, indeed, even future contexts. To be transferable in this way, such a framework has to be both capable of identifying what it is that is general to fertility change, while remaining flexible enough to cope with an almost infinite variety of circumstance; also it must avoid the sterility of merely truistic formulation of a kind that cannot generate fruitful, refutable lines of empirical inquiry and application.

Bearing in mind these considerations, this study of the history of changing fertility in modern Britain may be able to offer some generalisable lessons for policy-makers and for those studying fertility in other times and places. Such lessons are relatively few in number and certainly do not relate to specific aspects of the history of falling fertility in Britain. Indeed, as the foregoing has repeatedly stressed, there are no *specific* events, 'factors' or 'variables' which can be said to have had a general influence upon the fertility behaviour of all social groups and communities, even just in England, let alone elsewhere.

[145] Keynes, *The general theory*, p. 383.

The lessons are really meta-lessons of methodology, rather than specific potions promising guaranteed fertility change. They mainly specify the investigative preliminaries that are essential before the framework of perceived relative childrearing costs can be usefully deployed: the rich base of empirical information necessary for a proper understanding of the fertility behaviour of any community. As such they probably do no more than formalise the best practice that is already found among some students of contemporary fertility behaviour, several of which were mentioned in the course of the introductory review.

Reflection on the history of falling fertilities in modern Britain indicates that there are, perhaps, four of these methodological meta-lessons for the formulators and implementers of population policies. First, there is a need to identify the different communication communities within the target population. Ideally, policies have to be rendered appropriate to each of these groups' differing conceptions of the relative costs and benefits of childrearing. Where this is impractical it needs to be realised that measures which may encourage birth control among one of the social groups resident within the population may well have the opposite effects on others, given the intrinsically socially divisive forces involved when fertility behaviour changes significantly, as has been illustrated in the British historical case and also in the excellent local studies that have been made in two Italian communities. It follows that proper understanding of these divergent responses, dependent on proper identification of the relations of competition, conflict and co-existence between social groups within any community, is vital to accurate monitoring of the fertility effects of any policies that are instigated. For instance, if social groups within the target population alter their fertility in roughly equal and opposite ways as a result of a particular measure, then, unless they have been correctly identified, the entirely misleading and inaccurate conclusion might be drawn that the policy in question had no effect.

Secondly, there is the need to discover and identify the exact ways in which the groups within the target population perceive the relative costs and benefits of children and of childrearing. It is particularly to be noted that there are likely to be systematic (and, of course, mutually related) gendered differences in these perceptions. Attention is especially required to the examination of the varying indigenous definitions of notions such as childhood, parenthood and mothering – or their absence and the extant alternatives – rather than assuming that these are constants. This is essentially an ethnographic task, involving the patient observational techniques of anthropology, as exemplified in the work by C. Bledsoe and colleagues on fostering, lineage systems and intergenerational relations in West Africa, and by several of the articles in the collection edited by Carol P. McCormack.[146]

Thirdly, there is the need to examine the ways in which the communities in question already limit their fertility below the biological maximum. As surveys of

[146] For references, see ch. 1. n. 89.

the anthropological record have amply confirmed, in consequence of their established social and cultural institutions and adaptations to their physical environment all human societies limit their fertility to a greater or lesser extent by comparison with either some theoretical notion of 'total fecundability' or the Hutterite 'historical absolute' maximum fertility.[147] Only in Hutterite communities has any recorded human society come close to the situation of maximum fertility, where virtually all females are involved in bearing children for their entire fecund lives with as little gap as possible between confinements. It is by examining the ways in which communities depart from this maximum fertility pattern which can give vital clues as to the means by which the society in question already sanctions and practices birth control in some form and for some reason, whether those reasons be articulated and consciously appreciated by individuals in the community or not.[148] For those wishing to encourage the increased regulation of fertility in any society, this is most likely to be facilitated if these extant practices, once identified, can initially be extended or adapted in some way, rather than by attempting to impose upon the culture in question an entirely novel and alien set of practices and behaviours.

Hence, in the British historical case the principal structural fertility regulator before the modern period was the late marriage régime. This restricted the expression of maximum fertility through abstinence from sexual intercourse among young adults of both sexes. It has been argued here that a re-examination of the historical evidence on falling fertility in modern Britain, in the light of this insight, confirms that it was an extension of this long-practised indigenous method, in the form of attempted abstinence after marriage as well as before, which was the principal means of birth control initially adopted throughout most British communities. Obviously in other societies, either in Europe or elsewhere, it could be any of a range of other possible methods which were principally involved in the early stages, such as prolonged lactation, coitus interruptus, abortion, celibacy, plant and herbal concoctions, barrier methods, low coital frequency or ritual or migratory periods of abstinence.[149]

Fourthly, the knowledge learned from these three necessary preliminary investigative tasks has to be integrated and combined with an understanding of the full range of political and ideological forces operating in and upon the communities in question. Socio-political relations at the local level have been much emphasised in this and the previous chapter, the formal and practical

[147] Apart from Carr-Saunders's pioneering compilation of anthropological studies of fertility behaviour, subsequent important works include Krzywicki, *Primitive society*; Ford, 'Fertility controls in underdeveloped areas'; Devereux, *A study of abortion*; Nag, *Factors affecting human fertility*.

[148] A helpful, systematic discussion of many of the possibilities is contained in Davis and Blake, 'Social structure and fertility'. On the distinction between individuals' conscious rationality and the observable systemic rationality in a demographic régime, of which they may be unaware, see Wrigley, 'Fertility strategy'.

[149] All of these methods and many more are detailed in the reviews cited in n. 147 above.

politics of communication communities. But every bit as important is an assessment of the politics of the state and of its external and internal relations. The former refers to the economic implications and ideological influences of the state's international trading and geopolitical position. The latter refers to its relationship with local government, regional structures and all the forms of 'party' (using the term in the Weberian sense to refer not only to electoral parties, but to all the institutions and associations which exist for purposes of representation of the interests of different groups within a given society).

As was argued in chapter 1, there is much need in this field, both in historical and in contemporary research, for a much more sophisticated understanding of the role and character of 'the state' in relationship to fertility behaviour. As Johansson has forcefully argued, 'the state' is powerfully influencing fertility even when – indeed especially when – it has no positive policies to influence fertility.[150] But beyond this, there is also a need to incorporate some of the important recent revisionist theoretical and historical work on the nature of the state.[151]

In particular, Michael Mann has drawn attention to the critical significance of local power structures and provincial forms of 'party' in determining the relative strength of the central state and its capacity to influence its society. Michael Mann's notion of the 'polymorphous' modern state is a potentially fruitful one. This envisages the state as something composed not simply and primarily of a central administrative body but also of an equally important radiating network of executive tentacles, which may even be relatively informal in their relationship with the centre.[152] Indeed, it is the effectiveness of the remote agencies to carry through policies of the central state which is determinative of the true power of the state and which is essentially conditional and problematic. This is because the local efficacy, powers and respect accorded these agencies typically and critically depend on their capacity to be seen by locals to represent provincial, as much as central, interests: to speak the parochial community's language. Mann's conception of the nature of the central state's powers and its relationships with the peripheries clearly has affinities with Eric Wolf's emphasis on the importance and nature of 'brokers', as mentioned in chapter 9.[153] The foregoing account has tried to bring out the importance of the expanding range of public service professionals employed by local government and the great density of genteel charities and of plebeian voluntary associations in creating an extremely complex form to 'the state' in Britain. This needs to be taken into account in all its local diversity when explaining fertility change. However, such a great density of voluntary associations as in England is not typically found in many other

[150] Johansson, '"Implicit" policy'.

[151] For instance: Anderson, *Imagined communities*; Corrigan and Sayer, *The great arch*; Evans, Rueschmeyer and Skocpol *et al.* (eds.), *Bringing the state back in*; Mann, *The sources of social power I and II*; Torstendahl and Burrage (eds.), *The formation of professions*.

[152] Mann, *The sources of social power II*, especially ch. 3. [153] See pp. 523–4.

comparable societies, from an Australia to a France or a Germany, so that their historical developments were different; furthermore, the recognised powers of local agents of the central state to influence fertility practices differ enormously when comparing a culture such as China's with those of many of the sub-Saharan African societies, in which lineage loyalties take precedence over state authority and officials in such matters.

Ultimately, an understanding of the full range of political influences and considerations within each specific local community is required. In addition to 'the state' and to formal political institutions, this should include that which Mike Savage has defined as the constitutive forces of 'practical politics'. It is this analysis which will facilitate identification of the gendered and generational lines of power which so strongly influence perceptions of the relative costs and benefits of childrearing, through the definitions of individuals' familial and social roles, norms and expectations among different communication communities. It is these influences which may often result in the 'costs' of childrearing being born disproportionately by the quieter and more subordinate members of the population. The interaction between all forms of national, state power and local politics is what determines who these subordinate groups are and why they have to bear the burdens expected of them. As shown here, above, and in Nancy Folbre's research in the Philippines (pp. 44–5), the state's legal framework can be highly influential over the differential entitlements (in Amartya Sen's sense) and bargaining powers of these different groups.

Thus, it follows that in designing a policy to entice any population voluntarily into extending any of the fertility-regulating practices identified under the third heading, above (as occurred with the extension of abstinence in the British historical case) the rationales behind extant forms of fertility regulation have to be understood. These must then be carefully related to the component communication communities' various extant ways of evaluating the costs and, equally importantly, the positive benefits of children and childrearing, which in turn depends on correctly identifying the roles and meanings of parenthood, childhood, etc. This can provide the detailed knowledge of how to construct the kind of incentives which the communities understand for extending further the birth regulating practices which they already possess. It also suggests which kinds of contraceptive methods would be most appropriate to encourage initially.

But none of this will necessarily work unless full account has been taken of the fourth category, the relative powers of the 'carrying' forces of political representation of the various social groupings and lines of division within the local communities, as exemplified in the historical work of Kertzer and Hogan on Italy. Full recognition of the range of political forces involved under this heading will necessarily involve the investigator in coming to an appreciation of the highly conditional relationship obtaining between the central state and the different communication communities within a specific locality, and also of the unequal relationships between and within these social groups themselves, in each specific locality.

Thus, approached from this perspective it can be seen that even in a country like contemporary Kenya, which until very recently recorded the highest overall fertility rate of any African country, fertility regulation has always been and continues to be practised. Women did not typically begin to bear children immediately after menarche and, in common with much of East Africa, births were always deliberately spaced. This was achieved by moderate abstinence from intercourse because, although children are highly prized, too rapid childbearing has always been considered 'animal-like'.[154] In addition to their high fertility, Kenyan parents are also typically distinguished by an 'insatiable demand for education' for their children.[155] There are a number of historical reasons for this, including competing missionaries' emphases on literacy and learning and the abundance of relatively well-paying bureaucratic posts, especially after Nairobi's rise to prominence in the 1970s as the regional centre for all international organisations, following Kampala's demise under the disastrous régimes of Obote and Amin in Uganda.

Within the limits of the briefest of thumbnail sketches such as this, a number of important potentially fertility-restraining forces can be clearly identified even in this high-fertility society: namely the high evaluation of education and the recognition of the value of spacing births. Obviously, much more than this would need to be established from detailed investigation regarding the national and the local power structures influencing any specific Kenyan community: including its patterns of landholding and loyalties, the associated differentiation into distinct social groups and communication communities, complicated by the tribal and lineage systems, and the perceptions of gender and age relations held by each of these. This would be vital information for any specific policy in any part of the country designed to adjust Kenyans' perceptions of their relative childrearing costs and benefits. The point here is merely to suggest with a short example the outline of the kinds of specific policy implications which can legitimately be drawn from the historical study of changing fertility behaviour by following through the methodology of the suggested general framework of the perceived relative costs of childrearing.

It is to be noted that much of this is highly compatible with the broad thrust of the important policy suggestions which have recently been put forward by Partha Dasgupta, approaching the same intellectual problem from within the field of the contemporary economics discipline, rather than from that of British history, as here.[156] In examining the high fertility of much of sub-Saharan Africa and South

[154] Robinson, 'Kenya enters the fertility transition', p. 454, citing the research of Molnos, *Cultural source material*.

[155] Robinson 'Kenya', p. 456, citing Lockhart, 'The economics of nine years' education'.

[156] Dasgupta (unpublished paper). See also Dasgupta, *An inquiry into well-being*, especially chs. 11–12.

Asia Partha Dasgupta has particularly emphasised that there is a range of positive environmental, economic and cultural reasons why it is genuinely in the interests of individual parents to have high fertility, despite the fact that there may well be consequent disadvantages for the community as a whole. This is an example of a common category of paradox in economics and game theory, known as the 'Prisoner's Dilemma', which was generalised by Garrett Hardin, in application to social phenomena, as 'the tragedy of the commons'.[157]

This conflict between the interests of individuals and the overall interests of the community results from the existence of several specifiable forms of 'externalities', where parental fertility decisions are concerned.[158] Externalities are situations where the full economic costs of a particular decision – here the choice of whether or not to have another child – are not borne by the decision-taker. An important example of this has been documented by the Caldwells in showing that because of the character of the lineage systems in sub-Saharan West Africa, while reproductive decision-making is largely in the hands of husbands, they bear no part of the economic burden of childraising because of the separate budgets operated by the two spouses.[159] As Dasgupta notes, and as the Caldwells have documented, when this is further combined with a strongly patriarchal culture, then women will usually perceive themselves as having few reasons not to bear many children and many positive reasons to do so. Included in the latter set of reasons, in relatively poor societies, are first the need by parents to insure themselves for their old age by ensuring that they have the support of (often preferably male) children; and, secondly, the need for much labour in the onerous necessity of continuous fetching and carrying of water, fuel and food, which are the poor household's lifeblood, and which are tasks which would often otherwise fall to the female spouse.

The crucial innovatory emphasis in Dasgupta's policy proposals is his insistence that effective policies to reduce fertility must address the problem of offering substitutes for the *positive* benefits of having children, in the eyes of parents.[160] Previous policies have provided contraceptive information and appliances, have attempted to raise the costs of children through education programmes, for instance, and have even tried to enhance female autonomy through emphasis on female education. However, none of this is quite the same as measures which are aimed at replacing the positive services supplied by children. A policy of this sort has to be premised on a specific understanding of the positive values of children to parents in the community in question, including the associated externalities in a particular setting. This, therefore, entails the successful completion of the three preliminary, ethnographic, investigative steps outlined above: to achieve an

[157] *New Palgrave dictionary of economics*, 'The prisoner's dilemma'.
[158] Dasgupta (unpublished paper), pp. 21–4.
[159] Caldwell and Caldwell, 'The cultural context'.
[160] Dasgupta (unpublished paper), p. 27.

understanding of the perceived relative costs of childrearing in any given society or community.

Dasgupta correctly sees that proper appreciation of the values and virtues of high fertility to individual parents will typically require that policies aimed at reducing fertility will devise measures for the collective provision of substitutes for the children's positive functions. In poor societies this may well, for instance, require infrastructural investment, so that the bringing of water and energy into the home does not depend on a small army of little hands. In this context, the tendency for water and energy accessibility to become more difficult when poor and marginal communities face environmentally induced ecological pressures (because the rights of access of the poor are typically compromised first in such circumstances) should be especially worrying for those policy-makers who wish to encourage parents in such communities to have fewer children. The greater difficulty of access to these basics will actually encourage the poor to have more children; and this may be a generalisable proposition regarding the effect of primary ecological scarcity of many kinds on the fertility of the poor.[161]

In addition to water and energy delivery, the social security provided by pensions and a health system for protection in old age would also be very effective policies, in substituting for the positive values placed on having children. Dasgupta sums up his reasoning and policy strategy thus:

> It would certainly be unjust of governments to insist on parents sending their children to schools for so many years if this requirement further impoverished poor households. But it would not be unjust if the complementary household production inputs were made available through the provision of family-planning and public health services, and infrastructural investment and for governments then to make free school attendance compulsory.[162]

This formulation exemplifies an important implication of Johansson's argument: because of the functional values of children to parents in most poor societies, the relative absence of state measures to substitute for these functions constitutes a powerful policy – by default – in favour of high fertility.[163] However, to carry out such policies effectively will require taking into account all the political issues outlined, above, under the fourth category of considerations, including the international relations of the state and ideological influences upon it. Ironically, it seems likely that policies that give priority to the kind of infrastructural investments advocated by Dasgupta are least likely to be adopted in those countries most dependent upon or influenced by those powerful international aid agencies, governments and advisers in the west who, on ideological grounds, favour 'market' models of economic development and who look with great suspicion on the planned provision of goods or services by the state as an

[161] For an exploration of some implications of a range of ecological scarcities, see Homer-Dixon, 'Environmental scarcities'.

[162] Dasgupta (unpublished paper), p. 26.

[163] Johansson, '"Implicit" policy and fertility'.

invitation to wasteful inefficiencies. However, as Dasgupta's invocation of the Prisoners' Dilemma paradox indicates, this absence of collective intervention and provision may therefore represent collective folly, from the point of view not just of the longer term interests of the individual parents, but also of the state and, indeed, of the international community and its aid agencies, too.

Social science and history

The present study in all its Parts has, in effect, documented an object lesson in the insidious way in which the persistence of a 'good model' – in the pragmatic sense of a popular, widely used simplifying representation of a phenomenon – can impede and constrain investigative research in the social and historical sciences. Such models as the professional model of fertility decline are found to be useful on account of their ability to simplify complex data and issues and because of their intuitive intelligibility, often achieved through allusive and rhetorical linguistic or metaphorical facets (in this case the notion of a linear, graded social status hierarchy). As Ian Hacking has observed, models involve 'an odd mix of the pictorial and the mathematical'.[164]

Models such as these appear to be offering a reasoned account of social phenomena by appeal to superficially plausible and elegant logical principles or metaphors, giving 'order' and manageability to the subject of inquiry. In fact, acceptance of these representations or conceptual devices typically entails the users' acceptance of a system of implied epistemological and ontological, as well as socio-cultural assumptions. The history of the study of 'fertility decline' is particularly impregnated with such models and conceptual devices. They are the debris of decades of policy-related research conducted for predictive and, broadly, administrative purposes. Apart from the professional model itself, important other examples, which have been encountered above, during the course of this study, include: the grand dichotomy between 'traditional' and 'modern' societies or demographic régimes; the proposition that 'natural' and 'controlled' fertility are conceptually and empirically distinct opposites; the presumption that prudential marriage is a chronological and functional alternative to birth control within marriage; the notion that 'stopping' and 'spacing' are mutually exclusive strategies, which can be clearly empirically distinguished from each other; the assumption that abstinence and coitus interruptus are each precisely identifiable, singular and undifferentiated methods of birth control, which are quite distinct from each other, if not positively antithetical.

These are all conceptual devices which selectively abstract from a more complex and messy empirical reality. Abstraction is, of course, integral to the process of analytical inquiry. But this does not mean that all forms of abstraction and

[164] Hacking, *Representing and intervening*, p. 216.

representation are equally valid and justifiable: they may obscure or constrain inquiry as much as they can illuminate and facilitate it. In any field of investigation, there needs to be a preparedness to modify and revise pre-formed, overly neat analytical categories and models in recognition of the diversity of different contexts and of empirical findings.

Most of the conceptual devices listed above are, in fact, reductively simple abstractions or models: polarised dichotomies. Their deployment produces simple conceptions of fertility variation and simple explanations of change. Such beguiling dichotomies have to be discarded if the phenomena which they address are to be explored more thoroughly – both analytically and empirically. It has, for instance, been shown that more can be learned about how fertility changed in Britain by investigating the nature of the interactive relationship between marital fertility control and late marriage during the period 1860–1940 than simply by treating them as analytically separate features, whose histories have a supposedly distinct chronology. More variegated, sophisticated and realistic (meaning more complex, like the subject matter which they analyse) analytical concepts and forms of explanation need to be formulated. This will, no doubt, result in a diverse range of explanatory concepts and interpretations coming to be applied to changing fertility in different specific contexts. These context-dependent analyses may not appear to be as elegant, 'powerful' and universally applicable as the dramatic dichtomies – 'natural' versus 'controlled' fertility, for instance. But, neither will they perpetuate an essentially sciolistic approach, which preserves the integrity and elegance of 'cross-cultural' analytical concepts and metaphors, at the expense of advancing the sophistication and discriminatory powers of our synthetic, historical and empirical understanding of fertility change in any particular time and place.

Much of this book has been involved in attempting to expose the intellectual limitations which have been imposed upon the study of falling fertilities in modern Britain by a particularly seductive, quiet and all-pervasive model: the notion of a unitary national hierarchy of social classes. This professional model of social structure has dominated decades of research into fertility and is still retained to this day in the official publications of the Registrar-General.

Part II recounted the manner in which this *idea*, that British society could be represented as a unitary hierarchy of male occupations graded into a small number of classes, became infused into and embedded within the historiographical tradition of British empirical social science. This initially occurred through the medium of early twentieth-century attempts to explain demographic change in terms of elegant mechanistic systems, according to the Newtonian and positivistic paradigms still dominant in empirical social science at that time.[165] As Part II showed this model of society reflected both the common-sense views and the

[165] On the Newtonian influence upon classical Humean positivism, as further refined by J. S. Mill, see Hacking, *Representing and intervening*, p. 46.

national beliefs of the culturally dominant (though not necessarily the economically or industrially dominant) social status group within British society: the liberal arts trained cadres, who comprised most of the late Victorian and Edwardian British 'state' in all its Mannian polymorphic manifestation: the legislature, the judiciary, the organs of central government, the professions, local government and many philanthropic and voluntary associations, besides. The professional model, as chapter 3 showed, was the analogue, in terms of social structure, to this caste's teleological, evolutionary belief in national progress through their own rational, scientific and liberal leadership of society. Hence, its characteristic limitations corresponding to their ideological biases and preferences, which can be exposed to view through the intellectual exercise of 'deconstruction' which has been performed in Parts II and III, above.

Once established, the professional model of society has exhibited remarkable staying power, so that attempts to explain the historical events of falling fertility, in many other countries as well as in Britain, have continued to be premised, at an almost unconscious level, on the derivative class-differential theory of fertility decline. This directs attention towards finding unidimensional and generalisable causal factors to explain the phenomenon: diffusion was the first such form of explanation. Apparently, this is a far from unusual state of affairs. Ian Hacking reports, citing the work of Nancy Cartwright on physics, that 'models tend to be robust under theory change, that is, you keep the model and dump the theory'.[166]

However, Part III initially demonstrated that the primary source of demographic evidence which has always been considered to have confirmed this orthodox model, the 1911 census, in fact offers very little statistically significant support for such a theory. In order to show this, it was necessary to construct comparative fertility indices for 195 of the most important male occupations distinguished at the 1911 census, the fundamental taxonomic units from which the graded social classes were formed by aggregation. It was found that about half of the component couples and occupations of the graded classes failed to record fertility levels consonant with their class membership.

Once emancipated from this notion of a unitary hierarchy, the occupational fertility and nuptiality differentials have been further explored in an attempt to discern sensible alternative social patterns in this rich data source. The evidence suggests a much more complex and variegated pattern of multiple fertility declines among the different communication communities of the nation. This implies that no single factor or national set of events can explain 'the' fertility decline. However, a complex set of relationships, involving local and central government initiatives, plebeian and patrician voluntary associations and the divergent, variously gendered working practices in local labour markets, are all indicated as potentially important areas to be researched in the future, preferably

[166] Hacking, *Representing and intervening*, p. 47. See below, pp. 600–1, on models.

through properly contextualised comparative local studies. Notable among the influences accounting for divergences in fertility behaviour, suggested by the analysis above, were: the relative political organisation of male workers in a town or industry; the relative segregation of the sexes in the workforce; and associated power relationships or 'bargaining positions' between the sexes in the community in question and within the conjugal unit. These sources of differentiation interacted with the various contingent cultural, political and economic forces which have been addressed and which acted to change the perceived relative childrearing costs of children, principally by altering the characteristics and meanings of the primary familial and social roles of childhood, motherhood and fatherhood.

In many fields of inquiry the capacity to inspect much more closely than ever before the form of the phenomenon under investigation has had important implications for understanding of the causal forces involved: the use of the telescope for exploration of the firmament. Forms of causation which seemed plausible when objects and processes were viewed from a certain distance or with relatively poor, low-resolution observational tools became unrealistic and obsolete once the objects and their relationships could be discerned and interrogated in much greater detail, revealing processes, features and forces which were previously simply unavailable for study and for thought. In all empirically grounded subjects of study, whose explanatory goals are premised on the prior construction of the 'objects' whose relationships are to be elucidated, such observational transformations tend to be among the most powerful and important sources of new ideas and approaches. Within more analytical and reflective fields of study the construction and acquisition of new linguistic resources – concepts and articulations with which to describe and to deal intellectually with a given subject of thought and inquiry – can occur more autonomously. Nevertheless, the necessary, dialectical and limiting relationship between the available descriptive terms at our disposal and the analytical possibilities available, remains essentially similar in all spheres of thought and inquiry. As Wittgenstein apophthegmatically pronounced in 1921 in the *Tractatus logico-philosophicus*, on the dependent relationship between what cognitive anthropologists have distinguished as the 'etic' (signifying) and the 'emic' (signified) aspects of culture, 'Whereof one cannot speak, thereon one must remain silent.'[167]

If we continue to adhere doggedly to a particular view or model of the phenomenon of falling fertility which insists that the object of study be primarily conceived as a singular, socially graded national process, this inevitably restricts and impoverishes the range of explanatory concepts and approaches that can be brought to bear. Of course, in empirically premised subjects of inquiry such as this, there always remains the problem of the invention of the telescope itself: if for some

[167] For an accessible introduction to the emic/etic concepts, see Littleton, 'Lucien Lévy-Bruhl'. For further reading, see Headland, Pike and Harris, *Emics and etics*.

technical reason it is not possible to look more closely or in a different way at an object of study, then students must do the best they can with the currently available observational resources.[168] However, any such field of study which has remained content with the same representation of its object of study where the opportunity exists for alternatives is failing in its primary epistemological duty, which is to explore such possibilities and test the descriptive and conceptual constraints. Such a failure may well account for the difference between what Imre Lakatos has characterised as a progressive, as against a degenerating research programme.[169]

The problem with the history of the study of the causation involved in Britain's falling fertility would seem to be that it has long ago more or less exhausted the relatively limited range of possible alternative explanations which are consonant with a continued adherence to the professional model of unitary fertility decline. As Part I argued, there has in fact been remarkably little conceptual advance in the last fifty years, beyond the limited range of alternative explanations to account for the evidence which had already appeared before the Second World War. Yet there has been no significant move towards a different and potentially more productive programme for research or towards a new conception of the phenomenon itself.

Why has the exhaustion of explanatory possibilities not previously led to a re-examination of the construction of the phenomenon, its representation? No doubt the answers to this are complex and much to do with the sociology of the relationship between the intellectual disciplines charged with investigating this subject: social scientists of various kinds – principally demographers, sociologists and economists – and historians. It seems that a principal problem has been that of the largely unacknowledged rhetorical claims of those seeking to investigate the problem: unexamined assumptions about why the problem is important at all; and therefore what kind of approach is or is not appropriate. The nature of the most important unexamined assumption is that the object of explanation – falling fertility – has been an event of *national* import and that therefore it must be studied first and foremost with rhetorical reference to the life-history of the nation. This

168 Indeed, this is a limitation which applies in principle at all times to all forms of rational inquiry, as there is always the possibility of the next observational revolution, which may render obsolete the current agenda of investigative preoccupations. However, all specific fields of inquiry labour within this limitation. This only means that there is all the more a duty to exploit to the full all available ways of looking at a problem within the extant observational limitations, striving to overcome these regrettable and inevitable constraints.

169 For Lakatos a progressive scientific programme is one which has the capacity continuously to spawn significant new theoretical issues and debates capable of transforming the conceptualisation of the problems being addressed. In other words, these are extremely flexible heuristic frameworks not tied too closely to any specific observational technology or any specific formulation of the phenomena to be explained. Indeed, it seems to be entailed by Lakatos's formulation that these are programmes of intellectual activity which contain a drive towards exhausting the range of possibilities for causal explanation within the limitations of any given observational technology *and also* generating fruitful indications for the further conceptual transformation (in the construction of the object of study) which must eventually appear (otherwise, by definition they become degenerating or moribund programmes). Lakatos, *The methodology of scientific research programmes.*

'methodological nationalism' has taken on the form of an all too direct imperative and constraint. Not only has the phenomenon been almost exclusively studied as a national, unitary process, using only those sources of evidence which can supply a directly national picture. But also there has been a consistent rhetorical downgrading and ignoring in the mainstream of the literature of any pieces of research or approaches which do not purport to offer methods, results or conclusions, which can be seen to have a national remit or to report results which can be represented as having an explanatory scope directly generalisable to the nation as a whole.

The problem therefore is that, ever since the issue of falling fertility was first scientifically addressed, its students have not simply being trying to explore, investigate and explain the causation involved in the most open-minded and methodologically flexible way possible. They have instead, without noticing the conflation of two not necessarily compatible aims, been intent on explaining how *national* fertility fell, thereby automatically introducing a dramatic constraint on the conceptualisation of the nature of the problem to be explained, as well as an entailed set of limitations on the range of ways in which we might approach the problem as a subject for inquiry: its modelling, or representation.

The nation will, of course, long remain an object for reverence and fascination in the social and historical sciences, ultimately because of its role in the fundamental process of identity formation in the 'imagined community' of the researchers and their audience.[170] This is both a general problem for the social sciences and it also afflicts this particular case of the study of falling fertility. Any study purportedly pronouncing upon the course of a nation's historical fertility decline will never cease to have cultural significance and receive a hearing, regardless of that study's power to produce anything genuinely novel or compelling in a *scientific* sense about the causation involved. This is because it counts first as a cultural contribution, however scientifically unoriginal or uncompelling, to the rich mainstream of highly varied, rhetorical discourse on *the nation* – its past, present and future; and therefore it has a guaranteed minimal significance by virtue of the cultural centrality of that discourse. A researcher's unconscious primary aim in these circumstances is in fact to say something general and relatively authoritative about the nation, via the medium of a 'scientific' study of its fertility behaviour. This is the opposite of a truly and *merely* scientific set of priorities, which should be aimed exclusively and flexibly at elucidating the causation involved in changing fertility in the recent past, regardless of 'the nation'.

The unitary, hierarchical 'professional' model of fertility decline is in fact a direct consequence of this assumed and unexamined commitment to the explanatory rhetoric of nationism. It is a classificatory means for reducing empirically observed social and behavioural variations within a national population to an

[170] For this formulation of the historical construction and significance of 'nations', see Anderson, *Imagined communities*. 'Methodological nationalism' is analogous to Lukes's methodological individualism: see ch. 4, n. 185.

apparently simple, ordered unidimensional scale. This is a representation which marshals the anarchy of empirical variety into such a form as to give it the most coherent appearance of integrated order on a national basis. It is a representation which conveys to the maximum extent a particular gloss on the empirical data. It suggests that the data confirm that both the population itself and the behavioural phenomenon of varied and changing fertility behaviour exhibit a coherence of overall form which means that they can be treated as unitary national objects, *not* exhibiting the signs of any significant degree of further variety and complexity of structure or form, which might call forth the need for untidy and rhetorically unsatisfying explanations lacking a 'national' remit and resonance.

There is, finally, a need for a discussion of what conception of scientific inquiry is being invoked in an historical investigation of large-scale behavioural change, such as falling fertility in modern Britain. There are several possible philosophies of science, embracing the historical and social sciences. These broadly fall into three types: deductivist; contextualist; and realist.[171] The first is most associated with the 'positivist' or logical empiricist, 'covering laws' school of thought, which envisages the process of rational inquiry and the formulation of explanations as a singular kind of intellectual activity, which is termed 'science'.[172] Following the thrust of the logical positivist school and the early Wittgenstein of *Tractatus logico-philosophicus*, it is claimed that truly scientific methods of inquiry can take on only one absolute and proper form, although it may always remain a matter of conjecture – subject to critique and revision – to specify exactly what that general form comprises. Certain subject matters are more or less amenable to this singular approach at any time, which makes for more or less effective pursuit of 'science' in different fields of inquiry.

Contextualist or hermeneutic or interpretative models of scientific explanation have been associated with a diametrically opposed view, which has argued, following the late Wittgenstein of *Philosophical investigations*, that the meaning and authority of any explanation or activity, including that of 'scientific inquiry' itself, is crucially dependent on historically contingent aspects of a non-absolute and highly variable communication context.[173] The cultural and technological, linguistic

[171] These distinctions follow Roy Bhaskar's contributions to the *Macmillan dictionary of the history of science* (1981), especially articles on 'Aristotle's theory of cause'; 'Explanation'; 'Naturalism'; 'Positivism'; and 'Realism'. See also Lloyd, *Explanation in social history*, Part II.

[172] Carl Gustav Hempel is probably considered to be the most influential and sophisticated modern exponent of the logical empiricist 'covering laws' school, expounded in his *Studies in the logic of explanation* and *Aspects of scientific explanation*. For an introduction see Ryan, *The philosophy of the social sciences*, ch. 3; Lloyd, *Explanation in social history*, chs. 3–4; see also, above, ch. 4, n. 147.

[173] The most accessible and widely read exposition in English of the contextualist or interpretative position has been Winch, *The idea of a social science*. This anti-positivist philosophy of social science has a particularly strong tradition in much German thought, from Wilhelm Dilthey (1833–1911), author of *Introduction to the human sciences* (1883), and through the critical theory of the 'Frankfurt School' Institute for Social Research (founded in 1923), whose leading lights have included Max Horkheimer, Walter Benjamin, Theodor Adorno, Herbert Marcuse and most contemporarily, Jürgen Habermas, author of *Knowledge and human interests* (published in German in 1968 and first translated into English in 1972).

and power relations of any real historical community strongly condition the kind of explanations – both scientific and otherwise – available to its participatory agents. A strong relativism is therefore implied in this school of thought, as developed, for instance, in either the work of P. K. Feyerabend, or the Edinburgh 'strong programme' of 'externalist' influences on science.[174]

Realists comprise a more varied range of positions standing somewhere between these first two.[175] Realists such as Nancy Cartwright and Ian Hacking argue that as problem-solving rational scientists (whether in the natural, the social or the historical fields of inquiry) we create from the chaos of 'reality' an artificial order with which to work analytically and theoretically, by constructing representations and models of the phenomena to be studied. Scientific inquirers, according to Hacking, are first *homo depictor*.[176] We never can access and study 'reality' directly and unmediated, in all its messy, manifest complexity. There is always a necessary process of selection of certain 'essential' or 'important' aspects, while simultaneously excluding as 'noise' or ephemera an enormous range of other aspects of that same 'reality' (in a sense this form of scientific realism is all about drawing out the methodological implications of Werner Heisenberg's uncertainty principle).

There can, therefore, be no unmediated, direct articulation between theory and its validating observations: models, or representations, are the necessary, articulating intermediary. The incredible flexibility of this mediating process, as a technological and semantic bridge between 'theory' and 'observations', means that models and representations occupy an absolutely pivotal place in the process of rational, scientific inquiry. It is actually these models which contain and specify the crucial conceptual content of any empirically engaged scientific or interpretative work. This is because, as Ian Hacking has inferred from Nancy Cartwright's study of physics, 'models are doubly models. They are models of the phenomena, and they are models of the theory. That is, theories are always too complex for us to discern their consequences, so we simplify them in mathematically tractable models. At the same time these models are approximate representations of the universe.'[177] Therefore the process of construction, application, validation, critique and replacement of models, the representations of the problems to be studied, must form the centrepiece of any process of rational, empirical inquiry, as it has done in the foregoing historical study of changing fertility in modern Britain.

[174] Feyerabend, *Against method*; Barnes, *Scientific knowledge and sociological theory*. Note that Lakatos had first offered the distinction between 'external' (social, cultural, psychological, etc.) influences upon scientific activity and its 'internalist' cognitive development, as a post-Kuhnian response in order to emphasise the significance of the latter, 'internalist' growth of scientific knowledge, as a history supposedly distinct from the former category of 'externalist' influences. Hacking, *Representing and intervening*, ch. 8, esp. pp. 122–3; and see above, ch. 5, n. 147.

[175] On various other realisms, apart from that of Cartwright and Hacking discussed in the text here, see, for instance, Bhaskar, *A realist theory of science* and Bhaskar, *The possibility of naturalism*; see also Lloyd, *Explanation in social history*, chs. 7–8.

[176] Hacking, *Representing and intervening*, p. 132.

[177] Hacking, *Representing and intervening*, pp. 216–17, referring to Cartwright, *How the laws*.

If the engineered world of physics, as analysed by Nancy Cartwright, can be characterised in this way, as dealing through its models in self-referential knowledge, this is all the more true of the field of modern demographic social science, with its heavy reliance on the inscribed and encoded social data created by the technology of the census.[178] From this highly socially constructed data, models of society and demographic change are derived, for which we then seek theories of explanation, premised on those representations. Exercises in self-critical validation are therefore all the more essential in this field. Fortunately in the particular historical case studied here, T. H. C. Stevenson published, alongside his own professional model, a relatively comprehensive record of the evidence collected in 1911, tabulated according to enumerated male occupations. This has enabled an exercise of validation to be mounted, testing the adequacy of the professional model and the associated array of dichotomous explanatory concepts. The availability of this evidence has also enabled alternative social representations and explanatory concepts to be developed.

In this study, it has been argued that the incumbent, national, unitary, professional model of fertility decline has imposed an unhelpful set of inter-related conceptual and epistemological limitations on the study of fertility change. It has been argued that a superior form of general model is provided by the heuristic framework of perceived, relative childrearing costs. This phrase unpacks into a comprehensive theoretical position; but it has the virtue of committing the researcher to relatively little in the way of a particular social morphology or ontology. This is particularly appropriate to elucidation of the phenomena in question, since it has been shown that the varying social and political contexts – the overlapping communication communities and their interaction with the agencies of 'the state' – are a vital area for inquiry (rather than something to be excluded from study, which is one of the several intellectually unhelpful consequences of the professional model, since it is, in effect, a crude device for 'controlling' for this range of influences, obviating the need to investigate them).

The study of the causes of falling fertilities in modern British history is

[178] For an extensive exposition of the 'technological' creation of social and economic statistics, see Desrosières, *La Politique*; Brian, *La Mesure*; also Anderson, *The American census*; and for a study which addresses the more general social and political forces lying behind this, see Porter, *Trust in numbers*. Note that scientific realists do not hold that because science 'creates', through the engineered environment of the laboratory and through its observational technology, its own representation of the objects which it studies – and so is, ultimately, a self-referential activity – that therefore there can be no way of validating its 'findings'. Nancy Cartwright and Ian Hacking have argued that it is by experimentally manipulating (intervening with) the created 'objects' or models, so as to produce predicted 'effects', that scientists gain confidence both that their representations of the 'objects' and that their understanding of the relationships between them are valid. Furthermore, it follows, from logical criteria of consistency, correspondence and conciliance, that greatest confidence can be placed in those phenomena and their respective properties which can be created, observed or manipulated in a number of technologically independent ways. According to Hacking, therefore 'our notions of reality are formed from our abilities to change the world'. Hacking, *Representing and intervening*, pp. 146, 35–8.

simultaneously a scientific and an historical inquiry. The present contribution has brought an historian's eye and investigative techniques to the primary sources of demographic and social evidence, while maintaining a commitment to the scientific project, from which much of this evidence was originally created, of understanding and elucidating the causes of this demographic change. However, it has been argued in the course of this volume that the pursuit of such an understanding takes the study of fertility change away from the narrow, 'covering laws' philosophy of scientific research, which has historiographically dominated the subject's intellectual formation and which informed the provenance of the historical sources themselves. An alternative, realist philosophy of science, sketched above, has much more in common with the historical interpretation offered in this account.[179] Just as this scientific realism rejects any radical relativism, there is no sense in which it is being argued here that the phenomenon of falling fertilities can be deconstructed out of existence. As shown here, the historical and historiographical approach can, however, relativise the received scientific wisdom, by identifying the nature of the models that structure the authoritative, quantitative evidence: their mode of influence, their historical origins and their intellectual implications.

The key scientific and historical issue is: what representation of the phenomena we accept as the premise for our collective work of understanding and explanation. Social phenomena such as falling fertility can be represented in a wide manner of ways, from the artistic, as on the cover of this book, through any number of literary discourses and cultural constructions, one of which is the quantitative and statistical. All carry important, diverse meanings embracing manifold aspects of the phenomena. But if the primary aim is, as it is here, the specifically delimited, scientific one of the analysis of the causes of such historical change in fertility, then it is the numerical representation which carries a particular significance and an intellectual priority where demographic change is concerned. Hence, all the attention lavished upon this question in this study.

New ways of representing falling fertilities in modern Britain and an associated set of new explanations have been presented in the course of this study, all of which are compatible with a new general theory or approach to fertility change: through analysing the perceived relative costs of childrearing. But the most generalisable conclusion to emerge from this study is the exhortation that all who examine fertility change do so with as explicit and unblinking a critical awareness as is possible of the conceptual significance and epistemological ties of the models and representations which they necessarily use in pursuing this subject, whether they borrow them from the past or create them for themselves.

[179] This is, perhaps, not surprising, since, following Kuhn, its exponents have formed their philosophy of science from a primarily *historical* reconstruction of the activities of scientists (rather than, for instance, the analytical approach of Popper and Lakatos, or the 'anthropological', ethnographic approach of Latour and Woolgar).

APPENDICES

APPENDIX A COPY OF 1911 CENSUS HOUSEHOLD SCHEDULE

EXAMPLES OF THE MODE OF FILLING UP THE SCHEDULE.

Example	Name and Surname (1)	Relationship to Head of Family (2)	Age (last Birthday) and Sex: Males (3)	Females (4)	Particulars as to Marriage (5)	Number of Years Married (6)	Children of present Marriage: Total (7)	Living (8)	Dead (9)	Personal Occupation (10)	Industry or Service with which Worker is connected (11)	Whether Employer, Worker, or Working on own Account (12)	Whether Working at Home (13)	Birthplace (14)	Nationality of every Person born in a Foreign Country (15)	Infirmity (16)
1st Example	Henry Chapman	Head	[illegible]	—	Married	[illegible]	—	—	—	Bootmaker (Dealer)		Employer		Sussex, Brighton		
	Rachel Chapman	Wife	—	[illegible]	Married	[illegible]	[illegible]	[illegible]	[illegible]	Assisting in the business				India, Bombay (Resident)		
	Martin Marshall	Nephew	[illegible]	—	Single					Confectionery Sugar Boiler	Chocolate Manuf.	Worker		Huntingdon, St. Ives		
	George Roberts	Assistant	[illegible]	—	Single					Boot Repairer		Worker		Cardigan, Aberystwith		
	Emily Dart	Servant	—	[illegible]	Single					General Servant (Domestic)				Guernsey (Resident)		
2nd Example	Robert Taylor	Head	[illegible]	—	Widower					Bricklayer	Cotton Spinning	Worker		Lancs., Rochdale		
	Jessie Taylor	Sister	—	[illegible]	Single					Dressmaker		Own Acct.	At Home	Cumberland, Alston		
	Margaret Taylor	Daughter	—	[illegible]						School part time, Worsted Spinner		Worker		Lancs., Rochdale		
	Frederick Taylor	Son	[illegible]	—										Lancs., Rochdale		Totally deaf from birth
3rd Example	Andrew Lindsay	Head	[illegible]	—	Married	[illegible]	[illegible]	[illegible]	[illegible]	Farmer		Employer		Fife, St. Andrews		
	Florence Lindsay	Wife	—	[illegible]	Married									France (Resident)	Brit. sub. by parentage	
	Thomas Lindsay	Son	[illegible]	—	Single					Farmer's Son working on Farm		Worker		Bucks., Halstead		
	Elizabeth Lindsay	Daughter	—	[illegible]	Single					Farmer's Daughter, Dairy work		Worker		Bucks., Halstead		
	Samuel Blake	Servant	[illegible]	—	Single					Waggoner on Farm		Worker		Bucks., Braintree		
	Mary Clark	Servant	—	[illegible]	Single					General Servant (Domestic)		Worker		Suffolk, Sudbury		
4th Example	Daniel Sullivan	Head	[illegible]	—	Widower					Night Watchman	Chemical Manuf.	Worker		Kerry, Tralee (Resident)		
5th Example	Richard Croft	Head	[illegible]	—	Married	[illegible]	[illegible]	[illegible]	[illegible]	Coal Miner, Hewer		Worker		Yorks., Hemsworth		
	Eliza Croft	Wife	—	[illegible]	Married									Yorks., Lofthouse		
	Isaac Croft	Son	[illegible]	—	Single					Colliery Horsekeeper (below ground)		Worker		Yorks., Hemsworth		
	Ada Croft	Daughter	—	[illegible]										Yorks., Hemsworth		Totally blind, 5 yrs. old
6th Example	Grace Ward	Head	—	[illegible]	Married	[illegible]	None			Boarding House Keeper		Employer		London, Paddington		
	Harold Simpson	Boarder	[illegible]	—	Single					Accountant	Boro' Council			London, Chelsea		
	Charles Howard	Boarder	[illegible]	—	Single					Manager of Railway Co.				U.S. of America (Visitor)	U.S.A. citizen	
	Lal Mansukar	Boarder	[illegible]	—	Married					Law Student				India, Madras (Visitor)		
	Mabel Vincent	Visitor	—	[illegible]	Single					Gold Embroiderer	Military Tailoring	Worker		Malta (Visitor)		
	Hannah Webb	Servant	—	[illegible]	Single					Cook (Boarding House)		Worker		Lincoln, Louth		
	Sophia Orr	Servant	—	[illegible]	Single					Housemaid (Boarding House)		Worker		Wilts., Devizes		
	Carlo Barbieri	Servant	[illegible]	—	Single					Waiter (Boarding House)		Worker		Italy (Resident)	Italian	
7th Example	Morris Goldman	Head	[illegible]	—	Married	[illegible]	[illegible]	[illegible]	[illegible]	Tailor (Maker)		Worker	At Home	Russian Poland (Resident)	Natd. Brit. sub. (1900)	
	Leah Goldman	Wife	—	[illegible]	Married					Sewing Machinist, Tailoring		Worker	At Home	London, Whitechapel		
	David Goldman	Son	[illegible]	—						School				London, Whitechapel		
	Jacob Goldman	Son	Under 1 month	—										London, Whitechapel		

CENSUS

OF

ENGLAND AND WALES,

1911.

SCHEDULE.

Prepared pursuant to the Census (Great Britain) Act, 1910.

This space to be filled up by the Enumerator.

Number of Registration District ....

Number of Registration Sub-District ....

Number of Enumeration District ....

Name of Head of Family or Separate Occupier ....

Postal Address ....

NOTICE.

This Schedule must be filled up and signed by, or on behalf of, the Head of the Family or other person in occupation, or in charge, of the dwelling (house, tenement or apartment).

If a house be let or sub-let to two or more occupiers each occupier of a part of the house must fill up a Schedule for his part of the house. Boarders are not to be considered as separate occupiers.

In the case of Hotels, Boarding Houses, Clubs, and other similar establishments, the Keeper, Manager or other person in charge must fill up a Schedule with respect to all the inmates.

The Schedule will be called for on MONDAY, APRIL 3rd, by the appointed Enumerator; in order that he may not be delayed it must be ready with the answers written in the proper columns early on the morning of that day.

If the answers are incomplete or inaccurate, the Enumerator may ask any questions necessary to enable him to correct the Schedule.

If any person whose duty it is to give information refuses to do so, or wilfully gives false information as to any of the required particulars, he will be liable on conviction to a fine not exceeding FIVE POUNDS.

If the Head of the Family or other person responsible is unable to deliver the Schedule personally to the Enumerator, he may instruct another person to do so. If desired it may be put under cover.

The contents of the Schedule will be treated as strictly confidential.

BERNARD MALLET,
Registrar-General.

Approved by the Local Government Board.

JOHN BURNS,
President.

INSTRUCTIONS

For filling up the Columns headed "Profession or Occupation."

COLUMN 10.

1. DESCRIPTION OF PERSONAL OCCUPATION.—Describe the Occupation fully in Column 10. If more than one Occupation is followed, state that by which living is mainly earned.

2. DEALERS, SHOPKEEPERS OR SHOP ASSISTANTS as distinct from MAKERS, PRODUCERS OR REPAIRERS.—All such persons should be so described as to leave no doubt whether they are Dealers or Makers. In many cases "Tailors," "Bootmakers," "Hatters," "Watchmakers," "Goldsmiths," "Silversmiths," "Jewellers," "Chemists," "Bakers," "Seedsmen," "Florists," &c., and their Assistants are not Makers or Producers: in such cases the word "Dealer," "Shopkeeper," or "Shop Assistant" should be added to the occupational name. A person who both makes and deals should be described as "Maker," if chiefly Maker, or "Dealer" if chiefly Dealer.

3. OUT OF WORK.—If out of work or disengaged at the time of the Census, the **usual occupation must be stated.**

4. THE OCCUPATIONS OF WOMEN engaged in any business or profession, including women **regularly engaged in assisting relatives in trade or business,** must be fully stated. No entry should be made in the case of wives, daughters, or other female relatives wholly engaged in domestic duties at home.

5. CHILDREN AT SCHOOL AND STUDENTS.—For all persons over ten years of age attending school write "School," and for those attending colleges, evening schools, or other instructional classes, or receiving instruction privately, write "Student." If studying for any profession, state the profession, as "Law Student," "Medical Student."

If attending school or other classes half time or part time only, write "School part time," or "Student part time."

If also engaged in any employment state the employment, as "School, Newsboy"; "School, Grocer's Errand Boy"; "School part time, Cotton Roving Frame Doffer."

6. RETIRED OR PENSIONED.—If retired or pensioned state the fact, and add former Occupation, as "Retired Farmer," "Retired Butcher," "Police Pensioner," &c. **The present occupation,** if any, of pensioners should also be stated in all cases, as "Army Pensioner, Bank Porter," &c.

7. PRIVATE MEANS.—For persons neither following nor having followed a profession or occupation, but deriving their income from private sources, or allowances, write "Private Means."

8. VAGUE OR INDEFINITE TERMS MUST NOT BE USED ALONE, such for example as Apprentice, Assistant, Canvasser, Collector, Contractor, Foreman, Inspector, Labourer, Machinist, Manager, Manufacturer, Mechanic, Millhand, Overlooker, Superintendent (see also paragraphs a to r below). Care should be taken that no occupational name common to different industries is used without a full and distinctive description; an Enameller should be described as a "Pottery Enameller," "Watch-dial Enameller," "Cycle Enameller," &c.; a Painter as a "Painter (Artist)," "Ship Painter," "House Painter," &c.; a Rivetter, as a "Boiler Rivetter," "Ship Plate Rivetter," "Boot Rivetter," &c.

(a) ARMY, NAVY, CIVIL SERVICE, MUNICIPAL SERVICE, &c. State the service and rank or grade.

(b) CLERGYMAN, PRIEST, MINISTER. State whether "Clergyman (Established Church)," "Roman Catholic Priest," "Wesleyan Methodist Minister," &c. Clergymen who are also Schoolmasters should be returned as Schoolmasters. In the case of Local or Occasional Preachers, the ordinary occupation only should be given.

(c) LEGAL PROFESSION. State whether "Barrister," "Solicitor," "Solicitor's Articled Clerk," "Law Clerk," &c.

(d) AGENT, BROKER, BUYER, MERCHANT, SALESMAN, COMMERCIAL TRAVELLER. State particular kind of business or trade, as "Cycle Agent," "Sugar Broker," "Coal Merchant," "Commercial Traveller, Millinery."

(e) CLERK. State whether "Bank Clerk," "Insurance Clerk," "Law Clerk," "Bookstall Clerk," "Hotel Clerk," "Railway Clerk," "Theatre Clerk," &c.

(f) ENGINEERING AND METAL TRADES. State precise branch of trade and nature of operation, as "Engineer's Pattern Maker," "Ship Plater's Helper." "Iron Worker" is too indefinite; state whether employed at Blast Furnace, Puddling Furnace, Iron Foundry, &c.

(g) ENGINEMAN, ENGINE DRIVER, STOKER, FIREMAN. State whether "Railway Engine Stoker," "Traction Engine Driver," "Stationary Engineman," "Gas Stoker," "Furnace Stoker at Potteries," &c.

(h) COTTON, WOOL, SILK OR OTHER TEXTILE OPERATIVE, DYER, BLEACHER, &c. State the material and the precise occupation, as "Bobbin Carrier in Cotton Spinning Room," "Silk Throwster's Piecer," "Plaiter in Cotton Finishing Works."

(j) MINER, QUARRYMAN. State kind of mine or quarry, and nature of work, as "Coal Miner, Hewer," "Colliery Horsekeeper (below ground)," "Colliery Lamp Room Labourer (above ground)," "Colliery Labourer (above ground)," "Onsetter in Ironstone Mine," "Dresser in Stone Quarry," "Rockman in Slate Quarry."

(k) FARMER. State whether "Farmer," "Grazier," or "Farm Bailiff." Farmers' sons or other relatives assisting in the work of the farm should be returned as "Farmer's Son working on Farm," "Farmer's Brother working on Farm," "Farmer's Daughter, Dairy work," &c.

(l) FARM SERVANT. State nature of work, and indicate if mainly in charge of horses, cattle, &c., as "Horseman on Farm," "Waggoner on Farm," "Cowman on Farm," "Shepherd." A Labourer on a Farm whose work is of a general character should be described as "Farm Labourer," **not simply as a Labourer.**

(m) LABOURER, PORTER, &c. State nature of employment, as "Bricklayer's Labourer," "Dock Labourer," "Railway Contractor's Labourer," "Farm Labourer," "General Labourer," "Coal Porter," "Railway Porter," &c. **The terms "Labourer," "Porter," should never be used alone.**

(n) DOMESTIC SERVICE. State nature of service, as "Cook (Domestic)," "Housemaid (Domestic)," "Gardener (Domestic)," "Coachman (Domestic)," "Nursery Governess."

(o) SERVANTS, WAITERS &c., IN HOTELS, CLUBS, RESTAURANTS AND BOARDING HOUSES. State nature of employment and service in which engaged, as "Hotel Cook," "Hall Porter at Club," "Hotel Waiter," "Restaurant Waitress."

(p) NURSE. State whether "Nurse (Domestic)," "Monthly Nurse," "Sick Nurse," &c.

(q) GARDENER. State whether "Gardener (Domestic)," "Market Gardener," "Jobbing Gardener," "Nurseryman," &c.

(r) COACHMAN, GROOM, MOTOR-CAR DRIVER. State whether employed by Cab, Omnibus, Domestic, or other service, as "Coachman (Domestic)," "Chauffeur (Domestic)," "Motor-Bus Driver," "Tramway Motor Man."

COLUMN 11.

9. INDUSTRY OR SERVICE WITH WHICH CONNECTED.—The information asked for in this column is required in order to ascertain for each industry or service how many persons are employed therein, or in connection therewith, although following a distinct occupation. Thus, for instance, for breweries it is desired to know how many coopers, blacksmiths, bricklayers, &c., are in the direct employment of the brewery, as well as the numbers actually engaged in brewing processes. Further, it is desired to ascertain the number of persons directly employed by central or local government authorities, whether in administration or in undertakings such as tramways, gasworks, &c. Following are examples of cases in which entries should be made in Column 11 as well as in Column 10.

Column 10 Personal Occupation	Column 11 Industry or Service with which worker is connected	Column 10 Personal Occupation	Column 11 Industry or Service with which worker is connected	Column 10 Personal Occupation	Column 11 Industry or Service with which worker is connected	Column 10 Personal Occupation	Column 11 Industry or Service with which worker is connected
Blacksmith's Striker	Loco. Dept. Rly. Co.	Copper Roller Engraver	Calico Printer	Housekeeper	Drapery Warehouse	Shop Fitter	Harbour Board
Bricklayer	Blast Furnace	Cotton Drawing Frame Tenter	Carpet Manufacture	Iron Founder	General Engineer	[illegible]	Insurance Company
Cardboard Box Maker	Soap Manufacture	Head Teacher	County Council	Iron Founder	Stove Grate Maker	Typefounder	Type Foundry
Carter	General Carrier	Hotel Manager	Railway Company	Iron Founder	Gas Council	Type-founder	General Printers
Carter	Railway Company	House Painter	Builder	Lighterman	Cement Works	Wood Pin Maker	[illegible] Works
Carter on Sewage Farm	Urban Dist. Council	House Painter	Chemical Manufa.	Maltster's Labourer	Maltster	Wood Sawyer	[illegible] Works
Clay Miner	Pottery Manufacture	House Painter	Hotel Company	Maltster's Labourer	Brewer	Wood Sawyer	[illegible] Works
Coal Porter, Gasworks	Borough Council			Railway Engine Driver	Brewer	Wood Sawyer	[illegible] Carriage Wks.

(M266) Wt 22313—54 9,050,000 12/10 [illegible]

Harrison & Sons, Printers, St. Martin's Lane, London, W.C.

CENSUS OF ENGLAND AND WALES, 1911.

Number of Schedule ________
(To be filled up by the Enumerator after collection.)

Before writing on this Schedule please read the Examples and the Instructions given on the other side of the paper, as well as the headings of the Columns. The entries should be written in Ink.

The contents of the Schedule will be treated as confidential.** Strict care will be taken that no information is disclosed with regard to individual persons. **The returns are not to be used for proof of age, as in connection with Old Age Pensions, or for any other purpose than the preparation of Statistical Tables.

	NAME AND SURNAME	RELATIONSHIP to Head of Family.	AGE (last Birthday) and SEX.		PARTICULARS as to MARRIAGE.					PROFESSION or OCCUPATION of Persons aged ten years and upwards.				BIRTHPLACE of every person.	NATIONALITY of every Person born in a Foreign Country.	INFIRMITY.
	of every Person, whether Member of Family, Visitor, Boarder, or Servant, who (1) passed the night of Sunday, April 2nd, 1911, in this dwelling and was alive at midnight, or (2) arrived in this dwelling on the morning of Monday, April 3rd, not having been enumerated elsewhere. No one else must be included. (For order of entering names see Examples on back of Schedule.)	State whether "Head," or "Wife," "Son," "Daughter," or other Relative, "Visitor," "Boarder," or "Servant."	For Infants under one year state the age in months as "under one month," "one month," etc.		Write "Single," "Married," "Widower," or "Widow," opposite the names of all persons aged 15 years and upwards.	State, for each Married Woman entered on this Schedule, the number of:—				Personal Occupation.	Industry or Service with which worker is connected.	Whether Employer, Worker, or Working on Own Account.	Whether Working at Home.	(1) If born in the United Kingdom, write the name of the County, and Town or Parish. (2) If born in any other part of the British Empire, write the name of the Dependency, Colony, etc., and of the Province or State. (3) If born in a Foreign Country, write the name of the Country. (4) If born at sea, write "At Sea." NOTE.—In the case of persons born elsewhere than in England or Wales, state whether "Resident" or "Visitor" in this Country.	State whether:— (1) "British subject by parentage." (2) "Naturalised British subject," giving year of naturalisation. Or (3) If of foreign nationality, state whether "French," "German," "Russian," etc.	If any person included in this Schedule is:— (1) "Totally Deaf," or "Deaf and Dumb," (2) "Totally Blind," (3) "Lunatic," (4) "Imbecile," or "Feeble-minded," state the infirmity opposite that person's name, and the age at which he or she became afflicted.
						Completed years the present Marriage has lasted. If less than one year write "under one."	Children born alive to present Marriage. (If no children born alive write "None" in Column 7).			The reply should show the precise branch of Profession, Trade, Manufacture, &c. If engaged in any Trade or Manufacture, the particular kind of work done, and the Article made or Material worked or dealt in should be clearly indicated. (See Instructions 1 to 8 and Examples on back of Schedule.)	This question should generally be answered by stating the business carried on by the employer. If this is clearly shown in Col. 10 the question need not be answered here. No entry needed for Domestic Servants in private employment. If employed by a public body (Government, Municipal, etc.) state what body. (See Instruction 9 and Examples on back of Schedule.)	Write opposite the name of each person engaged in any Trade or Industry, (1) "Employer" (that is employing persons other than domestic servants), or (2) "Worker" (that is working for an employer), or (3) "Own Account" (that is neither employing others nor working for a trade employer).	Write the words "At Home" opposite the name of each person carrying on Trade or Industry at home.			
			Ages of Males.	Ages of Females.			Total Children Born Alive.	Children still Living.	Children who have Died.							
	1.	2.	3.	4.	5.	6.	7.	8.	9.	10.	11.	12.	13.	14.	15.	16.
1																
2																
3																
4																
5																
6																
7																
8																
9																
10																
11																
12																
13																
14																
15																

(To be filled up by the Enumerator.)

I certify that:—
(1.) All the ages on this Schedule are entered in the proper sex columns.
(2.) I have counted the males and females in Columns 3 and 4 separately, and have compared their sum with the total number of persons.
(3.) After making the necessary enquiries I have completed all entries on the Schedule which appeared to be defective, and have corrected such as appeared to be erroneous.

Initials of Enumerator ________

Total		
Males.	Females.	Persons.

(To be filled up by, or on behalf of, the Head of Family or other person in occupation, or in charge, of this dwelling.)

Write below the Number of Rooms in this Dwelling (House, Tenement, or Apartment). Count the kitchen as a room but do not count scullery, landing, lobby, closet, bathroom; nor warehouse, office, shop.

____

I declare that this Schedule is correctly filled up to the best of my knowledge and belief.

Signature ________

Postal Address ________

APPENDIX B

Copy of sample pages from 1911 census *Fertility of Marriage Report*, Part 2, Tables 30 and 35 (respectively, the tabulations for incomplete and completed fertility for male occupations)

TABLE 30. ENGLAND AND WALES.—Marriages where the Wife had not attained the Age of 45 years at Census.—Families and Mortality therein, classified by Occupation of the Husband, Duration of Marriage, and Age of Wife at Marriage (see Note on page 2.)—*continued.* (*See Note on page 28 as to figures in sub-headings.*)

Duration of Marriage in Years.	Age of Wife at Marriage.	Husband's Occupation. Soldiers and Non-Commissioned Officers. II. 1 (3). (IV.)			Officers of the Navy and Marines (Effective and Retired). II. 2 (1, 2, 4, 5). (I.)			Men of the Navy and Marines. II. 2 (3, 6). (IV.)			Clergymen (Established Church). III. 1 (1). (I.)		
		Couples.	Children Born.	Children Dead.	Couples.	Children Born.	Children Dead.	Couples.	Children Born.	Children Dead.	Couples.	Children Born.	Children Dead.
0-2	15-19	175	77	6	5	1	—	136	53	5	6	4	—
	20-24	1,021	421	31	73	16	1	1,034	316	21	122	27	1
	25-29	611	215	11	79	19	1	722	190	11	241	78	3
	30-34	185	52	4	44	8	1	215	46	1	170	38	—
	35-44	60	7	1	15	1	—	79	11	—	156	17	1
	All Ages.	2,052	772	53	216	45	3	2,186	616	38	695	164	5
2-5	15-19	296	403	43	13	7	—	335	440	51	18	20	3
	20-24	1,324	1,752	154	96	100	4	1,736	1,920	170	212	243	10
	25-29	780	937	80	100	78	—	1,080	1,087	86	364	386	12
	30-34	227	220	23	56	37	—	307	264	19	295	255	6
	35-44	65	47	6	23	10	—	89	55	3	208	123	5
	All Ages.	2,692	3,359	306	288	232	4	3,547	3,766	329	1,097	1,027	36
5-10	15-19	324	808	106	9	9	2	499	1,095	160	24	57	2
	20-24	1,391	3,220	307	134	220	12	2,125	4,235	502	380	721	23
	25-29	882	1,890	202	125	189	9	1,338	2,405	257	649	1,223	62
	30-34	302	554	50	60	91	9	380	583	70	485	726	40
	35-44	49	61	4	22	17	—	46	54	11	179	198	11
	All Ages.	2,948	6,533	669	350	526	32	4,388	8,372	1,000	1,717	2,925	138
10-15	15-19	189	737	110	14	23	—	392	1,307	241	43	113	6
	20-24	713	2,460	348	84	162	19	1,333	3,983	587	414	1,062	73
	25-29	409	1,207	155	118	214	22	710	1,769	264	697	1,644	85
	30-34	70	175	32	36	49	5	118	222	44	342	719	36
	All Ages.	1,381	4,579	645	252	448	46	2,553	7,281	1,136	1,496	3,538	200
15-20	15-19	166	824	163	6	19	2	229	986	200	55	160	17
	20-24	401	1,849	278	84	211	20	654	2,371	386	475	1,484	141
	25-29	127	474	74	63	126	4	222	682	96	400	1,116	102
	All Ages.	694	3,147	515	153	356	26	1,105	4,039	682	930	2,760	260
20-25	15-19	61	379	73	21	74	20	111	510	106	60	221	19
	20-24	90	460	97	59	138	15	185	759	153	232	766	77
	All Ages.	151	839	170	80	212	35	296	1,269	259	292	987	96
25-30	15-19	6	45	15	15	62	10	22	125	29	28	131	20
All Durations.	15-19	1,217	3,273	516	83	195	34	1,724	4,516	792	234	706	67
	20-24	4,940	10,162	1,215	530	847	71	7,067	13,584	1,819	1,835	4,303	325
	25-29	2,809	4,723	522	485	626	36	4,072	6,133	714	2,351	4,447	264
	30-34	784	1,001	109	196	185	15	1,020	1,115	134	1,292	1,738	82
	35-44	174	115	11	60	28	—	214	120	14	543	338	17
	All Ages.	9,924	19,274	2,373	1,354	1,881	156	14,097	25,468	3,473	6,255	11,532	755

Duration of Marriage in Years.	Age of Wife at Marriage.	Ministers, Priests, of other Religious Bodies. III. 1 (3). (I.)			Itinerant Preachers, Scripture Readers, Mission Workers. III. 1 (4). (II.)			Church, Chapel, Cemetery-Officers, etc. III. 1 (6). (II.)			Barristers. III. 2 (1). (I.)			Solicitors. III. 2 (2). (I.)		
		Couples.	Children Born.	Children Dead.	Couples.	Children Born.	Children Dead.	Couples.	Children Born.	Children Dead.	Couples.	Children Born.	Children Dead.	Couples.	Children Born.	Children Dead.
0-2	15-19	4	1	—	—	—	—	3	1	—	—	—	—	10	1	—
	20-24	84	26	1	33	15	1	42	16	—	39	16	1	176	57	3
	25-29	217	55	2	66	15	2	47	14	2	60	18	1	266	76	1
	30-34	146	29	1	36	6	—	34	8	2	32	6	—	151	29	1
	35-44	88	12	2	23	2	—	24	4	1	23	2	—	97	16	—
	All Ages.	539	123	6	158	38	3	150	43	5	154	42	2	700	179	5
2-5	15-19	7	11	1	1	—	—	11	18	2	5	4	—	13	13	1
	20-24	147	172	10	53	56	2	101	129	19	63	72	2	273	296	10
	25-29	355	366	22	99	103	7	84	79	6	71	75	4	470	459	18
	30-34	218	220	12	71	73	4	58	40	9	37	28	2	247	212	4
	35-44	82	47	3	34	23	3	28	9	2	29	9	—	114	49	4
	All Ages.	809	816	48	258	255	16	282	275	38	205	188	8	1,117	1,029	37
5-10	15-19	12	25	6	4	4	—	30	92	20	7	14	1	16	21	1
	20-24	256	493	30	97	180	13	213	477	47	97	176	7	458	840	48
	25-29	501	846	65	190	355	43	197	427	52	143	265	13	634	1,049	47
	30-34	330	515	44	82	142	13	76	127	17	72	107	8	312	437	20
	35-44	65	61	4	19	22	3	23	16	2	17	13	1	79	84	6
	All Ages.	1,164	1,940	149	392	703	72	539	1,139	138	336	575	30	1,499	2,431	122
10-15	15-19	15	46	7	8	25	2	59	235	50	15	32	3	22	67	4
	20-24	259	706	73	125	366	47	264	849	141	95	233	13	451	1,149	81
	25-29	539	1,393	157	155	428	48	236	666	98	114	261	14	671	1,522	102
	30-34	188	401	30	62	117	13	56	121	18	41	63	5	205	384	26
	All Ages.	1,001	2,546	267	350	936	110	615	1,871	307	265	589	35	1,349	3,122	213
15-20	15-19	29	113	14	18	84	15	54	273	52	7	14	3	31	97	13
	20-24	278	987	138	129	512	89	338	1,476	256	94	247	18	522	1,460	114
	25-29	275	789	80	85	292	36	166	531	90	64	151	7	431	1,105	103
	All Ages.	582	1,889	232	232	888	140	558	2,280	398	165	412	28	984	2,662	230
20-25	15-19	38	184	40	16	109	28	68	434	87	8	22	5	46	113	9
	20-24	127	587	88	63	308	61	180	894	174	41	109	10	222	677	62
	All Ages.	165	771	128	79	417	89	248	1,328	261	49	131	15	268	790	71
25-30	15-19	7	48	12	9	54	15	20	131	28	1	—	—	16	58	10
All Durations.	15-19	112	428	80	56	276	60	245	1,184	239	43	86	12	154	370	38
	20-24	1,151	2,971	340	500	1,437	213	1,138	3,841	637	429	853	51	2,102	4,479	318
	25-29	1,887	3,449	326	595	1,193	136	730	1,717	248	452	770	39	2,472	4,211	271
	30-34	882	1,165	87	251	338	30	224	296	46	182	204	15	915	1,062	51
	35-44	235	120	9	76	47	6	75	29	5	69	24	1	290	149	10
	All Ages.	4,267	8,133	842	1,478	3,291	445	2,412	7,067	1,175	1,175	1,937	118	5,933	10,271	688

TABLE 35. ENGLAND AND WALES.—Marriages where the Age of the Wife exceeded 45 Years at Census.—Families and Mortality therein, classified by Occupation of the Husband, Duration of Marriage and Age of Wife at Marriage (see Note on page 2).

(*See Note on page 28 as to figures in sub-headings.*)

Husband's Occupation.

Age of Wife at Marriage.	Duration of Marriage in Years.	Civil Service Officers and Clerks. I. 1 (1, 2, 5). (I.)			Post Office Officers and Clerks (other than Telegraphists and Telephone Operators). I. 1 (2). (I.)			Postmen. I. 1 (3). (IV.)			Civil Service Messengers, etc. (including Post Office.) I. 1 (4, 6). (IV.)			Civil Service Officers and Clerks (excluding Post Office). I. 1 (5.) (I).			Police. I. 2 (1.) (IV).			Poor Law Service. I. 2 (2.) (II).			Municipal, Parish and other Local or County Officers. I. 2 (3.) (II).			Army Officers (effective and retired). II. 1 (1, 2.) (I).		
		Couples.	Children Born.	Children Dead.	Couples.	Children Born.	Children Dead.	Couples.	Children Born.	Children Dead.	Couples.	Children Born.	Children Dead.	Couples.	Children Born.	Children Dead.	Couples.	Children Born.	Children Dead.	Couples.	Children Born.	Children Dead.	Couples.	Children Born.	Children Dead.	Couples.	Children Born.	Children Dead.
15–19	25–30	176	972	186	84	494	91	109	768	177	107	633	158	83	423	83	95	662	146	34	202	49	178	1,124	256	45	182	33
	30–40	282	1,702	344	121	734	145	160	1,179	248	181	1,274	335	157	947	198	68	469	91	108	707	166	349	2,395	617	196	940	219
	40–50	47	422	101	26	249	60	37	335	94	19	159	48	20	167	40	9	74	19	44	342	89	192	1,504	468	160	956	251
	50–60	10	83	21	8	70	20	1	—	—	—	—	—	2	13	1	1	3	2	5	51	20	29	228	84	44	321	99
	60–	—	—	—	—	—	—	1	6	3	—	—	—	—	—	—	—	—	—	—	—	—	—	—	—	3	38	12
	25–	515	3,179	652	239	1,547	316	308	2,288	522	307	2,066	541	262	1,550	322	173	1,208	258	191	1,302	324	748	5,251	1,425	448	2,437	614
20–24	20–25	826	3,139	493	411	1,625	257	512	2,421	452	285	1,246	231	380	1,374	222	653	3,183	561	168	602	110	453	1,950	339	159	440	53
	25–30	1,566	6,601	1,100	732	3,131	540	808	4,282	811	579	3,068	639	795	3,275	527	775	4,207	835	352	1,446	241	1,012	4,904	1,010	361	1,187	136
	30–40	1,187	6,138	1,228	540	2,899	605	609	3,556	779	472	2,806	678	628	3,153	613	241	1,426	288	467	2,515	509	1,379	7,825	1,855	574	2,429	507
	40–50	151	1,026	227	78	334	115	81	570	143	49	335	118	73	492	112	21	147	42	141	926	238	520	3,520	1,092	319	1,697	424
	50–60	24	168	55	14	99	31	6	38	6	2	11	3	10	60	24	1	8	4	15	125	39	66	498	149	63	366	105
	60–	—	—	—	—	—	—	—	—	—	1	13	2	—	—	—	—	—	—	—	—	—	1	13	6	1	1	1
	20–	3,754	17,072	3,103	1,775	8,288	1,548	2,016	10,867	2,191	1,388	7,479	1,671	1,886	8,363	1,498	1,691	8,971	1,730	1,143	5,614	1,137	3,431	18,710	4,451	1,477	6,120	1,246
25–29	15–20	568	1,483	183	263	698	96	313	915	134	193	651	131	276	709	79	610	2,146	354	117	289	57	312	938	136	111	217	26
	20–25	1,342	4,165	612	621	1,948	293	683	2,424	405	432	1,568	264	672	2,057	292	1,024	3,951	682	321	973	188	792	2,558	454	276	623	92
	25–30	801	2,880	451	357	1,260	209	364	1,414	250	284	1,175	250	428	1,554	233	248	1,088	205	239	915	166	530	2,010	411	224	575	91
	30–40	508	2,175	368	227	992	153	232	1,141	239	221	998	226	276	1,158	211	94	446	98	264	1,120	243	614	2,814	614	332	1,158	191
	40–50	59	287	62	31	177	35	38	189	57	14	72	22	28	110	27	7	31	6	87	400	106	197	1,035	275	132	557	146
	50–60	15	81	25	7	43	13	—	—	—	1	3	1	8	38	12	—	—	—	11	61	18	26	144	54	27	113	39
	60–	—	—	—	—	—	—	—	—	—	—	—	—	—	—	—	—	—	—	—	—	—	2	6	4	—	—	—
	15–	3,293	11,071	1,701	1,506	5,118	799	1,630	6,083	1,085	1,145	4,467	894	1,688	5,626	854	1,983	7,662	1,345	1,039	3,758	778	2,473	9,505	1,948	1,102	3,243	585
30–34	10–15	190	333	31	76	128	13	120	231	45	67	126	21	106	184	17	157	304	44	58	84	10	123	245	44	64	76	14
	15–20	487	976	111	231	469	47	307	723	127	193	436	81	230	463	60	432	1,097	207	162	330	65	320	686	108	138	217	25
	20–25	340	809	109	128	299	34	148	389	68	125	296	60	195	465	64	174	477	100	102	222	50	218	592	110	123	203	31
	25–30	189	508	79	81	219	36	80	201	38	76	196	49	104	270	38	40	126	34	79	198	35	150	402	81	60	127	12
	30–40	117	374	73	55	174	42	46	154	39	49	145	32	61	193	29	8	25	2	57	176	36	177	544	143	101	255	36
	40–50	15	51	10	7	27	6	10	37	6	6	13	2	8	24	4	—	—	—	9	36	7	35	99	32	35	111	21
	50–60	1	1	1	1	1	1	—	—	—	—	—	—	—	—	—	—	—	—	2	7	1	2	5	—	4	15	8
	60–	—	—	—	—	—	—	—	—	—	—	—	—	—	—	—	—	—	—	—	—	—	—	—	—	—	—	—
	10–	1,339	3,052	414	579	1,317	179	711	1,735	323	516	1,212	245	704	1,599	212	811	2,029	387	469	1,053	204	1,025	2,573	518	525	1,004	147
35–44	0–2	10	—	—	2	—	—	1	—	—	1	—	—	6	—	—	4	—	—	—	—	—	4	—	—	3	—	—
	2–5	50	4	—	20	1	—	29	2	—	19	2	—	27	2	—	28	12	1	15	2	—	25	6	—	25	4	—
	5–10	210	122	16	84	52	7	99	56	8	104	69	14	112	58	7	121	111	17	58	37	4	123	88	12	77	33	1
	10–15	242	199	18	103	83	8	163	178	30	131	123	28	138	116	10	153	174	29	87	57	7	220	191	31	103	83	10
	15–20	172	172	16	71	67	10	103	109	11	74	62	10	94	96	6	69	88	16	55	61	9	162	155	25	81	54	7
	20–25	94	128	26	34	59	13	44	66	12	49	61	15	58	68	13	23	36	2	31	45	10	102	135	33	56	49	6
	25–30	44	49	11	15	13	5	36	64	14	17	38	4	28	35	6	6	6	3	25	21	4	75	79	18	32	33	3
	30–40	36	42	9	11	12	3	15	22	6	14	28	9	24	29	6	2	3	—	15	23	8	58	115	25	41	84	19
	40–50	2	4	2	1	4	2	—	—	—	—	—	—	1	—	—	—	—	—	5	4	1	7	30	8	11	12	5
	50–60	—	—	—	—	—	—	—	—	—	—	—	—	—	—	—	—	—	—	—	—	—	—	—	—	—	—	—
	All Durations.	860	720	98	341	291	48	490	497	81	409	383	80	488	404	48	406	430	68	291	250	43	776	799	152	429	352	51
45 and upwards.	0–2	49	—	—	23	—	—	30	—	—	31	1	—	25	—	—	32	—	—	15	—	—	40	—	—	21	1	—
	2–5	70	—	—	33	—	—	32	—	—	28	3	—	35	—	—	27	2	—	26	—	—	71	—	—	40	—	—
	5–10	61	5	—	25	3	—	31	—	—	40	4	1	32	2	—	23	3	—	28	4	1	86	—	—	45	2	—
	10–15	24	—	—	9	—	—	28	—	—	22	—	—	15	—	—	10	—	—	13	—	—	43	—	—	26	—	—
	15–20	11	—	—	3	—	—	6	—	—	8	—	—	8	—	—	2	—	—	7	—	—	27	—	—	21	—	—
	20–25	7	1	—	—	—	—	5	—	—	8	1	—	7	1	—	3	—	—	3	—	—	24	—	—	18	—	—
	25–30	3	—	—	1	—	—	2	—	—	—	—	—	2	—	—	—	—	—	—	—	—	12	1	—	6	—	—
	30–40	1	—	—	—	—	—	—	—	—	1	—	—	1	—	—	—	—	—	—	—	—	1	1	—	3	—	—
	40–50	—	—	—	—	—	—	—	—	—	—	—	—	—	—	—	—	—	—	—	—	—	—	—	—	—	—	—
	All Durations.	226	6	—	94	3	—	134	—	—	138	9	1	125	3	—	97	5	—	92	4	1	304	2	—	180	3	—
All Ages.	0–2	59	—	—	25	—	—	31	—	—	32	1	—	31	—	—	36	—	—	15	—	—	44	—	—	24	1	—
	2–5	120	4	—	53	1	—	61	2	—	47	5	—	62	2	—	55	14	1	41	2	—	96	6	—	65	4	—
	5–10	271	127	16	109	55	7	130	56	8	144	73	15	144	60	7	144	114	17	86	41	5	209	88	12	122	35	1
	10–15	456	532	49	188	211	21	311	409	75	220	249	49	259	300	27	320	478	73	158	141	17	386	436	75	193	159	24
	15–20	1,238	2,631	310	568	1,234	153	729	1,747	272	468	1,149	222	608	1,268	145	1,113	3,331	577	341	680	131	821	1,779	269	351	488	58
	20–25	2,609	8,242	1,240	1,194	3,931	597	1,392	5,300	937	899	3,172	570	1,312	3,965	591	1,877	7,647	1,345	625	1,842	358	1,589	5,235	936	632	1,315	182
	25–30	2,779	11,010	1,827	1,270	5,117	881	1,399	6,729	1,290	1,063	5,110	1,100	1,440	5,557	887	1,164	6,089	1,223	729	2,782	495	1,957	8,520	1,776	728	2,104	295
	30–40	2,131	10,431	2,022	954	4,811	948	1,062	6,052	1,311	938	5,251	1,280	1,147	5,480	1,057	413	2,369	479	911	4,541	962	2,578	13,694	3,254	1,247	4,866	972
	40–50	274	1,790	402	143	991	218	166	1,131	300	88	579	190	130	793	183	37	252	67	286	1,708	441	951	6,188	1,875	657	3,333	847
	50–60	50	333	102	30	213	65	7	38	6	3	14	4	20	120	37	2	11	6	33	244	78	123	875	287	138	815	251
	60–	—	—	—	—	—	—	1	6	3	1	13	2	—	—	—	—	—	—	—	—	—	3	19	10	4	39	13
	All Durations.	9,987	35,100	5,968	4,534	16,564	2,890	5,289	21,470	4,202	3,903	15,616	3,432	5,153	17,545	2,934	5,161	20,305	3,788	3,225	11,981	2,487	8,757	36,840	8,494	4,161	13,159	2,643

8989. 2 G 2

APPENDIX C MALE OCCUPATIONS RANK ORDERED BY COMPLETED FERTILITY INDEX, AM2/81–5

Posn	AM2/81–5	RANK/ AM1	RANK/ AM3	RANK/ PRUDMARR	ID	Class	Occ. name	Size	Percent	Cum pcent
Panel 1										
1	3.16216	2	4	36	17	I	barristers	2,481	0.044	0.044
2	3.20824	3	2	97	204	I	private means	28,159	0.500	0.545
3	3.28809	5	3	103	9	I	army officers (incl. retired)	9,974	0.177	0.722
4	3.46715	1	10	85	11	I	officers of navy, marine (incl. ret.)	3,657	0.065	0.787
5	3.48329	8	14	3	20	I	physicians, surgeons, regd GPs	15,638	0.278	1.065
6	3.51579	9	18	6	18	I	solicitors	11,055	0.196	1.262
7	3.54983	15	6	78	188	II	lodging, boarding house keepers	7,396	0.131	1.393
8	3.61828	6	5	2	46	I	banks – officials, clerks	15,393	0.273	1.667
9	3.70701	14	7	16	25	I	civil, mining – engineers	4,465	0.079	1.747
10	3.73016	4	1	136=	29	II	actors	4,876	0.086	1.833
11	3.76230	18	15	46	26	I	painters, sculptors, artists	4,043	0.071	1.905
12	3.85294	11	22	25	24	I	scientific pursuits	2,401	0.042	1.948
13	3.92381	20	34	30	21	I	dentists (incl. assistants)	4,185	0.074	2.022
14	3.93750	12	9	47	185	II	tobacconists	7,540	0.134	2.156
15	4.00842	7	31	5	13	I	clergy (C of E)	15,552	0.276	2.433
16	4.00935	26	11	9	31	III	dom. indoor servants (not in hotels, etc.)	11,718	0.208	2.642
17	4.01818	13	20	11	27	I	architects	4,878	0.086	2.728
18	4.03871	16	26	45	40	I	merchants (commodity undefined)	3,595	0.063	2.792
19	4.04846	17	16	21	43	I	accountants	6,146	0.109	2.902
20	4.05104	45	8	175	201	II	retired from business (not army or navy)	169,955	3.022	5.925
21	4.07321	28	21	7	22	I	teachers (schools and universities)	36,683	0.652	6.577
22	4.10795	39	30	28	7	II	Poor Law service	8,588	0.152	6.730
23	4.11950	23	32	14	5	I	civil serv. – officers, clerks (not PO)	16,850	0.299	7.029
24	4.14231	19	23	38	122	II	dealers in jewellery, watches, gold, etc.	7,066	0.125	7.155
25	4.27732	25	38	10	2	I	PO officers and clerks (not telecomms.)	18,393	0.327	7.482
26	4.28235	21	17	26	19	I	law clerks	13,485	0.239	7.722
27	4.28821	10	12	39	23	I	authors, editors, journalists	7,109	0.126	7.849
28	4.29006	30	36	34	44	I	auctioneers, valuers, house agents	11,991	0.213	8.062

29	4.30273	29	29	8	148	I	chemists, druggists	13,688	0.243	8.305
30	4.30994	34	27	63	37	III	college, club – service	7,639	0.135	8.441
31	4.39002	41	47	22	42	I	commercial travellers	60,363	1.073	9.515
32	4.39498	36	56	12	14	I	clergy (nonconf.)	9,409	0.167	9.682
33	4.43783	31	44	33	41	I	brokers, agents, factors	28,468	0.506	10.189
34	4.44505	38	28	37	169	II	textile fabrics – other dealers	19,455	0.346	10.535
35	4.45149	37	25	20	45	I	commercial, business clerks	131,225	2.334	12.869
36	4.47635	46	51	18	38	II	hospital, benevolent soc. – service	9,559	0.170	13.039
37	4.48721	27	39	13	168	II	drapers, linen mercers	30,192	0.537	13.576
38	4.49014	43	19	96	39	IV	caretakers (not govt)	19,148	0.340	13.916
39	4.52414	61	33	52	173	II	boot, shoe, clog dealers	12,389	0.220	14.137
Panel 2										
40	4.53783	53	41	17	47	I	insurance – officials, clerks, etc.	21,454	0.381	14.518
41	4.59449	67	45	27	117	II	ironmongers/hardware merchants	14,899	0.265	14.783
42	4.61048	33	35	23	49	I	railway – officials, clerks	46,189	0.821	15.605
43	4.61810	42	49	31	183	II	grocers, dealers in beverages	79,922	1.421	17.026
44	4.63508	40	46	105	189	II	hotel keepers/publicans/off-licences	69,261	1.231	18.258
45	4.66357	47	40	167	202	II	pensioners	46,852	0.833	19.092
46	4.69767	32	13	99	28	II	musicians, music teachers	13,690	0.243	19.335
47	4.70631	55	42	54	162	VI	wool, worsted – weaving processes	13,594	0.241	19.577
48	4.73159	49	58	35	171	II	clothiers, outfitters	13,446	0.239	19.816
49	4.76793	57	43	40	161	VI	wool, worsted – spinning processes	6,241	0.111	19.927
50	4.78947	52	67	24	197	II	pawnbrokers	4,812	0.085	20.013
51	4.84039	72	24	75	187	II	cafes, restaurants – keepers	13,349	0.237	20.250
52	4.84585	48	48	48	8	II	municipal, parish, county officers	24,962	0.444	20.694
53	4.86441	24	68	44	15	II	itinerant preachers, missionaries, etc.	3,125	0.055	20.750
54	4.91647	62	72	61	176	II	cheesemongers, provision dealers	11,017	0.195	20.946
55	4.92112	69	37	111	119	II	goldsmiths, silversmiths	10,244	0.182	21.128
56	4.94560	51	62	57	182	II	bakers, confectioners (dealers)	30,984	0.551	21.679
57	5.02069	64	77	32	32	IV	dom. – coachmen, grooms	39,131	0.696	22.375
58	5.02211	83	52	86	208	VI	'wool, worsted – carding, others, undefined'	25,847	0.459	22.835
59	5.04293	57	50	94	139	II	furniture dealers	15,346	0.272	23.108
60	5.08369	73	86	104	120	II	watchmakers, clockmakers	9,056	0.161	23.269
61	5.09174	22	83	4	12	IV	men of the navy, marine	25,407	0.451	23.721
62	5.11638	85	78	49	180	II	corn, flour, seed – merchants, dealers	11,362	0.202	23.923
63	5.12975	84	54	101	121	III	piano, organ makers	7,892	0.140	24.063
64	5.13295	77	57	56	154	III	printers – hand compositors	21,401	0.380	24.444
65	5.13599	60	64	55	48	I	insurance – agents	39,602	0.704	25.148

Posn	AM2/81–5	RANK/ AM1	RANK/ AM3	RANK/ PRUDMARR	ID	Class	Occ. name	Size	Percent	Cum pcent
66	5.13636	63	82	41	103	III	electricians (undefined)	11,829	0.210	25.359
67	5.14634	35	88	87	190	IV	barmen	8,504	0.151	25.510
68	5.18289	120	89	64	114	III	motor car – chassis makers and mechanics	17,874	0.317	25.828
69	5.19084	57	73	79	158	VI	cotton – winding processes	11,231	0.199	26.028
70	5.20000	115	98	88	90	II	coal, coke – merchants, dealers	19,170	0.340	26.369
71	5.20403	75	87	77	123	I	builders	31,021	0.551	26.920
72	5.25116	44	65	19	191	III	waiters (not dom.)	9,935	0.176	27.097
73	5.28935	70	63	80	155	III	others in printing	36,464	0.648	27.746
74	5.29113	74	75	42	35	IV	dom. gardeners	68,806	1.223	28.970
75	5.29879	59	80	43	4	IV	civil service messengers (incl. PO)	12,485	0.222	29.192
76	5.29950	76	76	15	3	IV	postmen	29,972	0.533	29.725
77	5.31845	66	55	91	16	II	church, chapel, cemetery officers, etc.	6,062	0.107	29.833
78	5.36462	88	59	71	159	VI	cotton – weaving processes	38,620	0.686	30.520
Panel 3										
79	5.38787	122	85	149	196	II	general shopkeepers, dealers	22,984	0.408	30.928
80	5.40205	116	61	100	207	VI	'cotton – card room, others, undefined'	22,768	0.404	31.333
81	5.42704	54	53	176	164	VI	lace manfre	8,229	0.146	31.480
82	5.42839	50	106	1	6	IV	police	38,980	0.693	32.173
83	5.43243	117	108	83	52	III	signalmen	20,594	0.366	32.539
84	5.43322	153	93	109	142	II	timber merchants	6,588	0.117	32.657
85	5.44156	114	128	129	66	II	merch. service/seamen – navigators	22,111	0.393	33.050
86	5.45631	129	115	82	115	III	coach, carriage makers	14,123	0.251	33.301
87	5.45714	68	79	29	34	III	motor car drivers (dom. and non-dom.)	24,325	0.432	33.734
88	5.45882	87	84	62	80	IV	nursery, seedsmen, florists	14,502	0.257	33.992
89	5.47722	78	66	117	30	II	performers, showmen, sportsmen	13,859	0.246	34.238
90	5.48413	92	90	69	209	VI	'textiles – bleachers, printers'	10,850	0.192	34.431
91	5.49584	91	60	93	138	III	upholsterers	9,119	0.162	34.593
92	5.50909	80	71	66	174	III	hairdressers, wig makers	21,302	0.378	34.972
93	5.52200	107	135	59	51	III	railway guards	17,713	0.315	35.287
94	5.53048	81	99	50	175	II	milksellers, dairymen	25,953	0.461	35.749
95	5.53935	102	100	102	186	IV	brewers	17,426	0.309	36.059
96	5.55403	97	70	112	166	VI	textile dyers	14,714	0.261	36.321
97	5.57131	155	94	146	184	II	greengrocers, fruiterers	31,809	0.565	36.886
98	5.59310	93	113	124	57	II	stable keepers/coach, cab proprietors	8,054	0.143	37.030

99	5.60224	94	92	118	98	III	erectors, fitters, turners	80,033	1.423	38.453
100	5.62729	131	74	187	163	VI	hosiery manfre	8,173	0.145	38.599
101	5.64536	89	105	89	132	III	plumbers	35,280	0.627	39.226
102	5.65207	112	69	76	167	VI	textiles – calenderers, finishers	10,495	0.186	39.413
103	5.66450	146	112	136=	87	I	coal – mineowners, agents, managers	4,730	0.084	39.497
104	5.69473	90	142	58	73	II	farmers, graziers	161,867	2.879	42.376
105	5.69559	113	114	74	125	III	carpenters, joiners	130,069	2.313	44.690
106	5.70399	106	121	65	50	III	railway engine – drivers, stokers, cleaners	43,587	0.775	45.465
107	5.71646	119	91	95	157	VI	cotton – spinning processes	32,474	0.577	46.042
108	5.72628	118	97	67	64	III	trams – others	8,439	0.150	46.193
109	5.72894	101	165	92	53	IV	pointsmen, level crossing operators	10,369	0.184	46.377
110	5.73462	125	101	68	153	III	saddlers, harness makers	12,638	0.224	46.602
111	5.73728	110	102	98	116	III	wheelwrights	14,418	0.256	46.858
112	5.74141	137	133	73	179	IV	millers/cereal food manfre	14,531	0.258	47.117
113	5.74547	109	117	116	170	III	tailors	70,097	1.246	48.364
114	5.74590	99	109	148	70	IV	harbour, dock, lighthouse – officials, servant	14,877	0.264	48.628
115	5.74718	121	123	177	178	II	fishmongers, poulterers	22,980	0.408	49.037
116	5.75040	95	131	60	177	II	butchers, meat salesmen	59,695	1.061	50.099
117	5.75501	96	120	110	82	IV	other gardeners (not dom.)	45,324	0.806	50.905
Panel 4										
118	5.76282	79	119	108	58	V	coach, cabmen (not dom.)	21,185	0.376	51.282
119	5.77227	108	130	120	81	IV	market gardeners (incl. labourers)	20,775	0.369	51.651
120	5.79634	86	129	70	56	V	rail – porters	31,386	0.558	52.209
121	5.81870	138	104	106	133	III	gasfitters	10,149	0.180	52.390
122	5.86607	127	96	53	194	IV	electricity supply	9,753	0.173	52.563
123	5.86673	126	116	90	112	III	rail – coach, wagon makers	23,839	0.424	52.987
124	5.86848	134	134	125	110	III	shipwrights	16,113	0.286	53.274
125	5.89863	140	148	194	105	III	cutlers/scissors makers	8,284	0.147	53.421
126	5.90635	141	150	114	193	IV	waterworks service	6,643	0.118	53.540
127	5.92203	82	107	132	67	II	merch. serv./seamen – engineers	17,295	0.307	53.847
128	5.92615	98	95	81	102	III	electrical apparatus – makers, fitters	28,612	0.508	54.356
129	5.97570	133	136	121	131	III	painters, decorators	115,275	2.050	56.407
130	5.99124	147	81	139	136	III	cabinet makers	28,476	0.506	56.913
131	6.00157	105	127	122	72	V	messengers, watchmen (not rail or govt)	34,447	0.612	57.526
132	6.03161	135	146	113	59	V	horsekeepers, stablemen (not dom.)	24,199	0.430	57.956
133	6.05570	65	132	84	113	III	cycle makers	13,816	0.245	58.202
134	6.05667	132	118	154	104	III	tool makers	13,881	0.246	58.449

Posn	AM2/81–5	RANK/ AM1	RANK/ AM3	RANK/ PRUDMARR	ID	Class	Occ. name	Size	Percent	Cum pcent
135	6.06091	104	153	72	181	II	bakers – biscuits, cakes	36,583	0.650	59.099
136	6.08608	136	143	164	172	III	boot, shoe makers	89,687	1.595	60.695
137	6.10292	100	152	119	54	V	rail – platelayers, gangers, packers	37,828	0.672	61.368
138	6.11637	148	110	130	99	III	metal machinists	22,050	0.392	61.760
139	6.12254	157	122	135	140	IV	sawyers, wood-cutting machinists	22,746	0.404	62.164
140	6.16277	130	126	123	75	III	farm – bailiffs, foremen	17,502	0.311	62.476
141	6.18569	124	144	107	36	III	gamekeepers	11,297	0.200	62.677
142	6.19298	71	137	51	62	III	trams – drivers	11,771	0.209	62.886
143	6.21748	111	111	151	107	IV	tinplate goods makers	9,708	0.172	63.059
144	6.22212	151	159	126	97	III	blacksmiths, strikers	75,365	1.340	64.399
145	6.24777	165	149	155	95	III	iron – others (moulders, fettlers, etc.)	39,014	0.693	65.093
146	6.26000	171	140	153	106	IV	wire workers	10,173	0.180	65.274
147	6.27523	149	156	152	200	IV	engine (not rail, agro, marin) – drivers, etc.	79,205	1.408	66.683
148	6.27636	103	124	140	147	IV	manfring chemists	13,397	0.238	66.921
149	6.27655	139	160	133	100	V	engineering – undefined labourers	11,910	0.211	67.133
150	6.30678	145	169	134	128	III	masons	31,610	0.562	67.695
151	6.31455	142	162	127	61	V	carmen, carters (not farm)	181,401	3.226	70.922
152	6.31810	123	141	144	55	V	rail – labourers (not of rail contractors)	15,299	0.272	71.194
153	6.32215	150	154	128	150	V	grease, soap, manure manfre	7,396	0.131	71.326
154	6.33654	144	147	145	151	V	rubber, gutta percha workers	7,056	0.125	71.451
155	6.35610	128	158	188	198	V	costermongers, hawkers	29,077	0.517	71.968
156	6.37045	168	138	165	141	IV	coopers	8,752	0.155	72.124
Panel 5										
157	6.41408	172	157	171	101	III	boilermakers	28,519	0.507	72.631
158	6.42718	177	145	142	108	IV	brass, bronze workers	7,811	0.138	72.770
159	6.49828	169	151	159	145	IV	china, pottery manfre	21,715	0.386	73.156
160	6.50837	175	176	131	89	IV	stone – miners, quarriers	23,410	0.416	73.573
161	6.53042	160	139	160	152	IV	tanners, curriers	15,124	0.269	73.842
162	6.53113	187	179	170	130	III	plasterers	17,284	0.307	74.149
163	6.56421	143	193	180	195	V	refuse disposal	10,597	0.188	74.338
164	6.56556	164	174	157	96	V	ironfoundry labourers	16,646	0.296	74.634
165	6.58723	178	186	172	144	V	plaster, cement manfre	6,028	0.107	74.741
166	6.59105	162	161	183	137	III	french polishers	9,743	0.173	74.915
167	6.61384	154	163	156	93	IV	steel – manfre, smelting, founding	23,253	0.413	75.328

168	6.64157	166	171	174	126	III	bricklayers	72,263	1.285	76.614
169	6.65926	161	175	163	135	V	road labourers	31,262	0.556	77.170
170	6.68782	180	177	150	192	IV	gas works service	41,558	0.739	77.909
171	6.69231	185	103	181	149	V	oil (veg.) – millers, refiners	5,908	0.105	78.014
172	6.70227	191	185	161	134	V	navvies	10,140	0.180	78.194
173	6.70251	152	180	138	78	VIII	agrolab. i/c horses	56,539	1.005	79.200
174	6.72386	167	178	162	199	V	general labourers	145,624	2.590	81.790
175	6.74137	158	166	115	77	VIII	agrolab. i/c cattle	30,628	0.544	82.335
176	6.75563	186	182	190	111	V	shipyard labourers (undefined)	8,636	0.153	82.489
177	6.78571	156	187	143	76	IV	shepherds	13,371	0.237	82.726
178	6.78665	159	189	168	79	VIII	agrolab. duties not distinguished	180,643	3.213	85.939
179	6.81422	174	155	189	83	IV	fishermen	15,586	0.277	86.217
180	6.82213	183	188	195	68	V	bargemen, lightermen, watermen	17,918	0.318	86.535
181	6.83048	179	173	169	143	V	brick, terracotta makers	25,727	0.457	86.993
182	6.86081	163	167	178	69	V	dock, wharf labourers	61,815	1.099	88.093
183	6.86872	173	184	173	86	VII	coal – mineworkers above ground	39,218	0.697	88.790
184	6.87132	176	170	158	124	V	builders' labourers	41,212	0.733	89.523
185	6.92572	184	125	184	146	IV	glass, manfre	13,392	0.238	89.761
186	6.94345	190	168	147	129	V	masons' labourers	8,134	0.144	89.906
187	6.96547	170	172	182	71	V	coalheavers, coalporters	21,105	0.375	90.281
188	7.02869	182	164	141	94	IV	tinplate manfre	9,383	0.166	90.448
189	7.03828	194	183	186	109	III	ship – platers, riveters	17,034	0.302	90.751
190	7.05085	192	194	193	88	VII	iron – miners, quarriers	12,919	0.229	90.981
191	7.06213	181	190	166	127	V	bricklayers' labourers	40,871	0.726	91.708
192	7.08857	188	192	192	85	VII	coal – mineworkers below ground	111,290	1.979	93.688
193	7.10592	189	181	179	92	V	puddlers/iron, steel rolling mills	30,530	0.543	94.231
194	7.29142	193	191	185	91	V	pig iron manfre (blast furnace)	13,455	0.239	94.470
195	7.60287	195	195	191	84	VII	coal – mineworkers at the face	310,906	5.530	100.000

APPENDIX D MALE OCCUPATIONS: INDUSTRIAL ORDERS AND EMPLOYMENT STATUS VARIABLES

Posn	AM2/81–5	ID	Class	Occ. name	Order	Suborder	RANK/ OEMP	R/ OWNEMP	RANK/ EMPLOY	R/ EMPLOY	RANK/ OACC	R/ OWNACC
Panel 1												
1	3.16216	17	I	barristers	III	2	—	—	—	—	—	—
2	3.20824	204	I	private means	XXIII	1	—	—	—	—	—	—
3	3.28809	9	I	army officers (incl. retired)	II	1	—	—	—	—	—	—
4	3.46715	11	I	officers of navy, marine (incl. ret.)	II	2	—	—	—	—	—	—
5	3.48329	20	I	physicians, surgeons, regd GPs	III	3	—	—	—	—	—	—
6	3.51579	18	I	solicitors	III	2	—	—	—	—	—	—
7	3.54983	188	II	lodging, boarding house keepers	XX	4	30	1.02830	27	1.98614	26	2.132
8	3.61828	46	I	banks – officials, clerks	V	3	—	—	—	—	—	—
9	3.70701	25	I	civil, mining – engineers	III	6	—	—	—	—	—	—
10	3.73016	29	II	actors	III	7	—	—	—	—	—	—
11	3.76230	26	I	painters, sculptors, artists	III	7	—	—	—	—	—	—
12	3.85294	24	I	scientific pursuits	III	5	—	—	—	—	—	—
13	3.92381	21	I	dentists (incl. assistants)	III	3	—	—	—	—	—	—
14	3.93750	185	II	tobacconists	XX	2	7	0.59506	22	1.57516	6	0.956
15	4.00842	13	I	clergy (C of E)	III	1	—	—	—	—	—	—
16	4.00935	31	III	dom. indoor servants (not in hotels, etc.)	IV	1	—	—	—	—	—	—
17	4.01818	27	I	architects	III	7	—	—	—	—	—	—
18	4.03871	40	I	merchants (commodity undefined)	V	1	—	—	—	—	—	—
19	4.04846	43	I	accountants	V	1	—	—	—	—	—	—
20	4.05104	201	II	retired from business (not army or navy)	XXIII	1	—	—	—	—	—	—
21	4.07321	22	I	teachers (schools and universities)	III	4	—	—	—	—	—	—
22	4.10795	7	II	Poor Law service	I	2	—	—	—	—	—	—
23	4.11950	5	I	civil serv. – officers, clerks (not PO)	I	1	—	—	—	—	—	—
24	4.14231	122	II	dealers in jewellery, watches, gold, etc.	XI	5	15	0.70445	8	1.17943	18	1.749
25	4.27732	2	I	PO officers and clerks (not telecomms.)	I	1	—	—	—	—	—	—
26	4.28235	19	I	law clerks	III	2	—	—	—	—	—	—
27	4.28821	23	I	authors, editors, journalists	III	5	—	—	—	—	—	—
28	4.29006	44	I	auctioneers, valuers, house agents	V	1	—	—	—	—	—	—

29	4.30273	148	I	chemists, druggists	XV	3	21	0.78295	12	1.25298	24	2.087
30	4.30994	37	III	college, club – service	IV	3	—	—	—	—	—	—
31	4.39002	42	I	commercial travellers	V	1	—	—	—	—	—	—
32	4.39498	14	I	clergy (nonconf.)	III	1	—	—	—	—	—	—
33	4.43783	41	I	brokers, agents, factors	V	1	—	—	—	—	—	—
34	4.44505	169	II	textile fabrics – other dealers	XVIII	7	38	1.45890	26	1.96572	53	5.658
35	4.45149	45	I	commercial, business clerks	V	2	—	—	—	—	—	—
36	4.47635	38	II	hospital, benevolent soc. – service	IV	3	—	—	—	—	—	—
37	4.48721	168	II	drapers, linen mercers	XVIII	7	24	0.83717	11	1.22970	32	2.623
38	4.49014	39	IV	caretakers (not govt)	IV	3	—	—	—	—	—	—
39	4.52414	173	II	boot, shoe, clog dealers	XIX	1	17	0.72812	10	1.22273	20	1.800
Panel 2												
40	4.53783	47	I	insurance – officials, clerks, etc.	V	4	—	—	—	—	—	—
41	4.59449	117	II	ironmongers/hardware merchants	X	11	23	0.82004	9	1.21884	31	2.506
42	4.61048	49	I	railway – officials, clerks	VI	1	—	—	—	—	—	—
43	4.61810	183	II	grocers, dealers in beverages	XX	1	16	0.72409	20	1.48428	14	1.414
44	4.63508	189	II	hotel keepers/publicans/off-licences	XX	4	18	0.73564	23	1.57898	13	1.377
45	4.66357	202	II	pensioners	XXIII	1	—	—	—	—	—	—
46	4.69767	28	II	musicians, music teachers	III	7	—	—	—	—	—	—
47	4.70631	162	VI	wool, worsted – weaving processes	XVIII	2	77	7.07782	66	8.25745	80	49.545
48	4.73159	171	II	clothiers, outfitters	XIX	1	14	0.70272	6	1.01934	27	2.262
49	4.76793	161	VI	wool, worsted – spinning processes	XVIII	2	65	4.98485	51	5.16368	92	143.937
50	4.78947	197	II	pawnbrokers	XXII	4	22	0.80336	5	1.01731	41	3.820
51	4.84039	187	II	cafes, restaurants – keepers	XX	4	5	0.56711	15	1.36114	7	0.972
52	4.84585	8	II	municipal, parish, county officers	I	2	—	—	—	—	—	—
53	4.86441	15	II	itinerant preachers, missionaries, etc.	III	1	—	—	—	—	—	—
54	4.91647	176	II	cheesemongers, provision dealers	XX	1	26	0.91640	24	1.82013	23	1.846
55	4.92112	119	II	goldsmiths, silversmiths	XI	—	45	1.89261	38	3.03236	48	5.035
56	4.94560	182	II	bakers, confectioners (dealers)	XX	1	3	0.521	2	0.855	11	1.336
57	5.02069	32	IV	dom. – coachmen, grooms	IV	2	—	—	—	—	—	—
58	5.02211	208	VI	'wool, worsted – carding, others, undefined'	XVIII	2	84	9.851	75	10.667	90	128.724
59	5.04293	139	II	furniture dealers	XIII	1	27	0.927	25	1.879	22	1.830
60	5.08369	120	II	watchmakers, clockmakers	XI	2	28	0.992	45	3.966	10	1.323
61	5.09174	12	IV	men of the navy, marine	II	2	—	—	—	—	—	—
62	5.11638	180	II	corn, flour, seed – merchants, dealers	XX	1	29	1.013	19	1.447	38	3.377
63	5.12975	121	III	piano, organ makers	XI	3	42	1.664	53	5.970	28	2.308
64	5.13295	154	III	printers – hand compositors	XVIII	2	—	—	—	—	—	—
65	5.13599	48	I	insurance – agents	V	4	—	—	—	—	—	—
66	5.13636	103	III	electricians (undefined)	X	4	40	1.527	33	2.479	42	3.973

Posn	AM2/81–5	ID	Class	Occ. name	Order	Suborder	RANK/ OEMP	R/ OWNEMP	RANK/ EMPLOY	R/ EMPLOY	RANK/ OACC	R/ OWNACC
67	5.14634	190	IV	barmen	XX	4	—	—	—	—	—	—
68	5.18289	114	III	motor car – chassis makers and mechanics	X	10	43	1.668	32	2.401	51	5.462
69	5.19084	158	VI	cotton – winding processes	XVIII	1	102	108.833	102	145.111	99	435.333
70	5.20000	90	II	coal, coke – merchants, dealers	IX	2	13	0.680	17	1.420	9	1.304
71	5.20403	123	I	builders	XII	1	20	0.755	3	0.919	47	4.948
72	5.25116	191	III	waiters (not dom.)	XX	4	—	—	—	—	—	—
73	5.28935	155	III	others in printing	XVII	2	—	—	—	—	—	—
74	5.29113	35	IV	dom. gardeners	IV	2	—	—	—	—	—	—
75	5.29879	4	IV	civil service messengers (incl. PO)	I	1	—	—	—	—	—	—
76	5.29950	3	IV	postmen	I	1	—	—	—	—	—	—
77	5.31845	16	II	church, chapel, cemetery officers, etc.	III	1	—	—	—	—	—	—
78	5.36462	159	VI	cotton – weaving processes	XVIII	1	92	24.669	90	25.610	102	671.556
Panel 3												
79	5.38787	196	II	general shopkeepers, dealers	XXII	4	11	0.665	35	2.565	4	0.897
80	5.40205	207	VI	'cotton – card room, others, undefined'	XVIII	1	80	8.735	71	8.993	96	304.386
81	5.42704	164	VI	lace manfre	XVIII	5	59	3.410	44	3.937	70	25.500
82	5.42839	6	IV	police	I	2	—	—	—	—	—	—
83	5.43243	52	III	signalmen	VI	1	—	—	—	—	—	—
84	5.43322	142	II	timber merchants	XIII	2	19	0.750	13	1.287	21	1.800
85	5.44156	66	II	merch. service/seamen – navigators	VI	3	88	17.818	93	29.731	77	44.464
86	5.45631	115	III	coach, carriage makers	X	10	47	2.129	40	3.152	55	6.554
87	5.45714	34	III	motor car drivers (dom. and non-dom.)[a]	—	—	—	—	—	—	—	—
88	5.45882	80	IV	nursery, seedsmen, florists	VII	1	37	1.432	28	2.115	44	4.438
89	5.47722	30	II	performers, showmen, sportsmen	III	8	—	—	—	—	—	—
90	5.48413	209	VI	'textiles – bleachers, printers'	XVIII	6	87	14.651	84	16.390	91	138.144
91	5.49584	138	III	upholsterers	XIII	1	39	1.514	43	3.840	30	2.499
92	5.50909	174	III	hairdressers, wig makers	XIX	1	1	0.319	1	0.761	1	0.550
93	5.52200	51	III	railway guards	VI	1	—	—	—	—	—	—
94	5.53048	175	II	milksellers, dairymen	XX	1	8	0.607	16	1.407	8	1.067
95	5.53935	186	IV	brewers	XX	3	70	5.769	54	6.072	88	115.565
96	5.55403	166	VI	textile dyers	XVIII	6	83	9.567	80	11.794	81	50.657
97	5.57131	184	II	greengrocers, fruiterers	XX	1	2	0.506	18	1.439	3	0.780
98	5.59310	57	II	stable keepers/coach, cab proprietors	VI	2	10	0.661	14	1.287	12	1.360
99	5.60224	98	III	erectors, fitters, turners	X	3	98	57.107	101	132.862	86	100.158

100	5.62729	163	VI	hosiery manfre	XVIII	5	67	5.450	59	7.301	68	21.503
101	5.64536	132	III	plumbers	XII	1	32	1.229	29	2.129	35	2.910
102	5.65207	167	VI	textiles – calenderers, finishers	XVIII	6	81	9.076	81	12.450	75	33.490
103	5.66450	87	I	coal – mineowners, agents, managers	IX	1	57	3.302	42	3.767	72	26.739
104	5.69473	73	II	farmers, graziers	VII	1	12	0.679	4	0.950	29	2.375
105	5.69559	125	III	carpenters, joiners	XII	1	56	3.196	63	7.858	50	5.386
106	5.70399	50	III	railway engine – drivers, stokers, cleaners	VI	1	—	—	—	—	—	—
107	5.71646	157	VI	cotton – spinning processes	XVIII	1	89	17.843	85	18.248	103	804.308
108	5.72628	64	III	trams – others	VI	2	—	—	—	—	—	—
109	5.72894	53	IV	pointsmen, level crossing operators	VI	1	—	—	—	—	—	—
110	5.73462	153	III	saddlers, harness makers	XVI	2	33	1.293	34	2.515	33	2.661
111	5.73728	116	III	wheelwrights	X	10	41	1.599	39	3.104	37	3.30
112	5.74141	179	IV	millers/cereal food manfre	XX	1	46	2.023	36	2.692	60	8.14
113	5.74547	170	III	tailors	XIX	1	35	1.302	30	2.190	36	3.21
114	5.74590	70	IV	harbour, dock, lighthouse – officials, servant	VI	4	—	—	—	—	—	—
115	5.74718	178	II	fishmongers, poulterers	XX	1	6	0.570	21	1.557	5	0.90
116	5.75040	177	II	butchers, meat salesmen	XX	1	9	0.655	7	1.122	17	1.58
117	5.75501	82	IV	other gardeners (not dom.)	VII	1	52	2.534	91	28.221	34	2.78
Panel 4												
118	5.76282	58	V	coach, cabmen (not dom.)	VI	2	—	—	—	—	—	—
119	5.77227	81	IV	market gardeners (incl. labourers)	VII	1	25	0.899	31	2.378	15	1.45
120	5.79634	56	V	rail – porters	VI	1	—	—	—	—	—	—
121	5.81870	133	III	gasfitters	XII	1	63	4.352	83	14.191	54	6.28
122	5.86607	194	IV	electricity supply	XXI	1	103	113.889	104	170.833	97	341.67
123	5.86673	112	III	rail – coach, wagon makers	X	10	101	104.873	100	120.072	104	828.50
124	5.86848	110	III	shipwrights	X	9	85	12.486	87	21.713	73	29.38
125	5.89863	105	III	cutlers/scissors makers	X	5	53	2.721	55	6.604	45	4.63
126	5.90635	193	IV	waterworks service	XXI	1	109	578.400	110	723.000	109	2,892.00
127	5.92203	67	II	merch. serv./seamen – engineers	VI	3	106	202.080	107	459.273	98	360.86
128	5.92615	102	III	electrical apparatus – makers, fitters	X	4	74	6.304	70	8.940	67	21.38
129	5.97570	131	III	painters, decorators	XII	1	48	2.282	46	4.343	46	4.81
130	5.99124	136	III	cabinet makers	XIII	1	44	1.742	41	3.337	40	3.65
131	6.00157	72	V	messengers, watchmen (not rail or govt)	VI	5	—	—	—	—	—	—
132	6.03161	59	V	horsekeepers, stablemen (not dom.)	VI	2	—	—	—	—	—	—
133	6.05570	113	III	cycle makers	X	10	31	1.190	37	2.694	25	2.13
134	6.05667	104	III	tool makers	X	5	71	5.785	69	8.654	64	17.44
135	6.06091	181	II	bakers – biscuits, cakes	XX	1	55	3.155	52	5.329	57	7.74
136	6.08608	172	III	boot, shoe makers	XIX	1	34	1.298	48	4.785	19	1.78

Posn	AM2/81–5	ID	Class	Occ. name	Order	Suborder	RANK/ OEMP	R/ OWNEMP	RANK/ EMPLOY	R/ EMPLOY	RANK/ OACC	R/ OWNACC
137	6.10292	54	V	rail – platelayers, gangers, packers	VI	1	—	—	—	—	—	—
138	6.11637	99	III	metal machinists	X	3	104	124.596	103	158.024	101	589.00
139	6.12254	140	IV	sawyers, wood-cutting machinists	XIII	2	86	12.639	86	18.323	76	40.74
140	6.16277	75	III	farm – bailiffs, foremen	VII	1	—	—	—	—	—	—
141	6.18569	36	III	gamekeepers	IV	2	—	—	—	—	—	—
142	6.19298	62	III	trams – drivers	VI	2	—	—	—	—	—	—
143	6.21748	107	IV	tinplate goods makers	X	8	51	2.529	56	6.635	43	4.09
144	6.22212	97	III	blacksmiths, strikers	X	3	50	2.435	47	4.390	52	5.47
145	6.24777	95	III	iron – others (moulders, fettlers, etc.)	X	3	91	21.361	89	23.720	95	214.75
146	6.26000	106	IV	wire workers	X	8	64	4.617	68	8.445	63	10.19
147	6.27523	200	IV	engine (not rail, agro, marin) – drivers, etc.	XXII	5	—	—	—	—	—	—
148	6.27636	147	IV	manfring chemists	XV	3	60	3.940	50	5.023	66	18.28
149	6.27655	100	V	engineering – undefined labourers	V	3	—	—	—	—	—	—
150	6.30678	128	III	masons	XII	1	61	4.034	65	8.231	59	7.91
151	6.31455	61	V	carmen, carters (not farm)	VI	2	58	3.394	73	9.262	49	5.36
152	6.31810	55	V	rail – labourers (not of rail contractors)	VI	1	—	—	—	—	—	—
153	6.32215	150	V	grease, soap, manure manfre	XV	4	72	6.012	60	7.348	74	33.06
154	6.33654	151	V	rubber, gutta percha workers	XV	4	68	5.657	62	7.434	69	23.66
155	6.35610	198	V	costermongers, hawkers	XXII	4	4	0.564	58	7.160	2	0.61
156	6.37045	141	IV	coopers	XIII	2	66	5.262	78	11.211	62	9.92
Panel 5												
157	6.41408	101	III	boilermakers	X	3	95	33.618	95	45.995	89	124.93
158	6.42718	108	IV	brass, bronze workers	X	8	73	6.237	74	9.708	65	17.45
159	6.49828	145	IV	china, pottery manfre	XIV	1	82	9.272	76	11.174	82	54.46
160	6.50837	89	IV	stone – miners, quarriers	IX	1	93	26.736	96	50.350	83	57.01
161	6.53042	152	IV	tanners, curriers	XVI	1	76	6.752	64	7.944	78	44.98
162	6.53113	130	III	plasterers	XII	1	54	3.068	49	5.017	58	7.90
163	6.56412	195	V	refuse disposal	XXI	2	99	70.897	105	184.333	87	115.21
164	6.56556	96	V	ironfoundry labourers	X	3	108	567.200	109	709.000	108	2,836.00
165	6.58723	144	V	plaster, cement manfre	XIV	1	90	20.808	88	23.522	94	180.33
166	6.59105	137	III	french polishers	XIII	1	49	2.324	57	6.961	39	3.49
167	6.61384	93	IV	steel – manfre, smelting, founding	X	1	94	27.946	92	29.411	100	561.08
168	6.64157	126	III	bricklayers	XII	1	69	5.679	82	13.608	61	9.75

169	6.65926	135	V	road labourers	XII	2	97	41.704	99	92.313	84	76.07
170	6.68782	192	IV	gas works service	XXI	1	107	299.714	106	372.978	105	1,525.82
171	6.69231	149	V	oil (veg.) – millers, refiners	XV	4	75	6.401	61	7.388	79	47.91
172	6.70227	134	V	navvies	XII	2	—	—	—	—	—	—
173	6.70251	78	VIII	agrolab. i/c horses	VII	1	—	—	—	—	—	—
174	6.72386	199	V	general labourers	XXII	5	—	—	—	—	—	—
175	6.74137	77	VIII	agrolab. i/c cattle	VII	1	—	—	—	—	—	—
176	6.75563	111	V	shipyard labourers (undefined)	X	9	—	—	—	—	—	—
177	6.78571	76	IV	shepherds	VII	1	—	—	—	—	—	—
178	6.78665	79	VIII	agrolab. duties not distinguished	VII	1	—	—	—	—	—	—
179	6.81422	83	IV	fishermen	VIII	1	36	1.315	67	8.263	16	1.56
180	6.82213	68	V	bargemen, lightermen, watermen	VI	3	62	4.266	79	11.699	56	6.71
181	6.83048	143	V	brick, terracotta makers	XIV	1	79	8.239	72	9.194	85	79.28
182	6.86081	69	V	dock, wharf labourers	VI	4	—	—	—	—	—	—
183	6.86872	86	VII	coal – mineworkers above ground	IX	1	—	—	—	—	—	—
184	6.87132	124	V	builders' labourers	XII	1	—	—	—	—	—	—
185	6.92572	146	IV	glass manfre	XIV	1	78	7.804	77	11.176	71	25.86
186	6.94345	129	V	masons' labourers	XII	1	—	—	—	—	—	—
187	6.96547	71	V	coalheavers, coalporters	VI	5	—	—	—	—	—	—
188	7.02869	94	IV	tinplate manfre	X	2	—	—	97	70.844	—	—
189	7.03828	109	III	ship – platers, riveters	X	9	105	130.262	108	497.364	93	176.48
190	7.05085	88	VII	iron – miners, quarriers	IX	1	—	—	—	—	—	—
191	7.06213	127	V	bricklayers' labourers	XII	1	—	—	—	—	—	—
192	7.08857	85	VII	coal – mineworkers below ground	IX	1	—	—	—	—	—	—
193	7.10592	92	V	puddlers/iron, steel rolling mills	X	1	100	71.748	98	74.140	106	2,224.20
194	7.29142	91	V	pig iron manfre (blast furnace)	X	1	96	35.140	94	35.693	107	2,266.50
195	7.60287	84	VII	coal – mineworkers at the face	IX	1	—	—	—	—	—	—

[a] This occupational category was, uniquely, an amalgamation of two occupations drawn from two different Industrial Orders, hence no information in the 'Order' and 'Suborder' columns.

APPENDIX E MALE OCCUPATIONS RANK ORDERED BY INCOMPLETE FERTILITY INDEX, AM2/01–5

Posn	ID	Occ. name	AM2/01–5	AM3/01–5	RANK/AM3	IMR (rate)	PRNUPREG (rank)
Panel 1							
1	29	actors	1.39954	1.10256	1	128	126
2	9	army officers (incl. retired)	1.57584	1.52088	12	44	70
3	26	painters, sculptors, artists	1.60335	1.46995	5	27	95
4	204	private means	1.63728	1.46121	4	50	91
5	11	officers of navy, marine (incl. ret.)	1.64179	1.51200	11	41	2
6	31	dom. indoor servants (not in hotels, etc.)	1.67050	1.41061	2	147	180
7	40	merchants (commodity undefined)	1.67296	1.78065	61	30	25
8	46	banks – officials, clerks	1.70210	1.47361	6	54	3
9	23	authors, editors, journalists	1.70406	1.52703	14	54	108
10	27	architects	1.70632	1.61491	29	73	112
11	25	civil, mining – engineers	1.71368	1.55814	20	61	7
12	22	teachers (schools and universities)	1.71647	1.54340	18	58	24
13	24	scientific pursuits	1.76190	1.56522	22	68	1
14	122	dealers in jewellery, watches, gold, etc.	1.76641	1.67653	40	—	60
15	44	auctioneers, valuers, house agents	1.77718	1.69094	43	71	145
16	21	dentists (incl. assistants)	1.77848	1.57049	23	73	69
17	20	physicians, surgeons, reg'd GPs	1.78843	1.73581	55	39	85
18	43	accountants	1.79412	1.52163	13	55	105
19	201	retired from business (not army or navy)	1.79891	1.45355	3	—	184
20	5	civil serv. – officers, clerks (not PO)	1.80722	1.61228	27	—	30
21	17	barristers	1.81443	1.85315	75	63	28
22	19	law clerks	1.82490	1.55315	19	73	5
23	39	caretakers (not gov't)	1.83237	1.47977	8	137	195
24	18	solicitors	1.83406	1.65457	37	41	9
25	159	cotton – weaving processes	1.84666	1.47814	7	—	59
26	15	itinerant preachers, missionaries, etc.	1.85567	1.86842	79	87	23
27	45	commercial, business clerks	1.86402	1.58155	24	81	13
28	148	chemists, druggists	1.86536	1.56181	21	71	47

29	2	PO officers and clerks (not telecomms.)	1.86901	1.66364	39	—	81
30	173	boot, shoe, clog dealers	1.88667	1.73278	54	83	54
31	185	tobacconists	1.89065	1.53721	15	84	123
32	13	clergy (C of E)	1.89737	1.88444	83	48	62
33	42	commercial travellers	1.90204	1.64475	32	86	130
34	158	cotton – winding processes	1.91439	1.49708	10	—	20
35	49	railway – officials, clerks	1.91448	1.59563	25	82	45
36	14	clergy (nonconf.)	1.92578	1.68862	41	69	67
37	28	musicians, music teachers	1.93077	1.64797	35	120	116
38	162	wool, worsted – weaving processes	1.95161	1.48927	9	—	12
39	187	cafes, restaurants – keepers	1.95502	1.61465	28	145	156
Panel 2							
40	171	clothiers, outfitters	1.96004	1.73180	53	84	61
41	47	insurance – official, clerks, etc.	1.96246	1.69925	47	71	38
42	41	brokers, agents, factors	1.97503	1.64605	33	122	46
43	168	drapers, linen mercers	1.97892	1.65913	38	97	87
44	120	watchmakers, clockmakers	1.98066	1.82044	66	—	84
45	12	men of the navy, marine	1.99294	1.79746	64	120	42
46	117	ironmongers/hardware merchants	2.00195	1.70351	48	82	31
47	183	grocers, dealers in beverages	2.00298	1.69252	44	101	21
48	8	municipal, parish, county officers	2.00335	1.65332	36	80	79
49	7	Poor Law service	2.01282	1.63776	31	80	33
50	197	pawnbrokers	2.02709	1.75260	58	109	4
51	37	college, club – service	2.02928	1.60520	26	80	189
52	154	printers – hand compositors	2.03158	1.69076	42	—	151
53	169	textile fabrics – other dealers	2.05290	1.62238	30	70	41
54	161	wool, worsted – spinning processes	2.05882	1.54178	17	—	6
55	208	wool, worsted – carding, others, undefined	2.06257	1.69814	45	—	26
56	139	furniture dealers	2.07986	1.71364	50	76	129
57	103	electricians (undefined)	2.08061	1.77855	60	100	50
58	188	lodging, boarding house keepers	2.11732	1.54106	16	67	185
59	189	hotel keepers/publicans/off-licences	2.12196	1.84514	72	142	190
60	48	insurance – agents	2.12363	1.82277	67	122	162
61	207	cotton – card room, others, undefined	2.13098	1.64721	34	—	138
62	182	bakers, confectioners (dealers)	2.13493	1.85339	76	—	82
63	202	pensioners	2.15455	1.74694	56	—	188
64	123	builders	2.16949	1.90093	88	98	161
65	176	cheesemongers, provision dealers	2.17608	1.87555	81	99	102

Posn	ID	Occ. name	AM2/01–5	AM3/01–5	RANK/AM3	IMR (rate)	PRNUPREG (rank)
66	157	cotton – spinning processes	2.18143	1.69816	46	—	22
67	3	postmen	2.18209	1.88794	84	85	96
68	163	hosiery manfre	2.18476	1.74922	57	111	8
69	121	piano, organ makers	2.18868	1.71814	51	93	132
70	166	textile dyers	2.19174	1.80709	65	—	11
71	34	motor car drivers (dom. and non-dom.)	2.19674	1.92866	98	—	19
72	174	hairdressers, wig makers	2.20027	1.85737	77	112	103
73	119	goldsmiths, silversmiths	2.21236	1.77844	59	—	55
74	35	dom. gardeners	2.22281	1.85158	74	80	117
75	155	others in printing	2.22306	1.79688	63	—	48
76	209	textiles – bleachers, printers	2.23302	1.83063	69	—	90
77	38	hospital, benevolent soc. – service	2.23817	1.86906	80	120	136
78	191	waiters (not dom.)	2.23911	1.96667	110	120	120
Panel 3							
79	98	erectors, fitters, turners	2.23943	1.85088	73	114	83
80	16	church, chapel, cemetery officers, etc.	2.23944	2.16751	146	77	187
81	180	corn, flour, seed – merchants, dealers	2.24072	2.03947	127	83	64
82	90	coal, coke – merchants, dealers	2.24346	1.82671	68	99	158
83	32	dom. – coachmen, grooms	2.25050	1.98302	114	81	148
84	138	upholsterers	2.25101	1.86430	78	119	76
85	114	motor car – chassis makers and mechanics	2.25462	1.89184	86	73	29
86	52	signalmen	2.25624	1.92912	99	94	71
87	167	textiles – calenderers, finishers	2.25737	1.70942	49	—	74
88	87	coal – mineowners, agents, managers	2.25820	1.72727	52	122	181
89	177	butchers, meat salesmen	2.25983	1.99256	117	106	40
90	4	civil service messengers (incl. PO)	2.26148	1.94026	102	101	170
91	132	plumbers	2.26849	1.90875	90	97	78
92	133	gasfitters	2.27553	1.90037	87	106	92
93	125	carpenters, joiners	2.28231	1.96210	109	101	134
94	164	lace manf're	2.29774	1.79182	62	118	124
95	153	saddlers, harness makers	2.29960	1.92522	95	110	177
96	51	railway guards	2.30000	1.93787	100	102	186
97	30	performers, showmen, sportsmen	2.30154	1.95908	108	140	141
98	6	police	2.30398	2.05694	129	92	110

99	116	wheelwrights	2.30942	1.92708	96	113	121
100	102	electrical apparatus – makers, fitters	2.31394	1.91560	91	108	109
101	175	milksellers, dairymen	2.31568	1.98252	113	104	57
102	142	timber merchants	2.32361	1.88294	82	104	179
103	112	rail – coach, wagon makers	2.34061	1.92737	97	—	174
104	110	shipwrights	2.34937	2.11706	137	106	17
105	170	tailors	2.35342	1.91846	92	100	98
106	62	trams – drivers	2.35476	1.98950	115	—	194
107	104	tool makers	2.35871	1.84179	70	115	66
108	115	coach, carriage makers	2.36244	1.84448	71	—	93=
109	66	merch. service/seamen – navigators	2.36623	1.99165	116	—	101
110	53	pointsmen, level crossing operators	2.36675	1.94215	103	130	140
111	196	general shopkeepers, dealers	2.37078	1.93897	101	140	165
112	172	boot, shoe makers	2.37312	1.97180	112	127	73
113	184	greengrocers, fruiterers	2.38195	1.94653	105	126	114
114	57	stable keepers/coach, cab proprietors	2.38686	2.12360	139	100	169
115	81	market gardeners (incl. labourers)	2.38922	2.00518	120	—	34
116	194	electricity supply	2.39031	2.12684	141	111	93=
117	50	railway engine – drivers, stokers, cleaners	2.39363	2.00870	131	107	86
Panel 4							
118	80	nursery, seedsmen, florists	2.39664	1.92026	93	—	35
119	178	fishmongers, poulterers	2.40111	1.90499	89	116	150
120	181	bakers – biscuits, cakes	2.40551	1.95530	107	—	44
121	113	cycle makers	2.41630	1.96677	111	129	65
122	136	cabinet makers	2.42546	1.89085	85	103	100
123	56	rail – porters	2.43106	2.06545	121	—	53
124	105	cutlers/scissors makers	2.43333	2.14170	143	134	27
125	99	metal machinists	2.44168	1.94536	104	148	75
126	107	tinplate goods makers	2.45407	1.95418	106	137	10
127	151	rubber, gutta percha workers	2.45466	2.01458	122	144	63
128	193	waterworks service	2.46004	2.04777	128	122	131
129	140	sawyers, wood-cutting machinists	2.46131	2.00415	119	112	72
130	179	millers/cereal food manf're	2.46496	2.22401	157	—	49
131	64	trams – others	2.46605	2.06387	130	123	154
132	131	painters, decorators	2.46694	2.02848	123	147	119
133	190	barmen	2.47151	2.19820	152	—	106
134	82	other gardeners (not dom.)	2.47627	2.03294	124	116	68
135	186	brewers	2.47754	2.03432	126	70	97

Posn	ID	Occ. name	AM2/01–5	AM3/01–5	RANK/AM3	IMR (rate)	PRNUPREG (rank)
136	36	gamekeepers	2.50545	2.35688	175	70	111
137	58	coach, cabmen (not dom.)	2.51329	2.20050	153	125	193
138	97	blacksmiths, strikers	2.51787	2.07505	133	116	115
139	72	messengers, watchmen (not rail or gov't)	2.52323	2.11314	135	132	125
140	152	tanners, curriers	2.52989	2.16879	149	123	43
141	128	masons	2.53534	2.12619	140	128	183
142	75	farm – bailiffs, foremen	2.53683	2.21640	154	66	168
143	67	merch. serv./seamen – engineers	2.53731	2.03390	125	—	58
144	95	iron – others (moulders, fettlers, etc.)	2.53963	2.11429	136	120	118
145	141	coopers	2.55221	2.16556	145	127	128
146	200	engine (not rail, agro, marin) – drivers, etc.	2.56184	2.14038	142	136	160
147	54	rail – platelayers, gangers, packers	2.56432	2.16817	148	121	164
148	73	farmers, graziers	2.56758	2.29534	169	75	155
149	59	horsekeepers, stablemen (not dom.)	2.57629	2.26808	163	122	127
150	147	manf'ring chemists	2.59694	1.99661	118	143	149
151	137	french polishers	2.61080	2.14286	144	140	167
152	192	gas works service	2.61587	2.23395	159	147	191
153	108	brass, bronze workers	2.62222	2.08667	134	174	15
154	126	bricklayers	2.62743	2.23771	160	113	142
155	106	wire workers	2.63297	1.92254	94	139	18
156	70	harbour, dock, lighthouse – officials, servant	2.63399	2.22340	156	150	166
Panel 5							
157	101	boilermakers	2.63932	2.27717	165	134	113
158	150	grease, soap, manure manf're	2.64078	2.18827	151	120	107
159	145	china, pottery manf're	2.65428	2.07416	132	172	135
160	55	rail – labourers (not of rail contractors)	2.65839	2.28526	167	—	163
161	100	engineering – undefined labourers	2.66160	2.16763	147	150	171
162	61	carmen, carters (not farm)	2.66794	2.24161	161	147	143
163	130	plasterers	2.67625	2.17851	150	110	175
164	83	fishermen	2.68172	2.28989	168	139	88
165	89	stone – miners, quarriers	2.69449	2.32298	170	110	147
166	86	coal – mineworkers above ground	2.69990	2.21851	155	—	51
167	78	agrolab. i/c horses	2.70663	2.33996	172	—	52
168	198	costermongers, hawkers	2.70905	2.11937	138	196	182

169	94	tinplate manf're	2.71378	2.48182	183	143	39
170	143	brick, terracotta makers	2.71635	2.22525	158	140	99
171	93	steel – manf're, smelting, founding	2.72484	2.34116	173	139	133
172	77	agrolab. i/c cattle	2.73059	2.36177	176	—	56
173	76	shepherds	2.74220	2.47420	181	71	144
174	79	agrolab. duties not distinguished	2.74638	2.48102	182	—	36
175	144	plaster, cement manf're	2.75610	2.52358	187	129	16
176	96	ironfoundry labourers	2.76416	2.28483	166	171	159
177	68	bargemen, lightermen, watermen	2.79448	2.55280	191	161	146
178	129	masons' labourers	2.79652	2.37543	177	145	80
179	149	oil (veg.) – millers, refiners	2.80635	2.27228	164	152	14
180	135	road labourers	2.82390	2.34389	174	112	176
181	71	coalheavers, coalporters	2.82680	2.43796	178	147	157
182	146	glass manf're	2.82877	2.33407	171	156	77
183	85	coal – mineworkers below ground	2.84849	2.49474	184	—	37
184	199	general labourers	2.85114	2.45728	180	167	152
185	92	puddlers/iron, steel rolling mills	2.85381	2.44734	179	153	139
186	88	iron – miners, quarriers	2.85413	2.59064	193	108	32
187	124	builders' labourers	2.86603	2.54134	189	139	178
188	134	navvies	2.87123	2.50592	185	187	104
189	127	bricklayers' labourers	2.87751	2.50701	186	146	173
190	111	shipyard labourers (undefined)	2.91436	2.69456	195	137	153
191	195	refuse disposal	2.92654	2.26429	162	192	192
192	109	ship – platers, riveters	2.94555	2.54982	190	136	89
193	84	coal – mineworkers at the face	2.95531	2.63361	194	—	122
194	91	pig iron manf're (blast furnace)	2.97022	2.53968	188	166	137
195	69	dock, wharf labourers	3.00189	2.57737	192	172	172

APPENDIX F MALE OCCUPATIONS RANK ORDERED BY AM25PC20

(the extent to which older-marrying couples restrict fertility more than younger-marrying couples)

Posn	AM25PC20	ID	Occ. name	AM2/ 01–5	AM3/ 01–5	RANK/ AM2	RANK/ AM3	AMRATIO2	RANK/ AMRAT2
Panel 1									
1	0.728	188	lodging, boarding house keepers	2.117	1.541	58	16	0.865	20
2	0.730	106	wire workers	2.633	1.923	155	94	2.392	176
3	0.749	161	wool, worsted – spinning processes	2.059	1.542	54	17	1.329	73
4	0.757	167	textiles – calenderers, finishers	2.257	1.709	87	49	1.432	82
5	0.763	162	wool, worsted – weaving processes	1.952	1.489	38	9	1.153	52
6	0.765	87	coal – mineowners, agents, managers	2.258	1.727	88	52	1.167	54
7	0.769	147	manf'ring chemists	2.597	1.997	150	118	1.993	146
8	0.773	207	cotton – card room, others, undefined	2.131	1.647	61	34	1.557	98
9	0.774	195	refuse disposal	2.927	2.264	191	162	2.382	174
10	0.778	157	cotton – spinning processes	2.181	1.698	66	46	1.584	102
11	0.780	136	cabinet makers	2.425	1.891	122	85	1.853	130
12	0.780	164	lace manf're	2.298	1.792	94	62	2.472	180
13	0.781	115	coach, carriage makers	2.362	1.844	108	71	1.432	81
14	0.781	104	tool makers	2.359	1.842	107	70	2.039	151
15	0.781	145	china, pottery manf're	2.654	2.074	159	132	2.269	166
16	0.782	158	cotton – winding processes	1.914	1.497	34	10	1.226	59
17	0.782	198	costermongers, hawkers	2.709	2.119	168	138	2.491	182
18	0.785	121	piano, organ makers	2.189	1.718	69	51	1.559	99
19	0.788	29	actors	1.400	1.103	1	1	2.221	163
20	0.790	169	textile fabrics – other dealers	2.053	1.622	53	30	1.057	41
21	0.791	37	college, club – service	2.029	1.605	51	26	1.050	40
22	0.793	178	fishmongers, poulterers	2.401	1.905	119	89	1.907	136
23	0.796	108	brass, bronze workers	2.622	2.087	153	134	2.400	177
24	0.796	107	tinplate goods makers	2.454	1.954	126	106	2.054	152
25	0.797	99	metal machinists	2.442	1.945	125	104	1.918	138
26	0.800	159	cotton – weaving processes	1.847	1.478	25	7	1.501	90
27	0.801	163	hosiery manfre	2.185	1.749	68	57	1.646	111
28	0.801	80	nursery, seedsmen, florists	2.397	1.920	118	93	1.322	70

29	0.802	67	merch. serv./seamen – engineers	2.537	2.034	143	125	2.019	148
30	0.804	119	goldsmiths, silversmiths	2.212	1.778	73	59	1.776	126
31	0.808	39	caretakers (not gov't)	1.832	1.480	23	8	1.000	32
32	0.808	201	retired from business (not army or navy)	1.799	1.454	19	3	0.670	7
33	0.808	155	others in printing	2.223	1.797	75	63	1.459	84
34	0.810	149	oil (veg.) – millers, refiners	2.806	2.272	179	164	3.119	194
35	0.810	142	timber merchants	2.324	1.883	102	82	1.261	61
36	0.811	202	pensioners	2.155	1.747	63	56	0.898	23
37	0.813	181	bakers – biscuits, cakes	2.406	1.955	120	107	1.731	122
38	0.813	185	tobacconists	1.891	1.537	31	15	1.319	69
39	0.814	7	Poor Law service	2.013	1.638	49	31	0.751	12
Panel 2									
40	0.814	113	cycle makers	2.416	1.967	121	111	2.373	173
41	0.814	130	plasterers	2.676	2.179	163	150	2.588	186
42	0.814	90	coal, coke – merchants, dealers	2.243	1.827	82	68	1.265	62
43	0.814	140	sawyers, wood-cutting machinists	2.461	2.004	129	119	2.132	158
44	0.814	100	engineering – undefined labourers	2.662	2.168	161	147	1.902	135
45	0.815	170	tailors	2.353	1.918	105	92	1.720	121
46	0.817	184	greengrocers, fruiterers	2.382	1.947	113	105	1.637	110
47	0.818	196	general shopkeepers, dealers	2.371	1.939	111	101	1.703	116
48	0.819	143	brick, terracotta makers	2.716	2.225	170	158	2.169	161
49	0.820	209	textiles – bleachers, printers	2.233	1.831	76	69	1.539	94
50	0.821	53	pointsmen, level crossing operators	2.367	1.942	110	103	1.731	124
51	0.821	151	rubber, gutta percha workers	2.455	2.015	127	122	2.411	178
52	0.821	137	french polishers	2.611	2.143	151	144	2.743	191
53	0.821	82	other gardeners (not dom.)	2.476	2.033	134	124	1.226	58
54	0.821	186	brewers	2.478	2.034	135	126	1.581	101
55	0.822	86	coal – mineworkers above ground	2.700	2.219	166	155	2.092	153
56	0.822	131	painters, decorators	2.467	2.028	132	123	1.836	129
57	0.823	208	wool, worsted – carding, others, undefined	2.063	1.698	55	45	1.385	79
58	0.823	112	rail – coach, wagon makers	2.341	1.927	103	97	1.682	115
59	0.824	139	furniture dealers	2.080	1.714	56	50	1.327	71
60	0.824	97	blacksmiths, strikers	2.518	2.075	138	133	1.651	112
61	0.825	166	textile dyers	2.192	1.807	70	65	1.716	120
62	0.825	146	glass manf're	2.829	2.334	182	171	2.490	181
63	0.825	8	municipal, parish, county officers	2.003	1.653	48	36	0.893	21
64	0.826	187	cafes, restaurants – keepers	1.955	1.615	39	28	1.381	78
65	0.826	98	erectors, fitters, turners	2.239	1.851	79	73	1.633	109
66	0.827	96	ironfoundry labourers	2.764	2.285	176	166	2.324	172

Posn	AM25PC20	ID	Occ. name	AM2/ 01–5	AM3/ 01–5	RANK/ AM2	RANK/ AM3	AMRATIO2	RANK/ AMRAT2
67	0.828	102	electrical apparatus – makers, fitters	2.314	1.916	100	91	1.714	119
68	0.828	138	upholsterers	2.251	1.864	84	78	1.555	97
69	0.829	150	grease, soap, manure manf're	2.641	2.188	158	151	2.225	165
70	0.830	135	road labourers	2.824	2.344	180	174	1.959	142
71	0.831	172	boot, shoe makers	2.373	1.972	112	112	1.853	131
72	0.832	154	printers – hand compositors	2.032	1.691	52	42	1.188	56
73	0.832	193	waterworks service	2.460	2.048	128	128	1.475	85
74	0.833	95	iron – others (moulders, fettlers, etc.)	2.540	2.114	144	136	2.026	150
75	0.833	35	dom. gardeners	2.223	1.852	74	74	1.040	37
76	0.833	41	brokers, agents, factors	1.975	1.646	42	33	1.046	38
77	0.833	49	railway – officials, clerks	1.914	1.596	35	25	0.945	29
78	0.834	116	wheelwrights	2.309	1.927	99	96	1.327	72
Panel 3									
79	0.835	38	hospital, benevolent soc. – service	2.238	1.869	77	80	0.912	25
80	0.835	133	gasfitters	2.276	1.900	92	87	1.915	137
81	0.835	200	engine (not rail, agro, marin) – drivers, etc.	2.562	2.140	146	142	2.008	147
82	0.837	64	trams – others	2.466	2.064	131	130	1.499	89
83	0.837	153	saddlers, harness makers	2.300	1.925	95	95	1.306	68
84	0.837	148	chemists, druggists	1.865	1.562	28	21	0.850	18
85	0.837	72	messengers, watchmen (not rail or gov't)	2.523	2.113	139	135	1.618	105
86	0.838	168	drapers, linen mercers	1.979	1.659	43	38	0.804	15
87	0.839	128	masons	2.535	2.126	141	140	1.548	96
88	0.839	114	motor car – chassis makers and mechanics	2.255	1.892	85	86	1.984	145
89	0.839	50	railway engine – drivers, stokers, cleaners	2.394	2.009	117	121	1.652	113
90	0.839	81	market gardeners (incl. labourers)	2.389	2.005	115	120	1.514	91
91	0.840	61	carmen, carters (not farm)	2.668	2.242	162	161	2.386	175
92	0.841	132	plumbers	2.268	1.909	91	90	1.498	88
93	0.842	66	merch. service/seamen – navigators	2.366	1.992	109	116	1.523	93
94	0.843	51	railway guards	2.300	1.938	96	100	1.203	57
95	0.844	70	harbour, dock, lighthouse – officials, servant	2.634	2.223	156	156	1.628	107
96	0.844	174	hairdressers, wig makers	2.200	1.857	72	77	1.731	123
97	0.844	31	dom. indoor servants (not in hotels, etc.)	1.670	1.411	6	2	0.729	10
98	0.845	62	trams – drivers	2.355	1.990	106	115	1.633	108
99	0.845	183	grocers, dealers in beverages	2.003	1.693	47	44	1.099	48

100	0.846	54	rail – platelayers, gangers, packers	2.564	2.168	147	148	1.626	106
101	0.848	43	accountants	1.794	1.522	18	13	0.736	11
102	0.848	45	commercial, business clerks	1.864	1.582	27	24	1.005	33
103	0.849	141	coopers	2.552	2.166	145	145	1.871	133
104	0.849	129	masons' labourers	2.797	2.375	178	177	1.962	143
105	0.850	56	rail – porters	2.431	2.065	123	131	1.747	125
106	0.851	117	ironmongers/hardware merchants	2.002	1.704	46	48	1.060	42
107	0.851	19	law clerks	1.825	1.553	22	19	0.929	26
108	0.851	30	performers, showmen, sportsmen	2.302	1.959	97	108	2.025	149
109	0.852	126	bricklayers	2.627	2.238	154	160	2.094	154
110	0.854	28	musicians, music teachers	1.931	1.648	37	35	1.276	64
111	0.854	83	fishermen	2.682	2.290	164	168	2.590	187
112	0.854	192	gas works service	2.616	2.234	152	159	1.890	134
113	0.855	103	electricians (undefined)	2.081	1.779	57	60	1.445	83
114	0.855	52	signalmen	2.256	1.929	86	99	1.300	67
115	0.855	91	pig iron manf're (blast furnace)	2.970	2.540	194	188	2.532	185
116	0.856	175	milksellers, dairymen	2.316	1.983	101	113	1.589	104
117	0.857	152	tanners, curriers	2.530	2.169	140	149	1.944	141
Panel 4									
118	0.858	92	puddlers/iron, steel rolling mills	2.854	2.447	185	179	2.435	179
119	0.858	4	civil service messengers (incl. PO)	2.261	1.940	90	102	1.115	50
120	0.858	48	insurance – agents	2.124	1.823	60	67	1.273	63
121	0.859	69	dock, wharf labourers	3.002	2.577	195	192	2.502	184
122	0.859	93	steel – manf're, smelting, founding	2.725	2.341	171	173	2.294	168
123	0.860	55	rail – labourers (not of rail contractors)	2.658	2.285	160	167	2.171	162
124	0.860	125	carpenters, joiners	2.282	1.962	93	109	1.494	87
125	0.862	199	general labourers	2.851	2.457	184	180	2.101	155
126	0.862	176	cheesemongers, provision dealers	2.176	1.876	65	81	1.114	49
127	0.862	89	stone – miners, quarriers	2.694	2.323	165	170	1.860	132
128	0.862	71	coalheavers, coalporters	2.827	2.438	181	178	2.495	183
129	0.863	101	boilermakers	2.639	2.277	157	165	2.142	159
130	0.865	78	agrolab. i/c horses	2.707	2.340	167	172	2.224	164
131	0.865	197	pawnbrokers	2.027	1.753	50	58	1.154	53
132	0.865	42	commercial travellers	1.902	1.645	33	32	0.938	27
133	0.865	77	agrolab. i/c cattle	2.731	2.362	172	176	2.113	156
134	0.865	3	postmen	2.182	1.888	67	84	1.290	66
135	0.866	109	ship-platers, riveters	2.946	2.550	192	190	2.680	188
136	0.866	46	banks – officials, clerks	1.702	1.474	8	6	0.619	5

Posn	AM25PC20	ID	Occ. name	AM2/ 01–5	AM3/ 01–5	RANK/ AM2	RANK/ AM3	AMRATIO2	RANK/ AMRAT2
137	0.866	47	insurance – officials, clerks, etc.	1.962	1.699	41	47	1.068	43
138	0.868	182	bakers, confectioners (dealers)	2.135	1.853	62	76	1.368	76
139	0.870	189	hotel keepers/publicans/off-licences	2.122	1.845	59	72	1.237	60
140	0.871	127	bricklayers' labourers	2.878	2.507	189	186	2.296	169
141	0.873	134	navvies	2.871	2.506	188	185	2.160	160
142	0.874	75	farm – bailiffs, foremen	2.537	2.216	142	154	1.564	100
143	0.876	58	coach, cabmen (not dom.)	2.513	2.201	137	153	1.707	117
144	0.876	85	coal – mineworkers below ground	2.848	2.495	183	184	2.722	190
145	0.876	123	builders	2.169	1.901	64	88	1.093	46
146	0.877	14	clergy (nonconf.)	1.926	1.689	36	41	0.511	2
147	0.878	34	motor car drivers (dom. and non-dom.)	2.197	1.929	71	98	1.669	114
148	0.878	191	waiters (not dom.)	2.239	1.967	78	110	1.492	86
149	0.880	105	cutlers/scissors makers	2.433	2.142	124	143	2.308	170
150	0.880	59	horsekeepers, stablemen (not dom.)	2.576	2.268	149	163	1.814	128
151	0.881	32	dom. – coachmen, grooms	2.250	1.983	83	114	1.341	75
152	0.882	177	butchers, meat salesmen	2.260	1.993	89	117	1.376	77
153	0.883	21	dentists (incl. assistants)	1.778	1.570	16	23	1.036	36
154	0.884	171	clothiers, outfitters	1.960	1.732	40	53	1.048	39
155	0.887	124	builders' labourers	2.866	2.541	187	189	2.114	157
156	0.888	24	scientific pursuits	1.762	1.565	13	22	1.027	35
Panel 5									
157	0.889	190	barmen	2.472	2.198	133	152	2.293	167
158	0.890	57	stable keepers/coach, cab proprietors	2.387	2.124	114	139	1.539	95
159	0.890	194	electricity supply	2.390	2.127	116	141	1.515	92
160	0.890	2	PO officers and clerks (not telecomms.)	1.869	1.664	29	39	0.758	13
161	0.891	84	coal – mineworkers at the face	2.955	2.634	193	194	3.260	195
162	0.892	5	civil serv. – officers, clerks (not PO)	1.807	1.612	20	27	0.784	14
163	0.892	204	private means	1.637	1.461	4	4	0.994	31
164	0.893	6	police	2.304	2.057	98	129	1.179	55
165	0.894	73	farmers, graziers	2.568	2.295	148	169	0.897	22
166	0.896	23	authors, editors, journalists	1.704	1.527	9	14	0.944	28
167	0.899	22	teachers (schools and unversities)	1.716	1.543	12	18	0.629	6
168	0.901	110	shipwrights	2.349	2.117	104	137	1.982	144

169	0.902	12	men of the navy, marine	1.993	1.797	45	64	1.588	103
170	0.902	18	solicitors	1.834	1.655	24	37	0.722	9
171	0.902	179	millers/cereal food manf're	2.465	2.224	130	157	1.713	118
172	0.902	76	shepherds	2.742	2.474	173	181	1.811	127
173	0.903	79	agrolab. duties not distinguished	2.746	2.481	174	182	1.926	139
174	0.908	88	iron – miners, quarriers	2.854	2.591	186	193	2.312	171
175	0.909	25	civil, mining – engineers	1.714	1.558	11	20	0.907	24
176	0.910	180	corn, flour, seed – merchants, dealers	2.241	2.039	81	127	1.285	65
177	0.914	68	bargemen, lightermen, watermen	2.794	2.553	177	191	2.851	192
178	0.915	94	tinplate manf're	2.714	2.482	169	183	1.930	140
179	0.916	144	plaster cement manf're	2.756	2.524	175	187	2.708	189
180	0.917	26	painters, sculptors, artists	1.603	1.470	3	5	0.978	30
181	0.918	173	boot, shoe, clog dealers	1.887	1.733	30	54	1.132	51
182	0.919	120	watchmakers, clockmakers	1.981	1.820	44	66	1.428	80
183	0.921	11	officers of navy, marine (incl. ret.)	1.642	1.512	5	11	1.072	44
184	0.925	111	shipyard labourers (undefined)	2.914	2.695	190	195	3.029	193
185	0.941	36	gamekeepers	2.505	2.357	136	175	1.330	74
186	0.946	27	architects	1.706	1.615	10	29	0.835	17
187	0.949	122	dealers in jewellery, watches, gold, etc.	1.766	1.677	14	40	1.095	47
188	0.951	44	auctioneers, valuers, house agents	1.777	1.691	15	43	0.834	16
189	0.965	9	army officers (incl. retired)	1.576	1.521	2	12	0.855	19
190	0.968	16	church, chapel, cemetery officers, etc.	2.239	2.168	80	146	1.081	45
191	0.971	20	physicians, surgeons, reg'd GPs	1.788	1.736	17	55	0.563	3
192	0.993	13	clergy (C of E)	1.897	1.884	32	83	0.586	4
193	1.007	15	itinerant preachers, missionaries, etc.	1.856	1.868	26	79	0.511	1
194	1.021	17	barristers	1.814	1.853	21	75	0.678	8
195	1.064	40	merchants (commodity undefined)	1.673	1.781	7	61	1.026	34

APPENDIX G FEMALE OCCUPATIONS RANK ORDERED BY INCOMPLETE FERTILITY INDEX, AM2/01–5

Posn	AM2/01–5	ID	Occ. name	RANK/ AM3	AM3/ 01–5	FM25PC20	Size	PC2/ 01–5	PC3/ 01–5
1	1.185	211	fem. med., lit., sc. pursuits and artists	5	1.136	0.959	1,249	—	—
2	1.201	218	wood, furniture, decorns makers/workers	2	0.859	0.715	2,320	—	—
3	1.247	219	brush, broom makers/hair bristle workers	3	0.917	0.735	1,857	—	—
4	1.255	217	french polishers and upholsterers	1	0.857	0.683	2,353	—	—
5	1.400	29	actors	4	1.103	0.803	3,540	0.814	0.829
6	1.497	230	milliners	6	1.147	0.766	3,501	—	—
7	1.568	210	midwives and nurses	11	1.337	0.853	11,867	—	—
8	1.637	204	private means	17	1.461	0.964	23,724	0.784	0.847
9	1.670	31	dom. indoor servants (not in hotels, etc)	12	1.411	0.688	2,396	0.772	0.629
10	1.716	22	teachers (schools and universities)	25	1.543	0.867	11,557	0.672	0.648
11	1.734	226	textiles: bleachers, printers, dyers, finishers	7	1.240	0.715	1,961	—	—
12	1.735	236	jam, preserve, sweet makers	8	1.295	0.747	2,051	—	—
13	1.755	225	carpet, rug, felt manfre	9	1.321	0.753	1,229	—	—
14	1.779	222	dealers in stationery, books, newspapers	30	1.596	0.897	5,115	—	—
15	1.805	229	hat manfre: felt, cloth cap, other hats	14	1.423	0.788	2,060	—	—
16	1.812	231	dressmakers	16	1.439	0.794	33,276	—	—
17	1.847	159	cotton – weaving processes	19	1.478	0.733	53,691	0.945	0.866
18	1.857	239	coffee, eating, boarding house keepers	15	1.432	0.771	25,992	—	—
19	1.858	233	silk manfre	18	1.463	0.788	3,714	—	—
20	1.859	235	dealers in dress	29	1.594	0.857	7,308	—	—
21	1.864	45	commercial, business clerks	27	1.582	0.650	1,753	0.694	0.532
22	1.869	2	PO officers and clerks (not telecomms.)	36	1.664	0.789	2,824	1.007	0.893
23	1.891	185	tobacconists	23	1.537	0.802	3,147	0.894	0.882
24	1.914	158	cotton – winding processes	22	1.497	0.701	15,395	0.881	0.790
25	1.927	232	stay, corset makers	42	1.708	0.887	1,869	—	—
26	1.931	28	musicians, music teachers	33	1.648	0.810	3,096	0.724	0.687
27	1.952	162	wool, worsted – weaving processes	20	1.489	0.695	12,670	0.713	0.650
28	1.979	168	drapers, linen mercers	35	1.659	0.852	8,483	0.850	0.864
29	2.002	117	ironmongers/hardware merchants	41	1.704	0.864	1,339	1.033	1.049

30	2.003	183	grocers, dealers in beverages	38	1.693	0.813	21,112	0.961	0.925
31	2.013	7	Poor Law service	31	1.638	0.856	2,326	0.639	0.672
32	2.022	227	other textiles workers	10	1.324	0.655	5,674	—	—
33	2.043	214	farmers, graziers; & daughters, relatives	45	1.775	0.869	2,944	—	—
34	2.059	161	wool, worsted – spinning processes	24	1.542	0.679	6,170	0.920	0.834
35	2.063	208	wool, worsted – carding, others, undefined	39	1.698	0.636	2,181	0.919	0.709
36	2.110	238	tobacco manfre	13	1.418	0.672	1,863	—	—
37	2.111	233	shirt makers and seamstresses	21	1.490	0.706	10,359	—	—
38	2.119	237	other food manfre	26	1.550	0.732	3,621	—	—
39	2.122	189	hotel keepers/publicans/off-licences	52	1.845	0.841	31,285	0.958	0.927
40	2.131	207	cotton – card room, others, undefined	32	1.647	0.679	13,387	0.843	0.740
41	2.135	182	bakers, confectioners (dealers)	53	1.853	0.836	18,449	0.857	0.825
42	2.138	220	paper and stationery manfre	28	1.585	0.741	2,814	—	—
43	2.181	157	cotton – spinning processes	40	1.698	0.687	10,637	0.944	0.833
44	2.182	221	cardboard box makers	34	1.652	0.757	3,904	—	—
45	2.185	163	hosiery manfre	44	1.749	0.685	7,022	0.928	0.794
46	2.223	155	others in printing	49	1.797	0.663	2,749	0.865	0.710
47	2.225	228	straw hat, plait, bonnet manfre	47	1.788	0.804	3,509	—	—
48	2.242	215	other females in agriculture	37	1.690	0.753	4,000	—	—
49	2.259	216	metals, machines, jewellery, sc. instruments	43	1.740	0.770	16,670	—	—
50	2.260	177	butchers, meat salespersons	62	1.993	0.859	7,307	0.952	0.928
51	2.263	213	laundry workers, washerwomen	46	1.786	0.789	47,697	—	—
52	2.282	212	charwomen	54	1.856	0.813	37,441	—	—
53	2.298	164	lace manf're	48	1.792	0.730	6,265	1.111	1.040
54	2.300	153	saddlers, harness makers	58	1.925	0.854	1,561	0.902	0.920
55	2.316	175	milksellers, dairywomen	61	1.983	0.920	4,055	0.902	0.970
56	2.353	170	tailors	57	1.918	0.756	21,334	0.881	0.816
57	2.373	172	boot, shoe makers	60	1.972	0.726	9,416	0.829	0.724
58	2.382	184	greengrocers, fruiterers	59	1.947	0.756	9,465	0.923	0.854
59	2.401	148	fishmongers, poulterers	56	1.905	0.792	4,346	0.906	0.904
60	2.432	234	glove makers	55	1.874	0.770	2,326	—	—
61	2.435	240	rag – gatherers, dealers	50	1.828	0.751	1,651	—	—
62	2.455	151	rubber, gutta percha workers	63	2.015	0.686	1,087	0.742	0.620
63	2.472	190	barpersons	66	2.198	0.750	1,236	0.562	0.474
64	2.653	224	canvas, sailcloth, sacking, net manfre	51	1.829	0.689	1,768	—	—
65	2.654	145	china, pottery manf're	64	2.074	0.656	7,601	0.902	0.757
66	2.709	198	costermongers, hawkers	65	2.119	0.776	7,713	0.892	0.885

APPENDIX H

Estimate of the scale of effect of differing infant mortality levels on reported fertility after 7.5 years of marriage

If it is assumed that the 1911 low-fertility occupations generally exhibited infant mortality rates (IMRs) of approximately 50 per thousand (see Appendix E) while the pre-1837 population exhibited a typical level of 150 per thousand (see Wrigley and Schofield, *Population history*, Table 7.19), the following simple calculation demonstrates the maximum likely scale of the effect of this difference in infant mortality on recorded fertility over the first 7.5 years of marriage.

The calculation is based on the following further assumptions.

(i) That both populations breast-fed for a full twelve months, giving the same exposure to the effect of lactational amenorrhoea.

(ii) That all the infant mortality occurred at the beginning of the first year of life. This is, of course, grossly unrealistic but it simplifies the calculation. As it will bias the outcome so as to overestimate the extent of the infant mortality effect, it does not call into question the conclusion reported in the text that the effect is exceedingly small; indeed, it substantially strengthens that conclusion.

(iii) According to Bongaarts's summary of the available evidence, twelve months' breast-feeding increases the period of postpartum infertility by an average of eight months (see above, ch. 8, n. 57). It has therefore been set in the calculation below that the birth interval is eight months shorter among those experiencing an infant death.

(iv) In setting the typical birth intervals for those experiencing and those not experiencing an infant death, the findings of Chris Wilson on the pre-1837 parish register reconstitution data have been used as a guide. Wilson has found that average birth intervals were normally thirty months for those not experiencing an infant death and the average interval was reduced to twenty-two months following an infant death. These figures are derived from Figure 8.6 in Wilson, 'The proximate determinants of marital fertility in England 1600–1799'. This, therefore, is consistent with assumption (iii) and the findings reported by Bongaarts.

Calculation

(1A) A hypothetical population of 1,000 continually fecund women in which the IMR is 50/000 can be envisaged for the purposes of the calculation as two subpopulations:

(a) 950 whose average birth interval is 30 months
(b) 50 whose average birth interval is 22 months

(1B) Over 7.5 years of marriage (90 months), the average fertility of this population can be calculated as follows:
(a) 90/30 = 3.000; 3.000 × 950 = 2850.00 births
(b) 90/22 = 4.091; 4.091 × 50 = 204.55 births
(a) + (b) = 3054.55 births
Therefore average fertility is 3054.55/1,000 = 3.055 births per woman

(2A) A hypothetical population of 1,000 continually fecund women in which the IMR is 150/000 can be similarly envisaged as two subpopulations:
(a) 850 whose average birth interval is 30 months
(b) 150 whose average birth interval is 22 months

(2B) Over 7.5 years of marriage (90 months), the average fertility of this population can be similarly calculated:
(a) 90/30 = 3.000; 3.000 × 850 = 2550.00 births
(b) 90/22 = 4.091; 4.091 × 150 = 613.65 births
(a) + (b) = 3163.65 births
Therefore average fertility is 3163.65/1,000 = 3.164 births per woman

(3) Hence, on the above assumptions, the difference between the low IMR and the high IMR populations in their average fertility after 7.5 years of marriage is:
3.164 − 3.055 = 0.109 births per woman.

This last figure, 0.109, represents 3.445% of the fertility figure for the high IMR population (3.164).

Conclusion

Thus, according to this hypothetical calculation, the difference between the higher infant mortality rates prevailing in the pre-1837 parish register populations and those prevailing among the lower fertility occupations of 1911 would have accounted for the latter recording average fertility levels 3.45% lower than the former after 7.5 years of marriage. Given the assumptions made, this can be considered to be a maximum estimate of the scale of the effect.

Bibliography

Primary sources and unpublished work

Manuscript sources

Official papers
Public Record Office RG 19/1–123; RG26/1–94; RG29; MH 13.
Office of Population Census and Survey Departmental Archive.

Private papers
Beveridge Papers (London School of Economics and Political Science).
Carr-Saunders Papers (Wellcome Contemporary Medical Archives Centre).
Galton Papers (D.M.S. Watson Library, University College, London).
Mallet Papers (Wittersham House, Kent).
Pearson Papers (D.M.S. Watson Library, University College, London).

Official published papers

Annual Reports and Decennial Supplements of the Registrar-General, 1837–1919.
Censuses of England and Wales, 1841–1931.
Report of the Committee Appointed by the Treasury to Inquire into Certain Questions Connected with the Taking of the Census (with Minutes of Evidence and Appendices), PP 1890 LVIII.
Royal Commission on Physical Training (Scotland), PP 1903 XXX, Cd 1507 (Report); Cd 1508 (Evidence).
Interdepartmental Committee on Physical Deterioration, PP 1904 XXXII, Cd 2175 (Report); Cd 2210 (Evidence).
Census of Ireland, 1911, General Report, PP 1912–13 CXVIII.
Census of Scotland, 1911, Vol. III, PP 1914 XLIV.
Census 1911, Vol. XIII, *Fertility of Marriage Report*, Part 1, PP 1917–18 XXXV, Cd 8678.
Census 1911, Vol. XIII, *Fertility of Marriage Report*, Part 2, (HMSO 1923), Cd 8491.
Registrar-General's Statistical Review of England and Wales, 1920–39.
Final Report of the Royal Commission on Venereal Diseases, PP 1916 XVI, Cd 8189.
Lewis-Faning, E., *Report on an Enquiry into Family Limitation and its Influence on Human Fertility during the Past Fifty Years*, Papers of the Royal Commission on Population, Vol. I (HMSO 1949).

Report of the Royal Commission on Population, PP 1948–9 XIX, Cd 7695 (1949); and Papers, 6 volumes (HMSO 1949–54).

Unpublished secondary sources

Belfiore, G. M., 'Family strategies in Essex textile towns 1860–95: the challenge of compulsory elementary schooling' (DPhil thesis, University of Oxford 1987).
Benson, B., 'Mortality variation in the North of England 1851–60 to 1901–10' (PhD thesis, Johns Hopkins University 1980).
Brändström, A., 'Medical professionalisation and its value as an explanatory tool. Midwifery in nineteenth century Sweden' (unpublished mimeo. paper to workshop on 'The state of social history of medicine today' held at University of Essex, 8–9 January 1993).
Dasgupta, P., 'The population problem', paper prepared for Population Summit of the World's Scientific Academies, New Delhi, India, 24–7 October 1993.
Dowling, W. C., 'The Ladies Sanitary Association and the origins of the health visiting service' (MA thesis, University of London 1963).
Dupree, M., 'Family structure in the Staffordshire Potteries 1840–1900' (DPhil thesis, University of Oxford 1981).
Gittins, D., 'The decline of family size and differential fertility in the 1930s' (MA thesis, University of Essex 1974).
Hope, K., 'The political conception of merit' (unpublished typescript, 203pp., dated 1977).
Johansson, S., 'The demographic transition in Cornwall 1800–1900' (PhD thesis, University of California, Berkeley, 1974).
Johnson, P., 'Savings, fertility behaviour and economic development in nineteenth-century Britain and America', *CEPR Discussion Paper* 203 (Centre for Economic Policy Research 1987).
Kabir, M., 'Multivariate study of reduction in child mortality in England and Wales as a factor influencing the fall in fertility' (PhD thesis, University of London 1979).
Kemmer, D., 'The marital fertility of Edinburgh professionals in the later nineteenth century' (PhD thesis, University of Edinburgh 1989).
Millward, R., and Sheard, S., 'Government expenditure on social overheads and the infrastructure in England and Wales, 1870–1914', University of Manchester Working Papers in Economic and Social History No. 23 (1993).
Szreter, S. R. S., 'The decline of marital fertility in England and Wales', (PhD thesis, University of Cambridge 1984).
Tosh, J., 'Fatherhood and middle-class masculinity in Victorian England', paper given to the Second Carleton Conference on the Family, Ottawa, May 1994.
Walker, S. P., 'Occupational expansion, fertility decline and recruitment to the professions in Scotland, 1850–1914 (with special reference to the Chartered accountants of Edinburgh)' (PhD thesis, University of Edinburgh 1986).
Watkins, D. E. (now D. Porter), 'The English revolution in social medicine' (PhD thesis, University of London 1984).
Wilkinson, A. (now A. Hardy), 'The beginnings of disease control in London: the work of the medical officers in three parishes 1856–1900' (DPhil thesis, University of Oxford 1980).
Williams, P. (now Thane, P.), 'The development of old age pensions in Great Britain 1878–1925' (PhD thesis, University of London 1970).
Wilson, J. F., Sheard, S., and Millward, R., 'Trends in local authority loan expenditure in England and Wales 1870–1914', University of Manchester Working Papers in Economic and Social History No. 22 (1993).
Wooldridge, A., 'Child study and educational psychology in England, 1880–1950' (DPhil thesis, University of Oxford 1985).

Yeo, E., 'Social science and social change: a social history of some aspects of social science and social investigation in Britain 1830–90' (PhD thesis, University of Sussex 1972).
Young, R. K. F. J., 'Sanitary administration under the L.G.B. 1871–88' (BLitt thesis, University of Oxford 1964).

Principal works of reference

Aldrich, R., and Gordon, P., *Dictionary of British educationists* (1989).
Bullock, A., and Stallybrass, O., *The Fontana dictionary of modern thought* (1986).
Bullock, A., and Woodings, R. B., *The Fontana dictionary of modern thinkers* (1983).
Bynum, W. F., Browne, E. J., and Porter, R., *Macmillan Dictionary of the history of science* (1981).
Cook, C., and Stevenson, J., *The Longman handbook of modern British history 1714–1980* (1983).
Dictionary of National Biography.
Drabble, M. (ed.), *The Oxford companion to English literature* (5th edn, Oxford 1985).
Encyclopaedia Britannica, The (11th edn, 1910–11).
Kuper, A., and Kuper, J. (eds.), *The social science encyclopaedia* (1985).
Munk's *Roll of the Royal College of Physicians of London*.
Palmer, A., *The Penguin dictionary of twentieth-century history, 1900–1982* (1983).
Plarr's *Lives of the Royal College of Surgeons of England*.
Who was who

Secondary sources

ABBREVIATIONS
AHR American Historical Review
BHM Bulletin of the History of Medicine
CJE Cambridge Journal of Economics
CSSH Comparative Studies in Society and History
EcHR Economic History Review
EHR English Historical Review
FR Feminist Review
FS Feminist Studies
G&H Gender and History
HJ Historical Journal
HW History Workshop
INED Institut National d'Etudes Démographiques
IUSSP International Union for the Scientific Study of Population
JFH Journal of Family History
JHI Journal of the History of Ideas
JIH Journal of Interdisciplinary History
JRSS Journal of the Royal Statistical Society
JSH Journal of Social History
JSSL Journal of the Statistical Society of London
OH Oral History
PDR Population and Development Review
PI Population Index
P&P Past and Present
PS Population Studies
SH Social History

SHM Social History of Medicine
SR Sociological Review
VS Victorian Studies

Place of publication is London unless otherwise stated.

Abrams, P., *The origins of British sociology 1834–1914* (Chicago 1968).
Ackernecht, E. H., 'Hygiene in France, 1815–48' *BHM* 22 (1948), 117–55.
Medicine at the Paris Hospital (Baltimore 1967).
Alexander, S., 'Women, class and sexual differences in the 1830s and 1840s' *HW* 17 (1984), 125–49.
Alford, B. W. E., *British economic performance 1945–75* (1988).
Allen, G. A., *Thomas Hunt Morgan: the man and his science* (Princeton 1978).
Anderson, B., *Imagined communities* (1983; revised edn 1991).
Anderson, M., *Family structure in nineteenth century Lancashire* (Cambridge 1971).
'Household structure and the industrial revolution: mid-nineteenth century Preston in comparative perspective', in P. Laslett and R. Wall (eds.) *Household and family in past time* (Cambridge 1972), 215–35.
Anderson, M., and Morse, D. J., 'High fertility, high emigration, low nuptiality: adjustment processes in Scotland's demographic experience, 1861–1914', Parts I and II, *PS* 47 (1993), 5–25; 319–43.
Anderson, M. J., *The American census: a social history* (1988).
Anderson, O., *Suicide in Victorian and Edwardian England* (Oxford 1987).
Anderton, D. L. and Bean, L. L., 'Birth spacing and fertility limitation: a behavioral analysis of a nineteenth century frontier population' *Demography* 22 (1985), 169–83.
Andorka, R., 'Family reconstitution and types of household structure', in J. Sundin and E. Söderland (eds.), *Time, space and man: essays in microdemography* (Stockholm 1979), 11–33.
'La Prévention des naissances en Hongrie dans la région Ormansang depuis la fin du XVIIIe siècle' *Population* 26 (1971), 63–78.
Annan, N. G., *The curious strength of Positivism in English political thought* (1959).
'The intellectual aristocracy', in J. H. Plumb (ed.), *Studies in social history* (1955; reprinted New York 1969), 241–87.
Leslie Stephen: his thought and character in relation to his time (1951).
Ansell Jr, C., *On the rate of mortality at early periods of life, the age at marriage, the number of children to a marriage, the length of generation, and other statistics of families in the upper and professional classes* (1874).
Arensburg, C. M., and Kimball, S. T., *Family and community in Ireland* (1940; 2nd edn 1965).
Ariès, P., *L'Enfant et la vie familiale sous l'ancien régime* (Paris 1960); translated by R. Baldick as *Centuries of childhood* (1962).
Arnold, M., 'A French Eton', Pt I, *Macmillan's Magazine* 8 (1863), 353–62; Pt II, *Macmillan's Magazine* 9 (1863–4), 343–55.
Arthur, W. B., and McNicoll, G., 'An analytical survey of population and development in Bangladesh' *PDR* 4 (1978), 23–80.
Atkin, P. J., 'White poison? The social consequences of milk consumption' *SHM* 5 (1992), 207–27.
Bailey, P., 'Parasexuality and glamour: the Victorian barmaid as cultural prototype' *G&H* 2 (1990), 148–72.
'"Will the real Bill Banks please stand up?" Towards a role analysis of mid-Victorian working-class respectability' *JSH* 12 (1978), 336–53.
Balfour, T. G., 'Inaugural address' (untitled) *JRSS* 51 (1888), 683–700.
Ball, S., *The moral aspects of socialism*, Fabian Tract 72 (1896).
Bamford, T. W., *The rise of the public schools* (1967).

Banks, J. A., *Prosperity and parenthood. A study of family planning among the Victorian middle classes* (1954).

'The social structure of England as seen through the census', in R. Lawton (ed.), *The census and social structure* (1978), 173–223.

Victorian values, secularism and the size of families (1981).

Banks, J. A., and Banks, O., *Feminism and family planning in Victorian England* (Liverpool 1964).

Banks, O., *The biographical dictionary of British feminists*, 2 vols. (Brighton 1985–90).

Faces of feminism: a study of feminism as a social movement (Oxford 1981).

Parity and prestige in English secondary education. A study in educational sociology (1955).

Banton, M., 'Analytical and folk concepts of race and ethnicity' *Ethnic and Racial Studies* 2 (1979), 127–38.

The idea of race (1977).

Barker Benfield, G. J., *The horror of the half-known life. Male attitudes towards women and sexuality in nineteenth century America* (New York 1976).

'The spermatic economy; a metabolic view of sexuality' *FS* 1 (1972), 45–74.

Barnes, D., *Scientific knowledge and sociological theory* (1974).

Barret-Ducrocq, F. (transl. J. Howe), *Love in the time of Victoria. Sexuality, class and gender in nineteenth-century London* (1991).

Barrett, J. C., and Marshall, J., 'The risk of conception on different days of the menstrual cycle' *PS* 23 (1969), 455–61.

Bartrip, P., 'Expertise and the dangerous trades, 1875–1900', in MacLeod (ed.), *Government and expertise*, 89–109.

Bean, L. L., Mineau, G. P., and Anderton, D. L., *Fertility change on the American frontier: adaptation and innovation* (Berkeley 1990).

Beaud, J-P., and Prévost, J-G., 'La Classification canadienne des occupations pendant l'entre-deux-guerres: réflexion sur un cas d'indépendance statistique' *Canadian Journal of Political Science/Revue canadienne de science politique* 25 (1992), 489–512.

Bebbington, D. W., *Evangelicalism in modern Britain. A history from the 1730s to the 1890s* (1989).

Becker, G. S., 'An economic analysis of fertility', *Universities-national bureau committee for economic research* (Princeton 1960), 209–31.

A treatise on the family (Cambridge, Mass., 1981; 2nd edn 1991).

Beddoe, J., *The races of Britain: a contribution to the anthropology of western Europe* (Bristol 1885).

Beeton, I. A., *The book of household management* (1st edn 1861).

Behlmer, G. K., *Child abuse and moral reform in England, 1870–1908* (Stanford 1982).

Bell, (Lady) F., *At the works. A study of a manufacturing town* (1985; originally published 1907).

Bellamy, C., *Administering local–central relations 1871–1919. The Local Government Board in its fiscal and cultural context* (Manchester 1988).

Beller, S., *Vienna and the Jews 1867–1938. A cultural history* (Cambridge 1989).

Benn, J. M., *The predicaments of love* (1992).

Bennett, J., 'Feminism and history' *G&H* 1 (1989), 251–72.

Benson, J., *British coalminers in the nineteenth century: a social history* (New York 1980).

The penny capitalists. A study of nineteenth-century working-class entrepreneurs (1983).

The working class in Britain, 1850–1939 (1989).

Bernstein, B., 'Class and pedagogies; visible and invisible', in Karabel and Halsey (eds.), *Power and ideology*, 511–34.

'Social class, language and socialisation', in Karabel and Halsey (eds.), *Power and ideology*, 473–86.

Bertillon, J., *Cours élémentaire de statistique administrative* (Société d'études scientifiques, Paris 1895).

Beveridge, W. H., 'The fall of fertility among the European races' *Economica* 5 (1925), 10–27.

'Mr Keynes' evidence for overpopulation' *Economica* 4 (1924), 1–20.

'Population and unemployment' *Economic Journal* 33 (1923), 447–75; with reply from J. M. Keynes, 476–86.

Unemployment. A problem of industry (1909).

Bhaskar, R., *The possibility of naturalism* (Brighton 1979).

A realist theory of science (2nd edn, Brighton 1978).

Biagini, E., 'British trade unions and popular political economy 1860–1880' *HJ* 30 (1987), 811–40.

Liberty, retrenchment and reform. Popular liberalism in the age of Gladstone 1860–80 (Cambridge 1992).

Biagini, E., and Reid, A. J. (eds.), *Currents of radicalism. Popular radicalism, organised labour and party politics in Britain, 1850–1914* (Cambridge 1991).

Bill, E. G. W., and Mason, J. F. A., *Christ Church and Reform 1850–1867* (Oxford 1970).

Blake, J., 'Are babies consumer durables?' *PS* 22 (1968), 5–26.

'The fertility transition: continuity or disconuity with the past?', in *IUSSP International population conference, Florence 1985* Vol. IV (Liège: IUSSP 1985), 393–405.

'Income and reproductive motivation' *PS* 21 (1967), 185–206.

Bland, L., '"Cleansing the portals of life": the venereal disease campaign in the early twentieth century', in M. Langan and B. Schwarz (eds.), *Crises in the British state 1880–1930* (1985), 192–208.

'Feminist vigilantes of late-Victorian England', in C. Smart (ed.), *Regulating womanhood. Historical essays on marriage, motherhood, and sexuality* (1992), 33–52.

'Marriage laid bare: middle-class women and marital sex, c. 1880–1914', in Lewis (ed.), *Labour and love*, 123–46.

'The married woman, the "New Woman" and the feminist sexual politics of the 1890s', in J. Rendall (ed.), *Women's politics 1800–1914* (Oxford 1987), 141–64.

Blaug, M., *Economic theory in retrospect* (3rd edn, Cambridge 1983).

Bledsoe, C., 'The politics of children: fosterage and the social management of fertility among the Mende', in Handwerker (ed.), *Births and power*, 81–100.

Bledsoe, C., and Isiugo-Abanihe, U., 'Strategies of child fosterage among Mende grannies in Sierra Leone', in R. Lesthaeghe (ed.), *Reproduction and social organisation in sub-Saharan Africa* (Berkeley 1989), 442–74.

Bloch, I., *The sexual life of our time in its relation to modern civilisation*, transl. from the 6th German edition by M. Eden Paul (1908).

Bloch, J. M., 'Rousseau and Helvétius or innate and acquired traits: the final stages of the Rousseau–Helvétius controversy' *JHI* 40 (1979), 21–42.

Bolin-Hort, P., *Work, family and the state: child labour and the organisation of production in the British cotton industry, 1780–1920* (Lund 1989).

Boltanski, L., *The making of a class. Cadres in French society*, transl. A. Goldhammer, (Cambridge 1987).

Boner, H., *Hungry generations* (New York 1955).

Bonfield, L., Smith, R. M., and Wrightson, K. (eds.), *The world we have gained. Histories of population and social structure* (Oxford 1986).

Bongaarts, J., 'The proximate determinants of natural marital fertility', in R. A. Bulatao and R. D. Lee (eds.), *Determinants of fertility in developing countries*, vol. I (1983), 103–38.

Booth, C., 'Enumeration and classification of paupers and state pensions for the aged' *JRSS* 54 (1891), 600–43.

'Inhabitants of Tower Hamlets' *JRSS* 50 (1887), 326–401.

Life and labour of the people in London, Series 2, 10 vols. (1892–7).

Life and labour of the people. Series 3, 17 vols. (1902).

'Occupations of the people of the United Kingdom, 1801–81' *JSSL* 49 (1886), 314–435;

436–44 ('Discussion').
Old age pensions and the aged poor: a proposal (1899).
Pauperism, a picture: and the endowment of old age, an argument (1892).
(ed.) *Life and labour of the people,* Series 1, 2 vols. (1889). Vol. I East London; Vol. II London continued. (Note that Vol. II of Series 1 is confusingly titled *Labour and life of the people.*).
Booth, W. (and W. T. Stead), *In darkest England and the way out* (1890).
Borell, M., 'Biologists and the promotion of birth control research, 1918–1938' *Journal of the History of Biology* 20 (1987), 51–87.
Bornat, J., 'Lost leaders: women, trade unionism and the case of the General Union of Textile Workers 1875–1914', in John (ed.), *Unequal opportunities,* 207–33.
Bosanquet, B. (ed.), *Aspects of the social problem* (1895).
Bott, E., *Family and social network: roles, norms and external relationships in ordinary urban families* (1957; 2nd edn 1971).
Bourdieu, P., 'Cultural reproduction and social reproduction', in Karabel and Halsey (eds.), *Power and ideology,* 486–510.
Outline of a theory of practice, transl. R. Nice (Cambridge 1977).
Bourgeois-Pichat, J., 'The general development of the population of France since the eighteenth century', in Glass and Eversley (eds.), *Population in history,* 474–506.
Bourke, J., 'Housewifery in working-class England' *P&P* 143 (1994), 167–97.
Working-class cultures in Britain, 1890–1960 (1994).
Bourne, J. M., *Patronage and society in nineteenth century England* (1986).
Bowlby, J., *Child care and the growth of love* (Harmondsworth 1953).
Bowler, P. J., *Evolution. The history of an idea* (revised edn, Berkeley 1989).
'Holding your head up high: degeneration and orthogenesis in theories of human evolution', in J. R. Moore (ed.), *History, humanity and evolution. Essays for John C. Greene* (Cambridge 1989), 329–54.
Bowley, A. L., 'The improvement of official statistics' *JRSS* 71 (1908), 459–95.
The nature and purpose of the measurement of social phenomena (1915).
Bracher, M., 'Breastfeeding, lactational infecundity, contraception and the spacing of births: implications of the Bellagio consensus statement' *Health Transition Review* 2 (1992), 19–47.
Bradley, H., *Men's work, women's work* (Oxford 1989).
Branca, P., *Silent sisterhood. Middle-class women in the Victorian home* (1975).
Brand, J. L., *Doctors and the state. The British medical profession and government action in public health, 1870–1912* (Baltimore 1965).
Brandt, A., *No magic bullet: a social history of venereal disease in the United States since 1880* (Oxford 1987).
Brewer, J., *The sinews of power. War, money and the English state, 1688–1783* (1989).
Brewer, J., and Porter, R. (eds.), *Consumption and the world of goods,* vol. I (1993).
Brian, E., *La Mesure de l'Etat* (Paris 1994).
Briggs, A., 'The language of "class" in early nineteenth-century England', in A. Briggs and J. Saville (eds.), *Essays in labour history* (1960) 43–73.
Social thought and social action: a study of the work of Seebohm Rowntree (1961).
Bristow, E. J., *Vice and vigilance. Purity movements in Britain since 1700* (Dublin 1977).
Brookes, B., *Abortion in England 1900–1967* (1988).
'Women and reproduction *c.* 1860–1919', in Lewis (ed.), *Labour and love,* 149–71.
Brown, J., 'Charles Booth and labour colonies 1889–1905' *EcHR* 21 (1968), 349–60.
Brown, J. W., Greenwood, M. and Wood, F., 'The fertility of the English middle classes. A statistical study' *Eugenics Review* 12 (1920–1), 158–211.
Brown, K. D., *John Burns* (1977).
Brown, L., *The Board of Trade and the Free Trade movement* (Oxford 1958).

Brown, P., *The body and society: men, women, and sexual renunciation in early Christianity* (New York 1988).

Brownlee, J., 'The history of birth and death rates in England and Wales taken as a whole from 1570 to the present time' *Public Health* 29 (1915–16), 211–22; 228–38.

Brundage, A., *England's Prussian Minister: Edwin Chadwick and the politics of government growth* (1988).

Bryder, L., *Below the magic mountain. A social history of tuberculosis in twentieth-century Britain* (Oxford 1988).

Buer, M. C., *Health, wealth and population in the early days of the industrial revolution* (1926).

Bulmer, M., 'The development of sociology and of empirical social research', in Bulmer (ed.), *Essays in the history*, 3–36.

(ed.), *Essays in the history of British sociological research* (Cambridge 1985).

(ed.), *Mining and social change* (1978).

Burawoy, M., *Manufacturing consent* (Chicago 1979).

The politics of production (1985).

Burke, P., *History and social theory* (Oxford 1992).

Burman, S. (ed.), *Fit work for women* (1979).

Burnett, J. (ed.), *Destiny obscure: autobiographies of childhood, education and family from the 1820s to the 1920s* (Harmondsworth 1982).

Burns, A. F., and Mitchell, W. C., *Measuring business cycles* (1946).

Burrow, J. W., *Evolution and society* (Cambridge 1966).

Busfield, J., and Paddon, M., *Thinking about children. Sociology and fertility in post-war England* (Cambridge 1977).

Butterfield, H., *The Whig interpretation of history* (1931).

Bynum, W. F., 'Darwin and the doctors: evolution, diathesis, and germs in nineteenth-century Britain' *Gesnerus* 40 (1983), 43–53.

Bythell, D., *The sweated trades: outwork in nineteenth-century Britain* (1978).

Cain, M., 'The economic activities of children in a village in Bangladesh' *PDR* 3 (1977), 201–27.

'The household life cycle and economic mobility in Bangladesh' *PDR* 4 (1978), 421–38.

Caine, B., *Victorian feminists* (Oxford 1992).

Cairnes, J. E., *Some leading principles of political economy, newly expounded* (1874).

Caldwell, J. C., *Theory of fertility decline* (1982).

'Towards a restatement of demographic transition theory' *PDR* 2 (1976), 321–66.

Caldwell, J. C., and Caldwell, P., 'The cultural context of high fertility in sub-Saharan Africa' *PDR* 13 (1987), 409–37.

Limiting population growth and the Ford foundation contribution (1986).

'The role of marital sexual abstinence in determining fertility: a study of the Yoruba in Nigeria' *PS* 31 (1977), 193–217.

Caldwell, J. C., Hill, A. G., and Hull, V. J. (eds.), *Micro-approaches to demographic research* (1988).

Caldwell, J. C., Orubuloye, I. R., and Caldwell, P., 'Fertility decline in Africa: a new type of transition?' *PDR* 18 (1992), 211–42.

Calhoun, C. J., 'Community: towards a variable conceptualisation for comparative research' *SH* 5 (1980), 105–29.

Cantlie, J., *Degeneration amongst Londoners* (1885).

Physical efficiency (1906).

Caradog Jones, D. 'Some notes on the census of occupations for England and Wales' *JRSS* 78 (1915), 55–78; 78–81 ('Discussion').

Carballo, M., Cleland, J., Carael, M., and Albrecht, G., 'A cross national study of patterns of sexual behaviour' *Journal of Sex Research* 26 (1989), 287–99.

Carlsson, G., 'The decline of fertility: innovation or adjustment process', *PS* 20 (1966), 149–74.

Carr-Saunders, A. M., 'Differential fertility', in M. Sanger (ed.), *Proceedings of the world population conference, Geneva* (1927), 130–42.

The population problem (Oxford 1922).

Carr-Saunders, A. M., and Jones, D. C., *A survey of the social structure of England and Wales* (Oxford 1927).

Cartwright, N., *How the laws of physics lie* (Oxford 1983).

Cashdollar, C. D., *The transformation of theology, 1830–1890: Positivism and Protestant thought in Britain and America* (Princeton 1989).

Chadwick, E., *Report on the sanitary condition of the labouring population of Great Britain* (Edinburgh 1965; originally published 1842).

Chamberlin, J. E., and Gilman, S. L. (eds.), *Degeneration: the dark side of progress* (New York 1985).

Chandrasekhar, S., *'A dirty, filthy book': the writings of Charles Knowlton and Annie Besant on reproductive physiology and birth control and an account of the Bradlaugh–Besant trial* (1981).

Chapman, S. J., and Abbott, W., 'The tendency of children to enter their fathers' trades' *JRSS* 76 (1913), 599–604.

Chapman, S. J., and Marquis, F. J., 'The recruiting of the employing classes from the ranks of the wage-earners in the cotton industry' *JRSS* 75 (1912), 293–306.

Charbit, Y., *Du Malthusianisme au populationnisme. Les économistes français et la population 1840–70* (INED, Travaux et documents no. 90, Paris 1981).

Charles, E., *The practice of birth control: an analysis of the birth control experiences of nine hundred women* (1932).

The twilight of parenthood. A biological study of the decline of population growth (1934).

Chesnais, J.-C., *La Transition démographique* (INED, Travaux et documents no. 113, Paris 1986); translated by E. Kreager and P. Kreager as *The demographic transition. Stages, patterns and economic implications* (Oxford 1993).

Chesser, E., *The sexual, marital and family relationships of the English woman* (1956).

Childs, M. J., *Labour's apprentices: working-class lads in late Victorian and Edwardian England* (1992).

Chinn, C., *They worked all their lives. Women of the urban poor in England, 1880–1939* (Manchester 1988).

Chodorow, N., *The reproduction of mothering: psychoanalysis and the sociology of gender* (Berkeley 1978).

Clapham, J. H., *An economic history of modern Britain. Volume I The early railway age 1820–50* (Cambridge 1926).

Clark, A., 'The rhetoric of Chartist domesticity: gender, language and class in the 1830s and 1840s' *Journal of British Studies* 31 (1992), 62–88.

Clark, G. K., '"Statesmen in disguise": reflections on the history of the neutrality of the civil service' *HJ* 2 (1959), 19–39.

Clarke, P. F., *Lancashire and the New Liberalism* (Cambridge 1971).

Liberals and social democrats (Cambridge 1978).

Clegg, H. A., Fox, A., and Thompson, A. F., *A history of British trade unions since 1889. Vol. I 1889–1910* (Oxford 1964).

Cleland, J., and Wilson, C., 'Demand theories of the fertility transition: an iconoclastic view' *PS* 41 (1987), 5–30.

Coale, A. J., 'Age patterns of marriage' *PS* 25 (1971), 193–214.

'The demographic transition reconsidered', in *International population conference, Liège*, Vol. I (Liège: IUSSP 1973), 53–72.

'Factors associated with the development of low fertility: an historic survey', in *Proceedings of the World Population Conference, Belgrade 1965*, Vol. II (UN, New York 1967), 205–9.

'T. R. Malthus and the population trend of his day and ours' *Encyclopaedia Britannica Lecture, 1978* (Edinburgh 1978).

'The voluntary control of human fertility' *Proceedings of the American Philosophical Society* 111 (1967), 164–9.

Coale, A. J., and Hoover, E. M., *Population growth and economic development in low-income countries* (Oxford 1958).

Coale, A. J., and Trussell, T. J., 'Model fertility schedules: variations in age structure of child-bearing in human populations' *PI* 40 (1974), 205–58; and 'Erratum', *PI* 41 (1975), 572.

'Technical note: finding the two parameters that specify a model schedule of marital fertility' *PI* 44 (1978), 203–13.

Coale, A. J., and Watkins, S. C. (eds.), *The decline of fertility in Europe* (Princeton 1986).

Cockburn, C., *Brothers: male dominance and technological change* (1983).

Cocks, E., 'The Malthusian theory in pre-civil war America, an original relation to the universe' *PS* 20 (1967), 343–63.

Coghlan, T. A., *The decline of the birth rate of New South Wales and other phenomena of child birth* (Government Printer, Sydney 1903).

Cohen, D. A., 'Private lives in public spaces: Marie Stopes, the Mothers' Clinics and the practice of contraception' *HW* 35 (1993), 95–116.

Coleman, D. A., and Salt, J., *The British population: patterns, trends and processes* (Oxford 1993).

Coleman, S., *Family planning in Japanese society: traditional birth control in a modern urban culture* (Princeton 1983).

Coleman, W., *Death is a social disease. Public health and political economy in early industrial France* (Madison 1982).

Georges Cuvier, zoologist: a study in the history of evolution theory (Cambridge, Mass., 1964).

Colley, L., *Britons. Forging the nation 1707–1837* (1992).

Collini, S., *Arnold* (Oxford 1988).

'Hobhouse, Bosanquet and the state: philosophical idealism and political argument in England, 1880–1918' *P&P* 72 (1976), 86–111.

Liberalism and sociology (Cambridge 1979).

Public moralists. Political thought and intellectual life in Britain 1850–1930 (Oxford 1991).

Collini, S., Winch, D., and Burrow, J., *That noble science of politics* (Cambridge 1983).

Cominos, P. T., 'Late-Victorian sexual respectability and the social system' *International Review of Social History* 8 (1963), 18–48.

Conk (now Anderson), M., *The United States census and labor force change. A history of occupation statistics 1870–1940* (Ann Arbor 1978).

Connell, K. H., *The population of Ireland 1750–1845* (Oxford 1950).

Cooter, R. (ed.), *In the name of the child. Health and welfare 1880–1940* (1992).

Corbin, A., *Women for hire: prostitution and sexuality in France after 1850*, transl. A. Sheridan (Cambridge, Mass., 1990).

Corfield, P. J., 'Class by name and number in eighteenth-century Britain' *History* 72 (1987), 38–61.

(ed.), *Language, history and class* (Oxford, 1991).

Corrigan, P., and Sayer, D., *The great arch. English state formation as cultural revolution* (Oxford 1985; revised edn 1991).

Cowan, R. S., 'Nature and nurture: the interplay of biology and politics in the work of Francis Galton' *Studies in the History of Biology* 1 (1977), 133–208.

Crafts, N. F. R., 'British industrialisation in international context' *JIH* 19 (1989), 415–28.

'Duration of marriage, fertility and women's employment opportunities in England and Wales in 1911' *PS* 43 (1989), 325–35.

Craig, F. W. S., *British electoral facts 1832–1987* (1989).

Crombie, A. C., *Styles of scientific thinking in the European tradition: the history of argument and explanation especially in the mathematical and biomedical sciences and arts*, 3 vols. (1994).

Cronin, J. E., *The politics of state expansion: war, state and society in twentieth-century Britain* (1991).

Crook, R., '"Tidy women": women in the Rhondda between the wars' *OH* 10 (1982), 40–6.
Crossick, G., *An artisan elite in Victorian society. Kentish London 1840–80* (1978).
'From gentlemen to the residuum: languages of social description in Victorian Britain', in P. J. Corfield (ed.), *Language, history and class* (Oxford 1991), 150–78.
(ed.), *The lower middle class in Britain 1870–1914* (1977).
Crossick, G., and Haupt, H.-G. (eds.), *Shopkeepers and master artisans in nineteenth-century Europe* (1984).
Crowther, M. A., *The workhouse system 1834–1929* (1981).
Crowther, M. A., and White, B. M., 'Medicine, property and the law in Britain 1800–1914' *HJ* 31 (1988), 853–70.
Crozier, D., 'Kinship and occupational succession' *SR* 13 (1965), 15–43.
Cruikshank, M., *Children and industry. Child health and welfare in north-west textile towns during the nineteenth century* (Manchester 1981).
Cullen, M. J., 'The making of the Civil Registration Act of 1836' *Journal of Ecclesiastical History* 25 (1974), 39–59.
The statistical movement in early Victorian Britain (Hassocks 1975).
Cunningham, A. R., 'The "New Woman Fiction" of the 1890s' *VS* 17 (1973), 177–86.
Curtin, P. D., *The image of Africa: British ideas and action 1780–1850*, 2 vols. (Wisconsin 1964).
D'Aeth, J. W., 'Present tendencies of class differentiation' *SR* 3 (1910), 267–76.
D'Arcy, F., 'The Malthusian League and the resistance to birth control propaganda in late Victorian Britain' *PS* 31 (1977), 429–48.
Darley, G., *Octavia Hill* (1990).
Darwin, C., *The descent of man* (1871).
The origin of species by means of natural selection (1859).
Dasgupta, P., *An inquiry into well-being and destitution* (Oxford 1993).
Daunton, M. J., *Royal Mail* (1985).
Davenport-Hines, R., *Sex, death and punishment. Attitudes to sex and sexuality in Britain since the Renaissance* (1990).
Davey, C., 'Birth control in Britain during the interwar years: evidence from the Stopes correspondence' *JFH* 13 (1988), 329–45.
David, P. A., *Technical choice, innovation and economic growth* (Cambridge 1975).
David, P. A., and Mroz, T. A., 'Evidence of fertility regulation among rural French villagers, 1749–1789' *European Journal of Population* 5 (1989), 1–26.
David, P. A., and Sanderson, W. C., 'The emergence of a two-child norm among American birth-controllers' *PDR* 13 (1987), 1–41.
'Rudimentary contraceptive methods and the American transition to marital fertility control 1855–1915', in S. L. Engerman and R. E. Gallman (eds.), *Long term factors in American economic growth* (Chicago 1986), 307–79.
Davidoff, L., *The best circles. Society, etiquette and the season* (1973).
'Class and gender in Victorian England', in Newton *et al.* (eds.), *Sex and class*, 17–71.
'Mastered for life: servant and wife in Victorian and Edwardian England' *JSH* 8 (1974), 406–28.
'The separation of home and work? Landladies and lodgers in nineteenth and twentieth century England', in Burman (ed.), *Fit work for women*, 64–97.
Davidoff, L., and Hall, C., *Family fortunes. Men and women of the English middle class 1780–1850* (1987).
Davidson, R., *Whitehall and the Labour problem in late-Victorian and Edwardian Britain. A study in official statistics and social control* (1985).
Davidson, R., and Lowe, R., 'Bureaucracy and innovation in British welfare policy, 1870–1945', in W. J. Mommsen (ed.), *The emergence of the welfare state in Britain and Germany* (1981), 263–95.

Davies, C., 'The health visitor as mother's friend' *SHM* 1 (1988), 39–59.

Davin, A., 'Imperialism and motherhood' *HW* 5 (1978), 9–65.

Little women. The childhood of working-class girls in late nineteenth-century London (1993).

Davis, J., 'Jennings' Buildings and the Royal Borough. The construction of the underclass in mid-Victorian England', in Feldman and Stedman Jones (eds.), *Metropolis London*, 11–39.

Davis, John, *Reforming London. The London government problem 1855–1900* (Oxford 1988).

Davis, K., 'The world demographic transition' *Annals of the American Academy of Political and Social Science* 237 (1945), 1–11.

Davis, K., and Blake, J., 'Social structure and fertility: an analytic framework' *Economic Development and Cultural Change* 4 (1956), 211–35.

de Mause, L., (ed.), *The history of childhood* (1974).

Degler, C., *At odds. Women and the family in America from the Revolution to the present* (Oxford 1980).

'What ought to be and what was: women's sexuality in the nineteenth century' *AHR* 79 (1974), 1467–90.

Demeny, P., 'Social science and population policy' *PDR* 14 (1988), 451–769.

Dennis, N., Henriques, F., and Slaughter, C., *Coal is our life* (1956).

Dennis, R., *English industrial cities of the nineteenth century. A social geography* (Cambridge 1984).

Desmond, A., *The politics of evolution: morphology, medicine and reform in radical London* (1989).

Desrosières, A., *La Politique des grands nombres. Histoire de la raison statistique* (Paris 1993).

Devereux, G., *A study of abortion in primitive societies* (New York 1955).

Diamond, I., and Clarke, S., 'Demographic patterns among Britain's ethnic groups', in Joshi (ed.), *The changing population*, 177–98.

Dicey, A. V., *Law and public opinion in England during the nineteenth century* (1905).

Digby, A., *Making a medical living: doctors and patients in the English market for medicine 1720–1911* (Cambridge 1994).

Digby, E., 'The extinction of the Londoner' *Contemporary Review* 86 (1904), 115–26.

Donajgrodzki, A. P. (ed.), *Social control in nineteenth-century Britain* (1977).

Donzelot, J., *The policing of families* (New York 1979).

Drage, G., 'Alien immigration' *JRSS* 58 (1895), 1–35.

Drake, B., *Women in trade unions* (Labour Research Dept 1920).

Dublin, L. I., and Lotka, A. J., 'On the true rate of natural increase as exemplified by the population of the U.S., 1920' *Journal of the American Statistical Association* 20 (1925), 305–39.

Duman, D., *The English and colonial bars in the nineteenth century* (1983).

Dumont, A., *Dépopulation et civilisation: étude démographique* (Paris 1890).

La Morale basée sur la démographie (Paris 1901).

Natalité et démocratie (Paris 1898).

Dupâquier, J., *Pour la démographie historique* (Paris 1984).

Dupâquier, J., and Lachiver, M., 'Sur les débuts de la contraception en France ou les deux malthusianismes' *Annales ESC* 24 (1969), 1391–406.

Dupree, M., *Family structure in the Staffordshire Potteries 1840–1880* (Oxford 1994).

Dwork, D., *War is good for babies and other young children* (1987).

Dyhouse, C., *Feminism and the family in England 1880–1939* (Oxford 1989).

Girls growing up in late Victorian and Edwardian England (1981).

Dyson, K. H. F., *The state tradition in western Europe. A study of an idea and institution* (Oxford 1980).

Easterlin, R. A., 'The economics and sociology of fertility: a synthesis', in C. Tilly (ed.), *Historical studies of changing fertility* (Princeton 1978), 57–133.

'Towards a socio-economic theory of fertility: a survey of recent research on economic factors in American fertility', in S. J. Behrman *et al.* (eds.), *Fertility and family planning: a world view* (Ann Arbor 1969), 127–56.

Eaton, J., and Mayer, A. J., 'The social biology of very high fertility among the Hutterites. The demography of a unique population' *Human Biology* 25 (1953), 205–64.

Ebery, M., and Preston, B., *Domestic service in late Victorian and Edwardian England 1871–1914* (Reading 1976).

Ehrlich, P., *The population bomb* (New York 1968).

Ehrlich, P., and Ehrlich, A., *The population explosion* (1990).

Eicholz, N., 'The alleged deterioration of physique' *British Journal of Nursing* (19 Nov. 1904), 409–11.

Elbaum, B., and Lazonick, W. (eds.), *The decline of the British economy* (Oxford 1986).

Elderton, E., 'Report of the English birth rate. Part I England north of the Humber' *Eugenics Laboratory Memoirs* 19, 20 (1914).

Elderton, E., Barrington, A., Jones, N., Lamotte, E., Laski, H., and Pearson, K., 'On the correlation of fertility with social value. A cooperative study' *Eugenics Laboratory Memoirs* 18 (1913), 1–72.

England, L. R., 'Little Kinsey: an outline of sex attitudes in Britain' *Public Opinion Quarterly* 13 (1949), 587–600.

Ensor, R. C. K., *England 1870–1914* (Oxford 1936).

Ericksen, J. A., *et al.*, 'Fertility patterns and trends among the old order Amish' *PS* 33 (1979), 255–76.

'Response to Louis Henry' *PS* 34 (1980), 565.

Erickson, A. L., 'Introduction' to A. Clark, *Working life of women in the seventeenth century* (1992; first published 1919), vii–lv.

Evans, P., Rueschmeyer, D., and Skocpol, T. (eds.), *Bringing the state back in* (Cambridge 1985).

Eversley, D. E. C., *Social theories of fertility and the Malthusian debate* (Oxford 1959).

Eyler, J. M., 'Poverty, disease, responsibility: Arthur Newsholme and the public health dilemmas of British Liberalism' *Milbank Quarterly* 67, Supplement 1 (1989), 109–26.

'The sick poor and the state: Arthur Newsholme on poverty, disease and responsibility', in D. Porter and R. Porter (eds.), *Doctors, politics and society: historical essays* (Amsterdam 1993), 188–211.

Victorian social medicine: the ideas and methods of William Farr (Baltimore 1979).

'William Farr on the cholera: the sanitarian's disease theory and the statistician's method' *Journal of the History of Medicine* 28 (1973), 79–100.

Fancher, R. E., 'Francis Galton's African ethnology and its role in the development of his psychology' *British Journal of the History of Science* 16 (1983), 67–79.

Farr, W., 'Mortality of children in the principal states of Europe' *JSSL* 29 (1866), 1–35.

'On the construction of life-tables; illustrated by a new life-table of the healthy districts of England' (abstract) *Proceedings of the Royal Society of London* 9 (1857–9), 717–21.

'On infant mortality and on alleged inaccuracies of the census' (Part I) *JSSL* 28 (1865), 125–49. (Part II is to found in the same volume under 'Miscellanea', as 'Mortality at different stages of life', 402–13).

Farrall, L. A., 'The history of eugenics: a bibliographical review' *Annals of Science* 36 (1979), 111–23.

Faulkner, E., '"Powerless to prevent him". Attitudes of married working-class women in the 1920s and the rise of sexual power' *Local Population Studies* No. 49 (1992), 51–61.

Feinstein, C. H., 'What really happened to real wages?: trends in wages, prices and productivity in the United Kingdom' *EcHR* 43 (1990), 329–55.

Feldman, D. M., and Stedman Jones, G. (eds.), *Metropolis London. Histories and representations since 1800* (1989).

Feldman, D. M., *Englishmen and Jews: social relations and political culture, 1840–1914* (1994).

Femia, J. V., *Gramsci's political thought* (Oxford 1981).

Ferguson, H., 'Cleveland in history: the abused child and child protection, 1880–1914', in Cooter (ed.), *In the name of the child*, 146–73.

Feyerabend, P. K., *Against method* (1975).

Field, J., 'British historians and the concept of the labor aristocracy' *Radical History Review* 19 (1978–9), 61–85.

Fildes, V., *Breasts, bottles and babies: a history of infant feeding* (Edinburgh 1986).

(ed.), *Women as mothers in pre-industrial England* (1990).

Finer, S. E., *The life and times of Sir Edwin Chadwick* (1952).

Finlayson, G. B. A. M., *The Seventh Earl of Shaftesbury* (1981).

Finnegan, F., *Poverty and prostitution* (1979).

Flandrin, J.-L., 'Contraception, marriage and sexual relations in the Christian West', in R. Forster and O. Ranum (eds.), *Biology of man in history*, transl. E. Forster and P. Ranum (Baltimore 1975), 23–47.

Families in former times. Kinship, household and sexuality, transl. R. Southern (Cambridge 1979).

Sex in the western world: the development of attitudes and behaviour (Chur 1991).

Fleury, M., and Henry, L., *Des registres paroissiaux à l'histoire de la population. Manuel de dépouillement et d'exploitation de l'état civil ancien* (Paris 1956).

Flinn, M. W., 'Introduction' to E. Chadwick, *Report on the sanitary condition of the labouring population of Great Britain* (Edinburgh 1965).

Flinn, M. W. (ed.), *Scottish population history from the 17th century to the 1930s* (Cambridge 1977).

Florence, L. S., *Birth control on trial* (1930).

Floud, R., Wachter, K., and Gregory, A., *Height, health and history. Nutritional status in the United Kingdom, 1750–1980* (Cambridge 1990).

Folbre, N., 'Household production in the Philippines: a neo-classical approach' *Economic Development and Cultural Change* 32 (1983–4), 303–30.

'Of patriarchy born: the political economy of fertility decisions' *FS* 9 (1983), 261–84.

Who pays for the kids? Gender and the structure of constraint (1994).

Ford, C. S., *A comparative study of human reproduction* (New Haven 1945).

'Fertility controls in underdeveloped areas', in *Proceedings of the World Population Conference 1954*, Paper 1 (New York 1955).

Ford, C. S., and Beach, F. A., *Patterns of sexual behaviour* (New York 1951).

Foucault, M., *The history of sexuality*, transl. R. Hurley, 3 vols. (Harmondsworth 1990); Vol. I published in French in 1979 as *La Volonté de savoir*; Vols. II and III published in French in 1984 as *L'Usage des plaisirs* and *Le Souci de soi*.

The order of things. An archaeology of the human sciences (1970; first published in French as *Les Mots et les choses* in 1966).

Frankel, C., *The faith of reason* (New York 1948).

Fraser, D., *The evolution of the British welfare state* (2nd edn 1984).

Freeden, M., *The New Liberalism. An ideology of social reform* (Oxford 1978).

(ed.), *J. A. Hobson: a reader* (1988).

Freeman, D., *Margaret Mead and Samoa* (Harmondsworth 1984).

Freeman-Williams, J. P., *The effect of town life on the general health* (1890).

Friedson, E., *Professional powers. A study of the institutionalisation of formal knowledge* (Chicago 1986).

Fryer, P., *The birth controllers* (1967; first published 1965).

Fulcher, J., 'Gender, politics and class in the early nineteenth-century English reform movement' *Historical Research* 67 (1994), 57–74.

Galton, F., *Hereditary genius* (1892 edition; originally published 1869).

'Hereditary talent and character', Pts I and II, *Macmillan's Magazine* 12 (1865), 157–66; 318–27.

Memories of my life (London 1908).

'Proposal to apply for anthropological statistics from schools' *Journal of the Anthropological Institute* 3 (1873–4), 308–11.

'The relative supplies from town and country families to the population of future generations' *JSSL* 36 (1873), 19–26.

'Statistical inquiries into the efficacy of prayer' *Fortnightly Review*, New Series, 12 (1872), 125–35.

Gardner, P., *The lost elementary schools of Victorian England* (1984).

Garrard, J. A., *The English and immigration. A comparative study of the Jewish influx 1880–1910* (Oxford 1971).

Garrett, E., and Reid, A., 'Satanic mills, pleasant lands: spatial variation in women's work, fertility and infant mortality as viewed from the 1911 census' *Historical Research* 67 (1994), 156–77.

Garrett, E. M., 'The trials of labour: motherhood versus employment in a nineteenth-century textile centre' *Continuity and Change* 5 (1990), 121–54.

Gatrell, V. A. C., 'The decline of theft and violence in Victorian and Edwardian England and Wales', in V. A. C. Gatrell, B. Lenman and G. Parker (eds.), *Crime and the law: the social history of crime in western Europe since 1500* (1980), 238–370.

Gautier, E., and Henry, L., *La Population de Crulai, paroisse normande. Etude historique* (Paris 1958).

Gay, P., *The bourgeois experience*, Vol. I; *Education of the senses* (Oxford 1984).

The bourgeois experience, Vol. II; *The tender passion* (Oxford 1986).

Gayer, A. D., Rostow, W. W., and Schwartz, A. J., *Growth and fluctuations of the British economy, 1790–1850: an historical, statistical and theoretical study of Britain's economic development*, 2 vols. (Oxford 1953).

Georgescu-Roegen, N., *The entropy law and the economic process* (Cambridge, Mass., 1971).

Giddens, A., *The constitution of society* (Cambridge 1984).

Giddens, A., and Held, D. (eds.), *Classes, power and conflict. Classical and contemporary debates* (1982).

Giffen, R., 'The progress of the working classes in the last half century' *JSSL* 46 (1883), 593–622.

Gigerenzer, G., *et al.*, *The empire of chance. How probability changed science and everyday life* (Cambridge 1989).

Gilbert, B. B., *The evolution of national insurance in Great Britain: the origins of the welfare state* (1966).

'Health and politics: the British physical deterioration report of 1904' *BHM* 39 (1965), 143–8.

Gillis, J. R., 'Gender and fertility decline among the British middle classes', in Gillis *et al.* (eds.), *The European experience*, 31–47.

'Servants, sexual relations and the risks of illegitimacy in London, 1801–1900' in Newton *et al.* (eds.), *Sex and class*, 114–45.

Youth and history: tradition and change in European age relations 1770 – present (1974).

Gillis, J. R., Tilly, L. A., and Levine, D. (eds.), *The European experience of declining fertility. A quiet revolution 1850–1970* (1992).

Gini, C., 'Premières recherches sur la fécondabilité de la femme' *Proceedings of the Mathematical Congress* (Toronto 1924), 889–92.

Gittins, D., *Fair sex: family size and structure 1900–1939* (1982).

'Married life and birth control between the wars', *OH* 3 (1975), 53–64.

Glass, D. V., *Numbering the people. The eighteenth-century population controversy and the development of census and vital statistics in Britain* (Farnborough 1973).

Population policies and movements in Europe (Oxford 1940).

Glass, D. V., and Eversley, D. E. C. (eds.), *Population in history. Essays in historical demography* (1965).

Glass, D. V., and Grebenik, E., *The trend and pattern of fertility in Great Britain. A report on the family census of 1946*, Papers of the Royal Commission on Population 1944–9, Vol. VI (1954).

Goffman, E., *Asylums: essays on the social situation of mental patients and other inmates* (New York 1961).
'The nature of deference and demeanour', in E. Goffman, *Interaction ritual. Essays on face-to-face behaviour* (Harmondsworth 1972), 47–95.
Goldberg, D., 'The fertility of two-generation urbanites' *PS* 12 (1959), 214–22.
Goldman, L., 'A peculiarity of the English? The Social Science Association and the absence of sociology in nineteenth-century Britain' *P&P* 114 (1987), 133–71.
'The Social Science Association, 1857–86: a context for mid-Victorian Liberalism' *EHR* 101 (1986), 95–134.
'Statistics and the science of society in early Victorian Britain: an intellectual context for the G.R.O.' *SHM* 4 (1991), 415–34.
Goldstone, J. A., 'The demographic revolution in England: a re-examination' *PS* 49 (1986), 5–33.
Goldthorpe, J. H., and Hope, K., *The social classification of occupations: a new approach and scale* (Oxford 1974).
Goldthorpe, J. H., Llewellyn, C., and Payne, C., *Social mobility and class structure in modern Britain* (Oxford 1980).
Gordon, L., *Woman's body, woman's right: a social history of birth control in America* (New York 1976).
Gorer, G., *Exploring English character* (1955).
Sex and marriage in England today (1971).
Gorham, D., 'The "Maiden tribute of modern Babylon" re-examined: child prostitution and the idea of childhood in late Victorian England' *VS* 21 (1978), 353–79.
Goubert, P., *Beauvais et les Beauvaisis de 1600 à 1730. Contribution a l'histoire sociale de la France du XVIIe siècle* (Paris 1960).
Gould, S. J., *The mismeasure of man* (Harmondsworth 1984; first published 1981).
Ontogeny and phylogeny (Cambridge, Mass., 1977).
Gramsci, A., *Selections from the prison notebooks*, edited and translated by Q. Hoare and G. Nowell Smith (1971).
Graves, P. M., *Labour women: women in British working-class politics, 1918–1939* (Cambridge 1994).
Gray, B. Kirkman, *Philanthropy and the state, or social politics* (1908).
Gray, R. Q., *The labour aristocracy in Victorian Edinburgh* (Oxford 1976).
Grebenik, E., 'Demographic research in Britain 1936–86', in M. Murphy and J. Hobcraft (eds.), *Population research in Britain*, a supplement to *Population Studies* 45 (1991), 3–30.
Green, S. J. D., 'The religion of the child in Edwardian Methodism: institutional reform and pedagogical reappraisal in the West Riding of Yorkshire' *Journal of British Studies* 30 (1991), 377–98.
Greene, J. C., 'Darwin as a social evolutionist' *Journal of the History of Biology* 10 (1977), 1–27.
Greenhalgh, S., 'Toward a political economy of fertility: anthropological contributions' *PDR* 16 (1990), 85–106.
Greenhow, E. H., 'Illustrations of the necessity for a more analytical study of the statistics of public health' *Transactions of the National Association for the Promotion of Social Science* (1857), 365–87.
Papers relating to the sanitary state of the people of England (1858).
Greer, G., *Sex and destiny: the politics of human fertility* (1984).
Greven, P., *The Protestant temperament. Patterns of child-rearing, religious experience and the self in early America* (New York 1977).
Griffith, G. T., *Population problems of the age of Malthus* (Cambridge 1926).
Guest, R., and John, A. V., *Lady Charlotte. A biography of the nineteenth century* (1989).
Hacking, I., *Representing and intervening. Introductory topics in the philosophy of natural science* (Cambridge 1983).
Haeckel, E., *Generelle Morphologie der Organismen*, 2 vols. (Berlin 1866).

Hagen, E. E., *On the theory of social change* (1962).

Haines, M., *Fertility and occupation. Population patterns in industrialisation* (1979).

'Industrial work and the family life cycle, 1889–1890' *Research in Economic History* 4 (1979), 289–356.

'Occupation and social class during fertility decline: historical perspectives', in Gillis *et al.* (eds.), *The European experience*, 193–226.

'Social class differentials during fertility decline: England and Wales revisited' *PS* 43 (1989), 305–23.

Hajnal, J., 'Age at marriage and proportions marrying' *PS* 7 (1953–4), 111–36.

'European marriage patterns in perspective', in Glass and Eversley (eds.), *Population in history*, 101–43.

'The study of fertility and reproduction: survey of the last 30 years', in *Thirty years of research in human fertility: retrospect and prospect*, Papers presented at the 1958 annual conference of the Milbank Memorial Fund (New York 1959).

'Two kinds of preindustrial household formation system' *PDR* 8 (1982), 449–94.

Hakim, C., 'Social monitors: population censuses as social surveys', in Bulmer (ed.) *Essays on the history*, 39–51.

Hall, C., 'The tale of Samuel and Jemima: gender and working-class culture in nineteenth-century England', in Kaye and McClelland (eds.), *E. P. Thompson*, 78–102.

Hall, L. A., *Hidden anxieties: male sexuality 1900–50* (Cambridge 1991).

Halliday, R. J., 'The sociological movement, the sociological society and the genesis of academic sociology in Britain' *SR* 16 (1968), 377–98.

Hamilton, C., *Marriage as a trade* (1909).

Hamlin, C., *A science of impurity: water analysis in nineteenth century Britain* (Bristol 1990).

Hammerton, A. J., *Cruelty and companionship. Conflict in nineteenth-century married life* (1992).

Hammond, J. L., and Hammond, B., *The town labourer* (1917).

The village labourer (1911).

Handwerker, W. Penn (ed.), *Births and power: social change and the politics of reproduction* (Boulder, Colo., 1990).

Hanham, H. J., *The nineteenth century constitution 1815–1914* (Cambridge 1969).

Harben, H. D., *The endowment of motherhood*, Fabian Tract 149 (1910).

Hardin, G., 'The tragedy of the commons' *Science* 162 (1968), 1243–8.

Hardy, A., *The epidemic streets. Infectious disease and the rise of preventive medicine 1856–1900* (Oxford 1993).

'Public health and the expert: the London Medical Officers of Health, 1856–1900', in MacLeod (ed.), *Government and expertise*, 128–42.

Harris, J., 'Political thought and the welfare state 1870–1940: an intellectual framework for British social policy' *P&P* 135 (1992), 116–41.

Private lives, public spirits (1993).

Unemployment and politics. A study in English social policy 1886–1914 (Oxford 1972).

'The Webbs, the C.O.S. and the Ratan Tata Foundation: social policy from the perspective of 1912', in M. Bulmer, J. Lewis and D. Piachaud (eds.), *The goals of social policy* (1989), 27–63.

Harrison, J. F. C., *The early Victorians* (1971).

Harrison, R. (ed.), *The independent collier: the coal miner as archetypal proletarian reconsidered* (1978).

Harrison, R., and Zeitlin, J. (eds.), *Divisions of labour. Skilled workers and technological change in nineteenth century England* (Brighton 1985).

Harvie, C., *The lights of Liberalism. University Liberals and the challenge of democracy 1860–86* (1976).

Hawthorn, G. P., *The sociology of fertility* (1970).

(ed.), *Population and development* (1978).

Hay, J. R., *The origins of the Liberal welfare reforms 1906–14* (revised edn 1983).
Headland, T. N., Pike, K. L., and Harris, M., *Emics and etics. The insider/outsider debate* (1990).
Heckscher, E. F., 'Swedish population trends before the industrial revolution' *EcHR* 2 (1949), 266–77.
Hempel, C. G., *Aspects of scientific explanation* (New York 1965).
Studies in the logic of explanation (New York 1948).
Hendrick, H., *Images of youth. Age, class and the male youth problem 1880–1920* (Oxford 1990).
Hennock, E. P., *British social reform and German precedents. The case of social insurance 1880–1914* (Oxford 1987).
'Concepts of poverty in the British social surveys from Charles Booth to Arthur Bowley', in M. Bulmer, K. Bales and K. Kish Sklar (eds.), *The social survey in historical perspective 1880–1940* (Cambridge 1991), 189–216.
'The measurement of urban poverty: from the metropolis to the nation, 1880–1920' *EcHR* 40 (1987), 208–27.
'Poverty and social theory in England: the experience of the 1880s' *SH* 1 (1976), 67–91.
Henry, L., 'Some remarks on the paper by J. Ericksen et al.' *PS* 34 (1980), 564.
Herf, J., *Reactionary modernism: technology, culture, and politics in Weimar and the Third Reich* (Cambridge 1984).
Heron, D., 'On the relation of fertility in man to social status and on the changes in this relation that have taken place in the last fifty years' *Drapers Company Research Memoirs. Studies in National Deterioration* 1 (1906), 3–22.
Hewitt, M., *Wives and mothers in Victorian industry* (1958).
Hicks, N., *This sin and scandal: Australia's population debate 1891–1911* (Canberra 1978).
Higginbotham, A. R., '"Sin of the age": infanticide and illegitimacy in Victorian London' *VS* 32 (1989), 319–37.
Higgs, E., 'Disease, febrile poisons and statistics: the census as a medical survey, 1841–1911' *SHM* 4 (1991), 465–78.
'Domestic service and household production', in John (ed.), *Unequal opportunities*, 125–50.
Making sense of the census (1989).
'The struggle for the occupational census, 1841–1911', in MacLeod (ed.), *Government and expertise*, 73–86.
'Women, occupations and work in the nineteenth century censuses' *HW* 23 (1987), 59–80.
Hill, C. P., 'Pottage for freeborn Englishmen: attitudes to wage labour in the sixteenth and seventeenth centuries', in C. H. Feinstein (ed.), *Socialism, capitalism and economic growth* (Cambridge 1967), 338–50.
Hill, R., Stycos, J. M., and Back, K., *The family and population control* (Chapel Hill 1959).
Hilton, (A. J.) B., *The age of atonement. The influence of Evangelicalism on social and economic thought 1785–1865* (Oxford 1988).
'Manliness, masculinity and the mid-Victorian temperament', in L. Goldman (ed.), *The blind Victorian. Henry Fawcett and British Liberalism* (Cambridge 1989), 60–70.
Hilts, V. L., 'William Farr and the human unit' *VS* 14 (1970), 143–50.
Himes, N. E., 'British birth control clinics' *Eugenics Review* 20 (1928), 158–62.
'Editor's introduction' to Francis Place, *Illustrations and proofs of the principle of population* (1930; first edn 1822).
A medical history of contraception (Baltimore 1936).
Himmelfarb, G., 'The Victorian Trinity: religion, science and morals', in G. Himmelfarb, *Marriage and morals among the Victorians* (1975), 50–75.
Hobsbawm, E. J., 'The labour aristocracy in nineteenth century Britain', in Hobsbawm, *Labouring men*, 272–315.
Labouring men. Studies in the history of labour (1964).

'The making of the working class 1870–1914', in Hobsbawm, *Worlds of labour*, 194–213.

Worlds of labour. Further studies in the history of labour (1984).

Hodgson, D., 'Demography as social science and policy science' *PDR* 9 (1983), 1–34.

'Orthodoxy and revisionism in American demography' *PDR* 14 (1988), 541–69.

Hoffmann, W. G., *British industry 1700–1950*, translated by W. O. Henderson and W. H. Chaloner (Oxford 1955).

Hofsten, E., and Lundström, H., *Swedish population history. Main trends from 1750 to 1970*, Urval No. 8 (Stockholm 1976).

Hogben, L. (ed.), *Political arithmetic. A symposium of population studies* (1938).

Hoggart, R., *The uses of literacy* (1957).

Holcombe, L., *Wives and property. Reform of the married women's property law in nineteenth-century England* (Toronto 1983).

Holley, J. C., 'The two family economies of industrialisation: factory workers in Victorian Scotland' *JFH* 6 (1981), 57–69.

Hollis, P., *Ladies elect. Women in English local government 1865–1914* (Oxford 1987).

Holton, S., *Feminism and democracy: women's suffrage and reform politics, 1900–18* (Cambridge 1986).

Holtzman, E., 'The pursuit of married love: women's attitudes towards sexuality and marriage in Great Britain 1918–39' *JSH* 16 (1982), 39–51.

Homer-Dixon, T. F., 'Environmental scarcities and violent conflict: evidence from cases' *International Security* 19 (1994), 5–40.

Honey, J. R. de S., *Tom Brown's universe* (1977).

Honigsbaum, F., *The division in British medicine. A history of the separation of general practice from hospital care 1911–68* (1979).

Hooker, R. H., 'Modes of census-taking in the British dominions' *JRSS* 57 (1894), 289–368.

Hope, K., *As others see us: schooling and social mobility in Scotland and the United States* (Cambridge 1984).

Hopkin, W. A. B., and Hajnal, J., 'Analysis of the births in England and Wales, 1939, by father's occupation', Parts I and II, *PS* 1 (1947), 187–203; 275–300.

Horn, P., *The rise and fall of the Victorian servant* (1975).

Horsman, R., *Race and manifest destiny: the origins of American racial Anglo-Saxonism* (Cambridge, Mass., 1981).

Hosgood, C. P., 'The "pigmies of commerce" and the working-class community: small shopkeepers in England, 1870–1914' *JSH* 22 (1989), 439–60.

Hostetler, J. A., *Hutterite society* (Baltimore 1974).

Houghton, W. E., *The Victorian frame of mind* (New Haven 1957).

Houlbrooke, R., *The English family 1450–1700* (1984).

English family life 1576–1716 (Oxford 1988).

Howell, D., *British workers and the Independent Labour party, 1888–1906* (Manchester 1990).

Howkins, A., *Reshaping rural England. A social history 1850–1925* (1991).

Hudson, D., *Munby, man of two worlds* (1972).

Humphreys, N. A., 'Class mortality statistics' *JRSS* 50 (1887), 255–92.

'How far may the average death-rate of a population be considered an efficient test of its sanitary condition?' *Transactions of the National Association for the Promotion of Social Science* (1884), 485–96.

'The Registrar-General's decennial supplement 1881–90' *JRSS* 59 (1896), 543–6.

'Results of the recent census and estimates of population in the largest English towns' *JRSS* 54 (1891), 311–30; and 'Discussion', 331–40.

'The value of death rates as a test of sanitary conditions' *JSSL* 37 (1874), 437–77.

Vital statistics: a memorial volume of selections from the reports and writings of William Farr (1885).

Humphries, J., 'Class struggle and the persistence of the working-class family' *CJE* 1 (1977), 241–58.

'Protective legislation, the capitalist state and working class men: the case of the 1842 Mines Regulation Act' *FR* 7 (1981), 1–33.

Humphries, J., and Rubery, J., 'The reconstitution of the supply side of the labour market: the relative autonomy of social reproduction' *CJE* 8 (1984), 331–46.

Humphries, S., *A secret world of sex* (1988).

'Steal to survive: the social crime of working class children 1890–1940' *OH* 9 (1981), 24–33.

Humphries, S., and Gordon, P., *A labour of love* (1993).

Hunt, E. H., *British labour history 1815–1914* (1981).

Regional wage variations in Britain 1950–1914 (Oxford 1973).

Hunt, F. (ed.), *Lessons for life. The schooling of girls and women 1850–1950* (Oxford 1987).

Hunt, L., *The family romance of the French revolution* (1992).

(ed.), *The invention of pornography, 1500–1800* (1994).

Hurt, J. S., *Elementary schooling and the working classes, 1860–1918* (1979).

Hyam, R., *Empire and sexuality. The British experience* (Manchester 1990).

Hynes, S., *The Edwardian turn of mind* (Princeton 1968).

Innes, J. W., 'Class birth rates in England and Wales, 1921–31' *Milbank Memorial Fund Quarterly* 19 (1941), 72–96.

Class fertility trends in England and Wales 1876–1934 (Princeton 1938).

Ittmann, K., 'Family limitation and family economy in Bradford, West Yorkshire 1851–81' *JSH* 25 (1992), 547–73.

Jalland, P., and Hooper, J. (eds.), *Women from birth to death. The female life cycle in Britain 1830–1914* (Atlantic Highlands, N.J. 1986).

Jeffreys, J. B., *Retail trading in Britain, 1850–1950* (Cambridge 1954).

Jeffreys, S., *The spinster and her enemies: feminism and sexuality 1880–1930* (1985).

Jenkyns, R., *The Victorians and Ancient Greece* (Oxford 1980).

Johansson, S. Ryan, '"Implicit" policy and fertility during development' *PDR* 17 (1991), 377–414.

John, A. V., *By the sweat of their brow. Women workers at Victorian coal mines* (1980).

(ed.), *Unequal opportunities. Women's employment in England 1800–1918* (Oxford 1986).

Johnson, P., *Saving and spending. The working-class economy in Britain 1870–1939* (Oxford 1985).

Johnson, R., 'Adminstrators in education before 1870: patronage, social position and role', in Sutherland (ed.), *Studies in the growth*, 110–38.

Jones, G., *Social Darwinism and English thought* (Brighton 1980).

Social hygiene in twentieth-century Britain (1986).

Jones, H. R., 'The perils and protection of infant life' *JRSS* 57 (1894), 1–98; 99–103 ('Discussion').

Jordan, E., 'The exclusion of women from industry in nineteenth-century Britain' *CSSH* 31 (1989), 273–96.

'Female unemployment in England and Wales 1851–1911: an examination of the census figures for 15–19 year olds' *SH* 13 (1988), 175–90.

Joshi, H. (ed.), *The changing population of Britain* (1989).

Joshi, H., and Owen, S., 'How long is a piece of elastic? The measurement of female activity rates in British censuses, 1951–81' *CJE* 11 (1987), 54–74.

Joyce, P., *Visions of the people. Industrial England and the question of class, 1848–1914* (Cambridge 1991).

Work, society and politics. The culture of the factory in later Victorian England (1980).

Kadish, A., *The Oxford economists in the late nineteenth century* (Oxford 1982).

Kaelble, H., *Social mobility in the 19th and 20th centuries. Europe and America in comparative perspective* (Leamington Spa 1985).

Kaplan, M. A., *The making of the Jewish middle class: women, family and identity in Imperial Germany* (Oxford 1991).
Karabel, J., and Halsey, A. H. (eds.), *Power and ideology in education* (New York 1977).
Kaye, H. J., and McClelland, K. (eds.), *E. P. Thompson. Critical perspectives* (Oxford 1990).
Keeling, F., *Child labour in the United Kingdom* (1914).
Kent, R. A., *A history of British empirical sociology* (Aldershot 1981).
Kent, S. K., 'The politics of sexual difference: World War I and the demise of British feminism' *Journal of British Studies* 27 (1988), 232–53.
Sex and suffrage in Britain, 1860–1914 (Princeton 1987).
Kertzer, D. J., and Hogan, D. P., *Family, political economy and demographic change. The transformation of life in Casalecchio, Italy 1861–1921* (Madison 1989).
Kevles, D. J., *In the name of eugenics* (Harmondsworth 1986; first published 1985).
Keynes, J. M., *The economic consequences of the peace* (1919).
The general theory of employment, interest and money (Royal Economic Society edn 1973; originally published 1936).
Kiernan, V., 'Evangelicalism and the French Revolution' *P&P* 1 (1952), 44–56.
Knight, P., 'Women and abortion in Victorian and Edwardian England' *HW* 4 (1977), 57–69.
Knodel, J., *The decline of fertility in Germany* (Princeton 1974).
Demographic behaviour in the past: a study of fourteen German village populations in the eighteenth and nineteenth centuries (Cambridge 1988).
'Demographic transitions in German villages', in Coale and Watkins (eds.), *The decline of fertility*, 337–89.
'Espacement des naissances et planification familiale: une critique de la méthode Dupâquier–Lachiver' *Annales ESC* 36 (1981), 473–88; and response: J. Dupâquier and M. Lachiver, 'Du contresens à l'illusion technique', 489–92; with further reply from J. Knodel, 493–4.
'Starting, stopping and spacing during the early stage of fertility transition: the experience of German village populations in the nineteenth and twentieth centuries' *Demography* 21 (1987), 143–62.
Knodel, J., and van de Walle, E., 'Lessons from the past: policy implications of historical fertility studies' *PDR* 5 (1979), 220–37.
Knodel, J., and Wilson, C., 'The secular increase in fecundity in German village populations: an analysis of reproductive histories of couples married 1750–1899' *PS* 35 (1981), 53–84.
Koditschek, T., *Class formation and urban industrial society. Bradford 1750–1850* (Cambridge 1990).
'The dynamics of class formation in nineteenth-century Bradford', in A. L. Beier, D. Cannadine and J. M. Rosenheim (eds.), *The first modern society* (Cambridge 1989), 511–48.
Koot, G. M., *English historical economics, 1870–1926. The rise of economic history and neomercantilism* (Cambridge 1987).
Koutsoyiannis, A., *Theory of econometrics: an introductory exposition* (2nd edn 1977).
Koven, S., and Michel, S., 'Womanly duties: maternalist policies and the origins of welfare states in France, Germany, Great Britain and the United States 1880–1920' *AHR* 95 (1990), 1076–108.
(eds.), *Mothers of a new world. Maternalist politics and the origin of welfare states* (1993).
Kroeber, A. L., 'Diffusionism', article in *Encyclopaedia of the Social Sciences*, ed. E. R. A. Seligman (New York 1949).
Krzywicki, L., *Primitive society and its vital statistics* (1934).
Kuczynski, R. R., *The measurement of population growth* (1935).
Kuhn, T. S., *The structure of scientific revolutions* (1962).
Kuklick, H., *The savage within. The social history of British anthropology, 1885–1945* (Cambridge 1991).

Kula, W., *Measures and men*, transl. R. Szreter (Princeton 1986; first published as *Miary i ludzie*, Warsaw 1970).

Kussmaul, A., *Servants in husbandry in early modern England* (Cambridge 1981).

'When shall we marry?', ch. 2 in A. Kussmaul, *A general view of the rural economy of England 1538–1840* (Cambridge 1990).

La Berge, A. F., 'The early nineteenth-century French public health movement: the disciplinary development and institutionalisation of Hygiène Publique' *BHM* 58 (1984), 363–79.

'Edwin Chadwick and the French connection' *BHM* 62 (1988), 23–41.

Labov, W., *The social stratification of English in New York City* (Washington 1966).

Lachenbruch, P. A., 'Frequency and timing of intercourse: its relation to the probability of conception' *PS* 21 (1967), 23–31.

Lakatos, I., *The methodology of scientific research programmes*, ed. J. Worrall and G. Currie, (Cambridge 1978).

Lambert, R. J., 'Central and local relations in mid-Victorian England: the Local Government Act Office, 1858–71' *VS* 6 (1962–3), 121–50.

Sir John Simon 1816–1904 and English social administration (1963).

Land, H., 'The family wage' *FR* 6 (1980), 55–77.

Landers, J., 'Fertility decline and birth spacing among London Quakers', in J. Landers and V. Reynolds (eds.), *Fertility and resources* (Cambridge 1990), 92–117.

Landry, A., *La Révolution démographique. Etudes et essais sur les problèmes de la population* (Paris: INED 1982; first edn 1934).

'Les Trois Théories principales de la population', reprinted in A. Landry, *La Révolution démographique* (1982), 169–92. (First published in *Scientia* in 1909.)

Langer, W. L., 'Origins of the birth control movement in England in the early nineteenth century' *JIH* 5 (1975), 669–86.

Langford, C. M., 'Birth control practice in Great Britain: a review of the evidence from cross-sectional surveys', in M. Murphy and J. Hobcraft (eds.), *Population research in Britain*, Supplement to *PS* 45 (1991), 49–68.

Lankester, E. Ray, *Degeneration: a chapter in Darwinism* (1880).

Laqueur, T., 'Orgasm, generation and the politics of reproductive biology', in C. Gallagher and T. Laqueur (eds.), *The making of the modern body. Sexuality and society in the nineteenth century* (1987), 1–41.

'The Queen Caroline Affair: politics as art in the reign of George IV' *Journal of Modern History* 54 (1982), 417–66.

Religion and respectability. Sunday schools and working class culture 1780–1850 (1976).

Laslett, P., *Family life and illicit love in earlier generations* (Cambridge 1977).

The world we have lost (1965; new edn 1983).

Laslett, P., and Oostereven, K., 'Long-term trends in bastardy in England' *PS* 27 (1973), 255–86.

Laslett, P., Oostereven, K., and Smith, R. M., (eds.), *Bastardy and its comparative history*. (1980).

Latour, B., and Woolgar, S., *Laboratory life. The construction of scientific facts* (1979).

Lazarsfeld, P. F., 'Notes on the history of quantification in sociology – trends, sources and problems' *Isis* 52 (1961), 277–333.

Lazonick, W., 'Industrial relations and technical change: the case of the self-acting mule' *CJE* 3 (1979), 231–62.

Le Roy Ladurie, E., *Montaillou. Cathars and Catholics in a French village 1294–1324*, transl. B. Bray (Harmondsworth 1980; first edn Paris 1978).

Leathard, A., *The fight for family planning. The development of family planning services in Britain 1921–74* (1980).

Lécuyer, B., 'Médecins et observateurs sociaux: les annales d'hygiène publique et de médecine légale (1820–50)', in INED, *Pour une histoire de la statistique* (INED, Paris 1977), 445–76.

Ledbetter, R., *A history of the Malthusian League, 1877–1927* (1976).

Leibenstein, H., *Economic backwardness and economic growth* (New York 1957).

'Relaxing the maximisation assumption in the economic theory of fertility', in C. Hohn and R. Mackensen (eds.), *Determinants of fertility trends: theories re-examined* (Bad Homburg 1980), 35–48.

A theory of economic-demographic development (Princeton 1954).

Lesthaeghe, R. J., *The decline of Belgian fertility 1800–1970* (Princeton 1977).

'On the social control of human reproduction' *PDR* 6 (1980), 527–48.

Lesthaeghe, R. J., and Wilson, C., 'Modes of production, secularization and the pace of the fertility decline in Western Europe, 1870–1930', in Coale and Watkins (eds.), *The decline of fertility*, 261–92.

Levine, D., *Reproducing families. The political economy of English population history* (Cambridge 1987).

Levine, D., and Wrightson, K., *The making of an industrial society. Whickham 1560–1765* (Oxford 1991).

Levine, P., *Victorian feminism 1850–1900* (1987).

Lewis, J., 'Gender, the family and women's agency in the building of "welfare states": the British case' *SH* 19 (1994), 37–55.

'Intimate relations between men and women: the case of H. G. Wells and Amber Pember Reeves' *HW* 37 (1994), 76–97.

'Parents, school fees and the London School Board 1870–1890' *History of Education* 11 (1982), 291–312.

The politics of motherhood: child and maternal welfare in England, 1900–39 (1980).

Women in England 1870–1950 (Brighton 1984).

(ed.), *Labour and love. Women's experience of home and family, 1850–1940* (Oxford 1986).

Lewis, J., and Lockridge, K. A., '"Sally has been sick": pregnancy and family limitation among Virginia gentry women, 1780–1830' *JSH* 22 (1988), 5–19.

Lewis, R. A., *Edwin Chadwick and the public health movement* (1952).

Leybourne, G. G., and White, K., *Education and the birth-rate. A social dilemma* (1940).

Light, A., *Forever England: femininity, literature and Conservatism between the Wars* (1992).

Lilienfeld, A. M., *Foundations of epidemiology* (New York 1976).

Lindert, P. H., *Fertility and scarcity in America* (Princeton 1978).

Litchfield, R. Burr., 'The family and the mill: cotton mill work, family work patterns and fertility in mid-Victorian Stockport', in Wohl (ed.), *The Victorian family*, 180–96.

Littleton, C. Scott, 'Lucien Lévy-Bruhl and the concept of cognitive relativity', Introduction to Lucien Lévy-Bruhl, *How natives think*, transl. L. A. Clare (Princeton 1985), v–lviii.

Liveing, S., *A nineteenth-century teacher, John Henry Bridges* (1926).

Livi-Bacci, M., *A century of Portuguese fertility* (Princeton 1971).

'Social group forerunners of fertility control in Europe', in Coale and Watkins, *The decline of fertility*, 182–200.

Llewellyn Davies, M., *Life as we have known it* (1931).

Maternity. Letters from working women (1915; reprinted 1984).

Lloyd, C., *Explanation in social history* (Oxford 1986).

Loane, M. E., *From their point of view* (1908).

Outlines of routine in district nursing (1905).

Lockhart, J., 'The economics of nine years' education for all', in A. Killick (ed.), *Papers on the Kenyan economy* (1981), 279–86.

Lockridge, K. A., *The fertility transition in Sweden: a preliminary look at smaller geographical units, 1855–1890*, Report No. 3 from the Demographic Data Base, University of Umea (Umea 1983).

Longstaff, G. B., 'Rural depopulation' *JRSS* 56 (1893), 380–442.

Studies in statistics, social, political and medical (1891).

Lorimer, D. A., *Colour, class and the Victorians: English attitudes to the negro in the mid-nineteenth century* (Leicester 1978).

'Theoretical racism in late-Victorian anthropology, 1870–1900' *VS* 31 (1988), 405–30.

Lorimer, F., *Culture and human fertility* (Paris: UNESCO 1954).

Loudon, I., *Death in childbirth: an international study of maternal care and maternal mortality, 1800–1950* (Oxford 1992).

'Maternal mortality 1880–1950: some regional and international comparisons' *SHM* 1 (1988), 183–228.

Medical care and the general practitioner, 1750–1850 (Oxford 1987).

'On maternal and infant mortality 1900–1960' *SHM* 4 (1991), 29–73.

Lovell, J., *British trade unions 1875–1933* (1977).

Lowe, N. V., 'The legal status of fathers: past and present', in McKee and O'Brien (eds.), *The father figure*, 26–42.

Lowe, R., 'Eugenicists, doctors and the quest for national efficiency: an educational crusade 1900–39' *History of Education* 8 (1979), 293–306.

'Eugenics and education: a note on the origins of the intelligence testing movement' *Educational Studies* 6 (1980), 1–8.

Luckin, B., 'Evaluating the sanitary revolution: typhus, and typhoid in London 1851–1900', in R. Woods and J. Woodward (eds.), *Urban disease and mortality in nineteenth-century England* (1984), 102–19.

Lukes, S., *Individualism* (Oxford 1973).

Lummis, T., 'The historical dimensions of fatherhood: a case study 1890–1914', in McKee and O'Brien (eds.), *The father figure*, 43–56.

Lystra, K., *Searching the heart: women, men and romantic love in nineteenth-century America* (New York 1989).

Macaulay, T. B., *Critical and historical essays, contributed to the Edinburgh Review*, 3 vols. (1843).

The history of England from the accession of James II, 5 vols. (1858–61).

McBriar, A. M., *An Edwardian mixed doubles. The Bosanquets versus the Webbs. A study in social policy 1890–1929* (Oxford 1987).

Fabian socialism and English politics 1884–1918 (Cambridge 1966).

McBride, T., 'As the twig is bent: the Victorian nanny', in Wohl (ed.), *The Victorian family*, 44–58.

McCalman, I., *Radical underworld. Prophets, revolutionaries and pornographers in London, 1795–1840* (Cambridge 1988).

McCance, R. A., Luff, M. C., and Widdowson, E. E., 'Physical and emotional periodicity in women' *Journal of Hygiene* 37 (1937), 571–609.

McCann, P. (ed.), *Popular education and socialisation in the nineteenth century* (1977).

McClelland, K., 'Some thoughts on masculinity and the "Representative Artisan" in Britain 1850–1880' *G&H* 1 (1989), 164–77.

McClelland, K., and Reid, A., 'Wood, iron and steel: technology, labour and trade union organisation in the shipbuilding industry, 1840–1914', in Harrison and Zeitlin (eds.), *Divisions of labour*, 151–84.

McCloskey, D. N., *Econometric history* (1987).

McCormack, C. P. (ed.), *Ethnography of fertility and birth* (1982).

MacDonagh, O., 'The nineteenth-century revolution in government: a reappraisal' *HJ* 1 (1958), 52–67.

Macfarlane, A., *Marriage and love in England 1300–1840* (Cambridge 1986).
The origins of English individualism (Oxford 1978).

McGregor, O. R., *Divorce in England* (1957).

McHugh, P., *Prostitution and Victorian social reform* (1980).

McKee, L., and O'Brien, R. (eds.), *The father figure* (1982).

McKendrick, N., Brewer, J., and Plumb, J. H., *The birth of a consumer society: the commercialization of eighteenth-century England* (1983).

MacKenzie, D. A., *Statistics in Britain 1865–1930. The social construction of scientific knowledge* (Edinburgh 1981).

MacKenzie, J., and MacKenzie, N., *The first Fabians* (1977).

McKeown, T., and Brown, R. G., 'Medical evidence related to English population change in the eighteenth century' *PS* 9 (1955), 119–41.

McKibbin, R., 'Class and poverty in Edwardian England', in R. McKibbin, *The ideologies of class. Social relations in Britain 1880–1950* (Oxford 1990), 167–96.
'Why was there no Marxism in Great Britain?' *EHR* 99 (1984), 297–331.

McLaren, A., *Birth control in nineteenth-century England* (1978).
'Contraception and its discontents: Sigmund Freud and birth control' *JSH* 12 (1979), 513–29.
A history of contraception. From antiquity to the present day (1990).
Reproductive rituals. The perception of fertility in England from the sixteenth century to the nineteenth century (1984).
'The sexual politics of reproduction in Britain', in Gillis *et al.* (eds.), *The European experience*, 85–98.
'A woman's work and regulation of family size: the question of abortion in the nineteenth century' *HW* 4 (1977), 70–82.

McLeod, H., *Religion and the working class in nineteenth century Britain* (1984).

MacLeod, R. M., 'The frustration of state medicine 1880–1899' *Medical History* 11 (1967), 15–40.
'Introduction', in MacLeod (ed.), *Government and expertise*, 1–24.
Treasury control and social administration (1968).
(ed.), *Government and expertise. Specialists, administrators, and professionals, 1860–1919* (Cambridge 1988).

Macnicol, J., 'Family allowances and less eligibility', in P. Thane (ed.), *The origins of social policy* (1978), 173–202.

McNicoll, G., 'The economic activities of children in a village in Bangladesh' *PDR* 3 (1977), 201–27.
'The household life cycle and economic mobility in Bangladesh' *PDR* 4 (1978), 421–38.
'Population and development: outline for a structuralist approach', in Hawthorn (ed.), *Population and development*, 79–99.

McNicoll, G., and Cain, M. (eds.), *Rural development and population. Institutions and policy*, Supplement to *PDR* 15 (Oxford 1990).

MaHood, J., and Wenburg, K. (eds.), *The Mosher survey: sexual histories of 45 Victorian women* (New York 1980).

Mallet, B., *British budgets 1887–1913* (1913).
'Is England in danger of racial decline?' *National Review* (Feb. 1922), 843–53.
'Reform of vital statistics. Outline of a National Registration' *Eugenics Review* 21 (1929–30), 87–94.
'Registration in relation to eugenics' *Eugenics Review* 14 (1922), 23–30.

Mallet, B., and George, C. O., *British budgets*, 3rd Series, 1921–2 to 1932–3 (1933).

Malthus, T. R., *An essay on the principle of population as it affects the future improvement of society* (1st edn, 1798; 2nd edn, 1803).

Mandler, P., *Aristocratic government in the age of reform: Whigs and Liberals 1830–52* (Oxford 1990).

Mann, M., *The sources of social power*, Vol. I: *A history of power from the beginning to* A.D. *1760* (Cambridge 1986)

The sources of social power, Vol II: *The rise of classes and nation-states, 1760–1914* (Cambridge 1993).

Marcus, S., *The other Victorians. A study of sexuality and pornography in mid-nineteenth-century England* (1966; first published 1964).

Marks, L., '"Dear old mother Levy's": the Jewish maternity home and sick room helps society 1895–1939' *SHM* 3 (1990), 61–88.

Marsden, W. E., *Unequal educational provision in England and Wales: the nineteenth-century roots* (1987).

Marshall, A., *The economics of industry* (1879).

'The housing of the London Poor: where to house them' *Contemporary Review* 45 (1884), 224–31.

'Some aspects of competition', Presidential Address to British Association, Section F, *Report of the British Association* (1890), 898–915.

Marshall, T. H., 'The population problem during the industrial revolution: a note on the present state of the controversy' *Economic History* 1 (1926–9), 429–56. (Published in January 1929 in a supplement to the *Economic Journal*.)

Martin, B., *A sociology of contemporary cultural change* (Oxford 1981).

Martin, K., *Harold Laski* (1953).

Mason, M., *The making of Victorian sexual attitudes* (Oxford 1994).

The making of Victorian sexuality (Oxford 1994).

Mass-Observation, *Britain and her birth-rate* (1945).

Masterman, C. F. G., *The condition of England* (1909).

Mathias, P., *The retailing revolution* (1967).

Matthew, H. C. G., *Gladstone 1809–74* (Oxford 1986).

Maurice, Sir (J.) F., 'National health: a soldier's study' *Contemporary Review* 83 (1903), 41–56.

(pseud. 'Miles'), 'Where to get men' *Contemporary Review* 81 (1902), 78–86.

Maynard, J., *Charlotte Brontë and sexuality* (Cambridge 1984).

Victorian discourses on sexuality and religion (Cambridge 1993).

Mazumdar, P. M. H., 'The eugenists and the residuum: the problem of the urban poor' *BHM* 54 (1980), 204–15.

Meacham, S., *A life apart. The English working class 1890–1914* (1977).

Toynbee Hall and social reform, 1880–1914: the search for community (New Haven 1987).

Melman, B., *Women and the popular imagination in the twenties. Flappers and nymphs* (Basingstoke 1988).

Michels, R., *First lectures in political sociology* (New York 1965).

Miles, A., and Vincent, D., 'A land of "boundless opportunity"?: social mobility and stability in nineteenth-century England', in S. Dex (ed.), *Life and work history analyses; qualitative and quantitative developments*, Sociological Review Monograph 37 (1991), 43–72.

Mill, J. S., *Principles of political economy with some of their applications to social philosophy* (1st edn 1848).

A system of logic (1843).

Miller, W. B., and Goodwin, R. K., *Psyche and demos* (Oxford 1977).

Millerson, G., *The qualifying associations* (1964).

Milward, A. S., *War, economy and society 1939–45* (1977).

Mintz, S., *A prison of expectations. The family in Victorian culture* (1983).

Mitch, D. F., *The rise of popular literacy in Victorian England. The influence of private choice and public policy* (Philadelphia 1992).

Mitchell, B. R., and Deane, P., *Abstract of British historical statistics* (Cambridge 1962).

Mitchell, W. C., *Business cycles* (Berkeley 1971; originally published 1913).

Mohr, J. C., *Abortion in America: the origins and evolution of national policy, 1800–1900* (Oxford 1978).

Molnos, A., *Cultural source material for population planning in East Africa*, 4 vols. (Nairobi: Ford Foundation 1972).

Mommsen, W. J., and Husung, H.-G. (eds.), *The development of trade unionism in Great Britain and Germany, 1880–1914* (1985).

Mommsen, W. J., and Mock, W. (eds.), *The emergence of the welfare state in Britain and Germany 1850–1950* (1981).

Moore, G. E., *Principia ethica* (Cambridge 1903).

Moore, J., 'Deconstructing Darwinism: the politics of evolution in the 1860s' *Journal of the History of Biology* 24 (1991), 353–408.

'Socialising Darwinism: historiography and the fortunes of a phrase', in L. Levidow (ed.), *Science as politics* (1986), 38–80.

Moore, R., *Pit-men, preachers and politics. The effects of Methodism in a Durham mining community* (Cambridge 1974).

More, C., *Skill and the English working-class, 1870–1914* (1980).

More, H., *An estimate of the religion of the fashionable world* (1790).

Thoughts on the importance of the manners of the great to general society (1788).

Morgan, E., *The Puritan family: religion and domestic relations in seventeenth-century New England* (1944; new edn 1966).

Morgan, K., and Morgan, J., *Portrait of a progressive. The political career of Christopher, Viscount Addison* (Oxford 1980).

Morris, R. J., *Class, sect and party. The making of the British middle class 1820–50* (Manchester 1990).

'Clubs, societies and associations', in Thompson (ed.), *Cambridge Social History* III, 395–443.

'Voluntary societies and British urban elites, 1780–1850: an analysis' *HJ* 26 (1983), 95–118.

Mort, F., *Dangerous sexualities: medico-moral politics in England since 1830* (1987).

Moscucci, O., *The science of woman. Gynaecology and gender in England 1800–1929* (Cambridge 1990).

Mosk, C., 'Fertility and occupation: mining districts in prewar Japan' *Social Science History* 5 (1981), 293–315.

Mowat, C. L., 'Charity and case work in late Victorian London: the work of the C.O.S.' *Social Service Review* 31 (1957), 258–70.

The Charity Organisation Society 1869–1913. Its ideas and work (1961).

Mumford, K. J., '"Lost manhood" found: male sexual impotence and Victorian culture in the United States', in J. C. Fout (ed.), *Forbidden history: the state, society and the regulation of sexuality in modern Europe* (Chicago 1992), 75–99.

Musgrove, F., *Youth and the social order* (1964).

NBRC, *The declining birth-rate. Its causes and effects* (1916).

Nag, M., *Factors affecting human fertility in non-industrial societies: a cross-cultural study* (New Haven 1966).

Namboodiri, N. K., 'Some observations on the economic framework for fertility analysis' *PS* 26 (1972), 185–206.

Nardinelli, C., 'Child labor and the Factory Acts' *Journal of Economic History* 40 (1980), 739–55.

Neale, R. S., 'The standard of living 1780–1844: a regional and class study' *EcHR* 19 (1966), 590–606.

Nelson, R. R., 'A theory of the low-level equilibrium trap in underdeveloped economies' *American Economic Review* 46 (1956), 894–908.

Neuman, R. P., 'Masturbation, madness and the modern concepts of childhood and adolescence' *JSH* 8 (1975), 1–27.

Newby, H., *The deferential worker. A study of farm workers in East Anglia* (Harmondsworth 1977).

Newman, G., *Infant mortality* (1906).

Newsholme, A., *The declining birth rate: its national and international significance* (1911).

The elements of vital statistics (1st and 2nd edns 1889; 3rd edn 1899).

Fifty years in public health (1935).
The last thirty years in public health (1936).
'The national importance of child mortality' *Journal of the Royal Sanitary Institute* 31 (1910), 326–48.
'A national system of notification and regulation of sickness' *JRSS* 59 (1896), 1–28.
Newsome, D., *Godliness and good learning* (1961).
Newton, J. L., Ryan, M. P., and Walkowitz, J. R. (eds.), *Sex and class in women's history* (1983).
Nissenbaum, S., *Sex, diet, and debility in Jacksonian America: Sylvester Graham and health reform* (1980).
Noonan, J. T., *Contraception. A history of its treatment by the catholic theologians and canonists* (1965; enlarged edn 1986).
Norton, B., 'Psychologists and class', in Webster (ed.), *Biology, medicine, and society*, 289–314.
Notestein, F. W., 'Notes on the report of the royal commission on population (Great Britain)' *PI* 15 (1949), 304–11.
'Population – the long view', in T. W. Schultz (ed.), *Food for the world* (Chicago 1945), 36–57.
'The report of the royal commission on population: a review' *PS* 3 (1949), 232–40.
O'Day, R., and Englander, D., *Mr Charles Booth's inquiry. Life and labour reconsidered* (1993).
O'Gráda, C., *Ireland before and after the famine: explorations in economic history, 1800–1925* (Manchester 1988).
'New evidence on the fertility transition in Ireland, 1880–1911' *Demography* 28 (1991), 535–48.
Offer, A., *Property and politics 1870–1914: landownership, law, ideology and urban development in England* (Cambridge 1981).
Ogburn, W. F., *Social change with respect to culture and original nature* (New York 1922).
Ogle, W., 'Discussion' (part contribution) *JRSS* 49 (1886), 438.
'Discussion' (part contribution) *JRSS* 57 (1894), 683.
'On the alleged depopulation of the rural districts of England' *JRSS* 52 (1889), 206–32; 233–40 ('Discussion').
'On certain conditions of life of workmen in London' *Bulletin de l'Institut Internationale de Statistique* 6, 1 (Rome 1892), 180–7.
Okun, B. S., 'Evaluating methods for detecting fertility control: Coale and Trussell's model and cohort parity analysis' *PS* 48 (1994), 193–222.
Olby, R., 'Mendel no Mendelian' *History of Science* 17 (1979), 53–73.
Olson, M., *The logic of collective action: public goods and the theory of groups* (Cambridge, Mass., 1965).
Opie, I., and Opie, P., *The language and lore of school children* (Oxford 1967).
Osterud, N. G., 'Gender divisions and the organisation of work in the Leicester hosiery industry', in John (ed.), *Unequal opportunities*, 45–68.
Ottosson, J. O., 'Legal abortion in Sweden: thirty years' experience' *Journal of Biosocial Science* 3 (1971), 173–92.
PEP (Political and Economic Planning), *Population policy in Great Britain. A report by PEP* (1948).
Page, H. J., 'Patterns underlying fertility schedules: a decomposition by both age and marriage duration' *PS* 39 (1977), 85–106.
Pahl, R. A., *Divisions of labour* (Oxford 1984).
Parkin, F., 'Strategies of social closure in class formation', in F. Parkin (ed.), *The social analysis of class structure* (1974), 1–18.
Parsons, G. (ed.), *Religion in Victorian Britain*, 4 vols. (Manchester 1988).
Parsons, T., *The social system* (New York 1951).
The structure of social action: a study in social theory with special reference to a group of recent European writers (Glencoe, Ill. 1937).
Parsons, T., and Shils, E. (eds.) *Toward a general theory of action* (Cambridge, Mass., 1951).
Parton, C., 'The infant welfare movement in early twentieth-century Huddersfield' *Journal of Regional and Local Studies* 3 (1983), 69–77.

Passmore, J., *The perfectibility of man* (1970).

Pastore, N., *The nature–nurture controversy* (New York 1949).

Pateman, C., *The sexual contract* (Cambridge 1988).

Paul, D., 'Eugenics and the left' *JHI* 45 (1984), 567–90.

Peacock, A. T., Wiseman, J. (and Veverka, J.), *The growth of public expenditure in the United Kingdom* (revised edn 1967; first published 1961).

Pearson, K., 'Contributions to the mathematical theory of evolution. Note on reproductive selection', communicated by F. Galton, *Proceedings of the Royal Society of London* 59 (1895–6), 301–5.

The grammar of science (1892).

'Reproductive selection', in K. Pearson, *The chance of death and other studies in evolution*, Vol. I (1897), 63–102.

Pedersen, S., 'The failure of feminism in the making of the British welfare state' *Radical History Review* 43 (1989), 86–110.

Family, dependence, and the origins of the welfare state. Britain and France 1914–45 (Cambridge 1993).

Peel, J., 'The manufacture and retailing of contraceptives in England' *PS* 17 (1963), 113–25.

Peel, J. D. Y., *Herbert Spencer: the evolution of a sociologist* (1971).

Pelling, H. M., 'The concept of the labour aristocracy', in H. M. Pelling, *Popular politics and society in late Victorian Britain* (1968), 37–61.

A history of British trade unionism (Harmondsworth 1963; 5th edn 1992).

Social geography of British elections 1885–1910 (1967).

Pelling, M., *Cholera, fever and English medicine, 1825–65* (Oxford 1978).

Pennington, S., and Westover, B., *A hidden workforce. Homeworkers in England 1850–1985* (1989).

Perkin, H., *The rise of professional society. England since 1880* (1989).

Perry, C. R., *The Victorian Post Office. The growth of a bureaucracy* (Woodbridge 1992).

Peter, K. A., 'The certainty of salvation: ritualisation of religion and economic rationality among Hutterites' *CSSH* 25 (1983), 222–40.

Peterson, M. J., *Family, love and work in the lives of Victorian gentlewomen* (Bloomington 1989).

The medical profession in mid-Victorian London (Berkeley 1978).

Pfeffer, N., *The stork and the syringe. A political history of reproductive medicine* (Cambridge 1993).

Phelps Brown, E. H., *The growth of British industrial relations. A study from the standpoint of 1906–14* (1959).

Phillips, R., *Untying the knot. A short history of divorce* (Cambridge 1991).

Pick, D., *Faces of degeneration. A European disorder c. 1848 – c. 1918* (Cambridge 1989).

Pinchbeck, I., *Women workers and the industrial revolution* (1930).

Pinchbeck, I., and Hewitt, M., *Children in English society*, Vol. II: *From the eighteenth century to the Children Act 1948* (1973).

Pivar, D. J., *Purity crusade: sexual morality and social control, 1868–1900* (Westport 1973).

Plumb, J. H., 'The new world of children in eighteenth century England' *P&P* 67 (1975), 64–93.

Polanyi, K., *The great transformation: the political and economic origins of our time* (1946).

Pollack, S., 'Sex and the contraceptive act', in H. Homans (ed.), *The sexual politics of reproduction* (Aldershot 1985), 64–77.

Pollak, R. A., and Watkins, S. C., 'Cultural and economic approaches to fertility: proper marriage or *mésalliance*' *PDR* 19 (1993), 467–96.

Pollard, S., *Britain's prime and Britain's decline. The British economy 1870–1914* (1989).

The development of the British economy 1914–90 (1992).

Pollock, L., *Forgotten children: parent–child relations from 1500–1900* (Cambridge 1983).

A lasting relationship: parents and children over three centuries (1987).

Poovey, M., *Uneven developments. The ideological work of gender in mid-Victorian England* (1989).
Popper, K. R., *Conjectures and refutations. The growth of scientific knowledge* (1963).
Porter, D., '"Enemies of the race": biologism, environmentalism, and public health in Edwardian England' *VS* 35 (1991), 159–78.
Porter, D., and Porter, R., 'What was social medicine? An historiographical essay' *Journal of Historical Sociology* 1 (1988), 90–106.
Porter, R., *The making of geology: earth science in Britain, 1660–1815* (Cambridge 1977).
'Mixed feelings: the Enlightenment and sexuality in eighteenth-century Britain', in P.-G. Boucé (ed.), *Sexuality in eighteenth-century Britain* (Manchester 1982), 1–27.
(ed.), *Patients and practitioners. Lay perceptions of medicine in pre-industrial society* (Cambridge 1985).
Porter, R., and Hall, L., *The facts of life. The creation of sexual knowledge in Britain, 1650–1950* (1995).
Porter, T. M., *The rise of statistical thinking 1820–1900* (Princeton 1986).
Trust in numbers: the pursuit of objectivity in science and public life (Princeton 1995).
Prest, J., *Liberty and locality. Parliament, permissive legislation, and ratepayers' democracies in the mid-nineteenth century* (Oxford 1990).
Prest, W. (ed.), *The professions in early modern England* (1987).
Prochaska, F., 'A mother's country: mothers' meetings and family welfare in Britain, 1850–1950' *History* 74 (1989), 379–99.
Women and philanthropy in nineteenth-century England (Oxford 1980).
Provine, W. B., *The origins of theoretical population genetics* (Chicago 1971).
Sewall Wright and evolutionary biology (Chicago 1986).
Pugh, M., *Women and the women's movement in Britain 1914–59* (1992).
Quaife, G. R., *Wanton wenches and wayward wives: peasants and illicit sex in early seventeenth century England* (1979).
Quétel, C. *History of syphilis*, transl. J. Braddock and B. Pike (Oxford 1990).
Quetelet, L. A. J., *Anthropométrie ou mésure des différentes facultés de l'homme* (Brussels 1870).
Rabinowicz, L., *Le Problème de la population* (Paris 1929).
Rapp, D., 'The early discovery of Freud by the British general educated public, 1912–19' *SHM* 3 (1990), 217–43.
Raymond, J., 'Science in the service of medicine' *Society for Social History of Medicine Bulletin* 37 (1985), 43–5.
Read, D., *The age of urban democracy. England 1868–1914* (rev. edn 1994).
Reader, W. J., *Professional men* (1966).
Reay, B., 'Before the transition: fertility in English villages 1800–1880' *Continuity and Change* 9 (1994), 91–120.
Reddy, W. H., *The rise of market culture: the textile trade and French society 1750–1900* (Cambridge 1984).
Redford, A., *Labour migration in England 1800–1850* (Manchester 1926).
Reed, J., *From private vice to public virtue: the birth control movement and American society since 1830* (New York 1978).
Reid, A., 'Intelligent artisans and aristocrats of labour: the essays of Thomas Wright', in J. M. Winter (ed.), *The working class in modern British history* (Cambridge 1983), 171–86.
'The labour aristocracy in British social history' *Our History* 5 (1979), 3–6.
'Politics and economics in the formation of the British working class: a response to H. F. Moorhouse' *SH* 3 (1978), 347–61.
Social classes and social relations in Britain 1850–1914 (1992).
Reid, D. A., 'The decline of Saint Monday 1766–1876' *P&P* 71 (1976), 76–101.
Rendall, J., *The origins of modern feminism* (1985).
Renfrew, C., *Archaeology and language: the puzzle of Indo-European origins* (1987).
Retherford, R. D., *The changing sex differential in mortality* (Westport 1975).

Richards, E., 'The "Moral Anatomy" of Robert Knox: the interplay between biological and social thought in Victorian scientific naturalism' *Journal of the History of Biology* 22 (1989), 373–436.

Richardson, B. W., *Diseases of modern life* (1875).

The health of nations: a review of the works of Edwin Chadwick, 2 vols. (1887).

Hygiea: a city of health (1876).

A ministry of health and other essays (1879).

Richter, M., *The politics of conscience: T. H. Green and his age* (1964).

Riddle, J. M., *Contraception and abortion from the ancient world to the Renaissance* (1992).

'Oral contraceptives and early-term abortifacients during classical antiquity and the middle ages' *P&P* 132 (1991), 3–32.

Riesman, D. (with N. Glazer and R. Denney), *The lonely crowd* (New Haven 1950).

Riley, D., *War in the nursery: theories of the child and mother* (1983).

Rindfuss, R. R., and Morgan, S. P., 'Marriage, sex, and the first birth interval in Asia' *PDR* 10 (1983), 259–78.

Roach, J., *Public examination in England 1850–1900* (Cambridge 1971).

Robb-Smith, A. H. T., 'A history of the College's nomenclature of diseases: its reception' *Journal of the Royal College of Physicians of London* 4 (1969), 5–26.

Roberts, C., *A manual of anthropometry* (London 1878).

'Memorandum on the medical inspection of and physical education in secondary schools' *Report of the Royal Commission on Secondary Education in England*, Vol. V, pp. 352–74, PP 1895 XLVII, Cd 7862-iv.

'The physical development and the proportions of the human body' *St George's Hospital Reports* 8 (1874–6), 1–48.

'The physical requirements of factory children' *JSSL* 39 (1876), 681–733.

'On the uses and limitations of anthropometry' *Bulletin de l'institut International de Statistique* 6, 1 (Rome 1892), 13–18.

Roberts, D., 'The paterfamilias of the Victorian governing classes', in Wohl (ed.), *The Victorian family*, 59–81.

Paternalism in early Victorian England (1979).

Roberts, E., *A woman's place. An oral history of working class women 1890–1940* (Oxford 1984).

Women's work 1840–1940 (1988).

'Working class standards of living in Barrow and Lancaster 1890–1914' *EcHR* 30 (1977), 306–21.

Roberts, R., *The classic slum* (1971).

Robinson, W. C., 'Kenya enters the fertility transition' *PS* 46 (1992), 445–57.

Rogers, E., *Diffusion of innovations* (Glencoe 1962).

Rose, J., *Marie Stopes and the sexual revolution* (1992).

Rose, John, *The Edwardian temperament 1895–1919* (1986).

'Willingly to school: the working-class response to elementary education in Britain, 1875–1918' *Journal of British Studies* 32 (1993), 114–38.

Rose, L., *Massacre of the innocents. Infanticide in Great Britain 1800–1939* (1986).

Rose, M. E. (ed.), *The poor and the city: the English Poor Law in its urban context 1834–1914* (Leicester 1985).

Rose, N., *The psychological complex. Psychology, politics and society in England, 1869–1939* (1985).

Rose, P., *Parallel lives. Five Victorian marriages* (1984).

Rose, S. O., *Limited livelihoods. Gender and class in nineteenth-century Britain* (1992).

'Respectable men, disorderly others: the language of gender and the Lancashire weavers' strike of 1878 in Britain' *G&H* 5 (1993), 382–97.

Ross, E., *Love and toil. Motherhood in outcast London 1870–1918* (Oxford 1993).

'Mothers and the state in Britain', in Gillis *et al.* (eds.), *The European experience*, 48–65.

'"Not the sort that would sit on the doorstep": respectability in pre-World War I London neighbourhoods' *International Labour and Working-Class History* 27 (1985), 39–59.
Rostow, W. W., *The stages of economic growth: a non-Communist manifesto* (Cambridge 1960).
Rothblatt, S., *The revolution of the dons* (1968).
Rothman, E., *Hands and hearts: a history of courtship in America* (New York 1984).
Routh, G., *Occupation and pay in Great Britain 1906–60* (Cambridge 1965).
Rowbotham, J., *Good girls make good wives: guidance for girls in Victorian fiction* (Oxford 1989).
Rowe, J., *Wages in practice and theory* (1928).
Rowntree, B. S., *Poverty: a study of town life* (1901).
The poverty line: a reply (1903).
Rowntree, B. S., and Kendall, M., *How the labourer lives. A study of the rural labour problem* (1913).
Rowntree, B. S., and Lavers, G. R., *Poverty and the welfare state* (1951).
Rubin, M., and Westergaard, H., *Ægteskabsstatistik paa Grundlag af den sociale Lagdeling* (*Statistics of Marriages*) (Copenhagen 1890). This was also published in German as *Statistik der Ehen auf Grund der socialen Gliederung der Bevölkerung* (Jena 1890).
Rubinstein, D., *Before the suffragettes. Women's emancipation in the 1890s* (Brighton 1986).
School attendance in London 1870–1904: a social history (Hull 1969).
Rubinstein, W. D., 'Cutting up rich: a reply to F.M.L. Thompson' *EcHR* 45 (1992), 350–61.
Men of property (1981).
'New men of wealth and the purchase of land in nineteenth-century Britain' *P&P* 92 (1981), 125–47.
'Wealth, elites, and the class structure of modern Britain' *P&P* 76 (1977), 99–126.
Rumsey, H. W., *Essays on state medicine* (1856).
'On certain fallacies in local rates of mortality' *Transactions of the Manchester Statistical Society* (1871–2), 17–39.
Ryan, A., *The philosophy of the social sciences* (1970).
Ryder, N. B., 'Fertility', in P. M. Hauser and O. D. Duncan (eds.), *The study of population: an appraisal and inventory* (Chicago 1959), 400–36.
'Notes on the concept of a population' *American Journal of Sociology* 69 (1964), 447–63.
Santow, G., 'Coitus interruptus and the control of natural fertility' *PS* 49 (1995), 19–43.
Sargant, W. L., 'On certain results and defects of the Registrar-General' *JSSL* 27 (1864), 170–221.
Sarsby, J., *Missuses and mouldrunners* (Milton Keynes 1988).
Savage, G., '"The wilful communication of a loathsome disease": marital conflict and venereal disease in Victorian London' *VS* 34 (1990), 35–54.
Savage, M., *The dynamics of working class politics. The labour movement in Preston 1880–1940* (Cambridge 1987).
'Women and work in the Lancashire cotton industry, 1890–1939', in M. Jowitt and A. J. McIvor (eds.), *Employers and labour in the English textiles industry 1850–1939* (1988), 203–23.
Schellekens, J., 'Wages, secondary workers, and fertility: a working-class perspective of the fertility transition in England and Wales' *JFH* 18 (1993), 1–17.
Schelling, T., *Micromotives and macrobehaviour* (New York 1978).
Schmeichen, J. A., *Sweated industries and sweated labour. The London clothing trades, 1860–1914* (1984).
Schneider, J., and Schneider, P., *Culture and political economy in Western Sicily* (New York 1976).
'Demographic transitions in a Sicilian rural town' *JFH* 9 (1984), 245–73.
'Going forward in reverse gear: culture, economy and political economy in the demographic transitions of a rural Sicilian town', in J. R. Gillis *et al.*, *The European experience* (1992), 146–74.
Schofield, M., *The sexual behaviour of young adults* (1968).
The sexual behaviour of young people (1965).

Schofield, R. S., 'Family structure, demographic behaviour and economic growth', in J. Walter and R. Schofield (eds.), *Famine, disease and the social order in early modern society* (Cambridge 1989), 279–304.

Scholliers, P. (ed.), *Real wages in 19th and 20th century Europe. Historical and comparative perspectives* (Oxford 1989).

Schweber, S., 'The origin of the "Origin" revisited' *Journal of the History of Biology* 10 (1977), 229–316.

Scott, J. C., *Domination and the arts of resistance* (1990).

Scott, J. W., *Gender and the politics of history* (Oxford 1988).

Scull, A. T., *Museums of madness: the social organisation of insanity in nineteenth-century England* (1979).

'Museums of madness revisited' *SHM* 6 (1993), 3–23.

Searle, G. R., 'Eugenics and class', in Webster (ed.), *Biology, medicine and society*, 217–42.

'Introduction' to reprint of A. White, *Efficiency and empire* (1973).

The quest for national efficiency: a study in British politics and thought 1899–1914 (Oxford 1971).

Seccombe, W., *A millennium of family change. Feudalism to capitalism in Northwestern Europe* (1992).

'Patriarchy stabilised: the construction of the male breadwinner norm' *SH* (1986), 53–75.

'Starting to stop: working class fertility decline in Britain' *P&P* 126 (1990), 151–88.

Weathering the storm. Working-class families from the industrial revolution to the fertility decline (1993).

Secord, J. A., *Controversy in Victorian geology: the Cambrian–Silurian dispute* (Princeton 1986).

Sedgwick, E. Kosofsky, *Between men: English literature and male homosocial desire* (New York 1985).

Segal, L., 'Look back in anger: men in the fifties', in R. Chapman and J. Rutherford (eds.), *Male order. Unwrapping masculinity* (1988), 69–96.

Seidman, S., 'The power of desire and the danger of pleasure: Victorian sexuality reconsidered' *JSH* 23 (1990), 46–67.

Romantic longings: love in America, 1830–1980 (New Brunswick, N.J. 1991).

Semmel, B., *Imperialism and social reform. English social-imperial thought 1895–1914* (1960).

Sen, A. K., *Poverty and famine. An essay on entitlement and deprivation* (Oxford 1981).

Sewell, W. H., 'How classes are made: critical reflections on E. P. Thompson's theory of working class formation', in Kaye and McClelland (eds.), *E. P. Thompson*, 50–77.

Work and revolution in France: the language of labor from the Old Regime to 1848 (Cambridge 1980).

Shanley, M. L., *Feminism, marriage and the law in Victorian England* (Princeton 1989).

Sharlin, A., 'Urban–rural differences in fertility in Europe during the demographic transition', in Coale and Watkins (eds.), *The decline of fertility*, 234–60.

Sherard, R., *The child slaves of England* (1905).

Shils, E., 'On the eve: a prospect in retrospect', in Bulmer (ed.), *Essays in the history*, 165–78.

Shonfield, Z., *The precariously privileged. A professional family in Victorian London* (Oxford 1987).

Shorter, E., *The making of the modern family* (1976).

Showalter, E., *Sexual anarchy. Gender and culture at the Fin de Siècle* (1990).

Shryock, R. H., *The development of modern medicine* (1948).

Silberling, N. J., 'British prices and business cycles, 1779–1850' *Review of Economic Statistics* 5, Supplement (1923), 219–61.

Simey, T. S., and Simey, M. B., *Charles Booth* (Oxford 1960).

Simon, B., *Education and the labour movement 1870–1918* (1965).

Studies in the history of education 1780–1870 (1960).

Simon, H. A., 'From substantive to procedural rationality', in F. Hahn and M. Hollis (eds.), *Philosophy and economic theory* (Oxford 1979), 65–86.

Simons, J., 'Reproductive behaviour as religious practice', in C. Hohn and R. Mackensen (eds.), *Determinants of fertility trends: theories re-examined* (Liège 1980), 131–45.

Slater, E., and Woodside, M., *Patterns of marriage: a study of marital relationships in the urban working class* (1951).

Sloan, D. G., 'The extent of contraceptive use and the social paradigm of modern demography' *Sociology* 17 (1983), 380–7.

Smelser, N., *Social change in the industrial revolution* (1959).

Smith, D. Scott, 'Family limitation, sexual control and domestic feminism in Victorian America' *FS* 1 (1973), 40–57.

Smith, F. B., *The retreat of tuberculosis 1850–1950* (1988).

Smith, G. E., *Culture: the diffusion controversy* (New York 1927).

Smith, H. L. (ed.), *British feminism in the twentieth century* (Aldershot 1990).

Smith, J. V., and Hamilton, D. (eds.), *The meritocratic intellect. Studies in the history of educational research* (Aberdeen 1980).

Smith, R. M., 'Transfer incomes, risk and security: the roles of the family and the collectivity in recent theories of fertility change', in D. A. Coleman and R. S. Schofield (eds.), *The state of population theory. Forward from Malthus* (Oxford 1986), 188–211.

'Welfare and the management of demographic uncertainty', in M. Keynes (ed.), *The political economy of health and welfare* (1988), 108–35.

Smith-Rosenberg, C., 'The female world of love and ritual: relations between women in nineteenth-century America' *Signs* 1 (1973), 58–72.

Snedecor, K., and Cochran, W. G., *Statistical methods* (6th edn, Iowa 1967).

Soffer, R. N., 'The revolution in English social thought 1880–1914' *AHR* 75 (1979), 1938–64.

Soloway, R. A., *Birth control and the population question in England 1877–1930* (Chapel Hill 1982).

Demography and degeneration. Eugenics and the declining birthrate in twentieth-century Britain (Chapel Hill 1990).

Prelates and people. Ecclesiastical social thought in England 1783–1852 (1969).

Spencer, H., *The principles of sociology*, 3 vols. (1876).

Social statics: or the conditions essential to human happiness specified, and the first of ten developed (1851).

The study of sociology (1873).

Spengler, J. J., *France faces depopulation* (Raleigh, N.C., 1938).

'French population theory since 1800' Parts I and II *Journal of Political Economy* 44 (1936), 577–611; 743–66.

Springhall, J., *Coming of age: adolescence in Britain, 1860–1960* (Dublin 1986).

Stanley, L., *The diaries of Hannah Cullwick* (1984).

Stearns, P. N., and Knapp, M., 'Men and romantic love: pinpointing a 20th-century change' *JSH* 26 (1993), 769–95.

Stedman Jones, G., 'Class expression versus social control? A critique of recent trends in the social history of "leisure"', in *Languages of class*, 76–89.

'Class struggle and the industrial revolution', in *Languages of class*, 25–75.

'The "cockney" and the nation, 1780–1988', in Feldman and Stedman Jones (eds.), *Metropolis London*, 272–324.

'From historical sociology to theoretical history' *British Journal of Sociology* 27 (1976), 295–305.

Languages of class. Studies in English working-class history 1832–1982 (Cambridge 1983).

Outcast London (Oxford 1971; 2nd edn, Harmondsworth 1984).

'Rethinking Chartism', in *Languages of class*, 90–178.

'Working class culture and working class politics in London 1870–1900; notes on the remaking of a working class' *JSH* 8 (1974), 460–508.

Steedman, C., 'Bodies, figures and physiology. Margaret McMillan and the late nineteenth-century remaking of working-class childhood', in R. Cooter (ed.), *In the name of the child*, 19–44.

Childhood, culture and class. Margaret McMillan 1860–1931 (New Brunswick, N.J. 1990).

Steiner, Z., *The Foreign Office and foreign policy 1898–1914* (Cambridge 1969).
Stepan, N., *The idea of race in science. Great Britain 1800–1960* (1982).
Stevenson, T. H. C., 'The fertility of various social classes in England and Wales from the middle of the nineteenth century to 1911' *JRSS* 83 (1920), 401–44.
'The graphic method of constructing a life table illustrated by the Brighton life table 1891–1900' *Journal of Hygiene* 3 (1903), 297–304.
'The laws governing population' *JRSS* 88 (1925), 63–90.
'A method of estimating populations' *Journal of Hygiene* 4 (1904), 207–16.
'Suggested lines of advance in English vital statistics' *JRSS* 73 (1910), 685–713.
'The vital statistics of wealth and poverty' *JRSS* 91 (1928), 207–30.
Stevenson, T. H. C., and Newsholme, A., 'The decline of human fertility in the U.K. and other countries as shown by corrected birth rates' *JRSS* 69 (1906), 34–87.
'An improved method of calculating birth-rates' *Journal of Hygiene* 5 (1905), 175–84.
Stewart, J., 'Ramsay MacDonald, the Labour party, and child welfare, 1900–1914' *Twentieth Century History* 4 (1993), 105–25.
Stewart, R., *Henry Brougham 1778–1868. His public career* (1985).
Stigler, S. M., *The history of statistics* (Cambridge, Mass., 1986).
Stix, R., and Notestein, F. W., *Controlled fertility. An evaluation of clinic service* (Baltimore 1940).
Stocking, G. W., 'Introductory essay', to J. C. Prichard, *Researches into the physical history of man* (Chicago 1973).
Victorian anthropology (1987).
'What's in a name? The origins of the Royal Anthropological Institute (1837–1871)' *Man* 6 (1971), 369–90.
Stokes, E., *The English utilitarians and India* (Oxford 1959).
Stone, L., *The family, sex and marriage 1500–1800* (1977).
Stone, L., and Stone, J., *An open élite? England 1540–1880* (Oxford 1984).
Stopes, M., *Contraception: its theory, history and practice* (1923).
Early days of birth control (1921).
Married love. A new contribution to the solution of sex difficulties (1918).
(ed.), *Mother England: a contemporary history* (2nd edn 1930).
Strachey, R., *The cause: a short history of the women's movement in Great Britain* (1928).
Stycos, J. M., 'Culture and differential fertility in Peru', *PS* 16 (1963), 257–70.
Family and fertility in Puerto Rico. A study of the lower income group (New York 1955).
Human fertility in Latin-America: sociological perspectives (Ithaca 1968).
Stycos, J. M., Back, K., and Hill, R., 'Problems of communication between husband and wife on matters relating to family limitation' *Human relations* 9 (1956), 207–15.
Stycos, J. M., and Weller, R. H., 'Female working roles and fertility' *Demography* 4 (1967), 210–17.
Supple, B. E., 'Fear of failing: economic history and the decline of Britain' *EcHR* 47 (1994), 441–58.
The history of the British coal industry, vol. 4: 1913–1946, the political economy of decline (Oxford 1987).
Sutherland, G., *Ability, merit and measurement. Mental testing and English education 1880–1940* (Oxford 1984).
'Education', in F. M. L. Thompson (ed.), *The Cambridge social history of Britain* III (1990), 119–69.
'The movement for higher education of women 1840–1880', in Waller (ed.), *Politics and social change*, 91–116.
Policy-making in elementary education 1870–95 (Oxford 1973).
(ed.), *Studies in the growth of nineteenth-century government* (1972).
Sutter, J., 'Un démographe engagé: Arsène Dumont (1849–1902)' *Population* 8 (1953), 79–92.
Szreter, R., 'The origins of full-time compulsory education at five' *British Journal of Educational Studies* 13 (1964), 16–28.

Szreter, S. R. S., 'The first scientific social structure of modern Britain 1875–1883', in Bonfield *et al.* (eds.), *The world we have gained*, 337–54.

'The G.R.O. and the historians' *SHM* 4 (1991), 401–14.

'The G.R.O. and the public health movement 1837–1914' *SHM* 4 (1991), 435–63.

'Healthy government? Britain *c.* 1850–1950' *HJ* 34 (1991), 491–503.

'The idea of demographic transition: a critical intellectual history' *PDR* 19 (1993), 659–701.

'The official representation of social classes in Britain, United States and France: the professional model and "les cadres"' *CSSH* 35 (1993), 285–317.

Tanner, J. M., *A history of the study of human growth* (Cambridge 1981).

Tarde, G., *The laws of imitation*, transl. E. C. Parsons (New York 1903).

Taylor, A., *Annie Besant: a biography* (Oxford 1992).

Taylor, B., *Eve and the New Jerusalem. Socialism and feminism in the nineteenth century* (1983).

Teitelbaum, M. S., *The British fertility decline. Demographic transition in the crucible of the industrial revolution* (Princeton 1984).

Thane, P., 'The debate on the declining birthrate: the menace of an ageing population in Britain, 1920–50' *Continuity and Change* 5 (1990), 283–305.

The foundations of the welfare state (1982).

'Late Victorian women', in T. R. Gourvish and A. O'Day (eds.), *Later Victorian Britain 1867–1900* (1988), 175–208.

'Towards equal opportunities? Women in Britain since 1945', in T. R. Gourvish and A. O'Day (eds.), *Britain since 1945* (1991), 183–208.

'Visions of gender in the making of the British welfare state: the case of women in the British Labour party and social policy, 1906–45', in G. Bock and P. Thane (eds.), *Maternity and gender policies. Women and the rise of the European welfare states 1880s–1950s* (1991), 93–118.

'Women in the British Labour party and the construction of state welfare 1906–39' in S. Koven and S. Michel (eds.), *Mothers of a new world. Maternalist politics and the origin of welfare states* (1993), 343–77.

Thirsk, J., *Economic policy and projects: the development of a consumer society in early modern England* (Oxford 1978).

Thomas, D. S., *Social aspects of the business cycle* (1925).

Thomas, K., 'The double standard' *JHI* 20 (1959), 195–216.

Thomas, N., 'Land, fertility and the population establishment' *PS* 45 (1991), 379–97.

Thompson, Dorothy, *The Chartists* (1984).

Thompson, D., 'Courtship and marriage in Preston between the wars' *OH* 3 (1975), 39–44.

Thompson, E. P., *Customs in common* (1991).

The making of the English working class (1963).

Thompson, F. M. L., 'Life after death: how successful nineteenth-century businessmen disposed of their fortunes' *EcHR* 43 (1990), 40–61.

The rise of respectable society. A social history of Britain 1830–1900 (1988).

'Social control in Victorian Britain' *EcHR* 33 (1981), 189–208.

'Stitching it together again' *EcHR* (1992), 362–75.

(ed.), *Cambridge social history of Britain 1750–1950*, 3 vols. (1990).

Thompson, P., *The Edwardians. The remaking of British society* (1975).

'Women in the fishing: the roots of power between the sexes' *CSSH* 27 (1985), 3–32.

Thompson, T., *Edwardian childhoods* (1981).

Thompson, W. S., 'Population' *American Journal of Sociology* 34 (1929), 959–75.

Population problems (3rd edn, New York 1942).

Thomson, D., 'Welfare and the historians', in Bonfield *et al.* (eds.), *The world we have gained*, 355–78.

Titmuss, R. M., and Titmuss, K., *Parents revolt. A study of the declining birth rate in acquisitive societies* (1942).

Tomes, N., 'A "Torrent of abuse": crimes of violence between working-class men and women in London. 1840–75' *JSH* 11 (1978), 328–45.

Tosh, J., 'Domesticity and manliness in the Victorian middle class. The family of Edward White Benson', in M. Roper and J. Tosh (eds.), *Manful assertions: masculinities in Britain since 1800* (1991), 44–73.

Treble, J. H., *Urban poverty in Britain 1830–1914* (1979).

Trumbach, R., *The rise of the egalitarian family* (New York 1978).

Trussell, J., Menken, J., and Coale, A. J., 'A general model for analysing effects of nuptiality on fertility', in L. T. Ruzicka (ed.), *Nuptiality and fertility*, IUSSP Conference Papers, Bruges (1979), 7–28.

Turner, F. M., *Contesting cultural authority. Essays in Victorian intellectual life* (Cambridge 1993).

The Greek heritage in Victorian Britain (1980).

Turner, S. P., 'Forms of patronage', in S. E. Cozzens and T. F. Gieryn (eds.), *Theories of science in society* (Bloomington 1990), 185–211.

'The survey in nineteenth-century American geology: the evolution of a form of patronage' *Minerva* 25 (1987), 282–330.

Valverde, M., '"Giving the female a domestic turn": the social, moral and legal regulation of women's work in British cotton mills 1827–50' *JSH* 21 (1988), 619–34.

Van de Walle, E., *The female population of France in the nineteenth century: a reconstruction of 82 départments* (Princeton 1974).

'Fertility transition, conscious choice and numeracy' *Demography* 29 (1992), 487–502.

Vann, R. T., and Eversley, D., *Friends in life and death. The British and Irish Quakers in the demographic transition* (Cambridge 1992).

Veit-Wilson, J. H., 'Paradigms of poverty: a rehabilitation of B. S. Rowntree' *Journal of Social Policy* 15 (1986), 69–99; and ensuing debate with P. Townsend and H. McLachlan, 497–507.

Vincent, D., *Literacy and popular culture, England 1750–1914* (Cambridge 1989).

Vincent, J. R., *The formation of the British Liberal Party, 1857–68* (Harmondsworth 1972).

Pollbooks: how Victorians voted (Cambridge 1967).

Vlassof, C., 'The value of sons in an Indian village: how widows see it' *PS* 44 (1990), 5–20; and subsequent exchange with Mead Cain: *PS* 45 (1991), 519–28; 529–35.

Waddington, I., *The medical profession in the industrial revolution* (Dublin 1984).

Wahrman, D., '"Middle-class" domesticity goes public: gender, class and politics from Queen Caroline to Queen Victoria' *Journal of British Studies* 32 (1993), 396–432.

Waites, B., *A class society at war. England 1914–18* (Leamington Spa 1987).

Walby, S., *Patriarchy at work. Patriarchal and capitalist relations in employment* (Cambridge 1986).

Walker, S. P., *The Society of Accountants in Edinburgh 1854–1914* (1988).

Walkowitz, J., *Prostitution and Victorian society. Women, class and the state* (Cambridge 1980).

'Science, feminism and Romance: the Men and Women's Club, 1885–89' *HW* 21 (1986), 37–59.

Waller, P. J., 'Democracy and dialect, speech and class', in Waller (ed.), *Politics and social change*, 1–33.

Democracy and sectarianism. A political and social history of Liverpool 1868–1939 (Liverpool 1981).

(ed.), *Politics and social change in modern Britain* (Brighton 1987).

Town, city and nation. England 1850–1914 (Oxford 1983).

Wandersee, W. D., *Women's work and family values 1920–40* (Cambridge, Mass., 1981).

Ward, J. T., *The factory movement 1830–1850* (1962).

Watkins, S. C., *From provinces into nations. Demographic integration in western Europe 1870–1960* (Princeton 1991).

'Regional patterns of nuptiality in western Europe', in Coale and Watkins (eds.), *The decline of fertility*, 314–36.

Weatherill, L., *Consumer behaviour and material culture in Britain, 1660–1760* (1988).
Webb, S., *The decline of the birth rate*, Fabian Tract 131 (1907).
The difficulties of individualism, Fabian Tract 69 (1896).
Webb, S., and Webb, B., *English local government from the revolution to the Municipal Corporations Act*, 9 vols. (1906–29).
The history of trade unionism 1666–1920 (1920).
Weber, G., 'Science and society in nineteenth century anthropology' *History of Science* 12 (1974), 260–83.
Weber, Max, 'Religious ethics and the world: sexuality and art', in Max Weber, *Economy and society*, transl. G. Roth and C. Wittich (Glencoe 1968).
Selections in translation, ed. W. G. Runciman, transl. E. Matthews (Cambridge 1978).
Webster, C. (ed.), *Biology, medicine, and society 1840–1940* (Cambridge 1981).
Weeks, J., *Coming out: homosexual politics in Britain from the nineteenth century to the present* (1977).
Sex, politics and society. The regulation of sexuality since 1800 (1981).
Weinstein, M., Wood, J. W., Stoto, M. A., and Greenfield, D. D., 'Components of age-specific fecundability' *PS* 44 (1990), 447–67.
Weir, D., 'New estimates of nuptiality and marital fertility in France, 1740–1911' *PS* 48 (1994), 307–31.
Weismann, A., *The germ plasm. A theory of heredity*, transl. W. Newton Parker and H. Ronfeldt (1893).
Wellings, K., Field, J., Johnson, M., and Wadsworth, J., *Sexual behaviour in Britain. The National Survey of Sexual Attitudes and Lifestyles* (Harmondsworth 1994).
Welton, T. A., *England's recent progress* (1911).
'Occupations in England and Wales 1881 and 1901' *JRSS* 73 (1910), 164–6.
'On the classification of the people by occupations; and on other subjects connected with population statistics' *JSSL* 32 (1869), 271–87.
Werskey, G., *The visible college. A collective biography of British scientists and socialists of the 1930s* (1978).
Whetham, C. D., and Whetham, W. C. D., *The family and the nation: a study in natural inheritance and social responsibility* (1909).
Whipp, R., *Patterns of labour. Work and social change in the pottery industry* (1990).
'Women and the social organisation of work in the Staffordshire pottery industry, 1900–30' *Midland History* 12 (1987), 103–21.
White, A., *The destitute alien* (1892).
The problems of a great city (1887).
White, J. L., *The limits of trade union militancy: Lancashire textiles workers 1910–14* (Westport 1978).
Williams, K., *From pauperism to poverty* (1981).
Williams, R., *Culture and society 1780–1950* (1958).
Willis, P., *Learning to labour. How working class kids get working class jobs* (1977).
Wilson, C., 'The proximate determinants of marital fertility in England 1600–1799', in Bonfield *et al.* (eds.), *The world we have gained*, 203–30.
Wilson, C., Oeppen, J., and Pardoe, M., 'What is natural fertility? The modelling of a concept' *PI* 54 (1988), 4–20.
Wilson, C., and Woods, R., 'Fertility in England: a long-term perspective' *PS* 45 (1991), 399–415.
Wilson, C. H., *England's apprenticeship 1603–1763* (1965).
Wilson, D. J., 'Arthur O. Lovejoy and the moral of *The Great Chain of Being*' *JHI* 41 (1980), 249–65.
Wilson, E., *Women and the welfare state* (1977).
Winch, P., *The idea of a social science and its relation to philosophy* (1958; 2nd edn 1990).
Winstanley, M. J., *The shopkeeper's world 1830–1914* (Manchester 1983).
Winter, J. M., *The Great War and the British people* (1985).

Wittgenstein, L., *Philosophical investigations*, transl. G. E. M. Anscombe (Oxford 1953).
Tractatus logico-philosophicus (1923).
Wohl, A. S., *Endangered lives. Public health in Victorian Britain* (1983).
(ed.), *The Victorian family, structures and stresses* (1978).
Wolf, E. R., 'Aspects of group relations in a complex society: Mexico', in T. Shanin (ed.), *Peasants and peasant society* (Harmondsworth 1971), 50–68.
Woodruffe, K., 'The Charity Organisation Society and the origin of social casework' *Historical Studies* No. 33 (1959), in Vol. 9 (1959–61), 19–29.
Woods, R., 'Debate: working class fertility decline in Britain', Comment; and Reply by W. Seccombe, *P&P* 134 (1992), 200–11.
'The fertility transition in nineteenth-century England and Wales: a social class model?' *Tijdschrift voor Economische en Sociale Geografie* 76 (1985), 180–91.
Woods, R., and Smith, C. W., 'The decline of marital fertility in the late nineteenth century: the case of England and Wales' *PS* 37 (1983), 207–25.
Woods, R., Watterson, P. A., and Woodward, J. H., 'The causes of rapid infant mortality decline in England and Wales, 1861–1921', Part I, *PS* 42 (1988), 343–66; Part II, *PS* 43 (1989), 113–32.
Wright, M., 'Treasury control 1854–1914', in Sutherland (ed.), *Studies in the growth*, 195–226.
Wright, T., *Some habits and customs of the working classes* (1867).
Wright Mills, C., *The sociological imagination* (New York 1959).
Wrightson, K., *English society 1580–1680* (1982).
'Estates, degrees, and sorts: changing perceptions of society in Tudor and Stuart England', in Corfield (ed.), *Language, history and class*, 30–52.
Wrightson, K., and Levine, D., *Poverty and piety in an English village. Terling 1525–1700* (1979).
Wrigley, E. A., *Continuity, chance and change* (Cambridge 1988).
'The fall of marital fertility in nineteenth-century France: exemplar or exception' *European Journal of Population* 1 (1985), 31–60; 141–77.
'Family limitation in Colyton in pre-industrial England' *EcHR* 19 (1966), 82–109.
'Fertility strategy for the individual and the group', in C. Tilly (ed.), *Historical studies of changing fertility* (Princeton 1978), 133–54.
Wrigley, E. A., and Schofield, R. S., *The population history of England 1541–1871. A reconstruction* (1981).
Wrigley, E. A., *et al.*, *English population history from family reconstruction, 1580–1830* (Cambridge 1996).
Young, M., and Willmott, P., *Family and kinship in East London* (Harmondsworth 1957).
Young, R. M., 'Darwinism *is* social', in D. Kohn (ed.), *The Darwinian heritage* (Princeton 1985), 609–38.
Darwin's metaphor. Nature's place in Victorian culture (Cambridge 1985).
Mind, brain and adaptation in the nineteenth century: cerebral localization and its biological context from Gall to Ferrier (Oxford 1970).
Yule, G. U., 'Changes in marriages and birth rates in England and Wales in the last half century' *JRSS* 69 (1906), 88–132.
The fall of the birth-rate (Cambridge 1920).
Zeitlin, J., 'Engineers and compositors: a comparison', in Harrison and Zeitlin (eds.), *Divisions of labour*, 185–250.
Zeldin, T., *France, 1848–1945. Vol. I: Ambition, love and politics* (Oxford 1973).
France 1848–1945. Vol. II: Intellect, taste and anxiety (Oxford 1977).
Zelizer, V. A., *Pricing the priceless child. The changing social value of children* (New York 1985).
Zimmeck, M., 'The "new woman" in the machinery of government: a spanner in the works?', in MacLeod (ed.), *Government and expertise*, 185–202.
Zweig, F., *The worker in an affluent society* (1961).

Index

Explanatory note: the index entries refer to material which is *either* in the text *or* in the footnotes on any page that is referenced. There is no index entry for fertility or for the *Fertility of Marriage Report* of the 1911 census, the principal primary source, because their relevance is almost ubiquitous in this book. Authors of secondary sources are only referred to in the index where they are mentioned by name in discussion in the text or footnotes: there is therefore no comprehensive page index to the sources in the consolidated bibliography.

Cambridge Studies in Population, Economy and Society in the Past Time

0 *The population history of England 1541–1871* E. A. WRIGLEY and R. S. SCHOFIELD*
1 *Land, kinship and life-cycle* edited by RICHARD M. SMITH
2 *Annals of the labouring poor: social change and agrarian England 1660–1900* K. D. M. SNELL*
3 *Migration in a mature economy: emigration and internal migration in England and Wales 1861–1900* DUDLEY BAINES
4 *Scottish literacy and the Scottish identity: illiteracy and society in Scotland and Northern England 1600–1800* R. A. HOUSTON
5 *Neighbourhood and society: a London suburb in the seventeenth century* JEREMY BOULTON
6 *Demographic behavior in the past: a study of fourteen German village populations in the eighteenth and nineteenth centuries* JOHN E. KNODEL
7 *Worlds within worlds: structures of life in sixteenth-century London* STEVE RAPPAPORT
8 *Upland communities: environment, population and social structure in the Alps since the sixteenth century* PIER PAOLO VIAZZO
9 *Height, health and history: nutritional status in the United Kingdom 1750–1980* RODERICK FLOUD, KENNETH WACHTER and ANNABEL GREGORY
10 *Famine, disease and the social order in early modern society* edited by JOHN WALTER and ROGER SCHOFIELD*
11 *A general view of the rural economy of England, 1538–1840* ANN KUSSMAUL*
12 *Town and country in pre-industrial Spain: Cuenca 1540–1870* DAVID REHER
13 *A stagnating metropolis: the economy and demography of Stockholm 1750–1850* JOHAN SODERBERG, ULF JONSSON and CHRISTER PERSSON
14 *Population and nutrition: an essay on European demographic history* MASSIMO LIVI-BACCI*
15 *Istanbul households: marriage, family and fertility 1880–1940* ALAN DUBEN and CEM BEHAR
16 *A community transformed: the manor and liberty of Havering-atte-Bower 1500–1620* MARJORIE KENISTON MCINTOSH
17 *Friends in life and death: the British and Irish quakers in the demographic transition* RICHARD T. VANN and DAVID EVERSLEY
18 *A rural society after the Black Death: Essex 1350–1525* L. R. POOS
19 *London in the age of industrialisation: entrepreneurs, labour force and living conditions, 1700–1850* L. D. SCHWARZ
20 *Death and the metropolis: studies in the demographic history of London 1670–1830* JOHN LANDERS
21 *Family and social change: the household as a process in an industrializing community* ANGELIQUE JANSSENS
22 *Industry in the countryside: Wealden society in the sixteenth century* MICHAEL ZELL
23 *The Demography of Roman Egypt* ROGER S. BAGNALL and BRUCE W. FRIER
24 *Making a medical living: Doctors and patients in the market for medicine 1730–1911* ANNE DIBGY
25 *Patriarchy, property and death in the Roman family* RICHARD P. SALLER
26 *Men at work: Building in labour in northern England 1450–1750* DONALD WOODWARD
27 *Fertility, class and gender in Britain, 1860–1940* SIMON SZRETER

Titles available in paperback are marked with an asterisk